NEW PERSPECTIVES ON
Microsoft® Windows® 7 for Power Users

ADVANCED

Harry L. Phillips
Santa Rosa Junior College

COURSE TECHNOLOGY
CENGAGE Learning™

Australia • Brazil • Japan • Korea • Mexico • Singapore • Spain • United Kingdom • United States

COURSE TECHNOLOGY
CENGAGE Learning™

**New Perspectives on Microsoft Windows 7
for Power Users, Advanced**

Vice President, Publisher: Nicole Jones Pinard

Executive Editor: Marie L. Lee

Associate Acquisitions Editor: Amanda Lyons

Senior Product Manager: Kathy Finnegan

Product Manager: Leigh Hefferon

Associate Product Manager: Julia Leroux-Lindsey

Editorial Assistant: Jacqueline Lacaire

Director of Marketing: Cheryl Costantini

Senior Marketing Manager: Ryan DeGrote

Marketing Coordinator: Kristen Panciocco

Developmental Editors: Lisa Ruffolo, Mary Pat Shaffer

Content Project Manager: Heather Hopkins

Composition: GEX Publishing Services

Art Director: Marissa Falco

Text Designer: Althea Chen

Cover Designer: Roycroft Design

Cover Art: © Masterfile

Copyeditor: Mark Goodin

Proofreader: Kathy Orrino

Indexer: Alexandra Nickerson

Some of the product names and company names used in this book have been used for identification purposes only and may be trademarks or registered trademarks of their respective manufacturers and sellers.

Microsoft and the Office logo are either registered trademarks or trademarks of Microsoft Corporation in the United States and/or other countries. Course Technology, Cengage Learning is an independent entity from the Microsoft Corporation, and not affiliated with Microsoft in any manner.

Disclaimer: Any fictional data related to persons or companies or URLs used throughout this book is intended for instructional purposes only. At the time this book was printed, any such data was fictional and not belonging to any real persons or companies.

ISBN-13: 978-1-111-52649-8

ISBN-10: 1-111-52649-4

Course Technology
20 Channel Center Street
Boston, MA 02210
USA

Cengage Learning is a leading provider of customized learning solutions with office locations around the globe, including Singapore, the United Kingdom, Australia, Mexico, Brazil, and Japan. Locate your local office at:
international.cengage.com/global

Cengage Learning products are represented in Canada by Nelson Education, Ltd.

To learn more about Course Technology, visit **www.cengage.com/course technology**

To learn more about Cengage Learning, visit **www.cengage.com**

Purchase any of our products at your local college store or at our preferred online store **www.cengagebrain.com**

Printed in the United States of America
1 2 3 4 5 6 7 17 16 15 14 13 12 11

Preface

The New Perspectives Series' critical-thinking, problem-solving approach is the ideal way to prepare students to transcend point-and-click skills and take advantage of all that Microsoft Windows 7 has to offer.

In developing the New Perspectives Series, our goal was to create books that give students the software concepts and practical skills they need to succeed beyond the classroom. We've updated our proven case-based pedagogy with more practical content to make learning skills more meaningful to students.

With the New Perspectives Series, students understand *why* they are learning *what* they are learning, and are fully prepared to apply their skills to real-life situations.

About This Book

This book provides extensive coverage of Microsoft Windows 7, and includes the following:

- Complete coverage of Windows 7 basics, guiding students through managing folders and files, developing search techniques, creating desktop and Internet shortcuts, optimizing and enhancing the security of their computers, monitoring and evaluating system performance, troubleshooting problems, installing 32-bit and 64-bit Windows 7, and backing up a computer so they quickly learn to work independently
- Thorough explanations of the concepts, techniques, and advanced skills students need to become power users of Windows 7 in particular and operating systems in general
- In-depth coverage of new features, including graphical user interface features, libraries, search operators, Action Center, Problem Steps Recorder, system images, system repair disc, Windows XP Mode, Device Stage, and HomeGroup networking

New for this edition!

- Each session begins with a Visual Overview, a new two-page spread that includes enlarged screenshots with numerous callouts and key term definitions, giving students a comprehensive preview of the topics covered in the session, as well as a handy study guide.
- New ProSkills boxes provide guidance for how to use the software in real-world, professional situations, and related ProSkills exercises integrate the technology skills students learn with one or more of the following soft skills: decision making, problem solving, teamwork, verbal communication, and written communication.
- Important steps now include attached margin notes to help students pay close attention to completing the steps correctly and avoid time-consuming rework.

System Requirements

This book assumes a standard installation of Microsoft Windows 7 Ultimate on a networked or standalone computer with Windows Aero enabled. Most tasks in this text can also be completed with a standard installation of the Windows 7 Home Premium, Professional, and Enterprise Editions. Users with the Windows 7 Starter Edition can perform some of the basic operations presented. The book also assumes a standard installation of the Internet Explorer 8 Web browser.

www.cengage.com/ct/newperspectives

The New Perspectives Approach

Context

Each tutorial begins with a problem presented in a "real-world" case that is meaningful to students. The case sets the scene to help students understand what they will do in the tutorial.

Hands-on Approach

Each tutorial is divided into manageable sessions that combine reading and hands-on, step-by-step work. Numerous screenshots help guide students through the steps. **Trouble?** tips anticipate common mistakes or problems to help students stay on track and continue with the tutorial.

VISUAL OVERVIEW

Visual Overviews

New for this edition! Each session begins with a Visual Overview, a new two-page spread that includes enlarged screenshots with numerous callouts and key term definitions, giving students a comprehensive preview of the topics covered in the session, as well as a handy study guide.

PROSKILLS

ProSkills Boxes and Exercises

New for this edition! ProSkills boxes provide guidance for how to use the software in real-world, professional situations, and related ProSkills exercises integrate the technology skills students learn with one or more of the following soft skills: decision making, problem solving, teamwork, verbal communication, and written communication.

KEY STEP

Key Steps

New for this edition! Important steps now include attached margin notes to help students pay close attention to completing the steps correctly and avoid time-consuming rework.

INSIGHT

InSight Boxes

InSight boxes offer expert advice and best practices to help students achieve a deeper understanding of the concepts behind the software features and skills.

Margin Tips

Margin Tips provide helpful hints and shortcuts for more efficient use of the software. The Tips appear in the margin at key points throughout each tutorial, giving students extra information when and where they need it.

REVIEW

APPLY

Assessment

Retention is a key component to learning. At the end of each session, a series of Quick Check questions helps students test their understanding of the material before moving on. Engaging end-of-tutorial Review Assignments and Case Problems have always been a hallmark feature of the New Perspectives Series. Brief descriptions accompany the exercises, making it easy to understand both the goal and level of challenge a particular assignment holds.

REFERENCE

TASK REFERENCE

GLOSSARY/INDEX

Reference

Within each tutorial, Reference boxes appear before a set of steps to provide a succinct summary and preview of how to perform a task. In addition, a complete Task Reference at the back of the book provides quick access to information on how to carry out common tasks. Finally, each book includes a combination Glossary/Index to promote easy reference of material.

Our Complete System of Instruction

Coverage To Meet Your Needs

Whether you're looking for just a small amount of coverage or enough to fill a semester-long class, we can provide you with a textbook that meets your needs.

- Brief books typically cover the essential skills in just 2 to 4 tutorials.
- Introductory books build and expand on those skills and contain an average of 5 to 8 tutorials.
- Comprehensive and Advanced books are great for a full-semester class, and contain 9 to 12+ tutorials.

So if the book you're holding does not provide the right amount of coverage for you, there's probably another offering available. Go to our Web site or contact your Course Technology sales representative to find out what else we offer.

CourseCasts – Learning on the Go. Always available…always relevant.

Want to keep up with the latest technology trends relevant to you? Visit our site to find a library of podcasts, CourseCasts, featuring a "CourseCast of the Week," and download them to your mp3 player at http://coursecasts.course.com.

Our fast-paced world is driven by technology. You know because you're an active participant—always on the go, always keeping up with technological trends, and always learning new ways to embrace technology to power your life.

Ken Baldauf, host of CourseCasts, is a faculty member of the Florida State University Computer Science Department where he is responsible for teaching technology classes to thousands of FSU students each year. Ken is an expert in the latest technology trends; he gathers and sorts through the most pertinent news and information for CourseCasts so your students can spend their time enjoying technology, rather than trying to figure it out. Open or close your lecture with a discussion based on the latest CourseCast.

Visit us at http://coursecasts.course.com to learn on the go!

Instructor Resources

We offer more than just a book. We have all the tools you need to enhance your lectures, check students' work, and generate exams in a new, easier-to-use and completely revised package. This book's Instructor's Manual, ExamView testbank, PowerPoint presentations, data files, solution files, figure files, and a sample syllabus are all available on a single CD-ROM or for downloading at http://www.cengage.com/coursetechnology.

SAM: Skills Assessment Manager

SAM is designed to help bring students from the classroom to the real world. It allows students to train and test on important computer skills in an active, hands-on environment.

SAM's easy-to-use system includes powerful interactive exams, training, and projects on the most commonly used Microsoft Office applications. SAM simulates the Office application environment, allowing students to demonstrate their knowledge and think through the skills by performing real-world tasks, such as bolding text or setting up slide transitions. Add in live-in-the-application projects, and students are on their way to truly learning and applying skills to business-centric documents.

Designed to be used with the New Perspectives Series, SAM includes handy page references, so students can print helpful study guides that match the New Perspectives textbooks used in class. For instructors, SAM also includes robust scheduling and reporting features.

Content for Online Learning

Course Technology has partnered with the leading distance learning solution providers and class-management platforms today. To access this material, visit www.cengage.com/webtutor and search for your title. Instructor resources include the following: additional case projects, sample syllabi, PowerPoint presentations, and more. For students to access this material, they must have purchased a WebTutor PIN-code specific to this title and your campus platform. The resources for students might include (based on instructor preferences): topic reviews, review questions, practice tests, and more. For additional information, please contact your sales representative.

Acknowledgments

Many dedicated individuals at Course Technology actively participated in the planning, development, writing, reviewing, editing, testing, and production of this book. Their efforts reflect Cengage Learning's strong commitment to the highest quality college textbooks for instructors and students, and to all of them I owe many thanks. I extend my sincere thanks to all the members of the New Perspectives team who assisted with the development and production of this textbook.

Special thanks go to Mary Pat Shaffer and Lisa Ruffolo, Developmental Editors, who guided this textbook project and contributed their invaluable insight and experience to the development and scope of the textbook. Kathy Finnegan, Senior Product Manager, also deserves special thanks for planning, coordinating, and contributing her expertise and ideas to this textbook. I thank Marie Lee, Executive Editor, New Perspective Series; Julia Leroux-Lindsey, Associate Product Manager; Jacqueline Lacaire, Editorial Assistant; Heather Hopkins, Content Project Manager; Mark Goodin, Copyeditor; Marisa Taylor, Senior Project Manager, GEX Publishing Services; Louise Capulli, Project Manager, GEX Publishing Services; as well as Christian Kunciw, Manuscript Quality Assurance Supervisor, and Quality Assurance Testers John Freitas, Serge Palladino, Susan Pedicini, Danielle Shaw, Teresa Storch, Ashlee Welz Smith, and Susan Whalen.

I especially thank the following reviewers, whose invaluable comments and insight helped shape and improve the focus of this text: Robert Caruso, Santa Rosa Junior College; Ronald Norman, Grossmont College; Richard Pollak, Minneapolis Community and Technical College; Judy Scheeren, Westmoreland County Community College; and Leslie Vincent-Martinez, Delaware Technical and Community College.
– Harry L. Phillips

www.cengage.com/ct/newperspectives

BRIEF CONTENTS

WINDOWS

TABLE OF CONTENTS

TUTORIAL 1

OBJECTIVES

Session 1.1
- Learn about operating system software
- Examine PC operating systems and operating environments
- Compare the Windows operating systems

Session 1.2
- Work with features of the Windows 7 desktop
- Learn about the importance of Windows Aero
- Enable single-click activation on your computer
- Find Help information in Windows Help and Support

Session 1.3
- Navigate your computer's disk and folder structure
- Examine the importance and use of filenames
- View properties of your computer system
- Evaluate your computer's Windows Experience Index
- Compare options for shutting down your computer

Exploring the Windows 7 Operating System

Evaluating Windows 7

Case | *Deep Earth GeoThermal Systems, Ltd.*

Deep Earth GeoThermal Systems, Ltd., is a rapidly growing Seattle-based company that locates and develops new sources of geothermal energy stretching along the west coasts of North America, Latin America, and South America in a part of the Pacific Rim called the Ring of Fire. Juliann Chapin, a network specialist at Deep Earth GeoThermal Systems, is supervising the upgrade of company computers to Windows 7. Many of the company's employees are also ready to upgrade their laptops to Windows 7 so that they can take advantage of new features that allow them to work more efficiently and productively. Juliann works with you and other employees to explore some new and important Windows 7 features, to provide you with important information on how to properly assess the performance of Windows 7, and to identify what types of hardware and software work with your edition of Windows 7.

In this tutorial, you will examine the importance, role, and functions of operating system software, and then look at specific PC operating systems and their features. This overview will not only provide a historical perspective on the development of the Windows operating system, but it will also explore the new Windows 7 user interface and new technologies, including ongoing support for Windows Aero. You will also explore the use of Windows Help and Support to locate online information on using and evaluating new Windows 7 features. Finally, you will navigate your computer, view its properties, and evaluate the performance of Windows 7 on your computer.

STARTING DATA FILES

There are no starting Data Files needed for this tutorial.

SESSION 1.1 VISUAL OVERVIEW

Windows 95 was the first Windows operating system to use Plug and Play (PnP) hardware. **Plug and Play** refers to a set of specifications—developed by Microsoft, Intel, and a broad base of other companies, including hardware manufacturers—for automatically detecting and configuring hardware.

An **operating environment** is software that performs many of the same functions as an operating system, but requires an operating system to boot the computer and manage disks, drives, folders, and files.

DOS, an abbreviation for Disk Operating System, was the operating system used on IBM's first PC, introduced in 1981.

The first PC operating system was a **command-line operating system** that used a **command-line interface** through which you interacted with the operating system by manually entering and executing **commands**, or instructions.

Windows ME included a **System Restore utility**, or program, for rolling back a computer to an earlier point in time where everything worked properly.

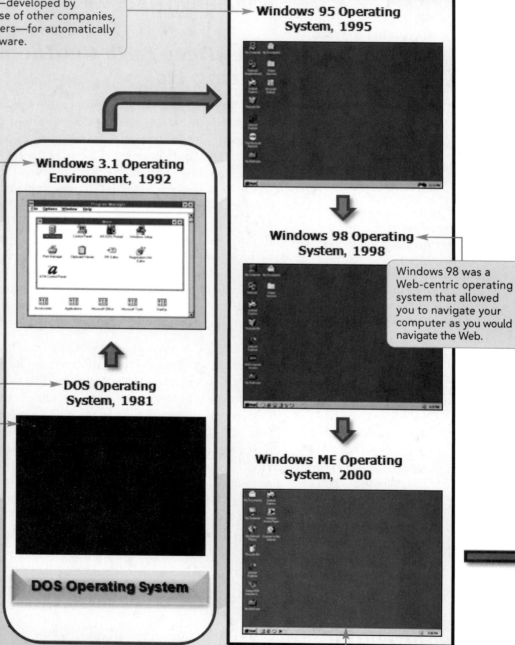

Windows 9x Product Line

Windows 95 Operating System, 1995

Windows 98 Operating System, 1998

Windows 98 was a Web-centric operating system that allowed you to navigate your computer as you would navigate the Web.

Windows ME Operating System, 2000

Windows 3.1 Operating Environment, 1992

DOS Operating System, 1981

DOS Operating System

WINDOWS TIMELINE

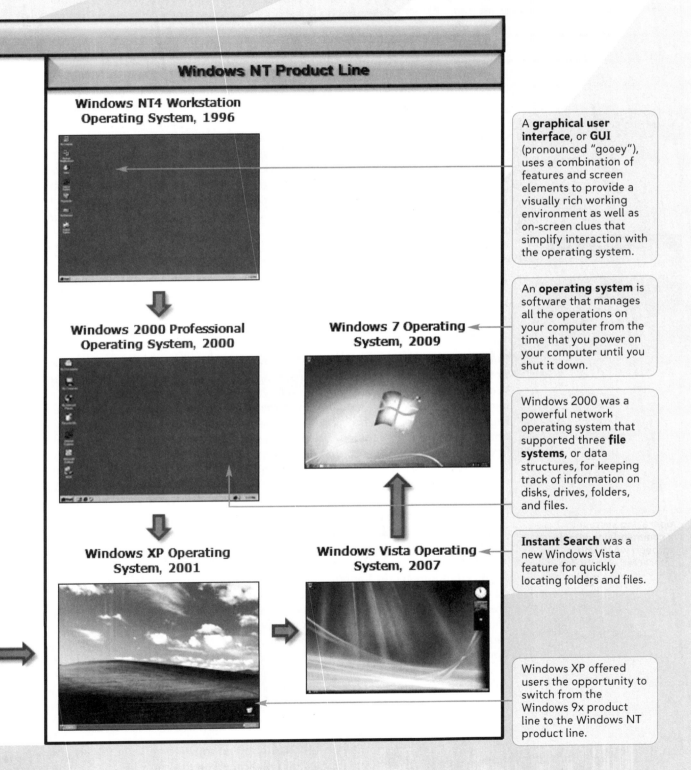

Windows NT Product Line

Windows NT4 Workstation Operating System, 1996

A **graphical user interface**, or **GUI** (pronounced "gooey"), uses a combination of features and screen elements to provide a visually rich working environment as well as on-screen clues that simplify interaction with the operating system.

Windows 2000 Professional Operating System, 2000

Windows 7 Operating System, 2009

An **operating system** is software that manages all the operations on your computer from the time that you power on your computer until you shut it down.

Windows 2000 was a powerful network operating system that supported three **file systems**, or data structures, for keeping track of information on disks, drives, folders, and files.

Windows XP Operating System, 2001

Windows Vista Operating System, 2007

Instant Search was a new Windows Vista feature for quickly locating folders and files.

Windows XP offered users the opportunity to switch from the Windows 9x product line to the Windows NT product line.

The Importance of Operating System Software

After Juliann and her support staff upgrade every staff member's computer, she schedules a hands-on workshop to familiarize everyone with the important role that the Windows operating system software plays in the proper functioning of each of their computer systems. She also schedules time in this workshop to cover new Windows 7 features that meet the specific needs of Deep Earth GeoThermal Systems.

Operating system software consists of a collection of programs, some of which are loaded into memory when you start up a computer, and some of which are loaded only when needed. Among the many different tasks it performs, the operating system manages the interaction of software and hardware so that all the software and hardware work together (where possible), and it provides support to other software that you use on your computer, including application software, Web browsers, email software, utilities, games, and even custom software designed for special tasks required in a business. Furthermore, the operating system includes settings and data for managing your computer and its operation. For example, after booting, the operating system stores settings about which drive it booted from; which drive and folder contains operating system files; which drive and folder contains installed applications, utilities, and games; which drive and folder contains settings and files for user accounts; and even information about the features of the processor.

Over the years, operating system software has evolved and become increasingly complex in order to adapt to newer types of hardware and software technologies and to support the ever-changing needs of businesses and home users. As the complexity of operating system software increases, computer users must become more savvy and knowledgeable about the use of the operating system on their computers.

Operating system software is responsible for the following types of operations on a computer:

- **Booting a computer**—The operating system plays a major role in booting a computer. **Booting** refers to the initial startup operations that get your computer up and running. When you press the power button to start your computer, you are performing a **cold boot** and starting your computer from scratch. During the initial stages of a cold boot, **routines** (or small programs) stored on a flash memory chip called the **BIOS** (pronounced "bye os"), or **System BIOS**, on the motherboard inside the system unit perform a series of important startup operations. BIOS is an abbreviation for basic input/output system. An initial routine performs a **Power-On Self-Test (POST)** and determines whether the hardware devices for booting the computer are present and functioning. You will examine the BIOS and booting in more detail in Tutorial 8.
- **Locating and loading the operating system**—One specific BIOS routine locates the operating system software on the hard disk and starts the process of loading the operating system. **Loading** refers to copying software from the hard disk into RAM so that you have a working copy of that software in addition to the permanent copy stored on disk.

    RAM (**random access memory**), also referred to as **system memory**, consists of computer chips stored on **memory modules** inside the system unit, and it is the predominant and most important type of memory within a computer. RAM stores the components of the operating system needed to manage your computer and provide support for all the other tasks you perform while you are using a computer. RAM also stores currently used programs, device drivers, documents, and data. RAM therefore provides a high-speed, temporary workspace for your use. RAM is **volatile**, or dependent on the availability of power. That means any programs and data that are stored in RAM are erased when you shut down your computer, but you have a fresh start at the next boot. RAM is also referred to as temporary memory. In contrast, storage space on a hard disk is referred to as permanent memory, because the hard disk stores a copy of the operating system software, all other installed software, all your folders and files, and the data structures used to track information about the hard disk itself. If the power fails while you are working on your computer, anything in RAM is lost, but when power is restored, you can power up your computer, and the operating system loads back into memory from the hard disk. Once up and running, you can reload from the hard disk any applications and files that you had open when the power failed. If someone asks you how much memory your computer has, they are asking about the amount of RAM installed on your computer, not the storage space of your hard disk.

After the BIOS routine loads core operating system files into memory, the operating system takes control of the computer, loads and configures the remainder of the operating system software, allocates system resources to hardware **devices** (hardware components in a computer), and completes the booting of the computer, including loading specific programs, such as Internet security software, critical to securing and protecting a computer. If you encounter a problem while using your computer, such as an unresponsive or slowly responding program, you can perform a **warm boot** to restart your computer without shutting down power to the computer and hardware devices. A warm boot skips the Power-On Self Test (POST), and is faster than a cold boot.

INSIGHT

Understanding the Relationship Between the BIOS and Operating System Software

Computer systems require the BIOS to start a computer because the operating system is not yet active when you first turn on a computer. Therefore, the BIOS plays an essential role in booting your computer because it provides access to a set of specific routines needed for the initial boot process, and it initiates the loading of whatever operating system is installed on a computer. That also means that the BIOS is operating-system independent. For example, you might have a dual-boot computer that provides an option for either starting Windows 7 or Windows Vista (or some other operating system, such as Linux, which is briefly covered later in the tutorial). Even on a dual-boot or multiboot computer, there is only one BIOS, and it performs its initial startup operations before it loads any operating system. In some instances, you might boot from a DVD, a CD, or even a flash drive to load and work with an operating system, such as Linux, or to troubleshoot problems with the operating system installed on your hard drive. Your Windows DVD is an example of a removable disk that you can use to boot your computer system if you need to reinstall or repair Windows on your computer.

Understanding the relationship between the operating system and the BIOS allows you to more effectively identify the source of a problem (i.e., the BIOS or the operating system), and save time and effort troubleshooting that problem.

- **Configuring a computer**—During the early stages of booting, the operating system detects the hardware in your computer and **configures** (or modifies) itself to support that hardware by loading the appropriate device drivers. A **device driver** is a file that contains program code that enables the operating system to communicate with, and manage the use of, a specific hardware device. To support each hardware device, the operating system must load one or more device drivers designed for use with each hardware device. When you attach a new hardware device to your computer, the operating system automatically detects the device during the early stages of booting. The operating system then locates and loads the device drivers for the hardware device and configures the hardware so it is ready to use. If the operating system cannot locate the device drivers for a hardware device, it prompts you to search online for, or to insert a disk with, the device drivers and other software for that hardware device. Then it installs that software, loads the device drivers, and configures the hardware so you can use it. You will examine hardware in more detail in Tutorial 12.

- **Customizing a computer**—While the process of configuring a computer prepares a computer for use by the operating system, the process of customizing a computer prepares it to meet your specific needs and preferences. Towards the end of the booting process, the operating system **customizes** your computer by loading optional programs that you want to use on your computer, and applying settings for your personal preferences. For example, it's common practice today to use antivirus software to protect a computer system from many different types of malicious software. However, unlike the operating system, this software is not required because while you can use your computer without antivirus software, you cannot boot or operate your computer without an operating system.

  Malicious software, also referred to as **malware**, consists of one or more programs designed to interfere with the operation and performance of your computer, render a computer inoperable, or compromise a computer's security and your privacy. The operating system loads your antivirus software as early as possible during booting so that the software can check your computer for malware before it becomes active. Once your computer boots, your Internet security software or antivirus software also monitors your computer while you work, checks each disk you access, and checks each program, folder, and file you open.

- **Displaying a user interface**—After your computer boots, the operating system displays a **user interface,** which allows you to interact with your computer. A user interface includes hardware, such as the monitor, keyboard, and mouse, as well as other features, such as a touchscreen, that enable you to interact with the operating system and other software on a computer. The type of user interface presented by the operating system, and its ease of use, have become increasingly important to users because they rely on it to simplify the tasks they perform on a computer and maintain the proper functioning and security of a computer.

- **Providing support services to applications**—The operating system provides important support services to software applications and other programs that you use. For example, if you need to create a document, such as a report, you open a program, such as Microsoft Word, and create the document. At some point, you instruct the program to save your document. The program prompts you for the disk where you want to store the document, the folder where you want to store the document, and the filename for the document. The operating system locates storage space on the disk for the file, and mediates the transfer of a copy of the document from RAM to the disk, folder, and file you designated. If you want to make changes to that document later, you open the same program and instruct it to open the file by identifying the disk and folder where the file is stored, and then selecting the file that contains the document. The operating system then mediates the transfer of a copy of that file from disk into RAM so that you can change that document. You therefore have a working copy stored in a RAM and a permanent copy on disk. Because RAM is volatile you need to periodically save your documents and data to disk in the event a power failure or computer problem occurs; otherwise, you run the risk of losing all or part of your work.

  Almost every program provides you with an option for saving and retrieving documents stored in files; therefore, it makes sense to delegate this task to the operating system rather than include the same program code for saving and retrieving files in every program. This approach also provides consistency across different applications so that the process for saving and retrieving files uses the same approach and same user interface components (i.e., the Open and Save As dialog boxes). Furthermore, this approach to handling the saving and retrieving of files is a security feature that protects access to the drive, folders, and files on your computer. You will examine software in more detail in Tutorial 11.

- **Handling input and output**—The operating system manages all input and output. **Input** refers to instructions and data that you provide a program so that it can accomplish some task for you, and **output** refers to the results produced by a program. When you work on a computer, you typically use your keyboard and mouse to input changes to a document and to input the command for saving your document. The final document shown on the screen is an example of output that results from your input.

  Printing is another example of output. When you print a document, the operating system uses a process called **spooling** to store the processed document in a temporary file called a **spool file** on disk, and to transmit the contents of the document in the spool file to the printer in the background, so that you can continue to work in your application and perform other tasks, such as checking email. Also, by spooling documents to disk, the operating system can print a set of documents one after the other while you continue to work. The operating system stores the documents in a **print queue** (a list of print jobs), and prints the documents in the order in which you submit them. Without spooling, you would have to wait until each document printed before you could do anything else. Once printing is complete, the Windows operating system deletes spool files.

- **Managing a computer's file system**—Your computer's **file system** consists of the operating system components and data structures that the operating system uses to keep track of all the disks, drives, folders, files, and data on your computer. Drives, folders, and files are organized into a **hierarchy**, or ordered structure or view, that starts with disks at the top of the hierarchy, and works its way down to the individual drives and folders to files and data. A hierarchy therefore shows and describes the logical relationship between components of a computer system. Figure 1-1 shows a partial view of the contents on Juliann's hard drive and the organization of folders in her user account.

Figure 1-1   **A partial view of the folder structure on Juliann's computer**

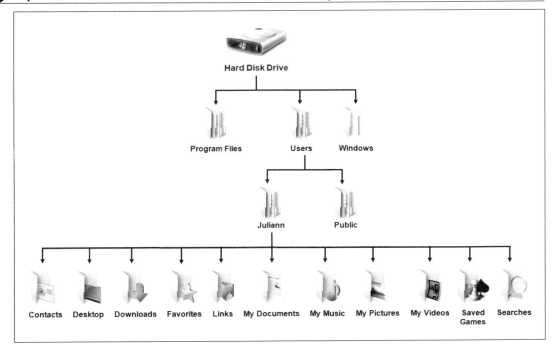

Juliann can navigate to her personal folders by opening a Computer window, opening drive C, opening the Users folder (which keeps track of each user's personal folders on a computer), and then opening her user folder. Another way for Juliann to access her personal folders is to click her user name on the Start menu.

Although your computer might only have one physical hard disk, it might be subdivided into one or more partitions that are treated as **logical disks**. A **partition** is a subdivision of a physical hard disk; each partition appears as a separate hard disk that is identified by a drive name. A **drive name** consists of a letter of the alphabet followed by a colon (**:**), such as C: for the hard drive, that Windows 7 assigns to a drive. The colon is a required part of the drive name, and when referring to the drive, you can say "C:" (pronounced "C colon"), or you can say "drive C" (the reference to the colon is assumed). For example, you might have one physical hard disk in your computer, but it might be partitioned or subdivided into two drives named C: (for drive C) and D: (for drive D). With this type of setup, your computer's operating system and other software are typically stored on drive C, and drive D stores user files. Or, perhaps you have a dual-boot computer, with one operating system installed on one hard drive, and another operating system installed on the other hard drive. If your computer has only one physical hard disk, and if it is not partitioned, then you have one drive (most likely identified as drive C) that stores your computer's operating system, other software, and your personal files. It is also possible to have more than one physical hard disk in a computer. Each hard disk would then have a different drive name. You will examine file systems in more detail in Tutorial 5.

- **Working with folders and files**—The operating system provides features and tools for organizing, locating, and using programs, folders, files, and data on your computer quickly and easily. For example, you can search for all files that contain information on a specific topic within the file itself so that you can locate the files you need for a specific project, or you can search for all files created by a coworker. You can also create **shortcuts**, or files that point to other files, programs, folders, and Web sites, so that you can open them with a single click. You will examine folder and file management in more detail in Tutorial 3 and shortcuts in more detail in Tutorial 4.

- **Managing system resources**—As noted earlier, the operating system manages all the hardware and software on your computer so that everything works properly together— a major feat because of the wide spectrum of hardware and software products and the constant introduction of new hardware and software technologies. One especially important resource managed by the operating system is memory. When you open an application, Web browser, utility, or game, the operating system loads or copies that program from disk into RAM and, in the process, allocates a certain amount of memory to that program so that you can use the program. When you exit an application, utility, or game, the operating system reclaims the memory used by that program so it can make that memory available to the next program you use. Furthermore, Windows supports **multitasking** so you can open and work with more than one program, folder, or file window at the same time. If your computer does not have enough RAM for multitasking and the programs you use, the operating system can set aside unused storage space on your hard drive for use as additional memory, or what's called **virtual memory**, thereby increasing the total amount of memory available to the operating system and programs. You will examine in more detail how the Windows 7 operating system manages memory in Tutorial 9.

- **Resolving system errors and problems**—The operating system must handle and, if possible, resolve errors as they occur on a computer. The errors can range from simple to very complex. The operating system attempts to identify the error, corrects the error, checks online for the solution to the problem, or requests that you correct the problem. The operating system also provides specific troubleshooting utilities, which are tools for identifying the cause of a problem and for correcting the problem. For example, you might use a Windows 7 utility to check the hard disk for errors and, when possible, to repair those errors. You will examine troubleshooting strategies and techniques in more detail in Tutorial 8.

- **Optimizing system performance**—Operating systems also include a variety of utilities or tools for analyzing, evaluating, and optimizing the performance of your computer. For example, you might use a utility to improve the speed of accessing data on a disk by rearranging how programs, folders, and your document files are stored on that disk. You might use another utility to evaluate memory usage on your computer and help you decide whether you need to add more RAM to your computer. Your operating system can also automatically perform preventive maintenance on your computer to optimize its performance. You will examine options for optimizing your hard disk in Tutorial 6.
- **Backing up your computer**—Operating systems provide tools for backing up your entire computer system or just your important personal files. **Backing up** refers to the process of storing a duplicate copy of the programs, folders, and files on another disk. If you lose an important file, or if your hard disk fails, you can restore copies of important files from a backup, or you can use a backup copy to restore your entire hard disk. Most people concentrate on backing up just their files. However, to further protect your computer, the operating system can restore a complete image (or backup) of your hard disk and thereby rebuild your computer by rolling back changes to your computer and restoring it to an earlier point in time when it was working properly. Furthermore, it keeps copies of all previous versions of folders and files so that you can retrieve an earlier version of the hard disk, a folder, or one or more files. You will examine options for backing up a computer and restoring previous versions of files in more detail in Tutorial 10.
- **Power management**—The operating system manages power to all the hardware devices in a computer. It can reduce power consumption to devices when they are not in use and then restore power to those devices when you need to use them. The operating system can also place your entire computer into a low-power state when you are not using your computer and then restore it to a full working state when you need to use it again. These power management features not only conserve power but also extend the useful lifetime of your computer and save energy. You will examine power management in more detail in Tutorial 2.

- **Computer and Internet security**—The operating system provides access to a computer via user accounts. A **user account** identifies you to Windows 7; provides you with access to specific programs, folders, and files on your computer; and allows you to specify custom settings for using the computer. Furthermore, your user account determines what types of operations you can perform on your computer. To gain access to your user account, you provide your user name and password. The operating system then uses that information to verify that you are authorized to use the computer. If more than one person uses the same computer, the operating system allows each user to set up and customize their own user account. Each user's files and settings are kept separate from each other.

   The operating system also prevents changes to important operating system files and folders to protect the integrity of your computer. When you are connected to the Internet or another network, the operating system includes features that prevent malicious software, Web sites, and hackers from gaining access to your computer. The operating system also ensures that malicious or questionable software already installed on your computer does not attempt to access a Web site on the Internet without your knowledge. In addition, you can set up your computer so that the operating system automatically checks for and installs important updates to the operating system, including updates that enhance the security of your computer. You will examine computer and Internet security and privacy in more detail in Tutorial 6.
- **Networking**—The operating system detects, sets up, and configures computers connected together via a wireless or wired network. The operating system also enables users to access other computers and hardware on a network, share resources (including hardware, folders, and files), modify network settings, monitor network performance, and troubleshoot network problems. You will examine networking in more detail in Tutorial 12.

• **Providing Help**—Operating systems typically include a Help system that provides you with information about the use of the operating system and its features. The Help system replaces the use of printed manuals and provides access to the content typically found in those manuals for ease of access while you're working. Help systems provide links to explanations of specific features as well as wizards, online videos, and online help. These various features identify the steps you need to perform an operation, troubleshoot a problem, or locate the help you need. A **wizard** is a tool that asks you a series of questions about what you want to do and what settings or features you want to use, and then completes the operation for you. Links found in a Help system work the same way as links that you use on a Web site to jump to another Web page. While some links are to specific Web sites, other links take you to other parts of the Help system or to specific tools on your computer. You will examine the Windows 7 Help and Support in more detail later in this tutorial.

The operating system is an indispensable component of your computer. While you might purchase a computer without an operating system, the first task you need to perform in order to use your computer is to install an operating system. As you work with application software, or other types of software, such as Web browsers, utilities, and games, the operating system manages the moment-to-moment operation of your computer in the background, from when you initially power on the computer until you shut it down. Furthermore, because the operating system handles important operations, such as disk, drive, folder, file, and data management, as well as all input/output functions, application software can focus on what it is designed to do best, and the operating system can focus on core functions required of all programs. As you examine desktop operating systems in general and Windows 7 in particular, you will learn about other ways in which the operating system manages your computer and provides you with the tools you need to work effectively and productively.

PC Operating Systems

The predominant operating systems used on PCs today are ones developed by Microsoft Corporation, and they therefore share a common history and many common features. Features, concepts, and techniques introduced with earlier operating systems remain important to the effective use of later operating systems. Therefore, you should be familiar not only with the operating system used on your computer, which may be one of the editions of Windows 7, but also with other editions of Windows 7 and versions of the Windows operating system that preceded Windows 7. Furthermore, command-line features are critical to the use of Windows 7 and other Windows versions even today.

The DOS Operating System

In 1981, IBM contracted with Microsoft Corporation, then a small company in Seattle, to provide the operating system for its first IBM PC. Microsoft purchased an operating system from Seattle Computer Products for use on the IBM PC. DOS 1.0 from Microsoft was the first version of the DOS operating system. Microsoft and IBM developed three related versions of the DOS operating systems: PC-DOS, IBM-DOS, and MS-DOS. Although there were subtle differences between these three DOS operating systems, all managed the hardware and software resources within a computer in similar ways, provided access to similar types of features, and included similar utilities for accessing, managing, and enhancing a computer system. Once you knew how to use MS-DOS, you also knew how to use IBM-DOS, and vice-versa.

Because the first IBM PCs did not have a hard drive, but rather two floppy disk drives, the DOS operating system was stored on, and loaded from, a floppy disk in the first floppy disk drive (drive A). The floppy disk in the second floppy disk drive (drive B) stored user files. Within the following year, hard drives with storage capacities of 5 MB, 10 MB, and 20 MB appeared in the marketplace for use on PCs, and then DOS was installed on, and loaded from, the first hard drive (drive C).

The DOS operating system, which preceded the Windows operating system, used a command-line interface that enabled you to communicate with the operating system by typing a command after an on-screen prompt referred to as an **operating system prompt**, a **command prompt**, or a **DOS prompt**. After you powered on a computer that used a DOS operating system, it displayed a prompt (usually C:\> for drive C) on the screen, unless someone had already customized the startup process to make the computer easier to use. Next to the operating system prompt was a blinking cursor (_) that identified your current working position for entering a command. See Figure 1-2. (Although Figure 1-2 is cropped to save space, the remainder of your view on the monitor consisted of a black background with no other features.)

| Figure 1-2 | DOS command-line user interface |

command prompt

The operating system prompt indicated that the computer had booted successfully from C: (the hard drive), that the operating system loaded into memory, and that it used a specific drive and folder as a reference point (namely, C:\). (*Note*: On the earliest PCs, which used two floppy disk drives, DOS booted from drive A, and displayed A:\> on the screen.)

The backslash (\ ) following the drive name is a special notation for the **root directory**, or what is now referred to as the top-level folder on a drive. Under the Windows operating system, the **top-level folder** is the folder you access once you open a drive from a Computer window. Under DOS, the term **subdirectory** was used to refer to a subfolder. Even today, when working in a command-line environment, you use the terms *directory* and *subdirectory* instead of *folder* and *subfolder*.

The DOS operating system did not display any other on-screen clues to help you figure out what to do next. You had to know what command to use, and you also had to know the proper syntax for entering each command. **Syntax** refers to the proper format for entering a command in a command-line environment or window, including the spelling of the command and any optional parameters or switches, as well as the spacing within a command. A **parameter** is an optional or required item of data used with a command, such as the name of a drive. A **switch** is an optional parameter that changes the way in which the command works. For example, Figure 1-3 shows a variation of the command for the CHKDSK program, which checks a disk for errors under the DOS operating system; the /F switch (for Fix) in this figure specifies that it repairs disk errors as it checks the disk.

| Figure 1-3 | DOS CHDSK command |

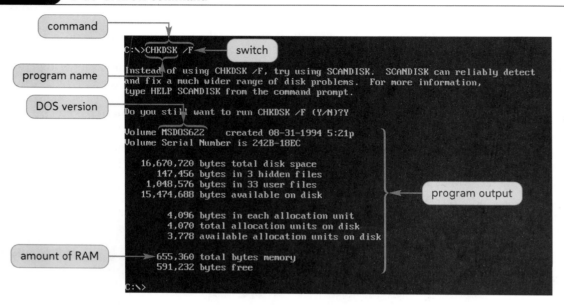

command

C:\>CHKDSK /F ← switch

program name

Instead of using CHKDSK /F, try using SCANDISK. SCANDISK can reliably detect
and fix a much wider range of disk problems. For more information,
type HELP SCANDISK from the command prompt.

DOS version

Do you still want to run CHKDSK /F (Y/N)?Y

Volume MSDOS622   created 08-31-1994 5:21p
Volume Serial Number is 242B-18EC

   16,670,720 bytes total disk space
      147,456 bytes in 3 hidden files
    1,048,576 bytes in 33 user files
   15,474,688 bytes available on disk

        4,096 bytes in each allocation unit
        4,070 total allocation units on disk
        3,778 available allocation units on disk

program output

amount of RAM

      655,360 total bytes memory
      591,232 bytes free

C:\>

After you enter a DOS command, the operating system locates and loads the program for that command. Then that program performs a specific action; in this example, it checked a disk for problems. In this case, it found no problems. When the program completed its operation, the operating system redisplays the command prompt so that you can enter another command to start another program.

Microsoft has included a CHKDSK disk analysis and repair utility in every version of the DOS operating system and in every version of the Windows operating system, including Windows 7. You will examine the use of this important command-line utility in more detail in Tutorial 6.

Not surprisingly, because of the simplicity of the user interface and the need to know the names of the operating system commands and their proper syntax, users found it difficult to use the DOS operating system. As a result, many users relied on computer technicians to set up their computers so that the DOS operating system automatically displayed a custom menu from which the user could select an installed application or perform some common operation, such as **formatting** or preparing a disk for use on a computer. Another limitation of the DOS operating system was that you could only perform one task at a time. For example, you could only use one program at a time, and you could only print one document at a time, and you could not do anything else until printing was complete.

An important feature of command-line interface operating systems is that they operate in text mode. In **text mode**, the operating system displays only text, numbers, symbols, and a small set of graphics characters, such as line drawing symbols like ╠, using white, amber, or green characters on a black background, or perhaps black characters on a white background. Because text mode does not need to display a user interface with complex graphics, the DOS operating system and present-day command-line operating systems are fast and require far less memory and other system resources than contemporary computers that rely on a graphical user interface. Because it operates in text mode, the user interface in a command-line operating system is also referred to as a **Text User Interface** (or TUI, and pronounced "two-ie").

INSIGHT

The Importance of Command-Line Skills

Command-line concepts and skills that are derived from the DOS operating system are still important today, especially for network administrators, network specialists, network technicians, telecommunication specialists, computer and network troubleshooters, computer consultants, and trainers. In fact, command-line skills are an invaluable resource in almost any job. In some cases, command-line tools enable you to perform operations that are not possible in the Windows graphical user interface. Command-line tools allow you to troubleshoot a computer system when Windows cannot boot to the desktop. For example, in Windows 7, Microsoft has introduced a variation on the POWERCFG command that analyzes power usage on a computer and produces a Power Efficiency Diagnostics Report, which identifies power problems that affect the performance of a computer. This report also provides technical details on the power management capabilities of Windows 7 and your hardware. You will find command-line features like this one essential in analyzing the power status and power problems on a computer.

The Windows Operating Environments

TIP

An OS environment is also referred to as a *wrapper* because it simplifies the use of DOS.

In 1985, Microsoft introduced Windows 1.0, the first in a series of Windows operating environments, and seven years later, Windows 3.1 became the most commonly used version of the Windows operating environment. An operating environment performs the same functions as an operating system except for configuring and customizing a computer system during booting and handling the storage and retrieval of files on a disk. The Windows operating environments therefore required a version of the DOS operating system be installed on the computer to handle booting and basic file functions. The Windows operating environments were the first versions of Windows to use a graphical user interface that was originally derived from a graphical user interface used on Apple and Xerox computers, and similar to today's Windows graphical user interface. Later, Microsoft introduced networking capabilities in Windows 3.1 for Workgroups (distinct from its predecessor Windows 3.1) and Windows 3.11 for Workgroups.

Although DOS was the predominant PC operating system for the 14 years from 1981–1995, the Windows operating environments were important because they eventually led to the development of the Windows operating system. In fact, Microsoft referred to the Windows operating environments as operating systems, anticipating the day when Windows would be a full-fledged operating system that no longer required DOS. The DOS operating system is still available, and you can install and use it in a virtual environment under a Windows operating system. A **virtual environment** is a simulation of a complete computer system, or in other words, a **virtual machine**.

The Windows Operating Systems

The first Windows operating system was Windows 95, and it marked a revolutionary change in operating system technology. The following list describes some Windows 95 features that are still quite important in current Windows operating systems:

- **Graphical user interface**—The Windows operating systems all rely on a graphical user interface. The graphical user interface uses colors; **fonts** (different character design styles); special screen design elements, such as shading, shadows, and **translucency** (or transparency); and animation to provide a more interesting working environment. Windows displays **icons**, or pictures, on the desktop to represent hardware and software components, as well as system tools, that you can open and use. Although icons are designed to identify their purpose, it is not always obvious to users what feature is associated with a specific icon, so icons have **icon titles**, or labels under the icon, that describe their purpose. For example, Windows 7 displays a recycle bin icon on the desktop with the *Recycle Bin* icon title so that you can glean the purpose of this icon.

The Windows graphical user interface relies on the use of **windows**, or work areas on the screen, that are designed to organize your view of disks, drives, folders, applications, documents, and data. Every time you open a program, that program appears within a program or **application window**. If you open more than one program, each program is displayed within its own window. Likewise, for many applications, each document you open in an application appears within its own **document window**.

Windows also uses **menus** to list options for performing different types of command operations. Like a restaurant menu, a Windows menu displays your choices so that you can easily make a selection from the list. Once you select a menu option, Windows might display a **dialog box** that includes additional options that you must examine, check, or select before completing that operation. In a graphical user interface, the mouse plays an important role. You use the mouse to open programs, to point to and select icons, and to select options in windows, on menus, and in dialog boxes. Unlike a command-line operating system, Windows operates in graphics mode rather than text mode. In **graphics mode**, Windows can display text in a variety of fonts and colors, as well as support the use of graphic images, video, and animation; however, the use of graphics mode requires far more memory and system resources than text mode.

- **Object-oriented interface**—The Windows operating systems treat components of the graphical user interface and the computer as objects. Hardware and software components, such as disks, drives, folders, files, programs, and data are represented on your computer with the use of icons, and therefore are objects. Objects have actions and properties. **Actions** are operations you can perform on an object. For example, you can open and explore the contents of your hard drive, share a drive on your network, create a link to quickly access the drive, and rename the drive by changing the **volume label** (the electronic name) assigned to the drive. Each object has a default action, such as Open, associated with it to save you time and effort. A **default action** is the action that Windows automatically takes when you double-click the object. You can view a list of other actions specific to an object by right-clicking the object to display the object's **shortcut menu**, or **context menu**. **Properties**, on the other hand, are characteristics of, or settings for, an object. You can view, and in many cases, change the properties of objects by right-clicking the object and selecting Properties on the object's shortcut menu. An **object** can therefore be defined as a visible element of the user interface that you can right-click.

TIP

To learn more about an object, right-click it, and then examine the options on the shortcut menu.

Because every object has a shortcut menu associated with it, you use the same approach to locate and perform actions on an object and examine its properties, whether the object is a drive, a piece of clip art pasted into a document, a word in a document, an icon in the notification area on the taskbar, a desktop shortcut, a Web page, or the desktop itself. When working in an application window or a document window, you right-click objects to access their actions and properties. Shortcut menus therefore provide a consistent way to work with different type of objects and clearly identify the actions available for an object.

The single most important and effective way to use your computer, Windows, and all the software on your computer, and become a power user, is to consider that each and every element you see on your screen might be an object (or part of another object) that has actions and properties.

- **Multitasking, task switching, and multithreading**—As noted earlier, the Windows operating systems support multitasking and allow you to open multiple programs and multiple folders, each of which appears in a different window. The Windows operating systems also supports task switching and multithreading. When you switch from one open task to another by clicking a taskbar button for a new task, such as to switch from one program window to another program window, from one folder window to another folder window, or from a program window to a folder window (or vice-versa), you are **task switching**.

Multithreading refers to the ability of Windows operating systems to **execute**, or carry out, the instructions contained within units of program code (called **threads**) within a program. For example, the Windows operating system can execute instructions in two different threads in two different programs almost simultaneously. Or it can execute instructions in two different threads within the same program, or two of the same threads in the same program. The term **process** refers to an open and running program that consists of one or more threads and associated data structures. True multithreading requires a multicore processor. **Multicore processors** contain one or more **execution cores**, each of which acts as a separate processor. The processor cores are located side by side within the same processor chip for faster processing. That means that two different tasks execute simultaneously as two different threads on two different processor cores (provided the program that you are using supports multithreading). Multicore processors are therefore useful for resource-intensive applications that spawn multiple threads. In contrast, a processor with one execution core is called a **single-core processor** and supports the processing of one thread at a time. That means each task must wait its turn. However, some Intel single-core processors supported a feature called **hyperthreading** that enabled the single-core processor to handle two threads almost simultaneously. While dual-core processors are commonplace today, Intel and AMD (Advanced Micro Designs), two well-known processor manufacturers, currently have triple core, quad-core (or four-core), hex-core (or hexa-core or six-core) processors, and eight-core processors. Quad-core processors generally perform better and faster than dual-core processors; however, benchmark tests on different types of multicore processors show that their performance spans a broad range, and the performance of quad-core and dual-core processors overlap. That makes sense because processor manufacturers produce a wide array of different types of processors with different capabilities and features.

Multitasking, task switching, and multithreading improve the performance of your computer and allow you to be more productive, especially on computers with multicore processors.

In contrast, the DOS operating system only supported **single-tasking**. That meant that you could perform only one task at a time, so you had to wait until that task was complete before you could perform another task. For example, you could only open one program at a time. To use another program, you had to close the program you were currently using before opening the next program.

- **Document-oriented approach**—The graphical user interface in the Windows operating systems makes it easier to use a document-oriented approach, rather than an application-oriented approach, to open files that contain documents that you want to use. When using an **application-oriented approach**, you first open the software application, and then you locate and open the document you want by using an Open dialog box. This approach was the only one available with the DOS operating system, and is still commonly taught and used today. In contrast, when using a **document-oriented approach**, you open the folder where a file is located, and then you double-click (or click) the file icon. Next, the operating system opens the application associated with the type of file you're opening, and then it opens the document within the file. This approach is useful if you are working in a folder that contains a group of files; you can open each file as needed from within the folder. You don't have to go through the lengthy process of using the Start menu and All Programs menu to locate and open the program for each different type of file in the folder, nor do you need to open a file from within a program. The document-oriented approach is a faster and more efficient way to work with files. Although the document-oriented approach was available with the Windows operating environments, it did not come into its own right until the release of Windows 95, and then it provided a different and unique way for working with files. However, as pointed out, it was not always obvious to a user then that they could open a file by double-clicking on it. That is also sometimes the case today.

- **Long filenames**—Under the DOS operating system, folder and filenames were limited to eight characters, and an optional three characters called an **extension** or **file extension** separated from the main part of the filename by a period. For example, under DOS, if you created an annual report, you used a filename like ANNRPT, ANN_RPT, or ANNUAL.RPT. (DOS used only uppercase characters, and file extensions were not required.) Because you could not include spaces in the filename, you had to use an underscore or dash between different parts of the same filename to make it easier to read. The limitations on naming files under DOS meant that you had to be creative when naming files and develop some type of naming scheme so that you could later identify the file you needed.

  Windows 7 supports **long filenames**, or filenames up to 255 characters in length. Long filenames can include spaces and certain types of symbols, and they typically include a file extension separated from the main part of the filename by a period (usually referred to as a "**dot**"). To save typing, most people use much shorter filenames that are perfectly adequate. Later in this tutorial, you will examine filenames in more detail.

INSIGHT

Understanding the Importance of File Extensions

Under the Windows operating system, the file extension is important because it identifies the application you use to open the file. For example, if you create an annual report, you might store it in a file named "Annual Report.docx". Unlike DOS, this example of a filename clearly identifies the content contained in the file (i.e., an annual report), and the file extension (*docx*) identifies it as a document file that was most likely created by Microsoft Office Word 2007 or Microsoft Word 2010. DOS file-naming conventions are still used today in assigning names to program files and many of the other files included with a software product, even the Windows operating system, so that problems do not arise when a Windows computer is connected to a network.

- **Shortcuts**—Under any version of the Windows operating system you can create shortcuts (or links) to programs, drives, folders, files, Web sites, and to components of the graphical user interface so that you can quickly open and access these objects. Tutorial 4 focuses on the use of shortcuts to work smarter.
- **Plug-and-Play**—The Windows operating systems support Plug-and-Play hardware. Once you add a new Plug-and-Play hardware device to your computer, the operating system automatically detects and configures the hardware device either during booting or when the computer is already on, with little or no intervention on your part. In contrast, **legacy** or **non-Plug-and-Play devices** are older types of hardware components that do not meet the specifications of the Plug-and-Play standard and that may require manual installation. Fortunately, Plug-and-Play hardware is the standard today.
- **Backward compatibility**—The ability of the Windows operating systems to work with older hardware, as well as software designed for earlier versions of the Windows operating system, is called **backward compatibility**. While not perfect, this capability improves the chances that you can keep your current computer system and its hardware and software without having to purchase a new computer system or upgrade your hardware and software when you purchase a new version of Windows.

The Windows 95, Windows 98, and Windows ME Operating Systems

In the summer of 1995, Microsoft released Windows 95, the first Windows operating system, for home users. After being installed on a computer that already had an installed version of the DOS operating system, Windows 95 replaced DOS as the operating system. If the computer also included an installed version of a Windows operating environment, such as Windows 3.1, Windows 95 replaced that as well. Microsoft later introduced four other upgrades of Windows 95 that added support for newer types of hardware devices, included new or updated components, and provided fixes that corrected problems in earlier versions of Windows 95. For example, the OEM Service Release 2.1 update to Windows 95B in 1997 added basic support for USB devices, and later Windows versions increased support for USB. **OEM** stands for **Original Equipment Manufacturer**. **USB** (**Universal Serial Bus**) is a technology for the high-speed transfer of data between hardware devices. Over the years, USB became the standard for newer types of hardware devices, including flash drives, and it is still a reliable and widely used technology. Rapid changes in hardware and software technologies have been and remain an important driving force in developing new versions of the Windows operating system.

Windows 95 was also the first Internet-oriented operating system because it enabled millions of users to access the Internet and its benefits without having to know the details of how their computers and Windows operated. Windows 95 users were therefore among the first to access resources available on Internet and Web servers around the world and to exchange email. If you examine statistics on the growth of the Internet and the World Wide Web at Hobbe's Internet Timeline (*www.zakon.org/robert/internet/timeline/#Growth*), you will see that the rapid increase in Internet use occurred right after the introduction of Windows 95. The line charts in the next two figures were created by plotting information derived from that Web site. Although data is only available through the end of 2006, the data shows early trends in the growth of the Internet and World Wide Web. The chart in Figure 1-4 shows the growth of the Internet by plotting the number of computers on the Internet over time. As you can see, the sharp rise in the curve occurred right after Microsoft released Windows 95, which resulted in the wide-spread use and rapid development of the Internet. With its graphical user interface, Windows 95 simplified the process for connecting to the Internet. By double-clicking a desktop icon, a user connected to an online service and could then browse the Internet.

Figure 1-4   **Growth of the Internet**

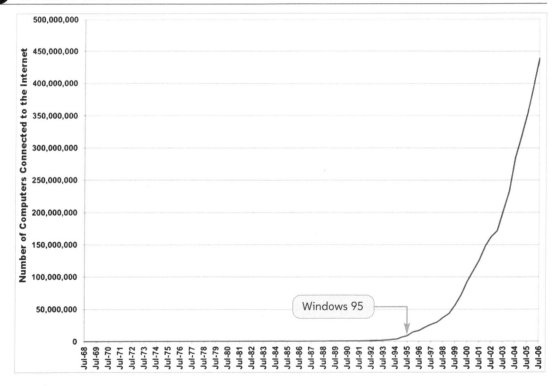

The chart in Figure 1-5 shows the growth of the World Wide Web, a component of the Internet, by plotting the number of Web sites over time.

Figure 1-5 **Growth of the World Wide Web**

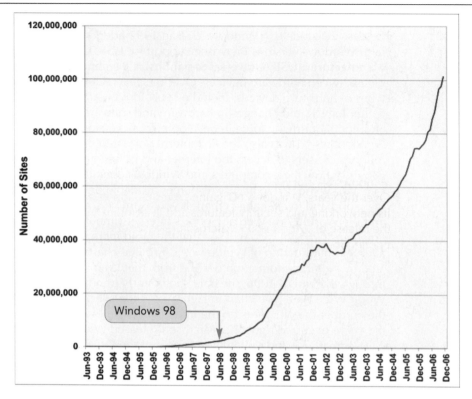

The rapid increase in the number of Web sites on the Internet occurred after Microsoft released Windows 98 and then Windows 2000. After the release of Windows 95, an increasing number of users learned how to navigate the Internet and use its resources, and then acquired the skills for designing Web pages and setting up Web sites. This rise in the number of Web sites peaked during the first half of 2002; after that, the number of Web sites declined briefly. The period from early 2000 to late 2003 is referred to as the dot-com crash. Many Internet companies went out of business because they were overvalued and were not showing a profit. By the end of 2002 and the beginning of 2003, the growth of the World Wide Web improved, and has continued to experience rapid growth.

In the summer of 1998, Microsoft released Windows 98 for home users. Like Windows 95, Windows 98 included support for newer types of hardware, such as DVD drives, and new Windows components and features, including utilities and tools for optimizing and troubleshooting your computer. Microsoft later released an improved edition of Windows 98 known as Windows SE (for *Second Edition*), which enabled Windows 98 to manage power to hardware devices. An **edition** is a different version of the same Windows operating system.

In late 2000, Microsoft introduced the Windows ME operating system, or Windows Millennium Edition, for home users. One of the important new features introduced in Windows ME was the System Restore utility. This utility periodically saved changes to system files, device drivers, and system settings on your computer system so that if you installed new software or made a change to your computer that created a problem, you could *roll back* your computer to the point just before you made these changes, and restore a previous configuration that worked without any problems, essentially undoing the changes you made. This feature was designed so that the average user could easily resolve a problem that occurred from a change to the computer system. Microsoft has retained the System Restore utility as an important component in Windows XP, Windows Vista, and Windows 7.

Windows 95, Windows 98, and Windows ME fall into a Microsoft product line called the **Windows 9x product line**. These Windows operating systems were designed for home users, and provided users with easy access to the Internet and multimedia content on their computer. Although these Windows operating systems supported basic networking, they lacked the networking and security features required by businesses and companies.

The Windows NT Workstation 4.0, Windows 2000, and Windows XP Operating Systems

In 1993, Microsoft introduced an advanced network operating system named Windows NT (for *New Technology*) that was primarily used by companies and businesses. Over the years, Windows NT gained a reputation in corporate and industrial circles for its networking and security features and its stability. In the summer of 1996, a year after the release of Windows 95, Microsoft released the Windows NT Workstation 4.0 network operating system for use on desktop computers. Microsoft adapted part of the Windows 95 interface and included many Windows 95 features in Windows NT Workstation 4.0. This version of the Windows operating system did not initially support the Plug-and-Play standard, had limited multimedia support, and did not support as many hardware devices as Windows 95. However, its release was important because it introduced a network operating system for use on desktop computers and, even more importantly, it served as the precursor to the Windows 2000 Professional operating system.

In early 2000, Microsoft introduced the Windows 2000 Professional operating system. Microsoft had originally planned to call this release Windows NT Workstation 5.0, because it was an upgrade to Windows NT Workstation 4.0. However, the release of this Windows operating system was delayed, and Microsoft eventually changed its name to Windows 2000 Professional Edition. The final Windows 2000 Professional operating system proved to be a powerful, reliable, and stable desktop network operating system, and many of its features are found in Windows XP, Windows Vista, and Windows 7.

The Windows XP (for *Experience*) operating system marked another important and major change in the development of the Windows operating system. Like all previous versions of the Windows operating system, Windows XP supported and enhanced many of the features found in earlier versions of Windows and introduced many new features. Over a 5-year period, Microsoft released six editions of Windows XP for home and business users, including two 64-bit editions for newer types of processors that appeared in the marketplace. Later in the tutorial, you will examine the differences and requirements of 32-bit and 64-bit computer systems.

Windows NT Workstation 4.0, Windows 2000 Professional, and Windows XP fall into a Microsoft product line called the **Windows NT product line** for business use. Over the years, Microsoft tried to combine the Windows 9x and Windows NT product lines into one product, and they finally succeeded with Windows XP.

The Windows Vista and Windows 7 Operating Systems

In January 2007, Microsoft released six editions of the Windows Vista operating system. In October 2009, Microsoft released five editions of the Windows 7 operating system for the United States and one version for emerging markets in other countries. Windows Vista and Windows 7 are closely related and share many common features and improvements over previous versions of Windows. Microsoft introduced a new user interface in Windows Vista called **Windows Aero**, and then redesigned and improved on the Windows Aero user interface in Windows 7. (You will examine Windows Aero in more detail in the next session.) Microsoft substantially improved the search capability in Windows Vista, and introduced the Preview pane, an innovative feature for viewing file content in a folder window without having to open the file. (Both features are covered in

Tutorial 3.) In Windows Vista, Microsoft also introduced an important new feature called Previous versions that allows you to restore previous versions of a file, a folder, or an entire drive (covered in Tutorial 10). The new Windows Recovery Environment (WinRE) provided a mechanism for analyzing and resolving Windows startup problems. A user complaint with Windows Vista was the frequent appearance of prompts to verify whether a user wanted to perform an operation that modified the computer system or the operating system. In Windows 7, Microsoft modified this security feature (covered in Tutorial 7) to reduce the number of prompts. Device driver support, perceived as a problem in Windows Vista, improved in later Windows Vista updates and in Windows 7.

Windows 7 includes the following editions:

- **Windows 7 Starter** is a simple-to-use edition designed for, and available only on, netbooks; it is intended for users who are primarily interested in browsing the Web, checking their email and using instant messaging.
- **Windows 7 Home Basic** is an edition customized for emerging markets.
- **Windows 7 Home Premium** is for home users who want to focus on and enjoy the multimedia capabilities of their computer; with this version, users can easily set up a home network and share pictures, music, and videos.
- **Windows 7 Professional** is designed for businesses users and for individuals who want access to more advanced Windows 7 features for use at home and at work.
- **Windows 7 Ultimate** is the most complete edition of Windows 7, designed for more advanced users and professionals.
- **Windows 7 Enterprise** is a complete edition of Windows 7, adapted to the needs of IT professionals and the needs of larger businesses and organizations.

Unlike Windows Vista, each Windows 7 edition (from top to bottom in the list above) not only contains new features, but also all features found in all prior editions. Also, the Windows 7 Starter Edition is equivalent to the Windows Vista Home Basic Edition, and the Windows 7 Home Basic Edition is equivalent to the Windows Vista Starter Edition.

PROSKILLS

Decision Making: Choosing a Windows 7 Edition

Before you purchase a computer, carefully evaluate the different editions of Windows 7. The edition you choose will depend on how you and others will use the computers; what features are needed to support the different types of applications and tasks you will perform; how much memory (or RAM) you need for resource-intensive applications and multitasking; what type of hardware is currently installed; and how the computer might be used in the foreseeable future. At the Microsoft Windows 7 Web site (*www.microsoft.com/windows/windows-7/default.aspx*), you can examine and compare the features of different Windows 7 editions. You can also identify what applications and hardware are currently supported by each edition. You can download and install a free copy of the Windows 7 Upgrade Advisor, and use that program on each of your computers to determine which Windows 7 edition will work best. The Upgrade Advisor also identifies hardware and software problems as well as system settings and other problems, such as the amount of available hard disk storage space, that determine whether you can upgrade from a previous version of Windows or from one Windows 7 edition to another. The Windows 7 Upgrade Advisor provides a 32-bit and a 64-bit report for upgrading with a 32-bit or 64-bit processor (covered in more detail later in the tutorial). You can also use the Upgrade Advisor to identify any problems on Windows 7 computers that you already have and which Windows 7 edition you can upgrade to.

By making use of the decision-making tools that Microsoft provides and carefully considering the current and future potential uses of your computer, you can ensure that you will make the right decision about which edition of Windows 7 will best suit your needs.

The Linux, Mac OS, and Unix Operating Systems

Two competitors to the Windows operating systems are Linux and the Mac OS. Linux is a free or low-cost PC operating system similar to the UNIX operating system, which is a multiuser, multitasking operating system that has played an important role in the development of the Internet. Like Windows, Linux has a graphical user interface with a desktop and an underlying powerful command-line interface. The Mac OS is a graphical user interface operating system designed for computers developed by Apple Corporation, and it contains features comparable to those found in the Windows operating system. The Mac OS X also contains a command-line operating system based on the UNIX operating system.

In this session, you examined the importance, and features of, operating system software. You examined the DOS operating system and its command-line interface, the Windows operating environments that relied on the DOS operating system, and the Windows operating systems from Windows 95 through Windows 7.

REVIEW

Session 1.1 Quick Check

1. A(n) _____ is a software product that manages all the operations that occur in a computer from the time you start your computer until you shut it down.

2. Objects have _____ and _____.

3. What type of user interface requires you to interact with the operating system by entering and executing commands at a command prompt?

4. What Windows 7 feature enables you to open more than one program and folder window at the same time?

5. A file's _____ is important to Windows because it identifies the type of file and the application you use to open the file.

6. True or False. When you print a document, the operating system uses a process called spooling to store the processed document in a temporary file on disk, and then transmits the spool file to the printer in the background.

7. Your computer's _____ consists of the operating system components and data structures that the operating system uses to keep track of all disks, drives, folders, files, and data on your computer.

8. What type of software does the operating system load to provide support for hardware devices and to enable the operating system to communicate with and manage those devices?

SESSION 1.2 VISUAL OVERVIEW

Use **smooth scaling** to adjust desktop and folder icon sizes.

Shake the title bar and **Aero Shake** minimizes all other windows.

Recycle Bin

Windows Aero supports **translucency**, or partial transparency, of window frames, window backgrounds, and icons.

« Pictu... ▸ Sample ...

Organize ▼   Preview ▼   Share

☆ Favorites
    Desktop
    Downloads
    Recent Places

    Libraries
    Documents
    Music
    Pictures
    Videos

    Homegroup

    Computer
    Local Disk (C:)
    Local Disk (D:)
    DVD RW Drive (F:) V
    CLASSES (G:)
    VERBATIM (J:)

Pictures
Sample Pictur

Chrysan

Hydra

Computer   Sample Music   Sample Pictu

Color hot-track displays a glow effect on taskbar buttons with one or more open windows.

Windows 7 uses **taskbar grouping** to group windows opened with the same program.

WINDOWS 7 DESKTOP

The **active window** is the current window in which you are working.

In Large icons view, **thumbnails** display a clear view of the contents of a file.

Aero Snap vertically resizes a window.

Live Taskbar Thumbnails display thumbnail previews of the contents of open windows, including live video.

Use the Show Desktop button to invoke **Aero Peek** and render all windows transparent.

The Windows 7 Desktop, Taskbar, and Start Menu

To support the ever-changing ways in which individuals use their computers, Microsoft has implemented some important changes to the graphical user interface and the desktop in Windows 7 to promote efficiency and productivity and to make using a computer more enjoyable.

In this session, you will examine the Windows 7 startup process and new features of the Windows 7 desktop, Start menu, and taskbar.

Logging On Your Computer

Now that Juliann has helped you install Windows 7 on your laptop, you are ready to log on to your computer and examine the Windows 7 desktop and graphical user interface.

The figures in this book are derived from a computer that uses the Windows 7 Ultimate Edition. If you are using another edition of Windows 7, then you may not have all the features covered in this textbook. If a feature is not available in another edition of Windows 7, then the tutorial instructions will note this fact where possible. Also, you may notice differences between your screen views and the figures. Even if your edition of Windows 7 does not have all the features described in this textbook, and even if your computer hardware does not support certain Windows 7 features, it's still important to know about those features so that you can make an informed decision when you upgrade your computer, purchase a new computer, or provide tech support to other users.

In the next set of steps, you log on to your computer. If you are working in a computer lab at your college, your instructor or technical support staff will explain how to log on to the computers in your computer lab. If you are working in a college computer lab, check the computer before you press the Power button to make sure it is not in the low-power Sleep state; otherwise, you might end up shutting the computer down. If you press a key on the keyboard or move the mouse, and if the computer is in the Sleep state, you will wake it up, and Windows 7 will restore power to the computer.

To log on to your computer:

▶ **1.** If your computer is turned off, power on your computer. During booting, you might see a splash logo for your computer's manufacturer. Then you will briefly see a progress indicator. The next screen displays the Windows 7 logo. Next, depending on how your computer is set up, Windows 7 may display a Welcome screen so you can select or enter your user account name and enter your password, or your Windows 7 computer may boot directly to the desktop.

Trouble? If you are working in a computer lab at your college, your instructor and technical support staff will tell you what user account and password, if any, you should use to log on to a computer.

▶ **2.** If Windows 7 displays a Welcome screen, click your **user account** icon (if required), enter your **password** (if necessary), and then click the **Next** button ➡. Figure 1-6 shows a view of the Windows 7 desktop.

Trouble? If your user logon account does not have a password, then Windows 7 automatically displays the Windows 7 desktop after you select your user logon account.

Trouble? If you type an incorrect password or mistype the password, Windows 7 informs you that your user name or password is incorrect. Click the OK button to continue. Windows 7 then displays the Password box so you can try again. It also displays your password hint under the Password box to help you recall your password, and it includes a link for resetting your password. Type your password correctly, and then click the Next button ➡.

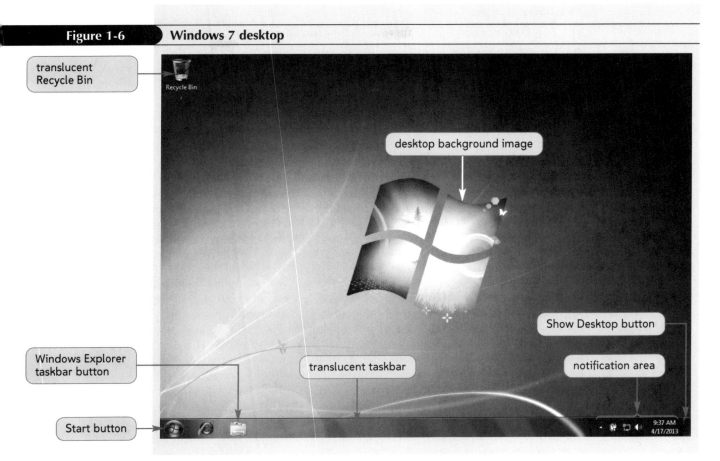

Figure 1-6   **Windows 7 desktop**

translucent Recycle Bin

desktop background image

Show Desktop button

Windows Explorer taskbar button

translucent taskbar

notification area

Start button

You may see a Switch User button for the Windows 7 Fast User Switching feature on the Welcome screen if more than one user has an account on the computer. **Fast User Switching** enables you to switch back to the Welcome screen without logging off your user account, and without closing any open programs or documents, so that you or someone else can log into another user account. Later, you can log back into your account and continue where you left off. All editions of Windows 7, except the Starter edition, support Fast User Switching Windows.

Exploring the Windows 7 Desktop

Like all other versions of the Windows operating system, the Windows 7 desktop is your starting point for accessing the resources and tools on your computer. In earlier versions of Windows, the image on the desktop was called wallpaper; however, in Windows 7, Microsoft refers to it as the **desktop background**. Although Windows 7 has a default image for the desktop background, you can change that image. Tutorial 2 shows you how to change your desktop background.

The icons that you see on the desktop depend on how you install Windows 7. If you upgrade from Windows Vista, your desktop should contain the same icons that it had prior to the upgrade. If you purchase a new computer with Windows 7, then the Recycle Bin is the only icon on the desktop, unless the manufacturer of your computer customized the desktop. Likewise, if you perform a **clean install** and erased everything on the hard drive where you installed Windows 7, then the only icon on the desktop is the Recycle Bin. As you install software and hardware, icons for opening those programs or for opening product documentation might also be placed on the desktop.

Windows 7 Aero

All of the Windows 7 editions, except the Starter and Home Basic Editions, support and improve on the Windows Aero user interface, which Microsoft introduced in Windows Vista. Windows Aero is hardware dependent, and if your computer hardware does not support Windows Aero, then Windows 7 adjusts the Windows Aero features in whole or in part.

In the Windows Aero user interface, elements of the graphical user interface—such as the taskbar, Start menu, windows, window frames, dialog boxes, some toolbars, and some toolbar buttons—are translucent, or partially transparent. Also, the Recycle Bin is partially translucent. That means that you can see the desktop background image under portions of the Recycle Bin icon. Furthermore, if you have multiple overlapping windows and if portions of those windows are translucent, you can view the background image through multiple windows. Windows Aero was also originally called **Aero Glass** because the translucency effects take on the appearance of translucent (or frosted) glass.

On computers that support Windows Aero, Windows 7 displays a shadow around windows and dialog boxes, animation effects (such as a window zooming out to a task-bar button as you minimize it), smooth scaling of icon sizes on the desktop and in folder windows, a glowing effect when you point to resizing buttons in a window or dialog box, and smooth visual refreshing (updating your view) of the Windows desktop.

If you open multiple application and folder windows, you can use two related Windows 7 features to view, locate, and select a window where you want to work. These two features are called Windows Flip and Aero Flip 3D. **Windows Flip** displays a pane with thumbnail views of open windows, including the desktop, while **Aero Flip 3D** (previously called Windows Flip 3D) displays a three-dimensional stacked view of open windows. To access each feature, you use a keyboard shortcut. A **keyboard shortcut** consists of one or more keys that provide an alternate method for performing a task. Individuals who are proficient at using a keyboard often prefer to use keyboard shortcuts rather than repeatedly move their right or left hand from the keyboard to the mouse and then back to the keyboard.

Juliann suggests that you try these features as she explains how to use them, starting with Windows Flip. First, you need to open a few windows.

To use Windows Flip:

▶ **1.** Close all open documents, applications, and windows.

▶ **2.** Click the **Windows Explorer** taskbar button 🔲, and then click the **Maximize** button 🔲 to maximize the Libraries window.

▶ **3.** Click the **Start** button 🔵, click **Control Panel**, and then click the **Maximize** button 🔲 (if necessary) to maximize the Control Panel window.

▶ **4.** Click the **Internet Explorer** button 🔵 on the taskbar to open an Internet Explorer window, click the **Maximize** button 🔲 (if necessary) to maximize the window, type **microsoft.com** in the Address bar, and then press the **Enter** key to navigate to the Microsoft Web site.

   Trouble? If Windows Internet Explorer is not installed on your computer, open your Web browser, maximize the Web browser window, type **microsoft.com** in the Address bar, and then press the **Enter** key to navigate to the Microsoft Web site.

▶ **5.** Move the mouse to the side of the desktop, press and hold the **Alt** key, and then press the **Tab** key. Windows 7 implements Windows Flip, and displays a pane with thumbnail views of each open window, and the desktop window. See Figure 1-7.

Figure 1-7	Invoking Windows Flip with Alt+Tab

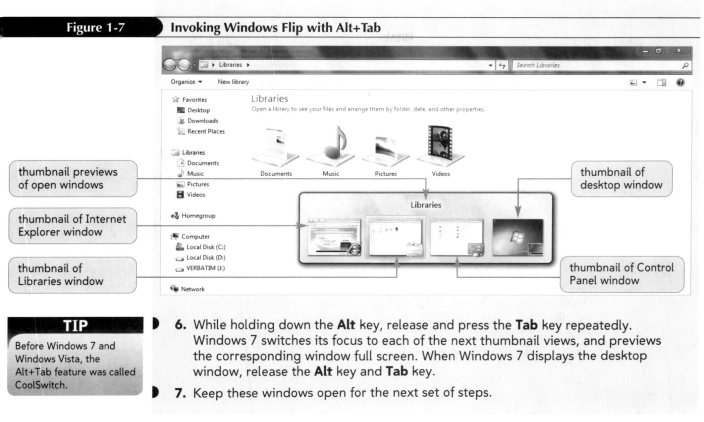

thumbnail previews of open windows

thumbnail of Internet Explorer window

thumbnail of Libraries window

thumbnail of desktop window

thumbnail of Control Panel window

TIP

Before Windows 7 and Windows Vista, the Alt+Tab feature was called CoolSwitch.

6. While holding down the **Alt** key, release and press the **Tab** key repeatedly. Windows 7 switches its focus to each of the next thumbnail views, and previews the corresponding window full screen. When Windows 7 displays the desktop window, release the **Alt** key and **Tab** key.

7. Keep these windows open for the next set of steps.

Another approach to selecting a window when using Windows Flip is to click one of the window thumbnails in the pane. If you want to view a full-screen preview of a window, then you can continue to hold down the Alt key while you use your mouse to point to each thumbnail. If you select the thumbnail of the desktop window, Windows 7 minimizes all open windows and returns to the desktop. You can use Windows Flip even if your Windows 7 version or your computer hardware does not support Windows Aero.

INSIGHT

Training New Computer Users

If you open multiple windows, the last window you open is the active window. If you click a visible portion of another window or click a taskbar button for a window that is hidden, that window comes to the foreground and becomes the active window. Other open windows are inactive windows. Windows 7 provides the active window with more resources than the inactive windows.

When training new computer users, it's important to point out not only what happens when you open and work with multiple windows, but also how to select another window that is not visible by using the taskbar button for that window. If a new user does not know how to find an open but not visible window, then they are likely to open the same window multiple times. By carefully explaining and demonstrating how to work with multiple windows and the corresponding taskbar buttons, you can ensure that new users are productive and have a good experience using Windows 7.

All the tutorials in this book include reference windows, like the one following this paragraph, that summarize what you performed in the previous set of numbered steps. Do not keystroke the steps listed in a reference window. Instead, you can use the reference windows later to quickly remind you of how to perform an operation.

REFERENCE

Using Windows Flip

- Open two or more application, folder, or document windows.
- Press and hold the Alt key and then press the Tab key to display a pane with thumbnail views of open windows and the desktop.
- While holding down the Alt key, release and press the Tab key repeatedly to switch focus to each of the next thumbnail views one at a time and preview each window full screen. Release the Alt key and Tab key to make the last window you select the current window.

or

- To preview each window full screen, continue to hold down the Alt key while you use your mouse to point to each thumbnail. Click one of the window thumbnails while you are holding down the Alt key to make that window the current window.
- If you select the thumbnail of the desktop window, then Windows 7 minimizes all open windows and returns to the desktop.

Next, try Aero Flip 3D. As its name suggests, this feature requires that your Windows 7 edition and your computer's hardware support Windows Aero.

To use Aero Flip 3D:

TIP

To identify the Windows key, look for the key with the Windows logo.

1. Click the **Windows Explorer** taskbar button 🖿 to restore the Libraries window.

2. Press and hold the **Windows** key, and then press the **Tab** key. Aero Flip 3D stacks all open windows, including the desktop window, at a three-dimensional angle on the desktop so that you can see more of the content of each of the windows, and select the window in which you want to work. See Figure 1-8.

Figure 1-8 Aero Flip 3D

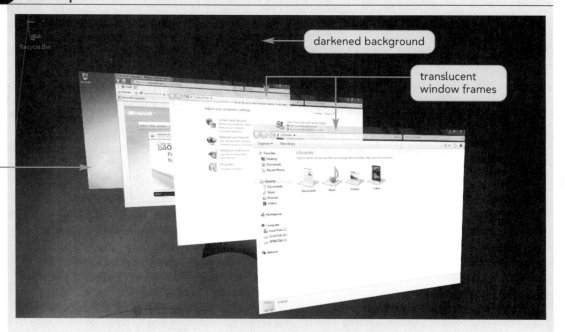

darkened background

translucent window frames

desktop window

The translucency of window borders and frames allows you to see through one window onto part of the next window, improving your view of all the windows. Furthermore, you can use your mouse scroll wheel to advance the windows forwards or backwards in the stack.

▶ **3.** While holding down the **Windows** key, release and press the **Tab** key repeatedly to adjust the view of the windows in the three-dimensional stack. Each time you press the Tab key, the first window moves to the back of the stack and each of the other windows move forward one window. If you release the Windows key, the window at the front of the stack becomes the current window.

▶ **4.** While still holding down the **Windows** key, move your mouse scroll wheel one notch *toward* you. The first window moves to the bottom of the stack and the next window moves to the front of the stack. If you keep moving the mouse scroll wheel toward you, you continue to scroll forward one window at a time and you can view each window at the front of the stack. Again, if you release the Windows key, the window at the front of the stack becomes the current window. Furthermore, you can move your mouse scroll wheel away from you to scroll backward one window at a time.

▶ **5.** Release the Windows key when the Libraries window is at the front of the stack.

Windows Vista contained a "Switch between windows" button on the Quick Launch toolbar to activate Windows Flip 3D, but Windows 7 no longer contains a Quick Launch toolbar.

REFERENCE

Using Aero Flip 3D

• Open two or more application, folder, or document windows.
• Press and hold the Windows key, and then press and hold the Tab key.
• While holding down the Windows key, release and press the Tab key repeatedly to switch to each of the next stacked windows and view a preview. Release the Windows and Tab keys so that the window at the front of the stack becomes the current window.

or

• While still holding down the Windows key, move your mouse scroll wheel one notch toward you to move the first window to the bottom of the stack and move all other windows forward, or move your mouse scroll wheel one notch away from you to scroll backward one window at a time. Release the Windows key so that the window at the front of the stack becomes the current window.

Another new Windows 7 feature is Aero Peek, which allows you to view the contents of the desktop, including gadgets, even if you have open windows on the desktop. **Gadgets**, first introduced in Windows Vista, are miniprograms that run on your desktop and that display easily accessible tools and information. When you use Aero Peek, each open window appears transparent so that you can see what's behind the window. This feature requires that your Windows 7 edition and computer hardware support Windows Aero.

To use Aero Peek:

1. Click the **taskbar** buttons for any minimized windows to restore those windows on the desktop, click the **Restore Down** button 🔲 for each of the three windows, and then drag each window's title bar to arrange the windows randomly around the desktop.

2. Point to the **Show desktop** button ▌ on the far-right side of the taskbar. Aero Peek changes the windows so they become translucent. See Figure 1-9.

| Figure 1-9 | Aero Peek |

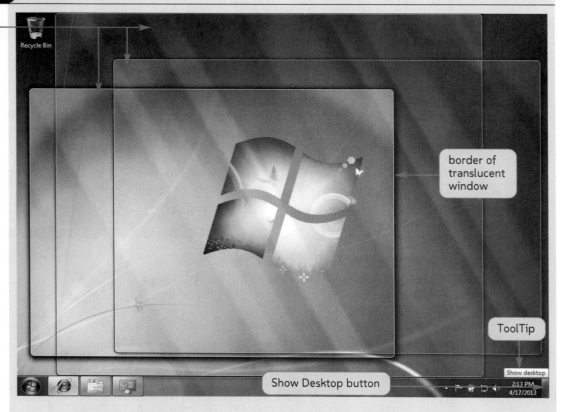

translucent windows

border of translucent window

ToolTip

Show Desktop button

Note that you can still see the faint outlines of the windows.

You may also see the "Show desktop" ToolTip. A **ToolTip** is a label Windows 7 displays when you point to an object that identifies the name of the object or explains its purpose. If you point to an object in an application window, such as a button, then the label displayed is called a **ScreenTip**.

To redisplay the windows, and then minimize all open windows:

1. Move your mouse pointer away from the Show desktop button ▌. Now you see the windows.

2. Click the **Show desktop** button ▌. Windows 7 minimizes all windows. You can also minimize all windows by pressing Windows+M. Windows+D also minimizes all windows, and if you press Windows+D again, Windows 7 restores all windows.

3. Click the **Show desktop** button ▌ again. Windows 7 restores all windows.

4. Keep the windows open for the next set of steps.

To turn off the Aero Peek feature, right-click the taskbar, click Properties, remove the check mark from the "Use Aero Peek to preview the desktop" check box on the Taskbar property sheet in the Taskbar and Start Menu Properties dialog box, and then apply the change with the OK button.

REFERENCE

Using Aero Peek

- Point to the Show desktop button on the far-right side of the taskbar so that all windows become translucent.
- Move your mouse pointer away from the Show desktop button to display the windows.
- Click the Show desktop button to minimize all windows.
- Click the Show desktop button again to restore all windows.

Aero Shake is another new Windows 7 feature that helps you position windows on the desktop so that you can see more of the contents of the window and work more easily. Aero Shake quickly minimizes (or restores) every open window except the active window when you shake the active window's title bar with your mouse.

To use Aero Shake:

1. If necessary, click the **Libraries** taskbar button ⊞ to bring the Libraries window to the foreground.

2. Point to the **Libraries window** title bar, hold down the mouse button, and quickly shake the window. Windows 7 minimizes all other open windows.

3. Again, point to the **Libraries window** title bar, hold down the mouse button, and quickly shake the window. Windows 7 restores all minimized windows.

The keyboard shortcut for these two operations is Windows+Home.

Another useful window management feature is Aero Snap, also just called Snap. This new Windows 7 feature allows you to quickly dock and resize windows in one of several different ways so that you can work more easily in one or two windows. First, use Aero Snap to dock a window.

To use Aero Snap to dock a window on the side of the desktop:

1. Close the Internet Explorer and Control Panel windows by clicking the **Close** button [X] on each window's title bar.

2. Point to the left side of the **Libraries window** title bar, hold down the mouse button, and drag the window's title bar to the left edge of the desktop, and then release the mouse when the mouse pointer reaches the desktop edge. Windows 7 places the window on the left side of the desktop and adjusts its size so that it fills up one-half of the desktop. See Figure 1-10.

    Trouble? If Windows 7 did not dock the window on the left side of the desktop, repeat Step 2, but make sure that the tip of the mouse pointer is at the edge of the desktop before you release the mouse button.

TIP

You can also right-click the taskbar and click "Show windows side by side" to achieve the same effect with two windows.

Figure 1-10	Aero Snap

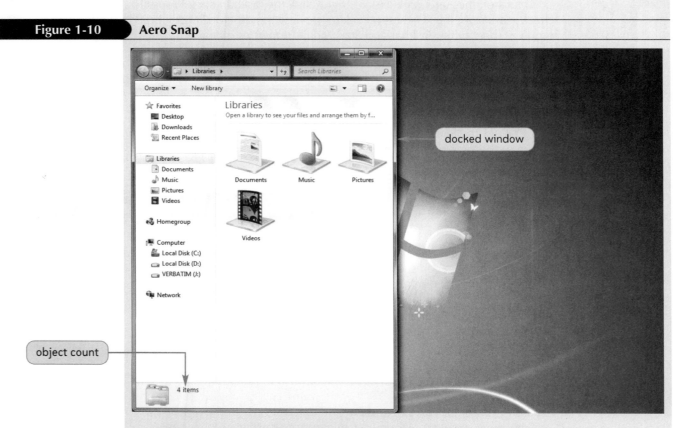

If you had a second window open, you could use Aero Snap to dock that window on the right side of the window and at the same time resize that window so that each of the two windows were side by side and equal in size.

3. Drag the **Libraries window** title bar away from the edge of the screen where the window is docked. Windows 7 restores the window.

The corresponding keyboard shortcuts for these two operations are Windows+left arrow and Windows+right arrow. If you hold down the Windows key and then keep pressing the right arrow or left arrow key, then Windows 7 cycles through three different window states: docking on one side of the desktop, restoring the window to its original size and placement, and docking on the other side of the desktop.

You can also use Aero Snap to maximize a window vertically. If you just use the Maximize button to maximize a window, that window fills the entire desktop; however, on computers with very wide flat screen monitors, the window may be far wider than you need. Instead, you may want to adjust the window so that it stays the same width but extends from the top of the desktop to the bottom of the desktop.

To use Aero Snap to vertically resize a window:

▶ **1.** Point to the very **top edge** of the Libraries window, and when the mouse pointer changes to a double-headed arrow pointing up and down ⇕, drag the **title bar** to the very top edge of the desktop, and then release the mouse button. Windows 7 then vertically resizes the window. See Figure 1-11.

Trouble? If you already tested the Windows+left arrow technique described before these steps, your Libraries window may already be vertically resized. Use the Windows+left arrow to undock the window, and repeat Step 1.

Figure 1-11	Aero Snap

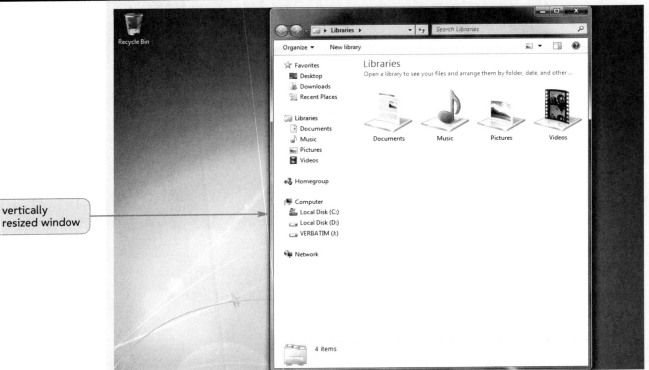

vertically resized window

With the increased height, you can see more of the contents of the window while keeping the window the same width. Like the option for docking a window on one side of the desktop, you have to make sure that you see a double-headed arrow ⇕ at the top edge of the window before you drag the window to the top of the desktop.

▶ **2.** To restore the window to its previous size and location on the desktop, point to the **top** of the window, and when the mouse pointer changes to a double-headed arrow pointing up and down ⇕, drag the window away from the top edge of the desktop.

▶ **3.** Close the Libraries window.

Windows 7 Help and Support notes that the Aero Snap feature might not work on some program windows, because those programs may have customized windows behaviors or settings.

REFERENCE

Using Aero Snap

- To dock a window on one side of the desktop and adjust its size so that it fills half of the desktop, point to the title bar of the window, hold down the mouse button, and drag the window's title bar to the left or right edge of the desktop and then release the mouse when the mouse pointer reaches the desktop edge. Repeat the same procedure to dock and resize a second window on the other side of the desktop. To restore a docked window, drag the title bar away from the edge of the screen where the window is docked.
- To maximize a window vertically, point to the very top edge of a desktop window, and when the mouse pointer changes to a double-headed arrow pointing up and down, drag the title bar to the very top edge of the desktop, and then release the mouse button. To restore the window to its previous size and location on the desktop, point to the top of the window, and when the mouse pointer changes to a double-headed arrow pointing up and down, drag the window away from the top edge of the desktop.

Because Windows Aero supports the smooth scaling of icon sizes on the desktop and in folder windows, you have greater control over adjusting icon sizes.

By default, desktop icons are set to a size called Medium icons; however, you can change this setting. Like every other software product that you use, Windows 7 uses predefined built-in settings, or **default settings**, that Microsoft assumes most individuals are likely to use and that the majority of businesses are likely to prefer. This in turn saves time and effort because these settings do not have to be changed.

Juliann recommends that you examine different desktop icon sizes to determine which settings work best for your job.

To change desktop icon sizes:

1. Right-click the **desktop background**, and point to **View** on the shortcut menu. The first three options on the cascading View menu—Large icons, Medium icons, and Small icons—determine icon sizes.

2. Click **Large icons**. Windows 7 increases the size of the desktop icons. On computers that support this feature, the translucency of desktop icons is more evident at this larger size. The simple action of right-clicking the desktop enables you to change a property of the desktop. See Figure 1-12.

| Figure 1-12 | Using Large Icons size for desktop icon |

resized translucent
Recycle Bin icon

Trouble? If your Recycle Bin is full, and if you want to empty the Recycle Bin so that you can observe its translucency at this icon size, right-click the Recycle Bin, and then click Empty Recycle Bin.

▶ **3.** Right-click the **desktop background**, point to **View** on the shortcut menu, and then click **Medium icons**. Windows 7 restores the default size of the desktop icons. The other View menu option, Small icons, reduces the size of the desktop icons to a very small size.

You can also use your mouse scroll wheel to adjust icon sizes along a continuum, or range, of sizes.

To adjust icon sizes with your mouse:

▶ **1.** Click the **desktop background**, hold down the **Ctrl** key (called the Control key) on the left side of the keyboard, and then move the mouse wheel one notch at a time *away* from you. Windows 7 gradually increases the size of the desktop icons. Figure 1-13 shows the Recycle Bin icon at its maximum size.

| Figure 1-13 | Desktop icon size increased with Ctrl key and mouse wheel |

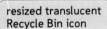

resized translucent Recycle Bin icon

Recycle Bin

By clicking the desktop background first, you changed the focus from wherever you last clicked to the desktop. By using the Ctrl key with the mouse scroll wheel, you have more flexibility in adjusting desktop icon sizes, and you can adjust icon sizes so that they are larger or smaller than what is available on the View short-cut menu.

▶ **2.** Click the **desktop background**, hold down the **Ctrl** key, and then move the mouse wheel one notch at a time *towards* you. Windows 7 gradually decreases the size of the desktop icons.

▶ **3.** To restore the default icon size, right-click the **desktop background**, point to **View** on the shortcut menu, and then click **Medium icons**.

You can use the Show desktop icons option on the View menu to turn off the display of all desktop icons so that you can view the desktop background, including any video that is running, and you can use this menu option to redisplay hidden desktop icons.

REFERENCE

Changing and Restoring Desktop Icon Sizes

- Right-click the desktop background, point to View on the shortcut menu, and click Large icons or Small icons.
- To restore desktop icon sizes, right-click the desktop background, point to View on the shortcut menu, and then click Medium icons.

or

- Click the desktop background, hold down the Ctrl key, and move the mouse wheel one notch at a time away from you to increase icon sizes or towards you to decrease icon sizes.
- To restore default desktop icon sizes, right-click the desktop background, point to View on the shortcut menu, and then click Medium icons.

Windows 7 automatically aligns icons to an invisible desktop grid so that icons are arranged evenly in columns and rows on the desktop. You can turn off the "Align icons to grid" option on the View menu so that you can place icons anywhere you want on the desktop. You can also use this same menu option to automatically realign desktop icons to the invisible desktop grid. If you enable the "Auto arrange icons" option on the View menu, Windows 7 arranges icons in columns from the left side to the right side of the desktop; with this option, you cannot move desktop icons to another location on the desktop away from the column arrangement. If you try, the icons automatically snap back to the left side of the desktop. However, you can move one icon and place it above another icon within a column. If you turn off this option by choosing it again, then you can reposition icons wherever you want on the desktop.

The Windows 7 Taskbar

One of the new features in Windows 7 is the change in the design and use of the Windows taskbar. Microsoft has made several major changes to the taskbar:

- **Icon sizes**—Icon sizes are larger than those found in previous versions of Windows.
- **Translucency**—If your edition of Windows 7 and your hardware support Windows Aero, the taskbar and taskbar buttons are partially translucent.
- **Color hot-track**—If you point to the Start button or a taskbar button for an open window, you see a glowing effect called Color hot-track. In the case of a taskbar button, the glowing color matches the predominant color of the icon on the button. The glowing effect is more evident for certain taskbar buttons. If you open a window from a taskbar button, the glowing effect disappears, but the taskbar button is still highlighted to indicate that the window is open. These features help you more easily locate taskbar buttons.
- **New taskbar button functionality**—Unlike previous versions of Windows, the Windows 7 taskbar does not display a button for each and every program, folder window, and document you open. Instead, similar types of windows are grouped together by program and are accessed via a single taskbar button. For example, the Windows Explorer button provides access to any and all open folder windows. If you click a taskbar button that has only one open window, then Windows 7 switches to that window. If you have opened multiple windows with the same program, and then click (or point to) that button, then you will see Live Taskbar Thumbnails (discussed next) so that you can pick which window to open for that program.
- **Live Taskbar Thumbnails**—If you minimize a window, you can point to the taskbar button for the program associated with that window, and Windows 7 will display a thumbnail preview of the window's contents with a label above the thumbnail that contains the name of the window or, in the case of a document window, the

document's filename and the program name. The thumbnail view is called a Live Taskbar Thumbnail (first introduced in Windows Vista, but enhanced in Windows 7). If you open several windows with the same program, and then point to the taskbar button for the program that opened those windows, Windows 7 displays a thumbnail for each open window (a feature not found in Windows Vista). If you point to a thumbnail, then Windows 7 displays a full-screen preview of the contents of that window (also new to Windows 7). If the window contains live content, such as video, Windows 7 plays back the video in the Live Taskbar Thumbnail. If Windows 7 displays thumbnails for several open windows, you can slide your mouse from one thumbnail to the next to preview the contents of each window. In Figure 1-14, Windows 7 displays Live Taskbar Thumbnails for three windows—the Sample Videos, Sample Pictures, and Sample Music folders.

| Figure 1-14 | Live Taskbar Thumbnail preview of minimized windows |

This figure shows the Sample Pictures window in the background so that you can compare views and verify that the Live Taskbar Thumbnail preview matches the contents of the window. If you minimize the Sample Pictures window and then point to the taskbar button for this window, you will see the Live Taskbar Thumbnails for all three windows. If you click one of the Live Taskbar Thumbnails, then you open the window. If you click the Live Taskbar Thumbnail Close button, then Windows 7 closes the window and the Live Taskbar Thumbnail Preview for that window.

- **Jump Lists**—If you right-click a taskbar button (or drag up on a taskbar button), then Windows 7 displays a jump list. A **jump list** is a menu that provides quick access to recently or frequently opened objects (such as a list of frequently opened windows, a list of recently opened documents for a specific program, or a list of frequently accessed Web sites), a list of tasks for a program (such as opening a new tab in a Web browser or playing music), the program, an option to pin or unpin a program from the taskbar, and an option to close a window or all windows. Figure 1-15 shows the Jump List for the Windows Explorer taskbar button. This feature in part replaces the Recent Documents option on the Start menu in previous versions of Windows and allows you to focus on program-specific files (such as all Microsoft Word files).

Figure 1-15   Taskbar button Jump List

The Windows 7 **notification area** shows the current date and time, a volume icon for adjusting the volume of speakers, a Network icon for showing the status of your network, and an Action Center button for displaying messages, notifications, and reminders. The Show Hidden Icons button displays a pop-up pane with icons for specific programs, such as the Safely Remove Hardware and Eject Media icon, and icons for other programs that you can access from this pane. To access information, options, settings, and properties for each button, you can click or right-click the button. As noted earlier, on the far-right side of the taskbar is the Show desktop button.

The Windows 7 Start Menu

Like Windows Vista, the Windows 7 Start menu contains two panes, each separated into groups. See Figure 1-16.

Figure 1-16   Start menu Jump Lists

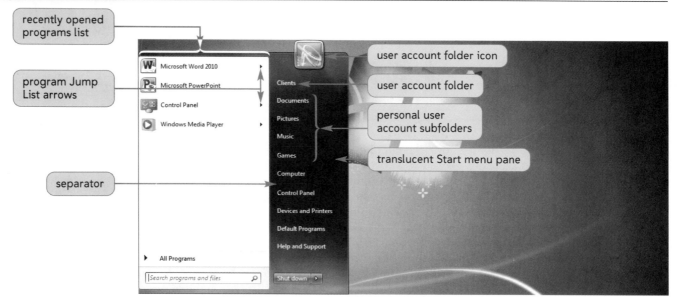

The left pane of the Start menu contains a list of recently used programs so that you can quickly return to a program you've used previously. The right pane of the Start menu contains three groups of options separated by a thin line called a **separator**. In the first group at the top right of this pane, Windows 7 displays options for opening some of your personal folders—Documents, Pictures, and Music. The very first option is the name of your user account folder. If you click your user account name, then Windows 7 opens your user account folder, and displays within that folder all your personal folders—Contacts, Desktop, Downloads, Favorites, Links, My Documents, My Music, My Pictures, My Videos, Saved Games, and Searches. See Figure 1-17. All of these folders are discussed in detail in Tutorial 3.

Figure 1-17 **User account folders**

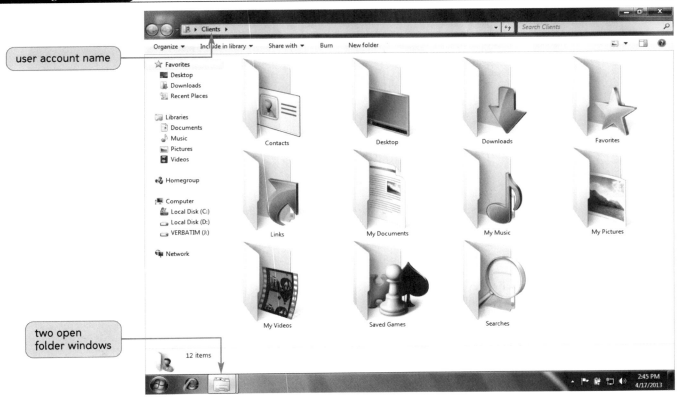

The second group on the Start menu contains links to the Games and Computer folders while the third group contains links to folders for system tools—the Control Panel, Devices and Printers, Default Programs, and Help and Support.

If you point to a program on the Start menu that you've previously opened and pause, then Windows 7 displays a Jump List in the right pane of the Start menu with shortcuts to files you've recently opened in that application, affording yet another easy way to access files with which you frequently work. (You can also point to the Jump List arrow button to immediately display the Jump List.) You can easily identify programs that have a Jump List because they contain a Jump List button to the right of the program. If you want to pin a file in the Jump List so that it is always available from the Jump List, point to the file and then click the Pin button to the right of the filename. Then you will see a new Pinned section on the Jump List with the name of the file you pinned. The items found on the Start menu Jump Lists for a specific program are the same as those on the taskbar Jump Lists for that same program.

When you point to All Programs at the bottom of the left pane, Windows 7 changes the left pane of the Start menu to display a list of individual programs in alphabetical order, followed by **group folders** that contain one or more programs for each software product you install on your computer. In Windows 7 (and Windows Vista), you do not see menus cascade to the right as you point to options on the All Programs menu. If you click a group folder for a specific software product, such as Microsoft Office, then Windows 7 expands the group and displays the programs included with that software product. See Figure 1-18.

Figure 1-18   Viewing the All Programs menu

If you find that you consistently use the same programs, you can pin, or attach, the programs to an area at the top of the left pane called the **Pinned items list** by right-clicking the program on the All Programs menu, or even the recently used programs list, and then choosing "Pin to Start Menu." Later, if you want to remove a program from the pinned items list, right-click the program in the pinned items list, and then click "Unpin from Start Menu."

At the bottom of the Start menu is a Search box for quickly locating programs, folders, and files on your computer using a feature called Instant Search. Like its name suggests, you can use this enhanced search feature in Windows 7 to quickly locate programs and files on your computer, so you can focus on getting your work done rather than waiting for Windows to find what you need. The Search feature also searches for email messages, saved instant messages, appointments, and contacts. Instant Search is the focus of Tutorial 3.

You can display icons for your user account folder as well as the Computer and the Control Panel on the desktop. The Computer window is an important resource because it displays a list of your hard drives and your removable disk drives, and allows you to access those drives. If there is no Computer icon on your desktop, complete the following steps to add the icon to your desktop. If you already have a Computer icon on the desktop, read, but do not keystroke, the following steps.

To place a Computer icon on the desktop:

1. Click the **Start** button 🔵 on the taskbar, and then right-click **Computer** on the Start menu. Windows 7 displays a shortcut menu for this object.

2. Click **Show on Desktop**, and then click the **Start** button 🔵 a second time to close the Start menu. Windows 7 now displays a Computer icon on the desktop.

TIP

You can also open and close the Start menu by pressing the Windows key.

If you later want to remove the Computer icon from the desktop, repeat the same steps to turn off this feature. The "Show on Desktop" option on the Computer's shortcut menu allows you to **toggle**, or switch, between displaying and not displaying the Computer icon. If you enable the option for displaying the Computer icon, and then display the Computer icon shortcut menu again, you'll notice that the option has a check mark next to it, indicating that it is enabled. If you turn off this feature, and then display the Computer icon shortcut menu, no check mark appears next to "Show on Desktop," indicating that this feature is turned off.

Using Single-Click Activation

By default, Windows 7, and all previous versions of Windows, are set up so that if you want to open a desktop object, folder, or file, you have to double-click the icon for the object. In contrast, if you single-click a desktop object, folder, or file, then Windows 7 selects that object. After you select an object, you can then perform some type of operation on the object such as moving, copying, renaming, or deleting the object. This way of using the mouse is the classic way in which most people typically use a mouse on their local computer system (and therefore it is part of what is referred to as **Classic Style** in earlier versions of Windows), but it's not the way that people use the mouse when they browse the Web. On the Web, if you want to go to a new Web page, you can single-click the link to that Web page. You don't have to double-click the link. Two questions immediately arise, "Why do I have to use two different ways of working with the mouse? Why can't I work with the objects on a local computer in the same way that I browse the Web?"

Windows 7, and previous versions of Windows, have an option called **single-click activation** that enables you to browse your local computer in the same way you browse the Web. After you enable this feature, you can use the same set of skills on your local computer that you use on the Web. If you want to open a desktop object, folder, or file, you simply single-click the object, folder, or file. If you want to select an object, folder, or file, you just point to (or hover above) the object, folder, or file. By using this feature, you eliminate almost all double-clicking, which some users find difficult anyway. You also eliminate all the single-clicking that you used to do when you selected an object. Most individuals do not realize the inordinate amount of double-clicking and single-clicking that they perform while working on a computer. By reducing the amount of double-clicking and single-clicking that you perform, you can save wear and tear on the muscles, tendons, and nerves in your hand, wrist, arm, and shoulder, thus reducing the chance of some type of permanent injury. Because single-click activation is similar to the way in which you browse the Web, it is part of what is referred to as **Web Style** that was introduced in earlier versions of Windows. Single-click activation makes navigating your computer simple and easy.

There are two ways to switch to Web Style:

- **Control Panel**—The Control Panel is a commonly used Windows tool for changing Windows settings. You can use the Folder Options link in the Appearance and Personalization section of the Control Panel to enable single-click activation on your computer. Once opened, this dialog box has three tabs for three different groups of settings—General, View, and Search. Each tab displays a group of related settings on what's called a **property sheet**. The General tab displays the General property sheet with the option for enabling single-click activation.
- **Folder window**—If you open any folder window, including a Computer window, you can click Organize on the **toolbar** (previously called the command bar in Windows Vista), and then click "Folder and search options" to access the General property sheet in the Folder Options dialog box.

Whichever approach you use to open the Folder Options dialog box, you then find that the option under the "Click items as follows" section labeled "Double-click to open (single-click to select)" is enabled by default for all versions of Windows.

If you work on a laptop, you may find that your mouse pointer automatically opens whatever you select, and therefore you could continue to work in Classic Style.

Juliann recommends that you try Web style and decide whether you can work more easily on your computer.

To enable single-click activation:

1. Click the **Start** button 🔵 on the taskbar, and then click **Control Panel**. Windows 7 opens the Control Panel window.

2. Click the **Appearance and Personalization** link. Windows 7 opens the Appearance and Personalization window.

3. Under Folder Options, click the **Specify single- or double-click to open** link. Windows 7 opens the Folder Options dialog box and displays the contents of the General property sheet. See Figure 1-19.

Figure 1-19 **Folder Options dialog box**

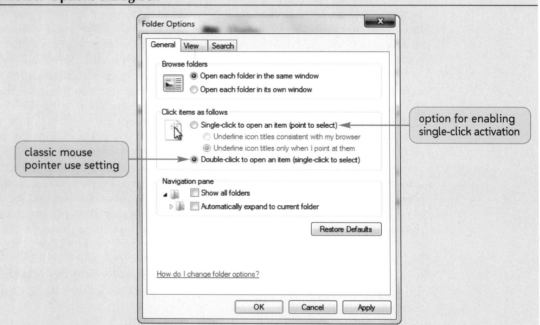

4. Under "Click items as follows" on the General property sheet, click the **Single-click to open an item (point to select)** option button if it is not already selected.

   As soon as you enable this option, two additional options under this setting become available. If you enable the option labeled "Underline icon titles consistent with my browser", then the icon titles for all desktop objects, folder icons, and file icons are underlined, similar to links on Web pages. The second option, labeled "Underline icon titles only when I point to them", only displays the underline when you point to a desktop object, folder icon, or file icon, and therefore does not change your view on your screen.

5. Click the **Underline icon titles only when I point at them** option button if it is not already selected, and then click the **OK** button.

6. Close the Appearance and Personalization window.

7. Point to, and rest the mouse pointer, on the **Computer** icon on the desktop. Windows 7 selects and highlights the Computer icon, and then displays an underline under the icon title. See Figure 1-20. The mouse pointer shapes changes to a Link Select pointer shape.

Figure 1-20	Using Web style

Link Select mouse pointer shape

point to select object

Note that you did not need to click the icon to select it. Also note that the mouse pointer appears as a hand with a finger pointing to the link, just as it does when you point to a link on a Web page.

▶ **8.** Click the **Computer** icon. Windows 7 opens a Computer window with a single-click.

▶ **9.** Close the Computer window.

Working in Web style with single-click activation is far easier than using the traditional Windows Classic Style. Furthermore, objects on your computer, such as desktop icons, folder icons, and files become links that require only one click to open. That means you navigate and open files the same way that you click links on a Web page.

REFERENCE

Using the Control Panel to Enable Single-Click Activation

- Click the Start button, and then click Control Panel.
- In the Control Panel window, click the Appearance and Personalization link.
- In the Appearance and Personalization window, click the blue "Specify single- or double-click to open" link under Folder Options.
- On the General property sheet, click the "Single-click to open an item (point to select)" option.
- Click the "Underline icon titles only when I point at them" option button, and then click the OK button.
- Close the Appearance and Personalization window.

At the beginning of every tutorial, you switch to single-click activation, and at the end of every tutorial, you restore double-click activation, so that other individuals who work in the same college computer lab and who are not familiar with this feature, are not affected. If you work on your own computer and prefer single-click activation, then you do not need to restore double-click activation on your computer.

Using Windows Help and Support

In her Windows 7 orientation, Juliann points out to employees that the **Windows Help and Support** center is a great resource for exploring Windows 7 features, finding quick answers to how-to questions, and accessing invaluable online resources. Windows Help and Support replaces the use of printed manuals and provides tools for locating online Help.

After you open Windows Help and Support, you can use the following techniques to locate information you need:

- **Use Help links**—After you open Windows Help and Support, you can use Help links to locate information on how to get started on your computer, learn about Windows Basics, or Browse Help topics. A **Help link** is similar to a link on a Web page, and therefore only requires a single click. If you use the Browse Help topics link, you will see a table of contents with a set of broad Help subject headings. If you click the link for one of these Help subject headings, then you will see links to a specific topic, such as "Working with files and folders," and to additional subject headings. By using this approach, you start with a general Help category, locate a more-specific Help category, and then choose a specific Help topic that provides you with the information you need. You can also use the Browse Help button on the Windows Help and Support toolbar to view a table of contents. These approaches are useful if you want to examine all the Help information related to a specific feature in an organized way, but it can take more time than other techniques to locate the Help you need because you may end up selecting one Help topic after another until you find what you want.
- **Search Help**—Searching Windows Help and Support is the fastest way to find Help information. You use one or more descriptive words called **keywords**, such as *Windows Aero*, to obtain a list of search results for all the Help topics that include the word or phrase you specified. This approach is similar to using an Internet search engine.
- **Ask button**—The Ask button on the Windows Help and Support toolbar displays more support options, such as using Windows Remote Assistance to get help from a friend over the Internet, asking experts and other Windows users at the Microsoft Answers Web site, by contacting technical support or customer support, by using the Windows Web site, and by using the Microsoft TechNet Web site for in-depth technical information.

PROSKILLS

Teamwork and Problem Solving: Using Remote Assistance

If you click the Ask button on the Windows Help and Support window toolbar, you can access and use a Windows 7 feature called **Remote Assistance** to obtain help from a coworker or expert, offer help to someone else, or work collaboratively on a team project using another computer. In a large business environment, Help Desk staff use Remote Assistance to help users with problems. To troubleshoot a problem or collaborate with a coworker, you can initiate a Remote Assistance session over the Internet or a network using the Easy Connect option within Remote Assistance or by using an invitation file. Easy Connect requires that both individuals have a Windows 7 computer. If one of the individuals has a computer with a different Windows version, then the person seeking help (called the User, or Novice) must extend an invitation to another person (called the Helper, or Expert) via email or by placing an invitation file in a network location. In both cases, a password is sent to the other person who then uses the password to make a connection to your computer. After a connection is established between the two computers, the other person can view your computer screen, use your computer to troubleshoot a problem, or work collaboratively on a project file on your computer. Using Easy Connect, you can build up a contact list to more easily access and work with other people.

You can also access Remote Assistance from the Maintenance group folder on the All Programs menu. If you search Windows Help for information on Remote Assistance, you will find a link to a video at the Microsoft Web site that describes the use of Remote Assistance.

By using Remote Assistance, you can more efficiently help coworkers in the same or a different location solve problems and improve teamwork by working together. You can also use Remote Assistance to support and collaborate online with clients.

Browsing and Searching Online Help

If Windows Help and Support is set to use Online Help, then Windows Help and Support searches online at the Microsoft Web site for Help information. You can also use Windows Help and Support to get online help from other Windows users, search the Microsoft Windows Web site, and invite someone to help you using Remote Assistance. In the latter case, you must configure Remote Assistance before you use it.

TIP

To open Windows Help and Support from the desktop, press the F1 key.

To open Help and Support and enable online Help:

▶ **1.** Click the **Start** button 🏵 on the taskbar, click **Help and Support** on the Start menu, and then maximize the Windows Help and Support window. Figure 1-21 shows the initial Help and Support window.

Figure 1-21   Windows Help and Support

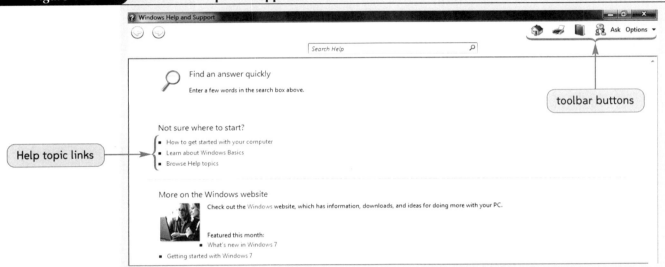

Help topic links

toolbar buttons

▶ **2.** Click the **Options** button on the right side of the toolbar, click **Settings** on the drop-down Options menu, and in the Help Settings dialog box, click the **Improve my search results by using online Help (recommended)** check box to select it, if necessary, and then click the **OK** button.

The table in Figure 1-22 identifies and describes buttons found on the Help and Support Window toolbar.

Figure 1-22 Windows Help and Support toolbar buttons

Button Name	Help Button	Use
Home	🏠	For returning to the starting Windows Help and Support page
Print	🖨	For printing a Help topic
Browse Help	📖	For opening the Table of Contents
Ask	 👥 Ask	For getting Help from a friend, expert, or Microsoft Customer Support, and for locating in-depth technical information at the Microsoft Web site and its Technet Web site
Options	Options ▾	For displaying a drop-down list with options for printing, browsing Help, changing the size of the text in Windows Help and Support, searching for information on a page, and changing Help settings

Next, Juliann recommends you browse for Help information on desktop gadgets so that you can decide whether you want to place any gadgets on your desktop to simplify the way you work or monitor the performance of your computer.

To open and browse Help and Support:

▶ 1. Click the **Learn about Windows Basics** link. Windows Help and Support displays categories of Help topics about basic Windows features and, under each category, lists specific Help topics.

▶ 2. Under Desktop fundamentals, click **Desktop gadgets (overview)**. The Desktop gadgets (overview) Help topic provides an explanation of gadgets and why you might want to use them. It also explains the use of specific gadgets, such as the Feed Headlines gadget for displaying updated news headlines from Web sites by subscribing to feeds, and how to add, remove, and organize gadgets on the desktop.

▶ 3. Under "In this article" on the right side of the window, click the **Adding and removing gadgets** link. This link takes you directly to the "Adding and removing gadgets" section in this Help topic so that you don't have to scroll.

▶ 4. Click the **To add a gadget** link. Windows Help and Support expands this Help topic and lists the two steps for performing this operation.

▶ 5. Click the **Minimize** button 🗕 to minimize the Windows Help and Support window.

▶ 6. Using the instructions for adding a gadget, right-click the **desktop background**, and then click **Gadgets** on the desktop shortcut menu. Windows 7 displays the Gadget Gallery dialog box. See Figure 1-23.

| Figure 1-23 | **Gadget Gallery** |

You can also open the Gadget Gallery by choosing Desktop Gadget Gallery on the All Programs menu.

▶ **7.** Click the **Show details** button ⊙ to expand the dialog box, and then click the **CPU Meter** gadget icon. Windows 7 informs you that the CPU meter provides information on the current computer CPU and system memory (RAM).

▶ **8.** Double-click the **CPU Meter** gadget icon. Windows 7 adds the CPU Meter to the desktop. On the left meter, the CPU Meter displays a percentage ranging from 0% to 100% to show you how busy the processor is. On the right meter, it shows the percentage of RAM currently in use. As you work on your computer, you can monitor how programs and operations that you perform affect the processor and use RAM on your computer, and thereby identify bottlenecks or potential performance problems.

▶ **9.** Close the Gadget Gallery dialog box.

From the Gadget Gallery dialog box, you can also look for more gadgets online.

REFERENCE

Browsing Windows Help and Support

- Click the Start button, and then click Help and Support (or press the F1 key from the desktop).
- Click the "Learn about Windows Basics" link to display Help topic links that provide information on the basic features and ways of working with Windows 7, and then click a specific Help topic link.
- To view a table of contents of subject headings, click the "Browse Help topics" link or the Browse Help button on the toolbar, click a subject heading, and then click a specific Help topic or click a Category to further narrow down and locate the Help topic with the information you need.
- If you want to quickly locate a section within a specific Help topic, click one of the links under "In this article" on the right side of the window. Then, if necessary, click a Help link to display the steps for performing a task.

Next, you'll search for Help information on Windows Aero.

To search Windows Help and Support using keywords:

▶ **1.** Click the **Windows Help and Support** taskbar button on the taskbar. Windows 7 restores the Windows Help and Support window.

▶ **2.** Click in the **Search Help** box in the Windows Help and Support window, type **aero**, and then click the **Search Help** button 🔍. Windows Help and Support displays a list of search results related to the keyword you specified. See Figure 1-24. Your search results may differ.

Figure 1-24 **Searching for Help**

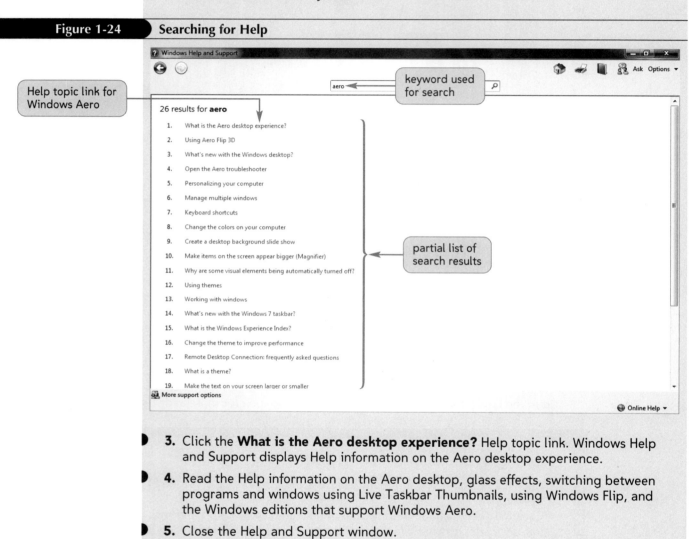

▶ **3.** Click the **What is the Aero desktop experience?** Help topic link. Windows Help and Support displays Help information on the Aero desktop experience.

▶ **4.** Read the Help information on the Aero desktop, glass effects, switching between programs and windows using Live Taskbar Thumbnails, using Windows Flip, and the Windows editions that support Windows Aero.

▶ **5.** Close the Help and Support window.

You can start a search from any location in the Windows Help and Support window. However, if you want to return to the initial view of the Windows Help and Support window, you can use the Home button on the Windows Help and Support window toolbar.

REFERENCE

Searching Windows Help and Support

- Click the Start button and then click Help and Support (or press the F1 key from the desktop).
- Click in the Search box in the Windows Help and Support window, type a keyword or phrase that identifies the Help topic you want to locate, and then click the Search Help button.
- In the list of Search results, click the Help topic you want to examine.
- If you want to return to the initial opening page to select another Help topic, click the Home button in the Windows Help and Support window.

Windows Help and Support provides Help information about Windows 7 features as well as programs that are part of Windows 7, such as Windows DVD Maker, but it does not provide Help for other programs, such as Microsoft Office programs or programs developed by companies other than Microsoft. Each of those programs has its own Help system where you can find more details about the use of that program.

REVIEW

Session 1.2 Quick Check

1. Windows uses _____, or predefined settings to simplify your use of a computer.
2. What new Windows 7 feature displays a menu of recently or frequently opened objects when you right-click a taskbar button or point to an application on the Start menu?
3. What Windows Aero feature does Windows 7 display when you point to a taskbar button for one or more windows open in the same application?
4. In Windows 7, what feature can you enable so that you can browse your local computer in the same way you browse the Web?
5. True or False. A group of related settings stored on a tab in a dialog box is called a property sheet.
6. True or False. The only way that you can locate Help information in Windows Help and Support is by browsing from one Help topic to another.
7. What is the difference between an active and an inactive window?
8. Explain the difference between Aero Peek, Aero Shake, and Aero Snap.

SESSION 1.3 VISUAL OVERVIEW

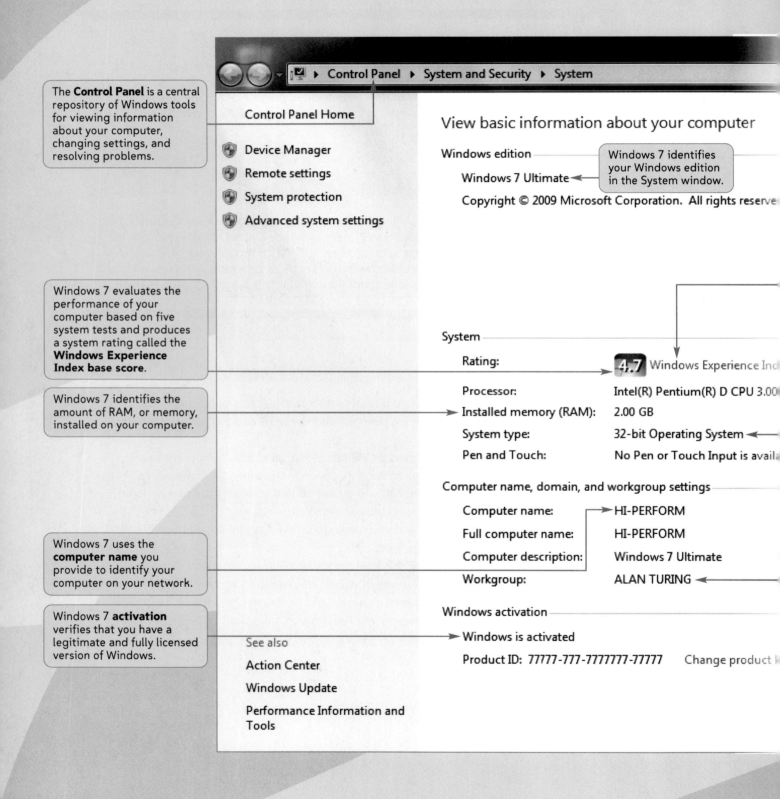

The **Control Panel** is a central repository of Windows tools for viewing information about your computer, changing settings, and resolving problems.

Windows 7 evaluates the performance of your computer based on five system tests and produces a system rating called the **Windows Experience Index base score**.

Windows 7 identifies the amount of RAM, or memory, installed on your computer.

Windows 7 uses the **computer name** you provide to identify your computer on your network.

Windows 7 **activation** verifies that you have a legitimate and fully licensed version of Windows.

▶ Control Panel ▶ System and Security ▶ System

Control Panel Home

🛡 Device Manager
🛡 Remote settings
🛡 System protection
🛡 Advanced system settings

View basic information about your computer

Windows edition

Windows 7 Ultimate ◄

Windows 7 identifies your Windows edition in the System window.

Copyright © 2009 Microsoft Corporation. All rights reserve

System

Rating: **4.7** Windows Experience Ind

Processor: Intel(R) Pentium(R) D CPU 3.00

Installed memory (RAM): 2.00 GB

System type: 32-bit Operating System ◄

Pen and Touch: No Pen or Touch Input is availa

Computer name, domain, and workgroup settings

Computer name: HI-PERFORM

Full computer name: HI-PERFORM

Computer description: Windows 7 Ultimate

Workgroup: ALAN TURING ◄

Windows activation

Windows is activated

Product ID: 77777-777-7777777-77777   Change product k

See also

Action Center

Windows Update

Performance Information and Tools

YOUR COMPUTER'S SYSTEM PROPERTIES

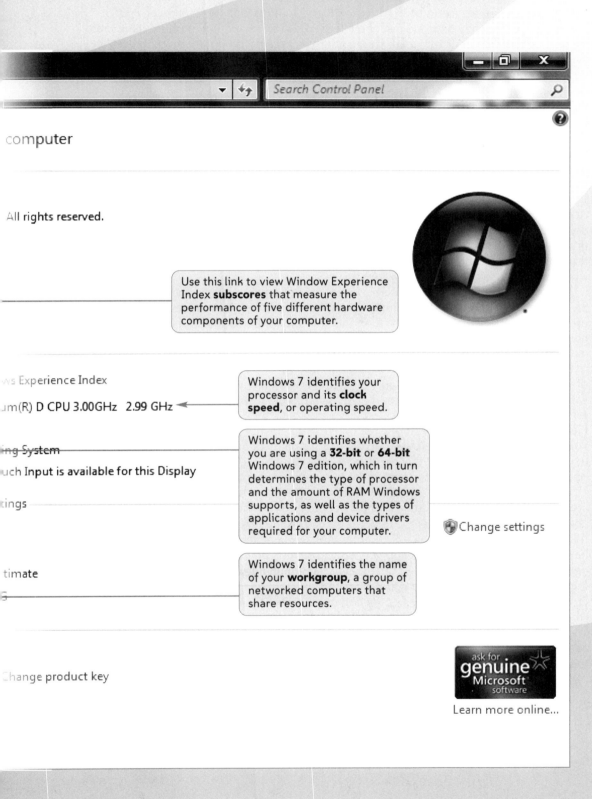

computer

Use this link to view Window Experience Index **subscores** that measure the performance of five different hardware components of your computer.

ws Experience Index

Windows 7 identifies your processor and its **clock speed**, or operating speed.

um(R) D CPU 3.00GHz   2.99 GHz

ng System

uch Input is available for this Display

Windows 7 identifies whether you are using a **32-bit** or **64-bit** Windows 7 edition, which in turn determines the type of processor and the amount of RAM Windows supports, as well as the types of applications and device drivers required for your computer.

tings

Change settings

timate

Windows 7 identifies the name of your **workgroup**, a group of networked computers that share resources.

Change product key

ask for
genuine
Microsoft
software

Learn more online...

Navigating Your Computer

To more effectively use Windows 7, you should be familiar with how Windows 7 organizes and provides access to disks, drives, folders, and files on your computer.

TIP

When purchasing a new computer, consider a combination DVD-Rewritable/CD-Rewritable drive so that you can record multiple times to both DVDs and CDs.

Computers typically have at least one internal hard drive and one or more removable drives, such as a DVD or CD drive. The hard drive contains the installed version of the Windows 7 operating system as well as all installed applications, utilities, and games on your computer, as well as your document files. Increasingly, individuals acquire software by downloading it from the Internet. However, if you purchase software at a local store, that software product includes a CD or DVD, which you must use to install the software. In order to do so, your computer must have an internal or external CD or DVD drive. Likewise, you might purchase software on a CD or DVD over the Internet, or you might want a CD or DVD with a copy of the software that you download. Because DVD drives can read or access the information on both DVDs and CDs, while CD drives can only read CDs, the better choice is a DVD drive.

The operating system assigns a unique drive name to each drive in your computer. According to conventions set in 1981 by IBM for the first IBM PC, the first hard drive is assigned the name C: and referred to as drive C. Any additional disk drives are assigned drive names starting with the next available drive letter; however, it is possible to change drive names on a computer with Windows 7 Disk Management console (which you examine in Tutorial 5).

USB flash drives (**UFDs**) are portable drives for storing documents. These type of drives are also referred to as pen drives, jump drives, key drives, keychain drives, disk-on-key drives, memory keys, thumb drives, flash memory drives, USB keys, and USB sticks (to name a few). When you attach a USB flash drive to a computer, Windows 7 assigns it a drive name, which is visible in the Computer window. When you detach, or safely remove, a USB flash drive from a computer, Windows 7 removes its drive name, and that drive name is no longer displayed in the Computer window. When you safely remove a USB flash drive, Windows 7 ensures that all data has been written to the disk before you remove it. To safely remove a USB flash drive, you click the Safely Remove Hardware and Eject Media icon in the notification area on the taskbar, choose the hardware device that you want to remove, and then wait for a Windows notification that informs you it is safe to remove the flash drive. If you don't use the Safely Remove Hardware and Eject Media option, but instead just pull the flash drive out, then you run the risk of losing data.

On hard disks, USB flash drives, DVD discs, and CD discs, software and documents are organized into folders. Although most people think of a folder as a container for files and perhaps even other folders, a **folder** is actually a file that keeps track of a group of related objects, such as subfolders and files that are all stored at different locations on the hard disk. Therefore, a folder is a logical concept, not a physical reality. Likewise, most people think of a **subfolder** as a folder contained within another folder. However, a subfolder is also a file that keeps track of a smaller set of related files within a larger, related group of files. A **file** consists of a collection of data, such as a program or a document, stored in a folder on a disk under a unique filename and, in most cases, a file extension. The operating system allocates a certain amount of disk storage space to each program and document file and associates each file's allocated space with the filename assigned to the file. Therefore, the primary function of folders is to organize related information so Although you (and the operating system) can easily find that information.

Although subfolders and files are not actually stored within a folder, it is common practice to think of files as being stored within folders (and subfolders stored within other folders) so that it is easier to understand and work with folders and files.

Using Long Filenames

Another important operating system feature is the support that it provides for assigning names to files. Most filenames consist of three parts: the main part of the name (sometimes called the **root name**), a period, and the file extension, which consists of the characters that follow the period. For example, the program that displays the desktop and the view that you see within a folder window is called Windows Explorer, which is a different program than Windows Internet Explorer. The Windows Explorer program is stored in a file with the filename Explorer.exe under the Windows folder. *Explorer* is the main part of the filename, and *exe* is the file extension. The *exe* file extension stands for *executable* and identifies this file as a program file whose program code can be loaded into memory and executed (or whose instructions can be carried out). The contents of an executable file are stored in a format that the processor can directly execute, and unlike the **source code** (or original program code) from which it was originally derived, you cannot read the contents of the file.

As noted earlier, with the Windows operating system, you can use descriptive filenames. These filenames can include spaces, periods, and symbols; however, the following nine symbols are not allowed because they have special meaning to the operating system: **: / \ | < > * ? "**

The colon (**:**) is used as part of a drive name, so you cannot use it in a filename. If you try to use one of these **reserved symbols** in a filename, Windows will not accept the symbol you type. Figure 1-25 lists examples of valid and invalid filenames.

Figure 1-25	Examples of valid and invalid filenames

Valid Filenames	Valid Characters
Five Year Sales Projection.xlsx	Spaces
PerformanceMeasurements.htm	Mixed case
NTFS vs. FAT Features.rtf	More than one period
CASHFLOW.XLS	All uppercase characters
bootmgr	No file extension
Resume #1.docx	Pound sign symbol (#) and number
Windows 7's System Requirements.docx	Apostrophe
Comparison of 32-bit & 64-bit Editions	Dashes, numbers, and ampersand (&)
Sales Commissions (1st Quarter).xlsx	Parentheses
@Innovator.com Privacy Policy.htm	@ symbol
Résumés	Accented characters (é)

Invalid Filenames	Invalid Characters
Drive C: Backup Report.docx	Reserved device name (C:)
Analysis: First Quarter Sales Performance.docx	Colon (:)
File Systems (NTFS/FAT/TFAT).ppsx	Slash (/)
Explorer\Advanced Registry Subkey.reg	Backslash (\ )
High Priority Projects.docx	Asterisk (*)
Potential Mergers?.doc	Question mark (?)
"Top-Notch" Sales Staff.docx	Quotation marks
<Client Mailing List>.accdb	Chevrons (< and >)
Level 1 l Level 2 l Level 3 Rating Systems.docx	Pipe symbol (l)

A filename might contain multiple periods; the last period in the filename is the one that separates the main part of the filename from the file extension. Windows programs typically assign file extensions to files you produce with those programs, and Windows 7 uses those file extensions to determine which application to open when you click (or double-click) a file icon. Also, file extensions serve to organize files by function and type, and when you choose the option to open a file from an application, that application displays a filtered view of the files within a folder, showing you only those filenames that have a certain file extension. If you want to view other file types (in other words, files with a different file extension), you must specify the file type. You can also specify that you want to view all files, regardless of their file extension. When you create and name a file, all you provide is the main part of the filename, and the program adds a file extension. Also, you do not need to type a period at the end of the filename you provide.

You can also use these long filenames, as they are called, for folders, but a folder name usually does not have a file extension (except for temporary folders used to install software) and, in some cases, files (such as operating system files) do not have file extensions. Because some network operating systems do not recognize long filenames, Microsoft uses names for its program files and other supporting files that follow the DOS conventions or rules for naming files. DOS filenames were limited to eight characters for the main part of the filename, followed by a period, and then three characters for the file extension (called an **8.3 filename**). Furthermore, unlike the Windows operating system, no spaces are allowed in a DOS filename, you can only use one period to separate the filename from the file extension, and the file extension cannot exceed three characters.

Since employees rely on the use of removable media to store backups of their important designs, Juliann recommends that each employee explore and become familiar with the drives and personal folders on their new computers, and develop their own visual model of how resources are organized under Windows 7.

To understand how Windows 7 organizes drives, folders, and files:

1. If you have already opened an application, drive, or folder window, close those windows.

2. Click the **Computer** icon on the desktop, and if necessary, maximize the Computer window.

3. Click the **More options** arrow ⊞ ▾ for the Change your view button on the toolbar, and then click **Tiles** (if necessary). The Tiles view provides information on available and total disk storage space for the hard drives. See Figure 1-26.

TIP

You can also use the Windows+E (for Explorer) keyboard shortcut to open the Computer window.

| Figure 1-26 | Viewing the contents of a Computer window |

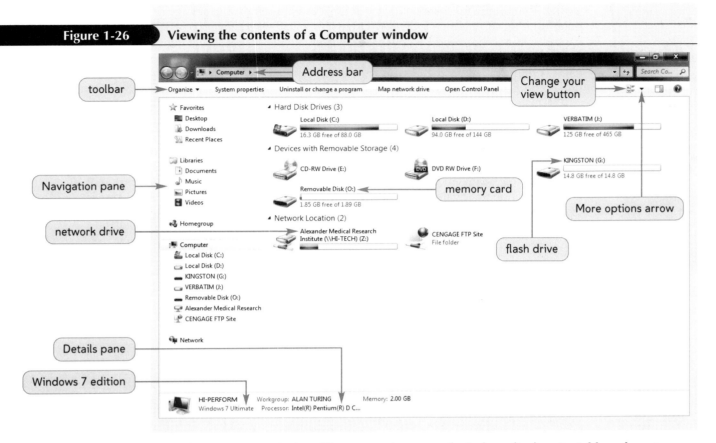

The Computer window, like every other type of window, displays its **Address bar** at the top of the window to identify your location on the computer. You can also use the Address bar to navigate around your computer. Window buttons located in the upper-right corner of the window let you minimize, maximize, restore down, and close a window. To the left of the Address bar is a Back button to back up to the previous window and a Forward button to undo moving back to a previous window. To the right of the Address bar is a Search box. Below the Address bar is a toolbar with a set of buttons for performing specific operations, such as changing your view in this window. The pane on the left side of the Computer window is the **Navigation pane**, and it contains links to other frequently used locations on your computer.

In Windows versions that preceded Windows Vista, there was a small program icon on the left side of the title bar in folder windows (and the title bar was more defined than in Windows Vista and Windows 7). If you click the program icon in a folder window in these earlier Windows versions, Windows displays a menu called the **control menu** that contained options for restoring, moving, sizing, minimizing, maximizing, and closing the window. Although Windows Vista and Windows 7 no longer include that program icon in folder windows, you can right-click the top border of a folder window to display the control menu. In contrast, program windows still retain the program icon, and a mere click displays the control menu.

In the main part of the Computer window, Windows 7 lists hard drives and removable disk drives in two separate groups. On the computer shown in Figure 1-26, Windows 7 identifies three hard drives. Local Disk (C:), Local Disk (D:), and Verbatim (J:). Drive J is an external hard drive assigned the name Verbatim by the manufacturer. Local Disk and Verbatim are example of **friendly names** that are assigned by Microsoft or hardware vendors so that you do not have to refer to drives using their drive names (such as drive C).

The Computer window identifies four devices with removable storage on the computer used for this figure—a CD-RW Drive (E:), a DVD RW Drive (F:), a 16 GB flash drive named Kingston (G:), and Removable Disk (O:), a memory card for a digital camera. Although this computer has three other drives for three other types of flash memory cards, Windows 7 does not identify those drives until a flash memory card is inserted in one of the memory card slots.

The Computer window also shows two network locations—Alexander Medical Research Institute (\\HI-TECH) (Z:), a network folder assigned the drive name Z:, and Cengage FTP Site, a link to an FTP site identified as a File folder.

The bars under each hard drive and the flash drive show the amount of free (or available) storage space and the total storage space. Beneath the bars, Windows 7 notes the amount of free space and the total storage capacity in GB (gigabytes) for each disk. **GB** is an abbreviation for gigabytes. A **gigabyte** is equal to approximately one billion bytes of storage. A **byte** is the storage space on disk or in RAM for one character. Figure 1-27 lists and defines storage capacity terms and their commonly used abbreviations.

Figure 1-27 Commonly used terms for measuring storage capacities

Term	Abbreviation	Equals	Bytes (Actual)	Power
Byte	B	1 character	1	2^0
Kilobyte	K or KB	1,024 bytes	1,024	2^{10}
Megabyte	M, MB, or megs	1,024 kilobytes	1,048,576	2^{20}
Gigabyte	G, GB, or gigs	1,024 megabytes	1,073,741,824	2^{30}
Terabyte	TB	1,024 gigabytes	1,099,511,627,776	2^{40}
Petabyte	PB	1,024 terabytes	1,125,899,906,842,624	2^{50}
Exabyte	EB	1,024 petabytes	1,152,921,504,606,846,976	2^{60}
Zettabyte	ZB	1,024 exabytes	1,180,591,620,717,411,303,424	2^{70}
Yottabyte	YB	1,024 zettabytes	1,208,925,819,614,629,174,706,176	2^{80}

The Power column shows the powers of 2 used to calculate the exact number of bytes. For example, 2^{10} is the same as multiplying 2 by itself 10 times and equals a total of 1,024 bytes.

In 2000, the International Electrotechnical Commission (a Swiss nongovernmental, nonprofit organization that defines and sets international standards for all electrical, electronic, and related technologies) published new standards, terms, and definitions for measuring storage capacities because the computer industry measured storage capacities in two different ways. For example, 4 GB of RAM is treated as 4,294,967,296 bytes (or 4 × 1,073,741,824 bytes). However, a 500 GB hard drive is treated as, and sold as, having 500,000,000,000 bytes (or 500 × 1,000,000,000 bytes). In the case of RAM, a gigabyte is treated as 2^{30}, while in the case of the hard drive, a gigabyte is treated as 10^9 (not the same). If you purchase a 500 GB disk drive, you expect to have 500 GB of storage, but Windows 7 reports the storage as 465 GB (500,000,000,000 bytes divided by 1024 three times). The hard disk manufacturer, on the other hand, treats the storage space as equal to 500,000,000,000 bytes divided by 1,000 three times (or 500 GB). Once a customer discovers that their hard disk has less storage space than they thought, they feel that they did not get what they paid for.

To standardize the measurement of storage capacities and prevent this confusion on the part of customers, the International Electrotechnical Commission proposed these new standards for measuring storage capacities. To distinguish, for example, between *giga*, which technically represents 1,000,000,000 (not 1,073,741,824 bytes), *gibi* now represents 1,073,741,824, and *giga* now represents 1,000,000,000. The new terms take the first two characters of the older terminology, and adds *bi* for *binary*, followed by *byte*. Therefore, gibibyte = *Gi* + *bi* + *byte* (pronounced "gih-bee-byte"). See Figure 1-28.

Figure 1-28   **International Electrotechnical Commission's standards for measuring storage capacities**

Term	Abbreviation	Equals	Bytes (Actual)	Power
Kibibyte	KiB	1,024 bytes	1,024	2^{10}
Mebibyte	MiB	1,024 kibibytes	1,048,576	2^{20}
Gibibyte	GiB	1,024 mebibytes	1,073,741,824	2^{30}
Tebibyte	TiB	1,024 gibibytes	1,099,511,627,776	2^{40}
Pebibyte	PiB	1,024 tebibytes	1,125,899,906,842,624	2^{50}
Exbibyte	EiB	1,024 pebibytes	1,152,921,504,606,846,976	2^{60}
Zebibyte	ZiB	1,024 exbibytes	1,180,591,620,717,411,303,424	2^{70}
Yobibyte	YiB	1,024 zebibytes	1,208,925,819,614,629,174,706,176	2^{80}

Figure 1-29 shows the new storage capacities for kilobyte, megabyte, gigabyte, terabyte, and so on.

Figure 1-29   **International Electrotechnical Commission's standards for measuring storage capacities**

Term	Abbreviation	Equals	Bytes (Actual)	Power
Kilobyte	K or KB	1,000 bytes	1,000	10^{3}
Megabyte	M, MB, or megs	1,000 kilobytes	1,000,000	10^{6}
Gigabyte	G, GB, or gigs	1,000 megabytes	1,000,000,000	10^{9}
Terabyte	TB	1,000 gigabytes	1,000,000,000,000	10^{12}
Petabyte	PB	1,000 terabytes	1,000,000,000,000,000	10^{15}
Exabyte	EB	1,000 petabytes	1,000,000,000,000,000,000	10^{18}
Zettabyte	ZB	1,000 exabytes	1,000,000,000,000,000,000,000	10^{21}
Yottabyte	YB	1,000 zettabytes	1,000,000,000,000,000,000,000,000	10^{24}

Increasingly, the new standards proposed by the International Electrotechnical Commission are being used in the United States alongside the older standards for defining storage capacities. To intelligently discuss and understand storage capacities with your peers and clients in the vast majority of other countries who have already adopted these standards, and to understand technical information provided at the Microsoft Web site, you need to understand and use these new standards for measuring storage capacities.

If you select a drive, then Windows 7 displays information about the drive in the **Details pane** at the bottom of the window.

To view details of your hard disk and then navigate to your personal user account folders:

▶ **1.** Point to the **Local Disk (C:)** icon (or the icon for your hard disk), but do not click this drive icon. Windows 7 selects the drive and displays a light blue border and light blue background around the drive. See Figure 1-30.

Figure 1-30 **Viewing hard drive information**

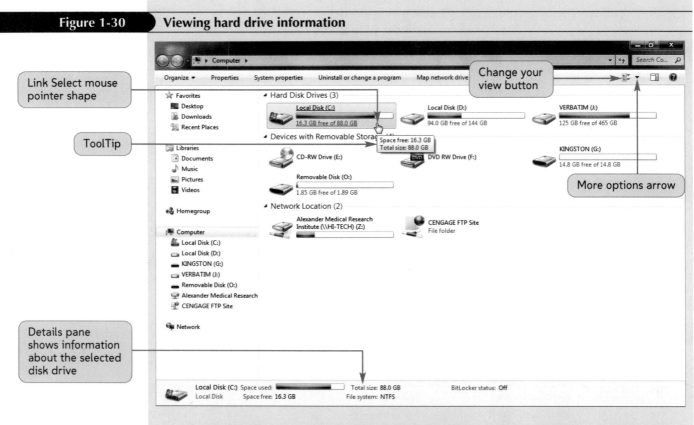

Link Select mouse pointer shape

ToolTip

More options arrow

Change your view button

Details pane shows information about the selected disk drive

In the Details pane, Windows 7 displays the same information shown in the main part of the window, but it also identifies the file system used on the disk drive and, in the case of Windows 7 Ultimate and Windows 7 Enterprise, its BitLocker status. The computer used for this figure has a hard disk that uses NTFS, a file system commonly used on disks with large storage capacities. BitLocker is an advanced feature for encrypting an entire drive (encoding and thereby securing the data). In Tutorial 5, you will examine file systems in more detail, and you will also examine BitLocker Drive Encryption.

TIP

To navigate to another drive, click the Address bar arrow to the right of Computer in the Address bar, and then choose the drive.

2. Click the **first Address bar** arrow ▶ to the left of Computer in the Address bar. Windows 7 displays a list of locations where you can navigate. See Figure 1-31.

Figure 1-31 **Navigating with the Address Bar**

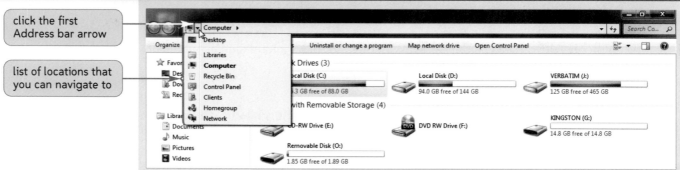

click the first Address bar arrow

list of locations that you can navigate to

You can navigate to your personal Desktop folder, the Computer window, the Recycle Bin window, the Control Panel, your personal user account folder with your user account name, the Libraries folder, the Homegroup folder, and the Network folder. You will examine these folders in more detail in Tutorial 3 and in later tutorials. The boldfacing applied to Computer in the drop-down list of locations indicates that it is the current folder (in other words, you are already in this folder).

3. Click your **user account name** in the drop-down location list. Windows 7 switches to your user account folder and displays your user account subfolders. Note that the Address bar now shows that you are in your user account. Although you can access your Downloads, Documents, Music, Pictures, and Videos folders from the Navigation pane, your user account folder allows you to access your other personal folders—Contacts, Desktop, Links, Saved Games, and Searches.

4. Click **Libraries** in the Navigation pane on the left side of the window, and then click the **Videos** icon in the File list pane on the right. Windows 7 opens the Videos library folder, which includes a Sample Videos folder. The Address bar now shows that the Videos folder is under Libraries. As described in Tutorial 3, Libraries allow you to consolidate the content of one or more folders.

5. Click the **Sample Videos** folder icon in the File list pane on the right. Windows 7 opens the Sample Videos folder, which contains a Wildlife video file. The Address bar now shows that the Sample Videos folder is under the Videos folder, which is in turn under the Libraries folder.

6. Click the **More options** arrow ▦ ▼ for the Change your view button on the toolbar, notice that the drop-down Views menu has a slider bar on the left, and then click **Extra Large Icons**. Windows 7 switches from Large Icons view to Extra Large Icons view. You can use the slider bar on the Views drop-down menu to adjust window icons to a custom size. See Figure 1-32.

Figure 1-32	Viewing a video file in the Videos library

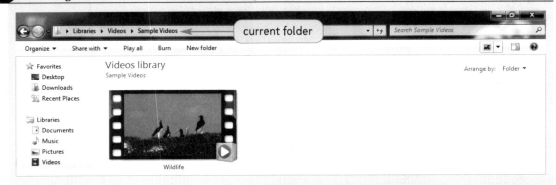

7. Press the **Alt** key. Above the toolbar, Windows 7 displays the classic menu bar found in earlier versions of Windows before Windows Vista.

Trouble? If you do not see the classic menu bar after pressing the Alt key, click the folder background, and then repeat this step.

8. Press the **Alt** key again. Windows 7 hides the classic Menu bar. If you are already familiar with the classic menu bar from earlier versions of Windows, this feature can save you time and effort. You can also use the F10 key to display the classic Menu bar.

9. Keep the window open for the next section of the tutorial.

TIP

To permanently display the classic Menu bar, click the Organize button on the toolbar, point to Layout, and then click Menu Bar.

When you are in a folder window, you can preview the contents of certain types of files, watch animation in a file that contains a PowerPoint presentation, and even play back video.

To view details of your hard disk and then navigate to your personal user account folders:

1. Click the **Show the preview pane** button 🔲 on the right side of the toolbar. Windows 7 displays a Preview pane to the right of the Wildlife video file.

2. Point to the **border** between the Details pane and the Preview pane, and when the mouse changes to a double-headed arrow ⟷ pointing to the right and left, drag the **Preview pane** border to the left until it's as wide as possible.

3. Click the **Play** button ▶ under the Wildlife video in the Preview pane to watch the video, and then point to the Sample Videos folder button on the taskbar. Windows 7 displays the Live Taskbar Thumbnail of the live video playing in the Live Taskbar Thumbnail. See Figure 1-33.

Figure 1-33   Viewing a video

4. Click the **More options** arrow 🔽 for the Change your view button on the toolbar, and then click **Large Icons** to restore the default icon size to the Sample Videos folder.

5. Close the Sample Videos folder window.

When using the Views menu to select an icon size, you can also use drag the slider tab on the slider bar to choose an icon size that is intermediate between one of the icon size options on the View menu, or as you did earlier with desktop icons, you can use the Ctrl key and your mouse wheel to adjust icon sizes in a folder window along a continuum (or range) of sizes. Depending on the window contents, you might be able to not only enlarge the icons but also fit all the icons within the window so you do not have to scroll.

REFERENCE

Navigating Your Computer

- Click the Start button, and then click the name of your personal user account, or click one of your personal user account folders, such as Documents, Pictures, or Music.
- Click one of the links in the Navigation pane, or click the Address bar arrow before or after the name of any window in the Address bar, and then click the location you want to access, or, if you want to view the contents of a specific subfolder within the current folder window, click the icon for that folder.
- Use the Change your view button, its menu options, and slider bar to adjust the sizes of icons in the folder window (or use the Ctrl key and your mouse wheel to scroll through a range of icon sizes).
- Press the Alt key or the F10 key to display the classic menu bar (or click Organize on the toolbar, point to Layout, and then click Menu Bar to permanently display the classic menu bar).

As a power user, you will want to become familiar with how Windows organizes folders on your hard drive so that you can quickly access whatever resources, folders, and files you need, and so that you can customize your folder structure and your access to those resources, folders, and files. This is especially important if you work with a Help Desk and assist other coworkers who are novices.

Viewing Properties of Your Computer

Whether you're a novice or power user, you should know how to find basic information about your computer, such as the operating system version and edition, the processor, and the amount of RAM installed in your computer. This information is particularly important if you are evaluating the performance of your computer, acquiring new hardware and software, or troubleshooting your computer.

In the case of the processor, Windows 7 provides information on the processor's clock speed (or operating speed) in GHz. Clock speed refers to the pace at which operations are performed by the processor. The abbreviation **GHz** stands for *gigahertz*. One **hertz** is one cycle per second, and one **gigahertz** is one billion cycles per second. The higher this value, the more operations the processor can perform in a given period of time. When evaluating a processor, this is one factor you consider; the other is the processor itself. Today's processors are designated as 32-bit or 64-bit processors because they support 32-bit and 64-bit processing. The term **bit** refers to each of the two digits in the binary numbering system; namely, 0 (zero) and 1 (one). The term *bit* is derived from *binary digit* by combining the *bi* in *binary* with the *t* in *digit*.

A 32-bit computer system uses a 32-bit processor, a 32-bit operating system, 32-bit applications (including utilities and games), and 32-bit device drivers. A 32-bit processor processes 32 bits (or data consisting of 32 zeroes and ones) in one operation. Operating systems, applications, and device drivers used on a 32-bit processor must support the capabilities of a 32-bit processor.

In contrast, a 64-bit computer system uses a 64-bit capable processor (or perhaps even a true 64-bit processor), a 64-bit operating system, 64-bit applications (including utilities and games), and 64-bit device drivers. A 64-bit processor can process 64 bits (or data consisting of 64 zeros and ones) in one operation. A **64-bit capable** processor not only supports either the 32-bit or 64-bit version of Windows 7, but also performs either 32-bit processing or 64-bit processing. Operating systems, applications, and device drivers used with a 64-bit processor must support the capabilities of a 64-bit processor.

To locate information about your computer, you view the properties of your computer system.

TIP

You can also use the Windows+Pause keyboard shortcut to open a System window.

To view basic information about your computer:

1. Right-click the **Computer** icon on the desktop, click **Properties** on the short-cut menu, and then maximize the System window (if necessary). As shown in Figure 1-34, Windows 7 reports information about your computer.

| Figure 1-34 | Viewing computer properties |

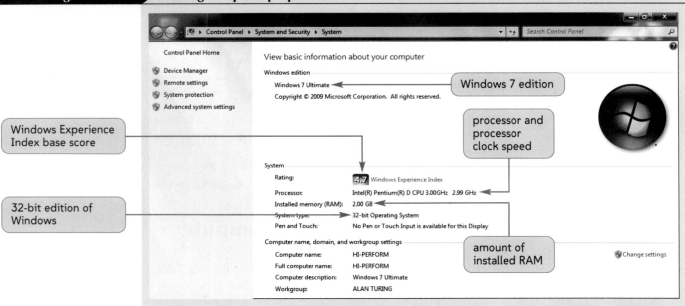

At the top of this window, Windows 7 displays the edition of Windows 7 used on your computer. In the System section, Windows 7 displays information about the processor and the amount of installed memory (or RAM). The System type in Figure 1-34 is identified as a "32-bit Operating System," which means it is running a 32-bit version of Windows 7. Also, under System, note that this computer has a Windows Experience Index rating of 4.7 (explained in the next section of the tutorial). Your computer's Windows Experience Index will differ, and your System type may differ.

2. Keep the System window open for the next section of the tutorial.

As shown in Figure 1-34, this computer has 2.00 GB of RAM and an Intel Pentium D CPU with a rated clock speed of 3.00 GHz, but which performs at 2.99 GHz. This processor is a dual-core processor that can process two sets of instructions from the same program or two different programs at the same time on different execution cores in the processor. **CPU** (which stands for **Central Processing Unit**) is an older term for *processor*.

Windows 7 requires a 32-bit (or **x86**) or 64-bit (or **x64**) processor with a clock speed of 1 GHz or more. Windows 7 also requires at least 1 GB of RAM.

PROSKILLS

Decision Making: Evaluating 32-Bit and 64-Bit Processors and Operating Systems

When you make a decision to purchase a new computer or upgrade a computer you must decide whether to purchase a 32-bit or a 64-bit computer system and use 32-bit or 64-bit operating system, applications, and device drivers.

Operating systems are designated as 32-bit or 64-bit because they are designed to work with a specific type of processor. If you buy a computer with a 32-bit processor, then you must install the 32-bit version of a Windows 7 edition. If you buy a computer with a 64-bit processor, you must install the 64-bit version of Windows 7. If you buy a computer with a 64-bit capable processor, then you can install either the 32-bit or 64-bit version of a Windows 7 edition.

A 32-bit version of the Windows 7 operating system requires 32-bit device drivers, and a 64-bit version of the Windows 7 operating system requires 64-bit drivers. Before you purchase hardware for a 64-bit computer system, you must make sure that there are 64-bit device drivers for that hardware. Before you upgrade your 64-bit capable computer from a 32-bit to a 64-bit version of Windows 7, you must make sure that there are 64-bit device drivers for all your hardware and when you purchase new hardware.

Another important consideration is the amount of RAM for your 32-bit or 64-bit computer system. In theory, a 32-bit processor supports up to 4 GB of RAM, and a 64-bit processor supports up to 16 EB (exabytes) (or 16 billion gigabytes) of RAM. However, Microsoft sets limits on the amount of RAM supported by different versions and editions of the Windows operating system, and the amount of RAM supported can vary by edition. Furthermore, computer manufacturers set limits on the amount of RAM you can install in a computer. The primary advantage of 64-bit editions of Windows 7 is that they support and can effectively utilize far more RAM than 32-bit editions of Windows 7.

All 32-bit applications are designed for 32-bit systems, and all 64-bit applications are designed for 64-bit computers. Some 32-bit applications may also work on a 64-bit system; however, they are limited to the amount of RAM that is supported for the 32-bit edition of Windows 7. If you upgrade from a 32-bit Windows version to a 64-bit Windows version, you must use or obtain a 64-bit version of your Internet security software or antivirus software.

By understanding the connection between processor type, operating system, software, device drivers, and hardware specifications, and carefully considering the needs of the end user, you can ensure that you will purchase a computer system that will support your needs for the immediate term as well as years down the line.

The Windows Experience Index

The Windows Experience Index (WEI) is a rating that is derived from an assessment of the performance of specific hardware components in your computer. This rating is called your computer's base score. A higher score indicates that your computer will perform better and faster, support the use of more resource-intensive applications and games, and support Windows 7 features such as Windows Aero. The Windows System Assessment Tool, or WinSAT, is the Windows 7 component that evaluates hardware and produces the Windows Experience Index.

From the System window, you can access more detailed information about the Windows Experience Index, including ratings, or subscores, for five separate hardware components in your computer: processor, memory (RAM), graphics, gaming graphics, and primary hard disk. The Processor subscore measures the computational capability of the processor. The Memory (RAM) subscore measures the rate of transfer of data in megabytes to and from RAM, and is also dependent on the amount of installed RAM. The Gaming graphics subscore measures the ability of the video graphics card to handle various textures. **Texture** refers to the detail applied to the surface of three-dimensional graphics. The Primary hard disk subscore is derived by measuring the number of megabytes of data transferred per second between the hard disk and RAM. The Windows Experience Index base score is not an average of the five subscores, but rather it is identical to the lowest subscore, which identifies the hardware component that limits the overall performance of the computer.

Using the Windows Experience Index for Purchasing New Hardware and Software

You can use the Windows Experience Index base score to evaluate the performance of your computer and determine whether, for example, you need to purchase more RAM or a higher performance video display card. When you do purchase new hardware or software for your computer, you can use this rating to make sure that you purchase hardware and software that will work with your version of Windows 7, and perform optimally on your computer. If you are purchasing a new computer, you can evaluate that new computer's capabilities by examining its Windows Experience Index to make sure the computer will meet your needs.

To view details on the Windows Experience Index:

1. Click the **Windows Experience Index** link. Windows 7 opens a Performance Information and Tools window with a table of subscores. See Figure 1-35.

Figure 1-35 **Viewing the Windows Experience Index subscores**

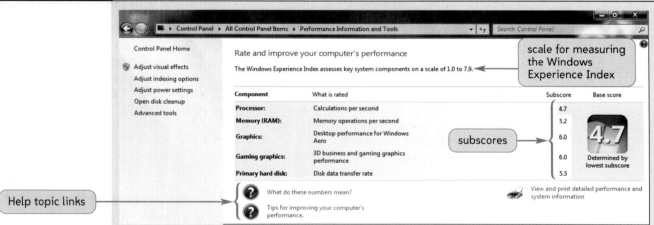

The table shows what hardware component is rated, how it is rated, and the subscore for each hardware component. On the computer used for this figure, the dual-core, high-performance processor is the limiting hardware component in the performance of this computer, and its rating determines the base score for the Windows Experience Index.

2. To understand the meaning of these subscores on your computer, click the **What do these numbers mean?** link, and maximize the Windows Help and Support window (if necessary). Windows 7 displays Help information on the Windows Experience Index. Windows Help and Support also notes that the scores currently range from 1.0 to 7.9 and that while the Windows Experience Index will support higher ratings as advances in computer hardware occur, standards for existing base scores will stay the same. The computer shown earlier in Figure 1-35 has a base score of 4.7 yet was a top-of-the-line system at the time of Windows Vista's release. Windows Vista rated the Windows Experience Index as 4.8, so as noted in Help and Support, new tests might be developed that result in lower scores.

▶ **3.** After you read the initial explanation on the Windows Experience Index, scroll down and click the **About your computer's base score** link. Windows 7 describes what kind of experience you can expect from your computer's base score. It notes that a computer with a base score of less than 2.0 can handle basic computing tasks, such as using office productivity software and searching the Internet; however, it also notes this base score is too low to support Windows Aero. A computer with a base score of 3.0 supports Windows Aero and many Windows 7 features, but only at a basic level (in other words, with reduced functionality). If a computer has a base score of 4.0 or 5.0, then it supports all new Windows 7 features and multitasking. If a computer has a base score of 6.0 or 7.0, it has a faster hard disk and supports high-end, graphics-intensive computing.

▶ **4.** Click the **About your computer's base score** link to collapse this Help topic.

▶ **5.** Click the **About your computer's subscore** link. Windows 7 expands this Help topic and explains how specific subscores affect your computer. It notes that high subscores for the processor and memory (RAM) are important if you use your computer for creating office documents, Web browsing, and email. Subscores of 2.0 or higher are usually sufficient for the other categories. If you use digital video-editing applications or realistic first-person games, then you need high subscores for the processor, memory (RAM), graphics, and gaming graphics categories, and subscores of 3.0 or higher for the hard disk category. If you use the Windows Media Center for more advanced types of multimedia operations, such as recording HDTV (high-definition TV) programming, then you need high subscores for the processor, hard disk, and graphics categories, and subscores of 3.0 or higher for the other categories.

▶ **6.** Close the Windows Help and Support window.

WinSAT checks your computer every week to determine whether your computer has new hardware and whether it needs to update the Windows Experience Index scores and subscores. If so, it operates in the background and updates your Windows Experience Index ratings. If your computer has never been rated, Windows 7 displays a "Rate this computer" link. Also, there are two ways in which you can initiate a reassessment of your computer. If you click the "Re-run the assessment" link in the Performance Information and Tools window, Windows 7 reevaluates the hardware on your computer and may update the Windows Experience Index base score and subscores. You can also use the Advanced tools link in the Performance Information and Tools window to open an Advanced Tools window where you can use the "Clear all Windows Experience Index scores and re-rate the system" link to force a complete rerun of all the Windows Experience Index tests.

To print information on your computer's Windows Experience Index, you can print a paper copy or produce an electronic copy. When you select the option to print, you can specify Microsoft XPS Document Writer as your printer, and Windows 7 will produce an XPS document file with the ".xps" file extension. XPS stands for *XML Paper Specification*. An **XML Paper Specification (XPS)** document is a type of electronic document format. Once you produce this file, you can view it with the Windows 7 XPS Viewer at any time. (The XPS Viewer is also available in Windows Vista and Windows XP).

To print a system summary report:

▶ **1.** In the Performance Information and Tools window, click the **View and print detailed performance and system information** link. Windows 7 displays another Performance Information and Tools window with a summary of your computer's Windows Experience Index base score and subscores as well as important specifications about your computer. See Figure 1-36.

Figure 1-36   **Viewing detailed information of a computer**

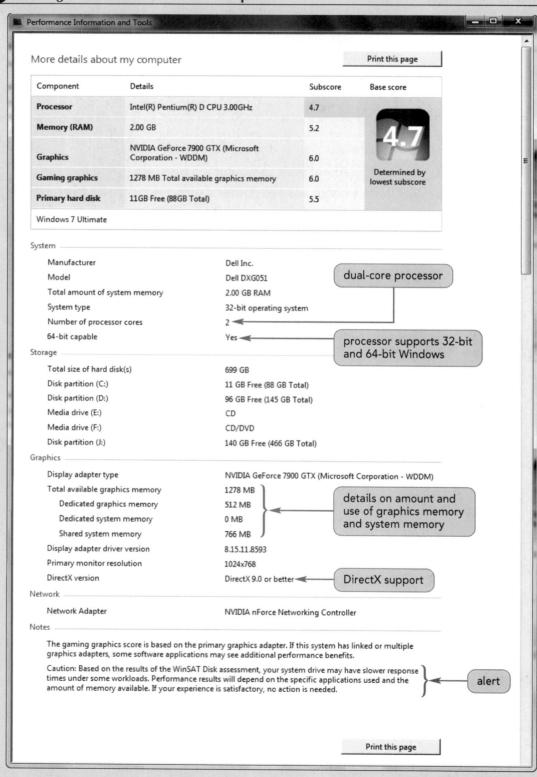

▶ **2.** Click the **Print this page** button, and after the Print dialog box opens, point to **Microsoft XPS Document Writer** under Select Printer on the General Property sheet, click the **Print** button. In the "Save the file as" dialog box, navigate to the Tutorial.01\Tutorial folder provided with your Data Files, click the **File name** box, type **WEI Summary**, and then click the **Save** button. After creating the XPS document file, Windows 7 opens the XPS document file in the XPS Viewer. If you want a printed copy as well, then you can use Print on the XPS Viewer File menu to print the document.

Trouble? If Windows 7 does not open the WEI Summary, then open your flash drive, click WEI Summary.xps, and then view the contents of the printed document.

▶ **3.** When you complete this tutorial, submit your XPS document via email, or your printed copy of the system summary report, to your instructor, as requested.

This report also includes additional information not found in the previous Performance and Information Tools window. For example, it identifies the video graphics card for the Graphics subscore and the total graphics memory for the Gaming graphics subscore, both of which are important in supporting the use of Windows Aero. In the System section, the report shows the computer's exact model, useful information when you need to download updates from a computer manufacturer's Web site. Also in the System section, the report identifies the number of processor cores.

The Graphics section of this report shows the total **dedicated graphics memory**, which consists of the video memory (or video RAM) available on the video display card itself or a portion of system memory dedicated exclusively for use by the Windows 7 graphics subsystem. **Shared system memory** consists of system memory (or RAM) that can be used by the graphics subsystem but which is not dedicated exclusively to that use. Both dedicated graphics memory and shared system memory are important in supporting the use of Windows. If you are purchasing a new computer, it is wise to acquire as much graphics memory as is available.

This section also shows the display adapter type and the DirectX version. Knowing your display adapter type is important in downloading updates for your video display adapter. **DirectX** refers to a set of Windows 7 technologies for handling multimedia software and content, including video, audio, 3D graphics, animation, and gaming on your computer's multimedia hardware devices. Windows 7 requires a video display adapter that supports at least DirectX 9 (or preferably DirectX 10), and a WDDM 1.0 driver. **WDDM** (**Windows Display Driver Model**) refers to specifications for a new type of video display adapter device driver required by Windows 7 to deliver high-performance and high-quality graphics and video, and thereby support the use of Windows Aero. Furthermore, this type of device driver provides far better multitasking, rapid updating of windows without visual artifacts (or defects), and increased overall system stability. Microsoft notes that you might need a graphics card that supports DirectX 10 or higher for some games and programs.

To complete your examination of system features:

▶ **1.** Close the WEI Summary.xps – XPS Viewer window.

▶ **2.** Close each of the two Performance Information Tools windows.

The Windows Experience Index is designed to make it easy for the average user to have a feeling for the overall performance of his or her computer and to act as an important guideline in purchasing a new computer, new computer hardware, and perhaps even new software.

Viewing the Windows Experience Index Base Score and Subscores

- Right-click the Computer desktop icon (or Computer on the Start menu), click Properties on the shortcut menu, maximize the System window, and then examine information on the Windows Experience Index base score.
- Click the Windows Experience Index link to open a Performance Information and Tools window, and then examine the Windows Experience Index subscores. Use the "What do these numbers mean?" link and the "About your computer's base score" link to locate Help information so that you can evaluate the Windows Experience Index base score and subscores.
- To view detailed performance information and then print a system summary report, click the "View and print detailed performance and system information" link, examine additional information about your computer system, click the "Print this page" button, select the printer you want to use (if necessary), and then click the Print button.

Restoring Your Computer

If you are working in a computer lab where you need to restore the computer to its original settings, or if you want to restore your computer to its original state (prior to starting this tutorial), complete the following steps.

To restore your computer's settings:

▶ 1. If you want to remove the CPU Meter from the desktop, right-click the **CPU Meter gadget**, and then click **Close gadget**.

▶ 2. If you want to remove the Computer icon from the desktop, click the **Start** button 🔵, right-click **Computer**, and then click **Show on Desktop** to remove the check mark.

▶ 3. If you want to turn off single-click activation, click the **Start** button 🔵 on the taskbar, type **folder options** in the Search box, press the **Enter** key, and in the Folder Options dialog box, click the **Double-click to open an item (single-click to select)** option button under "Click items as follows" on the General property sheet, and then click the **OK** button.

After restoring your computer, you can log off or turn it off.

Logging Off, or Turning Off, Your Computer

After you have finished using your computer, Windows 7 provides you with the following options for shutting down your computer or logging off your user account:

- **Shut down**—Windows closes all open programs, including Windows itself, and then completely turns off your computer, but you might need to manually shut the power off to your monitor and printer. Before you shut down your computer, you must save your work first. If you are planning on installing or replacing hardware in your system unit, completely shut down and unplug your computer before you open your system unit. If you are attaching a new hardware device to your computer, use the quick setup guide and other documentation for installing that hardware to determine whether you need to completely shut down your computer. If you see an orange shield icon with an exclamation mark on the Shut down button, then Windows 7 needs to install updates during the shutdown process.

- **Log off**—Windows 7 closes all windows, programs, and documents. If you want to use your computer later, you must log on under your user account again.
- **Lock**—Windows 7 locks your user account and then displays the Welcome screen. You must reenter your password to use your computer (assuming you use a password). This option is useful if you need to leave your computer for a while, but want to make sure it is secure. You can also use the Windows+L keyboard shortcut to lock your computer.
- **Restart**—Windows shuts down your computer and then restarts it. This option is useful if you notice that your computer responds slowly or if you encounter a problem. You may also need to use this option after installing a new software product or software update.
- **Sleep**—Windows 7 saves your work, turns off the monitor, and then reduces power consumption to all hardware components in your computer. Your computer appears off, but Windows 7 has actually placed your computer and its hardware in a low-power state called **Sleep**. When placed into the Sleep state, Windows 7 turns off power to the processor and most system hardware devices. Power is still provided to RAM in order to protect your open application and documents. Also, the mouse and keyboard remain powered on so that you can wake your computer up from the Sleep state. When you are ready to use your computer again, you can press the Power button on your computer. Windows 7 then restarts your computer and restores your computer to its previous state. It also opens any programs or files that you previously opened so that you are ready to work. Using this option is the fastest way to shut down your computer and the fastest way to restart it. Although Windows 7 saves any open documents, it's always a good idea to save your work manually in case you encounter an unexpected problem. You will examine Sleep in more detail after the bulleted points.
- **Hibernate**—If hibernation is enabled on your computer, then you will see this option on the Shut down menu. If you choose this option, Windows 7 saves the contents of RAM to a **hibernation file** on disk, shuts down your computer, and places it in **hibernation**. That means all devices, including the processor, are powered off. When you next power on your computer, Windows 7 restores the contents of RAM from the hibernation file so that your computer returns to the state it was in before you implemented hibernation. You do not need to save your work; however, that is always a good precaution against problems you might not anticipate.
- **Switch User**—If more than one person uses your computer and if each person has a different user account, then you will see this option on the Shut down menu. If someone else with an account on the same computer wants to use the computer, you can choose this option to have Windows 7 lock your user account and then display the Welcome screen so that user can log on under that user's account. Each user can set up their user account in different ways, use different Windows settings, keep their personal files separate from those of other users on the same computer, and, if required, use this option so that another person can quickly access his or her user account and complete a time-sensitive task and then log off so that you can log back on and pick up where you left off. This Windows 7 feature is called Fast User Switching.

Windows 7 (and Windows Vista) can implement one of two types of sleep states: Sleep and Hybrid Sleep. **Standby** mode in Windows XP is similar to Windows 7 Sleep. If your computer supports Sleep, you have to manually save your work before your computer enters the Sleep state. If a power failure occurs during Sleep and you have not saved your work, you will lose your work and the settings stored in RAM that are needed to restore your computer to its previous operating state.

In **Hybrid Sleep**, Windows 7 saves your computer's settings in memory and in a hibernation file on disk, turns off your monitor and hard disk, and reduces your computer's power usage. If you press a key or move the mouse, Windows 7 resumes power to the monitor and hard disk and you are ready to use your computer. However, if a power failure occurs, Windows 7 uses the hibernation file on disk to restore your computer to its previous operating state. Hybrid Sleep is automatically enabled on desktop computers, but not on mobile PCs. In Tutorial 2, you will examine power management settings, including those for turning on and turning off hibernation and Hybrid Sleep.

If you are working in a computer lab, do not shut down your computer unless your instructor or technical support staff specifically requests you to shut it down. College computer labs vary in their policies regarding shutting down computers, so if you are unsure as to what to do, check with your instructor or technical support staff.

To log off, or turn off, your computer:

▶ **1.** If you want to log off your own computer, or if you are working in a computer lab and want to log off the computer you are using, click the **Start** button ⊕, click the **Shut down menu button arrow**, and then click **Log off**.

▶ **2.** If you are using your own computer and want to place it into the Sleep state, click the **Start** button ⊕, click the **Shut down menu button arrow**, and then click **Sleep**.

▶ **3.** If you are using your own computer and want to completely shut down your computer, click the **Start** button ⊕ on the taskbar, and then click the **Shut down** button.

You can also open the Shut Down Windows dialog box by clicking the desktop background and then pressing the Alt+F4 keys. The Shut Down Windows dialog box includes the same options as the Start menu.

If you are working on a company network, or even on your computer, it is a good idea to log off when you finish your work so that no one else will be able to access files under your user account.

Juliann's coworkers thank her for the information she has shared with them, and they ask her to offer a monthly hands-on workshop that focuses on new features of interest to the staff, answer ongoing questions on the use of Windows 7, and provide them with additional tips to help them become more productive.

REVIEW

Session 1.3 Quick Check

1. The operating system assigns a unique _____ to each drive in a computer.
2. True or False. You can use the colon symbol (:) in certain types of folder names and filenames.
3. What two options in a folder window can you use to navigate around your computer?
4. What is the name of the rating that Windows 7 uses to measure the overall capability and performance of your computer hardware?
5. What Windows 7 state saves your computer's settings in memory, turns off the monitor and hard disk, and then reduces power usage to a level where the computer appears off?
6. In _____, Windows 7 saves your computer's settings in memory and in a hibernation file on disk, turns off your monitor and hard disk, and reduces your computer's power usage.
7. What is the difference between the terms gigabyte and gigahertz, and what do these terms measure?
8. Briefly describe the difference between a 32-bit and a 64-bit edition of Windows.

*Practice the skills
you learned in
the tutorial using
the same case
scenario.*

PRACTICE

Review Assignments

There are no Data Files needed for the Review Assignments.

Juliann has just hired a summer intern, Chad Cottrill, to assist her on a special project. Because Chad is already familiar with the use of Windows on computers at his high school, Juliann thinks he will adapt to Windows 7 quickly. While she is waiting for the go-ahead to implement the new project, she asks Chad to explore Windows 7 and become comfortable with the operating system. Since Chad is interested in animation, graphics, and music, and wants to eventually design special effects for movies, Juliann recommends that he explore the new features found in the Windows 7 Pictures and Music libraries.

As you complete each step, record your answers to questions so that you can submit them to your instructor. Use a word processing application such as Microsoft Word or the WordPad accessory to prepare your answers to these questions. If you change any settings on the computer you are using, make a note of the original settings so that you can restore them later. Complete the following steps:

1. If necessary, start Windows 7, and log on to your computer under your user account. Describe the process for logging on your computer. More specifically, does Windows 7 automatically display a Welcome screen and, if not, what happens? Is there only one user account, or are there multiple user accounts on the computer?

2. Describe the Windows 7 Aero features available with your Windows 7 edition, and then describe how you use these features.

3. If not already present, display the Computer icon on the desktop.

4. From the Start menu, click inside the Search box, and type **folder options**. What happens? Open Folder Options, enable the option for single-click activation, and apply this change to your computer.

5. Display the desktop View menu. Which options are enabled? Use the Esc key to close the View menu.

6. Open Windows Help and Support, and use the "Learn about Windows Basics" link to browse Help and find information that provides an overview of desktop gadgets. In the Help topic, examine information on the use of the Clock Gadget. Use the Windows Web site link to watch a video about desktop gadgets, and after the video finishes, close your Web browser window and the Windows Help and Support window.

7. Open the Gadget Gallery, double-click the Clock gadget in the Gadget Gallery dialog box, and then close the Gadget Gallery dialog box.

8. Right-click the Clock Gadget, and then choose Options. In the Clock dialog box, click the Next button under the view of the clock, examine each of the eight different styles for the clock, and then choose one of the eight styles. Click the "Show the second hand" check box to enable this option. Click the Time zone arrow, choose a different time zone than the one in which you reside, and note the name of that time zone. In the Clock name box, type the name of the time zone, or the name of a city in that time zone. Apply these settings and view the Clock gadget on the desktop. Briefly describe the appearance and features of your new Clock gadget, and indicate whether you would benefit from having two or more clocks for different time zones and, if so, how?

9. Use the Windows Help and Support Search feature to locate Help information on keyboard shortcuts. Select the Keyboard shortcuts link, and then select the "General keyboard shortcuts" link to view this Help topic. What keyboard shortcut can you use to undo an operation? What keyboard shortcut can you use to rename an object? What keyboard shortcut can you use to select everything in a document, or all the folders and files in a window? What keyboard shortcut can you use to rename an object, such as a desktop icon? What keyboard shortcut can you use to cancel the current task? Collapse the "General keyboard shortcuts" topic, and close the Windows Help and Support window.

10. Open the Computer window from the Computer desktop icon. List the friendly names, and drive names of your computer's hard drives and partitions, and identify any partitions or external drives. What is the storage capacity of your computer's hard drives? What is the available (or free) and used storage space on each hard drive? List and identify any devices with removable storage by type and by drive name.

11. Expand the Pictures library in the Navigation pane, expand the Public Pictures folder, and then open the Sample Pictures folder. Using the information in the Address bar, explain where the Sample Pictures folder is located in the folder structure of your computer. What type of view does Windows 7 use for the contents of this folder? What options are available on the toolbar? What other panes are visible in the Sample Pictures window?

12. Use the Change your view button to change the icon view to Extra Large Icons. What advantage(s) does this view have?

13. Point to one of the thumbnails in the Sample Pictures folder, and rest the mouse pointer on that thumbnail. Describe the two different ways in which Windows 7 displays information about the image in the file you selected.

14. Click one of the thumbnail images. What happens, and what program are you currently using? Why does Windows 7 use that program? Close the program window.

15. Open the Videos library from the Navigation pane, and then open the Sample Videos folder. Display the Preview pane, and then play the video in this folder from the Preview pane. Close the Sample Videos folder window.

16. Use the Computer icon on the desktop to open the System window and view properties of your computer. What edition of Windows 7 does your computer use? What is your system type? What type of processor does your computer use, and what is its clock speed? Is your processor a single-core or multicore processor? How much RAM is installed in your computer? What is your Windows Experience Index base score?

17. Use the Windows Experience Index link to view the subscores for each of the five components on which the Windows Experience Index is based. List your Windows Experience Index base score, and your five subscores (by component). What component is the most limiting factor in the performance of your computer? What component or components have the highest subscore? To improve the performance of your computer and improve your Windows Experience Index subscores, what change or changes could you make to your computer?

18. Choose the option to view and print detailed performance and system information. How many processor cores does your system have? Is your computer 64-bit capable? What is the total available graphics memory on your computer? What is the total dedicated graphics memory on your computer? What is the total dedicated system memory? How much shared system memory does your computer have? Close the two Performance Information and Tools windows.

19. Briefly list the features of the Windows 7 graphical user interface that you benefit the most from in order by most important feature, and briefly describe how you benefit (or make use of) these features.

20. Close the Clock gadget (to remove it from the desktop).

21. If you want to remove the Computer icon from the desktop, use the Start menu to turn off the display of the Computer icon on the desktop.

22. If you want to turn off single-click activation, open the Folder Options dialog box, choose the option to "Double-click to open an item (single-click to select)," and then apply this setting and close the dialog box.

23. Submit your answers to the questions in the Review Assignments to your instructor, either in printed or electronic form, as requested. Remember to include your name and any other information requested by your instructor on your assignment.

Use your skills to justify a software upgrade.

APPLY

Case Problem 1

There are no Data Files needed for this Case Problem.

Robotic Designs, Inc.   Kent Claypool works as a programmer for Robot Designs, Inc., a Delaware firm. One of his job's responsibilities is to prepare technical reference manuals on the design and use of robotic software. To produce these manuals, he must work with multiple applications, and assemble text, graphics, concept art, and illustrations from a variety of documents. Recently, Kent learned that the company's IT staff wants to upgrade the operating systems on the company's computers so that Kent and other employees can work more efficiently. Kent asks you to evaluate Windows 7 and prepare a report that identifies features of the Windows 7 operating system that will enable him and other employees to work more productively.

As you complete each step in this case problem, record your answers to questions so that you can submit them to your instructor. Use a word-processing application such as Microsoft Word or the WordPad accessory to prepare a report on your recommendations. Be specific and concise, and use boldface to enhance key terms, or key words, for features as you define and describe how an employee at Robotic Designs uses those features. Complete the following steps:

1. Identify five features of operating system software that support and simplify the process that Kent and his staff use to produce technical reference manuals. Describe each of the five features, and briefly explain in one paragraph what benefits employees at Robotic Designs might derive from using each of these features.

2. Describe six important criteria that the IT staff must consider when purchasing new computers and when upgrading hardware for use with Windows 7.

3. What Windows 7 edition or editions would best suit the needs of these employees and the type of products produced by this company? Why?

4. Submit your answers to this case problem to your instructor, either in printed or electronic form, as requested. Remember to include your name and any other information requested by your instructor on your assignment.

Use your skills to prepare a workshop on connecting to a network projector.

APPLY

Case Problem 2

There are no Data Files needed for this Case Problem.

Passos Marketing Analysts, Inc.   With its headquarters in Rio de Janeiro, Brazil, Passos Marketing Analysts, Inc., is a global Internet marketing firm specializing in full-service strategic market research and consulting for its clients. Alex Passos, the firm's owner, asks you to prepare a demonstration on using Windows 7 to connect to an overhead projector so that the company's professional marketing staff can set up effective market research presentations for clients. You decide to start by drawing on the resources in the Windows Help and Support Center.

As you complete each step in this case problem, record your answers to questions so that you can submit them to your instructor. Use a word-processing application such as Microsoft Word or the WordPad accessory to prepare your answers to these questions. If you change any settings on the computer you are using, make a note of the original settings so that you can restore them later. Complete the following steps:

1. Open Windows Help and Support, search for information on projectors, open the Help topic on connecting to a projector, and then use the Windows Web site link to watch a video on connecting to a projector.

✦ EXPLORE

2. Prepare a one-page report that describes the steps for connecting to a projector. Make sure you identify the three types of cable connections you can use, and the four ways in which you can display a desktop using your computer and a projector. What two ways are you most likely to use when connecting your computer to a projector? What shortcut key can you use to select a network projection display option? Describe an example of how you or someone else might use this feature in a workplace environment.

✦ EXPLORE

3. Locate and click the Help terms *video port* and *USB port* displayed in green in the Help topic to view definitions of these terms. Then, in the final paragraph of your report, list the definition for each of these terms. If the Help term includes an example, then describe that example.

4. In what other way might you use this procedure?

5. Submit your case problem report to your instructor, either in printed or electronic form, as requested. Remember to include your name and any other information requested by your instructor on your assignment.

Use your skills to determine the feasibility of upgrading a firm's computers.

APPLY

Case Problem 3

There are no Data Files needed for this Case Problem.

Pixel Dynamics, Inc. Imogene Maynard, the owner of Pixel Dynamics, and her staff use resource-intensive applications to design 3D graphics, animation, video, and online presentations for the Web sites of the company's business clients. She asks you to examine the feasibility of upgrading the company's computers from Windows Vista Business to Windows 7 Professional. The new computers must support Windows Aero to more efficiently and effectively meet the needs of their clients and to attract new clients. She asks you to prepare a report that summarizes your analysis and evaluation of upgrading the company's computers. As a starting point for analyzing the acquisition of new Windows 7 computer systems for Pixel Dynamics, Imogene recommends you evaluate your computer system first.

As you complete each step in this case problem, record your answers to questions so that you can submit them to your instructor. Use a word-processing application such as Microsoft Word or the WordPad accessory to prepare your answers to these questions. Complete the following steps:

1. What are the primary ways in which you use your computer?

2. Locate and list the Windows Experience Index base score and the Processor, Memory (RAM), Graphics, Gaming graphics, and Primary hard disk subscores for your computer.

⊕ EXPLORE

3. Use the "What do these numbers mean?" link in the Performance Information and Tools window to open Windows Help and Support and locate information on the Windows Experience Index. What is the base score for running Windows Aero? What base score should a computer have to support multitasking? What base score supports the use of high-end 3D graphics, animation, and video applications at Pixel Dynamics? What does the Windows Experience Index base score imply for the Processor, Memory (RAM), Graphics, Gaming graphics, and Primary hard disk subscores? Examine the Help information on a computer's subscores. What types of subscores support the types of computer tasks required of employees at Pixel Dynamics?

4. Using your computer's base score, rate your own computer's performance based on the information covered in this tutorial and in Windows Help and Support. Identify the current range used for the Windows Experience Index base score and subscores.

5. Examine the Windows Experience Index subscores, and identify the component that limits the performance of your computer. How do these subscores affect the performance of your computer?

6. Identify and list ways in which you can improve the performance of your computer by upgrading its hardware.

⊕ EXPLORE

7. In what other ways might you use the Windows Experience Index base score and subscores?

8. Close Windows Help and Support, and then close the Performance Information and Tools window.

9. Submit your answers to this case problem to your instructor, either in printed or electronic form, as requested. Remember to include your name and any other information requested by your instructor on your assignment.

Extend your skills to recommend the best strategy for managing files for a Web analysis company.

CHALLENGE

Case Problem 4

There are no Data Files needed for this Case Problem.

Web Stats, Inc. You have recently been hired as an information engineer by Web Stats, a company specializing in data mining and the analysis of large volumes of data for information. Serena Tusing, your supervisor, asks you to come up with a list of recommendations for improving how she and her workgroup employees can more efficiently share computers, folders, and files, and at the same time, enable staff members to keep certain folders and files separate and secure. One feature that immediately comes to mind is Fast User Switching.

As you complete each step in this case problem, record your answers to questions so that you can submit them to your instructor. Use a word-processing application such as Microsoft Word or the WordPad accessory to prepare your answers to these questions. Also, be specific and concise, and use boldface to enhance key terms, or key words, for features as you describe how employees at Web Stats can share certain files but keep other files private. Complete the following steps:

1. Use Windows Help and Support to locate information on frequently asked questions about user accounts, sharing files using the Public folders, and Fast User Switching.

2. Using information gleaned from Windows Help and Support as well as what you've learned in this tutorial, prepare a report containing a set of recommendations for managing access to the same computer by several employees and for sharing folders and files on the same computer. Address the following questions in your report:

⊕ EXPLORE

   a. What is a user account? What types of accounts does Windows 7 support, and how do they differ?

⊕ **EXPLORE**

    b. What are the advantages and disadvantages of having a separate user account, or sharing the same user account, on the same computer used by several employees?

    c. Where can employees store company files, downloads, and other types of files needed by all staff members who use the same computer? How can they organize different types of files for easy access?

    d. Where can employees store their business contacts, documents, downloads, and Internet shortcuts that only they need to access and use?

⊕ **EXPLORE**

    e. How can Fast User Switching enable several employees to share the same computer, and at the same time, keep their folders and files separate from other employees?

⊕ **EXPLORE**

    f. How can you as a single user of a computer benefit from the use of several accounts?

3. Submit your case problem report to your instructor, either in printed or electronic form, as requested. Remember to include your name and any other information requested by your instructor on your assignment.

ENDING DATA FILES

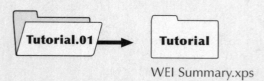

WEI Summary.xps

Customizing Windows 7

Customizing Desktops

OBJECTIVES

Session 2.1
- Select a desktop theme, desktop background, and window colors
- Examine mouse properties
- Use the ClearType Text Tuner
- Choose special visual effects

Session 2.2
- Customize the Start menu
- Customize the taskbar and notification area
- Create and customize taskbar toolbars

Session 2.3
- Adjust resolution, color depth, and refresh rate
- Adjust DPI scaling settings
- Evaluate power management features

Case | *Kimbrough & Co.*

Kimbrough & Co. is a global company that develops and sells pharmaceuticals around the world. Over the last 25 years, Kimbrough & Co. has developed new drugs in its research labs in Great Britain, France, and Sweden. Recently, Kimbrough & Co. opened a research facility in the United States that uses DNA splicing technology to accelerate the process for finding new classes of drugs. Furthermore, a new research group is exploring how to develop new pharmaceuticals from rain forests around the world. To increase the productivity of its staff, Kimbrough & Co. has purchased 100 top-of-the-line computers for its scientific, technical, office, and administrative support staff in its U.S. division. Over the next several weeks, you will work with Alejandro Castillo, a computer systems specialist at the new research facility, to help staff members customize their desktops. As Alejandro has discovered, employees are more productive if they can customize their working environment on their desktop and mobile computers.

In this tutorial, you select an Aero theme, and customize the desktop background image and window colors. You use the ClearType Text Tuner to sharpen text on the monitor, and you examine special visual effects that affect the performance and appearance of the graphical user interface. You customize the Start menu, the taskbar, and the notification area. You place toolbars on the taskbar, and you create a new taskbar toolbar from a folder. You examine how the settings for your screen resolution, color depth, refresh rate, and DPI scaling can improve the appearance of your desktop and windows. Finally, you examine power management settings and power plans on your computer.

STARTING DATA FILES

There are no starting Data Files needed for this tutorial.

SESSION 2.1 VISUAL OVERVIEW

Control Panel ▸ Appearance and Personalization ▸ Personalization

Control Panel Home

Change desktop icons

Change mouse pointers

Change your account picture

Use the "Change your account picture" link to change the image used for the icon displayed on the Start menu and Welcome screen for your user account and coordinate it with your desktop theme.

A **theme** consists of a set of elements that include a desktop background image (or combination of images), a screen saver, a window border color, and a sound scheme.

Windows 7 provides predefined Windows Aero themes for enhancing the graphical user interface. The Windows 7 theme is the default theme.

The Desktop Background window provides options for selecting and positioning a desktop background image (or images), specifying slide show settings for certain themes, and picking a background color.

Use Window Color to select, mix, and adjust the color intensity, hue, saturation, and brightness of windows, the Start menu, and the taskbar. **Hue** refers to the position of a color in the color spectrum, or what is typically thought of as a specific color, such as red. **Saturation** refers to the amount of gray in the color, and therefore determines the purity of a color.

See also

Display

Taskbar and Start Menu

Ease of Access Center

Change the visuals and sounds on your compute

Click a theme to change the desktop background, window color

My Themes (1)

My Custom Theme

Aero Themes (7)

Windows 7   Architecture   Ch

Scenes   United States

Desktop Background
Slide Show

Window Color
Custom

CUSTOM DESKTOPS

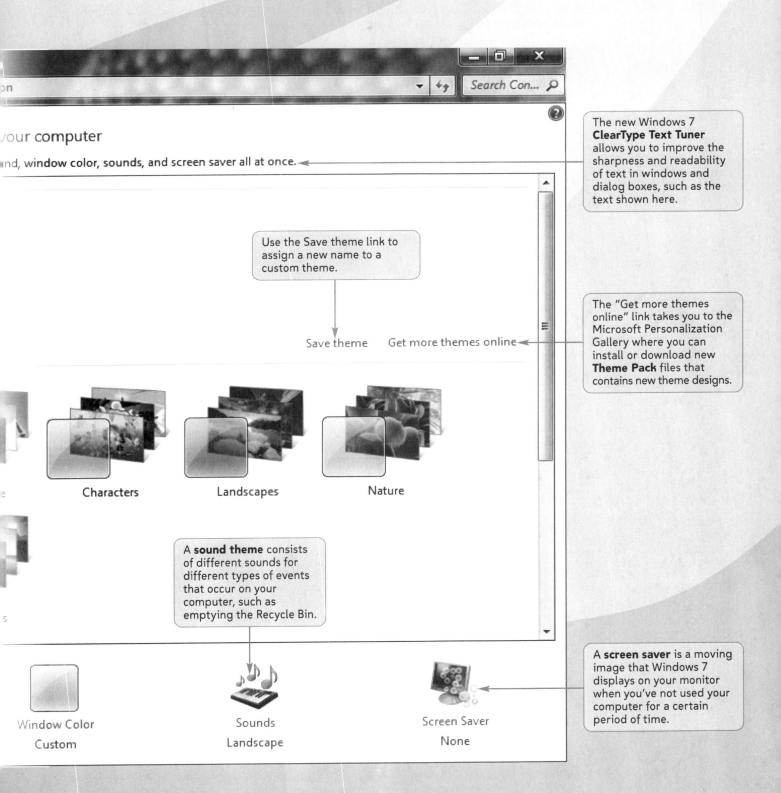

/our computer

nd, window color, sounds, and screen saver all at once.

The new Windows 7 **ClearType Text Tuner** allows you to improve the sharpness and readability of text in windows and dialog boxes, such as the text shown here.

Use the Save theme link to assign a new name to a custom theme.

Save theme   Get more themes online

The "Get more themes online" link takes you to the Microsoft Personalization Gallery where you can install or download new **Theme Pack** files that contains new theme designs.

Characters   Landscapes   Nature

A **sound theme** consists of different sounds for different types of events that occur on your computer, such as emptying the Recycle Bin.

A **screen saver** is a moving image that Windows 7 displays on your monitor when you've not used your computer for a certain period of time.

Window Color

Custom

Sounds

Landscape

Screen Saver

None

Setting Up Your Computer

To set up your computer for this tutorial, you should display the Computer icon on the desktop, and then switch your computer to Web style by enabling single-click activation. In the following steps, you will check and, if necessary, change those settings.

To set up your computer:

▶ 1. If Windows 7 does not display a Computer icon on the desktop, open the Start menu, right click **Computer**, click **Show on Desktop**, and then close the Start menu.

▶ 2. If you need to enable single-click activation, open the Start menu, type **folder options** in the Search box, and then press the **Enter** key to open the Folder Options dialog box.

▶ 3. Under "Click items as follows" on the General property sheet, click the **Single-click to open an item (point to select)** option button, and then click the **Underline icon titles only when I point at them** option button.

▶ 4. Click the **View** tab, and in the Advanced settings box, click the **Hide extensions for known file types** check box (to remove the check mark), and then click the **OK** button to close the Folder Options dialog box. Now you can view file extensions in folder windows.

Now, you're ready to look at themes and window color options for customizing the Windows 7 graphical user interface.

Customizing the Graphical User Interface

Like all earlier versions of Windows, Windows 7 provides a variety of options for customizing the graphical user interface. As you saw in Tutorial 1, Windows Aero provides a new user interface design that is richer than in previous versions of Windows. In the following sections, you examine different ways of customizing the Windows 7 graphical user interface.

Choosing a Theme

Windows 7 provides three types of themes—Aero themes, basic themes, and high-contrast themes—that provide a unified look for the graphical user interface, including the desktop. Aero themes combine Aero glass effects with a single desktop background image or with multiple desktop background images that are displayed as a slide show. You can change the interval of time for a theme's slide show effect so different desktop background images are displayed more frequently or in random order. Basic and high-contrast themes make it easier to see items on the monitor and improve the performance of your computer, but they do not include Aero glass effects. Some themes also include specific types of desktop icons and mouse pointers. Your computer might also have themes installed by your computer manufacturer or by other software products you acquire. In addition, you can create your own themes.

Businesses can create their own themes to provide a consistent look on company computers, display a company logo, improve access and use of a computer by individuals with visual limitations (such as color blindness), or display job-related information to employees. College computer labs sometimes use a custom theme to remind students of lab policies, and explain any limitations on printing (to contain printer and paper costs).

Alejandro recommends that you choose one of the Aero themes for your computer.

To choose a desktop theme:

▶ **1.** Right-click the **desktop background**, and then click **Personalize** on the desktop shortcut menu. Windows 7 opens the Personalization window, and displays the available themes on your computer, as shown in Figure 2-1.

Figure 2-1	Viewing the current Aero theme

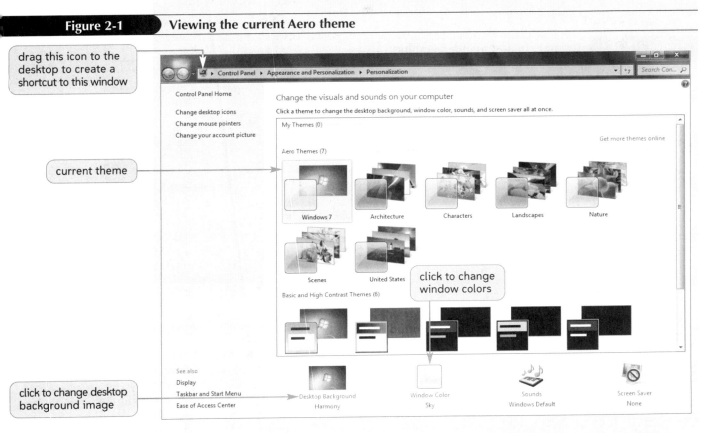

drag this icon to the desktop to create a shortcut to this window

current theme

click to change window colors

click to change desktop background image

Windows 7 displays a blue border and background around the current theme. On the computer used for this figure, the current theme is Windows 7, the default theme. The themes are organized into groups: My Themes (for ones you create), Aero Themes, and Basic and High Contrast Themes. All of the Aero themes, except Windows 7, include multiple desktop background images. If you choose the Windows Classic basic theme, the elements of the graphical user interface, including your desktop, windows, dialog boxes, Start menu, taskbar, and menus, appear similar to the way they appeared in much earlier versions of Windows. If your computer manufacturer or another software product installed themes on your computer, you will also see an Installed Themes category. At the bottom of this window, you can customize a theme you've chosen by selecting a different desktop background image (or a combination of images), a window color, a sound scheme, and a screen saver.

▶ **2.** Under Aero themes, click the **Architecture** theme, and then click the **Show desktop** button █ to minimize the Personalization window and view the new desktop theme. Windows 7 applies a theme as soon as you select it.

▶ **3.** Click the **Show desktop** button █ again to restore the Personalization window, and keep the Personalization window open for the next part of the tutorial.

You can use the "Change your account picture" link in the Personalization window to choose another icon for your user account so it fits with your theme.

Choosing a Desktop Background

One way to customize a theme is to change the desktop background image or images. You can use images stored in files with the file extension .bmp for Bitmap image, .jpg or .jpeg for JPEG image, .gif for GIF image, .png for PNG image, and .tif or .tiff for TIFF image. Each of these types of graphic file formats contains a bitmapped graphic. A **bitmapped graphic** is an image represented by a pattern of pixels, or picture elements, as shown in Figure 2-2.

Figure 2-2   **Example of a bitmapped graphic**

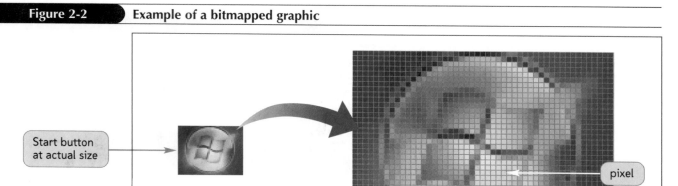

Start button at actual size

Start button magnified 800%

pixel

A **pixel** is the smallest unit on a monitor for displaying a specific color. Figure 2-2 shows the Windows logo on the Start menu button at actual size and at a magnification of 800%. As you can see, the image consists of an array of pixels, each of which is a different color. Each pixel consists of one or more dots, or points, that are treated as one logical unit on the monitor. Each dot in turn is composed of red, green, and blue (RGB) components that blend together to form a single color. At the maximum resolution for your monitor, (covered in the next section of the tutorial), one pixel equals one dot. The number of bits used for each pixel determines the number of colors available for a pixel (a feature you will also examine in the next section of the tutorial).

The Bitmap image file format (with the .bmp file extension) is one type of bitmapped graphic. It contains an image with thousands or millions of pixels in an uncompressed format, so file sizes can be quite large.

The **JPEG image** (for **Joint Photographic Experts Group**, and pronounced "jay peg") is a bitmapped graphic image file format with the .jpg or .jpeg file extension that stores images in a compressed format at a ratio of 10:1, 20:1, or greater by removing some of the detail in an image (changes that the human eye presumably cannot detect), and therefore it is called **lossy compression** and file sizes are relatively small. JPEG images are commonly used for real-life images, such as photographs of individuals or land-scapes, and for scanned images. Also, JPEG images are commonly used on Web pages and, because of their small size, the amount of time required to transmit them over the Internet is far less than for uncompressed Bitmap images.

GIF image (for **Graphics Interchange Format**, and pronounced "jiff" or "gif") is yet another bitmapped graphic file format. The GIF file format stores a bitmap image at a compression of 1.5:1 to 2:1 without any loss of detail in the image (called **lossless compression**). The actual amount of compression depends on the degree to which the same colors are repeated within the image itself. Also, GIF images are limited to a palette of 256 colors or less. A **palette**, or **color palette**, is a set of available colors used either by an application or by the operating system. GIF files are well suited for cartoon or line art, and for relatively small images with few colors and clearly defined borders between different parts of an image. As such, they are commonly used for buttons and small icons on Web pages.

The **PNG image** (for **Portable Network Graphics,** and pronounced "ping") is a newer type of high-quality bitmapped graphic file format that was designed as a replacement for the GIF file format. The PNG file format supports lossless compression with no loss of detail in the image, transparency, and up to 16.8 million colors (or almost all colors visible to the human eye), but unlike the GIF file format, it does not support animation. All the images for the figures in this textbook came from PNG files.

The **TIFF image** (for **Tag Image File Format**) is another important bitmapped graphic file format that supports the use of high-quality images, and therefore is commonly used in the publishing industry and for scanning images. Like the PNG file format, it supports lossless compression, transparency, and up to 16.8 million colors.

Next, you will customize the desktop background for the Architecture theme.

TIP

You can save a PowerPoint slide as a GIF, JPEG, PNG, or TIFF image.

To customize the desktop background for the Architecture theme:

▶ 1. Click the **Desktop Background** link at the bottom of the Personalization window. Windows 7 opens the Desktop Background window and displays the six desktop background images in the Architecture theme, as well as the desktop background images available in all of the other Aero themes. See Figure 2-3. Notice that each desktop background image under Architecture has a check mark in the check box located in the upper-left corner of the image.

| Figure 2-3 | Viewing images in an Aero slide show |

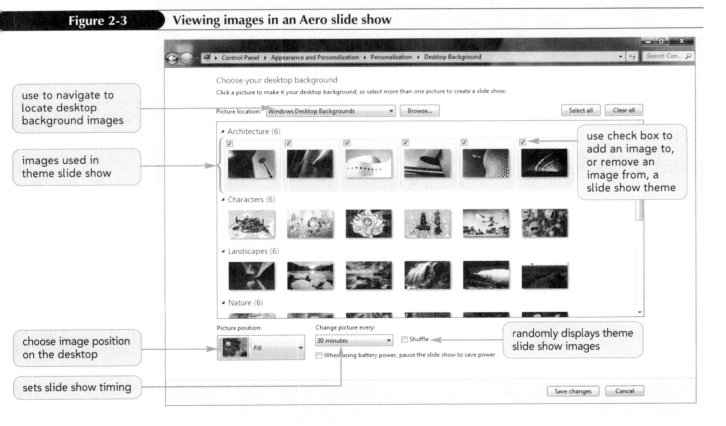

use to navigate to locate desktop background images

images used in theme slide show

use check box to add an image to, or remove an image from, a slide show theme

choose image position on the desktop

sets slide show timing

randomly displays theme slide show images

If you want to remove one or more desktop background images from a theme to create a custom theme, you remove the check mark from the check box for each desktop background image you want to remove. Likewise, if you want to add other images to your new custom theme, you point to the desktop background image you want to use, and after Windows 7 displays the check box for that image, click the check box. You can choose images from different themes to create a custom theme. For example, you might choose one or more images from the Landscape, Nature, Scenes, and United States Aero themes, or you might combine all of the images from all of the themes into a new custom theme.

The Picture location box shows that these images are Windows Desktop Backgrounds included with the built-in themes. From the Picture location list box, you can access the Pictures library to select photos stored in the My Pictures and Sample Pictures folders. The Top Rated Photos option on the Picture location menu selects images based on a ranking system assigned to the image. The Solid Colors option allows you to choose a single color for the desktop background. The Browse button allows you to locate other folders that contain images that you want to use for desktop backgrounds. Once you select another folder with the Browse button, that folder is subsequently listed in the Picture location box.

Windows 7 has five options for positioning an image on the desktop:

- **Fill**—Windows 7 resizes an image to fill the desktop, but maintains the ratio of its width to length. Windows 7 also crops any part of the image that does not fit on the desktop. For example, if the height of the image is greater than the width, Windows 7 resizes the image so the entire width of the image stretches across the desktop, and then crops the top and bottom parts of the image that do not fit on the desktop.
- **Fit**—Windows 7 stretches the image or video to fit either the width or length of the desktop, but maintains the ratio of the width to the length so there is no distortion. In some cases, the image may not fill the entire desktop, which leaves desktop space for icons.
- **Stretch**—Windows 7 stretches an image so it fills the entire desktop. That may mean altering the ratio of its width to length and introducing distortion; however, the distortion may look interesting and just reflect another way to look at the same image. In fact, a small amount of distortion might not even be discernable. If the height of an image is greater than its width, the height of the image or video fits the height of the desktop, and the width of the image or video is stretched to fit across the desktop.
- **Tile**—Windows 7 repeats the image at actual size across the desktop, starting in the upper-left corner of the desktop. Windows 7 displays the image with no distortion; however, only portions of the repeated image may be visible on the right and bottom edges of the desktop. This option is useful for files that contain a small graphic image because you can create a collage effect on the desktop.
- **Center**—Windows 7 centers an image at actual size on the desktop and maintains the ratio of its width to length with no distortion. In some cases, the image or video may not fill the entire desktop; however that can be useful because icons can be placed on the desktop outside the image or video. This option provides the sharpest view of an image.

If you add a check mark to the Shuffle check box, then the images in a theme's slide show are displayed in random order. If you are using a mobile computer that relies on battery power, or if you have a desktop computer with a backup power supply (as is the case for the computer used for these figures), you can choose the option to pause the slide show to save power. If you are using a desktop computer without a backup power supply, then this option is not available.

To further customize, and then view, your Aero theme:

▶ **1.** Click the **Picture position** button, and then click **Center**.

▶ **2.** Click the **Change picture every** button, click **10 seconds**, and then click the **Save changes** button. Windows 7 returns you to the Personalization window. All the changes you have made to the Architecture theme are stored under the name "Unsaved Theme" under My Themes.

▶ **3.** Click the **Show desktop** button ▮ to minimize the Personalization window and view the new desktop theme. Every 10 seconds you will see another desktop background image from the Architecture theme.

▶ **4.** Click the **Show desktop** button ▮ again to restore the Personalization window.

TIP

If you choose and apply an unsaved theme, then you can right-click the theme, and save the theme under another name.

Every time you change the theme on your computer, Windows 7 resets the interval of time for displaying the theme's slide show to the default setting of 30 minutes.

REFERENCE

Customizing a Theme's Desktop Background

- Right-click the desktop, and then click Personalize.
- In the Personalization window, click a theme under My Themes, Aero Themes, Basic and High Contrast Themes, or Installed Themes (if available).
- Click the Desktop Background link, and then click the Picture location button to view and select images from another location, such as Windows Desktop Backgrounds, Pictures Library, Top Rated Photos, Solid Colors, or another folder. Use the Browse button to locate a folder that contains images you want to use for a theme's desktop background.
- Click the Picture position button, and choose an option for displaying a desktop background.
- Click the "Change picture every" button, and select a time interval for displaying desktop background images in a theme's slide show.
- Click the Shuffle check box to display desktop background images randomly in a desktop slide show.
- Click the "When using battery power, pause the slide show to save power" check box to enable or turn off the option for pausing a slide show when using a computer with battery power or a battery power backup unit.
- Click the Save changes button to save your changes with the theme you chose.
- Close the Personalization window.

Specifying Window Colors

You can use the Window Color link in the Personalization window to open the Window Color and Appearance window and choose different color settings for window borders, the Start menu, and the taskbar. You can select a basic color and then change the color intensity, which determines the richness of the window color. You can also use a Color Mixer to adjust the hue, saturation, and brightness of a color.

Alejandro and you decide to examine the options for specifying and adjusting the color of window borders, window frames (such as the title bar, and in some instances, a translucent pane at the bottom of a window), window backgrounds (in some cases), the Start menu, the taskbar, and taskbar buttons. Then you can help other employees with visual limitations who need to customize these elements of the graphical user interface so those elements are easier to see.

To examine window color options:

1. Click the **Window Color** link at the bottom of the Personalization window. Windows 7 opens the Window Color and Appearance window. See Figure 2-4.

Figure 2-4 **Color options for window borders, the Start menu, and the taskbar**

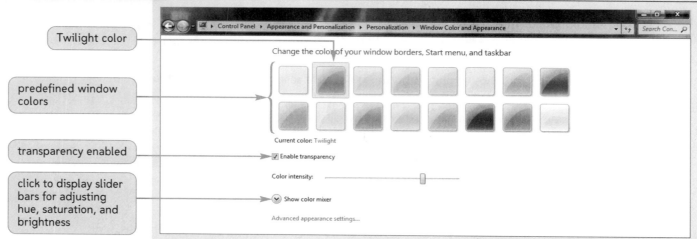

Twilight color

predefined window colors

transparency enabled

click to display slider bars for adjusting hue, saturation, and brightness

Windows 7 notes that the current color is Twilight (the default option for the Architecture theme), and in the palette of colors, it highlights the Twilight color with a blue border and blue background. Sky is the default color for the Windows 7 Aero theme.

The Enable transparency check box determines whether Windows 7 uses Windows Aero translucency. If you remove the check mark from this box, the Start menu, taskbar, window borders, and dialog boxes are no longer partially translucent.

2. Click the **Ruby** color, the bright red color on the right side of the first row of colors, and notice that Windows 7 applies this color to the borders and title bar of the Window Color and Appearance window as well as the taskbar and taskbar buttons. If you open the Start menu, you will notice that Windows 7 applies the same window color to the right panel and border of the Start menu. If you open a dialog box, Windows 7 applies the new window color to the frame and border of the dialog box.

3. Gradually drag the Color intensity slider tab ▯ to the right. Note that the intensity of the color increases in the window borders, the title bar, taskbar, and taskbar buttons.

4. Gradually drag the Color intensity slider tab ▯ to the left, and note that the color intensity decreases for the window borders, the title bar, taskbar, and taskbar buttons.

5. Click the **Ruby** color. Windows 7 restores the original Color intensity setting.

Next, use the color mixer to explore more options for adjusting window color.

TIP

If you point to a color, Windows 7 displays a ToolTip with the name of the color.

To examine window color mixer options:

▶ **1.** Click the **Show color mixer** expand button ⊙. Windows 7 displays slider bars for adjusting Hue, Saturation, and Brightness. See Figure 2-5.

| Figure 2-5 | Adjusting color intensity, hue, saturation, and brightness |

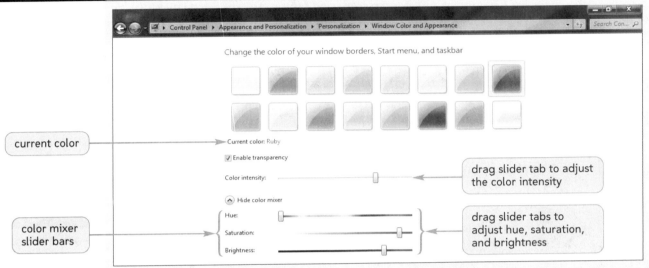

current color

color mixer slider bars

Notice that each slider bar shows how the color of the window borders, title bar, Start menu, taskbar, and taskbar buttons will change as you drag the slider tab to the left or right.

▶ **2.** Gradually drag the Hue slider tab to the right and then to the left. Windows 7 changes the color of the window's borders and title bar as well as the taskbar and taskbar buttons.

▶ **3.** Click the **Ruby** color to restore the default Hue setting for this color, and then gradually drag the **Saturation** slider tab to the left and then to the right. The shade of red in the window frame and borders gradually becomes lighter as you drag to the left, and it becomes darker as you drag to the right. To create this effect, the amount of gray in the color increases.

▶ **4.** Click the **Ruby** color to restore the default Saturation setting for this color, and then gradually drag the **Brightness** slider tab to the left along the slider bar. The amount of brightness in the color decreases, and the color changes to a darker color.

▶ **5.** Click the default **Twilight** color to restore the original color and original Brightness setting, and if necessary, click the **Save changes** button.

▶ **6.** Click the **Window Color** link to return to the Window Color window. If you click the Advanced appearance settings link in the Window Color and Appearance window, Windows 7 opens the Window Color and Appearance dialog box where you can select and customize individual elements of the graphical user interface, such as icon titles, menus, message boxes, and ToolTips (to name a few), but only if you have selected the Windows 7 Basic theme or a High Contrast theme.

▶ **7.** Keep the Window Color and Appearance window open for the next section of the tutorial.

REFERENCE

Adjusting Window Color Settings

- Right-click the desktop, click Personalization, and then click the Window Color link in the Personalization window.
- Click one of the 16 colors, and then drag the slider tab on the Color Intensity to adjust the intensity of the color.
- Click the Show color mixer expand button, and then drag the slider tab on the Hue, Saturation, and Brightness slider bars to fine-tune the color you prefer to use for window borders, the title bar, the Start menu, the taskbar, and taskbar buttons.
- If desired, click the Enable transparency check box to disable or enable Windows Aero translucency.
- Click the Save changes button to save your changes and apply your new window color settings.

Different themes have different sound schemes, so as you change themes, the sound scheme automatically changes. However, you can use the Sounds link in the Personalization window to choose another Windows 7 sound scheme.

INSIGHT

Enhance an Office's Security with a Screen Saver

While many people enjoy screen savers for their spectacular effects, you can also use a screen saver, such as the 3D text screen saver, to display your company's name and to enhance the security of your computer. For example, you can add a screen saver to your customized theme and then customize the screen saver so that Windows 7 not only displays the screen saver after a certain amount of time, but also prompts you for your password. You can use this feature to protect important documents with sensitive information that are displayed on your monitor when you are away from your computer. The screen saver prevents anyone else from viewing the contents of a document. If you also enable password protection for the screen saver, no one can access your computer while you are away from your desk. Furthermore, you can coordinate a screen saver with your power management plan (covered at the end of this tutorial) so the screen saver is active before Windows 7 turns off the display of your monitor, switches to a low-power usage state, or shuts down.

Saving a Theme and Creating a Theme Pack

Once you've chosen and customized a theme, you can save your changes to the theme. If you want to share that theme with someone else, then you can save the theme as a theme pack file, and then email the theme pack file to another person. A theme pack file has a .themepack file extension.

Alejandro asks you to save and then send your new custom theme pack via email to him so he can make it available to other staff members.

To save changes to your desktop theme and create a theme pack:

1. If necessary, click **Personalization** in the Address bar to return to the Personalization window.

2. Right-click the **Unsaved Theme** icon, and then click **Save theme**. Windows 7 opens the Save Theme As dialog box.

3. Type **Archetypal Designs** in the Theme name box, and then click the **Save** button. Figure 2-6 shows the new saved theme.

Figure 2-6　　Saving a new theme

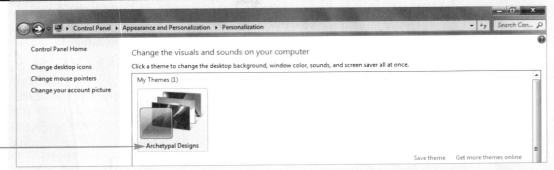

new saved theme

▶ **4.** To share this theme, right-click the **Archetypal Designs** theme icon, click **Save theme for sharing** on the shortcut menu, and in the Save Theme Pack As dialog box, type **Archetypal Designs** in the File name box. Windows 7 saves your theme pack in the Documents library unless you specify another location.

▶ **5.** To save the theme pack to your flash drive, click your flash drive in the Navigation pane, navigate to the **Tutorial.02\Tutorial** folder, click the Save button in the Save Theme Pack As dialog box, and then close the Personalization window.

▶ **6.** Click the Computer icon, and then click your flash drive icon. In your flash drive window, you will see your new theme pack file with the .themepack file extension.

▶ **7.** Close the flash drive window.

Now you can send that theme pack via email when you're ready. A company can use theme packs to deploy a standard corporate theme on all workplace computers and mobile computers.

REFERENCE

Saving a Theme and Creating a Theme Pack

- Right-click the desktop, and then click Personalize.
- To save changes to a theme, right-click the Unsaved Theme icon under My Themes, click Save theme, and in the Save Theme As dialog box, type a new name for your theme in the Theme name box, and then click the Save button.
- To save a theme as a theme pack, right-click a theme icon, and then click Save theme for sharing on the shortcut menu. In the Save Theme Pack As dialog box, use the Navigation pane to navigate to another folder (if necessary), type a name for your theme pack in the File name box, and then click the Save button.
- Close the Personalization window.

Any custom themes you create are shown under My Themes. If you want to delete one of these themes, you can right-click the theme icon, and then choose the option for deleting the theme. You cannot delete a custom theme that you are currently using. You first have to select and apply another theme before deleting the custom theme that was previously used. Before deleting a theme, save it as a theme pack in case you need it later.

Changing Mouse Properties

You can also customize your mouse so that you can work more effectively, make the use of the mouse more accessible and easier to use if you have limited use of your hands and fingers, and, just as importantly, reduce the risk of injury from prolonged use of the mouse. You can customize the use of your mouse in these five basic ways:

- **Mouse button configuration**—The **primary mouse button** is the one you use to select, click, and drag objects as well as position an insertion point in a document. The **secondary mouse button** is the one you use to right-click an object. The default mouse settings assume that you are right-handed, and that you use a right-handed mouse. If you are right-handed, you work with the mouse on the right side of your desk, and you use your index finger to click the left mouse button and your middle finger to click the right mouse button. If you are left-handed, you most likely will want to work with the mouse on the left side of your desk. You can swap the use of the left and right mouse buttons so you can use the index finger of your left hand to click with the right mouse button and the middle finger on your left hand to "right-click" with the left mouse button.
- **Double-click speed**—If you work in Windows Classic style with double-click activation, you can adjust the double-click speed of your mouse so double-clicking is easier, and so Windows 7 responds to two clicks as a double-click rather than two single-clicks (which can be a useful customization for individuals with limited use of their hands).
- **Pointer speed**—Depending on the type of work that you do, you may want to adjust the mouse pointer speed. For example, if you set the mouse pointer speed to a faster setting, a small movement of the mouse creates a greater movement of the mouse pointer across the screen. This feature is useful if you only have a small amount of desk space available for using the mouse. If you change the mouse pointer speed to a slower setting, the mouse pointer moves more slowly across the screen. A slower pointer speed gives you more control of the mouse pointer if, for example, you are using drawing software where you need precise control.
- **Mouse pointer shapes**—Windows 7 uses a set of default mouse pointer shapes to provide you with visual clues when pointing, selecting text, resizing a window, and clicking a link. Windows 7 also displays specific mouse pointer shapes to indicate that an application is busy and that you either can (1) continue to work, but the program you are using will respond slowly to your requests, or (2) you must wait until an operation is complete before you can do anything else on your computer. If you prefer, choose an alternate mouse point scheme so you can more easily identify where the mouse pointer is on the screen. You can also customize the individual mouse pointer shapes to make your use of the mouse more interesting.
- **Mouse wheel scrolling**—You can adjust the vertical scrolling and horizontal scrolling capability of the mouse wheel so you can scroll faster through windows, or zoom in more quickly on the contents of a document or a Web page, and then later zoom out.

Since you rely extensively on the use of a mouse as a graphics design specialist, Alejandro recommends you check and, if necessary, change your mouse settings.

Depending on the type of mouse you use, and what type of software support is installed for the mouse, your Mouse Properties dialog box might contain property sheets different from those shown in the figure. If this is the case, you might find the mouse properties that are described in the following steps on different property sheets, or these mouse settings might have slightly different names.

To view and change mouse properties:

▶ **1.** Open the **Start** menu, click **Control Panel**, and then click **Hardware and Sound**. The Hardware and Sound window opens. Under Devices and Printers, click **Mouse**. Windows 7 opens the Mouse Properties dialog box, and displays the Buttons property sheet. See Figure 2-7.

Figure 2-7	Viewing mouse properties (yours may differ)

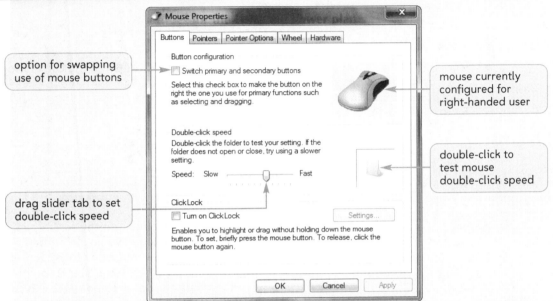

option for swapping use of mouse buttons

mouse currently configured for right-handed user

drag slider tab to set double-click speed

double-click to test mouse double-click speed

In the Button configuration section, you can switch the primary and secondary buttons if you are left-handed and prefer to use the mouse as a left-handed mouse. In the Double-click speed section, you can adjust the response recognition time for a double-click. If you use the Speed slider bar to specify a slower speed setting, you can double-click more slowly, and Windows 7 will interpret it as a double-click rather than two single clicks. When the ClickLock setting is enabled, you can highlight or drag without having to hold down a mouse button. You press the mouse button briefly, release it, and then move the pointer to select a group of folders or files, and then click a second time to complete the selection and turn off ClickLock. If you start to use this feature, and then change your mind, you can press the Esc key to cancel it.

▶ **2.** Drag the **Double-click speed** slider bar to a new position between Slow and Fast, and double-click the folder icon in the test area to determine how this change affects the use of the mouse. Try different settings to find the double-click speed setting that works best for you, and then apply the setting to your computer with the Apply button. If you set the slider bar closer to Slow, you can more leisurely double-click and save wear and tear on the tendons in your wrist and arm.

▶ **3.** Click the **Pointer Options** tab, or locate the property sheet that contains a Motion section. The Select a pointer speed setting controls the relative movement of the mouse pointer on the screen to the movement of the mouse across the desktop. See Figure 2-8.

Figure 2-8 | **Viewing mouse pointer option settings (yours may differ)**

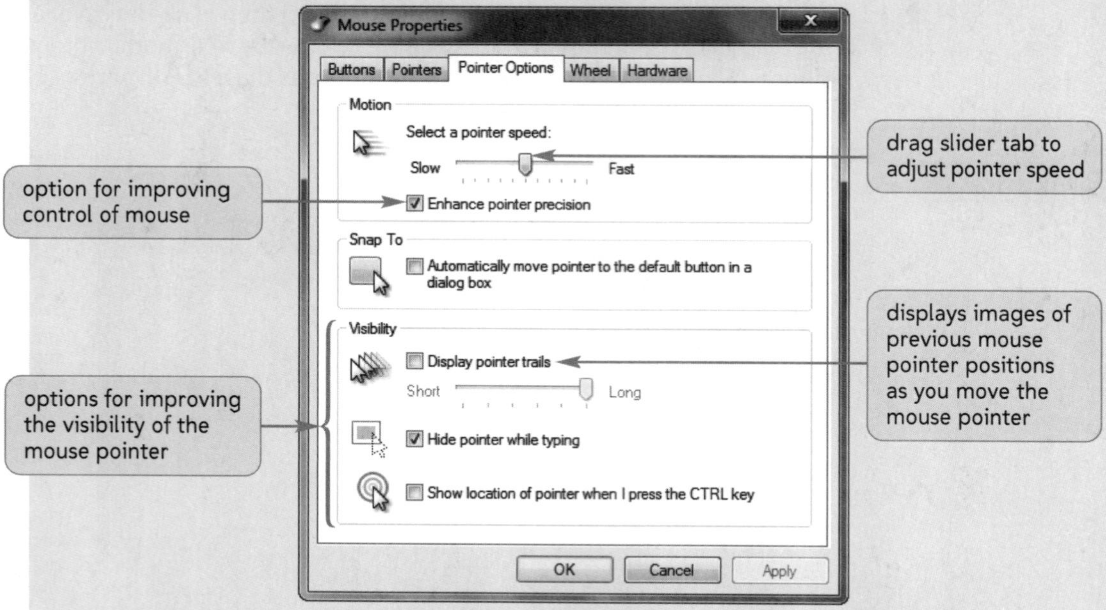

option for improving control of mouse

drag slider tab to adjust pointer speed

displays images of previous mouse pointer positions as you move the mouse pointer

options for improving the visibility of the mouse pointer

If you want greater control over mouse movement on the screen, adjust the mouse pointer speed to a slower setting. If you have only a limited amount of desktop space for moving the mouse, set the mouse pointer speed to a faster setting to accelerate it faster across the screen. The Enhanced pointer precision option, if available and enabled for your mouse, provides you with more control of the mouse pointer when you move the mouse a small distance, and the mouse pointer decelerates faster when you slow down or stop moving the mouse.

A Snap To option, if available for your mouse, moves the pointer to the default button in a dialog box, such as the OK button. If you have an option for displaying mouse trails (shown in the Visibility section) and if you enable this option, Windows 7 displays images of previous positions of the mouse pointer as you move the mouse, so it appears as if there is a trail on the screen. If available, the option for hiding the mouse pointer when you are typing is useful, because the mouse pointer does not inadvertently block your view of what's displayed on the screen when you type. The pointer disappears when you start typing, and reappears when you move the mouse. If available, you can also enable the option of showing the mouse pointer location when you press the Ctrl key. This feature is useful if you have difficulty locating the mouse pointer, or merely want to locate it quickly. This feature displays concentric circles that focus on the position of the mouse pointer.

To continue your examination of mouse settings:

▶ **1.** Click the **Wheel** tab (if available). On the Wheel property sheet shown in Figure 2-9, you can adjust the Vertical Scrolling setting for the mouse wheel so moving the wheel on the mouse one notch scrolls either a specific number of lines or one screen at a time. This option will simplify scrolling because you do not have to click vertical scroll bar arrows repeatedly or drag a scroll box to adjust your view within a window, document, or Web page.

| Figure 2-9 | Viewing mouse pointer wheel settings (yours may differ) |

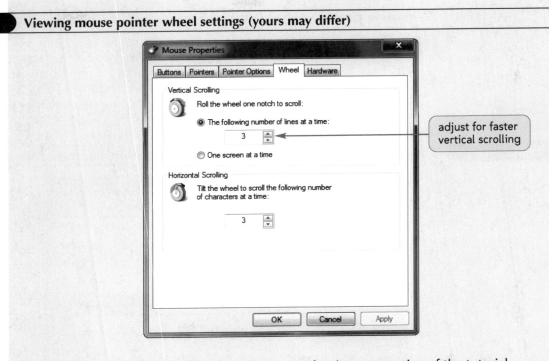

2. Keep the Mouse Properties dialog box open for the next section of the tutorial.

By adjusting mouse properties you can make it easier to use your computer at home or at work. By using Web style, choosing single-click activation, adjusting the double-click speed to a lower setting, and by adjusting other mouse settings, you might reduce or prevent problems that arise from using the mouse for extended periods of time. It's also important to know that other factors, such as how you use the keyboard, the type of desk and chair you use, and how you sit at your computer desk, can also play an important role in preventing and limiting work-related injuries.

Selecting a Mouse Pointer Scheme

Windows 7 works with two types of pointers: static cursors and animated cursors. A **static cursor** is a mouse pointer shape that does not change. For example, the Normal Select ▷ pointer shape, the one you see the majority of the time, is an example of a static cursor. In contrast, an **animated cursor** is a mouse pointer shape that plays back a short animation as you use the mouse pointer. For example, one of the animated cursors included with Windows 7 is the Aero Busy mouse pointer shape ◯. You can not only change individual mouse pointer shapes, but you can apply a **mouse pointer scheme**, which consists of a set of pointer shapes for common types of mouse operations.

Alejandro recommends that you examine other mouse pointer schemes to determine if another mouse pointer scheme works better for the type of work you do.

To choose pointer shapes and schemes:

1. Click the **Pointers** tab in the Mouse Properties dialog box. In the Scheme section on the Pointers property sheet, Windows 7 identifies the current scheme—Windows Aero (system scheme), the default mouse pointer scheme for your edition of Windows 7, or the last scheme you selected. As shown in Figure 2-10, Windows 7 also identifies the names of each of the default mouse pointer shapes included with your scheme.

Figure 2-10   Viewing the default (or current) mouse pointer scheme (yours may differ)

default Windows
Aero mouse
pointer scheme

default mouse
pointer names
and shapes

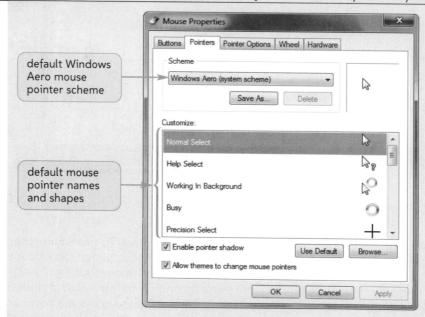

At the bottom are two options, "Enable pointer shadow" and "Allow themes to change mouse pointers," which are automatically enabled.

2. Scroll to the bottom of the Customize box, and examine the Link Select mouse pointer shape. You will recognize it as the mouse pointer shape for clicking links of Web pages and for selecting and opening objects on your computer if you are using single-click activation.

3. Click the **Scheme** button. Windows 7 displays pointer schemes available on your computer. See Figure 2-11.

| Figure 2-11 | Viewing a list of mouse pointer schemes (yours may differ) |

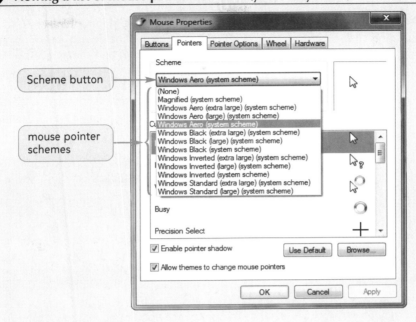

For the Windows Black, Windows Inverted, and Windows Standard schemes, you can use the standard, large, or extra-large mouse pointer shapes. The Magnified (system scheme) uses the standard mouse pointer shapes, but they are larger and more easily identifiable. Larger sizes are obviously useful for people with limited vision.

▶ 4. Click **Windows Inverted (extra large) (system scheme)** in the Scheme box, and then examine the mouse pointer shapes for this scheme in the Customize box.

▶ 5. Click the **Scheme** button, and then restore your original scheme.

▶ 6. Click the **OK** button if you have made changes to mouse properties and want to keep those changes; otherwise, click the **Cancel** button.

Changing Mouse Properties

- If you have a Control Panel menu, open the Start menu, point to Control Panel, and then click Mouse. If you do not have a Control Panel menu, open the Start menu, click Control Panel, click the Hardware and Sound link, and then click the Mouse link under Devices and Printers. If you are in the Personalization window, click the "Change mouse pointers" link.
- Click the Buttons tab, click the "Switch primary and secondary buttons" check box under Button configuration (and add a check mark) to enable left-handed use of the mouse, and, if necessary, adjust the double-click speed setting under "Double-click speed" to make it easier to use double-clicking.
- Click the Pointer Options tab, adjust the mouse pointer speed under Motion, and if necessary, click the "Enhance pointer precision" check box (and add a check mark) to improve control of the mouse pointer.
- Click the Wheel tab, and adjust the setting for Vertical Scrolling so you can scroll faster within a window.
- Click the Pointers tab, and use the Scheme button to display and select a mouse pointer scheme that helps you more easily see and identify mouse pointer shapes.
- Make and test any other changes you want to make to other mouse settings for your particular mouse.
- Click the OK button to close the Mouse Properties dialog box and, if necessary, close any other windows, such as the Hardware and Sound window or the Personalization window.

Customizing your mouse is an important part of using an operating system like Windows 7 that relies on a graphical user interface. Not only can you adjust mouse settings to improve your use, speed, and control of the mouse, but you can also implement options that prevent injury to your hand, wrist, arm, and shoulder, making it easier to perform your work.

Using the ClearType Text Tuner

To further enhance your use of Windows 7, you can choose from a variety of special visual display effects. One important feature is the ability to smooth the edges of screen fonts. A **font** consists of a specific typeface, point size, and weight or style. **Typeface** refers to the specific look or design style of a collection of characters, which includes the uppercase and lowercase letters of the alphabet, numbers, and symbols (such as the question mark). For example, the text of this paragraph uses the Optima typeface. **Point size** refers to the height of an uppercase character. One **point** is equal to 1/72 of an inch. Therefore, a character with a 72 point size appears one-inch tall when printed; however, it may appear larger on a monitor. A character with a 36 point size is one-half inch tall when printed. A font's **weight** or **style** refers to additional features applied to the font for emphasis, such as boldface, italics, or a combination of boldface and italics. A **screen font** is a specific typeface that Windows 7 uses to display text on the monitor (or screen). Many programs use *font* to refer to the typeface, *font size* to refer to the point size, and *font style* to refer to a font's weight or style.

The images that you see on a monitor are composed of thousands of very small pixels arranged in columns across the monitor's screen and rows down the monitor's screen. If you magnify what you see on the monitor, you will discover that the image consists of pixels (sometimes called dots) that blend together smoothly at regular magnification to form the final image. However, even at regular magnification, an image or icon on the monitor can appear uneven, as shown in Figure 2-12.

Figure 2-12  **Stair-step effect**

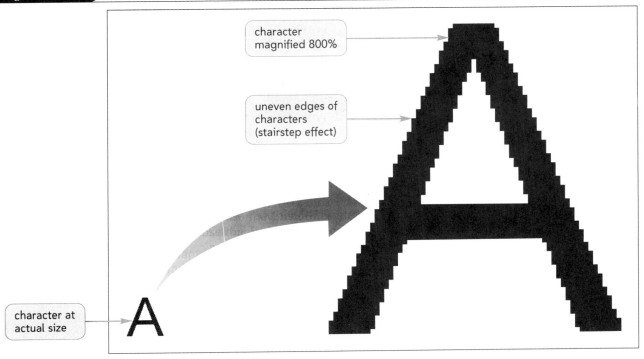

Notice that the sides of the uppercase character *A* in this figure are uneven and exhibit what's called a **stair-step effect**. This type of problem occurs with diagonal and curved lines but not with straight lines. To create a perfectly even diagonal or curved line, your video display adapter would need to illuminate only a portion of each pixel that forms the edge of a line or curve. That means it would illuminate a tiny portion of a pixel in some cases, and a larger portion of a pixel in other cases. Because that's not yet possible, this stair-step effect, or what's also referred to as a **jaggie**, occurs.

To handle this problem Windows 7 uses **ClearType** technology to display fonts as clearly and smoothly as is possible (a process called **font smoothing**). As shown in Figure 2-13, Windows 7 uses font smoothing to fill in pixels adjacent to a diagonal or curved line with increasingly lighter colors to simulate a smooth curve.

Figure 2-13	Font-smoothing reduces stairstep effect

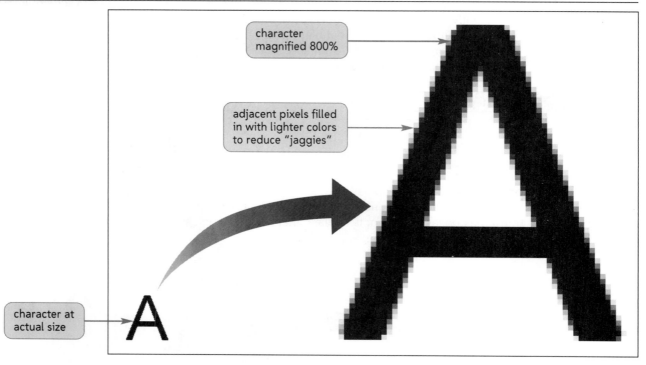

For example, in the case of an uppercase character A that is rendered in black, Windows 7 uses shades of dark brown, brown, light orange, and light yellow on the left diagonal edge of the stem of the letter A, and dark blue, bright blue, light blue, and faint blue for pixels located on the right diagonal edge of the stem of the letter A. The font smoothing produces a more even look at actual size, and reduces the stair-step effect or jaggies that is shown in Figure 2-12. This shading of adjacent pixels also produces a slight three-dimensional appearance.

If you examine the "before" and "after" of smoothing fonts with ClearType technology, as shown in Figure 2-14, then you can tell that the uppercase letter A on the right appears sharper.

Figure 2-14	How font smoothing affects the sharpness of characters

Microsoft introduced ClearType technology for LCD monitors, or flat panel displays, in Windows XP. On LCD monitors, pixels are composed of three vertical **subpixels**—a red, green, and blue subpixel, as shown in Figure 2-15.

| Figure 2-15 | Subpixels within an LCD pixel |

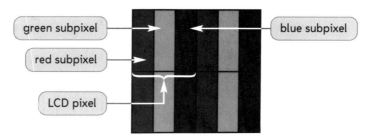

Windows XP, Windows Vista, and Windows 7 can use this ClearType technology to adjust the color of each subpixel so characters appear more even and sharper on the monitor. ClearType is automatically enabled on LCD monitors or flat panel displays.

Windows 7 includes a new feature called the ClearType Text Tuner that you can use to adjust the appearance of fonts on flat panel displays, such as an LCD or plasma display, in order to achieve the sharpest possible image.

Alejandro recommends that you use the ClearType Text Tuner to check the sharpness of your flat panel display.

To use the ClearType Text Tuner:

1. Right-click the **desktop**, click **Personalize** on the shortcut menu, and in the Personalization window, click the **Display** link under "See also" on the lower-left side of the Display window.

2. Click the **Adjust ClearType text** link on the left side of the window, and after Windows 7 opens the ClearType Text Tuner dialog box, close the Display window in the background. Windows 7 explains the value of ClearType technology in the ClearType Tuner dialog box, as shown in Figure 2-16. Notice that ClearType is automatically enabled in Windows 7.

| Figure 2-16 | ClearType Text Tuner dialog box |

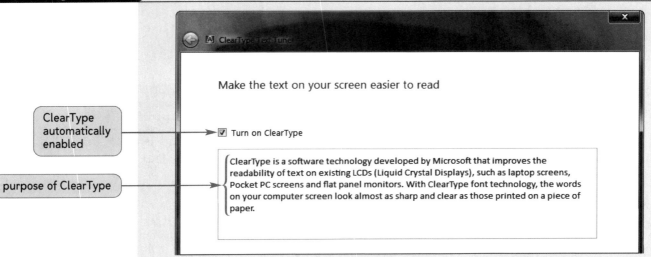

3. Click the **Next** button. In the next step, Windows 7 identifies your monitor model and notes whether the monitor is set to its native resolution.

4. Click the **Next** button. Windows 7 displays two text samples and asks you to pick the one that looks best.

▶ **5.** Click the **text sample** that looks best to you on the computer you are using, and then click the **Next** button. Windows 7 now displays six text samples, and highlights the one that it thinks look best.

▶ **6.** Examine each of the six text samples and, if necessary, select the one that looks best to you, and then click the **Next** button. Now you see three text samples.

▶ **7.** Examine each of the three text samples and, if necessary, select the one that looks best to you, and then click the **Next** button. Windows 7 again displays six text samples.

▶ **8.** Examine each of the six text samples and, if necessary, select the one that looks best to you, and then click the **Next** button. At the last step, Windows 7 informs you that you have finished tuning the text on your monitor.

▶ **9.** Click the **Finish** button.

Figure 2-17 illustrates the appearance of text before and after the use of ClearType and font smoothing.

Figure 2-17	Comparing text without and with ClearType

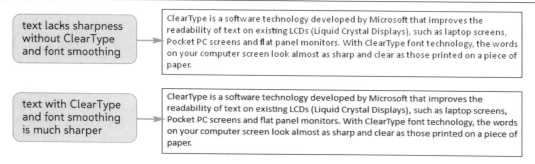

text lacks sharpness without ClearType and font smoothing

ClearType is a software technology developed by Microsoft that improves the readability of text on existing LCDs (Liquid Crystal Displays), such as laptop screens, Pocket PC screens and flat panel monitors. With ClearType font technology, the words on your computer screen look almost as sharp and clear as those printed on a piece of paper.

text with ClearType and font smoothing is much sharper

ClearType is a software technology developed by Microsoft that improves the readability of text on existing LCDs (Liquid Crystal Displays), such as laptop screens, Pocket PC screens and flat panel monitors. With ClearType font technology, the words on your computer screen look almost as sharp and clear as those printed on a piece of paper.

Notice how much sharper ClearType text appears, and how difficult it is to discern text that does not use ClearType and font smoothing.

Although Windows 7 enables ClearType and selects the best appearance for text on your monitor, you should use the ClearType Text Tuner to verify that it is using the best settings for your eyes (and eyeglasses). Whenever you change your video display settings, run the ClearType Text Tuner to make sure that you have the sharpest possible display.

REFERENCE

Using the ClearType Text Tuner

- Right-click the desktop, click Personalize on the shortcut menu, and in the Personalization window, click the Display link under "See also" on the lower-left side of the window.
- After Windows 7 opens the Display window, click the "Adjust ClearType text" link on the left side of the window. The ClearType Text Tuner dialog box opens. Click the Next button.
- Check the information on the resolution of your monitor and the model type, adjust your resolution (if needed), and then click the Next button.
- In each of the next four steps, click the text sample (if necessary) that looks best to you on the computer you are using, then click the Next button.
- When Windows 7 informs you that you have finished tuning the text on your monitor, click the Finish button, and then close the Display window.

Using an Administrator Account

An Administrator account is a type of user account that provides a user with the right to make changes to the system (such as installing new software) and troubleshoot problems, provides complete access to all the features that are part of the operating system, enables a user to manage other user accounts, and if necessary, allows a user to view other user's folders and files.

Certain types of operations that you perform on a computer in this and later tutorials require that you log on under an Administrator account or provide Administrator credentials (i.e., the Administrator account name and password). If you are working in a computer lab, you may already have access to an Administrator account so you can complete all your lab assignments.

Alejandro suggests that you determine the type of user account that you use on your own computer before you examine advanced visual effects settings that affect the performance of your computer.

To determine whether your user account is an Administrator or Standard user account:

▶ **1.** From the Start menu, click **Control Panel**, click the **User Accounts and Family Safety** link in the Control Panel window, and then click the **User Accounts** link in the User Accounts and Family Safety window. Windows 7 opens the User Accounts window. Next to your user account icon, and under your user name, Windows 7 identifies whether your account is an Administrator account or a Standard user account. As shown in Figure 2-18, Alejandro's user account is an Administrator account.

Figure 2-18	Checking your user account type

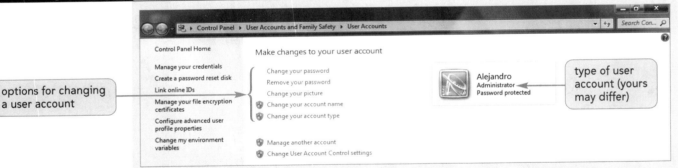

options for changing a user account

type of user account (yours may differ)

To the left of your user account icon are options for managing your user account and other user accounts. You can change your user account password and picture without Administrator credentials.

▶ **2.** Close the User Accounts window.

You will explore user accounts and new Windows 7 features for accessing and using user accounts in more detail in Tutorial 7.

Adjusting Visual Effects

To optimize the performance of your computer, or the appearance of the user interface, you can choose a combination of special visual effects that work best for you.

To complete the following steps, you must provide Administrator credentials. If you are not logged on under an Administrator account, or do not know the password for an Administrator account, do not keystroke the following steps, but instead read the steps, and examine the figures so you are familiar with the use of these advanced settings.

To examine a more comprehensive list of special visual effects:

TIP

You can also use the Windows+Break keyboard shortcut to open the System window.

1. Right-click the **Computer** icon on the desktop, and then click **Properties**. Windows 7 opens the System window.

2. Under Control Panel Home on the left side of the System window, click the **Advanced system settings** link, and if necessary, provide Administrator credentials. Windows 7 opens the System Properties dialog box and displays the contents of the Advanced property sheet. See Figure 2-19.

Figure 2-19 Viewing options for adjusting advanced system settings

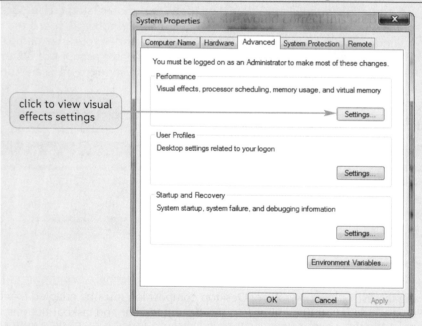

click to view visual effects settings

3. In the Performance section, click the **Settings** button. Windows opens the Performance Options dialog box, and displays the contents of the Visual Effects property sheet. See Figure 2-20.

Figure 2-20 Viewing options for selecting visual effects

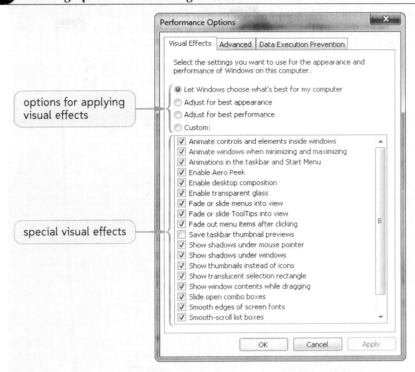

options for applying
visual effects

special visual effects

From the Custom box on this property sheet, you can adjust 20 different settings to improve the appearance of your user interface or to optimize the performance of your computer.

Most of the options are self-explanatory, and many of the options are Windows Aero options, including the following:

- **Enable Aero Peek**—By default, Windows 7 enables this setting so you can use the new Aero Peek feature that enables windows transparency to view the desktop.
- **Enable desktop composition**—A feature found in those editions of Windows 7 that support Windows Aero, **desktop composition** refers to the Windows 7 window-management technology for updating your view of the desktop and open windows, and for supporting the use of Windows Aero. Desktop composition must be enabled to view translucent window frames and borders, translucent taskbar and taskbar buttons, Live Taskbar Thumbnails, Windows Flip pane thumbnails and transparency, and Aero Flip 3D.
- **Enable transparent glass**—This option enables or disables translucency. Like Aero glass, *transparent glass* is a term that's commonly used to describe the glasslike translucency feature of window frames in the new Windows Aero user interface.
- **Show shadows under mouse pointer**—When enabled, Windows 7 displays a shadow under the mouse pointer, providing a three-dimensional perspective and making it easier to see and locate the pointer.

- **Show translucent selection rectangle**—When enabled, Windows draws a translucent, or partially transparent, light blue rectangle around folders or files in a window (or on the desktop) as you drag the mouse and select folders or files.
- **Use drop shadows for icon labels on the desktop**—When enabled, this feature further enhances the visibility and display of desktop icon titles or labels by providing a three-dimensional perspective.

Also included in the list of visual effects is "Smooth edges of screen fonts," which, as you saw earlier, is automatically enabled to render fonts using ClearType Technology.

PROSKILLS

Problem Solving: Balancing Appearance and Performance

At the top of the Visual Effects property sheet are three options: "Let Windows choose what's best for my computer," "Adjust for best appearance," and "Adjust for best performance." You can use these options to adjust settings for all the visual effects in the Custom box in one step. If you choose the "Adjust for best performance" option, Windows 7 turns off all the visual effects, and that in turn maximizes performance. If you choose the "Adjust for best appearance" option, Windows 7 enables all the visual effects, but that might reduce performance. If you choose the "Let Windows choose what's best for my computer," Windows 7 decides which visual effects to enable and which to turn off. The information provided by the latter option can help you determine the degree to which Windows 7 supports Windows Aero features and other features, and their impact on the performance of your computer.

If you notice that your computer is not performing optimally, then you should adjust the use of these visual effects for best performance, and then use your computer to determine whether they are the cause of your computer's slow performance. If Windows 7 turns off more than one visual effect when you choose the option to adjust your computer for best performance, then you can reenable one visual effect at a time to determine whether that visual effect is the source of the problem. By repeating this approach for each visual effect that Windows 7 turned off, you may be able to reenable one or more visual effects and enjoy the benefit of those extra features without affecting your computer's performance. In some cases, you might want to keep a specific visual effect because of its benefits, even if it slightly affects the performance of your computer.

To finish inspecting visual effects:

1. If you are working on your own computer, and want to make changes to one or more of these visual effects, adjust these settings using one of the first three options or by choosing specific options in the Custom box, click the **OK** button to close the Performance Options dialog box, click the **OK** button to close the System Properties dialog box, and then close the System window.

2. If you are working on your own computer and do not want to change any of these visual effects, click the **Cancel** button to close the Performance Options dialog box, click the **Cancel** button to close the System Properties dialog box, and then close the System window.

REFERENCE

Adjusting Visual Effects

- Right-click the Computer icon on the desktop (or on the Start menu), and then click Properties.
- Under Control Panel Home on the left side of the System window, click the "Advanced system settings" link, and if necessary, provide Administrator credentials.
- In the Performance section of the System Properties dialog box, click the Settings button.
- If you want Windows 7 to adjust your computer's settings for best performance, click the "Adjust for best performance" option button. If you want Windows 7 to adjust your computer's setting for the best appearance, click the "Adjust for best appearance" option button. If you want Windows 7 to choose the best settings for your computer, click the "Let Windows choose what's best for my computer" option button.
- If you want to specify a setting for each visual setting, then examine each visual setting in the Custom box and add a check mark to the check box to enable the option, or remove the check mark from the check box to turn off the option.
- Click the OK button to apply your changes and close the Performance Options dialog box, click the OK button to close the System Properties dialog box, and then close the System window.

In the next session, you explore options for customizing your computer's Start menu, taskbar, and notification area.

REVIEW

Session 2.1 Quick Check

1. What is the smallest unit on a monitor for displaying a specific color?
2. A(n) _____ consists of a set of elements, such as a desktop background, window color, screen saver, and sound scheme, that provide a unified look for your desktop and user interface.
3. What five common types of image file formats can you use as desktop backgrounds?
4. In Windows 7, you can save a custom theme as a(n) _____ so you can email it to a coworker or friend.
5. What is the name of the Microsoft technology for improving the appearance and readability of text on flat panel displays?
6. Windows 7 can control the color of each _____ on LCD or flat panel monitors so characters appear more even and sharper.
7. True or False. A bitmapped graphic is an image represented by a pattern of pixels.
8. _____ is the Windows 7 window-management technology for updating your view of the desktop and open windows and for supporting the use of Windows Aero.

SESSION 2.2 VISUAL OVERVIEW

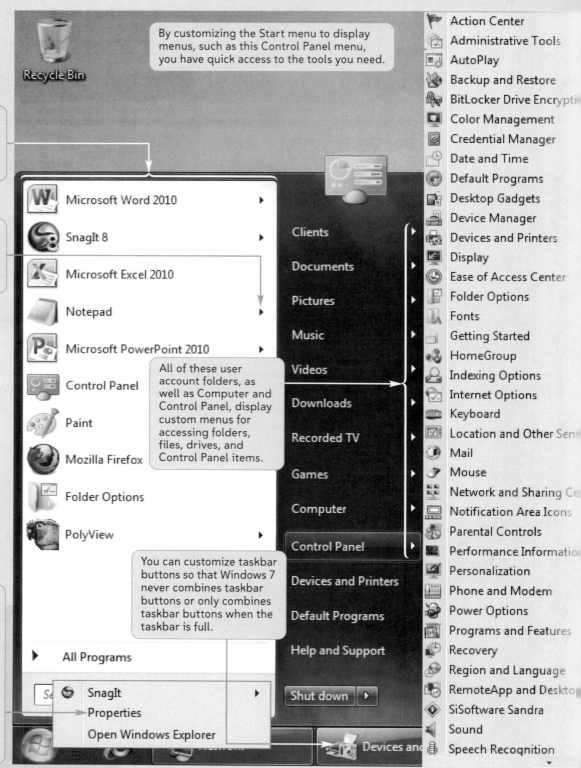

By customizing the Start menu to display menus, such as this Control Panel menu, you have quick access to the tools you need.

Adjust privacy actions for the Start menu to specify whether Windows 7 displays recently opened programs and items in the Start menu.

You can customize application **Jump Lists** on the Start menu and specify the number of recent items to display on application Jump Lists.

All of these user account folders, as well as Computer and Control Panel, display custom menus for accessing folders, files, drives, and Control Panel items.

You can customize taskbar buttons so that Windows 7 never combines taskbar buttons or only combines taskbar buttons when the taskbar is full.

You can change Start menu properties and specify a custom setting for the **Power action button** so Windows 7 automatically shuts down your computer, switches users, logs off your computer, locks your computer, restarts your computer, or places your computer in Sleep or Hibernation (if available) when you press your computer's power button.

CUSTOM MENUS

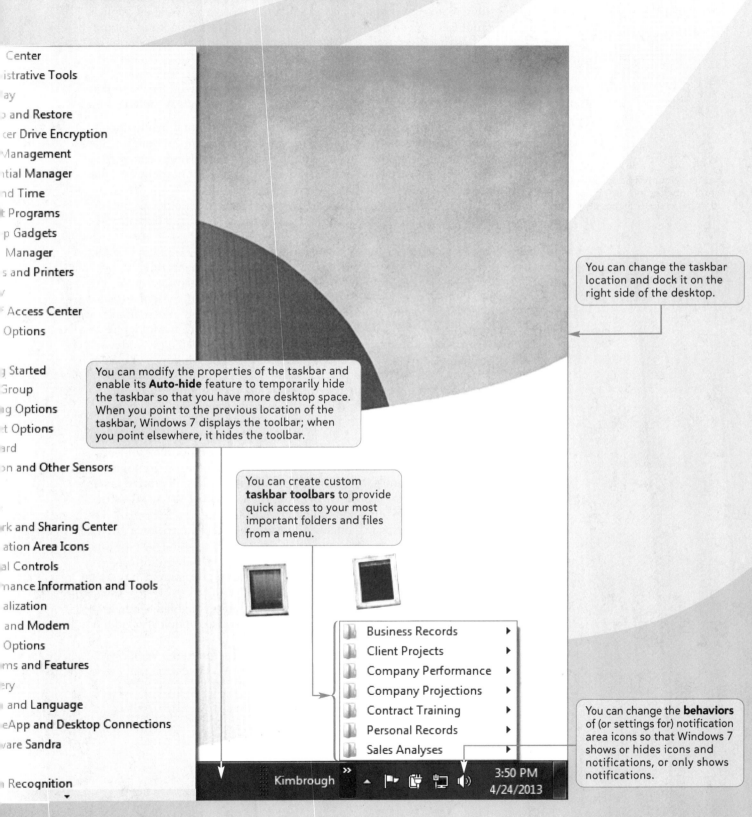

Center

istrative **Tools**

ay

and **Restore**

er Drive **Encryption**

Management

tial **Manager**

nd **Time**

Programs

p **Gadgets**

Manager

s and **Printers**

Access **Center**

Options

g **Started**

Group

g **Options**

t **Options**

ard

n and **Other Sensors**

rk and **Sharing Center**

ation **Area Icons**

al **Controls**

mance **Information and Tools**

alization

and **Modem**

Options

ms and **Features**

ery

and **Language**

eApp and **Desktop Connections**

vare **Sandra**

Recognition

You can change the taskbar location and dock it on the right side of the desktop.

You can modify the properties of the taskbar and enable its **Auto-hide** feature to temporarily hide the taskbar so that you have more desktop space. When you point to the previous location of the taskbar, Windows 7 displays the toolbar; when you point elsewhere, it hides the toolbar.

You can create custom **taskbar toolbars** to provide quick access to your most important folders and files from a menu.

Business Records ▶
Client Projects ▶
Company Performance ▶
Company Projections ▶
Contract Training ▶
Personal Records ▶
Sales Analyses ▶

You can change the **behaviors** of (or settings for) notification area icons so that Windows 7 shows or hides icons and notifications, or only shows notifications.

Kimbrough ▶▶ 3:50 PM 4/24/2013

Customizing the Start Menu

The Start menu still remains the central place for locating all properly installed applications, games, and utilities. Once you open an application, and assuming it has a Jump List with previously opened files used with that application, you can access options on the Jump List by pointing to the application on the Start menu or by right-clicking the application's taskbar button. The latter assumes you have opened the application or pinned the application to the taskbar, and that you've previously opened files with that application. You can also view and change Start menu properties, such as the following:

- **Privacy options**—By default, Windows 7 stores and displays a list of recently opened programs in the Start menu, as well as a list of recently opened items in both the Start menu and the taskbar; however, you can turn off both these options. You can also adjust the number of recently opened programs displayed on the Start menu and the number of recent items displayed in Jump Lists.
- **Power button action**—The default action for the power button is Shut down, but you can change that setting to Switch user, Log off, Lock, Restart, Sleep, or Hibernate (if available).
- **Start menu items**—You can specify whether Windows 7 displays Computer, Connect To, Control Panel, Default Programs, Devices and Printers, Documents (library), Downloads, Favorites, Games, Help (for Help and Support), Homegroup, Music, Network, Personal folder, Pictures, Recent Items, Recorded TV, Run, System administrative tools, and Videos on the Start menu. For some of these items, you can also specify whether Windows 7 displays the item as a link, which opens the folder, or as a menu, which displays a list of the options found in the folder. By default, Windows 7 displays these menu items as links and opens the corresponding window. For example, when you click Documents on the Start menu, Windows 7 opens the Documents library window so you can then work with your personal folders and files. If you display Documents as a menu instead, Windows 7 does not open the Documents folder, but instead it displays the folders found in the Documents library (by default, My Documents and Public Documents). Then, if you point to My Documents or Public Documents, Windows 7 displays the folders and files in the corresponding folder as items on a Documents menu. This same feature is also available for the Computer, Control Panel, Downloads, Games, Music, Personal folder, Pictures, Recorded TV, and Videos folders. If you choose to display the Favorites menu on the Start menu, you have yet another method for locating and opening Web sites that you've bookmarked with Internet Explorer (only). If you've organized your bookmarks into folders, then you will see those folders on the Favorites menu. If you are a member of the Administrators group, you will more than likely want to display System administrative tools on the Start menu and/or Programs menu so you can open tools for managing your computer and monitoring its performance.
- **Highlighting newly installed programs**—Windows 7 temporarily highlights newly installed programs on the Start menu in a different color so you can quickly find them; you can turn off this feature.
- **Opening submenus when you pause on them with the mouse pointer**—Windows 7 immediately displays the submenu for a menu option when you pause on that menu option; you can turn off this setting.

- **Enable context menus and dragging and dropping**—If you right-click a Start menu item, Windows 7 displays a shortcut menu, or context menu, with a list of options associated with that menu item. You can use drag and drop to rearrange some items on the Start menu. These options are automatically enabled; you can turn off these settings.
- **Use large icons**—By default, Windows 7 uses large icons for programs and tools in the left pane of the Start menu; however, you can turn this feature off so you can view more programs and tools in that same pane.

Alejandro points out that the Start menu is an important resource that you use every day, so you should take a few minutes to customize it to meet your needs.

To check and change Start menu settings:

▶ **1.** Right-click the **Start** button ⊛ on the taskbar, and then click **Properties**. Windows 7 opens the Taskbar and Start Menu Properties dialog box, and displays the Start Menu property sheet in the foreground. See Figure 2-21.

Figure 2-21   Options for changing Start Menu settings

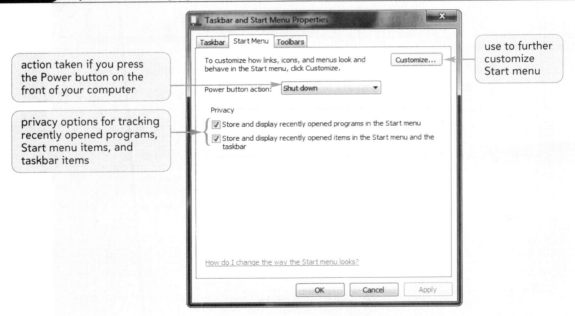

action taken if you press the Power button on the front of your computer

privacy options for tracking recently opened programs, Start menu items, and taskbar items

use to further customize Start menu

Under Privacy, you can specify whether you want Windows 7 to store and display a list of recently opened programs in the Start menu, and whether you want to store and display recently opened items in the Start menu and the taskbar.

▶ **2.** Click the **Power button action** button. Windows 7 displays a list of alternate options for specifying the default behavior of the power button. See Figure 2-22. Your options may vary and, for example, may include Hibernate.

Figure 2-22 Options for customizing the Power button

options for specifying what happens when you press the Power button (yours may differ)

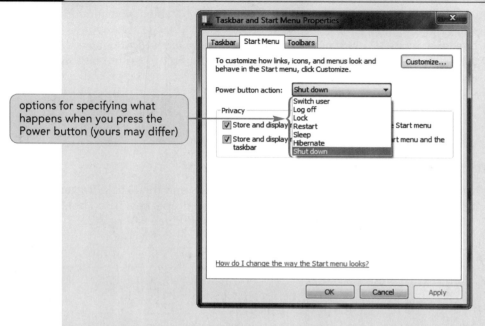

3. Click the **Power button action** button again to close the drop-down menu.

4. Click the **Customize** button on the Start Menu property sheet. Windows 7 opens the Customize Start Menu dialog box, and lists all the items described earlier for customizing the Start menu. See Figure 2-23.

Figure 2-23 Options for customizing the Start Menu

click to display Control Panel menu from Start Menu

option for displaying number of recently opened programs on Start Menu

option for displaying number of recently opened items in Start menu Jump Lists

option for restoring default Start Menu settings

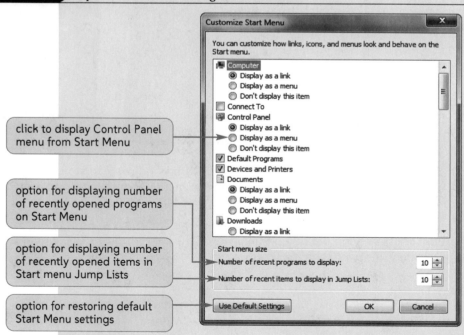

Under Start menu size, you can specify the number of recently used programs to display on the Start menu and the number of recent items to display in Start menu Jump Lists. You can use the "Use Default Settings" button to restore the Windows 7 default settings for the Start menu.

5. Under Control Panel, click the **Display as a menu** option button, click the **OK** button in the Customize Start Menu dialog box, and then click the **Apply** button in the Taskbar and Start Menu Properties dialog box.

6. Open the **Start** menu, and then point to **Control Panel**. Windows 7 displays a Control Panel menu that lists in alphabetical order all the options available from Control Panel. See Figure 2-24. This feature quickly puts everything you need at your fingertips, so you do not have to search for, or navigate to find the option you need in the Control Panel window.

Figure 2-24 Viewing the Control Panel menu

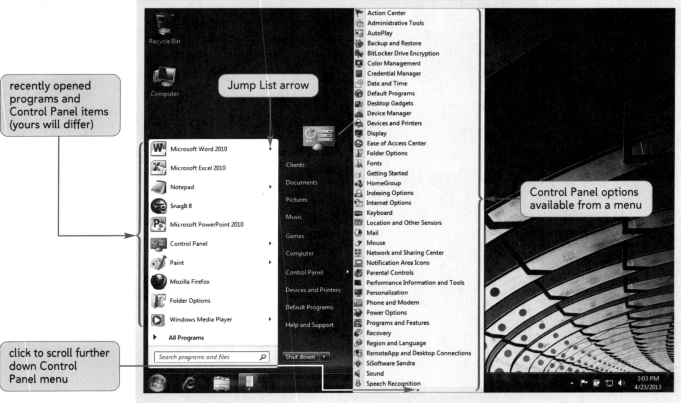

7. Click **Display** on the Control Panel menu. Windows 7 opens the Display window. Menu links like this one provide faster access to Windows tools.

8. Close the Display window, and then close the Taskbar and Start Menu Properties dialog box.

Since the Start menu provides you with access to all the software installed on your computer, it's important to be familiar with all the options for customizing the Start menu (and other components of the graphical user interface) so you can provide support to other users, whether as an IT professional, contractor, or as a friend. Furthermore, you can customize your own work (and home) computer to meet your specific needs as well as the way you prefer to work with your computer and access its resources. In addition to the features you just examined, you will examine more ways to customize the Start menu in Tutorial 4.

REFERENCE

Customizing the Start Menu

- Right-click the Start button, and then click Properties.
- Under Privacy on the Start menu property, you can turn off (or enable, if already turned off) two privacy settings for storing a list of recently opened programs on the Start menu and recently opened items in the Start menu and taskbar.
- If you want to change the default behavior of the Start menu power button, click the Power button action button, and then choose a shutdown option.
- Click the Customize button to open the Customize Start Menu dialog box so you can specify what the Start menu shows (such as using large or small icons), specify which options (such as Favorites or Downloads) appear on the Start menu, specify how to access certain options (such as via a direct link or a menu), and specify the number of recent programs to display on the Start menu and the number of recent items to display in Start menu Jump Lists.
- Click the OK button to close the Customize Start Menu dialog box, and then click the OK button in the Taskbar and Start Menu Properties dialog box to apply your changes.

By customizing your Start menu, you can make life easier and gain quick access to the options you need and frequently use in your line of work.

Customizing the Taskbar and Notification Area

Because the taskbar is another important desktop resource that you rely on, especially in Windows 7 where the focus has shifted from the Start menu to the taskbar, you can customize it in a variety of ways, including the following:

- **Lock or unlock the taskbar**—By default, the taskbar is locked so you cannot move or resize it, nor can you resize a toolbar on the taskbar; however, you can unlock the taskbar. This feature protects a new user from inadvertently making changes to the taskbar until they learn more about how to use Windows 7. If you need to move or resize the taskbar, or a toolbar on the taskbar, you must first unlock the taskbar. Then you can dock the taskbar on another edge of the desktop and increase its height so you can see more of the contents of the taskbar.
- **Use Auto-hide on the taskbar**—Although the taskbar is always visible by default, you can hide the taskbar to display more of the desktop or the window where you are working. When you hide the taskbar, it resizes itself to a very thin bar at the bottom of the desktop. When you point to this thin bar, Windows 7 immediately displays the taskbar so you can use the Start button, a taskbar button, an icon in the notification area, or just view the date and time. Then Windows 7 hides the taskbar when you move the mouse pointer away from the taskbar.

  If you previously increased the height of the taskbar by pointing to and dragging the top taskbar border so you can see taskbar buttons for multiple open programs, folders, files, and Web sites, you can still easily access a taskbar button for another open window, but with Auto-hide, you benefit from more desktop space for the program, folder, file or Web site in the active window. You can even use the Auto-hide feature in a workplace to hide taskbar buttons for minimized windows that are open, but not active, and thereby increase the privacy of your work.
- **Group similar taskbar buttons**—By default, Windows 7 automatically groups taskbar buttons for windows opened with the same program, and the buttons are stacked on the taskbar and offset slightly so you can tell there is more than one open taskbar button for that same program. However, you can only see the taskbar label for the taskbar button at the top of the stack. You then might assume that only one window remains open, and that all previously open windows for that same program are now closed;

however, that is not the case. As illustrated in Tutorial 1, if you point to a taskbar button, Windows 7 displays Live Taskbar Thumbnails for all open windows, so you can not only access a window, but also verify that it is still open. This taskbar option for handling taskbar buttons is called "Always combine, hide labels." You can modify this setting and choose one of two other settings: "Combine when taskbar is full" to combine similar taskbar buttons for the same program together when the taskbar is full, or the "Never combine" option to keep the taskbar button for each open window visible. One obvious advantage of this latter option is that it is easier to find what you need.

INSIGHT

Multitasking with the Taskbar

If you change the way Windows 7 displays taskbar buttons by choosing either "Never combine" or "Combine when taskbar is full," and if you open multiple program, folder, and document windows, you can increase the height of the taskbar so you can more easily see all the taskbar buttons and labels. First, you must make sure that you unlock the taskbar. Then point to the top edge of the taskbar, and when you see the mouse pointer shape change to a double-headed arrow pointing up and down, drag the top taskbar border up to increase its height. You will quickly discover that the height increases in increments of the default taskbar height. This feature is also useful if you add Windows toolbars or custom toolbars to the taskbar. The taskbar is essential when you multitask with multiple program windows, multiple document windows, multiple folder windows, and multiple windows onto Web sites. Increasing the size of the taskbar and choosing the option for displaying every taskbar button simplifies the process of switching from one window, one document, and one Web site to another as you work, and thereby increases your productivity and effectiveness because everything you need is at hand.

- **Preview desktop with Aero Peek**—You can turn off, or enable, the option for previewing the desktop with Aero Peek.
- **Customize the notification area**—You can decide which icons and notifications you want visible in the notification area. That includes both system icons as well as icons for programs that automatically load during booting or startup.
- **Displaying toolbars on the taskbar**—You can also display the Address, Desktop, Links, and Tablet PC Input Panel (for the Windows 7 Home Premium, Professional, and Ultimate Editions) toolbars on the taskbar. The Address toolbar provides an alternate method for navigating the Web, and the Desktop toolbar provides quick access to the contents of your desktop from the taskbar. (You will step through the use of these two features later.) The Links toolbar provides access to two new Windows Internet Explorer 8 features, Suggested Sites and the Web Slice Gallery. **Suggested Sites** is a Microsoft online service that provides suggestions for other Web sites that might be of interest to you based on the Web sites you frequently visit, thereby saving you time and effort in locating those Web sites. You can use the **Web Slice** option to subscribe to and view content located on a specific portion of a Web page that carries that information. With this feature, you can quickly access content that you want to view on a regular basis, whether it's for business or personal use, via a Web slice link on the Favorites bar. With the Tablet PC Input Panel, you can enter text by using a digital pen. Unlike previous versions of Windows, you no longer have a Quick Launch toolbar because its features have been incorporated into the taskbar.

Alejandro asks you to check your taskbar and notification area settings to ensure that they are set properly and meet your daily needs.

In the following steps, you will examine and change settings for the taskbar and notification area. If you change any additional settings not specified in these tutorial steps, make a note of the original setting so you can restore it later.

To check your taskbar settings:

▶ **1.** Right-click the **taskbar**, and then click **Properties** on the taskbar shortcut menu. Windows 7 opens the Taskbar and Start Menu Properties dialog box, and displays the Taskbar property sheet in the foreground. See Figure 2-25.

> **Trouble?** If you cannot see the taskbar, then Auto-hide is probably enabled. Point to the bottom edge of the desktop (or, if necessary, just below the desktop), and when the taskbar becomes visible, right-click the Taskbar, click Properties, and turn off the "Auto-hide the taskbar" option, and then click the OK button. If that's not the source of the problem, check the top, right, and left sides of the desktop to determine whether the taskbar was accidentally moved. It's possible that someone might have moved the taskbar and then enabled Auto-hide.

Figure 2-25 **Viewing taskbar settings**

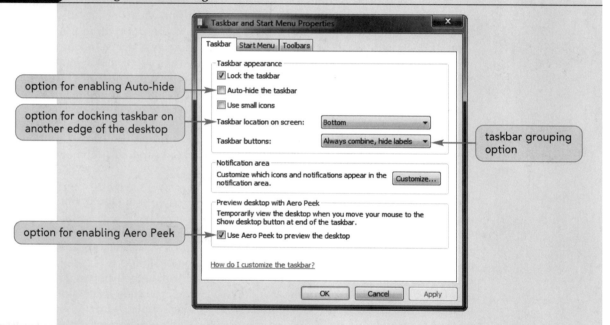

option for enabling Auto-hide

option for docking taskbar on another edge of the desktop

taskbar grouping option

option for enabling Aero Peek

TIP
You can also lock and unlock the taskbar directly from the Taskbar shortcut menu.

As shown in the Taskbar appearance section, the taskbar is automatically locked by default; however, you can unlock it if you want to resize the taskbar or dock it elsewhere on the desktop. You can also use Auto-hide on the taskbar and use small icons on the taskbar. In the "Preview desktop with Aero Peek" section, you can turn Aero Peek on (or off). Your taskbar settings may differ.

▶ **2.** Under Taskbar appearance, click the **Taskbar buttons** button, click **Combine when taskbar is full**, and then click the **Apply** button. If you have multiple folder windows or multiple document windows open, then you will see a taskbar button for each window, unless your taskbar is full. Windows 7 also displays labels (though you might not see the entire label) for each taskbar button so you know what is open where.

▶ **3.** To restore your previous setting, click the **Taskbar buttons** button, click **Always combine, hide labels**, and then click the **Apply** button.

▶ **4.** Click the **Taskbar location on screen** button, click **Right**, and then click the **Apply** button. Windows 7 moves the taskbar to the right side of the desktop, and if you have multiple windows or documents open in the same program, you will see vertical rather than horizontal Live Taskbar Previews as you point to each taskbar button. One advantage of placing the taskbar on the right side of the screen is that it is located closer to where you are using your mouse (assuming you are right-handed), so it takes less effort to move and position your mouse. Another advantage is that flat panel displays are far wider than they are tall, so you have more vertical space to view a document or Web page if the taskbar is on the side of the monitor.

▶ **5.** If your original setting for the taskbar was at the bottom of the screen, and if you want to restore that setting, click the **Taskbar location on screen** button, click **Bottom**, and then click the **Apply** button.

▶ **6.** In the **notification area**, click the **Customize** button. Windows 7 opens the Notification Area Icons window. See Figure 2-26.

Figure 2-26	Viewing notification area settings

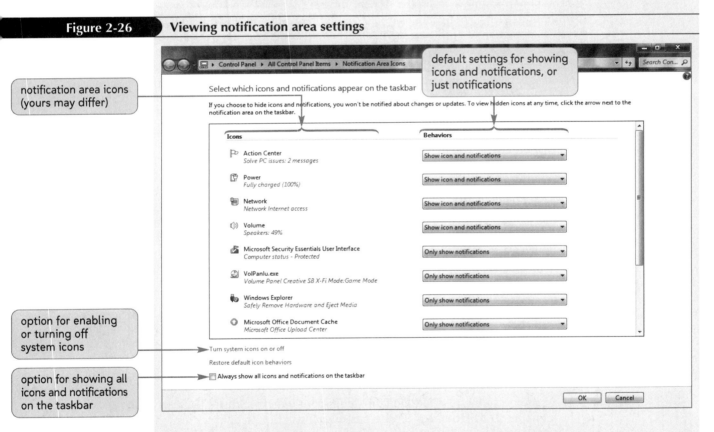

▶ **7.** Windows 7 displays options for modifying the behaviors of each program icon that currently appears or previously appeared in the notification area. Your notification area icon options and behaviors may differ. A faster way to customize icons and notifications as you work is to click the "Show hidden icons" button ▲, and then click the Customize link.

If you click the Behaviors button for the Action Center icon, or another notification area icon, you can choose "Show icon and notifications," "Hide icon and notifications," or "Only show notifications." Since the Action Center is a component of Windows 7 that notifies you of problems that arise on your computer, you probably will want to show both the icon and any notifications for problems that occur. Then you can click the notification to view information on the problem. You can also click the icon to see a message about the issue at hand or to open the Action Center. You can also right-click the icon to view options for viewing more information about the problem, or to resolve the problem, such as choosing "Open Action Center," "Troubleshoot a problem," and "Open Windows Update." However, for other notification area icons, you might want to hide both the icons and any program notifications so you are not interrupted while working with pop-up notifications about issues that are of low priority.

Problem Solving: Using the Notification Area to Stay on Top of Potential Problems

Since the notification area on the taskbar provides information about the status of your computer as well as notifications or alerts regarding changes to your computer system (such as detection of hardware devices), available updates, recommended maintenance and security tasks, incoming messages (such as email messages), network connectivity, and problems on your computer, it's important to customize its use so you have the information you need in order to stay on top of potential problems or issues that arise on your computer. By default, Windows 7 only displays system icons in the notification area. Other icons and notifications are not displayed in the notification area unless you take the time to customize icon behaviors. Also, other programs may make icons available via the notification area; however, you may not be aware of this change unless you periodically use the "Show hidden icons" button to periodically check for new program icons. For example, you might discover that your Internet security software has a message warning that you haven't run a scan on your computer for a while, and therefore your computer might be at risk. One easy way to resolve these types of problems is to choose the "Always show all icons and notifications on the taskbar" check box in the Notification Area Icons window. By making use of the options that Windows 7 provides for customizing the notification area, you ensure that you are aware of important issues concerning your computer and can quickly take action to solve any problems that develop.

The Notification Area Icons window also has a link for restoring default behaviors for icons.

To continue to check notification area settings:

1. At the bottom of the Notification Area Icons window, click the **Always show all icons and notifications on the taskbar** check box to enable this feature, and then examine your notification area. You may see icons in the notification area for programs other than system icons. All the Behaviors options in the Notification Area Icons window are now dimmed, and therefore unchangeable.

2. Click the **Turn system icons on or off** link. Windows 7 displays the System Icons window where you can turn on or off the display of system icons: Clock, Volume, Network, Power, and Action Center. See Figure 2-27. The Action Center is a central location for viewing alerts about problems or security issues with your computer.

Figure 2-27   **Options for enabling or turning off system icons**

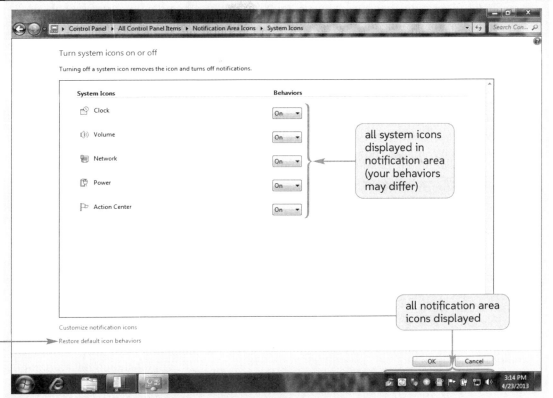

3. Click the **Customize notifications icons** link to return to the Notification Area Icons window.

4. If the "Always show all icons and notifications on the taskbar" option is not your computer's original setting, click the **Always show all icons and notifications on the taskbar** check box (to turn off the display of all icons and notifications).

5. If you have changed icon behaviors and want to restore their default behaviors, click the **Restore default icon behaviors** link.

6. Click the **OK** button to apply any changes you have made and close the Notification Area Icons window, and then close the System Icons window.

7. In the Taskbar and Start Menu Properties dialog box, click the **OK** button to apply any changes you have made and to close the Taskbar and Start Menu Properties dialog box.

If you want to display hidden notification area icons, you drag an icon to the notification area where you see the system icons so the previously hidden icon is always displayed. For example, you might want to use drag-and-drop to move the Safely Remove Hardware and Eject Media icon so it is always visible. Likewise, you can drag a visible icon in the notification area to the "Show hidden icons button," and place it with the other hidden icons.

REFERENCE

Customizing the Taskbar

- Right-click the taskbar, and then click Properties on the taskbar shortcut menu.
- To unlock (or lock) the taskbar, click the "Lock the taskbar" checkbox under Taskbar appearance.
- To use the Auto-hide feature (to hide or unhide) the taskbar, click the "Auto-hide the taskbar" check box.
- To use small icons for taskbar buttons, click the "Use small icons" check box.
- To change the taskbar's location on the screen, click the "Taskbar location on screen" button, and then choose Left, Right, Top, or Bottom.
- To change the way Windows 7 displays taskbar buttons, click the Taskbar buttons button; click "Never combine" to turn off taskbar grouping; click "Combine when taskbar is full" to display taskbar buttons (and labels, depending on the taskbar position on screen) for multiple program, folder, and document windows only when the taskbar is full; or to restore the default setting, click "Always combine, hide labels."
- To turn Aero Peek on or off, click the "Use Aero Peek to preview the desktop" check box.
- To customize the notification area icons and behaviors, click the Customize button under Notification area, and for each notification area icon, click the Behaviors button, and choose "Show icon and notifications," "Hide icons and notifications," or "Only show notifications" to control the behavior of each notification area icon.
- To display all icons and notifications, click the "Always show all icons and notifications on the taskbar" link.
- To restore the default settings for icon behaviors, click the "Restore default icon behaviors" link.
- To turn off or on the display of one or more system icons, click the "Turn system icons on or off" link and, in the System Icons window, click the Behaviors button for each system icon and choose On or Off.
- Click the OK button to close the Notification Area Icons window, and then click the OK button to close the Taskbar and Start Menu Properties dialog box.

Displaying and Creating Taskbar Toolbars

You can add built-in toolbars to the taskbar, or you can create a custom toolbar from a folder on your computer.

Alejandro offers to step you through the process for adding toolbars to the taskbar and creating a new toolbar from your Pictures and Videos folder.

To display and examine features of the Desktop toolbar:

▶ **1.** Right-click the **taskbar**, and if the taskbar is locked, click **Lock the taskbar** to remove the check mark; otherwise, if the taskbar is already unlocked, click the **desktop** to close the taskbar shortcut menu. It is easier to see the border of a toolbar on the taskbar when you unlock the taskbar.

▶ **2.** Right-click the **taskbar**, point to Toolbars on the taskbar shortcut menu, and then click **Desktop**. Windows 7 adds the Desktop toolbar to the taskbar, just to the left of the notification area.

3. Click the **Desktop toolbar** expand button ▌ to the right of the Desktop label for the new Desktop toolbar. Windows 7 displays a pop-up Desktop toolbar menu with options for viewing and accessing the contents of the Libraries, Homegroup, your current user account folder, Computer, Network, the Control Panel Jump List, Recycle Bin, and the Control Panel tool. See Figure 2-28. If you have other content on your desktop, such as folders, files, shortcuts, or Web pages, they also appear on the Desktop toolbar menu.

| Figure 2-28 | Viewing the Desktop toolbar menu |

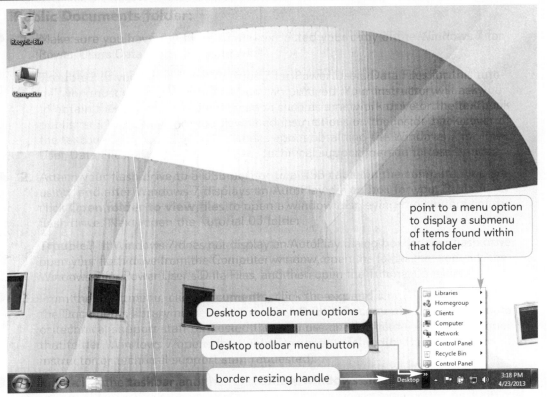

If you point to Libraries, you can access and view the contents of the Documents, Music, Pictures, and Video folders via cascading menus. If you point to Computer, then you can quickly access each of the different drives on your computer.

4. Press the **Esc** key to close the Desktop toolbar menu.

5. Point to the **border resizing handle** (which appears as a series of vertical dots) to the left of the Desktop title on the Desktop toolbar, and when the mouse pointer changes to ⟺, drag the left border to the left to display all the options (or as many options as possible) on the Desktop toolbar. Windows 7 displays buttons and a label for each option on the Desktop toolbar. When you click one of the Desktop toolbar buttons, the toolbar button opens a window onto one of these folders, just like a regular taskbar button.

6. Right-click the **Desktop** title (the name of the toolbar). Windows 7 displays a modified taskbar shortcut menu. At the top of this menu are options for adjusting the Desktop toolbar. You can use the View option to switch between Large Icons and Small Icons. You can use the Show Text option to turn off (or display) labels for each button and the Show title option to turn off (or display) the toolbar name.

7. Click **Close toolbar** on the shortcut menu, and then click the **OK** button in the Confirm Toolbar Close dialog box. Windows 7 closes the Desktop toolbar. If you need this toolbar later, you can add it to the taskbar again.

Another useful toolbar is the Address toolbar. You can use it to navigate to a Web site without first opening your Web browser.

To display the Address toolbar and navigate to a Web site:

1. Right-click the **taskbar**, point to **Toolbars** on the taskbar shortcut menu, and then click **Address**. Windows 7 adds the Address toolbar to the taskbar, again just to the left of the notification area.

2. Point to the **border resizing handle** just to the left of the Address title on the Address toolbar, and when the mouse pointer changes to ↔, drag the left border to the left to widen the Address box on this toolbar.

3. Click inside the Address box, type **microsoft.com**, and then press the **Enter** key. Windows 7 opens your default Web browser, and displays the home page for the Microsoft Web site.

4. Click inside the Address box, type **google.com**, and then press the **Enter** key. Your Web browser displays the home page for Google's Web site in a new tab (assuming your Web browser supports tabbed browsing).

5. Click the **Address toolbar** arrow ▾ to view a list of Web sites you visited.

6. Click the **URL** for the Microsoft Web site. Your Web browser opens the Microsoft home page.

7. Right-click the **Address toolbar title**, click **Close toolbar** on the shortcut menu, and then click the **OK** button in the Confirm Toolbar Close dialog box.

8. Close your Web browser window.

If you are right-handed, the Address toolbar location is more convenient than your Web browser Address bar.

As noted earlier, you can also create a new toolbar from a folder on your computer.

Since you frequently examine company videos in your line of work, Alejandro recommends that you create a toolbar to one of your folders that contains videos.

To create a new taskbar toolbar from a folder:

1. Right-click the **taskbar**, point to **Toolbars** on the shortcut menu, and then click **New toolbar**. As shown in Figure 2-29, Windows 7 opens a "New Toolbar – Choose a folder" dialog box so you can navigate to the folder you want to access from a toolbar.

| Figure 2-29 | Locating a folder for use as a taskbar toolbar |

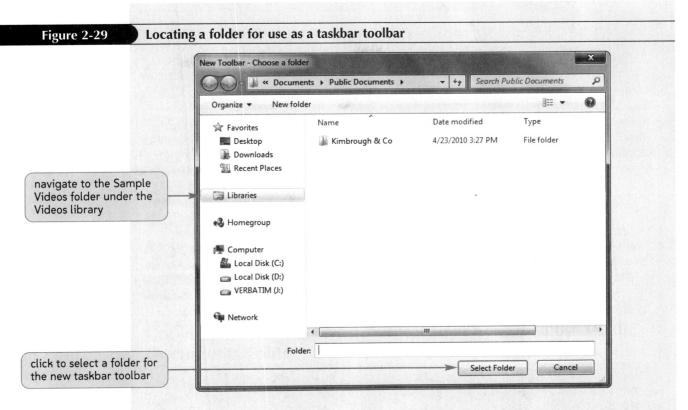

navigate to the Sample
Videos folder under the
Videos library

click to select a folder for
the new taskbar toolbar

> **2.** In the Navigation pane, point to **Libraries**, click the **expand** icon ▷ to the left of Libraries, click **Videos** under Libraries, and in the Contents pane on the right, point to the **Sample Videos** folder icon to select it, then click the **Select Folder** button. Windows 7 adds a Sample Videos toolbar on the right side of the taskbar.

> **3.** Point to the border resizing handle just to the left of the Sample Videos title on the Sample Videos toolbar, and when the mouse pointer changes to ⇔, drag the border to the left to widen the Sample Videos toolbar and display one or more videos in that folder.

> **4.** Click **Wildlife.wmv** (or another video) on the Sample Videos toolbar. Windows 7 opens this video in Windows Media Player and plays the video.

> **5.** After you view the video, close Windows Media Player.

> **6.** Right-click the **Sample Videos** toolbar title, click **Close toolbar** on the shortcut menu, and then click the **OK** button in the Confirm Toolbar Close dialog box.

If you frequently work with the contents of a folder, such as one that contains presentations, videos, or games, you can create a taskbar toolbar for that folder so you can access the files in that folder more quickly.

REFERENCE

Displaying and Creating Taskbar Toolbars

- Right-click the taskbar, and if the taskbar is locked, click Lock the taskbar to remove the check mark; otherwise, if the toolbar is already unlocked, click the desktop to close the taskbar shortcut menu.
- To add a built-in toolbar to the taskbar, right-click the taskbar, point to Toolbars on the taskbar shortcut menu, and then click one of the built-in toolbars on the Toolbars menu.
- To create a custom toolbar from a folder, right-click the taskbar, point to Toolbars on the shortcut menu, click New toolbar, use the Navigation pane to locate the folder you want to use, select the folder, and then click the Select Folder button.
- To widen a toolbar so you can display all the options on the toolbar, point to the border resizing handle just to the left of the toolbar title, and, when the mouse pointer changes to an arrow that points to the right and left, drag the left border to the left.
- Click the toolbar's expand button to the right of the toolbar label to view a menu of options for that toolbar, and then click the option you want to open.
- To display a menu of options for the toolbar, right-click the toolbar's title (the name of the toolbar), and then click one of the options at the top of the shortcut menu (such as View, Show text, and Show title).
- To close a custom toolbar, right-click the toolbar's title, click Close toolbar on the shortcut menu, and then click the OK button in the Confirm Toolbar Close dialog box.

With Alejandro's insights into customizing the taskbar and notification area and creating custom toolbars for the taskbar, you are ready to set up your desktop so you can more efficiently access the tools you need to work on your computer.

REVIEW

Section 2.2 Quick Check

1. How do you specify the default action for the power button?
2. You can customize certain Start menu options, such as those for Control Panel, so the Start menu option either _____ a window, or displays a(n) _____.
3. Windows 7 uses _____ to combine taskbar buttons for similar types of windows into one button.
4. True or False. If your computer supports Windows Aero, and if Aero Peek does not display translucent windows, then you can enable this setting on the Taskbar property sheet.
5. True or False. You can change the behavior of icons in the notification area, but you cannot change the notifications that are displayed.
6. What is a taskbar toolbar? What two ways can you create these toolbars?
7. How can you prevent a new user from making changes to the location of programs on the Start and All Programs menu by using drag and drop?
8. If the Aero Peek option for previewing the desktop is not available on a computer, how do you fix this problem?

SESSION 2.3 VISUAL OVERVIEW

Your monitor's screen **resolution** determines the sharpness and quality of the image displayed on your LCD. The video display adapter setting for your resolution determines the number of pixels displayed on the monitor, which in turn determines the sharpness of the image.

Use the Advanced settings link to open the properties dialog box so you can adjust the **color depth** setting, which determines the total number of colors that the video display adapter can display for any given pixel.

With this link, you can specify a password to be used in order to wake up a computer from a sleep, hybrid sleep, or hibernation power state.

You can create a custom power plan from one of the three Windows 7 power plans, and specify power management settings that meet your specific needs.

Display ▸ Screen Resolution

Search Con...

Change the appearance of your display

Detect

Identify

Display: 1. Dell 2007WFP (Digital)

Resolution: 1024 × 768

Orientation: Landscape

Advanced settings

Hardware and Sound ▸ Power Options

Search

Control Panel Home

Require a password on wakeup

Choose what the power button does

Create a power plan

Choose when to turn off the display

Change when the computer sleeps

Select and customize a **power plan**, or combination of power management settings, that improves your computer's performance and conserves energy.

Select a power plan

Power plans can help you maximize your computer's performa or conserve energy. Make a plan active by selecting it, or choo plan and customize it by changing its power settings. Tell me about power plans

Plans shown on the battery meter

⦿ **Balanced (recommended)**   Change plan setting
Automatically balances performance with energy consumption on capable hardware.

○ High performance   Change plan setting
Favors performance, but may use more energy.

VIDEO AND POWER MANAGEMENT

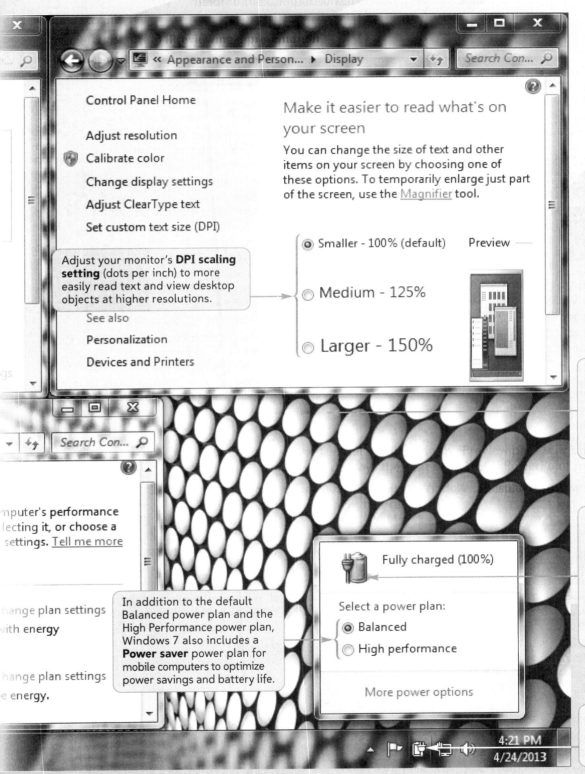

Adjust your monitor's **DPI scaling setting** (dots per inch) to more easily read text and view desktop objects at higher resolutions.

Your monitor's resolution determines the **aspect ratio** that compares the width of an image displayed on a monitor to its height, and determines whether you see a widescreen image.

In addition to the default Balanced power plan and the High Performance power plan, Windows 7 also includes a **Power saver** power plan for mobile computers to optimize power savings and battery life.

Newer, smart batteries for mobile computers include sensor circuitry for calculating the remaining battery charge and reporting that information to Windows 7. That in turn determines the icon that Windows 7 displays for the battery charge on the Power icon.

Use the **Power icon** in the notification area for quick access to power management settings.

Adjusting Your Video Display Settings

To optimize your investment in your flat panel display, you can check and adjust three important video display adapter and monitor settings—screen resolution, color depth, and DPI scaling.

Adjusting the Screen Resolution

One of the important characteristics of your monitor is its resolution, or the sharpness of the image that appears on the monitor. Your monitor's resolution is expressed by a combination of two numbers, such as 1680 × 1050. The first number refers to the number of pixels displayed across the width of your monitor, and the second number refers to the number of pixels displayed down its height. Therefore, at a resolution of 1680 × 1050, the video display adapter displays 1680 pixels across the width of the screen and 1050 pixels down the screen. If you multiply 1680 by 1050, you'll find that an image displayed on the monitor at this resolution is composed of 1,764,000 pixels.

LCD (liquid crystal display) monitors, or flat panel displays, on desktop computers and laptops, have a preset resolution called the **native resolution** that is the best resolution for the monitor. The native resolution is set by the manufacturer.

You can increase or decrease the resolution of your video display. For example, you might set your video display to a lower resolution, such as 1024 × 768, for a presentation before a group using an overhead projector so the presentation is easier for everyone to see. At the lower resolution, the video display adapter displays fewer pixels on the monitor, but they are larger in size. That means elements of the graphical user interface, such as text and icons, are easier for individuals in an audience to see because they are larger in size. Also, at lower resolutions, there's less room on the desktop for windows and dialog boxes because of the larger size of desktop objects.

In contrast, at higher resolutions, the video display adapter displays more pixels, and they are smaller in size, so elements of the graphical user interface are more difficult for individuals in an audience to see. However, if you are working on a project at your desk, you are closer to the monitor, and you can more easily see elements of the graphical user interface at much higher resolutions, and all the elements of the graphical user interface appear sharper. Also, there is more room for multiple open windows as well as dialog boxes on the desktop. You may have to strike a compromise, and select a resolution that provides a balance between how many objects you can fit on your desktop, and how easily you can see and locate those objects (as well as read their icon titles).

Another important feature of an image is its aspect ratio, a calculated value derived from the screen resolution by dividing the number of pixels across the monitor by the number of pixels from top to bottom.

For example, at a resolution of 1280 × 720, an LCD monitor has an aspect ratio of 16:9. A 16:9 aspect ratio means that the image on the monitor is 1.78 times wider than it is tall (16 ÷ 9 = 1.78, rounded off to two decimal places), or about twice as wide as it is tall. This aspect ratio is a standard high-definition TV (HDTV) resolution and a common widescreen video and movie format. In contrast, older TVs and older computer monitors display images using an aspect ratio of 4:3. With a 4:3 aspect ratio, the image is only 1.33 times wider than it is high (4 ÷ 3 = 1.33, rounded off to two decimal places), closer to a square image in appearance. Figure 2-30 lists examples of aspect ratios for different screen resolutions.

Figure 2-30 | Video display adapter resolutions with total number of pixels and aspect ratios

Resolution	Number of Pixels	Aspect Ratio	Decimal Value (up to 9 places)	Decimal Value (rounded off)
640 × 480	307,200	4.3	1.333333333	1.33
800 × 600	480,000	4:3	1.333333333	1.33
960 × 600	576,000	8:5	1.6	1.6
1024 × 768	786,432	4:3	1.333333333	1.33
1088 × 612	665,856	16:9	1.777777778	1.78
1152 × 648	746,496	16:9	1.777777778	1.78
1152 × 864	995,328	4:3	1.333333333	1.33
1176 × 664	780,864	16:9	1.771084337	1.77
1216 × 684	831,744	16:9	1.777777778	1.78
1280 × 720	921,600	16:9	1.777777778	1.78
1280 × 768	983,040	5:3	1.666666667	1.67
1280 × 800	1,024,000	8:5	1.6	1.6
1280 × 1024	1,310,720	5:4	1.25	1.25
1360 × 768	1,059,840	16:9	1.770833333	1.77
1440 × 900	1,296,000	8:5	1.6	1.6
1680 × 1050	1,764,000	8:5	1.6	1.6
2560 × 1600	4,096,000	8:5	1.6	1.6

For each resolution in Figure 2-30, the table lists the total number of pixels, the exact or closest aspect ratio (in whole numbers), an aspect ratio calculated up to nine decimal places, and a rounded-off aspect ratio. 640 × 480, 800 × 600, and 1024 × 768 are resolutions with an aspect ratio of 4:3 that were commonly used with earlier versions of the Windows operating system. The native resolution of the monitor used for these figures is 1680 × 1050 (the highest resolution), with an aspect ratio of 8:5 and a calculated ratio of 1.6. While the calculated value for the ratio of the 1176 × 664 resolution does not exactly match the calculated value for the 1280 × 720 resolution (which has a 16:9 aspect ratio), the values are so close that the aspect ratio for 1176 × 664 is listed as 16:9. Note that the 1440 × 900 and 1680 × 1050 resolutions have an increasingly common aspect ratio of 8:5 that is actually close to the 16:9 aspect ratio. The 1280 × 768 resolution has an aspect ratio of 5:3 that is also close to the 16:9 aspect ratio.

The manufacturer of the video display adapter for the computer used for this tutorial's figures notes that the video display adapter supports resolutions up to 2560 × 1600 with an aspect ratio of 8:5 (or 1.6); however, those resolutions are not available with the currently available device drivers. It should also be noted that LCD monitors support more resolutions than shown in this table. Furthermore, there are many manufacturers that produce LCDs with different resolutions.

The resolution that you use determines whether the video display adapter displays the image at one of these two common aspect ratios or at another aspect ratio. If you switch to a resolution that changes to a different ratio of the number of pixels for the width and height of the monitor, then certain desktop elements may exhibit distortion. Also, if you use an aspect ratio of 4:3 on a widescreen monitor, and if you adjust the image to remove distortion, then the image does not fill the width of the monitor. Instead, you see a black background on the left and right sides of a centered image. If you switch to a resolution that uses another aspect ratio, such as 16:9, then the image may fill the entire width of the monitor. The computer used for figures in this book is set for a lower resolution of 1024 × 768 so the details of an image are visible in the printed book.

To view and adjust your computer's resolution:

1. Right-click the **desktop**, and then click **Screen resolution** on the shortcut menu. Windows 7 opens the Screen Resolution window. See Figure 2-31.

| **Figure 2-31** | **Viewing monitor display settings** |

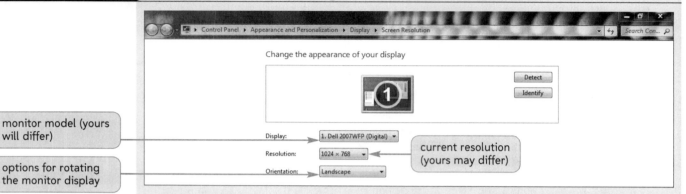

monitor model (yours will differ)

options for rotating the monitor display

current resolution (yours may differ)

Windows identifies the type of display, its current resolution, and its orientation. On the computer used for this figure, the orientation is currently set at Landscape (the default option); however, it can be changed to Portrait, Landscape (flipped), and Portrait (flipped) by using the Orientation button. If the monitor is physically rotated 90 degrees to the right, and if the Portrait orientation is selected, then the width of the monitor is far smaller than the height, and therefore it's possible to more easily view the contents of taller document windows. The Detect button checks for another monitor. The Identify button identifies which display you are using by number.

2. Note the current resolution so you can restore this setting later (if necessary).

3. Click the **Resolution** button. Windows 7 displays a drop-down slider bar for adjusting the resolution. See Figure 2-32. The lowest resolution for the display on this computer is 800 × 600. Your resolution options may differ.

| **Figure 2-32** | **Viewing options for changing the resolution** |

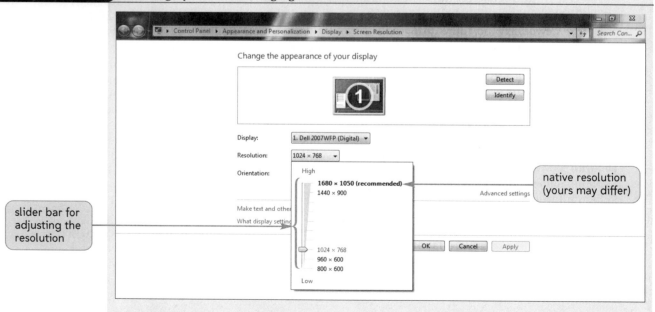

slider bar for adjusting the resolution

native resolution (yours may differ)

4. Drag the slider tab to the next lower resolution, and then click the **Apply** button. Windows 7 switches to a newer resolution, and displays a Display Settings dialog box asking if you want to keep these display settings. It also notes that it will revert back to the previous resolution in 15 seconds if you do not click the Keep changes button. After you change resolution, you can examine the desktop to determine if the resolution you chose will meet your needs.

Trouble? If your computer is already set to a low resolution, drag the slider tab to the highest resolution, and click the Apply button.

5. Let Windows 7 revert back to your original resolution. This option is also useful if you encounter an unexpected problem when changing the screen resolution because you can let Windows 7 automatically revert back to the previous resolution that worked.

6. Keep the Screen Resolution window open.

REFERENCE

Changing the Screen Resolution

- Right-click the desktop, and then click Screen resolution on the shortcut menu.
- Note the current resolution on your computer so you can restore this setting if necessary.
- Click the Resolution button, and drag the slider tab on the slider bar to another resolution you want to use.
- Click the Apply button, examine the appearance of the desktop at this new resolution, and either click the Keep changes button to apply this new setting, or click the Revert button to restore your previous resolution (or wait 15 seconds for Windows 7 to restore the previous resolution).
- Close the Screen Resolution window.

For certain resolutions, you can use the buttons on the front or side of your monitor to access a monitor's built-in menu so you can further adjust your display settings and, if necessary, eliminate distortion. For example, your default monitor display setting might be Fill (the image fills the entire monitor), and that option will work for most of your widescreen resolutions. However, you might have other options under a setting called Wide Mode, such as 4:3 (for a ratio of 1.33) and 1:1 (that keeps the same ratio of width to height). You can use these options, or whatever options are available with your monitor, to change the ratio of the image and reduce distortion. However, in some instances, the image may not fill the complete monitor. You can also use your monitor's built-in menu to adjust brightness, color settings, image mode settings (for example, Desktop Mode, Multimedia Mode, and Gaming Mode), and other display settings and to specify the input source for the image.

Adjusting the Color Depth

In addition to controlling resolution, you can typically set your video display adapter to use one of two color depth settings, each of which determines the maximum number of colors used to compose an on-screen image. Like the screen resolution, the color depth setting also determines the final quality of your monitor's image.

A **High Color** (16 bit) color depth setting means that your video display adapter uses 16 bits to display 65,536 colors. With 16 bits, there are a maximum of 2^{16} or 65,536 possible combinations of *0* (zero) and *1*. As you may already know, the *0* and *1* are the only two digits used in the binary numbering system. By combining 16 of these *0*s and *1*s in different ways, you can produce 65,536 codes, each of which uniquely defines a color.

With the **True Color** (32 bit) color depth setting, your video display adapter can use 24 bits to display 16,777,216 colors (or approximately 16.8 million colors). The other 8 bits (24 bits + 8 bits = 32 bits) supports transparency. Windows Aero requires a 32 bit color depth setting. Windows Vista and Windows XP referred to these two color depth settings as Medium (16 bit) for High Color and Highest (32 bit) for True Color.

The True Color option is the better of the two options because it improves the overall quality of the view that you see on your monitor. If your video display adapter does not have a sufficient amount of video RAM (i.e., RAM on the video card), and if you want to work at a much higher resolution, you may only be able to use the High Color setting.

To view and change the color setting:

▶ **1.** In the Screen Resolution window, click the **Advanced settings** link, and then click the **Monitor** tab in the dialog box for your monitor and video display adapter. As shown in Figure 2-33, the Colors button shows your current color depth setting.

Figure 2-33 Checking the color depth setting

▶ **2.** Click the **Colors** button. Windows 7 lists the color depth settings available for the video display adapter: High Color (16 bit) and True Color (32 bit).

▶ **3.** In the Colors list, click the next lower color depth setting (or next higher color depth setting) for your computer, click the **Apply** button, and wait a few seconds. Windows 7 displays a Display Settings dialog box and asks if you want to keep these display settings. See Figure 2-34.

Figure 2-34	Examining the effect of a lower color depth setting

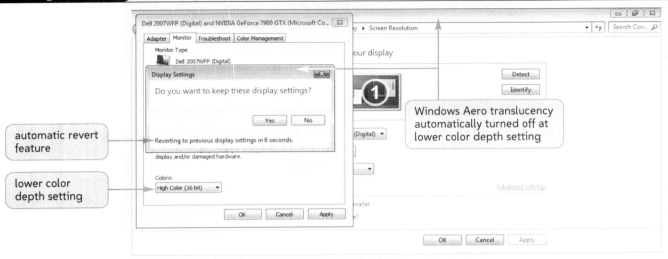

Examine the quality of the image on your monitor. On the computer used for Figure 2-34, Windows 7 turned off Windows Aero because it requires a 32-bit color depth setting. Therefore, window borders, the title bar, dialog boxes, task-bar, and taskbar buttons are no longer translucent. Also, other Windows Aero fea-tures, such as Live Taskbar Thumbnails, Windows Flip, and Windows Flip 3D, do not work in the same way or no longer work at all at the lower color depth setting.

4. Keep the dialog box for your monitor and video adapter display settings open for the next section of the tutorial.

As you will discover in Tutorial 8, you can change the way that Windows starts up, and some startup options use lower screen resolutions and color depth settings so you can troubleshoot problems on your computer that affect the video display. In some cases, you have no choice but to user lower resolution and color depth settings if you want to see an image on the monitor while you troubleshoot a problem.

REFERENCE

Changing the Color Depth Setting

- Right-click the desktop, click Screen resolution on the shortcut menu, and in the Screen Resolution window, click the Advanced settings link.
- Click the Monitor tab in the dialog box for your monitor and video display adapter display settings.
- Click the Colors button, click the color depth setting that you want to use, click the Apply button, examine the appearance of the desktop, and either click the Yes button to apply this new setting, or click the No button to restore your previous resolution (or wait 15 seconds for Windows 7 to restore the previous color depth setting).
- Click the OK button to close the dialog box for your monitor and video display adapter settings, and then close the Screen Resolution window.

Checking All Video Display Modes

You can also view all combinations of screen resolution settings, color depth settings, and refresh rates for your video display adapter. **Refresh rate** refers to the number of times per second that the image on the screen is redrawn by the video card, but it applies only to the older television-style **CRT** (**cathode ray tube**) monitors and is not an issue on modern-day LCD or flat panel displays. However, the refresh rate is still important for applications like the Windows Media Center that support a specific refresh rate for the TV-compatibility timing mode to record such things as HDTV broadcasts on your computer. If the refresh rate is too low on a CRT monitor, the image on the monitor flickers, which creates headaches and eyestrain. The recommended refresh rate for CRT monitors is 75 Hz (Hertz) because most people do not detect flicker at or above 75 Hz. However, because individuals differed in their ability to perceive flicker, it is generally recommended that individuals examine refresh rate settings in the range of 75 to 85 Hz. Refresh rates over 85 Hz serves no purpose because most individuals cannot detect flicker at these higher refresh rates. In some cases, a higher than needed refresh rate also results in a drop in resolution or color depth because video display adapters with limited video RAM do not support all combinations of resolutions, color depths, and refresh rates. Windows Vista requires the refresh rate be above 10 Hz (a rather low value) to support Windows Aero. The refresh rate for your monitor is shown on the Monitor property sheet where you examined the color depth setting.

PROSKILLS

Decision Making: Purchasing a Computer with Dedicated Graphics Memory

When purchasing a computer for your company's employees, you should make sure that the new computers contain an adequate amount of dedicated graphics memory, or video RAM, to support the types of tasks required by the end users. To handle graphics, a computer might use a video card that provides dedicated graphics memory, in other words, RAM devoted exclusively to graphics. Or a computer might use integrated graphics, and depend on a graphics processor chip on the motherboard to handle graphics. In the latter case, a portion of regular RAM, or system memory, must be used (or dedicated) for graphics, and that reduces the overall performance of your computer. The more dedicated graphics memory you have (such as 1–2 GB or more), the better your computer performs, and the more support you have for Windows Aero. Also, if you're into gaming, then you want to use dedicated graphics memory for the best possible performance. Not surprisingly, dedicated graphics memory is more expensive than integrated graphics memory, but it offers you better performance. The important point to remember is that you want to purchase a high-performance video display adapter with ample amounts of dedicated graphics memory, not only for Windows 7, but for all the other applications you use on your computer and all the other type of tasks you require of your computer. With the rapid growth of the Internet, and the rapid change in hardware technology and software applications, graphics memory is one of the major factors to consider when purchasing a computer. By carefully evaluating and comparing the video graphics memory available in different computers, you can ensure that you purchase a computer with enough dedicated video RAM to meet the current and future needs of the applications and features (like Windows Media Center) used by your company's employees.

Alejandro recommends that you examine all video display modes for your monitor.

To view all video display modes:

▶ **1.** In the properties dialog box for your monitor and video display adapter, click the **Adapter** tab. The Adapter property sheet has information about your video display adapter, including the Total Available Graphics Memory, Dedicated Video Memory, System Video Memory, and Shared System Memory (all of which are important to the use of Windows Aero under Windows 7). The Total Available Graphics Memory is the sum of Dedicated Video Memory, System Video Memory, and Shared System Memory. On the computer in Figure 2-35, the Dedicated Video Memory, or the total memory available on the video display card itself, is 512 MB.

| Figure 2-35 | Viewing information about the video card and the use of graphics memory |

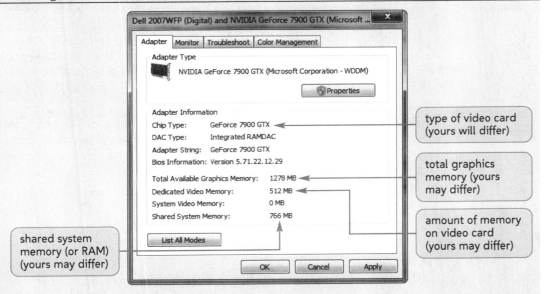

▶ **2.** Click the **List All Modes** button, and in the List All Modes dialog box, scroll to the top of the list of valid modes. Windows 7 lists all combinations of resolutions, color depth settings, and refresh rates that are supported on your computer, as shown in Figure 2-36. Your settings might differ.

Figure 2-36 **Viewing a list of valid display modes**

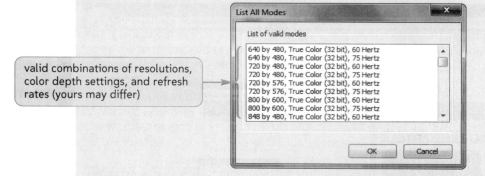

valid combinations of resolutions, color depth settings, and refresh rates (yours may differ)

> **List All Modes**
>
> List of valid modes
>
> 640 by 480, True Color (32 bit), 60 Hertz
> 640 by 480, True Color (32 bit), 75 Hertz
> 720 by 480, True Color (32 bit), 60 Hertz
> 720 by 480, True Color (32 bit), 75 Hertz
> 720 by 576, True Color (32 bit), 60 Hertz
> 720 by 576, True Color (32 bit), 75 Hertz
> 800 by 600, True Color (32 bit), 60 Hertz
> 800 by 600, True Color (32 bit), 75 Hertz
> 848 by 480, True Color (32 bit), 60 Hertz
>
> OK   Cancel

If you examine this list, you will discover screen resolutions lower than those that you examined earlier, such as 640 × 480, 720 × 480, and 720 × 576, as well as intermediate resolutions, such as 848 × 480 and 960 × 600. You will also find color depth settings, such as 256 colors that are not available on the Monitor property sheet. If you choose one of the modes in the List All Modes dialog box, Windows 7 will apply all three settings at once (if possible), and adjust the resolution, color depth, and refresh rate in one step.

3. Click the **Cancel** button to close the List All Modes dialog box without making any changes that you do not want, and click the **Cancel** button to close the Properties dialog box for your monitor and video display adapter without inadvertently making any changes.

4. Keep the Screen Resolution window open for the next part of the tutorial.

Although Windows 7 detects and uses the best possible display settings for your computer, it's a good idea to check those settings. Plus it's a good idea to be familiar with the specifics of your computer system, such as the type of video display adapter card and how memory is used on that card so you can apply that information to future purchases.

REFERENCE

Checking Video Display Settings

• Right-click the desktop, click Screen resolution, and then click the Advanced settings link in the Screen Resolution window.

• Click the Monitor tab in the dialog box for your monitor and video display adapter display settings, and then examine your monitor's Screen refresh rate.

• To view information about your video display adapter, including the Total Available Graphics Memory, Dedicated Video Memory, System Video Memory, and Shared System Memory (all of which are important to the use of Windows Aero under Windows 7), click the Adapter tab.

• To view a list of all combinations of resolutions, color depth settings, and refresh rates that are supported on your computer, click the List All Modes button on the Adapter property sheet, examine the list of valid modes, and then click the OK button to close the List All Modes dialog box.

• To apply any changes to display settings that you've made, click the OK button in the dialog box for your monitor and video display adapter settings. If you do not want to inadvertently make any changes to these display settings, click the Cancel button to close the Properties dialog box for your monitor and display adapter.

• Close the Screen Resolution window.

Adjusting DPI Scaling

If you want to use the native resolution of your monitor, or set your monitor to another high-resolution option, but at the same time want to more easily see desktop icons and the content of windows and dialog boxes, as well as the text of icon titles and menus, then you can adjust the DPI scaling setting for your computer. By default, the DPI scaling setting is 96 DPI (or 96 pixels per inch); in Windows 7 that translates to a value of 100% (or normal size). You can increase that value to 125% or 150% of normal size to increase the size of text and icons. You can define a custom DPI setting up to 500%. It is also possible to change icon font sizes; however, you have to use the Windows 7 Basic theme, or one of the Ease of Access themes, which means you do not have access to all of the Windows Aero features, such as translucency and Aero Flip 3D.

Alejandro recommends you examine these settings in case you decide to adjust your resolution to an even higher value than you already have.

When you change the DPI setting on a computer, you must log off the computer to implement the change. If you are working in a computer lab, you may not have the option of logging off your computer, and therefore you will not be able to change your computer's DPI setting. Instead, read the following steps and examine the options in the Custom DPI Setting dialog box but do not keystroke the following steps.

To adjust font sizes with the DPI scaling setting:

1. In the Screen Resolution window, click the **Make text and other items larger or smaller** link. Windows 7 displays three DPI settings on the right side of the window, as shown in Figure 2-37.

Figure 2-37 Viewing DPI Scaling options

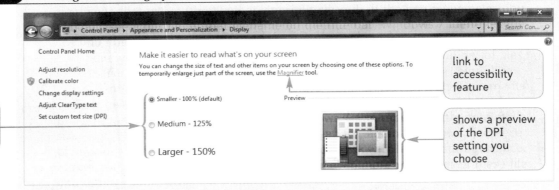

note differences in text size for different DPI scaling options

link to accessibility feature

shows a preview of the DPI setting you choose

If you choose one of the three DPI settings here, you then click the Apply button to apply the change to your computer, and Windows 7 will inform you that you have to log off your computer to apply these changes.

2. Click the **Set custom text size (DPI)** link on the left side of the window. In the Custom DPI Setting dialog box shown in Figure 2-38, Windows 7 shows you how the default 9 point Segoe UI font looks at 96 pixels per inch with the current DPI setting of 100%.

Figure 2-38 Viewing custom DPI scaling options

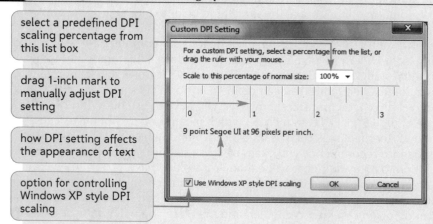

select a predefined DPI scaling percentage from this list box

drag 1-inch mark to manually adjust DPI setting

how DPI setting affects the appearance of text

option for controlling Windows XP style DPI scaling

Your DPI scaling may differ. You can change the current setting by selecting a DPI setting of 100%, 125%, 150%, or 200% from the "Scale to this percentage of normal use" box. Or you can point to the 1-inch mark on the ruler and drag it to the right (or left) to manually adjust the scaling to another value not available in the "Scale to this percentage of normal use" box. When you release the mouse pointer, the text below the ruler will change size. Windows 7 will list the number of pixels per inch at this new setting. If you set the DPI setting to higher than 144% while using Windows Aero, you might find that text in a program window does not appear sharp. To prevent this problem, make sure you enable "Use Windows XP style DPI scaling."

3. Click the **Scale to this percentage of normal size** arrow, select 125%, and then examine how the "9 point Segoe UI at 120 pixels per inch" setting looks on your computer.

4. Repeat this process, and test the options for 150% and 200% in the "Scale to this percentage of normal size" box.

5. If you want to use one of these DPI scaling options, or if you want to test a custom setting on your computer, click the **OK** button in the Custom DPI Setting dialog box, and then click the **Apply** button in the Display window. A Microsoft Windows dialog box then informs you that you must log off your computer to apply these changes, and it reminds you to save any open files and close all programs before logging off. If you want to apply the changes now, click the **Log off now** button and then log back onto your computer, or if you want to apply the change later, click the **Log off later** button. If you do not want to make a change to the DPI setting on the computer you are using, or if you are working in a computer lab where you cannot log off the computer, then click the **Cancel** button in the Custom DPI Setting dialog box.

6. Close the Display window.

If you work in a profession where you need to view documents at the same size as they will appear when printed, then you can place a real ruler on the monitor over the Custom DPI Scaling ruler, and drag and drop the 1-inch mark on the Custom DPI Scaling ruler so it matches a real inch.

REFERENCE

Adjusting the DPI Scaling

- Right-click the desktop, click Screen resolution on the shortcut menu, and then click the "Make text and other items larger or smaller" link.
- If you want to choose one of the three DPI settings shown in the Display window, click the option button for that DPI setting, and then click the Apply button.
- If you want to view more DPI scaling options, click the "Set custom text size (DPI)" link on the left side of the window. In the Custom DPI Setting dialog box, click the "Scale to this percentage of normal use" box, and select a DPI setting of 100%, 125%, 150%, or 200%, or point to the 1-inch mark on the ruler, and drag it to the right (or left) to manually adjust the scaling to another value.
- If you want to set the DPI setting to a value higher than 144% while using Windows Aero, make sure the "Use Windows XP style DPI scaling" check box contains a check mark (and is therefore enabled).
- To apply a new DPI setting, click the OK button in the Custom DPI Setting dialog box, click the Apply button in the Display window, and click the Log off now button in the Microsoft Windows dialog box. After Windows logs you off, then log back onto your computer. To apply the change later, click the Log off later button. If you do not want to make a change to the DPI setting on the computer you are using, click the Cancel button to close the DPI Custom Setting dialog box, and then click the Cancel button in the DPI Scaling dialog box.
- Close the Display window.

By adjusting your screen resolution, color depth setting, and DPI scaling, and by using the ClearType Text Tuner, you can fine-tune the appearance of your monitor's display and benefit from your monitor's capabilities. You can also improve the quality of the elements in the graphical user interface, text, and desktop background images so you can work effectively and comfortably. These types of settings are also important for individuals who need assistive features and technologies to make computers more accessible.

INSIGHT

Using Accessibility Features

The Ease of Access Center in Control Panel contains other accessibility settings and programs that are available in Windows 7. These features include a Start Narrator option for a program to read text on the screen out loud, and a Start Magnifier option for enlarging an area on the screen so it is more visible, as well as options for setting up other alternative input devices (other than the standard mouse and keyboard), adjusting mouse and keyboard settings, using text or visual alternatives for sounds (such as text captions or a flashing desktop, active window, or caption bar), and adjusting Windows settings for reading and typing. While designed for use by individuals who need assistive features and technologies, these same features can benefit anyone who wants to customize their computer for ease of use and optimal use.

Using Power Management

Kimbrough & Co., like many other global companies, depends on the power management features of Windows 7 to enhance the performance of its employee's computers, conserve energy, reduce energy-related costs, and protect the environment.

Windows 7 supports the **Advanced Configuration and Power Interface** (**ACPI**), a set of power-management specifications developed by Microsoft, Intel, and Toshiba that allow the operating system to control the amount of power that each device receives. Using these power-management specifications, Windows 7 monitors the power state of the computer, determines the power needs of applications and hardware devices, and increases or decreases the availability of power as needed.

In Windows 7, you can choose from one of three power plans and then customize it so you can take advantage of its features while adapting it to your specific needs. The three power plans are as follows:

- **Balanced** for matching power usage at any given time to system needs and performance. Balanced is the recommended power plan for both desktop and mobile computers.
- **Power Saver** for conserving power and maximizing battery life on mobile computers, even if it results in reduced performance.
- **High Performance** for maximizing power usage on mobile computers even if it means shorter battery life. You can also use the High Performance plan on a desktop computer if you rely heavily on multitasking or resource-intensive tasks.

The tutorial steps and explanations are designed primarily for desktop computers. If you are using a mobile computer, your power management settings may differ, and you may have additional settings.

> **TIP**
>
> Your computer's manufacturer may provide additional power plans.

To view Windows 7 power plans and power plan settings:

1. Click the **Power** icon ![icon] in the notification area, and then click the **More power options** link. In the Power Options window, Windows 7 displays two power plans—Balanced and Power saver, with a description of the primary purpose of each power plan. See Figure 2-39.

   Trouble? If Windows 7 does not display a Power icon in the notification area on your desktop computer, open the Start menu, point to Control Panel, and then click Power Options on the Control Panel menu.

Figure 2-39   **Viewing power plan options for conserving battery life and improving performance**

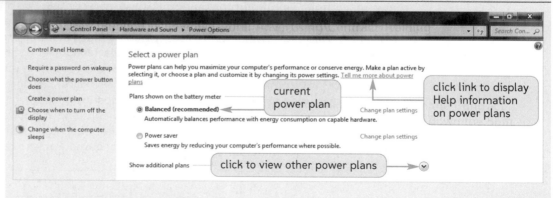

> **2.** To view additional plans, click the **Show additional plans** expand button ⊙. Microsoft keeps the High performance plan as a "hidden" additional plan to emphasize the importance of conserving energy by using either the Balanced or Power Saver plan.

> **3.** To the right of Balanced (recommended), click the **Change plan settings** link. In the Edit Plan Settings window, Windows 7 shows the settings for turning off the display and for putting the computer to sleep for this power plan. See Figure 2-40.

Figure 2-40   **Power management settings for the Balanced power plan**

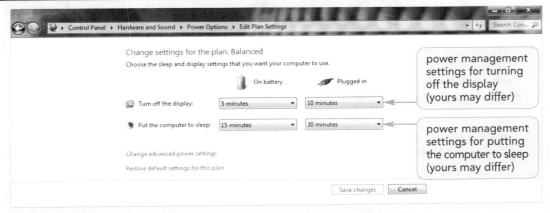

As shown on the desktop computer used for Figure 2-40, if the computer is plugged into a power outlet, Windows 7 will turn off the video display after 10 minutes of user and system inactivity, and put the computer to sleep after 30 minutes of user and system inactivity, by default. The computer in this figure is plugged into a UPS (uninterruptible power supply) unit, and therefore Windows 7 also displays options for operating "On battery." If the computer is operating on battery, or if the computer has a backup power supply, then Windows 7 turns off the video display after 5 minutes of inactivity, and puts the computer to sleep after 15 minutes. Your settings may differ. Notice that there is a link for restoring default settings of this plan.

> **4.** Click the **Change advanced power settings** link. In the Power Options dialog box, you can review and, if necessary, change specific power settings on the Advanced settings property sheet. If you click the "Change settings that are currently unavailable" link, and provide Administrator credentials, then Windows 7 will enable options (if any) in the Advanced settings dialog box that were previously dimmed, and you can then edit some options that you would not have otherwise been able to change without supplying Administrator credentials.

> **5.** Click the **expand** icon ⊞ to the left of Hard disk, and then click the **expand** icon ⊞ to the left of "Turn off hard disk after." On the computer in this figure, Windows 7 turns off the hard disk after 10 minutes of user and system inactivity on battery power. When plugged in, the computer turns off the hard disk after 20 minutes. See Figure 2-41. Your settings may differ. If you want to adjust either or both of these settings, click the setting, and then increase or decrease the setting.

Figure 2-41 **Viewing power management settings for the hard disk**

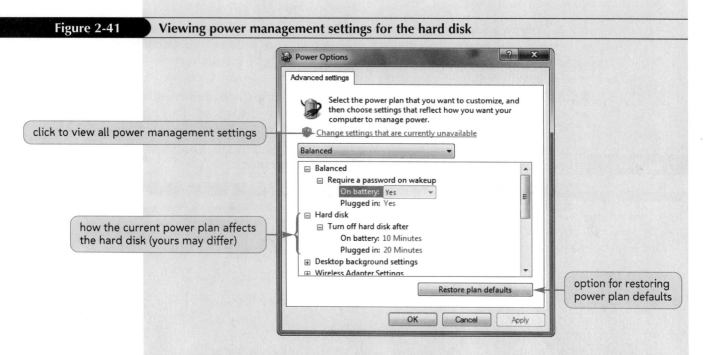

click to view all power management settings

how the current power plan affects the hard disk (yours may differ)

option for restoring power plan defaults

6. Click the **expand** icon 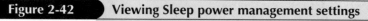 to the left of "Desktop background settings," then click the **expand** icon to the left of "Slide show." If the desktop theme includes multiple images that are displayed as a slide show, then by default Windows 7 pauses the slide show effect when the computer is operating on battery, and displays the slide show when plugged in.

7. Scroll down the Advanced settings box and then click the **expand** icon to the left of Sleep, and then click the **expand** icons to the left of "Sleep after," "Allow hybrid sleep," and "Hibernate after." See Figure 2-42.

Figure 2-42 **Viewing Sleep power management settings**

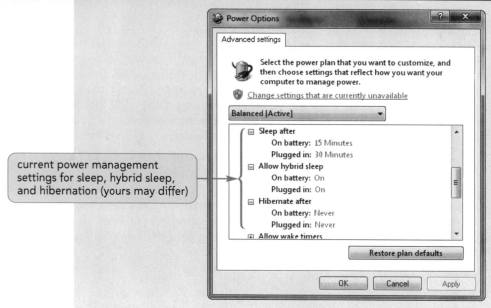

current power management settings for sleep, hybrid sleep, and hibernation (yours may differ)

As shown in this figure, Windows 7 automatically enables hybrid sleep when on battery and when plugged in for this computer. Also, since this computer is a desktop computer, the option for hibernation is "Never." Your settings may differ. By checking these sleep settings, you can determine whether hybrid sleep is enabled on your computer and you can enable hibernation. You can also adjust each of these settings manually. While the options in the Edit Plan Settings window that you previously examined allow you to select only certain intervals of time for sleep and turning off of the display, in the Power Options dialog box you can specify the exact number of minutes you want for a setting.

8. Examine other categories, and if you make changes to power management settings that you want to keep, click the **OK** button in the Power Options dialog box, and then click the **Save changes** button in the Edit Plan Settings window. If you want to restore default plan settings, click the **Restore default settings for this plan** link in the Edit Plan Settings window. If you have made changes to the power management settings that you do not want to keep, or if you are using a computer in a computer lab, click the **Cancel** button in the Power Options dialog box, and then click the **Cancel** button in the Edit Plan Settings window to avoid inadvertently changing any settings. Both the Cancel and the OK buttons in the Power Options dialog box return you to the Edit Plan Settings window.

9. In the Edit Plan Settings window, click the **Back** button ⬅ to display the Power Options window, and keep the Power Options window open.

In the Power Options dialog box, the Power Saving Mode option for the Wireless Adapter Settings on the Advanced settings property sheet is especially important for mobile computers because it determines whether the wireless adapter uses any power management features, and that in turn determines the speed at which the wireless adapter communicates with a wireless access point.

The Power button and lid settings specify what Windows 7 does when you press the power button on your computer. The lid setting specifies what Windows 7 does when you close the lid to a mobile PC, such as Take No Action, Shut Down, Sleep, or Hibernate.

The Multimedia settings on the Advanced settings property sheet apply to sharing media, such as music and videos. The "Allow the computer to enter Away Mode" option switches a computer to a state in which it appears off. However, the computer is still operational and can handle background tasks, such as recording TV broadcasts or sharing multimedia content.

To complete your examination of power plan settings:

1. If you made changes to power management settings that you want to keep, click the **Save changes** button in the Edit Plan Settings window. If you want to restore default plan settings, click the **Restore default settings for this plan** link in the Edit Plan Settings window. If you have made changes to the power management settings that you do not want to keep, or if you are using a computer in a computer lab, click the **Cancel** button in the Edit Plan Settings window to avoid inadvertently changing any settings.

2. In the Edit Plan Settings window, click the **Back** button ⬅ to display the Power Options window, but keep the Power Options window open.

On the left side of the Power Options window, there are four options for adjusting power management settings. The "Require a password on wakeup" and the "Choose what the power button does" options open the System Settings window where you can change both settings. The "Choose when to turn off the display" and the "Change when the computer sleeps" options are accessible from this window or from the Edit Plan Settings window for the current power plan's settings.

The "Create a power plan" option allows you to create and then modify a new power plan based on an existing power plan. Then, you can save your new power plan settings under a name of your choosing, so you can have all three of the original plans, and add any additional custom power plans you want.

To view these additional power option settings:

1. In the left pane, click the **Require a password on wakeup** link. Under "Password protection on wakeup" in the System Settings window, Windows 7 is set to automatically require a password. Options in this section require Administrator credentials and are therefore dimmed to prevent changes. See Figure 2-43.

Figure 2-43	Viewing Power button settings

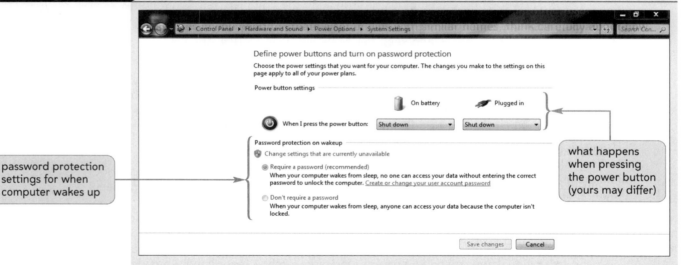

password protection settings for when computer wakes up

what happens when pressing the power button (yours may differ)

If you want to change these settings, you have to click the "Change settings that are currently unavailable" link. You can also change the Power button settings in this window, and specify what Windows should do when you press the power button on your computer.

2. To the right of "When I press the power button," click the **On battery** or **Plugged in** button to view the available options. You can specify that Windows 7 does nothing, places your computer in a sleep state or in hibernation, or shuts down your computer (the default). By changing this setting here, you don't have to choose the

option you most commonly use from the Start menu; instead, you just press the power button on your computer, and Windows 7 shuts your computer down in the way you specified here.

 ▶ **3.** To the right of "When I press the power button," click the **On battery** or **Plugged in** button a second time to close the list.

 ▶ **4.** Click the **Back** button ⊝ to return to the Power Options window.

 ▶ **5.** Click the **Create a power plan** link. In the Create a Power Plan window, you select one of the existing power plans to use as the basis for a new power plan, and you type a name for that power plan in the Plan name text box. After you click the Next button, you specify settings for turning off the display and putting the computer to sleep. Then you click the Create button (or click the Cancel button if you change your mind). If you create a new power plan, it appears with other available power plans and becomes the current power plan. Once you create this power plan, you can change its plan settings.

 ▶ **6.** Click the **Cancel** button, and then close the Power Options window.

INSIGHT

Strategy for Identifying a Monitor's Power State

It's not uncommon in workplaces, college computer labs, or even at home, for Windows 7 to automatically switch to a power saving mode that reduces power to the monitor. The monitor then appears to be turned off, and someone who does not realize that the monitor is in a low-power state will assume instead that the computer is off, and then press the power button. That turns off the computer. The user then will have to power the computer back on, and wait while the computer restarts. This same type of problem can also occur if someone has selected the Blank screen saver. Before you assume a computer is off, check the monitor's power button. If the power button is orange rather than green, then it's in a low-power state or the computer is off (but the monitor's power has not been turned off). If the monitor's power button is green, then the Blank screen saver is active. If you press a key on the keyboard, Windows 7 either wakes up the monitor if it's in a low power state and displays an image on the monitor or turns off the screen saver so you can see the desktop. If neither of these changes occur, then someone has probably turned off the computer. By taking into account a monitor's power state, you can avoid problems that might arise from improperly shutting down a computer that is already on and avoid wasting time and effort.

TIP

Mobile users can find more information by searching for "Conserving battery power" in Help and Support.

Power management is particularly important in the case of mobile computers because these features can double or triple the lifetime of a computer's battery. Furthermore, the use of power-saving features on PCs, now commonplace in offices and homes, can not only significantly reduce the cost of electricity to both business and home users but also improve the quality of the environment.

Managing Power Management Settings

- If Windows 7 displays a Power icon in the notification area, click the Power icon, and then click More Power options, or right-click the Power icon, and then click Power Options. If Windows 7 does not display a Power icon in the notification area on your desktop computer, open the Start menu, click Control Panel, click the System and Security link in the Control Panel window, and then click Power Options. If you have customized the Start menu to display a Control Panel menu, you can open the Start menu, point to Control Panel, and then click Power Options.

- In the Power Options window, select the power plan you want to use or change, click the "Change plan settings" link for that power plan, and in the Edit Plan Settings window, review and, if necessary, change the settings for turning off the display and putting the computer to sleep, and then click the Save changes button if you have made changes you want to keep.

- Click the "Change plan settings" link in the Power Options window for the power plan that you want to further change, click the "Change advanced power settings" link, and in the Power Options dialog box, review and, if necessary, change specific power management settings on the Advanced settings property sheet. If you want to keep any changes you have made, click the OK button in the Power Options dialog box, and then click the Save changes button in the Edit Plan Settings window. If you have made changes to power management settings that you do not want to keep, click the Cancel button in the Power Options dialog box, and then click the Cancel button in the Edit Plan Settings window to avoid inadvertently changing any settings. If you want to restore the default settings for your power plan, click the "Restore default settings for this plan" link, and in the Power Options dialog box, click the Yes button.

- Click the Back button to return to the Power Options window, click the "Require a password on wakeup" "Choose what the power button does" link, to open the System Settings window, view your current "Password protection on wakeup setting" and the action that Windows 7 takes when you press the power button, and if necessary, change that setting. If you change one or both of these settings and want to keep those changes, click the Save changes button; otherwise, click the Cancel button.

- To create a new power plan with your own custom settings, click the "Create a power plan" link in the Power Options window, choose an existing power plan as the basis for your new power plan, enter a Plan name for your power plan, click the Next button, specify settings for turning off the display and placing your computer in a sleep state, and then click the Create button. Then you can modify this new power plan in the same way as you modify other power plans.

- In the Power Options window, click the "Choose when to turn off the display" link or the "Change when the computer sleeps" link, and in the Edit Plan Settings window, examine and, if necessary, change one or both of the settings for turning off the display and for putting the computer to sleep. If you want to keep any changes you have made, click the Save changes button in the Edit Plan Settings window. If you have made changes to power settings that you do not want to keep, click the Cancel button in the Edit Plan Settings window to avoid inadvertently changing any settings.

- Close the Edit Plan Settings window, and then close the Power Options window.

Windows 7 provides many more options for fine-tuning the power management on your computer than earlier versions of Windows. Custom power management settings not only conserve power and optimize the performance of your computer, but also streamline your use of your computer and save you time and effort.

Restoring Your Computer's Settings

If you work in a computer lab, restore the original settings on the computer you used.

To restore your computer's settings:

▶ **1.** To restore the original desktop background settings, right-click the **desktop**, click **Personalize**, and then click the icon for your original theme. To restore the original Windows 7 theme, click **Windows 7** under Aero Themes.

▶ **2.** If you want to delete the Archetypal Designs theme and the Unsaved Theme under My Themes, right-click the **Archetypal Designs theme icon**, and then click **Delete theme**. Repeat this process for the Unsaved Theme, and then close the Personalization window.

▶ **3.** If you want to delete the theme pack you saved, click the **Windows Explorer** taskbar button ▭, click **Documents** under Libraries, right-click your theme pack file with the .themepack file extension, click **Delete**, click the **Yes** button in the Delete File dialog box, and then close the Documents library window.

▶ **4.** To restore the Start menu, right-click the **Start** button ⊕, click **Properties**, click the **Customize** button on the Start Menu property sheet in the Taskbar and Start Menu Properties dialog box, click **Display as a link** under Control Panel, click the **OK** button to close the Customize Start Menu dialog box, and then click the **OK** button to close the Taskbar and Start Menu properties dialog box.

▶ **5.** If you want to turn off single-click activation and hide the display of file extensions for known file types, open the Start menu, type **folder options** in the Search box, press the **Enter** key, and under "Click items as follows" on the General property sheet in the Folder Options dialog box, click the **Double-click to open an item (single-click to select)** option button, click the **View** tab, click the **Hide extensions for known file types** check box (to add a check mark), and then click the **OK** button to close the Folder and Options dialog box.

▶ **6.** To lock your taskbar, right-click the **taskbar**, and then click **Lock the taskbar**.

▶ **7.** If you want to remove the Computer icon from the desktop, open the Start menu, right-click **Computer**, click **Show on Desktop**, and then close the Start menu.

REVIEW

Session 2.3 Quick Check

1. _____ refers to the sharpness of the image on a monitor.
2. True or False. Color depth refers to the maximum number of colors used to compose an on-screen image.
3. Windows Aero requires a color depth setting of _____ bits.
4. What setting identifies the number of times per second that the image on the screen is redrawn by the video card?
5. True or False. You can use the DPI setting to improve readability of text at higher resolutions.
6. What is ACPI?
7. What is a power plan, and what are the names of the three Windows 7 power plans?
8. What three types of sleep states does Windows 7 support?

Practice the skills you learned in the tutorial using the same case scenario.

PRACTICE

Review Assignments

There are no Data Files needed for the Review Assignments.

Alejandro asks you to assist several new coworkers in customizing their computers.

If possible, choose another computer to complete the Review Assignments. As you complete the following steps, provide Administrator credentials (if required), and record your observations and answers to the questions so you can later prepare a one- to two-page report summarizing your findings. Use a word-processing application, such as Microsoft Word or the WordPad accessory, to prepare the report. If you change any settings on the computer you are using, note the original settings so you can restore them later. Complete the following steps:

1. What type of computer are you using? Are you using a desktop, laptop, notebook, netbook, or some other type of computer?

2. If necessary, switch to single-click activation so you can work in Web style.

3. Open Control Panel and check all user accounts on the computer you are using. Is your user account an Administrator account or a Standard user account? If you don't know the user name for the computer you are using, check the Start menu for the user account name. Close the User Accounts window.

4. Open the Personalization window from the desktop. What theme does Windows 7 currently use on your computer? Is that theme an Aero theme, a Basic and High Contrast Theme, or a theme of your own design? Is the desktop background for this theme a slide show?

5. From the Personalization window, select Desktop Background, then select Top Rated Photos from the Picture location box. Change the Picture position to Fill, change the interval of time for displaying the theme's slide show to 10 seconds, choose the Shuffle option, and save your changes.

6. From the Personalization window, select Window Color, and then display the color mixer. Which one of the 16 color options does Windows 7 currently use for this theme's window frame and borders, the Start menu, the taskbar, and taskbar buttons? Is transparency enabled on your computer?

7. Select another color from the palette of colors, adjust the color intensity, hue, saturation, and brightness. If you change your mind and want to restore the default color, how would you do so?

8. Save your new theme as **Top Rated Photos**, and then save it as a theme pack in the Tutorial.02\Review folder on your flash drive using **Top Rated Photos** as the filename.

9. In the Personalization window, choose the Display link, and then choose the option to Adjust ClearType text. Why would you want to use the ClearType Text Tuner? Step through the ClearType Text Tuner and adjust the appearance of text to suit your tastes. Close the Personalization window.

10. Open the System window, choose the option to view Advanced system settings, provide Administrator credentials, choose the Settings button for viewing Performance settings, and compare the options for letting Windows choose what's best for your computer, adjusting your computer for best appearance, and adjusting it for best performance. Is there any difference between the three approaches in terms of what visual effects Windows uses? Do you prefer only those visual effects that produce the best appearance or those for best performance? List up to five visual effects that are the most important to you. Close the Performance Options dialog box, close the System Properties dialog box, and then close the System window.

11. Right-click the Start button and choose the option for viewing Start menu properties. What is the current Power button action setting? What Power button action do you prefer, and why?

12. Use the Customize button to open the Customize Start Menu dialog box. Locate the options for the Music and Videos folders, and then choose the option for displaying each as a menu. Locate the Favorites menu option, and enable this option so it appears on the Start menu. Apply the setting as you close the Customize Start Menu dialog box, and then choose the option to apply the changes in the Taskbar and Start Menu Properties dialog box.

13. Open the Start menu, point to the Music menu, and then point to each of the options that appear in the cascading menus. Repeat this process for the Videos folder. Point to Favorites on the Start menu, and view the contents of the Favorites menu. Describe what happens as you examine these options. Would these options be useful to you on your home or work computers? Explain.

14. Open the Customize Start menu dialog box and restore the default settings for the Favorites menu, Music folder, and Videos folder. Then close the Customize Start Menu dialog box and Taskbar and Start Menu Properties dialog box to restore the default settings.

15. If necessary, unlock the taskbar, and then view the properties of the taskbar. Enable Auto-hide for the taskbar, and then apply this setting. What happens to the taskbar? Move your mouse pointer to the bottom of the desktop, and then move the mouse pointer to the middle of the desktop. What happens as you perform these two steps? Turn off Auto-hide for the taskbar, and then apply this setting. What happens next? What happens when you move the mouse pointer to the very bottom of the screen, and what happens when you move the mouse to the middle of the desktop? If necessary, restore and apply your computer's original setting for "Auto-hide the taskbar."

16. Do you prefer the default "Always combine, hide labels" option for taskbar buttons, or do you prefer the "Combine when taskbar is full," or "Never combine" option? Explain why.

17. Which system icons does Windows 7 display in your notification area? Have you added (or moved) any of the icons to the visible notification area, and if so, which ones?

18. Choose the option to customize the notification area. In the Notification Area Icons window, examine the Behaviors setting for each notification area icon. Is there an icon for your Internet security or antivirus software? If so, what is the name of this icon, and what is its default behavior? Are there any Behaviors that you would change on your computer and, if so, why? From the desktop, how can you change which icons are visible in the notification area and which icons are hidden?

19. Create a new toolbar for your computer's Libraries on the taskbar. If necessary, unlock the taskbar, and then resize the Libraries toolbar so you can see all the options on the toolbar. Right-click the toolbar, choose the option for viewing Large Icons, and turn off the display of the toolbar title and text. Readjust the width of the toolbar. Then try each of the toolbar buttons, and describe what happens when you click each button. Would this type of feature prove useful to you in your work or play? Are the icons sufficiently recognizable that you would not need a toolbar title and a text label for each toolbar button? Close the Libraries toolbar.

20. Right-click the desktop, and choose the option for adjusting your screen resolution. What is your current resolution? Change your screen resolution to the highest or the next lowest resolution on your computer, apply the setting, and then view the desktop. What resolution setting did you choose, and how did this change your view of the desktop and its contents? Let Windows 7 revert back to the original screen resolution, or if necessary, restore the computer's original resolution. Are there any other options in the Screen Resolution window that might prove useful to you now or in the future? Explain.

21. Click the link for viewing advanced settings. On the Adapter property sheet in the dialog box for your monitor and video display adapter settings, identify the chip type for the video display adapter used on the computer, the Total Available Graphics Memory, the Dedicated Video Memory, the System Video Memory, and the Shared System Memory. What would you do differently when considering video memory for your next computer purchase?

22. Select the Monitor tab. What type of monitor do you have? What is your computer's color depth setting? What is the screen refresh rate for your monitor? Close the properties dialog box for your video display adapter and your monitor settings without making any changes to the computer.

23. Choose Display in the Address bar to jump to the Display window. What is your current DPI scaling setting? Would a different setting work better with the screen resolution of your computer? Explain. What three options are available for changing the DPI scaling? Close the Display window.

24. Open the Power Options window by using the Power icon in the notification area or by using Control Panel. What power plan does your computer use? Does that power plan meet your needs? Choose the option to edit plan settings for that power plan. What settings does Window 7 use on your computer for turning off the display and putting the computer to sleep?

25. Choose the option for changing your advanced power settings. Expand the options labeled "Power buttons and lid" and then expand "Power button action." What is the default action for the power button on your computer? What other options might you use for the Power button action? Would any of those options prove useful to you? Explain. Use the Cancel button to close the Power Options dialog box without making any changes, and then click Cancel in the Edit Plan Settings window to avoid making any other changes.

26. Click the "Choose what the power button does" link. What options are available for changing what happens when you press the power button on your computer? Are these the same options that you examined in the previous step? Close the System Settings dialog box.

27. View properties of the Start menu button again. Does the "Power button action" button provide any additional options over those you examined in the two previous steps, and if so, what are they? Would any of these prove useful to you? Explain.

28. Submit your answers to the questions in the Review Assignments and the theme pack (if requested) to your instructor, either in printed or electronic form, as requested. Remember to include your name and any other information requested by your instructor on your assignment.

29. To restore your computer:
    - If necessary, restore your original theme for the desktop. If your instructor does not require you to submit your theme pack, and if you no longer need the theme pack you created, open the Public Documents folder and delete the theme pack.
    - If your taskbar was originally locked and if you want to restore that setting, then enable the "Lock the taskbar" option.
    - If necessary, turn off single-click activation.

Use your skills to customize display settings for a publishing firm.

APPLY

Case Problem 1

There are no Data Files needed for this Case Problem.

ePsionics Li-ying Yiu, the owner of ePsionics, a firm that publishes online science fiction and fantasy books, recently purchased several new Windows 7 computers for her employees to meet the increased demand for books in this genre. She asks you to set up these computers for her employees and help them customize display settings on these computers.

As you complete the steps in this case problem, use a word-processing application, such as Microsoft Word or the WordPad accessory, to record your answers to questions. If you change any settings on the computer you are using, note the original settings so you can restore them later. Complete the following:

1. What edition of Windows 7 does your computer use? What type of processor does your computer use, and what is its rated clock speed? How much RAM is installed on your computer? Are you using a 32-bit or a 64-bit version of Windows 7? Does your edition of Windows 7 support Windows Aero? Does your computer's hardware support Windows Aero?

2. What is your computer's Video RAM, Total Available Graphics Memory, Dedicated Video Memory, System Video Memory, and Shared System Memory?

3. Open the Personalization window, choose the Windows 7 Aero theme (if necessary) and apply it to your computer, and select the option for viewing desktop backgrounds. From the Windows Desktop Background picture location, choose a single desktop background image, choose the option to fit on your monitor, and then save your changes. Examine the quality and sharpness of the image that you placed on the desktop background.

4. What is the native resolution of your monitor, and what is its current resolution? What color depth setting and refresh rate does your computer use?

5. Test three of your computer's highest resolutions using your current color depth setting. List the screen resolutions you examined (and your computer's native resolution), calculate the aspect ratio for each resolution, and then briefly describe how the quality and sharpness of desktop icons and the desktop wallpaper change with each change in the screen resolution. Briefly describe what you think is the best resolution, and note any other Windows 7 options that you might use to enhance the view of the content on your desktop.

6. If necessary, switch back to your original or native screen resolution. Test each of the color depth settings available on your computer, using your current screen resolution and current theme. At each color depth setting, examine the image on the monitor, and describe how each of the color depth settings affects the quality and sharpness of the desktop background.

⊕ **EXPLORE**　7. View a list of the valid modes for your video display adapter. What is the highest combination of screen resolution, color depth setting, and refresh rate for your computer? What is the lowest combination of screen resolution, color depth setting, and refresh rate? Close the List All Modes dialog box, the dialog box for your monitor and video display adapter properties, and the Screen Resolution window.

8. What is the best resolution and color depth setting for your computer?

9. Restore your computer to its original screen resolution, color depth setting, desktop background, and if necessary, theme.

10. Submit your answers to this case problem to your instructor, either in printed or electronic form, as requested. Remember to include your name and any other information requested by your instructor on your assignment.

Use your skills to provide support to employees at a college.

APPLY

Case Problem 2

There are no Data Files needed for this Case Problem.

Evan Gates Community College Buster McFadden works for the Computer Help Desk at Evans Gate Community College in Wisconsin and provides technical computer support to employees all over campus. Employees work on computers with different types of hardware and software, including different Windows 7 editions. As Buster works with users to customize their computers and resolve problems, he adds the question or problem to a database, along with information on how to resolve the issue or problem so college employees can check online for answers to commonly asked questions.

As you complete the steps in this case problem, use a word-processing application, such as Microsoft Word or the WordPad accessory, to record your answers to questions. If you change any settings on the computer you are using, note the original settings so you can restore them later. Complete the following:

1. A new employee wants to delete a theme that he's created. Before you explain to him how to delete that theme, what question do you need to ask that employee? Then, how should the employee delete the theme?

2. An employee discovers that the image that she's chosen for her desktop background appears distorted. Explain how she would correct this problem.

3. Another employee has just noticed that his window frames, window borders, Start menu, taskbar, and taskbar buttons are no longer transparent. What would you recommend he do to correct these problems?

4. An employee who wears eyeglasses asks why the text and icons on her screen do not appear sharp. Is there any way that she can adjust the appearance of text and icons, and if so, how?

5. Another employee who works in the Applied Graphics Department wants to customize his Start menu so he can open a folder from his user account folder and also from his Documents folder without first opening a window for each of these folders. He also wants to be able to quickly access a drive from the Start menu without first opening the Computer window. Describe the steps this employee should follow to customize the Start menu on his computer.

6. A new research employee notices another employee using Aero Peek, so she asks that employee how to use that feature. When she returns to her computer, she finds that the Aero Peek feature does not work. When she calls for assistance, you explain that there are two ways to enable Aero Peek. Describe those approaches.

7. An intern asks you how to change his computer so it enters a sleep state when he presses the power button. Describe a simple approach to resolving this problem that is suitable for a beginning user.

8. A researcher who regularly backs up her research data to a flash drive asks you how she can display the Safely Remove Hardware and Eject Media icon in the notification area. Identify one way in which she can make this change to her computer.

9. Two employees who share the same computer and the same research data ask you how they can quickly access the Public Documents folder from the desktop. Explain how they can create a taskbar toolbar to that folder.

10. A new employee who works on a computer with a high screen resolution asks you how to enlarge the text and icons so they are easier to see. Explain how she can modify her computer.

11. A new employee is hired to replace an employee who took a new position. He notices that his computer automatically turns off the display every 5 minutes, and he asks you to change this setting. Describe the two options that you would check.

12. Submit your answers to this case problem to your instructor, either in printed or electronic form, as requested. Remember to include your name and any other information requested by your instructor on your assignment.

Extend your skills to develop a plan for customizing power settings.

CHALLENGE

Case Problem 3

There are no Data Files needed for this Case Problem.

Innovative Entrepreneurs   Selene Ochoa works as a technical support manager at Innovative Entrepreneurs, a firm that provides venture capital for entrepreneurs of new Internet companies. As one of the company's representatives, you rely on the use of your company laptop when you visit new clients. You want to adjust the power management settings on your laptop so you can conserve power while at the same time guaranteeing that your laptop is immediately available when you need to use it. Before you meet with Selene to discuss how best to adjust power settings on your computer, you decide to examine and document your laptop's current power management settings.

As you complete the steps in this case problem, use a word-processing application, such as Microsoft Word or the WordPad accessory, to record your answers to questions. If you change any settings on the computer you are using, note the original settings so you can restore them later. Complete the following:

1. What type of computer do you use? Desktop computer, laptop, notebook, netbook, or handheld? Do you use an uninterruptable power supply (or UPS unit)?

2. Open the Power Options window using the Power icon or using Control Panel. What type of power plan does your computer currently use? Does its approach to balancing performance with energy consumption meet your current needs? Explain.

3. Choose the option for viewing settings for your power plan. What settings does your computer use for turning off the display and putting your computer to sleep? What changes, if any, might you want to make to these settings, and why?

⊕ **EXPLORE**

4. Choose the option for changing advanced power settings. Examine and describe your power plan's settings for sleep, hybrid sleep, and hibernation. Are the settings appropriate to the type of computer you use? Explain. Is there any advantage to using hibernation on your computer? Explain.

5. Examine your computer's Power buttons and lids settings. What action does your computer take when you press the Power button on your system unit?

⊕ **EXPLORE**

6. If available, examine the Battery power management settings. What action does Windows 7 take when the battery reaches the Critical battery level? What percentage of battery capacity is set as the Critical battery level? Is Low Battery notification enabled? What is the low battery level? What action does Windows 7 take when the battery capacity reaches the low battery level? What is the Reserve battery level setting?

7. Close the Power Options dialog box and Edit Plan Settings window without making any changes.

8. Submit your answers to this case problem to your instructor, either in printed or electronic form, as requested. Remember to include your name and any other information requested by your instructor on your assignment.

Extend your skills to create custom toolbars for mortgage company.

CHALLENGE

Case Problem 4

There are no Data Files needed for this Case Problem.

Reliable Financiers, Inc.   Reliable Financiers, Inc. is a Hawaiian firm that provides fixed-rate mortgages for new homeowners and for homeowners who want to refinance adjustable rate mortgages. Kilani Kahalewai, a loan officer at Reliable Financiers, wants to create custom toolbars that will allow him to quickly access drives, folders, and files on his computer so he can then respond quickly to customer requests on the telephone. Since you've recently customized your computer, you offer to show him how to create toolbars that will simplify access to his computer.

As you complete the steps in this case problem, use a word-processing application, such as Microsoft Word or the WordPad accessory, to record your answers to questions. If you change any settings on the computer you are using, note the original settings so you can restore them later. Complete the following:

1. If necessary, unlock the taskbar.

⊕ **EXPLORE**

2. From the taskbar shortcut menu, choose the option for creating a new taskbar toolbar. In the New Toolbar - Choose a folder dialog box, select Local Disk (C:) (or your hard drive icon) in the Navigation pane, click the Users folder in the File list, click the folder for your user account, and then select, but do not open, the Favorites folder. Use the Select Folder button to create the taskbar toolbar.

⊕ **EXPLORE**

3. Display the pop-up menu for the new Favorites toolbar. What does Windows 7 display on the Favorites toolbar menu? Point to and click a Favorite bookmark on this menu. Explain what happens.

⊕ **EXPLORE**

4. Display the Favorites toolbar menu again and point to one of the folders. Explain what happens. Would this feature be useful to you in your work or play? Explain. Close any window (or windows) you opened, and close the Favorites pop-up menu.

⊕ **EXPLORE**

5. Choose the option to create a new taskbar toolbar; however, this time, select the Favorites folder from the Navigation pane on the left side of the Choose a folder dialog box, and then create the toolbar. Explain what you see on the new Favorites taskbar toolbar menu. Then select Recent Places from that menu. Explain what happens. Choose one or more items in the Recent Places window and explain what happens. Would this feature be useful to you in your work or play? Explain.

⊕ **EXPLORE**

6. Attach your flash drive and create a taskbar toolbar for the flash drive. View its menu, and explain what types of content you can access on your flash drive. Would this feature be useful to you in your work or play? Explain.

7. What other locations might you want to create taskbar toolbars for?

8. To restore your computer, close all three taskbar toolbars.

9. Submit your answers to this case problem to your instructor, either in printed or electronic form, as requested. Remember to include your name and any other information requested by your instructor on your assignment.

ENDING DATA FILES

Tutorial.02 ➡ Tutorial   Review

Archetypal Designs.themepack   Top Rated Photos.themepack

Managing Folders and Files

Organizing Client Files

Case | *Cabral Advertising, Inc.*

Maya Cabral operates a fast-growing advertising firm called Cabral Advertising, which provides a wide range of design and advertising services for her clients in the New Orleans area. She designs company logos, brochures, newsletters, annual reports, catalogs, ads, business cards, and expensive wine bottle labels. She scans and restores photos, creates illustrations and cartoons, designs eye-catching Web advertising, and offers contract training on the use of graphic software and advertising design principles. Maya stores the files for her client projects, contracts, proposals, and designs on her computer network. Because her business is growing and because turnaround times on projects are always tight, she asks you to help her develop a more effective strategy for organizing and locating files stored on her computer.

STARTING DATA FILES

Tutorial.03 →

Tutorial
- Business Records
- Client Projects
- Company Performance
- Company Projections
- Contract Training
- Personal Records
- Sales Analyses

Review
- Business Records
- Client Projects
- Company Performance
- Company Projections
- Contract Training
- Personal Records
- Sales Analyses

Case1

(none)

Case2
- Business Records
- Client Projects
- Company Performance
- Company Projections
- Contract Training
- Personal Records
- Sales Analyses

Case3
- Business Records
- Client Projects
- Company Performance
- Company Projections
- Contract Training
- Personal Records
- Sales Analyses

Case4
- Business Records
- Client Projects
- Company Performance
- Company Projections
- Contract Training
- Personal Records
- Sales Analyses

SESSION 3.1 VISUAL OVERVIEW

These files are organized into a **stack**, or group, because they share the same **tag**, or keyword, assigned to each file.

Windows 7 organizes user folders into **libraries** for ease of access. Each library can contain one or more folders, and the files for each folder in a library appear in one central location.

The Library pane provides options for **stacking**, or arranging, files by a shared property.

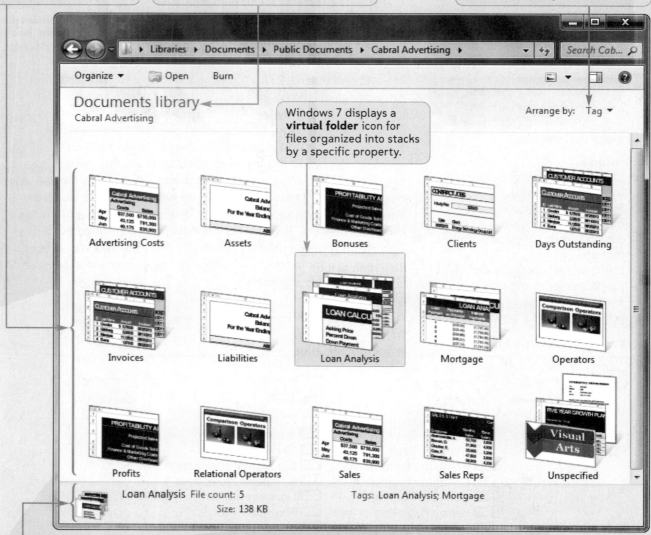

Windows 7 displays a **virtual folder** icon for files organized into stacks by a specific property.

Documents library
Cabral Advertising

Arrange by: Tag ▾

Advertising Costs

Assets

Bonuses

Clients

Days Outstanding

Invoices

Liabilities

Loan Analysis

Mortgage

Operators

Profits

Relational Operators

Sales

Sales Reps

Unspecified

Loan Analysis   File count: 5   Size: 138 KB   Tags: Loan Analysis; Mortgage

The **Details pane** provides information about files in the selected stack, including the number of files, the total size of all the files, and types of tags.

ORGANIZING FILES

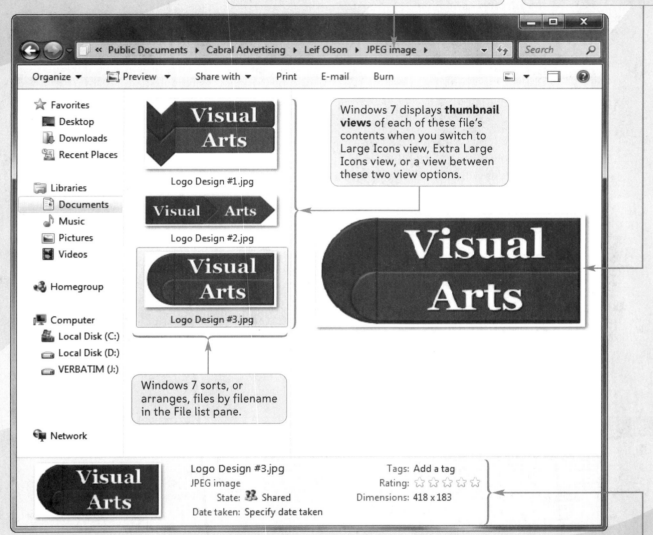

Windows 7 organizes files by file type in a JPEG image stack under another stack for a specific author. Each **file type** is associated with a specific application and has the same file extension.

Windows 7 displays a preview of a file's contents, including animation, in the **Preview pane**.

Windows 7 displays **thumbnail views** of each of these file's contents when you switch to Large Icons view, Extra Large Icons view, or a view between these two view options.

Windows 7 sorts, or arranges, files by filename in the File list pane.

In the Details pane, Windows 7 displays information about **file properties** of the file selected within this stack.

Organizing Folders and Files

One of the most important tasks you face is managing the disks, drives, folders, and files in your computer system. With the rapid increase in storage capacities of hard disks, newer types of software products, and increased reliance on downloading video, music, and other types of files from the Internet, the task of organizing folders and files becomes more important than ever. Fortunately, Windows 7 provides you with new approaches and features for organizing, accessing, and searching folders and files, and for locating information within files. However, you should also periodically analyze your current needs and reevaluate how Windows 7 and you organize your folders and files so you can simplify access to your personal files, improve your productivity, and optimize your computer's performance.

After Windows 7 installs itself on a computer, it creates a folder structure on the hard disk for the Windows operating system, for other installed software, and for each user account. Windows 7 then installs the majority of the files that constitute the operating system in a Windows folder. Windows 7 also creates a Program Files folder for all other installed software.

As you install new applications, utilities, and games on your computer, the installation program for each of those products usually installs the files for the software in a separate folder within the Program Files folder. If you are installing a new software product, and if the installation program proposes to install the software in a folder other than the Program Files folder, you can change the location of the installed software so it is also stored in the Program Files folder along with all of your other installed software. This approach guarantees that all your installed software is located in one folder on your hard disk. Although most of the files for the Windows 7 operating system are installed in the Windows folder, some components, such as Internet Explorer, are installed in subfolders under the Program Files folder.

Windows 7 also creates the Users folder on the hard disk, and within that Users folder, Windows 7 creates a user account folder for the first designated user of that computer. If several people use the same computer, each user can set up a user account with their own user account folder. That in turn enables each user to specify custom settings, such as desktop settings, and store their files separately from all other users of the same computer. Within each user account folder, Windows 7 creates a set of subfolders for storing specific types of files, as illustrated in Figure 3-1.

| Figure 3-1 | Folder structure for Maya's user account |

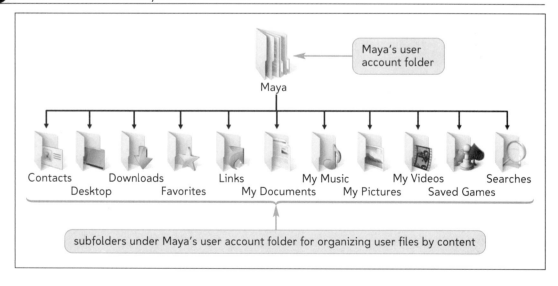

The following is a list of the folders that Windows 7 automatically creates within each user account folder:

- **Contacts**—The Contacts folder stores information on all your contacts, whether they are friends, family, coworkers, colleagues, business associates, companies, or organizations. This folder is also important for background compatibility when upgrading from Windows Vista, where it was first introduced. Within this folder, you can create a contact file where you store detailed information about each contact, including each person's name, nickname, family information, notes, and even digital IDs as well as personal and work email addresses, street addresses, phone numbers, and Web site addresses. A **digital ID** or **certificate** consists of information that verifies that an email message was actually sent by you, an increasingly important technique that protects the sender's and the recipient's privacy and the security of their computer systems. You can also use a digital ID to encrypt your email messages and thereby increase your privacy. Microsoft notes that email messages can be read and even altered in transit, so encryption helps protect those messages.

  The information for each contact is stored in a **contact file** with the .contact file extension. When creating a new user account, Windows 7 automatically creates a contact file for that user's account. For example, when Maya first created her user account, Windows 7 created a contact named *Maya.contact*. You can also customize contacts by adding a photo for each contact. Then you can select a contact by quickly examining pictures. You can also create a group contact, which combines multiple contacts. Then you can easily send the same message to each individual in your contact group in one simple operation. If you find that someone you know wants the information for one or more of your contacts, you can email those contact files as attachments to an email message. If you need to send a contact to someone who uses a different Windows version, you might need to **export**, or transfer, the information to another file format first. One common file format for storing exported data is **CSV** (for **comma-separated values**). In the exported file, which has a .csv file extension, the information for each contact is stored on one line, and each item of data is separated from the next by a comma. If an item of data contains one or more commas, it is enclosed within quotation marks. You can easily view the exported information by opening the file in Notepad.

- **Desktop**—Windows 7 stores any folders, files, shortcuts, or favorites that you place on your desktop in this folder. Windows 7 system desktop icons—Computer, Recycle Bin, User's File, Control Panel, and Network—are not displayed in this folder.

- **Downloads**—The Downloads folder is designed for storing software and files that you download from the Internet. By keeping downloaded software in one folder, you can quickly find software that you need to reinstall.

- **Favorites**—The Favorites folder contains any Internet shortcuts (or bookmarks) that you create with Internet Explorer.

- **Links**—When Windows 7 is first installed, the Links folder contains shortcuts to the Desktop, Downloads, and Recent folders, and these shortcuts appear in a folder's Navigation pane under Favorites; however, you can add more shortcuts to this folder for faster navigation around your computer (as you will see later in the tutorial).

- **My Documents**—The My Documents folder is designed as a central location for storing most of your personal files. By default, most applications save a document to a file in this folder. Likewise, if you open a file from an application, most applications also assume that the file you want to open is stored in the My Documents folder. Because most people prefer to store all their personal files in the My Documents folder, these default assumptions made by applications and other types of programs save you one important step in the process of selecting the right drive and folder for your document file. All you do is select (or create) the subfolder within the My Documents folder where you want to save the file. You can also override these default assumptions if you want to store a file in a folder other than the My Documents folder, or if you want to store a file on another disk drive, such as a flash drive. No matter where you store your personal files, you can create subfolders so you can organize your files into logical groups of related files. For example, you might store different versions of your resume in a folder called Resumes. All prior versions of Windows except Windows Vista referred to this folder as My Documents. In Windows Vista, this folder was named Documents. In Tutorial 5, you will see how Windows 7 resolves these differences so applications can locate specific system folders and files.

- **My Music**—You can use the My Music folder to store all your music and other audio files in one central location. This folder also contains a shortcut to the Sample Music folder (in the Public Music folder) that contains sample music files along with their cover art and other information about the music files, such as title name, album name, and contributing artists, plus whatever other information you want to display. You can play and listen to any music contained in this folder. Windows XP also referred to this folder as My Music; however, Windows Vista referred to this folder as Music.

- **My Pictures**—You can use the My Pictures folder to store all your digital photographs and other picture or image files in one central location. This folder contains a shortcut to the Sample Pictures folder (in the Public Pictures folder) with sample picture files that you can use as desktop backgrounds. You can also view the pictures in this folder as one continuous slide show. Windows XP referred to this folder as My Pictures; however, Windows Vista referred to this folder as Pictures.

- **My Videos**—You can use the My Videos folder to store all your video files in one central location. This folder contains a shortcut to the Sample Videos folder (in the Public Videos folder) with a sample video file that you can watch. You can play all videos you place in this folder. Windows XP referred to this folder as My Videos; however, Windows Vista referred to this folder as Videos.

- **Saved Games**—Windows 7 uses this folder to store information about games that you install on your computer.

- **Searches**—The Searches folder contains virtual folders with shortcuts to various types of files that are selected when you perform a search. Each virtual folder is a folder that organizes files from other folders into one central location for ease of access. Windows 7 also creates virtual folders as the result of some type of operation, such as searching for a set of files with some common characteristic.

Windows 7 creates a Public user account folder in the Users folder so two or more people using the same computer with different user accounts can share files. Also, all users can use these Public folders to share files with other users who are part of the same network. The Public folder contains the following subfolders (similar to those you just examined): Public Documents, Public Downloads, Public Music, Public Pictures, Public Videos, and Recorded TV (depending on your Windows 7 edition).

Getting Started

To complete this tutorial, you need to display the Computer icon on the desktop, switch your computer to single-click activation, and activate the option for displaying file extensions. In the following steps, you will check and, if necessary, change those settings.

To set up your computer:

1. If Windows 7 does not display a Computer icon on the desktop, open the **Start menu**, right-click **Computer**, click **Show on Desktop**, and then close the Start menu.

2. If you need to enable single-click activation, open the **Start menu**, type **folder options** in the Search box, press the **Enter** key, and under "Click items as follows" on the General property sheet in the Folder Options dialog box, click the **Single-click to open an item (point to select)** option button, and then click the **Underline icon titles only when I point at them** option button.

▶ **3.** Click the **View** tab, click the **Hide extensions for known file types** check box (and remove the check mark) to display file extensions, and then click the **OK** button to close the Folder Options dialog box and apply these changes. By changing this setting, Windows 7 displays file extensions with filenames for most types of files that you work with.

Now, as you work with files, you will see their file extensions so you can associate file extensions with specific programs on your computer. Understanding file extensions and their associations with one or more specific programs is key to becoming a power user.

Working with Libraries

To help you manage files and folders, Windows 7 goes a step further than previous versions of Windows and organizes User and Public folders into libraries so you can more easily access the folders and files on your computer system that contain similar types of content. A library is a virtual folder that consolidates files stored in different locations so you can work with all the files as a single group. Windows 7 automatically creates four default libraries, as follows:

- **Documents**—By default, the Documents library displays all files contained within the My Documents and the Public Documents folders. When you click Documents on the Start menu, Windows 7 opens the Documents library, not the My Documents folder. However, from the Documents library, you can view all the files you've stored in the My Documents folder under your user account as well as all the files in the Public Documents folder. And, if necessary, you can access the My Documents and Public Documents folders from the Navigation pane in the Documents library window. As shown in Figure 3-2, the Documents library (and the other three libraries), are nothing other than pointers, or links, to one or more folders under your user account and the Public user account (though the corresponding Public user accounts for each library, such as Public Documents, are not shown in the figure).

Figure 3-2   **Folder structure for Maya's user account**

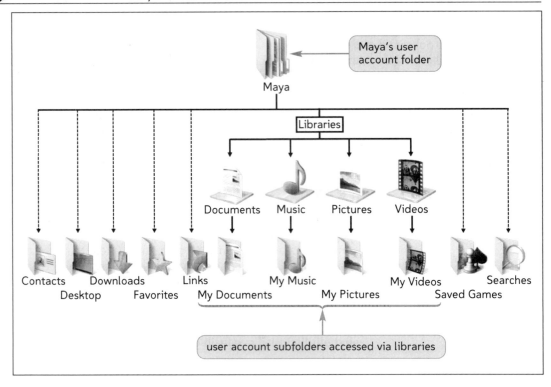

Maya's user account folder

Maya

Libraries

Documents   Music   Pictures   Videos

Contacts   Downloads   Links   My Music   My Videos   Searches
Desktop   Favorites   My Documents   My Pictures   Saved Games

user account subfolders accessed via libraries

- **Music**—The Music library displays all files contained within the My Music and the Public Music folders.
- **Pictures**—The Pictures library displays all files contained within the My Pictures and the Public Pictures folders.
- **Videos**—The Videos library displays all files contained within the My Videos and the Public Videos folder.

Windows 7 includes links to the Documents, Music, and Pictures libraries on the Start menu, and as you discovered in Tutorial 2, you can also add the Videos library link to the Start menu. If you click Documents on the Start menu (as noted earlier), or click Documents on the Windows Explorer Jump List (if available), you open the Documents library, which in turn displays the contents of the My Documents and the Public Documents folders together as if they were one folder. In Windows Vista, the Documents link on the Start menu opened the Documents folder. Before Windows Vista, all previous versions of Windows had a My Documents link on the Start menu that opened the My Documents folder.

You can expand each default library so it includes additional folders where you store similar content, and so the content is available as if it resided in a single folder. You can also create additional libraries of your own choosing, and add (or remove) one or more folders to each of those libraries. The folders that you include in a library can be ones on your hard disk drive(s), an external hard disk drive, a network, and your homegroup. A **homegroup** consists of a set of computers on a home network that shares documents, pictures, music, video, and one or more printers. Tutorial 12 covers the use of homegroups.

If you remove an external hard disk drive, the content in folders that are part of a library is no longer accessible until you reconnect the drive. Also, you should be aware of some limitations as to what you can include in a library. You cannot include folders on removable media such as a flash drive, a DVD, or a CD as part of a library, and you cannot include virtual folders with saved searches (which you will examine later in this tutorial) as part of a library. If you are working on a network, the contents of a network folder that's included in a library must be indexed. An **index** consists of information about folders and files, which enables Windows 7 to quickly search for specific folders and files you need.

Now that you've installed Windows 7 on your work computer, Maya recommends that you examine the Documents library and become familiar with how libraries work.

To examine the Documents library on your computer:

 1. From the Start menu, click **Documents**, and after Windows 7 opens the Documents window, click the **More options** arrow ▦ ▾ for the Change your view button on the toolbar, and then use the **slider bar tab** ▯ to adjust the view between Extra Large Icons and Large Icons. The Navigation pane on the left side of the window lists the Libraries available on the computer you are using. See Figure 3-3. The folders and files in your Documents library will differ.

Figure 3-3 **Viewing the contents of a Documents library**

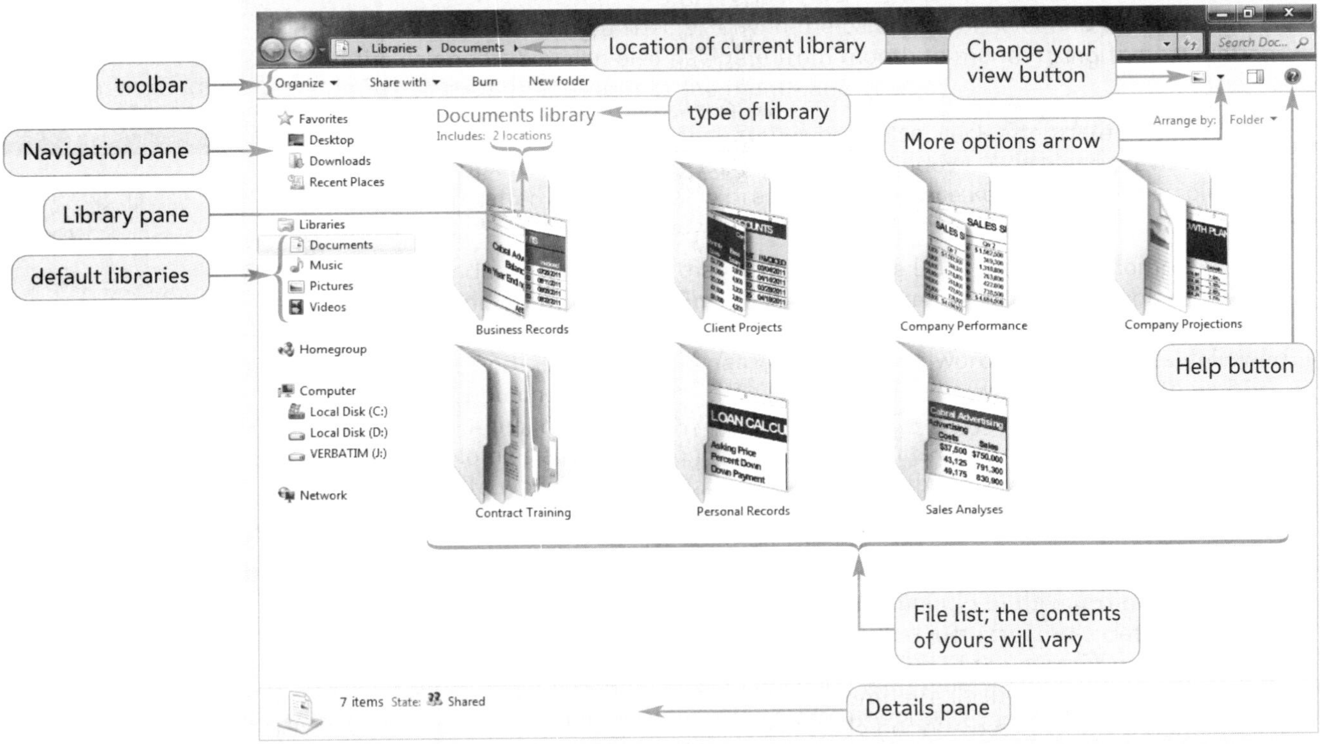

As noted earlier, Documents, Music, Pictures, and Videos are the default libraries built into Windows 7. The File list displays the content of a library or folder. The Library pane identifies the name of the library you're viewing; in this case, the Documents library. The Library pane also notes that two locations are included in the Documents library. The Details pane identifies how many items are in the Documents library on the computer used for Figure 3-3 and indicates that it is a shared folder. Windows 7 also displays information about drives, libraries, folders, files, your network, and your homegroup in the Details pane, but it depends on which window you open and what you select. You can use the Help button ⑦ on the toolbar to view information about managing folders.

> **2.** Click the **2 locations** link in the Documents Library pane. Windows 7 opens the Documents Library Locations dialog box and lists the folders that are included as part of this library—the My Documents folder and the Public Documents folder. See Figure 3-4. Your dialog box might differ if one or more other folders have already been added to this library.

Figure 3-4 **Viewing the default locations in the Documents library**

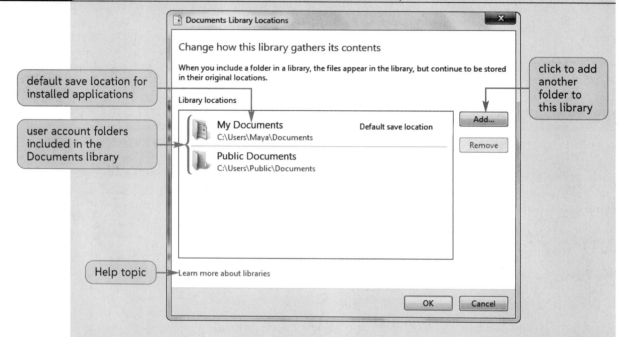

default save location for installed applications

user account folders included in the Documents library

click to add another folder to this library

Help topic

As noted in the dialog box, when you add a folder to a library, that folder's files appear in the library, but those files are still stored in their original locations.

The My Documents folder is designated as the default save location. If you open an application and save a document you've created, Windows 7 assumes you want to save the document in the My Documents folder within the Documents library.

You can use the Add button in the Documents Library Locations dialog box to add other folders on your local computer or shared folders on a computer in your network to a library. Use the Remove button to remove folders from a library. Another way to add a folder to a library is to right-click a folder, select "Include in library," and then either select a default library or create a new library on the spot.

To continue your examination of the Documents library:

> **1.** Click the **OK** button. Windows 7 closes the Documents Library Locations dialog box. The Navigation pane now displays the names of the two folders that are under the Documents library.

> **2.** Right-click **Documents** (not My Documents) under Libraries in the Navigation pane, and then click **Properties**. Windows 7 opens the Documents Properties dialog box and shows the locations that are included in this library—My Documents and Public Documents. See Figure 3-5. Your dialog box might differ if one or more other folders have already been added to this library.

Figure 3-5   **Viewing the properties of the Documents library**

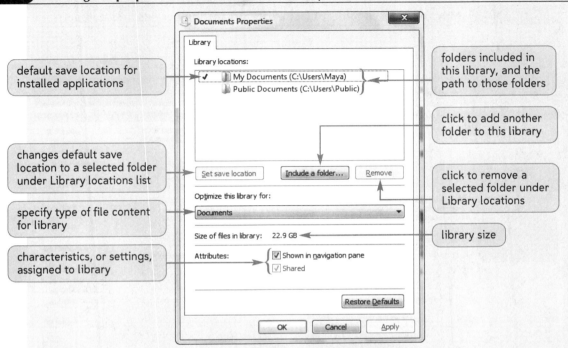

default save location for installed applications

changes default save location to a selected folder under Library locations list

specify type of file content for library

characteristics, or settings, assigned to library

folders included in this library, and the path to those folders

click to add another folder to this library

click to remove a selected folder under Library locations

library size

The check mark next to My Documents identifies it as the default save location. You can use the "Include a folder" button to add folders to this library. Windows 7 also shows you the total size of all the files in this library (or it might display "Calculating" as it determines the total size). Like files, libraries have settings called attributes assigned by the operating system, one of which is whether you want to show the library in the Navigation pane. You will examine attributes in more detail later in this tutorial and more extensively in Tutorial 5. You can also access this property sheet by right-clicking a library in the Windows Explorer Jump List.

▶ **3.** Click the **Optimize this library for** button. If you choose one of the options on this menu, Windows 7 customizes the window for a specific type of content—General Items (mixed context), Documents, Music, Pictures, or Videos—depending on the selected option. When you choose one of these options, Windows 7 uses a specific view (such as Details or Large Icons), changes options on the toolbar, and displays different types of information about the files in the folder.

▶ **4.** Click the **Optimize this library for** button to close the menu, verify that you did not inadvertently make any changes, close the Documents Properties dialog box, and then close the Documents window.

Libraries are a major step forward in changing the way you work with your computer. They present all the files you work with in one central location for ease of access. You do not need to navigate endlessly from one folder to another, and then back again, to access and use those files.

Organizing Your Personal Folders

If you operate a business, you will want to develop a plan for organizing your business folders so you can quickly find information for your clients, your customers, and your business. For example, suppose you operate a small business and perform contract work for various clients. Under the My Documents folder, you might create a subfolder named Clients to track all client information, as shown in Figure 3-6.

Figure 3-6   **Maya's proposed folder structure for organizing her business and personal files**

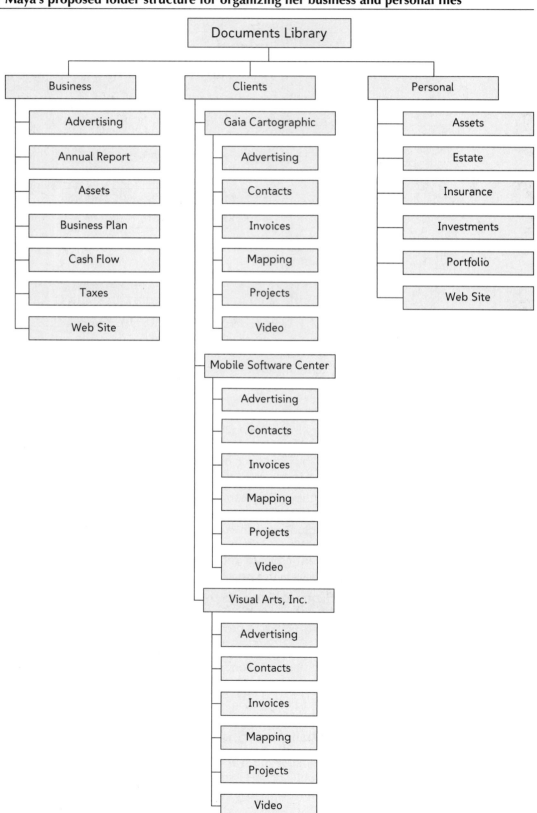

Within that folder, you might create a subfolder for each client. If you perform the same type of work for each client, you will more than likely have the same types of subfolders for each client so you can track similar information. For example, within each client folder, you might have separate folders for contracts, invoices, and projects. For certain clients, you might have additional folders where you store records specific to that client. You probably will also have a folder for your business records so you can track information important to maintaining your business, such as annual reports, assets, business plan, cash flow, and taxes. You might also have a personal folder for tracking important personal information, such as your personal portfolio, personal assets (useful for bank loans and insurance), investments, insurance information, and resumes (for use with project proposals where you or your client are seeking venture capital). If you work on multiple projects for a single client or employer, you might prefer to organize folders and files by project rather than by client.

If you efficiently organize your folder structure, you can quickly locate what you need, and you can store new files with other files that contain similar types of information. For example, if you need to locate a contract for a specific client, you know exactly where to find that document (i.e., in the Contracts folder for that client). If you need to finish preparing a monthly cash flow report for your business or update your database of personal assets, you know which folders contain each of those files. Another advantage of efficiently organizing your folders and files is that you can quickly back up important folders and files, and be assured that you have a copy of all your important documents. (You will examine backing up in more detail in Tutorial 10.) When searching for files, an organized folder structure gives you a head start on locating the exact document you need to meet a deadline.

Because the My Documents folder is now part of the Documents library in Windows 7, you have immediate access to the Clients folder and its contents when you open the Documents library.

INSIGHT

Organizing Your Class Files

You can use these same strategies and approaches to organize files for the college courses you take. For example, if you are taking six courses—Windows, Web Design, Electronic Portfolio, Gaming, Robotics, and Computer Forensics—you can create a separate folder for each course on the flash drive you use for your class work. Within each folder, you might have a Presentations folder where you store class videos, Adobe PDF files with class content, and perhaps even text files of class notes; a Lab Assignments folder for all your completed lab work; an Online Resources folder where you store links to, or saved copies of, Web pages that contain course information, the syllabus, class outlines, class handouts, and other course information materials such as recorded lectures; a Data Files folder where you store downloaded and extracted copies of the Data Files for a course; and a Bookmarks folder where you store bookmarks to Web sites, such as the Microsoft Support page, that you frequently visit for more information on class topics and for completing lab assignments. If you use your flash drive to store other information not related to the courses you take, you can create a Classes folder and store all the subfolders for all your classes within the Classes folder and keep all that information separate from the other contents of your flash drive.

Downloading, Extracting, and Copying Data Files

Some tutorials, like this one, require that you use Data Files to complete the steps and exercises. The next several sections explain in detail how to copy the Data Files from a flash drive, network folder, or the Documents folder to the Public Documents folder so you can complete the tutorial. In later tutorials where you need to work with Data Files, refer back to this section (if necessary) to review the process for copying the Data Files to the Public Documents folder. You can obtain these Data Files in one of two ways:

- **Downloaded file**—You can download a self-extracting executable file that contains the Tutorial.03 Data Files from Cengage Learning's Web site to the My Documents folder, the Public Documents folder, or to a flash drive, and then extract the contents of the self-extracting executable file to a subfolder within the My Documents folder, to the Public Documents folder on your hard disk, or to a flash drive. An **executable file** is a file that contains program code that Windows 7 can load into memory and run. A **self-extracting executable file** is an executable file that contains a set of folders and files stored in a compressed format to reduce the size of the file. It also contains a program for extracting the contents of the executable file (i.e., the folders and files contained with the self-extracting executable file). You can find the instructions for downloading the Data Files on the inside back cover of this book.
- **Network copy**—You can copy the Tutorial.03 Data Files from a network folder in your computer lab to a flash drive so you can complete this tutorial on your own computer. If you are going to complete this tutorial on a computer in your college's computer lab, you can copy the Tutorial.03 Data Files from the network folder directly to the My Documents folder or the Public Documents folder.

You are going to place a copy of the Data Files for this tutorial in the Public Documents folder (or another designated folder, such as the My Documents folder) on the computer that you are using so you can take advantage of Windows 7's Instant Search feature later in the tutorial. You can perform this operation in one of three ways:

- **Working on your own personal computer**—If you download the Tutorial.03 Data Files from Cengage Learning's Web site to your own computer, you can store the downloaded file in your My Documents or Public Documents folder, and then extract the Tutorial.03 Data Files to a subfolder in the My Documents folder or the Public Documents folder. The tutorial instructions assume you are using the Public Documents folder. If you choose to use the My Documents folder instead, you must adapt the instructions in the tutorial steps to take this slight difference into account. Both folders are easily accessible from the Documents library.
- **Working on a college lab computer**—If you are working on a computer in a computer lab, you can copy the extracted Data Files for this tutorial from your computer lab's network to the My Documents or the Public Documents folder on the computer you are using. The tutorial instructions assume you are using the Public Documents folder. If you choose to use the My Documents folder instead, you must adapt the instructions in the tutorial steps to take this slight difference into account. Both folders are easily accessible from the Documents library. Your instructor or technical support staff will provide you with any additional information you need to know to perform these operations and to work with the Tutorial.03 Data Files for this tutorial.
- **Using a flash drive**—If you download and extract the Tutorial.03 Data Files for this tutorial to your flash drive, you can copy the Tutorial.03 folder to your computer or to a computer in your college's computer lab. The tutorial instructions assume you are using the Public Documents folder. If you choose to use the My Documents folder instead, you must adapt the instructions in the tutorial steps to take this slight difference into account. Both folders are easily accessible from the Documents library.

The next three sections step you through the process for performing these three ways of copying the Tutorial folder for the Tutorial.03 Data Files to the Public Documents folder on the computer you are using. Decide which approach you want to use for working with these Data Files, and then complete the steps in that section only. After you copy the Tutorial folder to the Public Documents folder, continue with the "Renaming a Folder" section (you will be reminded). In later tutorials where you need to copy a working set of Data Files from your original downloaded Data Files, return to this tutorial if you need to refresh your memory on how to copy the Data Files.

Copying the Data Files from a Flash Drive to the Public Documents folder

If you downloaded and extracted the Tutorial folder provided with your Tutorial.03 Data Files to a flash drive, complete the following steps to copy the Tutorial folder to the Public Documents folder on your own computer, or to the My Documents folder (or another folder recommended by your instructor or technical staff) on a computer in your college's computer lab.

To copy the Tutorial folder from a flash drive to your computer's Public Documents folder:

▶ **1.** Make sure you have downloaded and extracted your copy of the Windows 7 for Power Users Data Files for this tutorial.

   Trouble? If you don't have Windows 7 for Power Users Data Files for this tutorial, you must obtain them before you can proceed. Your instructor will ask you to obtain them from a specified location such as a network drive or the textbook publisher's Web site using the download instructions on the inside back cover of the textbook. If you have any questions about obtaining the Windows 7 for Power User Data Files, ask your instructor or technical support person for assistance.

▶ **2.** Attach your flash drive to a USB port or to a USB cable on the computer you are using, and after Windows 7 displays an AutoPlay dialog box for your flash drive, click **Open folder to view files** to open a window displaying the contents of the flash drive. Next, open the Tutorial.03 folder.

   Trouble? If Windows 7 does not display an AutoPlay dialog box for your flash drive, open your flash drive from the Computer window, open the folder that contains the Windows 7 for Power User's Data Files, and then open the Tutorial.03 folder.

▶ **3.** From the Start menu, click **Documents**, click the **expand** icon ▷ to the left of the Documents library name, and then click **Public Documents**. If your instructor or technical support staff requested that you use another folder, locate and open that folder. Windows 7 opens the Public Documents folder (or the folder your instructor or technical support staff requested).

▶ **4.** Right-click the **taskbar** and then click **Show windows side by side**. Windows 7 adjusts the two folder windows so they are placed side by side on the desktop and are equal in size. Windows 7 places the last folder window that you opened on the left side of the desktop.

▶ **5.** In the Tutorial.03 folder window, drag the **Tutorial** folder to the **Public Documents** folder window (or to the folder recommended by your instructor or technical support staff), and then release your left mouse button. Windows 7 copies the Tutorial folder to the Public Documents folder window (or to the window for the folder recommended by your instructor or technical support staff).

▶ **6.** Close the Tutorial.03 folder window, but keep the Public Documents folder window (or the folder window recommended by your instructor or technical support staff), open.

▶ **7.** After reading the next three paragraphs in this section of the tutorial, continue with the tutorial section entitled "Renaming a Folder."

When you drag folders or files from one drive to another, Windows 7 makes a duplicate copy of the folders or files. If you hold down the Shift key while you drag, Windows 7 moves the folders or files instead.

If you drag folders or files from one folder window to another folder window on the same drive, including from one folder to another folder in the same library, or from one library to another library, Windows 7 moves the folders or files. If you hold down the Ctrl key while you drag, Windows 7 copies the files instead.

If you hold down the right mouse button as you drag folders or files from one window to another, or from one drive to another, Windows 7 displays a shortcut menu that includes the options for either moving or copying the folders or files. This latter approach guarantees that Windows 7 performs the type of operation that you want (i.e., either a move or a copy).

Copying the Data Files from the My Documents Folder to the Public Documents Folder

If you downloaded and extracted the Windows 7 for Power Users Data Files on your own computer, and now want to copy them from the My Documents folder (or any other folder) to your computer's Public Documents folder, complete the following steps.

To copy the Tutorial folder from the My Documents folder to your computer's Public Documents folder:

1. Make sure you have downloaded and extracted your copy of the Windows 7 for Power Users Data Files.

   Trouble? If you don't have Windows 7 for Power Users Data Files for this tutorial, you must obtain them before you can proceed. Your instructor will ask you to obtain them from a specified location such as a network drive or the textbook publisher's Web site using the download instructions on the inside back cover of the textbook. If you have any questions about obtaining the Windows 7 for Power User Data Files, ask your instructor or technical support person for assistance.

2. Close all open windows, right-click the **Windows Explorer** taskbar button, click **Documents** on the Jump List to open the Documents library, and in the Navigation pane on the left side of the Documents window, point to **Documents** under Libraries, click the **expand** icon ▷ to the left of the Documents library name, and then click **Public Documents**. Windows 7 opens the Public Documents folder.

3. From the Start menu, click **Documents** again to open the Documents library, and in the Navigation pane, point to **Documents** under Libraries, click the **expand** icon ▷ , and then click **My Documents** in the Navigation pane. Windows 7 opens the My Documents folder.

4. Locate and open the folder that contains the extracted Windows 7 for Power User Data Files, and then open the Tutorial.03 folder within that folder.

5. Right-click the **taskbar**, and then click **Show windows side by side**. Windows 7 adjusts the two open folder windows so they are placed side by side on the desktop and are equal in size. Windows 7 places the last folder window that you opened on the left side of the desktop.

6. Hold down the **Ctrl** key while you drag the **Tutorial** folder to the Public Documents folder window, and then release the mouse button. Windows 7 copies the Tutorial folder to the Public Documents folder.

   Trouble? If you accidentally moved the Tutorial folder, hold down the Ctrl key while you drag a copy of the Tutorial folder to the folder that contains the original downloaded and extracted Data Files.

7. Close the My Documents subfolder window that contains the extracted Windows 7 for Power Users Data Files, but keep the Public Documents folder window open.

8. After reading the next three paragraphs in this section of the tutorial, continue with the section entitled "Renaming a Folder."

If you drag folders or files from one folder window to another folder window on the same drive, including from one folder to another folder in the same library or from one library to another library, Windows 7 moves the folders or files. If you hold down the Ctrl key while you drag, Windows 7 copies the files instead.

When you drag folders or files from one drive to another, Windows 7 makes a duplicate copy of the folders or files. If you hold down the Shift key while you drag, Windows 7 moves the folders or files instead.

If you hold down the right mouse button as you drag folders or files from one window to another or from one drive to another, Windows 7 displays a shortcut menu that includes the options for either moving or copying the folders or files. This latter approach guarantees that Windows 7 performs the type of operation that you want (i.e., either a move or a copy).

Copying the Data Files from a Network Folder to the Public Documents Folder

If you are working on a computer in a computer lab and want to copy the Tutorial folder in the Tutorial.03 folder provided with the Windows 7 for Power Users Data Files from your computer lab's network to the Public Documents folder on the computer you are using or to another folder on that computer, complete the following steps. Your instructor will ask you to obtain the Data Files from a specific location. If you have any questions about obtaining the Windows 7 for Power Users Data Files, ask your instructor or technical support person for assistance.

To copy the Tutorial folder from a computer lab network to your computer's Public Documents folder:

1. Make sure you have downloaded and extracted your copy of the Windows 7 for Power Users Data Files.

Trouble? If you don't have the Windows 7 for Power Users Data Files for this tutorial, you must obtain them before you can proceed. Your instructor will ask you to obtain them from a specified network location. If you have any questions about obtaining the Windows 7 for Power User Data Files, ask your instructor or technical support person for assistance.

2. Close all open windows, right-click the **Windows Explorer** taskbar button, click **Documents** on the Jump List to open the Documents library, and in the Navigation pane on the left side of the Documents window, point to **Documents** under Libraries, click the **expand** icon ▷ to the left of the Documents library name, and then click **Public Documents**. Windows 7 opens the Public Documents folder.

3. From the Start menu, click **Documents** to open the Documents library again, and then follow the instructions provided by your instructor or technical support staff for opening the network folder that contains the Windows 7 for Power Users Tutorial.03 folder. Next, open the Tutorial.03 folder.

> **4.** Right-click the **taskbar**, and then click **Show windows side by side**. Windows 7 adjusts the two folder windows so they are placed side by side on the desktop and are equal in size. Windows 7 places the last folder window that you opened on the left side of the desktop.

> **5.** Drag the **Tutorial** folder from the network folder window to the Public Documents folder window (or to the folder recommended by your instructor or technical support staff), and then release the mouse button. Windows 7 copies the Tutorial folder to the Public Documents folder window (or to the window for the folder requested by your instructor or technical support staff).

> **6.** Close the network folder window, but keep the Public Documents folder window, or the window for the folder requested by your instructor or technical support staff, open.

> **7.** After reading the next paragraph, continue with the section entitled "Renaming a Folder."

If you drag folders or files from a network folder window to a folder window onto the computer you are using, Windows 7 always copies the folders or files.

Renaming a Folder

Next, you want to rename the Tutorial folder you just copied to the Public Documents folder (or to another folder requested by your instructor or technical support staff). First, make sure that the Public Documents folder does not contain a folder with the same name that you intend to use.

To rename the copied folder:

> **1.** Examine the names of folders in the Public Documents folder on the computer you are using (or in the window for the folder requested by your instructor or technical support staff).

> **2.** If you are working on your own computer, and find a folder named Cabral Advertising, right-click the **Cabral Advertising** folder name, click **Rename** on the shortcut menu, press the **Right Arrow** key to navigate to the end of the folder name, press the **Spacebar**, type **(Previous)** after the folder name, and then press the **Enter** key. Windows 7 adds "(Previous)" to the end of the existing folder name. If you are working in a computer lab and find a folder named Cabral Advertising, use the same approach just described, or follow the instructions recommended by your instructor or technical support staff for removing, renaming, or moving that folder.

> **3.** Point to the **Tutorial** folder you just copied to the Public Documents folder (or to the folder requested by your instructor or technical support staff), press the **F2** (Rename) key, type **Cabral Advertising**, and then press the **Enter** key. Windows 7 renames the folder and places it in alphabetical order with any other folders in your Public Documents folder.

Now you're ready to examine the Data Files for this tutorial.

Viewing the Contents of a Folder

Before she leaves for her next client meeting, Maya asks you to examine the folder structure and the files in the Cabral Advertising folder. She notes that you will be adding more files to the folder, so you need to be familiar with the folder structure and the location of important company files.

To view the contents of the Cabral Advertising folder:

▶ 1. Open the **Cabral Advertising** folder, and then maximize the window. Windows 7 displays the contents of the Cabral Advertising folder in alphabetical order.

▶ 2. If Windows 7 displays the folder contents in a view other than Extra Large Icons view, click the **More options** arrow [≣≣ ▾] for the Change your view button on the toolbar, and then use the **slider bar tab** to select a setting between Large Icons and Extra Large Icons so all folders are visible in the window. Using the new view setting, Windows 7 displays a partial view of the actual contents of documents within files on all the folder icons except for the Contract Training folder icon. See Figure 3-7. The Contract Training folder icon shows that this folder contains subfolders. Your view of this window may differ.

Trouble? If Windows 7 does not display a partial view of the folder contents in the folder icon, press the F5 (Refresh) key. If the folder content does not appear after you refresh the window, you can still complete the steps in this tutorial.

Trouble? If you are working at a lower resolution, adjust the icon view to a setting between Extra Large Icons and Large Icons view so all the folder icons fit within the Cabral Advertising folder window.

Trouble? If Windows 7 displays a Preview pane, click the "Hide the preview pane" button [▢] on the toolbar.

Figure 3-7	Viewing the contents of the Cabral Advertising folder

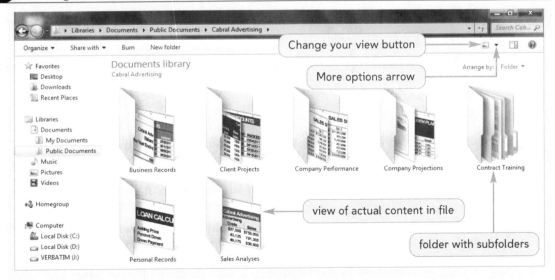

If Windows 7 does not display all the folders within a window, you can drag the slider tab along the Change your view menu slider bar and position it at an intermediate setting between Small Icons and Medium Icons, Medium Icons and Large Icons, or Large Icons and Extra Large Icons so you can see all the folder icons within the window. First introduced in Windows Vista, this feature for scaling icons in a folder, and displaying the content within files as part of folder icons, makes it easier to work and find what you need.

To continue your exploration of this folder:

1. Open the **Contract Training** folder, and then open the **Presentations** folder. Windows 7 displays thumbnail previews of each of the three files, and in the lower-right corner of each thumbnail, Windows 7 also displays a file icon that denotes the type of application associated with this file (in this case, Microsoft PowerPoint) and the type of file (in this case, an icon for a Microsoft PowerPoint Show). See Figure 3-8. The thumbnail preview helps you quickly spot content in a file that you want to use.

   Trouble? If Microsoft Office is not installed on your computer, the files in this folder might be associated with another type of application, and therefore display different file icons.

   Trouble? If you cannot see the three file icons in the Presentations folder, use the More options arrow ▣▾ for the Change your view button on the toolbar to further adjust your view.

Figure 3-8   **Viewing thumbnail previews of presentation files**

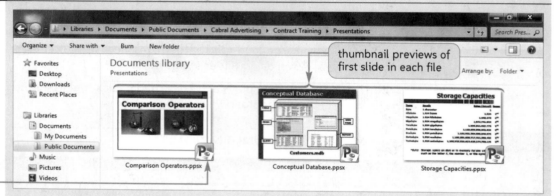

2. If you do not see a Preview pane on the right side of the window, click the **Show the preview pane** button 🔲 on the right side of the toolbar.

3. Point to the border between the Preview pane and the File list. When you see a double-headed arrow that points to the left and right ⟷, hold down the mouse button, and drag the border of the Preview pane to the left (or right) until it occupies about half of the space that the file icons previously occupied, or to a view that you prefer.

4. Click the **folder background** to remove the focus from any file you might have inadvertently selected by pointing with your mouse pointer.

5. Point to **Comparison Operators.ppsx** and watch the Preview pane. Windows 7 displays the first slide in this slide show, and displays the animation on this slide. Figure 3-9 shows the first slide in the Preview pane. If you are using a higher resolution than 1024 x 768, the arrangement of the file thumbnails in the File list will differ.

   Trouble? If you click the Comparison Operators.ppsx file icon and open the slide show, press the Esc key to close the slide show, and then repeat this step.

Trouble? If you miss the animation in the first slide of the Comparison Operators.ppsx file, click the folder background again, and then point to the Comparison Operators.ppsx file again.

Figure 3-9	Previewing a presentation

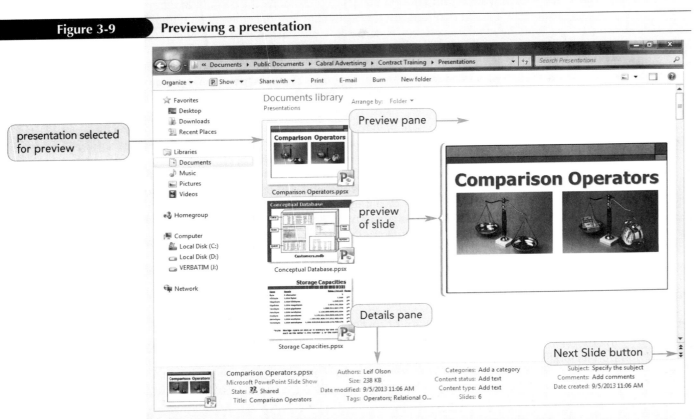

6. At the bottom of the vertical scroll bar in the Preview pane, click the **Next Slide** button. Windows 7 displays the next slide in this PowerPoint presentation file.

7. Point to **Conceptual Database.ppsx**. Windows 7 displays the one slide in this PowerPoint presentation in the Preview pane.

If you click the Organize button on the toolbar, you can point to Layout and then use the Layout menu to display or hide the Details, Preview, Navigation, and Library panes. You can also select "Menu bar" to display a classic menu bar similar to that found in previous versions of Windows before Windows Vista and Windows 7.

Using the Preview Pane to Work Smart

The Preview pane was first introduced with Windows Vista and provides you with a new way of working with files. If you need to examine the content of different files to locate content you might need for creating another document, you do not need to open each file in a folder, examine its contents, close the file, and then open the next file. Furthermore, you don't have to open different programs for each type of file you examine. For example, if you want to view the contents of a PowerPoint presentation, you can use the Preview pane to examine the contents of each slide within the PowerPoint presentation by just pointing to the file icon, and then you can scroll through the content of the file in the Preview pane. Furthermore, you can use the Preview pane to step through the mouse-controlled animation in a PowerPoint presentation. You can also copy the contents of what you view in the Preview pane, and then place that copy in a new document. For example, if you want to copy one of the slides in a PowerPoint presentation and use it in a new presentation, you just right-click the slide shown in the Preview pane, click Copy Slide, and then open a new presentation or switch to an existing presentation in Microsoft PowerPoint, and then paste the slide into the presentation. If you are previewing a Microsoft Word document, you can select and right-click text in the Preview pane, click Copy, and then paste the text into another open file. If you are previewing a Microsoft Excel spreadsheet that contains multiple sheets, you can click a sheet tab in the Preview pane to view a different part of the spreadsheet. While you cannot do in the Preview pane everything that you can do in an application window, the Preview pane can streamline the way in which you work, make you more productive, and make your work environment more interesting.

Windows 7 provides support for previewing the contents of some types of Office files (such as Microsoft Word, Microsoft Excel, and Microsoft PowerPoint files but not Microsoft Access database files), Web pages saved with different Web browsers, text files (including Rich Text Format files), email messages, email attachments, video files, and audio files. Software that you purchase and install on your computer might extend this preview capability of Windows 7 for specific types of files that you create with that software, such as Adobe Portable Document Format (PDF) files.

Checking Folder Options

Maya points out that you can customize your view by changing the way Windows 7 displays the content of folder windows as you browse and view folders and files. She recommends that you check these settings to make sure Windows 7 displays folders and files in the way you prefer.

To examine folder settings:

1. Click the **Organize** button on the toolbar, click **Folder and search options**, and then click the **View** tab in the Folder Options dialog box. In the Advanced settings list box on the View property sheet, Windows 7 displays a variety of settings for controlling the view and behavior of folders and files. See Figure 3-10.

Figure 3-10   Examining advanced folder view and behavior settings

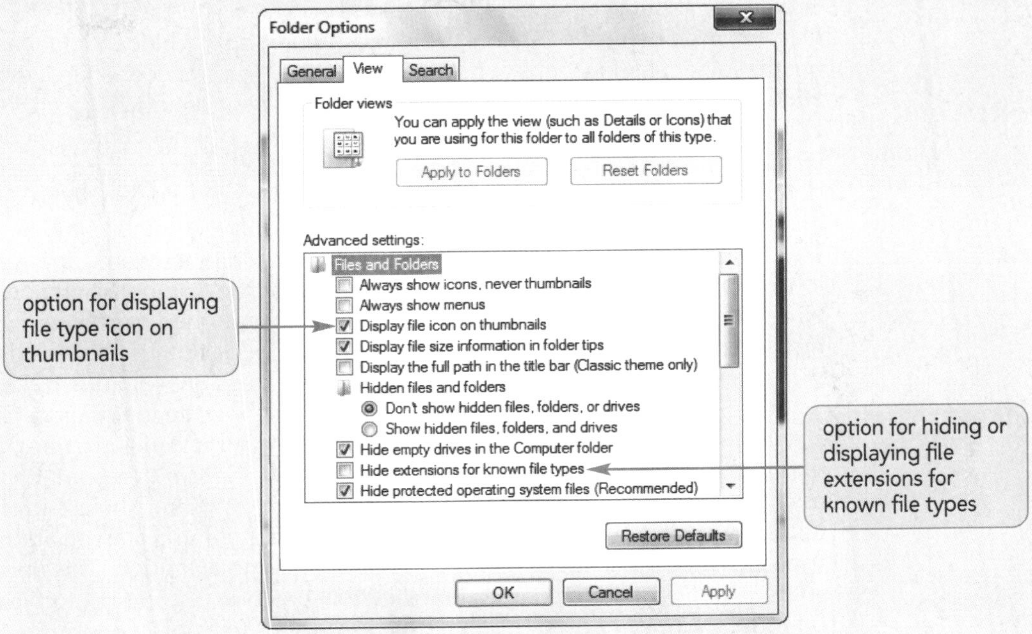

option for displaying file type icon on thumbnails

option for hiding or displaying file extensions for known file types

The following Advanced settings options improve the way you work with folders and files, as well as letting you choose an alternate, more preferable way to work:

- **Always show icons, never thumbnails**—By default, and where possible, Windows 7 displays thumbnails, or what are also called thumbnail previews, of files in a folder, rather than displaying just simple or static (that is, unchanging) file icons. Thumbnail previews help you quickly view and identify the content within a file. However, you can turn off this feature if you prefer the classic file icon view, or if you notice that it takes too long to display thumbnail previews of every folder and file within a window.

- **Always show menus**—By default, Windows 7 does not display the classic menu bar above the toolbar as in Windows XP and earlier versions of Windows. To always have access to the classic menu bar and its submenus, you can enable this feature. The toolbar will still be visible, so you can use either the toolbar or menu bar. If you prefer to not display the classic menu bar, but rather want only occasional access to the menu bar, you can override the default setting by pressing the Alt key or the F10 key to display the classic menu bar. Pressing the Alt key a second time hides the classic menu bar.

- **Display file icon on thumbnails**—Windows 7 includes a small file icon on the thumbnails of certain types of files, such as Microsoft Office or Adobe Acrobat files, so you can identify the types of files contained in a folder, and so you can identify the application associated with each file type. You can turn off this option if you prefer.

- **Display file size information in folder tips**—By default, when you point to a folder, Windows 7 displays only the date and time the folder was created. If you enable this option, Windows 7 not only displays the date and time the folder was created, but it also displays the size of the folder contents and a preview of filenames for files within the folder. In contrast, when you point to a file instead of a folder, Windows 7 always displays a ToolTip that contains information about the file, though the information displayed varies by file type. For example, for Microsoft Office PowerPoint files, Windows 7 displays the file type (such as a Microsoft PowerPoint Slide Show), the author, the document's title, the file size, and the date (and time) the file was last modified. In the case of JPEG files, Windows 7 displays the file type, rating, dimensions (in pixels wide by pixels tall), and file size.

- **Hidden files and folders**—By default, Windows 7 does not display user or system folders and files that are marked as hidden folders and files, and it does not display hidden drives. If you want to view hidden folders and files, whether to troubleshoot a problem or just to learn more about Windows 7 system folders and files, you can enable the "Show hidden files, folders, and drives" option. Windows 7 then displays hidden folder and file icons, but the folder and file icons appear fainter than regular folder and file icons.

- **Hide empty drives in the Computer folder**—This new Windows 7 feature hides removable drives in the Computer window when the drives do not contain media. For example, if your computer has one or more drives for memory cards, the drives are not displayed if there are no memory cards inserted in the drives. When you insert a memory card in a removable drive, the drive is displayed in the Computer window. This feature does not apply to DVD and CD drives; in other words, these drive icons are always displayed. Also note that Microsoft refers to the Computer window as a folder.

- **Hide extensions for known file types**—Though you turned off this setting when you first set up your computer earlier in the tutorial, this setting is enabled by default. When enabled, Windows 7 does not show file extensions for known file types, or what's also called registered files. A **registered file** is a file that is associated with an application or program on your computer. When you install a program, the installation program registers certain file types with Windows 7. From that point on, Windows 7 associates those file extensions with that program (assuming the associations do not change when you install another program). As part of the file association, Windows 7 uses the same file icon for all files with the same file extension. This option is enabled so users only see the filenames that they (or someone else) assign to files. If you turn off this option, Windows 7 displays file extensions for most types of files, and as noted earlier, you can use this information to help identify file types. In some cases, viewing the file extension helps you identify malicious software. Also, by displaying file extensions, you can associate specific types of file extensions with specific file types, and thereby learn more about file types as you work with different types of files. File extensions are critical to the functioning of the Windows operating system.

- **Hide protected operating system files (Recommended)**—Windows 7 hides important operating system files so a user cannot accidentally delete, move, rename, or modify a system file that Windows 7 needs to operate properly. Again, if you're troubleshooting a problem or want to view these operating system files, you can enable this feature. Windows 7 then displays these hidden system folder and file icons, though they appear fainter than regular folder and file icons.

- **Launch folder windows in a separate process**—If you enable this option, Windows 7 opens each folder window in a different part of memory. This option can increase the stability of Windows 7 and is obviously useful if you frequently encounter problems with opening folder windows or if your computer frequently crashes. When enabled, this option also slows down the performance of your computer.

- **Restore previous folder windows at logon**—If you enable this setting, Windows 7 restores any windows that were open when you last shut down your computer. This feature allows you to quickly return to those folders you were last working in.

- **Show drive letters**—When you open the Computer window, Windows 7 displays the friendly name of a drive, such as *Local Disk* for a hard disk drive, and it also displays the drive name in parentheses, such as (C:). If you turn off this setting, you will only see the friendly name, not the drive name.

- **Show encrypted or compressed NTFS files in color**—By default, Windows 7 displays these two types of files in a different color to distinguish them from files that are not encrypted or compressed (which usually are most files on your computer). Tutorial 5 covers encrypted and compressed files in more detail.

- **Show popup description for folder and desktop items**—By default, Windows 7 automatically displays a ToolTip when you point to a desktop item, folder, or file. However, sometimes these ToolTips momentarily obscure your view. If you turn off this option, Windows 7 does not display ToolTips.

- **Show preview handlers in preview pane**—**Preview handlers** are components of the Windows 7 operating system that display the contents of certain types of files in the Preview pane. If you turn off this feature, you will no longer be able to preview the content of files in the Preview pane. Although the performance of your computer might improve slightly, the ability to preview files will save you far more time and effort than is gained by the ever so slight improvement in your computer's performance.
- **Use check boxes to select items**—If you enable this feature, Windows 7 displays a small check box next to each folder or file icon when you point to the folder or file icon. You can then click this check box to select the folder or file, as shown in Figure 3-11. This option can be useful if you want to select a group of files, whether they are located side by side or scattered around the folder window, for some operations (such as copying, moving, or deleting). As you select a file's check box, you also see a ToolTip that identifies the file type, authors, title, size, and date modified. Another approach to selecting folders and files in a window is to hold down the Ctrl key as you point to each folder or file (assuming you are using single-click activation and not Classic style). However, if you Ctrl+click too fast in Classic style, (or if you Ctrl+drag), Windows 7 makes copies of the selected files. If you enable the use of check boxes, you cannot use the Ctrl key to select multiple files by pointing to them.

| Figure 3-11 | Selecting a file using its check box |

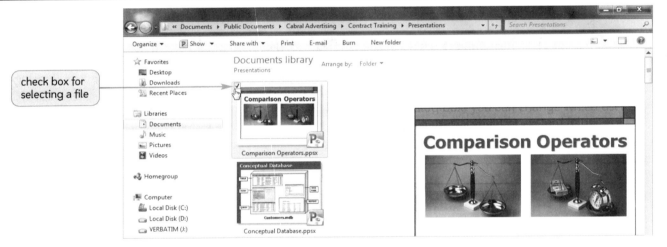

check box for selecting a file

- **Use Sharing Wizard (Recommended)**—By default, this option is enabled, and if you choose to share a folder (covered in Tutorial 12), Windows 7 uses a file-sharing wizard to simplify the process of sharing the contents of a folder with other people. If you turn off this option, you must use the Advanced Sharing option to share the contents of a folder (covered in Tutorial 12). The new Windows 7 HomeGroup feature (covered in Tutorial 12) replaces this previously used sharing feature retained from earlier versions of Windows.
- **When typing into list view**—By default, Windows 7 uses the "Select the typed item in the view" option under this category. When enabled, Windows 7 can perform a character search of the contents of a folder—another power user feature that is generally not known by most individuals. For example, if you want to quickly locate a folder or file in a folder window, you can type the first character of that folder and file, and Windows 7 then highlights the first folder or file that starts with that character. This feature saves an inordinate amount of time and effort because you do not have to scroll through a long list of folders or files to locate the one you want to use. If you switch this setting to "Automatically type into the Search box," then any character you type automatically appears in the folder's Search box at the top of the window. The latter option would be useful if you frequently use the Search feature (which you examine in more detail later in the second session of this tutorial) to locate folders and files in the current folder and its subfolders.

Microsoft removed the "Remember each folder's view settings" from the list of Advanced settings, because Windows 7 now automatically remembers view settings.

Under Folder Views on the View property sheet of the Folder Options dialog box, you can use the Apply to Folders button to apply the view of the current folder to every other folder with the same type of content (i.e., all folders that contain pictures). For example, if you prefer Extra Large Icons view, you can switch to that view, and then use this option in the Folder Options dialog box to apply that setting to other folders. However, this feature does not apply to libraries. You can use the Reset Folders to restore the default view settings for all folders. You can use the Restore Defaults button to restore all the options in the Advanced settings list box to their original settings. That feature is also useful if you forget what the default option is for a specific setting.

To continue your examination of this folder's contents:

▶ **1.** Click the **Cancel** button to close the Folder Options dialog box without making any changes to your computer.

▶ **2.** Point to the **Comparison Operators.ppsx** file icon to select that file, and then point to the **top border** of the Details pane, and after the mouse pointer changes to a double-headed arrow pointing up and down ⇕, drag the **Details pane border** up so you can see more information about the file. The Details pane provides more information than you see in a ToolTip. See Figure 3-12. In the case of this Microsoft PowerPoint Slide Show, the Details pane displays a count of the number of slides in the presentation.

Figure 3-12	**Using the Details pane to view file information**

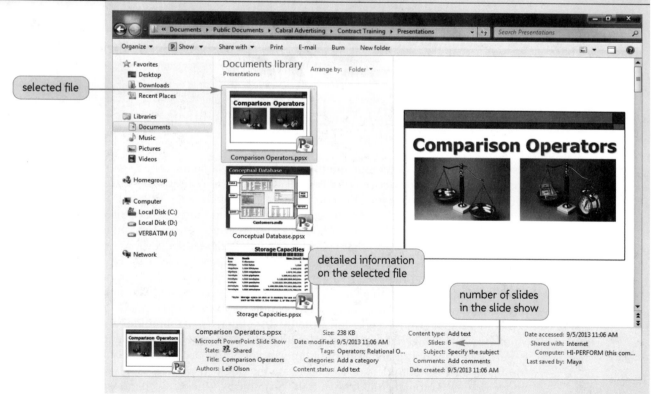

Another advantage of the Details pane is that after you select a file, you can make changes to the information about the file in the Details pane or specify new information. You will examine this use of the Details pane later in the tutorial. Microsoft introduced the Details pane in Windows Vista.

Viewing Properties of Files

Earlier, Maya noted that another way to view information about a file is to view its properties. You decide to compare this method with the use of ToolTips and the Details pane.

To view properties of a file:

▶ 1. Right-click **Comparison Operators.ppsx** and then click **Properties** on the shortcut menu. On the General property sheet of the Comparison Operators.ppsx Properties dialog box, Windows 7 shows a file icon for the file type, the full filename, the type of file (or file type), the name of the program that opens this file, the location of the file, the size of the file, the storage space that this file uses on disk, and the date the file was created, modified, and last accessed as well as the amount of time that has elapsed for each operation. See Figure 3-13.

Figure 3-13	Viewing properties of a file

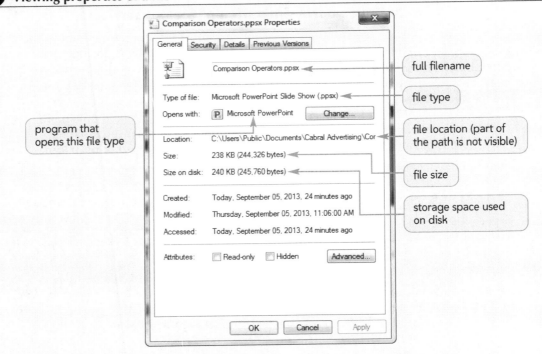

You can use the Change button to associate this file type with another application. Although you can't see the full location listed on the General property sheet, the location of the file on the computer used for this figure is:

C:\Users\Public\Documents\Cabral Advertising\Contract Training\Presentations

To view the rest of the location, click the location, and use the End key to move to the end of the path, the Home key to move to the beginning of the path, or the Right and Left arrow keys to move one character in either direction. To copy the path to a document, select the location by dragging from left to right, right-clicking the path, and then selecting Copy on the shortcut menu. You can then open a document, and use the Paste feature to copy the path into the document. Although you may use this feature only occasionally, it illustrates an important concept: The path is one of many objects on the property sheet that you can select and right-click. Objects are not limited to desktop, folder, and file icons. You will examine the concept and use of a path in more detail later in the tutorial. Likewise, you can use the same approach if you want to copy a URL from the Address bar of a Web browser window into an email message or an open document.

The file size is reported in KB (or kilobytes), and that information is then translated into bytes. If you divide 244,326 bytes by 1,024 (the number of bytes in a kilobyte), you obtain approximately 238 KB (rounded down). The difference between the number of bytes for "Size on disk" and "Size," (namely, 1434 bytes), is the amount of space allocated to the file, but not actually used by the file. You will examine how this allocation of storage space affects storage space on a hard disk in more detail in Tutorial 5.

The property sheet also contains check boxes labeled *Read-only* and *Hidden* next to *Attributes*. An **attribute** is a setting applied to a folder or file by the operating system; however, you can change these settings on the General property sheet or in a command-line environment. If you enable the Read-only attribute by adding a check mark to the Read-only check box, and then apply this setting, the program you use to open the file will open it in read-only mode. That means you cannot save any changes to the file under the original filename; however, you can save the changes to a file with a new filename. Read-only therefore protects a file from changes. If you enable the Hidden attribute, Windows 7 does not display the file icon in the folder unless you choose the option to "Show hidden files, folders, and drives" in the Folder Options dialog box described earlier.

To continue your examination of file properties:

1. Click the **Details** tab. Windows 7 provides more details about the properties of this file under the Description and Origin sections, including the author (in this case, Leif Olson, an employee at Cabral Advertising). See Figure 3-14.

Figure 3-14 Viewing details on file properties

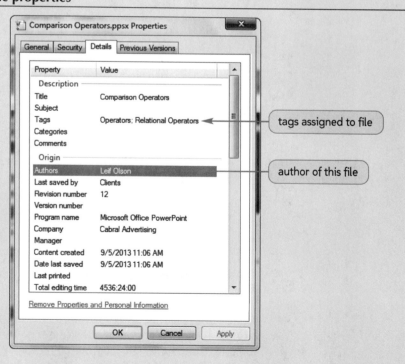

If you scroll to the Content section, Windows 7 displays information about the content of the file (for this file type, information such as the word count, paragraph count, number of slides, presentation format, and aspect ratio). Windows 7 displays more information about the file itself in the File section at the bottom of the Details property sheet, including the name of the computer on which this file is stored and who the file is shared with. You can also click some of these file properties, such as Title, Authors, and Company, and then alter the information.

▶ 2. Click the **Remove Properties and Personal Information** link at the bottom of the Details property sheet. Windows 7 opens a Remove Properties dialog box. See Figure 3-15.

Figure 3-15   Viewing options for removing file properties

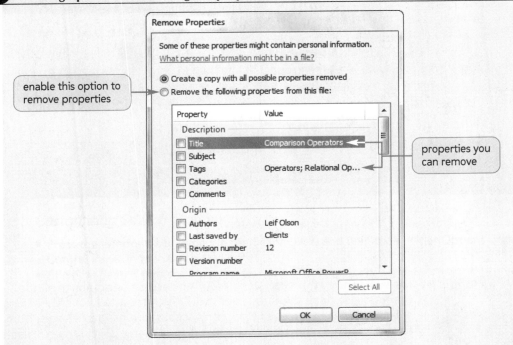

enable this option to remove properties

properties you can remove

At the top of this dialog box, Windows 7 notes that some file properties might contain personal information. Then, it displays two options. You can create a copy of this file with all possible properties removed, or you can choose which properties you want to remove from the file. After you click the "Remove the following properties from this file" option button, you can remove all the properties in the Description section, and some in the Origin and Content sections, but you cannot remove properties in the File section. For files produced with previous versions of an application (such as a previous version of Microsoft Office), you may not be able to remove any properties. Each file's property sheet identifies what properties are available and what file properties, if any, you can remove for that file.

▶ 3. Click the **Cancel** button in the Remove Properties dialog box and in the Comparison Operators.ppsx Properties dialog box.

▶ 4. Keep the Presentations folder window open for the next set of tutorial steps.

You can also view properties of a group of files.

TIP

You can use the Ctrl+A keyboard shortcut to select all the contents of a folder.

To view properties of a group of files:

▶ 1. Click the **Organize** button on the toolbar, and then click **Select all**. Windows 7 selects all the files in this folder. In the Details pane, Windows 7 lists information that applies to all the selected files. See Figure 3-16.

Figure 3-16   **Viewing details on group properties**

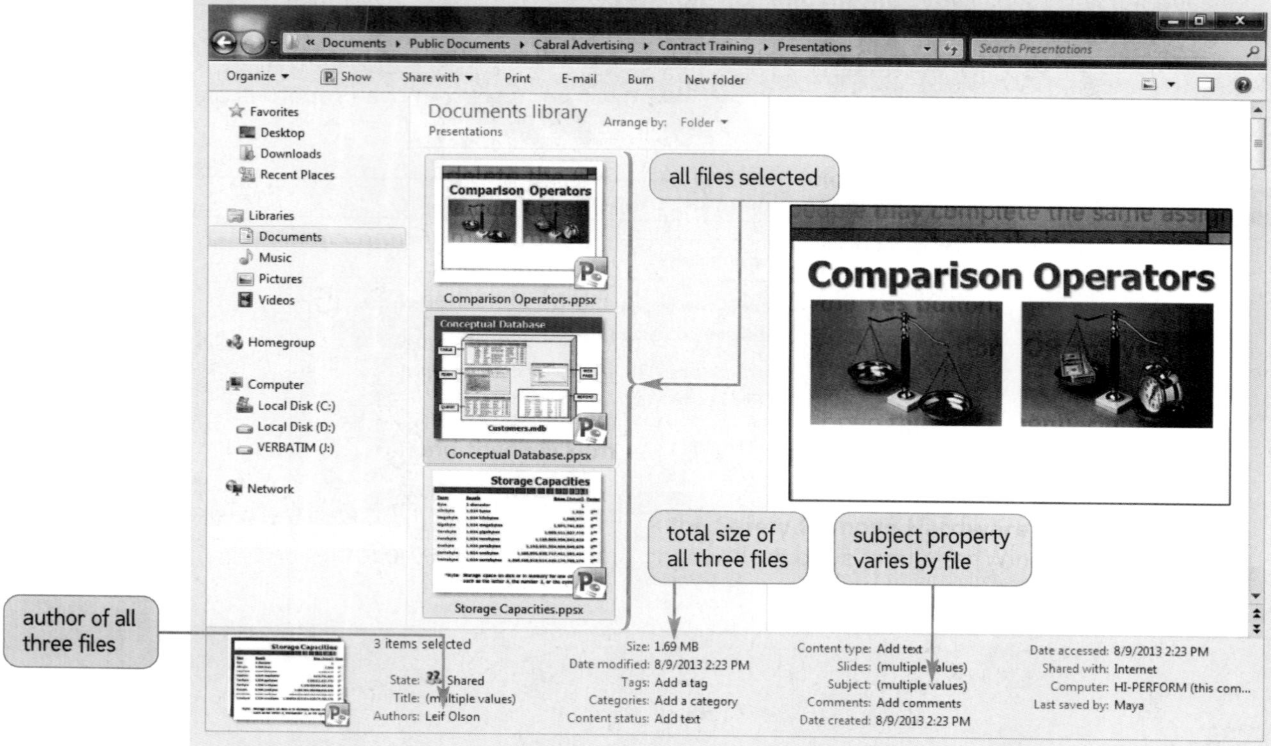

author of all three files

all files selected

total size of all three files

subject property varies by file

For example, in this case, Leif Olson is listed as the author of all the files, and the total size of all the files is about 1.7 MB, useful to know when copying files to another drive with limited storage space. Where properties vary from one file to another, such as the Title of the files (the filenames), Windows 7 displays "(multiple values)." Where it displays "Add a tag," "Add a category," "Add text," or "Add comments," you can enter or edit file properties.

 2. Carefully right-click **Conceptual Database.ppsx** without losing the selection for the three files, and then click **Properties** on the shortcut menu. On the General property sheet in the Conceptual Database.ppsx, ... Properties dialog box, Windows 7 displays group properties for all three files. See Figure 3-17.

Trouble? If you lose the selection for the three files, and if your Properties dialog box does not match that shown in Figure 3-17, click the Cancel button, click the Organize button on the toolbar, click Select all, click the Organize button again, and then click Properties.

Figure 3-17   Viewing group properties of three files

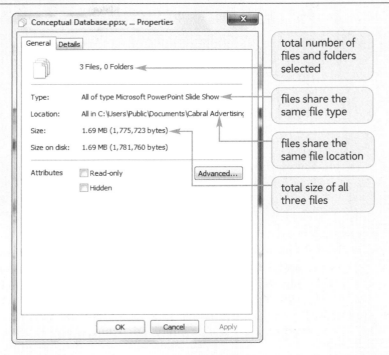

The ellipsis (…) after the beginning of the Properties dialog box name indicates that you are viewing a collection of files; however, you only see the name of the first file in that group (the file that you right-clicked). If the first filename is long, you only see a portion of that filename on the title bar. Windows 7 identifies the total number of files and folders that you are viewing properties for. That count is useful if you need to know the total number of folders or total number of files, or both. For Type, Windows 7 displays "All of type Microsoft PowerPoint Slide Show," and for Location, Windows 7 displays "All in C:\Users\Public Documents\ Cabral Advertising\Clients\Training\Presentations" (although you cannot see the entire path on the property sheet). Windows 7 also reports on the total file size and total size on disk required for all three files, again another useful piece of information if you are copying these files to a disk with limited storage space. From the Details property sheet, you can view even more properties of these files, and remove some properties from multiple files.

▶ **3.** Close the Conceptual Database.ppsx, … Properties dialog box.

As you can see, there are multiple ways in which you can view information about files. Each approach provides some of the same information and some new information (or perhaps a new way of looking at the same information), plus new options (for example, the option for removing properties and personal information).

REFERENCE

Viewing Properties of Files

- To view the property of a single file, select the file, and then examine the Details pane.
- To view properties of two or more files, hold down the Ctrl key as you point to, and select, each file, and then view the information of the selected files in the Details pane.
- To view properties of all the files in a folder, click Organize on the toolbar, click Select all, and then examine the Details pane.
- For more information, right-click a single file, a group of selected files, or all files, click Properties on the shortcut menu, and then examine the General and the Details property sheets. To remove properties or personal information from a file or a group of files, click the Remove Properties and Personal Information link at the bottom of the Details property sheet, choose the way in which you want to remove properties, select each available property that you want to remove, click the OK button to close the Remove Properties dialog box, and then click the OK button to close the Properties dialog box for the file or group of files.

If you want to copy a large file to a flash drive, you can examine the size of the file and the available space on the flash drive to determine if it has room for a copy of the file. Also, the ability to remove properties of a file can protect your privacy, especially if you decide to email a copy of a file to someone else.

Viewing Properties of Folders

In addition to viewing the properties of files, you can view properties of one or more folders using a similar approach.

To view properties of a folder:

1. Click the **Back** button ⊙ to return to the Contract Training folder, click the **Hide the preview pane** button ⬚ on the toolbar, right-click the **Presentations** folder icon, and then click **Properties** on the shortcut menu. On the General property sheet of the Presentations Properties dialog box, Windows 7 displays the icon used for this folder, the folder name (which you can change here), the type of folder (a File folder), and the location of the folder (C:\Users\Public\Documents\ Cabral Advertising\Contract Training), although not all of the path is visible. See Figure 3-18.

Figure 3-18   **View properties of a folder**

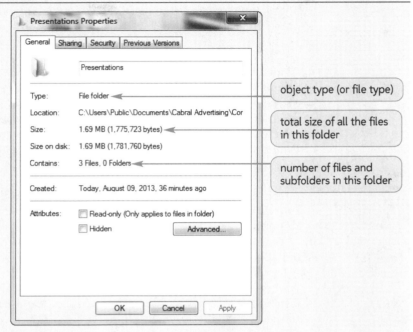

This property sheet also shows the size of the folder and its contents, the size on disk of the folder and its contents, the number of files and folders within this folder (three files, but no other folders), the date and time the folder was created, and any attributes assigned to the folder. Again, note that the size on disk is greater than the total size of the folder and its contents.

2. Close the Presentations Properties dialog box, but keep the Contract Training folder window open.

You can also view properties of a group of folders by selecting all the folders and choosing the option to view properties from the group folder shortcut menu or from the Organize menu.

REFERENCE

Viewing Properties of Folders

- To view the property of a single folder, right-click the folder, click Properties on the shortcut menu, and then examine the General property sheet.
- To view properties of two or more folders, hold down the Ctrl key as you point to, and select, each folder, right-click one folder, click Properties on the shortcut menu, and then examine the General property sheet.
- To view properties of all the subfolders within a folder, click the Organize button on the toolbar, click Select all, right-click one of the folders, click Properties on the shortcut menu, and then examine the General property sheet.

By viewing properties of one or more folders, you can determine the total storage capacity required of all those folders before you copy the folders to another disk, such as a flash drive. This is especially important if you need to make a backup, or duplicate copy, of important folders and their files, or to copy the folders and files to another computer that has limited storage space.

Understanding Paths

When you examined the properties of files and folders, Windows 7 displayed the location of the file, files, or folders on the General property sheet. For example, the location of the Presentations folder was listed as:

C:\Users\Public\Documents\Cabral Advertising\Contract Training

This notation is called a **path** because it identifies the exact location of the folder. The C: identifies the disk drive where the folder is located (namely, drive C, typically the hard disk drive). The backslash (\ ) symbol after the drive name C: is a special notation for the top-level folder on a disk drive. The top-level folder is the first folder created on a disk when the disk is formatted to store data, and once the top-level folder is created, you can create and store folders and files on the disk. After the notation for the top-level folder, Windows 7 displays the sequence of folders that you follow to find a specific folder or file. In this example, all of the backslashes other than the one that follows the drive name are called **delimiters**, because these backslashes serve to separate folder names. Only the backslash after the drive name refers to the top-level folder or what was called the **root directory** (in DOS). Basically, the full path describes the route (or path) that you or Windows 7 uses to locate a specific folder or file.

One way to navigate to this folder is to open a Computer window, open drive C, open the Users folder, open the Public folder, open the Documents folder, open the Cabral Advertising folder, and then open the Contract Training folder. If you use this approach, you are stepping through the path, one drive and folder at a time. You can use other and faster ways to access a folder as you've seen earlier, and as you will see in this and later tutorials.

In essence, the path is similar to the concept and use of a map. You use a map to determine the directions on how to get to a specific place. In the same way, the path points out how you navigate the folder structure of a disk to get to a specific folder or file.

If you open the Contract Training folder to view the Presentations folder, the sequence of folders shown in the Address bar path appears different from the path shown on the property sheet for the location of the current folder, as illustrated here:

▶ Libraries ▶ Documents ▶ Public Documents ▶ Cabral Advertising ▶ Contract Training

This path notation appears different from the previously described path because Windows 7 organizes the My Documents folder and Public Documents folder into the Documents library, so the library name is included in the path. There is a simple way to verify that these two different path notations essentially mean the same thing.

To view the path of the current folder:

▶ **1.** In the Address bar, click the **folder** icon 📁 to the left of Libraries. As shown in Figure 3-19, Windows 7 changes the display of the path to: C:\Users\Public\Documents\Cabral Advertising\Contract Training

The reference to ▶ Libraries ▶ Documents ▶ Public Documents changed to Public\Documents to identify the exact folder location. It's now clear that the Public folder is under the Users folder on drive C.

Trouble? If Windows 7 creates a Contract Training - Shortcut in the Contract Training folder, right-click the Contract Training - Shortcut, hold down the Shift key, click the Yes button in the Delete Shortcut dialog box to permanently delete this shortcut, and then release the Shift key.

Figure 3-19	Viewing the current folder's path

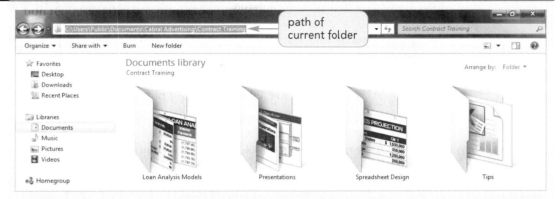

▶ **2.** To restore the previous path notation, press the **Enter** key while the path in the Address bar is highlighted. The path now returns to: ▶ Libraries ▶ Documents ▶ Public Documents ▶ Cabral Advertising ▶ Contract Training

This technique is a simple way to verify the actual path and learn how to navigate to a folder from the Computer window.

Although C:\Users\Public\Documents\Cabral Advertising\Contract Training is the path to the location of the folder that contains the Presentations folder, the actual path for the Presentations folder includes the name of that folder, as follows:

C:\Users\Public\Documents\Cabral Advertising\Contract Training\Presentations

Each file has its own path. For example, the path to the Comparison Operators file in the Presentations folder is: C:\Users\Public\Documents\Cabral Advertising\ Contract Training\Presentations\Comparison Operators.ppsx

The path of a file includes the full filename at the end of the path (with the file extension), and the filename is separated from the folder name where it is located by a backslash delimiter.

When you open a recently used file from a Jump List, Windows 7 uses the path to locate the file, and it also uses the path for the program associated with that file type to open the program that works with that file. For example, if you open the Presentations folder and click the Comparison Operators file icon (or thumbnail), Windows 7 opens the file in Microsoft PowerPoint and plays back (or runs) the presentation. The path to the Microsoft PowerPoint program (assuming you are using Microsoft Office 2010) is:

C:\Program Files\Microsoft Office\Office14\POWERPNT.EXE

Or, as shown in the Address bar:

▶ Computer ▶ Local Disk (C:) ▶ Program Files ▶ Microsoft Office ▶ Office14

In the latter case, the filename is not included.

POWERPNT.EXE is the name of the file that contains the Microsoft PowerPoint 2010 program. As noted earlier, files with the file extension .exe are executable files, which contain program code that Windows 7 can load into memory and run. In the Office14 folder, Windows 7 displays POWERPNT.EXE in uppercase because it follows the conventions for naming folders and files under the DOS operating system. Office14 also follows the same DOS conventions for naming folders and files. The next section describes these conventions for naming files under Windows and under DOS.

You should understand the concept and use of the path because it is critical to the proper performance of Windows 7. It uses the path to locate and open drives, folders (including virtual folders), programs, and files.

Using Long Filenames and Aliases

As noted in Tutorial 1, under any of the Windows operating systems, you can use long filenames to more clearly identify the contents and purpose of a file. You can also include special symbols or characters, such as the ampersand (&), pound sign (#), dollar sign ($), percentage symbol (%), single quotation marks (' and '), as well as opening and closing parentheses and spaces. You can also assign long folder names to folders so you can clearly identify the types of files stored within those folders.

Under the DOS operating system that preceded the Windows operating systems, filenames could be 1 to 8 characters in length. You could also use an optional file extension of up to 3 characters; however, the file extension was not needed by the operating system because DOS not did associate file extensions with a specific program. (Also, DOS did not use a mouse or other pointing device.) These types of filenames were called short filenames, or **8.3 filenames** (that is, names that allow eight characters, a period to separate the main part of the filename from the file extension, a three-character file extension, and no spaces in the filename or file extension). Like Windows filenames, the file extension was separated from the main part of the filename by a period (or what is typically called a "dot"). A DOS filename did not include spaces or more than one period, and as in the Windows operating system, you could not use certain symbols in a filename because those symbols were reserved for special operations performed by the operating system. For example, the plus sign symbol (+) was used as a **concatenation operator** to join together the contents of two or more simple text files by adding one file to the bottom of another file. Also, the DOS operating system used only uppercase characters for filenames.

If you assign a long filename to a file or a long folder name to a folder under Windows 7 (and previous versions of the Windows operating system), Windows creates an alias to provide backward compatibility with DOS and Windows 3.x applications (for example, applications designed for Windows 3.1 and 3.11) and with other network operating systems that do not recognize long filenames common to Windows. An **alias** is a filename that follows the rules and conventions for 8.3 filenames. Under the Windows operating system, an alias consists of the first six characters of the long filename (or a set of characters generated by Windows), followed by a tilde (~), a number, a period, and the first three characters after the last period in the long filename. Any spaces or symbols in a long filename are not used in the alias.

Take the Cabral Advertising folder name as an example. Windows 7 assigns it the alias CABRAL~1 (assuming no other file has that same alias). If another file in the same folder had already been assigned the alias CABRAL~1, Windows 7 then uses an **algorithm**, or a formula or procedure, to increment the number until it creates a unique alias. To continue with the example, Windows 7 checks to see if another folder, or file if the file has no file extension, used the alias CABRAL~2. If not, it would use this alias for the Cabral Advertising folder. Note that lowercase characters (which Windows 7 recognizes) are converted to uppercase characters (the default for the DOS operating system).

Suppose you have a folder that contains five or more files whose long filename starts with the same set of characters, as follows, and that are created in the order listed below:

Five Year Sales Projection.xlsx
Five Year Sales Analysis.xlsx
Five Year Growth Plan.xlsx
Five Year Growth Plan Template.xlsx
Five Year Budget Summary.xlsx

Also assume that no other files have the same six characters at the beginning of the filename (omitting spaces and symbols). Windows 7 creates the following short filenames, or aliases, (shown on the right and in Figure 3-20) for these files:

Five Year Sales Projection.xlsx	FIVEYE~1.XLS
Five Year Sales Analysis.xlsx	FIVEYE~2.XLS
Five Year Growth Plan.xlsx	FIVEYE~3.XLS

Five Year Growth Plan Template.xlsx   FIVEYE~4.XLS
Five Year Budget Summary.xlsx   FI0B6B~1.XLS
(The third character in the last filename is a zero.)

The command-line window in Figure 3-20 lists five Excel files created from the graphical user interface. In this figure, the last column displays the long filename of each file, while the next to last column displays the alias, or short filename, of each file. If you copy the folder with these files to another location on your hard disk, the short filenames remain the same except for the fifth file. Windows 7 assigns it a new alias during the copy operation.

| Figure 3-20 | Viewing aliases for long filenames |

Windows 7 uses the same approach to create aliases for the first four short filenames, but for each file after the fourth file, Windows 7 changes its approach. It uses the first two characters of the long filename, followed by four characters that are mathematically generated from the remainder of the characters in the long filename, and then a tilde followed by a unique number. Windows Vista and Windows XP use a similar approach, but the "calculated" values for filenames after the fourth file do vary.

The DOS operating system **truncated** filenames with more than eight characters and file extensions with more than three characters. In other words, if a filename exceeded eight characters, or if a file extension exceeded three characters, any extra characters were truncated (or removed). Today, many programs, including Microsoft Office, work with files that have more than three characters in the file extension. When Windows 7 creates an alias or short filename for a file with a file extension that exceeds three characters, as shown above for the five files with similar filenames, it removes any extra characters in the file extension so the alias or short filename only has three characters in the file extension. For these examples of Microsoft Excel 2010 files, the file extension is changed from ".xlsx" to ".xls".

You and the applications that you use cannot specify the alias that Windows 7 assigns for long filenames. Also, as noted in Tutorial 1, operating system and applications files follow the DOS naming conventions so they work properly when a Windows 7 computer is connected to a network containing other computers with operating systems that do not recognize Windows long filenames or that handle long filenames differently.

Under Windows 7, you might see a folder, shortcut, and file with the same name; however, the file extension (if present) differs, and each has a different alias if they are stored in the same location. Folders usually do not have a file extension (though temporary folders for installed software might have the .tmp extension for "temporary"). Shortcuts have the file extension .lnk (for link) or, in the case of shortcuts to DOS applications, ".PIF" (for Program Information File). (*Note:* The first character in the .lnk file extension is the lowercase letter *l*, not the numeral *1*.) Filenames have a file extension assigned by the program that created the file. That file extension depends on the file type the program uses or the file type that you choose during an open or save operation.

The short filename is also important in the rare event that you or someone else might use a DOS or Windows 3.*x* application under Windows 7 or an earlier version of the Windows operating system, because those applications do not recognize long folder names and long filenames. Instead, these applications can only "see" the alias (or short filename) for folders and files. Also, if you use a DOS application or a Windows 3.*x* application (such as an earlier version of Microsoft Word), you will only see the short filenames in Open and Save As dialog boxes. This limitation can make it difficult to know which folder or file to open, or which file to replace, because files like the ones described will have very similar short filenames. For example, how would you know whether FIVEYE~1.XLS, FIVEYE~2.XLS, FIVEYE~3.XLS, or FIVEYE~4.XLS contained the Five Year Growth Plan.xls that you want to open?

PROSKILLS

Problem Solving: Preventing Problems with Aliases and Filenames

You should understand how Windows 7 and other versions of the Windows operating system work with long and short filenames if you work with DOS, Windows 3.*x*, and applications designed for other versions of Windows on the same or different computer systems. You should also understand long and short filenames if you provide support to clients who might have a variety of software configurations on their computers, if you troubleshoot problems, and if you set up, configure, and customize computers for other users. In these instances, if you need to create a set of files with similar names, think carefully about how you name those files. One solution is to use names that begin with different characters. For example, instead of using the filenames Five Year Growth Plan.xlsx and Five Year Plan Template.xlsx, you could use the filenames Five Year Growth Plan.xlsx and Template for a Five Year Growth Plan.xlsx. Then you could easily tell these files apart using their short filenames (FIVEYE~1.XLS and TEMPLA~1.XLS).

Aliases are also important because the Windows Registry, which you examine in Tutorial 14, stores paths that use long folder names and filenames as well as paths that use aliases, or short filenames, for folders and files. Figure 3-21 shows a command for opening a Microsoft Access program. Note that the path to that program uses short filenames, such as PROGRA~1 for Program Files and MICROS~3 for Microsoft. If you are reconfiguring, customizing, or troubleshooting your computer using the Registry, you must know how to interpret and use aliases; otherwise, you might render your computer unusable. Likewise, applications may use aliases, or short filenames, in paths, when you create links between one application and another, such as inserting a link to the contents of a file created by another application. You might face a situation where you have to analyze and troubleshoot a problem posed by links that are not functioning properly, so understanding aliases and naming conventions for short filenames is important.

Figure 3-21 **Path in Registry uses short filenames for opening a program**

Organizing, Stacking, Grouping, and Sorting Files

Microsoft first introduced the concept and use of stacks in Windows Vista, and this feature carries over into Windows 7, but it is implemented in a different way. A stack is a virtual folder that contains a group of related files based on criteria you specify. If you have many files within a folder, you can use stacks to more quickly locate files that have a common feature, such as the same file type, or the same author.

To determine the usefulness of this feature in your job, and other coworkers you support, you decide to organize your work files into stacks.

To organize files into stacks by file type:

1. In the Address bar, click **Cabral Advertising**, click the **Client Projects** folder icon, click the **Visual Arts, Inc** folder icon, and then verify that the Library pane is visible at the top of the window.

   Trouble? If the Library pane is not visible at the top of the window, close the current window, open the Start menu, click Documents, click the expand icon ▷ to the left of the Documents library in the Navigation pane, click Public Documents in the Navigation pane, click the Cabral Advertising folder icon, click the Client Projects folder icon, and then click the Visual Arts, Inc folder icon. By navigating from the Public Documents folder in the Documents library to the folder you want to use, you guarantee that the Library pane is visible at the top of the folder window.

2. If necessary, use the **More options** arrow ⊞ ▾ for the Change your view button on the toolbar to adjust your view so you can see thumbnail previews of all the files in the window. Notice that the Arrange by option in the Library pane is set to Folder, the default setting used to organize folders in a window (however, this window has no subfolders).

3. In the Library pane, click the **Arrange by** button, and notice that you can arrange the contents of this folder by Author, Date modified, Tag, Type, and Name. You can also clear any changes you have made to this folder, and restore its default settings.

4. Click **Type**. Windows 7 organizes the files into three stacks (or virtual folders) by file type. See Figure 3-22.

Make sure the Library pane is visible at the top of the window; if not, complete the Trouble.

Figure 3-22   Files organized into stacks by file type

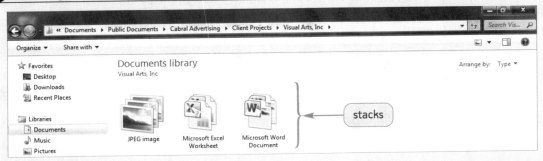

The three stacks are JPEG image, Microsoft Excel Worksheet, and Microsoft Word Document. The three file icons for the JPEG image stack indicate it contains three files in this stack, the two file icons for the Microsoft Excel Worksheet stack indicate that it contains two Microsoft Excel Worksheet files in this stack, and the two file icons in the Microsoft Word Document stack indicate it contains two Microsoft Word Document files.

5. Click the **JPEG image** stack, and if your view does not match that shown in Figure 3-23, click the **More options** arrow, and then click **Content**. Windows 7 displays the three files in this stack in Content view. See Figure 3-23.

| Figure 3-23 | Viewing files within a stack using Content view |

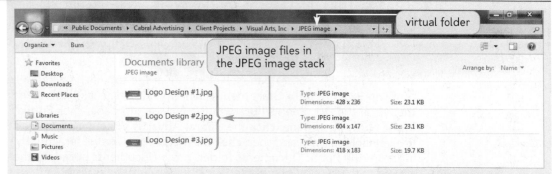

Windows 7 now displays dimensions (in pixels) of the JPEG images in the JPEG image files. As you can see, Content view provides more detail about folders and files than the other views. (Content view is not available in Windows Vista.) Notice that Windows 7 displays the name of this virtual folder at the end of the path notation in the Address bar.

6. Click the **Back** button. Windows 7 returns to the Visual Arts, Inc folder and redisplays the three stacks.

TIP

You can also press the Backspace key to return to the previous folder (or the previous Web page).

The Arrange by option is only available in Library windows and folders that are part of libraries, and it is not available, for example, for folders on a flash drive. The choices available on the "Arrange by" menu also vary by library and are therefore library-appropriate. For example, in the My Music folder, you can arrange files by Album, Artist, Song, Genre, and Rating. In the My Pictures folder, you can arrange files by Month, Day, Rating, and Tag. In the My Videos folder, you can arrange files by Year, Type, Length, and Name.

You can also create stacks within a stack.

To organize files into stacks by author:

1. Click the **Microsoft Word Document** stack, and if necessary, use the **More options** arrow on the Change your view button to switch to Content view. Windows 7 opens this stack and displays two files—Company Logo.docx and Logo Designs.docx—in Content view. Note also the setting for Arrange by is Name.

2. In the Library pane, click the **Arrange by** button, click **Author**, click the **More options** arrow for the Change your view button, and then click **Extra Large Icons**. Windows 7 displays two stacks for two authors—Leif Olson and Maya Cabral. See Figure 3-24.

Figure 3-24   **Viewing stacks within another stack**

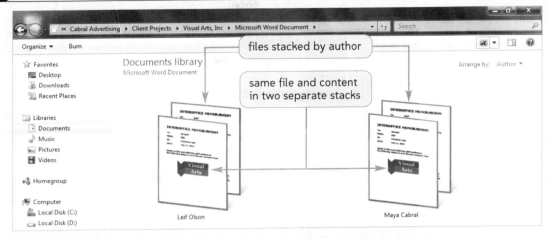

You are now viewing stacks within a stack. It's evident by examining the first file icon in each stack that the files are identical in content. That means the same file is in both stacks. Although not obvious, the other file is also in both stacks. But why does Windows 7 display the same two Microsoft Word Document files in each stack? Maya Cabral is a coauthor of two Microsoft Word Document files, and Leif Olsen is also a coauthor of the same two Microsoft Word Document files. But how can you confirm this information?

▶ **3.** Click the **Maya Cabral** stack, and then use the **More options** arrow ⊞ ▾ for the Change your view button to switch to Content view, if necessary. Windows 7 displays both Microsoft Word Document files in this stack in Content view. As shown under each filename, Maya Cabral is a coauthor on both files.

▶ **4.** Click the **Back** button ⬅, click the **Leif Olson** stack, and then use the **More options** arrow ⊞ ▾ on the Change your view button to switch to Content view, if necessary. Windows 7 displays the same two Microsoft Word Document files. Leif Olson is also a coauthor of both files.

▶ **5.** In the Address bar, click **Visual Arts, Inc**. Windows 7 returns to the Visual Arts, Inc folder.

▶ **6.** To remove the stacks, click the **Arrange by** button in the Library pane, and then click **Folder**.

▶ **7.** Keep the Visual Arts, Inc folder open for the next section of the tutorial.

Stacks are a powerful feature for organizing large numbers of files into smaller groups for ease of access. You can also use Content view to help you understand why Windows 7 displays the same file in more than one stack (i.e., because of multiple properties).

REFERENCE

Organizing Files into Stacks

- Right-click the Windows Explorer taskbar button, and then locate and open the folder that contains the files you want to organize into stacks.
- In the Library pane, click the Arrange by button, and then choose the property you want to use to create stacks.
- To view the contents of a stack, click the icon for that stack, and if necessary, use the Views button on the toolbar to select the view you want to use when examining the contents of a stack.
- If you want to organize stacks within a stack, click the Arrange by button in the Library pane, and choose another property for organizing the stack into stacks.
- To return to a previous folder or stack, click the Back button.
- To remove a stack, click the Arrange by button in the Library pane, and then click Folder.

You can also sort and group the contents of a folder in one of two ways. If you are working in Details view, you can sort and group files by using the column heading button above each column. If you click a column heading button, Windows 7 sorts the contents of the folder by that file property in ascending order, namely alphabetical, numerical, or date and time order. If you click the same column heading a second time, Windows 7 sorts the contents of the folder by that file property in descending order, namely reverse alphabetical, numerical, or date and time order. You can use this feature to quickly rearrange files in a folder so you can find what you want. Another way to sort and group files if you are working in another view (or even in Details view) is to right-click the folder background, and choose the Sort by or Group by option.

If you are working in Details view, you can also apply one or more **filters** that select specific files. For example, you could select a filter using the Type column heading button so Windows 7 only displays Microsoft Word Document files. You can also select multiple filters. For example, you might want to select all Microsoft Word Document files and all Microsoft Excel Worksheet files.

You decide to sort files and filter files by file type so you can compare these two options with the use of stacks.

To sort files and specify a file filter:

1. If Windows 7 is using a view other than Details view, click the **More options** arrow [▦ ▾] for the Change your view button on the toolbar, and then click **Details**. Windows 7 switches to Details view, and displays the Name, Date modified, Type, and Size columns.

2. Point to a file in the folder, and after Windows 7 selects the file, press the **Ctrl** key and the **plus sign (+)** on the numeric keypad to adjust all column widths for a best fit, or double-click the thin vertical border to the right of each column for a best fit of all the data in each column.

3. Click the **Size** column heading button. Windows 7 rearranges the files by file size, from the largest file size to the smallest file size (a descending sort). This option is useful if you need to locate the largest files in the folder because they are shown at the top of the column when in Details view.

4. Click the **Size** column heading button again. Windows 7 now arranges files from the smallest file size to the largest file size (an ascending sort). This option is useful if you want to identify the smallest files in a folder.

5. Click the **Name** column heading button to redisplay the files in order by filename.

6. Point to the **Type** column heading button, click the **Type button arrow** ⏷, and then click the **JPEG image** check box, and then click the **Type button arrow** ⏷ again to close the Type list. Windows 7 selects and displays only JPEG image files. See Figure 3-25.

Figure 3-25   **Filtering files by file type**

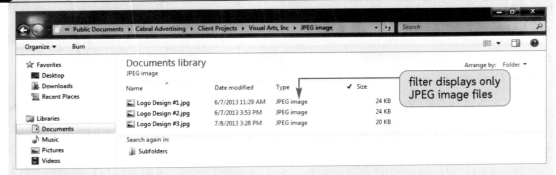

You can use the Subfolders link to locate other JPEG image files in any subfolders under the current folder. Windows 7 then displays any additional search results.

7. Click the **Type button arrow** ⏷ with the check mark, click the **JPEG image** check box (to turn off the display of JPEG image files), click the **Microsoft Excel Worksheet** check box, click the **Microsoft Word Document** check box, and then click the **Type button arrow** again to close the Type list. Windows 7 now displays both Microsoft Excel Worksheet and Microsoft Word Document files.

8. Click the **Type button arrow** ⏷ with the check mark, click the **JPEG image** check box, and then click the **Type button arrow** again to close the Type list. Windows 7 now displays all files in this folder.

9. Keep the Visual Arts, Inc folder open for the next section of the tutorial.

By sorting and filtering files, you can quickly select and focus on a smaller set of files for your work. If you right-click the background of the folder window, you will find on the shortcut menu a Sort by option with the same column headings as shown in the folder window. The shortcut menu also contains an Ascending and a Descending sort options.

Sorting and Filtering Files in a Folder

- Open the folder that contains the files you want to sort and filter.
- Click the More options arrow for the Change your view button on the toolbar, and then click Details.
- To adjust all column widths for a best fit of the longest entry in each column, point to a filename to select it, hold down the Ctrl key, and then click the plus sign (+) on the numeric keypad, or double-click the thin vertical border to the right of each column for a best fit of all the data in each column.
- To sort a column in ascending order (alphabetical, numerical, or date and time order), click the column heading button for that column, or right-click the folder background, point to Sort by, and then click Ascending.
- To sort a column in descending order (reverse alphabetical, numerical, or date and time order), and then click the column heading button for that column again (or twice if you have already applied a sort), or right-click the folder background, point to Sort by, and then click Descending.
- To filter files, click a column heading arrow button, and then click one or more of the check boxes for that column's categories. Repeat this process to remove all filters.

Next, you decide to group files.

To group files by file type:

1. Right-click the **background** of the folder window, point to **Group by**, and then click **Type**. Windows 7 organizes files into groups by file type and provides a count of the number of files in each group. See Figure 3-26.

Figure 3-26   **Grouping files by file type**

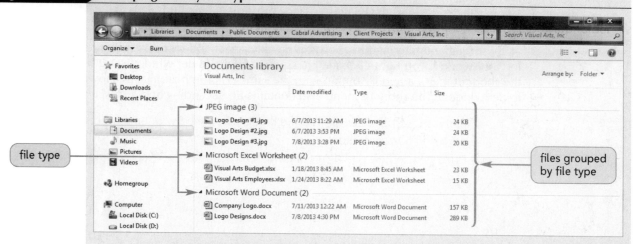

The files are listed in alphabetical order by filename within each file type group so you can easily locate groups of files. You can also use the collapse icon ◢ to hide files in a group.

▶ **2.** To restore your original view of the contents of this window, right-click the **Visual Arts, Inc** window background, point to **Group by**, and then click **(None)**. You can also choose "Clear changes" on the Arrange by menu, as you did earlier.

▶ **3.** Close the **Visual Arts, Inc** folder window.

If you store multiple file types in the same folder, the grouping option simplifies the process for identifying the types of files you want to use. It also provides a way for identifying which file extensions are associated with which file type.

REFERENCE

Grouping Files in a Folder

- Open the folder that contains the files you want to use, right-click the folder background, point to Group by, and then click the property you want to use.
- To adjust all column widths, point to a file, and after Windows 7 selects the file, press the Ctrl key and the plus sign (+) key on the numeric keypad, or double-click the thin vertical border to the right of each column for a best fit of all the data in each column.
- To restore your original view of the files in the folder, right-click the folder background, point to Group by, and then click (None).

All of these features—stacking, sorting, filtering, and grouping—provide you with a variety of tools and methods for organizing, locating, and examining files within folders.

REVIEW

Session 3.1 Quick Check

1. The majority of the Windows 7 operating system files are installed in the _____ folder, while application software, utilities, and games are typically installed in the _____ folder.
2. A(n) _____ is a virtual folder that consolidates files stored in two or more folders so you can work with all the files as a single group.
3. What is an executable file?
4. True or False. Ctrl+drag moves a file while Shift+drag copies a file.
5. A(n) _____ file is a file that is associated with an application or program on your computer.
6. True or False. The path is a notation that identifies the exact location of a folder or file.
7. What symbol does Windows 7 use to denote the top-level folder on a disk?
8. A(n) _____ is a virtual folder that contains a group of related files based on a property you specify.

SESSION 3.2 VISUAL OVERVIEW

The Windows 7 **Instant Search** feature creates a virtual folder that contains search results based on search criteria you specify in a folder's Search box.

The **parentheses Boolean operator** groups related search criteria, treats them as one logical condition, and performs that search comparison first.

All of the files match the **search criterion**, or search condition, that requires all files fall within the search filter date range.

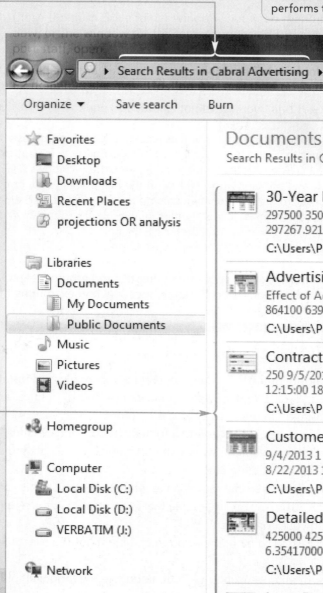

Search Results in Cabral Advertising ▸

Organize ▾   Save search   Burn

Favorites
- Desktop
- Downloads
- Recent Places
- projections OR analysis

Libraries
- Documents
  - My Documents
  - Public Documents
- Music
- Pictures
- Videos

Homegroup

Computer
- Local Disk (C:)
- Local Disk (D:)
- VERBATIM (J:)

Network

Documents library
Search Results in Cabral Advertising

30-Year Loan Model.xlsx
297500 350000 1 -232.07841531235056 -1797.396825 -2029.
297267.92158468766 0.15 2 -233.48055651179072 -1795.994
C:\Users\Public\Public Documents\Cabral Advertising\Co

Advertising Income.xlsx
Effect of Advertising on Sales 37500 750000 43125 791300 4
864100 63900 881400 72850 885800 Advertising Costs Sales
C:\Users\Public\Public Documents\Cabral Advertising\Sa

Contract Jobs.xlsx
250 9/5/2013 08:30:00 14:30:00 6 1500 9/6/2013 13:45:00 18:
12:15:00 18:00:00 5.75 1437.5 9/8/2013 08:00:00 13:00:00 5 1
C:\Users\Public\Public Documents\Cabral Advertising\Bu

Customer Accounts.xlsx
9/4/2013 1 5750 7/25/2013 41 2 3325 8/11/2013 24 3 11125 8
8/22/2013 13 5 3120 8/29/2013 6 6 2250 7/22/2013 44 7 4450
C:\Users\Public\Public Documents\Cabral Advertising\Bu

Detailed Loan Analysis.xlsx
425000 425000 0.1 0.1 42500 42500 382500 382500 7.624999
6.3541700000000001E-3 3573.0476553796166 250000 275000
C:\Users\Public\Public Documents\Cabral Advertising\Co

Loan Payment Analysis.xlsx
Loan Calculation 750000 0.1 75000 675000 4.7500000000000
-3521.1195213960418 Page 450000 500000 1 -566.16342930
C:\Users\Public\Public Documents\Cabral Advertising\Pe

9 items

BOOLEAN OPERATORS

Use a **search filter** to specify a condition for one or more file properties in your searches.

When you place the **quotation marks Boolean operator** around text in a search condition, you are specifying that you want an exact match.

This search filter uses a **date range operator** to select files that you worked on during a specific period of time.

(author:maya OR tags:="Loan Analysis") AND datemodified:9/1/2013..12/31/2013 ×

The **OR Boolean operator** in the Search box locates files that meet one of two or more conditions.

The **AND Boolean operator** combines two search conditions and requires that both conditions be met before selecting a folder or file for inclusion in the search results.

nge by: Top results ▾

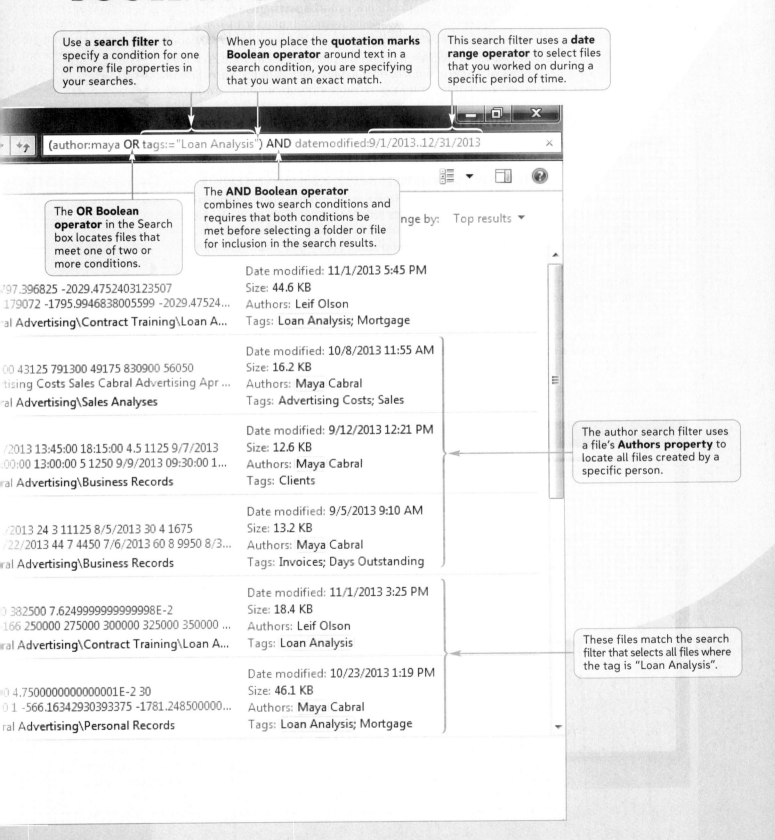

797.396825 -2029.4752403123507
179072 -1795.9946838005599 -2029.47524...
al Advertising\Contract Training\Loan A...

Date modified: 11/1/2013 5:45 PM
Size: 44.6 KB
Authors: Leif Olson
Tags: Loan Analysis; Mortgage

00 43125 791300 49175 830900 56050
ising Costs Sales Cabral Advertising Apr ...
al Advertising\Sales Analyses

Date modified: 10/8/2013 11:55 AM
Size: 16.2 KB
Authors: Maya Cabral
Tags: Advertising Costs; Sales

/2013 13:45:00 18:15:00 4.5 1125 9/7/2013
:00:00 13:00:00 5 1250 9/9/2013 09:30:00 1...
ral Advertising\Business Records

Date modified: 9/12/2013 12:21 PM
Size: 12.6 KB
Authors: Maya Cabral
Tags: Clients

The author search filter uses a file's **Authors property** to locate all files created by a specific person.

/2013 24 3 11125 8/5/2013 30 4 1675
/22/2013 44 7 4450 7/6/2013 60 8 9950 8/3...
ral Advertising\Business Records

Date modified: 9/5/2013 9:10 AM
Size: 13.2 KB
Authors: Maya Cabral
Tags: Invoices; Days Outstanding

0 382500 7.6249999999999998E-2
166 250000 275000 300000 325000 350000 ...
ral Advertising\Contract Training\Loan A...

Date modified: 11/1/2013 3:25 PM
Size: 18.4 KB
Authors: Leif Olson
Tags: Loan Analysis

These files match the search filter that selects all files where the tag is "Loan Analysis".

0 4.7500000000000001E-2 30
0 1 -566.16342930393375 -1781.248500000...
ral Advertising\Personal Records

Date modified: 10/23/2013 1:19 PM
Size: 46.1 KB
Authors: Maya Cabral
Tags: Loan Analysis; Mortgage

Using Search

All versions of Windows include a search feature for locating files; however, in Windows XP and prior versions of Windows, searches took time and were limited in scope. That all changed with Windows Vista and Windows 7. In Windows Vista, Microsoft introduced a new feature called Instant Search that remarkably improved the speed at which Windows located programs, folders, and files. Windows 7 also includes the Instant Search feature.

Now, when you start to enter the name of a program, folder, or file you want to locate in a Search box, either from the Start menu or a folder window, Windows 7 (and Windows Vista) immediately displays search results, and as you continue to type your search criteria, both versions of Windows continue to narrow your search results.

To provide search results quickly, the Windows 7and Windows Vista indexing service constantly indexes folder and filenames as well as the content and properties (or what's called metadata) of folders and files on your computer. A **service** is a Windows program that runs in the background and provides support to other programs. The Indexing service converts documents with different file formats into plain text so the Search service can then index, or catalog, the content. An **index** is a file that contains a collection of information about the folders and files on your computer. By cataloging and compiling data from programs, folders, and files in advance of when you will need it, Windows 7 (and Windows Vista) can more quickly locate what you need by using the index rather than by repeatedly searching the contents of each folder and file every time you do a search. **Metadata** is data about other data. A file's title, author, and company are examples of metadata associated with, and stored within, a file, such as a project report produced in Microsoft Word or a sales projection produced in Microsoft Excel. The Indexing service also extracts metadata, or file properties, for use in a search.

The Indexing service indexes the Start Menu folder because it contains shortcuts to all the installed software and Windows tools stored on your computer, including those available in the Control Panel. It also indexes all or some of the content of the Users folder. The Indexing service also indexes the **Offline Files cache**, a folder on your local computer that acts as a temporary storage location for copies of network files. The Offline Files folder provides you with faster access to those files as well as access to the files when a computer is not connected to the network. Once the connection is reestablished, Windows 7 and Windows Vista update the network copies of the files (or vice versa). You can also search the content of removable drives, such as flash drives.

The Indexing service does not index everything on your computer. For example, Windows 7 and Windows Vista exclude the ProgramData folder, which contains the Search index files, so the Indexing service does not index its own index. Also, protected operating system files are not indexed. Instead, the focus of the Windows 7 and Windows Vista Indexing service is to provide you with quick access to programs and your user folders and files. The Indexing service indexes folders and files when your computer is inactive (during idle periods), and does not interfere with your use of the computer.

You can initiate a search in one of several ways from the following locations:

- **Start menu**—The Search box on the Start menu is useful if you want to quickly locate programs on your computer. Once you start typing a program name, such as Calculator, or the name of a Control Panel feature, such as Power Options, Windows 7 immediately displays search results for the program or Control Panel feature.
- **Folder window**—For a more focused search, you can use the Search box in a folder window. It is useful if you want to search through the contents of a folder and all of its subfolders.
- **Search Results window**—If you press the F3 (Search) key from the desktop, or press the Windows+F keyboard shortcut from the desktop, Windows 7 opens a virtual folder window called Search Results so you can initiate a search in the same way you would initiate a search in a regular folder window. If you are working in a folder window, pressing the F3 Search key places you in the Search box for that window so you can specify your search criteria.

- **Searches folder**—As covered at the beginning of this tutorial, within your Users folder is a Searches folder where Windows 7 stores saved searches with specific search criteria. Later in this section of the tutorial, you will examine how to save a search and how to use a saved search.
- **Control Panel**—If you need to quickly locate Control Panel applets (or programs) or features, such as Backup and Restore, you can use the Search box in a Control Panel window.
- **Save As and Open dialog boxes**—If you are saving a file for the first time, assigning a new filename to a file, or saving a file in another folder or on another drive, you can use the Search box in the Save As or Open dialog box to locate another folder where you want to save the file. You can use the Search box to locate the filename of an existing file that you want to overwrite with the contents of the file you are saving. You can also use these same features in the Open dialog box to locate a folder that contains a specific file, a similar set of files, or files by a certain author. In essence, the Save As and Open dialog boxes serve as "folder windows" where you can not only perform searches, but you can also create a folder, rename files, move and copy files, and delete folders and files. Power users commonly use this feature and approach to locating, renaming, deleting, copying, and moving files.
- **Other dialog boxes**—Certain other dialog boxes that you open, such as the Change icon dialog box that you will examine in the next tutorial, provide a Browse button for locating a folder and file on your computer, and you can use the Search box in these dialog boxes to search for folders and files. Other dialog boxes provide a Search button, such as when you restore files from a backup (covered in Tutorial 10).

In the original version of Windows Vista, the Search option on the Start menu opened a Search Explorer for more advanced types of searches, but Microsoft removed it in the Windows Vista Service Pack Upgrade 1. This Start menu Search option is no longer included in subsequent Service Pack Upgrades of Windows Vista, and it is not included in Windows 7.

Searching from the Start Menu

If you need to find a program quickly, you search for that program from the Start menu. You can also search for folders and files, email contacts, email messages, Internet favorites (or bookmarks), and saved Web pages.

At Maya's request, you are putting together a timeline for a new client project. Because you need to know the number of days from the proposed project start date to the proposed completion date, you decide to open the improved Windows Calculator accessory, and calculate that value.

TIP

As you type more characters in the Search box, you narrow down the list of search results.

To locate a program using the Start menu Search box:

1. Press the **Windows** key. Windows 7 opens the Start menu, and as evidenced from the insertion point in the Search box, you can enter your search criteria.

2. Type **ca** and examine the search results. Notice that Windows 7 organizes search results into categories, including Programs and Control Panel. See Figure 3-27.

Figure 3-27	Searching for a program from the Start menu

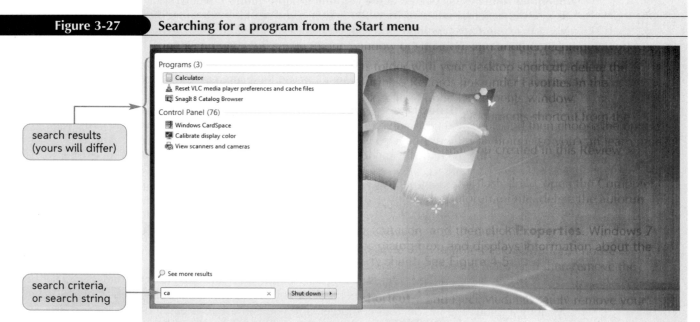

search results (yours will differ)

search criteria, or search string

If you wait for a second or two longer, Windows 7 adds search results for documents, music, pictures, and other types of files. Under Programs and Control Panel, Windows 7 lists programs or links that contain the character *ca* somewhere in the program name or link. Your search results may differ and may include more search results than shown in the figure. You can click the See more results link at the bottom of the Search Results pane to open a Search results window where Windows 7 can display more search results than is possible on the Start menu.

▶ 3. If Calculator is the first search result listed, press the **Enter** key; otherwise, click **Calculator** in the search results. Windows 7 opens the Windows Calculator.

▶ 4. Click **View** on the Calculator menu bar and pause. Note that the default settings for the Calculator are Standard and Basic. By selecting Scientific, Programmer, or Statistics, you can expand the capabilities of the Calculator to perform more complex and focused operations. You can also switch from Basic use to Unit conversion (so you can convert from one unit of measurement to another) and to Date calculation.

▶ 5. Click **Date calculation**. The Calculator window expands to include a Date calculation section. To calculate the number of days in a project, you have to specify the start and ending dates for that project.

▶ 6. Click the **From calendar button arrow**, and then select another date near the end of the current month or the beginning of the next month.

▶ 7. Click the **To calendar button arrow**, and use the calendar arrow ▶ to the right of the current month and year to advance 3 months, and then choose a date in that month.

▶ 8. Click the **Calculate** button. The Calculator determines the number of months, weeks, and days between the two dates and the total number of days.

▶ 9. To restore your default Calculator settings, click **View** on the menu bar, click **Basic**, and then close the Calculator.

The search criterion that you entered to locate the Calculator accessory is called a **search string**. A **string** is nothing other than a set of characters (or perhaps even a single character) treated exactly as you type them.

Performing a search from the Start menu is useful for locating programs that you do not use frequently and programs that you have difficulty locating on the All Programs menu or in the Control Panel.

Searching for Files

You can also use Search from the Start menu to locate folders, such as all folders with the word *Videos* in the folder name, as well as files on your computer. After you open a folder, you can then perform a search in the folder window to locate a file in the folder or one of its subfolders. In Windows 7 (but not Windows Vista), you can adjust the width of the Search box to make it easier to view more complex search criteria that consist of multiple conditions.

To quickly meet an important deadline during an especially busy day, Maya asks you to locate the Break-Even Analysis file for a new client.

As you complete the steps in the rest of this session, pay close attention so your results match as closely as possible the search results described in the steps and figures.

To search for a file in a folder window:

1. Click the **Windows Explorer** taskbar button 🖿, click **Documents** in the Navigation pane, click the **expand** icon ▷ to the left of the Documents library name, click **Public Documents** in the Navigation pane, and then click the **Cabral Advertising** folder icon. Windows 7 opens the Cabral Advertising window, and displays the Library pane. Although you could use the Search option on the Start menu to locate and open this folder, you would not have access to the Library pane and the Arrange by button.

   Trouble? If you already have another folder window open, right-click the Windows Explorer taskbar button 🖿, click Windows Explorer, click Documents in the Navigation pane, click Public Documents, and then click the Cabral Advertising folder icon.

   Trouble? If the Library pane is not visible, click the Organize button on the toolbar, point to Layout, and then click Library pane.

2. Right-click the **background** of the Cabral Advertising window, point to **Sort by**, and if Name is not already selected as the sort option, click **Name**. Windows 7 uses this option to display the contents of a window in alphabetical order by folder or filename.

3. Right-click the **background** of the Cabral Advertising window, point to **Sort by**, and if Ascending is not already selected as the sort order option, click **Ascending**. Windows 7 uses this option to display the name in alphabetical order from A to Z.

4. If Windows 7 displays the contents of the Cabral Advertising folder window in a view other than Content view, click the **More options** arrow ▤▾ for the Change your view button on the toolbar, and then click **Content**. You can use Content view to figure out how Windows 7 selected specific files for whatever search condition you specify.

5. Point to the **border** between the Address bar and Search box, and when the mouse pointer changes to a double-headed arrow pointing to the right and left ⟺, drag the **border** to the left, about halfway across the screen, to widen the Search box so you can more easily see its contents.

▶ **6.** Click in the **Search** box located in the upper-right corner of the window, type **b**, and then examine the search results. Windows 7 lists every file (in this example, 26 items) that contains the character *b* somewhere in the folder or filename, in the content of the file, in any of its file properties, or in the file's path. If the letter *b* is in a folder or filename, the visible contents of a file, or the path, Windows 7 highlights the character *b* or *B* in yellow so you can quickly spot those folder and filenames in the search results.

Searches are not case sensitive, so you can use lowercase, mixed case, or uppercase. If you scroll to the bottom of the window, Windows 7 provides you with the option to search again in the Documents library, all Libraries, Computer, and Homegroup windows, as well as perform a custom search and search the Internet. If you choose Computer, Windows 7 searches everything on your computer, including all indexed, nonindexed, system, and hidden folders and files. If you choose Custom, Windows 7 opens the Choose Search Location dialog box so you can select the location or locations you want to search by clicking a check box next to each location you want to use.

To narrow your search results:

▶ **1.** Click after the letter *b* in the Search box, type **re** (so your search criteria is *bre*), and examine the search results. Windows 7 narrows the selection to one file—Break-Even Analysis.xlsx, the one file that has the characters *bre* in the filename, document title, and the file contents. See Figure 3-28. After you locate a file, you can click the file's icon to open the file directly from the Search Results window.

| Figure 3-28 | Searching from a folder window |

first three characters of filename match search criteria

text that meets search criteria highlighted

search criteria or search string

▶ **2.** Right-click **Break-Even Analysis.xlsx** in the search results, and examine the shortcut menu. You can use Open, the first option shown in boldface on the shortcut menu, to open the file. See Figure 3-29.

Figure 3-29 Viewing actions on a file's shortcut menu

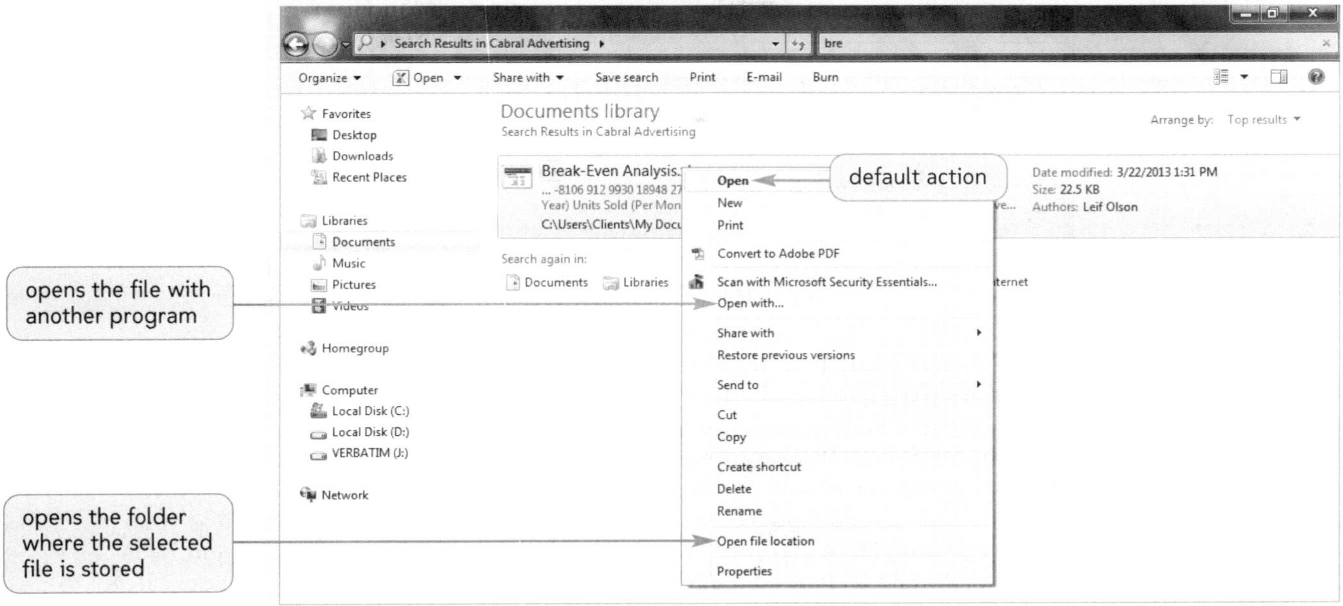

opens the file with another program

opens the folder where the selected file is stored

default action

You can use Print to print the document without first opening the file. Actually, Windows 7 opens the file and the application, prints the document, and then closes the application and document. You can use the "Open with" option to open the document in another program that supports the same file format. You can use the Send to menu option to send a copy of the file to another disk, such as a flash drive.

3. Click **Open file location**. Windows 7 opens the Client Projects folder window where the Break-Even Analysis.xlsx file is located. You can now create or work with any other files in the window (presumably ones related to the one that you searched for); however, you do not have access to the Library pane in the new window.

4. Click the **Back** button ⊙ to return to the Cabral Advertising folder. The Library pane is now available.

Trouble? If the Library pane is not visible, click the Organize button on the toolbar, point to Layout, and then click Library pane.

5. Keep the Search Results in Cabral Advertising window open for the next section of the tutorial.

Windows 7 displays the default action for any object in boldface on the object's shortcut menu. The **default action** is the operation that Windows 7 performs on a file if you click the file icon in Web style (or double-click it in Classic style).

Searching for Files Using All or Part of a Filename

When searching for files, the best approach is to enter a few characters of the filename to find the file rather than type the entire filename. The characters can be the characters at the beginning of the filename, or anywhere in the filename. You can also find what you want by entering some unique combination of characters found in the filename of the file you are looking for, but not likely to be found in other filenames. This approach simplifies searches, and finds what you need as quickly as possible.

Creating Searches Using File Properties and Search Filters

If you want to search using a file property, such as Authors, you can type all or part of the name of an individual, or you can precede the author's name with the name of the Authors property. For example, if you want to find all files by Maya Cabral, you could enter *author:Maya* or *author:Cabral*, or enter "author:Maya Cabral" (with quotation marks) in the Search box. The advantage of using *Cabral* is that you locate only those authors with that last name, and are likely to have fewer search results. If you use *Maya* or a more common first name, you locate all authors with the same first name, and your search results include more than you need. If you just specify *Cabral* without *author*, you locate every single file in the Cabral Advertising folder because Windows 7 includes all folders and files under the Cabral Advertising folder as that folder meets the search condition. Although the actual file attribute is *Authors* (with an *s*), you can enter the author property with or without the *s*. However, you *must always* use the colon after the name of the file property.

You can use the approach described in this paragraph to locate files by using one or more of 284 different file properties—including Closed captioning, Has attachments, and Meeting status. If you right-click a column header in Details view and then choose More, Windows 7 lists these properties in the Choose Details box, as shown in Figure 3-30.

| Figure 3-30 | Viewing a list of file properties |

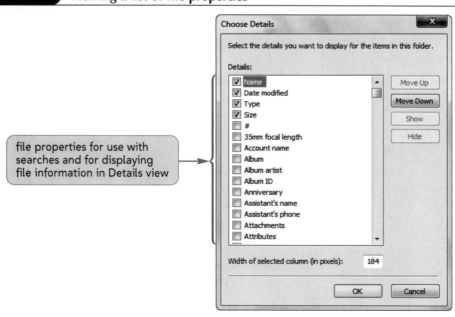

file properties for use with searches and for displaying file information in Details view

You can also use **search filters**, which include a file property, such as Authors, Type, Date modified, Size, Name, Folder path, Tags, and Title, along with an item of data selected from a drop-down menu, to simplify the process of constructing search criteria, especially more complex search criteria, and for selecting search criteria that fall within a range, such as a date range (e.g., last week) or a range of file sizes (such as "Gigantic" for file sizes exceeding 128 MB). These search filters are available from a Search menu after you start to type the name of the filter (such as author: or date:) in the Search box. When you type these filters, you must type a colon (:) after the filter; otherwise, Windows 7 assumes you want to locate all folders and files that have that search filter name in the folder or file-name, the file properties, or the path. If you select a search filter and then wait, Windows 7 displays a "Computing filters" message, and then compiles a list of all unique entries, such as all author names, for all files in the current folder and all subfolders. Then you can scroll down the list and select specific search criteria, such as a person's name, to complete the search criteria. Using this approach, you might discover content on your computer that you did not know about or that you might have long forgotten. (Unlike Windows 7, Windows Vista did not display search filters in a menu.)

As a precautionary note, when you type a search filter in the Search box, the Windows 7 search feature immediately starts searching for folders and files that match what you typed, even before you can complete what you want to type. Windows 7 might then respond either very slowly or block what you type, so you might need to wait and then reenter the search condition that you had tried to type.

Next, you want to display a list of Maya's files so you can make sure you have everything you need for the next project.

To search using the author property:

1. Click **bre** in the Search box to select this search condition, type **maya** to replace *bre*, and pause while Windows 7 locates the files that meet this search condition. Windows 7 lists 17 files. These 17 files contain *maya* in a file property or in the contents of the file. You do not need to press the Enter key after you type your search criteria in the Search box, but if you do so, Windows 7 closes the "Add a search filter" list.

> Make sure you type a colon (:) after *author*.

2. Click **maya** in the Search box, press the **Home** key, and then type **author:** before *maya* (so your search criteria reads *author:maya*). Windows 7 narrows the list to 15 files that contain *Maya* in the Authors property, either as the sole author or as a coauthor with Leif Olson. See Figure 3-31.

| Figure 3-31 | Searching for a specific author using the Authors property |

▶ **3.** Click after the last *a* at the end of the "author:maya" search condition in the Search box, and then press the **Backspace** key four times to delete *maya* from the search condition. Windows 7 compiles a list of all possible filters for this property and the available files, and lists Leif Olson, Maya Cabral, and Unspecified (where no author was specified). This feature is particularly useful because you know all possible choices for this file property.

▶ **4.** Click after the colon (:) at the end of **author:** in the Search box, press the **Backspace** key once to delete the colon, pause, and examine the search filters menu, which displays previous search criteria and lists the search filters for Authors, Type, Date modified, Size, Name, Folder path, Tags, and Title. The number of search filters that you see depends on the width of the Search box, which is why it's helpful to widen the Search box before searching.

▶ **5.** Click the **Back** button ⬅, click in the **Search** box, click **Type:** under Add a search filter, and then pause. After compiling search filters, Windows 7 displays a list of all available file types in this folder and its subfolders: **.docx, .jpg, .ppsx, .xlsx,** Directory, File folder, JPEG image, Microsoft Excel Worksheet, Microsoft PowerPoint Slide Show, and Microsoft Word Document (which is not visible unless you scroll). See Figure 3-32. That means if you wait for Windows 7 to list the filters, you can pick one from the filters list instead of typing it.

| Figure 3-32 | **Using the search filter feature to display a list of all file types** |

file types compiled for the type: search filter

search filter

▶ **6.** Click **.docx** in the search filter list. Windows 7 lists the three Microsoft Word Documents with the **.docx** file extension, no matter which folder contains these files. Notice that the search criteria in the Search box is: type:=.docx

If you enter type:-.docx (with a minus sign before **.docx**), Window 7 finds all folders and files except **.docx** files. If you select Microsoft Word Document from the filters list, the search criteria becomes type:="Microsoft Word Document" (with the quotation marks around the file type), and Windows 7 lists the same three files.

To locate only folders:

▶ **1.** Click to the right of type:=.docx in the Search box, use the **Backspace** key to delete =.*docx*, and after Windows 7 displays a list of search filters, click **File folder**. Windows 7 displays an alphabetical list of all the folders in the Cabral Advertising folder and its subfolders. Windows 7 found 12 folders using the search criteria type:="File folder" in the Search box. When you opened Cabral Advertising earlier, it contained only 7 folders. The additional 5 folders are subfolders of the folders under the Cabral Advertising folder. If you select the Directory search filter, Windows 7 lists the same folders.

2. Click **type:="File folder"** in the Search box, type **xlsx** and then examine the search results. Windows 7 finds all Microsoft Excel 2007 and Microsoft Excel 2010 Worksheet files (in this case, 21 files) with the **.xlsx** file extension. Notice that only the file extension of each file is highlighted in yellow.

3. Select **xlsx** in the Search box, press the **Delete** key, and under Add a search filter, click **Date modified**: and then pause. Windows 7 displays a calendar from which you can pick a date and a list of date range options: A long time ago, Earlier this year, Earlier this month, Last week, Earlier this week, and Yesterday. "A long time ago" extends from 1980 through the end of the previous year, "Earlier this year" extends from the first day of the current year to the end of the previous month, "Earlier this month" extends from the beginning of the current month through Saturday of the previous week, and "Earlier this week" extends from Sunday of the current week through the day before yesterday. These relative search filters allow you to specify a search condition relative to whatever period of time that you are examining, rather than selecting or entering a specific date range. You can also use the calendar to specify search criteria for the datemodified: search filter, such as selecting a specific day in the calendar, or selecting a date range in the calendar. You can also navigate from month to month using the navigation arrows to the left and right of the month and year.

Trouble? If you accidentally click somewhere else, click after *datemodified:* in the Search box to redisplay the calendar, or if Windows 7 displays previous search criteria, click after *datemodified:*, press the Backspace key to delete the colon, and then type the colon again.

4. In the calendar, click the **day** that you copied the Data Files to the computer you are using, and then press the **Enter** key to collapse the calendar so you can view the search results. Windows 7 displays a list of all folders for the day you select. The search condition consists of *datemodified:* (one word with no spaces) followed by the date you chose using the date format *m/d/yyyy* (where *m* = month with one or two digits, *d* = day with one or two digits, and *yyyy* with four digits for the year). No files are included in the search results because the files retain their modified date when copied. That is not the case, though, with folders.

5. Click the **Back** button 🔙 to clear the search criteria in the Search box.

6. Click in the Search box, click **Date modified:** under "Add a search filter," press and hold the **Shift** key, click the **date** for the beginning of the current month, press the **Enter** key, and release the Shift key. You just selected a date range starting from the current day going back to the first of the current month. Any folders or files created during the current month are included in the search results. Note that the date range includes two periods between the beginning and ending dates.

7. Use the **Back** button 🔙 to return to the Cabral Advertising folder. By returning to the Cabral Advertising folder, you remove any search criteria in the Search box and use the same folder as the starting point for all new searches.

With the use of file properties and search filters, you are no longer limited to searching for folders and files by name. Instead, these search features and others that you will examine in the rest of this session increase the options you have for locating folders and files on your computer. These features are increasingly important as the capacity of disk drives grows. To maximize the options available for searches, always open the library that contains the folder, and then open the folder.

Searching for Tags

To make it easier to organize your folders and files or perform a search, you can specify one or more tags to locate folders and files. For example, you can use tags to group files in a window, similar to the way you grouped files earlier in the tutorial by type and author. Tags also speed up searches. You can assign multiple tags to folders and files and cross-reference them. By assigning multiple tags to the same file, you can locate the file by using any word or phrase that comes to mind, as long as it matches one of the tags you specified.

Maya asks you to find the file that contains a list of the company's assets and liabilities.

To locate the file with the company's assets and liabilities:

▶ **1.** In the Search box, type **tags:** and pause. When Windows 7 displays a list of all available tags, click **Assets** in the list. Windows 7 displays the only file that contains the word *Assets* as a tag. See Figure 3-33. That file also has *Liabilities* as a tag.

Figure 3-33 Searching for a file using a tag

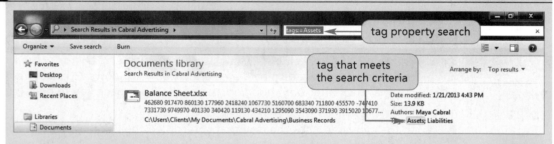

▶ **2.** Use the **Back** button ⬅ to return to the Cabral Advertising folder.

Searching Using a File Property, File Type, or Tags

REFERENCE

- Open the library that contains the folder where you want to start the search, and then open the folder.
- To search a folder using a file property, click in the Search box, select a search filter from the "Add a search filter" menu (or type the name of a property followed immediately by a colon), wait for Windows 7 to compile a list of search filters, and then click the search filter you want to use.
- To search for folders only, click in the Search box, click Type: under "Add a search filter," wait for Windows 7 to compile a list of file types, and then click the "File folder" search filter.
- To search for a tag, click in the Search box, type tags: and then wait for Windows 7 to compile a list of tags so you can select the tag you want to use.

To assign a tag to a file:

▶ **1.** In the Search box, type **five** and then press the **Enter** key. Windows 7 locates two files: Five Year Growth Plan.xlsx and Sales Projection Memo.docx (which contains the word *five* in the text of the document).

2. Point to the **Five Year Growth Plan.xlsx** file to select it. In the Details pane, Windows 7 displays information about this file. See Figure 3-34. The "Add a tag" entry for Tags in the Details pane indicates that no tags are assigned to this file.

Figure 3-34   **Using the Details pane to add a tag to a file**

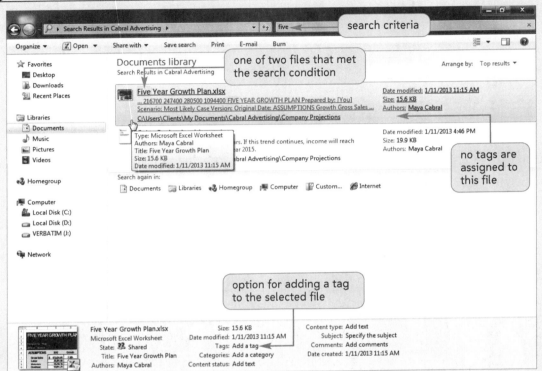

3. Next to the file property Tags in the Details pane, click **Add a tag**, type **Most Likely Case** in the Tags box, and then click the **Save** button in the Details pane. Windows 7 assigns this tag to the file and displays it with the other file properties in the column to the right of the filename. You can also press the Enter key instead of clicking the Save button, but if you do not click the Save button or press the Enter key, Windows 7 does not assign the tag as a file property.

   Trouble? If Windows 7 does not display *Most Likely Case* as the tag for the Five Year Growth Plan.xlsx file, repeat this step, making sure to click the Save button in the Details pane.

4. Check **Tags** in the Details pane, and verify that *Most Likely Case* is a tag for Five Year Growth Plan.xlsx (if not, repeat the previous step and save your change).

5. Use the **Back** button ⊙ to return to the Cabral Advertising folder.

6. To test your new tag, type **tags:case** in the Search box. Windows 7 finds one file, Five Year Growth Plan.xls, which contains the word *case* in the file's Tags. See Figure 3-35. You can also use the search criteria *tags:likely* and *tags:most* to locate the same file.

   Trouble? If Windows 7 does not locate the file, click the Back button ⊙, wait a few seconds, and then repeat this step.

Make sure you click the Save button after entering Most Likely Case in the Tags box in the Details pane.

Figure 3-35 **Searching for a file with a specific tag**

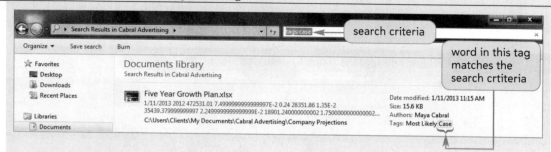

> **7.** Click the **Back** button ⬅ to return to the Cabral Advertising folder window.

You can assign more than one tag to a file. After you type a tag, you type a semicolon (;) to separate one tag from another. The semicolon acts as a delimiter (or separator) between tags. You can also select multiple files, and then add the same tag to all the files in one step (as part of a group property operation).

Assigning a Tag or Tags to a File

- Locate or search for the file that you want to assign a tag to, and then select the file.
- In the Details pane, click "Add a tag," and then type the first tag. If you want to assign more than one tag to the file, type each tag followed by a semicolon.
- Click the Save button in the Details pane or press the Enter key.

In the examples of the Microsoft Office files that you have examined thus far in the tutorial, you can enter, update, or change a file's Title, Authors, Tags, Category, Content status, Content type, Subject, and Comments properties in the Details pane. However, the properties that are available depend on the type of file. In addition, you cannot change certain types of file properties that are assigned by the operating system, such as Size, Date modified, or Date created, unless you locate a utility that provides this capability.

Specifying File Properties and Tags

Where available, tags are a great way to cross-reference files and find what you need quickly and efficiently. For some applications, you can enter or modify properties and tags for the file before you save it. You may also be able to specify or modify tags in the Save As dialog box. The approach that you use may also vary with the application, and perhaps even with the version of that application. For example, you specify file properties in different ways in Microsoft Office 2003, Microsoft Office 2007, and Microsoft Office 2010. For files created with applications developed before the introduction of Windows 7, the options for specifying file properties may be limited. For certain types of files, such as Rich Text Format files with the .rtf file extension and Text Document files with the .txt file extension, you cannot specify any file properties or tags.

Using Boolean Operators

Microsoft introduced the use of Boolean operators (also called Boolean filters in Windows Vista) so you can perform more precise searches and narrow a long list of possible search results more quickly. Those Boolean operators are also available in Windows 7.

The term *Boolean* is derived from George Boole, a British mathematician who invented a type of algebra in which every equation always resulted in a value of TRUE or FALSE. A Boolean operator (or **Boolean filter**) consists of a **search keyword** (also called a **logical operator**) or a symbol (called a **comparison operator** or **relational operator**) that allows you to specify one or more search conditions or perform a comparison between two items (whether numeric values or text). When working with more advanced features of certain programs, text is treated as a value (or string value).

When Windows 7 evaluates a Boolean operator, it determines whether the Boolean operator is TRUE or FALSE. If TRUE, Windows 7 includes the folder or file in the list of search results. If FALSE, Windows 7 does not include the folder or file in the search results. (If you want to test this logic, open an Excel spreadsheet, type the formula =1=1 in one cell to produce a TRUE result and verify that 1 actually does equal 1, and then type =1=2 in another cell to produce a FALSE result and verify that 1 does not equal 2.) In essence, these operators allow you to use simple logic to maximize the effectiveness of searches. Microsoft also uses the broad term **search operators** to refer to the various types of operators that you will examine in this tutorial. Note that different terms are used to refer to different types of search operators.

Whenever you use a search engine such as Google to search for information, you are performing a similar type of operation and using Boolean logic. The search engine compares the search criteria that you specify with the content of Web pages it examines to locate and display a list of search results that meet the criteria you specified. Rather than searching the Web each time you do a search, search engines rely on previously indexed information about Web sites to quickly locate and display the information you want. One problem with that indexed information is that the Web site might no longer exist, and if you try to access the Web site, your Web browser displays an error message to that effect. Windows 7 also uses indexes to locate previously catalogued information quickly. Again, one problem you might encounter with this index is that a folder or file might no longer exist, but information about it is still stored in the index.

Here's how the Boolean operators work:

- **AND**—This Boolean operator combines two different criteria and requires that any folders or files listed in the search results meet both conditions. For example, if you enter the search condition *company AND projection*, the search results includes all folders and files with both words, *company* and *projection*, somewhere in the folder name, the filename, the contents of the file, the file properties, or the path. *For the AND Boolean operator to work, you must type it in uppercase.* You can also substitute a plus sign (+) before *projection* to produce the same results. If you type *company projection*, AND is automatically assumed.
- **OR**—This Boolean operator combines two different criteria and requires that any folders or files listed in the search results meet only one of the two conditions. For example, if you enter the search condition *company OR projection*, the search results include all folders and files with one of the two words, *company* or *projection*, somewhere in the folder name, filename, the contents of the file, the file properties, or the path. If a folder or file contains both criteria in the folder or filename, the contents of the file, the file properties, or the path, the folder or file is included in the search results (because it met one of the two conditions). *For the OR Boolean operator to work, you must type it in uppercase.*

- **NOT**—This Boolean operator combines two criteria and requires that any folders or files listed in the search results meet the first condition but not the second condition. For example, if you enter the search condition *company NOT projection*, the search results includes all folders and files with the word *company*, but not the word *projection*, in the folder name, the filename, the contents of the file, the file properties, or the path. *For the NOT Boolean operator to work, you must type it in uppercase.* You can also substitute the minus sign (-) for negate before *projection* to produce the same results.
- **" "** **(quotation marks)**—If you enclose words or a phrase in quotation marks, the search results include exact matches. In other words, the search results include exactly what you type, in the order in which you type the words or phrase. For example, if you enter the search condition *"company projection"* with quotation marks around the two words, the search results includes any folder or file with the phrase *"company projection"* somewhere in the folder name, filename, the contents of the file, the file properties, or the path. In contrast, if you enter *company projection* without the quotation marks, the search results includes any folder or file that contains the two words in any order and in any location in the folder name, filename, the contents of the file, the file properties, or the path.
- **( )** **(parentheses)**—If you enclose a phrase in parentheses, the search results include all the words in the phrase; however, the words can be arranged in any order and can include other words between them. For example, if you enter *(Specialty Travel)* with the parentheses around the words or phrase as your search criteria, the search results include all folders and files with *Specialty Travel* or *Travel Specialty* in the folder name, the filename, the contents of the file, the file properties, or the path. The search results also include the two words separated by other words, such as *Travel Resort Specialty*.

When you use the AND, OR, and NOT Boolean operators, you *must* always type them in all uppercase for them to work properly. It's common practice to type text in lowercase (because it's simpler), so you might need to make a special effort to remember that uppercase is required for these Boolean operators.

Figure 3-36 lists other types of Boolean operators, or comparison operators for comparing two items; operators for locating nonexistent entries (such as no author) or any value; and an operator for locating a range of values. *Note*: Microsoft refers to these types of operators as Boolean operators when performing a search, though in other programs, such as Microsoft Access, they are referred to as comparison operators (a newer, friendlier term) or relational operators (a well-established term).

Figure 3-36 **Comparison operators**

Comparison Operators	Meaning	Example	Finds
>	Greater than	datemodified:>1/1/2013	All folders and files with a modified date after 1/1/2013
>=	Greater than or equal to	datemodified:>= 1/2/2013	All folders and files with a modified date of 1/2/2013 or later
<	Less than	size:<1 MB	All files with a size of less than 1 MB
<=	Less than or equal to	size:<=1 MB	All files with a size of exactly 1 MB, or a size of less than 1 MB
[ ]	No value, or null value	authors:[ ] authors:=[ ]	All folders and files that do not have an author in the Authors property **Note**: These empty braces do not contain a space.
−tag:=[ ] tag:−[ ]	Any value	−authors:=[ ] authors:−[ ]	All folders and files that have an author in the Authors property
start value .. end value	Range of values	datemodified: 1/2/2013 ..1/31/2013	All folders and files with a modified date from 1/2/2013 through 1/31/2013

Here's how these comparison operators work:

- **> (greater than)**—You can use the **greater than (>)** operator to determine if the value for a property exceeds another value, such as whether a file date or file size exceeds a certain date or size. If you specify the search condition *datemodified:>1/1/2013*, the search results include all folders and files modified after 1/1/2013. *Date Modified* is a file property, but when you specify it in the Search box, you do not include the space between *date* and *modified*; in other words, it's just one word: *datemodified*. When checking for dates, remember that Windows 7 keeps tracks of different types of file dates (such as date created, date modified, and date accessed) for each file, and you want to make sure you are using the correct date property.
- **>= (greater than or equal to)**—This operator is a variation of the previous operator, and functions in a similar way. You can use the greater than or equal to operator (**>=**) to determine if the value for a property exceeds another value or is equal to that value, such as whether a file date or file size exceeds a certain date or value or is equal to that file date or file size. This operator actually evaluates two separate conditions, namely, is it greater than, or is it equal to? For example, if you specify the search condition *datemodified:>=1/1/2013*, the search results include all folders and files modified after 1/1/2013 and on 1/1/2013. You can also use this operator to locate text that exceeds a specific value.
- **< (less than)**—Similarly, you can use the less than operator (**<**) to determine if a value for a property is less than another value, such as whether the file date precedes a certain date or whether a file size is less than a certain value. If you specify the search condition *size:<1 MB*, the search results include all files with a file size less than 1 MB. Unlike Windows Vista, Windows 7 excludes folders.
- **<= (less than or equal to)**—You can use the less than or equal to operator (**<=**) to determine if a value for a property is less than another value or equal to that value, such as whether the file date precedes a certain date or is equal to that date, or whether the file size is less than a certain value or is equal to that value. If you specify the search condition *size:<=1 MB*, the search results include all files with a file size less than 1 MB or equal to 1 MB.

  You must be careful when using these operators to locate files by file size because Windows 7 rounds off file sizes when reporting them in a folder window, but uses the actual file size when selecting it using operators. For example, if you have a file that is exactly 824.20315 KB in size but reported by Windows 7 as 825 KB in a folder window (such as the Comparison Operators.ppsx file in the Data Files for this tutorial), the search criteria *size:<824 KB* does not include this file in the search results, but the search criteria *size:<825 KB* does include this file in the search results.
- **[ ] (no value**, or **null value)**—You use this operator (also referred to as "empty braces"), which consists of two square brackets with no space between them, to locate properties that have no value. For example, if you specify the search condition *authors:[ ]*, the search results include all folders and files that do not have an author. To locate all authors (in other words, any value), you specify the following search condition: *-authors:[ ]* or *author:-[ ]*

  For this operator to work properly, you cannot include a space between the two square brackets.
- **.. (range of values)**—This operator selects a range of values, such as all folders and files with a date between two dates, and including the starting and ending dates. For example, if you specify the search condition *datemodified:1/2/2013..1/31/2013*, the search results include all folders and files modified between 1/2/2013 and 1/31/2013 as well as all folders and files modified on 1/2/2013 and 1/31/2013. In other words, the range is inclusive. Another approach to locating the same date range is to enter the search condition *datemodified:>=1/2/2013<=1/31/2013* using the greater than or equal to, and the less than or equal to, operators.

You can also combine these operators to create more complex criteria, as you will see later in this tutorial.

Maya asks you to locate and then print several files that she needs for a new client and for an upcoming workshop. Maya recommends that you use Boolean operators to quickly locate those files. She also notes that you can combine Boolean operators and file properties.

To locate this file with a Boolean operator:

▶ **1.** In the Cabral Advertising window, widen the Search box so you can see longer criteria.

▶ **2.** Type **"loan analysis" AND mortgage** in the Search box. Windows 7 locates two files with these criteria in the file's tags: 30-Year Loan Model.xlsx and Loan Payment Analysis.xls. See Figure 3-37.

> **Trouble?** If Windows 7 reports that "No items match your search," you typed AND in lowercase or mixed case rather than in uppercase. Repeat this step, but be sure to type AND in uppercase.

| Figure 3-37 | **Using the AND Boolean operator to find files** |

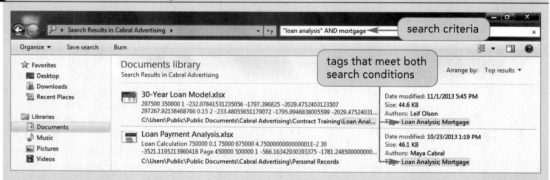

Because both files have *Loan Analysis* and *Mortgage* as a tag, you could have also specified the Tags property for both criteria, as follows: *tags:"loan analysis" AND tags:mortgage*

▶ **3.** Click the **search criteria**, and then type **projections OR analysis** in the Search box. Windows 7 locates 14 items (2 folders and 12 files) that contain either word in the folder name, filename, file content, or file properties, with one exception. See Figure 3-38.

> **Trouble?** If Windows 7 reports that "No items match your search," you typed OR in lowercase or mixed case rather than in uppercase. Repeat this step, but remember to type OR in uppercase.

Figure 3-38   **Using the OR Boolean filter to find files**

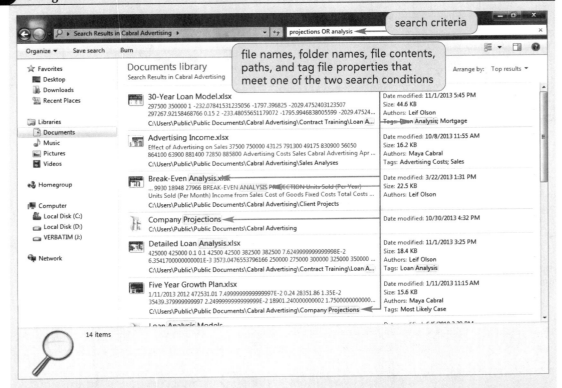

The one exception is a file that contains *analysis* as a name assigned to a cell in a Microsoft Excel Worksheet.

You have located all of the files Maya needs for spreadsheet projections and for analyzing sales. Because you might perform this same search again, you decide to save the search.

▶ **4.** Click the **Save search** button on the toolbar. Windows 7 displays a Save As dialog box and prompts you for a filename. It proposes to use your search criteria as the filename, and will add the **.search-ms** file extension to the filename. Windows 7 will save your search in your user account Searches folder. See Figure 3-39.

Figure 3-39 Saving the search criteria

search saved in user account Searches folder

proposed filename for saved search includes search criteria

file type and file extension

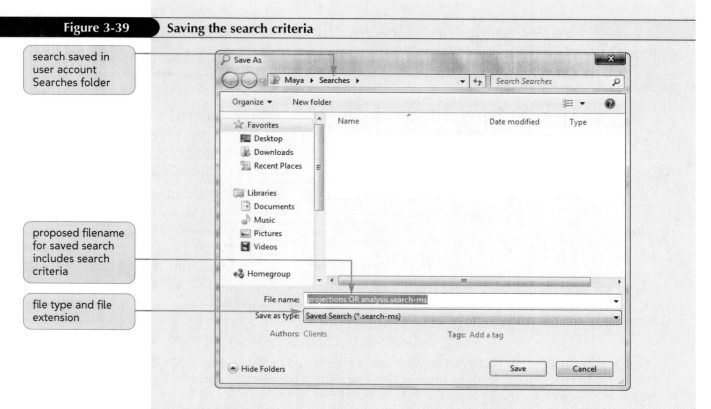

5. Click the **Save** button, and then click **Searches** in the Address bar. Windows 7 creates a virtual folder named "projections OR analysis" and places a link for the saved search under Favorites in the Navigation pane. See Figure 3-40.

Figure 3-40 Viewing a saved search in the Searches folder

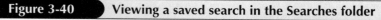

link to saved search

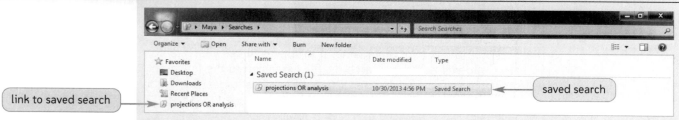

saved search

6. Click the **Recent Pages** button ⊽ to the left of the Address bar, and then click **Cabral Advertising** to return to this folder.

TIP

Windows 7 updates saved searches as you add, remove, and change folders and files so saved searches remain useful to you.

7. Click **projections OR analysis** under Favorites in the Navigation pane. Windows 7 opens the virtual folder for the saved search, and displays a copy of the files that it located with your search criteria. See Figure 3-41. Notice also it highlights that portion of the filename that meets one of the search conditions. The Address bar shows that you are now in that virtual folder, namely, Maya ▶ Searches ▶ projections OR analysis ▶

Figure 3-41	Using a saved search to locate folders and files

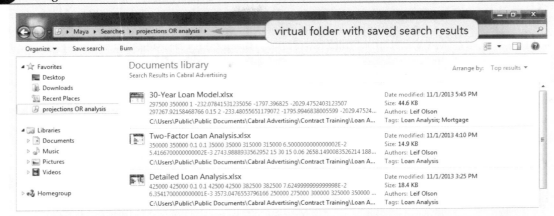

8. Use the **Back** button ⊙ to return to the Cabral Advertising folder, and then type **tags:models OR tips** in the Search box. Windows 7 locates the Excel Tips.xlsx file, the Sales Projection Models.xlsx file, and the Tips folder. See Figure 3-42.

   Trouble? If Windows 7 reports that "No items match your search," then you typed OR in lowercase or mixed case rather than in uppercase. Repeat this step, but remember to type OR in uppercase.

Figure 3-42	Combining a tag with a Boolean operator in a search

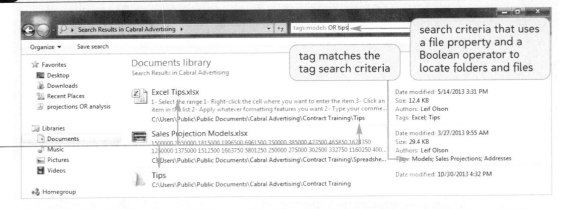

Here you used a tag with a Boolean operator. The criteria *tags:models* matched one file that contained the word *models* in a tag. The criteria *tips* matched one file that contained this word in the filename, and it matched one folder that contained this word in the folder name. The two files are the ones Maya needs to prepare for an upcoming training session.

TIP

To undo a move, right-click the folder background, and click Undo Move.

9. Drag the **Sales Projection Models.xlsx** file icon and drop it onto the Tips folder icon, and then click the **Tips** folder icon. Windows 7 moves the Sales Projection Models.xlsx file into the Tips folder, and then opens the Tips folder so you can verify the operation. Now Maya has the two files she needs for her contract training workshop.

10. Keep this folder open for the next section of the tutorial.

If you want to exclude the Tips folder from these search results for some reason, you can modify the search criteria, place parentheses around the OR criteria, and use the NOT Boolean operator to exclude folders, as follows:

(tags:models OR tips) NOT folder

By combining Boolean operators and file properties, you can quickly locate whatever combination of folders and files you need for a project. In some cases, you may discover valuable files that you have not used in a while, files that you were not able to locate previously, and ones that you no longer need.

Using Wildcards in File Specifications

To locate folders and files with specific patterns in their filenames under the DOS operating system and previous versions of the Windows operating system, you used wildcards to perform searches. You can also use these same wildcards in Windows 7. **Wildcards** are symbols that substitute for one character, a combination of characters, or even all characters in a folder name or filename. The two wildcards are the asterisk (*) and the question mark (?). The **asterisk wildcard** substitutes for all characters in a folder name or filename or a portion of a folder name or filename. For example, to search for all Microsoft Office Word Document files created with Microsoft Office 2007 or Microsoft Office 2010, you enter the criteria *.*docx* (pronounced "star dot doc x"). In this case, the asterisk wildcard substitutes for any and all characters in the filename before the period that separates the filename from the file extension.

The **question mark wildcard** substitutes for one character in a folder name or filename at the position of the wildcard. For example, to locate files with sales summaries for several years in a row, you can use the question mark wildcard to substitute for the last one or two digits of the year. For example, to locate a set of files with the filenames 2009 Sales Summary, 2010 Sales Summary, 2011 Sales Summary, and 2012 Sales Summary, you can enter the search condition *20?? Sales Summary*. In this instance, the two question marks instruct Windows 7 to look for any character in the third and fourth positions of the filename. You can also use *20*Sales Summary* to locate these same files. In this case, the asterisk substitutes for the last two digits of the year as well as the space between the year and *Sales Summary*. The search condition *.* selects all files. The first asterisk substitutes for any filename, and the second asterisk substitutes for any file extension. Open dialog boxes have an "All Files (*.*)" option so you can view all files in a folder rather than only files with a specific file extension.

Maya recommends that you experiment with wildcards so you can observe how they work.

To search using wildcards:

1. Click the **Back** button ⊙ twice (if necessary) to return to the Cabral Advertising folder.

2. In the Search box, type **"201? Sales Summary.xlsx"** (with the quotation marks) and then press the **Enter** key. Windows 7 locates two files, namely, 2011 Sales Summary.xlsx and 2012 Sales Summary.xlsx. See Figure 3-43. The only difference between the two files is a different character in the fourth position of the filename.

| Figure 3-43 | Using a wildcard in a search criteria |

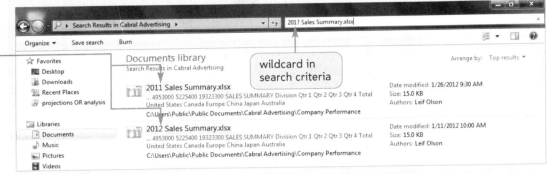

wildcard accepts any character in this position in the two filenames

wildcard in search criteria

▶ **3.** Click the **search criteria** in the Search box, and then type **2*Sales**. Windows 7 finds the same two files, illustrating that you have more than one way to specify a search condition for the same file or set of files. Here, the asterisk substitutes for the *01* (as part of 2011 and 2012), the digit *1* or *2* at the end of the year, and the space after *11* and *12*. This search condition is also less complex than the previous one you tried, and yet produces the same results.

▶ **4.** Click the **search criteria** in the Search box, type ***.*** and then press the **Enter** key. As shown in the Details pane, Windows 7 finds 42 items. Those 42 items include all the folders and all the files within the Cabral Advertising folder.

▶ **5.** Use the **Back** button 🔙 to return to the Cabral Advertising folder.

▶ **6.** In the Search box, type **.** (a period), and then press the **Enter** key. Again Windows 7 finds all 42 items. This period (called a "dot") is a special notation for the current folder, and selects everything in the current folder and all subfolders, producing the same results as *.* but with less typing.

▶ **7.** Close the Cabral Advertising folder window.

Wildcards add to the tools available for searching your computer, and can be used with file properties, tags, and Boolean operators. By combining search criteria that use file properties, search filters, tags, Boolean operators, and wildcards; by trying different types of search criteria; and by using a little bit of ingenuity you should be able to find anything on your computer.

You can also perform character searches using the following symbols (which are comparable to wildcards):

- ~< (**begins with**)—If you type a tilde (~) followed immediately by a less than symbol and then text, Windows 7 searches for all items that begin with the text you type. For example, if you specify the search condition ~<*type:microsoft*, the search results include all file types that begin with *Microsoft* in the file type description, such as Microsoft Word Document, Microsoft Excel Worksheet, Microsoft PowerPoint Presentation, Microsoft PowerPoint Slide Show, and Microsoft Access Database. This type of character search works in Windows 7, but not Windows Vista.

- ~> (**ends with**)—If you type a tilde (~) followed immediately by a greater than symbol and then text, Windows 7 searches for all items that end with the text you type. For example, if you specify the search condition ~>*type:document*, the search results include all files that end with *Document* at the end of the file type, such as Adobe Acrobat Document, Cascading Style Sheet Document, HTML Document, MHTML Document, Microsoft Office Word 97 - 2003 Document, Microsoft Word Document, and Text Document. This type of character search works in Windows 7, but not Windows Vista.

- ~~ (**contains**)—If you type two tildes (~~) one after another followed by text, Windows 7 searches for all items that contain the text you type. For example, if you specify the search condition ~~*name:Project*, the search results include all folders and files that contain *Project* in the folder name or filename, such as Client Projects, Company Projections, Research Projects, Regional Sales Projections.xlsx, Sales Projection Models.xlsx, Sales Projection Memo.docx, and Contract Income Projection.rtf. This type of character search works in Windows 7, but not Windows Vista.
- ~*? (**matches pattern**, or **pattern match**)—You can also combine wildcards with the tilde to search for folders and files where a property value matches a specific pattern. For example, if you specify the search condition ~*Logo?# then Windows 7 locates all files that contain the word *Logo* preceded by any or no character(s); any character after the word *Logo*, followed by a pound sign; and any or no character(s) in the remainder of the filename. That means it finds Logo #1.jpg, and Logo #1 Design.jpg, Company Logo #1.jpg, and Company Logo #1 Design.jpg.

Performing Relative Searches

You can also perform **relative searches** (meaning relative to a fixed reference, such as a day, month, or year). For example, the search condition *date:today* locates all folders and files with a folder or file date for the current day. *Date:yesterday* locates all folders and files with a folder or file date for the previous day. *Date:Friday* locates all folders and files with a folder or file date for the last Friday (or the current day if the current day is Friday).

Date:this week locates all folders and files with a folder or file date during the current week. *Date:Monday..Friday* locates all folders and files with a folder or file date for the last Monday through Friday (a date range). *Date:April* locates all folders and files with a folder or file date for the month of April. *Date:this month* locates all folders and files with a folder or file date for the current month. *Date:January..March* locates all folders and files with a folder or file date for the first quarter of the current year. *Date:this year* locates all folders and files with a folder or file date for the current year.

You can also specify other relative search conditions, such as *date:last week*, *date:last month*, or *date:past month* to perform comparable searches. *Date:last month* and *date:past month* produce the same results.

PROSKILLS

Decision Making: Locating Important Files Quickly

In many business situations, you find yourself working against tight deadlines and the need to locate important company or client files quickly. You can maximize your effectiveness, use your time more efficiently, and meet those tight deadlines by using the Windows 7 Instant Search feature and your logic skills to decide on the best approach for combining Boolean operators, comparison operators, file properties, search filters, wildcards, and relative searches. In certain instances, you might locate misplaced files by searching paths or by negating file properties to exclude what you know you already have. As you work with search criteria, you gain insight into alternative strategies for deciding how to define search criteria to locate folders and files.

Furthermore, evaluate what drives, folders, and files Windows 7 indexes (covered in the next section) on your computer, and then decide how to adjust these settings to make sure your searches cover every possible location that you or someone else might have used to save files. Examine the hundreds of file properties and decide how you might use file properties to more effectively locate files. Save your search criteria so you can quickly recall and use a previous search. You can also translate the skills you acquire using the Instant Search feature to online searches where you need to find that single important item from a vast amount of information.

Examining Search and Indexing Settings

Maya recommends that you examine your current indexing and search settings to determine whether you can optimize your searches by changing or customizing those settings.

To examine Indexing options:

▶ **1.** Press the **Windows** key, type **i** in the Search box, and then click **Indexing Options** under Control Panel in the search results. Windows 7 opens the Indexing Options dialog box. See Figure 3-44.

Figure 3-44 **Viewing indexing options, indexed locations, and excluded locations**

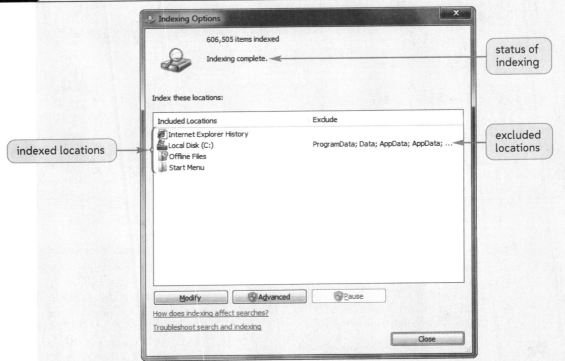

Windows 7 identifies the number of items that are indexed (yours will differ), and informs you that indexing is complete, that indexing speed is reduced because of user activity, or that indexing is in progress. In the "Index these locations" list box, Windows 7 identifies what locations are included in, and excluded from, indexing. By default, Windows 7 indexes your Internet Explorer history, folders on your hard disk drive, the Start Menu folder, the Offline Files folder, and the Users folder that contains all user account folders and files. The Start Menu folder is included because it contains shortcuts to all the installed software on your computer, plus access to Windows tools. If you add a location for indexing, Windows 7 displays the path to that location in this list box.

▶ **2.** Click the **Modify** button in the Indexing Options dialog box. Windows 7 opens the Indexed Locations dialog box. See Figure 3-45.

Figure 3-45 | **Viewing options for changing indexed locations**

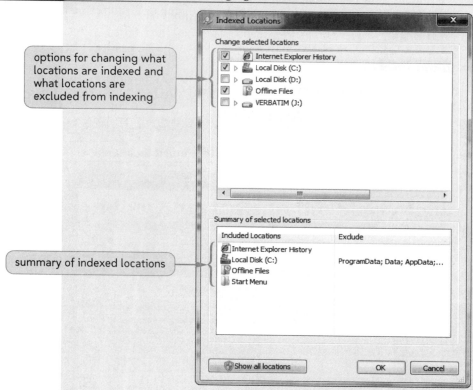

options for changing what locations are indexed and what locations are excluded from indexing

summary of indexed locations

In the Change selected locations list box, you can select those locations you want to include or exclude from indexing. The "Summary of selected locations" list box summarizes Windows 7 default settings and/or your choices of selected locations shown in the Indexing Options dialog box. Your settings may differ. To view all indexed locations, you must use the "Show all locations" button, and then provide Administrator credentials. You may also discover that Windows 7 automatically includes your backup set on an external hard disk drive as one of the locations to index.

3. If you are logged on as an Administrator, or can provide the password for an Administrator account, click the **Show all locations** button. Windows 7 then updates the contents of the Indexed Locations dialog box, and provides more details on indexed locations, as shown in Figure 3-46. Your settings may differ. Notice that Windows 7 automatically indexes Internet Explorer History and Offline Files for each user account.

Figure 3-46   **Viewing details on indexed locations**

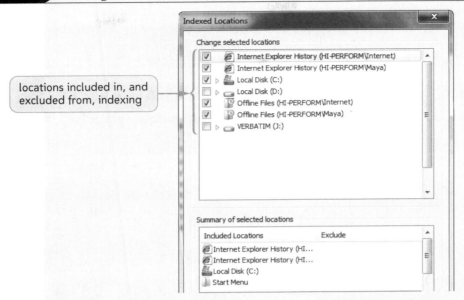

locations included in, and
excluded from, indexing

▶ **4.** In the Change selected locations list box, click the **expand** icon ▷ to the left of
Local Disk (C:) to expand the list for this drive, and then click the **expand** icon ▷
to the left of Users. Note that Windows 7 does not index the Windows folder, but
does index all user account folders, including the shared Public user account. See
Figure 3-47. Your settings will differ. In this dialog box, you can change which user
accounts are indexed and which folders within a user account or system folder are
indexed.

Figure 3-47   **Viewing details on indexed user accounts**

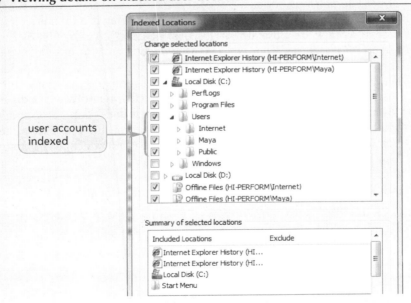

user accounts
indexed

5. Click the **Cancel** button to close the Indexed Locations dialog box without making any changes.

6. If you are logged on as an Administrator, or can provide Administrator credentials, click the **Advanced** button in the Indexing Options dialog box. Windows 7 opens the Advanced Options dialog box. See Figure 3-48.

Figure 3-48 **Viewing advanced index settings**

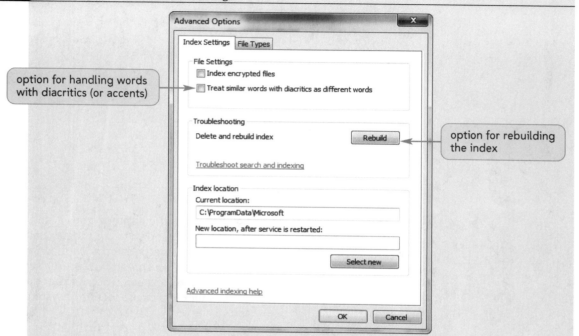

option for handling words with diacritics (or accents)

option for rebuilding the index

Under File Settings, indexing of encrypted files is disabled; however, you can enable this option. As noted previously, encryption is a technique for securing data in a file so only the authorized user has access to the file. By default, the option for treating similar words with diacritics as different words is not enabled. That means that similar words with diacritics (or accents), such as jalapeño and jalapeno, are considered the same words for indexing purposes, but you can change this setting if you want to treat words with and without diacritics as different words so each is indexed separately. Under Troubleshooting, you can delete and rebuild your index if you discover that it is not finding files and folders that you know you have. However, you should first check to make sure that those locations are included for indexing, because rebuilding an index can take hours. Under Index Location, Windows 7 shows the path to the folder where it stores the index. You have the option of specifying another location.

7. Click the **File Types** tab. Windows 7 displays a list of all file types that are included in the index. See Figure 3-49.

Figure 3-49   **Viewing file types included in indexing**

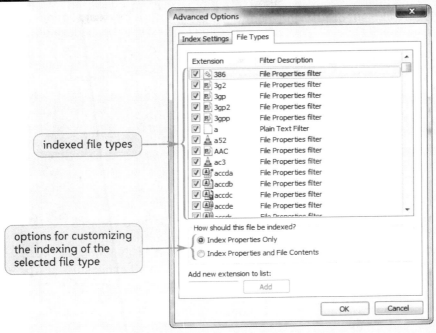

indexed file types

options for customizing
the indexing of the
selected file type

Here you can examine and, if necessary, change whether Windows 7 indexes a
specific file type (identifiable by file extension) and if so, whether it should index
only the file properties or both the file properties and file content. You can also
add new file extensions in the "Add new extension to list" box at the bottom of
the dialog box, and then customize the settings for that new file extension. For
each file type, Windows 7 identifies the type of filter (described after the next
step) used to extract information from a file's properties and its file content.

▶ **8.** Click the **Cancel** button in the Advanced Options dialog box to exit without making any change to the settings on your computer, and then close the Indexing
Options dialog box.

The Indexing service uses **IFilters**, components of the Windows search engine, to convert documents with different file formats into plain text so the Search service can then
index or catalog the content. IFilters also extract metadata, or file properties, for use in
a search. The title, author, and company are examples of metadata associated with, and
stored within, a file.

Examining Search and Index Settings

- Press the Windows key, type *i* in the Search box, click Indexing Options in the search results, and in the Indexing Options dialog box, examine the indexing status and information on indexed locations and locations excluded from indexing.
- In the Indexing Options dialog box, click the Modify button, and then review and, if necessary, add or exclude locations to index in the "Change selection locations" box of the Indexed Locations dialog box.
- Click the "Show all locations" button in the Indexed Locations dialog box, provide Administrator credentials, review and, if necessary, choose locations to index in the "Change selection locations" box of the Indexed Locations dialog box, and then click the OK button, or click the Cancel button to exit without making changes.
- In the Indexing Options dialog box, click the Advanced button, provide Administrator credentials, review and if necessary, change File Settings on the Index Settings property sheet, and then use the Rebuild button to reindex selection locations and rebuild the search index. Click the File Types tab, locate a file type in the Extension column, review and if necessary, change the option for indexing this file type, and then click the OK button, or click the Cancel button to exit without making changes.
- Close the Indexing Options dialog box.

You can also customize Search options by using the Folder Options dialog box.

To examine Search options:

1. Press the **Windows** key, type **f** in the Search box, and then click **Folder Options** under Control Panel in the search results.

2. Click the **Search** tab in the Folder Options dialog box. Under "What to search" on the Search property, Windows 7 searches both filenames and file contents for indexed locations. In nonindexed locations, it searches only filenames. See Figure 3-50.

Figure 3-50 **Viewing search settings**

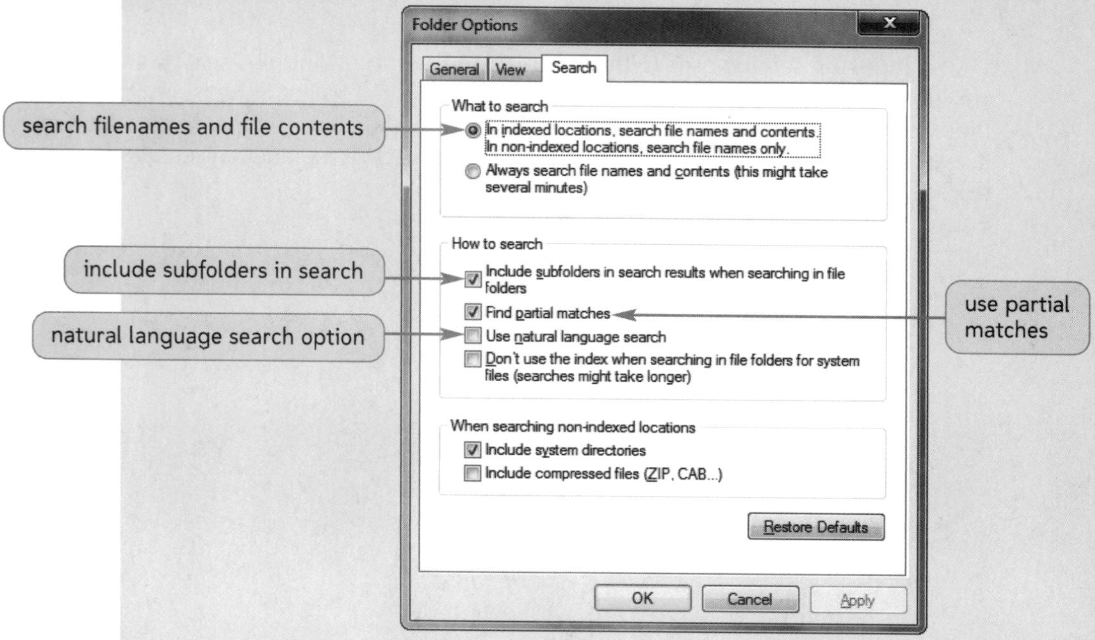

search filenames and file contents → In indexed locations, search file names and contents. In non-indexed locations, search file names only.

include subfolders in search → Include subfolders in search results when searching in file folders

natural language search option → Use natural language search

use partial matches → Find partial matches

You can specify that Windows 7 always search filenames and contents (which might be slow) or only search filenames (which is faster, but might not produce what you need). In the "How to search" section of the Search property sheet, Windows 7 is set to automatically search subfolders and to find partial matches, such as when you enter the first few characters of a folder or filename. If you specify that it use natural language search, Windows 7 interprets your search condition as a natural language query. For example, if you search for *email from Maya Cabral*, Windows 7 searches for and displays all email messages from Maya Cabral. You can also enable the option for not using the index when searching in file folders for system files to save time when searching.

As shown under "When searching nonindexed locations," Windows 7 automatically includes system directories (a command-line term for *folders*) but does not search compressed files. A **compressed file** is a single file that contains files, or folders and files, stored in a way that reduces the amount of storage space required on disk. You can also use the Restore Defaults button to restore the default Search settings listed in this dialog box.

To close the Folder Options dialog box:

▶ **1.** Click the **Cancel** button to close the Folder Options dialog box without making changes to your computer.

Customizing Search Options

- Press the Windows key, type *f* in the Search box, and then click Folder Options under Control Panel in the search results.
- Click the Search tab, and then review and, if necessary, change Search settings under "What to search," "How to search," and "When searching nonindexed locations."
- Use the Restore Defaults button to restore default Search settings.
- Click OK to close the Folder Options dialog box, or click Cancel to close the Folder Options dialog box without making any changes.

You have now examined the two locations where you can review, specify, change, or restore search settings.

Restoring Your Computer's Settings

If you are using your own computer, and want to restore the original settings, complete the following steps. If you are working in a computer lab or on a company network, and if the computers are not configured to restore their original settings with a simple restart, complete the following steps to restore the original display settings on your computer. If the computers in your computer lab are set up so a restart restores the computer to its previous states (and undoes all changes you've made to Windows 7), simply choose the option to restart your computer so the next person who uses the computer is not affected by the changes you have made to the computer.

To restore your computer's settings:

▶ **1.** To restore double-click activation, click the **Computer** icon on the desktop, click the **Organize** button on the toolbar, click **Folder and search options**, and on the General property sheet in the Folder Options dialog box, click the **Double-click to open an item (single-click to select)** option button.

2. To hide extensions for known file types, click the **View** tab in the Folder Options dialog box, click the **Hide extensions for known file types** check box if it does not contain a check mark, click the **OK** button to close the Folder Options dialog box and apply these changes, and then close the Computer window.

3. Right-click the **Windows Explorer** taskbar button 🖿 and then open the **Documents** library.

4. If you want to delete the Cabral Advertising folder from your computer, or if you are working in a computer lab where other people may complete the same assignment on the same computer, and therefore need to start with their own original copy of this folder, point to the **Cabral Advertising** folder icon, press the **Delete** key, and in the Delete Folder dialog box, click the **Yes** button.

5. Under Favorites in the Navigation pane, right-click **projections OR analysis**, and then click **Remove** on the shortcut menu.

6. To remove the Computer icon on the desktop, open the **Start menu**, right-click **Computer**, and then click **Show on Desktop**.

7. To remove your flash drive, click the **Show hidden icons** button ▲ on the left side of the notification area, click the **Safely Remove Hardware and Eject Media** icon 🖭, click the **Eject** option for your flash drive, and after Windows 7 displays a Safe to Remove Hardware notification, remove your flash drive.

Maya is impressed with the progress that you have made in using the Windows 7 search feature. Not only will it save time and effort, but it will help both of you meet critical client deadlines.

REVIEW

Session 3.2 Quick Check

1. A(n) _____ is a word or phrase that you assign as a property to a folder or file for the purpose of organizing and locating folders and files.

2. A(n) _____ is nothing other than a set of characters (or perhaps even a single character) treated exactly as you type it.

3. How can you identify the default option on a shortcut menu?

4. True or False. A Boolean operator consists of a word called a logical operator that allows you to specify one or more search conditions, or perform a comparison between two items.

5. Which Boolean operator can you use to specify that two conditions must be true to select a folder or file during a search? Which Boolean operator can you use to specify that one of two conditions must be true to select a folder or file during a search?

6. A(n) _____ includes a file property along with an item of data selected from a menu to simplify the process of constructing search criteria.

7. What search condition can you use to locate all files with a file size greater than 100 MB?

8. True or False. You cannot combine file properties with Boolean operators in search criteria.

*Practice the skills
you learned in
the tutorial using
the same case
scenario.*

PRACTICE

Review Assignments

For a list of Data Files in the Review folder, see page 153.

Maya recently hired Charlene Gosney to help her with special client projects. On Charlene's first day of work, Maya describes the types of client support that the two of them must provide to successfully complete their projects. Maya asks you to show Charlene the folder structure and file system used on your computer so Charlene can adapt a similar structure on the new computer she will use.

You will need to copy the Data Files in the Review folder to the computer you are using and allow Windows 7 a short amount of time to index the contents of this new folder.

As you complete each step in these Review Assignments, use a word-processing application, such as Microsoft Word or the WordPad accessory, to record your answers to questions. Also, if you change any settings on the computer you are using, note the original settings so you can restore them later. Complete the following:

1. If necessary, choose the option for displaying the Computer icon on the desktop, enable single-click activation, and display file extensions for known file types.

2. From the Start menu, open your user account folder (the menu option with your user account name). List the names of the folders Windows 7 created for your user account. Which folder contains the files that you work with every day? Have you implemented a folder structure for locating similar types of files? If so, briefly describe how you decided to organize that folder structure (for example, by file content, by file type, or by project). Close this window.

3. Open the Documents library from the Start menu. What are the names of the libraries on your computer? What folders are included in your Documents library? Are there any other folders that you might want to add to your Documents library? Have you created any other libraries? If so, briefly describe those libraries. What new types of libraries might you create in the future?

4. Open your copy of the Tutorial.03 folder. Open a second Documents library window, and then switch to the Public Documents folder. Choose the taskbar option to place the two windows side by side. Copy the Review folder with the Data Files for the Review Assignments to the Public Documents folder, and then close the Tutorial.03 folder with the original Data Files.

5. Check to make sure that the Public Documents folder does not contain a folder with the name *Special Projects*. If so, change the name of the folder by adding **(Original)** to the end of the folder name. Then rename the Review folder in the Public Documents folder to **Special Projects**.

6. Open the Special Projects folder. Use the Navigation pane to expand the folder structure of the Special Projects folder, and then examine the folder structure and files within each subfolder of the Special Projects folder. What suggestions, if any, would you recommend for modifying and improving the folder structure to more logically organize and quickly access the files? Prepare a diagram of the final folder structure you propose.

7. Open the Client Projects folder. If necessary, display the Preview pane, and adjust the Preview pane so it is approximately half of the window's width. Use the Change your view button to adjust your view of the folder's contents to a setting between Extra Large Icons and Large Icons view so all the folder icons fit within the window.

8. What is the path to the Client Projects folder? Assuming this folder is the only folder that contains the word *Client* at the beginning of the folder name, what (DOS) short filename or alias would Windows 7 likely use for this folder?

9. Examine and describe the current appearance of the file icons in this folder. From the Organize menu, choose Folder and search options, and then select the View tab. On the View property sheet, enable the option "Always show icons, never thumbnails," and then apply this change and close the Folder Options dialog box. Examine the files in this folder. Describe how the file icons changed. Open the View property sheet again and turn off the "Always show icons, never thumbnails" option, and then close the Folder Options dialog box, and apply this change.

10. What version of Microsoft Office, if any, is installed on the computer you are using? Select the Break-Even Analysis.xlsx file, and then examine the contents of the file in the Preview pane. Navigate from the Break-Even Analysis tab to the "Income from Sales vs Total Cost" tab in the Preview pane, and then to the "Units Sold Per Month" tab to examine the three worksheets in this file.

11. Examine the information in the Details pane on the Break-Even Analysis.xlsx file. What is the author's name? What is the file size? What is the modified date? Next to the Tags property, click Add a tag, and then type three tags: **Income from Sales; Total Cost; Units Sold**. Use the Save button to save and apply your changes.

12. Right-click the Break-Even Analysis.xlsx thumbnail, and choose the option for viewing its properties. What is this file's file type? What program opens this file? What is this file's size in KB and bytes? What is this file's size in KB and bytes on disk? How much storage space is wasted on disk for this file? What is the location for this file? (*Hint*: To make it easier to record this information, you can select the location by dragging and then, right-clicking the selected text, selecting Copy, switching to Microsoft Word or WordPad, and then clicking the Paste button.)

13. Switch to the Details property sheet, choose the "Remove Properties and Personal Information" option, and then choose the "Remove the following properties from this file" option. Under the Origin section, identify which properties you can remove and which properties you cannot remove. Use the Cancel button to close the Remove Properties dialog box and the Break-Even Analysis.xlsx Properties dialog box without making changes to the file's properties.

14. In the Client Projects window, use the Select all option on the Organize menu to select the contents of this folder, right-click one of the files, and choose the option to view properties. In the group properties dialog box, how many files and folders are stored in this folder? What is the total size of the contents of this folder in KB and bytes? How much storage space on disk in KB and bytes do the contents of this folder require? How much storage space is wasted? Close the group properties dialog box.

15. In the Client Projects folder, view properties of the Visual Arts, Inc folder. What type of object is this folder? What is its size? How much storage space does it use on disk? What does it contain? Close the Visual Arts, Inc Properties dialog box.

16. Right-click the background of the Client Projects folder window, and then choose the option to view its properties. What is the path to the location of this folder? Close the Client Projects Properties dialog box.

17. Open the Visual Arts, Inc folder. Turn off the display of the Preview pane, switch to Details view, and adjust the width of the columns for a best fit. If necessary, display the Date modified, Type, Size, Tags, and Authors headings. What happens when you click the Size column header button? How does this change affect your view of the files in this folder? What happens when you click the Size column header button again? How does this change affect your view of the files in this folder? What happens when you click the Name column header button? How does this change affect your view of the files in this folder? How might you benefit from these features?

18. What happens when you right-click the folder background and choose the option to group by Name? How does this change affect your view of the files in this folder? Click the Name column header button arrow, and then choose Q–Z. What happens, and how does this change affect your view of the files in this folder and the type of

information displayed in the Details pane? How might you benefit from this feature in a folder that contained many more files? Remove the option for grouping files by name.

19. Use Arrange by to stack files by Tag. What happens? How does this change affect your view of the files in this folder? Open the Hire Dates stack. What file does Windows 7 include in this stack? Use the Back button to return to the previous view of all stacks, and then open the Job Titles stack. What file does Windows 7 include in this stack? Go back to the previous folder, and then open the Salaries stack. What file does Windows 7 include in this stack? Explain how Windows 7 includes the same file in three different stacks. How might you benefit from assigning tags to files and then organizing files into stacks by tags? Return to the previous folder, and choose Arrange by Folder. Close the Visual Arts, Inc window.

20. Use the Windows key to open the Start menu, and then use the Search box to locate and open the Desktop Gadget Gallery in the Control Panel. What search string did you enter to locate the Desktop Gadget Gallery? Close the Desktop Gadget Gallery window.

21. If necessary, use the Windows Explorer taskbar button to open the Special Projects folder, and, if necessary, maximize the window, and switch to Details view.

22. Use the folder's Search box to find *only* the file with the filename Balance Sheet.xlsx. What search string did you enter to locate just this one file?

23. Use the folder's Search box to locate all files with *Olson* as part of the Authors property. How did you specify the search criteria? How many files did Windows 7 locate, and what feature did they have in common? Sort the files in ascending order by filename. What are the names of the first and last files?

24. In the folder's Search box, type **jpg**. How many files does Windows 7 find, and what features do these files have in common?

25. Add the Tags column to the folder window (if necessary). In the folder's Search box, use the tags property to locate all tags with *l* (the letter *L*) as the first character in a tag. What search criteria did you enter? How many files did Windows 7 find? What tags met the search criteria you specified? List one of the filenames found with this search criteria.

26. Modify the search criteria to locate only files with the *Loan Analysis* tag. What search criteria did you use, and how many files did Windows 7 find? List one of the filenames found with this search criteria.

27. In the Search box, enter * (an asterisk) as the search criteria to locate all folders and files under the Special Projects folder. How many items does Windows 7 find?

28. Locate and select the file named Conceptual Database.ppsx. In the Details pane, add **Database Concepts** to this file's Tags property. Use the folder's Search box to locate this file using each of the two parts of the tag separately. What search criteria did you use?

29. Use Boolean operators to locate all Excel files with Leif Olson as an author. What search string did you specify, and how many files did Windows 7 find?

30. Save the search. What is the name of the saved search in the Navigation pane under Favorites? Select and right-click the saved search you just created, and choose the option to remove the saved search.

31. In the Search box, enter **Customer Accounts** as the search criteria. Why does Windows 7 find two files with the same filename? Close the Search Results window.

32. Use the Start menu's Search box to open Indexing Options. How many files did Windows 7 index on your computer? What is the status of the indexing operation? What locations does Windows 7 include in the index? Close the Indexing Options dialog box.

33. If you are finished with this assignment, and no longer need the Special Projects folder, delete the Special Projects folder.

34. To restore your computer's default settings, choose the option for not displaying the Computer icon on the desktop, enable double-click activation, and hide file extensions for known file types.

35. If necessary, use Safely Remove Hardware and Eject Media to safely remove your flash drive.

36. Submit your answers to the questions in this Review Assignment to your instructor either in printed or electronic form, as requested. Remember to include your name and any other information requested by your instructor on your assignment.

Use your skills to set up a folder structure for a childcare agency.

APPLY

Case Problem 1

There are no Data Files needed for this Case Problem.

Coberley Child Care   Parents who are preparing themselves to reenter the job market rely on the childcare services provided by Coberley Child Care, a nonprofit agency. Federal, state, and county agencies, as well as corporations, fund the agency's programs with special grants and donations of computer equipment for its administrative staff. Recently, Jan Hostetler, the office manager, acquired a computer for a new employee, and asks you to set up its folder structure using the following guidelines:

- All the employee's folders and files should be stored in one central location and be easily accessible by not only Microsoft Office and other software applications, but by the new employee.
- The new employee will need to set up folders to keep track of the following information:
  - Services provided by Coberley Child Care, including childcare, job referrals, and job training workshops
  - Client support services, such as client counseling and support groups
  - Services offered by local community colleges, such as continuing education, adult reentry programs, and disability resources
  - Agency progress reports, including required federal, state, county, and city progress reports, as well as agency annual reports
  - Grant proposals and funding sources, such as federal, state, county, city, local, and corporate grants, plus small donor contributions
  - Budget documents, income and expense projections, and tax documents
  - Equipment donations, including computers, printers, and office furniture
  - Volunteer information, including volunteer schedules and performance appraisals
  - Email contact information for clients, donors, corporate sponsors, and volunteers as well as federal, state, city, and local officials
  - Software downloads
- Employees and volunteers will need to share certain documents on the agency's network.
- Certain files must be accessible by other users who also have an account on the same computer.

Use a word-processing application such as Microsoft Office Word, or the WordPad accessory, to prepare a list of recommendations on how you might implement these guidelines. In preparing your report, consider what types of folders Windows 7 provides for each user account and how they might be used to implement these guidelines. Describe how you would organize the final folder structure for the different types of documents listed above. Include a diagram of your proposed folder structure for the library where the employee will store the majority of the files that are not shared with other employees. Limit the folder structure to the first two levels under that library. Submit your answers to this case problem to your instructor, either in printed or electronic form, as requested. Remember to include on your assignment your name and any other information requested by your instructor.

Use your skills to sort, group, and create stacks for a mobile technology magazine.

APPLY

Case Problem 2

For a list of Data Files in the Case2 folder, see page 153.

Mobile Technology Plus, Inc.   Javier Estevez works as a writer for *Mobile Technology Plus*, a magazine that focuses on rapidly changing technologies for mobile devices. To meet tight publication deadlines, he asks you to help him sort, group, and create stacks so he can more quickly locate and assemble information from files for upcoming articles.

To complete this case problem, you must have an extracted copy of the Case2 folder in the Tutorial.03 folder. You will also need to allow Windows 7 time to index the contents of this new folder.

As you complete the steps in this case problem, use a word-processing application, such as Microsoft Word or the WordPad accessory, to record your answers to questions. Also, if you change any settings on the computer you are using, note the original settings so you can restore them later. Complete the following:

1. Copy the Case2 folder with the Data Files for this case problem to the Public Documents library, change the name of the Case2 folder to **Mobile Technology Plus**, open this folder, and then, if necessary, hide the Preview pane and switch to Details view.

 EXPLORE

2. Display the column headings for Date modified, Type, Authors, Size, and Tags (if necessary), remove the Folder path column heading (if necessary), and then choose the option for sizing all columns to fit.

3. In the Search box, enter search criteria for displaying all folders and files, change to Details view (if necessary), and then adjust column widths for a best fit. What search criteria did you use? How many items did Windows 7 find?

4. Arrange the search results in ascending order by Type, and then arrange the search results in order by Name. Compare each set of similar file types with the filenames. What happens when you sort first by Type, then by Name? What is the name of the first folder, and what is the name of the first file? Describe two ways you might benefit from sorting first by file type.

5. Arrange the search results in descending order by Size. What is the name of the largest file? Arrange the search results in ascending order by Size. What is the name of the smallest file?

6. Arrange the search results in descending order by Date modified. What is the most recent file? If you want to locate the oldest file, what would you do? How might this type of sort benefit you?

7. Return to the Mobile Technology Plus folder, open the Client Projects folder, and then open the Visual Arts, Inc folder.

8. Display the Authors column (if necessary), group the files by Authors, and if necessary, adjust column widths. What two groups does Windows 7 organize the files into? Do files appear in more than one group? If so, identify the files, and explain why. If not, explain why no files appear in both groups. Which file is assigned tags?

9. Change the grouping option to (None) to clear all changes, and then return to the Mobile Technology Plus folder.

10. Arrange the files in this folder and its subfolders by Tag. How many stacks does Windows 7 create? List the names of the first three stacks. Which stacks contain more than two files, and how can you tell? How does Windows 7 organize files that do not contain tags?

✛ **EXPLORE**　11. Open the Unspecified stack, and add the tag Logo to the Company Logo.docx, Logo Design #1.jpg, Logo Design #2.jpg, Logo Design #3.jpg, and Logo Designs.docx files. What happened to the files that you assigned a tag to? How can you verify this change? Remove all the stacks.

12. If you are finished with this case problem, and no longer need the Mobile Technology Plus folder, delete the Mobile Technology Plus folder.

13. If necessary, use Safely Remove Hardware and Eject Media to safely remove your flash drive.

14. Submit your answers to this case problem to your instructor, either in printed or electronic form, as requested. Remember to include on your assignment your name and any other information requested by your instructor.

Extend what you've learned to test search criteria for a training company.

CHALLENGE

Case Problem 3

For a list of Data Files in the Case3 folder, see page 153.

Yoshiko Learning Center, Inc.　Yoshiko Tanaka and her staff at Yoshiko Learning Center provide customized training for employees of companies in Tokyo. Recently, a new client contracted with Yoshiko Tanaka for a 3-day training session on how to perform searches. To prepare for this training session, Yoshiko asks you to test different search criteria and help her prepare a list of examples that she can use to demonstrate different search features. She intends to also use the information you compile as a handout for the training session.

As you complete the steps in this case problem, use a word-processing application, such as Microsoft Word or the WordPad accessory, to record your answers to questions. Also, if you change any settings on the computer you are using, note the original settings so you can restore them later. Complete the following:

1. Copy the Case3 folder with the Data Files for this case problem to the Public Documents folder, change the name of the Case3 folder to **Yoshiko Learning Center**, and then open this folder. Switch to Content view and, if necessary, close the Preview pane.

✛ **EXPLORE**　2. Enter the search criteria **name:projection** in the Search box. Switch to Content view (if necessary), and then list the names of the folders and files in the search results. Explain how Windows 7 selected each item.

✛ **EXPLORE**　3. Enter the search criteria **filename:projection** in the Search box. List the names of the folders and files in the search results. Compare these search results with those for the previous step. What conclusion do you draw about the last two search criteria?

✛ **EXPLORE**　4. Type **kind:** in the Search box, and wait for Windows 7 to display a list of file kind types, and then select Document from the dropdown list. Arrange the files by Type. List the names of the three file types in the search results. How might you use this feature to locate files?

✛ **EXPLORE**　5. What search criteria can you use to locate the following files?

a. Files with *loan* and *analysis* anywhere in their filenames. List the names of the folders and files in the search results. *Note:* The files you locate must contain both of these words in the filename. How could you narrow down these search results to locate folders and files?

b. Files with *loan* or *analysis* anywhere in their tags? List the names of the folders and files in the search results. *Note:* The files you locate must contain one of these words in the tag.

6. What search criteria can you use to locate all files with the exact phrase *Hire Dates* in their Tags property? What file does Windows 7 find with this search condition?

7. What search criteria can you use to locate all files with yesterday's date in the Date Modified property?

⊕ EXPLORE

8. What search criteria can you use to locate the following files?

   a. All files with a date earlier this month

   b. All files with sizes less than 10 MB

   c. All files authored only by Maya Cabral (and not coauthored by Leif Olson) with *clients* or *profits* in the Tags property. What file or files does Windows 7 find with this search criteria?

   d. All files with both the tags *days outstanding* and *invoices*. What are the names of the two files that Windows 7 finds?

9. If you are finished with this case problem and no longer need the Yoshiko Learning Center folder, delete the Yoshiko Learning Center folder.

10. If necessary, use Safely Remove Hardware and Eject Media to safely remove your flash drive.

11. Submit your answers to this case problem to your instructor, either in printed or electronic form, as requested. Remember to include on your assignment your name and any other information requested by your instructor.

Extend what you've learned to test search techniques for a financial investment company.

CHALLENGE

Case Problem 4

For a list of Data Files in the Case4 folder, see page 153.

Hamer Investment Group You work for the Help Desk at Hamer Investment Group, a multinational corporation with its headquarters in Berlin, Germany. To help staff locate important documents quickly, you rely on the use of Boolean operators, comparison operators, search filters, and file properties. To maximize the use of these features, you decide to test some new search criteria to determine their usefulness in your job.

As you complete the steps in this case problem, use a word-processing application, such as Microsoft Word or the WordPad accessory, to record your answers to questions. Also, if you change any settings on the computer you are using, note the original settings so you can restore them later. *Note*: Search conditions that you type are shown in **boldface**. Complete the following:

1. Copy the Case4 folder with the Data Files for this case problem to the Public Documents folder, change the name of the Case4 folder to **Hamer Investment Group**, and then open this folder. Switch to Content view and, if necessary, close the Preview pane.

2. Right-click the background of the Hamer Investment Group folder, and choose the option to view its properties. How many folders and files are contained in this folder? Add these values together. How many total objects are contained in this folder? Close the Hamer Investment Group Properties dialog box.

⊕ EXPLORE

3. Type the following search criteria in the Search box: *****. Without accidentally clicking the background of the folder window, examine the Details pane. How many items does Windows 7 find? Using the information you gleaned from Step 2 and this step, what do the search results tell you about the use of this search criteria?

4. Type the following search criteria in the Search box: **folder** Examine the Details pane. How many items does Windows 7 find? Using the information you gleaned from Step 2 and this step, what do the search results tell you about the use of this search criteria?

⊕ EXPLORE

5. Type the following search criteria in the Search box: **picture** Examine the Details pane. How many items does Windows 7 find? Using the information you gleaned from Step 4 and this step, what do the search results tell you about the use of this search criteria?

6. Type the **NOT word** search criteria in the Search box. How many items does Windows 7 find? Arrange the search results in order by type, and then examine the file types. What do the search results tell you about the use of this search criterion?

7. Switch to Content view (if necessary), and then type the **company** search criteria in the Search box. How many items does Windows 7 find? Choose the option for arranging the contents of this folder by Type. What types of objects and what file types are listed in these search results?

8. Delete your search criteria, and replace it with the following: **company NOT folder** How does this search criteria change the search results you found in the previous step?

⊕ EXPLORE

9. Perform the following searches, and use the search results to answer the questions about each search:

   a. What files does Windows 7 find if you enter **#?.jpg** in the Search box? Explain how Windows 7 found these specific files.

   b. What files does Windows 7 find if you enter **name:20** in the Search box? Explain how Windows 7 found these specific files. How did this search criterion benefit you? If you add more files to the Hamer Investment Group, what other files might this search criteria locate?

   c. What files does Windows 7 find if you enter **authors:(Maya AND Leif)** in the Search box? What feature do these two files have in common?

   d. What files does Windows 7 find if you enter **(name:sales OR name:summary)** in the Search box? Identify the three ways in which Windows 7 selected these specific files.

   e. What files does Windows 7 find if you enter **(name:sales OR name:summary) NOT folder** in the Search box? How does this search criteria change the search results you found in the previous step? Identify the four ways in which Windows 7 selected these specific files.

   f. Identify the files that Windows 7 finds when you enter this search condition: **(author:leif AND datemodified:9/1/2013..12/31/2013) NOT tags:="Loan Analysis"**

   Explain how Windows 7 applied this search criterion to the search results.

10. If you are finished with this case problem, and no longer need the Hamer Investment Group folder, delete the Hamer Investment Group folder.

11. If necessary, use Safely Remove Hardware and Eject Media to safely remove your flash drive.

12. Submit your answers to this case problem to your instructor, either in printed or electronic form, as requested. Remember to include on your assignment your name and any other information requested by your instructor.

ENDING DATA FILES

There are no ending Data Files needed for this tutorial.

TUTORIAL **4**

Creating and Customizing Shortcuts

Working Smart with Shortcuts

OBJECTIVES

Session 4.1
- Create shortcuts to a drive, folder, and file
- View shortcut properties
- Customize shortcuts
- Create shortcuts to programs
- Create a new shortcut from an existing shortcut
- Update a shortcut's path

Session 4.2
- Add a shortcut to the Start menu and taskbar
- Create a Control Panel shortcut
- Use the Create Shortcut Wizard
- Create a link in the Navigation pane
- Customize a drive icon
- Create Internet shortcuts
- Add a shortcut to the Startup folder

Case | *Upsilon Air*

Upsilon Air in San Diego, California, offers airline service to major vacation spots along the Pacific Rim and throughout Oceania. Lance Quattrone, an employee in the advertising group at Upsilon Air, develops custom advertising to showcase the company's travel packages. To increase his productivity, Lance relies on shortcuts to quickly locate documents, folders, files, and Web sites as well as Windows 7 resources on his desktop and laptop computers.

In this tutorial, you will create shortcuts to a drive, folder, and file; view shortcut properties; and customize shortcuts. You will create a shortcut to a program, create a new shortcut from an existing shortcut, and work with shortcut paths. You will customize the Navigation pane by creating a shortcut that is a link to a folder. You will add a shortcut to the Start menu, create Control Panel shortcuts, customize drive icons, and create and use Internet shortcuts. Finally, you will add a shortcut to your Startup folder.

STARTING DATA FILES

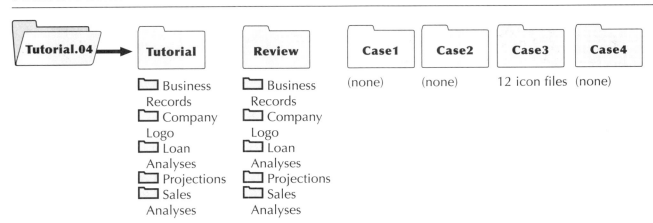

Tutorial.04 →	Tutorial	Review	Case1	Case2	Case3	Case4
	☐ Business Records ☐ Company Logo ☐ Loan Analyses ☐ Projections ☐ Sales Analyses	☐ Business Records ☐ Company Logo ☐ Loan Analyses ☐ Projections ☐ Sales Analyses	(none)	(none)	12 icon files	(none)

SESSION 4.1 VISUAL OVERVIEW

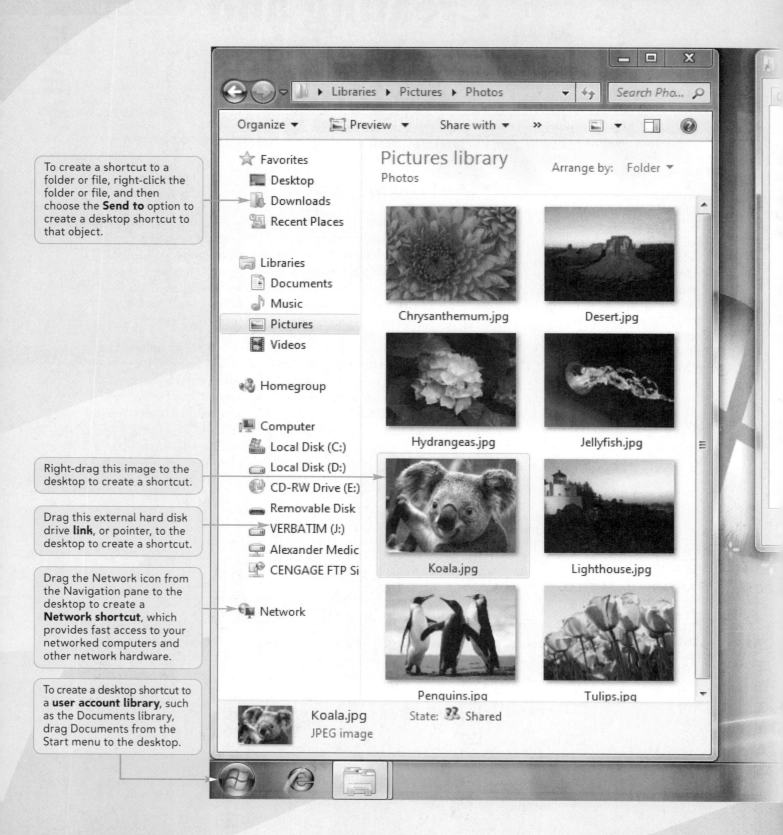

To create a shortcut to a folder or file, right-click the folder or file, and then choose the **Send to** option to create a desktop shortcut to that object.

Right-drag this image to the desktop to create a shortcut.

Drag this external hard disk drive **link**, or pointer, to the desktop to create a shortcut.

Drag the Network icon from the Navigation pane to the desktop to create a **Network shortcut**, which provides fast access to your networked computers and other network hardware.

To create a desktop shortcut to a **user account library**, such as the Documents library, drag Documents from the Start menu to the desktop.

DESKTOP SHORTCUTS

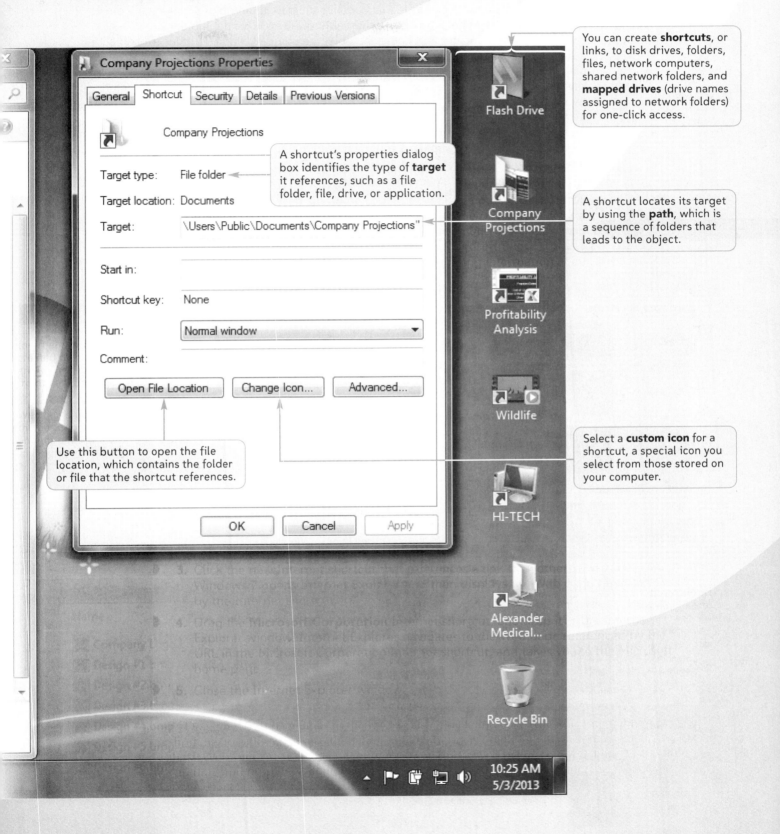

You can create **shortcuts**, or links, to disk drives, folders, files, network computers, shared network folders, and **mapped drives** (drive names assigned to network folders) for one-click access.

A shortcut's properties dialog box identifies the type of **target** it references, such as a file folder, file, drive, or application.

A shortcut locates its target by using the **path**, which is a sequence of folders that leads to the object.

Use this button to open the file location, which contains the folder or file that the shortcut references.

Select a **custom icon** for a shortcut, a special icon you select from those stored on your computer.

Using Shortcuts

A shortcut is a special type of file that contains the path to an object, making it a direct link to that object. When you click a shortcut in Web style (or double-click in Classic style), Windows 7 locates and opens the object referenced by the shortcut. The object of a shortcut might be a program, drive, library, folder, or file. An Internet shortcut is a special type of shortcut that contains the URL (Uniform Resource Locator) for a specific Web site, and therefore provides a direct link to a Web site. Network shortcut paths include two backslash characters at the beginning of the path. For example, \\HI-TECH identifies a computer on a network, and \\HI-TECH\Users\Lance identifies a user account folder on that same network. This type of path is called the **UNC path** (for Universal Naming Convention), and it is a standard approach used to reference servers, printers, and other resources on a network. Figure 4-1 and Figure 4-2 contain examples of different types of shortcuts that you can create on your computer. As you can tell from these figures, the shortcut icon is a small box with an arrow ![arrow icon] in the lower-left corner of the object's icon.

Figure 4-1	Examples of hardware, software, folder, and Control Panel shortcuts

Type of Shortcut	Shortcut	Path or Object Name
Hardware Shortcuts		
Drive C	Local Disk (C)	C:\
DVD Drive	CD Drive	D:\
Flash Drive	Removable Disk (G)	G:\
Software Shortcuts		
Microsoft Word 2010	Microsoft Word 2010	Microsoft Word 2010 ("C:\Program Files\Microsoft Office\Office14\WINWORD.EXE")
Microsoft Outlook 2010	Microsoft Outlook 2010	Microsoft Outlook 2010 "C:\Program Files\Microsoft Office\Office14\OUTLOOK.EXE")
Internet Explorer	Internet Explorer	"C:\Program Files\Internet Explorer\iexplore.exe"
Windows DVD Maker	Windows DVD Maker	"%ProgramFiles%\DVD Maker\DVDMaker.exe"
Command Prompt	Command Prompt	%windir%\system32\cmd.exe

Figure 4-1		Examples of hardware, software, folder, and Control Panel shortcuts (continued)

Type of Shortcut	Shortcut	Path or Object Name
Folder Shortcuts		
Documents Library		C:\Users\Clients\AppData\Roaming\Microsoft\Windows\Libraries\Documents.library-ms
Client Projects		"C:\Users\Clients\Documents\Client Projects"
Control Panel Shortcuts		
Folder Options		Control Panel\All Control Panel Items\Folder Options, OR %systemRoot%\system32\rundll32.exe %systemRoot%\system32\shell32.dll,Options_RunDLL 0
Sync Center		Control Panel\All Control Panel Items\Sync Center, OR %SystemRoot%\System32\mobsync.exe

Figure 4-2		Examples of document, network, and Internet shortcuts

Type of Shortcut	Shortcut	Path or Object Name
Document Shortcuts		
Sales Projection Memo.docx (Microsoft Word Document)		"C:\Users\Clients\Documents\Projections\Sales Projection Memo.docx"
Five Year Growth Plan.xlsx (Microsoft Excel Document)		"C:\Users\Clients\Documents\Projections\Five Year Growth Plan.xlsx"
Company Logo.jpg		"C:\Users\Clients\Documents\Logos\Company Logo.jpg"
Sleep Away		"C:\Users\Public\Music\Sample Music\Sleep Away.mp3"
Network Shortcuts		
Windows 7 Professional Computer		\\HI-TECH

Figure 4-2 Examples of document, network, and Internet shortcuts (continued)

Type of Shortcut	Shortcut	Path or Object Name
Alexander Medical Research Institute (HI-TECH) (Z) (Mapped Network Drive Z:)	 Alexander Medical Research Institute (HI-TECH) (Z)	Z:\
HP LaserJet network printer	 HP LaserJet (HI-TECH)	"\\HI-TECH\HP LaserJet"
Alexander Medical Research Institute network folder	 Alexander Medical Research Institute (HI-TECH)	"\\HI-TECH\Alexander Medical Research Institute"
Internet Shortcuts		
Course Technology Educator's Corner	 Course Technology Educator's Corner	http://cengagesites.com/academic/?site=3136
Microsoft Corporation	 Microsoft Corporation	http://www.microsoft.com/en/us/default.aspx

Shortcut icons to system objects, such as drives, are identical to the icon that Windows 7 uses for the object itself. The same is true for application shortcuts and document shortcuts. If you create a shortcut to a folder, Windows 7 uses the same type of folder icon. Likewise, if the shortcut references a system folder, such as My Pictures, it also has a custom icon. Shortcuts to network drives and folders have the same shortcut icon. Internet shortcuts use an icon that identifies the default Web browser used to open the Internet shortcut, or a custom icon created by the Web site.

You can place shortcuts on the desktop or in folders where you frequently work. For example, you might place a shortcut to your word-processing application, or even to a document that you work on daily, on the desktop or on the taskbar. You might store copies of the same shortcut in different places so you can quickly access the object from those locations. Shortcuts are also useful in networked environments because you do not have to browse the network looking for a network resource, such as a network folder; instead, you can use a shortcut to go directly to that resource from the desktop or taskbar.

Getting Started

To complete this tutorial, you need to display the Computer icon on the desktop, switch your computer to single-click activation, and activate the option for displaying file extensions.

To set up your computer:

▶ **1.** If Windows 7 does not display a Computer icon on the desktop, open the Start menu, right-click **Computer**, click **Show on Desktop**, and then close the Start menu.

▶ **2.** If you need to enable single-click activation, open the Start menu, type **folder options** in the Search box, press the **Enter** key, and under "Click items as follows" on the General property sheet in the Folder Options dialog box, click the **Single-click to open an item (point to select)** option button, and then click the **Underline icon titles only when I point at them** option button.

▶ **3.** Click the **View** tab, click the **Hide extensions for known file types** check box and remove the check mark to display file extensions, click the **OK** button to close the Folder Options dialog box and apply these changes, and then close the Computer window.

Copying Data Files to the Public Documents Folder

Next, you are going to copy the Tutorial folder from the Tutorial.04 folder provided with the Windows 7 for Power User Data Files from your flash drive, the Documents folder, or a network folder to the Public Documents folder.

To copy the Tutorial folder to your Public Documents folder:

▶ **1.** Make sure you downloaded and extracted your copy of the Windows 7 for Power User Data Files.

▶ **2.** Close all open windows.

▶ **3.** To copy the Tutorial folder from your flash drive, attach your flash drive to a USB port or to a USB cable on the computer you are using, and after Windows 7 displays an AutoPlay dialog box for the flash drive, click **Open folder to view files**. Next, open the Tutorial.04 folder.

   Trouble? If Windows 7 does not display an AutoPlay dialog box, click the Computer icon on the desktop, click the icon for your flash drive in the Computer window, open the folder that contains the Windows 7 for Power User's Data Files, and then open the Tutorial.04 folder.

▶ **4.** If you are not copying the Tutorial folder from a flash drive, open a window onto the Documents library or the network folder that contains a copy of the Tutorial folder under the Tutorial.04 folder.

▶ **5.** From the Start menu, open **Documents**, click the **Documents** library in the Navigation pane, point to **Documents** under Libraries, click the **expand** icon ▷ , and then click **Public Documents** in the Navigation pane, or if your instructor or technical support staff want you to use another folder, locate and open that folder. Windows 7 opens the Public Documents folder (or the folder your instructor or technical support staff requested).

▶ **6.** Right-click the **taskbar**, and then click **Show windows side by side**. Windows 7 adjusts the two folder windows so they are placed side by side on the desktop and are equal in size. Windows 7 places the last folder window that you opened on the left side of the desktop.

7. Drag the **Tutorial** folder from the flash drive folder or network folder window to the Public Documents folder window (or to the folder requested by your instructor or technical support staff), and then release the mouse button. Windows 7 copies the Tutorial folder to the Public Documents folder window (or to the window for the folder requested by your instructor or technical support staff).

8. Close the flash drive folder window, but keep the Public Documents folder window, or the window for the folder requested by your instructor or technical support staff, open.

9. To rename the Tutorial folder, select the **Tutorial** folder (if necessary), press the **F2** (Rename) key, type **Upsilon Air**, and then press the **Enter** key.

10. Close the Public Documents folder window, and the folder window that contains the original copy of the Tutorial folder.

Now you're ready to create shortcuts so you can access the folders, files, and features you use every workday.

Creating Shortcuts

If you want to create a desktop shortcut to a drive, folder, file, or program, you can use any of the following techniques:

- **Dragging**—To create a shortcut to a drive, you open the Computer window and drag a drive icon to the desktop. You can also drag a drive from the Navigation pane of a folder window to the desktop. However, you should not use this approach to create a shortcut to a folder that contains installed software or to a folder or file in your Documents library because Windows 7 will move the program, folder, or file instead of creating a shortcut. To be on the safe side, do not drag to the desktop the file icon for an application or any other type of program from a folder where it's installed.
- **Right-dragging**—If you right-drag the icon for a drive, folder, file, or program to the desktop, Windows 7 displays a shortcut menu, which includes an option for creating a shortcut.
- **Right-clicking**—If you right-click the icon for a drive, folder, file, or program, a shortcut menu opens from which you can choose the option for creating a shortcut to that object. If you perform this operation on a drive in the Computer window, Windows 7 places the shortcut on the desktop. If you perform this operation on the Windows folder or one of its subfolders or files, or if you perform this operation on one of the folders or files in the Program Files folder, Windows 7 informs you that it cannot create a shortcut in this location and asks if you want to place the shortcut on the desktop instead. If you perform this operation on a folder or file in the Documents library, Windows 7 creates the shortcut and stores it in the default save location (namely, the My Documents folder). You can then move the shortcut to the desktop.
- **Using the Send to menu**—If you right-click a library, folder, file, or program, and then point to Send to on the shortcut menu, you can choose Desktop (create shortcut) to place a shortcut to that object on the desktop. However, you cannot create a desktop shortcut to the Libraries folder. This approach is the easiest, fastest, and the safest one to use.

As you step through the tutorial, you will use these techniques and other techniques to create shortcuts. Then, as you work on your computer, you can use the technique that best suits your needs and your way of working.

Creating Shortcuts to Drives

To meet the increase in customer interest in its Pacific Rim flights, Upsilon Air hired you to assist Lance in the advertising department. After setting up your new computer, Lance suggests that you customize your computer and create the shortcuts you need for your new job. Lance recommends that you start by creating a desktop shortcut to your flash drive.

To create a desktop shortcut to your flash drive:

▶ 1. If necessary, attach your flash drive to the computer you are using. If Windows 7 displays an AutoPlay dialog box for your flash drive or opens a window or dialog box onto the flash drive, close the dialog box or window.

   Trouble? If you do not have a flash drive, you can create a shortcut to another disk drive, such as your hard disk drive, usually identified as Local Disk (C:) in the Computer window. The information you examine for another drive may differ from that described in the subsequent steps and from that shown in the figures.

▶ 2. Click the **Computer** icon on the desktop, and if Windows 7 maximizes the Computer window, click the **Restore Down** button [image], and then, if necessary, resize and drag the window to the right so you can see the left side of the desktop.

▶ 3. Drag your **flash drive** icon from the Computer window to the desktop. As you do, Windows 7 displays an icon for your flash drive: a ToolTip with a shortcut arrow icon [image], and the text "Create link in Desktop." See Figure 4-3.

Figure 4-3	Creating a drive shortcut using drag and drop

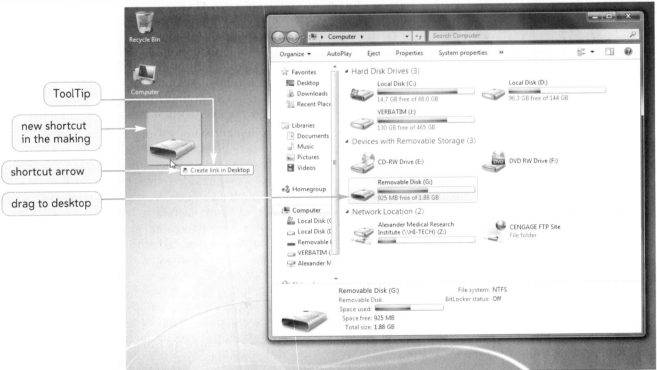

4. **Release the mouse button.** Windows 7 creates a desktop shortcut to your flash drive. See Figure 4-4. If the flash drive manufacturer or you have not assigned your flash drive a different name, Windows 7 names the flash drive shortcut "Removable Disk" followed by the actual drive letter in parentheses, a space, a dash, another space, and then the word "Shortcut", such as Removable Disk (G) - Shortcut. Your drive name may differ from that shown in Figure 4-4. Your flash drive icon might be identical to the default drive icon used for removable disk drives, as shown in Figure 4-4, or it might have a custom icon. Later in the tutorial, you will create a custom icon for your flash drive.

| Figure 4-4 | New Removable Disk drive desktop shortcut |

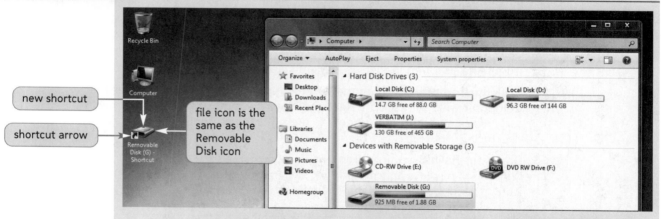

5. **Close the Computer window.**

6. **Point to the flash drive shortcut,** press the **F2** (Rename) key, type **Flash Drive**, and then press the **Enter** key to change the shortcut's name.

7. **Click the Flash Drive** shortcut icon. Windows 7 opens a window for your flash drive. Now you have one-step access to your flash drive.

8. **Close the window for your flash drive.**

Although Windows 7 displays an AutoPlay dialog box with an option for opening a folder for the flash drive when you first attach it to your computer, the flash drive short-cut on the desktop is still useful because you might close the flash drive window, and then later need to open it again, so the shortcut will speed up access to the flash drive. If your flash drive window is not open, and if you do not have this shortcut, you will need to click the Computer icon on the desktop, and then click the flash drive icon in the Computer window to view the contents of your flash drive. That operation would require two steps each time you opened a window onto your flash drive. Likewise, you can right-click the Windows Explorer taskbar button, and if the flash drive is in the Jump List, you can then open the flash drive. However, this approach also requires two steps each time you use it. If you do not have a Computer icon on the desktop, you must open the Computer window from the Start menu, requiring a total of three steps. In contrast, this shortcut requires only one step, saving you one or two steps each time you use it, and providing faster access to the contents of your flash drive. You can also drag the short-cut to the taskbar and pin it to Windows Explorer so you can quickly access your flash drive's contents while working in a maximized window that covers the desktop.

REFERENCE

Creating a Shortcut to a Flash Drive

- If necessary, attach your flash drive to the computer you are using. If Windows 7 displays an AutoPlay dialog box for your flash drive, or opens a window or dialog box onto the flash drive, close the dialog box or window.
- Click the Computer icon on the desktop, or open a Computer window from the Start menu.
- If the Computer window is maximized, click the Restore Down button, and resize and move the Computer window so you can also see the desktop.
- Drag the icon for your flash drive (or any other drive) from the Computer window to the desktop, release the mouse button, and if necessary, use the F2 (Rename) key to change the name of the shortcut to a more useful and shorter icon title.
- Close the Computer window.

Instead of creating drive shortcuts one at a time, you can select all of the drives for which you want to create shortcuts, and drag them to the desktop, or you can right-click one of the selected drives, and then click Create Shortcut. You can use any of the following approaches to select multiple objects in a window:

- **Using a selection rectangle**—If the objects you want to select are located next to each other, you can drag a selection rectangle around the objects with the mouse pointer. You can also use this feature when you are selecting objects on the desktop.
- **Using Ctrl+point**—If you want to select multiple objects that are not adjacent to each other, and if you are working in Web style with single-click activation, you select the first object by pointing to it until Windows 7 highlights it, hold down the Ctrl key, point to each of the next objects, and then release the Ctrl key. The selected objects constitute a **collection**; in other words, a group of objects that may or may not be located adjacent to each other. If you need to remove an object from a collection, you point to it again while you press and hold the Ctrl key.
- **Using Ctrl+click**—If you are working in Classic style with double-click activation, you click the first object, hold down the Ctrl key while you slowly click each of the next objects, and then you release the Ctrl key. If you click too quickly in a folder window, Windows 7 might make duplicate copies of all the objects you've selected.
- **Using Shift+point**—If you are working in Web style with single-click activation, and want to select objects adjacent to each other, point to the first object to select it, hold down the Shift key, point to the last object, and then release the Shift key. Windows 7 selects all the objects between the first and the last objects that you selected. The first and last objects in the selection can also be in different columns if you are working in Details view in a folder window.
- **Using Shift+click**—If you are using Classic style with double-click activation, and want to select objects adjacent to each other, click the first object to select it, hold down the Shift key, click the last object, and then release the Shift key. Windows 7 selects all the objects between the first and the last objects that you selected. The first and last objects in the selection can also be in different columns if you are working in Details view in a folder window. This feature is called **Shift clicking**, and you can also use it within application windows. For example, you can use it to select a sentence that spans more than one line, or to select a block of spreadsheet cells.
- **Using check boxes**—If you open the View property sheet in the Folder Options dialog box, and enable the option for using check boxes to select objects within a window, you can point to and click the check box for each object. You can also use this feature to select desktop objects.
- **Using Ctrl+A (Select All)**—If you want to select all the objects in a window, you can press Ctrl+A (or click Select All on the Organize menu).

After trying various selection techniques, you can decide which one you prefer. It's always a good idea to be familiar with multiple approaches for performing the same type of task in case you work on computers set up in different ways. You might also find that one technique works well in one window or situation, and another technique works better in another window or situation.

Viewing Properties of a Shortcut

Like any other type of object, you can right-click a shortcut, and then choose the option to view its properties. Lance encourages you to use this technique so you can learn more about how shortcuts work and how to customize shortcuts.

To view shortcut properties:

▶ **1.** Right-click the **Flash Drive** shortcut icon, and then click **Properties**. Windows 7 opens the Flash Drive Properties dialog box, and displays information about the shortcut on the Shortcut property sheet. See Figure 4-5.

| Figure 4-5 | Viewing properties of a flash drive shortcut |

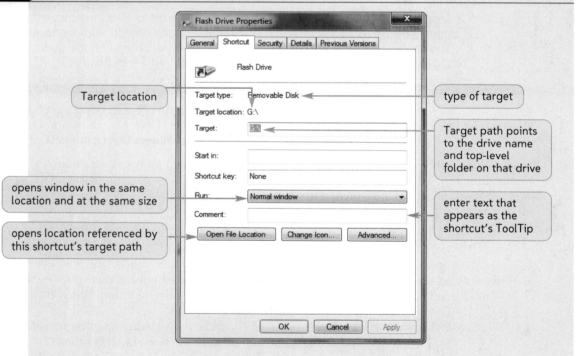

Windows 7 displays the shortcut's icon, the shortcut's name, the Target type (Removable Disk), the Target location (for example, G:\), and the Target's path (for example, G:\). Your Target location and Target path might differ. As you can tell from the backslash in the Target path box, the shortcut references the top-level folder of your flash drive.

In the Run box, Windows 7 displays "Normal window," indicating that Windows 7 displays the window at the same location and same size as the last time you opened or resized the window. From the Run list, you can also choose to open the object in a maximized window (full screen) or a minimized window (as a taskbar button). If you always work in a maximized window, adjusting this setting saves you yet one more step when setting up your computer for the work you're going to do. The minimized window option is useful if you open multiple windows when you first start working so you have access to everything you need, but do not plan on working in one or more of the windows until later. You can also define a keyboard shortcut for use with a shortcut, create a ToolTip by entering text in the Comment box, open the target's location, or customize the shortcut's icon.

To set the Run option, and specify a ToolTip:

▶ **1.** Click the **Run arrow button**, and then click **Maximized**. The next time you use this desktop shortcut, Windows 7 will maximize the flash drive window.

▶ **2.** In the Comment box, type **Open my flash drive** as the shortcut's ToolTip.

▶ **3.** Click the **Apply** button to apply these changes, but keep the Flash Drive Properties dialog box open for the next set of steps.

If you are customizing a computer for a beginning user who is not familiar with computers or with Windows 7, it's a good idea to include a ToolTip for desktop shortcuts you create for that person, and then show them how to display the ToolTip. They can then use the ToolTip to refresh their memories about a shortcut's purpose, or locate the shortcut they need as they work.

INSIGHT

Creating Keyboard Shortcuts for Desktop Shortcuts

If much of your computer work involves creating and modifying text files, such as word-processing documents and spreadsheets, you can save time by creating keyboard shortcuts for your desktop shortcuts. You can then use a flash drive desktop shortcut to access the files on your flash drive, for example, without leaving your document. To assign a keyboard shortcut, you open the Properties dialog box for the shortcut, click inside the Shortcut key box where you see "None", and type a character that you want to use for the keyboard shortcut (for example, *F* for *flash drive*). Windows 7 replaces "None" with Ctrl+Alt+F in the Shortcut box. To use this keyboard shortcut, you press and hold the Ctrl and Alt keys while you press the F key, and then release all three keys. Keyboard shortcut keys for shortcuts take precedence over the same key combination used in a Windows application. If you assign a keyboard shortcut and want to remove it later, click inside the Shortcut key box on the General property sheet of the shortcut, and then press the Backspace or Delete key. Windows 7 then displays "None" in the Shortcut key.

Besides viewing and changing general shortcut properties, you can examine the General property sheet for additional settings assigned to the shortcut and advanced attributes.

To locate the shortcut's target and view other shortcut properties:

▶ **1.** Click the **Open File Location** button. Windows 7 opens the Computer window and highlights the target for the desktop shortcut, namely, your flash drive. This feature is one way to quickly open the Target location or the location of the object.

▶ **2.** Close the Computer window.

▶ **3.** Click the **General** tab in the Flash Drive Properties dialog box. On the General property sheet, Windows 7 displays information about the shortcut name (you can change it to another name here), the type of file (Shortcut), a shortcut description, the shortcut file's location (the path to the folder with the shortcut), the shortcut's file size, the amount of storage space it uses on disk, and the dates and times the shortcut was created, modified, and accessed. Windows 7 also identifies what attributes are assigned to the object. See Figure 4-6. The details for your shortcut may differ.

Figure 4-6　　Viewing general flash drive shortcut properties

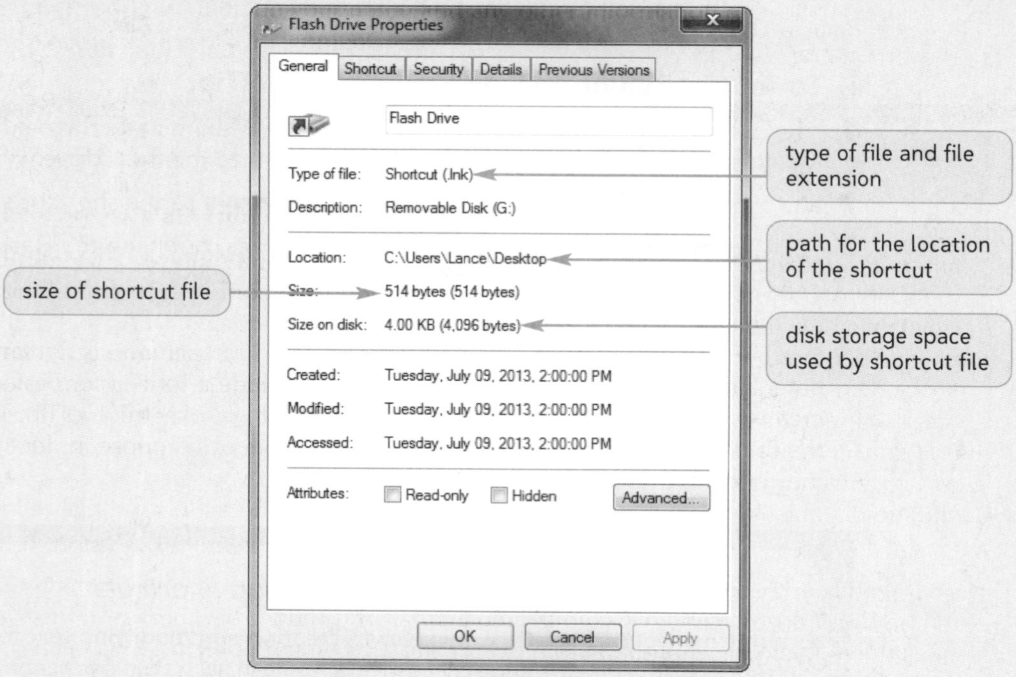

size of shortcut file

type of file and file extension

path for the location of the shortcut

disk storage space used by shortcut file

Windows 7 identifies the object as a Shortcut, and notes the shortcut's file extension as .lnk (with the lowercase letter *l*, not the number 1), which stands for *Link*, indicating that the shortcut is a link to another object. If you create a shortcut on the desktop, the path for the location of the shortcut points to the Desktop folder for your user account. On the computer used for this figure, the shortcut is stored in Lance's desktop folder—C:\Users\ Lance\Desktop. This shortcut, which is 474 bytes in size, is allocated 4,096 bytes (4.00 KB, or 4 × 1,024 bytes/kilobyte) on the disk; however, 3,622 bytes of the allocated disk space is not used by the shortcut and is therefore unavailable to any other file. In other words, the shortcut only uses 12 percent of the storage space allocated to it. The other 88 percent of the allocated storage space is wasted storage space. You will examine this issue in more detail in Tutorial 5.

To view advanced attribute settings:

▶ 1. Click the **Advanced** button. Windows 7 opens the Advanced Attributes dialog box. See Figure 4-7. Because you just created this shortcut, Windows 7 notes that your file is ready for archiving and that it is indexed for faster searching.

Figure 4-7   **Viewing advanced attributes**

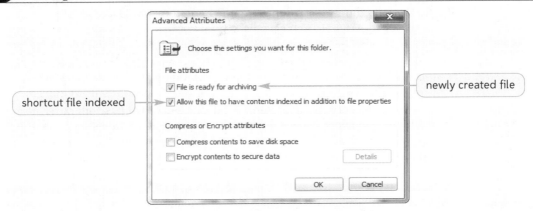

The "File is ready for archiving" means your backup software will automatically include this file in your next backup (covered in more detail in Tutorial 10). **Backup software** is software that copies folders and files from your hard disk drive to a disk or another hard disk drive. The resulting copy is called a **backup** and enables you to restore your files if needed.

To examine other settings:

▶ **1.** Click the **Cancel** button (or press the **Esc** key) to close the Advanced Attributes dialog box (without inadvertently making changes).

▶ **2.** Click the **Details** tab. On the Details property sheet, Windows 7 displays file properties for this shortcut. See Figure 4-8. Note that Windows 7 identifies the Owner of this file and the name of the Computer that contains this shortcut. Your file properties will differ. The "A" attribute stands for "Archive."

Figure 4-8   **Viewing details of flash drive shortcut properties**

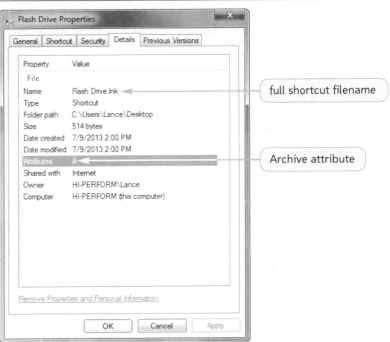

▶ **3.** Click the **Cancel** button to close the Flash Drive Properties dialog box.

▶ **4.** Point to the desktop shortcut, but do not click the shortcut icon. Windows 7 displays the ToolTip you created earlier.

The full filename for the Flash Drive shortcut is "Flash Drive.lnk". The alias, or short filename, for this shortcut is (most likely) FLASHD~1.LNK. By default, Windows does not display the file extension for desktop shortcuts.

Lance points out that by comparing the amount of storage space used on disk with the size of the shortcut, you can tell that shortcuts waste a disproportionate amount of space compared to their size; however, the trade-off is that they are very useful. One way to gain additional storage space on your hard disk is to remove shortcuts that you no longer use.

REFERENCE

Viewing Properties of a Shortcut

- Right-click a shortcut icon, and then click Properties.
- In the Properties dialog box for the shortcut, use the Shortcut property sheet to view a shortcut's target, specify a shortcut key, open the target window, include a comment for use as a ToolTip, and open the location where Windows 7 stores the shortcut file.
- Click the General tab to view information about the path, actual size, allocated space, and attributes of a shortcut, or to change the shortcut name and attribute settings.
- Click the Advanced button on the General property sheet to view information about advanced attributes, such as whether a file is ready for archiving and whether Windows 7 indexes the file for faster searching.
- Use the Details tab to view file properties that you can use when searching for this shortcut.
- Close the Properties dialog box for the shortcut.

Shortcuts simplify many routine tasks that you perform daily, and they allow you to work smarter. If you frequently work with other drives, including the hard disk drive itself, flash drives, a DVD drive, a CD drive, or drives for memory cards, you can create shortcuts for these drives, and thereby save yourself time and effort when you need to access their contents.

Creating Shortcuts to Folders

As noted earlier, when you create a shortcut to a folder, you *cannot* drag that folder to the desktop as you dragged the drive icon for your flash drive because Windows 7 will *move* the folder if the folder is on the same drive as the Desktop folder for your user account. Instead, you can right-click the folder, drag it to the desktop, and then choose the option to create a shortcut on the shortcut menu. You can also create the folder shortcut in the window that contains the folder and then drag the shortcut to the desktop; however, you must make sure you choose the correct object to drag (the shortcut, not the folder). If you are creating a shortcut to a folder that contains software (or even a document folder), it is *safer* to use the option for sending an object to the desktop as a shortcut. Then you will not inadvertently drag the original folder to the desktop by mistake.

Because your flash drive shortcut has proved useful, Lance suggests you create shortcuts to folders that you use every day, starting with your Documents library.

To create a shortcut to your Documents library:

1. Open the Start menu, and then drag **Documents** from the Start menu to the desktop. Windows 7 creates a desktop shortcut to your Documents library. As you drag Documents from the Start menu, Windows 7 displays a shortcut arrow icon 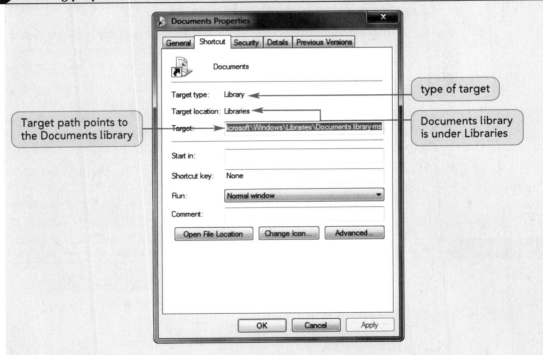 below the image of the Documents icon to provide a visual clue about the type of operation it will perform.

2. While the **Documents – Shortcut** icon is still selected, press the **F2** key, double-click **Shortcut** in the shortcut's name, press the **Backspace** key four times, and then press the **Enter** key. Windows 7 changes the shortcut name to "Documents."

3. Right-click the **Documents** shortcut, and then click **Properties**. Windows 7 opens the Documents Properties dialog box. See Figure 4-9.

Figure 4-9	Viewing properties of the Documents library shortcut

Windows 7 notes that the Target type is Library and the Target location is Libraries. The path to the Target is: C:\Users\Lance\AppData\Roaming\Microsoft\Windows\Libraries\Documents.library-ms

Notice that the shortcut's name is Documents.library-ms, the same type of name that Windows 7 creates when you create a saved search (as previously covered in Tutorial 3). Your user account name will differ; however, the target is still the Documents library. The full filename of this shortcut is Documents.lnk.

4. Click the **Open File Location** button. Windows 7 opens the Libraries window and displays the four default libraries.

5. Close the Libraries window, and then click the **General** tab in the Documents Properties dialog box. Note that the Documents shortcut is larger than the Flash Drive shortcut, but takes up the same amount of storage space on disk.

6. Close the Documents Properties dialog box.

You can create this Documents shortcut in two other ways: (1) You can open the Start menu, right-click Documents, point to Send to, click "Desktop (create shortcut)," and then close the Start menu; or (2) you can right-click the Windows Explorer taskbar button and then drag Documents from the Jump List to the desktop.

Because everyone needs quick access to their Documents folder and its subfolders and files, this desktop shortcut provides fast access to that folder and its contents—faster than the Start menu and the Windows Explorer Jump List. Furthermore, like Windows Vista, but not previous Windows versions, Windows 7 does not include a Start menu option for displaying the Documents icon on the desktop, so you can use this shortcut instead. (However, if you right-click your user account name on the Start menu, and then click Show on Desktop, you can display an icon for your user account on the desktop, and then access the My Documents folder by first opening your user account folder from its desktop icon.) You can also create desktop shortcuts to specific folders within the Documents library.

To create a shortcut to the Upsilon Air folder:

▶ **1.** Click the **Documents** shortcut, right-click **Upsilon Air**, point to **Send to** on the shortcut menu, click **Desktop (create shortcut)**, close the Documents library window, and then change the name of the Upsilon Air - Shortcut to **Upsilon Air**.

▶ **2.** Click the **Upsilon Air** desktop shortcut. Windows 7 opens the Upsilon Air folder. This shortcut not only saves you steps in opening this folder, but in the case of a folder window that contains many folders and files, you do not have to scroll to locate the folder you want. Scrolling is time consuming and causes unnecessary wear and tear on the tendons in your arm.

▶ **3.** Close the Upsilon Air folder window, right-click the **Upsilon Air** shortcut, and then click **Properties**. Windows 7 opens the Upsilon Air Properties dialog box. See Figure 4-10. The Target box on the Shortcut property sheet shows the path for the target: "C:\Users\Public\Documents\Upsilon Air".

Figure 4-10   **Viewing properties of the Upsilon Air folder shortcut**

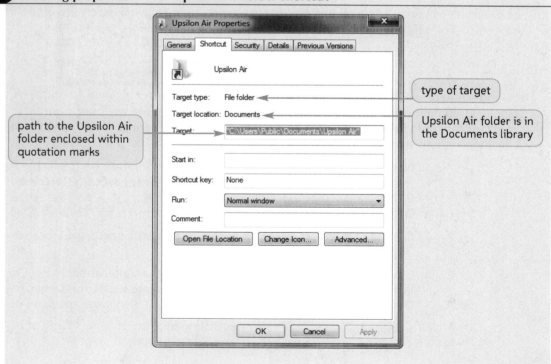

▶ **4.** Click the **General** tab. Notice that this shortcut is even larger than the Documents shortcut, but again, it takes up the same amount of space on disk as the other two shortcuts you created. Shortcut sizes vary slightly because they point to objects stored in different locations on your computer, and thereby their path is different. Also, metadata stored as file properties, such as the path to the file with the shortcut icon or a comment, affect shortcut file sizes.

▶ **5.** Click the **Details** tab. The full filename of the shortcut is Upsilon Air.lnk.

▶ **6.** Keep the Upsilon Air Properties dialog box open for the next set of steps.

If you create desktop shortcuts to more than one folder, you will find that some of them show custom icons while others show the same folder icon. In the latter case, it takes you more time to locate the folder shortcut that you need. To more easily distinguish desktop folder shortcuts, you can change the icon Windows 7 uses for a shortcut.

To change the icon for a shortcut:

▶ **1.** Click the **Shortcut** tab in the Upsilon Air Properties dialog box, and then click the **Change Icon** button. In the Change Icon dialog box, Windows 7 displays the path to a file named imageres.dll. See Figure 4-11.

Figure 4-11   **Choosing a custom icon for the Upsilon Air shortcut**

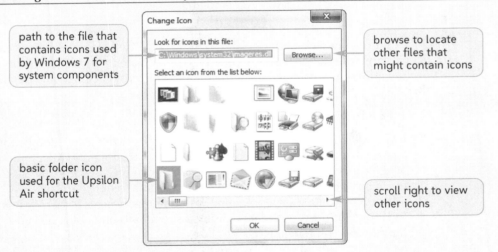

path to the file that contains icons used by Windows 7 for system components

browse to locate other files that might contain icons

basic folder icon used for the Upsilon Air shortcut

scroll right to view other icons

This file is located in the System32 folder under the Windows folder, and the icons it contains are ones that Windows 7 uses for various system components. The selected icon has a blue background (see the fourth icon in the first column). As you can see if you compare this icon to the one for your desktop shortcut, Windows 7 customizes this basic folder icon to reflect the type of content in the Upsilon Air folder (i.e., multiple subfolders). You can select another icon contained within this file or you can browse for another file.

▶ **2.** Use the horizontal scroll bar to scroll to the right and view all the icons.

▶ **3.** Scroll to the far right of the box containing icons, locate and click the **icon** that shows plotted data on a monitor 📊, and then click the **OK** button. Windows 7 closes the Change Icon dialog box and displays the new shortcut icon on the Shortcut property sheet.

TIP

You can also use the F5 (Refresh) key to update your desktop view.

4. Click the **OK** button to close the Upsilon Air Properties dialog box, right-click the **desktop background**, and then click **Refresh** to update your view of the desktop. Windows 7 now displays the new custom icon for the Upsilon Air shortcut.

You can find custom icons in files with the .exe (for executable), .dll (for dynamic link library), .ico (for Icon), .icl (for Icon Library), or .pif (for Program Information File) file extension; however, not all .exe and .dll files contain icons. A **dynamic link library** is a file that contains program code that one or more programs can use. Windows 7 identifies executable files as programs, and dynamic link library files as libraries.

REFERENCE

Creating a Shortcut to a Folder and Customizing the Shortcut Icon

- Locate the folder you want to create a shortcut for.
- Right-click the folder icon, point to "Send to" on the shortcut menu, and then click "Desktop (create shortcut)".
- Close the folder window.
- If you want to change the shortcut's icon, right-click the shortcut, click Properties, click the Change icon button on the Shortcut property sheet, and locate and select a new icon (or browse for an icon file).
- Once you've selected and clicked an icon, click the OK button to close the Change Icon dialog box, and then click the OK button to close the Properties dialog box for the shortcut.

It's not uncommon for people to move a folder that contains their documents to the desktop for ease of access. However, if you create a shortcut to that folder, you can leave the folder in its original location, and perhaps avoid accidentally deleting the folder.

Creating a Shortcut to a File

If you work with the same file every day, or work with a specific file for the duration of a project, you can create a desktop shortcut to that file so you can immediately open it after your computer opens the desktop. You can use the same approach to create a short-cut to a file as you used to create a shortcut to a folder.

Because you are experimenting with different designs for a new company logo, Lance recommends that you create a desktop shortcut to one of the files that contains a design for the new company logo.

To create a shortcut to a file:

1. Click the **Upsilon Air** shortcut, maximize the window (if necessary), and then click the **Company Logo** folder.

2. Right-click **Logo #1.jpg**, point to **Send to**, click **Desktop (create shortcut)**, and then close the Company Logo folder window. Windows 7 creates a shortcut to this JPEG image file on the desktop.

Notice that the name of the shortcut includes the file extension, which can be misleading, because you might think this object was the actual file unless you noticed the shortcut arrow icon 🔁. You can remove the file extension from the shortcut name without affecting the shortcut or the file that it references.

3. Change the **Logo #1.jpg - Shortcut** name to **Logo** (without the file extension).

▶ **4.** Click the **Logo** shortcut. Windows 7 opens the image in the file using Windows Photo Viewer.

   Trouble? If Windows opens the file in another application, the .jpg file extension on the computer you are using is associated with that application. That's fine. The important point is that the shortcut worked. Continue with Step 5.

▶ **5.** Close the Windows Photo Viewer window (or other application window) displaying the contents of the Logo #1 file.

▶ **6.** Right-click the **Logo** shortcut, and then click **Properties**. Windows 7 opens the Logo Properties dialog box. Note that this Target type is a JPEG image. The Target location is Company Logo, the folder that contains this file.

   Trouble? If Windows 7 displays "JPEG File" instead of "JPEG image" for the Target path, the "jpg" file extension is associated with another program other than the default Windows Photo Viewer.

▶ **7.** Click the **path** in the Target box, and then press the **Home** key. Windows 7 moves the insertion point to the beginning of the path.

▶ **8.** Press the **End** key. Windows 7 moves to the end of the path, and now you can see the remainder of the path. See Figure 4-12.

| Figure 4-12 | Viewing properties of a file shortcut |

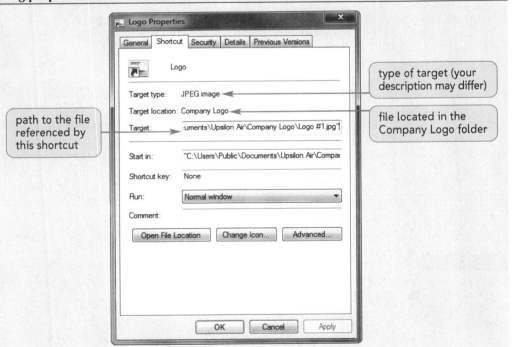

The path to the file referenced by this shortcut is "C:\Users\Public\Documents\Upsilon Air\Company Logo\Logo #1.jpg". If a path includes folder names or filenames with spaces, Windows encloses the entire path within quotation marks so a space between two parts of a folder name or filename is not interpreted as a delimiter (such as the backslash). The path in the "Start in" box is "C:\Users\Public\Documents\Upsilon Air\Company Logo". The "Start in" box identifies the folder that contains the object or related files that a program might need.

▶ **9.** Click the **Details** tab. On the Details property sheet, Windows 7 shows that the full filename of this shortcut is Logo.lnk.

▶ **10.** Close the Logo Properties dialog box.

For each project you work on, you can create a set of shortcuts to folders and files that you need to open. After your computer opens the desktop, a single-click means you are ready to work. The use of shortcuts simplifies the process for locating and opening files.

PROSKILLS

Teamwork: Using Shortcuts for Team Projects

To improve collaboration while working on a team project, provide fast access to project resources, and work efficiently and meet tight deadlines, team members can create and share a set of shortcuts to folders and files so each team member has access to all available joint resources. These shortcuts can also include shortcuts to shared network locations where all project resources and documents are stored for ease of access. Each team member can create their own project shortcuts on their desktop computer, laptop, and home computer to provide access to tools they need on that particular computer system and to tools that enable them to fulfill their role as a team member. Also, each team member can create shortcuts to a company's FTP site for uploading and downloading ongoing project documents and files. These FTP shortcuts are also useful for team members who are traveling or working at different company locations, and even while working at home. Using a set of standard shortcuts is especially helpful for people who are contracted to participate in the team project but live in another location.

Creating a Shortcut to an Application

Even though you can open all the installed software on your computer from the All Programs menu or from Jump Lists on the taskbar or Start menu, using these options requires more steps to locate and open a program. Instead, you can create shortcuts to applications, utilities, and games on your computer so you can open them directly from the desktop.

You can use several approaches to create shortcuts for installed software. If you know the location and name of the program file, you can open the folder where the program file is stored, right-click the program file icon, and then use the option on the Send to menu for creating a desktop shortcut—just as you did when creating shortcuts to folders and document files.

Another approach is to use the Create Shortcut Wizard to browse for the program file and customize the shortcut at the same time. You will examine this option in the next session of the tutorial.

TIP

You can also use the Create Shortcut Wizard to create an Internet shortcut to a Web site.

INSIGHT

Understanding Program Filenames

With a little understanding of how Microsoft and software developers name their program files, you can usually figure out the filename of a program file while browsing for that program manually or with the Create Shortcut Wizard. Program files for applications, utilities, and games have the file extension .exe (for Executable program file). Because the main part of the filename for a program file is limited to eight characters, you might have to guess the main part of the filename or search for a name that is similar to your guess. For example, in the Microsoft Office suite, the program file for Microsoft Excel is Excel.exe, the Microsoft Outlook program file is Outlook.exe, the Microsoft PowerPoint program file is Powerpnt.exe, the Microsoft Access program file is Msaccess.exe, and the Microsoft Word program file is Winword.exe (for Windows Word).

The All Programs menu is the obvious first place to check for a shortcut for an application, utility, or game because the All Programs menu has a complete list of all the software installed on your computer. You can send a copy of the shortcut for a program from the All Programs menu to the desktop. If you use the Start menu Search box to locate a program, you can right-click the program file, point to Send to, and then click "Desktop (create shortcut)." If a taskbar button Jump List has a shortcut to a program, you can also use the Send to option to create a desktop shortcut.

Because you commonly use the Calculator utility in Scientific mode to perform quick computations in your job, you decide to create a desktop shortcut to this utility.

To create a shortcut to a program:

▶ **1.** Open the Start menu, point to **All Programs**, click **Accessories**, right-click **Calculator**, point to **Send to**, click **Desktop (create shortcut)**, and then click the **Start** button again to close the Start menu. Windows 7 places a Calculator shortcut on the desktop.

You might wonder why you didn't just drag Calculator from the Accessories menu to the desktop to create the shortcut—similar to how you created the Documents library shortcut. If you drag Calculator from the Accessories menu, Windows moves the Calculator shortcut, and the Calculator shortcut no longer appears on the Accessories menu. If you accidentally drag a program off any part of the All Programs menu, right-click the desktop, click Undo Move, and then provide Administrator credentials to verify the operation. Windows moves the program shortcut from the desktop back to the Accessories menu.

You could also right-click the program shortcut, right-drag it to the desktop, and choose the option to create a desktop shortcut. Another option is to hold down the Ctrl key while you drag the shortcut to the desktop. Windows 7 then copies the program shortcut rather than moving it.

To view properties of this program shortcut:

▶ **1.** Right-click the **Calculator** desktop shortcut, and then click **Properties**. Windows 7 opens the Calculator Properties dialog box. As you can see from the Shortcut property sheet, the Target type is "Application" and the Target location is "system32". See Figure 4-13.

Figure 4-13   Viewing properties of the Calculator accessory shortcut

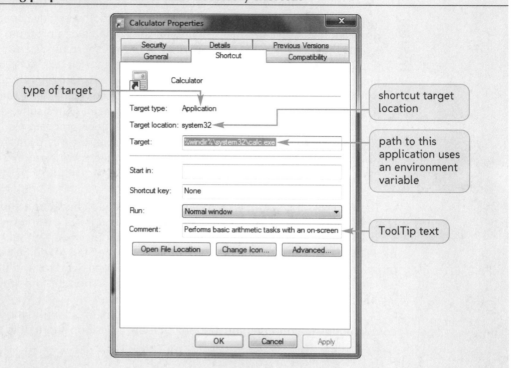

The System32 folder under the Windows folder contains close to a thousand executable programs. The Target box shows that the path for the Calculator shortcut is %windir%\system32\calc.exe. Windows 7 displays the text in the Comment box as a ToolTip when you point to or rest the mouse pointer over the shortcut.

2. Click the **Details** tab. On the Details property sheet, Windows 7 shows that the full filename of this shortcut is Calculator.lnk.

3. Keep the Calculator Properties dialog open for the following explanation of environment variables.

The windir enclosed within percent symbols is an example of an environment variable. An **environment variable** is a name assigned to a Windows 7 system setting. The name of the environment variable (in this case, windir) and its associated setting are stored in an area of memory called the **Windows environment**. Under the DOS operating system, that area of memory was referred to as the **DOS environment**—yet another example of how features from the DOS operating system were carried over into the Windows operating system.

Windows 7 and other programs check the Windows environment for settings. The percent symbols before and after an environment variable identify it as an environment variable and indicate it is a placeholder for a setting that can vary. When a path includes %windir%, Windows 7 substitutes the actual setting for the environment variable. If the Windows folder is on drive C (as is typically the case), the setting for the windir environment variable is C:\Windows. When opening the Calculator utility using the shortcut, Windows 7 substitutes C:\Windows for %windir% in the path to derive the actual path, namely: C:\Windows\system32\calc.exe

On another computer, Windows 7 might be installed on drive D, so the path to the Windows folder on that drive would be "D:\Windows" rather than "C:\Windows". The setting for the %windir% variable would then be "D:\Windows". When that computer starts up, Windows 7 can locate files for programs such as Calculator because "D:\Windows" is assigned to the windir environment variable. The use of environment variables provides flexibility for different types of installations and configurations of Windows 7, and guarantees that the operating system and other programs work properly.

If you use this feature to create shortcuts on your flash drives to quick and easy access to commonly used Windows utilities, you can use these shortcuts on your PC at home, your laptop, and even in a computer lab PC where Windows 7 might be installed on a different drive.

To test your Windows Calculator shortcut:

▶ **1.** Close the Calculator Properties dialog box.

▶ **2.** Click the **Calculator** desktop shortcut. Windows 7 opens the Calculator utility. When opened for the first time, the Calculator utility uses a view called Standard view. If you set Calculator for Scientific view, the features found in that mode are immediately available.

▶ **3.** Close the Calculator window.

If a program is installed in the Program Files folder, Windows 7 will use the %ProgramFiles% environment variable in the path so it can locate the Program Files folder whether it is installed on drive C or another drive along with the operating system. You will examine environment variables in more detail in Tutorial 8.

REFERENCE

Creating a Shortcut to an Application

- From the Start menu, point to All Programs, and then locate the application or program you want to create a shortcut for.
- Right-click the application or program name, point to "Send to", and then click "Desktop (create shortcut)".
- Click the Start button to close the Start menu.

The All Programs menu is the easiest way to locate shortcuts for applications, utilities, games, and other programs.

Creating a Shortcut from an Existing Shortcut

You can make a copy of an existing shortcut and change its path to create a new shortcut. If you change the path so it points to a different type of object, Windows 7 changes the new shortcut's icon.

Because you also need to work with other files in the Company Logo folder, Lance recommends you create a shortcut to that folder from the Logo shortcut because the target of the Logo shortcut contains the path to the Company Logo folder.

To create a Company Logo folder shortcut from the Logo file shortcut:

▶ **1.** Right-click the **Logo** shortcut, and then click **Copy** on the shortcut menu.

▶ **2.** Right-click the **desktop**, and then click **Paste** on the shortcut menu. Windows 7 creates a copy of the Logo shortcut and names it "Logo - Copy."

3. With the shortcut still selected, press the **F2** (Rename) key, type **Company Logo**, and then press the **Enter** key. Windows 7 changes the name of the new desktop shortcut to "Company Logo" but as evidenced by the shortcut icon, the shortcut still points to the Logo #1 file.

4. Right-click the **Company Logo** shortcut, and then click **Properties**. Windows 7 opens the Company Logo Properties dialog box, displays the Shortcut property sheet, and highlights the target of the shortcut. The path is currently set to "C:\Users\Public\Documents\Upsilon Air\Company Logo\Logo #1.jpg". Note that the Target type is still JPEG Image.

5. Press the **End** key, press the **left arrow** key once to position the insertion point to the left of the closing quotation mark, and then use the **Backspace** key to delete "\Logo #1.jpg" from the target's path.

6. Verify that the new path is "C:\Users\Public\Documents\Upsilon Air\Company Logo".

7. Click the **OK** button. Windows 7 now displays a custom folder icon for the Company Logo shortcut (with hints of files containing graphics images). See Figure 4-14.

Figure 4-14   **Viewing a new folder shortcut created from a file shortcut**

new folder shortcut created by modifying the path of a shortcut to a file

8. Right-click the **Company Logo** shortcut and then click **Properties**. The Company Logo Properties dialog box now identifies the Target type as "File folder" instead of JPEG image. See Figure 4-15.

Figure 4-15   **Viewing the Company Logo shortcut's properties**

Windows 7 updated the target type

path to the Company Logo folder

Company Logo folder located in the Upsilon Air folder

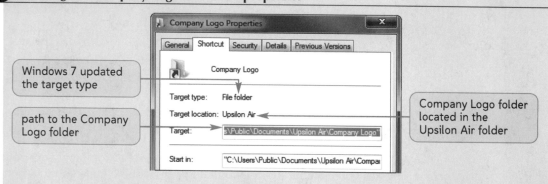

9. Close the Company Logo Properties dialog box.

10. To verify that the shortcut works, click the **Company Logo** shortcut, examine the contents of the Company Logo folder window, and then close the window.

If you are familiar with the use of the Windows path, you can easily create new shortcuts from existing shortcuts.

Automatic Updating of Shortcut Paths

As you've just discovered, when you create a shortcut to an object, Windows 7 stores the path to that object as part of the shortcut. If you change the name of the object to which the shortcut points or if you move the object, the shortcut still works. In each case, Windows 7 updates the path so the shortcut still points to the same object.

Lance informs you that senior management wants to redesign Logo #1.jpg and use it to create a new company logo. He asks you to change the name of the Logo #1 file to Company Logo.

To change the name of the Logo #1 file:

 1. Click the **Company Logo** shortcut. Windows 7 opens the Company Logo folder.

 2. In the Files list, point to **Logo #1.jpg**, press the **F2** (Rename) key, change the name from "Logo #1" to **Company Logo**, and then press the **Enter** key.

 3. Close the Company Logo folder window.

 4. Click the **Logo** shortcut. Windows 7 opens the Company Logo file for previewing in Windows Photo Viewer (or the application associated with this file type on your computer). The new filename is shown on the title bar. The shortcut works; in other words, it finds its target.

    Trouble? If Windows 7 opens the file in another program, that's okay. The point is that the shortcut still works.

 5. Close the Windows Photo Viewer window.

Next, view the path for the Logo desktop shortcut.

To view the path for the Logo shortcut:

 1. Right-click the **Logo** shortcut and then click **Properties**. Note that Windows 7 updated the path so it includes the new name of the file—namely, Company Logo.jpg. See Figure 4-16. Notice that the Target location is Company Logo.

Figure 4-16   **Target path updated after renaming the target file**

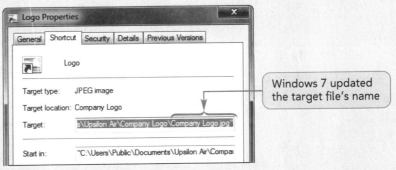

Windows 7 updated the target file's name

▶ **2.** Close the Logo Properties dialog box.

Next, you decide to move the Company Logo file to a new folder.

To move the Company Logo file to a new folder:

▶ **1.** Click the **Company Logo** shortcut, right-click the **Company Logo.jpg** file, and then click **Cut**.

TIP

You can also create a new folder by right-clicking the folder background, pointing to New, and then clicking Folder.

▶ **2.** Click **Upsilon Air** in the Address bar, click the **New folder** button on the toolbar, type **Annual Report** for the new folder's name, and then press the **Enter** key. Windows 7 assigns a name to this new folder.

▶ **3.** Click **Annual Report**, right-click the **folder background**, and then click **Paste**. Windows 7 moves the Company Logo.jpg file to this folder.

▶ **4.** Close the Annual Report folder window.

TIP

If you move a file to another folder, Windows 7 updates the path in all shortcuts that reference the file.

▶ **5.** Click the **Logo** shortcut. Windows 7 again opens the Company Logo file for previewing in Windows Photo Viewer (or the application associated with this file type on your computer). The shortcut still works; in other words, it finds its target.

▶ **6.** Close the Windows Photo Viewer window.

▶ **7.** Right-click the **Logo** shortcut, and then click **Properties**. Note that Windows 7 again updates the path to include the name of the Annual Report folder where this file now resides. See Figure 4-17. The Target location is now Annual Report.

Figure 4-17 | **Updated path includes new folder name for the target file**

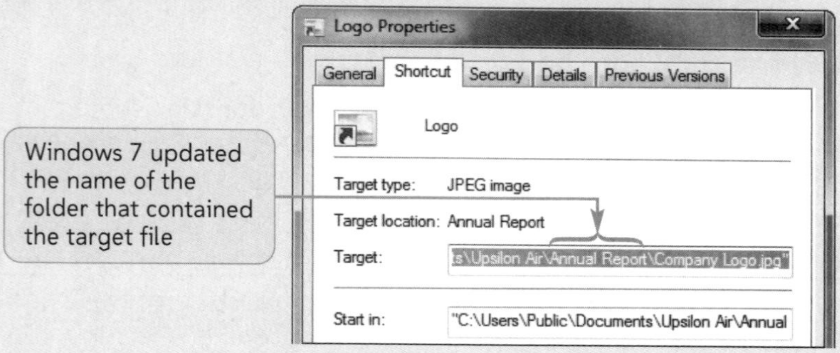

Windows 7 updated the name of the folder that contained the target file

▶ **8.** Close the Logo Properties dialog box.

Later, you accidentally delete the Company Logo file, and then discover the problem when you attempt to use the Company Logo desktop shortcut.

To delete the Company Logo file:

▶ **1.** Click the **Upsilon Air** shortcut, open the **Annual Report** folder, point to **Company Logo.jpg**, press the **Delete** key, and in the Delete File dialog box, click the **Yes** button to move the file to the Recycle Bin.

▶ **2.** Close the Annual Report folder window.

▶ **3.** Click the **Logo** shortcut. Windows 7 displays a Problem with Shortcut dialog box. See Figure 4-18.

Figure 4-18 **Problem locating the file for a shortcut**

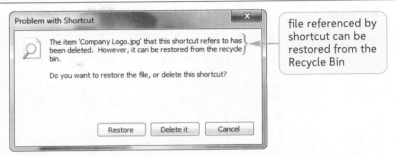

4. Click the **Restore** button. Windows 7 restores the deleted file to the folder where it was previously located, and then opens the Company Logo file that the desktop shortcut points to in Windows Photo Viewer.

5. Close the Windows Photo Viewer window.

As you rename, copy, and move files and folders around on your computer, Windows 7 updates the path that shortcuts use to reference these objects so your shortcuts continue to work.

REVIEW

Session 4.1 Quick Check

1. How does a shortcut find its target?
2. What is the file extension for a desktop shortcut, and what does that file extension imply about the shortcut?
3. True or False. Unlike other types of files, shortcuts do not waste storage space on disk.
4. What types of files are associated with the .exe, .dll, and .ico file extensions?
5. A(n) _____ is a name assigned to a Windows 7 system setting.
6. True or False. If you rename or move a file referenced by a shortcut, the shortcut no longer works.
7. What type of path do network shortcuts use?

SESSION 4.2 VISUAL OVERVIEW

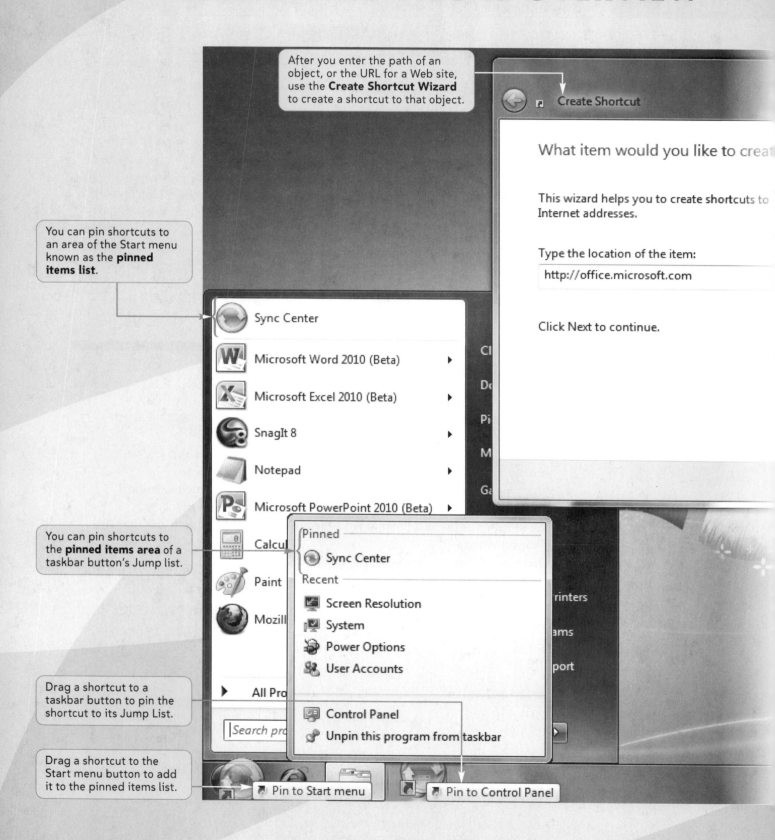

After you enter the path of an object, or the URL for a Web site, use the **Create Shortcut Wizard** to create a shortcut to that object.

Create Shortcut

What item would you like to creat

This wizard helps you to create shortcuts to Internet addresses.

Type the location of the item:

http://office.microsoft.com

Click Next to continue.

You can pin shortcuts to an area of the Start menu known as the **pinned items list**.

Sync Center

Microsoft Word 2010 (Beta)

Microsoft Excel 2010 (Beta)

SnagIt 8

Notepad

Microsoft PowerPoint 2010 (Beta)

You can pin shortcuts to the **pinned items area** of a taskbar button's Jump list.

Calcu

Paint

Mozill

Pinned
Sync Center

Recent
Screen Resolution
System
Power Options
User Accounts

Control Panel
Unpin this program from taskbar

Drag a shortcut to a taskbar button to pin the shortcut to its Jump List.

All Pro

Search pro

Drag a shortcut to the Start menu button to add it to the pinned items list.

Pin to Start menu

Pin to Control Panel

CUSTOM SHORTCUTS

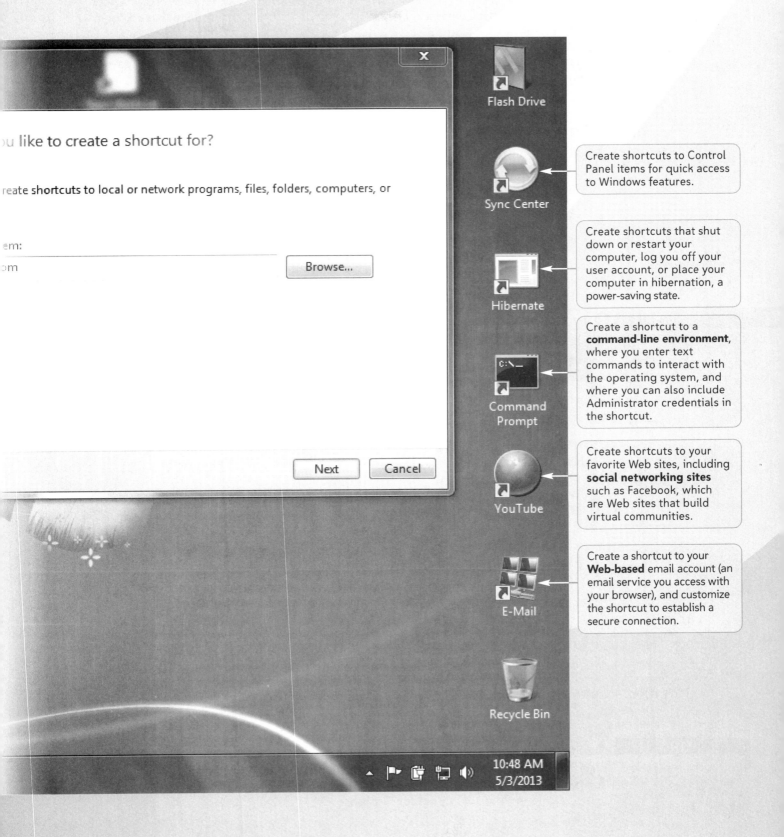

x

ou like to create a shortcut for?

reate **shortcuts to local or network programs, files, folders, computers, or**

em:

om   Browse...

Next   Cancel

Flash Drive

Sync Center

Create shortcuts to Control Panel items for quick access to Windows features.

Hibernate

Create shortcuts that shut down or restart your computer, log you off your user account, or place your computer in hibernation, a power-saving state.

Command Prompt

Create a shortcut to a **command-line environment**, where you enter text commands to interact with the operating system, and where you can also include Administrator credentials in the shortcut.

YouTube

Create shortcuts to your favorite Web sites, including **social networking sites** such as Facebook, which are Web sites that build virtual communities.

E-Mail

Create a shortcut to your **Web-based** email account (an email service you access with your browser), and customize the shortcut to establish a secure connection.

Recycle Bin

10:48 AM
5/3/2013

Creating a Control Panel Shortcut

If you find that you use a Control Panel tool or applet frequently, you can create a desktop shortcut to that Control Panel applet so you don't have to navigate to that applet in the Control Panel.

While working with you, Lance notices that you frequently open the Folder Options dialog box to make changes to folder and file settings. He suggests that you can save time and effort if you create a shortcut to that dialog box in the Control Panel.

To create a Control Panel shortcut:

▶ **1.** From the Start menu, click **Control Panel**, but do not maximize the Control Panel window. If necessary, resize and drag the window to the right so you can see the left side of the desktop. By default, Windows 7 organizes Control Panel applets by category.

▶ **2.** Click the **View by** button in the upper-right part of the window, and then click **Small icons** so you can see all the Control Panel options in the All Control Panel Options window. In this view you can see all or most of the Control Panel items without having to open one category after another by clicking links. See Figure 4-19.

| Figure 4-19 | Locating Folder Options in the Control Panel |

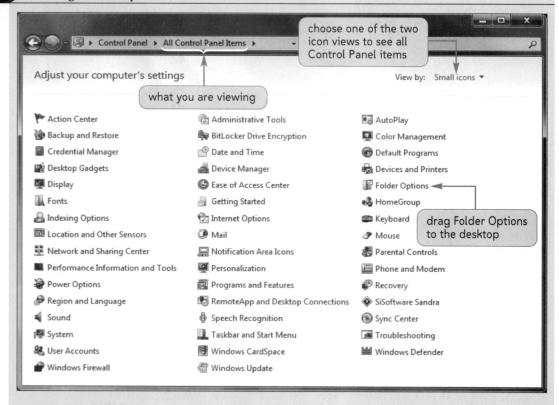

▶ **3.** Drag **Folder Options** to the desktop, and then close the Control Panel window. Windows 7 places a desktop shortcut to Folder Options in the Control Panel.

▶ **4.** Select the **Folder Options** shortcut, and then change its name from Folder Options - Shortcut to **Folder Options**.

TIP

In Category view, you can drag a Control Panel link to the desktop to create a shortcut.

▶ **5.** Click the **Folder Options** shortcut. Windows 7 opens the Folder Options dialog box. This shortcut saves multiple steps because you don't have to open Control Panel and search for Folder Options or open a folder window and use the Organize menu to open the Folder Options dialog box.

▶ **6.** Close the Folder Options dialog box.

▶ **7.** Right-click the **Folder Options** shortcut, and then click **Properties**. Windows 7 opens the Folder Options Properties dialog box. See Figure 4-20. In the Target box on the Shortcut property sheet, Windows 7 displays the target used by this shortcut as Control Panel\All Control Panel Items\Folder Options (although the entire path is not visible). The target is also dimmed, which means you cannot change it.

Figure 4-20 **Viewing properties of the Folder Options shortcut**

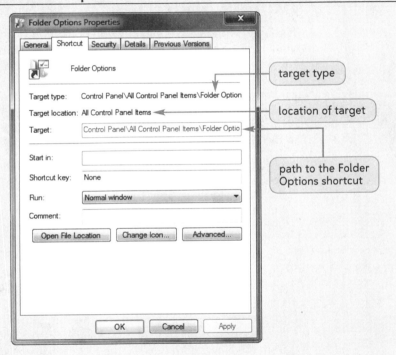

▶ **8.** Click the **Details** tab. On the Details property sheet, Windows 7 shows the filename of this shortcut: Folder Options.lnk. The shortcut file's size is 146 bytes, smaller than the previous shortcuts you've examined, but notice that the General property sheet shows the shortcut also takes up the same amount of storage space on disk as your previous shortcuts.

▶ **9.** Close the Folder Options Properties dialog box.

Creating a Control Panel Shortcut

- Open the Control Panel from the Start menu, click the View by button, and then click Large icons (or Small icons).
- Drag a Control Panel applet to the desktop.

or

- Open the Control Panel from the Start menu, locate the link you want to use for your shortcut, and then drag the Control Panel link to the desktop.

If you open a Control Panel applet and then decide to create a desktop shortcut to that applet, you can drag the icon in the Address bar to the desktop.

Adding Shortcuts to the Start Menu

If you are working in a maximized application window such as Microsoft Word, or viewing a Web page with Windows Internet Explorer, you might not want to minimize the window just to locate and click a desktop shortcut, and then later have to maximize the window. However, the Start button and taskbar are always accessible. If you place or pin a shortcut to the Start menu or on a taskbar toolbar, you can leave your application window maximized, and then still locate and use the shortcut.

If you want to customize the Start menu, you can add new group folders and shortcuts to the Start menu, All Programs menu, and other menus in the following ways:

- **Using the Taskbar and Start menu Properties dialog box**—In Tutorial 2, you opened the Taskbar and Start menu Properties dialog box, and then customized the Start menu to include those options that you need for your work.
- **Pinning programs and shortcuts to the Start menu**—If you find that you consistently use the same programs, you can pin the programs to an area on the Start menu known as the pinned items list, and you can pin the same programs to the taskbar. Then you can access these items from the Jump Lists on either the Start menu or taskbar. You can also drag desktop shortcuts and drop them on the Start menu, and then Windows 7 adds them to the pinned items list. You can pin certain types of shortcuts to the taskbar.
- **Using drag and drop**—You can use drag and drop to rearrange, move, or copy group folders and program shortcuts on the Start and All Programs menus, as well as dragging them from one menu to another. If you open a folder window, you can drag a folder from the Navigation pane or the Details list, and drop the folder on the Start menu button or taskbar to create a new shortcut to that folder. Windows 7 then pins the folder shortcut to the Start menu or Jump List Pinned items list. You can also use drag and drop to rearrange taskbar buttons as well as items pinned to a Jump List so they are arranged in a logical and easy-to-access location.
- **Using the Start menu folder**—You can also open the Start menu folder for your user account, create new group folders and shortcuts, or reorganize the existing group folders and shortcuts for your user account.

The approach you use depends on how you prefer to work, the types of changes you want to make, and the degree to which you want to customize the Start and All Programs menus.

Pinning Shortcuts to the Start Menu and Taskbar

To add a desktop shortcut to your Start menu, you drag it from the desktop and drop it on the Start button. Windows 7 then copies the shortcut to the Start menu and places it in the pinned items list. The original shortcut remains on the desktop. You can also pin certain types of shortcuts to the taskbar.

Lance invariably finds that he needs to switch to his Upsilon Air folder while he is working in an application window or examining a Web site with Internet Explorer. Rather than switch to the desktop to access the Upsilon Air shortcut, and later restore the window where he was working, he decides to add the Upsilon Air shortcut directly to the Start menu and the taskbar so he can access the shortcut more easily. He asks you to also add the Upsilon Air desktop shortcut to your Start menu and taskbar.

To add a desktop shortcut to the Start menu:

▶ **1.** Drag the **Upsilon Air** shortcut from the desktop to the Start button, release the mouse button, and then click the **Start** button if Windows 7 does not automatically open the Start menu. As you drag the shortcut to the Start button, Windows 7 displays a shortcut arrow 🔗 and a Pin to Start menu ToolTip. Notice that Windows 7 added a copy of the Upsilon Air shortcut to the pinned items list. See Figure 4-21. If you want to manually place this shortcut at a specific location on the Start menu, drag the shortcut to the Start button, wait for the Start menu to open, and then drag the shortcut to where you want to place it on the Start menu.

Figure 4-21	Pinning a shortcut to the Start menu

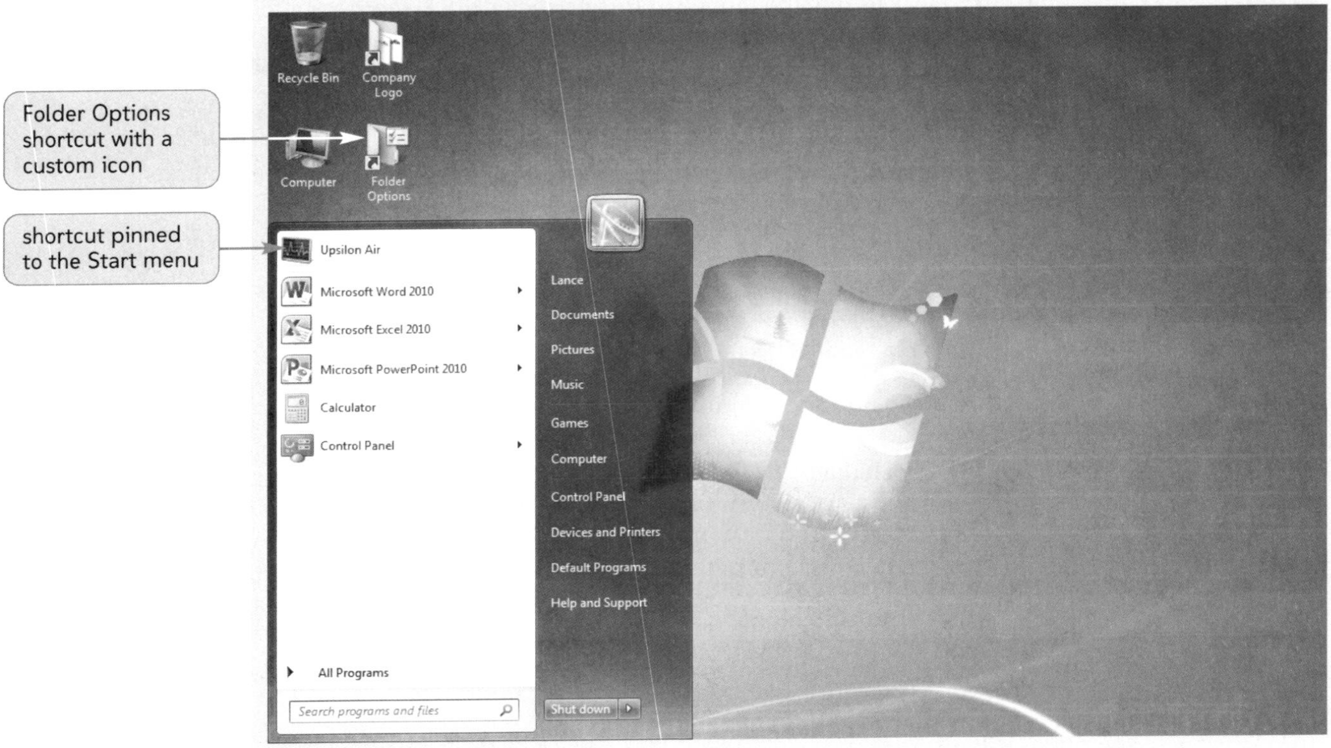

▶ **2.** Click **Upsilon Air** on the Start menu. The Upsilon Air shortcut on the Start menu works just like the desktop shortcut, and opens the Upsilon Air folder.

▶ **3.** Close the Upsilon Air window.

▶ **4.** Drag the **Upsilon Air** shortcut to the taskbar and pause. Windows 7 displays a "Pin to Windows Explorer" ToolTip.

▶ **5.** Release the mouse button. Windows 7 opens the Windows Explorer Jump List and highlights the Upsilon Air shortcut in the Jump List. See Figure 4-22. Now you have two ways to open the Upsilon Air folder, and each way requires two steps.

Figure 4-22 **Pinning a folder shortcut to the Windows Explorer Jump List**

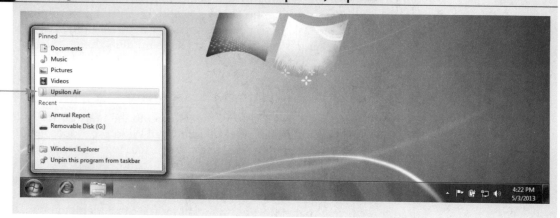

folder shortcut pinned to the Windows Explorer Jump List

If you inadvertently pin the wrong desktop shortcut to the Start menu, you can open the Start menu, right-click the shortcut in the pinned items list, and then click "Remove from this list." Likewise, you can remove a pinned item from a Jump List by displaying the Jump List, right-clicking the pinned item, and then click "Unpin from this list."

Pinning a Desktop Shortcut to the Start Menu and Taskbar

- To pin a desktop shortcut to the Start menu's pinned items list, drag the desktop shortcut to the Start button, and then release the mouse button.
- To remove a Start menu pinned item, right-click the pinned item shortcut, and then click "Remove from this list."
- To pin a desktop shortcut to a taskbar Jump List's pinned items list, drag the desktop shortcut to the taskbar, and then release the mouse button.
- To remove a pinned item from a Jump List, right-click the pinned item, and then click "Unpin from this list."

If you drag the Calculator shortcut to the taskbar, Windows 7 will create a Calculator taskbar button in the same way that it does for any other program. If you drag the Folder Options shortcut to the taskbar, Windows 7 will display a Not Allowed icon to warn you that you cannot perform this operation. To pin a Control Panel applet to the taskbar, you have to first pin the Control Panel window to the taskbar. After Windows 7 displays a taskbar button for the Control Panel window, you can pin a Control Panel shortcut to the taskbar. Then a Control Panel button remains on the taskbar, and you now have access to a Jump List with Control Panel applets that you've previously opened.

To pin the Folder Options shortcut to the taskbar:

1. Open the Start menu, and then right-click **Control Panel**. The Control Panel shortcut menu does not have an option for pinning Control Panel to the taskbar.

2. Click **Control Panel** to open the Control Panel window. Now you can pin Control Panel to the taskbar.

3. Right-click the **Control Panel** taskbar button, and then click **Pin this program to taskbar**.

4. Close the Control Panel window. Control Panel is now pinned to the taskbar.

▶ **5.** Drag the **Folder Options** desktop shortcut to the Control Panel taskbar button, and when you see a Pin to Control Panel ToolTip, release the left mouse button. Windows 7 adds the Folder Options shortcut to the pinned items area on the Jump List.

▶ **6.** Right-click the **Control Panel** taskbar button. Windows 7 displays a Jump List of recently opened Control Panel applets, including Folder Options.

You can use this same approach to pin other Control Panel desktop shortcuts to the Control Panel taskbar button.

REFERENCE

Pinning a Control Panel Desktop Shortcut to the Taskbar

- To pin Control Panel to the taskbar, open the Start menu, open Control Panel, right-click the Control Panel taskbar button, and then click "Pin this program to taskbar."
- To pin a Control Panel desktop shortcut to the Control Panel taskbar button, drag the Control Panel desktop shortcut to the Control Panel taskbar button, and when you see the Pin to Control Panel desktop shortcut, release the mouse button.
- To remove a pinned item from the Control Panel taskbar button, right-click the Control Panel taskbar button, right-click the pinned item, and then click "Unpin from this list."

After you pin the Control Panel to the taskbar, you can drag Control Panel links from the Control Panel window to pin new Control Panel items to the Control Panel taskbar button Jump List.

Using the Create Shortcut Wizard

Because you frequently use the Windows 7 On-Screen Keyboard on your mobile computer, you want to create a shortcut to the On-Screen Keyboard program. Lance recommends you use the Create Shortcut Wizard, and then specify the path to the osk.exe program in the Windows System32 folder.

To create a desktop shortcut with the Create Shortcut Wizard:

▶ **1.** Right-click the **desktop**, point to **New** on the desktop shortcut menu, and then click **Shortcut**. Windows 7 opens the Create Shortcut dialog box and explains you can use this wizard to create shortcuts to local or network programs, files, folders, computers, and even Web sites. See Figure 4-23. You can type the location of the item if you know its path or URL, or you can use the Browse button.

Figure 4-23   **Using the Create Shortcut Wizard**

how you can use this wizard

enter the path for the new shortcut

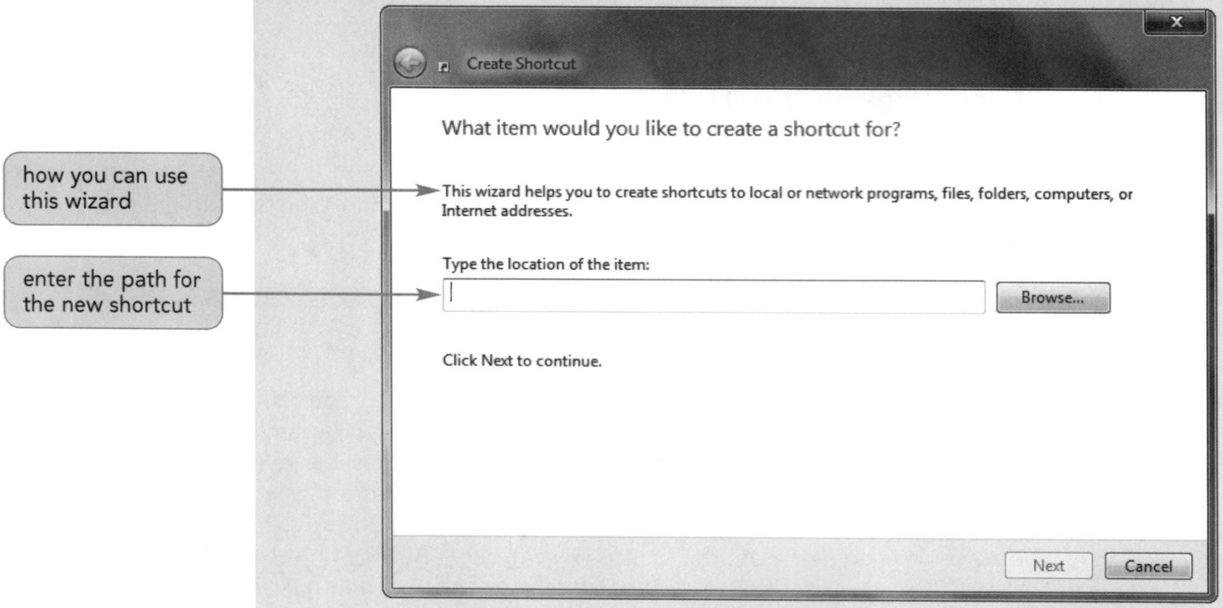

2. In the "Type the location of the item" box, type **c:\windows\system32\osk.exe** (without any spaces). (*Hint:* As you start typing, you can select the path to the System32 folder from a drop-down box.)

3. Verify that you have entered the path correctly.

4. Click the **Next** button in the Create Shortcut dialog box. Windows 7 prompts for a shortcut name.

5. In the "Type a name for this shortcut" box, type **On-Screen Keyboard**, and then click the **Finish** button. Windows 7 creates a desktop shortcut to the On-Screen Keyboard program. See Figure 4-24. Notice that Windows 7 uses a custom icon for this Windows 7 accessory.

Figure 4-24   **New program shortcut created by the Create Shortcut Wizard**

new program shortcut

6. Click the **On-Screen Keyboard** shortcut. Windows 7 opens the On-Screen keyboard. Instead of using your regular keyboard, you can use your mouse to click on-screen keyboard buttons.

7. Close the On-Screen Keyboard.

You can also drag this keyboard shortcut to the taskbar and pin it to the taskbar.

REFERENCE

Creating a Desktop Shortcut with the Create Shortcut Wizard

- Right-click the desktop (or background of a folder window), point to New on the desktop shortcut menu, and then click Shortcut.
- In the "Type the location of the item" box, type the path to a program, or browse and locate and select the program file, and then click the Next button.
- Type a name for the shortcut in the "Type a name for this shortcut" box, and then click the Finish button.

The Create Shortcut Wizard is yet another way for creating desktop shortcuts, but it does require that you know or can locate the path to the program that you want to create a shortcut to. You can also use this wizard in a folder window.

Customizing the Navigation Pane

The Navigation pane in folder windows contains links to commonly used locations on your computer, including the desktop, libraries, the Downloads folder, your network and homegroup, and saved searches. If you frequently use other folders, you can use Recent Places to locate those folders. You can also add those folders under Favorites in the Navigation pane. Windows 7 then creates shortcuts to those folders in your user account Links folder. Favorites in the Navigation pane are Windows Explorer Favorites (or links to other locations), not Internet Explorer Favorites (or bookmarks).

As you work, you need to quickly switch between the Documents library and other locations to the Upsilon Air folder. You decide to create a link to the Upsilon Air folder in the Navigation pane.

To create a link to the Upsilon Air folder in the Navigation pane:

1. Click the **Upsilon Air** shortcut. Windows 7 opens a window onto the Upsilon Air folder.

2. Click **Public Documents** in the Address bar. Windows 7 switches to the Public Documents folder, one folder level up, and highlights the Upsilon Air folder.

3. Drag the **Upsilon Air** folder to place it in alphabetical order under the Recent Places link under Favorites, as shown in Figure 4-25. As you drag, Windows 7 displays a horizontal black bar that indicates where the new link will be positioned when you release the mouse button. Windows 7 also displays a ToolTip with a shortcut arrow and the text "Create link in Favorites."

Figure 4-25 **Creating a Favorites Link using drag and drop**

dragging the Upsilon Air folder from the Folders list to Favorites

horizontal black bar identifies where Windows 7 will create the link

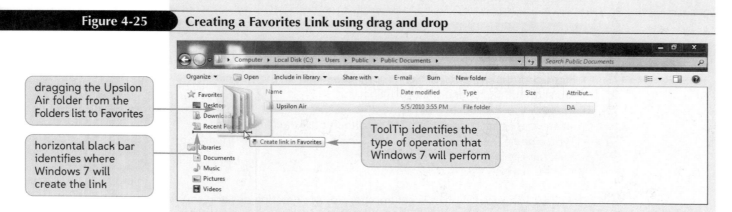

ToolTip identifies the type of operation that Windows 7 will perform

4. Release the mouse button. Windows 7 creates an Upsilon Air link under the Favorites link. See Figure 4-26. If you are working with files in another folder, you can now use the Upsilon Air link to quickly switch to the Upsilon Air folder.

Figure 4-26 **Newly created Favorite link**

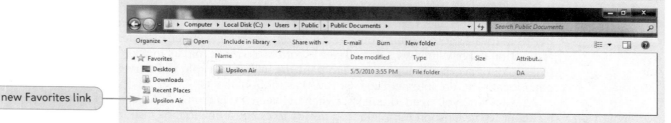

new Favorites link

TIP

After you create a link to a folder, you can drag the link to another location under the Favorites link.

5. Click **Computer** in the Address bar, and then click **Upsilon Air** under Favorites in the Navigation pane. Windows 7 opens the Upsilon Air folder.

Next, you decide to view the shortcut for your new Upsilon Air link.

To view the shortcut for the Upsilon Air link:

1. In the Address bar, click the **Location button arrow** ▶ to the left of "Public", and then click your **user account name**. Windows 7 switches to your user account folder.

2. Click the **Links** folder icon, and if necessary, click the **More options** arrow ☷ ▾ for the Change your view button on the toolbar, and then click **Large icons**. Windows 7 opens the Links folder and switches to Large icons view. The link to the Upsilon Air folder under the Favorites link in the Navigation pane is actually a shortcut in the Links folder. See Figure 4-27.

Figure 4-27 **Viewing shortcuts in the Links folder**

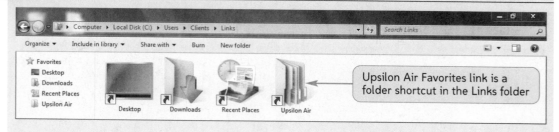

Upsilon Air Favorites link is a folder shortcut in the Links folder

▶ **3.** Click the **Upsilon Air** shortcut in the Files list of the Links folder window. Windows 7 opens the Upsilon Air folder.

▶ **4.** Use the **Back** button ◐ to return to the Links folder.

▶ **5.** Right-click the **Desktop** shortcut, and then click **Properties**. On the Shortcut property sheet in the Desktop Properties dialog box, Windows 7 identifies the Target type as a File folder, and shows the full path to the desktop in the Target box. This shortcut references the Desktop folder under your user account.

▶ **6.** Click the **Open File Location** button, and if necessary, click the **More options arrow button** ▤ ▾ for the Change your view button on the toolbar, and then switch to Tiles view. Windows 7 opens the Desktop folder, and displays not only the shortcuts that you've created but links to Libraries, Homegroup, Computer, Network, Control Panel, and Recycle Bin, all of which are identified as System Folders. None of these System Folders except the Recycle Bin are on the desktop. Furthermore, there are no options for examining the properties of the Libraries, Homegroup, Control Panel, and your user account System Folders.

▶ **7.** Close the Desktop window, and then close the Desktop Properties dialog box.

▶ **8.** Right-click the **Recent Places** shortcut, and then click **Properties**. On the Shortcut property sheet in the Recent Places Properties dialog box, Windows 7 identifies the Target location as Desktop and the Target as Recent Places. The Target is dimmed, so you cannot change this setting. If you examine the Details property sheet, you will discover that the full filename of this shortcut is Recent Places.lnk.

▶ **9.** Click the **Open File Location** button. Windows 7 opens the same Desktop folder that you examined in Step 6. There is no Recent Places shortcut in this folder despite the fact that Windows identifies its Target location as Desktop.

▶ **10.** Close the Desktop window, close the Recent Places Properties dialog box, and then close the Links folder.

Lance points out that if you no longer need a link under the Favorites link, you can remove it from the Links folder. He suggests that you remove the Upsilon Air link so you know how to remove links under Favorites, and then you can add it back to your Favorites later.

To remove the new Upsilon Air link:

▶ **1.** Click the **Documents** desktop shortcut to open the Documents library window, right-click the **Upsilon Air** link under the Favorites link in the Navigation pane, and then click **Remove**. Windows 7 deletes the Upsilon Air link under the Favorites link, and the Links folder no longer contains an Upsilon Air shortcut.

▶ **2.** Right-click the **Documents folder background**, and then click **Undo Delete**. Windows 7 restores the Upsilon Air link under Favorites, and displays the Upsilon Air shortcut in the Links folder.

▶ **3.** Close the Documents library window.

If you perform a task, such as deleting a shortcut, file, or folder, and then switch to another drive, folder, or the desktop, you can right-click the background of the current folder and undo the last task you performed (or use the Ctrl+Z Undo keyboard shortcut), as long as you performed that operation on the hard disk drive. You cannot undo, for example, a file you deleted from your flash drive. In fact, when you delete the file from your flash drive, Windows 7 will ask you if you are sure that you want to *permanently* delete this file.

REFERENCE

Adding and Removing Links in the Navigation pane

- To add a link to a folder under Favorites, drag the folder and drop it under Favorites in the Navigation pane.
- To move a link under Favorites, drag the link to another location under Favorites in the Navigation pane.
- To remove a Favorites link, right-click the Favorites link in the Navigation pane, and then click Remove.

As you work in different folders on your computer, you can add links to other folders in the Navigation pane to streamline access to important folders.

Customizing a Drive Icon

If you have several removable disk drives in your computer, Windows 7 uses the default Removable Disk icon for each of those drives. For example, you might have one or more memory card drives and one or more flash drives, all of which are identified in the same way in the Computer window. Although you can distinguish one drive from another by each drive's name (e.g., F: and G:), you can also specify a custom icon for each drive to more easily distinguish one from another. Windows 7 will also use that same icon for your flash drive desktop shortcut. To specify a custom icon for a flash drive, you must first locate or create a small icon file with the .ico file extension or .bmp (Bitmap Image) file extension.

Next, you create a folder named autorun in the top-level folder of your flash drive and put the icon file in the autorun folder. Finally, you use Notepad to create an autorun.inf file where you designate the location of the file icon. For example, if your icon file is named Upsilon Air.ico, you first put that file in a newly created autorun folder, and then you set up the autorun.inf file exactly as follows:

    [autorun]
    icon=autorun\Upsilon Air.ico

[autorun] is a section name, and icon= specifies the path for the location of the icon file. In this example, the autorun folder is assumed to be under the top-level folder of the same drive as the autorun.inf file. If you create this autorun.inf file on a flash drive, Windows 7 uses the icon in the autorun folder as the default icon for the flash drive when you attach it to your computer, and uses that same icon for any shortcuts to that flash drive.

When creating an autorun folder or an autorun.inf file, the case of the text does not matter. In other words, you can use all lowercase (which is easier to type).

Lance offers to step you through the process for creating your first autorun.inf file.

To copy an icon file to your flash drive:

▶ **1.** If necessary, attach your flash drive to the computer you are using, and then close any dialog box or window that opens.

▶ **2.** Click the **Flash Drive** desktop shortcut, and if necessary, adjust the size of the flash drive window so you can see the Upsilon Air shortcut on the desktop. Windows 7 opens the top-level folder of your flash drive, and as shown in the Navigation pane and Address bar, your flash drive window may be named Removable Disk or may have another name.

▶ **3.** Click the **Upsilon Air** desktop shortcut, and then click the **Company Logo** folder icon.

▶ **4.** Right-click the **taskbar**, and then click **Show windows side by side**. Windows 7 places the Company Logo window, the last opened window, on the left side of the desktop and the flash drive window on the right side of the desktop.

▶ **5.** Drag the **Upsilon Air.ico** file from the Company Logo folder window to the flash drive window, and if necessary, switch to Large icons view in your flash drive window. Windows 7 copies the Upsilon Air.ico file to the top-level folder of your flash drive.

▶ **6.** Close the Company Logo folder window, and then maximize your flash drive window.

Now you're ready to create the autorun folder and an autorun.inf file.

You must first make sure that Windows 7 displays file extensions for known file types; otherwise, you will encounter a problem creating and then renaming your autorun.inf file.

To create an autorun.inf file and specify a custom icon for your flash drive:

▶ **1.** Click the **Organize** button on the toolbar, click **Folder and search options**, click the **View** tab, if necessary, remove the check mark from the "Hide extensions for known file types" check box, and then click the **OK** button.

▶ **2.** Click the **New folder** button on the toolbar, type **autorun** and then press the **Enter** key.

▶ **3.** Drag the **Upsilon Air.ico** file, and drop it onto the **autorun** folder. Windows 7 moves the Upsilon Air.ico file into the autorun folder.

▶ **4.** Right-click the **folder background** of your flash drive window, point to **New** on the shortcut menu, click **Text Document**, and after Windows 7 creates a new file named "New Text Document.txt," type **autorun.inf** and use the **Delete** key to delete the **.txt** file extension. If the Windows 7 setting for hiding extensions for known file types was enabled when you performed this operation, you would not know that your final filename was autorun.inf.txt, and your autorun file would not work.

▶ **5.** Press the **Enter** key. In the Rename dialog box, Windows 7 warns you that changing a file's extension may make the file unusable.

▶ **6.** Click the **Yes** button. Windows 7 displays a custom icon for the autorun.inf file. See Figure 4-28. In the Details pane, Windows 7 identifies this .inf file as a Setup Information file.

Figure 4-28 | **Viewing the autorun Setup Information file icon**

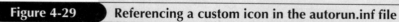

Setup Information file with custom icon

autorun folder with icon referenced in the autorun.inf file

Windows 7 identifies the file type of the selected file

autorun.inf
Setup Information
Date modified: 5/7/2010 9:16 AM
Size: 0 bytes
Date created: 5/7/2010 9:16 AM

7. Click the **autorun.inf** file icon. Windows 7 opens the file in Notepad.

8. Type **[autorun]** (with the square brackets) on the first line, press the **Enter** key, type **icon=autorun\Upsilon Air.ico** on the second line, and then press the **Enter** key.

9. Compare what you've entered with Figure 4-29, and if necessary, make any corrections.

Figure 4-29 | **Referencing a custom icon in the autorun.inf file**

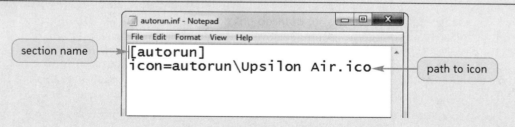

section name

path to icon

```
[autorun]
icon=autorun\Upsilon Air.ico
```

10. Click **File** on the Notepad menu bar, click **Save**, close the Notepad window, and then close the Removable Disk window.

To test your autorun.inf file, you have to remove your flash drive, and then reattach it.

To view your flash drive's custom icon:

▶ **1.** Examine the current icon used for your Flash Drive desktop shortcut.

▶ **2.** Click the **Computer** icon on the desktop and the current icon used for your flash drive.

▶ **3.** Click the **Show hidden icons** button ▲ in the notification area of the taskbar, click the **Safely Remove Hardware and Eject Media** icon 🔌 in the notification area, click the **Eject USB Mass Storage Device** option for the flash drive that contains the autorun.inf file, and after Windows 7 displays a Safe To Remove Hardware dialog box informing you this device can be safely removed, remove your flash drive.

> **Trouble?** If Windows 7 displays a Problem Ejecting USB Mass Storage Device dialog box, and informs you that the device is currently in use, close any programs or windows that might be accessing content on the drive, including the drive window itself, or close any file you might have opened from the flash drive, and then try this step again.

TIP

If you attach your flash drive to another computer, you will see the same custom icon.

▶ **4.** Attach your flash drive, and if necessary, close the AutoPlay dialog box or any other dialog box or window that opens. Windows 7 displays the new custom icon used for your flash drive in the Computer window. See Figure 4-30.

Figure 4-30   **Viewing a flash drive's custom icon**

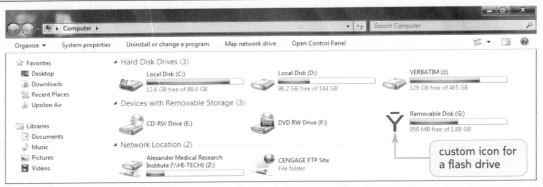

▶ **5.** Close the Computer window. Notice that your Flash Drive desktop shortcut still uses the previous Removable Disk icon.

▶ **6.** Right-click the **Flash Drive** shortcut icon, and then click **Properties**. Windows 7 opens the Flash Drive Properties dialog box. Windows 7 displays the Upsilon Air icon for the flash drive in the upper-left corner of the Shortcut property sheet.

▶ **7.** On the Shortcut property sheet, click the **Change Icon** button. Windows 7 opens the Change Icon dialog box, and displays the path to the icon in the Upsilon Air. ico file on your flash drive: G:\autorun\Upsilon Air.ico (Your drive name may differ.) See Figure 4-31.

Figure 4-31	Viewing the icon in the icon file

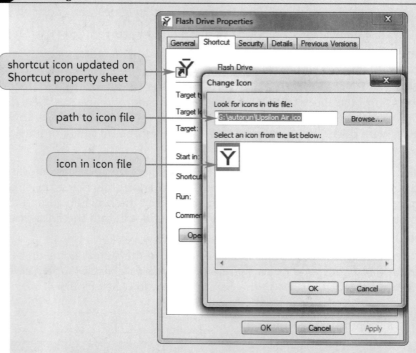

shortcut icon updated on Shortcut property sheet

path to icon file

icon in icon file

▶ **8.** Click the **OK** button in the Change Icon dialog box, and then click the **OK** button in the Flash Drive Properties dialog box. Windows 7 updates the icon for the Flash Drive desktop shortcut. See Figure 4-32.

Figure 4-32	Viewing the updated icon for the desktop shortcut

updated icon for flash drive shortcut

▶ **9.** Click the **Flash Drive** shortcut on your desktop. In the Removable Disk window, Windows 7 displays the custom icon for this drive on the left side of the Address bar, similar to the way Internet Explorer displays custom icons for Web sites. See Figure 4-33.

| Figure 4-33 | Viewing how Windows 7 uses custom icons in the Address bar |

flash drive custom icon appears in Address bar

▶ **10.** Close the Removable Disk window.

Microsoft has limited the features in the autorun.inf file that were previously available for use in earlier versions of Windows to provide more security for your computer system, and it may apply further limitations to its use in the future. See the "Securing AutoPlay in Windows 7" Insight box later in this tutorial.

REFERENCE

Customizing a Flash Drive Icon

- Open a window onto your flash drive, locate or create an icon file (with the .ico file extension), and copy or move the file to the top-level folder of your flash drive.
- Click the Organize button on the toolbar, click Folder and search options, click the View tab, and if necessary, remove the check mark from the "Hide extensions for known file types" check box, and then click the OK button.
- Click New folder on the toolbar, type autorun and then press the Enter key.
- Drag the icon file icon onto the autorun folder.
- Right-click the flash drive folder background, point to New, click Text Document, and after Windows 7 creates a new file named "New Text Document.txt", type autorun.inf and delete the .txt file extension. Press the Enter key, and when prompted about changing the file's extension, click the Yes button in the Rename dialog box.
- Click the autorun.inf file icon to open the file for editing.
- Type [autorun] (with the square brackets) on the first line, press the Enter key, type icon=autorun\ followed immediately by the filename of the icon file (for example, icon=autorun\Upsilon Air.ico) on the second line, and then press the Enter key.
- Click File on the Notepad menu bar, click Save, close the Notepad window, and then close the flash drive window.
- Click the "Show hidden icons" button in the notification area of the taskbar, click the Safely Remove Hardware and Eject Media icon in the notification area, click Eject USB Mass Storage Device for your flash drive, and after Windows 7 displays a Safe To Remove Hardware dialog box informing you this device can be safely removed, remove your flash drive.
- To view your custom icon in a Computer window, open a Computer window, attach your flash drive, and if necessary, close the AutoPlay dialog box or any other dialog box or window that opens.

Setup Information files with the .inf file extension are commonly used by Windows 7 to install device drivers for hardware on your computer, but as you can see, you can also use them to customize drive icons. You can go to the Microsoft Web site and search using the search criteria *autorun.inf* to locate a link to an Autorun.inf Entries Web page that provides more information on how to customize an autorun.inf file.

Securing AutoPlay in Windows 7

You can add commands in an autorun.inf file to open programs or install software on your computer. Unfortunately, some people have taken advantage of this feature to install malicious software from a flash drive onto other people's computers. Two famous examples of this problem are Conflicker, also referred to as Downadup (and pronounced "down and up"), and Kido. Conflicker is an Internet worm that was discovered in November 2008, and it quickly became one of the two most prevalent threats during the first half of 2009. Conflicker infected millions of computers via flash drives using a modified autorun.inf file that references a hidden folder on the flash drive containing the malicious software. When a user attached the flash drive to a computer, the AutoPlay dialog box displayed an additional "Open folder to view files" option. That new option, found only on DVDs and CDs for installing software, also used the standard folder icon to further confuse the user. If a user clicked that option, the user inadvertently installed Conflicker on their computer. In this respect, Conflicker relied on social engineering techniques, which take advantage of how people typically react in a given situation, to gain access to a computer system. To stem this problem, Microsoft modified the AutoPlay feature in Windows 7 so users do not see an additional option for installing software from a flash drive. Instead, Windows 7 only displays content from programs installed on your computer, not on flash drives or other types of removable media with two exceptions, namely, DVDs and CDs.

Creating Internet Shortcuts

An Internet shortcut is similar to a desktop shortcut, except that the target is the address (or URL) of a Web site. When you visit a Web site with Internet Explorer, you can use the Add to Favorites option to create an Internet shortcut to the current Web site. That Internet shortcut, called a **favorite** (or **bookmark** in other Web browsers) is stored in your Favorites folder. When you open Internet Explorer, you can then select an Internet shortcut for the Web site you want to visit by using the Add to Favorites button, or if you are already in the Favorites folder or have added the Favorites menu to your Start menu, you can click an Internet shortcut to open Internet Explorer and connect your computer to the Web site referenced by the Internet shortcut. You can also copy an Internet shortcut from the Favorites menu or Favorites folder and paste it onto the desktop so you have a direct link to a Web site you visit regularly. With the Windows 7 taskbar, you can pin Internet shortcuts to the Internet Explorer taskbar button so you always have easy access to Web sites you visit every day. Furthermore, you can copy shortcuts to your flash drive so, no matter where you are, you can quickly visit your favorite Web sites wherever you have access to a computer. Also, you can store Internet shortcuts for your online classes, or Internet shortcuts for opening Web pages posted by your instructor for your in-person class, on your flash drive.

If you right-click the background of a Web page, you can create a desktop shortcut to that Web page, or you can drag the icon to the left of the URL in the Address bar to the desktop to create an Internet shortcut. You can also drag the Address bar icon to the taskbar to pin the Web page to Internet Explorer.

Even if you regularly use another Web browser, the next set of tutorial steps calls for you to use Internet Explorer. You can then adapt what you learn using Internet Explorer to other Web browsers.

Because you frequently check the Microsoft Web site for the latest news on Windows 7 and its other products, as well as for technical troubleshooting information, you decide to create an Internet shortcut to the Microsoft Web site.

To create an Internet shortcut to Microsoft's Web site:

▶ **1.** Click the **Internet Explorer** taskbar button ⬡. Internet Explorer displays your home page.

▶ **2.** If the Internet Explorer window is maximized, click the **Restore Down** button ⬡, and if necessary, resize and reposition the window so you can see part of the content of the Internet Explorer window and your desktop background.

▶ **3.** Click the **Address bar** icon to the left of the URL for your home page to select the entire URL (this icon varies depending on your home page), type **microsoft.com**, press the **Enter** key, and if necessary, close any pop-up windows after Internet Explorer displays the Microsoft home page.

TIP

You can also right-click the background of a Web page and choose Create Shortcut.

▶ **4.** Drag the **Microsoft** icon on the left side of the Address bar to the desktop. Windows 7 creates a Microsoft Corporation Internet shortcut and uses the custom icon. See Figure 4-34. Your Internet shortcut name may differ.

Figure 4-34 | Internet shortcut created by dragging Web page Address bar icon to desktop

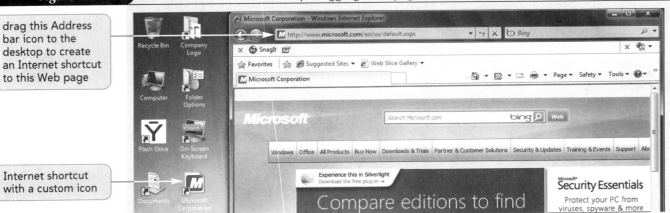

drag this Address bar icon to the desktop to create an Internet shortcut to this Web page

Internet shortcut with a custom icon

▶ **5.** Close the Internet Explorer window, and then click the **Microsoft Corporation** Internet shortcut. Internet Explorer (or your default Web browser) displays Microsoft's home page.

▶ **6.** Close the Internet Explorer window.

Next, view properties of the Microsoft Corporation Internet shortcut so you can compare it to the properties of other desktop shortcuts.

To view properties of an Internet shortcut:

▶ **1.** Right-click the **Microsoft Corporation** Internet shortcut, and then click **Properties**. Windows 7 opens the Microsoft Corporation Properties dialog box. See Figure 4-35. On the Web Document property sheet, the URL box contains the complete Web address for the Microsoft home page. Notice that you have the option of changing the icon for the Internet shortcut, and you can specify a keyboard shortcut.

Figure 4-35   **Viewing the Web document properties of an Internet shortcut**

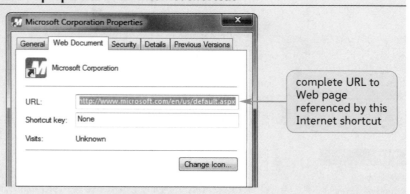

complete URL to
Web page
referenced by this
Internet shortcut

2. Click the **General** tab. On the General property sheet, Windows 7 shows the type
of file (Internet Shortcut), the location of the file (the Desktop folder for your user
account), and other details about the shortcut. See Figure 4-36. As shown on
this property sheet, the file extension for an Internet shortcut is .url. However,
Windows 7 does not display the URL file extension for Internet shortcuts. Notice
that Internet shortcuts, like regular desktop shortcuts, are relatively small in size
and use a disproportionate amount of storage space on disk relative to their size.

Figure 4-36   **Viewing General properties of an Internet shortcut**

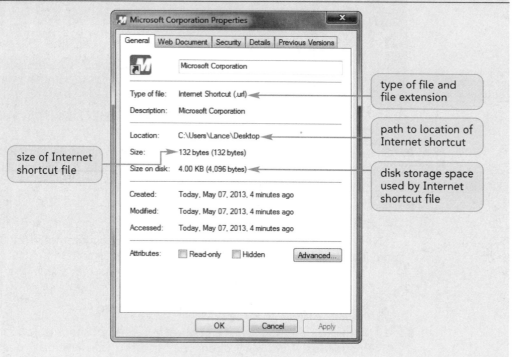

type of file and
file extension

path to location of
Internet shortcut

size of Internet
shortcut file

disk storage space
used by Internet
shortcut file

3. Close the Microsoft Corporation Properties dialog box.

The filename of the Microsoft Corporation Internet shortcut is Microsoft Corporation.url, and its short filename is most likely MICROS~1.URL

If you browse to a Web site and notice a link to another Web page or Web site, you can drag that link to your desktop to create an Internet shortcut to that Web page or Web site. This feature is useful if you don't have time to visit that Web page or Web site and add it to your Favorites list.

To create a shortcut to a link on a Web page:

▶ **1.** Click the **Microsoft Corporation** Internet shortcut.

▶ **2.** Locate a link of interest to you on Microsoft's home page (such as the link to the Microsoft Support Web page), drag that link to the desktop, and when Internet Explorer displays a Windows Security dialog box that asks if you want to allow files from this Web site to be copied to your computer, click the **OK** button, and then close the Internet Explorer window. On the computer used for this figure, Windows 7 created an Internet shortcut to the Microsoft Support Home page. See Figure 4-37. Your shortcut may differ. The Microsoft Support Home page and its Knowledge Base are useful Web sites for locating information about Windows 7 features or for troubleshooting a problem.

| Figure 4-37 | Creating an Internet shortcut using a Web page link |

Internet shortcut created by dragging an Address bar icon from the Web page

Web link dragged to the desktop to create an Internet shortcut

▶ **3.** Click the new Internet shortcut that references a link to another Web page. Windows 7 opens Internet Explorer and then displays the Web page referenced by the Internet shortcut.

▶ **4.** Drag the **Microsoft Corporation** Internet shortcut, and drop it in the Internet Explorer window. Internet Explorer navigates to the Web page referenced by the URL in the Microsoft Corporation Internet shortcut, and takes you to the Microsoft home page.

▶ **5.** Close the Internet Explorer window.

Dragging Web page links to the desktop is a quick and easy way to create Internet shortcuts to other Web sites that you might want to visit without having to navigate to those Web sites. Also, by having Internet shortcuts to Web pages you frequently visit, you can drag and drop those Internet shortcuts into your Web browser window to quickly go to another Web site.

PROSKILLS

Problem Solving: Logging on to Email Securely

Some Web-based email accounts only use secure connections for accessing your email. Others provide an option for a secure connection; however, the default connection is not a secure one. To prevent or reduce the chance that a malicious Web site or hacker can compromise your email account, you must make sure you have a secure connection when logging on that account. Secure connections are encrypted, reduce the chances of third-party eavesdropping, and prevent a third party from seeing your user logon name and password and from reading your email.

To protect your access to your email account, you can create a shortcut to the Web site and guarantee that you log on securely every time. First, you must make sure you have the right URL for your email shortcut. Open your Web browser, navigate to the Web site you use for email, select the option for logging into your email account, select the option for a secure connection, and then create an email shortcut on your desktop by dragging the Address bar icon to the desktop. Then, whenever you need to quickly access your email, all you have to do is to click the email desktop shortcut to access a secure connection and log on to your email account. Because the option for a secure connection is built into your email shortcut, you do not have to run the risk of not choosing that option.

This approach to accessing your email helps protect your communications with employers, clients, and personal contacts as well as documents that you attach to your email messages.

You can copy your Internet shortcuts to a flash drive and carry them with you wherever you go so you can quickly access Web sites that you frequently visit using whatever computer and Web browser is available.

INSIGHT

Using Internet Shortcuts in Different Web Browsers

You might use more than one Web browser to access resources and software updates on the Internet, to design Web pages, and to take advantages of features built into specific Web browsers, such as tabbed browsing, speed, or security. Rather than having a copy of one important Internet bookmark in only one of the Web browsers, you can copy Favorites or bookmarks from one Web browser to another so you have Internet shortcuts to every Web site you might need to access in each Web browser. If you also have Internet shortcuts on your desktop or in a folder on your desktop, you can use the same Internet shortcuts in different Web browsers by dragging them into whichever Web browser you are using. For example, if you are using the Firefox Web browser, you can drag and drop an Internet Explorer shortcut in the Firefox window. The Firefox Web browser then navigates to the site referenced by the URL in the Internet Explorer shortcut. Likewise, you can drag a Firefox Internet shortcut and drop it in an Internet Explorer window, and Internet Explorer navigates to the site referenced by the URL in the Firefox Internet shortcut.

Using the Create Shortcut Wizard

You can create an Internet shortcut on the fly using the Create Shortcut Wizard if you know the URL for the Web site.

To create an Internet shortcut with the Create Shortcut Wizard:

▶ **1.** Right-click the **desktop**, point to **New** on the desktop shortcut menu, and then click **Shortcut**. Windows 7 opens the Create Shortcut dialog box.

▶ **2.** In the "Type the location of the item" box, type the following URL: **http://google.com**

   You can also type www.google.com but you must type either *http://* or *www*, or the Create Shortcut Wizard will report that it cannot find the file.

▶ **3.** Verify that you have entered the path correctly, and then click the **Next** button in the Create Shortcut dialog box. Windows 7 prompts for a shortcut name.

▶ **4.** In the "Type a name for this shortcut" box, type **Google**, and then click the **Finish** button. Windows 7 creates an Internet shortcut on the desktop to the Google Web site.

▶ **5.** Click the **Google** Internet shortcut. Windows 7 opens the Google Web site using your default Web browser.

▶ **6.** Close your Web browser window.

TIP

You can press the Enter key if you want to keep your hand on the keyboard.

Lance points out that by being familiar with different ways to create and customize Internet shortcuts, you can maximize your use of Internet shortcuts.

Customizing Startup with Shortcuts

If you place desktop shortcuts or Internet shortcuts in the Startup folder for your user account, Windows 7 will automatically open the programs, drives, folders, files, dialog boxes, and Web sites referenced by those shortcuts after your computer boots to the desktop. The use of the Startup folder therefore represents one more way in which you can customize the use of your computer. Likewise, if you check email the first thing every day, or visit a specific Web site every day (such as a news Web site), you can place Internet shortcuts in the Startup folder, and Windows 7 opens those Web sites immediately after displaying your desktop. In some cases, software you install on your computer places program shortcuts in the Startup folder so specific programs automatically open after you power on your computer and perform a full start but not after you wake your computer from Sleep or Hibernation. You can check the Startup folder for these types of programs, and decide whether you want them to automatically start each time you start up your computer.

When you place shortcuts in your personal Startup folder, you can copy or move existing shortcuts you have on your desktop, Start menu, taskbar, and Favorites folder.

You decide to place a copy of the Google Internet shortcut in your Startup folder so you can quickly access the Internet and perform a search after your computer boots. First, you need to open the Startup folder.

To copy the Google Internet shortcut to your Startup folder:

▶ 1. Open the Start menu, point to **All Programs**, locate and right-click the **Startup** folder, and then click **Open** on the shortcut menu. Windows 7 opens the Startup folder for your user account (each user has their own Startup folder). The generic path to this folder is as follows:

   C:\Users\[your user account name]\AppData\Roaming\Microsoft\Windows\Start Menu\Programs\Startup

▶ 2. If necessary, restore down, resize, or reposition the Startup folder window so you can see your Google desktop shortcut.

▶ 3. Hold down the **Ctrl** key while you drag the Google Internet shortcut into the folder, release the mouse button, and then release the **Ctrl** key. Windows creates a copy of the Google Internet shortcut in the Startup folder.

▶ 4. If you are working on a computer in a college computer lab whose lab policy does not permit you to log off and then log back on your computer, does not allow you to restart your computer, or if your college's computers restore their original settings after a restart, right-click the **Google** Internet shortcut, click **Delete** on the shortcut menu, and in the Delete Shortcut dialog box, click the **Yes** button, and then close the Startup folder window.

▶ 5. If you are working on your own computer and want to log off and log back onto your user account or want to restart your computer so you can see how Windows 7 automatically opens Google's Web page in your Web browser after your computer starts up, close the Startup folder window, and then choose the Start menu option for logging off and then logging back on your computer, or the option for restarting your computer.

▶ 6. If you are working on your own computer and want to remove the Google Internet shortcut from your Startup folder, open the Start menu, point to **All Programs**, locate and right-click the **Startup** folder, click **Open** on the shortcut menu, right-click the **Google** Internet shortcut, click **Delete** on the shortcut menu, and in the Delete Shortcut dialog box, click the **Yes** button, and then close the Startup folder window.

▶ 7. If necessary, use Safely Remove Hardware and Eject Media to safely remove your flash drive.

By placing important shortcuts in your Startup folder, whether they are Internet, application, drive, folder, or file shortcuts, you can maximize the performance of your computer, have what you need at your fingertips when your computer starts, be ready to work at a moment's notice, and meet critical deadlines.

REFERENCE

Adding Shortcuts to Your Startup Folder

• Open the Start menu, point to All Programs, locate and right-click the Startup folder, and then click Open.

• Hold down the Ctrl key while you drag a desktop shortcut or an Internet shortcut into the Startup folder, or use the Create Shortcut Wizard to create a desktop or Internet shortcut in the Startup folder.

• To remove a desktop or Internet shortcut from the Startup folder, open the Startup folder, right-click the desktop or Internet shortcut, click Delete, and in the Delete Shortcut dialog box, click the Yes button.

• Close the Startup folder window.

Shortcuts unlock the power of Windows 7 by bypassing many of the intermediate steps that you would otherwise perform as you work on your computer and taking you directly to what you need to use in a single step, whether it's on your computer, another computer, or the Web.

Restoring Your Computer's Settings

If you are working in a computer lab, or if you want to restore your desktop computer to the settings established prior to working on this tutorial, complete the following steps.

To restore your computer's settings:

▶ **1.** Click the **Upsilon Air** desktop shortcut, and after Windows 7 opens the Upsilon Air folder, right-click **Upsilon Air** under Favorites in the Navigation pane, and then click **Remove**.

▶ **2.** To delete the Upsilon Air folder, click **Public Documents** in the Address bar, right-click the **Upsilon Air** folder, click **Delete**, click the **Yes** button in the Delete Folder dialog box, and then close the Public Documents folder window.

▶ **3.** If you want to remove the custom icon for your flash drive, click the **Flash Drive** desktop shortcut, hold down the **Ctrl** key, point to the **autorun** folder, point to the **autorun.inf** file, release the **Ctrl** key, press the **Delete** key, click the **Yes** button in the Delete Multiple Items dialog box, and then close your flash drive window.

▶ **4.** To hide extensions for known file types, click the **View** tab in the Folder Options dialog box, click the **Hide extensions for known file types** check box if it does not contain a check mark, and then click the **OK** button to close the Folder Options dialog box and apply these changes.

▶ **5.** To remove your desktop shortcuts, hold down the **Ctrl** key while you point to the **Flash Drive** shortcut, the **Documents** shortcut, the **Upsilon Air** shortcuts, the **Logo** shortcut, the **Calculator** shortcut, the **Company Logo** shortcut, the **On-Screen Keyboard** shortcut, the **Microsoft Corporation** shortcut, the **Microsoft Support Home** shortcut (or the shortcut to a link on Microsoft's Home page), and the **Google** shortcut, release the **Ctrl** key, press the **Delete** key, and then click the **Yes** button in the Delete Multiple Items dialog box.

▶ **6.** To remove Folder Options from the Control Panel taskbar button, right-click the **Control Panel** taskbar button, right-click **Folder Options** in the pinned items section of the Control Panel Jump List, click **Unpin from this list**, and then press the **Esc** key to close the Control Panel Jump List.

▶ **7.** To remove the Control Panel taskbar button, right-click the **Control Panel** taskbar button, and then click **Unpin this program from taskbar**.

▶ **8.** To clean up your Windows Explorer Jump List, right-click the **Windows Explorer** taskbar button, right-click **Upsilon Air** in the pinned items section of the Windows Explorer Jump List, click **Unpin from this list**, right-click **Removable Disk** (or the option for your flash drive), click **Remove from this list**, right-click **Annual Report**, click **Remove from this list**, right-click **Company Logo**, click **Remove from this list**, right-click **Desktop**, and then click **Remove from this list**.

If necessary, complete the next section to restore other default sections and remove your flash drive.

To restore other default settings and remove your flash drive:

▶ **1.** To restore double-click activation, click the **Folder Options** desktop shortcut, and on the General property sheet in the Folder Options dialog box, click the **Double-click to open an item (single-click to select)** option button, click the **OK** button, and then delete the **Folder Options** desktop shortcut.

▶ **2.** To remove the Computer icon from your desktop, open the **Start menu**, right-click **Computer**, and then click **Show on Desktop**.

▶ **3.** Use the Safely Remove Hardware and Eject Media icon to remove your flash drive.

REVIEW

Session 4.2 Quick Check

1. What Windows folder contains shortcuts for the items listed under Favorites in the Navigation pane?
2. The file extension for a desktop shortcut is _____, and the file extension for an Internet shortcut is _____.
3. Internet Explorer stores Internet shortcuts in your _____ folder.
4. True or False. You cannot create an Internet shortcut to a Web site by dragging a link on a Web page to the desktop.
5. What file extension does Windows use for Setup Information files?
6. True or False. If you want to automatically open a Web page right after you start your computer and log on your account, you can place an Internet shortcut to that Web site in the Startup folder.

Practice the skills you learned in the tutorial using the same case scenario.

PRACTICE

Review Assignments

For a list of Data Files in the Review folder, see page 239.

Lance recently hired another advertising associate, Elsa Vandenberg, to help him with client projects. On her first day of work, Lance explains to Elsa how he works with Windows 7, and he describes the types of support that his department must provide for other employees. Since time is always at a premium, Lance asks you to create shortcuts to the drives, applications, folders, and files that Elsa will be using on a daily basis.

As you complete each step in these Review Assignments, use a word-processing application, such as Microsoft Word or the WordPad accessory, to record your answers to questions. Also, if you change any settings on the computer you are using, note the original settings so you can restore them later. If you are using another browser, adapt the instructions to that browser. Complete the following:

1. If necessary, display the Computer icon on the desktop, switch to Web style with single-click activation, and choose the option to display file extensions for known file types.
2. Copy the Review folder under the Tutorial.04 folder to the Public Documents folder, and then change the name of the Review folder to **Clients**.
3. Open the Computer window, and then adjust the size and placement of the window so you can also see part of the desktop.
4. Create a desktop shortcut to your DVD or CD drive, and then close the Computer window. Which drive did you use for the shortcut? What name did Windows 7 assign to the drive? What name did Windows 7 assign to the desktop shortcut? Change the name of the desktop shortcut to **DVD Drive** if you created a shortcut to your DVD drive. If you created a desktop shortcut to your CD drive, change its name to **CD Drive**. What type of icon does Windows 7 use? Open the Properties dialog box for the DVD Drive or CD Drive. What is the target type? What is the shortcut's target? What file extension does this shortcut have? What is the full filename of the shortcut (including the file extension)? What is the size of the shortcut? How much disk storage space does the shortcut use? How much storage space does the shortcut waste on disk? Use the option to open the file location. What window does Windows 7 open? Close the DVD Drive or CD Drive Properties dialog box, and then close the newly opened window.
5. If you created a DVD Drive shortcut, insert a DVD in the DVD drive. What type of disc did you insert? What categories and options are shown in the AutoPlay dialog box? Close the AutoPlay dialog box. Click the DVD Drive shortcut. Briefly explain what happens. Close any window or dialog box that opens.
6. If you created a CD Drive shortcut, insert a CD in the CD drive. What type of disc did you insert? What categories and options are shown in the AutoPlay dialog box? Close the AutoPlay dialog box. Click the CD Drive shortcut. Briefly explain what happens. Close any window or dialog box that opens.
7. Open the Documents library, open the Clients folder, create a desktop shortcut to the Projections folder within the Clients folder, close the Projections folder window, and then change the name of the desktop shortcut to **Projections**. Describe the appearance of the Projections shortcut icon. Click the Projections shortcut, and explain what happens. Close the window that Windows 7 opened.
8. Open the Properties dialog box for the Projections shortcut. What is the target type? What is the Target location? What is the shortcut's target? What file extension does this shortcut have? What is the full filename of the shortcut (including the file extension)? What is the size of the shortcut? How much disk storage space does the shortcut use? How much storage space does the shortcut waste on disk?

9. On the Shortcut property sheet, choose the option for changing the icon used for the shortcut, and then choose one of the icons contained in the imageres.dll file, apply the change, close the Projections Properties dialog box. If necessary, right-click the desktop, and then choose Refresh to update the icon for the shortcut. What happens when you click the Projections shortcut?

10. Create a desktop shortcut to the Five Year Growth Plan.xlsx file, and then close the Projections folder window. What type of icon does Windows 7 use for the shortcut? Change the name of the shortcut to **Five Year Growth Plan**. If you have Microsoft Excel 2007 or later installed on your computer, click the Five Year Growth Plan shortcut, and after you examine the spreadsheet, close the Microsoft Excel window.

11. Open the Properties dialog box for the Five Year Growth Plan shortcut. What is the target type? What is the target location? What is the shortcut's target? What file extension does this shortcut have? What is the full filename of the shortcut (including the file extension)? What is the size of the shortcut? How much disk storage space does the shortcut use? How much storage space does the shortcut waste on disk? Close the Five Year Growth Plan Properties dialog box.

12. From the Start menu, open the All Programs menu, click Accessories, right-click Snipping Tool, and then use the Send to option to create a desktop shortcut. What is the name of this shortcut, and what type of icon does Windows 7 use for this new shortcut? What happens when you click this new shortcut? *Optional*: Use the Snipping Tool to select part of the desktop view, and then close the Snipping Tool window without saving the image.

13. Open the Properties dialog box for the Snipping Tool shortcut. What is the target type? What is the target's location? What is the shortcut's target? What environment variable does this shortcut use in the path for its target? What setting does this environment variable represent? What file extension does this shortcut have? What is the full filename of the shortcut (including the file extension)? What is the size of the shortcut? How much disk storage space does the shortcut use? How much storage space does the shortcut waste on disk? Close the Snipping Tool Properties dialog box.

14. Create a shortcut to the Control Panel on the desktop. What type of icon does Windows 7 use for the Control Panel shortcut? What happens when you click the shortcut? Close the window opened by the Control Panel shortcut.

15. On the desktop, create a copy of the DVD Drive or CD Drive shortcut. Open the Properties dialog box for this new shortcut. Replace the target in the Target box with the following path: **C:\Users\Public\Documents** What happens as you type this new path? Close the DVD Drive (or CD Drive) Properties dialog box, and apply the changes. Explain what happened to the shortcut icon.

16. Change the name of the DVD Drive (or CD Drive) shortcut to **Public Documents**, and then view its properties. What is the target type now? What is the new Target location? Close the Public Documents Properties dialog box. Click the Public Documents shortcut. What happens? Close the window opened by the shortcut.

17. Open the Control Panel, switch to Large icons view, create a desktop shortcut to the Mouse applet, and then close Control Panel. Click the Mouse shortcut, and then identify each of the property sheets in the Mouse Properties dialog box. What types of options can you access with the Mouse shortcut? Close the Mouse Properties dialog box.

18. Open the Properties dialog box for the Mouse shortcut. What is the target type? What is the shortcut's target? What file extension does this shortcut have? What is the full filename of the shortcut (including the file extension)? What is the size of the shortcut? How much disk storage space does the shortcut use? What is the Folder path (on the Details property sheet)? How much storage space does the shortcut waste on disk? Close the Mouse Properties dialog box.

19. Drag the Public Documents shortcut, and drop it on the Start menu button. Open the Start menu. Where did Windows 7 place the Public Documents shortcut? Click the Public Documents shortcut on the Start menu. Explain what happens. Close the window opened by this shortcut.

20. Drag the Snipping Tool to the taskbar. Explain what happens.

21. Right-click the desktop background, and then choose the option to create a new shortcut using the Create Shortcut Wizard. Type **C:\Windows\System32\desk.cpl** in the "Type the location of the item" box. Assign the name **Screen Resolution** to the new desktop shortcut. Describe the appearance of the new desktop shortcut. Click the Screen Resolution shortcut. What window did this shortcut open, and what options are available in this window? Close the window opened by the shortcut. *Note*: Control Panel applets in the Windows folder have the .cpl file extension.

22. View properties of the Screen Resolution shortcut. What is the target type? What is the target location? What is the path to the target? What is the full filename of this shortcut (with the file extension)? How much disk storage space does the shortcut use? How much storage space does the shortcut waste on disk? On the General property sheet, what program does Windows 7 use to open this shortcut? Close the Screen Resolution Properties dialog box.

23. Open the Projections folder with your desktop shortcut. Use the Address bar to switch to the Clients folder, and then create the link in the Navigation pane to the Business Records folder. Open the Projections link. What is the name of the file (or files) that Windows 7 displays in this folder window? Close this folder window.

24. Attach and open your flash drive. Create an autorun folder in the top-level folder of your flash drive. Open the Company Logo folder under the Clients folder, choose the option to display the two windows side by side, and then drag the Upsilon Air.ico file from the Company Logo folder to the autorun folder. Close the Company Logo folder. Create a new Text Document file in the top-level folder of the flash drive, name it **autorun.inf**, open autorun.inf in Notepad, set up the autorun.inf file as explained in the tutorial and specify Upsilon Air.ico as the file containing the icon to use for the flash drive icon, and then save and close the autorun.inf file. Close the flash drive window, open a Computer window, safely remove and reattach your flash drive, and if necessary, close the AutoPlay dialog box. What happens to your flash drive icon? Close the Computer window.

25. Open Internet Explorer (or another Web browser), navigate to the http://google.com/images Web page, adjust the size and placement of the Internet Explorer window so you can see a portion of the desktop, and then drag the icon located on the left side of the Address bar to the desktop. What is the name of the Internet shortcut? Close your Web browser, and then click the Internet shortcut. What happens? If necessary, drag the browser window to the right so you can see the Internet shortcut on the desktop.

26. Drag the Maps link to the desktop. Close your Web browser window, change the name of the Maps link to **Google Maps**, click the Google Maps link, and describe what happens. Drag the Google Images shortcut, and drop it in your Web browser window, and then describe what happens. Close your Web browser window. *Optional:* If you have Firefox or another Web browser installed on your computer, open that Web browser and then drag the Google Maps shortcut from the desktop into that Web browser's window. Does the shortcut work in the same way as it does in Internet Explorer?

27. View properties of the Internet shortcut to the Google Images page. What is the URL for this Internet shortcut? What file extension does Windows use for this Internet shortcut? What is the full filename of the shortcut (including the file extension)? What is the size of the shortcut? How much disk storage space does the shortcut use? How much storage space does the shortcut waste on disk? Close the Google Images Properties dialog box.

28. Explain how you would modify your computer system so it automatically opens the Screen Resolution desktop shortcut and the Google Maps shortcut when you start your computer and log onto your user account.

29. To restore your computer:

    • Open the Public Documents folder with your desktop shortcut, delete the Clients folder, remove the Business Records link under Favorites in the Navigation pane, and then close the Public Documents window.

    • Open the Start menu and remove the Public Documents shortcut from the pinned items area.

    • Delete the desktop and Internet shortcuts that you created in this Review Assignment.

    • If you no longer want the custom icon for your flash drive, open the Computer window, open your flash drive, delete the autorun.inf file, delete the autorun folder, and then close the flash drive window.

    • Eject the DVD or CD that you have in your DVD or CD drive.

    • If necessary, switch to Classic style with double-click activation, choose the option to hide file extensions for known file types, and then remove the Computer icon from the desktop.

30. If necessary, use Safely Remove Hardware and Eject Media to safely remove your flash drive.

31. Submit your answers to the questions in this Review Assignment to your instructor either in printed or electronic form, as requested. Remember to include your name and any other information requested by your instructor on your assignment.

Use your skills to create shortcuts to resources at a learning center.

APPLY

Case Problem 1

There are no Data Files needed for this Case Problem.

Toulumney Learning Center   The Toulumney Learning Center provides highly focused courses for people seeking to hone their college entry skills, prepare for certification exams, and develop basic computer skills. Lynsey Bivins, the manager, wants to create shortcuts on the classroom computers that students use so they can quickly access the programs and resources they need for their coursework. Because the upcoming session is only a week away, she asks you to help her determine which shortcuts students need and then create the shortcuts.

As you complete each step, record your answers to questions so you can submit them to your instructor. Use a word-processing application, such as Microsoft Word or the WordPad accessory, to prepare your answers to these questions. Also, if you change any settings on the computer you are using, make a note of the original settings so you can restore them later. Complete the following steps:

1. Open the Documents library, and create a shortcut to the Downloads folder under Favorites in the Navigation pane by using the Send to option on the shortcut menu for the Downloads folder. Close the Documents library. Describe the appearance of the icon used for the Downloads shortcut. Change the name of the Downloads desktop folder to **Toulumney Learning Center Downloads**.

2. View properties of the Toulumney Learning Center Downloads shortcut. What is the target for this shortcut? What is the target's location? What is the full filename of the shortcut (including the file extension)? What is the size of the shortcut? How much disk storage space does the shortcut use? How much storage space does the shortcut waste on disk? Where does Windows 7 get the icon for this shortcut? List the full path. Close the Toulumney Learning Center Downloads Properties dialog box.

3. Make a copy of the Toulumney Learning Center Downloads shortcut, change its name to **Toulumney Learning Center Videos**, and then view its properties. On the Shortcut property sheet, change the path shown in the Target box to **C:\Users\ Public\Videos\Sample Videos**, and then click the OK button. Describe the change in the icon for this new shortcut. Test the shortcut and verify that it works, play the video within this folder, and then close this folder window. Change the icon for the My Videos folder to another icon in the imageres.dll file in the Windows system32 folder. What icon did you use? What advantage does this type of shortcut confer (other than accessing videos)?

4. From the Start menu, drag Devices and Printers to the desktop. Describe the icon used for this shortcut. Click the Devices and Printers shortcut, and then describe what Windows 7 displays in the Devices and Printers window. Close the Devices and Printers window.

5. View properties of the Devices and Printers desktop shortcut. What is the Target location? What is the full filename of this shortcut? What happens when you click the Open File Location button? What options are available from this window? Close this window.

6. Create a desktop shortcut to the Ease of Access Center in the Control Panel. What method did you use to create a shortcut to the Ease of Access Center? What type of icon does Windows 7 use for this shortcut? What happens when you click the Ease of Access Center shortcut? What options are available? Click the Ease of Access Center link. What happens? Close the window.

7. Open the Documents library, open the Public Documents folder, and then create a folder named **Toulumney Learning Center Resources**. Create a desktop shortcut to the Toulumney Learning Center Resources folder. Describe the method that you used to create this shortcut. Close the Public Documents window. View properties of the Toulumney Learning Center Resources desktop shortcut. What is the target for this shortcut? Why is the path enclosed within quotation marks? What is the target's location? Choose a custom icon for this shortcut, and then close the Toulumney Learning Center Resource Properties dialog box.

EXPLORE

8. Drag the Toulumney Learning Center Downloads, Toulumney Learning Center Videos, Devices and Printers, and Ease of Access shortcuts and drop them on the My Resources shortcut. Click the Toulumney Learning Center Resources shortcut, and then explain what happened when you dropped the desktop shortcuts onto the Toulumney Learning Center Resources shortcut. How did Windows 7 put these desktop shortcuts into this folder?

9. Click the Devices and Printers shortcut in the Toulumney Learning Center Resources folder. Describe what happens. Close the Toulumney Learning Center Resources folder.

10. If necessary, attach your flash drive to your computer, and then send a copy of the Toulumney Learning Center Resources folder to your flash drive. Does Windows 7 move or copy this folder?

11. Can you think of why it would be useful to have a Resources folder for storing desktop shortcuts? Can you think of a way in which you might adapt this feature to your work or play? Explain.

12. What new features did you learn from this case problem?

13. If necessary, use Safely Remove Hardware and Eject Media to safely remove your flash drive.

14. To restore your computer, open the Documents library, delete the Toulumney Learning Center Resources folder, close the Documents library window, and then delete the Toulumney Learning Center Resources desktop shortcut.

15. Submit your answers to the questions in this case problem to your instructor, either in printed or electronic form, as requested, and, if also requested, a copy of your shortcuts by placing them in a drop folder on your computer lab's network. Remember to include your name and any other information requested by your instructor on your assignment.

Use your skills to create shortcuts for a computer troubleshooting firm.

APPLY

Case Problem 2

There are no Data Files needed for this Case Problem.

On the Edge Troubleshooting On the Edge Troubleshooting is a Milwaukee firm that uses cutting-edge computer troubleshooting techniques for its clients. Brice McCray, a networking systems specialist, provides his clients with fast, reliable, and effective network, computer, and laptop support and troubleshooting. Furthermore, he offers top-notch services for optimizing and tweaking the performance of networks and comput-ers. Brice carries on his flash drive shortcuts to common operating system folders and troubleshooting utilities as well as Internet shortcuts to resources at the Microsoft Web site. Since you are working this summer as one of his interns, he recommends that you put together a tool kit of shortcuts that you can use to assist clients seeking information on new trends in operating system software.

As you complete each step, record your answers to questions so you can submit them to your instructor. Use a word-processing application, such as Microsoft Word or the WordPad accessory, to prepare your answers to these questions. If you cannot find spe-cific Web site links described in the case problem steps, substitute another Web site link from the Web page you are examining, and identify any substitutions you made in your responses to the questions. Also, if you change any settings on the computer you are using, make a note of the original settings so you can restore them later. Complete the following steps:

⊕ EXPLORE

1. Right-click the desktop, choose the option to create a new folder on the desktop, name it **Troubleshooting**, and then open the Troubleshooting folder.

2. Open Internet Explorer (or your Web browser), and arrange the Troubleshooting and Web browser windows so they are side by side. Navigate to the Microsoft Web site, and then under Support, locate and drag the Microsoft Support Home, Knowledge Base, MSDN, and TechNet links from Microsoft Corporation's home page into the Troubleshooting folder. If Microsoft has changed its home page, use the Search feature to locate links to each of these Web pages, and then drag the link to the desktop.

3. Drag the MSDN Internet shortcut into the Internet Explorer window. Describe what happens.

4. At the MSDN Web page, drag the Library link into the Resources folder, and then change the name of the Library Internet shortcut to **MSDN Library**.

5. Go back to the Microsoft home page and search for **Windows 7** topics using the Search box. Locate and drag the link for the Windows 7 Upgrade Advisor link to the desktop. View the properties of this Internet shortcut. What is the URL to this Web site? (*Hint*: You can right-click the URL, select Copy from the shortcut menu, and then paste the URL into your Word or WordPad document.) Close the Windows 7 Upgrade Advisor Properties dialog box.

6. Close the Internet Explorer window (or your Web browser).

7. Right-click the background of the Troubleshooting folder window, use the Create Shortcut Wizard to create a shortcut to the Symantec Web site (http://symantec.com), and name the shortcut **Symantec**. What icon does Windows 7 use for this shortcut? View properties of the Symantec Internet shortcut. What file did Windows 7 use for

the Symantec Internet shortcut icon? Use the Symantec Internet shortcut to navigate to Symantec's home page, locate and drag the "View All Viruses And Risks" link (or another link) to the Troubleshooting folder. How does this Internet shortcut icon differ from that for the Symantec Internet shortcut? Test this shortcut, and then close your Web browser window.

8. Drag the Symantec Internet shortcut to the Start button. Open the Start menu. Where does Windows 7 place this shortcut? Close the Start menu. Drag the Symantec Internet shortcut from the Resources folder to the taskbar. Where does Windows 7 pin this Internet shortcut?

9. From the Start menu, drag Control Panel to the Resources folder.

10. Use the Control Panel shortcut to open the Control Panel, switch to Large icons view (if necessary), and then drag System to the Resources folder. Test the System shortcut. What does this shortcut open? Why would this shortcut be useful if you were troubleshooting problems on a computer? Close the window opened by this shortcut, and close the Control Panel window.

⊕ **EXPLORE** 11. In the Troubleshooting folder window, use the Create Shortcut Wizard to create a new desktop shortcut. When prompted for the location, type **%SystemRoot%** and then advance to the next step and name the shortcut **SystemRoot**. What is %SystemRoot%? After examining the icon for this shortcut, what would you expect this shortcut to open? Click the SystemRoot shortcut. Examine the Address bar. What is the target of the SystemRoot shortcut? Why would it be useful to use an environment variable in a shortcut rather than specify an exact location for the Windows folder using C:\Windows? Close the window opened by this shortcut.

12. What other types of shortcuts would you place in this Troubleshooting folder if you were responsible for troubleshooting computers?

13. To restore your computer, remove the Symantec shortcut from the pinned items list on the Start menu, and then unpin the Symantec shortcut from the Jump List of the Internet Explorer taskbar button.

14. If you want to keep the Troubleshooting folder and the shortcuts you created, attach your flash drive, and hold down the Shift key while you use the Send to option to move the Troubleshooting folder to your last drive.

15. If you do not want to keep the Troubleshooting folder, delete it.

16. If necessary, use Safely Remove Hardware and Eject Media to safely remove your flash drive.

17. Submit your answers to the questions in this case problem to your instructor, either in printed or electronic form, as requested, and, if also requested, a copy of your shortcuts by placing them in a drop folder on your computer lab's network. Remember to include your name and any other information requested by your instructor on your assignment.

Use your skills to create shortcuts for a toy company.

APPLY

Case Problem 3

For a list of Data Files in the Case3 folder, see page 239.

Next Generation Toys Julio Vargas, a sales rep for Next Generation Toys, depends on his company laptop to keep in touch with his company's headquarters as he travels and meets with prospective clients. Since he depends on his laptop for his business, he makes every effort to safeguard and improve his computer's performance. He asks you for ideas on how to customize the Start menu on his laptop so he can quickly access important Windows options for maintaining, troubleshooting, and improving the performance of his computer. He also asks you to help him create these shortcuts and add them to a folder on his All Programs menu.

As you complete each step, record your answers to questions so you can submit them to your instructor. Use a word-processing application, such as Microsoft Word or the WordPad accessory, to prepare your answers to these questions. Also, if you change any settings on the computer you are using, make a note of the original settings so you can restore them later. Complete the following steps:

1. If necessary, choose the option to display file extensions for known file types. Attach your flash drive to your computer, and after Windows 7 displays the AutoPlay dialog box, note the drive name for your flash drive on the computer you are using, and then close the AutoPlay dialog box.

2. Copy the Case3 folder from the Tutorial.04 folder to the Public Documents folder, change the name of the Case3 folder to **Icon Files**, open the Icon Files folder, and then minimize the window.

3. Use the Create Shortcut Wizard to create a desktop shortcut to your flash drive. Specify the path to the top-level folder of your flash drive, and use **Flash Drive** as the name for your new shortcut. What path did you specify?

4. Use the Flash Drive shortcut to open a window onto your flash drive.

5. Maximize the Icon Files window, and then arrange the Icon Files window and your flash drive window so they are displayed side by side.

6. Create an **autorun** folder on your flash drive, drag one of the icon files from the Icon Files window and drop it on the autorun folder, and then close the Icon Files window.

7. In your flash drive window, create a new Text Document file, name it **autorun.inf**, and then open the autorun.inf file.

⊕ EXPLORE   8. Enter an **[autorun]** section on the first line of the autorun.inf file, enter an **icon** command on the second line that references the location of the icon file you copied to the autorun folder, and on the third line, enter the following command: **label="Next Generation Toys"**

9. List the three commands that you entered in the autorun.inf file.

10. Save the autorun.inf file, close the flash drive window, safely remove your flash drive, open a Computer window, reattach your flash drive, and, if necessary, close the AutoPlay dialog box. Examine the flash drive in the Computer window, and then describe the two features that Windows 7 applied to your flash drive.

11. To update the flash drive shortcut icon on your desktop, close the My Computer window, open the Properties dialog box for your flash drive shortcut, click the Change Icon button, and then click the OK button twice to close the Change Icon dialog box and then the Properties dialog box for your flash drive shortcut. Describe how your flash drive's shortcut icon changes.

12. Describe how these features might benefit you in your everyday life.

13. To restore your computer, open the Public Documents folder, delete the Icon Files folder, close the Public Documents window, open your flash drive with your flash drive desktop shortcut, delete the autorun folder, delete the autorun.inf file, close the flash drive window, and delete the flash drive desktop shortcut.

14. If necessary, use Safely Remove Hardware and Eject Media to safely remove your flash drive.

15. Submit your answers to the questions in this case problem to your instructor, either in printed or electronic form, as requested, and, if also requested, a copy of your autorun.inf file via email or by placing it in a drop folder on your computer lab's network. Remember to include your name and any other information requested by your instructor on your assignment.

Extend what you've learned to create shortcuts for a Buenos Aires news show.

CHALLENGE

Case Problem 4

There are no Data Files needed for this Case Problem.

Buenos Aires Live   Sofia Castillo works as a news anchor for the TV news show Buenos Aires Live. Sofia is looking for ways to save time performing routine operations on her computer. You offer to show her how to create desktop shortcuts for logging off, restarting, and shutting down her computer. If Sofia decides to activate hibernation on her computer, you can create another shortcut for placing her computer in hibernation.

As you complete each step, record your answers to questions so you can submit them to your instructor. Use a word-processing application, such as Microsoft Word or the WordPad accessory, to prepare your answers to these questions. Also, if you change any settings on the computer you are using, make a note of the original settings so you can restore them later. In the following steps, you will create and test shortcuts for restarting, shutting down, and logging off. If you work on your own computer, you can create and keep these shortcuts on your desktop. If you are working on a computer in a computer lab that restores the computer (and the desktop) every time the computer is started up, you will have to create the shortcuts on your flash drive; otherwise, you will lose the desktop shortcuts you create. To test the shortcut for logging off a computer, your computer must be set up to include that option (which may not be the case in a college computer lab).

1. Create a new folder named **Shutdown Shortcuts** on your desktop or on your flash drive, and then open the Shutdown Shortcuts folder.

⊕ EXPLORE

2. Use the Create Shortcut Wizard to create a shortcut for restarting your computer. When prompted for the location of the program to use, enter the following command: **%SystemRoot%\system32\shutdown.exe /r**
Note: /r is a switch for restarting a computer.

3. Verify that you have entered the path correctly, and then use **Restart** as the name for this shortcut. Why would it be useful to use an environment variable in a shortcut rather than specify an exact location for the Windows folder using C:\Windows?

4. View properties of this shortcut and then provide the following information about this shortcut: Target type, Target location, Start in path, Type of file, Description, Size, Size on disk, and full filename (with file extension). Close the Properties dialog box for this shortcut.

5. Before you test this shortcut, save your work and close all open programs, and then use the Restart shortcut to shut down and restart your computer. As shown in Figure 4-38, Windows 7 displays a "You are about to be logged off" dialog box that informs you that it will shut down your computer in less than a minute. Click the OK button and wait for Windows 7 to shut down and then restart your computer. After your computer restarts, log on your user account, and if you are creating shortcuts in a folder on your flash drive, open that folder.

Figure 4-38   **Warning dialog box displayed after using a shutdown shortcut**

warning about upcoming log off

warning about when Windows will shut down computer

⚠ You are about to be logged off

⚠ Windows will shut down in less than a minute.

Close

⊕ EXPLORE　6. Right-click the Restart shortcut, click Copy, click the Shutdown Shortcuts folder background, and then click Paste. Change the name of the copy of that shortcut to **Shutdown**, view properties of the Shutdown shortcut, and modify the path in the target by changing /r to /s (for Shutdown). Verify that you have entered the path correctly, and then close the dialog box and apply the changes.

7. View properties of this shortcut and then provide the following information about this shortcut: Target type, Target location, Start in path, Type of file, Description, Size, Size on disk, and full filename (with file extension). Close the Properties dialog box for this shortcut.

8. Before you test this shortcut, save your work and close all open programs, and then use the Shutdown shortcut to shut down your computer. Again, Windows 7 displays a "You are about to be logged off" dialog box that informs you that it will shut down your computer in less than a minute. Click the OK button and wait for Windows 7 to shut down your computer. After Windows 7 shuts down your computer, manually power on your computer, log on your user account, and if you are creating shortcuts in a folder on your flash drive, open that folder.

⊕ EXPLORE　9. *Optional:* If your computer supports logging off and the use of a Welcome screen, make a copy of the Restart shortcut, change the name of the copy of that shortcut to **Log Off**, view properties of the Shutdown shortcut, and modify the path in the target by changing /r to /l (for Log Off). Make sure you type the letter *l* and not the number *1* for the switch. Verify that you have entered the path correctly, and then close the dialog box and apply the changes.

10. If your computer supports logging off and the use of a Welcome screen, you can test this shortcut. First, save your work and close all open programs, and then use the Log Off shortcut to log off your computer. After Windows 7 displays the Welcome screen, log back onto your computer, and if you are creating shortcuts in a folder on your flash drive, open that folder.

⊕ EXPLORE　11. If you created your shortcuts on the desktop and want to keep them, hold down the Shift key while you use the Send to option to move the Shutdown Shortcuts folder to your flash drive.

12. If you do not want to keep your desktop shortcuts, delete the Shutdown Shortcuts folder.

13. If you created the shortcuts on your flash drive and do not want to keep those shortcuts, open a window onto your flash drive, and then delete the Shutdown Shortcuts folder.

14. If necessary, use Safely Remove Hardware and Eject Media to safely remove your flash drive.

15. Submit your answers to this case problem to your instructor, either in printed or electronic form, as requested, and, if also requested, a copy of your shortcuts by placing them in a drop folder on your computer lab's network. Remember to include your name and any other information requested by your instructor on your assignment.

ENDING DATA FILES

There are no ending Data Files needed for this tutorial.

TUTORIAL **5**

OBJECTIVES

Session 5.1
- Develop an understanding of the concept and use of a file system
- Review the process for formatting a hard disk
- Compare details and features of the NTFS and FAT file systems
- Use Disk Management to view information about disks and partitions

Session 5.2
- Compress and uncompress folders and files
- Create and extract compressed folders
- Encrypt and decrypt folders and files
- Examine BitLocker Drive Encryption

Comparing Windows 7 File Systems

Managing NTFS File System Data

Case | *Cooper & Bauman*

Cooper & Bauman, a corporation with its headquarters in Melbourne, Australia, produces a variety of consumer products, including household and personal care products, as well as small household appliances. As Cooper & Bauman's information systems expert, Cadence Soubeiran is responsible for managing the handling, storage, and protection of vital company information. Cadence determines not only which employees have access to information but also what type of access. She also develops guidelines for securing, protecting, and releasing company information. Cadence and her staff are constantly evaluating and learning how to implement Windows 7 features to increase the security of the company's computers and their data. Her current focus is on the Windows 7 NTFS file system and its support for managing data on high-performance, high-capacity drives.

STARTING DATA FILES

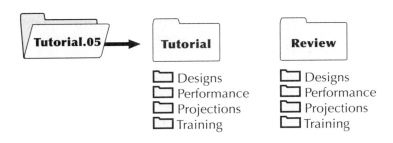

Tutorial.05 → Tutorial
- Designs
- Performance
- Projections
- Training

Review
- Designs
- Performance
- Projections
- Training

SESSION 5.1 VISUAL OVERVIEW

A **drive**, a logical concept, consists of all or part of a single disk, or a volume, that uses a specific file system, and is assigned a drive name. The terms drive and volume are frequently used interchangeably because the hard disk is usually devoted to one contiguous volume and one drive on that volume.

You, or the manufacturer of a disk, can assign a **volume label**, or electronic label, to a disk to identify its purpose.

A **file system** consists of the data structures that an operating system uses to track information about folders and files stored on a disk as well as information about the disk and file system.

Basic disks are physical disks, such as a hard disk, DVD disc, or flash drive, that contain one or more primary partitions, extended partitions, or logical drives.

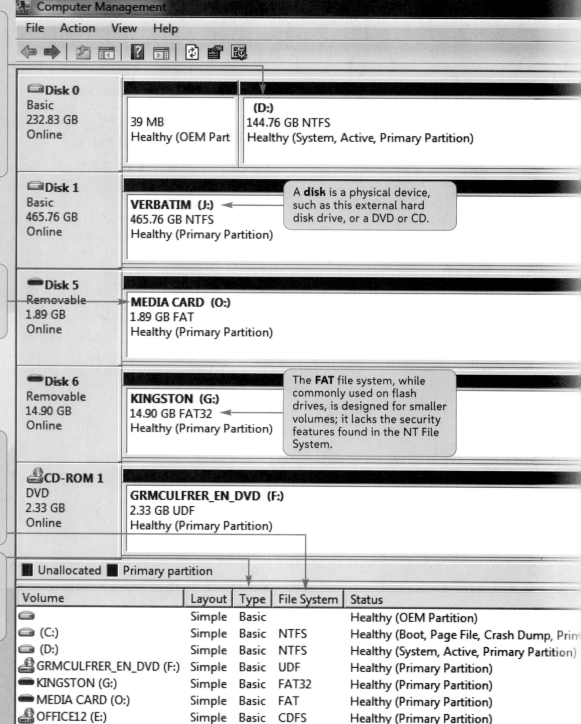

A **disk** is a physical device, such as this external hard disk drive, or a DVD or CD.

The **FAT** file system, while commonly used on flash drives, is designed for smaller volumes; it lacks the security features found in the NT File System.

DISK MANAGEMENT

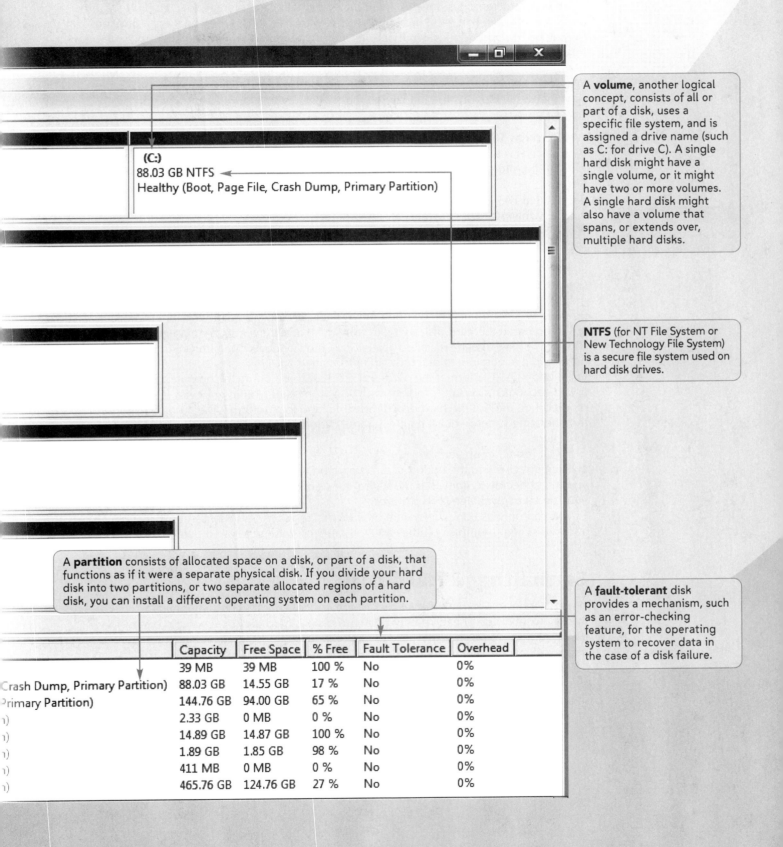

(C:)
88.03 GB NTFS
Healthy (Boot, Page File, Crash Dump, Primary Partition)

A **volume**, another logical concept, consists of all or part of a disk, uses a specific file system, and is assigned a drive name (such as C: for drive C). A single hard disk might have a single volume, or it might have two or more volumes. A single hard disk might also have a volume that spans, or extends over, multiple hard disks.

NTFS (for NT File System or New Technology File System) is a secure file system used on hard disk drives.

A **partition** consists of allocated space on a disk, or part of a disk, that functions as if it were a separate physical disk. If you divide your hard disk into two partitions, or two separate allocated regions of a hard disk, you can install a different operating system on each partition.

A **fault-tolerant** disk provides a mechanism, such as an error-checking feature, for the operating system to recover data in the case of a disk failure.

	Capacity	Free Space	% Free	Fault Tolerance	Overhead
	39 MB	39 MB	100 %	No	0%
Crash Dump, Primary Partition)	88.03 GB	14.55 GB	17 %	No	0%
Primary Partition)	144.76 GB	94.00 GB	65 %	No	0%
)	2.33 GB	0 MB	0 %	No	0%
)	14.89 GB	14.87 GB	100 %	No	0%
)	1.89 GB	1.85 GB	98 %	No	0%
)	411 MB	0 MB	0 %	No	0%
)	465.76 GB	124.76 GB	27 %	No	0%

The Windows 7 File Systems

A file system determines how an operating system allocates storage space to folders and files, how effectively it uses the storage space on a disk, what type of access it provides to specific folders and files, what options are available for maintaining and restoring the integrity of the file system, and any additional features unique to that file system. You can use different types of file systems on different types of disks, and different versions of the Windows operating systems differ in their support for specific file systems.

Windows 7 supports the following types of file systems for different types of storage media:

- **NTFS (New Technology File System)** for internal and external hard disk drives as well as flash drives
- **FAT (File Allocation Table)**, or **FATFS (File Allocation Table File System)**, for USB flash drives
- **Extended FAT file system (exFAT)** for mobile devices
- **UDF (Universal Disk Format)** for DVD discs
- **CDFS (Compact Disc File System)** for CD discs
- **Live File System**, for DVDs and CDs file system (first introduced in Windows Vista)

> **TIP**
>
> *Disc* is used instead of *disk* to refer to DVDs and CDs.

Before you can use a disk, the operating system or another application or utility must prepare the disk so Windows can record data to, and retrieve data from, the disk. That includes hard disks, DVDs, CDs, and flash drives. Unless you request otherwise when purchasing a computer, the computer manufacturer or dealer will have already formatted or prepared the hard disk so it can store data, and the computer manufacturer or dealer will have already installed a version of the Windows operating system on the disk. However, it is possible to purchase an unformatted hard disk and then use a Windows 7 installation DVD to format the hard disk first before installing the operating system. Also, if you encounter a serious problem with your computer, you might need to make copies of important files on the hard disk (if possible) and then reformat the hard disk, reinstall the operating system, reinstall all your applications, and restore your personal data from a backup.

If you install an upgrade to your existing operating system, then the installation program might give you the option of also upgrading to a newer file system. In some cases, you might decide to convert a file system for a specific disk to a different file system so you can take advantage of its features.

You can only use one file system on a drive. However, you can partition or subdivide a hard disk into multiple volumes and format each volume to use a different file system.

Formatting a Hard Disk

When Windows 7 formats a hard disk, it creates concentric recording bands known as **tracks** on each side of each platter of a hard disk. A hard disk may contain one or more **platters** for storing data. Both sides of each platter store data. Each track is subdivided into small storage compartments referred to as **sectors**, and each sector is typically 512 bytes in size. Tracks located at the same position on different platters are known as cylinders. A **cylinder** is therefore a three-dimensional way of viewing multiple tracks on different platters, while a track is a two-dimensional way of viewing single concentric recording bands on a platter. See Figure 5-1.

Figure 5-1   **Cylinders, tracks, and sectors on a hard disk**

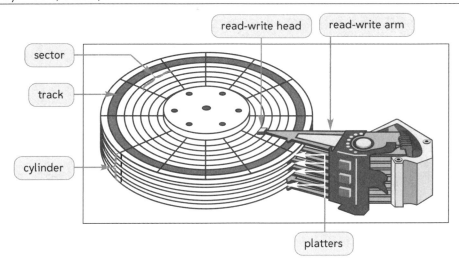

Although a sector is the basic storage compartment on a disk, the Windows 7 operating system does not allocate storage space on a sector-by-sector basis. Instead, Windows 7 allocates storage space on a cluster-by-cluster basis. A **cluster** (or **allocation unit**) consists of one or more sectors of storage space that Windows 7 allocates as a single unit or block to all or part of a file (depending on the file size). The number of sectors per cluster depends on several factors, including the file system used on the disk, the size of the volume, and the operating system itself. For example, on a particular 32 GB USB flash drive, a cluster may consist of 32 sectors, while on a 1 TB (1 terabyte, or 1,000 GB) hard disk, a cluster may consist of only 8 sectors. If you create a one-page document that requires 7 sectors of storage space on a disk, and if you save that document to a file on the 32 GB USB flash drive just described, then Windows 7 allocates 1 cluster of storage space for that file. If each cluster on that USB flash drive consists of 32 sectors, then that file uses 32 sectors of storage space even though it only requires 7 sectors. That means that the extra 25 sectors of storage space are wasted storage space that no other file can use. Storage space allocated to a file, but not used by that file, is called **slack**. If you save that same file to the 1 TB hard disk with 8 sectors per cluster, then Windows 7 still allocates 1 cluster of storage space for that file. However, if each cluster on that hard disk consists of 8 sectors, then that same file would use only 7 sectors of storage space. Unlike on the USB flash drive, only 1 sector of storage space is wasted space, or slack, that no other file can use. As you examine each file system later in this section of the tutorial, you will compare how the file system affects cluster sizes and slack.

On the nearly obsolete 3½-inch HD (high-density) floppy disk, each cluster consisted of 1 sector, making this type of disk more efficient for storing data with the least amount of wasted storage space, or slack. If you saved a one-page document that required 7 sectors of storage space to a file on a floppy disk, then Windows 7 would allocate 7 clusters for the file. If the file did not fill the last sector of storage space in the last cluster, then that would be the only wasted storage space. However, not only was the total amount of storage space on floppy disks limited, but floppy disks had a short useful life.

During the formatting process, Windows 7 verifies that it can write to and read from each sector on the disk. If it discovers sectors that it cannot write to or read from, it marks the clusters that contain those defective sectors as unusable, and does not store data in those clusters. Clusters with one or more defective sectors are called **bad clusters**.

At the end of the formatting process, Windows creates a file system on the disk and a top-level folder. The top-level folder (or root directory) is the first folder (or directory) created on a disk after Windows 7 formats the disk. When you open a Computer window, and click (or double-click) an icon for a disk drive, then the window opens onto the top-level folder of that disk.

Low-level formatting refers to the initial steps for creating tracks and sectors on a disk, while **high-level formatting** refers to the final steps for creating a file system on the disk.

After a disk has a file system and top-level folder, you can install software onto the disk and add your own personal folders and files. However, if you are formatting a hard disk while installing an operating system, the installation wizard installs the operating system as soon as the format is complete.

INSIGHT

Using Solid-State Drives (SSDs)

Solid-state drives use a flash memory chip for storage rather than a magnetic or optical disk. The flash memory chip consists of memory cells organized into arrays or blocks. Each cell stores 1 bit (a *0* or *1*) for single-level chips (SLC) or 2 or more bits for multi-level chips (MLC). Data is read from and written to the flash memory chip in fixed size blocks. Proprietary software on a controller chip in the solid-state drive reads and writes from the file system to the actual flash memory chip, and thereby emulates a hard disk drive interface. A solid-state drive, and another type of flash device such as a flash drive and memory cards, are formatted for a specific file system (FAT16, FAT32, or NTFS) just like a traditional hard disk drive, and the file system handles data as clusters (or allocation units) that consist of a specific number of sectors. The flash devices have the same type of file system problems, including slack or waste space. However, the design, capabilities, speed, and features of flash devices vary by manufacturer and type of device. Flash devices have no moving parts, and therefore they are less susceptible to problems that arise from mechanical parts that move. Flash memory speeds exceed the time it takes to access data on a moving physical disk, so flash devices provide far better performance. It's no surprise that flash memory is used not only on desktop computers and mobile computers, but also cell phones, music players, digital cameras, global position systems (GPS), and wireless communication devices.

Understanding the Role of the Master Boot Record

When Windows 7 prepares a disk for use with a specific file system, it creates a Master Boot Record (MBR) at the beginning of the hard disk drive. The **Master Boot Record** (**MBR**) is a critical data structure that plays an important role in the booting process. The MBR contains information about the hard disk's partitions. You can create up to four partitions on a hard disk that uses the MBR partitioning style, so that you can install more than one operating system (each on a different partition), or have a separate partition for software and for your personal files.

Within the Master Boot Record is a table called the Hard Disk Partition Table that contains the information about the partitions on the hard disk. The **Hard Disk Partition Table** identifies where each partition starts and ends, and it identifies which partition is the partition for booting the computer. That partition (usually drive C) contains the Windows 7 operating system files for loading the operating system. The Master Boot Record also contains a boot program called the **Master Boot Code**, which locates the bootable partition, and which then transfers control to the boot sector of the volume that contains the installed operating system. The **boot sector**, or **boot record**, is the sector at the beginning of a partition, and it contains information about the layout of the volume, the file system structures, and in the case of a bootable volume, code for locating and loading the operating system files, which then start the process of loading a specific operating system.

When your computer finds the hard disk during booting, it reads the Master Boot Record, finds the location of the boot drive (usually drive C), and then locates and loads the operating system from the hard disk. If you have a dual-boot computer with two different versions of Windows installed on two different partitions, you select the version that you want to use during the early stages of booting, and then that version of the Windows operating system loads from the partition where it is installed.

Examining the Native File System of Windows 7

NTFS, the native file system for Windows 7 and its predecessors in the Windows NT product line (including Windows Vista, Windows XP, and Windows 2000 Professional), relies on the use of a **Master File Table (MFT)** to keep track of folders and files as well as information about the volume and the Master File Table itself. The Master File Table contains at least one **record** (or listing) for each file on disk. Each record in this table consists of a row of file information organized into columns.

When Windows 7 prepares a hard disk to use NTFS, it creates the Master Boot Record on the hard disk, and then creates an NTFS boot sector for the volume where you install Windows 7, as well as the Master File Table and other NTFS data structures. Windows 7 keeps a second copy of the first four records or entries (or the first cluster, whichever is larger) in the Master File Table as a backup in the event of a problem that damages access to critical information stored in those records of the MFT. This backup copy is referred to as the **Master File Table Mirror (MFTMirr)**. These first four records contain information about the MFT, the MFTMirr, a transaction log file used for recovery (covered later), and the volume. If the first four records in the MFT are damaged, then Windows 7 may be able to recover from the damage, and replace the first four records of the MFT with the first four records from the MFTMirr.

The first 16 records in the MFT consist of **metadata**, or data about data, and include not only information about the first four records described in the previous paragraph but also information about which clusters are available and which clusters are in use, which clusters are bad clusters, and other key information needed by NTFS.

The NTFS boot sector contains information about the volume formatted for NTFS, including:

- The number of bytes per sector
- The number of sectors per cluster
- A **media descriptor**, or a setting that identifies the type of disk
- The total number of sectors
- The location of the Master File Table
- The location of the Master File Table Mirror
- The number of clusters used for each record in the Master File Table
- The volume serial number

The NTFS **transaction log file** contains a record of operations performed on a volume, such as renaming or deleting a file. Each operation is called a **transaction**. If a problem occurs, then Windows 7 uses the information in the transaction log file to roll back operations that were not completed, and thereby restore the integrity of the file system. Any operations listed as complete in the transaction log file are repeated to ensure that the corresponding changes were actually made on disk. Although this recovery approach might result in a slight loss of data, the integrity of the file system is more important. In Windows 7 and Windows Vista, NTFS automatically detects and, where possible, repairs file system problems—a feature called **self-healing**.

Comparing MFT Attributes

The Master File Table also includes **attributes**, or settings assigned to files by the operating system to indicate a specific state, such as:

- **Archive**—Windows 7 assigns the **archive attribute** to newly created or newly modified files so a backup utility can identify which files should be backed up. (This attribute is covered in more detail in Tutorial 10 on backing up folders and files.) If you display the Attributes column in a folder window, or view attributes in a command-line window, folders and files with this attribute are identified by the code letter *A*. See Figure 5-2.

Figure 5-2	Attributes of system folders and system files

Local Disk (C:)	Archive	Read-Only	Hidden	System	Directory	Symbolic Link	Not Content Indexed	Type of Symbolic Link	Points To
$Recycle.Bin			H	S	D				
Documents and Settings			H	S	D	L	I	<JUNCTION>	
Program Files		R			D				
ProgramData			H		D		I		
Users		R			D				
Windows					D				
hiberfil.sys	A		H	S			I		
C:\Users									
All Users			H	S	D	L	I	<SYMBLINKD>	C:\ProgramData
Default User			H	S	D	L	I	<JUNCTION>	C:\Users\Default
Public		R			D				
Libraries									
Documents	A						I		
Music	A						I		
Pictures	A						I		
Videos	A						I		

- **Read-only**—If a file is assigned the **read-only attribute**, you can open and view (or read) the contents of the file, but you cannot save changes to the file under the same filename. On the hard disk, the Program Files and Users folders are assigned this attribute. In the Users folder, the Public folder is assigned this attribute. In each user account folder, the Contacts, Desktop, Downloads, Favorites, Links, My Documents, My Music, My Pictures, My Videos, Saved Games, and Searches folder are also assigned the read-only attribute. If you display the Attributes column in a folder window, or view attributes in a command-line window, folders and files with this attribute are identified by the code letter *R*. See Figure 5-3.

Figure 5-3	Attributes of system folders for a user

C:\Users\ Cadence	Archive	Read- Only	Hidden	System	Directory	Symbolic Link	Not Content Indexed	Type of Symbolic Link	Points To
AppData			H		D		I		
Application Data			H	S	D	L	I	<JUNCTION>	C:\Users\Cadence\ AppData\Roaming
Contacts		R			D				
Cookies			H	S	D	L	I	<JUNCTION>	C:\Users\Cadence\ AppData\Roaming\ Microsoft\Windows\ Cookies
Desktop		R			D				
Downloads		R			D				
Favorites		R			D				
Links		R			D				
Local Settings			H	S	D	L	I	<JUNCTION>	C:\Users\Cadence\ AppData\Local
My Documents		R			D				
My Documents			H	S	D	L	I	<JUNCTION>	C:\Users\Cadence\ Documents
My Music		R			D				
My Pictures		R			D				
My Videos		R			D				
Recent			H	S	D	L	I	<JUNCTION>	C:\Users\Cadence\ AppData\Roaming\ Microsoft\Windows\ Recent
Saved Games		R			D				
Searches		R			D				
SendTo			H	S	D	L	I	<JUNCTION>	C:\Users\Cadence\ AppData\Roaming\ Microsoft\Windows\ SendTo
Start Menu			H	S	D	L	I	<JUNCTION>	C:\Users\Cadence\ AppData\Roaming\ Microsoft\Windows\ Start Menu

The folder path shown for the title of the first column and the actual path shown for specific folders assume that the user account is called "Cadence".

- **Hidden**—If a folder or file is assigned the **hidden attribute**, Windows 7 does not display the folder or file in folder windows (unless you choose the option to display all hidden folders and files). Even then, the icons for hidden folders and files are fainter in appearance to remind you that they are assigned this attribute. On Local Disk (C:), the hidden $Recycle.Bin folder and hiberfil.sys, the hibernation file, are assigned this attribute. In a user account folder, the SendTo and Start Menu folders are assigned this attribute. If you display the Attributes column in a folder window or view attributes in a command-line window, folders and files with this attribute are identified by the code letter *H*, as shown in Figure 5-2 and Figure 5-3.
- **System**—Folders and files with the **system attribute** are operating system files. Typically, system files are also assigned the hidden attribute and in some cases the read-only attribute (for obvious reasons, namely, to protect them). In Local Disk (C:), the $Recycle.Bin folder and hiberfil.sys, the hibernation file, are assigned the system attribute. If you display the Attributes column in a folder window, or view attributes in a command-line window, folders and files with the system attribute are identified by the code letter *S*, as shown in Figure 5-2 and Figure 5-3.
- **Compress**—Any folders and files that you explicitly choose to compress (to use disk storage space more efficiently) are assigned the **compress attribute**. If you display the Attributes column in a folder window, or view attributes in a command-line window, folders and files with this attribute are identified by the code letter *C*. Later in this tutorial, you will compress and uncompress files.
- **Encrypt**—Any folders and files that you explicitly choose to encrypt (or encode for security) are assigned the **encrypt attribute**. If you display the Attributes column in a folder window, or view attributes in a command-line window, folders and files with this attribute are identified by the code letter *E*. Later in this tutorial, you will encrypt and unencrypt files.
- **Not Content Indexed**—Folders and files with this attribute are excluded from indexing. The Documents, Music, Pictures, and Videos libraries are assigned this attribute. The hibernation file is an example of a file that is not indexed for faster searching. If you display the Attributes column in a folder window, or view attributes in a command-line window, folders and files with this attribute are identified by the code letter *I*. Windows Vista displays the code letter *N* for this same attribute. In a command-line window in either Windows 7 or Windows Vista, files with the Not Content Indexed attribute are identified by the code letter *I*.
- **Directory**—Directories (or folders), junction points (each of which acts as a link to a folder), and symbolic links (each of which act as a link to a folder or file) are assigned this attribute. Three examples are the Windows folder, the hidden Start Menu junction point in your user folder that references the actual Start Menu folder you opened in the previous tutorial, and the All Users folder symbolic link in the Users folder. If you display the Attributes column in a folder window, folders and junction points with this attribute are identified by the code letter *D*, as shown in Figure 5-2 and Figure 5-3.
- **Symbolic link**—Symbolic links, also called **symlinks**, were introduced in Windows Vista. Symbolic links are similar to junction points in that they act as links to a folder or file. Windows 7 uses symbolic links to redirect an application to a specific folder or file in a new version of Windows because of changes Microsoft made to the names and locations of some system folders from one version of Windows to the next. Desktop shortcuts and symbolic links are similar in concept, but you can think of symbolic links as file-system shortcuts. The hidden Recent, SendTo, and Start Menu symbolic links to the corresponding user folders are assigned this attribute. If you display the Attributes column in a folder window, or view attributes in a command-line window, files with this attribute are identified by the code letter *L*, as shown in Figure 5-2 and Figure 5-3. The hidden Recent, SendTo, and Start Menu folders are assigned the hidden, system, directory, Not Content Indexed, and symbolic link attributes.

Examining NTFS Cluster Sizes and Volume Sizes

The type of file system used on a disk affects cluster sizes as well as volume sizes. Figure 5-4 shows cluster sizes for NTFS volumes with different storage capacities.

Figure 5-4	Cluster sizes for NTFS volumes

Volume Size		Cluster Size		
From	To	Sectors/Cluster	Bytes	Kilobytes (KB)
7 MB	512 MB	1	512	0.5
513 MB	1 GB	2	1,024	1
1 GB+	2 GB	4	2,048	2
2 GB+	2 TB	8	4,096	4

Notice that, as the size of a volume increases, the number of sectors per cluster increases. Smaller volumes have smaller cluster sizes (with fewer sectors per cluster), and larger volumes have larger cluster sizes. Smaller volumes therefore use storage space more efficiently. The limit of 2 TB for a volume size is not a shortcoming of NTFS, but rather a limitation imposed by the Hard Disk Partition Table in the Master Boot Record, the most commonly used system for partitioning hard disks. The Master Boot Record table only supports a total of four partitions per disk, and can only store information on volumes up to 2 TB. To work with NTFS volumes over 2 TB, you must use a different system to partition a hard disk known as GPT (Globally Unique Identifier Partition Table) that can support up to 128 partitions per disk and, in theory, up to 16 EB (exabytes, or approximately 18 million terabytes) of storage space. If you have an MBR disk, you can convert it to a GPT disk with the Disk Management tool, but you cannot convert a GPT disk back to an MBR disk. Windows 7, Windows Vista, and 64-bit versions of Windows XP support the GPT disk-partitioning system.

Theoretically, NTFS supports volume sizes of 2^{64} clusters (less one cluster), for a total of 18,446,744,073,709,551,615 clusters. As currently implemented, NTFS supports volume sizes of 2^{32} clusters (less one cluster) using 64 KB clusters (or 128 sectors per cluster), for a total volume capacity of 256 TB (or 281,474,976,710,656 bytes, less one cluster). At the default cluster size of 8 sectors per cluster, the maximum size for an NTFS volume is 16 TB less 4 KB. 16 TB is equal to approximately 16,384 GB.

INSIGHT

Determining the Number of Sectors in a Cluster

Cluster sizes are commonly expressed as kilobytes (KB) rather than the actual number of sectors per cluster. If you need to convert cluster sizes expressed as KB to the number of sectors per cluster, you use the following approach:

To convert a 64 KB cluster size into the number of sectors per cluster:

64 KB × 1,024 bytes per KB = 65,536 bytes

65,536 bytes ÷ (512 bytes per sector) = 128 sectors

Likewise, if you know the number of sectors per cluster and want to express the cluster size in KB (kilobytes), you use the following approach:

To convert 8 sectors per cluster into kilobytes per cluster:

8 sectors per cluster × 512 bytes per sector = 4,096 bytes

4,096 bytes ÷ (1,024 bytes per KB) = 4 KB

Being familiar with both approaches to expressing cluster sizes is important when analyzing disk space usage on your computer and when choosing a file system for a disk so storage space is used efficiently.

Examining Other NTFS Features

NTFS has additional features that extend the capabilities of this file system and that are not available in the FAT file systems (which you will examine next), including the following:

- **Folder and File Permissions**—A **permission** is a rule that determines who has access to a resource, such as a folder or file, and how they can use the resource. For example, someone with Administrator privileges might deny you access to a specific folder, assign you read-only access, or permit you to create, modify, and delete files in a folder. This feature is important to maintaining the security of data on networked and even nonnetworked computers.

- **GUIDs**—Windows and applications create unique GUIDs for objects as needed. A **GUID** (**globally unique identifier**), also referred to as an **UUID** (**universally unique identifier**), is a unique randomly generated 128-bit (or 16-byte) number. If you raise two to the 128th power (2^{128}), then you will discover that there are a total of 340,282,366,920,938,000,000,000,000,000,000,000,000 (or 340 billion, billion, billion, billion) possible numbers. The chances that another object might be assigned the same GUID is improbable.

- **Multiple data streams**—NTFS supports files that contain multiple data streams. A **data stream** consists of a set of data stored within a file. All files have a main data stream that consists of the actual data stored in the file by the file's creator, and that data stream is visible to all file systems, but additional **alternate data streams**, such as file properties, a thumbnail of the file's contents, or additional content added by you or someone else, can be attached to a file. Other than the main data stream, each additional data stream has its own name so the application (or you) that created the data stream can access what is stored in the data stream.

- **Disk quotas**—If several users share the same computer, an Administrator can specify how much storage each user can have on the hard disk.

- **Mounted drives**—Using the Disk Management tool (which you will examine later in this tutorial), you can mount, or attach, a drive, such as a USB flash drive, to an empty folder that you have already created on an NTFS volume (for example, to an empty folder under the Documents folder). You can then access the contents of the drive (such as a flash drive) by opening the folder on your NTFS volume. The mounted drive appears as part of a group of related folders and provides a way for extending storage for files outside the current volume. You might use this feature if you do not have enough storage space on your hard disk for the contents of the other disk. Mounted drives, also called **volume mount points** or **drive paths**, are assigned a label or name instead of a drive letter.

- **Hard links**—A **hard link** is a link to a file on an NTFS volume. When you create a hard link, you assign a filename to the hard link. You now have two ways to open the same file: You can open the original file, or you can use the hard link to open the file (which may be in another folder). In fact, for all practical purposes, the hard link looks like and acts like the actual file. For example, if you had a file named Project Status.xlsx in a folder on your hard disk, you could create in another folder a hard link named Project Status.xlsx to the actual file named Project Status.xlsx. You can then open the same file from either folder. Any changes you make are made to the actual file (not its hard link). One advantage of using a hard link is that you do not need to keep two copies of the same file in two different folders and run the risk of updating one copy of the file without updating the other copy of the file. For example, you might need to reference the same document for each of your clients. Rather than having a duplicate copy of the same file stored in different client folders, you can reference the same document stored in the same location. Any updates to that document using the original file or a hard link are then applicable to all your clients. That also prevents inadvertently making a change to one copy of that document and rendering the other copies of the same document for the other clients outdated. This feature also reduces the need to keep switching folders to find the file you need.

TIP

If you rename a copy of an Office 2007 or Office 2010 document, and add .zip to the end of the filename, you can open the file and view its component parts.

A hard link can have the same name as the file that it points to if it is stored in another folder. The hard link can also have a different name than the file that it points to, whether it's stored in a different folder or the same folder as the original file. As you've seen, a shortcut enables you to quickly access a file. However, if you permanently delete the original file that a shortcut points to, then you've lost the entire file. The shortcut still exists, but it obviously cannot find the file it references. In contrast, if you permanently delete the original file that you've created a hard link to, you can still access the file's contents via the hard link. If you need to remove a file, you must also locate and remove all its hard links.

- **Sparse files**—Certain files, such as catalog files used for indexing files, contain not only specific data, but also contain long runs of zeroes in the file. Rather than allocate disk storage space to those portions of the file that contain the long runs of zeroes, Windows 7 can mark the file as a **sparse file**, and only allocate disk storage space to the meaningful data in the sparse file and not allocate disk storage space to long runs of zeroes. That means that potentially very large files can be stored more efficiently on disk, and take up less disk storage space. When accessing the file, Windows 7 can restore the sparse file to its original state.
- **Encryption**—As you will discover in the second session of this tutorial, you can encrypt (or encode) folders and files so only you have access to your files.
- **Compression**—As you will discover in the second session of this tutorial, you can compress folders and files so they use less storage space on disk.

NTFS is a complex yet full-featured file system that supports current and future disk storage capacities. Plus, its security features make it the file system of choice.

Understanding the FAT File System

The FAT file system was introduced with the first version of the DOS operating system and used in Windows 95 and subsequent versions in the Windows 9x product line. The FAT file system relies on the use of a file allocation table (FAT) to keep track of cluster usage on disk. There are actually several variations of the FAT file system, which you will examine after you examine components of the FAT file system. When Windows formats a disk with the FAT file system, it creates the following four tables in the system area of the disk:

- Boot record
- File allocation table #1 (or FAT1)
- File allocation table #2 (or FAT2)
- Directory table

The **system area** is the outer track of a disk (namely, Track 0), and it is used exclusively for these data structures. Right after the system area is the **files area** where you store your document files. The following sections describe each of these four tables.

The Boot Record

The boot record (sometimes called the boot sector) is a table that contains the name and the version number of the operating system used to format the disk, as well as information on the physical characteristics of the disk, including the following:

- Number of bytes per sector
- Number of sectors per cluster
- Number of file allocation tables
- Maximum number of files allowed in the top-level folder or root directory
- Total number of sectors
- Media descriptor, which identifies the type of disk

- Number of sectors for the FAT
- Number of sectors per track
- Number of sides formatted
- Drive number
- Volume serial number (calculated from the date and time on the computer)
- Volume label (an electronic label)
- Type of file system
- Number of hidden, reserved, and unused sectors

The boot sector also contains a **bootstrap loader** program for loading the operating system from a FAT volume.

When different versions of Windows access a drive with a disk that uses the FAT file system, they read the boot record so they know how to work with and allocate storage space on that disk drive. The boot sector is important because different types of disks (including hard disks) have different storage capacities and allocate storage space differently.

The File Allocation Tables

After the boot sector, the operating system creates two copies of a table called the **file allocation table** to keep track of which clusters (or allocation units) are available or unused, which ones store the contents of files and are therefore used, which are defective and unusable, and which are reserved for use by the operating system. Figure 5-5 shows a diagrammatic representation of a file allocation table.

Figure 5-5   **Cluster usage in the file allocation table**

File	Cluster		FAT
Sales Projections.xlsx	1500	pointer to next cluster in file	1501
	1501		1502
	1502	first cluster for a file	1503
	1503		1504
	1504		1505
	1505	end-of-file code	EOF
My Resume.docx	1506		1507
	1507		1508
	1508		1509
	1509		1510
	1510		EOF
	1511	unused cluster	Available
	1512		Available
	1513		Available
	1514	cluster with defective sector(s)	Bad Cluster

In Figure 5-5, the two files shown use clusters 1500–1505 and 1506–1510. Each cluster contains the number of the next cluster (called a **pointer**) for that same file (shown in the column labeled *FAT*). The last cluster of a file contains an **end-of-file** (**EOF**) code or marker. Because the operating system can easily determine the cluster number by counting the entries in the table, the file allocation table only contains the information shown in the last column.

The operating system places two copies of the file allocation table on a disk. One copy is called **FAT1**, the other, **FAT2**. Each time the operating system saves a new or modified file to a disk, it updates both tables. FAT2 is therefore a backup of FAT1. If FAT1 is damaged, then Windows can use FAT2 to access information about the use of clusters on disk.

The Directory Table

The **directory table** keeps track of information on the folders and files stored in the top-level folder or root directory. This table contains the names of folders and files, as well as information on their sizes, dates and times of creation, last accessed date, dates and times of modification, and any special attributes assigned to the folder or file by the operating system. Figure 5-6 contains a partial view of the contents of a directory table.

Figure 5-6   Directory table for top-level folder

	Filename	Extension	Attributes	File time	File Date	Starting Cluster	Size (Bytes)
folder (or directory) →	Portfolio		D	08:30:02	10/14/2013	156	
	Brochure	docx	A	10:31:58	10/25/2013	157	3,175,968
	Company Logo	jpg		16:32:19	03/21/2013	298	1,312,335
files →	Display Ad	jpg	A	09:27:43	02/07/2013	835	2,693,712
	Sales Projection	xlsx		14:01:32	11/15/2013	1890	521,690

The directory table only keeps track of the folders and files located in the top-level folder. This table does not keep track of the folders and files contained within subfolders below the top-level folder. Each subfolder below the top-level folder is actually a directory table, like the one for the top-level folder, and each directory table tracks the folders and files contained within that subfolder. In essence, the operating system divides the labor of tracking folders and files on a hard disk among different directory tables.

When you save a file, you specify not only the drive where you want to store the file, but also the folder. Because you consider the folder as a container for a file, you visualize the file as being stored within the folder. However, that is not the case. A folder is a file that keeps track of other files, and it's stored at a certain location on disk, just like any other file. When you save a file in a folder, you are really designating the directory table or folder file that will keep track of the file. So, a folder is a logical concept.

In the FAT file system, the directory table keeps track of the archive, read-only, hidden, system, and directory attributes (described earlier for NTFS).

Another important feature of the directory table is that it contains the number of the starting cluster for each folder and file on a disk. By using the directory table and the file allocation table, Windows can locate all the clusters used by a folder or file on a FAT volume and reassemble a file so you can work with the document in that file.

Comparing FAT12, FAT16, and FAT32

FAT12 is the file system that was used by small media, namely, floppy disks and volumes less than 32 MB in size. FAT12 supports a maximum of 4,096 clusters (or 2^{12} clusters) on a floppy disk. All versions of the Windows operating system support FAT12.

The original version of Windows 95 and Windows 95a used the **FAT16** file system. FAT16 supports a maximum of 65,536 clusters (or 2^{16} clusters) on a disk. Some clusters are reserved; therefore, the actual limit is 65,524 clusters. Another feature of the FAT16 file system is that the boot record, file allocation table #1, file allocation table #2, and directory table are fixed in size. The size of the file allocation tables cannot exceed 128 KB; that, in turn, affects the usage of storage space on hard disks because the file allocation table can only track a specific number of clusters, no matter how large the disk. As hard disk storage capacities increase, the number of sectors per cluster must therefore increase because the number of clusters cannot increase. When users purchased larger hard disk drives for more storage space, they quickly discovered that they did not gain that much storage space, because cluster sizes increased.

Figure 5-7 shows cluster sizes on different-sized volumes that use FAT16.

Figure 5-7	Cluster sizes for FAT16 volumes

Volume Size		Cluster Size		
From	**To**	**Sectors/Cluster**	**Bytes**	**Kilobytes (KB)**
7 MB	16 MB	4	2,048	2
17 MB	32 MB	1	512	0.5
33 MB	64 MB	2	1,024	1
65 MB	128 MB	4	2,048	2
129 MB	256 MB	8	4,096	4
257 MB	512 MB	16	8,192	8
513 MB	1 GB	32	16,384	16
1 GB	2 GB	64	32,768	32

Notice that, for hard disks that range in capacity from 1 GB up to 2 GB, each cluster is 64 sectors in size. If you examine a flash drive with 2 GB or less of total storage, Windows 7 will identify the file system used on the disk as FAT (for FAT16). FAT16 volumes can actually support up to 4 GB of storage (at 128 sectors per cluster or 64 KB clusters); however, applications might not work properly on volumes of that size. As you will discover, the theoretical and practical storage limits of file systems vary because it depends on the support Microsoft builds into each version of the Windows operating system for each file system, and takes into accounts other issues, such as support by applications.

The directory table for the top-level folder of a hard disk that uses FAT16 is fixed in size, so it can only track a total of 512 folders and files. With FAT16, you must also limit the use of long filenames for folders and files in the top-level folder, because long folder names and filenames take more than one directory entry in the Directory table, and therefore use up the available **directory space**. That's why it's important to organize files into folders on disks that use FAT16 so the top-level folder or root directory does not become full.

FAT32, a variation on the FAT file system, was introduced in Windows 95B and was supported in all later versions of Windows except for Windows NT Workstation 4.0. FAT32 supported even larger volumes than FAT16, and FAT32 used disk storage space more efficiently than FAT16.

The boot record on FAT32 drives is larger and contains a backup of critical data structures. Furthermore, a backup of the boot sector is stored elsewhere on the volume. Unlike FAT16, the file allocation tables and directory table in the FAT32 file system are not fixed in size, and these system files can "spill over" from the system area to the files area of the disk where you store document folders and files.

FAT32 supports a maximum of 268,435,456 clusters (or 2^{28} clusters) on a hard disk, so cluster sizes can be smaller. Although FAT32 uses 32 bits for each entry in the file allocation table, and therefore would theoretically support a maximum of 4,294,967,296 clusters (or 2^{32} clusters), the first 4 bits of each entry are reserved.

Figure 5-8 shows cluster sizes on different-sized volumes that use FAT32.

| Figure 5-8 | Cluster sizes for FAT32 volumes |

Volume Size			Cluster Size	
From	To	Sectors/Cluster	Bytes	Kilobytes (KB)
33 MB	64 MB	1 sector	512	0.5
65 MB	128 MB	2 sectors	1,024	1
129 MB	256 MB	4 sectors	2,048	2
257 MB	8 GB	8 sectors	4,096	4
8 GB	16 GB	16 sectors	8,192	8
16 GB	32 GB	32 sectors	16,384	16

On a 2 GB flash drive that uses FAT32, a cluster consists of only 8 sectors (as compared to 64 sectors for the same-sized volume under FAT16). FAT32 can support much larger hard disks, theoretically up to 8 TB (terabytes); however, FAT32 volumes are limited to 32 GB in size because Windows can only create FAT32 volumes up to 32 GB. For volumes larger in size than 32 GB, you must use NTFS.

Comparing Slack in FAT16, FAT32, and NTFS

Although large files obviously take a lot of storage space on a volume, small files waste a lot of storage space relative to their size. For example, on a 2 GB flash drive that uses FAT16, a 256-byte shortcut requires only a half-sector of storage space, but actually uses 64 sectors of storage space because the operating system allocates one cluster (or 64 sectors) to the shortcut. So, that shortcut wastes 63½ sectors (which now becomes slack), as illustrated in Figure 5-9.

| Figure 5-9 | How file systems affect slack |

Volume Size	File System	Shortcut Size	Allocated	Cluster Size	Slack
2 GB	FAT16	1/2 sector	1 cluster	64 sectors	63½ sectors
2 GB	FAT32	1/2 sector	1 cluster	8 sectors	7½ sectors
2 GB	NTFS	1/2 sector	1 cluster	4 sectors	3½ sectors

Size of a Single Cluster

FAT16=64 sectors

FAT32=8 sectors

NTFS=4 sectors

Legend

Disk space required for the shortcut (1/2) sector

Slack (wasted storage space)

On a 2 GB flash drive that uses the FAT32 file system, the operating system still allocates one cluster to a shortcut of the same size, but because a cluster contains 8 sectors, only 7½ sectors of storage space are wasted (and end up as slack). On a 2 GB volume that uses NTFS, the operating system would again allocate one cluster of storage space; however, because a cluster contains 4 sectors for a 2 GB volume, only 3½ sectors of storage space are wasted (and become slack). From Figure 5-9, it's clear that FAT32 is far more efficient than FAT16 on small volumes, and that NTFS uses storage space more efficiently and thereby reduces slack when compared to either FAT16 or FAT32.

> **TIP**
>
> You can store more files on FAT16 and FAT32 flash drives if you use 8.3 filenames instead of long filenames.

If you compare the largest-size volume supported by FAT32, namely 32 GB, with a similar 32 GB volume that uses NTFS, it's even more obvious that as volume sizes increase, NTFS is far more efficient at using disk storage space. Continuing with the previous example of a shortcut that only requires a half-sector of storage space, Windows allocates one cluster of storage space to the shortcut, but on a 32 GB volume that uses FAT32, the cluster size consists of 32 sectors, so 31½ sectors of storage space are wasted. On a 32 GB volume that uses NTFS, the cluster size is smaller and only consists of 8 sectors, so the same shortcut only wastes 7½ sectors of storage space on disk. See Figure 5-10.

Figure 5-10	How FAT32 and NTFS affect slack

Volume Size	File System	Shortcut Size	Allocated	Cluster Size	Slack
32 GB	FAT32	1/2 sector	1 cluster	32 sectors	31½ sectors
32 GB	NTFS	1/2 sector	1 cluster	8 sectors	7½ sectors

Size of a Single Cluster

FAT32=32 sectors

NTFS=8 sectors

Legend

 Disk space required for the shortcut (1/2) sector

 Slack (wasted storage space)

NTFS is the only Windows file system that supports larger capacity hard drives. Furthermore, even as hard disk storage capacities increase, it still uses storage space efficiently.

The exFAT, TFAT, and TexFAT File Systems

Microsoft introduced the **exFAT** (or **Extended FAT**) file system in the Windows Vista Service Pack 1 upgrade to provide support for larger storage capacities on flash memory storage devices. The exFAT file system is also an important file system for mobile devices. In theory, exFAT supports increased volume sizes up to 64 ZB (zettabytes, or approximately 64 billion terabytes); however, in practice, exFAT supports volumes up to 512 TB (terabytes) in size. exFAT also supports cluster sizes up to 32 MB (megabytes) and up to approximately 2.8 billion files per directory. Furthermore, the file system overhead is approximately 99% less than NTFS.

You can use Windows 7 to format a flash drive for the exFAT file system, but you will not be able to use it on a computer with a version of Windows that does not support exFAT.

TFAT (for **transaction-safe FAT**), introduced for mobile devices in Windows CE in 2003, uses two copies of the file allocation table (FAT1 and FAT0) to update the file system and protect the file system against problems that might occur if a file system transaction is not completed. Changes to the file system are first made to FAT1; once FAT1 is updated, then FAT0 is replaced with a copy of FAT1. That completes the process of updating the file system. If a change to the file system is not completed as the result of some problem, then FAT1 is replaced with a copy of FAT0, restoring the file system to its previous state. This is a simple but effective mechanism for guaranteeing the integrity of the file system.

TexFAT (for **transaction-safe exFAT**) is an enhancement to the exFAT file system that replaces the TFAT file system. TexFAT functions in a similar way to TFAT in terms of updating the file system and guaranteeing the integrity of the file system; however, it is designed to support larger file sizes and larger partitions.

Checking the File System of a Drive

If you want to find out what file system your computer currently uses for a specific drive or volume, you can view properties of that drive or volume. The General property sheet for a drive or volume identifies the file system and provides other information, such as the amount of used space, the amount of free space, and the total capacity of the drive or volume. Windows 7 or any operating system works more slowly with a disk that is full or nearly full than one that has plenty of free space, so this information can help you manage your computer resources and improve performance.

On the General property sheet, you can assign a name to a disk by entering a volume label (an electronic label). You can select a volume label that identifies the contents or purpose of the drive. In the case of a flash drive, you can enter all or part of your last name to identify that you own the disk in case you misplace it and need to claim it later. For NTFS volumes, you can use up to 32 characters for the volume label. You can also use symbols as part of the volume label, and you can use mixed case, lowercase, and uppercase. In contrast, FAT volume names are limited to 11 characters, and you cannot use periods or other symbols not allowed in a DOS filename. In addition, characters are converted to uppercase (to correspond to the naming conventions in the DOS operating system).

In response to a request by an employee in the Advertising Department, Cadence asks you to evaluate the file systems and storage capacities on that employee's computer to make sure they meet that employee's needs and that they ensure the privacy and security of the data on the hard drive.

To check the file systems used on your computer:

▶ 1. If necessary, display the Computer icon on the desktop, and use the Folder Options dialog box to switch your computer to single-click activation (or Web style) and activate the option for displaying file extensions.

▶ 2. Click the **Computer** icon to open a Computer window and, if necessary, change to Tiles view. Windows 7 displays an indicator that gives you an idea of how much storage space is used on the hard drive(s) as well as any removable drives. It also shows the amount of free storage space used out of the total storage space available on each drive.

▶ **3.** Point to the Local Disk (C:) icon or the icon of your hard disk. (Your drive C friendly name may differ if you or your computer manufacturer changed it.) Windows 7 displays information about this hard drive in the Details pane, including the file system used on the hard drive, namely NTFS.

▶ **4.** Right-click the **Local Disk (C:)** icon (usually drive C), and then click **Properties**. Windows 7 opens the Local Disk (C:) Properties dialog box and displays information about the hard drive on the General property sheet. In Figure 5-11, Windows 7 reports that the file system used on Local Disk (C:) is NTFS.

Figure 5-11   **Viewing hard disk drive properties**

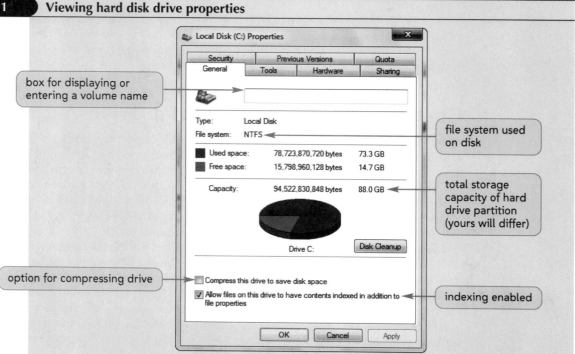

box for displaying or entering a volume name

file system used on disk

total storage capacity of hard drive partition (yours will differ)

option for compressing drive

indexing enabled

If you, a manufacturer, or a dealer does not assign a name to the hard disk, then Windows 7 uses the default name for the drive, namely Local Disk. If you or your computer manufacturer changed the default name for drive C from Local Disk, then the new name appears on the title bar of the dialog box and in the text box to the left of the drive icon. The pie chart visually represents the amount of used space and free space for the total storage capacity of the volume. As you can tell from this property sheet, Windows 7 automatically indexes this drive for faster searching. NTFS volumes also contain a check box for compressing the drive to conserve storage space.

From this dialog box, you can examine more information about all the disk drives.

To examine more properties of the disk drives:

▶ **1.** Click the **Hardware** tab, and in the "All disk drives" box, click a disk drive in the Name column, and then hold down the **Ctrl** key while you press the **plus sign** on the numeric keypad. Windows 7 adjusts the width of each column for the longest entry in each column (called a "best fit"). On the Hardware property sheet, Windows 7 lists all the disk drives in your computer, including removable drives not listed in the Computer window because they are empty (such as memory card readers). See Figure 5-12. You drives will differ and might include references to attached flash drives and other types of USB devices.

Trouble? If the column width does not change, you pressed the key with the plus sign on the main keyboard. Repeat this step, but use the plus sign on the numeric keypad (if available).

Trouble? If your keyboard does not have a numeric keypad, you can double-click the thin separator between each column for a best fit of the contents of that column; however, you have to repeat this process for each column, and you have to double-click the separator after the last column.

| Figure 5-12 | Viewing a list of disk drives on a computer |

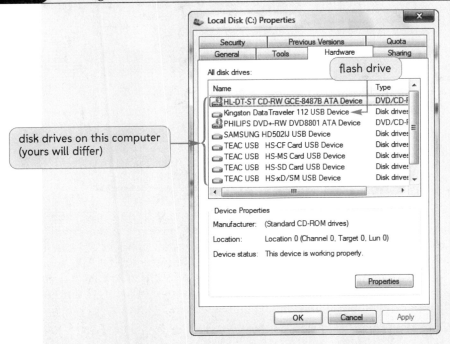

The Type column identifies the drive type, such as DVD/CD-ROM drives. Although Windows 7 identifies drives in the Computer window, this property sheet has the added advantage of identifying the manufacturer and model of each drive, if that information is known. If you select a drive in the "All disk drives" box, then the Device Properties section identifies the manufacturer, the physical location, and the device status (whether the device is working properly). If you select a drive in this list and then click the Properties button, Windows 7 opens a Properties dialog box that provides more information for that drive. You will examine hardware properties in more detail in Tutorial 12.

2. Close the Local Disk (C:) Properties dialog box.

3. If your flash drive is not already attached to your computer, attach your flash drive and, if necessary, close any window or dialog box that opens.

4. Right-click your **flash drive** icon, and then click **Properties**. Windows 7 opens a Properties dialog box for that drive. See Figure 5-13.

Figure 5-13 **Viewing properties of a USB flash drive**

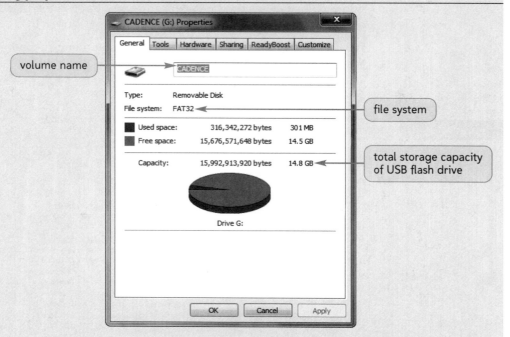

If you or the manufacturer assigned a volume label to this drive, then the volume label appears in the title bar and in the Name box next to the drive icon on the General Property sheet, as well as in the Computer window. For the flash drive used in Figure 5-13, Windows 7 reports the file system as FAT32. Your flash drive file system may be NTFS. If your flash drive (or SD memory card) uses the FAT16 file system, then Windows 7 reports the file system as just FAT (for FAT16), so you can easily distinguish between FAT16 and FAT32 volumes.

5. Close the Properties dialog box for your flash drive.

You can also view the file system used for other types of drives, including DVD and CD drives.

To examine the file systems used on other types of drives:

1. If you have a DVD drive on your computer and have a DVD available, insert a DVD into the DVD drive, wait a moment, and if Windows 7 displays an AutoPlay dialog box, close the AutoPlay dialog box, right-click the **DVD drive** icon in the Computer window, and then click **Properties**. On the General property sheet for the DVD drive, Windows 7 identifies the drive type as a CD drive, and the file system as UDF (explained after the steps below). See Figure 5-14. For the DVD-RW drive used on this computer, the total storage capacity of the DVD that contains the software for Windows 7 Ultimate is 2.32 GB. Your DVD properties will differ.

Figure 5-14	Viewing properties of a DVD drive

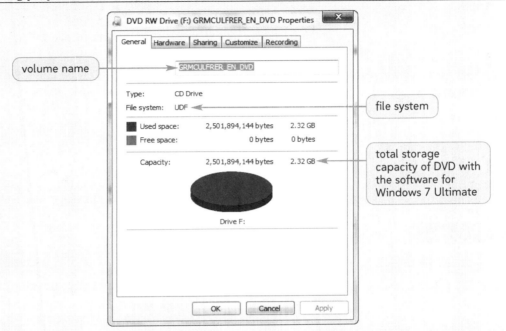

volume name

file system

total storage capacity of DVD with the software for Windows 7 Ultimate

▶ **2.** Close the DVD Drive Properties dialog box.

▶ **3.** If you have a CD drive or DVD/CD drive on your computer and a CD available, insert the CD into the drive, wait a moment, and if Windows 7 displays an AutoPlay dialog box, close the AutoPlay dialog box, right-click the **CD drive** icon in the Computer window, and then click **Properties**. See Figure 5-15.

Figure 5-15	Viewing properties of a CD drive

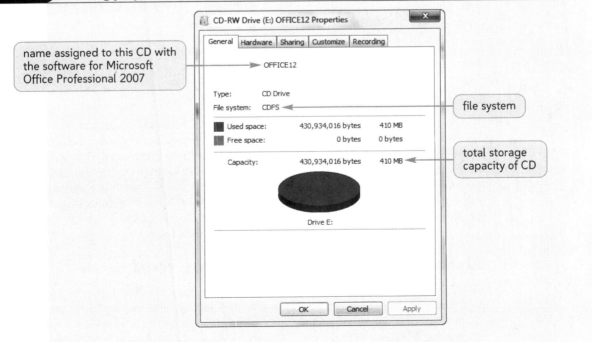

name assigned to this CD with the software for Microsoft Office Professional 2007

file system

total storage capacity of CD

> In Figure 5-15, Windows 7 identifies the file system as CDFS. For the CD-RW drive used on this computer, the total storage capacity of the Microsoft Office Professional 2007 CD is 410 MB. Office12 is the name assigned to the CD and the name of the folder where this version of Office is installed. Your CD properties will differ.
>
> ▶ **4.** Close the CD drive's Properties dialog box, and then close the Computer window.

The **Universal Disk Format (UDF)** file system is a successor to the **Compact Disc File System (CDFS)** originally designed for CDs. UDF provides support for long filenames (greater than 64 characters) and a multitier folder structure. These two file systems do not support compression.

Figure 5-16 shows a Removable Disk Properties dialog box for a 2 GB SD (Secure Digital) media card (or memory card) used to store photos in a digital camera. Notice that Windows 7 identifies the file system as FAT (for FAT16).

Figure 5-16	Viewing properties of a memory card

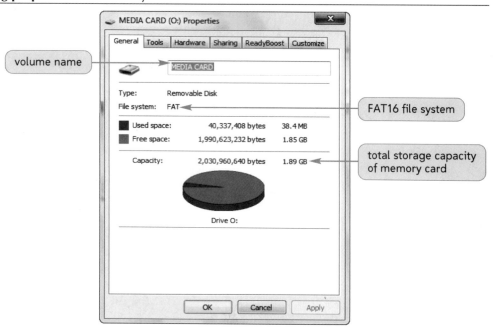

The **Live File System** used by Windows 7 and Windows Vista allows you to work with DVDs and CDs as if they were flash drives. That means that you can add, copy, replace, and delete files on a DVD or CD using drag-and-drop as you work. You no longer have to select a group of files, indicate that you want to copy them to a DVD or CD, and then wait for Windows to burn the files on the DVD or CD. The Live File System is compatible with Windows XP and Windows Vista. Windows 7 and Windows Vista report CDs prepared with the Live File System as having the UDF file system.

Using the Disk Management Tool

With an Administrator account, you can open a system administrative tool known as Computer Management and then use Disk Management to display more detailed information about disks and drives on your computer. Computer Management is a console within the Microsoft Management Console (MMC), which is a Windows component that provides access to administrative tools created by Microsoft and other software manufacturers so you can manage hardware, software, and networks.

The Disk Management tool identifies the type of file system each volume uses and whether a volume is a primary partition or a logical drive on an extended partition. As noted earlier, a primary partition is a partition on a basic disk, a physical disk that uses a Master Boot Record and a Hard Disk Partition Table to identify the active partition— the partition that contains the files for booting a computer. A basic disk can contain up to four primary partitions, or three primary partitions and one extended partition. An extended partition is a partition that contains one or more logical drives.

In the Windows 7 Professional, Ultimate, and Enterprise editions, you can convert a basic disk into a dynamic disk using the Disk Management tool. A **dynamic disk** is a physical hard disk that contains dynamic volumes, which support features described below that are not available on basic disks. A **dynamic volume** is a volume that you create on a dynamic disk. One of the primary differences between basic disks and dynamic disks is that on dynamic disks, you can extend a volume beyond one physical disk. In contrast, basic disks are limited to one physical disk and, as noted earlier, the storage capacity of a basic disk is limited. Dynamic disks use an operating-specific database to keep track of disks and volumes and provide features that are not available on basic disks (however, basic disks are simpler to manage). You can create one of the following types of dynamic volumes:

- **Simple volume**—A **simple volume** consists of a single region of storage space on one physical disk, or multiple regions of storage space on one physical volume. You can use Windows 7 to create simple volumes on basic disks as well as simple volumes on dynamic volumes.
- **Spanned volume**—A **spanned volume** combines unused storage space from more than one physical hard disk into one logical volume. That means the volume extends across more than one physical hard disk, so you must have at least two physical hard disks to create this type of volume. If one of the two physical hard disks fails, you lose all the data on the volume.
- **Striped volume** (also known as **RAID-0**)—A **striped volume** records data across two or more physical hard disks in a pattern known as **stripes**. Because reading from and writing to the different disks occur simultaneously, data can be accessed more quickly on this type of volume.

Simple, spanned, and striped volumes are not fault tolerant. Obviously, if the disk that contains a simple volume fails, you cannot access data on the simple volume. If one disk in a spanned or a striped volume fails, then you cannot access data on the spanned or striped volume.

RAID stands for **redundant array of independent disks** and, like a striped volume, provides a way of storing data on more than one disk, either to improve performance or to improve reliability.

There are two other types of dynamic volumes:

- **Mirrored volume** (also known as **RAID-1**)—A **mirrored volume** consists of two physical hard disks, one of which contains an identical copy of the contents of the other hard disk. By duplicating data on another volume (called **data redundancy**), this type of dynamic disk is fault tolerant. If one physical hard disk fails, then the operating system uses the second physical hard disk, which has a duplicate copy of the contents of the physical hard disk that failed. That means your computer continues to operate without problems if one physical hard drive fails.
- **RAID-5 volume**—A **RAID-5** volume stores data and parity information in stripes across three or more physical hard disks, and therefore is fault tolerant. **Parity** is a calculated value derived from data. This error-checking technique feature enables the operating system to reconstruct lost data if one physical hard disk fails. After restoring the lost data on the failed physical hard disk, your computer continues to operate without problems.

At a weekly meeting, Cadence and her staff examine and discuss features of the Windows 7 Disk Management tool. She asks you to set up a demonstration of this important tool for an upcoming meeting for IT staff.

You can access the Computer Management console in one of three ways, either by right-clicking Computer on the desktop (the fastest way), right-clicking Computer on the Start menu, or by adding Administrative Tools to the Start menu. The first approach is faster, but the last option provides you with access to more tools, and it is the more useful and preferred option if you are managing a computer on a day-to-day basis.

If you want to add Administrative Tools to your Start menu and All Programs menu now so it is always available, complete the following steps.

To add Administrative Tools to the Start menu:

▶ **1.** Right-click the **Start** button ⊞, click **Properties**, and on the Start Menu property sheet, click the **Customize** button.

▶ **2.** In the Customize Start Menu dialog box, scroll down to locate System Administrative Tools, and then click the **Display on the All Programs menu and the Start menu** option button to select it, click the **OK** button to close the Customize Start Menu dialog box, and then click the **OK** button to close the Taskbar and Start Menu Properties dialog box. After you apply the changes you have made, the Start menu will have an Administrative Tools option.

To complete the next section of the tutorial, your user account must be an Administrator account, or you must provide the password for an Administrator account. If your user account is not an Administrator account, and if you do not know the user name and password for an Administrator account, read the following steps and examine the figures so you are familiar with this important tool, but do not keystroke the steps.

If you are working in a college computer lab, ask your instructor and technical support staff whether you have permission to use the Disk Management tool to view information about volumes on the computers in your lab.

Now you're ready to open Computer Management and view information about the drives in your computer.

To open Computer Management:

▶ **1.** Right-click the **Computer** icon on the desktop (or on the Start menu), click **Manage**, provide Administrator credentials (if necessary), and then maximize the Computer Management window. The left pane is called the Console tree pane, and it provides access to built-in consoles for managing Windows 7. In the center is the Details pane where you view information for a specific console. The pane on the right side of the window is the Action pane where you can choose specific operations that you want to perform on an item selected in the Details pane.

▶ **2.** Under Storage in the Console tree, click **Disk Management**, and wait for Windows 7 to load disk configuration information. Windows 7 then displays information about the volumes and disks on your computer in the Details pane. See Figure 5-17. At the top of the Details pane is the Volume List area, and at the bottom is the Graphical View area. The computer used for this figure differs from most other computers because it has two partitions on the hard disk, identified in the figure as (C:) for the Windows 7 partition and (D:) for the Windows Vista partition. The view in your Details pane will differ.

Figure 5-17 Information on disks, partitions, volumes, and drives, as seen in Windows 7

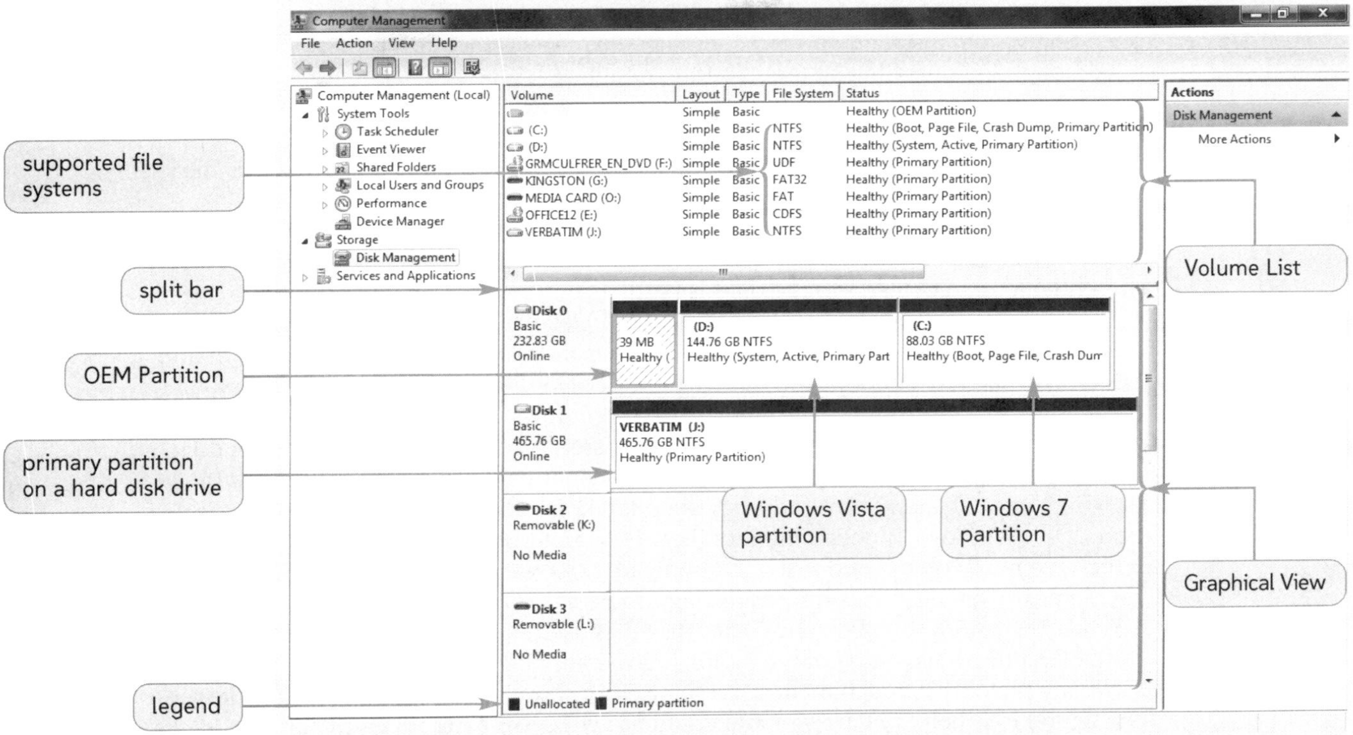

3. To adjust your view of the Volume List and Graphical View area, point to the horizontal split bar between the Volume List and Graphical View area, and when the mouse pointer changes to ⇕, drag the split bar up or down.

   Trouble? If you cannot find the split bar, it may be displayed under a horizontal scroll bar in the Volume List area.

4. To more clearly identify these two areas in the Details pane, click **View** on the menu bar, and click **Customize**. The Customize View dialog box opens, displaying the actual names of GUI components in the Computer Management window.

5. Click the **Description bar** check box to enable this feature, and then click the **OK** button. The Description bar at the top of the Details pane identifies the two views in the Details pane (i.e., Volume List + Graphical View). The Customize View dialog box displays the actual names of GUI components within this window.

6. If Windows 7 displays a horizontal scroll bar in the Volume List area at the top of the Details pane, scroll to the right to view the other information reported by this console, and then scroll left to view the Volume column. Disk Management also shows the capacity of each disk or partition, the amount of free space, the percent free, whether or not a disk or partition is fault tolerant, and the overhead. Overhead identifies the amount of storage space on a drive required for the fault tolerance feature.

In Figure 5-17, the legend on the Status bar at the bottom of the Details pane identifies the disk regions shown in the Graphical View area as either Unallocated area or as a Primary partition. The Graphical View area right above the legend shows one hard disk that is identified as Disk 0 with a storage capacity of 232.83 GB. Disk 0 is divided into three primary partitions: a hidden partition set up by the computer manufacturer (and identified as the OEM Partition in the Volume List), an internal hard disk partition identified as D: (for drive D), and an internal hard disk partition identified as C: (for drive C). On the computer used for this figure, both partitions have a different Windows operating system installed on them. If you have two internal hard disk partitions, but only one operating system installed on your computer, the drive C partition is listed first.

Although the operating systems are not identified for the different partitions on this computer, drive D is the partition where Windows Vista is installed, and drive C is the partition where Windows 7 is installed. If you boot this computer with Windows Vista instead of Windows 7, then drive C is the Windows Vista partition and drive D is the Windows 7 partition.

Both drive D and drive C use NTFS. All three partitions are identified as "Healthy", meaning that the volumes are accessible and do not have any known problems. There is presently no unallocated storage on this hard disk.

As shown in the Volume List at the top of the Details pane, drive C (where Windows 7 is installed) and drive D (where Windows Vista is installed) are simple volumes on a basic disk (one that supports the Master Boot Record disk-partitioning approach). In both the Volume List and the Graphical View area, Windows 7 identifies drive C as the boot partition (where the Windows 7 operating files are stored). Windows 7 identifies drive D as the system partition because it contains the Windows 7 operating system files for booting the computer. The Windows Vista operating boot files are also on the same partition as the Windows 7 operating boot files. This dual-boot setup illustrates a situation in which the boot volume and system volume are not one and the same. (The ProSkills box on the next page describes how to distinguish these two volumes.)

Disk 1 is a 465.76 GB external hard disk that uses NTFS. Disks 2, 3, and 4 (not shown in the Graphical View area of the figure) are memory card slots, which currently do not have any memory cards in them. Disk 5 (also not shown in the Graphical View area of the figure) is a memory card slot that contains a 1.89 GB memory card that uses the FAT file system. Here, FAT means FAT16. Disk 6 is a 14.90 GB flash drive (sold as a 16 GB flash drive). As shown in the Volume List, drive F is a DVD drive that uses the UDF file system, and drive E is a CD drive that uses the CDFS file system. Depending on the format applied to the DVD disc you inserted, Windows 7 may identify it as using the CDFS file system. At the bottom of the Graphical View area (not visible in the figure), the CD drive is identified as CD-ROM 0, and the DVD drive is identified as CD-ROM 1. **ROM** stands for read-only memory. The DVD, CD, flash, and media card drives are all identified as healthy, primary partitions as illustrated by the alphabetical list of drive names in the Volume column in the Volume List.

If you boot this computer with Windows Vista instead, and then open Computer Management, Disk Management reports that drive C is both the boot and the system volume, as shown in Figure 5-18.

| Figure 5-18 | Information on disks, partitions, volumes, and drives, as seen in Windows Vista |

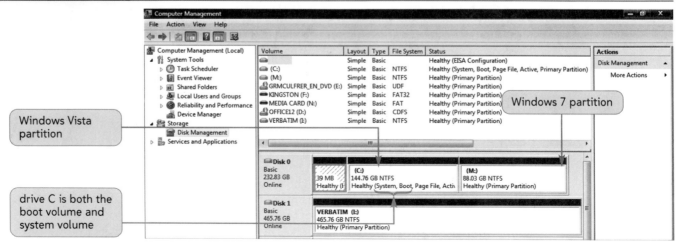

That means that the Windows Vista boot files and the Windows Vista folder, with the remainder of the operating system software, are on the same volume (identified as (C:) in the figure). In contrast, as shown in the previous Figure 5-17, the Windows 7 boot files are located on the drive identified as (D:) while the Windows 7 folder is located on the drive identified as (C:).

PROSKILLS

Problem Solving: Distinguishing the Boot Volume and System Volume

The **boot volume** is the volume that contains the Windows 7 operating system files located in the Windows folder. The **system volume** is the volume that contains the files and data structures for loading Windows 7. In other words, the files and data structures required to start your computer are stored on the system volume rather than the boot volume (logically backwards). Likewise, the operating system files are stored in the Windows folder on the boot volume, not the system volume (also logically backwards). Fortunately on most computers, the boot volume and system volume are usually one and the same, but they can be different. If you have one hard disk, and if there is only one volume on that disk (typically identified as drive C), then the boot volume and system volume are the same. It's important to understand this distinction if you plan on setting up a computer as a dual-boot or multiboot computer, whether for yourself, for a coworker, or for a client. Then, you can more effectively plan full-system backups that include an entire disk, including operating system files, in the event you will need to restore an entire computer. Understanding how Windows 7 uses boot and system volumes is also important for troubleshooting problems.

If you compare Windows 7's view of disks, drives, and partitions in Figure 5-17 with Windows Vista's view of the same disks, drives, and partitions in Figure 5-18, you can see how remarkably similar the information is. What differs is which operating system you use to start up your computer. You can click a column button in the Volume List area to sort a column in ascending (or descending order).

To change the Volume List to a Disk List view:

▶ 1. Click **View** on the menu bar, point to **Top**, and then click **Disk List**. The view at the top of the Details pane now lists disks by disk number or CD-ROM number. See Figure 5-19.

Figure 5-19 Using Disk Management to view information on disks

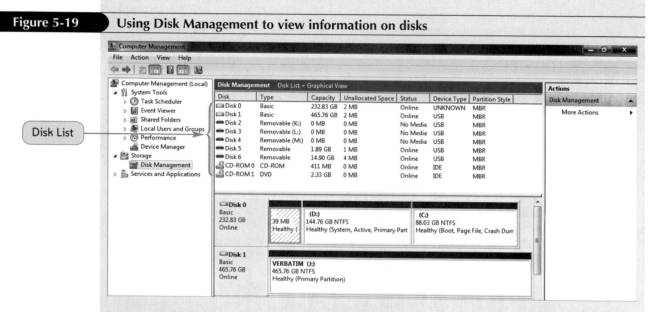

The Status column identifies whether a disk is online, which means that the disk is available and does not contain any errors, or whether it contains no media. The Device Type column identifies the type of connection (IDE for Integrated Drive Electronics, UNKNOWN for the OEM partition, and USB for a USB hardware device). The Partition Style column identifies all these disks as MBR disks, or disks that use a Master Book Record. Your details will differ.

2. In the Graphical View area, right-click the **partition** where Windows 7 is installed (typically identified as drive C). Windows 7 displays a shortcut menu for this drive. Notice that there are options for extending and shrinking a volume, adding a mirror volume, formatting a volume, and deleting a volume. You can also open or explore a volume, and you can view properties of a volume. Dimmed options are not available for a variety of reasons. For example, you cannot format the system volume where Windows stores its boot files or the boot volume where Windows 7 is installed. However, you can format an external hard drive. The Mirror option is available if you have a second hard drive. These same options are available by right-clicking a disk in the Volume List and Disk List views, and these options and other options are available from the Action pane on the right.

3. To restore your default settings before closing the Computer Management window, click **View** on the menu bar, point to **Top**, and then click **Volume List**.

4. Next, click **View** on the menu bar, click **Customize**, and in the Customize View dialog box, click the **Description bar** check box to disable this feature, click the **OK** button, and then close the Computer Management window.

You can use the Disk Management tool to perform a variety of tasks on disks, partitions, volumes, and logical drives, including identifying and troubleshooting problems. Under Windows 7 and Windows Vista, you can extend a simple or spanned volume (but not a striped volume) to use additional unallocated disk storage space, or you can shrink the size of a simple or spanned volume (but not a striped volume) so you can use unallocated disk storage space as a new partition. If you shrink a partition or logical drive, files are moved (if necessary) so you do not lose any data. In Windows 7, you use unallocated storage space or unused storage space on a disk (depending on the type of operation you want to perform) to create a simple volume, spanned volume, or striped volume. If you open Help from the Computer Management window, and then select Disk Management on the Contents tab, you can access detailed information on how to perform these operations. You can also use Windows 7 Help and Support as well as the Microsoft, TechNet, and MSDN Web sites and their libraries. Another valuable resource for IT staff is the Windows 7 Resource Kit, which is a 1,709-page comprehensive guide to Windows 7 that you can purchase online from Microsoft Corporation.

REFERENCE

Using the Disk Management Tool

- Right-click the Computer icon on the desktop (or Start menu), click Manage, and then click Disk Management under Storage in the Console tree in the left pane of the Computer Management window.
- To more clearly identify the two areas in the Details pane, click View on the menu bar, click Customize, and in the Customize View dialog box, click the Description bar check box to enable this feature, and then click the OK button.
- To view disk information by disk number and CD number, click View on the menu bar, point to Top, and then click Disk List.

Windows 7 also supports a new type of disk called a virtual hard disk (VHD). A **virtual hard disk** is a file with the .vhd file extension. You can use the Disk Management tool to create and attach (or **mount**) a virtual hard disk so Windows 7 treats it as a physical disk drive.

REVIEW

Session 5.1 Quick Check

1. A(n) _____ is a physical device, such as a hard disk, whereas a(n) _____ consists of all or part of a disk, uses a specific file system, has a drive name, and may span multiple hard disks.
2. A(n) _____ is a subdivision of a track and stores 512 bytes, whereas a(n) _____ is the smallest amount of storage space that Windows 7 allocates to a file or part of a file.
3. Storage space allocated to a file, but not used by that file, is called _____.
4. What table does NTFS use to keep track of folders and files on a hard disk?
5. What file system supports copying to a DVD or CD on an as-need basis in Windows 7 and Windows Vista?
6. What is the difference between the boot volume and the system volume?
7. What is the Hard Disk Partition Table, and what purpose does it serve?
8. What is the purpose of the NTFS transaction log file?

SESSION 5.2 VISUAL OVERVIEW

NTFS encryption encodes folders, such as this Finances folder, so that the folder's contents are secure and protected from individuals who do not have the proper encryption key for accessing the encrypted folder. You can also encrypt individual files.

NTFS compression compresses folders, such as this Logo Designs folder, so the folder's contents use less storage space on disk. You can also compress individual files.

The directory attribute is assigned to folders. If you display the Attributes column in a folder window, Windows 7 identifies folders by the code letter *D* for *directory*.

The encrypt attribute is assigned to an encrypted folder (or file). If you display the Attributes column in a folder window, Windows 7 identifies encrypted folders and files by the code letter *E* for *encrypt*.

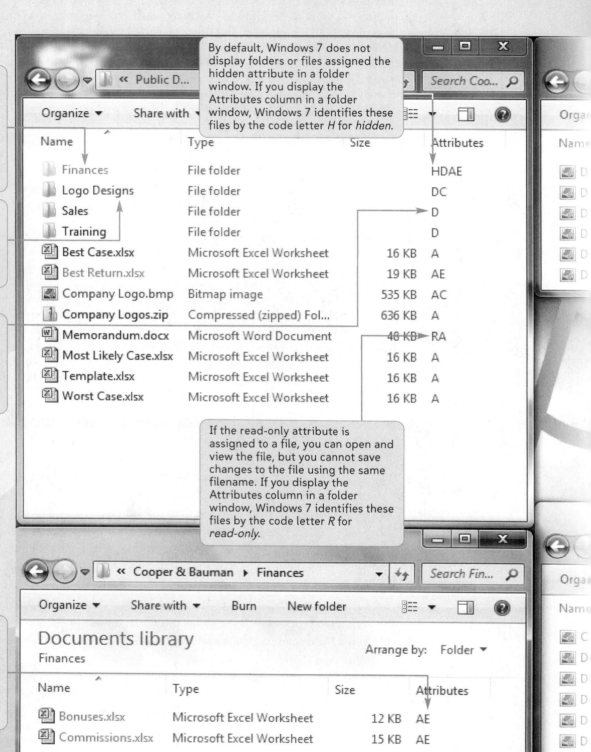

By default, Windows 7 does not display folders or files assigned the hidden attribute in a folder window. If you display the Attributes column in a folder window, Windows 7 identifies these files by the code letter *H* for *hidden*.

If the read-only attribute is assigned to a file, you can open and view the file, but you cannot save changes to the file using the same filename. If you display the Attributes column in a folder window, Windows 7 identifies these files by the code letter *R* for *read-only*.

ATTRIBUTES

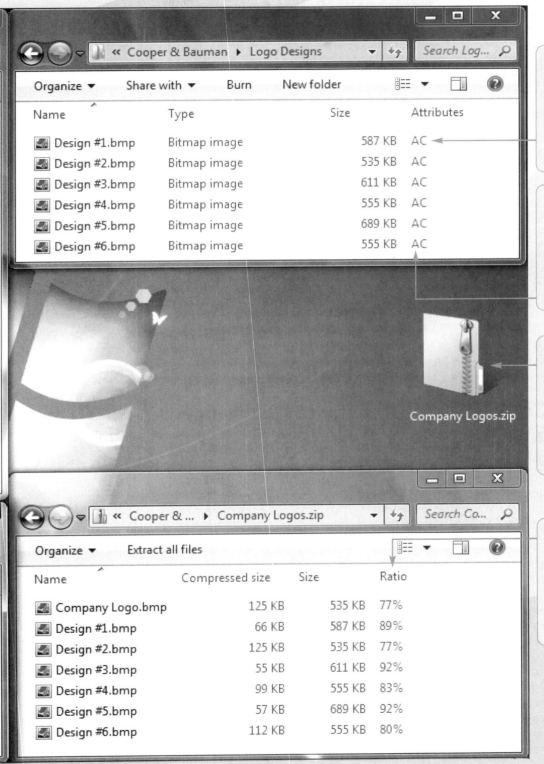

The compress attribute is assigned to compressed folders (or files). If you display the Attributes column in a folder window, Windows 7 identifies compressed folders and files by the code letter *C* for *compress*.

The archive attribute is assigned to newly created, newly copied, and newly modified files. If you display the Attributes column in a folder window, Windows 7 identifies these files by the code letter *A* for *archive*.

A Compressed (zipped) folder is a file that contains a group of files, or one or more folders and files, within a single file. compressed (zipped) folders have the .zip file extension, and you can open them like you open a folder.

The Ratio column in a Compressed (zipped) folder shows the percent compression of each file. The Size column shows the original size of each file, and the Compressed size column shows the compressed size of each file.

Getting Started

In this section of the tutorial, you are going to examine the process for compressing and uncompressing folders and files, creating and extracting the contents of Compressed (zipped) folders, encrypting and decrypting folders and files, and BitLocker Drive Encryption.

Next, you will copy the Tutorial folder provided with the Windows 7 for Power User Data Files from a flash drive, the My Documents folder, or a network folder to the Public Documents folder.

To copy the Tutorial folder to your Public Documents folder:

▶ **1.** Make sure you have downloaded and extracted your copy of the Windows 7 for Power User Data Files.

▶ **2.** Close all open windows, attach your flash drive (if necessary), open the Tutorial.05 folder, and copy the Tutorial folder to the Public Documents folder on your hard drive, or to the folder requested by your instructor or technical support staff. If you need to review the steps for performing these operations, refer to the detailed steps found in Tutorial 3.

▶ **3.** Close all other windows except the Public Documents folder window or the window for the folder requested by your instructor or technical support staff.

▶ **4.** If the computer you are using already has a Cooper & Bauman folder, rename that folder to **Cooper & Bauman (Previous)**, and then change the name of the Tutorial folder to **Cooper & Bauman**.

Now you're ready to examine the folder and file compression feature of NTFS.

Compressing and Uncompressing Folders and Files

On an NTFS volume, you can compress files, folders, or even an entire drive. This compression option is not available on FAT volumes. Once a file is compressed, NTFS handles the decompression and recompression of files as you work with them. Windows 7 follows certain rules when you copy or move uncompressed or compressed folders and files from one location to another within an NTFS volume:

- When you *move* a folder or file to another folder, the folder or file keeps its compression state after the move. For example, if you move a compressed folder or file to an uncompressed folder, then the folder or file remains compressed. Likewise, if you move an uncompressed folder or file to a compressed folder, then the folder or file remains uncompressed.
- When you *copy* a folder or file to another folder, the folder or file takes on the compression state of the folder. For example, if you copy a compressed folder or file to an uncompressed folder, then the file is uncompressed. Likewise, if you copy an uncompressed folder or file to a compressed folder, then the file is compressed.
- If you copy a file to a folder and that folder contains a file by the same name, then the copied file takes on the compression state of the file already stored in that folder. The filename and file extension do not change.

If you copy a file from a folder on a FAT volume to a folder on an NTFS volume, then the file takes on the compression state of the folder on the NTFS volume. If you copy a compressed folder or file from an NTFS volume to a FAT volume, then the folder or file is uncompressed. Likewise, if you email a file that is compressed on your computer, the person who receives that message receives an uncompressed file attached to the message.

NTFS compression is available in the Windows 7 Starter, Home Basic, Home Premium Professional, Ultimate, and Enterprise editions.

In the following steps, you are going to compress and uncompress a folder on an NTFS volume. If you are working in a college computer lab, ask your instructor or technical support staff whether you can compress and uncompress a folder. If you do not have permission to use the NTFS compression feature on a volume, read the steps and examine the figures so you are familiar with this feature, but do not keystroke the following steps.

Cadence asks you to show a new employee how to compress folders and files on his computer so he can archive important files and free up valuable storage space.

To compress a folder and its contents:

1. If necessary, use the Change your view button ▤ ▾ on the toolbar to switch to Large Icons view.

2. Open the Cooper & Bauman folder, right-click the **Performance** folder icon, click **Cut**, click the **Back** button ◐, click the **Organize** button on the command bar, and then click **Paste**. Windows 7 moves the Performance folder and all its contents from the Cooper & Bauman folder to the Public Documents folder.

3. Right-click the **Cooper & Bauman** folder, and then click **Properties** on the shortcut menu. On the General property sheet in the Cooper & Bauman Properties dialog box, Windows 7 reports that this folder and its subfolder and files are 4.63 MB (or 4,865,515 bytes) in size, use 4.67 MB (or 4,902,912 bytes) of storage space on the disk, and currently contain 22 files in 3 folders. See Figure 5-20. That means this folder and its subfolders and files waste 37,397 bytes of storage space on the disk because of slack.

> **TIP**
>
> If a folder or file is already selected, you can press Alt+Enter to open the folder or file's Properties dialog box.

Figure 5-20 | **Viewing properties of the Cooper & Bauman folder**

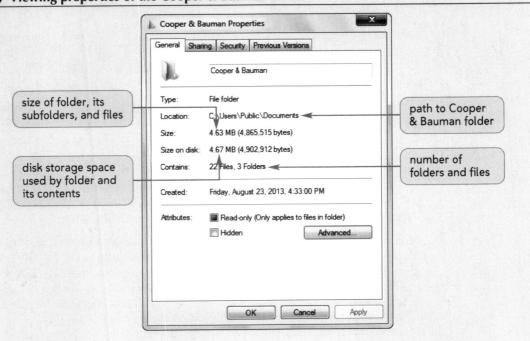

4. Click the **Advanced** button. Windows 7 opens the Advanced Attributes dialog box. See Figure 5-21. Under the Compress or Encrypt attributes section is an option for compressing the contents of the folder to save disk space (and an option for encrypting data, which you will use later).

Figure 5-21 Advanced Attributes dialog box

option for compressing and uncompressing folders and files

option for encrypting or decrypting folders and files

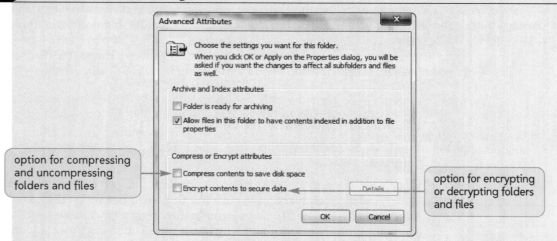

5. Click the **Compress contents to save disk space** check box, click the **OK** button in the Advanced Attributes dialog box, and then click the **Apply** button in the Cooper & Bauman Properties dialog box. In the Confirm Attribute Changes dialog box, Windows 7 informs you that you have chosen to apply the compress attribute. See Figure 5-22.

Figure 5-22 Confirm Attribute Changes dialog box

attribute to apply

choose how to apply attribute

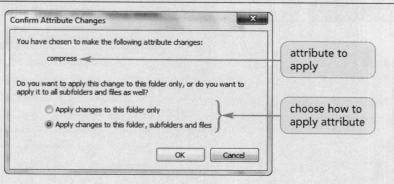

You have the option of applying this change to only the Cooper & Bauman folder, or you can apply the change to the Cooper & Bauman folder and all its subfolders and files. Windows 7 automatically selects the latter option by default.

6. If it is not already selected, click the **Apply changes to this folder, subfolders and files** option button, and then click the **OK** button. On the General property sheet in the Cooper & Bauman Properties dialog box, Windows 7 reports that this folder and its subfolders and files are still 4.63 MB (or 4,865,515 bytes) in size, but the folder and its subfolders and files now use only 2.16 MB (or 2,273,648 bytes) of storage space on the disk. See Figure 5-23.

| Figure 5-23 | Viewing properties of a compressed folder |

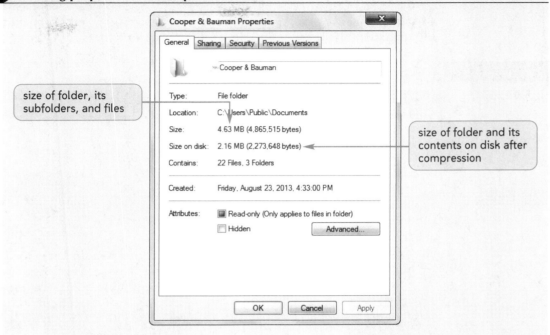

size of folder, its
subfolders, and files

size of folder and its
contents on disk after
compression

Windows 7 has reduced the amount of disk space used by this folder by 2,629,264
bytes (or 2.5 MB). That means that Windows 7 compressed the folder by almost
46% so the folder is about 54% of its original size. That's a substantial reduction in
the amount of storage space the folder and its contents now use on disk.

7. Click the **OK** button to close the Cooper & Bauman Properties dialog box, click
the **folder window background**, and notice that the Cooper & Bauman folder
name is displayed in bright blue to indicate that the folders contents are compressed. In contrast, the Performance folder is uncompressed, as shown by the
black color used for the folder name.

Trouble? If Windows 7 does not display compressed folders and files in bright
blue, click the Organize button on the toolbar, click Folder and search options,
click the View tab, and in the Advanced settings list box, locate and add a check
mark to the "Show encrypted or compressed NTFS files in color" check box, and
then click the OK button to close the Folder Options dialog box, and apply the
new setting.

TIP

If a folder or file is already
selected, you can press the
Enter key to quickly open
the folder or file.

8. Open the Cooper & Bauman folder, and if the folders are not displayed in Details
view, click the **More options** arrow ▤ ▾ for the Change your view button, and
then click **Details**. Notice that the subfolder names are also shown in bright blue.

You can also view attributes to verify the compression status of a file and to view other
attributes assigned to folders and files.

To view attributes:

1. Right-click a **column heading**, click **More** on the shortcut menu, locate and click
the **Attributes** check box in the Choose Details dialog box, and click the **OK**
button.

2. Right-click a **column heading**, and then click **Size All Columns to Fit**. In the Attributes column, Windows 7 displays *C* for all the folders to indicate that they are assigned the compress attribute (see Figure 5-24), and *D* in the Attribute column identifies these subfolders as directories (or folders).

Figure 5-24 | **Viewing compressed folders**

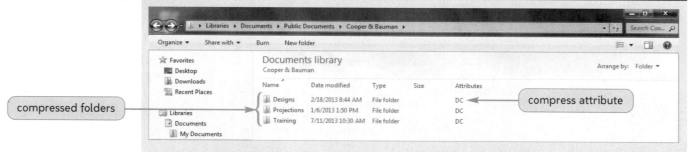

3. Open the **Projections** folder, right-click a **column heading**, and then click **Size All Columns to Fit**, and notice that all the filenames are also displayed in bright blue to indicate that they are compressed. See Figure 5-25. All these files are assigned the Archive attribute, indicated by *A*, because you earlier copied the Tutorial folder and all its folders and files to the Public Documents folder.

Figure 5-25 | **Viewing compressed files**

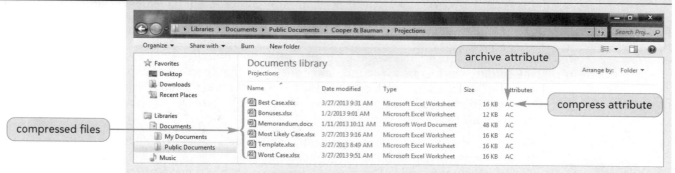

4. Click **Public Documents** in the Address bar to return to the Public Documents folder.

Next, you want to move the Performance folder back to the Cooper & Bauman folder, and then copy the Projections folder from the Cooper & Bauman folder to the Public Documents folder.

To move the Performance folder to the Cooper & Bauman folder:

1. Drag the **Performance** folder, and drop it onto the Cooper & Bauman folder icon. Windows 7 moves the Performance folder into the Cooper & Bauman folder.

2. Open the **Cooper & Bauman** folder, and if necessary, change to Details view. Because you moved the Performance folder rather than copying it, Windows 7 did not compress it after the move (the folder name is shown in black rather than blue). See Figure 5-26. Instead, the folder retained its original uncompressed state. Also, the Attributes column does not contain a *C* for compressed. That means the Performance folder is not compressed.

Figure 5-26   **Viewing the compression status of folders**

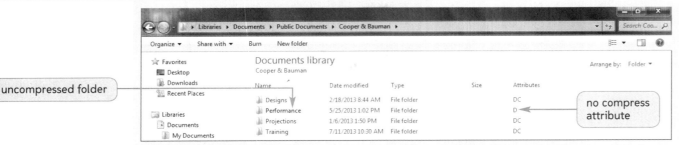

3. Open the **Performance** folder. The files in this folder are not compressed (the filenames are shown in black rather than blue).

4. Click the **Back** button ⬅, right-click the **Projections** folder, click **Cut**, click **Public Documents** in the Address bar, right-click the **background** of the Public Documents window, and then click **Paste**. Notice that the Projections folder retains its compression state when moved from the Cooper & Bauman folder to the Public Documents folder (the folder's name is shown in bright blue).

5. Open the **Projections** folder and, if necessary, click **Details view**. All the files within this folder are still compressed.

6. Click **Public Documents** in the Address bar, and then drag the **Projections** folder and drop it on the **Cooper & Bauman** folder. Windows 7 moves the Projections folder back into the Cooper & Bauman folder. If you open the Cooper & Bauman folder, you will find that the Projections folder still retains its original compressed state (as you would expect).

You've just discovered that moving a folder or file to another folder does not change the compression state of the folder or file. Next, you are going to copy a folder from the Cooper & Bauman folder, and then copy an uncompressed file into the Cooper & Bauman folder to determine how Windows 7 handles the compression state of a folder or file when copied (rather than when moved).

To copy a compressed folder and its files from a compressed folder:

1. Open the **Cooper & Bauman** folder, right-click the **Training** folder, click **Copy**, click the **Back** button ⬅, right-click the **background** of the Public Documents window, and then click **Paste**. The copy of the previously compressed Training folder is now uncompressed (it takes on the compression state of the current folder, and the folder name is now shown in black).

2. Open the **Training** folder. Notice that the files within this folder are now uncompressed.

3. Right-click the **Spreadsheets.pptx** file, click **Copy**, click the **Back** button ⬅, open the **Cooper & Bauman** folder, right-click the **background** of the folder window, and then click **Paste**. The Spreadsheets.pptx file now takes on the compression state of the current folder, and the filename is displayed in blue (it's now compressed).

4. Keep this folder open for the next set of steps.

In the next set of steps, you will copy a file from the Cooper & Bauman folder to your flash drive.

To copy a compressed file to a flash drive:

1. If necessary, attach your flash drive and close any window or dialog box that opens.

2. Right-click **Spreadsheets.pptx** in the Cooper & Bauman folder, point to **Send to**, and then click the **option for your flash drive** on the Send to menu. Windows 7 copies this compressed file to your flash drive.

3. Click the **Address bar arrow** ▶ to the left of Libraries in the Address bar, click **Computer**, and then click your **flash drive** icon. Windows 7 opens a window onto your flash drive. The Spreadsheets.pptx file is uncompressed. After copying this file, you change your mind, and want to remove it from your flash drive.

4. Right-click the **background** of your flash drive window, click **Undo Copy**, and in the Delete File dialog box, click the **Yes** button. Windows 7 removes the copy of the Spreadsheets.pptx file from your flash drive.

5. Click the **Recent Pages** button ▾, and then click **Public Documents**.

6. Right-click the **Training** folder icon, click **Delete**, and in the Delete Folder dialog box, click the **Yes** button. Windows 7 deletes this duplicate copy of the Training folder.

7. Open the Cooper & Bauman folder, right-click **Spreadsheets.pptx**, click **Delete**, and in the Delete File dialog box, click the **Yes** button. Windows 7 deletes this duplicate copy of the Spreadsheets.pptx file.

8. Click the **Back** button ⬅ to return to the Public Documents folder.

9. Keep the Public Documents folder window open for the next set of steps.

TIP

You can also undo an operation by using the Ctrl+Z keyboard shortcut.

You've just discovered that a folder or file takes on the compression state of the folder where you copy the folder or file to.

Now, you are going to reverse the compression process, and uncompress the Cooper & Bauman folder and its contents.

To uncompress a folder and its contents:

1. Right-click the **Cooper & Bauman** folder, click **Properties** on the shortcut menu, and on the General property sheet of the Cooper & Bauman Properties dialog box, click the **Advanced** button.

2. In the Advanced Attributes dialog box, click the **Compress contents to save disk space** check box to remove the check mark, click the **OK** button, and then click the **Apply** button in the Cooper & Bauman Properties dialog box. Windows 7 displays the Confirm Attribute Changes dialog box, notes that you have chosen to apply the uncompress attribute, and asks how you want to apply this change.

3. Click the **Apply changes to this folder, subfolders and files** option button (if necessary), and then click the **OK** button. On the General property sheet in the Cooper & Bauman Properties dialog box, Windows 7 reports that this folder and its subfolder and files are 4.73 MB (or 4,964,045 bytes) in size, and the 27 files and 4 folders now use 4.77 MB (or 5,009,408 bytes) of disk storage space.

4. Click the **OK** button to close the Cooper & Bauman Properties dialog box.

5. Keep the Public Documents folder open for the next section of the tutorial.

In summary, if you *copy* a file (compressed or uncompressed) to a folder on an NTFS volume, the file takes on the compression state of the folder (compressed or uncompressed). If you *move* a compressed or uncompressed file from one folder to another on an NTFS volume, the file remains as it originally was (compressed or uncompressed), no matter whether the folder is compressed or uncompressed. The ability to compress and uncompress folders and files is a feature of NTFS volumes and is not available on FAT volumes.

REFERENCE

Compressing and Uncompressing a Folder and Its Contents

- Locate the folder you want to compress, right-click that folder, click Properties, and then click the Advanced button on the General property sheet in the Properties dialog box for that folder.
- In the Compress or Encrypt attributes section of the Advanced Attributes dialog box, add a check mark to the "Compress contents to save disk space" check box to compress the folder and its contents or remove the check mark from the "Compress contents to save disk space" check box to uncompress the folder and its contents, click the OK button in the Advanced Attributes dialog box, and then click the OK button in the Properties dialog box for the folder.
- In the Confirm Attribute Changes dialog box, click the "Apply changes to this folder, subfolders and files" option button, and then click the OK button.

You just successfully compressed and then uncompressed a folder and its contents.

INSIGHT

Maximizing the Use of Disk Storage Space by Compressing Files

If you want to keep important files that you no longer use on a daily basis but want to minimize their impact on the available storage space on your hard disk, you can compress them so they use less storage space on your hard disk, and you can still access them in the same way you used to access them. If you want to compress all the folders and files on your hard disk, except for certain operating system files, you can open the Computer window, view properties of the hard drive, and then choose and apply the option to compress the drive to save disk space. By using this strategy for your work or personal computer, you can retain important files, maximize the availability of storage space, and can quickly identify compressed files by their color.

Using Compressed (Zipped) Folders

Windows 7 supports the use of Compressed (zipped) folders on *both* NTFS and FAT volumes. Any folders or files you place within a Compressed (zipped) folder are compressed and therefore require less storage space on disk.

If you need to send someone a set of files, you do not have to attach each and every file separately to an email message. Instead, you might be able to store the files in a single Compressed (zipped) folder, and attach that one file to your email message if your email software supports the use of files with the .zip file extension. The person who receives your email message saves the attachment with the .zip file extension on the hard disk, opens the Compressed (zipped) folder, and then chooses the option to extract the folders and files within the Compressed (zipped) folder.

Because it's possible for someone to package malicious software in a Compressed (zipped) folder, your email software may remove files with the .zip file extension before transmitting or receiving an email message. If this is the case, you can remove the .zip file extension from the Compressed (zipped) folder before you attach it to an email message, and inform the recipient that they have to add the .zip file extension back to the filename to access the contents of the Compressed (zipped) folder.

When you create a Compressed (zipped) folder, Windows 7 uses a custom icon with a zipper for the Compressed (zipped) folder. The Compressed (zipped) folder behaves exactly like a zip file created with a file compression utility such as WinZip. When you copy a Compressed (zipped) folder to another computer with a pre-Windows XP version of Windows that does not support the Compressed (zipped) Folder feature, the Compressed (zipped) folder appears simply as a zip file with the .zip file extension, and you have to use a file compression utility such as WinZip to extract the contents of the zip file. Even though Windows XP, Windows Vista, and Windows 7 support the Compressed (zipped) Folder feature, some individuals download a file compression utility such as WinZip and use that instead because it offers more features than the support provided in Windows for this file type.

PROSKILLS

Teamwork: Posting Files on an FTP Site

When working collaboratively on a project with coworkers, clients, and contractors, you can package files together in a single Compressed (zipped) folder, and then post it on an FTP site so everyone only has to download one file. Likewise, they can use the same approach when providing you with project files. Once you, your coworkers, or a client downloads a Compressed (zipped) folder, the compressed files can be extracted from the Compressed (zipped) folder. This approach is also useful for transferring very large files that cannot be sent as email attachments because of their size. Another advantage of using an FTP site is that all project files are stored in one central location for ease of access to everyone involved in a project. By using this approach, everyone can work together effectively, meet tight deadlines, and stay on top of everything that occurs on a project.

Cadence asks you to convert the Cooper & Bauman folder into a Compressed (zipped) folder so she can post the entire folder on the company's FTP site. She also asks you to help another coworker extract the files for use on her computer.

If you have a file compression utility (such as WinZip) installed on your computer, then that utility might be associated with the file extension used for Compressed (zipped) Folders, and Windows 7 might prompt you how you want to handle extracting the file. If the latter occurs, and you do not know how to extract the files with that program on the computer you are using, read the following steps and examine the figures, but do not keystroke the steps.

To create a Compressed (zipped) folder:

1. Right-click the **Cooper & Bauman** folder, point to **Send to**, click **Compressed (zipped) folder**, and then press the **Enter** key to accept the default filename.

2. Right-click a **column heading**, and then click **Size All Columns to Fit**. Windows 7 creates a Compressed (zipped) folder named *Cooper & Bauman.zip*. See Figure 5-27. Notice that you still have your original Cooper & Bauman folder.

Figure 5-27   Compressed (zipped) folder with a custom folder icon

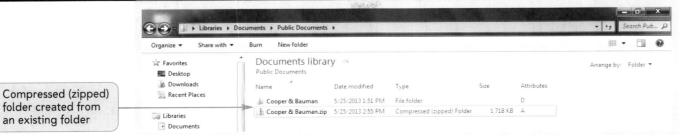

Compressed (zipped) folder created from an existing folder

3. Right-click the original **Cooper & Bauman** folder, click **Delete**, and then click the **Yes** button in the Delete Folder dialog box.

4. Right-click **Cooper & Bauman.zip**, and then click **Properties**. In the Cooper & Bauman.zip Properties dialog box, Windows 7 reports that the size of this folder and its contents is now 1.67 MB (or 1,758,782 bytes) and that its size on disk is now 1.67 MB (or 1,761,280 bytes). See Figure 5-28.

Figure 5-28   Viewing properties of a Compressed (zipped) folder

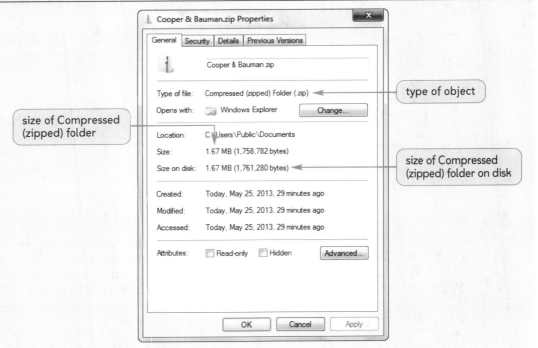

type of object

size of Compressed (zipped) folder

size of Compressed (zipped) folder on disk

When you last examined the size of the uncompressed Cooper & Bauman folder and its contents, Windows 7 reported that this folder and its subfolder and files were 4.73 MB (or 4,964,045 bytes) in size, and used 4.77 MB (or 5,009,408 bytes) of disk storage space (wasting 45,363 bytes of storage space). The Compressed (zipped) folder is 3,205,263 bytes (or approximately 3.1 MB) smaller in size, and it uses 3,248,128 bytes (or approximately 3.1 MB) less storage space on disk. Also, it wastes far less storage space on disk, namely, 2,498 bytes; in other words, it has 94% less slack than the uncompressed folder. Windows 7 compressed this folder and its subfolders and files by 65% so the Compressed (zipped) folder is only 35% of the size of the original Cooper & Bauman folder.

In contrast, NTFS compression only compressed the folder and its contents by 46%, leaving the folder and its contents about 54% of its original size. That means you get better compression by using a Compressed (zipped) Folder, and this compression is also available on drives that use the FAT file system (which is not the case for NTFS compression).

5. Close the Cooper & Bauman.zip Properties dialog box, and then click **Cooper & Bauman.zip**. Windows 7 opens the Compressed (zipped) folder just like it opens a regular folder. Within this Compressed (zipped) folder is the original Cooper & Bauman folder. Now that you've opened the Compressed (zipped) folder, the toolbar now has an "Extract all files" option.

6. Click the **Cooper & Bauman** folder. Within this folder are all the Cooper & Bauman subfolders.

7. Click the **Designs** folder icon, right-click a **column heading**, and then click **Size All Columns to Fit**. Notice that Windows 7 reports on the original size of each file (in the Size column), the compressed size, and a ratio that shows the percent compression. See Figure 5-29.

| Figure 5-29 | Examining the compression of bitmap image files |

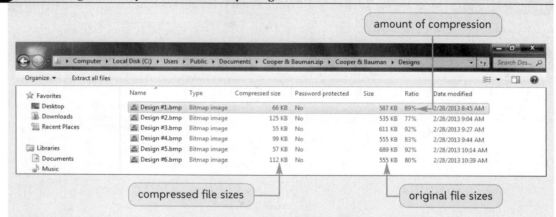

Windows 7 compressed these Bitmap image files by 77% to 92% so the files range from 8% to 23% of their original size.

8. Click the **Back** button ⬅, click the **Training** folder icon, right-click a **column heading**, and then click **Size All Columns to Fit**. Notice that for other types of files, compression varies, and is less than that for Bitmap image files. See Figure 5-30.

Figure 5-30 | **Comparing file compression for different file types**

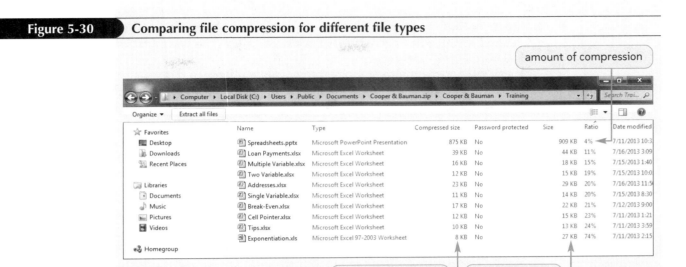

For example, Spreadsheets.pptx was only compressed 4%, and compression for all of the other files except for Exponentiation.xls, ranges from 11% to 24%. Exponentiation.xls was compressed by 74%.

After examining the contents of this Compressed (zipped) folder, you're ready to extract its contents.

To extract everything in a Compressed (zipped) folder:

1. Click the **Extract all files** button on the command bar. In the Extract Compressed (Zipped) Folders dialog box, Windows 7 prompts you for the name of the folder where it will store the extracted files. See Figure 5-31. Windows 7 proposes to use the path: "C:\Users\Public\Documents\Cooper & Bauman", and it is set to show the extracted files after the extraction.

Figure 5-31 | **Extract Compressed (Zipped) Folders dialog box**

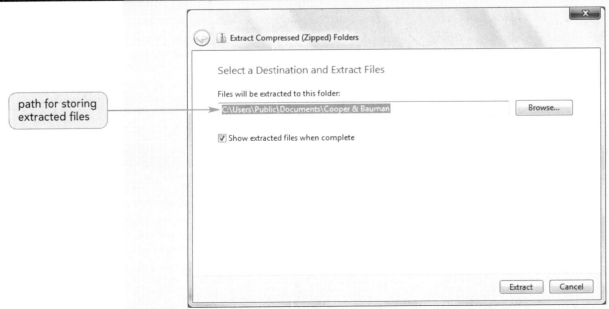

▶ **2.** Press the **End** key to move the insertion point to the end of the path, and then delete Cooper & Bauman as well as the backslash so the final path reads: C:\Users\Public\Documents

If you did not change the path and remove the reference to the Cooper & Bauman folder, then the extracted Cooper & Bauman folder would be placed within another Cooper & Bauman folder.

TIP

You can also extract folders and files by copying them from a Compressed (zipped) folder.

▶ **3.** Click the **Extract** button. Windows 7 extracts the files, and then opens a new Public Documents window where you now have an extracted copy of the Cooper & Bauman folder. If you had not removed the previous copy of the Cooper & Bauman folder, then Windows 7 would have prompted you to replace the previous copy with the extracted copy.

▶ **4.** Point to the **Windows Explorer** taskbar button 🖳, point to the **Training** thumbnail on the left, and then click that thumbnail's **Close** button ⊠.

Make sure you delete the Compressed (zipped) folder so you do not have to create and rename a new copy of the Cooper & Bauman folder.

▶ **5.** Since you no longer need the Cooper & Bauman Compressed (zipped) folder, right-click **Cooper & Bauman.zip**, click **Delete**, and in the Delete Folder dialog box, click the **Yes** button.

▶ **6.** Keep the Public Documents window open for the next set of steps.

Once you create a Compressed (zipped) folder, you can copy or move files to or from the Compressed (zipped) folder, and you can delete folders and files within a Compressed (zipped) folder. You can open a file from a Compressed (zipped) folder; however, the file has the read-only attribute. If you make changes to the file, you cannot save the changes to the file in the Compressed (zipped) folder. Instead, you have to save the changes in a file with a new filename in another location.

REFERENCE

Creating and Extracting a Compressed (Zipped) Folder

- To compress a folder, locate the folder you want to compress, right-click that folder, point to Send to, and then click Compressed (zipped) folder.
- To extract a Compressed (zipped) folder, open the Compressed (zipped) folder, click the "Extract all files" button on the toolbar, adjust the path in the Extract Compressed (Zipped) Folders dialog box (if necessary), and then click Extract.

Compressed (zipped) folders are also useful if you need to transport a set of folders and files, or just files, from one location to another with your flash drive, whether it uses the FAT or NTFS file system. As noted earlier, NTFS compression is only available on NTFS volumes; however, you can create and work with Compressed (zipped) Folders on *both* NTFS and FAT volumes.

Encrypting and Decrypting Folders and Files

With the Windows 7 **Encrypting File Service** (**EFS**), you can encrypt and decrypt folders and files on hard disks to protect your important files. In fact, you can encrypt an entire volume. However, you cannot encrypt system files. **Encryption** encodes data so only the original user can access that data. If several individuals use the same computer and if each user has their own user account, each user can encrypt their own folders and files, so each user cannot access another user's encrypted folders and files. If you copy encrypted folders and files to a flash drive that uses NTFS, then only the original user can access their encrypted data. Encryption can be important if you share your computer with other users, use a mobile computer, or connect your computer to a larger network, including the Internet. However, you have to take every measure possible to guarantee that you can access your encrypted folders and files should a problem develop later.

The Encrypting File Service works with NTFS, and therefore it is only available on NTFS volumes. The Professional, Ultimate, and Enterprise editions of Windows 7 fully support the Encrypting File Service (EFS); however, encryption is not fully supported in the Starter, Home Basic, and Home Premium editions of Windows 7.

If you open an encrypted file, NTFS uses the Encrypting File Service to automatically decrypt the file. When you save a file to disk, NTFS uses the Encrypting File Service to automatically reencrypt it. In other words, the process is transparent to you (just like NTFS compression), and you can work with the contents of your files just as if they were not encrypted. Although you can encrypt files one by one, a more effective approach is to encrypt the folder that contains your files, and then all files stored in that folder are automatically encrypted.

If you copy or move an unencrypted file to an encrypted folder on an NTFS volume, the unencrypted file is automatically encrypted. If you copy or move an encrypted file to an unencrypted folder on an NTFS volume, the file remains encrypted.

If you copy an unencrypted folder or file from a FAT volume to an encrypted folder on an NTFS volume, Windows 7 automatically encrypts the folder (and its contents) or the file. If you move or copy an encrypted folder or file to a FAT volume, Windows 7 removes the encryption because FAT volumes do not support encryption. If you attach an encrypted file to an email message, Windows 7 removes the encryption.

If you are working in a college computer lab, ask your instructor or technical support staff whether you have permission to encrypt and decrypt a folder and its files. If you do not have permission to use encryption on an NTFS volume, read the steps and examine the figures so you are familiar with this feature, but do not keystroke the following steps. Also, because this feature is only available on NTFS volumes, you cannot use a flash drive with the FAT file system. Instead, you must use an NTFS volume.

With the increasing attention paid to security, Cadence discusses with her staff the potential value of the Windows 7 Encrypting File Service. She asks you to encrypt and decrypt the Cooper & Bauman folder so you are familiar with this process, and provide her with feedback about the usefulness of this feature.

To encrypt a folder and its contents:

1. In the Public Documents folder, right-click the **Cooper & Bauman** folder, click **Properties**, and after Windows 7 opens the Cooper & Bauman Properties dialog box, click the **Advanced** button on the General property sheet. The Advanced Attributes dialog box includes an option for encrypting the contents of this folder under "Compress or Encrypt attributes."

   Trouble? If you find that you accidentally deleted the extracted Cooper & Bauman folder, copy the Tutorial folder from your set of Data Files to the Public Documents folder, rename it Cooper & Bauman, and then complete this step.

2. Click the **Encrypt contents to secure data** check box, click the **OK** button in the Advanced Attributes dialog box, and then click the **OK** button in the Cooper & Bauman Properties dialog box. The Confirm Attribute Changes dialog box informs you that Windows 7 will apply the encrypt attribute, and then prompt you to select how you want to apply this change.

3. Click the **Apply changes to this folder, subfolders and files** option button (if necessary), and then click the **OK** button. Windows 7 now displays an Applying attributes dialog box, and encrypts this folder and all the folders and files within this folder.

4. Click the **folder window** background, and notice that Windows 7 displays the Cooper & Bauman folder name in green to indicate it is encrypted.

Trouble? If Windows 7 does not display encrypted folders and files in green, click the Organize button on the command bar, click Folder and search options, click the View tab, and in the Advanced settings list box, locate and add a check mark to the "Show encrypted or compressed NTFS files in color" check box, and then click the OK button to close the Folder Options dialog box and apply the new setting.

5. Open the Cooper & Bauman folder, right-click a **column heading**, and then click **Size All Columns to Fit**. Notice that Windows 7 displays all the subfolder names in green to indicate that they are encrypted. See Figure 5-32. In the Attributes column, *E* indicates its encrypted, *D* indicates a directory (or folder), and *A* indicates the archive attribute.

Trouble? If Windows 7 does not display an Attributes column, right-click a column heading, click More, locate and click the Attributes check box (to add a check mark), and then click the OK button.

Figure 5-32	Viewing encrypted folders

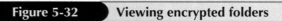

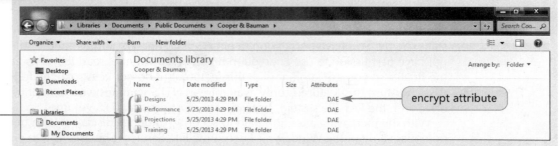

6. Open the Performance folder, right-click a **column** heading, and then click **Size All Columns to Fit**. Windows 7 displays all the filenames in green to indicate that they are encrypted. Also, all files are assigned the encrypt attribute, as evidenced by the *E* in the Attributes column.

Next, you will copy an encrypted file to an unencrypted folder.

To copy an encrypted file to an unencrypted folder:

1. Right-click **Best Return.xlsx**, click **Copy**, click the **expand** icon ▷ to the left of the Documents library in the Navigation pane (if necessary), and then click **Public Documents** in the Navigation pane.

2. Right-click the **background** of the folder window, and then click **Paste**. Windows 7 copies the encrypted file to the Public Documents folder. Notice that the file remains encrypted.

3. Right-click **Best Return.xlsx**, click **Properties**, click the **Advanced** button on the General property sheet, click the **Encrypt contents to secure data** check box (to remove the check mark), click the **OK** button in the Advanced Attributes dialog box, and then click the **OK** button in the Best Return.xlsx Properties dialog box. Windows 7 removes the encryption from the file.

▶ **4.** Drag **Best Return.xlsx** and drop it onto the encrypted Cooper & Bauman folder icon.

▶ **5.** Open the Cooper & Bauman folder, right-click a **column heading**, and then click **Size All Columns to Fit**. Windows 7 encrypted the unencrypted file after copying it to an encrypted folder.

▶ **6.** Click **Public Documents** in the Address bar, and then keep the Public Documents window open for the next set of steps.

You work with encrypted folders and files just as you work with unencrypted folders and files; however, Windows 7 does not index encrypted files (though, as covered in Tutorial 3, you can enable this option).

Now you're going to reverse this process, and decrypt the Cooper & Bauman folder and its contents.

To decrypt a folder and its subfolders and files:

▶ **1.** Right-click the **Cooper & Bauman** folder, click **Properties**, click the **Advanced** button on the General property sheet in the Cooper & Bauman Properties dialog box, click the **Encrypt contents to secure data** check box (to remove the check mark), click the **OK** button in the Advanced Attributes dialog box, click the **OK** button in the Cooper & Bauman Properties dialog box, click the **Apply changes to this folder, subfolders and files** option button (if necessary), and then click the **OK** button. Windows 7 removes the encryption from this folder and its subfolders and files.

▶ **2.** Click the folder window **background**, and notice that Windows 7 displays the Cooper & Bauman folder name in black to indicate that it is no longer encrypted.

▶ **3.** Open the **Cooper & Bauman** folder, and notice that the subfolder names and the Best Return.xlsx filename are now shown in black. Windows 7 removed the encryption that you applied earlier to the Cooper & Bauman folder. Also, in the Cooper & Bauman folder, Windows 7 no longer displays an *E* for *encrypt* in the Attributes column for the folders and the single file.

▶ **4.** To restore your computer, click **Documents** in the Address bar, point to the Cooper & Bauman folder (if it is not already selected), click **Delete**, and in the Delete Folder dialog box, click the **Yes** button.

▶ **5.** Close the Documents library window.

▶ **6.** If you want to empty the Recycle Bin of all the folders and files you deleted, right-click the **Recycle Bin** icon, click **Empty Recycle Bin**, and in the Delete Multiple Items, click the **Yes** button to permanently delete all the items in the Recycle Bin.

The process for encrypting a folder or file is similar to that for compressing a folder or file. However, they are mutually exclusive. In other words, you cannot apply both compression and encryption to the same folder or file.

REFERENCE

Encrypting and Decrypting a Folder

- Locate the folder you want to encrypt or decrypt, right-click the folder, click Properties, and then click the Advanced button on the General property sheet in the Properties dialog box for that folder.
- In the Compress or Encrypt attributes section of the Advanced Attributes dialog box, click the "Encrypt contents to secure data" check box, click the OK button in the Advanced Attributes dialog box, and then click the OK button in the Properties dialog box for the folder.
- In the Confirm Attributes dialog box, click the "Apply changes to this folder, subfolders and files" option button (if necessary), and then click the OK button.

You can use the Encrypting File System wizard to back up your file encryption certificates and encryption keys in the event the original certificates and keys are lost or corrupted; otherwise, you will not be able to access your files if a problem occurs. A **certificate**, issued by a certification authority (such as Microsoft), confirms your identity and contains information used to protect data or to establish secure network connections. Like the house key you use to lock and unlock the door to your home, an **encryption key** is a code that Windows 7 uses to encrypt and decrypt files. If you choose to back up your file encryption certificate and encryption key, Windows 7 will store this information in a file on a disk you specify (such as a USB flash drive).

To initiate this process, open the Control Panel, open User Accounts and Family Safety, open User Accounts, and then click the "Manage your file encryption certificates" link. That opens the Encrypting File System dialog box where Windows 7 explains that to encrypt files for additional security, you must have an encryption certificate and its associated decryption key on your computer (or on a smart card); otherwise, you cannot access your encrypted files without the certificate and key. You can use the wizard to select or create a file encryption certificate and key, back up the certificate and key so you do not lose access to your encrypted files, set up EFS to use a smart card, and update previously encrypted files to use a different certificate and key. In the next set of steps using the wizard, you select a certificate or create a new certificate, specify which type of certificate you want to create (such as a self-signed certificate stored on your computer), specify a backup location and a filename, enter and confirm a password, and finally select the folder (such as All Logical Drives) or folders (such as a local disk) that contain encrypted files that you want to associate with the new certificate and key. In the last step, the Encrypting File System wizard verifies that your encrypted files are updated, displays information about the certificate and its expiration date, and identifies the path to the certificate and key backup location. The certificate and key is stored in a file with the .pfx (Personal Information Exchange) file extension.

If you rely on NTFS encryption, you should make sure that you back up this critical information, and make sure that you have unencrypted backups stored in a secure location.

BitLocker Drive Encryption

BitLocker Drive Encryption, introduced in Windows Vista, and only available in the Windows 7 Ultimate and Windows 7 Enterprise editions, increases the security of a computer by encrypting the boot volume where the Windows 7 operating system files are located. BitLocker can also encrypt system files, such as the hibernation file, temporary files, paging file (covered in Tutorial 9), and Registry (covered in the last tutorial).

With BitLocker Driver Encryption, your computer system remains encrypted if someone removes your hard disk drive, and inserts it into the system unit of another computer with the intent of accessing your data on that computer. Your system is also protected if someone attempts to access the contents of your hard disk drive by installing or loading another operating system. If malicious software alters important Windows startup files, then BitLocker Drive Encryption can detect those changes and prevent access to your computer.

BitLocker uses a **Trusted Platform Module (TPM) microchip** on the motherboard to store and protect the information needed to encrypt and decrypt the boot volume. At each boot, the Trusted Platform Module microchip verifies that the correct hard disk is in the correct computer system, and that important system files have not been altered in any way before it unlocks access to the hard disk drive, the operating system, and your data.

It is also possible to use the Trusted Platform Module microchip with a USB flash drive to store a Startup Key that validates your identity; however, as many people discover, it's easy to forget or misplace a flash drive, and it's also easy for someone else to pick up a flash drive in a split second. You do have the option of storing a second copy of the Startup Key on another USB flash drive. You can also validate your identity using a PIN (or personal identification number).

If BitLocker detects a problem or a change to the hard disk or system files, then it boots in recovery mode, and you must enter a 48-character recovery password using the function keys on the keyboard to gain access to your computer. When setting up BitLocker you have the option of saving this password to a USB flash drive or a local or remote folder, and you can print the password.

For maximum security, BitLocker requires that your computer have an enabled Trusted Platform Module version 1.2 or later microchip. You must also have a BIOS that supports this feature, and you must enable the Trusted Platform Module via the BIOS. Also, your computer must have a separate NTFS system volume (which is unencrypted) with the hardware-specific files needed to boot your computer. This system volume can be relatively small in size.

If you are seriously considering the use of BitLocker Drive Encryption, you should examine the information that Microsoft makes available at its Web site prior to purchasing a computer and prior to installing Windows 7. Then you can verify that the computer contains the hardware needed to support this feature, and that you have the ability to create the partitions needed to implement BitLocker. These requirements depend on how you intend to implement BitLocker, and the degree of security that you want to use. Also, while you can use BitLocker on a computer that does not have a Trusted Platform Module microchip, BitLocker cannot verify the integrity of boot files, and therefore it cannot detect a hard disk moved to another computer.

If you need to upgrade or replace your motherboard or BIOS, repartition the hard disk, install a new operating system, or install updates to hardware firmware, then you can disable BitLocker first, and then reenable it afterwards. You can also remove BitLocker and then reencrypt your hard disk afterwards.

If a computer is at the end of its useful life, you can delete the BitLocker encryption keys from the volume so no one can *ever* access data on the hard disk.

BitLocker also prevents hackers from accessing information on your computer, such as passwords, and it is useful on laptops that contain sensitive data that might be easily misplaced or stolen. However, its use is more applicable to an enterprise environment where it can be implemented properly and where reliable security, backup, and recovery procedures are already in place.

You can combine the use of BitLocker Drive Encryption with NTFS encryption of folders and files to further protect a computer. BitLocker can encrypt system files. NTFS can encrypt your personal files, but not system files.

With Windows 7, you can use BitLocker To Go to encrypt removable drives. If you also use a removable drive with earlier versions of Windows, you can use the BitLocker To Go Reader to read encrypted files on the removable drive.

Restoring Your Computer's Settings

If you are working in a computer lab or if you want to restore your desktop computer to the settings that existed prior to working on this tutorial, complete the following steps.

To restore your computer's settings:

▶ **1.** To restore double-click activation, click the **Computer** icon on the desktop or Start menu, click the **Organize** button on the toolbar, click **Folder and search options**, and on the General property sheet in the Folder Options dialog box, click the **Double-click to open an item (single-click to select)** option button.

▶ **2.** To hide extensions for known file types, click the **View** tab in the Folder Options dialog box, click the **Hide extensions for known file types** check box if it does not contain a check mark, click the **OK** button to close the Folder Options dialog box and apply these changes, and then close the Computer window.

▶ **3.** To remove the Computer from the desktop, right-click **Computer** on the Start menu, and then click **Show on Desktop**.

▶ **4.** If necessary, use Safely Remove Hardware and Eject Media to safely remove your flash drive.

REVIEW

Session 5.2 Quick Check

1. Which file system(s) supports compression of folders and files and also supports encryption?

2. True or False. When you move a file on an NTFS volume to another folder on the same volume, the file takes on the compression state of the new folder.

3. True or False. When you copy a file on an NTFS volume to another folder on the same volume, the compression state of the file does not change.

4. What happens if you copy a compressed file from an NTFS volume to a FAT volume?

5. If you want to send a folder with a set of files as a single email attachment, or reduce the amount of disk storage space used by that folder and its contents, you can create a _____ from the folder.

6. True or False. If you copy or move an unencrypted file to an encrypted folder on an NTFS volume, the unencrypted file is automatically encrypted.

7. True or False. If you copy or move an encrypted file to an unencrypted folder on an NTFS volume, the file remains encrypted.

8. What happens if you add a compressed file as an attachment to an email message?

Practice the skills you learned in the tutorial using the same case scenario.

PRACTICE

Review Assignments

For a list of Data Files in the Review folder, see page 305.

Cadence just acquired several laptop computers for use by Cooper & Bauman staff members when they are traveling on company business. She asks you to examine the file systems used on those laptops and verify that employees can compress, uncompress, encrypt, and decrypt folders and files without any problems. She also asks you to create a Compressed (zipped) folder with your most recent folders and files for an upcoming conference.

As you complete each step in these Review Assignments, use a word-processing application, such as Microsoft Word or the WordPad accessory, to record your answers to questions. If you change any settings on the computer you are using, note the original settings so you can restore them later. Complete the following steps:

1. If necessary, display the Computer icon on the desktop, switch to single-click activation, choose the option for displaying file extensions, copy the Review folder from the Tutorial.05 folder to the Public Documents folder, change its name to Cooper & Bauman, attach your USB flash drive, close any open dialog boxes, and then close the Public Documents folder. *Note*: If the computer you are using already has a Cooper & Bauman folder, rename that folder to Cooper & Bauman (Previous).

2. Open a Computer window and view properties of your hard disk drive. Which drive name is assigned to your hard disk drive? What is the friendly name of your hard disk drive? What file system does Windows 7 use on your hard drive? How much used space, free space, and disk storage capacity does your hard drive have? Does Windows 7 index this drive for faster searching? Is the drive compressed or uncompressed?

3. Select the Hardware property sheet in the Properties dialog box for your hard drive. What type of hard drive is installed in the computer you are using? Close the Properties dialog box for your hard drive, and then close the Computer window.

4. If you are using an Administrator account or can provide Administrator credentials, open the Disk Management tool. What is the disk type and layout of your hard drive? Which drive is the boot volume? Which drive is the system volume? How many partitions are on your hard drive? Identify each partition and its purpose. Switch to Disk List view at the top of the Details pane. What partition style does your hard disk use? Is there any unallocated storage space on that disk? Switch back to Volume List view. Identify the file systems used for your DVD and CD drives. Close the Computer Management window.

5. Open the Cooper & Bauman folder in your Public Documents folder, open the Designs folder, and if necessary, remove the Preview pane, switch to Details view, and adjust column widths to the widest entry in each column.

6. Add the Attributes column to this folder window. What attributes are assigned to the files in this folder?

7. View the properties of the Design #5.bmp file. What is its size in KB and bytes? How much storage space does it use on disk in KB and bytes? How much slack does this file have? Close the Properties dialog box for this file.

8. Create a Compressed (zipped) folder from the Design #5.bmp file. What is the name of the new Compressed (zipped) folder? View properties of this file. What is the file's size in KB and bytes? How much storage space does it use on disk in KB and bytes? How much slack does this file have? How does this slack compare to that used by the original file? How much less disk storage space does the Compressed (zipped) folder use than the original file? What is the percent compression for this file? Close the Properties dialog box for this file.

9. Compress Design #5.bmp (using NTFS compression), and then view properties of the compressed file. What is the compressed file's size in KB and bytes? How much storage space does it use on disk in KB and bytes? What is the percent compression for this file? How much less disk storage space does the compressed file use than the original file? What attributes does this file have after compression? Remove the compression from Design #5.bmp, and then close the Properties dialog box for this file.

10. Prepare a table that lists the size and size on disk of the original uncompressed file, the Compressed (zipped) folder, and the NTFS compressed file, using the following format:

Filename	Size (KB)	Size on Disk (KB)	Percent Compression
Original Design #5.bmp			
Compressed (zipped) folder			
Compressed Design #5.bmp			

Calculate the percent compression for the Compressed (zipped) file by comparing it to the original uncompressed file size.

11. Using the data in this table, which file has the smallest file size? Which file uses the least storage space on disk?

12. Encrypt the compressed folder you created from Design #5.bmp. What attributes does this file have after encryption? Close the Properties dialog box for this file, and then delete the encrypted Compressed (zipped) folder.

13. Return to the Public Documents folder, switch to Details view (if necessary), size all columns to fit, and display the Attributes column (if necessary). What attributes, if any, are assigned to the Cooper & Bauman folder?

14. View properties of the Cooper & Bauman folder. What is the size of this folder and its contents in MB and bytes? How much storage space does this folder and its contents use on disk in MB and bytes? How many files and folders does the Cooper & Bauman folder contain? Close the folder's Properties dialog box.

15. Create a Compressed (zipped) folder from the Cooper & Bauman folder, and accept the filename proposed by Windows 7. What is the filename of the Compressed (zipped) folder that you just created? What attributes does the Compressed (zipped) folder have?

16. View properties of the Compressed (zipped) folder created from the Cooper & Bauman folder. What is the size of this Compressed (zipped) folder in MB and bytes? How much storage space does this Compressed (zipped) folder use on disk in MB and bytes? Close the compressed folder's Properties dialog box.

17. Compress the original Cooper & Bauman folder and its subfolders and files using NTFS compression. What attributes does this folder have after compression? View properties of the compressed Cooper & Bauman folder. What is the size of this folder and its contents in MB and bytes? How much storage space does this folder and its contents use on disk in MB and bytes? Close the compressed Cooper & Bauman Properties dialog box.

18. Prepare a table that lists the size and size on disk of the original uncompressed Cooper & Bauman folder, the Cooper & Bauman Compressed (zipped) folder, and the Cooper & Bauman folder that uses NTFS compression, using the following format:

Filename	Size (MB)	Size on Disk (MB)	Percent Compression
Original Cooper & Bauman Folder			
Cooper & Bauman.zip			
Compressed Cooper & Bauman Folder			

Calculate the percent compression for Cooper & Bauman.zip by comparing it to the original, uncompressed folder's size.

19. Using the data in this table, which folder or file has the smallest file size? Which folder or file uses the least storage space on disk?

20. Encrypt the compressed Cooper & Bauman folder, its subfolders, and files. Did the attributes of the Cooper & Bauman folder change after encryption? If so, what are the attributes? Are the Cooper & Bauman folder and its contents still compressed? Explain.

21. What edition of Windows 7 do you use? Does your edition of Windows 7 support BitLocker Drive Encryption and, if so, do you use BitLocker on your computer? What advantage(s) do you derive (or might you derive) from using BitLocker?

22. To restore your computer, delete the encrypted Cooper & Bauman folder and its contents, delete the Cooper & Bauman Compressed (zipped) folder, remove the Attributes column from Details view, and then restore your original view.

23. If you had a Cooper & Bauman folder before starting the Review Assignments, and if you renamed it to Cooper & Bauman (Previous), change its name back to Cooper & Bauman, and then close the Public Documents folder.

24. If necessary, use Safely Remove Hardware and Eject Media to safely remove your flash drive.

25. Submit your answers to the questions in this Review Assignment to your instructor either in printed or electronic form, as requested. Remember to include your name and any other information requested by your instructor on your assignment.

Use your skills to compile information for a PC users group meeting.

APPLY

Case Problem 1

There are no Data Files needed for this Case Problem.

Middletown PC Users Group   Each month, your local PC users group meets to discuss and share information on a specific topic. You have been asked to lead the discussion at the next meeting, which will focus on disks, partitions, volumes, and drives. You decide that now is a good time to compile information about your computer system so you can use that information to illustrate various concepts at the users group with the Disk Management tool.

To complete this case problem, you must provide Administrator credentials to open the Disk Management tool.

As you complete each step, record your answers to questions so you can submit them to your instructor. Use a word-processing application, such as Microsoft Word or the WordPad accessory, to prepare your answers to these questions. If you change any settings on the computer you are using, make a note of the original settings so you can restore them later. Complete the following steps:

1. Attach your USB flash drive to your computer, and if you have a media card reader, insert a memory card into the media card reader. Insert a DVD in your DVD drive (if available) and a CD in your CD drive (if available). Close any AutoPlay dialog boxes that open.

2. Use the Computer window and the Volume List, Disk List, and the Graphical View area in Disk Management to prepare a table of information on the hard drive, DVD or CD drive (or both), flash drive, and memory card (if available) in your computer. Include the following information (if available):
   - Type of drive (i.e., hard disk)
   - Drive name (or volume name)
   - Drive layout

- Drive type
- File system
- Status
- Fault tolerance
- Device type
- Partition style

3. Using the information provided by Disk Management, identify by drive name and by type of drive (i.e., flash drive) which volume or volumes are system volumes, boot volumes, and which are primary partitions or extended partitions. Also identify whether there is unallocated space on a volume, and include any other information you feel is pertinent or unique to the computer you are using.

4. If necessary, use Safely Remove Hardware and Eject Media to safely remove your flash drive.

5. Submit your answers to this case problem to your instructor, either in printed or electronic form, as requested. Remember to include on your assignment your name and any other information requested by your instructor.

Use your skills to evaluate the use of file systems on a flash drive.

APPLY

Case Problem 2

There are no Data Files needed for this Case Problem.

Carpelan & Thakur   Jatan Thakur is a partner in a computer-aided design/computer-aided manufacturing (CAD/CAM) business that manufactures machine parts for companies who want to replace worn-out components that are no longer made by the original manufacturer. As one of his close friends, he asks you to help him determine the best file system to use on his new 32 GB flash drive as well as his older 2 GB flash drive. Using the information covered in this tutorial, evaluate the use of the FAT16, FAT32, and NTFS file systems on these flash drives.

As you complete each step, record your answers to questions so you can submit them to your instructor. Use a word-processing application, such as Microsoft Word or the WordPad accessory, to prepare your answers to these questions. If you change any settings on the computer you are using, make a note of the original settings so you can restore them later. Complete the following steps:

1. Prepare a one- to two-page double-spaced report in which you evaluate each of the three file systems listed above for both flash drives.

2. In your evaluation, identify the cluster sizes on the 2 GB flash drive and 32 GB flash drive for each file system that is supported by those drives, and recommend the file system that you think would best use storage space on these flash drives. When you identify cluster sizes for each file system, list the cluster sizes as the number of sectors per cluster and as the number of kilobytes per cluster. Also, are there any of these file systems he could not use on these flash drives?

3. Evaluate and describe other features of each of the three file systems that enhance, and any problems that limit, the use of a particular file system on these flash drives.

4. If necessary, use Safely Remove Hardware and Eject Media to safely remove your flash drive.

5. Submit your answers to this case problem to your instructor, either in printed or electronic form, as requested. Remember to include on your assignment your name and any other information requested by your instructor.

Use your skills and the Internet to compile information on using virtual hard disks.

RESEARCH

Case Problem 3

There are no Data Files needed for this Case Problem.

Nguyen Mai Consulting   Nguyen Mai is a young professional computer consultant adept at finding the right solutions for her clients while working for an advanced degree in expert systems. Mai provides her enterprise customers with information on implementing new Windows 7 technologies. She asks you to prepare a fact sheet summary on the use of Windows 7 virtual hard disks (VHDs) that she can provide to customers.

As you complete each step, record your answers to questions so you can submit them to your instructor. Use a word-processing application, such as Microsoft Word or the WordPad accessory, to prepare your answers to these questions. If you change any settings on the computer you are using, make a note of the original settings so you can restore them later. Complete the following steps:

1. Use the Microsoft Web site to locate information in the Microsoft TechNet online libraries, including frequently asked questions, about the use of virtual hard disks in Windows 7, and then prepare a report that concisely answers the following questions. (*Note*: You may need to use keywords or phrases in each question to help you locate information.)

    a. What is a virtual hard disk?

    b. In what ways can you use a virtual hard disk?

    c. What file systems can you use on a virtual hard disk?

    d. What is the difference between a fixed and dynamically expanding virtual hard disk?

    e. What is a VHD with Native Boot, and what advantages does it offer?

    f. List three to five ways in which enterprises or businesses might benefit from the use of virtual hard disks.

    g. How do you create a virtual hard disk in Windows 7?

2. At the end of your report, list the sources that you used for the report. Include the article topic, the Web site name, and addresses (or URLs) of the Web pages you used to prepare your report.

3. If necessary, use Safely Remove Hardware and Eject Media to safely remove your flash drive.

4. Submit your answers to this case problem to your instructor, either in printed or electronic form, as requested. Remember to include on your assignment your name and any other information requested by your instructor.

Use your skills to assist coworkers with their computers.

APPLY

Case Problem 4

There are no Data Files needed for this Case Problem.

Video OnStream   Landon Evans works as a technical support person for Video OnStream, a video production firm in Los Angeles, California. Many Video OnStream employees work on mobile computers, and some employees work exclusively at home on company-supplied laptops or desktop computers. Employees often ask Landon for his advice on how to optimize the storage of files on their computer's storage devices and how to protect their data. Evaluate each of the following scenarios encountered by employees and explain what you think Landon should recommend.

As you complete each step, record your answers to questions so you can submit them to your instructor. Use a word-processing application, such as Microsoft Word or the WordPad accessory, to prepare your answers to these questions. If you change any settings on the computer you are using, make a note of the original settings so you can restore them later. Complete the following steps:

1. Erica just purchased a 16 GB USB flash drive and wants to know which file system it uses. What file systems are supported on a flash drive with that storage capacity, and what do you think would be the most likely file system used on that flash drive? How can Erica determine the file system used on that flash drive?

2. Alec's older flash drive has a storage capacity of 1 GB and uses the FAT16 file system. Would Alec benefit from reformatting the flash drive for FAT32? Explain.

3. Janine wants to compress a large folder and its contents on her flash drive, but the General property sheet does not have an Advanced button for accessing the option for compressing folders and files. What is the cause of this problem? Is there any other way for Janine to compress this folder and its contents?

4. Ivan wants to email several digital images that he's captured with his digital camera, but his digital images exceed the allowable size for file attachments. How can Ivan resolve this problem?

5. Selene just received an email message with an attachment that has the .zip file extension. She does not know the person that sent the email message, and she therefore wants to know whether it is safe to open the attachment. What type of file is this attachment, and what is the most likely content of this file? What would you recommend that Selene do?

⊕ EXPLORE

6. Trevor uses an external 1 TB (terabyte) hard disk that's partitioned into one volume. He wants to know which file system the disk uses, and whether Windows 7 would use disk storage space more efficiently if he partitioned, or subdivided, the hard disk into two volumes. What file system does this hard drive use? Would he benefit from partitioning the hard disk into two volumes? If so, how? If not, are there any other ways in which he might be able to improve the usage of disk storage space on this hard disk? How might Trevor protect the security of information on this drive?

7. If necessary, use Safely Remove Hardware and Eject Media to safely remove your flash drive.

8. Submit your answers to this case problem to your instructor, either in printed or electronic form, as requested. Remember to include on your assignment your name and any other information requested by your instructor.

ENDING DATA FILES

There are no ending Data Files needed for this tutorial.

WINDOWS

OBJECTIVES

Session 6.1
- Remove unneeded files with the Disk Cleanup utility
- Use the Error-checking tool and Check Disk utility
- Examine the problems posed by lost clusters and cross-linked files

Session 6.2
- Examine file and free space fragmentation
- Use Disk Defragmenter to analyze a hard disk drive
- Schedule tasks with Task Scheduler

Optimizing Your Hard Disk

Performing and Scheduling Preventive Maintenance

Case | *Celedon Global Marketing, Inc.*

Celedon Global Marketing, Inc., a technology marketing business in Princeton, New Jersey, provides its clients with the expertise to achieve success in global markets. Aaron Larsen, a business technology IT specialist, assists clients in understanding and maximizing the use of new technologies important to their businesses. As new employees join the firm, Aaron explains and demonstrates techniques for optimizing and maintaining their computers.

In this tutorial, you use the Disk Cleanup utility to check hard disk drives for files that can safely be deleted. You also learn when and how to use the Error-checking tool and the Check Disk utility to examine disks for errors, and how to use Disk Defragmenter to defragment a hard disk drive. In addition, you examine how to schedule routine computer maintenance tasks.

STARTING DATA FILES

There are no starting Data Files needed for this tutorial.

SESSION 6.1 VISUAL OVERVIEW

You can use the **Disk Cleanup** utility to locate unneeded files on your computer that can safely be removed, and thereby free up valuable storage space.

Whenever you access a Web page, all of the components on the Web page—including graphics, animation, music, video, and the HTML code for the Web page itself—are downloaded to the Temporary Internet Files folder. These files constitute what is commonly known as your **Internet cache**.

The Downloaded Program Files category includes ActiveX controls and Java applets. An **ActiveX control** is a module of program code, such as Windows Media Player, that provides access to interactive Web content. A **Java applet** is similar to an ActiveX control; however, the program is written in the Java programming language.

An application can create a **temporary file** in the same folder as the file you opened in order to process data. Applications close the temporary file after you close the program.

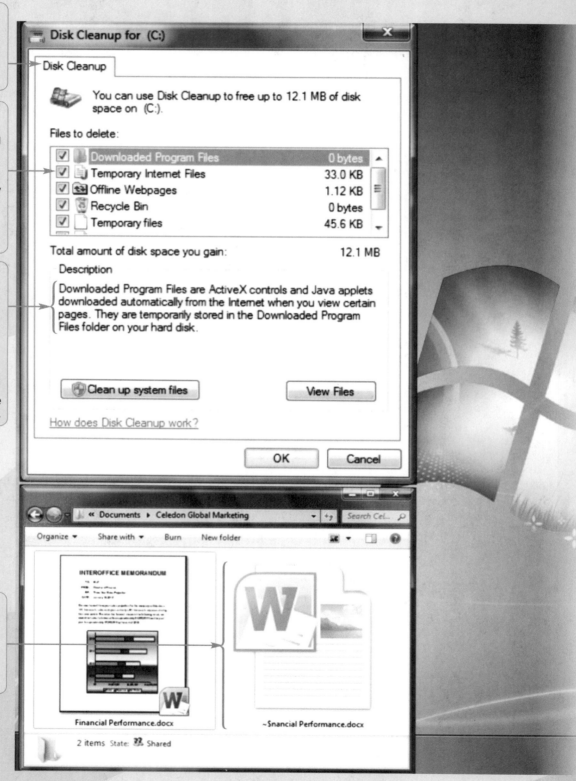

Disk Cleanup for (C:)

Disk Cleanup

You can use Disk Cleanup to free up to 12.1 MB of disk space on (C:).

Files to delete:

☑ Downloaded Program Files	0 bytes
☑ Temporary Internet Files	33.0 KB
☑ Offline Webpages	1.12 KB
☑ Recycle Bin	0 bytes
☑ Temporary files	45.6 KB

Total amount of disk space you gain: 12.1 MB

Description

Downloaded Program Files are ActiveX controls and Java applets downloaded automatically from the Internet when you view certain pages. They are temporarily stored in the Downloaded Program Files folder on your hard disk.

Clean up system files   View Files

How does Disk Cleanup work?

OK   Cancel

« Documents ▸ Celedon Global Marketing

Organize ▾   Share with ▾   Burn   New folder

INTEROFFICE MEMORANDUM

Financial Performance.docx   ~Snancial Performance.docx

2 items State: Shared

OPTIMIZING DISKS

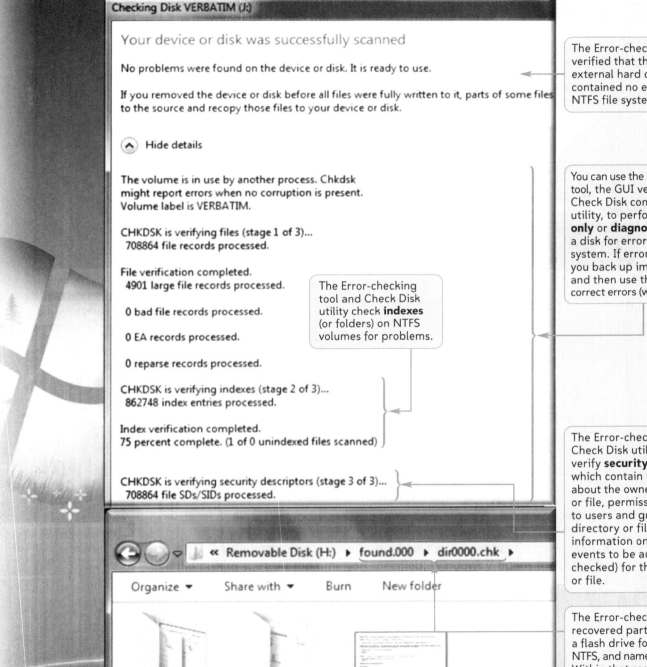

Checking Disk VERBATIM (J:)

Your device or disk was successfully scanned

No problems were found on the device or disk. It is ready to use.

If you removed the device or disk before all files were fully written to it, parts of some files
to the source and recopy those files to your device or disk.

⊙ Hide details

The volume is in use by another process. Chkdsk
might report errors when no corruption is present.
Volume label is VERBATIM.

CHKDSK is verifying files (stage 1 of 3)...
 708864 file records processed.

File verification completed.
 4901 large file records processed.

 0 bad file records processed.

 0 EA records processed.

 0 reparse records processed.

CHKDSK is verifying indexes (stage 2 of 3)...
 862748 index entries processed.

Index verification completed.
75 percent complete. (1 of 0 unindexed files scanned)

CHKDSK is verifying security descriptors (stage 3 of 3)...
 708864 file SDs/SIDs processed.

The Error-checking tool
verified that this 500 GB
external hard disk drive
contained no errors in its
NTFS file system.

You can use the **Error-checking**
tool, the GUI version of the
Check Disk command-line
utility, to perform a **read-only** or **diagnostic** check of
a disk for errors in its file
system. If errors are found,
you back up important files,
and then use this utility to
correct errors (where possible).

The Error-checking
tool and Check Disk
utility check **indexes**
(or folders) on NTFS
volumes for problems.

The Error-checking tool and
Check Disk utility check and
verify **security descriptors**,
which contain information
about the owner of the folder
or file, permissions granted
to users and groups for that
directory or file, and
information on security
events to be audited (or
checked) for that directory
or file.

⊙ ⊙ ⊽ ↧ « Removable Disk (H:) ▸ found.000 ▸ dir0000.chk ▸

Organize ▼   Share with ▼   Burn   New folder

Photocopy   Presentations   NTFS Links.docx

The Error-checking tool
recovered part of a folder on
a flash drive formatted for
NTFS, and named it found.000.
Within that recovered folder
is a recovered subfolder
named dir0000.chk, which in
turn contains folders and files.

The Importance of Optimizing Your Computer

To achieve the best performance from your computer and extend its useful lifetime, you can use Windows 7 utilities to periodically optimize your hard disk drive or drives. For example, you can:

- Search for and remove unneeded system files from your hard disk drive, and thereby reclaim valuable disk storage space.
- Identify and correct file system problems and hard disk drive errors that prevent access to files and that affect the stability and performance of the operating system itself.
- Optimize the storage of programs, folders, and files on disk.
- Schedule routine preventive maintenance tasks.

These utilities protect your investment in your computer, and reduce the risk of losing important information on your computer.

Using the Disk Cleanup Utility

The Disk Cleanup utility searches for, and can remove, the following categories of unneeded files and components if they are present on your computer:

- **Downloaded Program Files**—Downloaded program files consist of ActiveX controls and Java applets that Internet Explorer automatically downloads and stores in the Downloaded Program Files folder under the Windows folder. An example of an ActiveX control is the Adobe Systems Incorporated Shockwave Flash Object add-on that provides interactive Web content, and thereby increases functionality of the Windows Internet Explorer Web browser and other browsers such as Firefox, and Chrome, but not Apple's Safari.

  You can safely remove program files that Internet Explorer automatically downloads from Web sites to the Downloaded Program Files folder. The Downloaded Program Files folder does not contain programs that you download and then install for use on your computer. Nor does it include Web browser plug-ins, device drivers, or program updates (such as Adobe Systems Acrobat or Apple QuickTime updates) that you download and install on your computer. Furthermore, your Web browser does not store other types of files, such as clip art, images, video, or music that you download to your computer for your personal or professional use in the Downloaded Program Files folder. Do not confuse the Downloaded Program Files folder with the Downloads folder for your user account. The latter is where you store downloaded software you want to install on your computer.

- **Temporary Internet Files**—Temporary Internet files are files that Internet Explorer downloads and stores in the Temporary Internet Files folder for your user account. The contents of this folder therefore constitute that Web browser's Internet cache. A **cache** (pronounced "cash") is a folder or area of memory where a program or Windows 7 temporarily stores data. The Disk Cleanup utility can locate and remove all of these files, but it does not change your personalized settings for Web pages. When you use your Web browser to remove files that it has stored on your computer, your browser removes information that Web sites use to remember your personal preferences, such as login information or purchasing preferences that you might otherwise want to keep. You should weigh the pros and cons of removing all this information.

  Because the Disk Cleanup utility does not identify files cached by other browsers, such as Firefox, Chrome, and Safari, you must use those other Web browsers to remove temporary Internet files that they download and store locally on your computer. If you use a Web browser other than Internet Explorer, carefully examine the options for customizing that browser, including the options for removing temporary files that are stored on your computer.

Balancing Speed, Storage Space, and Security

Internet Explorer can open the files used to display Web pages from sites you visit repeatedly more quickly if you don't empty the Temporary Internet Files folder because it doesn't have to download them. Instead, it accesses the files for those Web pages in the Temporary Internet Files folder and, if necessary, updates them if the content of the Web page you visit has changed. To benefit from this performance boost while on the Web, you need to retain the contents of the Temporary Internet Files folder. If you frequently visit many different Web sites, the number of files in the Temporary Internet Files folder will increase and consume more storage space on your hard disk drive, which can impair the performance of your computer. Under these conditions, you can use the Disk Cleanup utility to periodically empty the Temporary Internet Files folder, reclaim valuable storage space, and improve the performance of your computer. You can also specify that Internet Explorer empty the Temporary Internet Files folder when you close your Web browser.

Another important reason for emptying the Temporary Internet Files is that this folder may contain potentially harmful malicious software that was downloaded to your computer when you viewed a Web page at a Web site.

You can apply the same concepts to other Web browsers, such as Firefox, that you use in conjunction with Internet Explorer so you can optimize the use of storage space of your computer and limit your exposure to malicious software.

- **Offline Webpages**—You can store Web pages on your local computer so you can work with them locally. Removing Offline Webpages does not affect your personalized settings for Web pages.
- **Recycle Bin**—You can also remove deleted folders and files from the Recycle Bin, but then they are no longer available if you need to restore these folders or files on your hard disk drive.
- **Temporary files**—Some programs use the Temp folder to store information in temporary files; however, programs typically delete those temporary files after you close the programs. The Disk Cleanup utility can remove any temporary files that have not been changed in over a week.

Applications also create temporary files for open documents, but they create them in the folder where the documents are located rather than in the Temp folder. When you complete an operation or close a program or a file, any temporary files created by the application are deleted from disk. However, if a power failure or some other type of problem occurs, any open temporary files remain on disk. You can recognize some types of temporary files (and temporary folders) because they have the .tmp file extension or a tilde (~) as the first character in the temporary file's filename, or both. You can view the process of creating a temporary file; however, you must first enable the options for showing hidden folders, files, and drives, as well as the option for displaying protected operating system files.

For example, assume you open a folder window and then open a file named Financial Performance.docx in Microsoft Word 2010. If you arrange the folder window and the Word document window so they are side by side, you can view the contents of both windows. After you open the file, Windows 7 updates the view of the folder window to show a temporary file called ~$nancial Performance.docx. See Figure 6-1.

Figure 6-1 Temporary file created after opening a Microsoft Word file

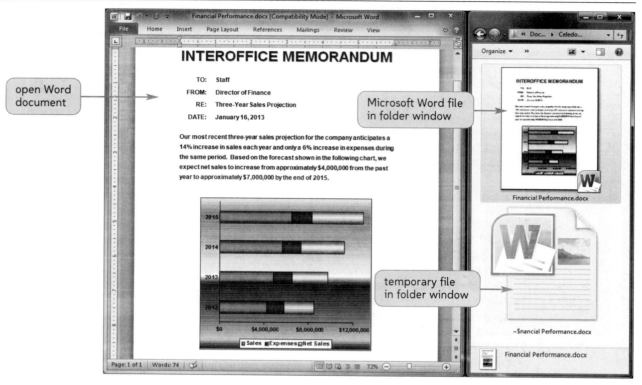

After you close Microsoft Word, Windows 7 again updates the folder window to show that the temporary file no longer exists. In some cases, Windows 7 does not update the window, but you can manually update a window by pressing the F5 Refresh key.

- **Thumbnails**—Windows 7 creates and keeps a copy of thumbnails for your picture, video, and document files so it can quickly redisplay the thumbnails when you open a folder. If you remove these thumbnails, Windows 7 re-creates them when you next open a folder.
- **Setup Log files**—Setup log files are created by Windows 7 during the installation of software.
- **Old Chkdsk files**—The Check Disk utility, which you examine later in this tutorial, checks a disk drive for file system errors, and where possible, repairs those errors. During a repair operation, it saves recovered file fragments that are no longer part of a file and that are no longer needed. These recovered file fragments have the .chk file extension. Selecting the "Old Chkdsk files" option instructs the Disk Cleanup utility to remove those recovered files from a disk drive and frees up valuable storage space.
- **Microsoft Office Temporary Files**—These files are used by Microsoft Office for diagnostic purposes. Because these files are created from previous Office sessions, the Disk Cleanup utility notes that they can be safely deleted.
- **System error memory dump files** and **System error minidump files**—Windows 7 creates these files when an error occurs so a Microsoft tech support person can analyze them for the source of a problem. Dump files are important because they contain information about the state of the operating system at the time a problem occurs.

- **Debug Dump Files**—Windows 7 creates these files when a problem occurs on your computer. If you encounter a problem, a Microsoft tech support person can use these files to help you with troubleshooting the problem.
- **Per user archived Windows Error Reporting Files**, **Per user queued Windows Error Reporting Files**, **System archived Windows Error Reporting Files**, and **System queued Windows Error Reporting Files**—Windows 7 creates and uses these files for reporting errors and checking for solutions to problems.
- **Temporary Windows installation files**—These files are installation files used by Windows 7 Setup. Because these files are left over from an installation of Windows 7, Microsoft notes that you can safely delete them.
- **Windows upgrade log files**—These files contain information for identifying and troubleshooting problems that occur when you install or upgrade Windows 7. If you remove these files, then troubleshooting Windows 7 installation problems might be difficult.
- **Files discarded by Windows upgrade**—These files are left over from a previous installation of Windows. If you are upgrading Windows, then Windows 7 keeps a copy of any nonsystem files that are not included with the upgrade to a new version of Windows. Microsoft notes that you can safely remove these files if you are sure that a user's personal files are not missing after the upgrade.
- **Game Statistics Files**—Windows 7 creates these files for tracking information about your use of games.

The Disk Cleanup utility automatically selects those types of files that are safe to delete. You also have the option of removing any additional types of files that it identifies, or keeping files that you think you might need.

Aaron asks you to show Kimberly, the company's graphic design specialist, how to use the Disk Cleanup utility so she can include it as part of her regular disk maintenance program.

In the following steps, you will determine how much storage space you can free on your hard disk drive. If you are working in a computer lab, the technical support staff might already use the Disk Cleanup utility on a regular basis, and might prefer that you not make any changes to the computer without their permission. Ask your instructor or technical support staff whether you can use the Disk Cleanup utility in your computer lab.

To run the Disk Cleanup utility:

1. If necessary, display the Computer icon on the desktop, switch your computer to single-click activation (or Web style), and activate the option for displaying file extensions.

TIP

You can use the Disk Cleanup utility on internal and external hard disk drives but not on removable drives.

2. Open a Computer window, right-click the **Local Disk (C:)** icon (your drive C name may differ), click **Properties**, and after Windows 7 opens the Local Disk (C:) Properties dialog box, click the **Disk Cleanup** button on the General property sheet. Windows 7 displays a Disk Cleanup dialog box informing you that the Disk Cleanup utility is calculating how much space you will be able to free on (C:), and it notes that this process might take a few minutes. After the Disk Cleanup utility scans files on your computer, it displays the Disk Cleanup for (C:) dialog box, as shown in Figure 6-2, and identifies files you can safely remove.

Figure 6-2 **Files selected for safe removal**

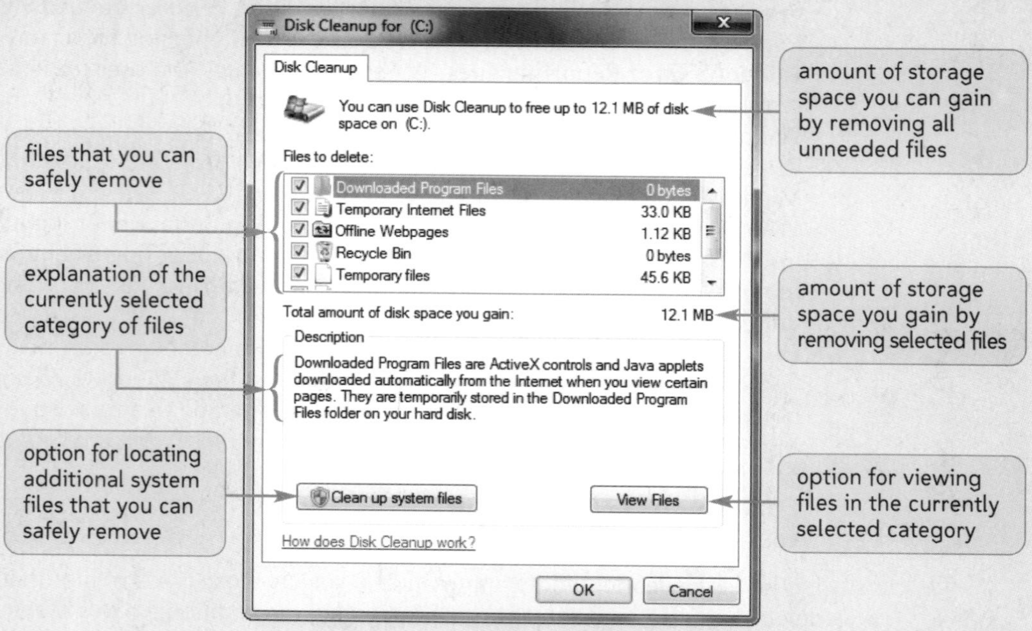

files that you can safely remove

explanation of the currently selected category of files

option for locating additional system files that you can safely remove

amount of storage space you can gain by removing all unneeded files

amount of storage space you gain by removing selected files

option for viewing files in the currently selected category

The options shown in the "Files to delete" box can vary, and depend on how your computer is set up, which file system Windows 7 uses for a drive, and what the Disk Cleanup utility finds. On the computer used for this figure, the Disk Cleanup utility lists these options: Downloaded Program Files folder, Temporary Internet Files, Offline Webpages, Recycle Bin, Temporary files, and Thumbnails (although the last option is not visible in this figure). The Disk Cleanup utility reports on the amount of space that you can free up on your computer if you remove just the selected files or all the files. If the Disk Cleanup utility does not select a category, then the files in that category might prove useful to you later. As noted earlier, keeping Windows upgrade log files might prove useful to you in troubleshooting a problem you encounter after installing a Windows 7 upgrade. Also, even if the Disk Cleanup utility identifies certain files that are safe to remove, you might want to keep them anyway. For example, you might want to keep offline Web pages so you can continue to work with them, and you might want to keep deleted files in the Recycle Bin in case you need to later recover a file.

If you select Downloaded Program Files, Temporary Internet Files, Offline Webpages, or Recycle Bin, then you can view the files contained in the corresponding folder to make sure you do not remove files you might want to keep, or you can examine what types of files are included in that category of files to delete so you better understand what is actually being put on your computer. You can also use the "Clean up system files" button to locate other files that are safe to delete. The security icon on this button indicates that you need to provide Administrator credentials.

In order to free up more storage space, Aaron recommends that you expand the scan to locate unneeded system files.

To also scan for unneeded system files:

1. If you are logged on under an Administrator account, or if you can provide the password for an Administrator account, then click the **Clean up system files** button, and provide Administrator credentials, if necessary. Windows 7 displays a Disk Cleanup dialog box that informs you that the Disk Cleanup utility is calculating how much space you will be able to free on (C:), and it notes that this process might take a few minutes. Then the Disk Cleanup utility displays another Disk Cleanup for (C:) dialog box with its findings. Now the "Files to delete" box shown in Figure 6-3 also includes System queued Windows Error Reporting Files for this computer. Your list of file types will differ.

   Trouble? If you do not know the password for an Administrator account, read but do not keystroke these tutorial steps.

Figure 6-3 Files selected for safe removal

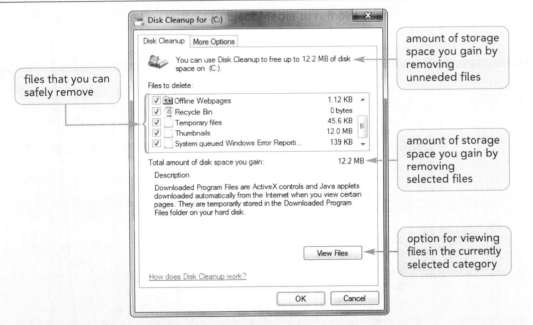

2. If you are working on your own computer and do not want to delete any of these files, or if you are working in a computer lab where you do not have permission to remove these files, click the **Cancel** button in the Disk Cleanup for (C:) dialog box.

3. If you are working on your own computer and want to free storage space by removing the categories of files identified by the Disk Cleanup utility as safe to remove, click the **check boxes** for any additional categories of files to delete, click the **OK** button, and in the Disk Cleanup dialog box, verify that you want to permanently delete these files by clicking the **Delete Files** button. If you choose the option for removing specific categories of files, the Disk Cleanup dialog box charts your progress.

4. Close the Local Disk (C:) Properties dialog box, and then close the Computer window.

TIP

If you're looking for other system utilities, then the System Tools menu is the first place to look.

You can also open the Disk Cleanup utility from the System Tools menu, which is found under Accessories on the All Programs menu. After you select this option for opening the Disk Cleanup utility, Windows 7 opens a "Disk Cleanup: Drive Selection" dialog box, and although it automatically selects (C:) for drive C by default, it asks you to select the drive you want to clean up. You can then choose that drive from the Drives drop-down box.

If you want to use the Start menu Search box to locate the Disk Cleanup utility, press the Windows key, type *disk*, and then click Disk Cleanup under Programs.

The easiest way to create a shortcut that opens the Disk Cleanup utility so you can quickly remove unneeded files is to right-click Disk Cleanup on the System Tools menu and use the Send to menu to create a desktop shortcut icon. If you view properties of this shortcut, you will discover that its target is:

> *%windir%\system32\cleanmgr.exe*

Windows 7 displays a custom icon for your new desktop shortcut, and when you click that desktop shortcut, Windows 7 automatically opens the Disk Cleanup utility and prompts you for the drive to clean up.

You can also modify the path of the Disk Cleanup shortcut so the Disk Cleanup utility scans for and includes additional system files, as follows:

> *%windir%\cleanmgr.exe tuneup*

The additional files included in this scan are Debug Dump Files, Previous Windows installation(s), System error memory dump files, System error minidump files, Temporary Windows installation files, Files discarded by Windows upgrade, and Windows upgrade log files. In the case of both shortcuts, the windir environment variable guarantees that you can open the Disk Cleanup utility if Windows 7 is installed on another drive.

REFERENCE

Using the Disk Cleanup Utility

- Open a Computer window, right-click an internal or hard disk drive icon, click Properties, and on the General property sheet click the Disk Cleanup button to check the selected drive for unneeded files.
- After the Disk Cleanup utility reports on its findings, review each type of file category listed under "Files to delete," and decide whether you want to remove that category of files. For some categories, you can use the View Files button to examine the folder with those files to make sure you do not remove files you want to keep.
- Make sure there is a check mark in each check box for each category of files you want to remove, and then click OK, or if you want to also locate and remove system files, click the "Clean up system files" button, provide Administrator credentials, and after the Disk Cleanup utility reports its findings, confirm that there is a check mark in each check box for each category of files you want to remove, and then click OK. If you do not want to remove any files with the Disk Cleanup utility, click the Cancel button.
- Close the Disk Cleanup for (C:) dialog box (or boxes).

The primary advantage of the Disk Cleanup utility is that it identifies files that are generally safe to remove, and it does so quickly. It is one simple way you can improve the use of storage space on your computer.

Deleting Your Browsing History

You can use Internet Explorer to delete your browsing history, Temporary Internet files (or your Internet cache), cookies, form data, and Web site passwords. A **cookie** is a simple text file that contains information about your visit to a Web site. Not all Web sites place cookies on your computer. In addition, you can delete files and settings created by

add-ons (or programs used with your Web browser). Aaron recommends you also show Kimberley this option.

These steps assume you are using Windows Internet Explorer 8.

To use Internet Explorer to empty the Internet cache:

TIP

You can open the same dialog box by clicking Internet Options from the Tools menu, and then clicking the Delete button under Browsing history.

1. Open Internet Explorer, click the **Safety** button on the Internet Explorer command bar, and then click **Delete Browsing History**. In the Delete Browsing History dialog box, you can delete Temporary Internet files, Cookies, History, Form data, Passwords, and InPrivate Filtering data, some of which you will examine in more detail in Tutorial 7. See Figure 6-4.

   Trouble? If the command bar is not visible, right-click the Favorites bar, and then click Command Bar.

Figure 6-4	Options for deleting your browsing history

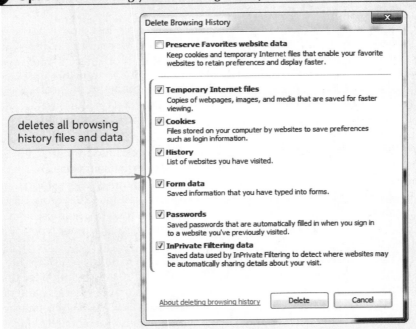

deletes all browsing history files and data

Internet Explorer notes that cookies are files placed on your computer by Web sites you visit to store your personal user preferences. It also notes that History contains a list of Web sites that you have visited, that Form data consists of data you've typed into forms, Passwords include passwords that are automatically entered when you revisit the same Web site, and InPrivate Filtering data includes data saved by a new Internet Explorer feature called InPrivate Filtering which attempts to detect which Web sites may be sharing details about your Web browsing visits. "Preserve Favorites website data" is another new option that retains temporary Internet files and associated cookies for your favorite Web sites so you can access those Web sites more quickly. This latter option is enabled in the Delete Browsing History dialog box because it is assumed that you would want to keep this information. You can pick and choose which of these categories of information you want to delete, or you can use the Delete all button to delete all these files and data that Internet Explorer saves on your hard disk drive.

> **2.** If you want to delete one or more of these categories of information, click the check box for deleting that category of information and verify the operation, and then click the **Delete** button and wait for Internet Explorer to remove this data on your browsing history. If you do not want to delete information from any of these categories, click the **Cancel** button.
>
> **3.** Close Internet Explorer.

If you choose to delete your browsing history, Internet Explorer does not delete your favorite bookmarked Web sites, and it does not delete feeds to which you have subscribed. A **feed** (also known as an **RSS feed**) consists of Web site content (such as news headlines or digital content, such as video) automatically delivered to your Web browser; other programs, such as email software; or your desktop.

Using the Check Disk Utility

Problems with the file system on a disk might arise from insufficient power, a power failure, a brownout (a diminished supply of power), a power surge, an improper shutdown, or a system lockup that requires a restart. File system problems can also arise from an infection by malicious software, faulty or failing hardware, software problems, and even limited disk storage space (because the disk is almost full). You might need to move folders and files that you are no longer using, but want to keep, from the hard disk drive to some type of permanent storage medium for long-term storage. You should also consider the use of an uninterruptible power supply or backup power unit that provides a steady supply of enough power to support your computer and all of its hardware.

To check for errors in the file system or the hard disk itself, you can use the Windows 7 command-line Check Disk utility or the Error-checking tool (the GUI version of the command-line Check Disk utility). Both tools fall into a category of software called disk analysis and repair utilities, both perform the same types of file system checks, and both help you protect your investment in your hard disk and other types of disks, including flash drives.

The Check Disk utility and the Error-checking tool examine a disk for file system errors and repair those errors where possible. They can also check the physical structure of a disk and evaluate the integrity of sectors on a disk's surface. Checking the file system is relatively fast; however, checking the integrity of a disk's surface is time consuming. Fortunately, you only need to check the physical integrity of a disk's surface if you suspect or encounter a major problem with the hard disk. If that happens, you should immediately back up important files on your computer before you run either utility. If you attempt to use these utilities on the system volume (the volume from which Windows 7 starts), Windows 7 will inform you that the drive is in use and asks if you want to schedule the disk check for the next time you start the system.

You can use the Check Disk utility and Error-checking tool in one of three ways:

- **Perform a diagnostic check**—If you run one of these utilities in read-only mode or diagnostic mode, it examines a disk for errors and reports on any errors that it finds, but it does not correct the errors. Instead, it reports what it would do if you decide to correct the file system errors. After using this approach, you can decide whether to immediately make a backup of the contents of your computer's hard disk drive before you correct the file system errors. Another advantage of this option is that you can check the system volume without restarting; however, Microsoft notes that a diagnostic check can report nonexistent errors because the volume must be in an unchanging state, and the only way to guarantee that is to lock the volume by using the /F (Fix) or /R (Repair) switches.

- **Check for and repair file system errors**—This option checks for and attempts to fix file system errors, but it does not check for bad sectors. If you are checking the system volume, you must restart the computer before Windows 7 checks the file system on the volume.
- **Check and repair file system errors and bad sectors**—Although this option is the most thorough, it is also the most time consuming. If you are checking the system volume, you must restart the computer. If either utility finds a bad sector that contains data, it attempts to recover the data from the cluster with the bad sector by moving the data to another cluster on the disk.

The Check Disk utility was introduced with the first version of the DOS operating system on the first IBM PCs in 1981 and was included in every subsequent version of the DOS operating system and every version of the Windows operating system in both the Windows 9.x and Windows NT product lines. This utility is still available in Windows 7. The Windows 9.x product line also contained a ScanDisk utility, which was introduced originally in the DOS operating system. Both utilities are disk analysis and repair utilities that work in a similar way; however, ScanDisk is typically used in the Windows GUI in the Windows 9.x product line, whereas Check Disk is used in a command-line window in both product lines. The Windows 9.x product line also had a command-line version of ScanDisk. Windows 7, Windows Vista, Windows XP, and Windows 2000 have a GUI version of Check Disk called the Error-checking tool.

PROSKILLS

Problem Solving: Troubleshooting with Check Disk

You can use the Error-checking tool and the command-line Check Disk utility to check for and resolve many types of problems that arise on a computer. For example, if you experience problems with a hardware device, such as problems viewing an image on the monitor, a problem with the file system might be interfering with the loading of a device driver for the video display. Or, if you experience problems accessing a drive, that drive may contain problems with the file system. Likewise, a file system problem might prevent you from opening a folder or file, or it might even lock up your computer. If you search for a file that you know you have and cannot find that file, there may be a problem with the file system.

Because file system problems are common, you must consider the likelihood of a file system problem whenever you encounter some type of problem on your computer. Therefore, if you experience a problem with hardware, software, folders, or files on your computer, first try the Error-checking tool or command-line Check Disk utility because the source of the problem may actually result from a problem with the file system. Also, don't assume a hardware problem means that the hardware is failing. These utilities take only a few minutes to run a read-only or diagnostic mode check of your computer, and if the problem you are experiencing results from a problem in the file system, these utilities can correct the problem in most instances and save you valuable time and money.

Microsoft has included (and updated) the Check Disk utility in every version of the DOS and Windows operating systems, which points to the value of this command-line utility in checking and repairing disk problems.

Using the Error-checking Tool on an NTFS Volume

Because the file systems for NTFS and FAT volumes differ, the Error-checking tool and Check Disk utility examine different data structures important to tracking folders and files on each type of volume.

If you use the Error-checking tool or command-line Check Disk utility on an NTFS volume, either in diagnostic mode or to repair errors, the utility makes three passes of the volume and examines all the data used to keep track of all the folders and files on a volume. As it does, it performs three types of checks:

- **File verification**—During the first pass or phase, the Error-checking tool and command-line Check Disk utility verify files. These utilities examine each file record segment in the volume's Master File Table (MFT) for internal consistency and identify which file record segments and clusters are in use. A file record segment (FRS) is a 1,024-byte entry in the Master File Table for a file or folder. At the completion of this phase, these utilities compare the information that they compile to information that NTFS maintains on disk to find discrepancies or problems, such as corrupted file record segments.
- **Index verification**—During the second pass or phase, the Error-checking tool and command-line Check Disk utility verify indexes, or NTFS directories (folders), on the volume. They examine each directory on the volume for internal consistency by making sure that every directory and file is referenced by at least one directory, and that the file record segment reference for each file and subdirectory (subfolder) in the Master File Table is valid. During this pass, these utilities also verify time stamps (file dates and times) and file sizes. From the information garnered during this phase, the Error-checking tool and command-line Check Disk utility can determine whether the volume contains any orphaned files. An **orphaned file** has a valid file record segment in the Master File Table but is not listed in any directory. An orphaned file might occur if the parent folder is overwritten or modified in some way, but the file record segment in the MFT for the orphaned file still refers to that parent folder. These utilities can restore an orphaned file to its original directory if that directory still exists. If that directory does not exist, the Error-checking tool and command-line Check Disk utility create a directory in the top-level folder or root directory for that file. If these utilities find a file record segment that is no longer in use or that does not correspond to the file in the directory, they remove the directory entry. This phase takes the most time.
- **Security descriptor verification**—In the third pass or phase, the Error-checking tool and command-line Check Disk utility verify the integrity of security descriptors for each folder and file. These utilities only verify that the security descriptors are properly formed, not whether they are appropriate.

If you specify the "Scan for and attempt recovery of bad sectors" option with the Error-checking-tool, or specify the **Repair switch (/R)** with the command-line Check Disk utility, these utilities step through two additional phases that determine whether they can read from, and write to, sectors in each cluster on disk. During the fourth phase, these utilities verify all used clusters (that contain data), and in the fifth phase, they verify all unused clusters (that do not contain data). These two phases are time consuming.

Before you run the Error-checking tool and command-line Check Disk utility, you should close all other programs and windows to make sure that no open program accesses folders or files on the disk that you intend to check; otherwise, that open program might interfere with the Error-checking tool and command-line Check Disk utility.

If the Error-checking tool and command-line Check Disk utility cannot lock (or prevent access to) the drive, they offer to check the hard disk drive the next time you start the computer. If the drive you are checking is not the system volume, the Error-checking tool and command-line Check Disk utility might be able to dismount the volume so it has exclusive access to the volume. When Windows 7 dismounts a volume, that volume is no longer available for use. Windows 7 automatically remounts a volume after it has checked the volume. If you do not want to or cannot dismount a volume, you can instead schedule the Error-checking tool and command-line Check Disk utility to check the disk the next time you start up the system.

When the Error-checking tool and command-line Check Disk utility detect and then repair errors in the file system, they may attempt to move data from bad clusters to good clusters. Because any utility that moves, recovers, or repairs data on disk is subject to potential errors, you should first back up your hard disk drive or at least your important files in case you need to restore files later.

Aaron emphasizes the importance of using the Error-checking tool regularly to check and maintain the integrity of hard disks that contain important company documents. He points out that it is easier to repair problems while they are relatively minor, rather than wait until the problems become more serious and perhaps impossible to repair. To become familiar with the Error-checking tool, Aaron suggests you use it to check your hard disk drive.

In the next set of steps, you will use the Error-checking tool to perform a diagnostic check of your hard disk drive. As noted earlier, the Error-checking tool is the version of the command-line Check Disk utility that operates in the graphical user interface. Later in the tutorial, you will use the command-line Check Disk utility so you can compare the two approaches. If Windows 7 cannot boot to the desktop for some reason, but rather boots to a command-line environment, you must use the command-line Check Disk utility to troubleshoot file system problems on your computer.

Although you are only going to perform a read-only check on a hard disk drive, make sure you first have a backup of all your important files on the drive you decide to check if you are working on your own computer.

If you are using a computer in a college computer lab, make sure that you have permission to use the Error-checking tool. If you don't have permission, do not keystroke the following steps but instead read the steps and examine the figures so you are familiar with the use of the Error-checking tool.

To use the Error-checking tool to perform a diagnostic check of a hard disk drive:

▶ **1.** Open a Computer window, right-click the **Local Disk (C:)** drive icon, click **Properties**, and then click the **Tools** tab in the Local Disk (C:) Properties dialog box. The first option on the Tools tab is the one you use to check this drive for errors. See Figure 6-5.

Figure 6-5 | **Local Disk (C:) Tools property sheet**

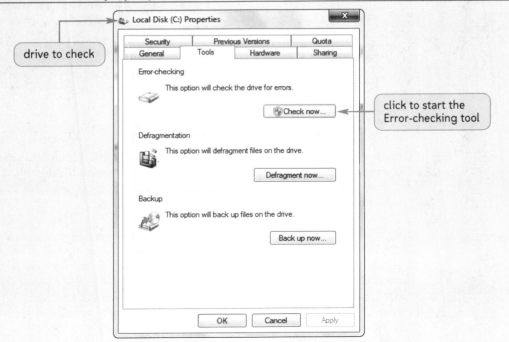

The security shield icon 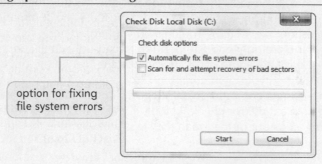 on the Check now button under Error-checking requires that you provide Administrator credentials if you are checking either a boot volume or system volume.

2. Under Error-checking, click the **Check now** button, and if necessary, provide Administrator credentials. Windows 7 displays a Check Disk Local Disk (C:) dialog box with two options for checking a disk. See Figure 6-6.

Figure 6-6 | **Verifying options for checking a hard disk drive**

option for fixing
file system errors

The first option, "Automatically fix file system errors," is already enabled. This option checks the file system, and if necessary, repairs file system errors. The second option, "Scan for and attempt recovery of bad sectors," is not enabled because it checks each sector on the disk, and if any defective sectors are found, the Error-checking tool attempts to recover the data from the bad sectors, and move the data to good sectors. That process is time consuming. You can use either option, both options, or neither option.

Make sure you remove the check mark from the "Automatically fix file system errors" and "Scan for and attempt recovery of bad sectors" check boxes.

3. To perform a read-only or diagnostic check of your hard disk drive, click the **Automatically fix file system errors** check box to *remove* the check mark, and make sure there is no check mark in the "Scan for and attempt recovery of bad sectors" check box, and then click the **Start** button.

Windows 7 immediately performs the check. As the disk is checked, the Error-checking tool will inform you that it's checking file records, index entries, SDs/SIDs, and finally USN bytes. Then Windows 7 displays a Checking Disk Local Disk (C:) dialog box, and as is the case for the computer used for this figure, reports that your device or disk was successfully scanned, and notes whether any problems were found.

In some instances, when operating in read-only or diagnostic mode, the Error-checking tool may report that some problems were found and fixed, but that is not actually the case. Instead, the Error-checking tool is just reporting what it would do if it were not operating in read-only or diagnostic mode.

The Error-checking tool may also note that any files that were affected by these problems were moved to a folder named FOUND on the device or disk. When the Error-checking tool creates a FOUND folder, the folder name includes an extension with three digits, starting with FOUND.000 for the first set of found files, and incrementing by one each time you perform another scan. If Windows 7 reports that an NTFS directory is corrupt and unreadable (which means you cannot open the folder), run the Error-checking tool or command-line Check Disk utility to recover the directory (or folder) and all its subfolders and files. After you open the FOUND.000 folder, you will find a folder named dir0000.chk that contains your recovered folder, its subfolders, and files, all of which are intact and functional (as shown in this session's Visual Overview). You can select this folder and copy its contents to a new location on your hard disk. Windows 7 might be able to recover all or some of your original folders and files. The Error-checking tool and Check Disk utility are far better at recovering orphaned directories and files on NTFS volumes than recovering lost clusters on FAT volumes.

To view details found by the Error-checking tool:

▶ **1.** Click the **See details** button ⊙ in the Checking Disk Local Disk (C:) dialog box. The Error-checking tool provides details on the check of the hard disk drive. If the Error-checking tool reports near the bottom of this dialog box that "Windows found problems with the file system," then it will also recommend that you "Run CHKDSK with the /F (Fix) option to correct these." See Figure 6-7. Your results will differ.

| Figure 6-7 | Results from checking a hard disk drive for errors |

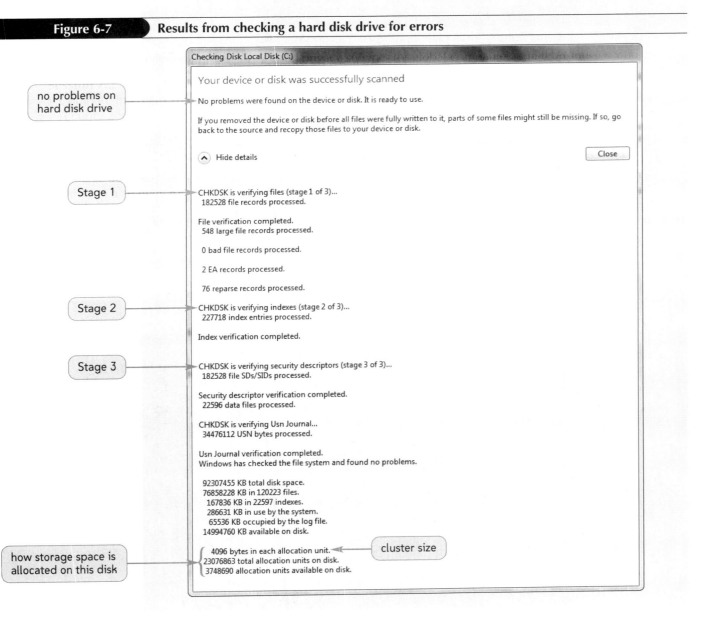

In the Checking Disk Local Disk (C:) dialog box, the Error-checking tool identifies the three stages used by CHKDSK (the Check Disk utility). In Stage 1 of 3, it verifies files, and shows the number of file records processed. In Stage 2 of 3, it verifies the indexes (or directories), shows the number of index entries processed, and indicates that index verification is completed. In Stage 3 of 3, it verifies security descriptors, shows the number of file SDs/SIDs (Security Descriptors/Security IDs) processed, notes that security descriptor verification is complete, and shows the number of data files processed.

Next, the Error-checking tool notes that CHKDSK is verifying the Usn Journal (also called the Change Journal), which keeps track of changes made to folders and files on an NTFS volume. The Error-checking tool examines the Usn Journal file record segment, shows the number of USN bytes processed, and notes that Usn Journal verification is complete.

Then the Error-reporting tool provides information on the usage of disk storage space and allocation units. First, the Error-checking tool reports on the amount of total disk space, the storage space used by files and the total number of files, the storage space used by indexes and the total number of indexes, the storage space used by the system, the number of kilobytes used by the log file, and the storage space still available on disk.

The last section shows how many bytes are found in each allocation unit (or cluster), the total number of allocation units (or clusters) on disk, and the total number of allocation units (or clusters) still available on disk. If you divide the number of bytes per allocation unit (or cluster), namely 4,096, by 512 (the number of bytes per sector), then there are 8 sectors per allocation unit (or cluster) on this NTFS volume.

To complete the operation:

▶ **1.** Click the **Close** button to close the Checking Disk Local Disk (C:) dialog box, and then click the **OK** button to close the Properties dialog box for that disk drive.

▶ **2.** Close the Computer window.

If the Error-checking tool, or the Check Disk utility, reports that Windows found problems on the disk, you should immediately make a backup of your hard disk drive and your important files, and then run the Error-checking tool or Check Disk utility and fix the file system problems. Later, if you discover that you are missing important files, then you can restore those important files from your backup. If you discover that an application does not work properly, then you can reinstall that application.

REFERENCE

Using the Error-checking Tool to Check the File System on a Hard Disk Drive

- Open a Computer window, right-click the Local Disk (C:) drive icon or the drive icon for an external hard disk drive, click Properties, and then click the Tools tab in the Properties dialog box for the specific drive you chose.
- Under Error-checking on the Tools tab, click the Check now button, and then provide Administrator credentials.
- After Windows 7 displays a Check Disk Local Disk dialog box (with the drive name), remove the check mark from the "Automatically fix file system errors" check box if you want to perform a read-only or diagnostic check, and make sure there is no check mark in the "Scan for and attempt recovery of bad sectors" check box, click the Start button, and after the Error-checking tool displays another Checking Disk Local Disk dialog box for that drive, examine the results of the disk check. If you want to fix file system errors, click the "Automatically fix file system errors" check box, click the Start button, and if Windows 7 displays a Microsoft Windows dialog box and informs you that it cannot check the disk while it's in use, click the "Schedule disk check" button, open the Start menu, click the Shut down button, click Restart, and after the Check Disk utility completes the disk check, examine the results of the disk check, and then restart your computer.

As noted in Tutorial 5, Windows 7 uses the self-healing feature of NTFS to detect and repair file system errors while your computer is up and running. This feature not only reduces the number of file system problems on NTFS volumes, but also reduces the likelihood that you (or someone with an Administrator account) might need to manually resolve those problems. This self-healing feature is especially useful in a business environment because a hard disk check is time consuming and can result in the loss of productivity when employees' computers are not available. If the self-healing capabilities of NTFS do not resolve file system problems, Windows 7 schedules a check of the disk by the Check Disk utility the next time the system starts up.

INSIGHT

The Importance of Preventive Maintenance

In Windows versions before Windows Vista and Windows 7, it was common practice to recommend a periodic check of the hard disk drive, preferably once a week, and at the very least, once a month, to check for and remove problems before they became more serious. Even though the NTFS self-healing feature of Windows 7 helps protect the hard disk drive, Microsoft still recommends periodic preventive maintenance. Microsoft notes that problems with the file system and disks commonly result in problems that are difficult to troubleshoot, and therefore they recommend the Check Disk utility as one of the first tools to diagnose and repair problems, especially if you have not made a change to your system's settings or configuration. By performing preventive maintenance, you improve the chances that your hard disk drives and flash drives will remain free of file system problems that might result in the loss of valuable data.

Using the Error-Checking Tool on FAT Volumes

The NTFS self-healing feature is not available in the FAT file system, so the use of the Error-checking tool or the command-line Check Disk utility on FAT volumes is more important. Flash drives typically use the FAT file system, and therefore you might need to check the file system if you experience problems with accessing data on the flash drive.

When checking the file system on a FAT volume, the Error-checking tool and command-line Check Disk utilities check the file allocation tables (FAT1 and FAT2), the directory table for the top-level folder (or root directory), the folder (or directory) structure, the integrity of files, and the validity of long filenames. As you may recall from Tutorial 5, the file allocation table contains information on cluster usage. Also, the operating system keeps and updates two copies of the file allocation table (FAT1 and FAT2). When these utilities examine the file allocation tables, they trace the chain for each file and account for all clusters in use by each file.

The directory table for the top-level folder (or root directory) in the FAT file system tracks information on the folders and files that are stored in the top-level folder of a disk, including the starting cluster for each file and its size. When checking the directory table, the Error-checking tool or command-line Check Disk utility verifies that the size of each file matches the total amount of storage space assigned to clusters for each file in the file allocation table.

Checking the folder or directory structure is also important because Windows 7 must be able to navigate to locate and store files on a disk. The Error-checking tool and command-line Check Disk utility therefore navigate the entire directory structure of a disk to ensure that it is functional and intact.

Checking for Lost Clusters

When the Error-checking tool and the command-line Check Disk utility verify the integrity of files, they look for lost clusters and cross-linked files. A **lost cluster** is a cluster on a FAT volume that contains data that once belonged to a program, document, or another type of file, such as a temporary file. In the file allocation table, there is no pointer to the lost cluster; therefore, the lost cluster is not associated with any file, and you cannot view the data in the lost cluster. (The pointer is the cluster number of the next available cluster for a folder or file.) The cluster is still allocated to the lost cluster, so the lost cluster wastes disk storage space.

Like other types of file system problems, lost clusters might develop when a power failure occurs, when you restart a computer system after it locks up, when a brownout or a power surge occurs, or when you do not properly shut down Windows 7. In these cases, lost clusters develop because the operating system might not be able to record any remaining information it has on the location of the clusters for a file in the file allocation table or the information it has on the starting cluster of the file in the folder or directory file.

Figure 6-8 illustrates this common problem on FAT volumes. Assume you are looking at the part of the file allocation table where Windows 7 tracks the usage of cluster numbers 1500 through 1512.

Figure 6-8 **How a lost cluster might occur on a FAT volume**

File	Cluster	Status		Cluster	Status	
Financial Analysis.xlsx	1500	1501		1500	1501	
	1501	1502		1501	1502	
	1502	1503		1502	1503	
	1503	1504		1503	1504	
	1504	1505		1504	1505	
	1505	EOF		1505	EOF	
Project Overview.docx	1506	1507		1506	1507	
	1507	1508		1507	1508	
	1508	1509		1508	1509	
	1509	1510		1509	EOF	a power failure modifies the FAT entry for cluster 1509
	1510	1511		1510	1511	
	1511	1512		1511	1512	
	1512	EOF		1512	EOF	one chain of lost clusters

In this example, assume that Windows 7 has assigned clusters 1500 through 1505 to a file named Financial Analysis.xlsx, and that it assigned clusters 1506 through 1512 to a file named Project Overview.docx. As a result of a power failure, assume the pointer for cluster 1509 for the Project Overview file changes to an end-of-file code (EOF). If you open the Project Overview file in the application that produced it, Windows 7 reads clusters 1506 through 1509 and then stops because it finds an end-of-file code for cluster 1509. If you examine the end of this file (assuming you can open it at all), you discover that part of the file is missing and that part of the file contains combinations of characters and symbols that make no sense. Clusters 1510 through 1512, which once belonged to the Project Overview file, are now lost clusters. In fact, they constitute one **chain** of lost clusters because they are derived from a single file. A chain of lost clusters is also called a **file fragment**. The file allocation table shows those clusters as being in use (i.e., they contain data). However, those clusters are not associated with any file on disk because the file allocation table does not contain a pointer to cluster 1510. The operating system cannot use or access the storage space occupied by these lost clusters, so they waste valuable storage space on disk. Because lost clusters arise so easily, they are the most common type of problem encountered on FAT volumes.

Likewise, if a power problem occurs near the end of a file save operation, you might end up with lost clusters on a disk, or the entire file that you had open may end up as lost clusters. In this case, Windows 7 might report the file size as 0 (zero). That means all of the clusters originally assigned to the file are now lost clusters. If a FAT volume has lost clusters, it might appear that all of the disk storage space is available because you cannot see the lost clusters in a folder window. However, the disk could have lost clusters that are not visible when viewing the contents of the disk. You can use the Error-checking tool or the command-line Check Disk utility to recover those lost clusters and free up valuable storage space on the disk. If a disk contains lost clusters, the command-line Check Disk utility will report that it found errors on the disk and then ask if you want to convert the lost chains to files. A **lost chain** is a sequence of lost clusters that once belonged to a single file. The Error-checking tool converts the lost chains to files without asking you.

As it recovers lost clusters, the Error-checking tool or command-line Check Disk utility creates a hidden system folder named FOUND.*nnn* in the top-level folder of the disk that it checks (where *nnn* is a sequential number, starting with 000) for each chain of lost clusters, and then stores the recovered clusters in a file named FILE0000.CHK within that folder. The file extension .chk stands for Check Disk. If these utilities find more than one chain of lost clusters, they name the second chain FILE0001.CHK, the third chain FILE0002.CHK, and so on. To view the FOUND.000 folder in a folder window, you have to open the Folder Options dialog box and choose the options for showing hidden files and folders and for displaying hidden, protected operating system files.

After recovering lost clusters, you can delete the FOUND.000 folder and recover the disk storage space used by lost clusters. Or, you can open the FOUND.000 folder, open each file with recovered lost clusters, and then attempt to determine if these files contain anything of value to you. You can open each file in Notepad to try to determine what type of content is contained in the file, close the file, and then open the program that you think created the file to determine if the file can be opened by that program and, if so, whether the file has any useful information you need. If you open a file in Notepad, you might not be able to distinguish what type of content is stored in the file; however, if you examine the beginning of the file, you will see a code, such as JPEG or GIF, which identifies the file type. Close Notepad, change the file extension to the appropriate file type, and open the file with the program associated with that file type. If the file contains useful information, and if you do not have a copy of that information elsewhere, you can save it using an appropriate filename related to its contents. If the file does not contain anything of value to you, or if you still cannot tell which application produced the file or what type of information was contained in the file (more than often the case), delete the file to recover the disk space used by the file. Later, if you discover that you are missing part of a file, you can restore the file from a backup.

Over time, lost clusters can increase in number on FAT volumes, waste more valuable disk space, and lead to further disk errors. In most cases, you should delete the files that contain lost clusters and reclaim valuable storage space on your hard disk drive. This is yet another reason for switching the file system to NTFS where feasible.

Checking for Cross-Linked Files

Another important but less common problem on FAT volumes is cross-linked files. A **cross-linked file** is a file that contains at least one cluster that belongs to or is shared by two (or perhaps more) files. For example, as shown in Figure 6-9, one file might be cross-linked with only one other file through one cluster.

Figure 6-9   **How a cross-link might occur on a FAT volume**

File	Cluster	Status
Financial Analysis.xlsx	1500	1501
	1501	1502
	1502	1503
	1503	1504
	1504	1505
	1505	EOF
Project Overview.docx	1506	1507
	1507	1508
	1508	1509
	1509	1510
	1510	1511
	1511	1512
	1512	EOF

Cluster	Status	
1500	1501	
1501	1502	
1502	1503	
1503	1504	
1504	1505	
1505	1510	a power failure modifies the FAT entry for cluster 1505
1506	1507	
1507	1508	
1508	1509	
1509	1510	clusters shared by two files
1510	1511	
1511	1512	
1512	EOF	

In this example, the problem that caused the file system error might modify the end-of-file code for one file so it points to a cluster that's part of another file.

Again, assume you are looking at cluster usage in the file allocation table for the same two files you examined earlier. Also, assume that as a result of a power problem, the end-of-file (EOF) code for the last cluster of the file Financial Analysis.xlsx changes so it points to a cluster assigned to the file Project Overview.docx. In this example, the end-of-file code for cluster 1505 now points to cluster 1510. Cluster 1509 for the Project Overview file also points to cluster 1510. If you open the Financial Analysis file (assuming you can open it at all), Windows 7 reads clusters 1500 through 1505, and then, because it finds a pointer to another cluster (and not an EOF code), Windows 7 reads clusters 1510 through 1512 (which were originally part of the Project Overview file). Windows then stops when it encounters the EOF code for cluster 1512. If you examine the Financial Analysis file (again assuming you can open it at all), you will discover lost data in the file where the cross-link occurs and perhaps in other parts of the file as well. If you open the Project Overview file (assuming you can open it), Windows reads clusters 1506 through 1512, the clusters originally assigned to this file before the cross-link occurred. Again, if you examine this file, you will discover combinations of characters and symbols that make no sense and that indicate possible loss of data where the cross-link occurs.

How do you repair cross-linked files? You can copy each file to a new location and remove the original files so the files are no longer cross-linked. You then open both files (if possible), examine them, and edit the files to remove unusable content and add any data that might have been lost. Or, you can use the Error-checking tool or command-line Check Disk utility to eliminate the cross-links between files by providing each file with a copy of the same cross-linked cluster(s). However, you will have to open and examine each file and then edit the contents of the file where the cross-link occurred.

Checking a Flash Drive with the Error-Checking Tool

Aaron recommends that you check your flash drive with the Error-checking tool so you become familiar with how to check other types of drives and disks.

Before you check your flash drive for errors (and repair any errors that are found), make sure you have backup copies (or duplicate copies) of any important files on your flash drive. To be on the safe side, you may first want to copy everything on your flash drive to a folder named Flash Drive in the Public Documents folder (just as you copied the Data Files to the Public Documents folder). In the following steps, you can also choose the option for performing a read-only or diagnostic check of your flash drive.

To use the Error-checking tool to check a flash drive:

▶ **1.** If necessary, attach a flash drive to your computer, and close any dialog boxes or windows that Windows 7 automatically opens.

▶ **2.** Open a Computer window, right-click your **flash drive** icon, click **Properties**, and then click the **Tools** tab in the flash drive's Properties dialog box.

▶ **3.** Under Error-checking, click the **Check now** button. Windows 7 opens the Check Disk Removable Disk dialog box.

▶ **4.** To perform a read-only or diagnostic check of your flash drive, click the **Automatically fix file system errors** check box to remove the check mark, make sure there is no check mark in the "Scan for and attempt recovery of bad sectors" check box, and then click the **Start** button.

> Make sure you remove the check mark from the "Automatically fix file system errors" and "Scan for and attempt recovery of bad sectors" check boxes.

▶ **5.** Click the **See details** button ⊙. The Checking Disk Removable Disk dialog box (with the drive name) expands to display information about the findings of the Check Disk utility. See Figure 6-10.

Figure 6-10 **Check Disk results for a FAT32 volume**

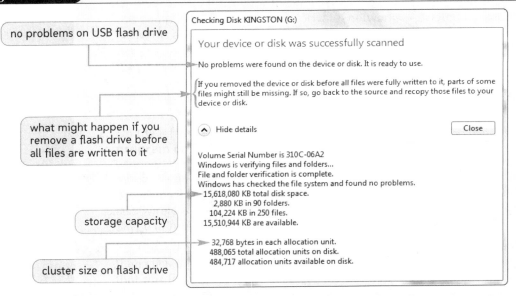

no problems on USB flash drive

what might happen if you remove a flash drive before all files are written to it

storage capacity

cluster size on flash drive

Checking Disk KINGSTON (G:)

Your device or disk was successfully scanned

No problems were found on the device or disk. It is ready to use.

If you removed the device or disk before all files were fully written to it, parts of some files might still be missing. If so, go back to the source and recopy those files to your device or disk.

⊙ Hide details   [Close]

Volume Serial Number is 310C-06A2
Windows is verifying files and folders...
File and folder verification is complete.
Windows has checked the file system and found no problems.
15,618,080 KB total disk space.
   2,880 KB in 90 folders.
104,224 KB in 250 files.
15,510,944 KB are available.

32,768 bytes in each allocation unit.
488,065 total allocation units on disk.
484,717 allocation units available on disk.

On the computer used for this figure, the Error-checking tool checked a 16 GB flash drive and found no problems with the file system. After the Error-checking tool examines the flash drive, it notes that it successfully scanned this disk, and that it found no problems. Then it reports on the total disk space in kilobytes; the amount of storage space used by folders and files as well as the total number of folders and files; and the amount of available disk storage space in kilobytes remaining on the disk. Finally, it reports that each allocation unit (or cluster) contains 32,768 bytes. If you divide that value by 512 bytes per sector, you find that this flash drive has 64 sectors per cluster. If you check the properties of this flash drive, you would discover that it uses the FAT32 file system. Finally, it reports the total and available number of allocation units (or clusters) on the flash drive.

▶ **6.** Click the **Close** button to close the Checking Disk dialog box for your flash drive, and then click the **OK** button in the Properties dialog box for your flash drive.

▶ **7.** Before you close the Computer window, note the drive name assigned to your flash drive because you will need this information in the next section of the tutorial.

You do not need to perform a surface scan of a flash drive because data is written to a flash drive in a different way than for a hard disk drive.

Using the Command-Line Check Disk Utility

You use the command-line Check Disk utility in a command-line environment either under the Windows 7 graphical user interface or by starting up Windows 7 in a command-line user interface. From the desktop, you can open a command-line window by using Command Prompt on the Accessories menu. In the command-line window, you enter one command at a time at the command-line prompt (or operating system prompt). Windows 7 locates and opens the program; the program performs its intended task and reports its results, and then Windows 7 displays another command-line prompt so you can enter another command.

Aaron asks you to show Kimberley how to check her flash drive with the command-line Check Disk utility and compare its use with the Error-checking tool.

In the following steps, you will open the command-line Check Disk utility and then use read-only or diagnostic mode to check your flash drive. To complete this next section, you need to know the drive name for your flash drive.

To use the Check Disk utility in a command-line window to check a flash drive:

TIP

You can also open a Command Prompt window by typing COMMAND in the Start menu search box and pressing Enter.

1. If you don't know the drive name for your flash drive, open a Computer window, locate the drive name for your flash drive, and then close the Computer window.

2. On the Start menu, point to **All Programs**, click **Accessories**, and then click **Command Prompt**. Windows 7 opens a Command Prompt window. See Figure 6-11.

| Figure 6-11 | Command Prompt window |

operating system prompt for current directory

Windows version

Windows 7 also identifies the Windows version, and then displays a command-line prompt. Windows 6.1.7600 is the original version of Windows 7. "C:\Users\Aaron>" is the command-line prompt where you enter a command for your user account (identified on this computer as Aaron). As you can tell, a command-line prompt includes the path to the current directory (or folder). The greater-than symbol (>) separates the path from the command you enter.

TIP

You can use lowercase or uppercase for a command and for any options that you specify with the command.

3. Type **CHKDSK** (in uppercase or lowercase), press the **Spacebar**, type the **drive name for your flash drive**, and then press the **Enter** key. For example, if your flash drive is identified as drive G in the Computer window, you type CHKDSK G: and then press the Enter key. The Check Disk utility checks the disk and then reports on its findings. See Figure 6-12. Your results will differ.

Trouble? If Windows 7 informs you that the command you entered "is not recognized as an internal or external command, operable program, or batch file," you mistyped the command, or did not include a space between the command and the drive name. Repeat Step 3 and enter the command properly.

Trouble? If Windows 7 informs you that it cannot open the volume for direct access, you typed a drive name for a nonexistent drive. If necessary, open a Computer window, verify the flash drive's drive name (or an empty drive that does not contain a disk), close the Computer window, and then repeat Step 3 with the correct drive name.

Trouble? If Windows 7 informs you that the file system is RAW, and that "CHKDSK is not available for RAW drives," then you specified a drive name for a DVD or CD drive that contains a DVD or CD. If necessary, open a Computer window, verify the flash drive name, close the Computer window, and then repeat Step 3 with the correct drive name.

Trouble? If Windows 7 informs you that access is denied because you do not have sufficient privileges and that you have to invoke this utility running in elevated mode, then you did not type a colon after the drive name letter. Repeat Step 3, and enter the drive letter followed by a colon.

| Figure 6-12 | Checking a flash drive with the Check Disk utility |

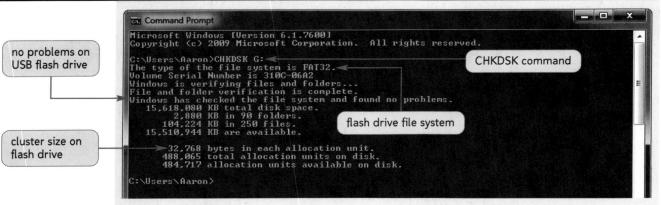

Note that this 16 GB flash drive uses the FAT32 file system, and it contains 90 folders and 250 files. After verifying files and folders, CHKDSK reports that Windows found no problems with the file system.

4. To close the Command Prompt window, type **EXIT** and press the **Enter** key.

If the Check Disk utility reports problems with a disk, you should back up your important files, and then use the Check Disk **Fix switch** (**/F**) to repair the problems with the file system (if at all possible). A switch is an optional parameter you use with a command to change the way the command works. Check Disk can also check the physical integrity of sectors on a disk if you use the Repair switch (/R). When you use this switch, Check Disk attempts to recover data stored in bad sectors before marking the clusters within those sectors as unusable. Any recovered data is recorded in other unused, but good, sectors on the disk (if possible). If you are using the Repair switch to check sectors on a disk, Check Disk can take a long time, making the disk volume unavailable until the Check Disk utility completes its check and repair of the disk. Microsoft recommends that you not interrupt the Check Disk utility once you start it, but allow it to complete its repair of the file system.

If Windows 7 detects a problem with a disk during start up, it automatically runs Autochk.exe, a version of Check Disk that runs only at the next start up, before Windows 7 loads the desktop. If you schedule a Check Disk for the next start up, Windows 7 runs Autochk.exe the next time the system starts up.

As you've discovered, the Error-checking tool and the Check Disk utility perform comparable operations. Figure 6-13 summarizes how you perform the three basic types of checks discussed at the beginning of the earlier section entitled "Using the Check Disk Utility."

Figure 6-13   **Comparison of Error-checking tool and Check Disk utility**

Operation	Error-checking tool	Check Disk utility
Read-only, or diagnostic, mode	Check Disk options: Remove check mark from the: • "Automatically fix file system errors" check box • "Scan for and attempt recovery of bad sectors" check box	CHKDSK [*drivename*] Example: CHKD SK C:
Fix file system errors	Check Disk options: • Add a check mark to the "Automatically fix file system errors" check box • Remove the check mark from the "Scan for and attempt recovery of bad sectors" check box	CHKDSK [*drivename*] /F Example: CHKDSK C: /F
Fix file system errors and recover bad clusters	Check Disk options: Add a check mark to the: • "Automatically fix file system errors" check box • "Scan for and attempt recovery of bad sectors" check box	CHKDSK [*drivename*] /F /R Example: CHKDSK C: /F /R

REFERENCE

Using the Check Disk Utility in a Command Prompt Window

- If necessary, open a Computer window, locate the drive name for the drive you want to check, and then close the Computer window.
- If you want to check a drive other than the system or boot volume, open the Start menu, point to All Programs, click Accessories, and then click Command Prompt. If you want to check the drive that is the system volume or boot volume, open the Start menu, point to All Programs, click Accessories, right-click Command Prompt, click Run as administrator, and then provide Administrator credentials.
- To perform a read-only or diagnostic check, type CHKDSK (in uppercase or lowercase), press the Spacebar, type the drive name for the drive (including the colon) you want to check, and then press the Enter key.
- To check and repair file system errors, type CHKDSK, press the Spacebar, type the drive name, press the Spacebar, type /F and then press the Enter key.
- To check and repair file system errors and bad sectors, type CHKDSK, press the Spacebar, type the drive name, press the Spacebar, type /F /R and then press the Enter key.
- After examining the status report and repairing file system errors and bad clusters, type EXIT and press the Enter key (or click the Command Prompt window's Close button) to close the Command Prompt window.

The Check Disk utility is a powerful tool for maintaining the integrity of the file system on a computer.

REVIEW

Session 6.1 Quick Check

1. True or False. Temporary files are files that applications create when you are working with a document, or that Windows creates while performing an operation.
2. What utility or utilities can you use to check a hard disk drive for errors, and where possible, repair those errors?
3. What happens when the Check Disk utility verifies indexes, or NTFS directories?
4. What NTFS file system component contains information about the owner of the folder or file, permissions granted to users and groups for that directory or file, and information on security events to be audited for that directory or file?
5. A(n) _____ is a cluster on a FAT volume that contains data that once belonged to a program, document, or another type of file, such as a temporary file, but which is no longer associated with any file.
6. A(n) _____ is an optional parameter that you use with a command in a command-line environment to change the way in which the command works.
7. What is the difference between the Check Disk utility's Fix (/F) and the Repair (/R) switches?
8. What is a cross-linked file?

SESSION 6.2 VISUAL OVERVIEW

You can use Disk Defragmenter to analyze and optimize the storage of files and folders on a disk.

Fragmentation on a disk consists of **fragmented files** and **fragmented folders** whose clusters are stored in one or more nonadjacent blocks in different locations on a disk.

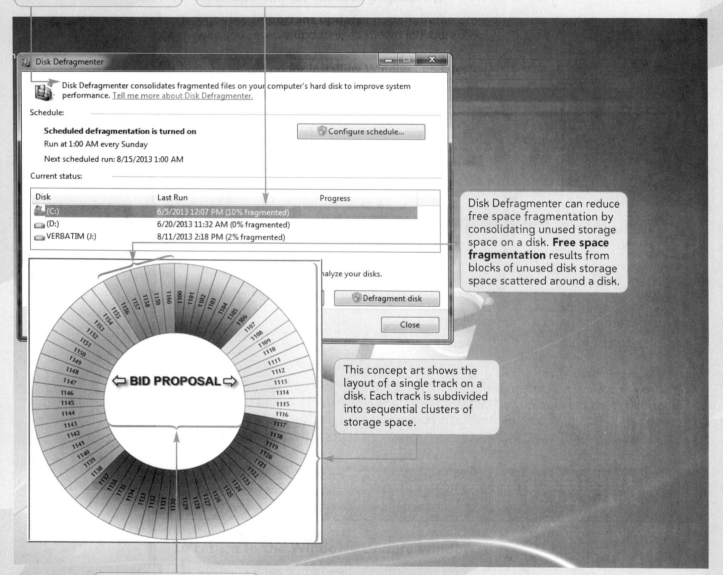

Disk Defragmenter

Disk Defragmenter consolidates fragmented files on your computer's hard disk to improve system performance. Tell me more about Disk Defragmenter.

Schedule:

Scheduled defragmentation is turned on

Run at 1:00 AM every Sunday

Next scheduled run: 8/15/2013 1:00 AM

Configure schedule...

Current status:

Disk	Last Run	Progress
(C:)	6/5/2013 12:07 PM (10% fragmented)	
(D:)	6/20/2013 11:32 AM (0% fragmented)	
VERBATIM (J:)	8/11/2013 2:18 PM (2% fragmented)	

...nalyze your disks.

Defragment disk

Close

BID PROPOSAL

Disk Defragmenter can reduce free space fragmentation by consolidating unused storage space on a disk. **Free space fragmentation** results from blocks of unused disk storage space scattered around a disk.

This concept art shows the layout of a single track on a disk. Each track is subdivided into sequential clusters of storage space.

The Bid Proposal file is stored in two blocks of clusters at different locations on a disk.

SCHEDULED TASKS

You can use Task Scheduler to create a **scheduled task** that automatically starts at a specific time on a specific date or in response to some event that occurs on the computer. Windows 7 has built-in scheduled tasks, including one for running Disk Defragmenter weekly.

A **trigger** is a set of criteria that specify when a task begins.

The **Create Basic Task** action starts a wizard that steps you through defining a scheduled task.

Windows 7 automatically runs the Autochk scheduled task if it detects that the hard disk volume is **dirty**, or contains errors.

Windows 7 has a **Disk Diagnostics** scheduled task that monitors the status of the hard disk and warns users of an impending failure.

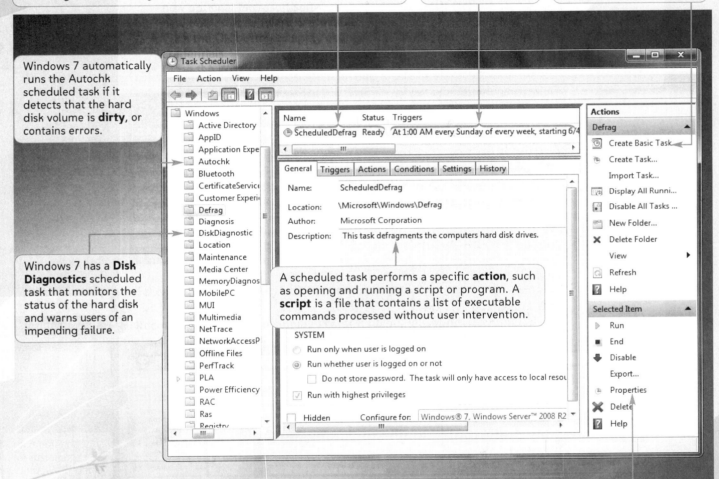

A scheduled task performs a specific **action**, such as opening and running a script or program. A **script** is a file that contains a list of executable commands processed without user intervention.

Each scheduled task has **properties**, such as a trigger, action, and history of events, that you can examine and, in some cases, customize.

Understanding File Fragmentation

As you create, modify, and save files to a hard disk drive, Windows 7 attempts to store the different parts of each file in **contiguous**, or adjacent, clusters; in other words, one right after the other. However, as you add, delete, and modify files, Windows 7 might then store different parts of the same file in **noncontiguous** or nonadjacent clusters that are scattered across the surface of a disk because the disk does not have enough space to store the file in contiguous clusters. The file is then called a fragmented file. It's normal and necessary for there to be fragmented files on your disk. However, over time, file fragmentation can build up, affect the performance of a hard disk drive, and as noted by Microsoft, place undue stress on the hard disk.

A hard disk's read/write heads retrieve data from and record data on the surface of the hard disk. Each time you instruct a program to retrieve a file from a hard disk, the hard disk must move the read/write heads to different positions on the hard disk to locate each cluster for a file and reassemble its contents so you can work with the file. When retrieving a file that is stored in contiguous clusters, the read/write heads can quickly reassemble the entire file from one location on the hard disk. However, when retrieving a fragmented file, the read/write heads must keep moving to different positions on the hard disk to locate and then reassemble the entire file. Therefore, the overall process of retrieving the file takes longer, and you spend more time waiting for a file to open before you can begin your work.

Likewise, when you issue a command to save a new or modified file to a disk, Windows 7 must locate available clusters for that file on disk. It begins writing your file in the first available cluster. If the file requires more than one cluster, it moves onto the next available cluster, even if that next available cluster is in a different physical location on the disk. If a file is stored in noncontiguous clusters, it takes the read/write heads longer to write the file to the disk because the read/write heads must move to different positions on the hard disk to record data. Obviously, the problem is compounded if all or most of the files on a disk are fragmented. Furthermore, as fragmentation builds up on a disk, it not only means that you spend more time waiting for files to open and save, it also results in more disk access, and that in turn causes increased wear and tear on the hard disk.

To understand how file fragmentation occurs, consider a simple example. Assume that over the last six months you added files to a hard disk drive, and you deleted and modified files on the same hard disk drive. Also assume that you created and saved a project overview report, a financial bid proposal, and a financial projection, and assume that these three files are each stored on the hard disk drive in contiguous clusters, one file after another.

As shown in Figure 6-14, the Project Overview report is stored in seven contiguous clusters (clusters 1100 through 1106), the Bid Proposal in 10 contiguous clusters (clusters 1107 thru 1116), and the Financial Projection in 21 contiguous clusters (clusters 1117 through 1137). Clusters 1138 through 1160 are currently unused clusters, and the remaining tracks on the hard disk drive store many other files that you have added to the hard disk drive over time.

Figure 6-14	Files arranged in contiguous clusters

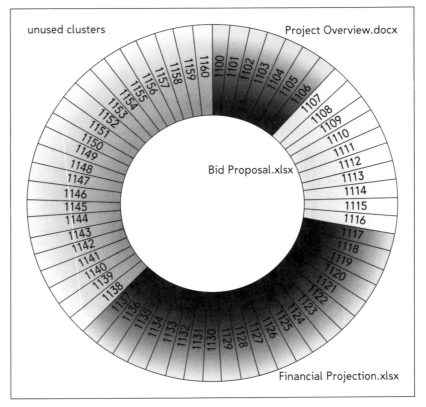

Continuing this example, assume you decide you no longer need the Bid Proposal, so you delete this file from your hard disk drive. By removing this file, you free up 10 clusters (clusters 1107 thru 1116), as shown in Figure 6-15.

Figure 6-15   **Clusters freed after deleting a file**

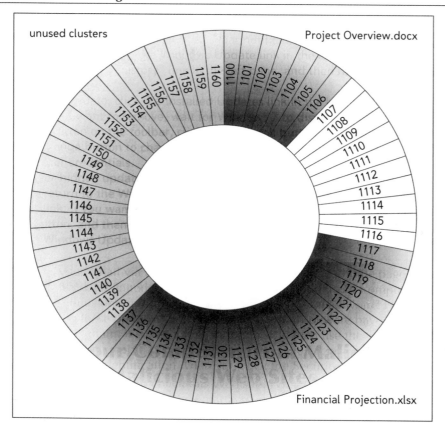

Next, you prepare and save a new Portfolio document for an upcoming project. Let's assume that this file initially requires 10 clusters and that Windows 7 uses the clusters that were previously occupied by the Bid Proposal. A short while later, you open the file again and add a new section to the Portfolio so the final file size requires 28 clusters of storage space on disk. When Windows 7 allocates storage space for the file with the Portfolio, it might use the next available set of contiguous clusters for the additional 18 clusters required for this file, right after the clusters for the file with the Financial Projection.

The Portfolio file is now a fragmented file because it is stored in two blocks of non-contiguous clusters. The first part of the file is stored in clusters 1107 through 1116, and the second part of the file is stored in clusters 1138 through 1155. Clusters 1156 through 1160 remain unused. See Figure 6-16. From this example, you can see that if you reduce the size of files or delete files from a disk, you free clusters that Windows 7 might use later for part of another file. If you increase the size of files or add new files to a disk, and the disk does not contain enough consecutive clusters to hold the entire file, Windows 7 stores the files in noncontiguous clusters. Over time, the number of fragmented files increases and the performance of your computer decreases.

| **Figure 6-16** | Fragmented file stored in two noncontiguous blocks |

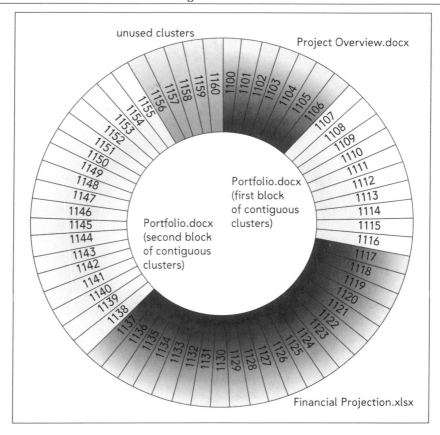

To reduce file fragmentation, you can use the Windows 7 Disk Defragmenter utility. Disk Defragmenter reorganizes the clusters assigned to each file so they are located in contiguous clusters, and it also rearranges files so they are stored one right after another. This latter operation reduces free space fragmentation by removing free space (or unused space) between files that would result in even more fragmentation later. This type of problem occurs when the available free space is scattered around the disk rather than consolidated in adjacent clusters in one area of the disk (usually the inner surface of a hard disk drive). If all of the clusters for a file are stored in adjacent clusters, the read/write heads can quickly retrieve the contents of that file, improving the response time and performance of your computer and reducing stress on your hard disk.

Unlike versions of Windows before Windows Vista, the Windows 7 Disk Defragmenter does not attempt to defragment a noncontiguous block in a file if the noncontiguous block is larger than 64 MB because the performance gain is minimal. Also, like Windows Vista, it does not graphically display the progress of analyzing and then defragmenting a disk.

Windows 7, unlike earlier versions of Windows, disables automatic defragmentation for solid-state drives (SSDs). A **solid-state drive (SSD)** is a storage device that stores data on flash memory, similar to a flash drive, and therefore has no moving parts. Accessing data on a solid-state drive is much faster than accessing data on traditional hard disk drives that use spinning platters. Solid-state drives are quieter, they enable a computer to start more quickly, and they do not require defragmentation. Because they have a set lifetime, in other words, a specific number of erase/write cycles, defragmentation shortens that lifetime.

INSIGHT

Optimizing Defragmentation

In previous versions of Windows, you opened Disk Defragmenter and then manually initiated the process of analyzing and defragmenting a disk. That process required that you back up your computer first, check the file system for errors next, and not use your computer during defragmentation, which could last for hours. In Windows Vista and Windows 7, defragmentation is automatically enabled, and Disk Defragmenter is scheduled to run every Wednesday at 1 a.m. to keep your hard disk drive optimized. If your computer is turned off at this time, Disk Defragmenter runs when you next start your computer. This feature guarantees a weekly defragmentation of your hard disk drive. You can continue to use your computer while defragmentation occurs in the background; however, defragmentation proceeds faster if the disk is not in use. You can change this schedule, and you can also manually perform a defragmentation of your hard disk drive. Before initiating a manual defragmentation, it's a good idea to check for and fix file system errors with the Error-checking tool or the Check Disk utility, and it's always a good idea to make sure you have a recent backup of your hard disk drive in case you need to restore files later.

Opening Disk Defragmenter

The time it takes to defragment a traditional hard disk drive depends on the size of the hard disk drive, the number of folders and files on the hard disk drive, the amount of storage space already in use on the hard disk drive, the amount of fragmentation that already exists on the hard disk drive, the available system resources (such as memory), and how often you run the defragmenting utility. The first time you optimize your hard disk drive with a defragmenting utility like Disk Defragmenter, it may take a long time to defragment the hard disk drive, but it is well worth the time and effort. If you run a defragmenting utility frequently, it takes less time to defragment the hard disk drive because most of the drive is already optimized. If fragmentation builds up quickly, the amount of time required to defragment the disk increases. Frequent use of the Disk Defragmenter or another defragmenting utility was important in previous versions of Windows, but as just noted, the Windows 7 and Windows Vista Disk Defragmenter automatically defragments hard disk drives every week, starting from your initial purchase of a computer, so your hard disks are constantly being optimized. Even if Windows 7 system utilities are preconfigured, it's always a good idea to verify that they are using the proper settings for your computer, operating properly, and producing the results you expect.

Disk Defragmenter does not defragment network locations, and if a program has exclusive access to a disk, then the disk cannot be defragmented. Also, the disk must use the NTFS, FAT32, or FAT file system; otherwise, you cannot defragment the disk.

Aaron recommends that you step Kimberley through the process of adjusting the schedule for Disk Defragmenter on her computer.

In the following steps, you will open Disk Defragmenter and view the current schedule for defragmenting your computer's hard disk drive. You will not defragment your hard disk drive in these steps because it could take anywhere from a few minutes to a few hours, and you have no way of knowing how long it will take. To change the schedule for defragmenting your hard disk drive, to analyze fragmentation on a drive, or to manually defragment the hard disk drive, you must log on under an Administrator account or provide Windows 7 the password of an Administrator account. If you are using a computer in a college computer lab, make sure that you have permission to open and use Disk Defragmenter. If you don't have permission, then read those steps that require Administrator credentials and examine the figures, but do not keystroke those steps.

To open Disk Defragmenter:

▶ **1.** From the Start menu, point to **All Programs**, click **Accessories**, click **System Tools**, and then click **Disk Defragmenter**. Windows 7 opens the Disk Defragmenter window. See Figure 6-17.

| Figure 6-17 | Viewing Disk Defragmenter settings |

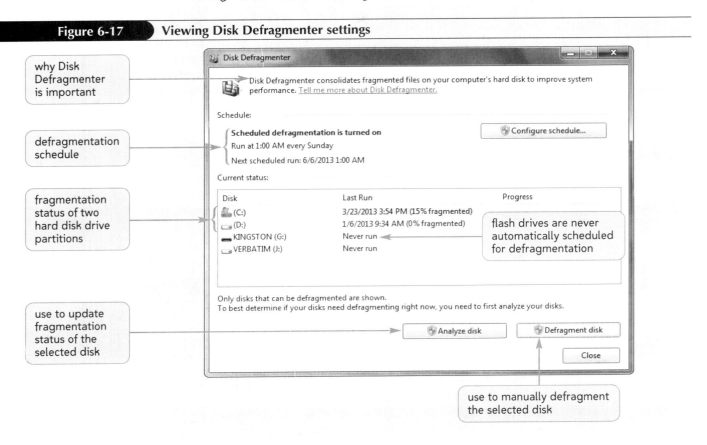

Windows 7 explains how Disk Defragmenter improves the performance of your computer by consolidating fragmented files, displays the current schedule for running Disk Defragmenter, displays the date and time of the next scheduled run, and identifies when Disk Defragmenter last defragmented each of the disks in your computer. Note that drive C has 15 percent file fragmentation, and drive D has 0 percent file fragmentation. Microsoft has recommended that you defragment a disk if file fragmentation is 10 percent or higher, so this disk is overdue for a defragmentation.

Flash drives are included in the Current status box because they can also contain fragmented files; however, Disk Defragmenter is set to never defragment a flash drive. Disk Defragmenter also notes that only disks that can be defragmented are shown under Current status. On the computer used for Figure 6-17, the schedule is the default schedule built into Windows 7. Your defragmentation schedule may differ. You can use the Configure schedule button to change the schedule and also select which drives you want to defragment on a regular basis. In Windows 7, but not Windows Vista, you can use the Analyze disk button to examine defragmentation on a disk before you defragment it. Then, if necessary, you can use the Defragment disk to initiate a defragmentation. Analyzing a disk is much faster than defragmenting a disk. Because defragmenting a disk can be time consuming, you can analyze it first and then decide whether to defragment the disk.

To examine Disk Defragmenter settings:

▶ **1.** Click the **Configure schedule** button, and if necessary, provide Administrator credentials. Windows 7 opens the Disk Defragmenter: Modify Schedule dialog box. See Figure 6-18.

Figure 6-18 | **Disk Defragmenter's schedule for defragmenting disks**

default schedule for defragmenting disks

option for selecting disk to defragment

The "Run on a schedule (recommended)" option is automatically enabled. From the Frequency box, you can choose Daily, Weekly, or Monthly. If you choose Monthly, you can choose a number from 1 to 31 using the Day menu to specify the day of the month to perform the defragmentation, or you can choose Last day for the last day of the month, whatever date that might be. If you stick with the default Weekly option, then you can choose the day of the week from the Day box. From the Time box, you can choose an hour of the day ranging from midnight to 11 pm.

▶ **2.** Click the **Select disks** button. Windows 7 opens the Disk Defragmenter: Select Disks for Schedule dialog box, and identifies all the disks currently connected to your computer that you can defragment. See Figure 6-19.

Figure 6-19 | **Disks selected for defragmentation**

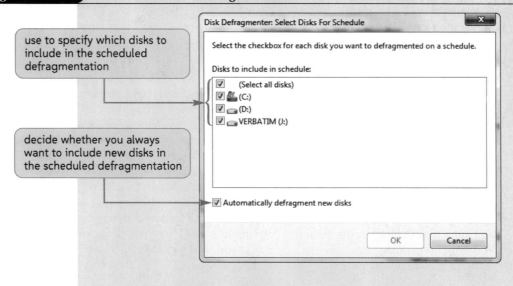

use to specify which disks to include in the scheduled defragmentation

decide whether you always want to include new disks in the scheduled defragmentation

If you click the (Select all disks) check box, then defragmentation is enabled for all disks listed in this dialog box. Or you can pick and choose which disks you want to defragment. The "Automatically defragment new disks" check box is automatically enabled; however, you can turn this option off if you prefer.

3. Click the **Cancel** button to close the Disk Defragmenter: Select Disks For Schedule dialog box without making any changes, and then click the **Cancel** button in the Disk Defragmenter: Modify Schedule dialog box without making any changes.

4. In the Current status box, select your hard disk drive (if necessary), click the **Analyze disk** button, and wait for Windows 7 to complete the disk analysis. Because you already provided Administrator credentials to configure the disk defragmentation schedule, you do not need to repeat this process to analyze or defragment a disk. Windows 7 starts analyzing the disk, and shows the percentage analyzed in the Progress column. After the analysis is complete, Windows 7 updates the date and time for the Last Run setting for the disk, and also shows the percentage fragmentation. See Figure 6-20. Drive C on the computer used for this figure is now estimated at 10 percent fragmented.

Figure 6-20	Updated fragmentation status of hard disk drive

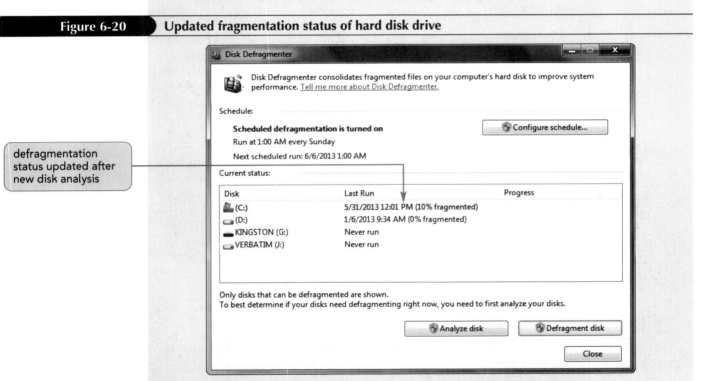

defragmentation status updated after new disk analysis

You can use the Defragment disk button to reduce the amount of fragmentation, or you can let Disk Defragmenter automatically handle fragmentation at the next scheduled run.

5. Close the Disk Defragmenter dialog box.

If you click the Defragment now button, you can close the Disk Defragmenter dialog box, and continue to work on your computer as Disk Defragmenter defragments the hard disk drive(s). Windows 7 will note that the defragmentation may take minutes or hours, depending on the amount of fragmentation on your hard disk drive(s). If you click the Defragment now button, and then change your mind, you can click the Cancel defragmentation button, and then close the Disk Defragmenter dialog box.

REFERENCE

Opening Disk Defragmenter

- From the Start menu, point to All Programs, click Accessories, click System Tools, and then click Disk Defragmenter.
- To configure the schedule for defragmenting a disk or disks, click the Configure schedule button, and if prompted, provide Administrator credentials, then decide whether to defragment disks on a schedule, and if so, use the Frequency box to specify Daily, Weekly, or Monthly. If you choose Weekly, then use the Day box to specify a day of the week. If you choose Monthly, then specify the number for the day when you want to defragment disks (or select Last day for the last day of the month). Click OK to apply any changes you made.
- To perform a disk analysis, select the disk you want to analyze in the Current status box, click the Analyze disk button, provide Administrator credentials (if prompted), wait for Windows 7 to complete the disk analysis, and then examine the percent fragmentation for that disk in the Last Run column of the Disk Defragmenter dialog box.
- If you want to perform a manual defragmentation as you work, click the Defragment disk button, and then click the Close button to close the Disk Defragmenter dialog box.

If you want to create a desktop shortcut that opens Disk Defragmenter so you can check Disk Defragmenter settings, examine the current status on defragmentation on different disks, perform a fragmentation analysis of a disk, and/or defragment a disk, right-click Disk Defragmenter on the System Tools menu, and use the Send to menu to create a desktop shortcut icon. If you view properties of this shortcut, you will discover that its target is:

%windir%\system32\dfrgui.exe

Windows 7 displays a custom icon for your new desktop shortcut, and when you click that desktop shortcut, Windows 7 automatically opens the Disk Defragmenter dialog box. Again, the windir environment variable guarantees that you can open Disk Defragmenter utility if Windows 7 is installed on another drive.

Defragmenting your hard disk drive(s) is an important process that extends the longevity of your hard disk and improves the performance of your computer and, fortunately, in Windows 7, it is now automated so you do not overlook this important type of preventive maintenance.

Using the Command-Line Defrag Utility

Windows 7, Windows Vista, and Windows XP also have a command-line utility for defragmenting a disk called Defrag. Unlike the graphical user interface version, you have more control over defragmentation using the command-line utility than you do with the graphical user interface version. Furthermore, Microsoft has expanded the capabilities of the Windows 7 Defrag utility. Using this command-line utility, you can:

- **Defragment a specific volume, all volumes, or all volumes except those specified**— You can defragment just one volume or you can defragment multiple volumes sequentially or simultaneously, the latter of which is a new Windows 7 feature. As noted earlier, by default, Disk Defragmenter only consolidates file fragments smaller than 64 MB. The option for defragmenting all volumes except those specified is also new to Windows 7.
- **Perform a fragmentation analysis of a specific volume**—The Defrag utility displays a fragmentation analysis report without defragmenting the volume. The report includes information about the volume, the amount of fragmentation, file fragmentation, folder fragmentation, free space fragmentation, and Master File Table (MFT) fragmentation. It also advises you whether you need to defragment the volume. You can also choose

which volume you want to examine. For example, you can analyze fragmentation on your hard disk drive or on an external hard disk drive. A related but new Windows 7 option allows you to also show the progress of the fragmentation analysis on a volume (i.e., the percentage completed).

- **Consolidate free space**—This new Windows 7 feature reduces free space fragmentation, consolidates most of the free space in one region, and reduces future fragmentation. That means that new files are laid down in contiguous clusters. This feature is also useful if you want to shrink a partition. When you instruct Windows 7 to shrink a partition using Disk Management, it reduces the size of the partition and, if necessary, relocates nonsystem files. Then you can set up a new partition using the space gained from shrinking an existing partition.

- **Specify normal or low priority**—If you are using your computer while also defragmenting it at the same time, then the defragmentation occurs in the background at a low priority and takes longer. This new Windows 7 option permits you to specify normal priority rather than the default priority if your computer is not currently being used for anything else and you would like to speed up the defragmentation process.

- **Force defragmentation of a volume when the free space is low**—To effectively defragment a hard disk drive, Disk Defragmenter must have access to enough unused disk space for defragmenting files. If the free space is low, defragmentation is not as effective. With this option, the Defrag utility can force defragmentation of a volume with a limited amount of free space. For effective defragmentation of a disk, Microsoft has noted that 15 percent of the hard disk drive should be free for use by Disk Defragmenter, and if possible, you should keep 30–50 percent of the hard disk drive free for sorting file fragments.

To produce a detailed fragmentation analysis report, you enter the DEFRAG command at the command prompt and then specify two switches: /A (for Analysis) and /V (for Verbose). The Analysis switch instructs the Defrag utility to analyze the volume rather than defragment it. The Verbose switch instructs the Defrag utility to provide more detailed information about the analysis than it would otherwise provide.

To use the command-line Defrag utility, you must open a Command Prompt window in Admin Approval Mode and provide Administrator credentials.

So you can more effectively analyze defragmentation on your computer, Aaron offers to demonstrate how to use the Defrag utility to produce a detailed fragmentation analysis report for your computer's hard disk drive.

In the following steps, you will open the command-line Defrag utility with Administrator credentials and produce a fragmentation analysis report for your computer's hard disk drive. If you are using a computer in a college computer lab, make sure that you have permission to open and use the command-line Defrag utility. If you don't have permission to open and use the command-line Defrag utility, or cannot provide Administrator credentials, read the following steps and examine the figures, but do not keystroke the steps.

To produce a fragmentation analysis report for a hard disk drive:

1. On the Start menu, point to **All Programs**, click **Accessories**, right-click **Command Prompt**, click **Run as administrator**, and when prompted, provide Administrator credentials. Windows 7 opens an Administrator: Command Prompt window (as evidenced by the title on the window's title bar).

2. Maximize the Administrator: Command Prompt window. Note that the Command Prompt window does not maximize in the same way that other windows maximize.

3. In the Administrator: Command Prompt window, type **DEFRAG C: /A /V** (in uppercase or lowercase) at the command-line prompt, press the **Enter** key, and wait for the fragmentation analysis report. Figure 6-21 shows a Post Defragmentation Report for a Windows 7 volume. Your fragmentation analysis results will differ.

TIP

You can also use DEFRAG C: -A -V to produce a fragmentation analysis report.

Trouble? If Windows 7 informs you that the command you entered "is not recognized as an internal or external command, operable program, or batch file," you mistyped the command, or did not include a space between the command and the drive name. Repeat Step 3, and enter the command properly.

Trouble? If Windows 7 displays a Defrag.exe - No Disk dialog box and reports there is no disk in the drive, you typed a drive name for a nonexistent drive. Click the Cancel button to close the Defrag.exe - No Disk dialog box. If necessary, open a Computer window, verify the hard disk drive's name, close the Computer window, and then repeat Step 3 with the correct drive name.

Trouble? If you see a message that informs you that the CD-ROM volumes cannot be defragmented, then you specified a drive name for a DVD or CD drive that contains a DVD or CD. If necessary, open a Computer window, verify the hard disk drive's name, close the Computer window, and then repeat Step 3 with the correct drive name.

Trouble? If you see a message that the given volume path is invalid, followed by help information on the DEFRAG command, then you did not type a colon after the drive name letter, or you typed a backslash rather than a regular slash before the switches *A* and *V*. Repeat Step 3 and enter the drive letter followed by a colon and make sure you use a regular slash before the switches *A* and *V*.

Figure 6-21 | **Fragmentation analysis of a hard disk**

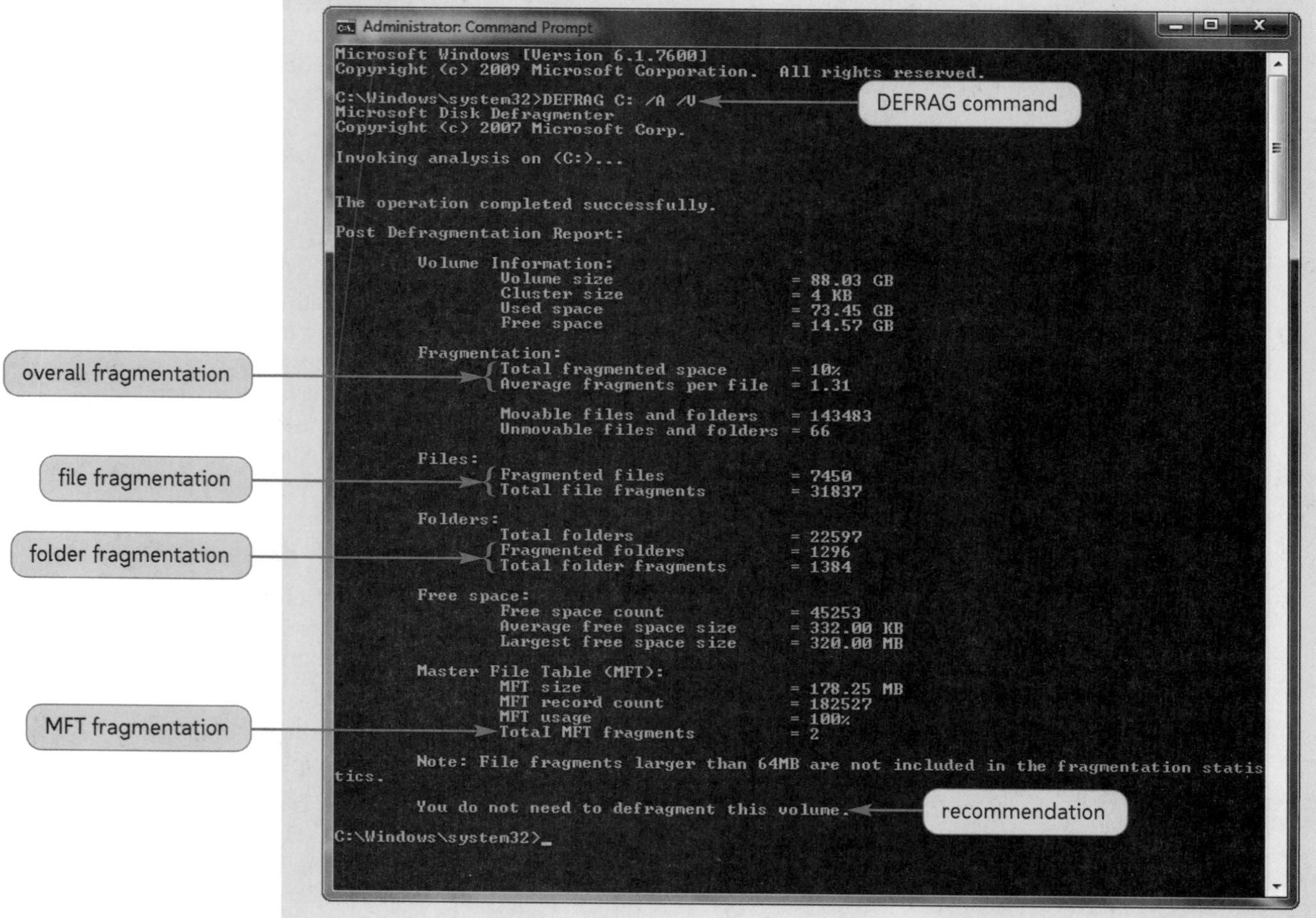

```
Administrator: Command Prompt
Microsoft Windows [Version 6.1.7600]
Copyright (c) 2009 Microsoft Corporation.  All rights reserved.

C:\Windows\system32>DEFRAG C: /A /V          ◄ DEFRAG command
Microsoft Disk Defragmenter
Copyright (c) 2007 Microsoft Corp.

Invoking analysis on (C:)...

The operation completed successfully.

Post Defragmentation Report:

        Volume Information:
                Volume size                  = 88.03 GB
                Cluster size                 = 4 KB
                Used space                   = 73.45 GB
                Free space                   = 14.57 GB

        Fragmentation:
                Total fragmented space       = 10%          ◄ overall fragmentation
                Average fragments per file   = 1.31

                Movable files and folders    = 143483
                Unmovable files and folders  = 66

        Files:
                Fragmented files             = 7450          ◄ file fragmentation
                Total file fragments         = 31837

        Folders:
                Total folders                = 22597
                Fragmented folders           = 1296          ◄ folder fragmentation
                Total folder fragments       = 1384

        Free space:
                Free space count             = 45253
                Average free space size      = 332.00 KB
                Largest free space size      = 320.00 MB

        Master File Table (MFT):
                MFT size                     = 178.25 MB
                MFT record count             = 182527
                MFT usage                    = 100%
                Total MFT fragments          = 2          ◄ MFT fragmentation

        Note: File fragments larger than 64MB are not included in the fragmentation statis
tics.

        You do not need to defragment this volume.          ◄ recommendation

C:\Windows\system32>_
```

The defragmentation analysis report is divided into these sections:

- **Volume Information**—The first section in the report provides information on the volume size, the cluster size (in kilobytes), the amount of used space, and the amount of free space. On the hard disk drive used for this fragmentation analysis shown in Figure 6-21, cluster sizes are 4 KB for the 88.03 GB Windows 7 volume (a partition on a 250 GB hard disk), meaning that there are 8 sectors per cluster (4 KB × 1,024 bytes/KB = 4,096 bytes, and 4,096 bytes ÷ 512 bytes/sector = 8 sectors per cluster.)
- **Fragmentation**—The second section of the report shows the total fragmented space, the average fragments per file, and the number of movable and unmovable files and folders. On the computer used for Figure 6-21, total fragmentation is 10 percent, the average fragments per file is 1.31, the total number of files that can be moved during fragmentation are 143,483, and the number of unmovable system files and system folders is 66. This hard disk drive's value of 1.31 indicates that 31 percent of the fragmented files, on average, are stored as two file fragments.
- **Files**—The third section of the report provides information on file fragmentation. On the hard disk drive used for Figure 6-21, there are only 7,450 fragmented files with a total of 31,837 file fragments. That translates to an average of over four fragments per fragmented file. While it might be ideal to have no fragmented files, the files that are fragmented represent only a very small fraction of the total number of files, and the files that have file fragments are likely to be greater than 64 MB in size.
- **Folders**—The fourth section of the report deals with folder fragmentation. Here, the Defrag utility reports on the total number of fragmented folders out of the total number of folders on the disk and the total number of folder fragments. On the computer used for Figure 6-21, there are 1,296 fragmented folders with a total of 1,384 folder fragments out of a total of 22,597 folders. That translates to approximately 6.1 percent folder fragmentation.
- **Free space**—The fifth part of the report focuses on free space fragmentation. On the computer used for Figure 6-21, there are 45,253 regions of free space with an average size of 332 KB per region of contiguous free space. The largest region of free contiguous space is 320 MB out of the 88.03 GB volume. The more consolidated free space you have on a disk, the less fragmentation builds up.
- **Master File Table (MFT)**—Finally, Defrag reports on the size of the MFT, the number of records within the MFT, the number of MFT records, the percentage of MFT usage, and total MFT fragments. On the computer used for Figure 6-21, the MFT is 178.25 MB in size, and contains 182,527 records. On the computer used for this figure, the MFT contains 2 file fragments.

At the bottom of this report, Windows 7 notes that file fragments larger than 64 MB are not included in the fragmentation statistics. More importantly, it informs you that you do not need to defragment this volume.

To end your command-line session:

▶ **1.** To close the Administrator: Command Prompt window, type **EXIT** and press the **Enter** key, (or click the Administrator: Command Prompt window Close button ▆▆▆).

If you decide that you want to defragment your hard disk drive after examining a defragmentation analysis, you enter the same command without the switches. You have to specify the drive. The basic command for defragmenting drive C is: DEFRAG C:
Remember that on a large volume, defragmentation can take hours.

REFERENCE

Producing a Fragmentation Analysis Report Using the Command-Line Defrag Utility

- On the Start menu, point to All Programs, click Accessories, right-click Command Prompt, and then click Run as administrator.
- In the User Account Control dialog box, click the Yes button if you are logged on under an Administrator account. If you are not logged on under an Administrator account, select an Administrator account, enter the password for that Administrator account, and then click the Yes button.
- In the Administrator: Command Prompt window, type DEFRAG C: /A /V (in uppercase or lowercase) at the command-line prompt, press the Enter key, and wait for the fragmentation analysis report.
- After examining the fragmentation analysis report, type EXIT and press the Enter key to close the Administrator: Command Prompt window.

Command-line tools can be quite powerful and can provide more options for examining, evaluating, and fine-tuning the performance of a computer. Tutorial 13 focuses on command-line tools and techniques.

Creating a Scheduled Task

You can use the Windows 7 Task Scheduler to schedule and thereby automate tasks on a computer. For example, you can schedule the Disk Cleanup utility to run at a specific time each week to guarantee that you do not forget to clean your disk of unneeded files. Like many other programs, the Disk Cleanup utility does not include a built-in scheduling feature, so you can use Task Scheduler to set up a schedule for the Disk Cleanup utility.

Aaron asks you to show Kimberley how to set up a scheduled task so she can run the Disk Cleanup utility weekly. Because you need to know the location and name of the program file for the Disk Cleanup utility to create the scheduled task, Aaron shows you how you can use the All Programs menu to locate this information.

To determine the location and program filename for the Disk Cleanup utility:

1. Open the Start menu, point to **All Programs**, click **Accessories**, click **System Tools**, right-click **Disk Cleanup**, and then click **Properties**. Windows 7 opens the Disk Cleanup Properties dialog box. See Figure 6-22.

Figure 6-22   **Locating the path to the Disk Cleanup program**

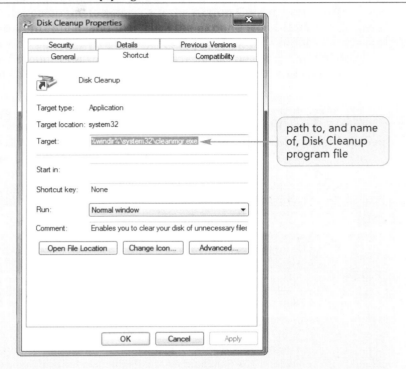

The Target box shows the full path to the Disk Cleanup utility program and the name of the program file: *%windir%\system32\cleanmgr.exe*

The program filename is cleanmgr.exe, and it is located in the System32 folder, which is located under %windir%. The windir environment variable contains the setting for the path to the folder where Windows 7 is installed. On most computers that setting is C:\Windows. Recall that the percent symbols identify *windir* as a replaceable parameter. In other words, Windows 7 replaces %windir% with the setting for the actual path to the Windows folder to determine the path for the Disk Cleanup utility program on any given computer.

▌ **2.** Close the Disk Cleanup Properties dialog box.

INSIGHT

Locating Program Names and Paths

Because the All Programs menu contains a list of all programs installed on your computer, including Windows 7 programs, you can easily locate the program name and program path for any program installed on your computer by viewing its properties. This allows you to determine not only what the program name and path is, but also to understand how the program loads. You can use this information to examine the other programs and files included with a specific program and to create scheduled tasks (which you will examine in the next session of this tutorial). This power user technique is a simple technique for locating valuable information about programs, troubleshooting programs, and modifying program properties.

Now that you know the location and name of the program for the Disk Cleanup utility, you are ready to create your scheduled task. So you can easily locate and, if necessary, modify the scheduled task later, Aaron recommends that you set up a folder for the scheduled task after you open Task Scheduler. Because you will need to open Task Scheduler in the future, Aaron recommends that you first place the Administrative Tools option on the All Programs menu and Start menu.

To place Administrative Tools on the Start and All Programs menus:

▶ **1.** Right-click the **Start** button, and then click **Properties**. Windows 7 opens the Taskbar and Start Menu Properties dialog box and displays the Start Menu tab in the foreground of the dialog box.

▶ **2.** Click the **Customize** button, scroll to the bottom of the box that lists options for customizing how links, icons, and menus look and behave on the Start menu, and under System administrative tools click the **Display on the All Programs menu and the Start menu** option button to select it (if necessary), click the **OK** button to close the Customize Start Menu dialog box, and then click the **OK** button to close the Taskbar and Start Menu Properties dialog box.

Before you create your scheduled task, Aaron suggests that you examine the scheduled task for defragmenting hard disk drives on your computer so you are familiar with how scheduled tasks are structured.

If you are working in a computer lab, ask your instructor or technical support staff whether you have permission to create a scheduled task. The lab staff might have already set up a regular maintenance schedule for each computer (including a scheduled task for the Disk Cleanup utility). If that is the case, read the steps and examine the figures so you are familiar with how to create and remove scheduled tasks, but do not keystroke the following steps.

To open Task Scheduler to view information on a scheduled task:

▶ **1.** Open the Start menu, point to **Administrative Tools**, click **Task Scheduler**, and then maximize the Task Scheduler window.

The Task Scheduler window is organized into three areas: a Scope pane on the left, an Actions pane on the right, and a Results pane in the center. See Figure 6-23.

TIP

You can also open the All Programs menu, click Accessories, click System Tools, and then click Task Scheduler.

Figure 6-23   **Task Scheduler window**

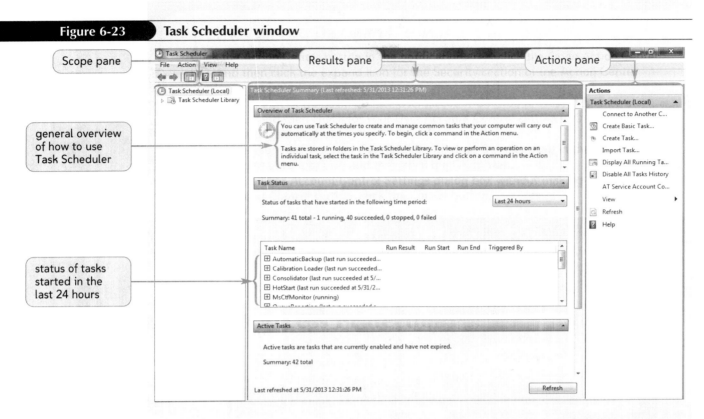

From the Scope pane, you access scheduled tasks or create scheduled tasks using the console tree (a hierarchy of folders that contain scheduled tasks). The Results pane displays detailed information about scheduled tasks. The Actions pane lists actions available to the user depending on what is selected in the Scope or Results panes.

When you first start Task Scheduler, it displays a Task Scheduler Summary in the Results pane. Under Overview of Task Scheduler, it informs you that you can use Task Scheduler to create and manage common tasks that your computer will carry out automatically at the times you specify. It also informs you that tasks are stored in folders in the Task Scheduler Library (shown in the Scope pane on the left), and that you can select a task from the Task Scheduler Library to view information about the task or to make changes to the task.

Under Task Status, Task Scheduler lists tasks (if any) that have started in the last 24 hours, and summarizes how many are running, how many succeeded, how many stopped, and how many failed. Then, you see a list of tasks by name. Note that on this computer, the last task was an automatically scheduled backup that was successfully completed.

Under Active Tasks in the Results pane, Task Scheduler notes that active tasks are ones that are currently enabled and have not expired. Your list of tasks will differ.

2. If the Scope pane is not wide enough, point to the **vertical split bar** to the right of the Scope pane toolbar, and when the mouse pointer changes to ⟺, drag the **vertical split bar** to the right so you can better see the contents of the Scope pane.

3. Click the **expand** icon ▷ to the left of **Task Scheduler Library** in the Scope pane on the left side of the window, click the **expand** icon ▷ to the left of **Microsoft**, and then click the **expand** icon ▷ to the left of **Windows** to display Windows scheduled tasks.

4. In the Scope pane, click **Defrag** under the Windows folder subnode, point to the **column border** between the Name and Status columns in the Task list at the top of the Results pane, and then double-click that **column border** to gain a best fit for the content in the Name column. Task Scheduler displays ScheduleDefrag, the name of the scheduled task in the Name column. See Figure 6-24.

Trouble? If Task Scheduler does not display any information in the Preview pane under the Task list, then click ScheduleDefrag in the Task list.

Figure 6-24   **Viewing a Windows scheduled task**

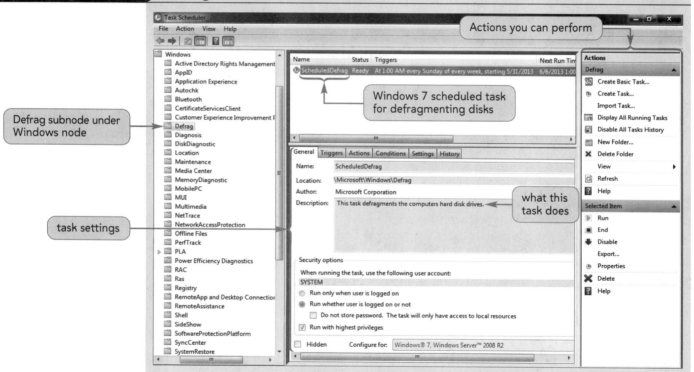

This task is set to run on the default schedule set in Windows 7. Under the Task list is a Preview pane that contains the properties and settings for a selected task. On the General tab in the Preview pane, Task Scheduler displays the name of the scheduled task, the path to the location of the scheduled task in the console tree, the task author (Microsoft Corporation), and a description identifying what the task does. Below that is an area with Security options that you'll examine later.

You can also use the same approach to view information about other scheduled Windows tasks so you better understand the conditions under which these tasks run.

REFERENCE

Viewing Information on a Windows Scheduled Task

- Open the Start menu, point to Administrative Tools, click Task Scheduler, and then maximize the Task Scheduler window.
- If the Scope pane is not wide enough, point to the vertical split bar to the right of the Scope pane toolbar, and when the mouse pointer changes to ◁➡▷, drag the vertical split bar to the right so you can better see the contents of the Scope pane.
- Click the expand icon to the left of Task Scheduler Library in the Scope pane on the left side of the window, click the expand icon to the left of the Microsoft folder subnode, and then click the expand icon to the left of the Windows folder subnode to display Windows scheduled tasks.
- In the Scope pane, click the folder subnode for a specific type of Windows task, click a task in the Task list at the top of the Results pane, and then examine the properties of the scheduled task in the Preview pane at the bottom of the Results pane.

Now you're ready to set up your scheduled task.

To create a folder subnode for your own scheduled tasks and for the Disk Cleanup scheduled task:

1. In the Scope pane, click the **collapse** icon ◢ to the left of the Windows subnode, click the **collapse** icon ◢ to the left of the Microsoft subnode, and then widen the Scope pane (if necessary).

2. Click **Task Scheduler Library** in the Scope pane, and then verify that you have selected the Task Scheduler Library node. By selecting this subnode, you ensure that the new subnodes you create are not included with the Windows folder subnodes for scheduled Windows tasks. Also, to create a task under the Windows folder subnode, you need to open Task Scheduler using Administrator credentials.

3. In the Actions pane on the right side of the window, click **New Folder**, and in the "Enter name of the new folder" dialog box, type **My Scheduled Tasks**, and then click the **OK** button. Windows creates a My Scheduled Tasks folder subnode under Task Scheduler Library.

4. Click the My Scheduled Tasks folder subnode, click **New Folder** in the Actions pane, and in the "Enter name of the new folder" dialog box, type **Disk Cleanup** in the Name box, click the **OK** button, click the **expand** icon ▷ to the right of the **My Scheduled Tasks** folder subnode, and then click the **Disk Cleanup** folder subnode.

Now, you're ready to set up the task. You can set a task to start and run daily, weekly, or monthly (common options), or you can specify that a task run only once, when the computer starts, when you log on, or when a specific event is logged. After you select the trigger for a task, you specify the name of the program or script that should run. In addition, you can include optional arguments for the program or script and specify where the task starts. A trigger can be a time-based trigger or an event-based trigger, and a scheduled task can have multiple triggers. You will examine these options as you set up a task.

TIP

To manually define a task without using the wizard, click Create Task in the Actions pane.

To create a scheduled task and specify the details for that task:

1. Click **Create Basic Task** in the Actions pane. Task Scheduler opens the Create Basic Task Wizard dialog box, as shown in Figure 6-25, and notes that you can use this wizard to quickly schedule a common task.

Figure 6-25 Specifying a name and description for a basic task

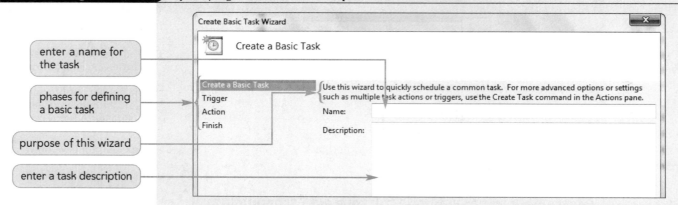

- enter a name for the task
- phases for defining a basic task
- purpose of this wizard
- enter a task description

It also notes that if you want to create a task that has multiple actions or triggers, you use the Create Task command. In this first dialog box, you type a name for the task and provide any additional information about the task in the Description box. On the left is a list of operations that you will perform as you define this task.

2. Type **Disk Cleanup** in the Name box, type **Run Disk Cleanup once a week** in the Description box, and then click the **Next** button. In the next step, you specify the Task Trigger. In other words, you specify the conditions under which you want the task to start. You can specify that the scheduled task run daily, weekly, monthly, one time, when the computer starts, when you log on, or when a specific event is logged. See Figure 6-26.

Figure 6-26 Choosing a trigger for a basic task

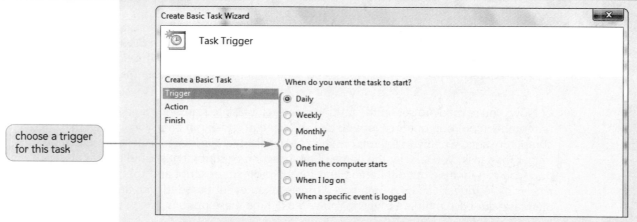

- choose a trigger for this task

3. Click the **Weekly** option button, and then click the **Next** button. In the next step, you specify the date and time for starting the task the first time, how frequently the task repeats (once a week, for example), and the day of the week for repeating the task. See Figure 6-27. In the Start box is the current date. You can use the Start arrow button to the right of the current date to display a navigable calendar so you can select the date on which you want the task to start.

Figure 6-27 Refining the trigger for a basic task

click to view a navigable calendar

choose a starting date and time, how frequently the task repeats, and a day of the week

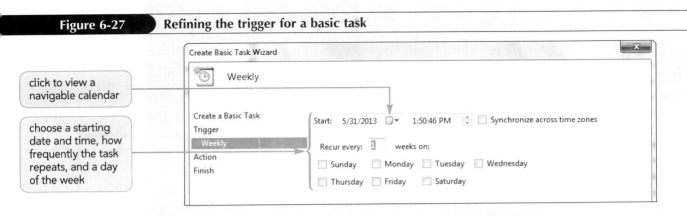

▶ **4.** Make sure the task is set to start on the current date, click the **minutes** in the time, use the **up** button to set the time so it is 5 to 10 minutes ahead of the current time (and so you can complete the remaining steps before the task is scheduled to start), click the **check box for the current day of the week**, and then click the **Next** button. In the next step, you specify what action you want the task to perform. See Figure 6-28. You can have the task start a program, send an email, or display a message.

Figure 6-28 Choosing an action for a task

pick an action for this basic task

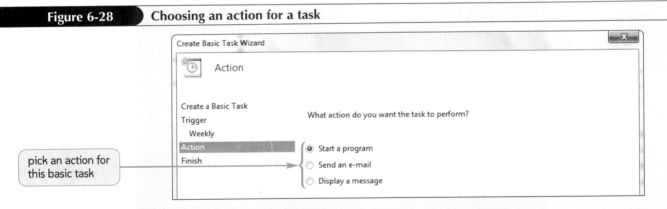

▶ **5.** Make sure the "Start a program" option button is already selected, and then click the **Next** button. In the next step, you specify the name of a program or script, and you can also add optional arguments for the program or script and specify where the task starts. See Figure 6-29.

Figure 6-29 Providing details on the program to start

enter the path to the program, or browse and locate the program

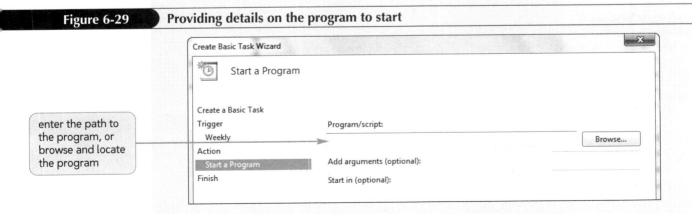

Options on this page depend on what you selected on the previous Action page. You now have to specify the path for the program that starts the Disk Cleanup utility. The program name is cleanmgr.exe, and it is stored in the Windows System32 folder. The System32 folder and its subfolders contain many of the programs and utilities provided with Windows 7, as well as important components of the operating system, such as dynamic link libraries, files with configuration settings, Control Panel components, device drivers, event logs, system files, and the Windows 7 Registry files (to name a few).

6. Click the **Browse** button. Windows 7 displays an Open dialog box and then displays the contents of the System32 folder (under the Windows folder). See Figure 6-30. Your Open dialog box may show a Date modified column.

Trouble? If Windows 7 opens a folder other than the System32 folder, then click Local Disk (C:) under Computer in the Navigation pane, click the Windows folder icon, click the System32 folder icon, and then continue with the next step.

Figure 6-30 Browsing for a program for a scheduled task

navigate to this folder (if necessary)

type the first few characters of the program filename to locate the program

7. In the File name box, type **cle** (for cleanmgr.exe), and after Windows 7 displays the program name in the Filename box, click **cleanmgr.exe**, and then click the **Open** button. Windows 7 displays the full path to the program for running the Disk Cleanup utility. See Figure 6-31.

Figure 6-31 Viewing the path to the program for this scheduled task

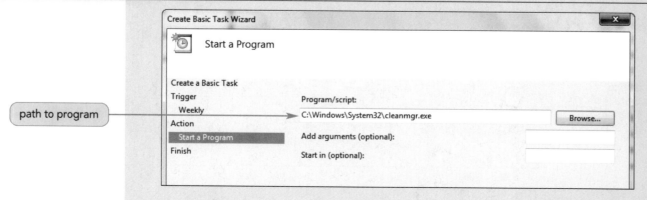

path to program

Trouble? If the path contains a program name other than cleanmgr.exe, then repeat this step and make sure you choose cleanmgr.exe before continuing to the next step.

In the Add arguments (optional) box, you can specify additional parameters, such as a switch, to change the way that a command works. For example, if you want a scheduled task to check an external hard disk drive in drive F, you would enter the Drive switch (/D) in the Add arguments (optional) box and specify the drive you want to check (/D F:). In the optional Start in box, you can specify the path to a folder where the program might need access to other files.

▶ **8.** Click the **Next** button. Windows 7 displays a summary of the options you specified for the task. See Figure 6-32. You can review these options, and if you want to make any last-minute changes, you can use the Back button to return to an earlier step, make the change, and then use the Next button to return to this summary.

Figure 6-32   **Viewing settings for a scheduled task**

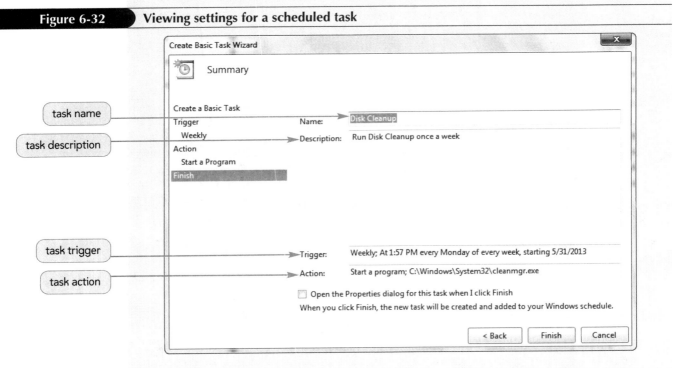

▶ **9.** Click the **Finish** button, minimize the Task Scheduler window, and then wait for the task to start. At the time you specified, Windows 7 opens the Disk Cleanup: Drive Selection dialog box. To run the Disk Cleanup utility, all you have to do is to select the drive, and then click the **OK** button.

▶ **10.** Now that you've tested the scheduled task, click the **Exit** button in the Disk Cleanup: Drive Selection dialog box.

The Create Basic Task Wizard is the easiest way to create a task.

REFERENCE

Creating a Scheduled Task

- Open the Start menu, point to Administrative Tools, click Task Scheduler, maximize the Task Scheduler window, and then click Task Scheduler Library in the Scope pane.
- In the Actions pane on the right side of the window, click New Folder, and in the "Enter name of the new folder" dialog box, type a name for a folder to hold your scheduled tasks (such as *My Scheduled Tasks*), and then click the OK button.
- In the Scope pane, click the folder subnode you just created for your own scheduled tasks, click New Folder in the Actions pane, and in the "Enter name of the new folder" dialog box, type a name for the folder subnode that will contain a specific scheduled task in the Name box, click OK, click the expand icon to the right of the folder subnode for your own scheduled tasks in the Scope pane, and then click the folder subnode for the new scheduled task you want to create.
- In the Actions pane on the right, click Create Basic Task.
- In the Create Basic Task Wizard dialog box, type a name for the task in the Name box, type a brief description about the task in the Description box (optional), and then click the Next button.
- In the next step, specify when you want the task to start by clicking the proper option button, and then click the Next button.
- In the next step, specify the trigger options for starting the task, and then click the Next button.
- In the next step, specify what action you want the task to perform (such as start a program, send an email, or display a message), and then click the Next button.
- In the next step, specify the details for the action you selected in the previous step (such as the path to a program and any optional parameters), and then click the Next button.
- In the next step, review the summary for the scheduled task, and if necessary, use the Back button to back up to a previous step to make a change, use the Next button to advance to this last step, and finally, click the Finish button.
- Close the Task Scheduler window.

Now, you can view the settings for your scheduled task.

TIP

To change settings for a scheduled task, click Properties in the Actions pane.

To view the settings for your scheduled task:

1. Click the **Task Scheduler** taskbar button to restore the Task Scheduler window.

2. Click **Disk Cleanup** in the Task list at the top of the Results pane, adjust column widths for a best fit so you can see everything in each column, and then examine the information about the task.

Task Scheduler shows the task name, the status of the task (Ready), its triggers, the next run time, the last run time, the last run result (if applicable), the author, and the date and time the task was created. (To view all these options, you must scroll to the right.) See Figure 6-33.

Figure 6-33 Viewing properties of a new task

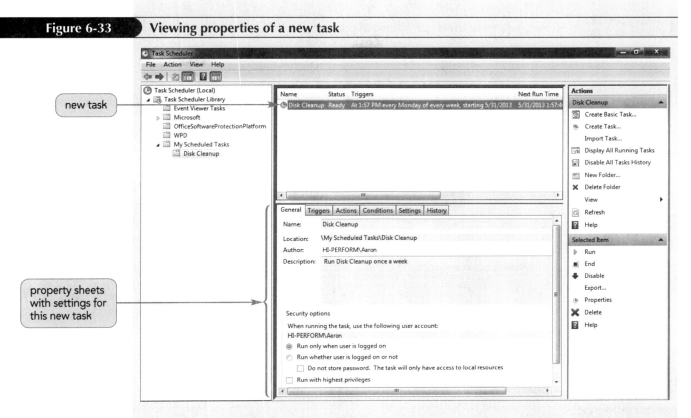

new task

property sheets with settings for this new task

In the Preview pane under the Task list, Task Scheduler displays the task name, task location (in Task Scheduler), the author, the task description, and security options associated with the task. This scheduled task is set to run only when the user is logged on the computer.

3. Click the **Triggers** tab. Task Scheduler shows how frequently the task is triggered, details on the task (including the time and day of the week the task is designated to start, the starting task date, and whether the task is enabled and active).

4. Click the **Actions** tab. Task Scheduler identifies the type of action performed by this task (in this case, start a program), and the path to the program opened by this task.

5. Click the **Conditions** tab. Task Scheduler identifies any other conditions associated with starting the task, such as how the task operates when the computer is idle, how the power state affects the task, and whether a network connection is needed. This scheduled task starts only if the computer is on AC power, and it stops if the computer switches to battery power.

6. Click the **Settings** tab. Task Scheduler lists any additional settings that affect the behavior of the task. This scheduled task runs on demand, the task will stop if it runs longer than three days, and if the task does not end when requested, Windows 7 will force it to stop.

7. Click the **History** tab, wait for Windows 7 to compile a list of events associated with this task, click **Information** under the Level column, and then adjust all column widths for a best fit. Task Scheduler identifies a list of events associated with this task, such as when the task was initially registered (defined), when the task started, and when the task completed. See Figure 6-34.

Trouble? If the History tab is labeled "History (disabled)," then click "Enable All Tasks History" in the Actions pane.

Figure 6-34 **History property sheet for scheduled task**

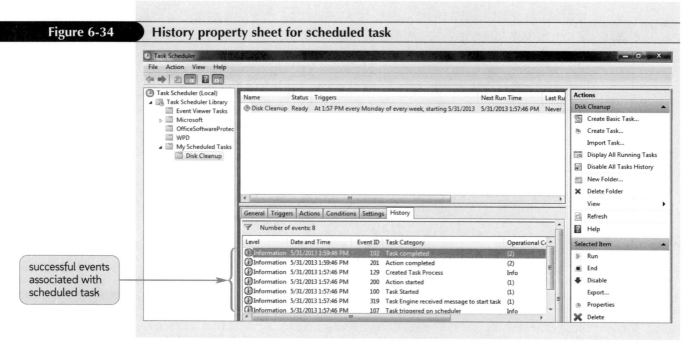

successful events
associated with
scheduled task

If you select a task, and then click Properties in the Actions pane, Task Scheduler will
display the same information in a Disk Cleanup Properties (Local Computer) dialog box,
as shown in Figure 6-35.

Figure 6-35 **Viewing properties of a scheduled task that you can edit**

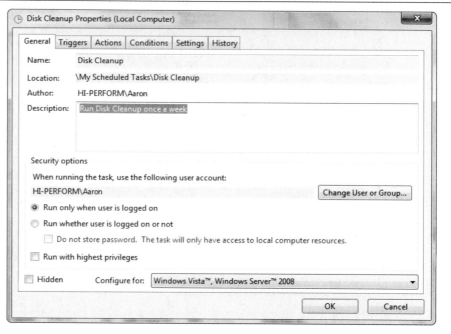

You can examine and make changes to the task from this task's Properties dialog
box. Options that were not available when you created the task with the Task Scheduler
Wizard are available here, so you can fine-tune settings for a task. You can also just
double-click the task in the Task List to access these same task properties.

REFERENCE

Checking Settings for a Scheduled Task

- From the Start menu, point to Administrative Tools, and click Task Scheduler.
- Click the expand icon to the left of Task Scheduler Library in the Scope pane on the left side of the window.
- Click the folder subnode where you stored the task, and if necessary, select the task in the Task list in the Results pane.
- Click the General, Triggers, Actions, Conditions, Settings, and History tabs to view detailed information about the task.
- To view properties of the task and modify task settings, click Properties in the Action menu, or double-click the scheduled task in the Task list in the Results pane, and then review details about the task.

After you create a scheduled task, you may want to delete it. In the next set of steps, you will delete the Disk Cleanup scheduled task to restore your computer to its original state.

To delete your scheduled task:

1. If you opened the Disk Cleanup Properties (Local Computer) dialog box, click its **Cancel** button to close it without applying any changes.

2. Click **Disk Cleanup** in the Task list in the Results pane, verify that you selected the Disk Cleanup task under the Disk Cleanup folder under the My Scheduled Tasks subnode, click **Delete** under Selected Item in the Actions pane, and in the Task Scheduler dialog box, click the **Yes** button.

3. Click the **Disk Cleanup** folder under the My Scheduled Tasks subnode in the Scope pane, verify that you selected the Disk Cleanup folder, click **Delete Folder** in the Actions pane, and then click the **Yes** button in the Task Scheduler dialog box.

4. Click the **My Scheduled Tasks** folder subnode under Task Scheduler Library in the Scope pane, verify that you selected the My Scheduled Tasks folder, click **Delete Folder** in the Actions pane, and then click the **Yes** button in the Task Scheduler dialog box.

5. Close the Task Scheduler window.

You might have more than one task in the same folder, so you should always select the folder, and then select and delete the task first. If the folder has only one task (and you've deleted that task), you can then delete the folder if you do not want to keep it.

Deleting a Scheduled Task

- From the Start menu, point to Administrative Tools, and click Task Scheduler.
- In the Task Scheduler window, click the expand icon to the left of Task Scheduler Library in the Scope pane on the left side of the window, and repeat this process to locate the folder subnode that contains the task you want to delete.
- Click the task name in the Task list in the Results pane, click Delete under Selected Item in the Actions pane, and in the Task Scheduler dialog box, click the Yes button.
- If there is only one task in the folder, and if you want to delete the folder subnode as well, click the folder subnode name in the Scope pane that contained the scheduled task, click Delete Folder in the Actions pane, and in the Task Scheduler dialog box click the Yes button.
- Close the Task Scheduler window.

The easiest way to create a Task Scheduler desktop shortcut is to right-click Task Scheduler on the Administrative Tools menu, and use the Send to menu to create a desktop shortcut with a custom icon. If you view properties of the shortcut, you will discover that the command for target of the Task Scheduler shortcut is:

%windir%\system32\taskschd.msc /s

Windows 7 displays a custom icon for your new desktop shortcut, and when you click that desktop shortcut, Windows 7 automatically opens Task Scheduler.

Problem Solving: Automating Routine Operations

You can schedule tasks for other important types of operations, such as sending a monthly email reminder about a staff or workgroup meeting, opening your email Web site at a specific time (or times) each day, opening a document or a set of documents at the same time each day, opening your Internet security or antivirus software so you can perform a full scan of your computer, opening Disk Defragmenter each month so you can initiate a defragmentation analysis of your hard disk drive, and opening Windows Update so you can manually check Windows Update and decide which ones you want to download (rather than have all updates downloaded and installed automatically). You can also modify predefined scheduled tasks, such as the one for defragmenting your hard disk drive. If you discover that you are routinely performing the same operation on a regular basis, you can create a scheduled task to start the program you use for this. By automating routine operations with scheduled tasks, you can use your time more efficiently and be more productive and focus on your work. Plus, scheduled tasks serve as a valuable reminder for performing certain tasks, such as preventive maintenance.

Restoring Your Computer's Settings

If you are working in a computer lab, or if you want to restore your desktop computer to the settings that existed prior to working on this tutorial, complete the following steps.

To restore your computer's settings:

▶ **1.** If necessary, use the Folder Options dialog box to turn off single-click activation (Web style) and the option for displaying file extensions, and then use the Start menu to turn off the display of the Computer icon on the desktop.

▶ **2.** If you want to remove Administrative Tools from the Start menu, right-click the **Start** button, click **Properties**, click the **Customize** button on the Start Menu property sheet, scroll to the bottom of the list of options for customizing the Start menu, click the **Don't display this item** option button under System administrative tools, click the **OK** button to close the Customize Start Menu dialog box, and then click the **OK** button to close the Taskbar and Start Menu Properties dialog box.

▶ **3.** Use Safely Remove Hardware and Eject Media to remove your flash drive.

REVIEW

Session 6.2 Quick Check

1. If a file is stored in noncontiguous clusters, the file is _____.
2. What two types of fragmentation can arise on a hard disk drive?
3. Microsoft recommends that you defragment a disk if the fragmentation is greater than _____.
4. How can you produce a fragmentation analysis report of a drive with the Defrag command-line utility?
5. True or False. The Master File Table (MFT) on an NTFS volume cannot be fragmented.
6. If you need to perform the same operation at regular intervals on your computer, what can you do to automate that operation?
7. What is an event?
8. What is a scheduled task trigger?

Practice the skills you learned in the tutorial using the same case scenario.

PRACTICE

Review Assignments

There are no Data Files needed for the Review Assignments.

Aaron just hired Michael Everett to assist him with his duties. After showing Mike his desk and his computer system, Aaron asks you to show Mike how to perform a thorough check of his computer and customize it for his new job.

If possible, use a computer that is different from the one that you used for the tutorial so you can compare your results with those from the tutorial. Also, to perform some of these operations, you must log on as Administrator or under a user account with Administrator privileges.

As you complete each step, record your answers to the questions so you can submit them to your instructor. Use a word-processing application such as Microsoft Word or the WordPad accessory to prepare your answers to these questions. If you change any settings on the computer you are using, make a note of the original settings so you can restore them later. Complete the following steps:

1. Open a Computer window, and if necessary, switch to Tiles view. If Windows 7 does not organize drives by type, right-click the folder window background, point to Group by, and then click Type. (*Note:* If Type is not available on the Group by menu, select More, choose Type in the Choose Details dialog box, and then apply the change.) How many hard disk drives does your computer have, and what are their names? Are these drives internal or external hard disk drives? Point to and select each hard disk drive icon, and then examine the information in the Details pane. What file system does each hard disk drive use? What is the total storage capacity of each hard disk drive?

2. If you have one hard disk drive, select it; if you have two or more hard disk drives, select a hard disk drive that you did not use in the tutorial, and then open and run the Disk Cleanup utility. What hard disk drive did you check? How much storage space can the Disk Cleanup utility free on your hard disk drive? What types of files does it propose to remove? If you can provide Administrator credentials, choose the option to "Clean up system files." How much storage space can you now recover, and what additional categories of files (if any) does the Disk Cleanup utility identify? After you finish using the Disk Cleanup utility, close it, and then close the Properties dialog box for the drive.

3. Suppose you open a file named Sales Projection Memo.docx, and then notice another file named ~$les Projection Memo.docx in the folder window with the Sales Projection Memo.docx file. What type of file is ~$les Projection Memo.docx? If you close Sales Projection Memo.docx, what happens to ~$les Projection Memo.docx?

4. Run the Error-checking tool on your flash drive in read-only or diagnostic mode by turning off the options for automatically fixing file system errors and for scanning for and attempting recovery of bad sectors. Then, view details of the scan. Did the Error-checking tool find any problems? If so, what were the problems? How many bytes of storage space are allocated in each cluster (or allocation unit)? How many sectors are in each cluster (or allocation unit) on the flash drive? After you finish using the Error-checking tool, close any open dialog boxes or windows.

5. Open and then maximize a Command Prompt window. Use the command-line Check Disk utility without any switches to check the same flash drive for errors in read-only or diagnostic mode (without making any changes to the flash drive). Make sure you specify the flash drive name as it may be different from the default drive used by Windows 7 in the Command Prompt window. What file system is used on your flash drive? Does Check Disk report any errors or problems? If so, what are they? What is the total disk space on the flash drive? Close the Command Prompt window.

6. Open Disk Defragmenter. Is Disk Defragmenter automatically enabled on your computer, and if so, what is its schedule? What disks can you defragment on your computer? What disks does it automatically check? Select your flash drive, provide Administrator credentials (if necessary), and then analyze the flash drive for fragmentation. What is the percentage of fragmentation? Close the Disk Defragmenter dialog box.

7. Open, and then maximize an Administrator: Command Prompt window. Enter the command for producing a fragmentation analysis report for your flash drive (using Verbose mode). What command did you enter to perform this operation? List your answers to the following questions:

   - What is the volume size?
   - What is the cluster size?
   - What is the total fragmented space?
   - What are the average fragments per file?
   - What is the total number of fragmented files?
   - What is the total number of fragmented folders?
   - What is the largest free space size?
   - Does Disk Defragmenter recommend that you defragment this volume?
   - If you wanted to defragment the flash drive, what command would you enter?

   Close the Administrator: Command Prompt window.

8. If you are working in a computer lab, before using Task Scheduler, obtain permission from your instructor or technical support staff to use the Task Scheduler to schedule a task. Open Task Scheduler, expand the Task Scheduler Library subnode in the Scope pane, create a new subnode folder named Clean Disks, and then select the Clean Disks folder.

9. Use the Start menu Disk Cleanup shortcut to determine the path for the Disk Cleanup utility. What is its path?

10. Use the Create Basic Task Wizard to schedule the following task:

    - Open the Clean Disks folder you created in Step 8, and then create a basic task named **Disk Cleanup** with a daily trigger.
    - Set the start time so it is five to ten minutes later than the current time (so you have enough time to finish creating the scheduled task before it starts).
    - Specify the action for starting a program, and then locate the cleanmgr.exe program by browsing.
    - Complete the process for creating this scheduled task.

11. Wait for Windows 7 to start the scheduled task. What drive(s) can you select? Close the Disk Cleanup Options dialog box.

12. Maximize the Task Scheduler window, select the newly scheduled Disk Cleanup task in the Results pane, and then answer the following questions:

    - Who is identified as the author on the General property sheet?
    - What user account does this task use when it runs?
    - Under Security Options, what condition must be met for this task to run?
    - Select the Conditions property sheet. Under what power conditions will the task start or stop? Does the task need a network connection?

13. Select and delete the Disk Cleanup task, delete the Clean Disks folder that you created for this task, and then close the Task Scheduler window.

14. Which of the techniques covered in this tutorial have you used in the last three months to optimize the storage of files on your hard disk drive and also optimize the performance of your computer? Are there any techniques or tasks that you want to implement in the future? Explain.

15. Use Safely Remove Hardware and Eject Media to remove your flash drive.

16. Submit your answers to the questions in this Review Assignment to your instructor, either in printed or electronic form, as requested. Remember to include on your assignment your name and any other information requested by your instructor.

Use your skills to analyze a hard disk drive for errors.

APPLY

Case Problem 1

There are no Data Files needed for this Case Problem.

Dubuisson International Foods, Inc. Jacquelyn Dubuisson is the owner and manager of Dubuisson International Foods, Inc. Like many small businesses, she and her staff depend on their computers to track and fulfill orders as well as manage all financial transactions. Recently, she's experienced some problems accessing files on her computer, so she asks you to check the hard disk drive on her computer to make sure it is functioning properly.

To complete this case problem, you may need to provide Administrator credentials to run the Error-checking tool on your hard disk drive and to open an Administrator: Command Prompt window and use the command-line Check Disk utility. If you are working in a computer lab, make sure you have permission to use the Error-checking tool and the command-line Check Disk utility to examine a computer's hard disk drive.

As you complete each step, record your answers to the questions so you can submit them to your instructor. Use a word-processing application such as Microsoft Word or the WordPad accessory to prepare your answers to these questions. If you change any settings on the computer you are using, make a note of the original settings so you can restore them later. Complete the following steps:

1. View the General property sheet for Local Disk (C:). What is the total storage capacity of this drive? How much storage space on the drive is already used? How much is available?

2. From the Tools property sheet for your hard disk drive, choose the option for running the Error-checking tool, provide Administrator credentials, and then turn off the option for automatically fixing file system errors so you can perform a read-only or diagnostic check of the drive, and then run the Error-checking tool. If you did not turn off the option for automatically fixing file system errors, what would happen?

3. After the disk check is complete, choose the option to view details of the operation. Did the Error-checking tool find any problems? If so, describe the problem(s).

4. From the detailed check disk results, answer the following questions:
   - How many file records did the Check Disk utility process?
   - How many index entries did it process?
   - How many files with security descriptors did it process?
   - How many kilobytes are in use by the system?
   - What is the size of each allocation unit (or cluster) in bytes and in sectors?

5. Close the Checking Disk Local Disk (C:) dialog box, close the Properties dialog box for Local Disk (C:), and then close the Computer window.

EXPLORE

6. Open and then maximize an Administrator: Command Prompt window. Enter the command **HELP CHKDSK** to display Help information on the use of the command-line Check Disk utility. What is the purpose of this utility? What does the /F switch do? What does the /R switch do? What does the /B switch do?

7. Enter the **CHKDSK C:** command. What file system does the Check Disk utility report for your hard disk drive? How do you know that Check Disk performed a read-only or diagnostic check of your hard disk drive? Did the Check Disk utility find any problems? If so, describe them. How many kilobytes in bad sectors are there on the hard disk drive? Do the Check Disk results match what you found by using the Error-checking tool?

8. If the Check Disk utility found a problem with the file system, what steps would you take to repair that problem?

9. Close the Administrator: Command Prompt window, and if necessary, use Safely Remove Hardware and Eject Media to remove your flash drive.

10. Submit your answers to this case problem to your instructor, either in printed or electronic form, as requested. Remember to include on your assignment your name and any other information requested by your instructor.

Use your skills to analyze disk fragmentation.

APPLY

Case Problem 2

There are no Data Files needed for this Case Problem.

McCuen Refinancing Specialists   Jarod McCuen assists homeowners in refinancing the mortgages on their homes so they can switch from an adjustable rate mortgage to a fixed rate mortgage. Recently, Jarod noticed a slowdown in the performance of his computer, so he asks you to help him analyze fragmentation on his computer. You decide to use the command-line Defrag utility because it provides more information than the Disk Defragmenter GUI version.

To complete this case problem, you must provide Administrator credentials to open an Administrator: Command Prompt window and use the command-line Defrag utility. If you are working in a computer lab, make sure you have permission to use the command-line Defrag utility to analyze a computer's hard disk drive.

As you complete each step, record your answers to the questions so you can submit them to your instructor. Use a word-processing application such as Microsoft Word or the WordPad accessory to prepare your answers to these questions. If you change any settings on the computer you are using, make a note of the original settings so you can restore them later. Complete the following steps:

1. View the General property sheet for your hard disk drive. What file system does this drive use? What is the total storage capacity of this drive? How much storage space on the drive is already used? How much is available?

2. Open an Administrator: Command Prompt from the Accessories menu, and then maximize the window.

⊕ EXPLORE

3. Enter the command **DEFRAG HELP** to display Help information on the use of the command-line Defrag utility. What is the purpose of this utility? What is the purpose of the /A switch? What is the purpose of the /V switch?

4. Enter the following command, and be patient: **DEFRAG C: /A /V**

5. Using the fragmentation analysis report, list your results for the following items in the Analysis report:
   - Volume size
   - Cluster size
   - Total fragmented space
   - Average fragments per file
   - Fragmented files
   - Total file fragments
   - Total folders
   - Fragmented folders
   - Total folder fragments
   - Average free space size
   - Largest free space size
   - MFT size

- MFT record count
- Total MFT fragments

6. From the information you've examined thus far, calculate the following information:
   - Cluster size (in sectors/cluster)
   - Percentage of used disk space
   - Percentage of unused disk space
   - Average number of file fragments per fragmented file
   - Average number of folder fragments per fragmented folder

7. Using the information in the Analysis report, answer the following questions and note which information in the fragmentation analysis report led you to your conclusion:
   - What would you conclude about file fragmentation on your computer?
   - What would you conclude about folder fragmentation on your computer?
   - What would you conclude about free space fragmentation on your computer?

8. Do you need to defragment this volume? Explain how you arrived at this conclusion.

9. Close the Administrator: Command Prompt window, and if necessary, use Safely Remove Hardware and Eject Media to remove your flash drive.

10. Submit your answers to this case problem to your instructor, either in printed or electronic form, as requested. Remember to include on your assignment your name and any other information requested by your instructor.

Use your skills to create a scheduled task.

APPLY

Case Problem 3

There are no Data Files needed for this Case Problem.

Vasquez Pharmaceuticals Vasquez Pharmaceuticals is a major distributor of low-cost pharmaceuticals and medical supplies for hospitals, clinics, and healthcare services throughout Latin America. Danielle Diaz, a healthcare services manager, wants to optimize the availability of disk storage space on her computer by removing unneeded files daily from not only her internal hard disk drive but also her external hard disk drive. She decides to create scheduled tasks that automatically start the Disk Cleanup Wizard each Friday afternoon and check a specific hard disk drive.

If you are working in a computer lab, make sure you have permission to use Task Scheduler to create a scheduled task.

As you complete each step, record your answers to the questions so you can submit them to your instructor. Use a word-processing application such as Microsoft Word or the WordPad accessory to prepare your answers to these questions. If you change any settings on the computer you are using, make a note of the original settings so you can restore them later. Complete the following steps:

1. If necessary, add Administrative Tools to the Start menu, and then open Task Scheduler.

2. In the Task Scheduler Library, create a new folder named **Preventive Maintenance** for these scheduled tasks, expand the Task Scheduler Library subnode, and then select the Preventive Maintenance subnode folder.

⊕ **EXPLORE**

3. In the Action pane, choose the Create Task option (*not* the Create Basic Task option).
   a. On the General property sheet, enter **Clean Up Drive C** as the task name, and enter **Check drive C for unneeded files** as the task description.
   b. Use the "Configure for" option to configure the task for Windows 7.

     c. Select the Triggers property sheet, and use the New button to specify the following conditions:

- Begin the task: On a schedule
- Settings: Daily, starting 10 minutes from the current time on the *current date*
- Close the New Trigger dialog box and save the settings you've specified.

     d. Select the Actions property sheet, and use the New button to specify the following action:

- Action: Start a program
- Program/script: Browse for, and select, the program cleanmgr.exe in the Windows System 32 folder, and then choose the option to open that program.
- To automatically check drive C, enter: **/D C:** in the Add arguments (optional) box, and then save the new action you specified.

     e. Select the Settings property sheet, and specify the following settings:
Enable: Run task as soon as possible after a scheduled start is missed

4. Save the settings you specified, and then wait for the scheduled task to begin. What types of files does the Disk Cleanup utility propose to remove from your computer, and how much storage space will you gain? Decide whether you want to remove the files identified by the Disk Cleanup utility, and then close the Disk Cleanup dialog box.

⊕ **EXPLORE**   5. Assume you have an external hard disk drive named Local Disk (D:), and you want to create a second scheduled task for the Disk Cleanup utility. What optional argument would you specify for the action of the second scheduled task? *Note:* If you have an external hard disk drive, and want to create a second scheduled task for this drive, adjust the trigger for the drive C scheduled task so it will start in about 5 or 10 minutes (depending on how long you think you will need to set up the second scheduled task). Create a second scheduled task using the same approach you used for the first scheduled task, and then set the trigger for the scheduled task so it starts shortly after the scheduled task for your internal hard disk drive. After the first task opens, complete that task, wait for the next scheduled task, and then complete that scheduled task.

6. What new features did you learn about by completing this case problem, and will these features benefit you in your job or on your own computer?

7. Delete the scheduled task(s) that you just created in the Preventive Maintenance folder, delete the Preventive Maintenance folder, and then close Task Scheduler. If necessary, use Safely Remove Hardware and Eject Media to remove your flash drive.

8. Submit your answers to this case problem to your instructor, either in printed or electronic form, as requested. Remember to include on your assignment your name and any other information requested by your instructor.

Use your skills to create shortcuts for optimizing a client's hard disk drive.

APPLY

Case Problem 4

There are no Data Files needed for this Case Problem.

Troy Hansen Computer Consulting As a self-employed computer consultant, Troy Hansen helps his clients customize and streamline their computer systems. Troy's newest client is always looking for new techniques that will allow him to access disk tools that optimize the performance of his computer. Troy asks you to show the client how to create shortcuts that will allow him to quickly clean up files on his internal and external hard disk drives.

As you complete each step, record your answers to the questions so you can submit them to your instructor. Use a word-processing application such as Microsoft Word or the WordPad accessory to prepare your answers to these questions. If you change any settings on the computer you are using, make a note of the original settings so you can restore them later. Complete the following steps:

⊕ **EXPLORE**

1. Use the Create Shortcut wizard to create a desktop shortcut for the Disk Cleanup utility. Use the following path to specify that it check drive C, and then name your shortcut **Clean Up Drive C:**

   %windir%\system32\cleanmgr.exe /d c:

   Note: This is the same path you specified for the Disk Cleanup scheduled task in the tutorial. However, it now includes a switch for specifying the drive to automatically check.

2. Test your new desktop shortcut and describe what happens. List the files the Disk Cleanup utility proposes to delete, and the total amount of storage space you will gain. Remove any files you no longer need.

3. Why might you use %windir% instead of C:\Windows in the path for this shortcut?

4. View properties of the shortcut, and identify where this shortcut gets its icon. What is the path for the file that contains this icon? Close the Change Icon and Clean Up Drive C Properties dialog boxes.

⊕ **EXPLORE**

5. If you have an external hard disk drive, make a duplicate copy of the Clean Up Drive C shortcut, and then change the name of the shortcut so it refers to the drive name for your external hard disk drive. View properties of this new shortcut, change the target path so it uses the drive name for your external hard disk drive. What is the final path for the shortcut's target? Close the shortcut's Properties dialog box, and save your changes. Test your new desktop shortcut, and describe what happens. List the files the Disk Cleanup utility proposes to delete, and the total amount of storage space you will gain. Remove any files you no longer need.

6. If you no longer need the two desktop shortcuts you created, select and delete them.

7. If necessary, use Safely Remove Hardware and Eject Media to remove your flash drive.

8. Submit your answers to this case problem to your instructor, either in printed or electronic form, as requested. Remember to include on your assignment your name and any other information requested by your instructor.

ENDING DATA FILES

There are no ending Data Files needed for this tutorial.

Enhancing Computer Security

Protecting Computer Data

OBJECTIVES

Session 7.1
- Use the Action Center to evaluate your computer's security
- Examine firewall settings
- Check Windows Update settings and update history
- Verify virus protection and spyware settings
- Explore user accounts and User Account Control
- Create a password reset disk

Session 7.2
- Compare Internet Explorer security zones
- Enable SmartScreen Filter, Pop-up Blocker, and InPrivate Filtering
- Manage add-ons
- Develop a strategy for managing cookies
- Delete your browsing history
- Use InPrivate Browsing

Case | *Joyner Security Consulting Services, Inc.*

Joyner Security Consulting Services specializes in computer security and privacy services for global companies, small businesses, and nonprofit organizations. Arielle Joyner, the founder and president, relies on a small staff of dedicated professionals and skilled contractors to handle the security needs of a variety of clients. To enhance your major in computer security with real-world experience, you have enrolled in a college work-experience program that recently placed you as an intern with Joyner Security. Arielle Joyner asks you to work directly with her to evaluate the computer security and privacy settings on the computer systems for a new client.

In this tutorial you evaluate your computer's security with the Windows 7 Action Center, and you check your firewall and Windows Update settings as well as your Windows Update history. You examine malware and other types of threats posed by malicious Web sites. You explore the importance and use of user accounts and User Account Control, and you create a password reset disk for your user account. You compare Internet Explorer security zones and Protected Mode. You enable the Internet Explorer SmartScreen Filter to identify unsafe Web sites, Pop-up Blocker to block pop-up windows, and InPrivate Filtering to identify content providers tracking your Web browsing habits from site to site. You examine Internet Explorer add-ons to determine their purpose and use, and you develop a strategy for managing cookies. Finally, you learn how to use InPrivate Browsing to browse the Internet without leaving any record of the Web sites that you visit.

STARTING DATA FILES

There are no starting Data Files needed for this tutorial.

SESSION 7.1 VISUAL OVERVIEW

The Windows 7 **Action Center** contains information about security settings and security problems on your computer.

A **firewall** is a program that protects your computer by monitoring incoming traffic from the Internet or a network and by monitoring outgoing traffic from your computer to the Internet or a network. Windows 7 provides its own firewall called Windows Firewall.

The Action Center identifies your virus protection status and your antivirus software. A **computer virus** is a program that can damage or adversely affect the performance of a computer or its security. **Antivirus software** protects you against computer viruses and other types of malicious software.

Spyware is software that monitors the Web sites you visit and sends information about your browsing habits to a Web site without your knowledge or consent.

User Account Control (UAC) is a Windows 7 security feature that prompts you for Administrator credentials when you attempt to perform an operation on your computer that changes system settings and affects its security.

A **security shield icon** identifies Windows 7 settings that require you to provide Administrator credentials before you can change those settings.

Network Access Protection (NAP) checks a computer's security settings and installed software to make sure it is secure before it's connected to a network, and if necessary, updates that computer's software and security settings.

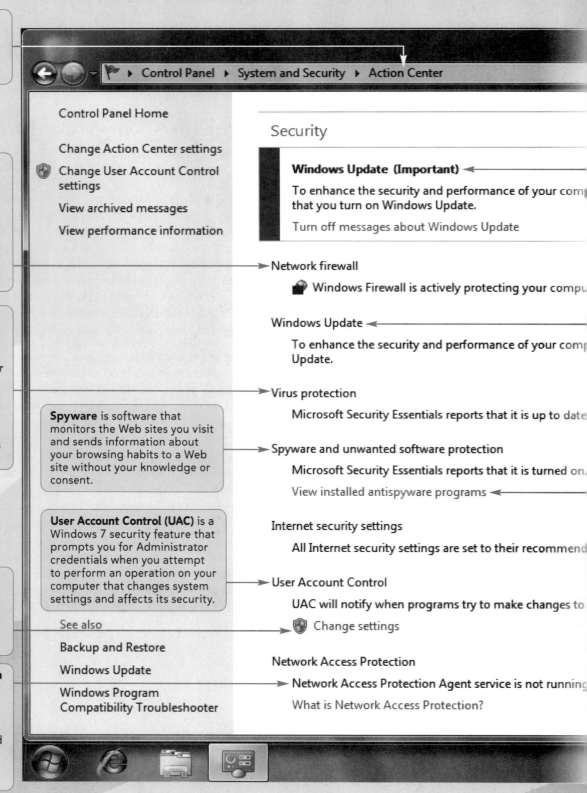

▸ Control Panel ▸ System and Security ▸ Action Center

Control Panel Home

Change Action Center settings

Change User Account Control settings

View archived messages

View performance information

See also

Backup and Restore

Windows Update

Windows Program Compatibility Troubleshooter

Security

Windows Update (Important)

To enhance the security and performance of your com that you turn on Windows Update.

Turn off messages about Windows Update

Network firewall

Windows Firewall is actively protecting your compu

Windows Update

To enhance the security and performance of your com Update.

Virus protection

Microsoft Security Essentials reports that it is up to date

Spyware and unwanted software protection

Microsoft Security Essentials reports that it is turned on.

View installed antispyware programs

Internet security settings

All Internet security settings are set to their recommend

User Account Control

UAC will notify when programs try to make changes to

Change settings

Network Access Protection

Network Access Protection Agent service is not running

What is Network Access Protection?

ACTION CENTER

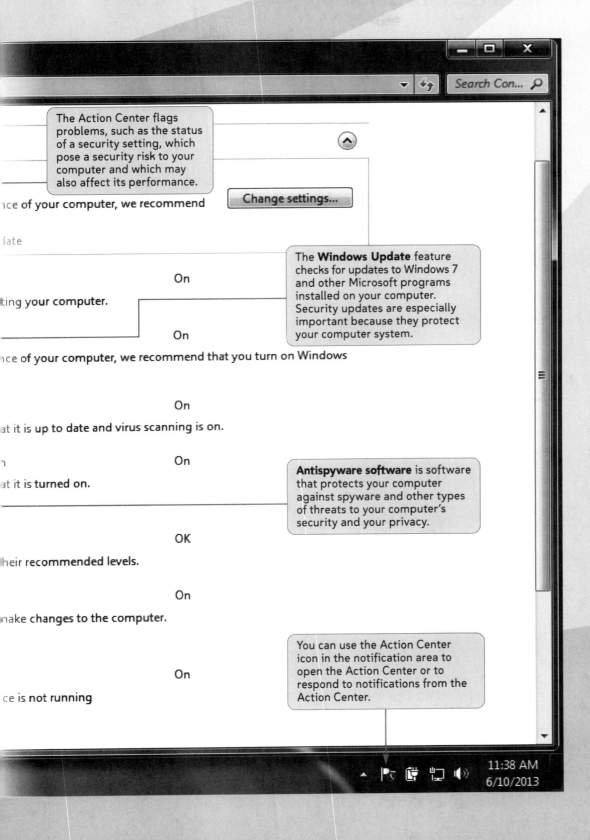

The Action Center flags problems, such as the status of a security setting, which pose a security risk to your computer and which may also affect its performance.

Change settings...

ce of your computer, we recommend

date

On

ting your computer.

On

ce of your computer, we recommend that you turn on Windows

The **Windows Update** feature checks for updates to Windows 7 and other Microsoft programs installed on your computer. Security updates are especially important because they protect your computer system.

On

at it is **up to date** and virus scanning is on.

On

at it is **turned on.**

Antispyware software is software that protects your computer against spyware and other types of threats to your computer's security and your privacy.

OK

heir recommended levels.

On

make changes to the computer.

You can use the Action Center icon in the notification area to open the Action Center or to respond to notifications from the Action Center.

On

ce is **not running**

11:38 AM
6/10/2013

Using the Action Center to Evaluate Your Computer's Security Settings

Today, computer security and privacy are the most important issues facing computer users connecting to the Internet and browsing the World Wide Web. In each new version of Windows and Internet Explorer, Microsoft Corporation has introduced new security and privacy features and enhanced existing security and privacy features. To effectively manage your privacy and the security of your computer, it's important to understand, check, and maximize your use of the privacy and security features in Windows 7.

You use the Windows 7 Action Center to examine the security settings on your computer. There you can verify the status of various security settings, make changes to your security settings, and identify and troubleshoot problems. The Action Center also provides information on maintenance that you need to perform on your computer. Any Action Center items identified by a red bar are ones that need your immediate attention, and any items identified by a yellow bar are suggestions you should consider. Windows 7 may also display alert messages in the notification area that you can click in order to open the Action Center and focus on the issue at hand.

After discussing the importance of periodically checking security systems with Arielle, you decide it's time to open the Action Center and examine the status of your computer's security settings.

To set up your computer and open the Action Center:

1. If necessary, display the Computer icon on the desktop, open a Computer window, enable single-click activation, and then close the Computer window.

2. In the notification area on the taskbar, click the **Action Center** button ▮▸ to open the Action Center dialog box, as shown in Figure 7-1.

   Trouble? If Windows 7 does not display an Action Center button in the notification area, press the Windows key, type *action* in the Search programs and files box, and when Windows 7 displays *Action Center* in the search results, press the Enter key if Action Center is the first item in the search results; otherwise, click Action Center.

Figure 7-1 **Viewing the computer's status**

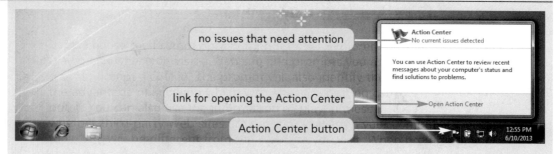

In Figure 7-1, the Action Center dialog box notes that there are *No current issues detected*. Your Action Center issues may differ.

TIP
To create an Action Center desktop shortcut, drag the Action Center icon in the Address bar to the desktop.

3. Click the **Open Action Center** link. Windows 7 opens the Action Center and displays two categories—Security, and Maintenance. See Figure 7-2.

Figure 7-2 | **Windows 7 Action Center**

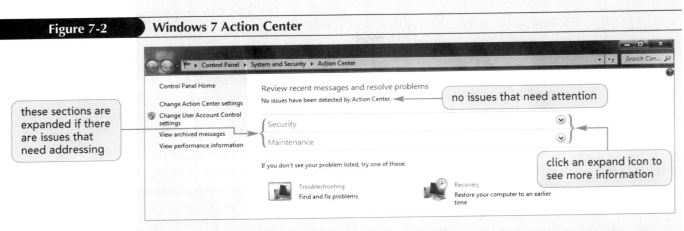

these sections are expanded if there are issues that need addressing

no issues that need attention

click an expand icon to see more information

If the Action Center expands one or both of the categories, then it identified a problem. For example, if the Action Center detects that a computer's files are not being backed up, it expands the Maintenance category, identifies the problem, and displays a Set up backup button for resolving this issue. There is also a link for turning off messages about Windows Backup.

▶ 4. If necessary, click the **expand** icon ⊙ for the Security section of the Action Center window. The Action Center now displays information on different security settings. On the computer used for Figure 7-3, the Action Center displays *On* or *OK* next to each type of security setting except Network Access Protection (which applies to corporate environments). If the first six settings are On or OK, then the Action Center has not identified any security problems on this computer.

Figure 7-3 | **Viewing security settings**

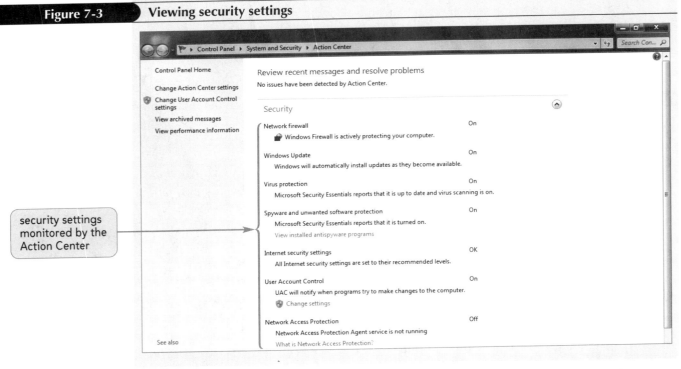

security settings monitored by the Action Center

Under the Network firewall security setting, the Action Center reports that Windows Firewall, a component of Windows 7, is actively protecting this computer.

Examining Firewall Settings

A firewall is software that protects your computer in two ways:

- **Monitors incoming traffic from the Internet or a network**—A firewall protects your computer from Web sites that attempt to install malicious software on your computer and from hackers that attempt to gain access to your computer while you are on the Internet. A firewall can also prevent worms from gaining access to your computer while you are connected to the Internet or another type of network. A **worm** is an independently functioning program that may adversely affect the performance of a computer, damage a computer, and compromise its security. You will examine worms in more detail later in the tutorial when you examine different types of malicious software.
- **Monitors outgoing traffic from your computer to the Internet or a network**—A firewall also prevents programs and malicious software already installed on your computer from connecting to the Internet, a Web site, or another computer network without your knowledge or permission.

In both instances, the firewall can permit or block incoming or outgoing traffic. For example, if you open your Web browser and initiate a request to visit a specific Web site, your firewall knows that this request originated from your computer. When the Web site responds, the firewall permits traffic from that Web site so you can view its Web page. If a hacker or worm attempts to access your computer, the firewall knows that you did not originate that request from your computer, so it blocks access and prevents the hacker or worm from gaining access to your computer. Likewise, if an unknown program on your computer attempts to connect to the Internet or to a Web site, your firewall will either prevent that outgoing communication or warn you of the problem and ask you what you want to do.

Arielle asks you to examine Windows Firewall so you can later compare it with other firewall products that you are considering. If your computer uses another firewall, you can examine the settings of that firewall and compare what's described in the following steps for Windows Firewall to your firewall.

To open Windows Firewall and examine your firewall settings:

> **TIP**
>
> Microsoft recommends you use only one firewall because two firewalls might conflict with each other.

1. In the Address bar of the Action Center window, click the **location** arrow ▶ just to the left of Action Center, and then click **Windows Firewall**. In the Windows Firewall window, Windows 7 displays Window Firewall settings for those networks to which you are connected. See Figure 7-4.

   Trouble? If your computer uses a different firewall, Windows 7 will inform you that your specific firewall is managing these settings. You may not be able to view or change these settings in the Windows Firewall window.

| Figure 7-4 | Viewing firewall settings |

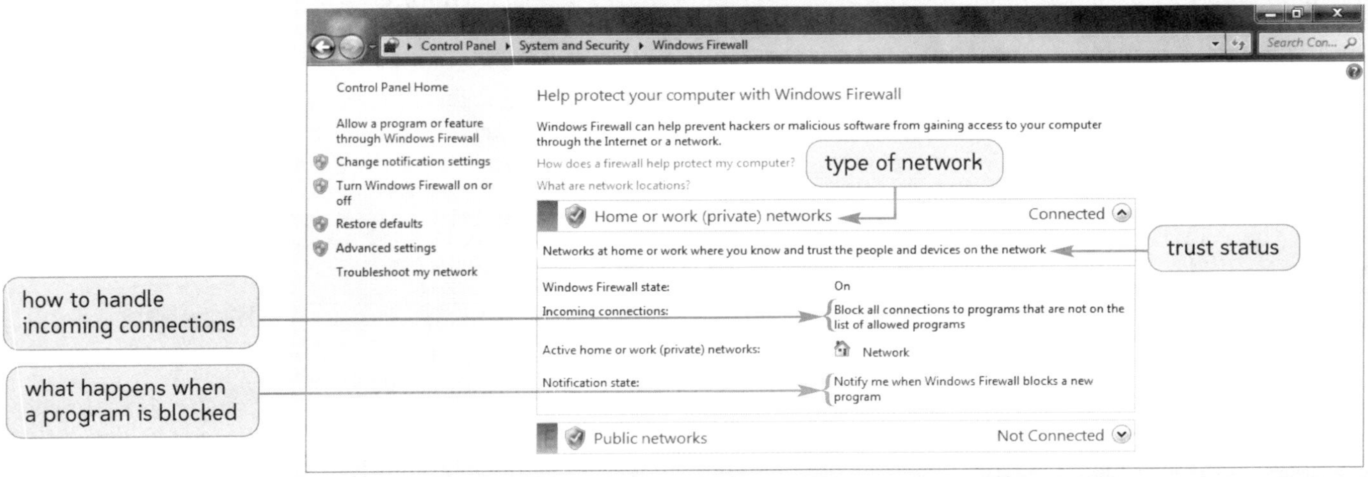

On the computer used for this figure, Windows Firewall shows its settings for this computer's Home or work (private) networks. As noted by Windows 7, these networks are ones at home or at work where you know and trust the people and devices on the network. Windows 7 notes the Windows Firewall is on, indicating that it is actively protecting your computer. Windows 7 also notes that it is set to block all incoming connections to programs that are not on a list of allowed programs. Finally, Windows 7 notes that it is set to notify you if Windows Firewall blocks a new program.

▶ **2.** On the left side of the window, under Control Panel Home, click the **Allow a program or feature through Windows Firewall** link. In the Allowed Programs window, Windows 7 identifies which programs and features are allowed to communicate through the Windows Firewall. This list includes not only Windows 7 programs (such as Internet Explorer and Windows Media Player) and services, but also wireless portable devices and installed applications like Microsoft Office or Skype (a program for making Internet video phone calls).

▶ **3.** Locate and click **Remote Desktop** under Allowed programs and features, and then click the **Details** button. The Remote Desktop Properties dialog box notes that this feature remotely accesses the desktop from another computer system.

▶ **4.** Click the **OK** button to close the Remote Desktop Properties dialog box. You can use the Change settings button to enable the option for making changes to these settings (after you provide Administrator credentials); otherwise, that option is disabled and the settings are dimmed. Once enabled, you can use the "Allow another program" button to open an Add a Program dialog box where you can add, or browse for, programs on your computer, such as Adobe Acrobat Reader, that you want to add to this list of allowed programs and features, and you can also specify the network location type (Home/Work (Private) or Public) for the added program.

▶ **5.** Click the **Back** button ⬅ to return to the Windows Firewall window.

The "Change notification settings" link and the "Turn Windows Firewall on or off" link allow you to access the same two groups of settings for specifying basic firewall settings.

To examine Windows Firewall notification settings:

1. Click the **Change notification settings** link in the left pane of the Windows Firewall window, and, if necessary, provide Administrator credentials. The Customize Settings window opens. Here you can customize settings for each type of network that you use. See Figure 7-5.

Figure 7-5   **Options for customizing Windows Firewall settings by network type**

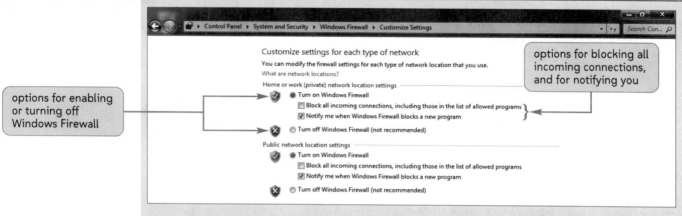

You can block all incoming connections—including those in the list of allowed programs—for both network location types, you can specify whether Windows Firewall notifies you when it blocks a new program, and you can turn Windows Firewall on or off. Turning off Windows Firewall is not recommended unless you are using another firewall.

2. Click the **Back** button ⬅ to return to the Windows Firewall window. You can use the Restore defaults link in the left pane to remove all Windows Firewall settings that you have configured for all network locations, but Windows 7 notes that this might cause some programs to stop working. The Advanced settings link provides a more detailed overview of firewall settings.

3. Click the **location** arrow ▶ to the right of System and Security in the Address bar, and then click **Action Center**.

4. Keep the Action Center open for the next section of the tutorial.

REFERENCE

Verifying Windows Firewall Settings

- Click the Action Center button in the notification area, and then click the Open Action Center link.
- If necessary, click the expand icon for the Security section of the Action Center window to view information on Security settings.
- Verify that the Network firewall setting is enabled on your computer, and verify the name of the firewall software that's actively protecting your computer.
- To view Windows Firewall settings, click the location arrow just to the left of Action Center in the Address bar, click Windows Firewall, and then examine settings for your Home or work (private) networks and Public networks.
- To change which programs or features can communicate through Windows Firewall, click the "Allow a program or feature through Windows Firewall" link under Control Panel Home, and then examine the list of Allowed programs and features. To change these settings, click the Change settings button, and then provide Administrator credentials. To view information on an item in the "Allowed programs and features" list box, select that program or feature, and then click the Details button.
- To add another program to this list of "Allowed programs and features," click the "Allow another program" button, and select (or browse for) a program listed under Programs in the Add a Program dialog box. Click the "Network location types" button, and in the Choose Network Location Types dialog box, specify the selected network locations for this program or port, click OK, and then click the Add button. Click the Back button to return to the Windows Firewall window.
- Click the "Change notification settings" link or the "Turn Windows Firewall on or off" link to examine Home or work (private) network and Public network settings for blocking all incoming connections, to notify you when Windows Firewall blocks a new program, and to turn off (or enable) Windows Firewall. Click the Back button to return to the Windows Firewall window.
- Click the Restore defaults link to remove all Windows Firewall settings that you have configured for all network locations. Click the Restore defaults button to make this change, or click the Back button to return to the Windows Firewall window.
- To return to the Action Center, click the location arrow to the right of System and Security in the Address bar, and then click Action Center.

If there is a problem with your firewall, then Windows 7 will indicate that your firewall is turned off or set up incorrectly, as shown in Figure 7-6.

Figure 7-6 **Problem with current Windows Firewall settings**

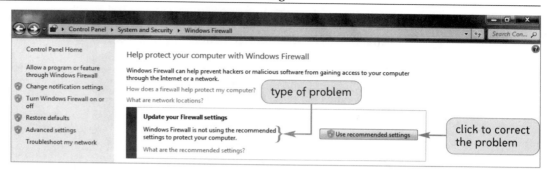

A valuable online resource for information on personal firewalls, security and utility suites, computer viruses, worms, Trojan horses, phishing, spam, mobile security, and privacy protection is the Home PC Firewall Guide (*www.firewallguide.com*). This Web site includes information on best practices, links to reviews for different types of security and anti-malware software, and information about commercial and free software products.

Using Windows Update

Another important tool for protecting your computer is Windows Update. This tool identifies the make and model of your computer, the Windows version on your computer, and any other Microsoft software on your computer. Then, it locates and installs software updates that enhance the security and privacy of your computer, improve its performance, and provide new features. Some updates are critical updates, such as security updates, and others, such as driver updates, are optional.

Windows 7 enables automatic updating on your computer to identify, download, and install security updates and other important updates. Optional updates are not automatically downloaded and installed; however, you might find some of the optional updates useful. Updates are identified, downloaded, and installed on your computer when you are connected to the Internet. Microsoft notes that the automatic updating of software does not interfere with other operations that you are performing on your computer or with Web browsing. If you disconnect your computer from the Web during a download, that same download picks up where it left off the next time you have an Internet connection.

If you turn off automatic updating, you must remember to periodically check for recommended and optional updates and download and install them on your computer to maintain its security and your privacy.

Checking Your Windows Update Settings

Windows updates are critical to protecting the security of your computer, so you should make sure that your computer is properly configured for receiving them. If you are using a mobile computer, it's important to have the most recent security updates as well as the proper software before you connect to your company's computer network. You may want to configure Windows Update so you can examine and decide on individual updates before they are installed on your computer. If you are troubleshooting a problem on your computer, you may need to examine your update history for potential problems.

Arielle recommends that you check the Windows Update settings on your laptop and examine your update history to ensure that Windows Update downloads and installs the latest security updates.

To view Windows Update settings:

TIP

To create a Windows Update desktop shortcut, drag the Windows Update icon in the Address bar to the desktop.

1. At the bottom of the left pane in the Action Center window, click the **Windows Update** link. In the Windows Update window, Windows 7 indicates whether or not there are any important updates available. It also displays the number of available optional updates, information about your most recent check for updates, the date when Windows 7 last installed updates, and what types of updates Windows 7 installs on your computer. See Figure 7-7. Your settings and available updates will differ.

Figure 7-7 Viewing the availability of Windows updates

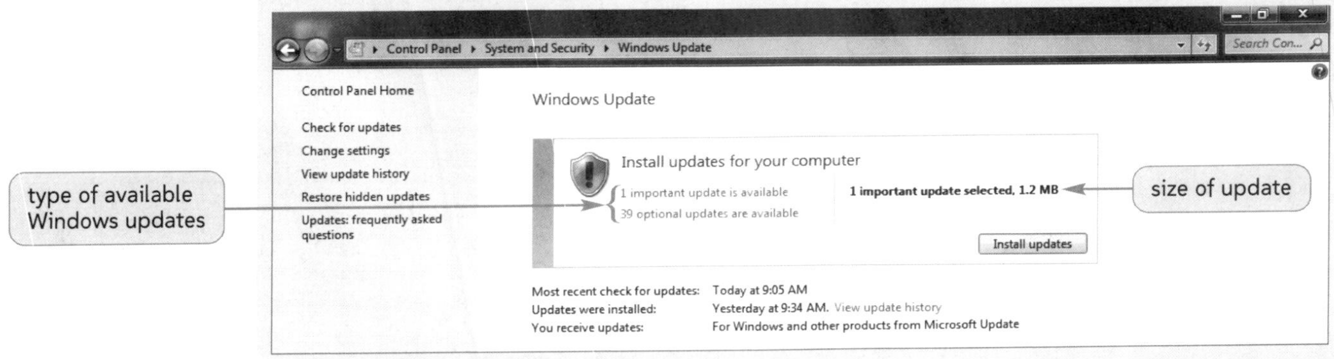

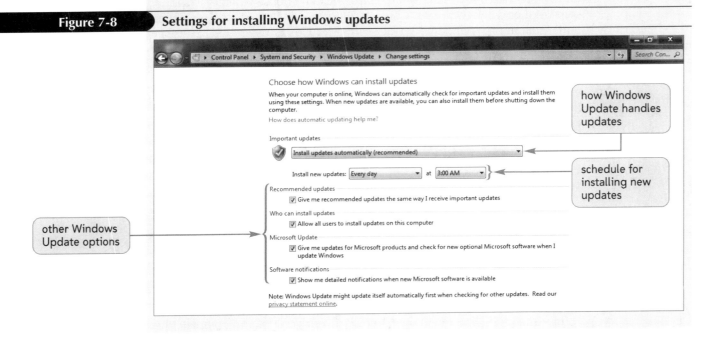

2. Click the **Change settings** link in the left pane. In the Change settings window, you can choose how Windows checks for and installs updates. By default, Windows 7 is set to check for, download, and install updates automatically, as shown by the setting under Important updates on the computer used for Figure 7-8. That is the recommended option to keep your computer updated.

Figure 7-8 Settings for installing Windows updates

By default, new updates are installed every day at 3:00 AM, or as soon as your computer is turned on and connected to the Internet. You can specify another day of the week and another time of day. Also by default, Windows 7 provides recommended updates at the same time you receive important updates. It also provides updates for Microsoft products and checks for new optional Microsoft software when you update Windows 7. Windows Update also shows detailed notifications when new Microsoft software is available. Windows 7 notes that Windows Update might first update itself before checking for other updates. Installing updates requires Administrator credentials.

To view options for handling updates:

▶ **1.** Click the **Important updates** button. In the drop-down list, you can change the way you receive updates, as shown in Figure 7-9.

Figure 7-9 **Choosing an option for installing Windows updates**

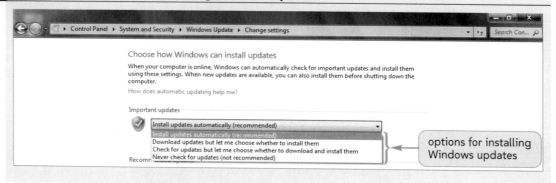

If you choose "Download updates but let me choose whether to install them," Windows Update will still automatically check for and download updates, but will notify you once updates are available so you can choose whether to install all or just some of them. If you choose "Check for updates but let me choose whether to download and install them," Windows Update will let you know when updates are available, but will not download and install them. Again, you can decide what you want to install. The advantage of the latter option is that you control which updates are installed on your computer. By choosing not to download updates that you may never install, you save valuable storage space on your hard drive. If you choose "Never check for updates (not recommended)," Windows Update will not check for updates. Instead, you will have to manually check for updates on a regular basis. Microsoft does not recommend this option because you might encounter a problem with your computer if you do not regularly check or if you forget to check for updates. To make changes to your Windows Update settings, you click the OK button and provide Administrator credentials to apply your changes.

To return to the Windows Update window:

▶ **1.** Click the **Back** button 🔙 to return to the Windows Update window.

▶ **2.** Keep the Windows Update window open for the next section of the tutorial.

In some cases, you might need to restart your computer to complete the installation of one or more updates. Also, in some cases, Windows Update might need to install an update on your computer before it can install other updates.

Checking Your Windows Update Settings

- Click the Action Center button in the taskbar notification area, click the Open Action Center link, and then click the Windows Update link in the lower-left pane.
- Click the Change settings link in the left pane, and then review your Windows Update settings.
- To change how Windows 7 handles updates, click the Important updates button, and then choose the option you want to use for handling Windows updates.
- Decide how you want Windows Update to give you recommended updates, whether all users can install updates, whether you want updates for Microsoft products and new optional Microsoft software, and whether you want detailed notifications when new Microsoft software is available.
- Click the OK button to apply changes you made, and then provide Administrator credentials.
- Close the Windows Update window.

Internet security software, antivirus software, antispyware software, and other types of software that you acquire from other software manufacturers should include an option for automatically checking for and downloading updates. It's a good idea to periodically check the settings for updating this software and verify that this software is working properly. You might need to visit the software manufacturer's Web site and manually check for updates and other software that might prove useful to you. By verifying update settings for software, you guarantee that you have the maximum amount of protection for your security and that you have access to new features included with updates that may prove useful to you.

If Windows Update is turned off, the Action Center will inform you of an issue with Windows Update, as shown in Figure 7-10, and recommend that you turn on Windows Update to enhance the security and performance of your computer.

| Figure 7-10 | Recommendation for resolving Windows Update settings |

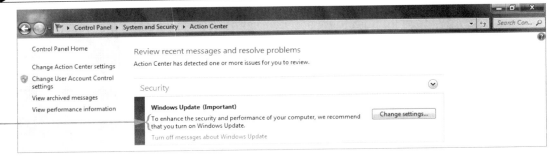

recommendation for installing Windows updates

Windows 7 also displays a notification area alert and displays a red circle with a white *X* on the Action Center icon to indicate a problem that you need to resolve or to show you the status of an operation, such as a backup in progress.

Checking Your Windows Update History

You might need to check your update history and verify that all important updates are installed, or you might want to remove updates if you encounter an unexpected problem after downloading and installing an update.

After downloading updates for your computer, you decide to take a moment to review a history of updates made to your laptop computer.

To view your update history:

1. In the left pane of the Windows Update window, click the **View update history** link. In the View update history window, Windows 7 lists the names of all successfully installed, pending, failed, and canceled updates. It also notes whether each update was an important, recommended, or optional update.

   On the computer used for Figure 7-11, Windows 7 shows successfully installed recommended and important updates as well as failed updates. Your update history will differ.

| Figure 7-11 | Viewing the Windows update history |

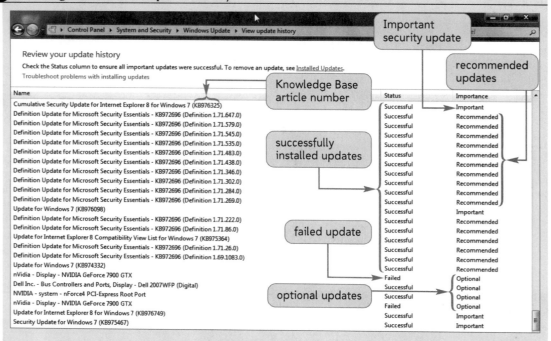

If you want to remove an update, you use the Installed Updates link at the top of the window. The "Troubleshoot problems with installing updates" link will open Help and Support so you can examine Help topics on resolving problems caused by installing updates.

Do not click an installed update while using single-click activation. If you do, Windows 7 might uninstall the update without prompting you for verification.

2. Click the **Installed Updates** link. In the Installed Updates window, Windows 7 organizes updates into groups, and it lists the update by name, which program the update applies to, the version (if available), the publisher of each update, and when the update was installed. See Figure 7-12.

Figure 7-12   **Viewing installed Microsoft Windows and Microsoft Office updates**

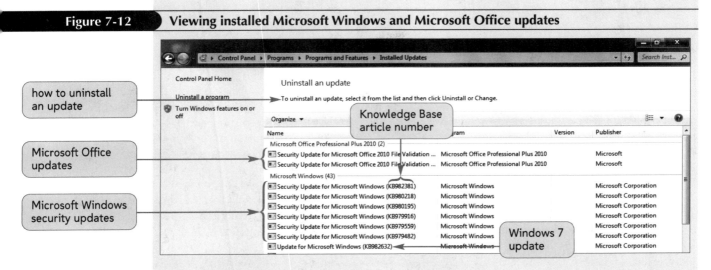

how to uninstall
an update

Microsoft Office
updates

Microsoft Windows
security updates

If you want to uninstall or change an update, you first select the update. Windows 7 will then display an Uninstall or Change button on the toolbar for you to use to remove the update or change its installation.

Microsoft Office and Microsoft Windows updates include a Knowledge Base article number after the update name in parentheses (with *KB* at the beginning of the Knowledge Base article number). If you select a Microsoft Windows update, in the Details pane at the bottom of the window, Windows 7 displays the URL for the Microsoft Support Web page where you can view information about the purpose and importance of the update. If you select a Microsoft Office update, you can then click the Support link URL in the Details pane to view the Knowledge Base article about the purpose and importance of the update.

▶ **3.** Click the **Back** button ⬅ twice to return to the Windows Update window.

The "Restore hidden updates" link in the left side of the window displays a list of updates that you had previously instructed Windows 7 not to automatically install or to notify you about. After you display hidden updates, you can choose to install them if you change your mind.

▶ **4.** Click the **location** arrow ▶ to the left of Windows Update in the Address bar, click **Action Center**, and keep the Action Center window open for the next section of the tutorial.

Because of the frequency with which Microsoft releases new security and critical Windows updates, you should choose either the option for downloading and installing updates or the option for having Windows 7 inform you of the availability of updates.

REFERENCE

Checking Your Windows Update History

- Click the Action Center button in the taskbar notification area, click the Open Action Center link, and then click the Windows Update link in the lower-left pane.
- Click the "View update history" link in the left pane, and then review your update history.
- To remove an update, click the Installed Updates link in the lower-left pane, select the update you want to remove, wait for Windows 7 to display an Uninstall button or Change button on the toolbar, click the Uninstall button to remove the update or click the Change button to change the installation of the update. If necessary, provide Administrator credentials.
- To check for hidden updates that you previously decided not to install, click the Back button to return to the Windows Update window, and click the "Restore hidden updates" link. If you want to restore a hidden update, select the update, click the Restore button, and then provide Administrator credentials.
- Close the Windows Update window.

The Automatic Updates feature is a convenient way to protect your computer and to improve the capabilities of Windows 7 and your other Microsoft software.

Protecting Your Computer from Malicious Software and Malicious Web Sites

To effectively protect the security of your computer and the privacy of information stored on it while using the Internet, you should be familiar with the types of threats that you may encounter and understand how best to handle them. Many of these threats result from **malware**, a catch-all term for different types of malicious software. The following list describes various types of malware that might infect your computer when you are browsing the World Wide Web and while you are using email:

- **Computer virus**—Computer viruses are programs that affect the security of your computer and that may also cause damage to your computer's hardware, software, and data. A computer virus requires a host (such as a program or file) to which it is attached, or it might be contained within an email attachment. When you open the program, file, or attachment that contains the computer virus, it becomes active, delivers its payload, makes copies of itself, and spreads to other computers. **Payload** refers to the actions a computer virus performs to damage a computer or compromise its security.
- **Worm**—Like a computer virus, a worm adversely affects the performance of a computer and may compromise its security. However, unlike a computer virus, a worm does not require a host, but instead is an independently functioning program. Also like a computer virus, it makes copies of itself and spreads from computer to computer via a network (such as the Internet). In the process, it ties up system and network resources and significantly slows down the performance of a computer. It can gain access to a computer via an email attachment or directly over your Internet connection. If you get an email message with an attachment that has the .vbs file extension, that attachment may very well be a worm. That's why it's important to know about, and pay attention to, file extensions of email attachments.
- **Trojan horse**—A **Trojan horse**, or **Trojan**, is a program that masquerades as a legitimate and useful program, but once you open the program, the Trojan horse performs some type of malicious action on the computer or compromises its security by placing a program called a **backdoor** on the computer so an intruder or hacker can gain access to a

computer without detection. Unlike computer viruses or worms, Trojan horses do not replicate or make copies of themselves. Instead, they are spread via computer viruses, worms, or downloaded software.

- **Spyware**—Spyware poses a security threat to your computer and your privacy because it monitors your activities on the Internet and reports information about your browsing habits to a third party, such as an advertising company, without your permission. Spyware might be installed on your computer without your consent, or it might be packaged with other software that you download and install on a computer (and actually agree to use). It is not uncommon for spyware to adversely affect the performance of a computer and even prevent you from connecting to the Internet. Also, a computer system can be infected by more than one spyware program. To complicate matters, some antispyware products that claim to remove spyware from your computer are spyware themselves. Spyware can be hard to remove and, in some cases, you might need to manually remove the software. Before downloading antispyware software, you might want to examine a useful Web site called Spyware Warrior (*www.spywarewarrior.com/ rogue_anti-spyware.htm*); it provides information on rogue or suspect antispyware software products and Web sites.

- **Adware**—Originally designed to display advertising in pop-up windows, **adware** can also be spyware that displays unsolicited advertising (usually in pop-up windows), monitors your activity on the Internet, and reports that information to a third party without your authorization or knowledge.

- **Browser hijacker**—A **browser hijacker** is malicious software that changes your Web browser's home page to the Web site of the maker of the browser hijacker software or to another Web site, hijacks your computer and takes it to that Web site without your permission, and prevents you from navigating to other Web sites and from changing your Web browser settings back to what you originally specified. A well-known example of this type of malicious software is CoolWebSearch, which hijacks your Web browser and takes it to the Web site for CoolWebSearch or to another associated Web site.

- **Keylogger**—A **keylogger** is malicious software that can monitor your computer, record keys that you press, capture screenshots, and send the information it compiles to a third party. That information may include passwords, PINs, a Social Security number, and credit card numbers. A keylogger can track and report your Web browsing habits, and it can become active when you connect to a secure Web site, such as your online banking Web site. There are also legitimate keylogger programs for monitoring other users' activities on a computer, including children.

- **Rootkits**—A **rootkit** is usually malicious software that, once installed on your computer, uses stealth techniques to hide itself from the operating system, other software, and you. Once installed, a rootkit integrates itself into the operating system and intercepts and filters operations performed by the operating system so it can hide itself and information about itself, such as its program files and references to it in the Windows Registry. A rootkit can also hide the activity of other malicious software, such as computer viruses, worms, and Trojan horses, as well as backdoors that permit an intruder or hacker to remotely control a computer.

TIP

A company can also include a rootkit in its software to detect copyright violations.

To remove a rootkit, you use Internet security software or a rootkit detector program to identify and, if possible, remove the rootkit. If your Internet security software cannot remove it, then you can search the Internet to determine if there is any software designed to specifically remove the rootkit or if there is any other known way to remove the rootkit. Once you remove a rootkit, you may also need to remove other malicious software hidden by the rootkit. If you cannot find a way to remove a rootkit, you must back up your document files, reformat your hard disk, and reinstall Windows 7 and your software. That approach may, in fact, prove to be the most reliable and least time-consuming way to resolve the problem, but it obviously requires that you keep backups of your valuable data up to date.

Arielle recommends you check the status of your virus protection and spyware software.

To view other installed software:

▶ **1.** If necessary, click the **expand** icon ⊗ for the Security section of the Action Center window to expand this category. The Action Center also reports on the status of the software you use for virus protection and for spyware and other unwanted software. On the computer used for Figure 7-13, Windows 7 reports that Virus protection and "Spyware and unwanted software protection" is on and that Microsoft Security Essentials reports it is up to date and virus scanning is on.

Figure 7-13	Virus and spyware protection program and status

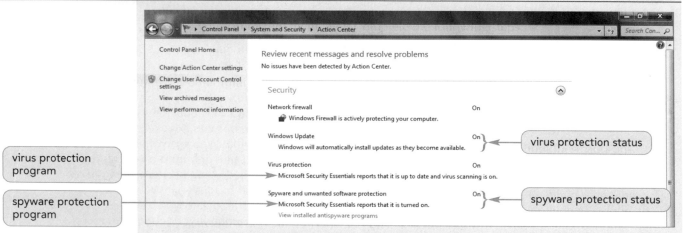

Microsoft Security Essentials, free for download from the Microsoft Web site, is designed to protect a computer against viruses, spyware, and other types of malicious software.

▶ **2.** If Windows 7 displays a link for viewing antispyware software products on your computer, then click the **View installed antispyware programs** link. On the computer used for Figure 7-14, Windows 7 lists two antispyware products, Microsoft Security Essentials and Windows Defender, also from Microsoft.

Figure 7-14	Installed spyware protection programs

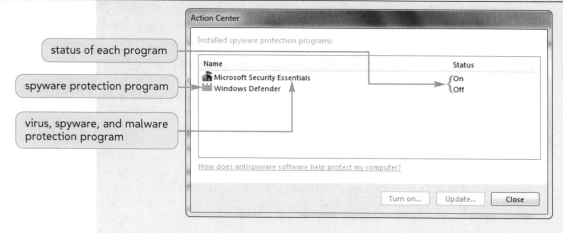

Windows Defender was introduced in Windows Vista and is available in Windows 7; however, you might need to enable Windows Defender if you want to use it.

▶ **3.** Close the Action Center dialog box, and then close the Action Center window.

Even after using software to remove malicious software from your computer, you might still have to manually remove files or Registry entries that remain on your computer. If you discover malicious software on your computer, or if your Internet security software and antivirus software find malicious software on your computer, you can check Web sites of companies, such as Symantec (*www.symantec.com*), that specialize in products that remove malicious software to find out what problems a malicious program poses, how it affects your computer, what steps to take to manually remove that malicious software, or how to remove whatever might remain after your Internet security or antivirus software removes the malicious software. Some Web sites, like the Symantec Web site, make available free tools for removing certain types of malicious software, including recently discovered malicious software that your Internet security or antivirus software might not yet detect.

INSIGHT

Reading License Agreements

For obvious reasons, most individuals prefer not to read the license agreement for software that they download and install on their computers. However, today, it's critical to examine the license agreement for each software product you download from the Internet to make sure that you are not agreeing to the download and installation of other programs that are packaged with that software product. This additional software might be spyware, other types of malicious software, or software that compromises your computer's security and your privacy. The time it takes to read a license agreement is far less than the time it might take for you to reinstall the programs on your computer and restore lost data.

The Action Center also identifies whether all Internet security settings are set to their recommended levels. You will examine these security settings in more detail in the next session.

The Importance of User Account Control

As noted in Tutorial 1, a user account is a collection of settings that identifies you to Windows 7 and determines what you can do on your computer. For example, a user account:

- Identifies which folders and files you can access
- Provides access to your personal settings (such as desktop and folder settings)
- Determines what types of changes you can make to the computer (such as installing software and hardware, updating software, and managing user accounts)
- Determines what types of system settings you can access, view, and change

Windows 7 supports three types of user accounts:

- **Administrator**—An **Administrator account** provides you with complete access to your computer. You can change system settings (including security settings); manage user accounts (your account and other users' accounts); install, configure, update, troubleshoot, and uninstall software and hardware; and access all folders and files on a computer (including folders and files of other users).

- **Standard user**—A **Standard user account** (called a Limited account in Windows XP) provides you with access to the full capabilities of a computer but prevents or restricts you from making changes to system settings; managing your user account and other user accounts; installing, configuring, updating, troubleshooting, and uninstalling software and hardware; and accessing other user's folders and files. A Standard user can use installed software and hardware, make certain changes to their own user account, specify personal desktop and folder settings, and create their own folders and files. But they cannot install software. Also, Standard users cannot access information about other user accounts.

- **Guest**—A **Guest account** is an account designed for a user (such as a visitor or friend) who needs temporary access to the features on your computer, such as the ability to use software, connect to the Internet, and browse the Web. A user of a Guest account faces the same restrictions as those for a Standard user account. However, a Guest account does not have a password, and a temporary user cannot specify a password. Because the Guest account is disabled by default, a user with Administrator credentials must enable the Guest account on a computer before a guest can use it, but that may only need to be done on an occasional basis (if at all).

When you install Windows 7 on a computer, it creates an Administrator account for setting up the computer. When you create that account, you provide a user account name, and you also provide a secure password for added protection of your computer. If you create additional user accounts for new users, Windows 7 automatically sets those accounts up as Standard user accounts. You specify a user name and provide a password for each of those user accounts. Each user can then change their password. Each person can also specify a password hint in case they forget their password. The password hint you choose should remind you of your password.

Windows 7 also includes an additional built-in Administrator account that is automatically disabled. However, under certain conditions (which you examine in the next tutorial), you have access to that Administrator account.

To enhance the security of Windows Vista over previous versions of Windows, Microsoft included in Windows Vista an important feature known as User Account Control (UAC). That same feature is continued in Windows 7. By default, User Account Control is automatically enabled on a computer. User Account Control prompts you (and any other users of the same computer) for permission, or for the user name and password of an Administrator account, before performing an operation that affects the operation of your computer or that affects other users.

By prompting for permission or Administrator credentials, User Account Control also prevents the installation of malicious software or spyware on your computer without your knowledge. Unlike Windows Vista, which gained a reputation for displaying too many User Account Control prompts, Microsoft improved Windows 7 so you are not unnecessarily and repeatedly prompted for Administrator credentials.

If you log on under a Standard user account and start an operation that requires Administrator credentials, Windows 7 switches to Secure Desktop Mode, dims the desktop, displays a User Account Control dialog box, and prompts for Administrator credentials. You must select an Administrator account, and provide the password for that account before you can perform the operation.

In **Secure Desktop Mode**, you can perform only one operation, namely, the specific operation that you initiated. Secure Desktop Mode, a new feature introduced with Windows Vista and not available in previous versions of Windows, prevents another operation that you might not even be aware of (such as malicious software attempting to install itself) from becoming active on your computer once you provide Administrator credentials for the operation you want to perform. Also, Secure Desktop Mode prevents other software from interacting with the user interface while you are performing an operation that requires Administrator credentials. Only Windows processes can access Secure Desktop Mode, preventing what are called silent installs of malicious software. **Silent installs** are ones performed without your knowledge or consent. This feature also applies when you are on the Internet or World Wide Web. Hackers or Web sites cannot silently install malicious software on your computer.

You can recognize when you will need to provide Administrator credentials because Windows 7 displays a security shield icon next to an option in a dialog box to let the user know that the option requires Administrator credentials. For example, as shown in Figure 7-15, the option for changing the date and time in the Date and Time dialog box requires Administrator credentials. This feature is designed to protect you or someone else from inadvertently or deliberately making a change to your computer that seriously affects its performance.

Figure 7-15   **Viewing Date and Time settings**

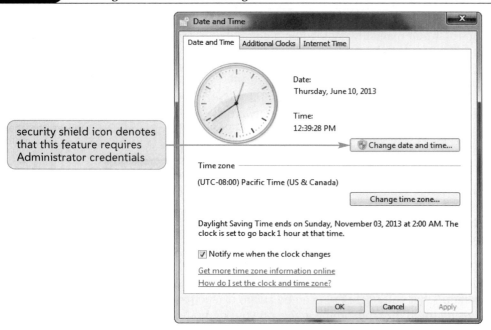

security shield icon denotes that this feature requires Administrator credentials

You might discover that certain older applications that you have do not run properly on your computer because they were originally designed to run with Administrator privileges on a prior version of Windows where it was assumed you automatically worked in an Administrator account. To correct this problem, you must upgrade to a newer version of that software product designed for Windows 7 that does not require Administrator privileges.

To view information about user accounts or to change settings for a user account, you open User Accounts from the Control Panel. You can also create a Password Reset Disk in case you later forget the password to your user account. That Password Reset Disk stores password recovery information. To create a Password Reset Disk, you can use a flash drive or a memory card.

After discussing the value of having a Password Reset Disk with other members of Arielle's staff, you decide to make one for your user account.

To open User Accounts and create a Password Reset Disk:

1. If necessary, attach your flash drive to your computer, and then close any dialog boxes or windows that open.

2. On the Start menu, click **Control Panel**, click the **User Accounts and Family Safety** link, and then click **User Accounts**. Windows 7 opens the User Accounts window and displays information about your user account. Figure 7-16 shows information about Arielle's user account.

Trouble? If you previously switched the Control Panel to view its contents by Large Icons or Small Icons, click the User Accounts link.

Figure 7-16   Viewing user account settings

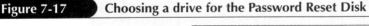

option for creating a password reset disk

options for changing your user account that require Administrator credentials

type of user account

options for changing your user account that do not require Administrator credentials

You can change or remove your password or change your account picture without Administrator credentials. If you want to change your account name, account type, manage another account, or change User Account Control settings, you must provide Administrator credentials, as evidenced by the security icon to the left of those options, or log on under an Administrator account.

▶ 3. In the left pane, click the **Create a password reset disk** link. Windows 7 opens the Forgotten Password Wizard dialog box. Windows 7 notes that you can use a password reset disk to create a new password for your account if you forget that password and are unable to log in under your user account. Windows 7 also notes that no matter how many times you change your password, you only need to create this disk once. Windows 7 warns you that anyone can use your password reset disk to reset the password and gain access to your user account. However, the trade-off is that you have a way to access your computer if you forget your password.

▶ 4. Click the **Next** button. The Forgotten Password Wizard prompts for the location of the disk and drive where it will store your password information. See Figure 7-17. You can use a removable disk, memory card, or an external hard disk drive, but not your internal hard disk drive.

Figure 7-17   Choosing a drive for the Password Reset Disk

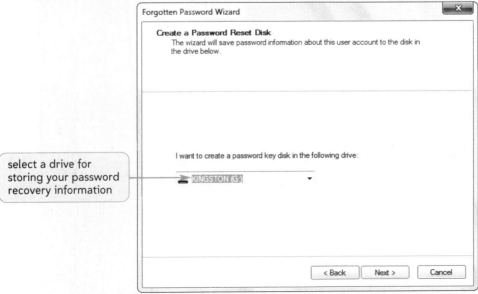

select a drive for storing your password recovery information

▶ **5.** Click the **I want to create a password key disk in the following drive** arrow, select the disk drive that contains your flash drive, and then click the **Next** button. At the next step, the Forgotten Password Wizard prompts for the password to your user account.

▶ **6.** In the Current user password box, type your **current password**, and then click the **Next** button. The Forgotten Password Wizard then displays a progress indicator to show the progress of creating the Password Reset Disk.

Trouble? If you already have a password reset disk for your user account, the Forgotten Password Wizard will display a Replace Previous disk dialog box, and explain that you will render the old (or previous) password reset disk unusable if you continue. You must then decide whether to continue or whether to cancel this operation.

Trouble? If a disk already contains password reset information, the Forgotten Password Wizard will display an Overwrite Existing Disk dialog box, and ask you whether you want to replace the existing information. You must then decide whether to continue or whether to cancel this operation.

▶ **7.** After the Forgotten Password Wizard notes that the operation is complete, click the **Next** button. In the last step, the Forgotten Password Wizard notes that you cannot use any previous password reset disk, and it recommends that you keep this disk in a safe place.

▶ **8.** Click the **Finish** button to close the Forgotten Password Wizard dialog box, and then close the User Accounts window.

TIP

After you create a password reset disk, test it to make sure it will work when you need it.

If you examine your flash drive, you will discover a new file with the name userkey.psw that contains information for resetting your user account password if you forget your password. If you change your password later, you can step through this same process using the same flash drive and overwrite the userkey.psw file.

REFERENCE

Creating a Password Reset Disk

- If necessary, insert a flash drive, and then close any windows that open.
- On the Start menu, click Control Panel, click the User Accounts and Family Safety link, and then click User Accounts.
- In the User Accounts window, click the "Create a password reset disk" link, and then read the information about creating a password reset disk in the Forgotten Password Wizard dialog box.
- Click the Next button, and then click the "I want to create a password key disk in the following drive" arrow, select a disk drive, and then click the Next button.
- At the next step, type your current password in the "Current user password" box, and then click the Next button.
- After the Forgotten Password Wizard creates a Password Reset Disk in the next step, click the Next button, and at the last step, click the Finish button to close the Forgotten Password Wizard dialog box.
- Close the User Accounts window.

If you attempt to log on under your user account and can't remember your password, check your password hint, and see if it helps you recall your password. If not, enter any password and then complete these steps:

- After Windows 7 informs you that the user name or password that you entered is incorrect, click the OK button.
- When prompted to log into the same account again, click Reset password.
- After Windows 7 opens the Password Reset Wizard dialog box, it explains the purpose of this wizard. When ready, advance to the next step where the Password Reset Wizard prompts you to insert your Password Reset Disk.
- Insert your Password Reset Disk, and then advance to the next step where the Password Reset Wizard prompts you to select the disk drive with your Password Reset Disk.
- Select the disk drive, and then advance to the next step where you reset your user account password and provide a new password hint. The Password Reset Wizard also notes that your new password will replace your old password, but everything else about your user account remains the same.
- Enter a new password in the "Type a new password" box, enter the same password again in the "Type the password again to confirm" box, enter a new hint in the "Type a new password hint" box, and then advance to the next step.
- The Password Reset Wizard informs you that you've successfully reset the password and notes that you can now log on with the new password. Click the Finish button to complete this process and return to the Welcome screen where you can log into your user account.

Many users occasionally forget account passwords, especially if they have many different types of accounts with different passwords and PINs (personal identification numbers). To guarantee access to your user account, you can make sure that you have a way back in if you forget your user account password.

Creating Strong Passwords and Passphrases

Windows 7 Help and Support recommends the following approach to creating strong passwords, and many of these recommendations are approaches currently practiced by many users:

- Create a password that contains eight or more characters (the more the better). In certain networked environments, you might need to limit the number of characters in a password. You can ask your network administrator if there are any restrictions or limitations for passwords.
- Do not use something obvious as a password, such as all or part of your real name, your user account name, or your company's name as a password. Likewise, do not use your child's name, your pet's name, or the name of someone close to you as a password. All of these make it too easy for others to guess.
- Do not use a complete word as your password; instead, modify it in some way that's easy for you to remember. For example, you might remove or replace certain characters or scramble the characters in some way.
- In your password, mix uppercase and lowercase characters (passwords, including email passwords, are always case sensitive), include one or more numbers and symbols, and include spaces to further reduce the chance of someone cracking the password. In fact, some password protected accounts require you to use one or more numbers and symbols as part of a password. You can also use numbers or other characters that resemble actual characters in a password. By randomly combining different characters, numbers, symbols, and spaces, you can create an even stronger password; however, the password also becomes more difficult to recall.
- Use misspellings in your password. In other words, substitute other characters for correctly used characters in a password.

A strong password will take into account all these guidelines; if one of these guidelines is not met, then the password is weak. If feasible, change your password on a regular basis. Make sure your next password is not similar to your previous password. Because people today rely on many different passwords for many different types of accounts and access systems, you may need to record your passwords on paper or in an encrypted or password protected file in case you forget a password. If you record a password on paper, make sure you do not identify it as a password or as a password for a specific account, but instead identify it using some personal association unique to the way you think.

In some cases, individuals use a passphrase instead of a password for added security. A **passphrase** consists of multiple words that are organized into a phrase for added security. Passphrases follow the same guidelines as passwords, but are typically 20–30 characters long, include spaces, do not contain words found in a dictionary, and do not contain phrases found in literature or music.

You can use the Microsoft Password Checker Web site (*www.microsoft.com/protect/fraud/passwords/checker.aspx*) to test the strength of your passwords and the Microsoft Strong Passwords Web site (*www.microsoft.com/protect/fraud/passwords/create.aspx*) to learn other helpful hints for creating strong passwords.

PROSKILLS

Decision Making: Creating Strong Passwords and Passphrases

One of the important decisions you make as an employee is choosing a strong password that will protect your computer (such as a company laptop) and not expose your company's computer network to a security breach. Your company's network administrator will take measures to protect the security of the company's network, such as requiring you to change your computer's password after some interval of time and not permitting the use of the same password again. But you also play an important role. No matter what type of account you have, you should decide on a strong password that reduces the chances that someone might guess your password, or that someone might use a program to crack your password. The latter applies to hackers and malicious Web sites, both of which keep becoming more resourceful and clever in accessing computers. You should also have different passwords for different computer accounts.

While it might prove a slight inconvenience to have to log onto your computer or to specify a complex but secure password, you should never use a computer without a strong password because you never know what circumstances might occur that allow an unauthorized person access to your computer. This applies equally to workplace computers, the use of mobile computers while traveling on company business, the use of your own computer at home for both personal and business use, such as telecommuting or contract work for an employer halfway around the world. By using the guidelines presented here, you can ensure that you decide on a password or passphrase that protects the security of your computer and your company's network.

Checking User Account Control Settings

Windows 7 makes it easy for you to check and change User Account Control settings. The following steps require Administrator credentials. If you cannot provide Administrator credentials, do not keystroke the steps, but instead read the steps and examine the figures.

To check User Account Control settings:

▶ **1.** In the notification area on the taskbar, click the **Action Center** button , click the **Open Action Center** link, and then click the **expand** icon for the Security section of the Action Center window (if necessary). Windows 7 reports on the status of your User Account Control setting, which should be set to On. Windows 7 also reports that User Account Control will always notify (you) and wait for a response.

▶ **2.** Click the **Change settings** link under User Account Control, and provide Administrator credentials. Windows 7 opens the User Account Control Settings dialog box, and displays the default or current User Account Control setting. See Figure 7-18. Your User Account Control setting may differ.

Figure 7-18   Viewing your User Account Control setting

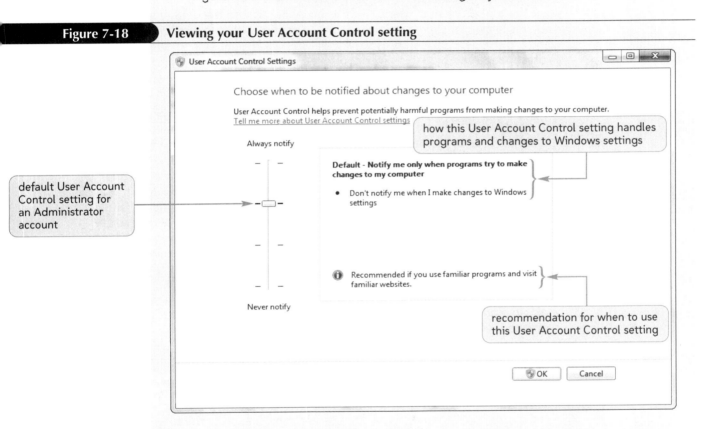

The User Account Control setting shown in this figure is the default for an Administrator account. Windows 7 always notifies you when programs try to make changes to your computer, but does not notify you when you make changes to Windows settings. This is the recommended setting if you use familiar programs and visit familiar Web sites.

Be sure you make a note of your computer's default User Account Control setting before you change it so you can restore it at the end of these steps.

▶ **3.** Note the default setting for User Account Control on your computer, and then drag the **slider tab** in the slider bar to the top of the slider bar (or click in the slider bar next to the top notch).

This is the default User Account setting for a Standard user account. With this User Account Control setting, Windows 7 always notifies you when programs try to install software or make changes to your computer, and Windows 7 always notifies you if you make changes to Windows settings. As shown in the dialog box, this is the recommended setting if you routinely install new software on your computer and visit unfamiliar Web sites that might pose a risk. This default setting is the most secure User Account Control setting.

▶ **4.** Drag the **slider tab** in the slider bar two notches down (or click the third notch from the top of the slider bar). This setting is identical to the default setting that you first examined except that Windows 7 does not dim your desktop. Because dimming the desktop is part of Secure Desktop Mode, you are not afforded the protection offered by Secure Desktop Mode. Although this setting is not recommended, you might want to choose this setting if it takes a long time to dim the desktop. If you are logged on under a Standard user account, Windows 7 displays an informational prompt ⓘ informing you that you must be logged on as an administrator to select this setting.

▶ **5.** Click the **slider bar notch** one notch down (or click the last notch at the bottom of the slide bar). With this setting, Windows 7 never notifies you if programs try to install software or make changes to your computer, and it never notifies you if you make changes to Windows settings. This setting is also not recommended because programs have the same access to your computer as you do. That means they might be able to access and change protected system areas and your personal files. Programs also might be able to transfer information to and from anything your computer connects to (such as the Internet). However, in rare circumstances, you might need to use this setting if you are using programs that are not certified for use with Windows 7 because they do not support the User Account Control feature. Your best bet in that case would be to upgrade your software and take maximum advantage of User Account Control. Like the previous setting, you must be logged on as an administrator to select this setting.

▶ **6.** Restore your original User Account control setting, and then close the User Account Control dialog box. If you do not recall your computer's User Account Control setting, click the **Cancel** button to restore your default User Account Control setting.

▶ **7.** Keep the Action Center window open for the next section of the tutorial.

One important reason for upgrading from Windows XP to Windows 7 is the added security offered by Windows 7 User Account Control.

REFERENCE

Checking User Account Control Settings

- Click the Action Center button in the notification area, click the Open Action Center link, and then click the expand icon for the Security section of the Action Center window.
- Click the Change settings link under User Account Control, provide Administrator credentials, and then check for your User Account Control setting in the User Account Control Settings dialog box.
- To change your User Account Control Setting, drag the slider tab in the slider bar to the setting you want to use, and then click the OK button.
- To close the User Account Control Settings dialog box without making changes to your User Account Control setting, click the Cancel button.

Because most tasks do not require an Administrator account or Administrator credentials, a single user can work under a Standard user account yet still provide Administrator credentials to perform tasks protected by User Account Control.

Network Access Protection

In the Action Center window, the Network Access Protection setting, designed for network administrators, determines what happens when a mobile computer such as a laptop (called a client computer) connects to, or communicates with, a corporate network. When Network Access Protection (NAP) is enabled, the corporate network verifies the client computer's identity and checks the client computer to determine whether or not the client computer has the most recent security updates (including updates for Internet security software or antivirus software), and that the client computer has the proper configuration settings, such as an enabled firewall. If not, the client computer is restricted from accessing the network until any necessary updates and software are installed on that computer and that computer's configuration settings are automatically updated by the company's network so it can have full access to that network. Network Access Protection is available not only in Windows 7, but also in Windows Vista.

Changing Action Center Settings

The Action Center is set up to provide you with information about problems that arise on your computer. You can examine those default settings and, if necessary, make changes.

To view Action Center settings:

▶ 1. In the left pane of the Action Center, click the **Change Action Center settings** link. As shown in the Change Action Center settings window in Figure 7-19, Windows 7 checks for security and maintenance problems and, if necessary, displays messages or alerts if problems are found. You can decide whether you want to receive security messages for each of the security categories monitored by the Action Center.

Figure 7-19 Options for handling security and maintenance problems and notifications

how Windows 7 handles maintenance problems and notifications

how Windows 7 handles security problems and notifications

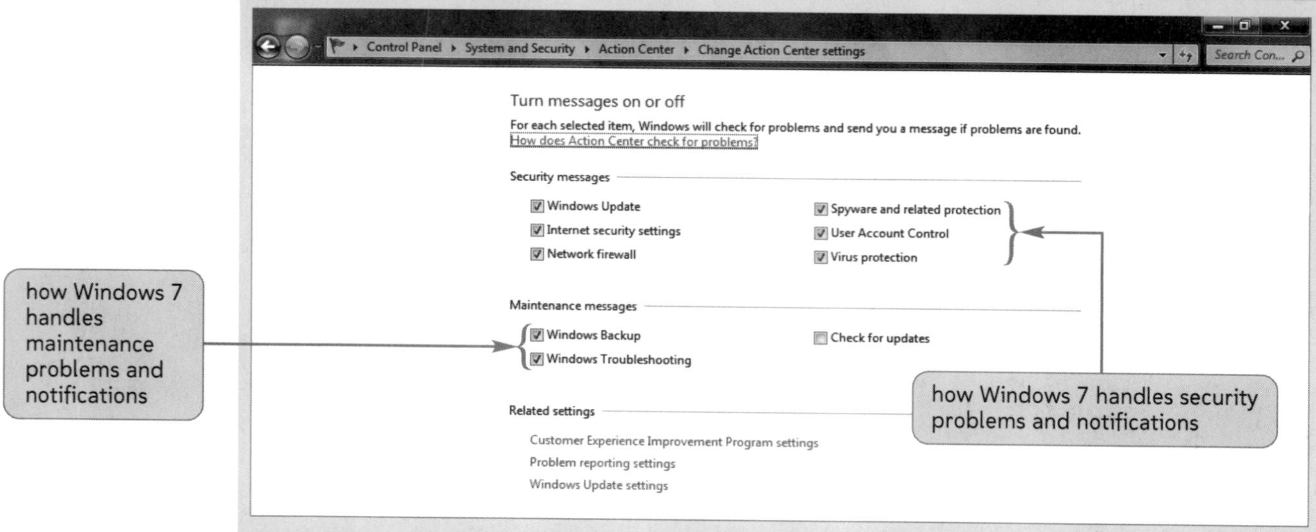

2. Click the **Problem reporting settings** link under Related settings. In the Problem Reporting Settings window, you can specify whether and how Windows 7 sends problem reports to Microsoft so you receive solutions as they become available. You can specify that Windows 7 automatically checks for solutions (the recommended option), checks for solutions and sends additional report data, prompts you first before checking for solutions to a problem, or never checks for solutions (the not recommended option). You can use the "Select programs to exclude from reporting" link to locate and add programs to exclude from the problem reporting feature of Windows 7. You also have the option of deciding whether to apply these report settings to all users.

3. Click the **OK** button twice to close the Problem Reporting Settings and Change Action Center Settings windows, and then close the Action Center window.

If you are experiencing a problem with your computer, then check the Action Center to determine whether Windows 7 has already identified the problem and whether it offers a solution. You can then troubleshoot a problem more effectively.

REFERENCE

Changing Action Center Settings

- Click the Action Center button in the notification area, click the Open Action Center link, and then click the Change Action Center settings link.
- Click the Problem reporting settings link under Related settings, and then specify how you want to handle security and maintenance messages for Action Center items.
- Click the OK button to close the Change Action Center settings window, and then close the Action Center window.

The Action Center is a useful and centralized resource for maintaining and protecting your computer and for providing information you need to make informed decisions about the security and privacy of your computer.

Session 7.1 Quick Check

REVIEW

1. What Windows 7 component can you use to check the status of your computer's firewall, Windows' automatic updating feature, your computer's malware protection, Internet settings, and User Account Control settings?

2. _____ software monitors incoming traffic from, and outgoing traffic to, the Internet or a network.

3. What is a Trojan horse?

4. What type(s) of software monitors a user's activities on the Internet and reports information about a user's browsing habits to a third party, such as an online marketing company, without that user's knowledge or consent?

5. _____ prompts you (and any other users of the same computer) for permission or for the user name and password of an Administrator account before performing an operation that affects the operation of your computer or that affects other users.

6. True or False. In Secure Desktop Mode, you can multitask and perform more than one operation.

7. _____ is a Windows 7 component or tool for identifying important updates for the Windows operating system, device driver updates, and other Microsoft software.

8. If you receive an email message with an attachment that has the .vbs file extension from someone you do not know or recognize, is it safe to open the file extension? Explain.

SESSION 7.2 VISUAL OVERVIEW

You can browse the Web in a Windows Internet Explorer 8 **InPrivate Browsing** window without leaving any record of the Web sites that you visit.

Web sites that use the **HTTPS protocol** display *https:* at the beginning of the Web site address to indicate that they provide a secure, encrypted connection.

Windows Internet Explorer 8 uses **domain highlighting** to highlight the part of a Web site's address that clearly identifies the Web site so you can verify that you are at the right Web site.

A **cookie** is a simple text file that contains information about your visit to a Web site. A **third-party cookie** is a cookie placed on your computer by a Web site that provides content to a Web site you visit.

A **first-party cookie** is a cookie placed on your computer by a Web site that you visit.

Pop-up Blocker is an Internet Explorer feature that blocks **pop-up windows** that display advertising from Web sites you visit and that may also place malicious software on your computer.

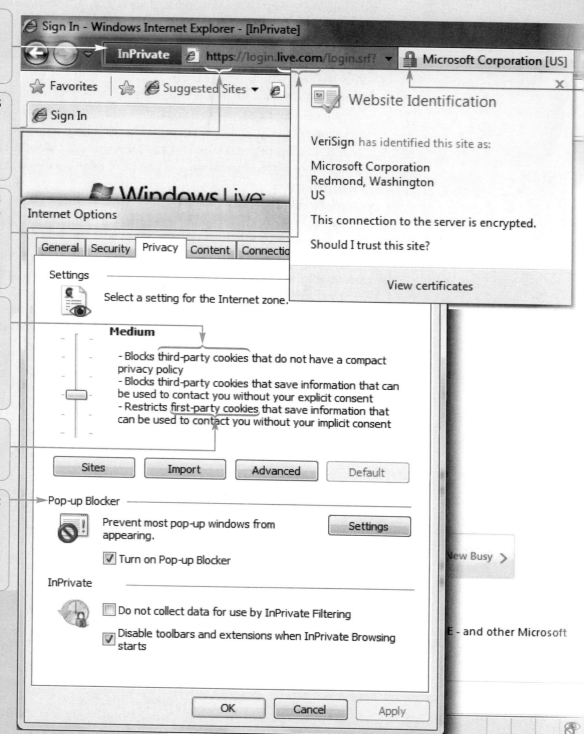

INTERNET SECURITY

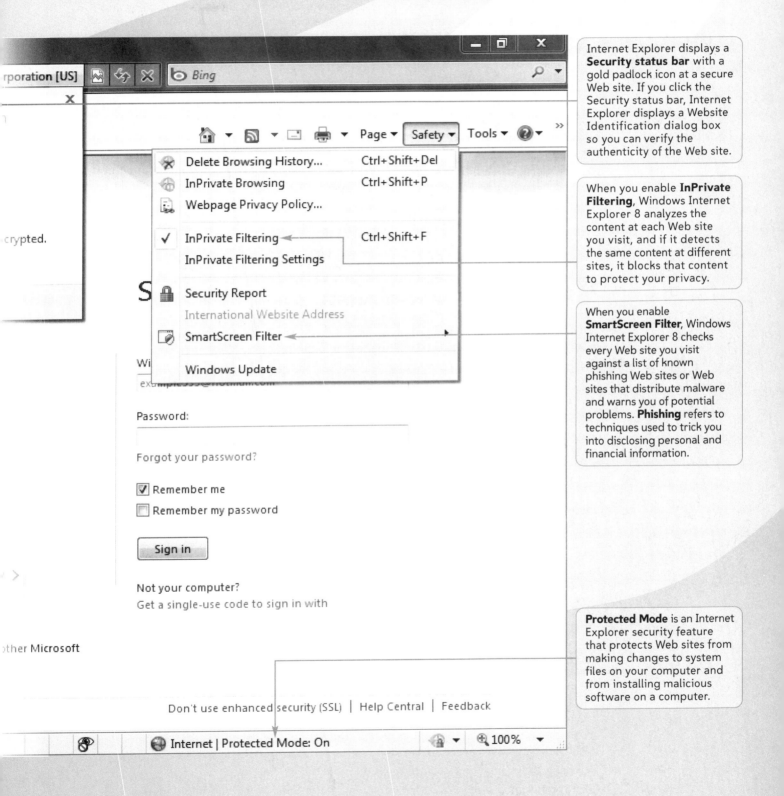

Internet Explorer displays a **Security status bar** with a gold padlock icon at a secure Web site. If you click the Security status bar, Internet Explorer displays a Website Identification dialog box so you can verify the authenticity of the Web site.

When you enable **InPrivate Filtering**, Windows Internet Explorer 8 analyzes the content at each Web site you visit, and if it detects the same content at different sites, it blocks that content to protect your privacy.

When you enable **SmartScreen Filter**, Windows Internet Explorer 8 checks every Web site you visit against a list of known phishing Web sites or Web sites that distribute malware and warns you of potential problems. **Phishing** refers to techniques used to trick you into disclosing personal and financial information.

Protected Mode is an Internet Explorer security feature that protects Web sites from making changes to system files on your computer and from installing malicious software on a computer.

Checking Internet Explorer Security and Privacy Settings

When using a Web browser, you should examine its security and privacy settings and verify that it is properly configured for your needs. If you use more than one Web browser, you should check each Web browser's security and privacy settings. You can check Internet Explorer settings in several ways:

- **Using Internet Explorer**—You can open Internet Explorer and use its Tools menu to examine Internet security and privacy settings and features, such as those for Pop-up Blocker and managing add-ons, both of which you will examine later in this session. In Internet Explorer 8, you can also use the Safety menu to enable InPrivate Browsing and to check InPrivate Filtering and SmartScreen Filter settings, all three of which you will examine later in this session of the tutorial.
- **Using the Control Panel**—You can open the Control Panel and use Internet Options to open the Internet Properties dialog box, where you can examine security and privacy settings.

For other Web browsers, such as Firefox, you must open the Web browser and locate, examine, and adjust its security and privacy settings.

Checking Internet Explorer Security Zone Settings

To reduce the risk that a Web site or a Web application might install malicious software on your computer, perform other types of malicious operations on your computer, or reconfigure your computer's settings, Internet Explorer organizes Web sites into four security zones, each of which determines the security settings for a Web site.

- **Local intranet**—**Local intranet sites** are Web sites that are part of your company's intranet. An **intranet** is a private network that relies on the use of Internet technologies and **protocols** (the rules and conventions for transmitting data over a network) and that is limited to a specific group of people, such as employees within a company. By default, these Web sites are secure Web sites that use the HTTPS protocol to encrypt and decrypt information that you transmit to the Web site. *HTTPS* stands for Hypertext Transfer Protocol over Secure Socket Layer or HTTP over SSL.
- **Trusted sites**—**Trusted sites** are Web sites that you trust to not damage your computer or its data. By default, this security zone is empty; however, Administrators can add trusted Web sites to this zone.
- **Restricted sites**—**Restricted sites** are Web sites that you do not trust and therefore are sites that could potentially damage your computer or its data. By default, this zone is empty; however, you can add a Web site to this zone if you do not trust the safety of the Web site, but need to visit that Web site.
- **Internet**—This security zone includes Web sites not included in the Trusted sites and Restricted sites zones. By default, these Web sites, which typically constitute the majority of Web sites that you access on the Internet, cannot make changes to your computer and cannot view private information on your computer. However, you can change this security zone's settings to download content that might otherwise be considered unsafe.

You can assign specific Web sites to the Local intranet sites, Trusted sites, and Restricted sites security zones and that, in turn, affects the security setting for those Web sites. Also, each security zone has its own default security level; however, you can change the security level for each security zone. The default security level for the four security zones are as follows:

- **Medium-high for the Internet zone**—Using this default setting, Internet Explorer prompts you before downloading potentially unsafe content from the Internet, and it does not download unsigned ActiveX controls that do not have a trusted digital signature. **ActiveX controls** are programs downloaded from a Web site you visit, and they run on your local computer to provide you with access to features at that Web site, such as interactive content. A **digital signature** is an electronic security mark added to a program to verify the publisher of the program (such as Microsoft) and to verify that the program has not been changed since it was last signed. However, even if a program has a valid digital signature, it does not mean it is harmless. Use your best judgment as to whether to trust the content in the program by deciding whether you trust the publisher and whether you trust the Web site that downloads the content. **Unsigned ActiveX controls** are ones that have not been verified as safe, and Internet Explorer prevents these from being downloaded to your computer with the default setting for this security zone. You can change the default setting for the Internet zone from Medium-high to Medium or High. A Medium setting is similar to Medium-high. The High setting provides the maximum safeguards from potentially harmful content from Web sites and disables less secure features. Microsoft also notes that Medium-high is appropriate for most Web sites, and that High is appropriate for Web sites that might have harmful content. The Medium, Medium-high, and High security levels determine the specific setting used for 48 different types of security settings, all of which you can manually adjust individually by using the Custom level button for a security zone.

- **Medium-low for Local intranet**—This setting is appropriate for Web sites on your company's intranet. With this setting, Internet Explorer does not prompt you in most cases before running content, but like the Internet zone, it does not download unsigned ActiveX controls. You can adjust this Security level setting to Low (to indicate that you have absolute trust in these type of Web sites), Medium (similar to Medium-low but with prompts), Medium-high, or High (for maximum safeguards).
- **Medium for Trusted sites**—Internet Explorer prompts you before downloading potentially unsafe content and does not download unsigned ActiveX controls. You can adjust this level to Low (to indicate that you have absolute trust in these type of Web sites), Medium-low (similar to Medium but without prompts), Medium-high, or High (for maximum safeguards).
- **High for Restricted sites**—This setting provides the maximum protection for your computer from Web sites that you suspect might contain harmful content, and it is the only available allowed level for this security zone.

Protected Mode is enabled for two of the four security zones—Internet and Restricted Sites, the sites that require the most protection. In Protected Mode, Internet Explorer operates with restricted privileges, and therefore cannot make changes to the Windows Registry, (which contains all hardware, software, network, user account, object, and system settings) as well as files in system and user folders. That, in turn, protects your computer from Web sites that attempt to install malicious software on your computer and from hackers or intruders who attempt to make changes to your computer system. However, Internet Explorer can make changes to specific locations, such as the Temporary Internet Files, History, Cookies, Favorites, and other temporary file folders so it can provide access to content from Web sites that you visit. Internet Explorer identifies on its status bar the Internet security zone of the Web site you're visiting, and displays the status of Protected Mode (On or Off). If a Web site or Web browser add-on requires more privileges than otherwise allowed by Protected Mode, a User Account Control dialog box prompts for Administrator credentials. An **add-on** is a program that works in conjunction with your Web browser to extend its capabilities. Also, Protected Mode does not apply to a Local intranet or Trusted sites because they are secure by design.

To protect the security and privacy of the company's computers, Arielle and her staff work with employees on an ongoing basis to make sure their security and privacy settings meet their needs and the company's needs. Arielle asks you to examine and configure Internet Explorer settings on your computer so they are appropriate for your use.

To examine Internet Explorer Security settings:

▶ **1.** Open Internet Explorer, click the **Tools** button on the toolbar, click **Internet Options**, and then click the **Security** tab in the Internet Options dialog box. Internet Explorer displays four security zones—Internet, Local intranet, Trusted sites, and Restricted sites. See Figure 7-20.

Figure 7-20 Internet Explorer security zones and security settings

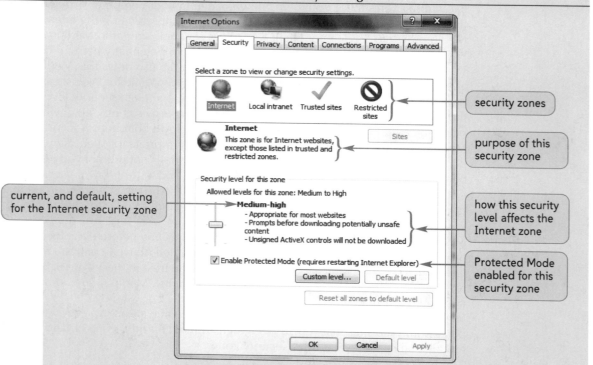

You can select a security zone to view (by clicking the zone's icon) and, if necessary, change security settings for that security zone. Once you select a security zone, Internet Explorer displays information about that security zone under the area that identifies the four security zones. Under "Security level for this zone," Internet Explorer shows the default (or custom) security level for the security zone selected at the top of the Security property sheet, and summarizes features of the security level setting. As noted above, the default setting for the Internet security zone is Medium-high, but you can change that setting to Medium or High, or you can specify more advanced settings by using the Custom level button. Notice that the Enable Protected Mode check box indicates that Internet Explorer uses Protected Mode for the Internet security zone.

▶ **2.** Click the **Trusted sites** icon. Notice that the Enable Protected Mode check box indicates that this feature is not enabled for the Trusted sites security zone because you trust Web sites you place in this zone not to harm your computer.

▶ **3.** Click the **Sites** button. In the Trusted sites dialog box, you can enter the URL for a specific Web site and add it to your Trusted sites security zone if it is a secure site that uses the HTTPS protocol. Internet Explorer automatically inserts the URL of the current Web site in the "Add this website to the zone" box. You might, for example, add your secure email logon Web page, similar to the one shown in Figure 7-21, or your online banking Web site to the Trusted sites security zone.

| Figure 7-21 | Option for adding a Web site to the Trusted sites security zone |

enter a Web site address
to add to Trusted sites

Internet Explorer notes that all Web sites in this zone will use this zone's security settings. Notice that Internet Explorer verifies whether the Web is a secure Web site, with *https:* at the beginning of the Web site address, before you can add it to the Trusted sites security zone. If you add a Web site to this security zone and then change your mind later, you can open this dialog box, select the Web site in the Websites box, and remove it from this security zone. You can also add Web sites to the Local intranet and Restricted sites security zones in the same way.

4. Click the **Close** button to close the Trusted sites dialog box, and then click the **OK** button to close the Internet Options dialog box.

To create a desktop shortcut to the Internet Options property sheet, open the Control Panel, locate Internet Options in the Network and Internet category, and then drag the Internet Options link to the desktop. You can now open the Internet Options property sheet without opening Internet Explorer.

REFERENCE

Checking Internet Explorer Security Settings

- Open Internet Explorer, click the Tools button on the toolbar, click Internet Options, and then click the Security tab in the Internet Options dialog box.
- To select a security zone, click the Internet, Local intranet, Trusted sites, or Restricted sites icon in the "Select a zone to view or change security settings," and then examine the security settings for that zone.
- To change a security zone's setting, drag the slider tab on the slider bar under "Security level for this zone" up or down to view each setting and pick a new setting.
- To check the status of, or change, Internet Explorer's use of Protected Mode, view the current setting in the Enable Protected Mode check box, make any changes you want, and, if necessary, restart your computer after you close Internet Explorer.
- Use the Custom level button to examine and, if necessary, change more advanced settings for a security zone.
- If you want to add a Web site to a security zone, select the security zone first, click the Sites button, enter the URL of the Web site (or verify the URL of the current Web site), click the Add button, and then click the Close button.
- Click the OK button to close the Internet Options dialog box.

By judiciously using these different security zones, you can apply the appropriate security zone settings for the Web sites that you visit.

Using the Security Status Bar

When you visit a Web site where you disclose confidential and personal information, such as logging onto secure email or an online banking Web site, the address for that Web site changes from *http* to *https* to indicate a secure connection that uses encryption to protect information transmitted to the Web site. In earlier versions of Internet Explorer or in other Web browsers, you typically saw a gold lock icon on the status bar of the Web browser window. In Internet Explorer 7 and 8, the Security status bar to the right side of the Address bar now identifies a secure Web site. When you click the Security status bar, Internet Explorer displays a Website Identification dialog box that identifies the name of the authority that certifies the authenticity of Web sites (such as VeriSign), identifies the Web site, and notes that the connection to the Web server at this Web site is encrypted. Figure 7-22 shows a Website Identification dialog box for Windows Live Web site after selecting the option for using enhanced security. To view this type of information, you click the Security Report button with the gold lock icon. Also, the Address bar and Security status bar have a green background to denote that the Web site is safe.

> **TIP**
>
> You can also open the Website Identification dialog box by clicking Safety on the toolbar and then clicking Security Report.

Figure 7-22	Verifying a Web site's identity

padlock identifies this site as a secure Web site

https verifies this site as a secure Web site that uses encryption

Security status bar

Safety button

verifies that Web site is what it claims to be and that it uses encryption

If you click the Security status bar and then click the View certificates link in the Website Identification dialog box, Internet Explorer opens the Certificate dialog box and provides more information on the certifying authority. That certificate also identifies the Web site and the purpose of the certificate

Using the Internet Explorer SmartScreen Filter

Two common threats users face are phishing and pharming. Phishing (pronounced "fishing") refers to a technique for tricking a user into disclosing personal and financial information, such as bank account numbers, PINs, Social Security number, or the user's mother's maiden name, in order to steal the user's assets or identity (or both). If you are the target of a phishing attempt, you might receive a forged email message that appears to be sent from a reputable company with which you do business, such as an ISP, bank, or credit card company. The email message informs you that you need to immediately update your account information, or your account will be closed or suspended, and you will not be able to access services or money (in the case of a bank). You are also informed that you must respond within a short time, or there will be dire consequences. This threat is intended to force you to panic and act quickly without thinking. It's important to these Web sites that you respond immediately because they evade detection by closing a Web site after a few days and then setting up another Web site.

The email message also includes a bogus URL that purports to take you to the Web site for the company with which you do business so you can update your account information. The URL and the fraudulent Web site looks similar or identical to that of the online business with which you have an account; however, if you point to the URL in the body of an email message with the mouse pointer and then examine the status bar at the bottom of the Web browser window, you see a completely different URL—the actual one that's used when you click the URL in the email message. You can use this simple but effective technique to quickly identify a phishing threat because the two URLs do not match. If you receive this type of email message, or if you are suspicious of an email message, do not respond to it. Rather than click the URL in the email message, contact the company in question by telephone, in person, or via its online support Web site to verify whether it requested you to update your account information and to let the company in question know about a potential problem that its customers face.

Pharming (pronounced "farming") is similar to phishing and relies on an email message that informs you to immediately update account information. However, pharming may use malicious software or tamper electronically with a URL to redirect your Web browser to a Web site that appears identical or very similar to that of a company with which you do business to obtain personal and financial information without your knowledge or permission. Again, do not click the URL in the message; instead, contact the company by telephone, in person, or via its online support Web site to verify whether the request is legitimate and to warn them of a potential problem.

INSIGHT

Protecting Your Identity and Assets

If you have been the victim of a phishing scam or identity theft, or if you want more information about preventing these types of problem, you can use the following online resources:

- **Anti-Phishing Working Group** (*www.antiphishing.org*)—This industry association Web site has information on avoiding phishing scams and, just as important, has detailed step-by-step lists of what you should do (and the order in which you should do it) and whom you should contact if you have given out financial information, such as information about your credit card, debit card, ATM card, bank account, or eBay account. It also lists steps to take if you downloaded a computer virus or Trojan horse that captured information off your computer, and steps to take if you've given out personal information, such as your Social Security number.
- **Federal Deposit Insurance Corporation (FDIC)** (*www.fdic.gov/consumers/ consumer/alerts/phishing.html*)—The FDIC site has information about phishing and phishing alerts.
- **Internet Crime Complaint Center (IC3)** (*www.ic3.gov/default.aspx*)—This site is the result of a partnership between the FBI and the National White Collar Crime Center (NW3C), and it focuses on cybercrime.

All of these Web sites contain a wealth of information that you can examine and compare to decide your best course of action in a given situation. You might very well discover that their information includes steps to take that you had never considered. As everyone knows, over time, Web sites and Web site URLs change, but you can use any search engine to locate these and other Web sites. You want to act quickly, but you also want to act effectively.

To counteract phishing and pharming as well as other types of threats posed by unsafe Web sites that install malicious software, Microsoft has included a SmartScreen Filter in Internet Explorer. The SmartScreen Filter checks Web sites that you visit against a list of unsafe Web sites verified by the Microsoft SmartScreen service. If you visit a Web site that is on a list of known phishing Web sites or Web sites that distribute malware,

Internet Explorer displays a Web page blocking access to that Web site and the Address bar appears in red. Then, you can bypass the unsafe Web site. The Microsoft SmartScreen service, with a constantly updated list of reported phishing and pharming Web sites, is essential because these Web sites appear for a short time and then move to a new location to evade detection.

The SmartScreen Filter protects you in three ways. First, it analyzes Web pages you visit and attempts to determine if the Web pages contain characteristics common to unsafe Web sites. If it detects such a Web page, then it displays a message and urges you to be cautious. Second, it checks these Web sites against a list of reported phishing Web sites and Web sites that distribute malicious software, then it blocks the Web site and the Address bar turns red to indicate a threat. That list of reported phishing and malicious Web sites is updated hourly. Third, the SmartScreen Filter checks files you download from Web pages against that same list, and if it finds that a file is unsafe, it blocks the download. To counter these threats, the SmartScreen Filter sends the following information to Microsoft via a secure encrypted connection so Microsoft can check whether these Web sites are safe:

- The address of the Web site that you visit, standard computer information (including your computer's IP address, Web browser type, Web browser language, and access times), and the SmartScreen Filter version number.
- Search terms, or data you enter in a form. Search terms might inadvertently include personal information; however, filters are used to remove this information (where possible). Microsoft does not use this information to identify or contact you or to target advertising to you.
- Periodically, information is sent to Microsoft about how you used the SmartScreen Filter (such as information about the time and total number of Web sites that you visited), along with the name and path of files that you download, your Web browser version, Web browser language, the use of Compatibility View, and a unique identifier (a randomly generated number) produced by Internet Explorer.

Compatibility View improves the display of Web pages designed for earlier versions of Internet Explorer so they appear as they would in an earlier version of Internet Explorer. Internet Explorer displays the Compatibility View button 🖼 on the Address bar if it detects a Web page that is not compatible so you can enable this feature.

In its Internet Explorer 8 privacy policy (*www.microsoft.com/windows/internet-explorer/privacy.aspx*), Microsoft notes that it only uses this information to analyze the performance of the SmartScreen Filter and to improve the quality of its products and services.

If Internet Explorer displays a message asking you if you are trying to visit a Web site, then that Web site exhibits features of an unsafe Web site, but that Web site is not on the list of reported unsafe Web sites. Though the Web site might be safe, you should proceed with caution and make sure you trust that Web site before providing personal or financial information.

Because of the widespread use of phishing and pharming techniques, Arielle recommends that you verify that the SmartScreen Filter is enabled.

To check the status of the Internet Explorer SmartScreen filter:

▶ 1. Click the **Safety** button on the Internet Explorer toolbar, and then point to **SmartScreen Filter**. Internet Explorer displays the SmartScreen Filter menu. If your SmartScreen Filter menu contains the option "Turn On SmartScreen Filter," then this filter is turned off, and Internet Explorer does not check the safety of the Web sites you visit. If your SmartScreen Filter menu contains the option "Turn Off SmartScreen Filter," then the SmartScreen Filter is turned on, and Internet Explorer is checking Web sites that you visit.

▶ **2.** If your SmartScreen Filter is turned off, and if you want to enable this filter, click **Turn On SmartScreen Filter**. Internet Explorer opens the Microsoft SmartScreen Filter dialog box and enables the option for using this filter. See Figure 7-23.

| Figure 7-23 | Microsoft SmartScreen Filter enabled |

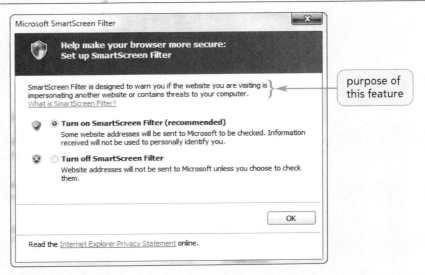

▶ **3.** If you opened the Microsoft SmartScreen Filter dialog box and want to enable this feature, choose the setting you want to use, and then click the **OK** button.

▶ **4.** Keep Internet Explorer open for the next section of the tutorial.

If you visit a Web site and want to determine whether it is an unsafe Web site, you can use the "Check This Website" option on the SmartScreen Filter menu. This option is also useful if you turned off the SmartScreen Filter, but then decide you want to check a Web site you visit. You can use the "Report Unsafe Website" option on the SmartScreen Filter menu to report the Web site you're visiting to Microsoft so it can determine whether it is an unsafe Web site.

REFERENCE

Using the SmartScreen Filter

- To turn the SmartScreen Filter on, click the Safety button on the Internet Explorer toolbar, point to SmartScreen Filter, and then click "Turn On SmartScreen Filter."
- To check a Web site to determine whether it's safe or unsafe, click the Safety button on the toolbar, point to SmartScreen Filter, and then click "Check This Website."
- To report a Web site you suspect is unsafe, click the Safety button on the toolbar, point to SmartScreen Filter, and then click "Report Unsafe Website."
- To turn off the SmartScreen Filter, click the Safety button on the toolbar, point to SmartScreen Filter, and then click "Turn Off SmartScreen Filter."

Internet Explorer 7 had a comparable safety feature called the Phishing Filter.

Problem Solving: Dealing with Email Hoaxes

Email hoaxes are another problem faced by individuals in a work environment as well as at home. A hoax is an email message sent from a coworker, friend, or family member warning you of a problem that poses a risk to your computer. The problem sounds plausible, and the email message usually includes technical information to make you believe it's true. Furthermore, the email message quotes an expert to make you believe the threat is real, and may also make claims about reputable companies who have verified the problem. The email message then recommends that you send an email message to everyone you know and warn them of the threat, and have them in turn send an email message to everyone they know, warning of a problem that does not actually exist. The end result can be that the email traffic overloads and might even shut down email servers of companies and businesses, as has occurred in the past. If you receive this type of message, first check its validity by visiting a Web site that contains information about email hoaxes (such as the Symantec Web site at *www.symantec.com/norton/security_response/threatexplorer/risks/ hoaxes.jsp*) before you forward that email message to everyone you know.

Make a point of knowing your company's email policies and paying attention to communications from your IT staff about malicious software, email phishing and pharming attempts, hoaxes, and spam. Work cooperatively with your IT staff to report problems and inform coworkers, friends, and family members of the potential problems caused by email hoaxes, phishing, pharming, and spam, and provide them with the necessary information for identifying email hoaxes. By complying with your company's email policies, you can reduce cyberattacks, prevent infections from malicious software, reduce user downtime and help desk calls, and improve overall productivity.

Using the Internet Explorer Pop-up Blocker

Pop-up windows are commonly used to display advertising from Web sites that you visit. The pop-up window may appear either in front of your Web browser window, blocking part of your view onto a Web page, or behind the Web browser window unknown to you. In the latter case, you do not see the pop-up window until you close or minimize your Web browser window. While many people find pop-up windows annoying when they are trying to browse the Web and view Web pages, Web sites can also use pop-up windows to place malicious software on your computer, so you need to control the use of pop-up windows.

Internet Explorer has a Pop-up Blocker that can prevent many different types of pop-up windows from automatically opening. However, if you deliberately click a link or button for a pop-up window, that pop-up window will open unless you adjust Pop-up Blocker settings. The Pop-up Blocker feature will also prevent pop-up windows that are larger than the viewable screen or outside the viewable screen area from opening.

Next, you want to examine your Pop-up Blocker settings as you continue your thorough check of your new company laptop.

TIP

Pop-up Blocker settings are also accessible from the Privacy property sheet in the Internet Options dialog box.

To view Pop-up Blocker settings:

1. In the Internet Explorer window, click the **Tools** button on the toolbar, and point to **Pop-up Blocker**. You can use the Pop-up Blocker menu to turn Pop-up Blocker on or off, and to view Pop-up Blocker settings.

2. Click **Pop-up Blocker Settings**. See Figure 7-24. Under Exceptions in the Pop-up Blocker Settings dialog box, Internet Explorer notes that most pop-ups are currently blocked.

Trouble? If Pop-up Blocker Settings on the Pop-up Blocker menu is dimmed, click Turn On Pop-up Blocker, click Yes in the Pop-up Blocker dialog box, click Tools on the menu bar, point to Pop-up Blocker, and then click Pop-up Blocker settings.

Figure 7-24 | **Viewing Pop-up Blocker settings**

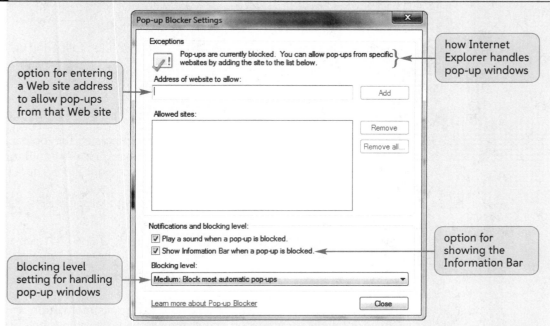

option for entering a Web site address to allow pop-ups from that Web site

how Internet Explorer handles pop-up windows

option for showing the Information Bar

blocking level setting for handling pop-up windows

Internet Explorer also notes that you can allow pop-up windows from a specific Web site by adding the site to the Allowed sites list box. You type the URL of the Web site in the "Address of website to allow" box, and then click the Add button to allow that Web site to display pop-up windows. Later, if you no longer want to allow pop-ups from an allowed site, you select that site in the Allowed sites box and click the Remove button.

Under Notifications and blocking level, you can specify whether you want a sound to play when a pop-up is blocked, and whether you want Internet Explorer to display an Information Bar when a pop-up window is blocked. (The Information Bar appears as a bar that extends across the top of the Web page you're examining.) You can use the Blocking level button to specify one of three settings for pop-up windows. The High setting blocks all pop-up windows, the Medium setting is the default and blocks most automatic pop-up windows, and the Low setting allows pop-up windows from secure sites. If you select the High setting, Internet Explorer will block all pop-up windows, even those that appear after you click a link or button.

When Pop-Up Blocker blocks a pop-up window from opening, Internet Explorer displays an Information Bar dialog box, such as the one shown in Figure 7-25, and displays the following message on the left side of the Information Bar: "Pop-up blocked. To see this pop-up or additional options click here".

Figure 7-25 **Pop-up window blocked**

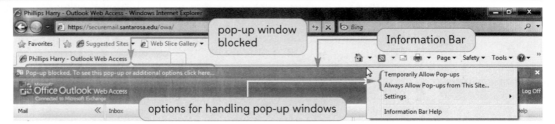

If you click the Information Bar, it displays a menu with the following options:

- Temporarily Allow Pop-ups
- Always Allow Pop-ups from This Site
- Settings
- Information Bar Help

If you open the Pop-up Blocker menu after selecting Tools on the toolbar, Internet Explorer lists the first two of the four options listed above. "Information Bar Help" opens Windows Help and Support and displays frequently asked questions about the Internet Explorer Information Bar.

If you point to Settings, you see a cascading menu with these options:

- Turn Off Pop-up Blocker
- Show Information Bar for Pop-ups
- More Settings

"Show Information Bar for Pop-ups" is enabled, and "More Settings" opens the Pop-up Blocker Settings dialog box.

Internet Explorer also uses the Information Bar to display information about security risks (such as installing an unsafe ActiveX control or security settings below recommended levels), downloads, and other activities (all of which are described in detail in Windows Help and Support).

Even if Pop-up Blocker is enabled, you might still see pop-up windows if spyware is installed on your computer. In this case, you have to use antispyware software to remove the spyware from your computer.

Troubleshooting Problems with Pop-up Windows

It's not uncommon for Web sites to use pop-up windows to display advertising, so your first inclination might be to block all pop-up windows. However, you might need to display certain types of pop-up windows from specific Web sites and to adjust Pop-up Blocker settings to accommodate your use of these pop-up windows. For example, your Web-based email software might display your Address Book with email addresses for your important contacts in a pop-up window, or your online banking Web site might display a pop-up window for logging on and conducting an online transaction. Or your email software may need to open a pop-up window for opening or downloading an email attachment. In these instances, you want to make sure that these Web sites can display pop-up windows by adding them to your Allowed sites list (or adjust your Pop-up Blocker settings). Also, if you experience problems accessing a feature at a Web site, Internet Explorer might be blocking a pop-up window that you need to access. Add that site to your Allowed sites list and determine whether that resolves the problem. If not, you can always remove the site from your Allowed sites list.

To close the Pop-up Blocker Settings dialog box:

▶ **1.** Click the **Close** button to close the Pop-Up Blocker Settings dialog box.

▶ **2.** Keep Internet Explorer open for the next section of the tutorial.

REFERENCE

Blocking Pop-up Windows with Pop-up Blocker

- Open Internet Explorer, click the Tools button on the toolbar, and point to Pop-up Blocker. On the Pop-up Blocker menu, click Turn On Pop-up Blocker to enable Pop-up Blocker, or click Turn Off Pop-up Blocker to turn off this feature.
- If you turn on Pop-up Blocker, or if Pop-up Blocker is already turned on, click the Tools button on the toolbar, point to Pop-up Blocker, and then click Pop-up Blocker Settings.
- To set the Blocking level, click the Blocking level button, and then click the High, Medium, or Low setting.
- To enable the Information Bar, add a check mark to the "Show Information Bar when a pop-up is blocked" check box.
- To allow pop-ups from a Web site, type the address of the Web site in the "Address of website to allow" box, and then click the Add button.
- To remove an Allowed site, click the name of the Web site in the Allowed sites list box, and then click the Remove button.
- Click the Close button to close the Pop-up Blocker settings dialog box.

The Pop-up Blocker is a useful tool because some Web sites overwhelm the user by displaying one pop-up window after another and block your view of a Web page or leave pop-up windows all over your desktop after you close your Web browser.

Managing Internet Explorer Add-ons

As noted earlier, add-ons are programs that work with Internet Explorer and expand the capabilities of the Web browser. You acquire add-ons from Web sites that you visit. Some add-ons require your permission before you install them; others are installed without your permission or knowledge. In the latter case, the add-on might be installed as part of another program that you download and install on your computer. Also, Windows 7 might install some add-ons.

From Internet Explorer, you can view information on different types of add-ons, and you can filter your view to show only those add-ons that are currently loaded, only those that run without your permission, only those that are downloaded controls, or all add-ons. You can also access information about the following categories of add-ons: Browser Helper Objects (BHO), Browser Extensions, Toolbars, Explorer Bars, and ActiveX Controls. A **Browser Helper Object (BHO)** is a dynamic link library (with the .dll file extension) that extends the capabilities of (or adds functionality to) a Web browser. A **Browser Extension** is a dynamic link library or program that also extends the capabilities of a Web browser. An ActiveX control is a program module that supports the use of interactive content such as multimedia and animation on Web pages. A Toolbar refers to an additional button that appears on the Internet Explorer toolbar, or one that you can access from the Toolbar options button ⮞ on the right side of the toolbar.

After discussing Internet Explorer add-ons with Arielle at your weekly staff meeting, you decide to use the Internet Explorer Add-on Manager to examine information about the add-ons on your mobile computer.

To view add-on settings:

▶ **1.** In Internet Explorer, click **Tools** on the toolbar, and then click **Manage Add-ons**. The Manage Add-ons dialog box lists categories of add-ons under Add-on Types, and displays add-ons that fall into the first category—Toolbars and Extensions. See Figure 7-26.

Figure 7-26 | **Viewing Internet Explorer add-ons**

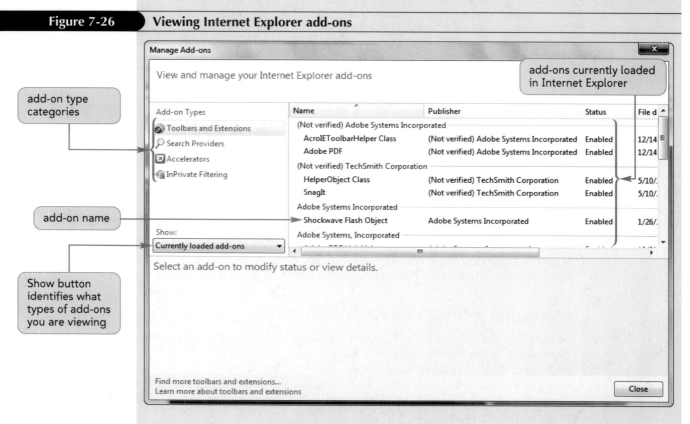

Add-ons are grouped by publisher and include the add-on name, the status, file date, version number, and load time in seconds (although not all these items are visible in Figure 7-26). Note also that the Show button under Add-on Types indicates that you are viewing currently loaded add-ons.

If you click an add-on in the Manage Add-ons dialog box, and then click the "Search for this add-on via default search provider" link in the bottom pane, you can view search results that pertain to that add-on, perhaps find out what it does, and possibly also determine whether it is safe.

Windows 7 provides a simple way for turning off all Internet Explorer add-ons. Instead of starting Internet Explorer using the taskbar Internet Explorer button, you open the All Programs menu, click Accessories, click System Tools, and then click Internet Explorer (No Add-ons).

TIP

To enable or disable an add-on, click the add-on name, and click the Enable or Disable button at the bottom of the Manage Add-ons dialog box.

To view information about an add-on:

▶ **1.** If you have an add-on for Adobe Systems, such as Adobe PDF Link Helper, double-click that **add-on name**, and then examine the information in the More Information dialog box; otherwise, select another add-on of interest to you, double-click the **add-on name**, and then examine the information in the More Information dialog box. See Figure 7-27 for information on the Adobe PDF Link Helper add-on.

Figure 7-27   **Viewing detailed information on a Browser Helper Object**

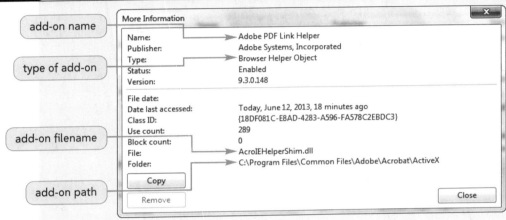

On the computer used for Figure 7-27, the More Information dialog box identifies the name of the add-on (Adobe PDF Link Helper), the publisher (Adobe Systems, Incorporated), the type of add-on (a Browser Helper Object), the status, version number, the name of the actual file for this add-on, and the path to the location of this add-on (the ActiveX folder). The Adobe PDF Link Helper is one type of add-on for opening PDF files in the Internet Explorer Web browser window.

Knowing the filename and path to where the add-on is stored is important if you want to find more information about an add-on or determine whether it is unsafe. A malicious program file might have the same name as a legitimate add-on, but it is stored in a different folder than the one containing the legitimate add-on.

To view more information about an add-on:

▶ **1.** In the More Information dialog box, click the **Close** button.

▶ **2.** In the Manage Add-ons dialog box, under Add-on Types, click the **Show** button, and then click **Run without permission**. You now see add-ons, such as Shockwave Flash Object and Adobe PDF Reader, which do not require permission to run. These add-ons are preapproved by Microsoft Corporation, a service provider, or your computer manufacturer.

▶ **3.** If you have an add-on for Adobe Systems, such as Shockwave Flash Object or Adobe PDF Reader, double-click that **add-on name**, and then examine the information in the More Information dialog box; otherwise, select another add-on of interest to you, double-click the **add-on name**, and then examine the information in the More Information dialog box.

On the computer used for Figure 7-28, the More Information dialog box identifies the name of the add-on (in this figure, Shockwave Flash Object), and provides information similar to what you examined for the previous add-on, except that in this case, the add-on is an ActiveX control.

| Figure 7-28 | Viewing detailed information on an ActiveX control |

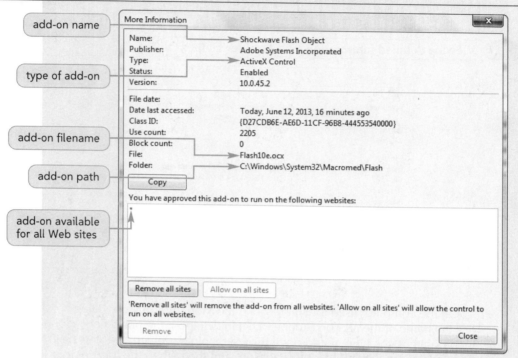

Under the Copy button, note that you are informed that you have approved this add-on to run on the following Web sites. The single asterisk indicates all Web sites.

4. Close the More Information dialog box for the add-on you selected.

5. Under Add-on Types, click the **Show** button, and then click **Downloaded controls**. The Manage Add-ons dialog box now shows any add-ons downloaded and stored on your computer. These downloaded controls are ActiveX controls.

6. Click the **Show** button, and then click **Currently loaded add-ons**. The Show list also contains an option for showing all add-ons.

You can also examine information on add-ons for Search Providers, Accelerators, and InPrivate Filtering. **Accelerators**, a feature introduced in Internet Explorer 8, allow you to access features of another Web site without having to navigate to that Web site. To use an accelerator, you select text on a Web page (such as the name of your college), and after a blue Accelerator icon ![icon] appears, you click that Accelerator icon to display a menu of options, such as Blog with Windows Live, E-mail with Windows Live, Map with Bing, Search with Bing, and Translate with Bing, and then select a menu option to access the feature of interest to you, such as a map for your college. InPrivate Filtering, a feature introduced in Internet Explorer 8, prevents Web sites from collecting information about the Web sites you visit. You will examine InPrivate Filtering later in this session of the tutorial.

To view information on other types of add-ons:

▶ **1.** Under Add-on Types, click **Search Providers**. The Manage Add-ons dialog box now lists any search provider add-ons, such as Bing.

▶ **2.** Under Add-on Types, click **Accelerators**. The Manage Add-ons dialog box lists accelerators that are available for use in Internet Explorer 8.

▶ **3.** Close the Manage Add-ons dialog box, but keep Internet Explorer open for the next section of the tutorial.

Because add-ons can pose a security and privacy risk, or might be malicious software, it's important to be familiar with the concept and use of add-ons used by your Web browsers.

REFERENCE

Examining Information on Add-ons

- Open Internet Explorer, click Tools on the toolbar, and then click Manage Add-ons.
- To view information about a currently loaded add-on in the Toolbars and Extensions Add-on Types group, double-click an add-on name to open the More information dialog box, and after examining details about the add-on, click the Close button.
- To view information about other types of add-ons, click the Show button, and then choose All add-ons, Run without permission, or Downloaded controls.
- To view information about other add-on Types, click Search Providers, Accelerators, or InPrivate Filtering under Add-on Types.
- To search for information about an add-on, click the add-on name, and then click the "Search for this add-on via default search provider" link in the bottom pane.
- To disable an add-on, click the add-on name, and then click the Disable button.
- Click the Close button to close the Manage Add-ons dialog box.

There are several approaches you can use to research information about add-ons:

- If the Manage Add-ons dialog box identifies the publisher, you could send an email message to the company's tech support personnel and ask for details about the add-on, including not only what does it do, but also why is it necessary.
- If the Manage Add-ons dialog box identifies the publisher, you can go to the support Web page of that publisher, and then search for information about that browser helper object, browser extension, toolbar, Explorer bar, or ActiveX control. To locate the type of information you want, you can also specify not only the add-on name but also the add-on type. Or you could search for the exact name of the add-on file. If you find no information, then you might want to try a more generalized search phrase, such as add-ons or add-ins.
- If the Manage Add-ons dialog box identifies the publisher, you can open the Help system for that software product on your computer and search for information on add-ons (or add-ins).
- There are specific Web sites, such as Sysinfo.org (*www.sysinfo.org*) that contain information about browser helper objects and other types of add-ons. These Web sites attempt to research and evaluate the purpose of add-ons and any problems that they might pose. It is a good idea to compare information from several Web sites that you consider reliable before you make a decision about how to handle an add-on.
- You could also use a search engine like Google. You might find one or more Web sites that identify the purpose of the add-on. You might also find a large number of Web sites where individuals like you are trying to find out more information about an add-on, or are suspicious of the add-on for one reason or the other (such as the publisher not being verified). This type of search might also produce no search results or far more search results than you can manage to examine.

Add-ons, especially browser helper objects and toolbars, are an easy medium for introducing malicious software to your computer, so individuals who troubleshoot computer problems must take into account these types of objects.

Developing a Strategy for Managing Cookies

Another potential privacy issue is the use of cookies, or simple text files, placed on your computer by Web sites you visit. A cookie contains the Web site's address as well as information about the date and time of a visit, which Web pages you examined, and other information, such as your preferred language or country setting or the expiration date and time for the cookie. A cookie might also contain personal information you provide a Web site, such as your user name and user preferences.

First introduced with the Netscape Web browser, cookies are used by many Web sites, including personal Web sites set up by individuals (and often hosted by their ISP). Some individuals create their own Web pages with online tools that automatically place cookies on visitor's computers, and the owners of those Web pages are not even aware of this practice. Although not all Web sites use cookies, their use by many Web sites has raised the issues of online profiling and online privacy and how information stored in a cookie might be used by the Web site that created the cookie, and perhaps by other Web sites. Although a piece of information about yourself may seem harmless, it might be used later in a way you never expect. **Online profiling** refers to techniques that Web sites use to gather information about your personal preferences without your knowledge or consent.

Advertising agencies are obviously interested in the use of cookies because they can develop a profile of your interests from the Web sites that you visit, and then use this information to develop more effective marketing strategies that promote products you are likely to find interesting, and that display that information on Web pages and in customized banner advertising. Web sites that sell products or provide services might allow other companies with related products or services to place advertising on their Web site, and more than likely, those other Web sites will place cookies on your computer as well. In some cases, Web sites might rely on income from such advertising to cover the costs of maintaining the Web site.

Cookies can also be useful to you, so you do not want to arbitrarily block all cookies. For example, if you frequently visit the same Web site, and if that Web site requires you to identify yourself, a cookie stored on your computer the first time you visit the site will expedite your access to that same site later. If you visit an interactive gaming site, and advance to different skill levels, that Web site can use a cookie on your computer to identify the skill level you last attained so you can pick up where you left off when you return. Cookies are also used to track information in online transactions, such as purchasing products or online banking, so you must allow cookies to be placed on your computer to perform those transactions. If you visit a Web site that sells products in different countries, that site might place a cookie on your computer that identifies your country (and therefore your language system). Also, your Web browser must accept cookies to access online email accounts.

If you decide that you do not want a Web site tracking information about you and developing an online profile of your interests, you can use your Web browser to remove and block future cookies from that Web site.

The next group of settings that you want to examine on your mobile computer is its privacy settings.

To examine Privacy settings:

▶ 1. Click the **Tools** button on the Internet Explorer toolbar, click **Internet Options**, and in the Internet Options dialog box, click the **Privacy** tab. Under Settings, Internet Explorer displays the current setting for handling cookies in the Internet security zone. See Figure 7-29.

Figure 7-29   **Internet Explorer default privacy settings**

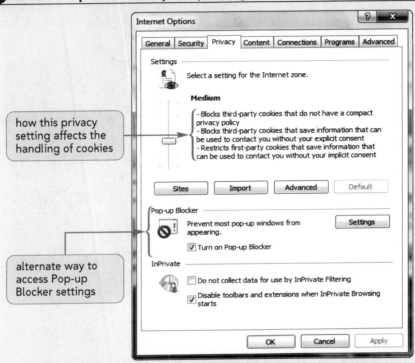

how this privacy setting affects the handling of cookies

alternate way to access Pop-up Blocker settings

The default Internet security zone setting is Medium; however, you can use the Settings slider bar to choose an alternate privacy setting, such as Block All Cookies, High, Medium High, Low, or Accept All Cookies. Notice that you can also access Pop-up Blocker settings from this same property sheet.

If the security level is set at Medium (the default setting), Internet Explorer blocks cookies from third-party Web sites that do not have a compact privacy policy, blocks cookies from third-party Web sites that save information that can be used to contact you without your explicit consent, and restricts cookies from first-party Web sites that save information that can be used to contact you without your implicit consent. A **compact privacy policy** is a condensed privacy statement that explains what information a Web site gathers about you, how it uses that information, and your options for managing that information. Usually there will be a link in fine print at the bottom of a Web page that will take you to the Web page that contains the compact private policy, and then you can use yet another link to view the complete privacy policy (instead of just a summary). A **first-party Web site** is a Web site whose Web page you are currently viewing, whereas a **third-party Web site** is another Web site that provides content (such as banner advertising) to the Web site you're viewing. **Explicit consent** means that you contacted the Web site and agreed (in some way) that the Web site can use information it collects about you to contact you. For example, you may have filled out a form at a Web site specifically requesting their newsletter. **Implicit consent** means that you have not informed a

Web site that you do not want it to use information it collects about you to contact you. In other words, you have not opted out. As you might imagine, what constitutes implicit consent can be hard to determine. For example, does your visit to a Web site constitute implicit consent?

Internet Explorer lets you override automatic cookie handling and decide whether to accept or reject a cookie when prompted. You can also specify whether you want to always allow **session cookies**—temporary cookies that expire and are deleted when you close Internet Explorer. In contrast, a **persistent cookie** is one that remains on your computer and that can be read by the Web site that created it when you next visit that Web site.

To further protect your mobile computer, you want to examine the options for overriding automatic cookie handling.

To override automatic cookie handling:

1. Click the **Advanced** button on the Privacy property sheet, and then click the **Override automatic cookie handling** check box. In the Advanced Privacy Settings dialog box, you can override automatic cookie handling by Internet Explorer and specify whether you want to accept or block first-party and third-party cookies, or whether you want Internet Explorer to always prompt you before accepting a cookie. See Figure 7-30.

Figure 7-30	Overriding automatic cookie handling

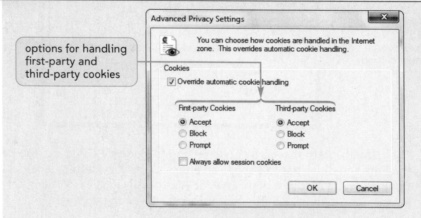

options for handling first-party and third-party cookies

If you choose the Prompt option, then Internet Explorer displays a Privacy Alert dialog box when you visit a Web site and prompts you as to whether or not you want to accept a cookie. The prompt will also identify the Web site, so you have the advantage of knowing which Web sites are putting cookies on your computer. You can also use the information display in these Privacy Alerts to find out whether third-party Web sites are putting cookies on your computers because their URL will be different from the Web site you visit. When prompted, you can choose to accept or reject each cookie, and you can choose whether you want to apply the same option to every cookie sent from a Web site. You can also specify whether you want to always allow session cookies.

2. Click the **Prompt** option button under First-party Cookies, click the **Prompt** option button under Third-party Cookies, click the **OK** button to close the Advanced Privacy Settings dialog box, and then click the **OK** button in the Internet Options dialog box.

▶ **3.** Browse to a Web site that you frequently visit, and if you see a Privacy Alert dialog box similar to the one shown in Figure 7-31, examine the information in the dialog box and verify the URL of the Web site attempting to place a cookie on your computer, click the **Apply my decision to all cookies from this website** check box, click the **Block Cookie** button to block all first-party cookies from this Web site, and then determine whether blocking cookies affects your access to that Web site. A first-party alert will include the domain name of the Web site, such as microsoft.com, that you entered in the Address bar.

Figure 7-31 **First-party privacy alert showing the domain name of the Web site you specified**

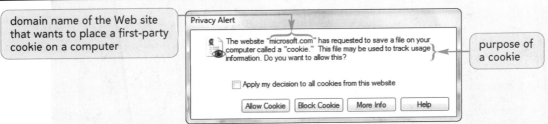

domain name of the Web site that wants to place a first-party cookie on a computer

Privacy Alert

The website "microsoft.com" has requested to save a file on your computer called a "cookie." This file may be used to track usage information. Do you want to allow this?

☐ Apply my decision to all cookies from this website

Allow Cookie | Block Cookie | More Info | Help

purpose of a cookie

▶ **4.** If you see another Privacy Alert dialog box while accessing that same site, examine the information to determine if the cookie comes from another Web site (a third-party Web site with a different domain name in the URL that does not correspond to the Web site you chose to visit), click the **Apply my decision to all cookies from this website** check box, and then click the **Block Cookie** button to block all third-party cookies from that particular third-party Web site. Because more than one third-party Web site might place cookies on your computer when you visit a Web site, you might see more Privacy Alert dialog boxes for other third-parties. You can use the information you glean from these Web sites in this step and the following step to allow or block Web sites in the next section.

▶ **5.** Use this same approach to visit several other Web sites that you frequently visit and to block cookies from both first-party and third-party Web sites while at the same time noting which Web sites are placing cookies on your computer. You can also use these addresses to visit the third-party Web sites to determine the company name and its business purpose, and then decide whether you want them to place cookies on your computer.

▶ **6.** To restore default privacy settings, click **Tools** on the Internet Explorer toolbar, click **Internet Options** on the Tools menu, click the **Privacy** tab in the Internet Options dialog box, click the **Advanced** button on the Privacy property sheet, click the **Accept** option button under First-party Cookies, click the **Accept** option button under Third-party Cookies, click the **Override automatic cookie handling** check box (to turn this feature off), click the **OK** button in the Advanced Privacy Settings dialog box, and then click the **Apply** button in the Internet Options dialog box. If you now visit the same Web sites you just visited, they will place cookies on your computer, and Internet Explorer will not display Privacy Alerts.

Now that you know some of the Web sites that place cookies on your computer, you can allow or block cookies from those specific Web sites. You might want to seriously consider the option of blocking all third-party cookies because the Web sites are only collecting information about your browsing habits and your personal interests.

To allow or block cookies from specific Web sites:

1. Click the **Sites** button on the Privacy property sheet. In the Per Site Privacy Actions dialog box, you can specify the addresses of Web sites that are always permitted to place cookies on your computer, and you can specify the addresses of Web sites that can never place cookies on your computer, regardless of their privacy policies. See Figure 7-32.

Figure 7-32 Specifying cookie usage by Web site

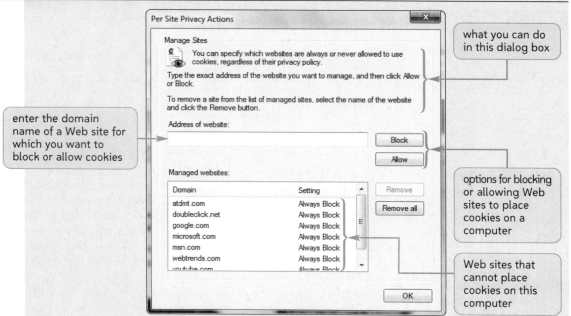

If you blocked first-party and third-party cookies from an earlier Web site, those Web sites are displayed in the Managed websites list box, and cookies from those Web sites are always blocked, as shown on the computer used for this figure.

2. In the Managed websites box, click the **address** of the Web site that you just visited, and then click the **Remove** button. Internet Explorer removes that Web site from the Managed websites list box, and if you visit that Web site again, Internet Explorer will accept first-party cookies from that Web site. If you also blocked cookies from a third-party Web site earlier, Internet Explorer will continue to block third-party cookies from that Web site.

3. In the Address of website box, type the **address** of the Web site that you just removed from the Managed websites list box, and then click the **Allow** button. The address for that Web site is added to the Managed websites list box, and Internet Explorer will now always accept first-party cookies from that Web site.

4. In the Per Site Privacy Actions dialog box, click the **OK** button, and in the Internet Options dialog box, click the **OK** button.

5. Navigate to yet another Web site that you frequently visit, and then use the **Back** button 🔙 to return to the previously visited Web site. You no longer see Privacy Alert dialog boxes for first-party and third-party cookies.

6. To restore your original privacy settings, click **Tools** on the toolbar, click **Internet Options**, click the **Privacy** tab, click the **Sites** button, either click the **Remove all** button to remove all Managed Web sites, or select individual Web sites one at a time in the Managed Web sites list box and click **Remove** to remove each Web site. Click the **OK** button in the Per Site Privacy Actions dialog box, and then click the **OK** button in the Internet Options dialog box.

7. Keep Internet Explorer open for the next section of the tutorial.

A long-established Web site with information about cookies and cookie demos is Cookie Central (*www.cookiecentral.com*).

REFERENCE

Controlling Cookie Usage

- Open Internet Explorer, click the Tools button on the Internet Explorer toolbar, click Internet Options, and in the Internet Options dialog box, click the Privacy tab, examine the current Privacy setting for the Internet zone, and, if necessary, use the Settings slider bar to adjust the setting for the Internet zone.
- To override automatic cookie handling, click the Advanced button on the Privacy property sheet, and then click the "Override automatic cookie handling" check box in the Advanced Privacy Settings dialog box. Click the Accept, Block, or Prompt option button under First-party Cookies and under Third-party Cookies. If you want to allow session cookies, click "Always allow session cookies." Click OK to close the Advanced Privacy Settings dialog box, and then click the Apply button to apply the changes you made.
- To allow or block cookies from a specific Web site, click the Sites button on the Privacy property sheet, type the address of a Web site in the "Address of website" box in the Per Site Privacy Actions dialog box, and then click the Block button to always block cookies from that Web site or click the Allow button to always allow cookies from that Web site. To remove a Web site from the Managed websites list box, click the address for the Web site under Domain, and then click the Remove button. Click the OK button to close the Per Site Privacy Actions dialog box, and then click the OK button to apply your changes and close the Internet Options dialog box.

Some Web site addresses in the Address bar are quite long and consist of many different parts, which in turn can confuse users and mask the fact that the user might be at a malicious Web site. To help users more easily identify the Web site, Internet Explorer uses a feature called domain highlighting to highlight that portion of the Web site address that identifies the Web site. Also, starting with Internet Explorer 7, each Web browser window must include the Address bar.

You can also view a Privacy Report for a Web site.

To view a Privacy report for the Microsoft Web site:

1. In the Address bar, type **microsoft.com** and then press the **Enter** key to navigate to the Microsoft Corporation home page. In the Address bar, Internet Explorer uses domain highlighting to display "microsoft.com" in black and the rest of the address in gray.

2. Click the **Safety** button on the toolbar, and then click **Webpage Privacy Policy**. In the Privacy Report dialog box, Internet Explorer informs you whether cookies are restricted or blocked based on your privacy settings. See Figure 7-33.

Figure 7-33   Viewing a privacy report

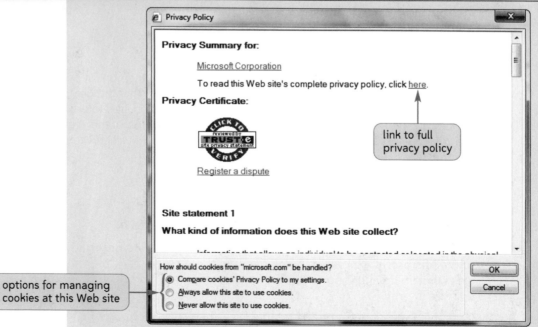

Web sites with content on the current Web page

current privacy settings do not restrict or block cookies

this first-party Web site can now place cookies on this computer

The Privacy Report also lists the addresses of Web sites that contribute content to the current page and identifies whether cookies are blocked or accepted for a specific Web site. You can use the Settings button to open the Privacy property sheet in the Internet Options dialog box so you can adjust your cookie settings.

3. In the Site column, click the URL for the Microsoft Web site, and then click the **Summary** button. Internet Explorer displays a Privacy Policy dialog box for Microsoft Corporation. Under the company name is a link to the complete privacy policy. The Privacy Policy describes what kinds of information this Web site collects, why the information is collected, who has access to the information, how long the information is retained, whether users have access to their own information, and how this Web site handles disputes about collected data. See Figure 7-34. You can also specify how your Web browser handles cookies from this Web site.

Figure 7-34   Viewing a Web site's privacy policy

Privacy Policy

Privacy Summary for:

Microsoft Corporation

To read this Web site's complete privacy policy, click here.

Privacy Certificate:

link to full privacy policy

Register a dispute

Site statement 1

What kind of information does this Web site collect?

options for managing cookies at this Web site

How should cookies from "microsoft.com" be handled?
- Compare cookies' Privacy Policy to my settings.
- Always allow this site to use cookies.
- Never allow this site to use cookies.

OK   Cancel

4. Close the Privacy Policy dialog box, and then close the Privacy Report dialog box, but keep Internet Explorer open for the next section of the tutorial.

Before you provide a Web site with information about yourself, you may want to first examine their privacy policy to determine which types of information they collect and how they claim to use this information.

Viewing the Privacy Report and Privacy Policy for a Web Site:

- Open Internet Explorer, and then navigate to the Web site whose privacy policy you want to examine.
- To view a Privacy Report, click the Safety button on the toolbar, click Webpage Privacy Policy, and in the Privacy Report dialog box, examine the list of Web sites that contribute content to the current page and the information about whether cookies are blocked or accepted from the current Web site.
- To view the Privacy Policy for a Web site, click the address of a Web site listed in the Site column, click the Summary button, and then examine the privacy summary for the company.
- Close the Privacy Policy dialog box, and then close the Privacy Report dialog box.

If you are interested in privacy issues and the impact of technology on privacy, then you may want to examine information at the Web site for the Electronic Frontier Foundation (*www.eff.org*).

Using InPrivate Filtering to Identify Content Tracking

Another tool for protecting your privacy and reducing online profiling is InPrivate Filtering. This feature blocks content, such as web measurement tools, placed by third-party Web sites on the Web pages of Web sites you visit in order to track your browsing habits across multiple Web sites. To accomplish this tracking, these third-party Web sites (also called content providers) place the same content on multiple Web sites. InPrivate Filtering therefore blocks cross-site tracking. In fact, if InPrivate Filtering discovers that the same content is identified on over 10 different Web sites, it provides you with the option to allow or block that content. You can also specify whether you want to automatically block all content providers or you can manually block specific content providers. Each time you open and use Internet Explorer, you *must* enable this feature if you want it to identify Web sites that track your visits to Web sites.

To enable InPrivate Filtering:

The InPrivate Filtering feature behaves differently the first time it is enabled, so carefully choose the correct steps to complete in Step 1.

1. To turn on InPrivate Filtering for the first time, click the **Safety** button on the Internet Explorer toolbar, click **InPrivate Filtering**, and then click **Let me choose which providers receive my information** link to open the InPrivate Filtering settings dialog box. If you have previously turned on InPrivate Filtering or previously turned off this feature, click the **Safety** button on the Internet Explorer toolbar. If InPrivate Filtering has a check mark next to it, click **InPrivate Filtering Settings**. If InPrivate Filtering does *not* have a check mark next to it, click **InPrivate Filtering** to add a check mark, click the **Safety** button on the Internet Explorer toolbar again, and then click **InPrivate Filtering settings**.

The InPrivate Filtering settings dialog box explains how this feature works, and allows you to automatically block all content tracking, choose the content that you want to block or allow, or turn off InPrivate Filtering. Figure 7-35 shows a list of five content providers who have placed the same content at eight or more Web sites. When you enable this feature for the first time, InPrivate Filtering reports under Content provider that there are no items to display.

Figure 7-35   **Viewing InPrivate Filtering settings**

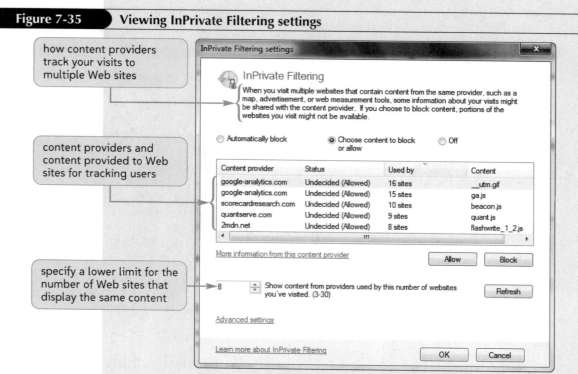

how content providers track your visits to multiple Web sites

content providers and content provided to Web sites for tracking users

specify a lower limit for the number of Web sites that display the same content

You can also specify a lower limit for the number of Web sites you've visited that show the same content from a provider. The Content provider column identifies the Web sites that provide the same content to other Web sites. The Content column shows the name of the actual file that contains the same content provided to different Web sites. The default setting for showing content from providers is 10; however, that value was reset to 8 to show at least five sites in the InPrivate Filtering settings dialog box in this figure. If you select a content provider and then click the "More information from this content provider" link, Internet Explorer opens a Web page for the Web site of that content provider.

▶ **2.** Click the **OK** button to close the InPrivate Filtering Settings dialog box.

▶ **3.** Click the **Tools** button on the Internet Explorer toolbar, click **Internet Options**, and then click the **Privacy** tab. Under the InPrivate section, you can choose to not collect data for use by InPrivate Filtering.

▶ **4.** Click the **OK** button to close the Internet Options dialog box, but keep Internet Explorer open for the next section of the tutorial.

In some cases, content placed on multiple Web sites by a content provider is visible, such as a visitor counter; however, more often than not this content is invisible by design so you do not know that your browsing habits are being tracked. This content is therefore similar to the use of Web beacons, which consist of a single transparent pixel placed on a Web page by a content provider to track and compile information about your activity at a Web site.

REFERENCE

Using InPrivate Filtering to Identify Content Tracking

- Open Internet Explorer, click the Safety button on the toolbar, and if you have never enabled (or turned off) InPrivate Filtering and if the Safety menu does not have a check mark next to InPrivate Filtering, then click InPrivate Filtering. If Internet Explorer displays an InPrivate Filtering dialog box, click the "Block for me" link to automatically block all content providers or click the "Let me choose which providers receive my information" link to specify which content providers you want to allow or block, to adjust the setting for specifying the number of Web sites that contain the same content from the same content provider, or to turn off InPrivate Filtering.
- If you have already enabled (or turned off) InPrivate Filtering previously and want to turn InPrivate Filtering on or off, click the Safety button on the toolbar, and then click InPrivate Filtering.
- To view or change InPrivate Filtering settings, click the Safety button on the toolbar, click InPrivate Filtering Settings, view information on content providers identified by InPrivate Filtering, automatically block all content providers or selectively block or allow individual content providers, adjust the setting for specifying the number of Web sites that contain the same content from the same content provider, and then click the OK button.

InPrivate Filtering is a useful tool because you can familiarize yourself with the types of Web sites that track content and the types of files used for content tracking. Also, if you adjust the number of sites required to identify the same content to the lowest setting, then you can identify content tracking sooner.

Deleting Your Browsing History

Another way to protect your privacy is to periodically delete your browsing history. **Browsing history** includes temporary Internet files, cookies, your history (a list of Web sites you've visited), form data (or information that you've entered into forms at Web sites), passwords that are automatically filled in when you visit the same Web site again, and InPrivate Filtering data (or data saved by this feature to determine where Web sites are sharing details about your visits).

Although retaining the various components of your browsing history can improve your browsing experience on the Web, your Web browser might download malicious software from a Web site you visit and store it in the Temporary Internet Files folder (or your Internet cache). To reduce the risk to your computer, you can empty the Temporary Internet files folder and remove that malicious software from your computer. Also, if you use a public computer, such as a library computer or college computer, you should delete your personal browsing history when you finish using that computer. You should also make sure you remember to sign out of your email software account; otherwise, the next person who uses the same Web browser on that computer right after you might have immediate access to your email after they open the same Web browser.

As part of raising the awareness of security and privacy issues for new clients, Arielle asks that you show your coworkers how to delete their browsing history.

To delete your browsing history:

1. Click **Safety** on the Internet Explorer toolbar, and then click **Delete Browsing History**. In the Delete Browsing History dialog box, you can pick and choose which components of your browsing history you want to delete, or you can delete all of them in one step. See Figure 7-36.

Figure 7-36 | Options for deleting your browsing history

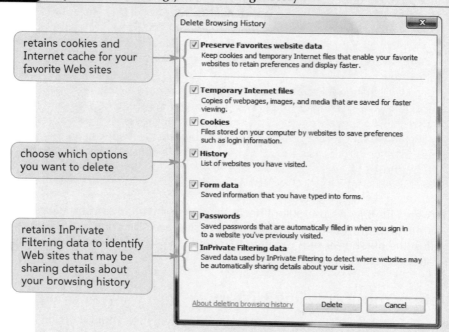

retains cookies and Internet cache for your favorite Web sites

choose which options you want to delete

retains InPrivate Filtering data to identify Web sites that may be sharing details about your browsing history

By default, Internet Explorer preserves Favorites website data. In other words, it keeps cookies and temporary Internet files for Web sites identified as Favorites so you can access those Web sites more quickly.

2. If you do not want to delete your browsing history or any of the items in the Delete Browsing History dialog box, click the **Cancel** button. Otherwise, make sure the items you want to delete are selected and the items that you do not want to delete are not selected, then click the **Delete** button for those items.

3. Keep the Internet Explorer window open for the next section of the tutorial.

TIP

After working on a public computer, restart that computer to remove your browsing history cached in RAM.

If you delete your browsing history, Internet Explorer does not delete your Favorite bookmarks, and it does not delete RSS feeds that you subscribe to. Also, if you use another Web browser (or if you use both Internet Explorer and another Web browser, such as Firefox), you must use the other Web browser's options for removing comparable content from your computer.

REFERENCE

Deleting Your Internet Explorer Browsing History

- Open Internet Explorer, click the Safety button on the toolbar, and then click Delete Browsing History.
- In the Delete Browsing History dialog box, add check marks to the check boxes of those items you want to remove, remove check marks from check boxes of those items you do not want to remove, decide whether to keep InPrivate Filtering data, decide whether to Preserve Favorites website data, click the Delete button, and then close Internet Explorer.

The Disk Cleanup utility you examined in Tutorial 5 also removes temporary Internet files and downloaded program files, but it does not remove cookies, your browsing history, form data, passwords, and InPrivate Filtering data.

Enabling InPrivate Browsing

InPrivate Browsing, a new Internet Explorer 8 feature, opens a new Web browser window, and as you browse the Web, Internet Explorer does not store any information about your browsing history, data and passwords you enter on forms, and Address bar and AutoComplete information. Internet Explorer does store the content of Web pages in the Temporary Internet Files folder, but it deletes that content when you close your Web browser. Cookies are stored in memory so you can access certain Web pages, but once you close your Internet Explorer, it removes all cookies.

Arielle offers to show you two approaches for opening an InPrivate Browsing window.

TIP

You can also use the Internet Explorer taskbar button Jump List to start an InPrivate Browsing session.

To open an InPrivate Browsing window:

1. Click **Safety** on the toolbar, and then click **InPrivate Browsing**. Internet Explorer opens a new Web browser window, and in the title bar, Address bar, and the background of the InPrivate Web page it identifies that you are using InPrivate (browsing). See Figure 7-37. Now you can browse the Web using InPrivate Browsing.

Figure 7-37	Using InPrivate Browsing

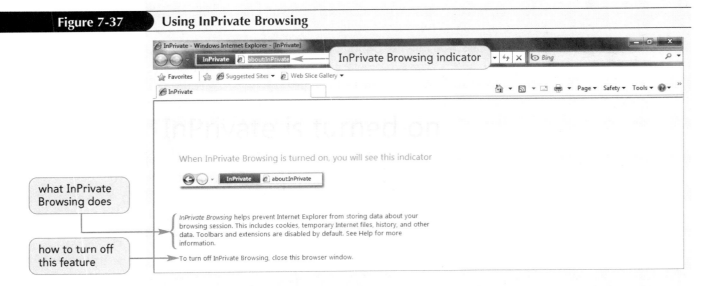

what InPrivate Browsing does

how to turn off this feature

▶ **2.** Click the **New Tab** button 🗔 to the right of the InPrivate tab. Internet Explorer also uses InPrivate Browsing for the new tab.

▶ **3.** Click the InPrivate Browsing window's **Close** button ▬▬x▬▬ , and then click the **Close all tabs** button in the Internet Explorer dialog box.

▶ **4.** In the previously opened Web browser window, click the **New Tab** button 🗔. Internet Explorer opens a new tab, but it's not using InPrivate Browsing. However, you can click the "Browse with InPrivate" link or the "Open an InPrivate Browsing window" link to open a separate InPrivate Browsing window. Internet Explorer then closes the new tab you opened in the other Internet Explorer window.

▶ **5.** Close the Internet Explorer window.

Windows 7 provides more security for your computer than previous versions of Windows, and Internet Explorer 8 offers many new security and privacy enhancements—all essential to safe browsing on the Internet.

Restoring Your Computer's Settings

If you are working in a computer lab, or if you want to restore your desktop computer to the settings that existed prior to working on this tutorial, complete the following steps.

To restore your computer's settings:

▶ **1.** If necessary, use the Folder Options dialog box to turn off single-click activation.

▶ **2.** If necessary, use the Start menu to turn off the display of the Computer icon on the desktop.

REVIEW

Session 7.2 Quick Check

1. What types of Web sites are included in the Internet security zone?
2. What is Protected Mode?
3. True or False. The Internet Explorer Security status bar provides information about whether a Web site provides a secure, encrypted connection.
4. What Internet Explorer feature can you use to help you identify phishing and other unsafe Web sites?
5. What two types of techniques rely on the use of email messages that appear to be sent from a reputable company in order to trick a user into disclosing personal and financial information and steal that user's assets and identity?
6. What is the difference between a first-party cookie and a third-party cookie? What type of cookie is used for online profiling?
7. What is the difference between InPrivate Filtering and InPrivate Browsing?
8. List one reason for deleting your browsing history and one reason for keeping your browsing history.

Practice the skills you learned in the tutorial using the same case scenario.

PRACTICE

Review Assignments

There are no Data Files needed for the Review Assignments.

In preparation for an upcoming training session on ways to protect a computer's security and privacy for employees of a new client, Arielle asks you to review what you will cover during that training session.

As you complete each step, record your answers to the questions so you can submit them to your instructor. Use a word-processing application such as Microsoft Word or the WordPad accessory to prepare your answers to these questions. If you change any settings on the computer you are using, make a note of the original settings so you can restore them later. Complete the following steps:

1. Open the Action Center. Does the Action Center identify any security or maintenance issues for you to review? If so, what are those issues?
2. Examine your security settings. What is the name of the firewall you use on your computer? What is the status of your firewall? If you use Windows Firewall on your computer, use the Address bar to navigate to Windows Firewall settings; otherwise, open your firewall program and examine its settings. How does your firewall handle incoming connections? What does your firewall do when it blocks a new program? What types of network location does your firewall protect?
3. Go back to the Action Center. What is the setting for Windows Update? Is this the default setting? How does Windows Update handle updates? Use the Windows Update link to switch to Windows Update. What types of updates are you scheduled to receive? What updates are available, if any?
4. View your update history. What types of updates has Windows Update installed on your computer? (Do not list every update, but rather summarize the types of updates by importance.)
5. Return to the Action Center and examine your security settings. What software do you use for virus protection and for protecting your system from spyware and other unwanted software?
6. What is the status of your Internet security settings?
7. What is the status of User Account Control? Use the Address bar to switch to User Accounts and Family Safety, and then open User Accounts. What type of account are you using? Is your account password protected? Does your account type permit you to install and remove software and hardware, change system settings, and manage other user accounts? How can you tell which options in User Accounts require Administrator credentials? Close the Action Center.
8. Open Internet Explorer, use the Tools menu to open the Internet Options dialog box, and then select the Security tab. What security level setting does Internet Explorer use for the Internet security zone? What advantage, if any, would the High security level settings have over your current security zone setting?
9. Select the Privacy tab. What is the purpose of Pop-up Blocker? Is Pop-up Blocker enabled? Choose the option to view Pop-up Blocker settings from the Privacy property sheet. What blocking level does your Pop-up Blocker use? What can you do to allow specific Web sites to display pop-up windows that might otherwise be blocked? Have you implemented this option, and if so, how? If not, how might you use it? Close the Pop-up Blocker Settings dialog box.
10. What is the advantage of using InPrivate Filtering? Using information on the Privacy tab, how does Internet Explorer handle InPrivate Filtering? What is the advantage of using InPrivate Browsing? What happens to toolbars and extensions when InPrivate Browsing starts? Close the Internet Options dialog box.

11. Use the Tools menu to view information on managing add-ons and, if necessary, choose Toolbars and Extensions under Add-on Types. What publishers have add-ons that are currently loaded in Internet Explorer? Select an add-on and then choose the option to view More information. For this add-on, list its name, the publisher, the specific type of add-on, its status, the add-on filename, and the add-on path's folder. Close the More Information dialog box. How can you disable an add-on shown in the Enabled list? Are there any add-ons that do not have a publisher listed, and if so, what are the names of the add-ons? How might you find information about these add-ons? Close the Manage Add-ons dialog box.

12. Open the Internet Options dialog box, and then select the Privacy property sheet. If you chose the option for blocking all cookies, can Web sites read cookies already stored on your computer? What advantage would the Medium-high setting have over the Medium setting? Use the Advanced button to view Advanced Privacy Settings. Would overriding automatic cookie handling be beneficial to you? How do you or would you implement the handling of first-party and third-party cookies if you used this option? Close the Advanced Privacy Settings dialog box. How can you allow first-party cookies and block third-party cookies from specific Web sites? Close any dialog boxes you've opened, including the Internet Options dialog box.

13. If you access your email via an online Web site, visit that site's home page or logon page. What options (if any) does your online email Web site have for remembering you on the computer you are using and remembering your password? How might you benefit from these options? Does your online email software have an option for a secure logon? Explain. If so, enable that option, and then use the Security status bar to view a security report. What information does the Security status bar provide about the Web site's identification when you click the Security status bar?

14. Use the SmartScreen Filter to check this Web site. What does the SmartScreen Filter report about this Web site? Close the SmartScreen Filter dialog box.

15. From the Safety menu, choose the option for deleting your browsing history. Which of the browsing history options or data do you delete from your computer, and which browsing options or data do you keep? Explain. Close the Delete Browsing History dialog box.

16. Close Internet Explorer.

17. Submit your answers to this case problem to your instructor, either in printed or electronic form, as requested. Remember to include on your assignment your name and any other information requested by your instructor.

Use your skills to evaluate Windows updates for a foundation.

APPLY

Case Problem 1

There are no Data Files needed for this Case Problem.

California Marine Protection Foundation In addition to handling the funding for specific marine protection projects along the California coast, Julianne Lauchland provides tech support for other employees who work at the California Marine Protection Foundation. Because she is currently faced with a tight deadline for submitting a funding proposal, she asks you to check another employee's laptop to make sure that the automatic Windows Update feature is providing him with the most recent security and hardware updates.

As you complete each step in this case problem, record your answers to the questions so you can submit them to your instructor. Use a word-processing application such as Microsoft Word or the WordPad accessory to prepare your answers to these questions. If you change any settings on the computer you are using, make a note of the original settings so you can restore them later. Complete the following steps:

1. Open the Action Center, switch to the Windows Update window, and then choose the option to view your computer's update history.
2. What is the first update identified in your update history, and what is its status and importance? Also note the Knowledge Base article number.
3. Click the Name column button to sort updates alphabetically by name. What categories of updates are listed (for example, Cumulative Security Updates).
4. Click the Date Installed column button to sort updates, and make sure the updates are listed in order from most recently installed. Double-click the last successfully installed Update for Windows in your update history to open the Windows Update dialog box. What is the name, update type, and purpose of this update? Click the More information link to view the Knowledge Base article. After examining the information on this Windows update, explain in more detail the purpose and value of this update. Close your Web browser window, and then close the Windows Update dialog box.
5. Sort updates by name. If available in your update history, examine information on a hardware update and identify the update name, the update type, and the purpose of that update. If you don't have a hardware update, then examine another type of update either for Windows 7, Internet Explorer, Microsoft Office, or other Microsoft software on your computer, and summarize the purpose and value of that update.
6. Sort updates by Status, and if available, double-click an update whose status is Failed. Click the "Get help with this error" in the Windows Update dialog box and, if possible, view Help information for the specific error code. What is the name of the update, and what is the likely cause for the failure to install this update? What, if anything, does Windows Help and Support recommend? Are there any other options for resolving this problem? Close Windows Help and Support, close the Windows Update dialog box, use the Date Installed column button to list updates in order from the most recently installed update to the oldest update, and then close the View update history window.
7. Submit your answers to this case problem to your instructor, either in printed or electronic form, as requested. Remember to include on your assignment your name and any other information requested by your instructor.

Use your skills to evaluate Web browser add-ons for a book company.

APPLY

Case Problem 2

There are no Data Files needed for this Case Problem.

Arenales Books Agustín Martínez manages the acquisition of books for Arenales Books, an online supplier of computer books that focus on computer security. Agustín also provides technical support for updating Arenales Books' Web site. To guarantee that this computer remains free of malicious software, he periodically checks add-ons that load with his Web browser. As his assistant, he asks you to help him document and research new add-ons on his computer.

As you complete each step in this case problem, record your answers to the questions so you can submit them to your instructor. Use a word-processing application such as Microsoft Word or the WordPad accessory to prepare your answers to these questions. If you change any settings on the computer you are using, make a note of the original settings so you can restore them later. Complete the following steps:

1. Open Internet Explorer, and then choose the option for viewing information about managing add-ons.

2. List information on three add-ons currently loaded in Internet Explorer on the computer you are using. If possible, provide information on add-ons from three different publishers. Include in your list the name of the add-on, its publisher, its status, its type, its filename, and the path to the folder where it is stored.

⊕ EXPLORE

3. Use a search engine, such as Google, to locate information about these add-ons. Use the information provided for each add-on (such as its name, publisher, type, filename, and folder location) in the Manage Add-ons dialog box to verify that you have located the right information for the add-on. (*Hint*: For example, when searching lists of browser helper objects, use only part of an add-on name, such as *Adobe*, to locate a list of related Adobe add-ons.) List the following types of information (where available) on each add-on you research:

   • Add-on name

   • Type of add-on (to verify the information provided by Internet Explorer)

   • Whether the add-on is a legitimate program or malicious software

   • How the add-on is installed (i.e., as part of a software product installed on your computer, or as part of some type of download, such as a toolbar)

   • Any other useful information you learn about the add-on

   • Addresses of the Web sites where you located information on the add-on

⊕ EXPLORE

4. If you use or have access to another Web browser, such as Firefox, describe how you would locate information on add-ons or plug-ins used by that browser. If that browser uses the same type of add-ons as Internet Explorer, then identify those add-ons.

5. Submit your answers to this case problem to your instructor, either in printed or electronic form, as requested. Remember to include on your assignment your name and any other information requested by your instructor.

Use your skills and the Internet to prepare a security report on rootkits.

RESEARCH

Case Problem 3

There are no Data Files needed for this Case Problem.

Talcott Security Systems Unlimited   As a computer security specialist working for Talcott Security Systems Unlimited in Saint Louis, Missouri, Zhi Lin is frequently called upon to present papers, prepare background information, and moderate conferences on various types of security threats and risks. For an upcoming forum on rootkits, Lin asks you to help him prepare background information on rootkits and rootkit detection software for participants and thereby set the stage for a more focused and in-depth discussion.

As you complete each step in this case problem, record your answers to the questions so you can submit them to your instructor. Use a word-processing application such as Microsoft Word or the WordPad accessory to prepare your answers to these questions. If you change any settings on the computer you are using, make a note of the original settings so you can restore them later. Complete the following steps:

1. From the Microsoft Web site (*www.microsoft.com*), search for information on rootkits.
2. In the first page of search results, locate and read information on RootkitRevealer or any other type of Microsoft Rootkit detection product.
3. Answer the following questions:
   a. What is a rootkit?
   b. What are the four types of rootkits?
   c. What is a persistent rootkit?
   d. How does RootkitRevealer (or any other type of Microsoft Rootkit detection product) detect a rootkit?
   e. How might a rootkit evade detection by RootkitRevealer (or another rootkit detection program)?
   f. How does RootkitRevealer evade detection from a rootkit when you open RootkitRevealer?
   g. List the names of at least three rootkits.
4. Return to the Microsoft home page, and search for information on the Strider GhostBuster Project. How does Strider GhostBuster detect rootkits, and what fundamental weakness of rootkits does it rely on to detect rootkits?
5. From the Microsoft home page, search for information on the Strider HoneyMonkey Project. What is Strider HoneyMonkey?
6. Include a list of resources that you used to prepare your report, including the address of Web sites that contained information on rootkits, Strider GhostBuster, and the Strider HoneyMonkey Project.
7. Submit your answers to this case problem to your instructor, either in printed or electronic form, as requested. Remember to include on your assignment your name and any other information requested by your instructor.

Use your skills and the Internet to evaluate the latest security threats and risks.

RESEARCH

Case Problem 4

There are no Data Files needed for this Case Problem.

Eberhardt Strategic Assessments   Corina Puzon, a specialist in computer security and privacy issues, works as a computer analyst for Eberhardt Strategic Assessments. As part of her job, she evaluates new threats and risks to identify new patterns in the development and distribution of these threats and risks. Recently, she's noticed a steep rise in new threats, and she asks you to help her evaluate them.

As you complete each step in this case problem, record your answers to questions so you can submit them to your instructor. Use a word-processing application such as Microsoft Word or the WordPad accessory to prepare your answers to these questions. If you change any settings on the computer you are using, make a note of the original settings so you can restore them later. Complete the following steps:

1. Visit the Symantec Web site (*www.symantec.com*), and locate (or search for) Threat Explorer (*www.symantec.com/norton/security_response/threatexplorer/index.jsp*) to view a list of the latest threats and risks.

2. Click one of the latest threats and view information on the Summary tab about that threat.

3. Prepare a summary that contains the following information:
   a. Threat name
   b. Date discovered
   c. Type of threat (e.g., computer virus, worm, Trojan horse)
   d. Infection length
   e. Systems affected (i.e., which Windows versions are affected)
   f. Basic operation (or actions)

4. Summarize the types of operations that it performs on a computer using the information on the Technical Details tab. (Do not copy this information, but rather sift through it and summarize the operations performed by this threat.)

5. Describe the basic approach (but not a detailed step-by-step list) for removing the threat.

6. Based on the information you examined, what do you conclude about this threat?

7. Include a list of resources that you used to prepare this paper, including addresses of Symantec Web sites (or other Web sites).

8. Submit your answers to this case problem to your instructor, either in printed or electronic form, as requested. Remember to include on your assignment your name and any other information requested by your instructor.

ENDING DATA FILES

There are no ending Data Files needed for this tutorial.

OBJECTIVES

Session 8.1
- Develop a strategy for troubleshooting problems
- Use Problem Steps Recorder to reproduce a problem
- Analyze your computer's stability with Reliability Monitor
- Create a restore point with System Protection
- Use Event Viewer to examine event logs

Session 8.2
- Use the BIOS Setup utility to view the boot sequence
- Examine the Windows 7 boot process and boot in Safe Mode
- Use Task Manager to view running processes and services
- Analyze startup programs and environment variables
- Examine System Recovery Tools

Troubleshooting Windows 7

Using Troubleshooting Tools

Case | *Carbon Sink, Unlimited*

Carbon Sink, Unlimited, is a Swiss consortium of international companies that work cooperatively to research and develop new strategies and technologies for removing carbon dioxide from the atmosphere and thereby tackling the immediate and long-term effects of global warming. Julien Cottier, a network specialist with a strong background in climate science, assists the scientists and research technicians with configuring, customizing, optimizing, and troubleshooting their computer systems.

In this tutorial, you examine a strategy for troubleshooting problems, reproduce a problem with Problem Steps Recorder, use Reliability Monitor to evaluate the current performance level of your computer, use Event Viewer to examine detailed information on events that occur on your computer, check System Protection settings, use System Protection to create a restore point, and use System Restore to view existing restore points. You open the BIOS Setup utility during booting and view your computer's boot sequence, and then you examine the Windows 7 boot process. You view running processes and services in Task Manager and learn how to shut down nonresponding programs. You use System Configuration and System Information to view information on startup programs and you learn how to use System Configuration to control the loading of those programs during booting. Finally, you examine System Recovery Tools provided with Windows 7.

WINDOWS

STARTING DATA FILES

There are no starting Data Files needed for this tutorial.

SESSION 8.1 VISUAL OVERVIEW

You can use the **Problem Steps Recorder** as a troubleshooting tool to document a problem and capture screenshots as you reproduce a problem.

Use **Reliability Monitor** to view a system stability chart that identifies and graphically illustrates the impact of problems on the stability of your computer.

Reliability Monitor plots **stability index** values, or reliability ratings, so you can assess changes in the stability and performance of your computer.

Reliability Monitor displays an Error icon on the chart for critical events, such as application failures, Windows failures, and miscellaneous failures that affect the stability of a computer and its reliability rating.

An Information icon indicates a successful operation, such as a successful Windows update.

In the Reliability details area, Reliability Monitor identifies the program that failed and the type of problem that occurred.

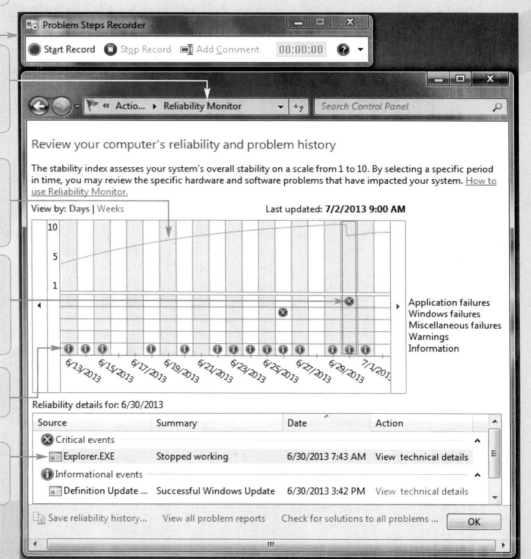

Problem Steps Recorder

● Start Record ● Stop Record ▣ Add Comment   00:00:00   ❓ ▾

« Actio... ▸ Reliability Monitor   ▾ | ↯   Search Control Panel   🔍

Review your computer's reliability and problem history

The stability index assesses your system's overall stability on a scale from 1 to 10. By selecting a specific period in time, you may review the specific hardware and software problems that have impacted your system. How to use Reliability Monitor.

View by: **Days** | Weeks   Last updated: **7/2/2013 9:00 AM**

Application failures
Windows failures
Miscellaneous failures
Warnings
Information

Reliability details for: 6/30/2013

Source	Summary	Date	Action
✖ Critical events			
Explorer.EXE	Stopped working	6/30/2013 7:43 AM	View technical details
ⓘ Informational events			
Definition Update ...	Successful Windows Update	6/30/2013 3:42 PM	View technical details

Save reliability history...   View all problem reports   Check for solutions to all problems ...   OK

TROUBLESHOOTING TOOLS

Event Viewer documents, and provides information on, events that occur on a computer. An **event** is a significant change in your computer system, such as an application failure.

Event Viewer organizes similar types of events into event logs, such as Application, Security, and System events. Each **event log** contains a record of a significant event that occurred on your computer, such as a successful Windows update or a problem with the file system.

For each event that occurs, Event Viewer identifies the type of event, such as an Application Error. You can **filter** event logs and specify criteria to show only specific types of events, such as all Critical events.

For each application failure, Event Viewer identifies the program that experienced a problem by filename so that you can detect problems with a specific application.

From the System window, you can open **System Protection** to create restore points on a computer so that later you can use **System Restore** to roll back your computer to an earlier point in time when it worked properly. A **restore point** is a snapshot of your computer at a specific point in time.

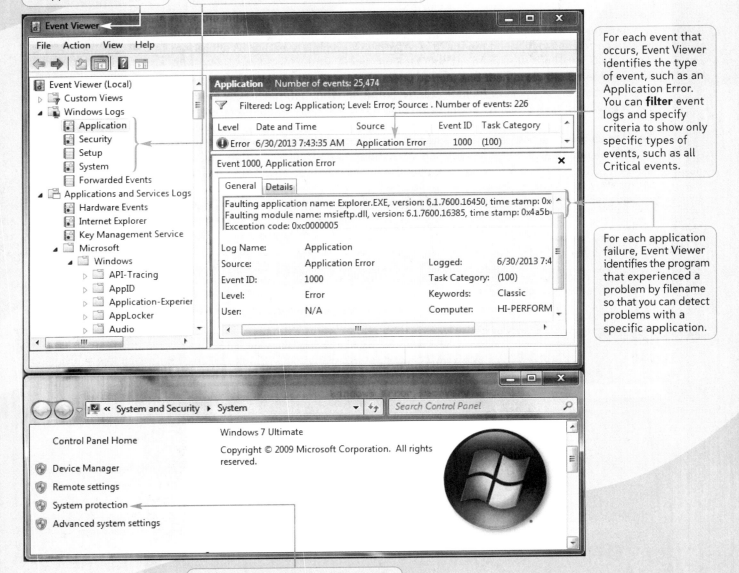

Developing a Troubleshooting Strategy

Since the recent formation of Carbon Sink, Unlimited, company research groups have been interviewing, hiring, and assembling staff with multidisciplinary backgrounds in climate science. Julien Cottier not only trains his staff in the latest troubleshooting tools and techniques, but he also determines how each new staff person can assist the specialized needs of the different research groups important to the company's mission. With each new employee, Julien discusses the importance of developing a troubleshooting strategy to quickly identify and resolve problems.

When faced with a problem on your computer system, you can adapt and apply the following approach for troubleshooting problems:

- **Define the problem**—First, make sure you know the exact nature of the problem. For example, if you observe a change in the performance of Windows 7, ask yourself questions that provide you with the information you need to clearly identify the nature and possible cause of the problem. For example, exactly how does this problem affect your computer system? Does Windows 7 display any error messages? If so, do the messages provide clues for troubleshooting the problem? Is this the first time you've encountered this type of problem? If you encountered the problem before, how did you resolve the problem? Did you or someone else recently make a change to an important Windows 7 setting or to its configuration? For example, did you recently download and install a new software product or device driver? Or is the source of the problem a recent Windows update? Or did you recently install new hardware or driver updates for existing or new hardware?

- **Analyze the problem**—Next, analyze the problem by evaluating your responses to the questions you ask yourself. For example, if you recently changed the configuration of your computer, such as downloading and installing a new video display driver, and then notice problems with your video display, did the problem result from the installation of the new video display driver? Or might some other type of error, such as a problem with the file system, be causing the problem? Could important system files be damaged?

- **Devise ways to test the possible cause of the problem**—To obtain more information about the nature of a problem, devise other tests that help you identify the cause of the problem. For example, if you experienced a problem with the video display after installing an update for a video display adapter and then discover a change to one of your video display settings, adjust that setting and determine whether it resolves the problem. If the problem persists, then restore the previously used device driver and determine whether that resolved the problem. (In Tutorial 12, you will examine the use of Roll Back Driver, which permits you to restore the previously used device driver for a hardware device.) If not, consider other possible sources for the problem, such as file system errors.

- **Draw on all the resources you have to resolve the problem**—What tools are available in Windows 7 for obtaining more information about the problem or for identifying and analyzing the problem? How can you best use those tools to help identify or solve the problem? For example, did Windows 7 send a problem report to Microsoft and, if so, what information does it provide in the Action Center on the nature of the problem and the availability of a solution?

Check hardware and software settings, and examine information about recent events that occurred on your computer. Check any reference manuals provided with your hardware or software or downloaded from the manufacturer's Web site. If the manufacturer of the product you purchased has a technical support line, call and talk to a technical support person about the problem. That person might know the answer immediately or might be able to replicate the problem and then determine how to resolve it. Many companies provide support and assistance via their Web sites, publish answers to frequently asked questions (FAQs), and post updates, such as device drivers, that users can download. Microsoft Help and Support and its online Knowledge

Base (*http://support.microsoft.com*) is another valuable source for information on Windows 7, Internet Explorer, Office applications, and other software products as well as problems identified by Microsoft.

- **Decide how best to proceed in resolving the problem**—For example, if you recently installed an update to your video display driver and if that is the only recent change made to your computer, evaluate what options are available for resolving the problem. Can you uninstall the driver update, or can you roll back the device driver to the previously used device driver? If you encounter a more serious problem, can you restore your entire computer to an earlier working state? After you decide on the best approach to take, make one change at a time, and ascertain whether the change resolved the problem and, if not, decide whether you want to (for example) use Windows Update to reinstall the update device driver, and then try the next logical troubleshooting option. If you decide to make a major change to your computer system, stop and make a backup first of important files and, if necessary, your computer system itself. Tutorial 10 covers ways to back up your computer system and your important files.
- **Consider other alternatives**—If you attempt to troubleshoot a problem and cannot resolve it, consider other possible causes, such as the possibility that your computer is infected with malicious software or that a Web site, hacker, or intruder might have gained access to your computer and modified it in some way.

If your field of specialty is technical support and troubleshooting, you might want to develop a system for reporting problems that includes the following:

- **A database of problems and solutions to those problems**—You can create a database of problems that users have already encountered or are likely to encounter, identify the operating systems and applications for each problem and solution, include specific steps for resolving each problem, and include warnings. You can design the database for yourself and other technical support staff who need to quickly consult this resource, and you can prepare an online version of this database for users so they can search for and resolve common problems that do not require major changes to the configuration of a computer, such as modifying the Registry. Cross-reference the information so users can more easily locate solutions to problems. You can also include links to the Microsoft Knowledge Base or other Web sites that provide troubleshooting information or assistance.
- **Online form for reporting problems**—Rather than rely on recording information via the telephone or after a conversation, you can create an online form for reporting problems that gathers all of the necessary information, provides the detail you need, and standardizes the reporting process. Show staff members how to use the Windows 7 Snipping Tool accessory or Alt+Print Screen to capture an image of a dialog box that identifies an error, and in the case of Alt+Print Screen, how to paste the image into a new document. If an employee can reproduce a problem, then recommend that the employee use Problem Steps Recorder to capture screen shots of the steps for performing an operation and the problem that occurs.
- **Remote control of user's screen**—If you encounter a problem with your computer, you might want to use a software tool, such as Windows Remote Assistance or Remote Desktop Connection, to request help from another person you trust or to troubleshoot a problem from another computer.

Because of the complexity of troubleshooting problems with an operating system, as well as all the other software and all the hardware on a computer, you will need to become familiar with the tools and features provided with the operating system for identifying, analyzing, and troubleshooting problems.

Getting Started

To complete this tutorial, you must display the Computer icon on the desktop, create a Control Panel desktop shortcut, switch your computer to single-click activation, and display Administrative Tools on the Start menu. In the following steps, you will check and, if necessary, change these settings.

To set up your computer:

▶ **1.** If necessary, display a Computer icon on the desktop.

▶ **2.** Click the **Start** 🔵 button, and then drag **Control Panel** from the Start menu to the desktop. Windows 7 creates a shortcut to the Control Panel.

▶ **3.** Press the **F2** (Rename) key, and then change the name of the Control Panel shortcut from *Control Panel - Shortcut* to **Control Panel**.

▶ **4.** If you need to enable single-click activation, double-click the **Computer** icon on the desktop, click the **Organize** button on the command bar, click **Folder and search options**, and under "Click items as follows" on the General property sheet in the Folder Options dialog box, click the **Single-click to open an item (point to select)** option button, click the **Underline icon titles only when I point at them** option button, click the **OK** button to close the Folder and Options dialog box, and then close the Computer window.

▶ **5.** If Administrative Tools is not displayed on the Start menu, right-click the **Start** button 🔵, click **Properties**, and on the Start Menu property sheet, click the **Customize** button, scroll to the bottom of the list of options for customizing the Start menu, and under System administrative tools, click the **Display on the All Programs menu and the Start menu** option button, click the **OK** button to close the Customize Start Menu dialog box, and then click the **OK** button to close the Taskbar and Start Menu Properties dialog box.

To get started, Julien suggests you investigate a tool called the Problem Steps Recorder.

Using the Problem Steps Recorder

If you are experiencing a problem on your computer and if you can reproduce that problem by going through the same steps again, then you can use the Problem Steps Recorder, a new Windows 7 tool, to record information about what happens when you repeat those steps and encounter the same problem. The Problem Steps Recorder not only records each step you perform but also captures images of the desktop, open program windows, and other open windows. Each step is listed as a numbered problem step, such as Problem Step 1, along with the date and time; the action you performed—such as entering text or right-clicking the Computer desktop icon—and a screen capture of the desktop. After each of the problem steps, there is an Additional Details section that identifies the open programs and details about how you used each program. You can also use the Add Comment button to add user comments any time during the process of recording a problem and thereby provide additional information about the operation. Note that the Problem Steps Recorder might not be able to capture screen shots for some full-screen programs, such as a game.

Julien suggests you use the Problem Steps Recorder to document a problem you've encountered with pinning the Control Panel option on the Start menu to the taskbar. You examined this problem in Tutorial 4, and used a workaround to add a Control Panel button to the taskbar by first opening a Control Panel applet. Let's assume you did not know about that workaround, and that you just encountered this problem for the first time.

TIP

You can also press the Windows key and type *psr* in the Search programs and files box to open the Problem Steps Recorder.

To use the Problem Steps Recorder to document a problem:

▶ **1.** Press the **Windows** key, type **record steps** in the Search programs and files box, and then click **Record steps to reproduce a problem** under Control Panel in the Search results. Windows 7 opens the Problem Steps Recorder as shown in Figure 8-1.

Figure 8-1	The Problem Steps Recorder dialog box

Once you start recording, the Start Record button changes to a Pause Record button so you can pause the process of recording steps, if necessary. If you click the Pause Record button, it changes to a Resume Record button so you can continue the process of recording steps when you are ready.

The Problem Steps Recorder toolbar also contains an Add Comment button that opens a Highlight Problem and Comment dialog box so you can type a comment and highlight the problem area on the screen. Once you continue, the area on the screen that you highlighted and your comment are recorded as a single problem step.

Now you're ready to perform the operations to reproduce the same error or problem you previously encountered.

▶ **2.** Click the **Start Record** button in the Problem Steps Recorder.

▶ **3.** Click the **Add Comment** button, drag the mouse pointer around the desktop Control Panel shortcut to identify where you will start this operation, release the mouse button, and in the Highlight Problem and Comment dialog box, type the following comment: **I want to drag and pin the Control Panel desktop shortcut to the taskbar.**

▶ **4.** Click the **OK** button in the Highlight Problem and Comment dialog box, drag the **Control Panel** desktop shortcut to an empty area of the taskbar, and then release the mouse button.

▶ **5.** Click the **Add Comment** button again, drag the mouse pointer around the area of the taskbar where you tried to pin the shortcut, release the mouse button, and in the Highlight Problem and Comment dialog box, type the following comment: **I tried to pin the desktop shortcut to an empty area of the taskbar.**

▶ **6.** Click the **OK** button in the Highlight Problem and Comment dialog box.

▶ **7.** Click the **Stop Record** button in the Problem Steps Recorder, and in the Save As dialog box, navigate to the Tutorial.08/Tutorial folder on your flash drive, type **Problem Pinning Control Panel Shortcut to Taskbar** in the File name box, notice that the Save as type problem defaults to saving the information in a ZIP file (*.zip), and then click the **Save** button.

You can use the Problem Steps Recorder Settings button [⊙ ▾] to send the file to Microsoft tech support or to anyone else you choose via email using your default email program. You can, of course, close the Problem Steps Recorder, open Microsoft Outlook or your Web-based email software, and attach the file with the recorded steps. There is also an option on that same menu to run the Problem Steps Recorder as an administrator for operations that require Administrator privileges.

The Settings button also contains a Settings option for specifying a default filename for the final recorded steps, an option for turning off the screen capture feature so any sensitive information, such as a view of an online bank transaction, is not recorded, and an option to set the number of recent screen captures to store as part of the final file (the default being 25 screens).

Now that you've recorded this problem, you're going to open the ZIP file and examine the information compiled by the Problem Steps Recorder.

To view the contents of the Problem Steps Recorder ZIP file:

▶ **1.** Click the Problem Steps Recorder **Close** button [X].

▶ **2.** Right-click the **Windows Explorer taskbar** button, and then click **Windows Explorer** on the Jump List. In the Libraries window, navigate to the Tutorial.08\Tutorial folder on your flash drive, click the **Hide the preview pane** button [□] on the toolbar (if necessary), and then use the **More options** arrow [▥ ▾] for the Change your view button to switch to Details view. Because of the .zip file extension, Windows 7 identifies this file as a Compressed (zipped) Folder.

▶ **3.** Click the **Problem Pinning Control Panel Shortcut to Taskbar.zip** file to open this file.

Inside the Compressed (zipped) Folder is an MHTML Document that you can open in Internet Explorer. MHTML is short for *Mime HTML*. This file format combines Web page components, such as images, along with HTML code in a single file. The filename consists of *Problem* followed by an underscore, then the current date followed by an underscore, the time the file was saved, and then the **.mht** file extension.

▶ **4.** Click the **Problem** file to open it. Internet Explorer opens the Recorded Problem Steps MHTML Document within this file in Internet Explorer, as shown in Figure 8-2, and you see part of what's included with Problem Step 1.

Figure 8-2 **Viewing the first recorded problem step**

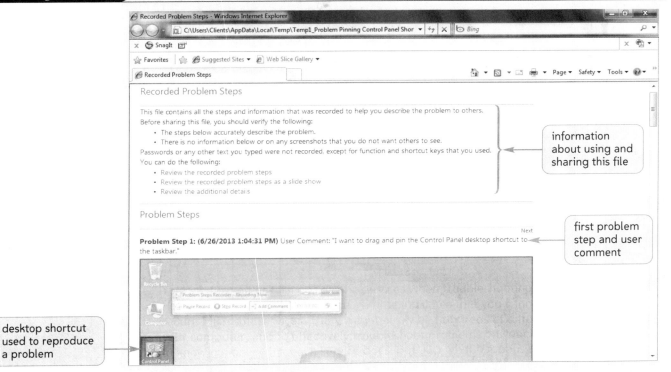

This file contains all the steps and information that the Problem Steps Recorder recorded so you can show and explain the problem you encountered to others. The text at the beginning of the file recommends that you verify that the steps shown in this file accurately describe the problem, and that there is no information below or on any screenshots that you do not want others to see. The Problem Steps Recorder does not record any password or text that you type as you encounter a problem, but it does record which function and shortcut keys you used. In this example, the Problem Steps Recorder includes the following steps:

- **Problem Step 1**—This step shows the view of the desktop after you immediately started recording and includes a User Comment with the text that you typed after you chose the option to add a comment. Note also that in Figure 8-2 the Control Panel shortcut contains a red border around it so the person examining this information knows where you started performing an operation.
- **Problem Step 2**—This step shows you selecting the Control Panel desktop shortcut (notice the Link Select mouse pointer shape over the Control Panel desktop shortcut) and the text for this step indicates that you, the user, started the process of dragging the Control Panel item. See Figure 8-3.

Figure 8-3 Viewing the second recorded problem step

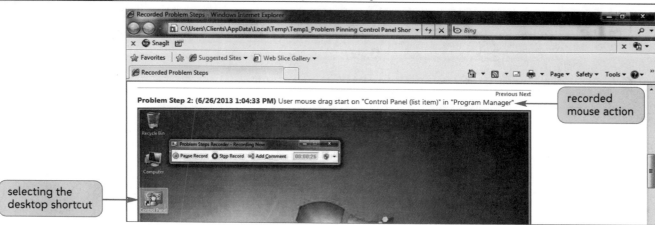

selecting the desktop shortcut

- **Problem Step 3**—This step shows that you dragged the Control Panel shortcut to an empty area of the taskbar, but you have not released the mouse button. See Figure 8-4.

Figure 8-4 Viewing the third recorded problem step

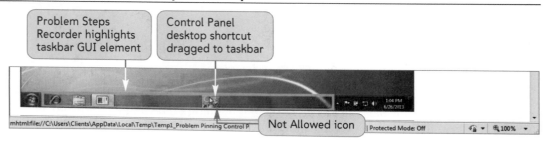

Problem Steps Recorder highlights taskbar GUI element

Control Panel desktop shortcut dragged to taskbar

Not Allowed icon

It also shows the Not Allowed icon next to the Control Panel shortcut icon. The text for this step notes that you used the mouse to drag the Control Panel shortcut to the toolbar (where other running applications are shown). The taskbar itself is surrounded by a green border that does not include the Start button or the notification area, two separate elements of the graphical user interface.

- **Problem Step 4**—This last step shows the area on the taskbar that you highlighted before adding a user comment to the effect that you tried to pin the desktop shortcut to an empty area of the taskbar. See Figure 8-5.

Figure 8-5 Viewing information on the last recorded problem step

taskbar area marked by the user when adding a comment

The Additional Details section contains additional information that was recorded to help find a solution to this problem, and as noted, it may contain text that is internal to programs, which only very advanced users or programmers may understand. See Figure 8-6.

| **Figure 8-6** | **Viewing additional details on recorded problem** |

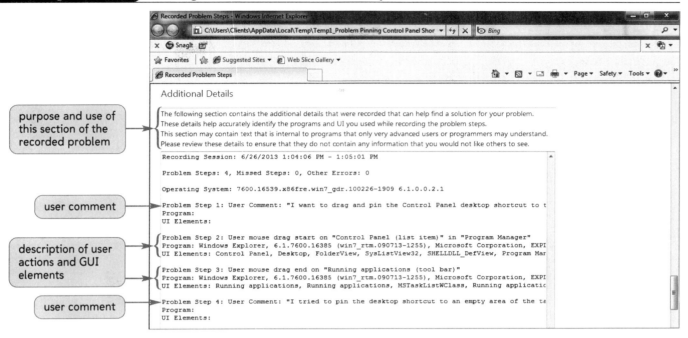

The Additional Details section shows the duration of the recording session; the number of problem steps, missed steps, and other errors; the Windows operating system version and edition; each problem step with a user comment or information about the task, the program in use (such as Windows Explorer); and UI (user interface) elements, such as Desktop, Control Panel, and FolderView. You can also edit the Additional Details section if there is information you want to exclude.

Each action you perform is recorded as a step, so the number of steps identified by Problem Steps Recorder may vary depending on the user or the way in which you attempt to repeat a step. Each click and user comment initiates a screen capture, which then becomes a step.

To close the ZIP file and delete your Control Panel desktop shortcut:

▶ **1.** Close the Internet Explorer window, and then close the Problem Pinning Control Panel Shortcut to Taskbar.zip window.

▶ **2.** Press and hold down the **Shift** key, right-click the **Control Panel** shortcut, click **Delete**, and when prompted to permanently delete this shortcut in the Delete Shortcut dialog box, click the **Yes** button, and then release the **Shift** key. When you use the Shift key to delete a folder or file, the folder or file is not placed in the Recycle Bin, but rather permanently deleted from your computer.

In Tutorial 4, you resolved this problem by opening the Control Panel and dragging an applet (such as Folder Options) to the Control Panel taskbar button, which then remained on the taskbar. You could then add pinned Control Panel items to that taskbar button's Jump List.

Using the Problem Steps Recorder

- Press the Windows key, type *record steps* in the Start menu Search programs and files box, and then click "Record steps to reproduce a problem" under Control Panel in the Search results.
- After Problem Steps Recorder opens, click the Start Record button, and then perform the same steps that you completed the last time you encountered a problem.
- If you want to add a comment at any point as you try to reproduce the problem, click the Add Comment button, drag the mouse pointer around the area that you want to comment on, release the mouse button, and in the Highlight Problem and Comment dialog box, type your comment, and then click the OK button.
- After completing the steps you want to reproduce, click the Stop Record button in the Problem Steps Recorder, and in the Save As dialog box, locate the folder where you want to save the ZIP file, type a filename for this file, click the Save button, and then close the Problem Steps Recorder.
- To view the problem steps recorded in the ZIP file, open the folder that contains the ZIP file, click the Problem file icon, examine the information in the ZIP file (and if necessary, modify that information), close the Problem file, and then close the ZIP file.

If you want to create a Problem Steps Recorder desktop shortcut, you can use one of the following paths: *%systemroot%\System32\psr.exe* or *%windir%\System32\psr.exe*. You can also create a Problem Steps Recorder shortcut by dragging the "Record steps to reproduce a problem" link from the Start menu Search results to the desktop.

Using Reliability Monitor

Reliability Monitor, introduced in Windows Vista and enhanced in Windows 7, is a tool that gathers, analyzes, and reports on the reliability and stability of your computer using data collected by the Reliability Analysis Component (RAC) of Windows 7. Reliability Monitor assigns a rating on a scale of 1 to 10 to reflect the current reliability of your computer. That reliability rating is called the stability index, or reliability index. (See the "How Windows 7 Assigns Stability Index Ratings" Insight on the next page for more information on how Windows 7 assigns this rating.)

If a problem arises as you use your computer, Reliability Monitor identifies the cause of the problem, such as an application failure, and you can view information about a specific problem that occurred on a specific day. You can also get a sense of the overall performance of your computer and determine whether its performance is improving or becoming worse over time.

Reliability Monitor provides information on five types of events that affect system stability:

- **Application failures**—Reliability Monitor reports on applications that stopped working.
- **Windows failures**—Reliability Monitor reports on problems encountered by the operating system.
- **Miscellaneous failures**—Reliability Monitor reports on other types of failures, such as an improper shutdown of Windows.
- **Warnings**—Reliability Monitor reports on failed Windows updates and unsuccessful driver installations.
- **Information** (also referred to as informational events)—Reliability Monitor reports on successful operations, such as successful Windows Updates, application installations, application updates, application reconfigurations, driver installations, and Windows installation.

INSIGHT

How Windows 7 Assigns Stability Index Ratings

Stability index ratings range from 1.0 (for least reliable and unstable) to 10.0 (for the highest degree of reliability and stability). On the day you install Windows 7, it assigns your computer a stability index value of 10 (the highest possible score). Whenever a problem occurs, Windows 7 lowers the stability index value, indicating that your computer is not as reliable and not as stable. If your computer does not experience any problems on a given day, Windows 7 increases your computer's stability index slightly. That means a single critical event affects the stability index (and therefore your computer's reliability and stability) more than a day in which your computer does not experience any problems. The stability index therefore reflects the overall performance and stability of your computer at any given point in time. When calculating the stability index, Reliability Monitor does not include days when your computer is off or in a sleep state. You can use changes to the stability index to identify ongoing problems or practices that you need to resolve or change to realize the best possible performance from your computer.

So you can monitor the health of your new computer, Julien recommends you use Reliability Monitor to produce a system stability report to use as a baseline for tracking changes to the performance of your computer.

To open Reliability Monitor and examine a system stability report for your computer:

1. In the notification area on the taskbar, click the **Action Center** button 🏳, and then click the **Open Action Center** link.

2. In the Action Center window, click the Maintenance section's **expand** icon ⓥ, and under "Check for solutions to problem reports," click the **View reliability history** link. Reliability Monitor produces a report, and then displays a chart with information about the stability of your computer. See Figure 8-7.

   Trouble? If Reliability Monitor reports *There are no reports in this view* in the lower Reliability details pane, then the date selected in the chart does not contain any events that affect the stability of the computer.

> **TIP**
>
> You can also type *perfmon /rel* in the Search programs and files box and then press the Enter key to open Reliability Monitor.

| Figure 8-7 | Viewing stability index ratings in Reliability Monitor |

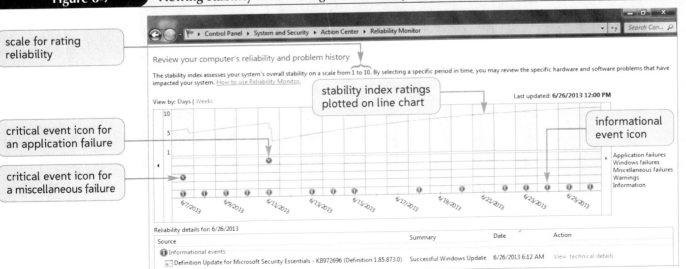

In the Reliability details area under the chart, Reliability Monitor displays information on any errors or events that occurred for the date where an error occurred. The horizontal axis shows the date range, and the left vertical axis displays the stability index (a rating from 1 to 10). The blue line in the chart plots your computer's stability index and shows changes to that value over time. Under the chart, there are five rows used to identify Application failures, Windows failures, Miscellaneous failures, Warnings, and Information (for successful events). Critical events or errors are identified by a red error icon, warnings are identified by warning symbol (a yellow triangle with a black exclamation mark), and information on successful events are identified by an information icon (a blue circle with a white *i*). On any given date, there may be no events or errors reported, or there might be one or more events or errors reported.

On the computer used for Figure 8-7, the stability and reliability continued to improve over a 15-day period from 3.42 to 9.55 (a substantial improvement). Although the Windows Vista Reliability Monitor showed the actual numbers for the stability index, that is not the case with Windows 7. Over the complete 20-day period shown, there was only one date on which an application failure resulted in a lower stability index. That application failure substantially lowered the stability index. There was one miscellaneous failure when Windows was not properly shut down, but its effect on the stability index was much less. Your system stability chart details will differ.

Although you cannot discern exact values from the chart, you can use the "Save reliability history" link at the bottom right of the window to create an XML (Extensible Markup Language) Document file with exact stability index measurements taken every hour since Windows 7 was installed on your computer. Then you can use Internet Explorer to view the content of that XML Document file. You will also discover that the file is quite large in size, but it has all the information you need for an extensive analysis of your computer.

You can use the left scroll arrow on the left side of the chart to view earlier dates, and you can use the right scroll arrow on the right side of the chart to view later dates. You can also use the Weeks link to display results for dates a week apart over a 20-week period.

Next, you examine information on the critical or warning errors on your computer to determine if you can spot problems with the use of specific applications.

To view information on a critical error:

1. If Reliability Monitor displays a red critical error icon ⊗ or a yellow warning icon ⚠ during the 20-day period, then click the red **critical error** icon ⊗ or the **warning** icon ⚠. On the computer used for Figure 8-8, Reliability Monitor displays information about four critical events where Internet Explorer stopped working.

   Trouble? If there is no red critical error icon ⊗ or yellow warning icon ⚠ for the time period displayed, use the scroll arrow on the left side of the chart to locate a date where a critical error or warning occurred. If there are no red critical error or yellow warning icons on your computer, then do not keystroke this step, but instead read the information in this step and examine the figure.

   Trouble? If you cannot see the entire entry in a column in the Reliability details, then double-click the column border on the right side of that column to widen the column for the longest entry in that column.

Figure 8-8	Viewing information on application failures

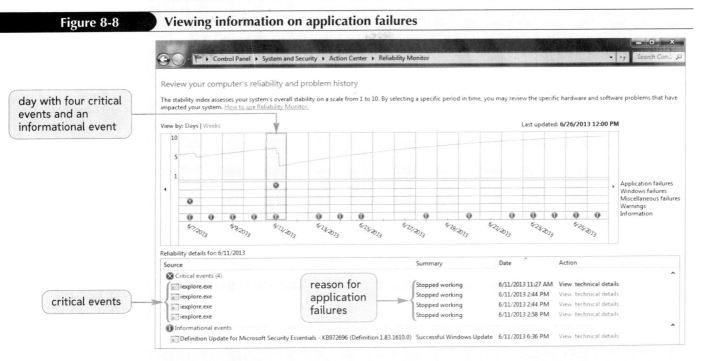

day with four critical events and an informational event

critical events

reason for application failures

Internet Explorer stopped working four times, causing a steep drop in the stability index on one day. Then the stability index rating substantially improved over the next 15 days.

The Action column may display either "Check for a solution" so you can check online for a solution to the problem, or "View technical details" so you can examine detailed information on the error condition, including the component of the program where the problem occurred. Obviously, if the same application failure appears repeatedly, then you need to follow up and research the cause of the problem. You may discover that removing an application and installing another application that performs the same function results in better performance.

▶ **2.** Close the Reliability Monitor window.

By examining critical events for application failures, you can more easily identify problems with specific programs or spot trends or changes in the performance of your computer that require your attention. The problems might relate to the specific software or to limited resources on your computer, such as RAM. You can also use Reliability Monitor Help for assistance in troubleshooting performance problems.

You can create a desktop shortcut with the path *%systemroot%\System32\perfmon.exe /rel* or the path *%windir%\System32\perfmon.exe /rel* to open Reliability Monitor.

REFERENCE

Using Reliability Monitor

- To open Reliability Monitor, click the Action Center button in the taskbar's notification area, click the Open Action Center link, click the Maintenance section expand icon in the Action Center window, and then click the "View reliability history" link under "Check for solutions to problem reports."
- Examine the change in the stability index on the chart produced by Reliability Monitor to obtain a sense of the performance, reliability, and stability of your computer.
- To view changes in the stability index by weeks, click the View by Weeks link above the chart.
- To create a reliability report, click the "Save reliability history" link, locate and click your flash drive (or the folder where you want to store this report) in the Navigation pane on the left side of the Export Reliability Report dialog box, type a name for the report in the File name box, and then click the Save button.
- To view information on a critical event, click the red critical error icon for an Application failure, Windows failure, or Miscellaneous failure, and then examine the information on the critical event or events in the Reliability details section.
- To view information on a warning, click the yellow warning error icon, and then examine the information on the warning or warnings in the Reliability details section.
- To view details on Information events, click the information icon with a blue circle, and then examine the information under Informational events.
- Close the Reliability Monitor window.

Reliability Monitor's chart showing changes in the stability index and the reliability report are two useful tools for identifying problems and trends and changes that affect the stability and performance of your computer.

Using System Restore and System Protection

If you encounter a problem after installing an operating system upgrade, a software product, or a device driver for a hardware device, you can use System Restore to roll back your computer to the point before you installed or updated that software on your computer. Likewise, if you make a change to a system setting, or if your computer sustains damage from malicious software, then you can use System Restore to roll back your computer to an earlier working state and then determine whether that corrected the problem.

System Protection is the Windows 7 component that creates and saves restore points so you can roll back your computer with System Restore and restore it to an earlier working state. Each restore point contains information about the state of system files and system settings, including Registry settings, on a computer at a specific point in time. System Protection creates restore points at specific intervals of time and when it detects an operation that changes the state of the computer. Although System Protection keeps track of changes to system files and system settings, *it does not save copies of your personal files, such as documents, photos, email messages, or favorites (bookmarks for Web sites)*. Instead, you use the Backup and Restore Center (covered in Tutorial 10) to make sure you have copies of important files and documents. Also, System Protection creates restore points on NTFS volumes, but not on FAT32 volumes, because FAT volumes do not support the use of shadow copies (also covered in Tutorial 10) used by System Protection.

System Protection creates restore points under the following conditions:

- **Before installing Windows updates**—System Protection creates a restore point before Windows Update installs any new service pack upgrade or other Windows update.

- **Before installing and uninstalling certain types of software**—System Protection creates a restore point before you install a program using Windows Installer or InstallShield. Windows Installer is a Windows service that manages the installation, configuration, and removal of programs on your computer. InstallShield is a software tool for packaging and reliably installing and uninstalling software. When you use System Restore to roll back your computer to a restore point created before installing a program, System Restore removes the installed software and Registry settings for the installed software and restores programs and system files that were altered during the installation of the new program. If you later decide you want to use a software product, you must reinstall it. System Protection does not create restore points for software installed without Windows Installer or an InstallShield Wizard, so you must create those restore points manually.
- **Before installing device drivers**—Because device drivers are a common source of problems, System Protection creates a restore point before installing a device driver. This is particularly important in the case of unsigned device drivers, or device drivers that have not been digitally signed or certified by Microsoft Corporation. If a problem arises after installing a device driver or a set of device drivers, you can use the restore point to roll back your computer and restore your previous device driver. In Tutorial 12, you will examine a feature called Roll Back Driver that allows you to replace a newly installed device driver with the device driver previously used on your computer.
- **Before restoring files from a backup**—System Protection creates a restore point before you back up or restore backed-up files using Windows Backup (or a third-party backup/restore program) because either operation might alter the state of the operating system.
- **Before restoring your computer using a restore point**—If you roll back your computer using a restore point, System Protection creates a new restore point first so if a problem develops after the restore operation, you can roll your computer forward to its original state before the restore operation. However, if you roll back your computer while in Safe Mode (described later in the tutorial) or in the Windows Recovery Environment (also covered later in the tutorial), System Protection does not create a restore point for undoing the restore operation.
- **When you create manual restore points**—You can use System Protection to manually create restore points before you make changes to your computer. For example, before you make changes to Registry settings or other system settings, or before you install a downloaded program that does not use Windows Installer, you can create a restore point in the event a problem develops.
- **Every week**—System Protection automatically creates restore points once every seven days if no other restore points were created during this time.

To save restore points, your computer must have at least 300 MB of free space on hard disks that are 500 MB or larger in storage capacity. System Restore will then use from 3 percent to 5 percent of the storage space on the hard disk drive for restore points. Once the disk storage space reserved for System Restore fills up, then older restore points are deleted to make room for newer restore points.

Windows 7 keeps fewer restore points than Windows Vista or Windows XP. Older restore points are not needed because you are not likely to roll back your computer a significant period of time, such as three months, six months, or a year or more, because you would unravel a substantial number of changes to your computer, such as removing all Windows updates, installed applications, and updated device drivers. Instead, you are more likely to roll back your computer to the most recent restore point first in the hope that it will resolve your problem with the minimum amount of change to your computer. If that does not resolve the problem, then you would perhaps try the previous restore point, or consider an alternative strategy to resolving the problems. That also means that more of your hard disk drive's storage space is available because you are not tying it up with restore points that you would never use.

Examining System Protection Settings

As a precautionary measure, Julien asks all of his support staff to make a manual restore point before modifying the Windows Registry on their own computers and on the computers used by the company's research staff.

Before you create a restore point in the following steps, you will examine the System Protection settings on the computer you are using. To complete the following steps, you need to provide Administrator credentials. If you cannot provide Administrator credentials, read the following steps and examine the figures so you are familiar with the use of System Restore, but do not keystroke the steps.

To open System Restore and view System Protection settings:

TIP
The Windows+Break keyboard shortcut also opens the System window.

1. Right-click the **Computer** desktop icon, click **Properties**, click the **System protection** link in the left pane of the System window, and if prompted, provide Administrator credentials. Windows 7 displays the System Protection property sheet in the System Properties dialog box. See Figure 8-9.

Figure 8-9 **Viewing System Protection settings**

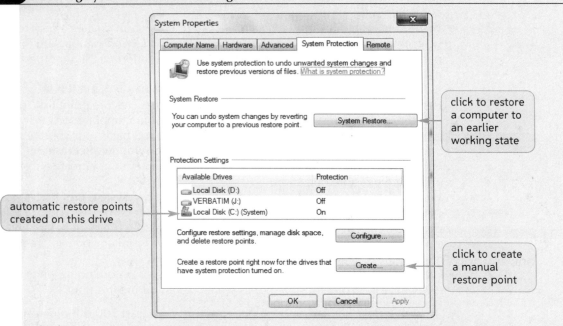

- click to restore a computer to an earlier working state
- automatic restore points created on this drive
- click to create a manual restore point

In the Protection Settings box, System Protection identifies the hard disk drives (internal and external) for which it creates restore points. On the computer used for this figure, System Protection creates restore points only for Local Disk (C:), the system volume. It does not create restore points for Local Disk (D:) and an external hard disk drive that stores automated daily backups. Your System Protection settings will differ.

2. Click **Local Disk (C:) (System)** in the Protection Settings box, and then click the **Configure** button. Windows 7 opens the System Protection for Local Disk (C:) dialog box. See Figure 8-10. Your drive C name may differ.

| Figure 8-10 | Viewing options for restoring settings and using disk space |

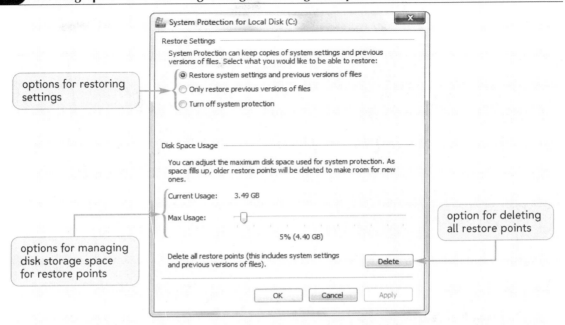

options for restoring settings

options for managing disk storage space for restore points

option for deleting all restore points

Under Restore Settings, Windows 7 notes that System Protection can keep copies of system settings and previous versions of files, and it prompts you to select what you would like to be able to restore. You can choose to restore both system settings and previous versions of files (the default option), restore only previous versions of files, or turn off system protection (for just this drive). In the Disk Space Usage section, you can specify the maximum amount of disk space used for system protection. On the computer used for this figure, the maximum usage is set at 5 percent of the total disk space, or 4.40 GB, and System Protection is currently using 3.49 GB of 4.40 GB storage space. Microsoft notes that Windows 7 uses up to 5 percent of the disk storage space for restore points on hard disk drives over 64 GB in size, or no more than 10 GB, whichever is less. For hard disk drives with a size of 64 GB or less, Windows 7 only uses up to 3 percent of the disk storage space for restore points. You can drag the slider tab to increase the space used by System Protection, or you can decrease that storage space. If you increase the amount of storage space, then you have more and older restore points available. If you decrease the amount of storage space, older restore points are deleted if System Protection is using the maximum amount of storage space. You can also use the Delete button to delete all restore points, and Windows 7 notes that this option includes both system settings as well as previous versions of files.

▶ **3.** To exit this dialog box without making any changes to your computer and its restore points, click the **Cancel** button.

▶ **4.** Keep the System Properties dialog box open for the next section of the tutorial.

You can use the Disk Cleanup utility if you want to delete all restore points except for the most recent restore point. To do so, you click the "Clean up system files" button, after you run the Disk Cleanup utility. You then provide Administrator credentials (if necessary), select the drive you want to check, select the More Options tab, and as shown in Figure 8-11, you click the Clean up button under "System Restore and Shadow Copies," click the Delete button, click the Delete Files button, and then click OK to complete the process. Think carefully before you delete these restore points because they might prove valuable later.

Figure 8-11 Disk Cleanup's option for removing restore points

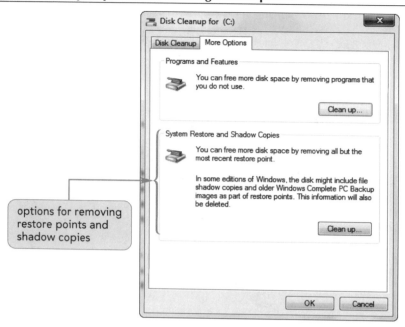

If you turn off System Protection, then System Restore deletes all existing restore points and does not create any new restore points.

To open System Protection from the desktop, you can create a shortcut with the path *%systemroot%\System32\SystemPropertiesProtection.exe* or *%windir%\System32\ SystemPropertiesProtection.exe*.

REFERENCE

Checking System Protection Settings

- To view System Protection settings, right-click the Computer desktop icon, click Properties, and in the left pane of the System window, click the System protection link, and then provide Administrator credentials.
- Examine the Protection Settings box to identify which drives are protected by System Protection. If you want to enable or turn off System Protection for a drive or want to adjust System Protection settings for a drive, click the drive listed under the Available Drives column, and then click the Configure button. Under Restore Settings, choose the option you want to use for System Protection. Under Disk Space Usage, check and, if necessary, use the slider tab to adjust the maximum amount of disk storage space used by System Protection for the drive you selected. The Delete button removes all restore points and previous versions of files. Click the OK button to save your changes, or click the Cancel button to close the System Protection dialog box for the selected drive without making any changes. *(Warning:* If you turn off the option for automatically creating restore points, then System Protection warns you that all existing restore points on the disk will be deleted and no new restore points will be created.) Then you will not be able to use System Restore to undo unwanted system changes on that drive. If you do not want to lose your existing restore points, then do not turn off System Protection.
- Click the OK button to close the System Properties dialog box and apply any changes you have made, or click the Cancel button to exit the System Properties dialog box without changing your system settings.

Although Windows 7 automatically enables System Protection for the system volume, you should check the System Protection settings to make sure it creates restore points for all the drives that you want to protect.

Using System Protection to Create a Restore Point

Although System Protection creates restore points automatically under certain conditions, you can also manually create a restore point before you make an important change to your computer that might cause a problem that you don't anticipate, such as changing a Registry setting.

Because many employees also carry work home and use their own computer systems, Julien asks you to show employees how to create manual restore points as a precautionary measure before they make a significant change to their computer.

To create a restore point:

▶ **1.** In the System Properties dialog box, click the **Create** button on the System Protection property sheet. System Protection prompts you to enter a description that identifies the purpose of the restore point. It also notes that it will automatically add the date and time to the description.

▶ **2.** Type **Manual Restore Point**, and then click the **Create** button. System Protection displays a dialog box to let you know that it is creating a restore point. When it finishes creating the restore point, it displays a dialog box to let you know that it successfully created the restore point.

▶ **3.** Click the **Close** button in the System Protection dialog box.

▶ **4.** Keep the System Properties dialog box open for the next section of the tutorial.

Rolling back your computer using a system restore point can result in a major change to the configuration of your computer, so you also have to weigh the effect that the restore point has on other changes you made to your computer during the same period of time.

INSIGHT

Naming Manual Restore Points

When you create a manual restore point, enter a description that clearly explains the purpose of restore point. For example, if you are going to install a new program that you've downloaded from the Internet, you could enter the description "Installation of" or "Before installing" followed by the actual name of the program. By being as specific as possible, you can locate the exact restore point you need later and easily distinguish it from the automatic restore points made by System Protection. That ensures you roll back your computer to the right point in time.

Although System Protection is designed to create restore points prior to operations that affect the use of your computer, such as installing new software, you can use System Protection to manually create restore points before you make changes to your computer. Furthermore, while System Protection is invaluable, it does not substitute for backups; you still must back up your important documents on a regular basis. Along with system restore points automatically made by System Protection, manual restore points improve the chances that you can restore your computer to an earlier functioning state and resolve a problem.

Creating a Manual Restore Point

- Right-click the Computer desktop icon, click Properties, and in the System window, click the System protection link, and provide Administrator credentials.
- In the System Properties dialog box, click the Create button on the System Protection property sheet, enter a description for the restore point in the System Protection dialog box, and click the Create button.
- After System Protection informs you that it successfully created a restore point, click the Close button in the System Protection dialog box, and then click the OK button to close the System Properties dialog box.

Viewing Restore Points

If you run into a problem on your computer and decide to roll back your computer, you must first save any open documents or files, and then close all programs and windows before you use System Restore to select a restore point and then roll back your computer.

TIP

You can also open System Restore from the System Tools menu under Accessories.

To view restore points:

1. In the System Properties dialog box, click the **System Restore** button on the System Protection property sheet, and wait for System Restore to start. System Protection displays a System Restore dialog box and explains that you can use System Restore to fix problems that might be making your computer run slowly or stop responding.

   It points out that choosing a restore point does not affect any of your personal documents, pictures, or data and that the process is completely reversible. It also warns you that recently installed programs and drivers might be uninstalled during the System Restore operation.

2. Click the **Next** button. In the next System Restore dialog box, System Restore displays a list of restore points, as shown in Figure 8-12. Your restore points will differ.

Figure 8-12 **Viewing recent restore points**

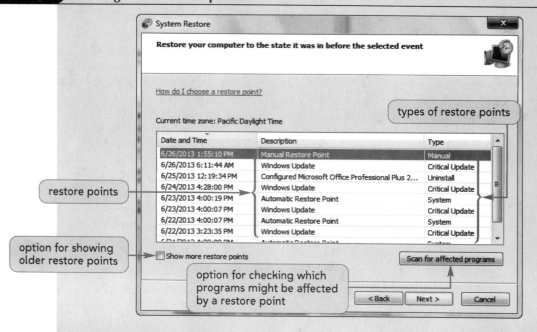

The Manual Restore Point that you just made is listed first. Although Windows 7 is supposed to create a restore point each day, you might only see the most recent restore point. All the restore points are listed in reverse date and time order. On this computer, four of the nine restore points resulted from Windows Update downloading and installing critical updates. Another three restore points were automatically created system restore points (identified as System under the Type column). One restore point resulted from uninstalling a component of Microsoft Office Professional Plus 2010. You may also see a System Image Restore Point identified as a Backup Type. This system image backup, which you will examine in more detail in Tutorial 10, has a copy of the entire contents of your hard disk drive or drives, and therefore is quite important. You can use the "Show more restore points" check box to view older restore points.

▶ 3. Click the **Scan for affected programs** button. After System Restore scans for affected programs and drivers, it displays another System Restore dialog box that lists any programs and drivers that will be deleted as well as any programs and drivers that might be restored based on the restore point you have selected. In some cases, none are found.

At the top of the System Restore dialog, System Restore notes that any programs added since the last restore point will be deleted and any programs that were removed will be restored. In the list of programs and drivers that might be restored (the second box), it notes that any programs and drivers that are restored might not work correctly after the restore operation, and you might need to reinstall them. This scan is useful so you do not end up with any surprises later.

> Do not click the Finish button when prompted to confirm your restore point. If you do, you will roll back your computer to an earlier state.

▶ 4. Click the **Close** button to close the System Restore dialog box, and then click the **Next** button. System Restore then prompts you to confirm your restore point. See Figure 8-13.

| Figure 8-13 | Confirming a restore point |

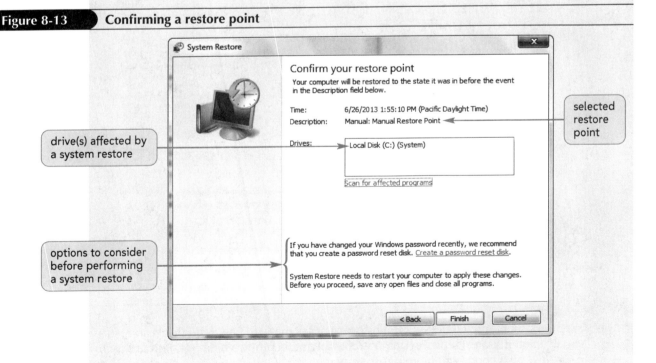

This window shows the date and time of the restore point, the type of restore point (Manual), the description for the restore point, and the drive or drives affected by the restore point. System Restore recommends that you create a password reset disk if you have recently changed your Windows password. Then it informs you that it needs to restart your computer to apply these changes, and it recommends that you save any open files and close all programs before you continue. If this is not the correct restore point, or if you change your mind about which restore point you want to use, then you can use the Back button to back up and pick another restore point.

▶ **5.** So you do not inadvertently roll back your computer to an earlier working state with a restore point that is not needed, click the **Cancel** button to cancel this operation.

▶ **6.** Close the System Properties dialog box, and then close the System window.

If you continue with the process of using a restore point by clicking the Finish button, System Restore warns you that once started, System Restore cannot be interrupted, and it asks if you want to continue. It also notes that you cannot undo the changes System Restore makes until after it restores your computer to the restore point you chose.

If you decide to proceed, next you will see a System Restore dialog box that displays the message *Preparing to restore your system*. Then you will see the message *Please wait while your Windows files and settings are being restored. System Restore is initializing.* After your computer reboots, you log on under your user account.

If you have already used a restore point to roll back your computer to an earlier point in time, then System Restore includes an option for undoing that restore operation in the System Restore dialog box the next time you open it, as shown in Figure 8-14.

Figure 8-14   **System Restore option for undoing a restore operation**

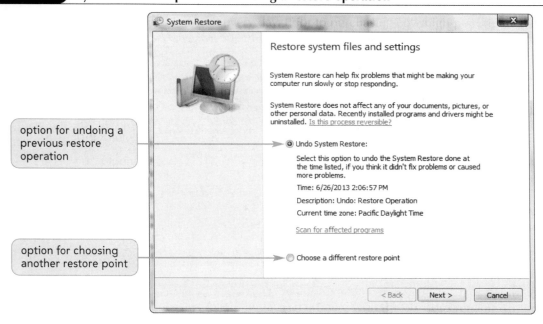

Under Undo System Restore, it notes that you can undo that restore operation if you think that the last system restore did not fix problems or caused more problems. You can also choose a different restore point.

If you want to open System Restore without first opening System Protection, you can open the All Programs menu, open the Accessories menu, open the System Tools menu, and then select System Restore and provide Administrator credentials.

You can create a desktop shortcut with the path *%systemroot%\System32\rstrui.exe* or *%windir%\System32\rstrui.exe* to open System Restore quickly. You can also use the Send to menu option or hold down Ctrl and drag to copy the System Restore shortcut from the System Tools menu to the desktop.

System Restore provides you with a powerful tool for reversing changes that affect the performance of your computer system; however, don't automatically assume that it will resolve every problem you encounter.

Using Event Viewer

Event Viewer provides detailed information about significant events that occur on a computer, such as an application failure, Windows boot failure, the successful completion of a Check Disk utility operation, or when you log onto your computer.

Events are recorded in files called event logs. You can use Event Viewer to access the information in event logs to check the status of your computer system and to troubleshoot problems that you are experiencing. Event Viewer creates event logs for the following types of events that occur on a computer:

- **Application events**—Depending on the nature of an event, Event Viewer organizes application or program events in one of three categories—Error, Warning, or Information. Errors, such as an application failure, are serious problems. Warnings are not as serious; however, they might be indicative of a more serious problem that could arise later. An Information event verifies the successful completion of some type of operation of an application or program, a device driver, or a service. As a reminder, a service, such as a Windows service, is a program that operates in the background and provides support to other programs on your computer.
- **Security events**—Event Viewer identifies a security-related event as an Audit Success or an Audit Failure. Examples of an Audit Success include a successful attempt by a user to log onto or log off their user account, a successful start of Windows Firewall, and a successful change in the system time. An example of an Audit Failure is a corrupt device driver for an installed program (which you could then uninstall).
- **Setup events**—This category contains information about events on a domain controller. A **domain controller** is a specially configured computer that functions as a server on an Active Directory network and provides services for other computers. An **Active Directory network** is one that manages user logons and provides access to network and shared resources.
- **System events**—Event Viewer displays information about events triggered by components of the Windows operating system. Examples of system events include the start or stop of system services (such as Security Center, Windows Update, Windows Search, Windows Error Reporting, and Windows Backup), the system uptime, and the start and completion of a Windows Defender scan. Windows Defender is Microsoft antispyware software product included with Windows Vista and Windows 7. Examples of system errors include a driver problem, the failure to assign a specific resource to a hardware device, recovery of a corrupted Registry entry for a specific user logon, an unexpected shutdown of the system, and a nonfunctioning device attached to the computer. System events are reported as Error, Warning, or Information.
- **Forwarded events**—These events are ones forwarded from another computer.

Event Viewer organizes events into two categories—Windows Logs, and Application and Services logs. These logs contain events that apply to the entire system and events for legacy applications, which are older programs designed for earlier versions of Windows. Windows Logs include Application, Security, and System logs as well as two new logs, the Setup log and Forwarded Events log. The latter log contains events collected from a remote computer. A **remote computer** is a computer that is not physically connected to your computer, but one that you can access over a network, including the Internet.

When you open Event Viewer, it displays a Summary of Administrative Events and groups specific types of events into one of six categories: Critical, Error, Warning, Information, Audit Success, and Audit Failure. You can expand one of these categories to view a list of events that fall in that category. Then, you can double-click an event to view more detail about that event.

To access all of the event logs or change settings in Event Viewer, you must provide Administrator credentials; otherwise, some event logs are not available to you, and you are limited to making changes to settings only in your user account.

After recently encountering a couple of problems on your computer, Julien and you decide to use Event Viewer to try to identify the source of those problems.

In the next set of steps, you must provide Administrator credentials as you open Event Viewer. Although you can open Event Viewer without Administrator credentials, the information displayed by Event Viewer differs, and you do not have access to all the information available in Event Viewer. Also, because Event Viewer tracks information on thousands of events on your computer, you may have to be patient while Event Viewer compiles information on those events.

To examine the Summary of Administrative Events:

1. From the Start menu, point to **Administrative Tools**, right-click **Event Viewer**, click **Run as administrator**, provide Administrator credentials, and after Windows 7 opens Event Viewer, click **Event Viewer (Local)** in the console tree pane on the left side of the window, and then maximize the window. Event Viewer compiles a Summary of Administrative Events in the Details pane in the center of the Event Viewer window, and organizes the event summary by Event Type. See Figure 8-15.

   Trouble? If you cannot provide Administrator credentials, open the Start menu, point to Administrative Tools, and then click Event Viewer. After you open Event Viewer, you will not see an Audit Success category in the Summary of Administrative Events, and the information displayed in the Recently Viewed Nodes box is limited; however, you can still follow the discussion and examine the figures.

Figure 8-15	Viewing the Summary of Administrative Events

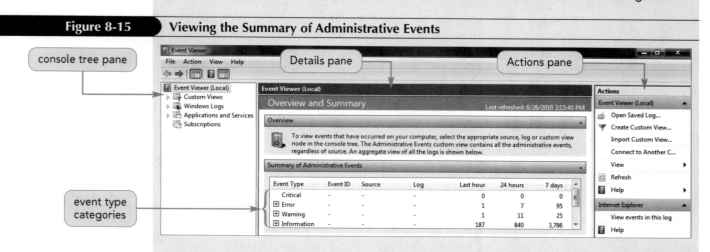

Critical, Error, and Warning are three groups of events that you want to examine and if possible, troubleshoot and resolve. In the Summary of Administrative Events, Event Viewer includes information about events that occurred within the last hour, the last 24 hours, and the last 7 days. The pane on the right side of the window is called the Action pane.

▶ **2.** If Windows 7 displays an expand icon ⊞ next to *Critical, Error,* or *Warning* under the Event Type column in the Summary of Administrative Events, then click an **expand** icon ⊞ to the left of one of these categories.

   Trouble? If Event Reviewer does not display an expand icon ⊞ to the left of any of these categories, and if there is an expand icon ⊞ next to the Information category, then click the Information expand icon ⊞; otherwise, read this and the following steps and examine the figures.

▶ **3.** If you want to adjust the width of each column in the Summary of Administrative Events for a best fit, then click an **Event Type** category, and press the **Ctrl key** and the **plus sign** on the numeric keypad, or double-click each column border.

▶ **4.** Double-click a specific **event name** under one of the Event Type categories, and double-click an **event** in the Summary page events list. Event Viewer opens an Event Properties dialog box for the event you selected. On the computer used for Figure 8-16, Event Viewer notes on the General property sheet that a backup did not complete because of an error writing to the backup location, and then it reports that the backup location could not be found or is not valid. Your event details will differ.

Figure 8-16   **Viewing details about a critical event**

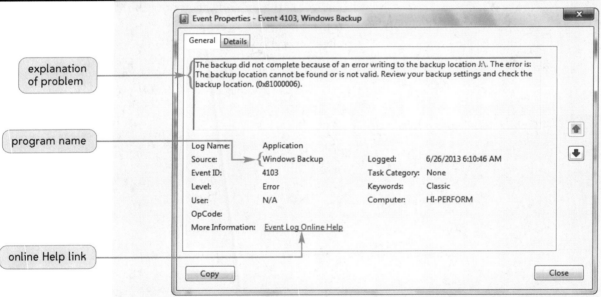

Event Viewer then suggests a review of the current backup settings and a check of the backup location. In this case, the problem occurred because the external hard disk used for the backup was turned off and temporarily removed from the computer system, so the problem is easily resolved by turning that drive on.

If you want to use Microsoft online assistance to provide you with more information about this specific event, you can click the Event Log Online Help link at the bottom of the General property sheet and verify that you want to send this information over the Internet.

▶ **5.** Click the Event Properties dialog box **Close** button.

▶ **6.** Use the **Back** button  on the Standard toolbar to return to the Event Viewer (Local) Overview and Summary.

▶ **7.** View an event in each of the other event categories so you are familiar with other types of events and then return to the Summary of Administrative Events.

▶ **8.** Keep Event Viewer open for the next section of the tutorial.

You can also choose to view a category of events, such as Application events, Security events, and System events. Furthermore, you can filter or select events by applying one or more criteria so you can focus on one specific type of event, such as all Application event errors.

To examine Application events:

▶ **1.** In the console tree pane on the left, double-click **Windows Logs**. Event Viewer expands this part of the console tree, and in the Details pane in the center of the window, Event Viewer lists the total number of events that appear in each of the five Windows logs.

▶ **2.** In the console tree pane, click **Application** under Windows Logs. Event Viewer displays a list of events that fall in this category and lists them from the most recent event to the oldest event.

▶ **3.** Choose and double-click an **Application event** under Application in the Details pane, and review the information reported on that event on the General property sheet. On the computer used for Figure 8-17, Event Viewer reports that the Windows Security Center Service has started. Your event and event details will differ.

| Figure 8-17 | Viewing details of an Information event |

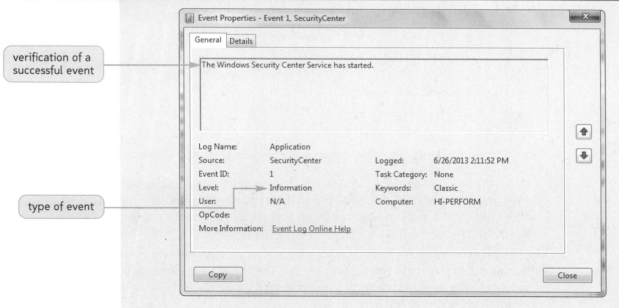

▶ **4.** Click the Event Properties dialog box **Close** button.

> **5.** In the Actions pane on the right, click the **Filter Current Log** link. Event Viewer displays a Filter Current Log dialog box. See Figure 8-18.

Filter Current Log dialog box for specifying filter criteria

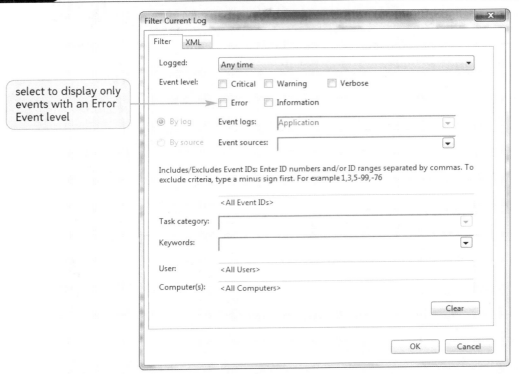

select to display only events with an Error Event level

You can now specify criteria for filtering events and thereby display only those events that meet the criteria you specify. For Application events, you can choose the Critical, Error, Warning, or Information check boxes under Event level.

> **6.** Under Event level, click the **Error** check box and then click the **OK** button. Event Viewer filters events and displays all events assigned the Error level.

> **7.** Click the **Source** column button to sort Application Error events in alphabetical order and, if necessary, press the **Home** key to view the first event listed. You can also drag the split bar between the list of Application events and the pane with detailed information on a specific event so you can either view more Application events or view more information on a specific event's properties within the Details pane.

> **8.** Click an **event** in the list of filtered Application Error events. Event Viewer displays information about that event on the General property sheet in the Details pane, as shown in Figure 8-19, and identifies the name of the application that encountered an error condition.

Figure 8-19 **Viewing details on a filtered event**

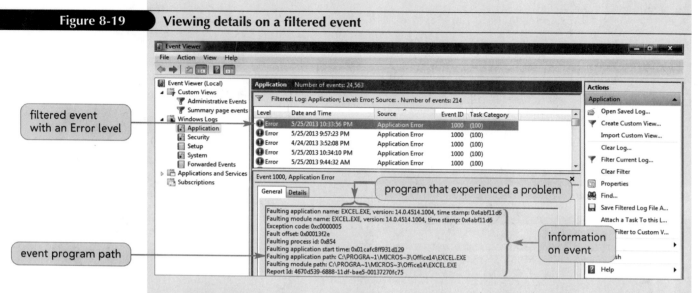

filtered event with an Error level

program that experienced a problem

information on event

event program path

In this case, the error occurred with Microsoft Office 2010 Excel, identified as EXCEL.EXE. It also identifies the application path using aliases: C:\PROGRA~1\ MICROS~3\Office14\EXCEL.EXE.

9. In the Actions pane, click **Clear Filter**. Event Viewer removes the filter you applied to the list of Application events, and then recompiles a list of Application events.

10. Keep the Event Viewer window open for the next section of the tutorial.

By examining application errors, you can identify problems with specific applications on your computer so you can troubleshoot and resolve those problems. You can use the same approach to examine system events so you can identify and evaluate problems with Windows and Windows services.

If you want to examine security-related problems, you must open Event Viewer with Administrator credentials. Then, if you select Security under Windows logs, Event Viewer displays a list of Security events in the Details pane. Under the Keywords column, Event Viewer identifies the event as an Audit Success or Audit Failure, and the Task Category column identifies the type of task, including, for example, Logon, Logoff, Other System Events (such as starting Windows Firewall), and User Account Management (such as changing a user account). If you want to view just Audit Failures, you click the Filter Current Log option in the Action pane, click the Keywords arrow on the Filter property sheet in the Filter Current Log dialog box, click the Audit Failure check box, and then apply the filter by clicking OK. Now you can focus on security-related problems.

Under Application and Services Logs in the console tree pane, you can view information on Hardware Events, Internet Explorer, Microsoft Office Alerts, and Microsoft services. If you expand the Microsoft node, and then expand the Windows node, you can select and view events related to a specific Windows service, such as Reliability Monitor's Reliability-Analysis-Engine, Task Scheduler, User Account Control (under UAC), and Windows Update (under WindowsUpdateClient).

Microsoft Office Alerts contain event logs that provide information about Microsoft Office events, such as performing a copy operation, saving changes to a file, results of a search and replace operation, and repairs to damaged files.

To examine events for a specific service:

▶ **1.** In the console tree pane on the left, double-click **Applications and Services Logs** to expand this category.

▶ **2.** Under Applications and Services Log in the console tree pane, double-click **Microsoft**, double-click **Windows**, and then use the horizontal scroll bar in the console tree pane to adjust your view so you can see the nodes under Windows.

▶ **3.** Locate and double-click **Reliability-Analysis-Engine**, and then click **Operational** under Reliability-Analysis-Engine in the console tree pane. In the Details pane, Event Viewer lists events for the Reliability Analysis component that updates information on your computer's stability index every day. See Figure 8-20.

| Figure 8-20 | Viewing Windows events for the Reliability-Analysis-Engine |

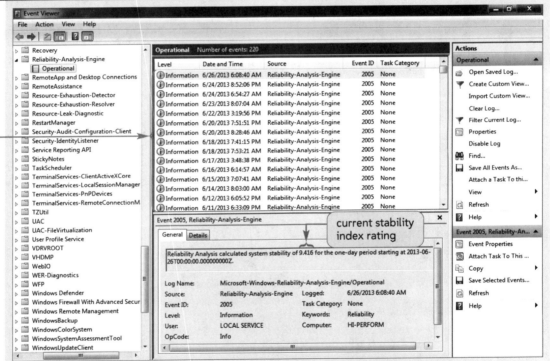

Reliability-Analysis-Engine events

current stability index rating

If you select an event, such as the first one shown in the figure, and examine the General tab, the event log shows the exact stability index value or rating that was calculated at a specific point in time. On the computer used for this figure, Event Viewer reports that Reliability Analysis calculated a system stability of 9.416 for the current day. Your event details will differ.

▶ **4.** Click the **collapse** icon ◢ to the left of the Microsoft node.

▶ **5.** If Microsoft Office is installed on your computer, locate and click **Microsoft Office Alerts**, **Microsoft Office Diagnostics**, or **Microsoft Office Sessions** in the console tree pane under Applications and Services Logs. Event Viewer displays event information for Microsoft Office operations. As an example, one Information event reported for Microsoft Word that errors were detected in a file, and that Microsoft Word was able to save the file by making repairs.

▶ **6.** Close the Event Viewer window.

Reliability Monitor is similar to Event Viewer; however, Reliability Monitor provides a visual overview of the performance of your computer and allows you to drill down to details for certain types of system events. In contrast, Event Viewer provides information about all events on a computer. You can combine the use of these two tools to grasp what's happening on a computer and then troubleshoot it. For example, you can use Reliability Monitor to quickly determine how long you've experienced problems with a specific application, and then you can use Event Viewer to find more information about that problem and, if possible, identify any related types of events that might help you troubleshoot and resolve the problem.

You can create a desktop shortcut with the path *%systemroot%\system32\eventvwr.msc* or *%windir%\system32\eventvwr.msc* to open Event Viewer. You can also use the Send to menu option or press and hold the Ctrl key and drag to copy the Event Viewer shortcut from the Administrative Tools menu to the desktop. To customize an Event Viewer desktop shortcut so it automatically runs as an Administrator, open the shortcut's Properties dialog box, and enable the "Run as administrator" option using the Advanced button on the Shortcut property sheet.

REFERENCE

Using Event Viewer

- To open Event Viewer with Administrator credentials, open the Start menu, point to Administrative Tools, right-click Event Viewer, click "Run as administrator," and then provide Administrator credentials. To open Event Viewer without Administrator credentials, open the Start menu, point to Administrative Tools, and then click Event Viewer.
- In the Summary of Administrative Events in the Details pane, click the expand icon to the left of each Event Type category you want to examine, examine the list of events, and if you want to view information about a specific type of event, double-click that event, click a specific event under Summary page events, and examine information about that event on the General property sheet. Use the Back button on the Standard toolbar to return to the Summary of Administrative Events.
- To view information on Application events, Security events, Setup events, System events, or Forwarded Events, expand the Windows Logs node in the console tree pane, click Application, Security, Setup, System, or Forwarded Events under Windows Logs, select an event in the Details pane, and review the information reported on that event on the General property sheet.
- To filter events, click the Filter Current Log link in the Actions pane on the right, and in the Filter Current Log dialog box, select or specify one or more criteria for filtering events, click the OK button, and then select and examine an event in the list of filtered events. To remove a filter, click Clear Filter in the Actions pane.
- To examine events for a specific Windows component or service, expand the Applications and Services Logs node in the console tree pane to expand this category, expand the Microsoft node, expand the Windows node, locate and expand the Windows component or service you want to examine, click Operational in the console tree pane under the Windows component or service you selected, and in the Details pane, review the information on events or select and examine specific events.
- If Microsoft Office is installed on your computer, locate and click the Microsoft Office Alerts node, and then examine the information on Microsoft Office events.
- Close the Event Viewer window.

Remember to examine Microsoft Office Alerts and Internet Explorer events when checking events for Microsoft software.

PROSKILLS

Problem Solving: Using Event Viewer to Identify Problems

To benefit from Event Viewer, you should examine events on a frequent basis so you can identify new problems that could become worse over time. Also, problems that keep reoccurring, such as problems with the same application not responding, affect the performance of your computer and indicate a limiting factor in the performance of your computer, such as insufficient RAM. In some cases, you might need to replace an application with one that performs better and that does not create problems on your computer.

To help you identify serious or ongoing problems, you can use filters to focus on the most serious events and resolve the problem when it occurs. Using filters as part of your troubleshooting strategy is important because Event Viewer records information on every single event that occurs on your computer, and the number of events recorded over time can easily become too extensive to examine one by one. However, this is also one of the assets of Event Viewer.

Under Custom Views in the console tree pane is a predefined filter named Administrative Events that displays all Critical, Error, and Warning events on a computer that require troubleshooting or action on the part of an Administrator, and thereby provides you with a head start on identifying and resolving problems. You must open Event Viewer with Administrative credentials to view information about all events.

By using Event Viewer on a regular basis, you can stay on top of problems that arise on your computer, combine the use of Event Viewer with other troubleshooting tools to resolve problems, identify the best software to use on your computer, evaluate whether you need to purchase additional hardware (such as RAM), and assure yourself that your computer system is working properly and optimally.

Session 8.1 Quick Check

REVIEW

1. What Windows 7 tool can you use to reproduce and document a problem so your IT support staff can better assist you?
2. What is Reliability Monitor?
3. What is a stability index?
4. What is the difference between System Protection and System Restore?
5. True or False. Windows 7 can create restore points on both FAT and NTFS volumes.
6. A(n) _____ is a significant change in your computer system that is documented by Windows 7 in _____.
7. To locate specific types of events, you can _____ events and thereby display only those that meet the criteria you specify.
8. List five types of events that trigger System Protection to create a restore point.

SESSION 8.2 VISUAL OVERVIEW

If you encounter a problem with starting Windows, you use the **Advanced Boot Options** menu to choose a different option for starting Windows so you can troubleshoot the problem under a different set of conditions. For example, you might need to remove a new video display driver so that you can view the image on the monitor when you perform a regular boot.

You can use this boot option to choose a troubleshooting tool such as Startup Repair from the **Windows Recovery Environment**, a special environment for troubleshooting computer startup problems.

```
                         Advanced Boot Options

     Choose Advanced Options for: Windows 7
     (Use the arrow keys to highlight your choice.)


        Repair Your Computer


        Safe Mode
        Safe Mode with Networking
        Safe Mode with Command Prompt

        Enable Boot Logging
        Enable low-resolution video (640x480)
        Last Known Good Configuration (advanced)
        Directory Services Restore Mode
        Debugging Mode
        Disable automatic restart on system failure
        Disable Driver Signature Enforcement


        Start Windows Normally


     Description: View a list of system recovery tools you can use to repair
                  startup problems, run diagnostics, or restore your system.


     ENTER=Choose                                          ESC=Cancel
```

Available in every version of Windows, **Safe Mode** is a boot option for troubleshooting problems that might be caused by device drivers, Windows services, startup programs, and video display problems. This option starts Windows 7 with a minimal set of services and drivers—ones that are safe and reliable—so that you can access your computer and troubleshoot a problem.

The **Last Known Good Configuration** boot option uses settings from your last successful boot to quickly and easily resolve a startup problem.

Start Windows Normally is the default boot option for performing a full boot with all Windows settings.

BOOT OPTIONS

You can use **System Configuration** to adjust boot settings, manage the loading of programs and services, and to troubleshoot problems caused by incompatible programs and malicious software.

Startup programs, identified as **Startup Items** in System Configuration, are programs, such as Internet security or antivirus software, that load during startup and that operate in the background as you use your computer.

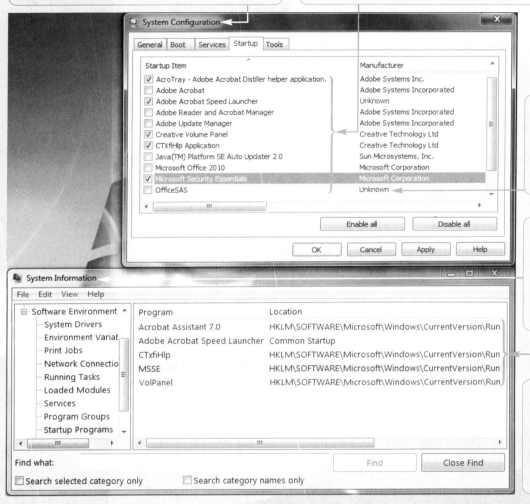

If you do not recognize a startup program or its manufacturer, or if information is not reported about a startup program, then you should research the program and determine its function, usefulness, and safety.

The **System Information** utility provides detailed information about your computer system; hardware devices, resources, and problem devices; and information about software, including device drivers and startup programs.

You can compare information reported by System Configuration and System Information on startup programs to identify how startup programs load, troubleshoot problems, and improve your computer's performance.

Using Your Computer's BIOS

As you discovered in Tutorial 1, the BIOS (basic input/output system) plays an important role during the initial stages of booting, including locating and loading the operating system on a computer. The BIOS also contains important system settings that are retained after you turn off the power to your computer and that are used during the next boot to help configure your computer. The term **firmware** refers to a hardware device, such as the BIOS, that contains embedded software that controls how the device interacts with the operating system.

To view and change BIOS settings, you open a computer's built-in BIOS Setup utility during booting by pressing a specific key (or combination of keys), such as F2 or F1. During the very early stages of booting, most computers (but not all) display a message on the initial startup screen to identify the key or keys to press to open the BIOS Setup utility, as shown in Figure 8-21 for a Dell computer.

| Figure 8-21 | Initial startup screen identifying hotkeys |

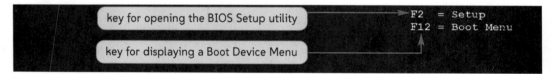

On some computers, the option for displaying these keys (also called **hotkeys**) is turned off to prevent someone from inadvertently opening the BIOS Setup utility and making changes that might adversely affect a computer. Over time, individuals might no longer remember what key or keys to press to open the BIOS Setup utility. If the latter happens, examine the startup screen as your computer boots for the name of the BIOS manufacturer, such as American Megatrends. Then search online for the *BIOS setup key* for that BIOS manufacturer.

The BIOS might also display a message that identifies which hotkey to press to open a Boot Device Menu. Figure 8-22 shows a Boot Device Menu from a Dell computer.

| Figure 8-22 | Viewing Boot Device Menu options |

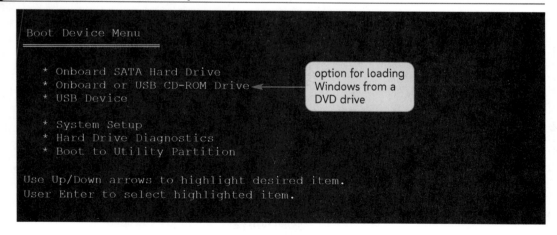

From the Boot Device Menu, you can choose which device to use to boot your computer. The Onboard or USB CD-ROM Drive option on this computer also supports booting from a DVD drive. Your Boot Device Menu might also display other options, including the option for entering System Setup (in other words, opening the BIOS Setup utility). You can customize this menu using the BIOS Setup utility.

After you open the BIOS Setup utility, you can view and change certain BIOS settings. However, you also want to make sure that you do not accidentally change a setting that might affect the performance of your computer system or prevent your computer from booting. Before you make a change, make a note of the original BIOS setting, the new setting, and the date of the change. That way, you can restore a setting that proves problematic later.

You can use the BIOS Setup utility to:

- **Check and change the boot sequence**—The **boot sequence** consists of a list of devices that the BIOS examines during booting in order to locate the operating system. Typically, the hard disk drive is listed first, followed by other devices, such as a CD drive or USB device. If you want to boot from a device other than the default (or first) device, you might need to change the boot sequence. For example, if you want to install Windows 7 from the Windows 7 DVD, you might need to adjust BIOS settings so your computer can boot from your DVD drive (as is the case for the computer used for figures in this tutorial).
- **Locate important information about your computer**—The BIOS contains detailed information about the computer system itself. For example, you can view information about the memory slots available in your computer, determine how much RAM is located in each memory slot, and determine which memory slots are used and which are empty.
- **Specify security settings**—If you want to prohibit an unauthorized user from changing BIOS configuration settings, you can specify an Admin password. If you want to prevent an unauthorized user from booting your computer, you can also specify a System password.
- **View and change power management settings**—For example, you can specify an Auto Power On setting to automatically turn your computer on every day, or only weekdays, at a specific time. You can also specify what happens after a power loss, namely, whether the system stays off, powers itself on, or returns to its previous state (on or off) after power is restored.
- **Adjust POST behavior settings**—As you may recall from Tutorial 1, POST (for Power-On Self-Test) refers to initial tests performed to verify the presence and working state of boot devices. You can specify whether your computer displays messages that identify which keys to press at startup to open the BIOS Setup utility or Boot Device Menu. You can also specify whether to display either the Setup or Boot Device Menu message, or specify that the BIOS display no messages so a new user does not know which keys to press to open the Setup utility or Boot Device Menu (and therefore does not inadvertently change BIOS settings). You can also specify whether the Num Lock key is on or off after your computer boots.

To open the Setup utility, you must reboot your computer or if your computer is already off, you must power on your system and identify the key or keys needed to open the Setup utility. As your computer starts up, pay close attention to the information displayed on the monitor so you know what you need to press to open the Setup utility. You must press the key or keys for opening the BIOS Setup utility at that point, before booting continues. Otherwise, you must let Windows 7 boot to the desktop, restart your computer, and then try again.

If you are working in a computer lab, your technical support staff may have already password-protected the Setup utility so only the technical support staff can access and change these settings. In some cases, you might be able to open a password-protected Setup utility but not make any changes to BIOS settings. If you are working in a computer lab, and if the Setup utility is not password-protected, do not perform the following steps without the permission of your instructor or technical support staff. If you cannot or prefer not to open the Setup utility on your computer until you are more familiar with this utility, read the following steps and examine the figures, but do not keystroke the steps.

Julien asks you to check and adjust BIOS settings on a new computer purchased for a new research scientist.

Read the following steps before you perform them, because you may not have enough time to read the steps and check the information displayed on the monitor at the same time.

To open the BIOS Setup utility:

1. If your computer is turned off, turn the power on to your computer. If you already logged on your computer, close all open applications, windows, and dialog boxes, and then restart your computer.

2. During booting or rebooting, watch the monitor for a message that identifies which key or keys to press to open the Setup utility, and then very quickly press that key or combination of keys.

   At that point, you may see the message *Entering Setup* displayed on the monitor, and then the BIOS Setup utility opens. Figure 8-23 shows BIOS settings for a Dell computer. Your view of BIOS settings may differ because different companies manufacture different types of BIOS chips, and they change and improve their BIOS chips over time.

Figure 8-23 BIOS settings

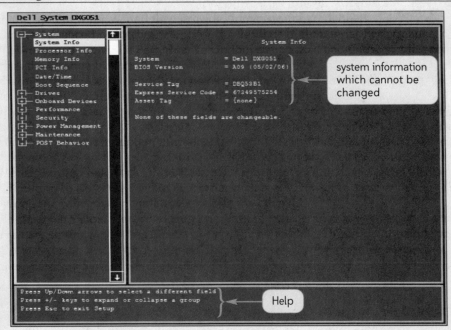

Trouble? If you see the Windows logo and the message that Windows is starting, you've passed the point at which you can open the BIOS Setup utility. Wait for Windows 7 to boot to the desktop, restart your computer, and then try again. In some cases, a computer might boot so quickly that you might not be able to see any messages displayed on the monitor. If your keyboard has a Pause key (which might be labeled Pause/Break), then you can press that key to temporarily halt booting so you can see what's displayed on the screen. To resume booting, press the Enter key. If you do not see a message on how to open Setup, check your computer documentation or the manufacturer's Web site for information on how to open the Setup utility, use a search engine to locate this information, or try pressing F2 or F1 in the first few seconds of the boot process. In the latter case, if the key you press is not the key for opening the Setup utility, you will have to wait until Windows 7 boots to the Welcome Screen or desktop, and then restart your computer and try another key.

On the computer used for Figure 8-23, the pane on the left side of the screen displays different categories from which you can access specific types of BIOS settings. On this computer, the BIOS Setup utility selects the first category, System, expands this category, highlights System Info, and in the right pane, displays System Info settings. On this computer, the System group contains basic system information as well as options for changing the date, time, and boot sequence. The System field identifies the exact Dell model, useful for searching for information about BIOS setting and locating user manuals at the manufacturer's Web site. A **field** refers to the name of a specific type of setting and the setting itself. At the bottom of the screen, the BIOS Setup utility displays information on how to select another field, expand or collapse a group, and exit the BIOS Setup utility. For example, on the computer used for this figure, you press the Up and Down arrow keys to select a different group or a different field, press the plus and minus keys to expand or collapse a group of settings, and press the Esc key to exit the BIOS Setup utility. (The Enter key also opens a group.) It also notes that you cannot change the fields in this category. While the BIOS on your computer might differ from the one shown in Figure 8-23, it will provide information on how to use the BIOS Setup utility, and it should also contain similar options, though they might be organized and labeled in a different way. However, the logic and techniques for working with different types of BIOS chips is the same.

Next you will examine your computer's boot sequence.

To examine your computer's boot sequence:

1. Examine each category of options available on your computer and locate and select the field that contains information on the boot sequence or boot order of your computer. After selecting Boot Sequence under the System group or category in the left pane on the computer used for Figure 8-24, the BIOS Setup utility lists five bootable devices. Some boot devices are not present; however, the settings shown are the manufacturer's settings.

Figure 8-24   **BIOS boot sequence settings**

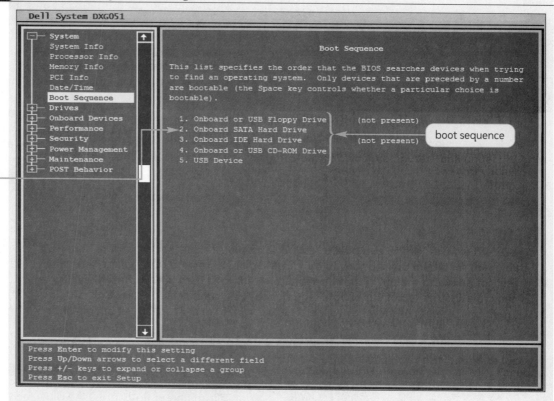

option for booting from hard disk

boot sequence

The Setup utility notes that only devices preceded by a number are bootable. In this case, it also informs you that you can use the Space key (in other words, the spacebar) to control whether a specific device is bootable. Your BIOS settings will differ.

On the computer used for this figure, the first bootable device present is the Onboard SATA Hard Drive, followed by an Onboard or USB CD-ROM Drive, and then a USB Device. **SATA** (for Serial ATA or Serial Advanced Technology Attachment) is a newer type of technology for connecting a hard disk to a computer to achieve faster data transfers than was possible with the previous **PATA** (for Parallel ATA or Parallel Advanced Technology Attachment) hard disks. PATA is often referred to simply as ATA.

When this computer boots, the BIOS routine responsible for locating and loading the operating system checks the SATA hard disk drive first, and because Windows 7 is installed on this hard disk drive, it boots the computer from that drive. However, if there is a problem with that drive that prevents the BIOS routine from accessing it, the BIOS routine will then examine the next drive listed in the boot sequence (and present in the computer) for the operating system. If it locates the operating system on that next drive, then it boots the computer; otherwise, it examines the next drive listed in the boot sequence. If you want to boot from another drive or from another type of bootable device, such as a DVD or CD drive, you can change the boot sequence so the DVD or CD drive is listed before the option for booting from the hard disk drive. Even if the DVD or CD drive is not listed first in the boot sequence, the BIOS might automatically detect it during booting if it contains a DVD or CD, and then prompt you to press a key to boot from that disc.

As shown in the Help pane at the bottom of the window, you can use the Enter key to change the boot sequence with this manufacturer's BIOS. You select the first boot device (in this example, the SATA hard drive), press the Enter key, use the Down and Up arrow keys to select another drive in the drop-down menu, and then press the Enter key.

Once you save changes to one or more BIOS settings, you use the Esc key to exit the BIOS Setup utility. As shown in Figure 8-25, the BIOS Setup utility used on this computer provides two options after pressing the Esc key: "Remain in Setup" and Exit.

Figure 8-25   **BIOS Exit options**

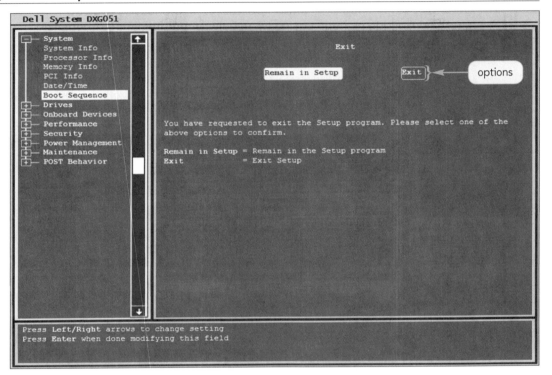

It prompts you to choose one of these options and it explains what each option does. Once you exit the BIOS Setup utility, your computer reboots with whatever new settings you specified.

To close the BIOS Setup utility and reboot your computer:

▶ **1.** If you changed your computer's BIOS settings, make a note of the changes you made in case you need to reverse those changes later, and then choose the option to save your changes and exit or choose the option to exit. If you did not make any changes to BIOS settings, or want to exit without saving changes, choose the option to exit without saving changes.

▶ **2.** After your computer reboots, log onto your user account.

You can also use the BIOS Setup utility to document important system settings, troubleshoot problems, or reconfigure your computer for new hardware.

REFERENCE

Changing the Boot Sequence

- If your computer is turned off, turn the power on to your computer. If you have already started Windows 7 and booted to the desktop, close all open applications, windows, and dialog boxes, and then restart Windows 7.
- During the initial stages of booting, watch the monitor for a message that identifies which key or keys to press to enter the BIOS Setup utility, then press the key or keys shown on the monitor before you see the screen with the Windows logo.
- Locate the category that contains the settings for changing your computer's boot sequence, examine and make a record of the current boot sequence order, and then change the boot sequence so it lists devices in the order in which you want the BIOS to search drives and boot your computer.
- Choose the option that allows you to save your changes, and exit the Setup utility.

Because BIOS settings are so important and because they affect the performance of your computer, you should check the materials that came with your computer to see if they contain any information on the options available on your computer. If not, visit the manufacturer's Web site and download manuals for your specific computer. You can also use a search engine to locate other Web sites that contain information about BIOS settings and about troubleshooting problems using the BIOS Setup utility.

Your BIOS documentation should also explain how to reset BIOS passwords (and therefore bypass existing password protection), how to clear and reset BIOS settings, and how to replace the battery that stores computer configuration settings and date and time information.

The Windows 7 Boot Process

Starting with Windows Vista, Microsoft Corporation changed the way that the Windows operating system boots a computer. Windows 7 and Windows Vista rely on the following system components to boot your computer:

- **Boot Configuration Data (BCD)**—On BIOS-based systems, this component is a database file that contains boot configuration settings and information about the location of boot files that in turn determine how Windows 7 loads from disk. The data in this file is stored in a format similar to that of the Windows Registry, so it is referred to as a registry file (also called a data store). On BIOS-based systems, the file that contains boot configuration data is named BCD and it is stored in the Boot folder under the top-level folder on the system volume (the volume from which Windows 7 boots). The path to this file is C:\Boot\BCD.
- **Windows Boot Manager**—This component starts the process of loading the Windows 7 operating system by examining the Boot Configuration Data (BCD) to determine whether there is another Windows operating system installed on the computer. If so, Windows Boot Manager displays an OS Choices menu so you can choose which operating system you want to use. Figure 8-26 shows a Windows Boot Manager menu for a computer set up for a dual boot between Windows 7 and Windows Vista.

Figure 8-26   Windows Boot Manager's OS choices menu

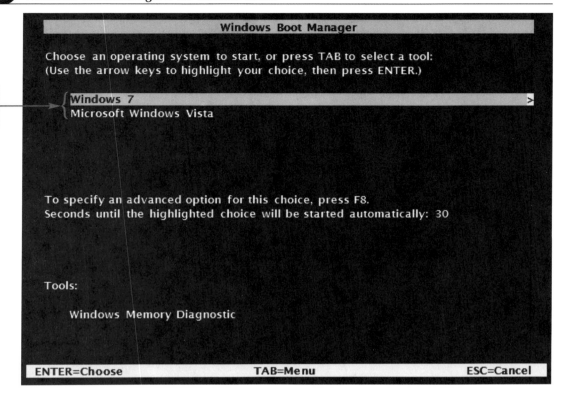

Windows versions on a dual boot computer

If you choose an operating system other than Windows 7, the Windows Boot Manager passes control to the operating system loader for that operating system. If there is no other operating system installed on the computer, then it passes control to either the Windows Boot Loader or Windows Resume Loader. If the Boot Configuration Data (BCD) data store does not contain information about a hibernation file, then it passes control to the Windows Boot Loader; otherwise, it passes control to the Windows Resume loader. The Windows Boot Manager is stored in a file named boot-mgr in the top-level folder of the system volume, and therefore its path is C:\bootmgr. Another important feature of Boot Manager is its ability to read supported file systems.

- **Windows Boot Loader**—The Windows Boot Loader, stored in a file named winload.exe in the Windows System32 folder, loads the Windows 7 operating system and basic hardware device drivers. The path to this file is C:\Windows\System32\winload.exe.
- **Windows Resume Loader**—The Windows Resume Loader, stored in a file named winresume.exe in the Windows System 32 folder, reads the hibernation file and restores Windows 7 to its previous state before Windows 7 switched to hibernation. The path to this file is C:\Windows\System32\winresume.exe.

These Windows components are hidden system folders and files. To view them, you must enable the options for displaying hidden files and folders and for displaying protected operating system files.

Figure 8-27 provides a general overview of the booting process on a basic volume that uses the MBR partition style (covered in Tutorial 5).

Figure 8-27 **Overview of booting process on a basic volume**

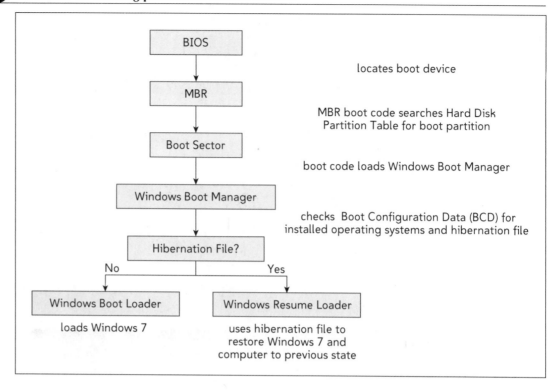

The BIOS uses boot sequence settings to locate the boot device (usually the hard disk drive). Then, it reads the Master Boot Record (MBR), loads the boot code and Hard Disk Partition Table contained in the Master Boot Record (MBR) into memory, and passes control to the MBR boot code. The Hard Disk Partition Table identifies which partition is the boot partition. The MBR code then locates and reads the boot sector on the boot partition to determine the location of the Windows Boot Manager. Next, it loads the Windows Boot Manager and checks the Boot Configuration Data in the BCD store for installing operating systems and the presence of a hibernation file. Windows Boot Manager starts the Windows Boot Loader or the Windows Resume Loader, which in turn loads Windows 7.

During the Boot Loader phase, the Windows 7 operating system kernel, ntoskrnl.exe, loads along with portions of the Windows Registry. Device drivers needed for booting load at this time using information in the Windows Registry. The path to the operating system kernel is C:\Windows\System32\ntoskrnl.exe.

The Boot Configuration Data (BCD) can also contain information on how to start the Windows Memory Diagnostic (\Boot\memtest.exe), data for loading the legacy ntldr boot loader in previous versions of the Windows NT product line (such as Windows XP), and data for starting a non-Microsoft boot loader. In other words, the BCD is customizable. Ntldr stands for "NT Loader."

Using the Advanced Boot Options Menu

At a weekly meeting with his assistants, Julien notes that staff members might occasionally encounter a problem booting Windows 7. When that situation occurs, they may have to troubleshoot the problem using the Advanced Boot Options menu. In the ensuing discussion, Julien and his assistants review the different options on the Advanced Boot Options menu with you. This menu, shown in Figure 8-28, contains a list of options that provide alternate approaches to booting Windows 7.

Figure 8-28	Advanced Boot Options menu

how to select a boot option

Safe Mode boot options

default boot option

explanation of selected boot option

```
                         Advanced Boot Options

Choose Advanced Options for: Windows 7
(Use the arrow keys to highlight your choice.)

     Repair Your Computer

     Safe Mode
     Safe Mode with Networking
     Safe Mode with Command Prompt

     Enable Boot Logging
     Enable low-resolution video (640x480)
     Last Known Good Configuration (advanced)
     Directory Services Restore Mode
     Debugging Mode
     Disable automatic restart on system failure
     Disable Driver Signature Enforcement

     Start Windows Normally

Description: View a list of system recovery tools you can use to repair
            startup problems, run diagnostics, or restore your system.

ENTER=Choose                                          ESC=Cancel
```

To display the Advanced Boot Options menu, you press the F8 function key after the initial startup screen before you see the Windows logo.

Once Windows displays the Advanced Boot Options menu, you can use the Up and Down arrow keys to highlight a boot option; a brief description of that boot option appears at the bottom of the Advanced Boot Options menu.

The Advanced Boot Options menu provides you with access to these boot options:

- **Start Windows Normally**—If you choose this option from the Advanced Boot Options menu, Windows 7 performs a full boot. The Start Windows Normally option is therefore the default boot option that Windows 7 uses when you don't display the Advanced Boot Options menu.
- **Enable Boot Logging**—This boot option is identical to the Start Windows Normally option, except Windows 7 creates a special startup log file named ntbtlog.txt (for NT Boot Log) in the Windows folder during booting and logs all the drivers that it loads (or fails to load). By examining the drivers that failed to load, you might be able to identify the exact cause of a problem. Be cautious in analyzing this data because not all device drivers listed as failing to load in ntbtlog.txt are required by Windows 7. You can, however, compare an ntbtlog.txt file created during a normal boot with one created using boot logging to find out what was not loaded in Safe Mode. That means you need a recent copy of the ntbtlog.txt file created by a normal boot before you encounter a problem. Figure 8-29 shows part of the NT Boot Log in the file ntbtlog.txt.

Figure 8-29 Viewing an NT boot log

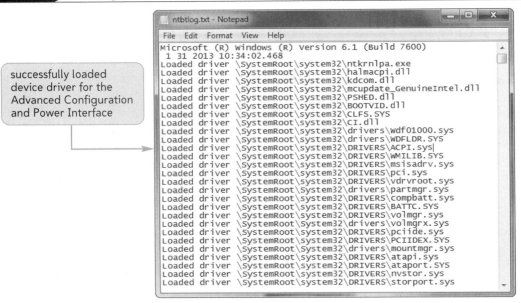

successfully loaded device driver for the Advanced Configuration and Power Interface

The path to this file is C:\Windows\ntbtlog.txt. To open this file on your computer, you can type *%windir%\ntbtlog.txt* in the Start menu Search programs and files box, and then press the Enter key.

- **Last Known Good Configuration (advanced)**—This boot option starts Windows 7 with the boot configuration saved in the Windows Registry by the operating system from the last successful boot. If you encounter startup problems or if your system is unstable, then a recent change to system settings, device drivers, or the Windows Registry might be the source of the problem, and you can use the Last Known Good Configuration to start your computer with settings that worked during your last successful boot. Because this boot option restores previously used device drivers and the previous set of Registry settings from the last successful boot, you could lose any changes to the configuration of your computer that you recently made. However, that may make all the difference if you are otherwise unable to boot your computer. Microsoft recommends that you use the Last Known Good Configuration boot option before you try other boot options because the other startup and troubleshooting options are more complex and the Last Known Good Configuration may immediately resolve the problem.

- **Enable low-resolution video (640x480)**—This boot option is similar to a normal boot but with one difference. Although it uses your current video display adapter device driver, it switches your video display to a low resolution (640 × 480 with an older aspect ratio of 4:3) so you can troubleshoot a problem with your video display settings or your video display driver. Therefore, if you install a new device driver for your video display adapter, or if a problem develops with your current video display adapter device driver, you can start your computer with this boot option and troubleshoot the problem. This boot option is also useful if you experience a problem that does not permit you to see an image on the monitor. With this boot option, you still have access to your network and to the Internet.

- **Safe Mode**—In Safe Mode, Windows 7 loads only basic device drivers as well as essential Windows services. This boot option also switches the video display to a lower resolution of 800 × 600. Once your computer is up and running, you can then attempt to troubleshoot the source of the problem or problems you were experiencing. You might use Safe Mode to troubleshoot problems caused by newly installed device drivers, newly installed software, software upgrades, startup background programs, or changes to system settings. Startup background programs (which you will examine in the next section of the tutorial) are programs that are automatically loaded at each boot and that operate in the background. However, in Safe Mode, Windows 7 does not load startup background programs because they might be the cause of the problem that you encountered when you booted your computer in normal mode.

If a problem that caused you to choose the Safe Mode boot option does not appear in Safe Mode, then basic device drivers and settings loaded by Windows 7 during Safe Mode are not the source of the problem. Rather, the problem is more likely to result from a new device that you've added to your computer or to a change in device drivers for a hardware component. When you boot in Safe Mode, you can use Event Viewer to identify system problems in the System logs. You can use the Error-Checking Tool to repair a problem with the file system. You can also use System Restore to roll back your computer, but because no restore points are created in Safe Mode, you cannot undo that restore operation.

If the source of the problem is a device driver, you might need to reinstall the device driver, replace a faculty device driver with a working device driver, or use Device Driver Rollback to replace the current device driver with the previously used device driver (covered in Tutorial 12). If you use Safe Mode before trying Last Known Good Configuration, you can still use Last Known Good Configuration later because Safe Mode does not make any changes to the Last Known Good Configuration settings stored in the Windows Registry, and therefore it remains a viable option.

When working in Safe Mode, you do not have a connection to other computers in your network, and you do not have Internet access. (You can verify these connections by examining the Network icon in the notification area.) If you point to the Network icon, a ToolTip will verify whether or not you have network and Internet access. Also, you may not have access to other features, such as audio.

- **Safe Mode with Networking**—This boot option is similar to Safe Mode; however, Windows 7 establishes network connections so you can troubleshoot a problem that requires network and Internet access.
- **Safe Mode with Command Prompt**—This boot option is similar to Safe Mode, but Windows 7 boots to a command prompt instead of booting to the desktop. That means you must have command-line skills so you can work in a command-line operating environment to troubleshoot system problems. After selecting this boot option, you are logged on as Administrator. Figure 8-30 shows the command-line environment after choosing the Safe Mode with Command Prompt boot option.

Figure 8-30   **Safe Mode with Command Prompt user interface**

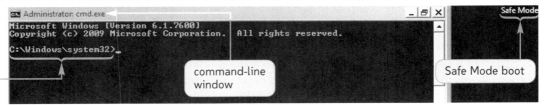

operating system prompt

command-line window

Safe Mode boot

You do not have access to your network or the Internet. To restart your computer, you type *shutdown /r* at the command prompt, and then press the Enter key.

- **Disable automatic restart on system failure**—When Windows 7 encounters an error that prevents it from booting, it automatically restarts, often only to encounter the same problem again. This boot option turns off the automatic restart feature so you can boot your computer and view any error codes or information needed to troubleshoot the problem. For example, if you see a **Blue Screen of Death (BSOD)**, then you've encountered a **Stop Error**, a fatal error from which Windows 7 cannot recover and which therefore requires a reboot. The reboot may resolve the problem or you might see the same BSOD again. If you disable the automatic restart on system failure, then you can view the BSOD, record the Stop Error codes, and then search Microsoft Support using another computer, if necessary, for information on the problem that might have caused the Stop Error. Also check the System log using Event Viewer for information on system failures.

If you want to turn off the automatic restart feature after Windows boots to the desktop, right-click the Computer icon on the desktop or Start menu, choose the option to view Properties, click the "Advanced system settings" link in the System window, provide Administrator credentials, click the Settings button under Startup and Recovery on the Advanced property sheet in the System Properties dialog box, and remove the check mark from the "Automatically restart" check box under System failure, and then apply this new setting and close the System window.

- **Disable Driver Signature Enforcement**—This boot option allows you to install device drivers that do not contain the proper driver signatures because those device drivers might be the only ones available for you to use. As noted previously, signed drivers have a digital signature (or electronic security mark) that identifies and verifies the integrity of the publisher of that software, and indicates whether the original contents of the driver software package has been changed. The use of signed drivers protects the stability and security of your computer, so you should make every effort to use signed drivers.

- **Directory Services Restore Mode**—This boot option applies only to Windows domain controllers on a server operating system. An administrator can use this option to restore the SYSVOL (system volume) directory and the Active Directory service on a domain controller. SYSVOL is a shared directory that stores the server copy of the domain's public files. A domain is a group of computers that are part of a network and that share a common directory database and security policy.

- **Debugging Mode**—This boot option is a more advanced troubleshooting option that enables an administrator to send debugging (or troubleshooting) information through a cable to another computer as Windows 7 starts so an administrator (or perhaps Microsoft tech support) can examine the information.

- **Repair your computer**—This boot option is displayed on the Advanced Boot Options menu so you can use the following system recovery tools for troubleshooting your computer:
  - Startup Repair (for repairing startup problems)
  - System Restore
  - System Image Recovery
  - Windows Memory Diagnostic
  - Command Prompt

You've already examined System Restore, and you will examine Startup Repair later in this tutorial. You will examine the process for creating a system image using Backup and Restore in Tutorial 10, the Windows Memory Diagnostic tool in Tutorial 9, and the Command Prompt in Tutorial 13.

Booting Your Computer in Safe Mode

To ensure you are familiar with Safe Mode in case you need to troubleshoot a problem, Julien recommends that you use the Advanced Boot Options menu to boot in this mode.

In the next set of steps, you will boot your computer in Safe Mode. If you are using a computer in your college computer lab, verify with your instructor or technical support staff that you have permission to boot in Safe Mode. Also, to complete the following steps, you must log on under an Administrator account. If you do not have permission to boot your computer in Safe Mode or if you cannot log on under an Administrator account or provide the password for an Administrator account, do not keystroke the steps, but instead read the steps and examine the figures.

When you reboot your computer, you need to press and *release* the F8 key after the initial startup screen and before you see the Starting Windows screen with the progress indicator. If you pass this point, Windows 7 boots to the desktop. Also, when you switch from one boot mode to another, Windows 7 boots your computer more slowly, so you must be patient. If you are unsure when to press the F8 key, you can press and release it several times during the initial stages of booting, but make sure you include a slight pause between each press of the F8 key so the BIOS does not display a keyboard error condition. Also, if you use the Up or Down Arrow key on the numeric keypad to choose an option from the Advanced Boot Options menu, you might need to first press the Num Lock key to turn Num Lock off.

To boot in Safe Mode:

▶ **1.** From the Start menu, choose the option to restart your computer from the Shutdown menu.

▶ **2.** After the initial startup screen with configuration information, and before you see the Starting Windows message and the Windows logo, press and release the **F8** key (several times, if necessary, with a slight pause between each press).

▶ **3.** Use the Up or Down arrow key to point to and highlight the **Safe Mode** menu option (if necessary), and then press the **Enter** key. Windows 7 system files are loaded and listed on the monitor on a line-by-line basis. At the Welcome screen, you are prompted to select your user name and enter your password.

▶ **4.** Log onto your computer under an Administrator account. After Windows 7 displays the desktop, it opens Windows Help and Support and explains that Safe Mode is a troubleshooting option that starts your computer in a limited state. Windows Aero user interface features are not available in Safe Mode. See Figure 8-31.

Figure 8-31	Help and Support window opens after booting in Safe Mode

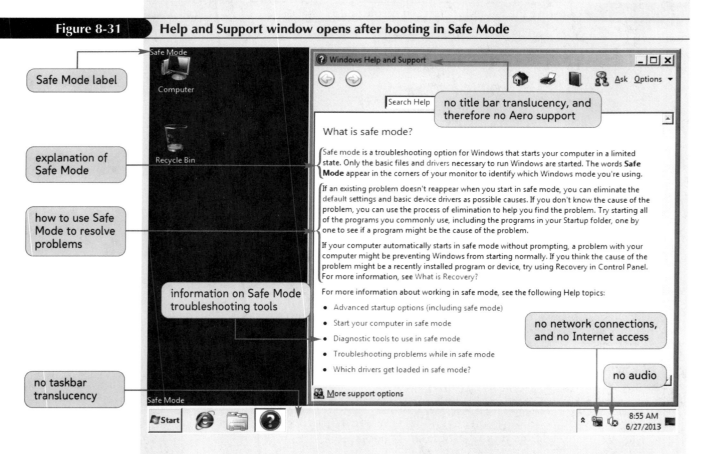

Windows 7 notes that if an existing problem does not appear in Safe Mode, then you can eliminate default settings and basic device drivers as possible causes of the problem. It further notes that if you don't know the cause of the problem, you can use the process of elimination to ascertain the problem by opening the programs that you typically use, including the programs in the Startup folder, one at a time to determine whether one of these programs caused the problem. If Windows 7 automatically starts in Safe Mode, then a recently installed program or device might prevent Windows 7 from starting normally. In this case, Windows 7 suggests you use System Restore to resolve the problem.

▶ 5. Close the Windows Help and Support window. In the four corners of the screen, Windows 7 displays the message "Safe Mode." Note also that Windows 7 no longer displays your wallpaper, and your view of windows, dialog boxes, and menus is more like the view found in what's called Classic View in earlier versions of Windows. At this point, you can implement the suggestions recommended in the Windows Help and Support window to determine the cause of the problem. You can also open the Control Panel to check, and if necessary, change system settings, and then restart Windows 7.

▶ 6. Right-click the **desktop**, and then click **Screen resolution**. As shown in the Screen Resolution dialog box on the computer used for Figure 8-32, Windows 7 is configured for a default monitor and a screen resolution of 800 × 600 pixels.

Figure 8-32	Viewing the Safe Mode screen resolution

If you use the Advanced settings link to open the "(Default Monitor) and Properties" dialog box, Windows 7 displays "<unavailable>" or "n/a" for video display adapter information. If you click the Monitor tab in the "(Default Monitor) and Properties" dialog box, you will see that the screen refresh rate is set at "Use hardware default setting" (the only option), and the color depth setting is True Color (32 bit). These display settings enable Windows 7 to boot the computer so you can see an image on the monitor.

▶ 7. Click the **Cancel** button to close the Screen Resolution dialog box without changing any video display settings.

▶ 8. From the Start menu, choose the option to restart your computer from the Shutdown menu, and after Windows 7 boots to the desktop, log on your computer under your user account (if necessary).

The first thing you might want to try after rebooting in Safe Mode is to simply restart Windows 7 to determine if it can rebuild damaged files and reconfigure itself. As noted earlier, if you are unable to repair a problem in Safe Mode, you can still use the Last Known Good Configuration boot option.

REFERENCE

Booting in Safe Mode

- Turn the power on to your computer, or if your computer is already up and running, open the Start menu and choose the option to restart your computer from the Shutdown menu.
- After the initial startup screen with information about the configuration of your computer, and before you see the Starting Windows message and the Windows logo, press and release the F8 key (several times, if necessary, with a slight pause between each press).
- After Windows 7 displays the Advanced Boot Options menu, use the Up or Down arrow key to highlight the Safe Mode menu option, and then press the Enter key.
- Log onto your computer under an Administrator account.
- After you examine the information on Safe Mode in the Windows Help and Support window, close this window.
- Use the approaches recommended in the Windows Help and Support window to locate the cause of the problem you encountered, or simply reboot your computer to see if Windows 7 automatically resolves the problem.
- After you have finished working in Safe Mode, choose the option to restart your computer, and after Windows 7 boots to the desktop, log on your computer under your user account.

Windows 7 might automatically boot in Safe Mode if it encounters a problem, so it's important to be familiar with this boot option. Windows 7 might also display a Windows Error Recovery screen during booting, as shown in Figure 8-33, indicating that it failed to start and noting that a recent hardware or software change might be the cause of this problem.

Figure 8-33   **Windows Error Recovery screen**

```
                        Windows Error Recovery
Windows failed to start. A recent hardware or software change might be the
cause.

If Windows files have been damaged or configured incorrectly, Startup Repair
can help diagnose and fix the problem. If power was interrupted during
startup, choose Start Windows Normally.
(Use the arrow keys to highlight your choice.)


      Launch Startup Repair (recommended)
      Start Windows Normally


Seconds until the highlighted choice will be selected automatically: 27
Description: Fix problems that are preventing Windows from starting
```

Windows 7 notes that if Windows files have been damaged or improperly configured, you can use Startup Repair to help diagnose and fix the problem. If the problem resulted from a power interruption, Windows 7 recommends that you choose the Start Windows Normally option instead.

Using Windows Task Manager

Whenever possible, you should shut down your computer properly. However, if you are using an application that stops responding or responds too slowly, first try to shut down the application before you shut down your entire computer system and run the risk of losing changes to other documents or damaging system files. You can use Windows Task Manager to shut down a nonresponding application or any other type of program. Windows Task Manager not only provides information about applications, but also information about processes, services, and processor and memory usage. As noted earlier, a process is an executable program, such as Windows Explorer, Microsoft Word, and Task Manager itself; a service, such as the Print Spooler service that handles the printing of files in the background; or a subsystem, such as the one for Windows 7 applications. A service is a program, routine, or process that provides support to other programs.

After you open Task Manager, you can view a list of running applications and determine whether a program is not responding. If so, you can instruct Windows 7 to shut it down so you can continue to use your computer.

To open Task Manager and view information about processes:

1. From the Start menu, point to **All Programs**, click **Accessories**, click **Paint**, and then minimize the Paint window.

2. From the Start menu, point to **All Programs**, click **Accessories**, click **WordPad**, and then minimize the WordPad window.

TIP

You can also press Ctrl+Shift+Esc to open Windows Task Manager.

3. Right-click the **taskbar**, click **Start Task Manager** on the shortcut menu, and then click the **Applications** tab (if necessary) in the Windows Task Manager window. On the Applications sheet of the Windows Task Manager window, Windows 7 displays a list of running applications in the Task column, including Untitled - Paint and Document - WordPad. See Figure 8-34.

Figure 8-34 **Viewing running applications with Task Manager**

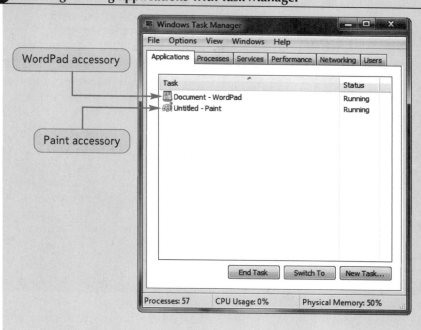

"Untitled" is the temporary filename for the new Paint document, and "Document" is the temporary filename for the new WordPad document. If you have other open applications or windows, as well as open documents, then they are also listed as tasks. In the Status column, Task Manager shows whether a process is running or is not responding. If it is not responding, you can select that process in the Task column, click the End Task button, and have Windows 7 shut it down so you can continue to use your computer. If you end a task, you lose any changes that you made to a document with that program. You can also use the Switch To button to switch to an application or document that you first select in the Task column. If you click the New Task button, Task Manager opens a Create New Task dialog box where you can enter the name of (or browse to locate) a program, folder, document, or Internet resource that you want to open.

At the bottom of the dialog box, Windows 7 lists information about the number of processes currently running on your computer, the percent of CPU usage, and the amount of physical memory in use. You will examine this information in more detail in Tutorial 9.

4. Click the **Processes** tab in the Windows Task Manager window, press and hold down the **Ctrl** key and press the **plus sign** key on the numeric keyboard to automatically adjust columns for a best fit (or manually double-click or drag the border after each column), drag the **right border** of the Windows Task Manager window to the right so you can see the Description column, drag the **bottom border** down to increase the height of this window so you can see all the processes, and then click the **Image Name** column button. Task Manager displays a list of running processes in alphabetical order by Image Name. See Figure 8-35. Your list of processes will differ.

Figure 8-35　Viewing running processes with Task Manager

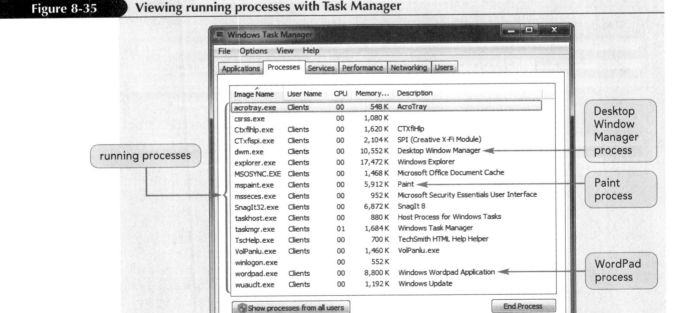

In the Image Name column, Task Manager lists mspaint.exe, the name of the file that contains the Paint program. At the bottom of this list of processes, Task Manager lists the newly opened program identified as wordpad.exe, the name of the file that contains the Windows WordPad Application. The dwm.exe image name is the Desktop Window Manager used in Windows 7 and Windows Vista, the explorer.exe image name is Windows Explorer, and the taskmgr.exe image name is Windows Task Manager. The Memory (Private Working Set) column shows the amount of memory exclusively used by each process.

▶ 5. Right-click the **Untitled - Paint** taskbar button, and then click **Close window**. After Paint closes, Task Manager updates its list of processes and no longer lists mspaint.exe as a running process.

▶ 6. Click the **Applications** tab in the Windows Task Manager window, note that Untitled - Paint is not listed as an open task, right-click the **Document - WordPad** taskbar button and then click **Close window**. After WordPad closes, Task Manager no longer lists WordPad as an open task.

▶ 7. Click the **Services** tab in the Windows Task Manager window, click the **Name** column button (if necessary) to display an alphabetical list of the names of services, and then adjust the width of all the columns for a best fit. In the Description column Task Manager identifies the nature of each service. If you examine the Status column, you can easily identify which services are currently running (such as the Print Spooler, Security Center, Task Scheduler, Windows Event Log, Windows Firewall, Windows Search, and Windows Update services) and which services are currently stopped (such as the Disk Defragmenter and Windows Installer services).

▶ 8. Close the Windows Task Manager window.

If you press the Ctrl+Shift+Esc keyboard shortcut, Windows 7 displays options for locking a computer, switching users, logging off, changing a password, and starting Task Manager.

You can create a desktop shortcut with the *%systemroot%\system32\taskmgr.exe* or *%windir%\system32\taskmgr.exe* path to open Task Manager quickly.

REFERENCE

Using Task Manager to Shut Down a Nonresponding Program

- Right-click the taskbar, and then click Start Task Manager.
- After Windows 7 opens the Windows Task Manager window, select the nonresponding program in the Task column on the Applications property sheet, click the End Task button, and then verify that you want to close the nonresponding program.
- Close the Windows Task Manager window.

Although you might only occasionally use Task Manager to shut down a nonresponding program, remember that it is available. It allows you to shut down a program that is tying up your computer system without affecting any other open programs, and without losing valuable documents or data in other windows. A complete shutdown, from turning off or rebooting, clears all memory, so it's better to try Windows Task Manager first. Task Manager is also useful if you want to see what applications are loaded when you notice that your computer is not performing optimally.

Using System Configuration

System Configuration is an important troubleshooting tool because it enables you to identify and, if necessary, turn off startup programs. As touched on earlier, a **startup program** (also referred to as a startup item) is a program that loads during booting and that operates in the background as you use your computer. For example, a startup program might provide you with quick access to a program for listening to music; however, if you do not use that program while you are working on other tasks, then you never really take advantage of the startup program, and therefore it wastes valuable resources and memory on your computer. In cases like this, you can open the program directly from the Start menu when you need it.

You can also use System Configuration to control the startup process by specifying which startup programs and services load during booting and to identify a malicious program that loads at every boot. You start by using its list of startup items to research the different startup programs on your computer to determine whether they are useful, necessary, or malicious. Also, if you suspect that a particular program is the source of a problem you're experiencing on your computer, you temporarily turn off the loading of that program with System Configuration so Windows 7 does not load it during the next boot. If the problem you experienced does not recur after you reboot your computer, you've identified the source of the problem. If the problem remains, the startup item that you turned off is not the source of the problem. You can restart your computer, turn on the option to load that startup program again, and then repeat the process with another startup program or service. Using this approach, you can identify and isolate the source of a problem.

Because staff members periodically run into problems with certain background programs, Julien sets aside some time to show you and his other assistants how to use System Configuration to identify and troubleshoot startup programs that cause problems.

To open System Configuration, you must provide Administrator credentials. If your account is a Standard User account and if you do not know the password for an Administrator account, read the following steps and examine the figures, but do not keystroke the steps.

TIP
You can also type *msconfig* in the Search programs and files box, and then press the Enter key to open System Configuration.

To examine your computer system's startup programs:

▶ 1. From the Start menu, point to **Administrative Tools**, click **System Configuration**, provide Administrator credentials, and then click the **General** tab (if necessary). Windows 7 opens the System Configuration dialog box. See Figure 8-36.

Figure 8-36   System Configuration startup options

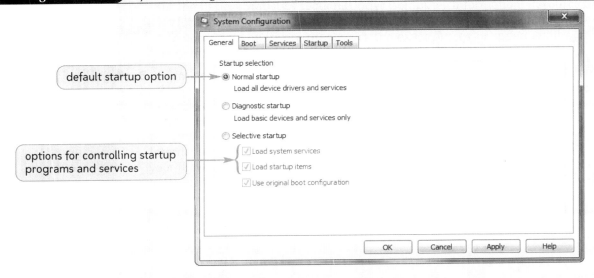

default startup option

options for controlling startup programs and services

Under Startup selection on the General property sheet, Normal startup is automatically selected as the default option for starting your computer unless you have already used System Configuration to modify the startup programs and services on your computer. As noted, Normal startup loads all device drivers and services. If you choose Diagnostic startup, a troubleshooting option, Windows 7 loads only basic devices and services during the next boot. This option also turns off the loading of all startup programs during the next boot. Selective startup, the most useful of these three options, allows you to pick which system services and startup items (also called startup programs) are loaded during booting.

▶ **2.** Click the **Boot** tab in the System Configuration dialog box. On this property sheet, Windows 7 identifies the operating system (or systems) used on your computer and lists advanced boot options. See Figure 8-37.

Figure 8-37 **Viewing installing operating systems**

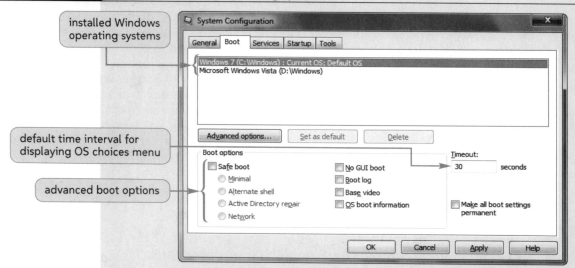

installed Windows operating systems

default time interval for displaying OS choices menu

advanced boot options

On the dual-boot computer used for this figure, the System Configuration utility lists Windows 7 and Microsoft Windows Vista as the two operating systems installed on this computer, shows the path where each operating system is installed, and identifies the current and default OS. On this computer, Windows 7 is installed in a Windows folder on drive C, and Windows Vista is installed in a Windows folder on drive D. Windows 7 is the current OS because Windows 7 booted this computer, and Windows 7 is the default OS. If you do not select an operating system from the OS Choices menu, Windows Boot Manager loads the default OS. The Timeout box lists the default time in seconds to wait before selecting the default OS; however, you can change that value to shorten the wait.

▶ **3.** Click the **Services** tab in the System Configuration dialog box, and then click the **Service** column button to sort services in alphabetical order by name (if necessary). This property sheet lists the names of all services that load during booting, lists the manufacturer (if known), identifies whether the service is currently running or stopped, and the date that you (or someone else) disabled a service. See Figure 8-38.

Figure 8-38	Viewing Microsoft and non-Microsoft services

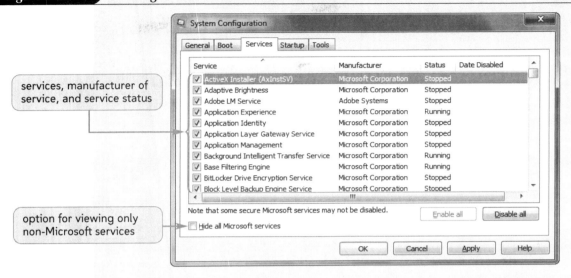

services, manufacturer of service, and service status

option for viewing only non-Microsoft services

You can turn off or turn on specific services when troubleshooting problems. However, under the list of services, a note indicates that you cannot disable some secure Microsoft services. There might easily be hundreds of different services on your computer, and to effectively troubleshoot problems on your computer, you need to know not only what each service does, but also what happens if you turn off the service and whether one service is dependent on the availability of another service.

To learn more about services, you can open Services from the Administrative Tools menu and view the names and descriptions of services as well as each service's status and startup type—Automatic, Automatic (Delayed Start), Disabled, or Manual. If you double-click a service in the Services window, you can modify settings for services and determine whether they depend on another service or services.

▶ **4.** Click the **Hide all Microsoft services** check box on the Services property sheet. Now you only see a list of non-Microsoft services (if any). When you troubleshoot system startup problems, and after you have already eliminated startup programs as the cause of the problem, consider the possibility that a non-Microsoft or third-party service might be the cause of the problem. Microsoft recommends that you not turn off the loading of a service unless you know that it is not an essential service.

▶ **5.** Click the **Hide all Microsoft services** check box on the Services property sheet to redisplay all services.

▶ **6.** Click the **Startup** tab in the System Configuration dialog box, and if the list of Startup items is not displayed in alphabetical order, click the **Startup Item** column button above the list of startup items, and then adjust all column widths for a best fit. In the Startup Item column, System Configuration lists startup items, or startup programs, that load during booting. See Figure 8-39.

Figure 8-39 Viewing startup programs

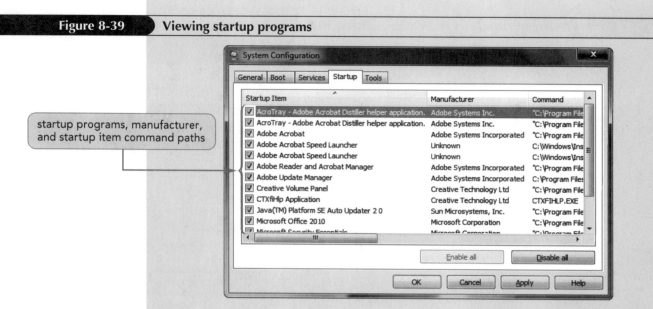

startup programs, manufacturer, and startup item command paths

The Startup Item name is important when you are troubleshooting a problem because you can use it to locate information on a startup program and verify its authenticity, usefulness, and safety. The Manufacturer column shows the name of the software developer (if known) and is also useful in verifying whether a program is a legitimate, useful, unnecessary, or malicious program.

In the Startup Item column, you may see common types of startup items from Adobe Systems, Inc., Microsoft Corporation, Sun Microsystems, Inc., and other software manufacturers. System Configuration may also report *Unknown* for the manufacturer of certain startup items, but the startup item name might identify the manufacturer. If you see the same startup item listed more than once, then that means the first occurrence of that startup item was disabled, only to be reinserted later as part of an update or from opening a program.

7. Use the horizontal scroll bar to adjust your view so you can see the information in the Command column. This column displays the full path or location for the startup program, and the name of the program file itself is shown in the path. This information is important if you are troubleshooting a problem because you may be able to verify whether a program is legitimate or malicious by its location.

8. Use the horizontal scroll bar to adjust your view so you can see the information in the Location column. This column shows how a startup item loads. Startup items whose locations start with HK are programs (including malicious software) that load from the Registry at each boot. If a path is shown for the Location, then the program loads directly from a folder on your computer, usually, the folder where the software product is installed or from a common Startup folder.

9. Keep the System Configuration dialog box open for the next set of tutorial steps.

If you have already disabled a startup program or item, then the date and time that you made that change is shown in the Date Disabled column.

When troubleshooting the use of startup programs, you may need to rely on all this information. Some startup programs display icons in the notification area, but this list provides a more complete accounting of startup programs.

To examine tools available from the System Configuration dialog box:

▶ **1.** Click the **Tools** tab in the System Configuration dialog box, and then click the **Tool Name** column button to sort tools in alphabetical order by name. From this property sheet, you have quick access to various tools for troubleshooting your computer—including the Action Center, Command Prompt, Computer Management, Event Viewer, Internet Options, System Properties, System Information (which you will examine in the next section of this tutorial), System Restore, Task Manager, and Windows Troubleshooting, to name a few. If you select a tool, then System Configuration displays the path to the program for that tool in the Selected command box. You can use these paths to create desktop shortcuts to commonly used tools.

▶ **2.** Click the **Cancel** button to close the System Configuration dialog box without making any changes.

> Do not click the OK or Apply buttons unless you want Windows 7 to restart your computer and apply any changes you might have made with System Configuration.

Trouble? If you make a change in the System Configuration dialog box and then click the OK button, another System Configuration dialog box informs you that you may need to restart your computer to apply the change. It also recommends that you close any open programs or files before doing so. Click the Exit without restart button to close the System Configuration dialog box without restarting your computer.

Although System Configuration provides an option for disabling the loading of startup items, you may be able to achieve the same effect by trying one of these options first:

- If a startup program displays an icon in the notification area, you can right-click the icon to determine if there is an option for disabling or closing the startup program. In some cases, you can merely click the icon to display a menu of options for that startup program. You may also be able to view an object's properties and permanently turn off the option for loading when Windows starts. The primary limitation with this approach is that most startup programs do not display an icon in the notification area.
- You can open the software product that displays an icon in the notification area or that loads a startup item and determine whether the software product contains an option for turning off the loading of the startup item when Windows 7 starts and whether it contains an option for displaying an icon in the notification area.
- For certain startup items, you might have to start the Setup program for a software product and uninstall a specific component that loads a startup item. This approach is especially useful for removing startup items that automatically reload themselves after you turn off the loading of those startup items with System Configuration.

You might also find yourself wondering how all these startup programs are installed on a computer. Some startup programs are installed when you install other programs, such as an application or office suite, and they are designed to quickly load the program, provide extra features, download updates, or verify that you are a licensed user of software installed on your computer. When you download software from a Web site, read the license agreement carefully before you agree to it so you know whether you are also agreeing to the installation of other programs (including malicious software) that you may not want or need. Also, once you start the installation program for a software product, you may also be able to choose which options you want to install.

Problem Solving: Developing an Effective Strategy for Troubleshooting Startup Programs

Startup items are a common source of problems, so developing an effective troubleshooting strategy helps you prevent or resolve problems. You can use these three approaches to locate the source of a problem that might be caused by a startup item:

- If you know the software manufacturer of a startup item, search their Web site for information about that startup item. You can also use a search engine (and perhaps even Microsoft Support) to locate and compare information about a startup item from multiple Web sites rather than rely on just one Web site. When analyzing startup items, you may need to use the startup name, manufacturer, command path, and location to verify that your startup item matches the information you find about a legitimate startup program. You also use this information to distinguish a startup item from a malicious startup program that might have the same or very similar (but disguised) startup item name or program name, but which loads from another location on a computer. You can then disable a startup item that you've identified as unnecessary, malicious, or unknown; restart your computer; and then determine whether your change corrected the problem you encountered. If not, you can restore that startup item and then test another questionable or unknown startup item until you've determined which (if any) caused the problem. If you determine that none of those startup items caused the problem, look at other startup items and non-Microsoft services.

- If you do not know which startup item might be the source of a problem, and if you do not want to test each one separately (each of which requires a reboot), you can reduce the amount of time that it takes to locate the startup item causing the problem by disabling the loading of half of the startup items and then restarting your computer. If the problem remains, you've eliminated half of the startup items you just disabled prior to rebooting because those startup items did not load during the reboot. You can open System Configuration and then test half of the remaining startup items using the same approach until you locate the one that is the source of the problem. If the problem no longer appears after you first disable half of the startup items and reboot, you know that the problem was caused by a startup item that you disabled and that did not load. Then you can use the same strategy by enabling half of the startup items you disabled until you find the startup item that caused the problem.

  This approach, referred to as "divide and conquer," is useful for reducing the number of reboots required to identify the problem. If you eliminate all the startup items as the source of the problem, then you next examine non-Microsoft services using the same approach.

- You can disable all the startup items and then reboot your computer. If the problem remains, you know that none of the startup items are the likely cause of the problem, and then you can examine non-Microsoft services using the same approach. If you disable all the startup items and the problem disappears, you know that the likely cause of the problem is one of the startup items. You can then use a similar approach to the previous one where you enable and load half of the startup items to determine the source of the problem.

  The only problem posed by these approaches is that you may turn off essential startup items or services and therefore lose some functionality of your computer. However, by carefully and thoroughly researching the startup items as described in the first approach, you might be able to minimize or eliminate this problem. As you make changes with System Configuration, make sure you document each change you make so you can reverse it later.

  Staying on top of startup programs and using an effective strategy to identify and troubleshoot problems caused by startup programs is one important way to protect the security of your computer and optimize its performance.

Among the many Web sites that contain information about startup programs (and Browser Helper Objects), Sysinfo.org (at *www.sysinfo.org*) has become a recognized and valuable resource for PC tech support staff and for users who want to troubleshoot performance problems on their computer. Also, Symantec (*www.symantec.com*) maintains a comprehensive list of threats posed by various types of malicious software.

If you discover that a startup program is the source of a problem on your computer and if you want the features available in that startup program, check for an upgrade or new version of the program that might function on your computer without causing any problems. Also, another software product might offer the same features without creating problems.

If you want a desktop shortcut for opening the System Configuration dialog box, you can use one of the following paths: *%windir%\system32\msconfig.exe* or *%systemroot%\system32\msconfig.exe.*

REFERENCE

Using System Configuration

- From the Start menu, point to Administrative Tools, click System Configuration, and then provide Administrator credentials.
- On the General property sheet in the System Configuration dialog box, choose the type of Startup selection you want to use. Use Normal startup to load all device drivers and services (as well as all startup items). Use Diagnostic startup to load only basic devices and services at the next boot when troubleshooting problems caused by startup items and services. Use Selective startup to specify whether you want to load startup items and/or services at the next boot.
- Use the Services property sheet as part of your troubleshooting strategy to specify which services load at the next boot as part of your troubleshooting strategy. Click the "Hide all Microsoft services" check box to view a list of non-Microsoft services that might be the source of a problem on your computer.
- Use the Startup property sheet to specify which startup items load at the next boot so you can identify and isolate a program that is the source of the problem.
- Use the Tools property sheet to open troubleshooting and diagnostic tools.
- Close the System Configuration dialog box and, if necessary, restart your computer to apply the changes you made for loading startup items and services.

If you need to restore the loading of all startup configuration files, services, and programs, choose Normal Startup on the General property sheet and restart your computer.

Using System Information

Another useful tool for locating information about your computer is System Information. In addition to a System Summary, it provides information on the use of hardware resources, hardware components, and your software environment. You can use the System Summary to verify the Windows edition on a computer.

Julien shows you an alternate approach for locating information on startup programs using System Information. In the process, he reviews how Windows 7 uses environment variables.

To open the System Information utility:

▶ 1. From the Start menu, point to **All Programs**, click **Accessories**, click **System Tools**, click **System Information**, and then maximize the System Information window.

In the Category pane on the left, System Information organizes information into three categories—Hardware Resources, Components, and Software Environment. In the Details pane on the right, System Information displays a System Summary that contains basic information about your computer, such as your Windows 7 Edition (e.g., Microsoft Windows 7 Ultimate), your Windows version and build (e.g., Version 6.1.7600 Build 7600 for the first version of Windows 7), the system manufacturer and model, the processor (including information on the number of logical processors), the BIOS version and date (which is also available via the BIOS Setup utility), the path for the Windows directory and the System directory, the boot device, the time zone, and memory usage details (which you will examine in Tutorial 9).

▶ 2. Click the **expand** icon ⊞ to the left of the Software Environment category. The Software Environment category provides detailed information on the software currently loaded in the computer's memory, such as system drivers, running tasks, startup programs, and loaded modules, as well as other related information.

▶ 3. Under Software Environment, click **Startup Programs**, and then adjust the column widths in the Details pane for a best fit of all columns. System Information displays information about startup programs. See Figure 8-40.

Figure 8-40	Viewing startup programs in System Information

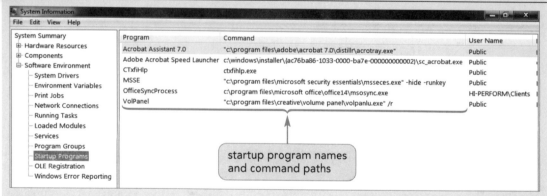

You can compare this information to that found on the Startup property sheet in the System Configuration dialog box. For example, System Information lists the first startup item shown on the computer in this figure as Acrobat Assistant 7.0; however, System Configuration identifies the startup item as "AcroTray – Adobe Acrobat Distiller helper application." Though the names are different, the program paths are identical and therefore refer to the same startup item. Likewise, the startup programs identified as CTxfiHlp, MSSE (for Microsoft Security Essentials), and VolPanel are the same ones identified with more friendly names in System Configuration.

> **4.** Under Software Environment, click **Environment Variables**, click **ComSpec** under the Variable column in the Details pane, and then adjust the width of all columns for a best fit. The Details pane lists environment variables and their corresponding values. See Figure 8-41.

Figure 8-41   **Viewing environment variables and their settings**

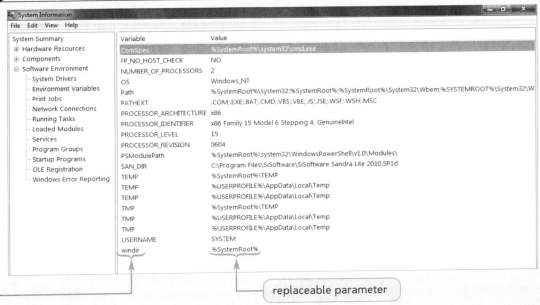

environment variable

replaceable parameter

Your environment variable names and settings might differ from those shown in the figure (and described after the figure). Notice that the windir environment variable's value is %SystemRoot%.

As you learned earlier, an **environment variable** is a symbolic name (such as OS) associated with a specific setting (such as Windows_NT for the OS environment variable). The environment variable therefore acts as a pointer to a setting, such as a system setting, an application setting, or a user-defined setting (one created by you). Environment variables and their settings are stored in an area of memory known as the **Windows environment** (previously known as the DOS environment under the DOS operating system). Windows 7, applications, and other programs check the Windows environment for settings, and you can create and assign settings to new environment variables.

Understanding these environment variables gives you a better sense of how Windows 7 works. You are already familiar with the windir and SystemRoot environment variables that identify the location of the Windows folder (or directory). The windir environment variable is assigned the value %SystemRoot%. (*Note:* In any sentence in this tutorial that contains a period or comma after an environment variable name, setting, or path, the period or comma is not part of the setting or path.) SystemRoot is the environment variable that refers to the folder that contains the Windows 7 operating system files. Though not shown here, the SystemRoot environment variable is assigned the path to the Windows folder, and although it's not listed in the System Information window, it is listed in the command-line environment when you view the contents of the Windows environment. If the Windows folder is located on drive C, then the value for the SystemRoot environment variable is C:\Windows. If the Windows folder is located on drive D, then the value for this variable is D:\Windows. Because the Windows folder might be located on a hard disk drive other than drive C on another computer, Windows assigns the setting for this environment variable during booting. Therefore, because the path for the Windows folder can vary, it's stored in an environment variable. When the environment variable is used in a path, it is enclosed within percent symbols to indicate that it is a **replaceable parameter**. In other words, it's a variable value (meaning it can change or be different on different computers) and that it is replaced by the actual path on a specific computer.

Other important environment variables include:

- **ComSpec**—This environment variable (a holdover from the DOS operating system) identifies the path of the **command interpreter**, the program that interprets commands you enter in a command-line environment. The setting for this environment variable is %SystemRoot%\system32\cmd.exe. As already noted, if the Windows folder is located on drive C, then the SystemRoot environment variable is assigned the setting C:\Windows. When interpreting a path that contains %SystemRoot%, Windows 7 replaces %SystemRoot% with C:\Windows so the final and actual path for ComSpec is C:\Windows\System32\cmd.exe (the exact path to this program on this computer). If you boot in Safe Mode with Command Prompt, Windows 7 automatically starts this program so you can work in a command-line environment. Also, you can open a command-line window by typing *cmd* in the Start menu Search programs and files box.

- **Path**—This environment variable (also a holdover from the DOS operating system) identifies a sequence of directories (or folders) that contain program files that Windows 7 searches to locate and load a program from disk. This path may differ on different computers because different computers have different software products installed on them. On the computer used for this figure, the path is as follows (all on one line without any spaces after the semicolons): %SystemRoot%\system32; %SystemRoot%;%SystemRoot%\System32\Wbem; %SYSTEMROOT%\System32\ WindowsPowerShell\v1.0\

When Windows 7 substitutes C:\Windows for %SystemRoot% in each part of the path that uses this replaceable parameter, the final path used by Windows 7 to locate programs is as follows (again all on one line and without spaces after the semicolons): C:\Windows\system32;C:\Windows;C:\Windows\System32\Wbem; C:\Windows\ System32\WindowsPowerShell/v1.0\

The path for each folder *must* be separated from the previous one by a semicolon. If you issue a command to use a specific program, Windows 7 searches the current folder first to see if the program file is contained in that folder. If it finds the program file, it loads the program into memory. If it does not find the program file, it checks the path defined by the Path environment variable, starting with the first folder listed in the path and proceeding from one folder in the path to the next folder in the path until it locates the program. For example, after checking the current folder for a program file, Windows 7 then checks the System32 folder (C:\Window\System32) because it is listed first in the path. If the program is not found in the System32 folder, then it checks the Windows folder next (in this case, C:\Windows). If the program is not found in the Windows folder, then it checks the Wbem folder (C:\Windows\System32\ Wbem). If the program is not found in the Wbem folder, then it checks the Windows PowerShell v1.0 folder (C:\Windows\System32\WindowsPowerShell\v1.0\).

- **PATHEXT**—This environment variable identifies a set of file extensions that are used to locate a program file, and therefore it is used in combination with the Path variable. For example, if you type a command for a program filename, a folder name, a path, or a URL in the Start menu Search programs and files box (or Run box), and press the Enter key, then Windows will open the program, folder, file, or Web site. If you enter the CMD command in the Search programs and files box, Windows 7 opens a command-line window. The CMD command that you type is actually the main part of the filename for the program file (for example, the program file for the CMD command is named CMD.EXE). Windows 7 then checks the current folder and each of the other folders listed in the path, in the order in which they are listed, for the program file. However, because program files can have different file extensions, Windows 7 looks for that program file using the command you type and different possible file extensions in each directory. In each folder Windows 7 checks, it looks for a program using the first file extension in the PATHEXT environment variable (in this case, .COM), and searches for a file named CMD.COM. If it finds a program by that name, it loads the program into memory so you can use it. If it does not find a program by this name, then it looks for a program using the next file extension in the PATHEXT variable (in this case, .EXE), and then searches for a file named CMD.EXE in the same directory. Because CMD.EXE is the name of the program for opening a command-line window, it finds and loads this program from the System32 folder, the first folder it checks in the path. If this folder did not contain a program by this name, then it would repeat the same process using the next file extension listed in the PATHEXT environment variable on a folder-by-folder basis until it locates the program.

Some computer viruses use the same filename as a legitimate program on your computer that has an .EXE file extension, but the computer virus filename uses the .COM file extension. Because the .COM file extension is the first one listed in the PATHEXT environment variable, this approach guarantees that Windows locates and loads this program file with the computer virus. Then the computer virus might pass control to the file with the .EXE file extension so it also loads and you are not even aware that a computer virus has been loaded into memory, but it now has access to your entire system. However, if you are more specific and type *CMD.EXE* in the Start menu Search programs and files box (or the Run box), Windows 7 searches for a file by that exact filename and file extension using the folders listed in the Path variable. That's why it pays to know about and enter the full filename of a program file.

The DOS operating system used the same technique for locating program files; however, it looked only for files with the .COM, .EXE, and .BAT file extensions (in that order). Those program file extensions were carried over to the Windows operating system, and additional file extensions are now included in the PATHEXT environment variable. The file extensions in the PATHEXT environment variable are ones that are currently considered unsafe and therefore potentially dangerous if they are the file extensions of an email attachment.

Other categories under Software Environment provide the following types of information:

- **System Drivers**—This category includes a list of the names of all system drivers, a description for each driver (such as FAT12/16/32 File System Driver, Ntfs, and Windows Firewall Authorization Driver), the path to the file that contains each driver, the type of driver (kernel driver or file system driver), whether the driver started (i.e., loaded), the Start Mode of each driver (Auto, Boot, Disabled, Manual, or System), and the State of each driver (Running or Stopped).
- **Running Tasks**—This category includes detailed information about all running tasks, most of which have the .exe file extension, and includes their filenames and their path (if known).
- **Loaded Modules**—This category includes detailed information on all loaded modules of program code, most of which have the .dll (for dynamic link library), .drv (for device driver), .exe (for executable file), and .cpl (for Control Panel extension) file extensions, and includes the names and paths to each module.

- **Services**—This category includes detailed information on all services, including the display name (such as Disk Defragmenter), the name (such as defragsvc), the State (Running or Stopped), the Start Mode (Auto, Disabled, or Manual), and the path.
- **Program Groups**—This category contains the group name (such as Start Menu, Start Menu\Programs, and Start Menu\Programs\Accessories) of all the group folders on the Start Menu for Default Users, the Public User, and the currently logged-on user.
- **Windows Error Reporting**—This category contains a list of errors that have occurred on the computer you are using and shows the date and time of each error, the type of error (such as Application Error, Application Hang, and Windows Error Reporting), and details on each error. This information is similar to what you saw earlier using Event Viewer except it is more easily accessible than Event Viewer. If you are trying to troubleshoot a problem with an application, you might want to examine this information.
- **OLE Registration**—This category contains a list of object types, such as Microsoft Word Document, Microsoft Excel Chart, and Microsoft PowerPoint Presentation and the path of the program associated with the object path.

At the bottom of the System Information window, you can use the Find what box to search for information, and you can specify whether to only search a selected category or only search category names.

System Information is yet another invaluable tool for locating information that will in turn help you identify and perhaps resolve problems you encounter on your computer. You can also use System Information to learn more about your own computer system.

To complete your examination of System Information:

▶ **1.** Close the System Information window.

You can create a desktop shortcut with the path *%windir%\system32\msinfo32.exe* or *%systemroot%\system32\msinfo32.exe* to open System Information more quickly. You can also use the Send to menu option or press and hold the Ctrl key and drag to copy the System Information shortcut from the System Tools menu to the desktop.

REFERENCE

Using System Information to View Information on Startup Programs and Environment Variables

- From the Start menu, point to All Programs, click Accessories, click System Tools, click System Information, and then maximize the System Information window.
- In the Category pane on the left, click the expand icon to the left of the Software Environment category, then click Startup Programs and examine the information on startup programs in the Details pane on the right.
- In the Category pane on the left, click Environment Variables under Software Environment, and in the Details pane, examine the information on environment variables and their settings.
- Close the System Information window.

Using the Windows Recovery Environment

If you experience a startup problem, such as a Windows 7 boot failure, then you can troubleshoot that problem in the Windows Recovery Environment (WinRE) using one of the following **System Recovery Tools**:

- **Startup Repair**—This recovery tool checks for, and automatically fixes, problems with boot and disk configuration settings and metadata (including the Master Boot Record, Hard Disk Partition Table, and boot sector), missing or damaged system files, damage to Registry hives (covered in Tutorial 14), device drivers, Windows service packs and updates, and file system problems that prevent your computer from starting properly (or at all). Startup Repair checks Windows event logs to identify recent changes to Windows. Startup Repair cannot repair problems with BIOS settings, improperly functioning hardware, incorrect hardware configuration, incorrect device driver settings, or hardware failures. It cannot repair hardware and BIOS problems, installation or upgrade problems, and problems caused by malicious software. Furthermore, it cannot help you recover your personal documents. It can detect, but not repair, problems caused by bad RAM or hard disk failures. After Startup Repair checks your computer, it creates a log file named SrtTrail.txt in the following location: %WINDIR%\System32\LogFiles\Srt. That log file contains diagnostic information and information about repairs made to a computer.
- **System Restore**—You can use this recovery tool to roll back your computer to an earlier working state. Also, Startup Repair might automatically start the process for restoring your computer using System Restore in order to repair a problem with starting Windows. You can also use this option if you change the password for an Administrator account and then forget that password, or if Windows 7 does not recognize the password for some reason. In addition, you can use System Restore if you make a change to an Administrator account that subsequently prevents you from logging on under that account (such as changing the Administrator account to a Standard User account). If you use System Restore from the System Recovery Options dialog box, you cannot undo the restore operation and roll your computer back to its original state. If you have other restore points, you can use System Restore to roll back your computer to one of those restore points.
- **System Image Recovery**—If you have created a system image using Windows Backup before you encounter a serious problem, you can use the system image to restore your entire computer. If you choose this option, then you lose any files that you created or modified since you created that system image; therefore, it's important to frequently update your system image.
- **Windows Memory Diagnostic Tool**—You can use this recovery tool to perform a thorough check of the RAM in your computer. This tool is stored in the \Boot folder; however, you can only run it in the Windows Recovery Environment.
- **Command Prompt**—With this recovery tool, you can use certain command-line tools, such as the Check Disk utility, to troubleshoot problems with a computer. Some types of command-line tools, including network command-line tools, are not available because Windows 7 is not running on the computer. Instead, you work in the Windows Recovery Environment (WinRE).

Windows 7 automatically installs the Windows Recovery Environment on a computer. If the hard disk drive where the Windows Recovery Environment is installed is inaccessible because of a problem with the Master Boot Record, the Hard Disk Partition Table, or boot sector on the hard disk drive, you can still start the Windows Recovery Environment from the Windows DVD or from a system repair disc that you created from Backup and Restore in the Control Panel (covered in Tutorial 10). That system repair disc must be created before the problem occurs.

To open the Windows Recovery Environment, you restart your computer, press the F8 function key to display the Advanced Boot Options menu, and then choose the option to repair your computer. To open the Windows Recovery Environment from your Windows DVD, you:

- Insert your Windows DVD into a DVD drive.
- Restart your computer.
- Use your Boot Device Menu to choose the option for booting from your DVD drive, and then wait for Windows to load.
- In the first Install Windows dialog box, verify and if necessary, change, the "Language to install," "Time and currency format," and "Keyboard or input method" settings, and then click the Next button.
- In the next Windows dialog box, click the "Repair your computer" link. Windows displays a System Recovery Options dialog box and searches for Windows installations.
- In the next System Recovery Options dialog box, click the operating system you want to repair, and then click the Next button. If Microsoft Windows 7 is not listed, use the Load Drivers button to load drivers for your hard disk drive.
- In the next System Recovery Options dialog box, shown in Figure 8-42, choose one of the five recovery tools described previously.

Figure 8-42 | **System Recovery Options dialog box**

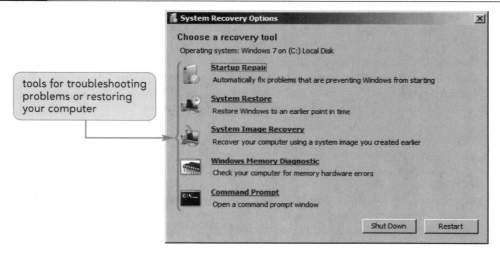

If Windows 7 did not start during your last boot, then the Startup Repair tool automatically starts, checks your computer for the possible source of the problem, and then, if possible, automatically fixes the problem. Or the Startup Repair tool might prompt you to restore your computer with System Restore. If the Startup Repair tool successfully diagnoses and repairs the problem, then it will display information about the nature of the problem. That information will include the source of the problem (if found) and how the problem was resolved.

Restoring Your Computer's Settings

If you are working in a computer lab, or if you want to restore your desktop computer to the settings that existed prior to working on this tutorial, complete the following steps.

To restore your computer's settings:

▶ 1. To remove Administrative Tools from the Start menu, right-click the **Start** button 🟦, click **Properties**, and on the Start Menu property sheet, click the **Customize** button, scroll to the bottom of the list of options for customizing the Start menu, and under System administrative tools, click the **Don't display this item** option button, click the **OK** button to close the Customize Start Menu dialog box, and then click the **OK** button to close the Taskbar and Start Menu Properties dialog box.

▶ 2. If necessary, restore double-click activation and remove the Computer icon from the desktop.

REVIEW

Session 8.2 Quick Check

1. _____ is a term commonly used to refer to a hardware device, such as the BIOS, which contains embedded software that interacts with the operating system.
2. What term is used to refer to the name of a BIOS setting and the setting itself?
3. _____ is a database that contains boot configuration settings and information about the location of boot files which in turn determine how Windows 7 loads from disk.
4. How can you use Last Known Good Configuration on the Advanced Boot Options menu?
5. What program can you use to shut down a nonresponding program?
6. What are startup programs, and how can you control the loading of those programs?
7. What is an environment variable?
8. What is the Windows Recovery Environment (WinRE)?

Practice the skills you learned in the tutorial using the same case scenario.

PRACTICE

Review Assignments

There are no Data Files needed for the Review Assignments.

Sencia Bacay, one of Julien's coworkers, recently downloaded and installed new software on her computer. Now she is experiencing problems with the performance of her computer. You offer to help her troubleshoot this problem.

To complete some of these steps in the Review Assignments, you must log on under an Administrator account or provide the password for an Administrator account. As you complete each step in the Review Assignments, record your answers to the questions so you can submit them to your instructor. Use a word-processing application such as Word or WordPad to prepare your answers to these questions. If you change any settings on the computer you are using, note the original settings so you can restore them later. Complete the following steps:

1. If necessary, display the Computer icon on the desktop, switch to single-click activation, and display Administrative Tools on the Start menu and All Programs menu.
2. What is the likely cause or source of the problems that Sencia is currently experiencing on her computer?
3. Outline the steps that Sencia should use to resolve the problem.
4. If Sencia notices that the same problem keeps reoccurring as she uses the new software she installed on her computer, what tool can she use to reproduce and document that problem so her company's tech support staff can help her? Briefly explain how this tool works.
5. Open Reliability Monitor. What would you estimate as the current stability index value (or reliability rating)? Describe how the reliability rating has changed over the time period represented on the system stability chart. Select the icon for the most recent Application, Windows, or Miscellaneous failure, or if there have been no failures, select the last icon for the most recent Warning or Information event. What type of event did you select? Using the information in the system stability report, describe the cause of the failure or the information about the Warning or Information event you selected. What, if anything, would you do next? Close the Reliability Monitor window.
6. Right-click the desktop Computer icon, and choose the option to view its properties. In the System window, select System protection in the left pane, provide Administrator credentials, and wait for System Protection to update information on Protection Settings. List the disks on your computer for which System Protection automatically creates restore points.
7. Use the Create button on the System Protection property sheet to create a manual restore point. Enter a description for the restore point (such as *Manual Restore Point*), and create the restore point. After System Protection creates the restore point, close the System Protection dialog box, and then close the System Properties dialog box and System window.
8. From the All Programs menu, select Accessories, select System Tools, and then open System Restore. After providing Administrator credentials, advance to the next step, or select the option for choosing a different restore point and then advance to the next step. Choose the option for showing more restore points. Identify the different types of restore points created by System Protection. Then close the System Restore dialog box without making any changes to your computer.
9. Open Event Viewer with Administrator credentials (if possible), and then expand the Critical category in the Summary of Administrative Events. Double-click one of the events with a Critical event type, or if there are no Critical event types, expand the Error, Warning, or Information category, and double-click one of the

event types. What Event Type did you choose? What is the Source of this event? What information does Event Viewer provide on the nature of this event?

10. In the Event Viewer console tree pane, double-click Windows Logs and then select Application. Use the Filter Current Log action to specify all events with a Critical event level and an Error event level. Also, use the Event sources list button to select Application Error and Application Hang event sources. Apply the filter, and then select one of the recent Application Hang events (if available) with a Critical or Error Event level. If there are no Application Hang events, choose an Application Error event. What type of event did you choose? In your own words, describe or summarize what caused this problem. What recommendations does Event Viewer suggest for troubleshooting the problem (if any)? Clear the filter.

11. In the Event Viewer console tree pane, open Applications and Services Logs, and then select Internet Explorer. Does Event Viewer report any Critical, Error, or Warning events for Internet Explorer? If so, explain. Why might Sencia examine this category of event logs? Close Event Viewer.

12. Read this step before you restart your computer so you know what types of information to collect during booting to answer the questions in this step. Close all open programs and windows, choose the option to restart your computer, and then open the BIOS Setup utility. (If you are not permitted to open the BIOS Setup utility in your college's computer lab, note that fact as your answer to this step.) What key or keys did you use to open the BIOS Setup utility? Is there a key for opening a boot menu and, if so, what key can you use? After opening the BIOS Setup utility, locate the startup sequence, and then list the drives and any other options for starting up your computer. Exit the BIOS Setup utility without making any changes to your computer, and then display the Advanced Boot Options menu as your computer restarts. If Windows 7 displays the desktop, then restart your computer and try again.

13. Choose the "Enable low-resolution video (640×480)" option on the Advanced Boot Options menu, and log on under your user account. View the Display settings for your computer's screen resolution and color setting. What is the current setting for resolution and color depth? What type of monitor and video display adapter does Windows 7 report? Close the Display Settings dialog box. Can you connect to the Internet if you needed to search for information on troubleshooting a problem? Restart your computer, let Windows 7 boot normally, and then log on your user account.

14. Open Internet Explorer and then open Windows Task Manager. What applications are running on your computer? View processes. Locate the Image Name iexplore.exe for the Internet Explorer task. How much memory does the Internet Explorer task use for its Private Working Set? Close Internet Explorer. What happens to the process(es) for Internet Explorer?

15. Select the Services property sheet, and then click the Description column header to alphabetize services by Description (you may have to click twice). Check the Status column for the Security Center, Windows Firewall, and Windows Event Log. What is the status of these services? If you use a firewall other than Windows Firewall, then note this information in your response to the question. Close Windows Task Manager.

16. Open System Configuration with Administrator credentials (if possible). What type of Startup selection does your computer use? View the Boot property sheet. What operating system or operating systems are installed on your computer? Select the Startup property sheet, adjust the width of all the columns so you can view all the information displayed in each. Arrange the startup items in alphabetical order. Which startup items, if any, load during booting on your computer? Which startup items, if any, are not loaded? What startup items, if any, are listed more than once, and why are these items listed multiple times?

17. Choose one of the startup items that automatically loads, and then list the startup item's name, the manufacturer's name (if known), the command for loading the startup item, and the location from which Windows 7 loads the startup item. How does this startup item load? Close the System Configuration dialog box without applying any changes to your computer.

18. Open System Information. In the System Summary, list the information provided by System Information for OS Name, Version, Processor, Windows Directory, System Directory, Boot Device, and Total Physical Memory on your computer.

19. In the Category pane, expand the Software Environment category, and then select Startup Programs. Widen the columns in the Details pane so you can view all the information in each column. List the names of the startup programs, and then examine the Location column. What location (or locations) does Windows 7 use to load these startup programs?

20. Select the Environment Variables category. What are the settings for OS, NUMBER_OF_PROCESSORS, and windir environment variables? What value does Windows 7 substitute for the replaceable parameter in the windir environment variable? Explain the purpose and use of the PATHEXT environment variable. Close System Information.

21. Submit the results of the preceding steps to your instructor, either in printed or electronic form, as requested.

Use your skills to troubleshoot problems using Reliability Monitor.

APPLY

Case Problem 1

There are no Data Files needed for this Case Problem.

Laskowski Analytics, Inc. Over the years, Hanna Laskowski's software testing and analysis firm has evaluated the performance of applications and utilities under different Windows operating systems. The computers used by her employees must therefore meet the highest performance standards in order to return reliable data about the performance of programs that they test every day. Prior to purchasing new high-performance computers to test new Windows operating systems and applications, she asks you to evaluate a new state-of-the-art computer.

As you complete each step in this case, record your answers to the questions so you can submit them to your instructor. Use a word-processing application such as Word or WordPad to prepare your answers to these questions. If you change any settings on the computer you are using, note the original settings so you can restore them later. Complete the following steps:

1. Open Reliability Monitor, and make sure you are viewing information by days. Then use the system stability chart to evaluate the performance of your computer by locating information to answer the following questions:

   a. What is the most recent date for which Reliability Monitor has information, and what is the approximate reliability rating (or stability index) of the computer you are using?

   b. Adjust your view in the system stability chart and select the earliest date shown on the system stability chart without scrolling to view previous dates. What date did you select, and what is the approximate reliability rating (or stability index)? How does this reliability rating compare with the previous reliability rating? What would you conclude, if anything, about the overall performance of your computer over this time period?

   c. Locate and select the date for the lowest reliability rating shown in the system stability chart over this same time period. What date did you select, and what is the approximate value for lowest reliability rating? Which failures or problems account for this lower reliability rating? If necessary, examine the previous time period to answer this question.

2. Switch to a view of information by weeks. Use the system stability report to evaluate problems on your computer, as follows:

   a. Examine Application failures. Identify the names and the types of events for the application failure, or combination of application failures, that most affected the performance of your computer over the time period you are examining.

   b. Examine Windows failures. Identify the type of event for the last Windows failure (if any) and how that failure affected the reliability index.

   c. Examine Miscellaneous failures. Identify the type of event for the last Miscellaneous failure (if any).

   d. Examine Warnings. If Reliability Monitor lists any warnings, select the last warning and identify the type of problem that occurred.

   e. Examine Information events. Select the last Information event, and identify the type of event, and explain the result of this event.

3. After analyzing the information you examined, summarize your impression of the performance of your computer over the period of time for which Reliability Monitor contains information on Application, Windows, and Miscellaneous failures as well as Warnings and Information events. Indicate in your analysis whether the performance of your computer is improving or becoming worse, and if the latter is the case, identify what you must troubleshoot to improve your computer's performance and what options you might explore.

4. Close Reliability Monitor.

5. Submit the results of the preceding steps to your instructor, either in printed or electronic form, as requested.

Use your skills to analyze events for a troubleshooting firm.

APPLY

Case Problem 2

There are no Data Files needed for this Case Problem.

Avant Garde Troubleshooters, Inc.   Toru Miyazaki and Isao Nagano cofounded and now manage a cutting-edge troubleshooting firm that helps customers resolve problems caused by different operating systems. Their employees rely on Event Monitor for up-to-date information about problems that arise on the computers they use to remotely troubleshoot problems. Toru asks you to use Event Viewer to evaluate System events on a computer used by one of his new employees.

As you complete each step in this case, record your answers to the questions so you can submit them to your instructor. Use a word-processing application such as Word or WordPad to prepare your answers to these questions. If you change any settings on the computer you are using, note the original settings so you can restore them later. Complete the following steps:

1. Open Event Viewer with Administrator credentials (if possible), open Windows Logs in the console tree pane, and then select System.

2. Create a filter that displays System events with a Critical event level, apply the filter, and then click the Source column header to list events in alphabetical order. How many System events does Event Viewer report for the Critical event level?

3. If there are any Critical-level events, list the different types of Sources for these events.

4. If there are any Critical-level events, select one event in each different type of Source, and summarize the following information about the events:

   • Level and Source

   • Nature of the problem, and recommended resolution (if any)

✦ **EXPLORE**

5. Open the current filter and change the filter to display Error-level events. If there are several error-level events, select one and summarize the following information about that event:
   - Level and Source
   - Nature of problem, and recommended resolution (if any)

6. Change the existing filter so it displays Warning-level events, and if necessary, alphabetize that list by Source. Select a Warning-level event, and summarize the following information about that event:
   - Level and Source
   - Nature of problem, and recommended resolution (if any)

7. Open Applications and Services Logs in the console tree pane, open the Microsoft node, open the Windows node, open WindowsUpdateClient, and then double-click Operational. Create a filter that displays events for the Critical, Error, and Warning levels. Click the Date and Time column header to sort events by date, select the most recent Critical, Error, or Warning event. What does Event Viewer report about the event level and the nature of this event? Clear the current filter, and then close Event Viewer.

8. How might you benefit from, or use, Event Viewer on your computer?

9. Submit the results of the preceding steps to your instructor, either in printed or electronic form, as requested.

Extend what you've learned to examine other important BIOS settings.

CHALLENGE

Case Problem 3

There are no Data Files needed for this Case Problem.

Euro-Russian Seed Vault Foundation   Olga Sergeyev is the director of the Euro-Russian Seed Vault Foundation, a joint Russian and European Community venture designed to store and protect seeds of all known crop and wildflower species in the world to guarantee future crop and wildlife diversity and to recover from ecological disasters and pathogens. As Olga's in-house computer specialist, she has asked you to examine and, if necessary, optimize the BIOS settings on the computers used by foundation staff.

As you complete each step in this case problem, record your answers to the questions so you can submit them to your instructor. Use a word-processing application such as Word or WordPad to prepare your answers to these questions. If you change any settings on the computer you are using, note the original settings so you can restore them later. Complete the following steps:

1. Restart your computer, and open the BIOS Setup utility.

2. Locate information about the processor and, if available, provide the following information:
   - Processor type, clock speed, bus speed, L2 cache (size), and L3 cache (size)
   - Multiple core capability
   - Hyperthreading capability
   - 64-bit technology

3. Locate information about the memory on your computer and, if available, provide the following information:
   - (Amount of) installed memory
   - Memory speed
   - Memory technology
   - (Type of) memory slot and amount of memory used in each memory slot

4. Locate the boot sequence on your computer, and then list the order in which the BIOS searches your computer to locate the drive with the operating system.

EXPLORE 5. Locate information about power management and, if available, indicate the purpose of each of the following settings and provide the following information:
- Auto Power On setting and options for this field
- AC Recovery setting and options for this field
- Suspend Mode setting and any other option(s) for this field

EXPLORE 6. Locate information about Execute Disable, if available. What does this setting do, what is the current setting for this field, and what is the factory default? (*Hint*: Check the Security category for this field.)

EXPLORE 7. Locate information about POST behavior and, if available, indicate the purpose of each of the following settings and provide the following information:
- Fast Boot setting
- Numlock Key setting
- POST Hotkeys

8. Exit the BIOS Setup utility without making any changes to BIOS settings.

9. After your computer restarts, log onto your computer, view properties of your computer, provide the following information, and then close the System window.
- Processor
- Memory (RAM)
- System type

10. Open System Information from the All Programs menu, and provide the following information from the System Summary:
- Processor
- Total Physical Memory

11. Select the Environment Variables category, provide the following information from environment variables, and then close the System Information window.
- Number of processors
- Processor architecture
- Processor Identifier

12. Submit the results of the preceding steps to your instructor, either in printed or electronic form, as requested.

Use your skills and the Internet to evaluate startup programs.

RESEARCH

Case Problem 4

There are no Data Files needed for this Case Problem.

Mostyn Excursions, Inc. Mostyn Excursions, a business located in Wales, provides unique travel tours and packages to exotic, unusual, and quaint locales throughout Wales, Scotland, Ireland, and England as well as the Hebrides, Orkney Islands, Shetland Islands, Rockall, and Isle of Man. Cedric Mostyn, the owner of Mostyn Excursions, asks you to evaluate the startup programs used on the computers at Mostyn Excursions to determine how best to optimize those computers.

To complete this case problem, you must log on under an Administrator account or know the password for an Administrator account. As you complete each step, record your answers to the questions so you can submit them to your instructor. Use a word-processing application such as Word or WordPad to prepare your answers to these questions. If you change any settings on the computer you are using, note the original settings so you can restore them later. Complete the following steps:

1. From the Administrative Tools menu, open System Configuration with Administrator credentials (if possible), select the Startup property sheet, widen all the columns, and then click the Startup Item column header to sort the startup items in alphabetical order.

2. Prepare a list that includes the name of five startup items, the program filename, and the name of the folder where the program file is located (where available). (*Hint:* You will have to extract this information from the path for each startup item. In some cases, you might want to specify enough of the path to make it clear where the program is installed, and in other cases, no path may be specified for the program filename.)

3. Use a search engine to locate one or more Web sites that contain information about startup programs. (*Hint:* Because Mostyn Excursions, Inc. is located in Wales, you might want to use the Sysinfo.org Web site (*www.sysinfo.org*), which contains information on tens of thousands of startup programs, as one of the Web sites you examine.)

4. For each startup item on your computer, use the startup name, program filename, and program file location to locate and record the following information (where available).

   - The purpose of the startup item
   - Whether the startup item is legitimate or malicious software
   - The recommended option for loading the startup item, such as:
     - Safe to load during booting
     - Required
     - Not required or not recommended
     - User's choice
     - Unknown
     - URL of Web site that contained information about the startup item

5. For each startup item you examined, explain whether you would enable or disable the loading of the program, and explain how you arrived at that decision.

6. Close the System Configuration dialog box.

7. Submit the results of the preceding steps to your instructor, either in printed or electronic form, as requested.

ENDING DATA FILES

Problem Pinning Control Panel Shortcut to Taskbar.zip

Evaluating System Performance

Monitoring Memory Usage

To monitor the
application
1. Click the U
Right-click
processe
nitor com
Display bu

OBJECTIVES

Session 9.1
- Examine RAM, virtual memory, and the paging file
- View virtual memory settings
- Monitor changes in system performance with Task Manager
- Use Resource Monitor to evaluate system performance
- Create a system health report

Session 9.2
- Use Performance Monitor to track performance changes on your computer
- Analyze, save, and print performance measurements
- Use Resource and Performance Monitor to examine memory usage
- Examine Windows ReadyBoost and SuperFetch

Case | *Allele Vigor, Inc.*

Allele Vigor, Inc. is a Boston-based biotech company that develops new species of plants by using interspecific, intraspecific, interfa-milial, intergeneric, and cross-species gene-splicing techniques. Over the years, these innovative efforts have resulted in new food crops and new ways of producing fibers for use in a wide array of products. Allele Vigor's employees rely on high-performance and resource-intensive gene modeling and analysis software to develop these new plant species. Cai Shuang, a tech specialist at Allele Vigor, checks and optimizes the performance of computer systems used by the research staff.

In this tutorial, you will examine the importance of RAM, virtual memory, and the paging file. Next, you examine virtual memory settings on your computer. You will use Windows Task Manager to study information on processor and memory usage. You will use Resource Monitor to evaluate system performance, and you will use Resource and Performance Monitor to create a system health report and identify potential problems. Then you will use Performance Monitor to track memory and processor usage as you work on your computer. Finally, you learn how you can use Windows ReadyBoost to optimize memory usage.

WINDOWS

STARTING DATA FILES

There are no starting Data Files needed for this tutorial.

SESSION 9.1 VISUAL OVERVIEW

Windows Task Manager, a Windows tool, provides an ongoing graphical update of processor activity and memory usage showing the CPU Usage, CPU Usage History, Memory, and Physical Memory Usage History so you can monitor and evaluate how programs affect the performance of the processor, its execution cores, and memory (including the use of RAM).

Resource Monitor, a Windows tool, provides valuable information on the use of memory in a computer. For example, In Use memory is the total amount of RAM currently used by the operating system, applications, Windows services, startup programs, and device drivers.

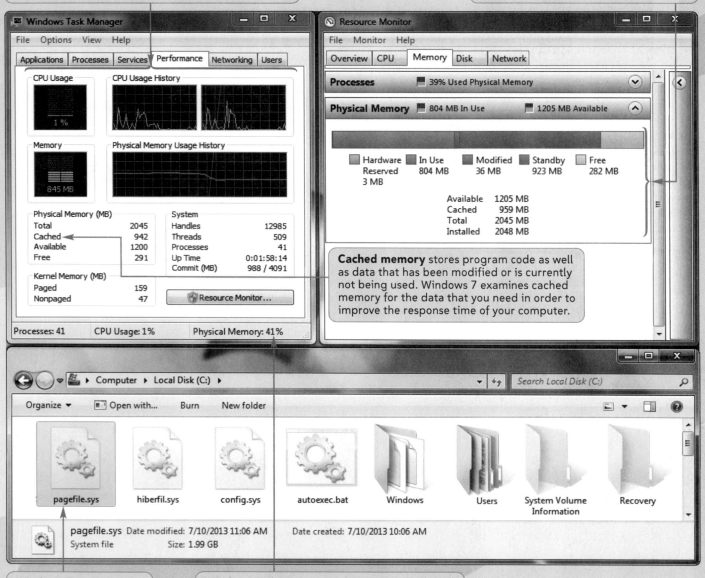

Cached memory stores program code as well as data that has been modified or is currently not being used. Windows 7 examines cached memory for the data that you need in order to improve the response time of your computer.

Windows 7 creates and constantly updates a special system file called the **paging file** for use as supplemental RAM.

Windows Task Manager and Resource Monitor report on the amount of Physical Memory, or RAM, currently in use. Windows 7 optimizes the use of RAM for the program that you are currently using, even while you are multitasking.

MEMORY USAGE

The Windows 7 **Resource and Performance Monitor** tool can produce a **System Diagnostics Report** that provides extensive information about the performance, security, and current status of your computer. The Warnings section of this report identifies problems, such as Windows Update being disabled, and describes how to resolve the problem.

The Informational section in the System Diagnostics Report identifies other issues of importance to the security and performance of your computer, such as the lack of antivirus software, and describes how to resolve the problem.

Resource Overview provides information on the status, utilization, and details of four basic system components: CPU, Network, Disk, and Memory.

The System Diagnostics Report includes small note icons that function like ToolTips to provide more information about system resources, such as the load on a network adapter or the number of disk reads and writes.

The Basic System Checks section in the System Diagnostics Report provides information on the status of five basic system checks, such as problems identified by the Security Center.

The Importance of RAM and Virtual Memory

One of the most important components of your computer that affects its overall performance is RAM (random access memory). If a computer has less than an optimal amount of RAM for a certain task you are trying to perform on your computer, the performance of your computer is adversely affected.

To increase the amount of memory available in a computer, and to handle multiple tasks, Windows 7 uses a paging file to enhance the performance and response time of your computer by swapping program code and data back and forth between RAM and the paging file. Together, the installed physical RAM and the paging file constitute what is called **virtual memory**.

For example, assume you open Microsoft PowerPoint and create a presentation. Then you decide to insert a pie chart from a Microsoft Excel spreadsheet into your PowerPoint presentation. After you open Microsoft Excel, Windows 7 temporarily transfers, or swaps, most of the Microsoft PowerPoint application and your presentation to the paging file on the hard disk to optimize the amount of physical RAM available to you while you are working in Microsoft Excel. After you open the spreadsheet that contains the graph you want to copy, you select that pie chart, copy it to the Office Clipboard, and then you switch back to Microsoft PowerPoint and your presentation and paste a copy of that pie chart into your presentation. When you switch back to Microsoft PowerPoint, Windows 7 transfers the Microsoft Excel application and the workbook to the paging file on disk and then transfers Microsoft PowerPoint and your presentation from the paging file to RAM in order to optimize the amount of physical RAM available to you while you are working in Microsoft PowerPoint. (*Note*: In the early versions of the Windows operating system in its Win9x product line, the paging file was called a swap file to emphasize how Windows used that file, and its presence was critical to booting the computer.)

The segments of memory that Windows 7 swaps to and from disk are called **pages,** and this process of swapping pages to and from RAM is called **paging**. Each page is 4 KB (or 4,096 bytes) in size and contains either program code or data. Windows 7 keeps track of how frequently each page is used; less frequently used pages are the first to be swapped to the paging file on disk.

By default, Windows 7 manages the size of the paging file. Windows 7 sets the minimize size of the paging file so it equals close to the amount of installed RAM. If your computer contains 4 GB of RAM, the minimize size of the paging file is almost 4 GB. The recommended size is 1.5 times that amount, namely, 6 GB. Therefore, Windows 7 can increase the amount of available memory you are using up to 10 GB (4 GB for RAM + 6 GB for the paging file). When needed, Windows 7 will further dynamically increase the size of the paging file up to a maximum size of three times the amount of installed RAM to support the operations you perform on your computer. If you start to close applications and documents and reduce the number and types of operations you perform on your computer, Windows 7 will then dynamically reduce the size of the paging file. This process is transparent to the user. The absolute minimum size for the paging file is 16 MB. Each time you start your computer, Windows 7 automatically creates the paging file, even if it is not needed.

If your computer uses a 32-bit edition of Windows 7 and if you install 4 GB of RAM (the maximum RAM supported in 32-bit editions of Windows 7), then part of the last gigabyte of RAM is reserved for use by the system and is not available to applications. However, that last gigabyte of RAM is still useful. If your computer uses a 64-bit edition of Windows 7, you can install and make use of more than 4 GB of RAM.

Although the use of a paging file provides you with the additional memory that you need to work with resource-intensive applications and multitask, it does pose a problem. Swapping programs and data to and from disk is slow compared to the speed with which your computer can access programs and data in RAM. If your computer has a limited amount of RAM, or does not have enough RAM for the types of applications that you use and the way in which you multitask, it functions more slowly as Windows 7 swaps pages from RAM to the paging file on disk, and from the paging file back into RAM. The more

RAM you have, the less you have to rely on virtual memory. The less your computer has to rely on virtual memory, the faster it runs. If you install more RAM on your computer, you immediately improve its performance.

PROSKILLS

Decision Making: Selecting the Right Amount of RAM for a Computer

It's a good idea to purchase the RAM you need for your computer when you first acquire that computer so you don't encounter performance problems. Try to anticipate how long you will keep your computer, and evaluate how you intend to use a new computer before deciding how much RAM you need. As part of this process, you should have some idea of the amount of memory required by the different types of programs you intend to use so you can purchase a computer with the amount of RAM that you need. These programs include not only the ones you use on an everyday basis, such as a Web browser and email software, as well as word-processing, spreadsheet, graphics, and database applications, but also the Windows 7 operating system and other programs that operate in the background, such as Internet security or antivirus software. Also take into account whether you intend to watch movies or videos, record TV broadcasts, listen to music, and work with graphics and animation on your computer, because all these activities require, and benefit from, more RAM. Furthermore, when you multitask and open multiple applications at the same time, Windows 7 must allocate memory to each application. Even if you are currently using a 32-bit edition of Windows 7 that is licensed for only 4 GB, you might find yourself switching to a 64-bit version of Windows 7 in the near future, so purchasing more than 4 GB in anticipation of that change in the near future is still a good investment. In fact, RAM is relatively inexpensive and well worth investing in up front.

If you increase the amount of installed RAM on your existing computer, you will see a marked improvement in the performance and speed of your computer, particularly when you are multitasking and have more than one application open at a time, and when you use resource-intensive applications. Note that other factors, such as the processor speed, also affect the performance of a computer. However, studies have shown that the single best way to boost the performance of a computer is to add more RAM.

The operating system not only allocates memory to applications that you use, but it is also supposed to reclaim memory after you close an application. However, some software developers design their applications so they leave program code in memory after you close the application. If you open the same application later, or use another application in the same office suite or same family of products that requires some of the same program code, then the application opens faster. Windows 7 and Windows Vista also makes use of a feature called SuperFetch to keep track of what applications you open and when you open them so Windows can automatically load applications into memory when it expects you will need them. However, if you don't open the same application again or don't work with another application in the same office suite or family of products, then that memory is tied up and unavailable. Furthermore, applications that remain in memory after you close them or that are preloaded by Windows can prevent you from performing certain operations, such as changing the name of the folder that contained a file you previously opened in that application.

This phenomenon, where allocated memory is not reclaimed by the operating system, but rather tied up by previously open applications or processes, is referred to as a **memory leak** (or **memory overuse**). A memory leak can also be caused by a poorly designed program that does not relinquish memory when you close it. One simple way to deal with this problem is to reboot. When you reboot, everything in RAM is erased, so the amount of memory available to the operating system and applications returns close to the level that was available when you first booted your computer. While not the preferable approach to reclaiming memory, it might be the best in certain situations, especially if your computer is performing very slowly or is unresponsive. A far better approach to this type of problem is to install updates for the program that causes memory leaks or switch to software that does not create memory leaks.

INSIGHT

Identifying Low Memory Problems

If you notice any of the following types of problems, your computer does not have a sufficient amount of memory for proper performance:
- Poor overall performance, including very slow responses to routine operations, such as opening windows, and opening and selecting options from a menu
- Display problems, such as the appearance of blank areas on the monitor after selecting an option on a menu or closing a dialog box
- Windows 7 notifications that inform you that your computer is low on memory or that it is out of memory
- Windows 7 or programs stop responding and lock up your computer

These problems might occur only under certain circumstances, such as when multitasking or using a resource-intensive application. When you observe these types of problems, then you need to evaluate whether you need to purchase and install more RAM in your computer and whether you need to adjust virtual memory settings on your computer. You should also consider whether a video display problem caused by a file system error might be the source of a problem, and use the Check Disk utility to check and repair errors in the file system.

Your computer must also have sufficient storage space available on the hard disk for virtual memory to work properly. If disk storage space is limited on your hard disk, you will experience problems opening and using applications.

Getting Started

To complete this tutorial, you must display the Computer icon on the desktop, switch your computer to single-click activation, display file extensions for known file types, choose the option to display hidden files and folders as well as protected operating system files, and display Administrative Tools on the Start Menu. In the following steps, you will check and, if necessary, change these settings.

To set up your computer:

1. If Administrative Tools is not displayed on the Start menu, right-click the **Start** button 🔘, click **Properties**, and on the Start Menu property sheet, click the **Customize** button, scroll to the bottom of the list of options for customizing the Start menu, and under System administrative tools, click the **Display on the All Programs menu and the Start menu** option button, click the **OK** button to close the Customize Start Menu dialog box, and then click the **OK** button to close the Taskbar and Start Menu Properties dialog box.

2. If necessary, display the Computer icon on your desktop, open the Folder Options dialog box; enable single-click activation; display file extensions; and display hidden folders, files, drives, and protected operating system files; and apply those changes as you close the Folder Options dialog box.

3. Keep the Computer window open for the next section of the tutorial.

Now you're ready to view the paging file on your computer.

Viewing the Paging File

By default, the paging file, which is named pagefile.sys, is stored in the top-level folder of the boot volume where Windows 7 is installed (usually drive C). As you will discover later in the tutorial, you can move the paging file to another drive that has more storage space or that is faster in order to improve the performance of your computer. If you have multiple hard disks in your computer, you can create a paging file on each hard disk. Then it's possible to process multiple I/O requests concurrently on multiple disks.

Shuang asks you to help her perform a thorough check of several newly acquired computer systems for staff research scientists. As you examine these computer systems, Shuang discusses with you the importance of maximizing memory usage on these computers, and if necessary, adjusting the size of the paging file. To acquaint you with important system files used by the Windows 7 operating system, the two of you examine the hidden and protected paging file on one of the new computers.

To view the paging file:

▶ **1.** Open a window onto drive C (or your boot volume), and if necessary, click the **More options** arrow ▦ ▾ for the Change your view button to switch to Details view, right-click a **column heading** and choose the option for displaying Attributes, adjust the columns for a best fit, and slightly increase the height of the Details pane to show more information and make that information easier to read.

▶ **2.** Locate and point to **pagefile.sys**, and then examine the information on the paging file in the Details Pane. On the computer used for Figure 9-1, Windows 7 reports that the paging file is 1.99 GB in size. Your paging file size may differ.

   Trouble? If you do not see pagefile.sys in the top-level folder of drive C, make sure that your computer is set to display hidden files, folders, and drives as well as protected operating system files. Also, the paging file might be located on another drive. If necessary, examine your other drive(s) and locate the paging file.

Figure 9-1	Viewing the paging file on the system volume

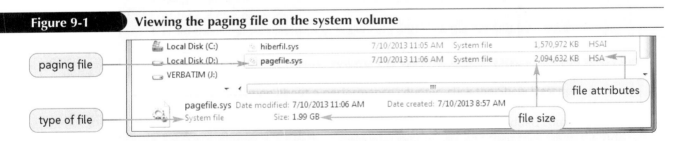

Because this computer contains 2 GB of RAM, Windows 7 sets the minimum size of the paging file close to that. In the Details pane, Windows 7 also identifies this file as a System file, and the Attributes column shows this file is a hidden system file with the archive attribute enabled. On the computer used for this figure, hibernation is enabled, and the hiberfil.sys hibernation file is 1.49 GB in size. This file is also a hidden system file with the archive attribute enabled, plus it is assigned the Not Content Indexed attribute (I) indicating that it is not indexed for searching. The paging file and the hibernation file are typically the largest files in the top-level folder of the boot volume.

▶ **3.** Examine other system folders and system files in this folder. Bootmgr is the Windows Boot Manager. The Boot folder contains the Boot Configuration Data (BCD). On the computer used in Figure 9-1, Bootmgr and the Boot folder are not visible because they are stored on a different partition identified as drive D, the one where Windows Vista is installed, because the computer is set up to perform a dual-boot between Windows 7 and Windows Vista. The Windows 7 and Windows Vista boot files are on that same partition.

▶ **4.** Close the Computer window.

It is easier to understand the concept and use of virtual memory if you can associate it with something physical on your computer, such as installed RAM and the paging file.

In the next section of the tutorial, you will examine how to change the size of the paging file.

Examining Virtual Memory Settings

Another way to manage memory is to examine which drives Windows 7 uses for paging files. If your computer has more than one drive, Windows 7 maintains a paging file on only one drive, namely, the boot volume. You can use the Computer window to find out whether another drive on your computer has more storage space for the paging file. If that drive is accessed less frequently than drive C, is a faster drive, and has more storage space, it might make more sense to use that drive for the paging file, and thereby free up valuable storage space on your boot volume for installed applications and the operating system and reduce disk access. (*Note*: You should be able to locate the speed of your hard disk drive on the order or invoice for your computer, or by searching the Internet for a utility that measures drive speed.)

Microsoft recommends that you do not put a paging file on the same drive as the system files, and it also recommends that you do not put multiple paging files on different partitions of the same physical hard disk. Although you can specify no paging file, Microsoft also recommends against that option. Unless you have enough physical memory, or RAM, you need at least one paging file on one of the drives to provide virtual memory. Windows 7 also uses the paging file to store information on serious error conditions that occur on your computer so you can send an error report with that information to Microsoft for analysis at the next successful boot of your computer.

As you examine virtual memory settings in the tutorial steps, you will discover that the default setting for managing the paging file is "System managed size." That means that Windows 7 manages the size of the paging file to optimize the performance of your computer, so you may never need to change your virtual memory settings.

Shuang asks you to check and, if necessary, adjust virtual memory settings on the new computers so Windows 7 can take maximum advantage of virtual memory.

To complete the following steps, you must provide Administrator credentials. If you are not logged on under an Administrator account or cannot provide the password for an Administrator account, read the following steps and examine the figures, but do not keystroke the steps.

To view virtual memory settings:

1. Right-click the **Computer** icon, click **Properties**, click the **Advanced system settings** link on the left side of the System window, and then provide Administrator credentials (if necessary). Windows 7 opens the System Properties dialog box and displays the Advanced property sheet in the foreground.

2. Under Performance, click the **Settings** button, and then click the **Advanced** tab. You can adjust the setting for processor scheduling and view virtual memory settings. By default, Windows 7 enables the Programs option under Processor scheduling to provide more processor resources to the foreground program (e.g., the active program) than background services. As a result, your foreground program performs more smoothly and faster. If you select the Background services option under Processor Scheduling, all programs and background services receive an equal amount of processor resources. Windows 7 also shows the total paging file size for all drives under the Virtual memory section.

3. Under Virtual memory, click the **Change** button. Windows 7 opens the Virtual Memory dialog box, as shown in Figure 9-2.

| Figure 9-2 | Viewing virtual memory settings |

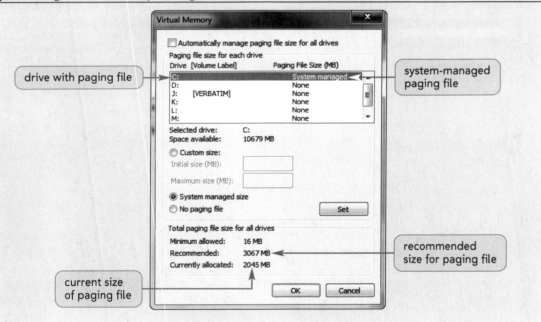

At the bottom of the Virtual Memory dialog box, Windows 7 summarizes the total paging file size for all drives. On the computer used for this figure, the recommended size is 3,067 MB (or approximately 3 GB), which is 50 percent higher than the amount of installed 2 GB of RAM. The currently allocated size is 2,045 MB (or approximately 1.99 GB). The minimum allowed size is 16 MB. Your virtual memory settings may differ.

By default, Windows 7 automatically manages paging files on all drives; however, if you turn off the "Automatically manage paging file size for all drives" option, then you can select a drive in the "Paging file size for each drive" box, and specify a custom size by entering a minimum and maximum size in MB after you choose the Custom size option button. Once you specify a custom size, you click the Set button to apply that setting. You can also specify no paging file, but that is not recommended for reasons mentioned earlier.

To close the Virtual Memory dialog box without making changes:

1. Click the **Cancel** button to close the Virtual Memory dialog box without making changes, click the **Cancel** button to close the Performance Options dialog box, click the **Cancel** button in the System Properties dialog box, and then close the System window.

As you change the way you work with your computer, you can adjust these virtual memory settings and optimize the use of paging files on multiple physical hard disk drives. If you routinely use programs that demand a lot of memory and if you also discover that Windows 7 consistently uses more than 70 percent of the paging file, you can increase the size of the paging file to provide extra memory and thereby optimize performance or, better yet, you can install more RAM.

If you want to move the paging file from one drive to another, you select the other drive and specify a paging file. Then you select the drive from which you want to remove the paging file and choose the "No paging file" option button for that drive.

REFERENCE

Viewing Virtual Memory Settings

- Right click the Computer icon, click Properties, click the Advanced system settings link in the System window, and then provide Administrator credentials.
- On the Advanced property sheet, click the Settings button under Performance, click the Advanced tab in the Performance Options dialog box, and under Virtual memory, click the Change button.
- Examine the virtual memory settings for your computer in the "Total paging file size for all drives" section at the bottom of the Virtual Memory dialog box.
- If you want to specify your own virtual memory settings, remove the check mark from the "Automatically manage paging file size for all drives" check box, select a drive, click the Custom size option button, enter an Initial size and Maximum size in MB for the paging file for the selected drive, click the Set button, click OK to close the Virtual Memory dialog box, click OK to close the Performance Options dialog box, click the OK button to close the System Properties dialog box, close the System window and, if necessary, reboot your computer to apply the changes.
- To close the Virtual Memory dialog box without making any changes to your virtual memory settings, click the Cancel button. Click the Cancel button in the Performance Options dialog box, click the Cancel button in the System Properties dialog box, and then close the System window.

In Windows Vista, the minimum size of the paging file is the same size as the amount of installed RAM, plus 300 MB, and the maximum size of the paging file was three times the amount of installed RAM. In Windows XP, the size of the paging file is 1.5 times the amount of installed RAM, similar to what's recommended for Windows 7.

Using Windows Task Manager to View System Performance

Windows Task Manager, commonly referred to as just Task Manager, is a Windows 7 tool for viewing information on changes in CPU (or processor) usage as well as memory usage on your computer. You can also view details on the use of physical memory, kernel memory, and the system. **Kernel memory** is memory reserved for use by the operating system.

Next, Shuang and you decide to use Windows Task Manager to check the overall performance of one of the new computers.

To view information on the performance of your system:

▶ **1.** Right-click an empty area of the taskbar, and then click **Start Task Manager**. Windows 7 opens the Windows Task Manager window.

▶ **2.** Click the **Performance** tab. In the upper-left corner of the Performance property sheet, Windows Task Manager displays a vertical bar graph that shows the percent of CPU in use. See Figure 9-3.

Figure 9-3 Examining performance data in Windows Task Manager

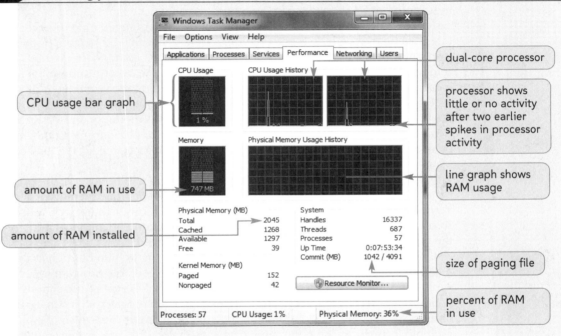

After an earlier spike in processor usage on each execution core, processor activity dropped and stayed at an idle level (near 0 percent). Because the amount of installed RAM in each computer can vary, because each computer is configured differently, and because the information shown on the Performance property sheet changes as you use your computer, your view and details will differ.

The computer used for this computer has a dual-core processor, so Task Manager displays two line graphs under CPU Usage History that show the change in (or history of) CPU usage for each of the two execution cores in the dual-core processor. Under the graphs for CPU Usage and CPU Usage History, Task Manager displays graphs for the current level of Memory usage and the Physical Memory Usage History, both of which measure the change in RAM usage.

The CPU Usage graph reflects the activity of the processor at any given point in time. If you use Task Manager on a regular basis to examine the performance of your computer, you will find that CPU Usage is low, unless you are performing an operation, such as clicking the Start button, opening a Computer window, opening an application, or connecting to the Internet; then it peaks momentarily before it drops again to an idle level. If the value for CPU Usage remains high, some program might be unduly burdening the CPU with requests for processing, which affects the performance of your computer. As you discovered in Tutorial 8, you might be able to use the System Configuration

TIP

To enlarge the two sets of CPU usage graphs, double-click a graph. Double-click a graph again to return to regular view.

utility to identify a program or service adversely affecting the performance of your computer. Once you locate that program (or service), you can prevent it from loading, remove it from your computer, or replace it with another program that does not adversely affect your computer. You can also use Performance Monitor (which you will examine in the second session of this tutorial) to identify programs that affect processor activity.

The Memory bar graph on the computer used for Figure 9-3 shows that 747 MB of RAM is currently used on this computer. On the status bar at the bottom of the Task Manager window, Task Manager reports for Physical Memory that 36 percent of the installed RAM is currently in use.

Under the Physical Memory (MB) section, Windows Task Manager lists the total amount of installed RAM, the amount of cached RAM, and the amount of free RAM. On the computer used for Figure 9-3, the amount of installed RAM is 2045 MB, or almost 2 GB. (The total amount is not exactly 2,048 MB because 3 MB is reserved for the BIOS and hardware drivers.) The Cached value refers to the system cache. The **system cache** is the amount of RAM used to store pages of open files. By maintaining past pages in the system cache, Windows 7 can find information that you need more quickly. In fact, hit rates can be in the high 90 percent range. That means that 90 percent or more of the time Windows 7 finds the data you need in the system cache and therefore does not need to retrieve the data from the hard disk. That translates into faster response times and reduces wear and tear on the hard disk drive, thereby extending the useful life of your hard disk.

The Available value refers to memory that can be used immediately by processes, drivers, or the operating system. The Free value is the amount of unused RAM. Available (memory) plus Cached (memory) also includes the amount of memory used by data swapped to the paging file on disk, and therefore exceeds the total amount of installed RAM.

Kernel memory refers to the memory used by core components of the operating system and by device drivers. On this computer, paged kernel memory is 152 MB. **Paged kernel memory** is that portion of kernel memory that can be paged, or swapped, to disk so other programs can use that memory. **Nonpaged kernel memory** is available only to the operating system, and these pages cannot be paged to disk.

Under the System section, Task Manager reports on the number of handles, threads, and processes. As you may recall, a process is an executable program, a service, or a subsystem. A **thread** is an object within a process that executes instructions (or program code). Windows 7 supports multiple threads for each program so it can execute instructions from different parts of the same program at the same time. Also, it can execute multiple instructions from the same part of the same program at the same time. On a computer which has a multicore processor, such as a dual-core with two execution cores, a quad-core processor with four execution cores, or a computer with multiple processors, different parts of the same program can run concurrently on different execution cores or different processors. If a program creates threads and does not release those threads when you close the program, you have found the source of a memory leak.

A **handle** is an ID that uniquely identifies a resource, such as a file or Registry setting, so a program can access that resource. The Up Time shows the amount of time that the computer has been up and running. Commit (MB) shows two values, the first of which is the size of the paging file, and the second of which shows a value close to twice the amount of installed RAM. As you work on a computer, the paging file size constantly changes as Windows 7 adjusts how memory is used at any given moment.

Shuang points out that you can use Windows Task Manager to monitor changes in your system so you have a better idea of what resources your system uses and needs. For example, after you open an application, you can evaluate the change in CPU usage and memory usage and review the detailed statistics that Task Manager provides.

To monitor memory usage on your computer:

▶ **1.** Click **Options** on the Windows Task Manager menu bar, and if the Always On Top option does not have a check mark next to it, click **Always On Top**; otherwise, click **Options** a second time to close the menu. The Windows Task Manager window will now remain on top of any other open windows.

▶ **2.** Click **Options** on the Windows Task Manager menu bar, and if the Minimize On Use option has a check mark next to it, click **Minimize On Use**; otherwise, click **Options** a second time to close the menu. This option keeps Windows Task Manager from minimizing its window when you open an application.

▶ **3.** If Microsoft Word is installed on your computer, open that application; otherwise, open another application that you commonly use. As shown in Figure 9-4, CPU Usage History shows a large spike in processor usage on one execution core and a much smaller spike on the other execution core as Microsoft Word opens, and then processor activity returns to an idle level.

Figure 9-4   **Changes in memory usage after opening Microsoft Word**

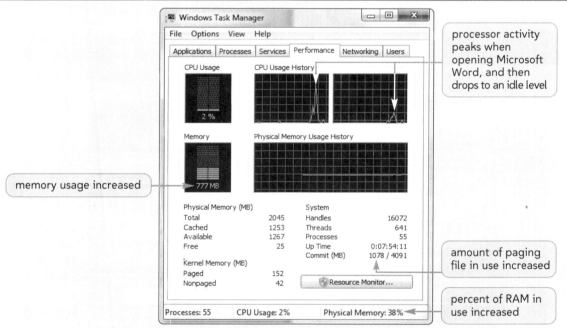

On the computer shown in this figure, memory usage increased from 747 MB (as shown in Figure 9-3) to 777 MB (as shown in Figure 9-4), an increase of 30 MB when opening Microsoft Office Word 2010. As shown by Commit (MB), the amount of the paging file in use increased from 1,042 MB to 1,078 MB (an increase of 36 MB). Your details will differ.

On the computer used for this figure and the following figures, a screen capture program was operating in the background to capture and save a figure for each step, so the use of memory may differ somewhat from the pattern exhibited on your computer. Also, if you have one or more other programs still open in the background on your computer, and if you access those programs as you complete these steps, then your results will show a different pattern. Likewise, if you have previously opened Microsoft Word, then your results will differ from what you would see if you had opened this program for the first time. Windows 7 services, such as Disk Defragmenter, may become active in the background, scheduled tasks may start as you monitor your computer, and Windows 7 may preload programs using SuperFetch, all of which obviously change memory usage. Another factor that affects the pattern you see as you open and close programs is the amount of RAM in your computer. The important point is that Windows 7 constantly adjusts the use of memory to provide programs with the memory they need as you work on your computer.

To continue to monitor memory usage on your computer:

1. Close Microsoft Word or the application that you first opened. On the computer used for Figure 9-5, CPU Usage History shows a small spike on each execution core as Microsoft Word closes. Your change in processor activity may differ.

Figure 9-5   Changes in memory usage after closing Microsoft Word

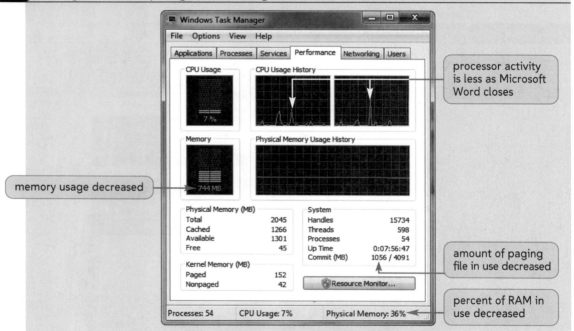

memory usage decreased

processor activity is less as Microsoft Word closes

amount of paging file in use decreased

percent of RAM in use decreased

Memory usage dropped from 777 MB (as shown in Figure 9-4) to 744 MB (as shown in Figure 9-5), a decrease of 33 MB when closing Microsoft Word 2007. The amount of the paging file in use decreased from 1,078 MB to 1,056 MB (a decrease of 32 MB). Your details will differ.

2. To restore Windows Task Manager settings, click **Options** on the Windows Task Manager menu bar, click **Always On Top** to remove the check mark and turn off this option, click **Options** on the Windows Task Manager menu bar again, and then click **Minimize On Use** to add a check mark and enable this option.

3. Close Windows Task Manager.

From this simple examination of memory usage, you can discern how Windows 7 manages memory usage on your computer:

- Windows 7 uses the majority of RAM after you start up your computer. During booting, Windows 7 allocates RAM to itself and to startup programs. During this process, Windows 7 loads device drivers and the program code required for each hardware device on your computer. While the amount of RAM allocated after booting varies with the configuration of your computer system, you should know what Windows 7 requires just to boot your computer. If you want to limit the amount of RAM allocated to startup programs, you can use the System Configuration utility you examined in Tutorial 8 to control the loading of those startup programs.
- Each time you open an application or another type of program, such as a Web browser, email software, game, or utility, or after you load a player to watch video or listen to music, Windows 7 allocates RAM to that program. That same principle applies to opening folder windows, such as the Computer and Documents library windows. During this process, Windows 7 pages currently unused programs to disk so the program you are currently using has access to as much RAM as possible. As a result, the size of the paging file increases, and the amount of available RAM increases. The processor usage also spikes momentarily as you open an application, and then it drops back down to an idle level.
- Each time you close an application or another program, Windows 7 reclaims RAM. That same principle applies to closing folder windows, such as the Computer and Documents library windows. As you close programs and windows, the size of the paging file decreases.
- After you close all open applications or programs, the amount of RAM in use may not return to its original level after booting your computer because Windows 7 may not be able to reclaim all of the originally allocated RAM.

As Windows 7 manages memory, the number of processes, threads, and handles changes, and the size of cached, available, and free memory also changes.

REFERENCE

Using Task Manager to Monitor System Performance

- Right-click the taskbar, click Start Task Manager, and then click the Performance tab in the Windows Task Manager window.
- To keep Windows Task Manager on top of all other open programs and windows, click Options on the Windows Task Manager menu bar, and if the Always On Top option does not have a check mark next to it, click Always On Top; otherwise, click Options a second time to close the menu.
- To keep the Windows Task Manager window from minimizing itself after you open a program, click Options on the Windows Task Manager menu bar, and if the Minimize On Use option has a check mark next to it, click Minimize On Use; otherwise, click Options a second time to close the menu.
- As you open and close applications or windows, check the CPU Usage, CPU Usage History, Memory, and Physical Memory Usage graphs on the Performance property sheet for changes in processor activity and memory usage on your computer. Also examine information on the number of processes, handles, and threads as well as the size of the paging file, identified as Commit (MB), and the percent of Physical Memory in use.
- After monitoring the performance of your system, close Windows Task Manager.

Windows Task Manager is a simple but useful way to obtain an overview of how processor and memory usage changes as you work on your computer.

Using Resource Monitor to Evaluate System Performance

Resource Monitor is a Windows 7 feature that displays information about the use of CPU, disk, network, and memory resources. You can use Resource Monitor not only to provide you with an overview of the performance of your computer, but also to identify one or more processes affecting the performance of your computer. (*Note*: In Windows Vista, Resource Monitor is called Resource Overview.)

Next, you and Shuang use Resource Monitor to examine details on the performance of one of the new computers.

To complete the following steps, you must provide Administrator credentials. If you cannot provide Administrator credentials, read the following steps and examine the figures so you are familiar with the use of Resource Monitor, but do not keystroke the steps.

To open Resource Monitor:

1. From the Start menu, point to **Administrative Tools**, and then click **Performance Monitor**. Windows 7 opens the Performance Monitor window, and under Overview of Performance Monitor, Windows 7 notes that the new Resource Monitor displays detailed information about the performance of hardware resources, such as the processor, disk, and memory, as well as system resources used by the operating system, services, and running applications.

TIP
You can also open Resource Monitor from the Windows Task Manager Performance property sheet.

2. Click the **Open Resource Monitor** link, provide Administrator credentials (if necessary), and then maximize the Resource Monitor window. In the Chart pane on the right side of the window, Resource Monitor displays four graphs that measure CPU (or processor), disk, network, and memory usage in real time over a 60-second time frame. See Figure 9-6. Resource Monitor may expand the CPU section and show details about CPU usage.

| Figure 9-6 | Viewing CPU, disk, network, and memory activity |

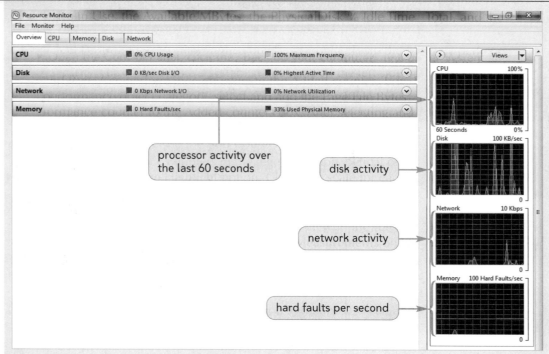

On the computer used for this figure, Resource Monitor shows that CPU usage, measured on a scale of 0 to 100 percent, varies, and that disk I/O activity, measured on a scale of 0 to 100 KB/second, is present and that it also peaks periodically. Network activity is minimal. Memory usage is measured as the number of hard faults/per second. Your details will differ.

A **hard fault** (or **hard page fault**, or **page fault**) refers to a condition in which the operating system must retrieve a page from the paging file on the hard disk because the page is no longer available in physical memory.

In the main part of the window, Resource Monitor provides access to detailed information about each of these resources

To examine details on resource usage:

1. If necessary, click the **expand** icon ⊙ for the CPU section, and if you cannot see all of the detail in this section, then point to the bottom border of the CPU section and when you see a vertical double-headed arrow ⬍, double-click the **section border** to view all the detail in this section. You can also drag the border up or down to adjust the view manually. To adjust column widths, click Monitor on the menu bar, and then click Auto-Fit Columns in Window.

Under CPU, Resource Monitor displays information on programs and processes using CPU resources, and it constantly updates the list of programs and processes using the processor.

In the Resource Monitor window, the content under each section and on each tab is referred to as a table, and the first table on each tab is called the **key table**. The Image column in the CPU table on the Overview tab lists the file names of executable processes, the PID column lists the Process ID for each process, the Description column identifies the process with an easy-to-understand description, the Status column indicates whether a process is running or terminated, the Threads column lists the number of active threads for each process, the CPU column lists the current percent of CPU usage, and the Average CPU column lists the percent load placed by each process on the CPU within the last 60 seconds. If you rest your mouse pointer on a column name, a ToolTip will identify the type of detail shown in the column or explain what resource is measured and how it is measured.

If you want to pause Resource Monitor so it does not continue to update data and so you can examine, evaluate, or save data, you can choose the Stop Monitoring option on the Monitor menu. You can resume Resource Monitor by choosing Start Monitoring on the Monitor menu.

If you want to locate information about a process or service and determine not only its purpose and function in your computer, but also determine whether it's critical to the operation of your computer, you can right-click the process or service, and then click Search Online. That opens Internet Explorer, and your default search engine displays search results on that process or service.

To examine details on CPU usage:

1. Click the **Description** column name. Resource Monitor sorts and then displays process descriptions in alphabetical order. Desktop Window Manager (identified by the process named dwm.exe) updates the Windows Aero desktop window and provides access to Windows Aero features. The Average CPU value for the Resource and Performance Monitor process indicates that it is currently placing the greatest load on the computer used for Figure 9-7. Your details may differ.

| Figure 9-7 | Viewing processes that are using the CPU |

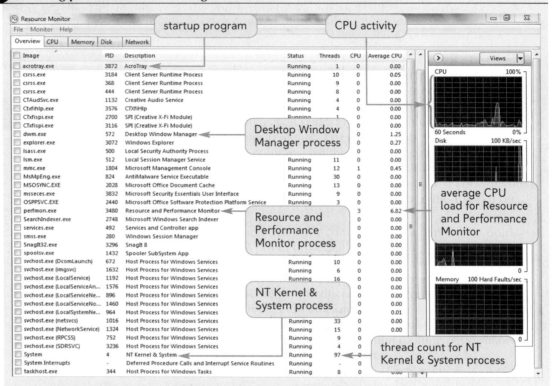

The component using the most threads is the NT Kernel & System process. Your details may differ. You can click any of the column headings to sort data so you can examine the data in a different way. For example, if you click the CPU or Average CPU column name, you can quickly locate the process that most affects processor usage. This information may also help you identify programs and services on your computer that you do not need or want.

2. Click the **collapse** icon ⊗ for the CPU section, click the **expand** icon ⊗ for the Disk section, and if necessary adjust the height of this section so you can see all (or most of) the detail. This section provides details on disk activity, and it can vary from moment to moment. See Figure 9-8.

Figure 9-8	Viewing processes reading and writing to files on disk

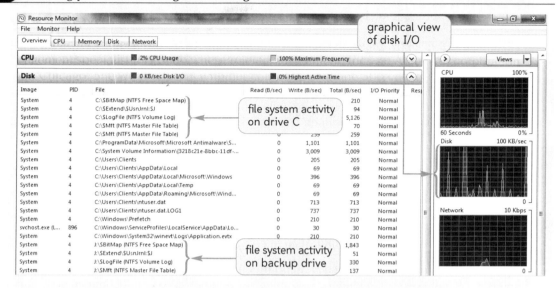

The File column lists the path of the file that is currently being read from, or written to, disk. The Read (B/sec) and Write (B/sec) shows the number of bytes being read from, or written to, the file on disk in the last minute. The Total (B/sec) measures the average number of bytes for reads and writes to the file in the last minute. The I/O Priority column shows the task's priority (such as Normal or Background), and the Response Time column shows the disk response time in milliseconds for each process.

On the computer shown in Figure 9-8, Resource Monitor identifies file system activity on drive C and on an external backup hard disk drive. Your details will differ. You might see system processes for C:\$Mft (NTFS Master File Table) and the C:\$LogFile (NTFS Volume Log).

▶ **3.** Click the **collapse** icon ⊙ for the Disk section, click the **expand** icon ⊙ for the Memory section, and then adjust the height of this section so you can see all (or most of) the detail.

This section provides details on memory usage by each program or process. For example, SearchIndexer, the main component of the Windows search engine, is active because the computer is relatively idle. See Figure 9-9. Your details will differ.

Figure 9-9 Viewing processes and their memory usage

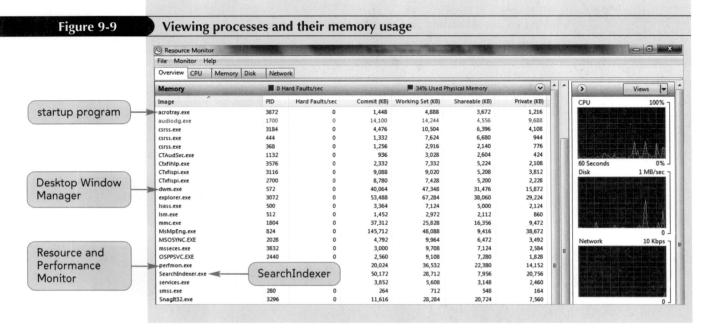

The Hard Faults/sec column shows the average number of hard faults per second in the last minute. As noted earlier, a hard fault occurs when a page is no longer available in physical memory but has instead been paged to disk and therefore requires a disk read. If disk paging consistently exceeds 70 percent of total disk activity, then you are experiencing a high-level of hard faults, and your computer probably does not have enough RAM for the way in which you use your computer.

The Commit (KB) column lists in kilobytes the amount of virtual memory reserved by the operating system for a process. The Working Set (KB) column lists the amount of physical memory currently used by a process. The Shareable (KB) column lists the amount of memory allocated to a process that can be shared with other processes. The Private (KB) column lists the amount of memory in exclusive use by a process (it cannot be shared).

The CPU, Memory, Network, and Disk tabs provide even more detailed information.

To view more detailed information on CPU usage:

1. Click the **CPU** tab. Resource Monitor includes sections on processes, Windows services, associated handles, and associated modules. The Chart pane includes graphs that measure total CPU usage and Service CPU Usage as well as graphs for each processor or, in the case of multicore processors, each execution core. Cores are identified sequentially by number, starting with 0 for the first execution core. So the execution cores for a dual-core processor are identified as CPU 0 and CPU 1.

Handles are pointers to system components, such as Registry entries (covered in Tutorial 14), folders (identified as directories), files, and even events. **Modules** are program files, such as dynamic link library files (with the .dll file extension) and other types of helper files that work in conjunction with other program files. If you add a check mark to the check box for a process (such as Desktop Window Manager) listed under the Processes section, then Resource Monitor expands the Associated Handles and Associated Modules sections and identifies the handles and modules used by that process.

To view information on services and their effect on CPU usage:

1. If necessary, click the **collapse** icon for the Processes section, click the **expand** icon ⊙ for the Services section, click the **Description** column heading to list the services in alphabetical order so it is easier to locate a service, adjust the height of this section so you can see all (or most of) the detail, and then adjust the width of the columns for a best fit. This table identifies which services are running and which are stopped, as well as current CPU consumption in the CPU and Average CPU columns. See Figure 9-10.

Figure 9-10	Viewing the effects of services on CPU usage

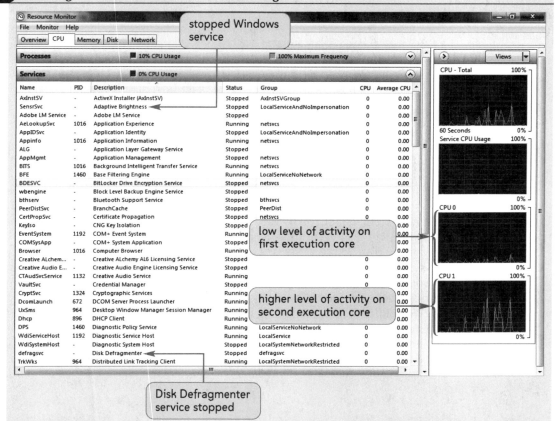

For example, on the computer used for this figure, the Adaptive Brightness and Disk Defragmenter services are currently stopped, and the Desktop Window Manager Session Manager service is running. Your details may differ.

Note also that one of the second of the two execution cores shows more CPU usage.

You can use this information to not only find out which services are active on your computer but also to decide whether or not to enable or disable a service. For example, if you do not use Windows Media Player, but rather use one or more other players, you can turn the Windows Media Player feature and its corresponding services off (as you will discover in Tutorial 11). In addition, if you turn off Windows Media Player, you also turn off Windows Media Center because the latter depends on Windows Media Player.

▶ **2.** Click the **Memory** tab, click the **collapse** icon Ⓐ for the Processes section, if necessary, and then click the **expand** icon Ⓥ for the Physical Memory section to view graphical information on memory usage. On the computer used for Figure 9-11, the Physical Memory horizontal bar shows that 767 MB of RAM is in use and that 1,246 MB of RAM is still available. Your details will differ.

| Figure 9-11 | Viewing information on how physical memory is used |

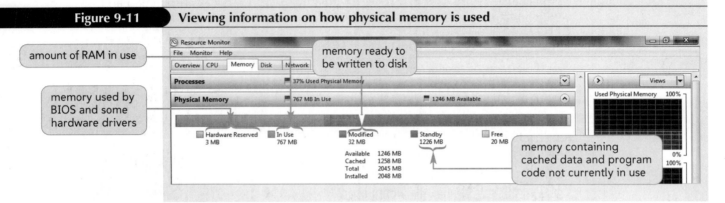

amount of RAM in use

memory ready to be written to disk

memory used by BIOS and some hardware drivers

memory containing cached data and program code not currently in use

In the Chart pane, Resource Monitor displays three graphs that provide an overview of the percent of Used Physical Memory (over the last 60 seconds), Commit Charge, and Hard Faults/sec.

Under the Physical Memory section, Resource Monitor graphically displays how physical memory, or RAM, is used at this point in time. **Hardware Reserved memory** is memory reserved for use by the BIOS and some hardware drivers. In Use memory is the total amount of RAM in use. **Modified memory** is the amount of memory that must be written to disk before it can be used for another purpose. **Standby memory** is memory that contains cached data and code that is currently not being used. **Free memory** is the amount of memory that can be immediately used by the operating system, drivers, and processes.

The total amount of Available memory is the sum of Standby memory and Free memory. Cached memory is the sum of Standby memory and Modified memory. Total memory is the sum of In Use, Modified, Standby, and Free memory, and does not include Hardware Reserved memory. The total Installed memory is the total amount of physical RAM.

To view more detailed information on Disk usage:

▶ **1.** Click the **Disk** tab, and if necessary, click the **expand** icon Ⓥ for the Processes with Disk Activity section, then click the **expand** icon Ⓥ for the Disk Activity section to view processes and their corresponding files that are being accessed on disk. Resource Monitor displays a graph at the top of the Chart pane for overall disk activity and then a graph showing Queue length for each disk drive in your computer system. Queue length refers to the number of pending read/write requests for a disk at a given time.

▶ **2.** Click the **expand** icon Ⓥ for the Storage section. Resource Monitor displays a list of logical drives by logical drive name and their corresponding physical disk numbers. On the computer used for Figure 9-12, Resource Monitor provides information about disk activity by the file system and paging file. Your details will differ.

Figure 9-12   **Viewing information on disk activity, processes, and storage**

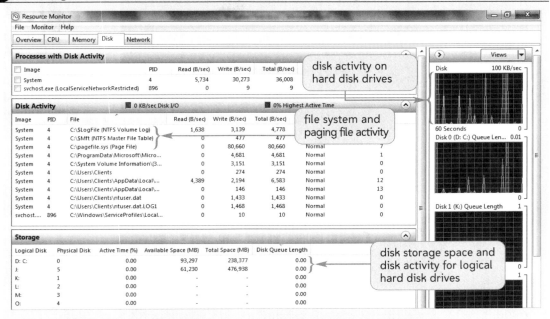

The graphs in the Chart pane show overall disk activity and disk activity by logical disk drive. The Storage section identifies disks by logical disk drive letter(s) and physical drive number, and it includes information on the percentage of time the disk is not idle in the Active Time (%) column, Available Space (MB), Total Space (MB), and the average Disk Queue Length by logical disk(s).

3. Close the Resource Monitor window, and then close the Performance Monitor window.

The Network tab in Resource Monitor lists processes with network activity, network activity (such as information on your ISP connection), TCP connections, and listening ports. **TCP/IP (Transmission Control Protocol/Internet Protocol)** is a standard protocol for transferring data in packets with a source and destination address over the Internet or a private network. **TCP (Transmission Control Protocol)** controls the transfer of data between a program on one computer and a program on another computer. The Network section on the Overview tab provides information on how much data is being transmitted over a network by different processes.

Using Resource Monitor to Evaluate Memory Usage and System Performance

- From the Start menu, point to Administrative Tools, click Performance Monitor, click the Open Resource Monitor link in the Performance Monitor window, and then provide Administrator credentials.
- On the Overview tab, examine the graphs on CPU, Disk, and Network activity as well as the Memory graph showing hard faults. Expand the CPU, Disk, Network, and Memory sections to view information on processes that affect these resources.
- Click the CPU tab to view graphical and detailed information on how processes and services affect processor usage. Select a process under Processes to view more detailed information on that process in the Services, Associated Handles, and Associated Modules sections.
- Click the Memory tab to view a summary of information on how processes use memory and to view information on how physical memory is used.
- Click the Disk tab to view information on processes with disk activity, including the number of bytes read and written per second by process, and the total number of bytes for both operations by process. Examine the Disk Activity section to view more detailed information by each file used by a process. Examine the Storage section for information on logical disks, their physical disk number, percent active time, available and total storage space, and average disk queue length.
- Click the Network tab to view information about processes with network activity, network activity addresses, TCP connections, and listening ports with information on firewall status by process.
- To focus on a specific process and display more detailed information about that process, click the check box in the key table (the first table) on the Overview, CPU, Disk, Memory, or Network tab.
- When you have finished evaluating the performance of your system, close the Resource Monitor window, and then close the Performance Monitor window.

You can use one of the following paths to create a desktop shortcut for Resource Monitor: *%systemroot%\System32\resmon.exe, %windir%\System32\resmon.exe, %systemroot%\System32\perfmon.exe /res,* or *%windir%\System32\perfmon.exe /res.*

Creating a System Health Report

You can use Resource and Performance Monitor to create a system health report to identify any potential problem with the performance or security of your computer and to produce a detailed analysis that you can then use to further investigate potential problems.

Shuang asks you to produce a system health report for your computer.

To complete the following steps, you must provide Administrator credentials. If you are not logged on under an Administrator account or cannot provide the user name and password for an Administrator account, read the following steps and examine the figures so you are familiar with the use of Resource and Performance Monitor, but do not keystroke the steps.

To create a system health report:

1. Right-click the **Computer** desktop icon, click **Properties**, click the **Performance Information and Tools** link in the System window, click the **Advanced tools** link, click the **Generate a system health report** link, provide Administrator credentials (if necessary), and then maximize the Resource and Performance Monitor window.

Windows 7 starts a System Diagnostics test and notes that this analysis takes 60 seconds. Under System Diagnostics, Resource and Performance Monitor notes that this report provides detailed information on the status of local hardware resources, system response times, and processes as well as system information and configuration data. Furthermore, this report includes suggestions for ways to maximize the performance of your computer and streamline its operation. After the test is complete, you see a System Diagnostics Report. See Figure 9-13.

Figure 9-13 Viewing a System Diagnostics Report

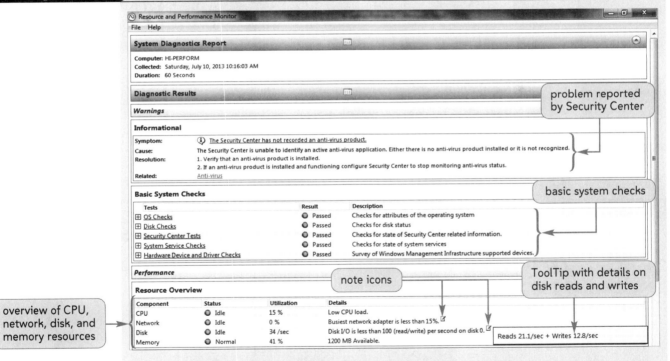

Under Diagnostic Results, Resource and Performance Monitor displays any warnings and reports on any problems that it found; explains the symptom, cause, and steps for resolving the problem; and includes any related links to help you quickly resolve problems. Your System Diagnostics Report details will differ.

If the Security Center has not recorded an antivirus software product, as is the case for the computer used in Figure 9-13, then Resource and Performance Monitor will note that it is unable to identify an active antivirus application and that either there is no antivirus product installed or it is not recognized (the latter of which is the case for the computer used for this figure). If Windows Update is turned off, then Resource and Performance Monitor reports this information and recommends that you run Windows 7 with Windows Update enabled. Under Basic System Checks, Resource and Performance Monitor identifies the results of OS Checks, Disk Checks, Security Center Checks, System Service Checks, and Hardware Device and Driver Checks, and indicates whether the checks passed or failed. You can expand each category and examine the status of each individual test. You can use Hardware Device and Driver Checks to identify hardware and driver problems.

Under Resource Overview in the Performance section, Resource and Performance Monitor shows Idle or Normal for the CPU, Network, Disk, and Memory components of the computer, and reports on the amount of memory utilized and available. If you see a small note icon, then you can point to that note icon to display a ToolTip with more details. As shown in Figure 9-13, the Disk note reports on the number of Reads and Writes per second.

To examine the system health report:

▶ **1.** Click the **collapse** icons ⊝ for the Warnings section and the Performance section, click the **expand** icon ⊝ for the Software Configuration details section, click the **expand** icon ⊝ for the Startup Programs section, and then, if necessary, adjust your view so you can see all your startup programs. Resource and Performance Monitor displays a list of startup programs and the paths with the commands for starting those programs. See Figure 9-14. Your details will differ. The information shown here is similar to that found using System Information (covered in Tutorial 8).

Figure 9-14 **Viewing information on startup programs**

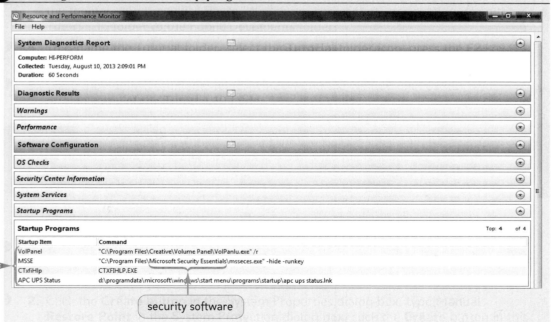

startup programs

security software

▶ **2.** Click the **collapse** icon ⊝ for the Software Configuration section, click the **expand** icon ⊝ for the Disk section, click the **expand** icon ⊝ for Hot Files, adjust your view so you can see all the reported Hot Files, and then click the **expand** icon ⊞ to the left of C:\$Mft (or if not available, another file). Resource and Performance Monitor identifies the files that cause the most disk I/Os. See Figure 9-15.

Figure 9-15	Viewing Hot Files that cause the most disk I/O

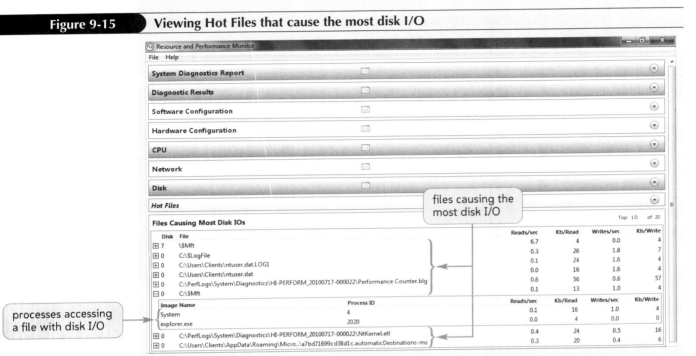

processes accessing a file with disk I/O

files causing the most disk I/O

▶ **3.** Click the **collapse** icon ⊝ for the Disk section, click the **expand** icon ⊝ for the Memory section, and then click the **expand** icon ⊝ for the Process section. Resource and Performance Monitor lists individual processes, including explorer (which displays the desktop and folder windows), SearchIndexer, and dwm (Desktop Window Manager), and shows the Commit (KB), Working Set (KB), Shareable (KB), and Private (KB) for each process.

▶ **4.** Click the **collapse** icon ⊝ for the Memory section, click the **expand** icon ⊝ for the Report Statistics section. Under Computer Information, Resource and Performance Monitor identifies the number of processors (which might be execution cores on a multicore processor), the exact processor speed in MHz, the amount of RAM, and the type of platform (i.e., 32 bit).

▶ **5.** Examine any other diagnostic results of interest to you, close the Resource and Performance Monitor window, and then close the Advanced Tools window. You can also use Save As on the File menu to save the System Diagnostics Report as an HTML file.

Shuang notices that the System Diagnostics Report also contains information about memory usage, but she decides to examine that information in more detail after the two of you use Performance Monitor to examine specific performance factors on this computer.

You can use one of the following paths to create a desktop shortcut for Resource and Performance Monitor: *%systemroot%\System32\perfmon.exe /report* or *%windir%\System32\perfmon.exe /report.*

REFERENCE

Creating a System Health Report

- Right-click the Computer desktop icon, click Properties, click the Performance Information and Tools link in the System window, click the Advanced tools link, click the Generate a system health report link, and then provide Administrator credentials.
- After Resource and Performance Monitor completes a System Diagnostics test and displays a System Diagnostics Report, examine any warnings displayed under Diagnostic Results and use this information to improve the performance or security of your computer.
- Under Basic System Checks, check for any Failed results for OS Checks, Disk Checks, Security Center Tests, System Service Checks, and Hardware Device and Driver Checks.
- Under the Performance section, examine the information in the Resource Overview on the status, utilization, and details of the CPU, Network, Disk, and Memory components.
- If you see a small note icon to the right of a Resource Overview entry, then point to that note icon to display a ToolTip with more detail about that component.
- Expand each section and subsection to view more details about the performance of your computer. If you want to examine information on startup programs, expand the Software Configuration details section and then expand the Startup Programs section. If you want to identify the files that cause the most disk I/O, expand the Disk details section and then expand Hot Files.
- Close the Resource and Performance Monitor window and the Advanced Tools window.

You can use the System Diagnostics Report to identify and correct problems and to view information about the status of your computer so you can decide whether there might be ways to improve the performance of your computer.

Session 9.1 Quick Check

REVIEW

1. Windows 7 creates a special system file on your hard disk called a(n) _____ for use as supplemental RAM.
2. True or False. If Windows 7 relies too heavily on the paging file, then you may not have enough RAM to support the ways in which you use your computer.
3. The phenomenon where allocated memory is not reclaimed by the operating system, but rather tied up by previously open applications or processes, is called a(n) _____.
4. Windows 7 uses the _____ to store pages of open files to improve the chances that it can locate data that you might need later.
5. A(n) _____ occurs when a page is no longer available in physical memory, but has instead been paged to disk, and therefore requires a disk read.
6. The installed physical RAM and the paging file constitute what is called _____.
7. What is paged and nonpaged kernel memory?
8. What is a process's working set?

SESSION 9.2 VISUAL OVERVIEW

Performance Monitor, a Windows 7 tool, plots performance values that show the change in disk activity as an application is opened. The plotted values showing Pages/sec reflects the number of disk reads and writes.

As an application opens, the amount of overall memory in use increases, as shown by the plot of **Committed Bytes**.

The **% Processor Time** counter, which shows the level of processor activity, spikes when opening an application, and after the application is open, processor activity returns to a low level.

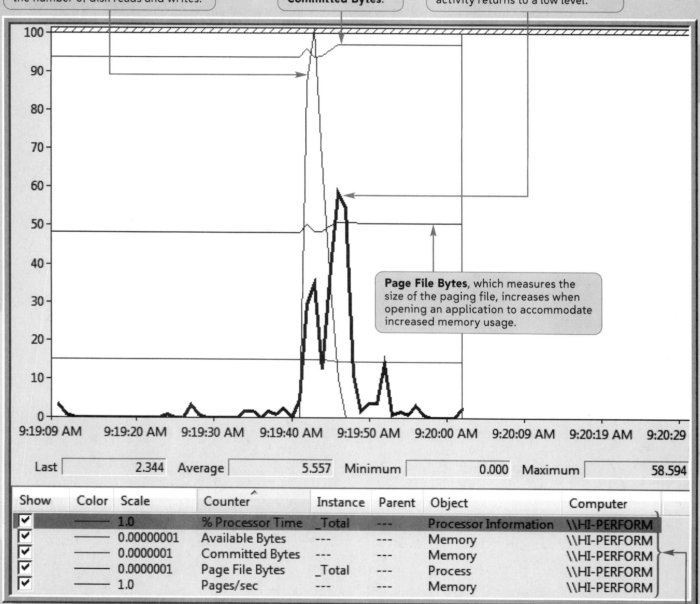

Page File Bytes, which measures the size of the paging file, increases when opening an application to accommodate increased memory usage.

Show	Color	Scale	Counter	Instance	Parent	Object	Computer	
☑	———	1.0	% Processor Time	_Total	---	Processor Information	\\HI-PERFORM	
☑	———	0.00000001	Available Bytes	---	---	Memory	\\HI-PERFORM	
☑	———	0.0000001	Committed Bytes	---	---	Memory	\\HI-PERFORM	
☑	———	0.0000001	Page File Bytes	_Total	---	Process	\\HI-PERFORM	
☑	———	1.0	Pages/sec	---	---	Memory	\\HI-PERFORM	

Last 2.344   Average 5.557   Minimum 0.000   Maximum 58.594

Performance counters allow you to evaluate the performance of your computer and to monitor processor activity, memory usage, disk activity, and the size of the paging file.

MEMORY USAGE

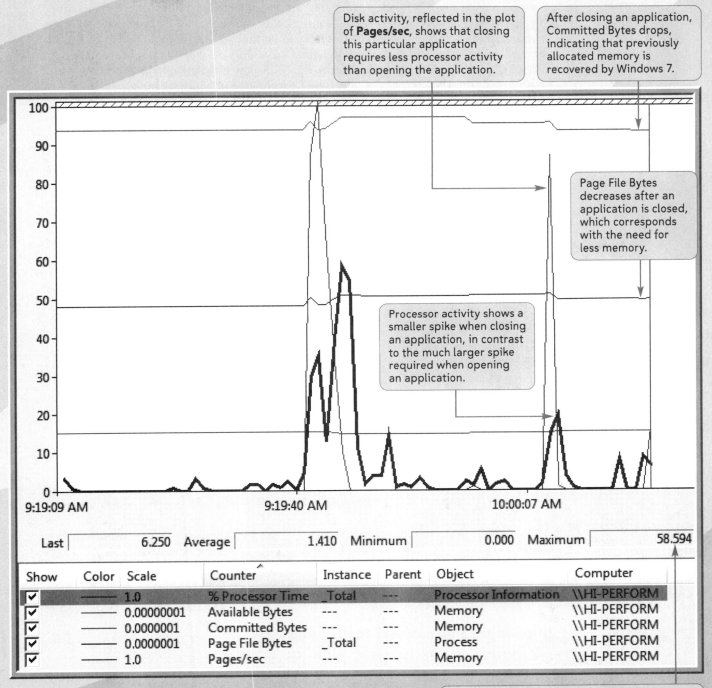

Disk activity, reflected in the plot of **Pages/sec**, shows that closing this particular application requires less processor activity than opening the application.

After closing an application, Committed Bytes drops, indicating that previously allocated memory is recovered by Windows 7.

Page File Bytes decreases after an application is closed, which corresponds with the need for less memory.

Processor activity shows a smaller spike when closing an application, in contrast to the much larger spike required when opening an application.

Show	Color	Scale	Counter	Instance	Parent	Object	Computer
☑	——	1.0	% Processor Time	_Total	---	Processor Information	\\HI-PERFORM
☑	——	0.00000001	Available Bytes	---	---	Memory	\\HI-PERFORM
☑	——	0.0000001	Committed Bytes	---	---	Memory	\\HI-PERFORM
☑	——	0.0000001	Page File Bytes	_Total	---	Process	\\HI-PERFORM
☑	——	1.0	Pages/sec	---	---	Memory	\\HI-PERFORM

Last: 6.250 Average: 1.410 Minimum: 0.000 Maximum: 58.594

Performance Monitor tracks the highest value for a performance counter so you have an idea of the magnitude of the impact of an operation. In this graph, Performance Monitor shows that processor activity peaked at close to 60% when opening an application.

Using Performance Monitor to Evaluate System Performance

Shuang points out that you can use Performance Monitor, another Windows 7 tool, to more closely monitor the performance of your computer, evaluate the use of resources (such as memory), and identify bottlenecks or other problems that interfere with your use of your computer. Unlike with other tools, with Performance Monitor, you can pick and choose which performance factors you want to monitor and thereby focus on resolving a specific problem. Also, because information is displayed graphically in real time, it's easier to visualize how programs affect the performance of your computer system.

When using Performance Monitor, you start by selecting a performance object. A **performance object** is a broad category that contains a set of related performance counters for measuring the performance of some aspect of your computer system. For example, the Memory performance object contains a variety of options for measuring the use of memory on a computer, and the Processor Information performance object provides a variety of options for measuring the effect of programs on the processor.

After you select a performance object, you select a performance counter that allows you to measure the performance of an object in a specific way. For example, you can choose to measure allocated memory and available memory—two different performance counters under the Memory performance object category. Performance counters consist of Windows 7 performance counters as well as performance counters added by applications.

For some performance counters, you can also select an instance. An **instance** allows you to sample a performance counter in a specific way. For example, the Process performance object contains options for measuring the effects of one or more programs on a resource (such as memory or the processor). Under the Process performance object, you can use the % Processor Time performance counter to monitor how all programs or how one specific program affects the processor. If you want to measure % Processor Time for all programs, you select the _Total instance. If you want to measure % Processor Time for a specific program, such as Microsoft Word, you select that program's name (for Microsoft Word, you would select WINWORD). By measuring the effect of an individual program on processor usage, you can identify programs that tie up the processor and force it to perform unneeded operations.

Shuang relies on Performance Monitor to track changes in processor and memory resources, two components that significantly affect the performance of computer systems. She asks you to open Performance Monitor and measure the use of processor and memory resources on this new computer. She also suggests you save the performance measurements on your flash drive.

It's a good idea to reboot your computer and log on again before you use Performance Monitor so you can obtain a better idea of how your computer performs and what Windows 7 needs in order to start your computer. Rebooting also clears RAM so your performance measurements show the real effect of opening a program for the first time.

To open the Performance Monitor window:

▶ **1.** Restart your computer, log on under your user account, attach your flash drive to the computer you are using and, if necessary, close any open windows or dialog boxes.

▶ **2.** From the Start menu, point to **Administrative Tools**, and then click **Performance Monitor**. In the middle of the right pane of the Performance Monitor window, Performance Monitor displays a System Summary with the UNC path for your computer.

In the System Summary section, under Memory, Performance Monitors reports on the % Committed Bytes in Use, the Available MBytes, and the Cache Faults/sec. Committed Bytes is the amount of committed virtual memory, and therefore it is used to measure the amount of memory your computer is using at any given time. Available MBytes is the amount of physical memory, or RAM, available for use. Cache Faults/sec refers to the rate at which pages are not found in the system cache and therefore must be retrieved from disk (a hard fault) or from somewhere else in memory (a soft fault).

Under Network Interface, Performance Monitor shows the total number of bytes per second for your ISP, your Local Area Connection, and your network adapter. Under Physical Disk, Performance Monitor shows the total % Idle Time and Avg. Disk Queue Length for all drives and for each individual drive. The Avg. Disk Queue Length is the average number of read and write requests for all disk drives or for a specific disk drive during a specific interval of time.

Under Processor Information, Performance Monitor shows information on % Interrupt Time, % Processor Time, and Parking Status for all processors or processor execution cores as well as information on each processor or processor core. % Interrupt Time refers to the amount of time that hardware devices request a service of the processor or inform the processor that a task is completed, and therefore it is a measure of the activity of hardware devices. Parking Status refers to a power management feature where a processor or processor core is in a low power state or powered off.

To start Performance Monitor and specify performance counters:

▶ **1.** Under Monitoring Tools in the console tree pane on the left side of the Performance Monitor window, click **Performance Monitor**. As shown in the Details pane on the right, Performance Monitor is already plotting values on a line graph for the % Processor Time performance counter. See Figure 9-16.

| Figure 9-16 | Performance Monitor plotting % Processor Time values |

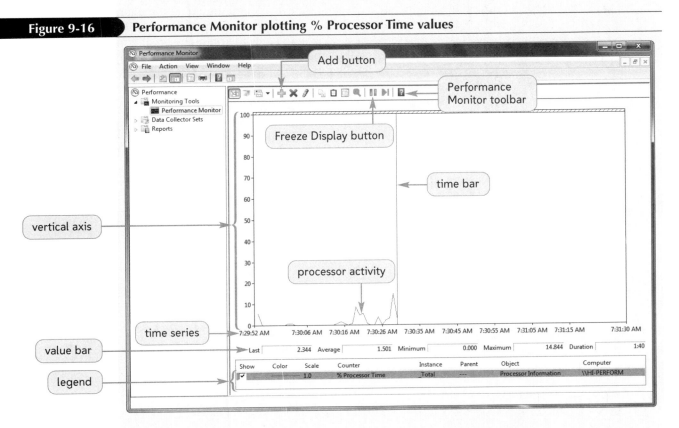

When a computer is on but not in use, processor activity is usually relatively low. The small spikes in processor activity on the computer used for this figure result from the use of a background program that captures the screen, and then saves the screen capture. Your details will differ.

In the **legend** at the bottom of the Details pane, Performance Monitor identifies the names of the counters, instances, and objects that it measures. In this case, Performance Monitor is measuring the _Total instance for the % Processor Time performance counter that in turn falls within the Processor Information performance object category. In the legend, Performance Monitor also identifies the name of the computer where it is measuring performance counters, the color code for the corresponding line that represents plotted values in the line graph, and the scale used for this performance counter. The values shown on the vertical axis (also referred to as the y-axis or value axis) on the left are scaled for the plotted values in the line graph. For example, if the % Processor Time is 100 percent, then the value plotted on the line graph matches the 100 mark on the vertical axis and indicates that the processor is working at its maximum capacity. The horizontal axis is called the Time axis and shows intervals of time. The Show check box in the legend allows you to decide whether or not you want to show the plot of a performance counter on the line graph.

The **value bar** above the legend and below the graph lists the last value, average value, minimum value, and maximum value for the performance counter you select in the legend. The value bar also shows the duration for plotting performance values. Samples are taken every second (by default), and Performance Monitor plots 100 samples for each counter on the graph (by default). Thus the duration of 1:40 represents 1 minute 40 seconds, or 100 seconds (one second for each sample). The **time bar** is the red vertical bar that slowly moves to the right as Performance Monitor samples values each second, plots those values on the graph, and adds the last, average, minimum, and maximum values for that performance counter to the value bar. After sampling 100 values, Performance Monitor plots subsequent samples starting at the left side of the line graph (replacing data already plotted on the graph), and the time bar follows the sampling of the next 100 values from left to right across the line graph.

% Processor Time measures the percentage of elapsed time that the processor spends processing instructions and data for a process. When you are not using the computer, the computer is idle, and the % Processor Time is quite low unless background programs, services, or scheduled tasks become active. If you open a resource-intensive application, % Processor Time can increase up to 100 percent momentarily or for a short period of time until the application finishes the process of loading into memory. Then % Processor Time typically drops back to a low level. When evaluating the performance of your computer, the % Processor Time performance counter is important because it is the primary indicator of processor activity.

PROSKILLS

Problem Solving: Troubleshooting High % Processor Times

If % Processor Time peaks and remains high for a short time before dropping down to an idle level, then you might be using a resource-intensive application that would work better on a computer with a newer and faster processor. If % Processor Time remains high and does not drop as you are examining the effect of a single program on your computer, then you've identified a program that is unduly burdening the processor with repeated requests for processing data. You can uninstall that program and, if necessary, replace it with a program that does not tie up the processor.

If you cannot identify a specific program as the cause of the problem, then it's time to open the system unit and clean the dust that's built up inside the system unit and around the fan. In fact, you might want to try this option before you invest valuable time trying to find that one single program that's causing high processor times. Dust buildup around the fan can prevent proper circulation of air within the system unit, and dust buildup on the system board acts as insulation to trap heat that can then damage electronic components. Check the manual that came with your computer for the proper approach for opening the system unit and reattaching it later. Also check that manual for the proper techniques for cleaning the system unit and other computer components, such as your monitor. Compressed air is a simple and straightforward way to blow dust out of the inside of a system unit without accidentally touching or damaging a component (such as RAM) on the system board.

When evaluating the performance of your computer or attempting to resolve performance problems, use % Processor Time to determine if the problem resides with overuse of the processor by a program.

Because Shuang also wants to monitor memory, disk, and page file usage on this computer, she recommends that you add the Available Bytes performance counter to measure available memory, the Committed Bytes performance counter to measure allocated memory, the Pages/sec performance counter to measure disk I/O, and the Page File Bytes performance counter to measure changes in the size of the paging file.

Now that you have given your computer time to return to an idle state, you are ready to add performance counters and monitor the performance of your computer.

To add performance counters:

1. Click the **Add** button ⊞ on the Performance Monitor Toolbar directly above the line graph (not the toolbar for the Performance Monitor window). In the Add Counters dialog box, you specify which performance counters you want to track. See Figure 9-17.

Figure 9-17 **Add Counters dialog box for selecting performance counters**

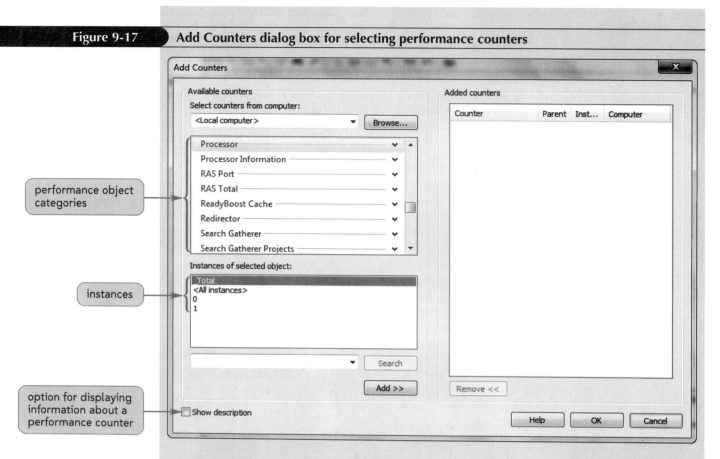

performance object categories

instances

option for displaying information about a performance counter

Under the Available counters section, you can use local computer counters or counters from a specific computer on a network. Performance Monitor also displays a list of performance object categories from which you can choose specific performance counters. Note that Performance counters are listed in alphabetical order. Because the types of performance objects depend in part on the type of software installed on a computer, your list of performance objects will differ.

Under "Instances of selected object," Performance monitor shows four instances for the currently running % Processor Time performance counter, namely Total, <All instances>, 0, and 1.

2. If <Local computer> is not displayed in the "Select counters from computer" box, click the arrow and select **<Local computer>**.

3. Below the "Select counters from computer" box, use the vertical scroll bar to locate the Memory performance object in the list of available counters, click the **expand** icon ⌄ to view a list of performance counters under the Memory performance object, adjust your view so you can see this section better, click **Available Bytes**, and then click the **Show description** check box (lower-left corner of dialog box). The Add Counters dialog box expands to show the Description section at the bottom of the dialog box. See Figure 9-18.

Figure 9-18   **Viewing information on the Available Bytes performance counter**

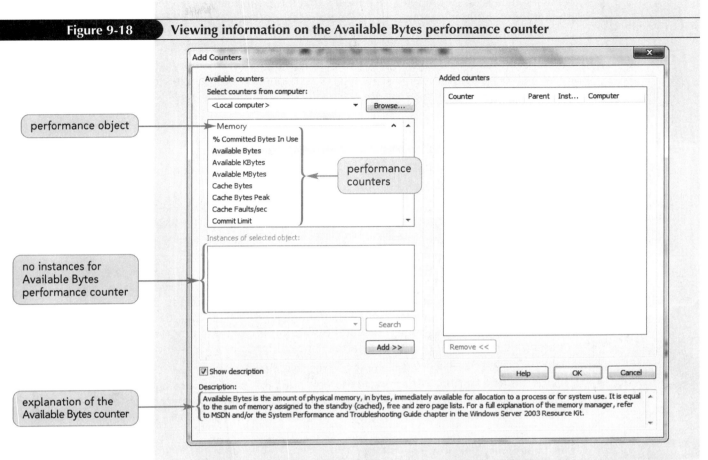

performance object

no instances for
Available Bytes
performance counter

explanation of the
Available Bytes counter

Performance Monitor explains that the Available Bytes performance counter measures the amount of physical memory in bytes that Windows 7 can immediately allocate to a process or for use by the system. Performance Monitor then provides more detail on what constitutes Available Bytes. There are no instances for this performance counter, as shown by the dimmed "Instances of select object" box.

▶ **4.** Click the **Add** button in the Add Counters dialog box. Performance Monitor lists this performance counter in the Added counters box on the right.

▶ **5.** Under Memory, locate and click **Committed Bytes**. In the Description section, Performance Monitor explains that Committed Bytes is the amount of committed virtual memory. Then it explains that committed memory is physical memory for which space has been reserved in the paging file in case it's needed. It further notes that each physical disk can have one or more paging files.

▶ **6.** Click the **Add** button. Performance Monitor adds this performance counter to the list of Added counters.

▶ **7.** Under Memory, locate and click **Pages/sec**. In the Description section, Performance Monitor explains that Pages/sec measures the number of pages read from or written to disk to resolve hard faults.

As noted earlier, a hard fault occurs when a process requires program code or data that is not in its working set or elsewhere in physical memory, and therefore must be retrieved from the paging file on disk. A working set is the physical memory allocated to and used by a process. A **page fault error (PFE)**, or **invalid page fault**, occurs when Windows 7 is unable to find data in the paging file. Performance Monitor also notes that this performance counter is the primary indicator of hard page faults that result in systemwide delays on a computer. That means that this performance counter is especially important for monitoring paging activity. Possible causes for an excessive number of hard page faults include an insufficient amount of RAM, an insufficient amount of available disk storage space, a memory conflict between two applications where one attempts to access data used by the other, a problem in translating virtual memory addresses to physical memory addresses, some other type of corruption or problem in virtual memory, or turning off or reducing the size of the paging file.

To continue to add performance counters:

1. Click the **Add** button. Performance Monitor adds the Pages/sec performance counter to the Added counters box.

2. In the list of available counters, locate the Process performance object, click the **expand** icon ✔ to view a list of performance counters under the Process performance object, locate and click **Page File Bytes**, and make sure the **_Total** instance is selected under "Instances of selected object." In the Description section, Performance Monitor notes that this performance counter measures the current amount of virtual memory in bytes that all the processes have reserved for use in the paging file. It also notes that the paging file stores pages of memory used by these processes that are not contained in other files, and that because all processes share the paging file, an insufficient amount of storage space in a paging file can interfere with the performance of other processes and their use of physical memory (or RAM).

3. Click the **Add** button. Performance Monitor adds this performance counter to the Added counters box. Note that the performance factors are organized by performance object category. See Figure 9-19.

| Figure 9-19 | Choosing memory performance counters |

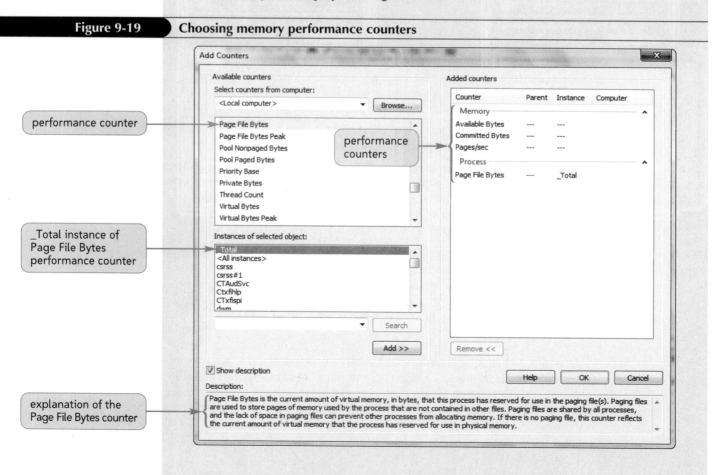

- performance counter
- _Total instance of Page File Bytes performance counter
- explanation of the Page File Bytes counter

▶ **4.** Click the **OK** button to add these counters to your performance plot. Performance Monitor now plots values for the five performance counters that you have selected.

Plotted values for some of the performance counters are not easily visible because they do not fit within the range of values shown on the vertical axis. To correct this problem, you can adjust settings for performance counters.

To examine and adjust your view of performance counters:

▶ **1.** Click the **% Processor Time** counter in the legend, and then press the **Ctrl key** and the **plus sign** key on the numeric keypad to create a best fit of the data in all the columns of the legend, and then if necessary, adjust the width of any column in the legend so you can clearly see column headings. If your keyboard does not have a numeric keypad, then you can double-click the right border of a column to adjust the column width for a best fit.

▶ **2.** Click the **Counter** column button. Performance Monitor arranges the performance counters in alphabetical order by counter name—% Processor Time, Available Bytes, Committed Bytes, Page File Bytes, and Pages/sec.

Trouble? If the performance counters are listed in descending order (reverse alphabetical order), then click the Counter column button a second time.

Trouble? If you are missing one of the five performance counters just described, use the Add button ⊞ to locate and add that performance counter to the set of performance counters that you are measuring, and then click the Counter column button to sort them in alphabetical order by Counter name.

Trouble? If the same performance counter is listed twice, Performance Monitor might produce spurious results if you do not remove one of the counters. Select one of the two performance counters, and then click the Delete button ✖ on the Performance Monitor toolbar (or press the Delete key).

▶ **3.** Click the **Highlight** button 🖉 on the Performance Monitor toolbar. Because the % Processor Time counter is selected in the legend, Performance Monitor highlights the line in the graph that contains plotted values for that counter. The Highlight button is useful not only in separating a single performance measurement from all others so you can examine just that one counter, but it also more easily displays plotted values that are represented by lines with a light color (such as yellow) that are otherwise difficult to see.

Trouble? If Performance Monitor highlights the plotted values for another counter, click the % Processor Time counter in the legend.

4. Click the **Available Bytes** counter in the legend. Performance Monitor highlights the line in the graph that contains plotted values for this counter. Because the plotted values for the Available Bytes counter lie outside the range of values represented on the vertical axis, the line for this counter appears as a dark line at the top of the graph. Note that the scaled value for this counter is 0.000001, as shown in the legend. That means that the actual values plotted on the line graph for this counter are divided by 0.000001 before being plotted on the graph. Fortunately, the value bar shows the actual value which, for example, might be close to 1,500,000,000 bytes. To determine where to plot this value on the graph, Performance Monitor multiplies the actual number of bytes by 0.000001 to produce a value in megabytes (in this example, approximately 1,500 megabytes) that is plotted on the graph. Because 100 is the highest value on the vertical axis, the plotted values do not fit within the graph.

5. Right-click the **Available Bytes** counter in the legend, and click **Scale Selected Counters** on the shortcut menu. Performance Monitor changes the scale for this plotted counter so it lies within the range of values on the vertical axis. Note that the scale for this counter is now 0.00000001 (you may have to widen the Scale column to see the entire value). Your value for the scaled counter may differ. If you examine where a plotted value intersects the vertical axis, you might, for example, come up with an estimate of 15 for Available Bytes. However, to obtain the actual number of bytes with this new scale, you have to divide 15 by 0.00000001. Your estimate would then yield a value of approximately 1,500,000,000 bytes (or approximately 1.5 GB). Again, the exact value in bytes is shown in the value bar. The Available Bytes performance counter is important because it shows the amount of RAM that remains after Windows 7 and all other device drivers and startup programs load during booting.

6. Click the **Committed Byte**s counter in the legend, notice that the plotted value lies outside the upper limit of the vertical axis, right-click the **Committed Bytes** counter in the legend, and click **Scale Selected Counters** on the shortcut menu. Performance Monitor changes the scale for this plotted counter so it lies within the range of values on the vertical axis. Committed Bytes now shows the amount of memory in use at any given point in time.

7. Click the **Page File Bytes** counter in the legend, notice that the plotted value lies outside the upper limit of the vertical axis, right-click the **Page File Bytes** counter in the legend, and click **Scale Selected Counters** on the shortcut menu. Note that the plotted values are now visible on the graph. This performance counter is important because it monitors changes in the size of the paging file.

If you want to scale more than one counter and if the counters are listed one right after the other in the legend, you click the first counter, hold down the Shift key while you click the last counter, right-click the group, and choose Scale Selected Counters. If the counters are not located one after the other, then hold down the Ctrl key while you click each counter you want to scale, right-click the group (now called a collection), and choose Scale Selected Counters.

INSIGHT

Understanding the Scaling of Plotted Values

If the scale for a counter is 1, that means the values plotted on the line graph for the counter are the actual values. You can therefore use the values on the vertical axis to estimate the actual value for a point on the line graph, such as a momentary peak in a value, and your estimated value would be very close to the actual value. For example, if the % Processor Time jumps to 80 on the vertical axis after you open an application, then the actual value for % Processor Time is 80 percent.

If the scale for a counter is 10, then the values plotted on the line graph are 10 times larger than the actual values, and you must divide the estimated value you derive from the vertical axis by 10 to determine the actual value for a measurement plotted on the line graph. For example, if you change the vertical axis so the values range from 0 to 1000, and if you notice that the % Processor Time jumps to 800 after opening an application, then the % Processor Time is actually 80 percent (800 divided by 10).

If the scale for a counter is 0.1, then the values plotted on the line graph are one-tenth of the actual values, and you must multiply the estimated value that you derive from the vertical axis by 10 to determine the actual value for a momentary peak in the line graph. For example, if the vertical axis values range from 0 to 10 and if you notice that the % Processor Time jumps to 8 after opening an application, then the % Processor Time is actually 80 percent (8 times 10).

Simpler yet, you can obtain the actual values from the value bar no matter what scale is used or use the value bar to confirm your estimated value.

Next, you are going to save your line graph with your starting performance values.

To save performance measurements:

TIP

You can also press the Ctrl+F keys to freeze or unfreeze the display.

1. Click the **Freeze Display** button ⏸ on the Performance Monitor toolbar (not the Performance Monitor window toolbar). Performance Monitor stops plotting counter values so you can save the data, analyze the data, select different performance counters in the legend, and examine the details of each measurement in the value bar. Once you click the Freeze Display button it becomes the Unfreeze Display button ▷.

2. Right-click the **line graph**, click **Save Image As** on the shortcut menu, and if necessary, click the **Browse Folders** button ⊙ in the Save As dialog box to display the Navigation pane. Note that your performance measurements will be saved as an image file with the .gif file extension.

3. Locate and click your **flash drive** in the Navigation pane and navigate to the Tutorial.09\Tutorial folder, type **Initial Performance Measurements** in the File name box, and then click the **Save** button.

4. Click the **Unfreeze Display** button ▷ on the Performance Monitor toolbar. Performance Monitor resumes plotting counter values.

Now you have a record of baseline values for specific performance counters on your computer. Baseline values are important so you have a sense of the current state and performance level of the computer after booting or at the point in time where you start measuring the performance of the computer. Before you start the next set of steps, wait a short time for your computer to idle down and for performance counters to return closer to the levels they were before you saved the performance data. You can check the plotted values, and when they do not change or change only slightly, you are ready to continue.

Shuang recommends that you examine each of these performance counters so you have an idea of the level of processor activity when your computer is idle, how your computer uses memory, and the level of disk activity when your computer is idle.

To examine information on specific counters:

1. Click **% Processor Time** in the legend, click the **Freeze Display** button ⏸, and then examine the Maximum value for % Processor Time in the value bar. That is the highest value for % Processor Time, and if your computer has been idle, then that value will likely be under 5 percent. If it's much higher and does not drop, then you've identified a program (such as a background program) that's forcing the processor to stay busy.

2. Click the **Available Bytes** counter in the legend, and then examine the last reported value for this performance counter in the value bar. If you convert this value to gigabytes, then you have an estimate of the amount of RAM that is available after starting the computer, opening Performance Monitor, and adding performance counters. That also makes it easier for you to compare it with the total amount of RAM installed in your computer.

3. Click the **Committed Bytes** counter in the legend, and then examine the last reported value for this performance counter in the value bar. If you also convert this value to gigabytes, then you have the amount of memory that is in use after starting the computer, opening Performance Monitor, and adding performance counters.

4. Click the **Page File Bytes** counter in the legend, and then examine the last reported value for this performance counter in the value bar. If you also convert this value to gigabytes, then you have an estimate of the amount of storage space used in the paging file by all processes. For best performance, Windows 7 should not be using more than 70 percent of the paging file.

5. Click the **Pages/sec** counter in the legend area. When your computer is idle, and you are not opening any programs or files, you expect no disk activity. If you see a lot of disk activity, then your hard disk drive might be too slow in handling paging.

6. Click the **Unfreeze Display** button ▷ to resume plotting performance data.

Typically, you check these baseline values after you boot your computer so you can capture information on performance counters and thereby be able to evaluate the performance of your computer as you continue to work or as you troubleshoot problems.

Now you're ready to evaluate the performance of this computer by opening and then closing a program on your computer. Again, before you start the next set of steps, wait a minute for the performance data on the computer that you are using to "quiet down."

To monitor the performance of your computer as you open an application:

1. To clear the plotted performance data, right-click the **graph**, and then click **Clear**. If you clear the graph before performing another operation, then the values shown for the performance counters in the value bar relate to that new operation.

2. Click the **% Processor Time** counter in the legend.

3. Open **Microsoft Word** or another application on your computer (preferably one you depend on), click the **Performance Monitor** taskbar button to redisplay that window in the foreground, wait a few seconds for % Processor Time and Pages/sec to return to levels close to the previously displayed levels, and then click the **Freeze Display** button ▌▌.

Performance Monitor shows changes in all the performance counters after you opened the program. See Figure 9-20.

| Figure 9-20 | Viewing an increase in % Processor Time after opening Word |

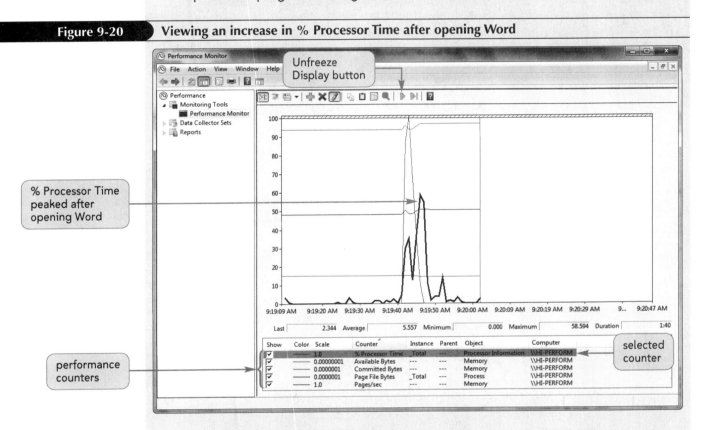

The second and higher of the two peaks on the graph corresponds to opening the Microsoft Word application.

4. On the graph, point to the **peak of processor activity**. Performance Monitor displays a ToolTip that identifies the performance counter, the value, and the time and date of the measurement. See Figure 9-21.

Figure 9-21 | **Viewing information about a plotted value for % Processor Time**

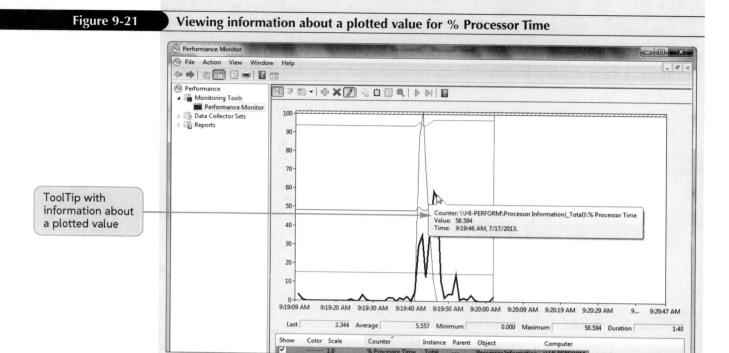

ToolTip with information about a plotted value

As shown by the information in the ToolTip and the Maximum value in the value bar on the computer used for this figure, % Processor Time spiked at 58.594 percent during the time when the processor was busy with the loading of Microsoft Word. Your details will differ. This spike in processor activity is higher the first time you open an application and then smaller when you reopen it later, indicating that some of the program code was already cached (or stored) in memory for possible use later. % Processor Time should drop and return to a low level after a program is loaded into memory.

If % Processor Time does not drop after loading a program, then you've identified a problem with that particular program affecting the performance of your computer.

5. Click the **Pages/sec** counter in the legend and examine the line graph. On the computer used for Figure 9-22, there was a large spike in disk activity (or disk I/O) as Windows 7 loaded Microsoft Word from disk into memory.

| Figure 9-22 | Viewing increased disk I/O when opening Microsoft Word |

Pages/sec peaked
after opening Word

selected counter

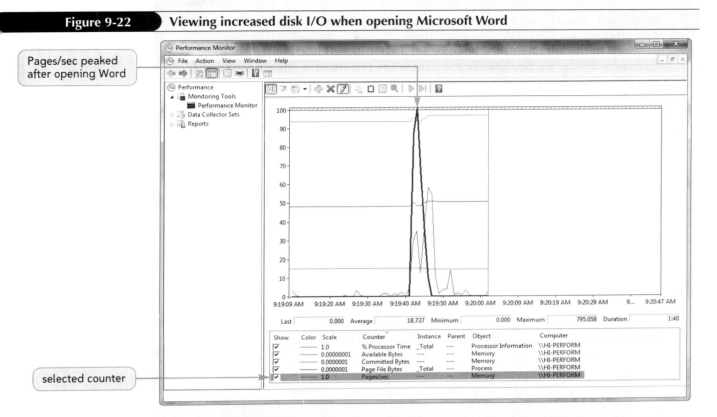

As shown in the value bar for the computer used for this figure, the peak in disk
I/O reached a maximum value of 795.058 pages per second on the computer used
for this figure, and then disk I/O dropped to 0 pages per second. Your details will
differ. If you had plotted Page Reads/sec and Page Writes/sec, then you would
discover that the vast majority of these Pages accessed per second correlated with
reading Microsoft Word from disk.

6. Click the **Committed Bytes** counter in the legend, and examine the graph and
value bar. To determine the change in memory usage, point to the "before" and
the "after" plot of committed bytes in the graph, and examine the information in
the ToolTip.

On the computer used for Figure 9-23, the amount of memory in use after loading Microsoft Word increased from approximately 894 MB to a maximum value
of 927 MB (a gain of 33 MB) because Windows 7 allocated memory to Microsoft
Word. The peak of processor activity coincided with the increase in memory
usage. Your details will differ.

Figure 9-23 **Viewing an increase in memory usage after opening Word**

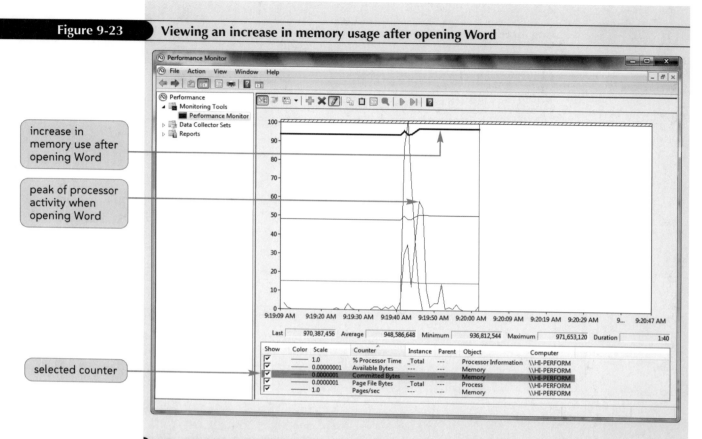

increase in memory use after opening Word

peak of processor activity when opening Word

selected counter

7. Click the **Available Bytes** counter in the legend, and examine the graph and value bar.

On the computer used for Figure 9-24, the amount of available memory after loading Microsoft Word decreased from 1.41 GB to 1.36 GB (a decrease of approximately 44 MB) because less RAM is available after Windows 7 allocated memory to Microsoft Word. The drop in memory occurred at the peak of processor activity when opening Word. Your details will differ.

Figure 9-24   Viewing a decrease in available memory after opening Word

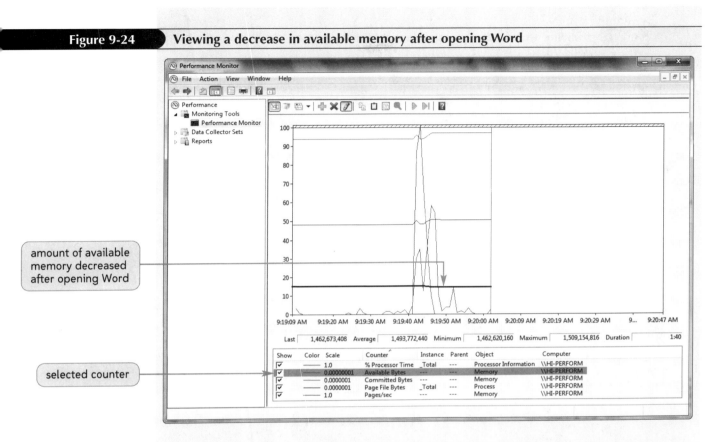

amount of available memory decreased after opening Word

selected counter

8. Click the **Page File Bytes** counter in the legend, and examine the graph and value bar. On the computer used for Figure 9-25, the amount of storage space used in the paging file after loading Microsoft Word increased from 460 MB to approximately 483 MB (a gain of 23 MB). Your details will differ.

Figure 9-25 | **Viewing an increase in page file usage after opening Word**

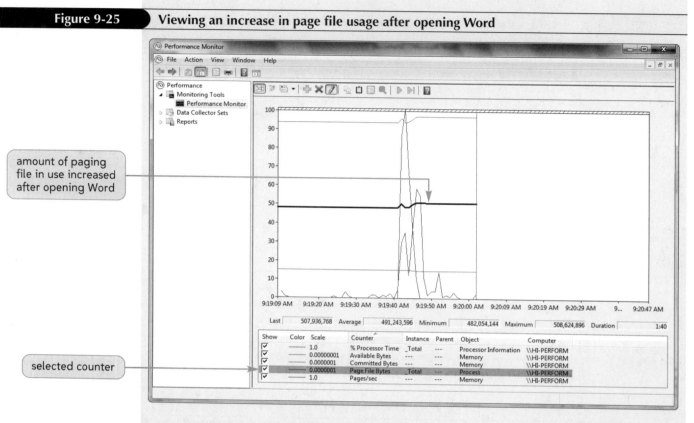

amount of paging file in use increased after opening Word

selected counter

That means data in RAM was swapped to the paging file to optimize the use of memory for Microsoft Word. Note also that the plotted values for Page File Bytes produce the same pattern as the plotted values for Committed Bytes. That indicates you are seeing a corresponding change in Committed Bytes and Page File Bytes, both of which report on usage of virtual memory.

Next, you want to save your graph with a record of performance values after opening Microsoft Word.

To save performance measurements:

1. Right-click the **line graph**, click **Save Image As** on the shortcut menu, navigate to the Tutorial.09\Tutorial folder, type **After Opening Microsoft Word** in the File name box, and then click the **Save** button.

Next, you'll close Microsoft Word and then examine changes in each of these five performance counters so you can evaluate how Windows 7 reclaims and handles these valuable resources.

To monitor the performance of your computer as you close an application:

▶ **1.** Click the **Unfreeze Display** button ▷ on the Performance Monitor toolbar to resume plotting performance counters.

▶ **2.** Right-click the **Microsoft Word** taskbar button (or the taskbar button for the application you opened), click **Close window** on the program Jump List, click **% Processor Time** in the legend, wait for several more seconds so Performance Monitor can plot the changes that just occurred, and then click the **Freeze Display** button ❚❚.

On the computer used for Figure 9-26, % Processor Time recorded a smaller spike of processor activity than what occurred when opening Microsoft Word. This spike reached a maximum value of 19.531 percent as compared to 58.594 percent when opening Microsoft Word. Your details will differ.

| Figure 9-26 | Viewing processor activity after closing Word |

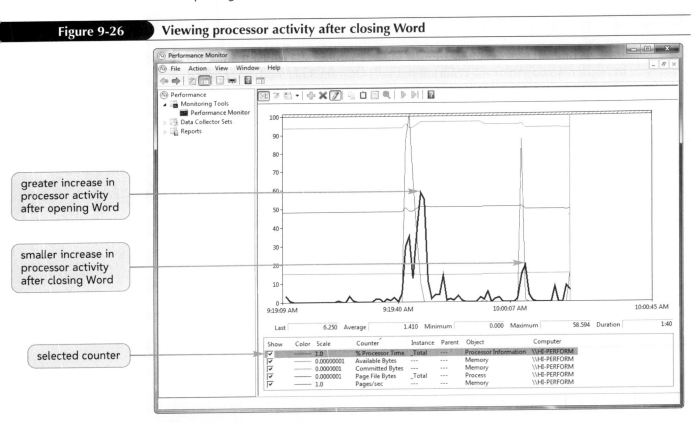

greater increase in processor activity after opening Word

smaller increase in processor activity after closing Word

selected counter

▶ **3.** Click the **Pages/sec** counter in the legend, and examine the graph and value bar. On the computer used for Figure 9-27, Pages/sec showed a smaller spike in disk activity as Microsoft Word closed. Pages/sec spiked at 87.005 Pages/sec as compared to 795.058 Pages/sec when opening Microsoft Word. Your details will differ. Less disk I/O is required for closing this program.

Figure 9-27 **Viewing disk I/O after closing Microsoft Word**

far more disk I/O when opening Word

Pages/sec resulted in less disk I/O after closing Word

selected counter

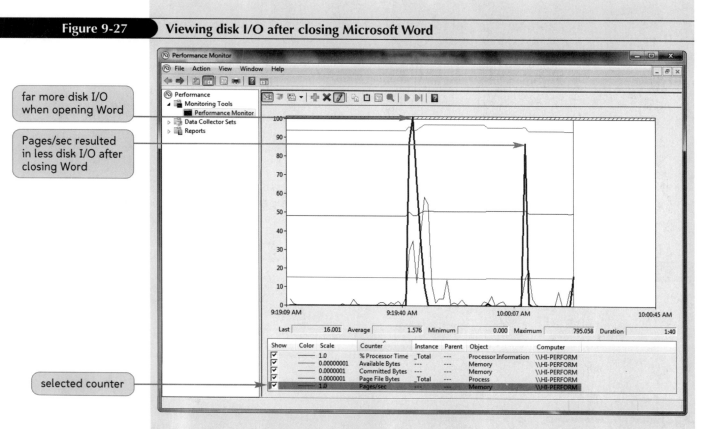

> **4.** Click the **Committed Bytes** counter in the legend, and examine the graph and value bar. On the computer used for Figure 9-28, the amount of memory in use decreased in two stages from 927 MB to approximately 893 MB for an overall decrease of 34 MB after closing Microsoft Word, and then was adjusted again shortly thereafter. Your details will differ.

Figure 9-28   **Viewing a decrease in memory usage after closing Word**

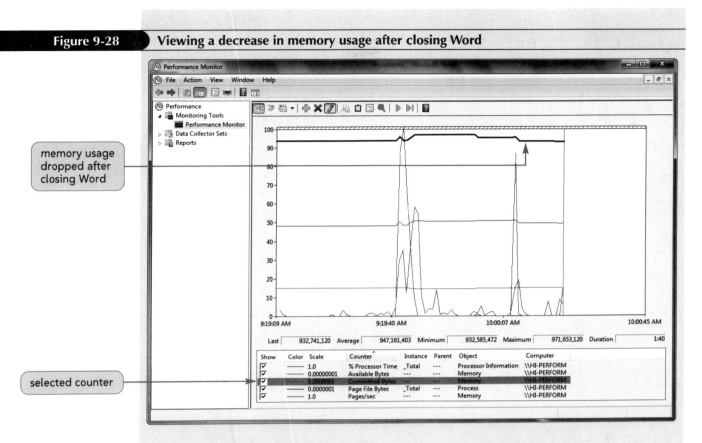

memory usage dropped after closing Word

selected counter

▶ **5.** Click the **Available Bytes** counter in the legend, and examine the line graph and value bar. On this same computer, the amount of available memory increased from 1.36 GB to 1.40 GB (a gain of 39.5 MB) after closing Microsoft Word. Your details will differ.

▶ **6.** Click the **Page File Bytes** counter in the legend, and examine the line graph and value bar. On the computer used for Figure 9-29, the amount of used storage space in the paging file decreased from 581 MB to approximately 538 MB (a decrease of 43 MB) after closing Microsoft Word. Your details will differ. Again note that the plotted values for Page File Bytes follows the same pattern as for Committed Bytes.

Figure 9-29 | **Viewing a decrease in page file usage after closing Word**

decrease in page file usage after closing Word

selected counter

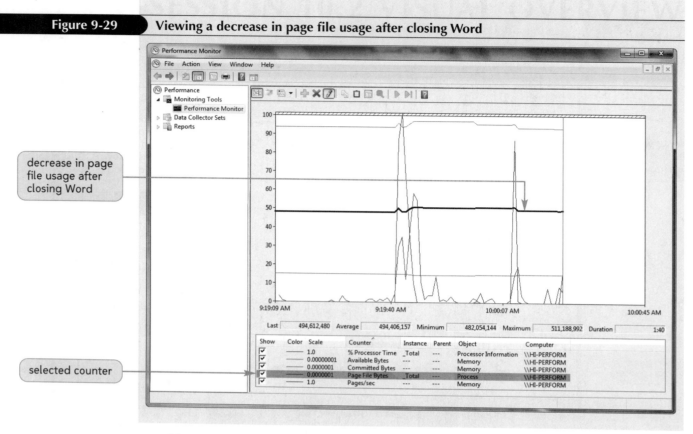

Next, you are going to save your graph so you have a record of performance values after closing Microsoft Word.

To save performance measurements:

▶ **1.** Click the **% Processor Time** counter in the legend.

▶ **2.** Right-click the **line graph**, click **Save Image As** on the shortcut menu, navigate to the Tutorial.09\Tutorial folder, type **After Closing Microsoft Word** in the File name box, and then click the **Save** button.

▶ **3.** Click the **Unfreeze Display** button on the Performance Monitor toolbar, and then close the Performance Monitor window.

Next, you will view and print two of the files that contain information about the performance of your computer after opening and closing Microsoft Word. Although you can open different applications to print the image files that contain a view of your graphs, you are going to use Paint in the following steps because the image files have the .gif file extension. Plus, Paint is included with the Windows 7 accessories and therefore is available on all computers.

To view and print performance measurements:

▶ **1.** Open a Computer window, and then open a window onto your flash drive.

▶ **2.** Navigate to the Tutorial.09\Tutorial folder, right-click **After Opening Microsoft Word.gif**, point to **Open with**, notice that you can open this file type in several different programs (including Internet Explorer, though the programs may vary from one computer to another), and then click **Paint**. Paint displays the contents of the image file.

▶ **3.** Click the **Paint menu** button to the left of the Home tab, point to **Print**, click **Page setup** in the right pane, click the **Landscape option** button under Orientation in the Page Setup dialog box (if it is not already selected), and then click the **OK** button.

▶ **4.** Click the **Paint menu** button, point to **Print**, and then click **Print preview**. Now that you switched to Landscape orientation, your graph will print on one page.

▶ **5.** Click the **Print** button on the Print Preview toolbar, verify that you have chosen the correct printer in the Print dialog box, and then click the **Print** button in the Print dialog box.

▶ **6.** Click the **Paint menu** button, click **Open**, navigate to the Tutorial.09\ Tutorial folder, and open the **After Closing Microsoft Word.gif** file.

▶ **7.** Click the **Paint menu** button, click **Print preview** to examine this image, click the **Print** button on the Print Preview tab, and then click the **Print** button in the Print dialog box.

▶ **8.** Close the Paint application window.

▶ **9.** If requested by your instructor, submit your printed or file copies of the Initial Performance Measurements.gif, After Opening Microsoft Word.gif, and After Closing Microsoft Word.gif image files.

If you compare the results for the performance counters after opening and then after closing Microsoft Word, you can determine whether Windows 7 was able to reclaim all of the memory allocated to Microsoft Word. If not, then you have a memory leak. Figure 9-30 shows the initial performance measurements on memory usage and the performance measurements on memory usage after opening and after closing Microsoft Word.

Figure 9-30 Comparing changes in memory usage

Memory Usage	Available Bytes	Committed Bytes	Page File Bytes
Initial Performance Measurements	1.41 GB	894 MB	460 MB
After Opening Microsoft Word	1.36 GB	927 MB	483 MB
After Closing Microsoft Word	1.40 GB	893 MB	538 MB

Available memory dropped from 1.41 GB to 1.36 GB after opening Microsoft Word. After closing Microsoft Word, available memory increased to 1.40 GB. That means that 0.01 GB (or 10.24 MB) of RAM was not reclaimed. After closing Microsoft Word, the value for Available Bytes should have returned to its original level prior to opening Microsoft Word; however, that did not occur. Therefore, Windows 7 did not completely reclaim all the memory used by this application. However, the next time you open Microsoft Word or another Office application during that same computer session, that application opens faster, so the program code that remained in memory proves useful.

By monitoring Committed Bytes and Available Memory, you can determine how much memory Windows 7 needs after booting and how much is still available for exclusive use with the current application. You can observe the demands on memory by the types of applications that you use and by the way you work (multitasking versus single task-ing). This information gives you a baseline value (or values) for the amount of memory that Windows 7 needs as you work on your computer. You can use this baseline value to decide whether to add more RAM to your computer, to estimate how much you might need to meet the most demanding applications that you use, and to handle multitasking of resource-intensive applications.

If Performance Monitor continually reports a high value for the Pages/sec performance counter, a memory or disk bottleneck might be degrading the performance of your computer. You can close application and folder windows you no longer use, turn off features that you use in applications (such as optional add-ons), or move the paging file to another disk with more space, less disk activity, and/or a faster speed. Because all pro-cesses share the paging file, Windows 7 might not be able to allocate memory to other processes if it cannot expand the size of the paging file when needed. You might need to add more physical memory (more RAM) to your computer to reduce the amount of pag-ing that occurs—paging that also makes excessive demands of your hard disk.

Furthermore, you should monitor the performance of your computer before you encounter problems so you know how resources are allocated from one session to the next, and from one way of working to another (such as multitasking versus single task-ing), so if problems develop, you can monitor the performance of your computer and compare its current performance to times when those problems did not occur.

Other useful options on the Performance Monitor toolbar include the following:

- **Change graph type button** [icon] ▼—The default graph type is Line, but you can use this toolbar button to switch to Histogram bar or Report. The Histogram bar displays the magnitude of values by the height of vertical bars. One nice feature of the Histogram bar is that you can visually see rapid changes in measurements for performance coun-ters (i.e., vertical column bars fluctuating rapidly in size and appearing and disappear-ing). The Report option displays the current values for performance counters, as shown in Figure 9-31. If you press the Ctrl+G keys, the keyboard shortcut for the Change graph type button, you can quickly switch between different graph types.

Viewing performance counters in Report view

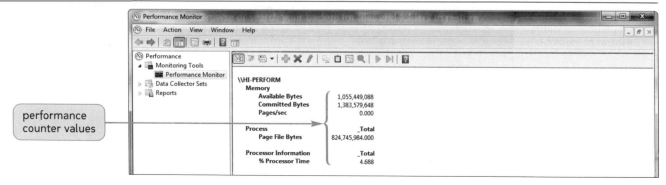

performance counter values

- **Properties button** ▣—You can use the Properties button to open the Performance Monitor Properties dialog box and customize your use of Performance Monitor. For example, you can specify which elements (such as the legend, value bar, or toolbar) you want to display, what you want to report for Report and Histogram data (default value, current value, minimum value, maximum value, or average value), whether to sample automatically, how frequently the sample occurs (in seconds), the duration of the sampling (in seconds), and whether you want to log (or copy) performance data to a file. You can also specify a minimum and maximum value for the vertical scale axis, specify the use of vertical and horizontal grids, specify the use of vertical scale numbers and time axis labels, specify colors for the graph background, choose fonts, and choose a border. You can also specify the line color, scale, line width, and line style for each performance counter. You can press the Ctrl+Q keys to quickly open the Performance Monitor Properties dialog box.
- **Update Data button** ▶|—If you freeze the display, you can use the Update Data button, or press the Ctrl+U keys, to manually plot one sample at a time.
- **Delete button** ✖—If you select a counter in the legend, then you can use this button to remove that counter from your graph.

REFERENCE

Using Performance Monitor to Track Performance

- Open the Start menu, point to Administrative Tools, click Performance Monitor, and after the Performance Monitor window opens, click the Performance Monitor node in the console tree pane.
- If you want to remove any existing performance counters, select each of those performance counters in the legend, and then click the Delete button on the Performance Monitor toolbar.
- If you want to add performance counters, click the Add button on the Performance Monitor toolbar to open the Add Counters dialog box, or right-click the graph, and click Add Counters.
- Select the option to use either local computer counters or counters for a specific computer on your network.
- From the list of Available counters, locate and click the expand icon for a Performance object.
- Locate and select the counter you want to use and, if necessary, locate and select the instance you want to measure from the "Instances of selected object" box.
- To view information about a performance counter, click the Show Description check box.
- Click the Add button to add the performance counter to the Added counters box.
- Repeat this process for each counter you want to use, and then click OK in the Add Counters dialog box.
- To focus on performance measurements for a specific counter, select that counter in the legend area or by clicking on its line in the line graph.
- If you want to highlight a specific performance counter in the graph, click the performance counter in the legend, and then click the Highlight button. Click the Highlight button a second time if you want to turn off the highlight.
- If you want to save the graph, click the Freeze Display button, right-click the graph, click Save Image As on the shortcut menu, select the drive and folder in the Save As dialog box where you want to save the performance information, type a filename in the File name box, and then click Save.
- Click the Unfreeze Display button again to view further updates to the graph.
- When you have finished your performance measurements, close the Performance Monitor window.

You can use one of the following paths to create a desktop shortcut for the Performance Monitor window: *%systemroot%\System32\perfmon.exe* or *%windir%\ System32\perfmon.exe*. In the Performance Monitor window, you can then select Performance Monitor in the console tree pane. To open Performance Monitor in stand-alone mode (in other words, in a window by itself), you can use one of the following paths for the desktop shortcut: *%systemroot%\System32\perfmon.exe /sys* or *%windir%\System32\perfmon.exe /sys*.

Then you're ready to add performance counters and start monitoring your computer.

Performance Monitor is a powerful tool for analyzing nearly every aspect of the performance of your computer. Because of the extensive number of performance counters and the ways that you can combine these performance counters to evaluate your computer, you could develop a career devoted exclusively to performance monitoring of computers.

Using Resource and Performance Monitor to Examine Memory Performance

In the first part of the tutorial, you used Resource and Performance Monitor to create a system health report to identify any potential problem with the performance or security of your computer and to also produce a detailed analysis so you could then further research potential problems. As part of the system health report, Resource and Performance Monitor also provides information on the current memory usage by reporting on the values of key performance counters.

Shuang asks you to create another system health report, and then she evaluates the information on memory usage with you.

To complete the following steps, you must provide Administrator credentials. If you are not logged on under an Administrator account or cannot provide the password for an Administrator account, read the following steps and examine the figures so you are familiar with the use of Resource and Performance Monitor, but do not keystroke the steps.

To create a system health report:

1. Right-click the **Computer** desktop icon, click **Properties**, click the **Performance Information and Tools** link, click the **Advanced tools** link, click the **Generate a system health report** link, provide Administrator credentials (if necessary), maximize the Resource and Performance Monitor window, and wait for the System Diagnostics Report.

2. Locate and click the **expand** icon ⊗ for the Memory section, click the **expand** icon ⊗ for the Counters section, and then adjust your view so you can see the details on the memory performance counters as shown in Figure 9-32.

| Figure 9-32 | Viewing memory performance data |

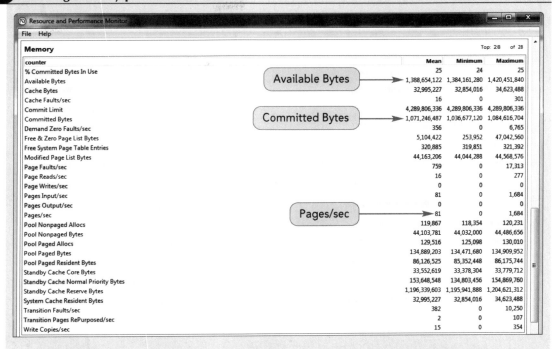

The Counter column includes the Available Bytes, Committed Bytes, and Pages/sec performance counters that you used with Performance Monitor as well as many other memory performance counters. The System Diagnostics Report also provides the mean, minimum, and maximum value for each of these memory performance counters.

The maximum value for Committed Bytes is 1,084,616,704 (or 1.01 GB) of memory currently in use. The minimum value for Available Bytes is 1,384,161,280 (or 1.28 GB) of memory available for use. Disk I/O ranges from 0 to 1,684 pages per second. Cache Bytes is the amount of memory set aside for storing pages read from disk and kept in the cache in case you need the data in these pages later. That in turn obviates the need for reading the pages from disk again (and again). Page Faults/sec, which ranges from 0 to 17,313, measures the number of requests for pages from either disk or physical memory. Your details will differ.

3. Right-click the **background** of the System Diagnostics Report that contains the Memory performance counters, and then click **Print Preview** on the short-cut menu. Print Preview displays the first of three pages for this report. See Figure 9-33. Your print preview may differ.

| Figure 9-33 | Previewing the first page of the System Diagnostics Report |

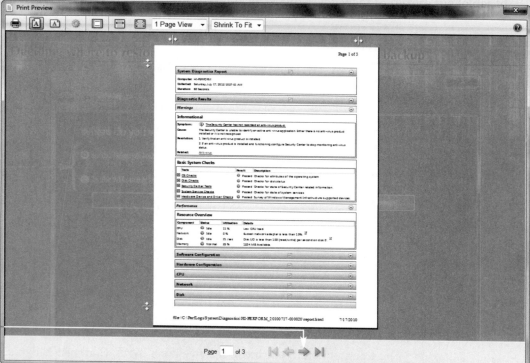

Next Page button

▶ **4.** Click the **Next Page** button ➡ to the right of the Page box on the status bar. The next page of this report contains the information on Memory Performance counters at the time you produced the System Diagnostics Report. You can print this report or you can return to the System Diagnostics Report.

▶ **5.** Close the Print Preview window, close the Resource and Performance Monitor window, and then close the Advanced Tools window.

When you right-click the Memory performance counter results in Resource and Performance Monitor, the shortcut menu may also contain an "Export to Microsoft Excel" option that copies the Memory performance counters and their mean, minimum, and maximum values to a new Microsoft Excel spreadsheet so you can analyze the data further. Figure 9-34 shows an Excel spreadsheet with performance data for performance counters exported from the Resource and Performance Monitor's System Diagnostics Report.

| Figure 9-34 | Viewing exported performance data in an Excel spreadsheet |

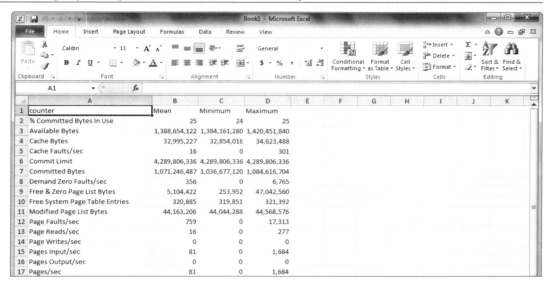

	A	B	C	D
1	counter	Mean	Minimum	Maximum
2	% Committed Bytes In Use	25	24	25
3	Available Bytes	1,388,654,122	1,384,161,280	1,420,451,840
4	Cache Bytes	32,995,227	32,854,016	34,623,488
5	Cache Faults/sec	16	0	301
6	Commit Limit	4,289,806,336	4,289,806,336	4,289,806,336
7	Committed Bytes	1,071,246,487	1,036,677,120	1,084,616,704
8	Demand Zero Faults/sec	356	0	6,765
9	Free & Zero Page List Bytes	5,104,422	253,952	47,042,560
10	Free System Page Table Entries	320,885	319,851	321,392
11	Modified Page List Bytes	44,163,206	44,044,288	44,568,576
12	Page Faults/sec	759	0	17,313
13	Page Reads/sec	16	0	277
14	Page Writes/sec	0	0	0
15	Pages Input/sec	81	0	1,684
16	Pages Output/sec	0	0	0
17	Pages/sec	81	0	1,684

In Figure 9-34, note that the column headings from the Resource and Monitor Performance window are listed on the first row, and that the data for each performance counter is listed in columns on a different row.

REFERENCE

Using the System Diagnostics Report to Examine Memory Performance Counters

- Right-click the Computer desktop icon (or Computer on the Start menu), click Properties, click the Performance Information and Tools link in the System window, click the Advanced tools link, click the Generate a system health report link, provide Administrator credentials, maximize the Resource and Performance Monitor window, and wait for Resource and Performance Monitor to produce the System Diagnostics Report.
- Locate and click the expand icon for the Memory section, click the expand icon for the Counters section, and then adjust your view so you can examine the memory performance counters.
- If you want to preview and then print the current view of the System Diagnostics Report, right-click the background of the System Diagnostics Report, click Print Preview on the shortcut menu, and examine the preview in the Print Preview window. Click the Print Document button on the Print Preview toolbar to print the report, or close the window to return to the System Diagnostics Report.
- If you want to copy the Memory performance counters and their mean, minimum, and maximum values to a new Microsoft Excel spreadsheet so you can analyze the data further, right-click the background of the System Diagnostics Report, and then click the "Export to Microsoft Excel" option.
- Close the Resource and Performance Monitor window, and then close the Advanced tools window.

The System Diagnostics Report is a snapshot of your computer at a specific point in time. If you are experiencing problems with your computer, such as a slow response time, you can produce a new System Diagnostics Report so you can examine memory usage and check for any other types of problems that Resource and Performance Monitor might report.

Using ReadyBoost with SuperFetch

When you purchase a flash drive, the product label might note that the flash drive is *Enhanced for Windows ReadyBoost*. **Windows ReadyBoost** is a Windows 7 (and Windows Vista) technology that uses high-speed storage space on a flash drive to boost the performance of your computer by storing cached data on the flash drive, including the paging file. Accessing and loading cached data on a flash drive is far faster than accessing and loading it from a slower hard disk drive. The cached data on the flash drive is backed up by the paging file on the hard disk, so if you remove the flash drive, then Windows 7 reverts back to using the paging file.

ReadyBoost can improve the performance of computers with 2 GB or less of RAM. ReadyBoost can also improve the performance of computers with slower hard disk drives that have a Windows Experience Index (WEI) subscore of less than 4.0.

When you insert a flash drive, a secure digital (SD) memory card, or a CF (CompactFlash) memory card with more than 256 MB of memory in a computer, Windows 7 will check the device to determine if all or a part of the storage space on the flash drive is fast enough to support Windows ReadyBoost. If so, it displays an AutoPlay dialog box similar to the one shown in Figure 9-35 with the "Speed up my system" option.

Figure 9-35 **Option for boosting performance with Windows ReadyBoost**

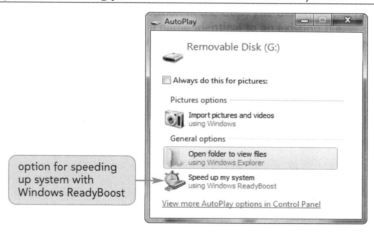

option for speeding up system with Windows ReadyBoost

If you select the "Speed up my system" option, then Windows 7 opens the Properties dialog box for the flash drive and displays the ReadyBoost property sheet, as shown in Figure 9-36. You can specify whether to use this flash drive to speed up your system by using storage space on the flash drive and, if so, then you can use the amount of available space recommended by Windows 7, or you can specify how much space to reserve for optimizing the speed of your system. Windows 7 supports the use of up to eight ReadyBoost flash drives simultaneously on a computer, and supports ReadyBoost flash drives with more than 4 GB of storage. The ReadyBoost cache cannot exceed 4 GB on ReadyBoost drives that use FAT32 and cannot exceed 32 GB on ReadyBoost drives that use NTFS. Microsoft recommends that you set aside at least 1 GB of available space before ReadyBoost can effectively speed up your computer.

On the computer used for Figure 9-36, Windows recommends that 4,094 MB (or almost 4 GB) of the 16 GB of storage space be used for a ReadyBoost cache. If you need more storage space for files on the flash drive, you can adjust the amount of space you want to reserve for the ReadyBoost cache on the ReadyBoost property sheet. However, as noted on the ReadyBoost property sheet, any extra storage space on the flash drive is not available for storing files if the flash device is currently used to optimize system speed.

Figure 9-36	Options for adjusting Windows ReadyBoost settings

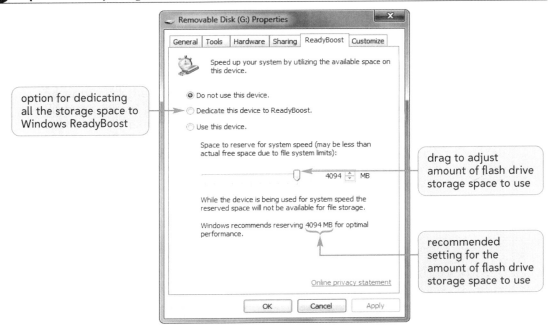

option for dedicating all the storage space to Windows ReadyBoost

drag to adjust amount of flash drive storage space to use

recommended setting for the amount of flash drive storage space to use

The "Dedicate this device to ReadyBoost" option uses the maximum available space on a flash drive or memory card that supports this feature. If your flash drive uses a combination of slow and fast memory, you may not be able to use all of the storage space on your flash drive for ReadyBoost.

Once you enable ReadyBoost, you will see a ReadyBoost Cache File with the filename ReadyBoost.sfcache on the flash drive when you view its contents. See Figure 9-37. The abbreviation *sf* stands for SuperFetch, a related technology described below.

Figure 9-37	Viewing the ReadyBoost cache file on a flash drive

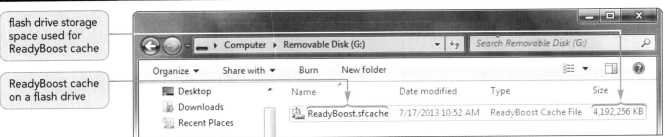

flash drive storage space used for ReadyBoost cache

ReadyBoost cache on a flash drive

The ReadyBoost cache created on the flash drive is specific to the computer that you used to enable this feature. However, you can remove the flash drive and use it on other computers to store files on that portion of the flash drive not used by the Windows ReadyBoost.sfcache file. Furthermore, the data stored on the flash drive by ReadyBoost is encrypted so other computers cannot read the data, and thereby your privacy is protected.

If you have a computer with a solid-state drive (SSD) for the hard disk, and if you attach a flash drive or flash memory card, then you may see a message to the effect that ReadyBoost is not enabled because the system disk (i.e., the hard disk) is fast enough that ReadyBoost would not provide any additional benefits.

SuperFetch, another Windows 7 (and Windows Vista) technology, monitors which system files, programs, and document files you use; the frequency with which you use those files; and the dates and times you use those files over a period of time in order to determine how you use your computer. Then, it preloads those programs so they are available when you need them. That also means that it can preload different applications on different days of the week and weekend so the appropriate programs are available to you.

SuperFetch performs another important function. If your computer is idle, system background processes (such as SearchIndexer) become active, and Windows 7 swaps your open applications and programs to the paging file. Once background processes complete their operations, then SuperFetch quickly restores your applications and programs from the paging file to RAM so they are ready for you to use. SuperFetch is also responsible for determining what data to cache to a flash drive (or flash drives) that support ReadyBoost.

Restoring Your Computer

If you are working in a computer lab, or if you want to restore your desktop computer to the settings that existed prior to working on this tutorial, complete the following steps.

To restore your computer's settings:

1. To remove Administrative Tools from the Start menu, right-click the **Start** button, click **Properties**, and on the Start Menu property sheet, click the **Customize** button, scroll to the bottom of the list of options for customizing the Start menu, and under System administrative tools, click the **Don't display this item** option button, click the **OK** button to close the Customize Start Menu dialog box, and then click the **OK** button to close the Taskbar and Start Menu Properties dialog box.

2. If necessary, use the Folder Options dialog box to restore double-click activation and not display hidden folders, files, and protected operating system files, and then remove the Computer icon from the desktop.

REVIEW

Session 9.2 Quick Check

1. What is the difference between a performance object and a performance counter?
2. A(n) _____ allows you to sample a performance counter in a specific way.
3. A(n) _____ is the physical memory allocated to and used by a single process or program.
4. What performance counter is the primary indicator of processor activity?
5. What performance counter is the primary indicator of hard page faults?
6. Name three ways in which memory usage changes when you open a program.
7. _____ is a Windows 7 feature that uses the high-speed storage space on a flash drive to improve the performance of your computer by caching frequently used data.
8. Windows 7's _____ feature keeps track of which programs and files you use and preloads them into RAM so they are available when you need them.

Practice the skills you learned in the tutorial using the same case scenario.

PRACTICE

Review Assignments

There are no Data Files needed for the Review Assignments.

In preparation for an upcoming staff training session on optimizing memory usage on a laptop, Shuang asks you to evaluate the performance of a laptop she recently acquired, and then prepare an analysis of its performance that she will use as background information in that training session.

As you complete each step in the Review Assignments, record your answers to the questions so you can submit them to your instructor. Use a word-processing application such as Microsoft Word or the WordPad accessory to prepare your answers to these questions. If you change any settings on the computer you are using, make a note of the original settings so you can restore them later. Complete the following steps:

1. If necessary, display a Computer icon on the desktop, enable single-click activation, display hidden files and folders, display protected operating system files, and display Administrative Tools on the Start menu.

2. Attach a flash drive to the computer and, if necessary, close any dialog boxes or windows that open.

3. Open a Computer window onto the drive that contains your computer's paging file, switch to Details view (if necessary), and then select and examine information about the paging file using the Details pane. What is the name of the paging file? What type of file is the paging file? How large is the paging file? What drive contains the paging file? Is that drive the boot volume or the system volume, or both? Close the Computer window.

4. Open the Virtual Memory dialog box so that you can examine your virtual memory settings. Does Windows 7 manage the paging file or have you (or someone else) set a custom initial size and maximum size, and if so, what are these sizes? On what drive is the paging file located? What is the recommended and currently allocated size of the paging file? What other drives, if any, are available on your computer for creating paging files? Use the Cancel button to close the Virtual Memory, Performance Options, and System Properties dialog box without making changes to your computer. Then close the System window.

5. Right-click the taskbar, select the option for starting Windows Task Manager, and then select its Performance sheet (if necessary). What is the total physical memory on your computer? What percent of that memory is in use? How much of that memory is cached, and how much is free? How much memory is currently available? What is the current size of the paging file, and what is the total possible page file size on your computer?

6. Open a resource-intensive application, such as Internet Explorer, Microsoft Access, Microsoft PowerPoint, Microsoft Outlook, Adobe Photoshop, or Adobe Dreamweaver, but preferably another application, utility, or game that you did not open in the tutorial. What program did you open? What changes occurred in CPU Usage and Memory Usage when you opened that application? What percent of physical memory is in use? What does Windows Task Manager report for Available Physical Memory and Free Physical Memory? What is the current Commit (MB) size for the paging file, and what is the maximum Commit (MB) size? What conclusions would you draw about how memory usage changed when you opened this application?

7. Close the program you just opened. What changes occurred in CPU Usage and Memory Usage when you closed that program? What percent of physical memory is now used? What does Windows Task Manager report for Available Physical Memory and Free Physical Memory? What is the current Commit (MB) size for the paging file, and what is the maximum Commit (MB) size? What conclusions would you draw about how memory usage changed when you closed this application?

8. Use the Resource Monitor button on the Windows Task Manager Performance tab to open Resource Monitor, and if necessary, select the Overview tab. Use the graphs to describe the changes in CPU, disk, and memory usage that are currently occurring on your computer. What percent of physical memory is currently used? Examine the CPU, Disk, Network, and Memory section bars, and list the percent Maximum Frequency for CPU usage, percent Highest Active Time for Disk I/O, percent Network Utilization, and percent Used Physical Memory.

9. Select the Memory tab, expand the Processes section (if necessary), sort the processes in alphabetical order by Image name, and then locate the Image name explorer.exe. What does Resource Monitor report for this program's Commit (KB), Working Set (KB), Shareable (KB), and Private (KB)? Expand the Physical Memory section (if necessary), and list the amount of Hardware Reserved, In Use, Modified, Standby, and Free physical memory. Then list the amount of Available, Cached, Total, and Installed physical memory. From the information you examined on the Windows Task Manager Performance tab and the Memory tab in Resource Monitor, briefly describe how your computer currently uses its memory and whether or not you might benefit from additional RAM. Close the Resource Monitor and Windows Task Manager windows.

10. Create a system health report. Does the System Diagnostics Report display any warnings and, if so, what are they? For each warning, describe the steps that Resource and Performance Monitor recommends to resolve the issue. Did Resource and Performance Monitor report that any basic system checks failed and, if so, what are they? If necessary, expand the Performance section. Under Resource Overview, how much of memory is currently used and how much is available? What is the status of the CPU and Disk? How would you rate the performance of your computer? Explain.

11. Expand the Memory section, and then expand the Counters section. What is the mean value for % Committed Bytes In Use? What is the mean value for Available Bytes, and how many megabytes or gigabytes does that represent? What is the mean value for Committed Bytes, and how many megabytes or gigabytes does that represent? What is the mean rate of Pages/sec? Close the Resource and Performance Monitor window and the Advanced Tools window (if necessary).

12. Open Performance Monitor. In the System Summary, what is the % Committed Bytes In Use, the Available MBytes, the PhysicalDisk % Idle Time _Total, and the % Processor Time _Total for Processor Information?

13. Select Performance Monitor in the console tree pane. From the Memory performance object category, select and add the Available MBytes, Committed Bytes, and Pages/sec performance counters to the Added counters box. From the Process performance object category, select and add the Page File Bytes _Total instance performance counter to the Added counters box. After selecting and adding these four performance counters to the existing % Processor Time performance counter, apply these changes and close the Add Counters dialog box.

14. Sort the performance counters in the legend in alphabetical order by Counter name, and then turn on the Highlight option. Check the scale for each counter and, if necessary, adjust a counter's scale so its plotted values appear within the visible area of the graph.

15. Freeze the display and save the current graph view in the Tutorial.09\Review folder in an image file named **Initial Performance Measurements** on your flash drive.

16. Choose each counter in the legend, and list its last recorded value and its maximum value. What performance counter or counters changed the most over this initial period of time?

17. Unfreeze the display, right-click the graph and choose Clear, and then open an application, utility, or game that you have not yet opened on your computer. Freeze the display after activity correlated with the opening of this program stabilizes, and then save the current graph view in the Tutorial.09\Review folder on your flash drive in an image file named **After Opening** followed by the name of the program. What

program did you choose? Select each counter in the legend again and *concisely* describe the changes in the performance counters and how each change affected your computer as Windows 7 opened the program you chose. What performance counter or counters changed the most while opening an application?

18. Unfreeze the display, close the program, and then freeze the display after activity correlated with the closing of this program stabilizes. Save the current graph view in the Tutorial.09\Review folder on your flash drive in an image file named **After Closing** followed by the name of the program.

19. Choose each counter in the legend, and list its last recorded value and its maximum value. Select each counter in the legend again, and *concisely* describe the changes in the performance counters and how each change affected your computer as the program closed. What performance counter or counters changed the most while opening an application?

20. Prepare a table that lists the last recorded value for Available MBytes, Committed Bytes, and Page File Bytes prior to opening a program, after opening a program, and then after closing a program. Examine the results. Was Windows able to reclaim all of the allocated memory, or was there a memory leak. Describe how the paging file changed. Are there any other conclusions that you can draw from this data? If so, concisely describe them.

21. Based on your observations of what happened when you opened and then closed a program, what would you expect to happen if you opened and then later closed a different program on your computer (one that you had not opened previously)? Close the Performance Monitor window.

22. Open a Computer window, right-click your flash drive, and choose the option to view its properties. Select the ReadyBoost property sheet. Does Windows 7 report that this flash drive supports the Windows ReadyBoost feature? If so, how much space is actually allocated for optimizing system speed, or how much space does Windows 7 recommend for optimizing the performance of your computer? How much total storage space does your flash drive have? Close the flash drive Properties dialog box.

23. Submit your answers to the questions in this Review Assignment to your instructor either in printed or electronic form, as requested. Remember to include your name and any other information requested by your instructor on your assignment.

Use your skills to evaluate the performance of a computer for a writer.

APPLY

Case Problem 1

There are no Data Files needed for this Case Problem.

Trent Danford   Trent Danford is a successful, self-employed writer who regularly contributes articles on innovative scientific and technological inventions to national magazines. Because Trent must meet frequent deadlines for contributing articles, he needs a reliable computer that is configured for optimal performance. He enlists your help in evaluating the performance of his computer during a typical workday.

As you complete each step in this case problem, record your answers to the questions so you can submit them to your instructor. Use a word-processing application such as Microsoft Word or the WordPad accessory to prepare your answers to these questions. If you change any settings on the computer you are using, make a note of the original settings so you can restore them later. Complete the following steps:

1. View the System Properties of your computer. What version of Windows 7 are you using? What is your computer's Windows Experience Index rating? What type of processor does your computer use, and what is its clock speed? How much memory (RAM) does your computer have? What is your System Type? Close the System window.

2. Open Performance Monitor, add the following performance counters, sort the legend in alphabetical order by counter name, and then scale the counters to automatically fit within the plotting area of the line graph:
   - Available Bytes for the Memory performance object
   - Committed Bytes for the Memory performance object
   - Page File Bytes Peak and _Total instance for the Process performance object
   - Virtual Bytes Peak and _Total instance for the Process performance object
   - % Usage Peak and _Total instance for the Paging File performance object

3. What do the _Total instances of the Page File Bytes Peak, Virtual Bytes Peak, and % Usage Peak performance counters measure, and why are they important?

4. Use the Delete button on the Performance Monitor toolbar to remove the % Processor Time performance counter.

5. Sort the legend in alphabetical order by counter name, and then scale the counters to automatically fit with the plotting area of the line graph.

6. After adding these performance counters, use the Change graph type button arrow on the Performance Monitor toolbar to switch to a Report graph, freeze the display, and then record the last measured value for each of the performance counters in a table. (You can switch to a Line graph as you perform an operation, and then switch back to a Report graph to record measurements.) List each activity you perform in the first column, and in the next five columns, list the performance measurements for each performance counter. Also, for long performance counter names, enter the names on two lines so you can include all columns in one table. Save a copy of your graph in an image file named **Initial Performance Measurements** in the Tutorial.09\Case1 folder.

7. For the remainder of your work session, use your computer as you typically would, but, where possible, note the basic types of tasks that you perform, such as checking email, browsing the Web, using an application, attaching and removing your flash drive, opening a folder, searching the Web, or playing a game. Switch to a Line graph, and after you open a program, freeze the display, switch to a Report graph, update the table of measurements that you are tracking by briefly describing the operation you performed and recording the last measured value for the other performance counters, and then unfreeze the display to continue plotting performance counters. Repeat this process for each activity you measure.

8. After you complete your work session, save your graph in an image file named **End of Session Performance Measurements** in the Tutorial.09\Case1 folder.

9. Analyze the information that you've collected on the performance of your computer. What conclusions can you draw about the effect of different types of operations (such as opening or closing applications, utilities, folders, and files) on the resources available in your computer? Describe your observations for each performance counter.

10. Was Windows 7 able to reclaim all of the memory it allocated during your work session, or was there a memory leak? Explain.

11. Were there any bottlenecks or problems? If so, what are they?

12. Are there any ways in which you might be able to improve the performance of your computer?

13. Submit your answers to this case problem to your instructor either in printed or electronic form, as requested. Remember to include your name and any other information requested by your instructor on your assignment.

Use your skills to evaluate the performance of a computer.

APPLY

Case Problem 2

There are no Data Files needed for this Case Problem.

Aschbacher Project Management, Inc. Shannon Longbotham works as a project management specialist for Aschbacher Project Management, Inc., an American corporation in Chicago. She works closely with her company's Fortune 500 clients to develop strategies for organizing, implementing, and evaluating company projects. Shannon needs a high-performance computer that is optimally configured so she can manage multiple client projects. She asks you to perform a thorough analysis of her computer.

To complete this case problem, you must work on a computer with Microsoft Office or one that has four major software applications.

As you complete each step in this case problem, record your answers to the questions so you can submit them to your instructor. Use a word-processing application such as Microsoft Word or the WordPad accessory to prepare your answers to these questions. If you change any settings on the computer you are using, make a note of the original settings so you can restore them later. Complete the following steps:

1. View the System Properties of your computer. What edition of Windows 7 are you using? What is your computer's Windows Experience Index rating? What type of processor does your computer use, and what is its clock speed? How much memory (RAM) does Windows 7 report for your computer? What is your computer's System Type?

2. View and then list your Windows Experience Index subscores. Close the System window.

3. Open Performance Monitor with Administrator credentials, and add performance counters for tracking available memory, allocated (or committed) memory, and the number of bytes used by all processes in the paging file. Verify that you have also included the performance counter for measuring the percent of processor time. List the names of the performance objects, their corresponding performance counters, and their instances (if any).

4. Sort the legend in alphabetical order by counter name, and then scale the counters to automatically fit within the plotting area of the line graph.

5. Read this step before you record performance data. Freeze the display, use the Change graph type button arrow on the Performance Monitor toolbar to switch to a Report graph, and then record the values for each of the performance counters in a table. In the first column, note that the measurements are your initial or starting performance measurements, and in the next three columns, list the names of the performance counters, and then record the initial or starting performance values you record for each performance counter on the next line in the table. (You can switch to a Line graph as you perform an operation, and then switch back to a Report graph to record measurements.)

6. Unfreeze the display and then open the following applications on your computer, one right after the other: Microsoft Word, Microsoft Excel, Microsoft PowerPoint, and Microsoft Access (if the latter is installed on your computer). List the names of the applications with the version of Microsoft Office that you are using (for example, Microsoft Word 2010). If you are using another Office suite, such as OpenOffice, then list the applications and suite version number.

7. Freeze the display and then record the values for each of the performance counters in your table. In the first column, note that the next set of measurements are ones taken after opening office suite applications.

8. Unfreeze the display, close all of the open applications, freeze the display again, and then record the current settings for your performance counters in your table. In the first column, note that the next set of measurements are ones taken after you closed all applications.

9. Analyze your performance measurements to determine the effect of Microsoft Office applications (or another office suite's applications) on your computer, and then answer the following questions:

   a. What was the effect on memory of opening three or four major software applications? Explain whether your results illustrate the type of pattern you expect when examining memory usage.

   b. After you closed all applications, did Windows 7 reclaim all of the memory it originally allocated before opening the applications, or was there a memory leak? Explain.

   c. What was the effect on the paging file of opening and multitasking with four major software applications?

   d. Does your computer have enough RAM installed to support multitasking of major applications? Explain.

10. Examine your Windows Experience Index subscores. What types of improvements, if any, could you make to your computer?

11. Submit your answers to this case problem to your instructor either in printed or electronic form, as requested. Remember to include your name and any other information requested by your instructor on your assignment.

Use your skills to identify tools for collecting information on a computer.

APPLY

Case Problem 3

There are no Data Files needed for this Case Problem.

Prescott Systems, Inc. Xavier Calderon works as a security specialist for Prescott Systems, Inc., a New York state consulting firm that provides network security services for local government agencies. One of Xavier's coworkers has noticed an extensive amount of disk I/O and thrashing (excessive paging) on his computer, and Xavier has asked you to help this coworker identify tools that he might use to collect more information about this potential problem

As you complete each step in this case problem, record your answers to the questions so you can submit them to your instructor. Use a word-processing application such as Microsoft Word or the WordPad accessory to prepare your answers to these questions. If you change any settings on the computer you are using, make a note of the original settings so you can restore them later. Complete the following steps:

1. Identify how Xavier's coworker might use each of the following Windows 7 tools to locate information about disk I/O and paging.

   a. Windows Task Manager

   b. Resource Overview

   c. System Diagnostics Report

   d. Performance Monitor

   Be as specific as possible when you provide information about the use of these tools.

2. Are there other tools that you examined in previous tutorials that Xavier's coworker might use to assist him?

3. Would the following factors affect overall disk I/O and, if so, how?

   a. RAM

   b. Paging File

   c. Windows ReadyBoost

   d. Processor

4. Submit your answers to this case problem to your instructor either in printed or electronic form, as requested. Remember to include your name and any other information requested by your instructor on your assignment.

Use your skills to create a system health report for a laptop.

APPLY

Case Problem 4

There are no Data Files needed for this Case Problem.

Portnoy Designs   Celeste Portnoy is a fashion designer who recently launched her own firm after working in the fashion industry for many years with other firms. Recently, she experienced problems with her laptop, and she asks you to ascertain the source of the problem. You decide to start by creating a system health report for her laptop.

As you complete each step in this case problem, record your answers to the questions so you can submit them to your instructor. Use a word-processing application such as Microsoft Word or the WordPad accessory to prepare your answers to these questions. If you change any settings on the computer you are using, make a note of the original settings so you can restore them later. Complete the following steps:

1. Create a system health report.

2. After examining the System Diagnostics Report for Celeste's desktop computer, you notice the following findings:

   - After opening Resource and Performance Monitor, you notice that the System Diagnostics Report includes the following warnings under Diagnostic Results:

   - The Security Center reports that Windows Update is disabled.

   - The Security Center has not recorded an antivirus product.

   - The Security Center reports that User Account Control is disabled.

   - Under Basic System Checks, Resource and Performance Monitor reports that the Security Center Tests failed. When you examine this category, the System Diagnostics Report shows that the User Account Control Enabled Check and the Windows Update Enable Check both failed.

   - Under Disk Hot Files, the System Diagnostics Report shows that ReadyBoost. sfcache is one of the files causing most disk I/Os.

   - Under Report Statistics, you discover that the laptop has 1,024 MB of RAM

3. After opening Reliability Monitor, you notice that the Stability Index value dropped over a 5-day period as a result of six critical events during which Explorer.exe stopped responding twice, Adobe Acrobat stopped working once, and three Office applications stopped working.

4. After reviewing these findings, what changes would you recommend to Celeste's desktop computer, and what tools would you recommend for further analysis of her computer? Also explain why you would make these recommendations.

5. Submit your answers to this case problem to your instructor either in printed or electronic form, as requested. Remember to include your name and any other information requested by your instructor on your assignment.

ENDING DATA FILES

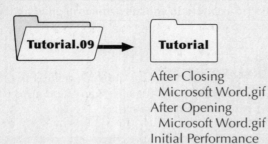

Tutorial

After Closing
  Microsoft Word.gif
After Opening
  Microsoft Word.gif
Initial Performance
  Measurements.gif

Review

After Closing
  [*Application name*].gif
After Opening
  [*Application name*].gif
Initial Performance
  Measurements.gif

Case1

End of Session Performance
  Measurements.gif
Initial Performance
  Measurements.gif

OBJECTIVES

Session 10.1
- Learn why backups are important
- Examine backup strategies
- Evaluate how backup software uses the archive attribute
- Back up folders and files

Session 10.2
- Restore folders and files from a backup
- Create a system image and system repair disc
- Examine how to restore a system image
- Restore previous versions of files

Backing Up and Restoring Files

Protecting Your Important Files

Case | *Gaia Cartographics*

Gaia Cartographics is a small company in Santa Fe, New Mexico, that specializes in aerial, satellite, and digital mapping. Thiago Ribeiro, a mapping specialist, is currently preparing maps of the Amazon River and the Brazilian rainforest, a biome that contains a greater variety of plant and animal life than any other region of the world. To ensure that he has backup copies of all his maps, Thiago relies on Windows Backup.

In this tutorial, you examine the importance of backing up your computer and explore backup strategies that combine the use of full backups with differential or incremental backups. You evaluate the use of the archive attribute in identifying files to include in a backup. You open the Backup and Restore Control Panel tool, and compare options for backing up folders and files, restoring folders and files, making a system image and system repair disc, and restoring a system image. You also view previous versions of files on your computer, and then restore files from a previous version.

STARTING DATA FILES

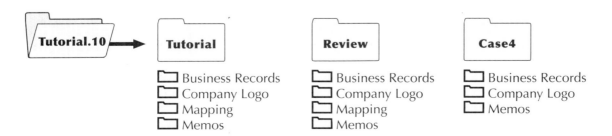

Tutorial.10 → Tutorial

📁 Business Records
📁 Company Logo
📁 Mapping
📁 Memos

Review

📁 Business Records
📁 Company Logo
📁 Mapping
📁 Memos

Case4

📁 Business Records
📁 Company Logo
📁 Memos

SESSION 10.1 VISUAL OVERVIEW

After you specify the settings you want to use for a backup, Windows Backup saves those settings and then performs a backup of your data. Each backup is stored in a **backup set** that contains daily, weekly, or manual backups of the same files using the same backup settings.

After you open Backup and Restore from the Control Panel, you can set up Windows Backup to back up your files on a regular basis. Your first backup is a **full backup** of all user files on your computer and therefore requires the most time and the most backup storage space. Subsequent backups update changes within files that have already been backed up.

Use the Help topic links in the Set up backup dialog boxes to help you decide which backup media to use, decide what files to include in the backup, and determine which files are automatically excluded so you can make the best possible choices for backing up your files.

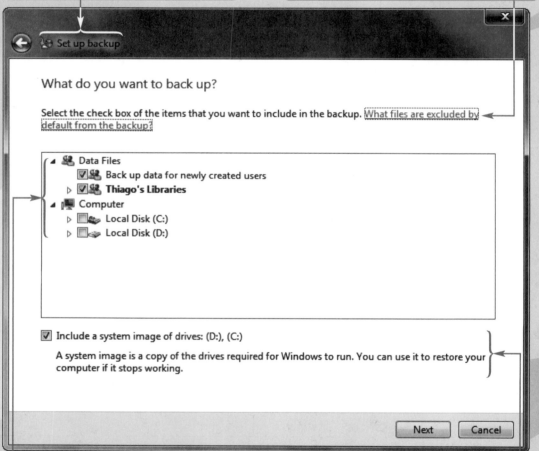

← Set up backup

What do you want to back up?

Select the check box of the items that you want to include in the backup. What files are excluded by default from the backup?

▲ 🖳 Data Files
   ☑🖳 Back up data for newly created users
  ▷ ☑🖳 **Thiago's Libraries**
▲ 🖳 Computer
  ▷ ☐ Local Disk (C:)
  ▷ ☐ Local Disk (D:)

☑ Include a system image of drives: (D:), (C:)

A system image is a copy of the drives required for Windows to run. You can use it to restore your computer if it stops working.

[Next]   [Cancel]

If you prefer to choose what to include in your backup rather than let Windows choose, Windows Backup lets you select specific libraries and folders, user accounts, and other locations, such as other drives and folders on the same or other drives.

You can include a system image in your backup if there is enough storage space on your backup media. A **system image** is a backup copy of the drives that Windows 7 requires in order to run properly. If necessary, you can use a system image to restore your entire computer.

BACKING UP

Windows Backup uses a progress indicator to provide you with information about the status of a backup. You can also use the View Details button to view the path and name of each file that is backed up as well as the percentage complete.

Windows Backup reports on the total amount of storage space on your backup media and the amount available so you can make sure there is enough storage space for your next backup or for a system image.

You can use the Back up now button to initiate a manual backup. Your next backup then follows the schedule you originally specified for Windows Backup.

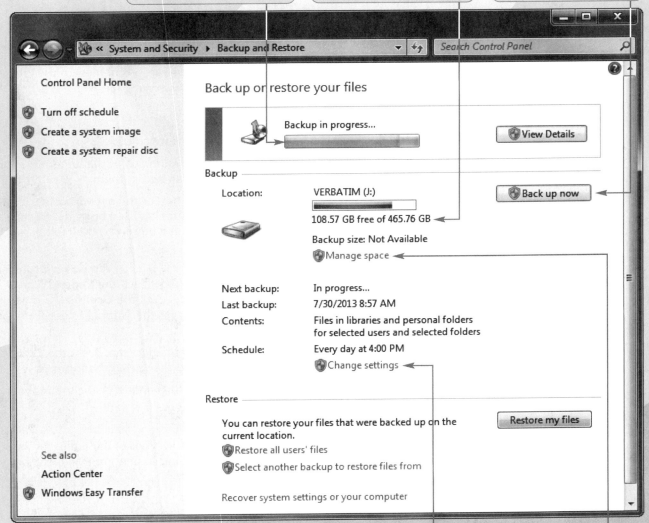

Control Panel Home

Turn off schedule
Create a system image
Create a system repair disc

« System and Security ▸ Backup and Restore   ▾ ↔   Search Control Panel

Back up or restore your files

Backup in progress...   View Details

Backup

Location: VERBATIM (J:)   Back up now
                     108.57 GB free of 465.76 GB
                     Backup size: Not Available
                     Manage space

Next backup: In progress...
Last backup: 7/30/2013 8:57 AM
Contents: Files in libraries and personal folders
                     for selected users and selected folders
Schedule: Every day at 4:00 PM
                     Change settings

Restore

You can restore your files that were backed up on the current location.   Restore my files

Restore all users' files
Select another backup to restore files from

Recover system settings or your computer

See also

Action Center

Windows Easy Transfer

After providing Administrator credentials, you can use the Change settings link to change your backup settings and select another backup location and specify what to back up.

After providing Administrator credentials, you can use the Manage space button to view a summary of how storage space is used on your backup media and to view details on specific backups (organized in backup periods). You can remove older backups to free up storage space on your backup media.

Getting Started

To complete this tutorial, it is recommended that you display the Computer icon on the desktop, and switch your computer to single-click activation. In the following steps, you will check and, if necessary, change these settings.

To set up your computer:

▶ **1.** If necessary, use the Start menu to display the Computer icon on the desktop.

▶ **2.** Open the Folder Options dialog box and enable single-click activation (if necessary); display hidden folders, files, and drives; and display hidden protected operating system files.

Next, you will copy the Data Files that you will need later in the tutorial to the Public Documents folder. In the second session of the tutorial, you will look at a feature called Previous Versions, which allows you to restore previous versions of files. To use Previous Versions, Windows 7 needs to make copies of currently existing files.

To copy the Data Files to your Public Documents folder:

▶ **1.** Make sure you have downloaded and extracted your copy of the Windows 7 for Power User Data Files and that your computer can access them.

▶ **2.** Open the Documents library, your flash drive folder, or the network folder that contains a copy of the Tutorial.10 folder, click **Tutorial.10** to open the folder, point to the **Tutorial** folder icon, click the **Organize** button on the toolbar, and then click **Copy**.

▶ **3.** Right-click the **Windows Explorer** taskbar button 🔲, click **Windows Explorer** to open the Libraries window in the Navigation pane, click the **expand** icon ▷ to the left of Documents, click **Public Documents**, click the **Organize** button on the toolbar, and then click **Paste**. Windows 7 copies the Tutorial folder from the Tutorial.10 folder to the Public Documents folder.

▶ **4.** To rename the Tutorial folder, select the **Tutorial** folder icon, press the **F2** key (the Rename key), type **Gaia Cartographics**, and then press the **Enter** key.

▶ **5.** Close the Public Documents folder window and the window that contains your original copy of the Tutorial.10 folder.

To improve the chances that you will have previous versions of these files for the second session of the tutorial, you will create a restore point. To perform this operation, you must provide Administrator credentials.

To create a restore point:

▶ **1.** Right-click the **Computer** desktop icon, click **Properties**, and in the System window, click the **System protection** link and, if necessary, provide Administrator credentials.

▶ **2.** Click the **Create** button in the System Properties dialog box, type **Manual Restore Point** in the System Protection dialog box, click the **Create** button in this same dialog box, wait for System Protection to create a restore point, and then click the **Close** button in the final System Protection dialog box.

▶ **3.** Click the **OK** button to close the System Properties dialog box, and then close the System window.

You have successfully created a restore point.

The Importance of Backing Up Files

Like other professionals who depend on their computers, Thiago understands the importance of regular backups. Several years ago, he accidentally deleted some important client contract files while he was rushing to meet a deadline. Fortunately, he had performed regular backups of his computer, so he was able to quickly restore those files from his backups and complete negotiations on a new contract. Without those backups, he would have had to reconstruct the contract documents from scratch.

Common causes of loss of documents and data include the following:

- User errors (such as accidentally deleting folders and files, or overwriting files)
- Malicious software, malicious Web sites, and hackers
- Power failures, power surges, or power brownouts
- Unresolved file system problems
- Hardware malfunction or failure
- Software problems
- Theft or vandalism of a computer
- Natural disasters, including fires, floods, and earthquakes

The potential for accidentally losing important files is far greater today because of the variety of risks posed by malicious software introduced to a computer via email attachments, Internet downloads, and malicious Web sites. If you do not back up your computer, the time required for restoring important personal or business documents can be substantial. If you operate a business and do not routinely back up important business and client records, and if you lose all your business and client records as a result of a problem, you could easily be out of business.

Even though the reliability and useful lifetime of hard disks has improved considerably, hard disks are still susceptible to damage and failure. As noted above, restoring the contents of a hard disk from scratch would be a formidable task (assuming it is even possible) and one that could cost you time and money. That's why it's important to regularly back up your hard disk drive. Think of a backup as an insurance policy that helps you protect your personal and business assets.

INSIGHT

Reducing the Risk of Problems on Your Computer

As you've discovered in previous tutorials, you can decrease the likelihood of problems on your computer by using Windows tools and features, such as the Check Disk utility to check and repair a hard disk drive file system, Disk Defragmenter to optimize the use of storage space on your hard disk drive, and the Disk Cleanup utility to remove unnecessary files on a regular basis. In addition, you should use and frequently update your Internet security software, antivirus software, antispyware software, and if necessary your firewall to protect your computer from malicious software, malicious Web sites, and hackers. You should rely on the Windows Update feature to automatically download and install critical security updates. Also, if you implement safe practices, such as using caution when opening email attachments, you further reduce the risk of problems on your computer.

It's critical for businesses, including small businesses and home-based businesses, to develop and implement an efficient and reliable backup strategy and to verify its effectiveness. Studies have found that a large percentage of those businesses that do not back up their data and experience a major loss of data end up closing their doors within a year or less. That in turn adversely affects employees who lose their jobs as well as adversely affecting the overall economy, which relies on the financial stability of companies. Digital data is increasingly important, and loss of even a portion of that data could represent a major financial loss for a business.

Approaches for Backing Up Files

The method you use to back up files on your computer depends on how you work, how much data you store on your hard disk, and how important the data in those files is to you. You can use different approaches to back up important files:

- **Copying files from a hard disk to some type of removable storage**—You can copy important folders and files to a flash drive, DVD, or CD. This approach guarantees that you have at least two copies of important folders and files in two different locations. This backup approach is also useful if you need to make a quick backup at the end of a busy day before you leave the office or before you finish work on your home computer or a mobile PC. However, one potential problem with this approach is that if you store the same file on your hard disk and on another drive or disk, you might find later that you have made different changes to both copies of the same file so you now have two versions of that same file. Then you are faced with the task of reconciling the differences between the two files, or you might inadvertently copy the older version of that file over the most recent version of that file, losing important changes. This problem is compounded if you work on multiple files on your home computer, copy them to a flash drive, and then later use another computer, such as your computer at work, to make revisions to those files. Then you must remember which files you changed on the flash drive so you can update those same files on your home computer (and vice versa). Also, if you use a DVD or CD to store copies of important files, you might need to use special software to first format the discs, a time-consuming operation that can take longer than a simple copy operation to a flash drive.
- **Copying files from a hard disk to an external hard disk drive or network folder**—External hard disk drives can easily provide enough storage space for backing up all your files or your entire computer, and this approach also guarantees that you have at least two copies in two different locations. If you have a home computer network, you can copy or back up files to a shared folder on another computer on the network. In fact, you might keep an older, but still useful, computer solely for this purpose. You might also purchase and employ newer technologies, such as Microsoft Home Server, to provided automated backups on networked computers.
- **Using a backup utility**—A **backup utility** is a program for copying the contents of a hard disk drive, whether it's everything stored on that drive or just selected folders and files, to another drive or disc to ensure that you have a duplicate copy of everything that you consider important. You can also use a backup utility to perform an **online backup** and back up folders and files to a Web site that provides storage space for backups. Backup utilities use storage space more efficiently than copying files to a disk, and they can compress files to reduce the amount of storage space or media needed for a backup. You can also use a variety of backup media, such as external hard disks, DVDs, CDs, or a flash drive. If you experience a problem that results in the loss of folders and files, or even one file, on your hard disk, you can restore those folders or files, or a single file, from a backup that you made with the backup utility. You can use Windows Backup from the Backup and Restore Center, or you can purchase a backup utility that meets your specific needs.
- **Using shadow copies**—Windows 7 automatically makes copies of all folders and files on your computer at periodic intervals of time, and these copies are known as shadow

copies. Later in this tutorial, you will learn more about shadow copy technology, and you will examine how to restore files and folders using shadow copies. While this backup feature is invaluable when you lose an important file, the downside is that the shadow copies are stored on your hard disk along with the original copies of all your folders and files. If your hard disk fails, then you have lost not only your original copies of your folders and files, but also your shadow copies of those same folders and files. That's why you need to make sure that you have at least one other copy of important files stored in a different location, such as on removable media, an external hard disk, or a network.

You may discover that a combination of these approaches serves your needs best, conveniently fits backups into your schedule, and guarantees that you can restore important files to your computer.

Organizing Folders and Files for Backups

Organizing your folders and files logically allows you to quickly select those folders and files that you want to include in a backup. At certain times, you might want to back up all your folders and files. If your folders and files are stored in a single folder, such as the Documents library, you can specify that you want to back up the Documents library, and then immediately start your backup. At other times, you might want to back up only certain folders and files. If you have already organized your files into groups and placed those files into groups of logically related folders, then you can more easily select the folders and files that you want to back up and be assured that you have a backup copy of all your important files. If you do not organize your files into folders and do not organize folders into logical groups as subfolders under one main folder, then you may need to perform the time-consuming task of locating all the folders and files that you want to back up and hope that you have found everything you need to include in the backup (including email messages). It's also important to periodically reevaluate how you organize files by folder because you may discover a more efficient and more logical approach that makes it easier for you to locate the files you need when you must change those files and when you want to back up the files.

You may also want to periodically perform a full backup in which you make a backup copy of everything stored on your hard disk, including files, folders, and software applications. Obviously, a full-system backup requires an external hard disk or some other type of backup medium that has enough storage space to store the full-system backup. If you later encounter a problem with your computer, you may need that full-system backup to restore your entire system, your software applications, or all your folders and files. Although it's easy to reinstall software from DVDs or CDs that contain the software you purchased or by downloading and installing another copy of the software from the Internet, you must then obtain all the updates for the software since you originally installed it on your computer. You also have to devote time to specifying and customizing software settings so the software is set up the way you prefer to use it. If you reinstall software from a backup, then you avoid the need for downloading all previous updates and you retain your custom settings.

Developing an Effective Backup Strategy

You should develop and implement an effective backup strategy for three reasons: (1) to reduce the time, effort, and media required for backups; (2) to guarantee that you have recent backups of important files that you work with daily; and (3) to simplify the processing of restoring folders and files.

One commonly used backup strategy is to make a full backup at regular intervals, such as every week, month, quarter, or perhaps even every day. The interval of time between each full backup is called the **backup cycle**, and it begins by backing up your whole system, or an important or major part of your computer (such as your Documents, Music, Pictures, and Videos libraries as well as your user account folders), and continues with backups of important files at shorter intervals of time within each backup cycle; this cycle ends with the next full backup. The length of your backup cycle depends on how important your files are to you, how frequently you change your files and add new files, and how frequently you make changes to your computer system. For example, if you use your computer every day, and create and modify many files within a day, you might opt for a weekly or daily backup cycle. The first backup in a backup cycle is typically called a full backup, or **normal backup**, because it includes all your folders and files (or per-haps everything on your computer).

Combining Differential Backups with a Normal Backup

If you perform a full or normal backup each month, you might want to perform either a differential or an incremental backup at the end of each week to streamline backups and save time, effort, and media. On the other hand, if you perform a full or normal backup each week, you might perform a differential or incremental backup at the end of every day. Differential and incremental backups are two different approaches for backing up folders and files, and they differ in how folders and files are selected for a backup.

Unlike a full backup, which includes all folders and files you select, a **differential backup** includes only new and modified files since your last full or normal backup. After you perform a full or normal backup, you have a copy of all your folders and files stored in your backup. However, then you continue to make changes to the folders and files on your hard disk and create new folders and files. So, you do not have a backup of the changes to the folders and files you've modified or created—until the next full or nor-mal backup. If you perform a differential backup between full or normal backups, then the first differential backup includes only those folders and files that you've modified or created since your last full backup. After the first differential backup, you have the most recent copy of every folder and file in either the full backup or the differential backup. Then you continue to make further changes to your folders and files and you create even newer folders and files that have not yet been backed up. So, you must continue to make additional differential backups during the backup cycle.

Each additional differential backup that you perform within the same backup cycle includes all the files you backed up during previous differential backups. For example, assume you perform a full or normal backup at the beginning of the month and then per-form differential backups at the end of each week. At the end of the first week after the full or normal backup, you perform your first differential backup. This backup includes all files that you created or modified during the first week, since the previous full or nor-mal backup. That differential backup does not include files that you did not change after the full or normal backup because copies of those files are in your full or normal backup.

At the end of the second week, you perform your second differential backup. This backup includes all files that you created or modified during the first *and* second weeks, again since the full or normal backup.

At the end of the third week, you perform your third and last differential backup. This backup will include all files that you created and modified during the first, second, *and* third weeks, again since the full or normal backup at the start of the backup cycle.

At the beginning of the next month, you perform a new full or normal backup that includes all files (including all those files created or modified since the start of the backup cycle). Then, you start a new backup cycle, and you continue with differential backups during the new backup cycle.

Figure 10-1 illustrates an example of this approach to combining a full or normal backup with differential backups within a backup cycle.

| Figure 10-1 | Using a backup strategy that combines full and differential backups |

Backup Cycle	New or Modified Files	Type of Backup	Files Backed Up
Beginning of backup cycle		Full backup #1	All folders and files in: • Projects folder • Portfolio folder
End of week 1	Portfolio 1.docx Portfolio 2.docx	Differential backup #1	Portfolio 1.docx Portfolio 2.docx
End of week 2	Portfolio 3.docx Portfolio 4.docx	Differential backup #2	Portfolio 1.docx Portfolio 2.docx Portfolio 3.docx Portfolio 4.docx
End of week 3	Portfolio 2.docx Portfolio 5.docx Portfolio Cover Letter.docx	Differential backup #3	Portfolio 1.docx Portfolio 2.docx Portfolio 3.docx Portfolio 4.docx Portfolio 5.docx Portfolio Cover Letter.docx
Start of a new backup cycle	Portfolio 1.docx	Full backup #2	All folders and files in: • Projects folder • Portfolio folder

Assume you regularly back up two important folders on your hard disk: a Projects folder and a Portfolio folder. At the beginning of the backup cycle, you back up all your projects records, including all your business portfolios. During the first week, assume you change two of your portfolios—Portfolio 1.docx and Portfolio 2.docx. That means that the copies of these two files in your full or normal backup are no longer your most recent copies of the files. However, after you perform your first differential backup, that differential backup will include these two files.

During the second week, you change Portfolio 3.docx and Portfolio 4.docx. Your second differential backup will include these two files plus the two you worked on during the first week; in other words, it contains Portfolio 1.docx, Portfolio 2.docx, Portfolio 3.docx, and Portfolio 4.docx. Typically, each differential backup is stored in a separate file.

During the third week, you change Portfolio 2.docx again, create a new portfolio called Portfolio 5.docx, and revise another existing file, Portfolio Cover Letter.docx. These three files, plus the others you worked on during the previous two weeks, are backed up when you perform your third differential backup. You now have a copy of Portfolio 2.docx in the files that contain your first, second, and third differential backups. The copy in your third differential backup is the most recent copy of the file.

During the last week of the backup cycle, assume you revise Portfolio 1.docx again. At the end of that fourth week, you start a new backup cycle with a new full or normal backup that includes all the files in your Projects and Portfolio folders plus any new or modified files. That full or normal backup also includes the revision you made to Portfolio 1.docx during the last week of the previous backup cycle (the fourth week of the previous month).

To better understand the concept of differential backups, you can think of each new differential backup after the first differential backup as a "cumulative backup" because each one contains all files included in previous differential backups.

One disadvantage of using a differential backup strategy is that differential backups increase the amount of time and media you need for backups. After the first differential backup, subsequent differential backups take longer because you are backing up more files. However, once you complete a differential backup, you do not need to keep the previous differential backups created in that same backup cycle (unless you want to err on the side of caution). Because you do not need to keep previous differential backups, a differential backup strategy is primarily used in those instances where you need to keep only the most recent version of files that you have worked on during the current backup cycle. For example, if you work in a profession that is constantly changing (such as computer sciences), then you might frequently update your files and may not need previous versions of those files. (However, if you decide to keep each of your differential backup sets, you might be able to find previous versions of some files in an earlier differential backup set.)

One advantage of differential backups is that it is easier to restore folders and files. For example, if you need to restore all the files in your Projects and Portfolio folders, you first restore all the files from your last full or normal backup, and then you restore all the files in the last differential backup for that backup cycle because it contains the most recent copy of all the files you changed after your last full or normal backup. The catch is that you spend more time backing up files than you do restoring files.

Combining Incremental Backups with a Full Backup

Instead of using a differential backup strategy with your full backups, you can combine a full backup with incremental backups. An **incremental backup** includes only those files that you create or change since your previous backup—whether it was a full backup *or* an incremental backup.

Again assume that you've just started a new backup cycle and that you've performed a full backup. After you perform a full or normal backup, you have a copy of all your folders and files. However, then you continue to make changes to the folders and files on your hard disk, but until you perform the next full or normal backup, you do not have a backup of any folders or files that you have created or modified. At the end of the first week, you perform your first incremental backup. This backup includes all the files that you created or modified during the first week, and is therefore identical to a differential backup at this point in your backup cycle.

At the end of the second week, you perform your second incremental backup. This backup includes all files that you created or modified during the second week *only*. This is the point at which an incremental backup strategy differs from a differential backup strategy. Unlike a differential backup, this next incremental backup would not include folders and files that you created or modified and backed up during the first incremental backup.

At the end of the third week, you perform your third and last incremental backup. This backup includes all files you created or modified during the third week *only*. It does not include folders and files you created or modified during the first and second weeks.

At the end of the month, you perform a new full or normal backup that includes all files, and you start a new backup cycle again followed by periodic incremental backups. This backup also includes any folders or files you created or modified during the last week of your previous backup cycle.

Figure 10-2 illustrates this use of incremental backups with full or normal backups. Again, assume you regularly back up two folders on your hard disk—a Projects folder and a Portfolio folder. At the beginning of the backup cycle, you perform a full or normal backup and back up all files in the Projects and Portfolio folders.

Figure 10-2	Using a backup strategy that combines full and incremental backups

Backup Cycle	New or Modified Files	Type of Backup	Files Backed Up
Beginning of backup cycle		Full backup #1	All folders and files in: • Projects folder • Portfolio folder
End of week 1	Portfolio 1.docx Portfolio 2.docx	Incremental backup #1	Portfolio 1.docx Portfolio 2.docx
End of week 2	Portfolio 3.docx Portfolio 4.docx	Incremental backup #2	Portfolio 3.docx Portfolio 4.docx
End of week 3	Portfolio 2.docx Portfolio 5.docx Portfolio Cover Letter.docx	Incremental backup #3	Portfolio 2.docx Portfolio 5.docx Portfolio Cover Letter.docx
Start of a new backup cycle	Portfolio 1.docx	Full backup #2	All folders and files in: • Projects folder • Portfolio folder

During the first week, you modify the Portfolio 1.docx and Portfolio 2.docx. Your first incremental backup at the end of the first week includes only those two files.

During the second week, you modify Portfolio 3.docx and create Portfolio 4.docx. Your second incremental backup at the end of that week includes *only* Portfolio 3.docx and Portfolio 4.docx. Unlike a differential backup, it does not include Portfolio 1.docx and Portfolio 2.docx, which you worked on during the first week; rather, the backups for these files are contained in your first incremental backup. If you don't work on Portfolio 3.docx and Portfolio 4.docx during the remainder of the backup cycle, then this backup is the only one that contains the latest versions of those files.

During the third week, you modify the Portfolio Cover Letter.docx and Portfolio 2.docx, and you also create Portfolio 5.docx. Your third incremental backup at the end of that week includes *only* those three files. It does not include Portfolio 1.docx, Portfolio 3.docx, and Portfolio 4.docx from the first two weeks. The copy of Portfolio 2.docx in your third incremental backup is a more recent version of Portfolio 2.docx than the one in your first incremental backup. So, you now have two versions of this file in your incremental backups (allowing you to return to an earlier version of the same file if needed). In contrast, with a differential backup strategy, you typically have only the most recent version of this file because you would typically recycle backup media sooner to keep costs down and to make sure there is enough available storage space for future backups. This latter consideration is especially important to businesses that perform more frequent and extensive backups to guarantee they have the backups they need in case they need to restore important business records after a major disaster and also to comply with federal law.

During the last week of this backup cycle, you revise Portfolio 1.docx. At the beginning of the next month, you start a new backup cycle with a new full or normal backup that includes all the files in your Projects and Portfolio folders (including any new or modified files that you worked on during the last week of the backup cycle). That backup also includes the revision you made to Portfolio 1.docx during the last week of the previous backup cycle (the fourth week of the previous month).

Incremental backups have some advantages and disadvantages over differential backups (and vice versa). Performing incremental backups is faster than differential backups because each new incremental backup includes fewer files than a corresponding differential backup. Also, because each incremental backup does not include files backed up during previous incremental backups, you do not need to use as much backup media. However, unlike a differential backup strategy, you need to keep all your incremental backups so you can restore all of the files you worked on during a backup cycle.

However, incremental backups take longer to restore. For example, if you need to restore all the files in your Projects and Portfolio folders, you would first restore all the files from your last full or normal backup, and then you would restore all the files in each of your incremental backup sets in the order in which you produced them during the last backup cycle.

Why do you need to restore folders and files from all the incremental backups? You might have created a new file during the second week of the backup cycle and not worked on that file during the remainder of the backup cycle. The only copy of that file is in the second incremental backup. If you just restore files from the full backup and the last incremental backup, you will not have that file in the second incremental backup, because it's not included in either the full or last incremental backups. If you use differential backups, that file is included automatically in the last differential backup, so you only need to restore the normal backup and the last differential backup.

Why not use a differential background strategy rather than an incremental one? If you've worked on a document every day during a backup cycle, each incremental backup will have a different version of the file that contains that document. Unlike a differential backup strategy, where you do not typically save previous differential backups, you can restore earlier versions of a file if you use an incremental backup strategy. You just choose the incremental backup that contains the version of the file you want to restore. Also, because incremental backups are faster and require fewer backup media, they are the most common types of backups that businesses and individuals make. Plus, as noted earlier, you spend more time backing up files than you do restoring files, so incremental backups make more effective use of your time.

If you are faced with the daunting task of performing full or normal backups that require a substantial amount of time, such as 24 hours, then you might combine full or normal backups on a less frequent basis with both differential and incremental backups. For example, you might do a full or normal backup at the beginning of the month, and perform differential backups on a daily basis, except for the end of each week when you perform an incremental backup. The daily differential backups ensure that you have a "cumulative" backup of every folder and file that you create or modify during the week. The end-of-week incremental backups include all the folders and files you created or modified during the week, and in essence, act like a weekly full or normal backup but require less time. Furthermore, unlike differential backups, incremental backups turn off the archive attribute on all the folders and files that you created or modified during the week so you can start with a new set of differential backups the following week that only back up data during that next week. (You will examine the archive attribute shortly.) If you need to restore all the data on your computer from these backups, you restore the last full backup, the last incremental backup, and then the last differential backup.

Making Copy and Daily Backups

Even if you employ the use of a differential or incremental backup strategy with full backups, you might also want to implement other types of backups, such as a copy backup and a daily backup. A **copy backup** backs up all the files you select without affecting other types of backups that you create during a backup cycle. You might use a copy backup to make an extra backup within a backup cycle so you can store the copy backup off site. For example, if you combine a full backup with an incremental backup strategy, you can use a copy backup at any point during the backup cycle to back up specific files that you select. Any new or modified files that are included in the copy backup are also backed up in the next incremental backup.

In contrast, a **daily backup** backs up all files that have been created or modified the day you perform the daily backup. Like the copy backup, a daily backup does not interfere with an incremental or differential backup strategy. Again, you might use a daily backup to make an extra backup within a backup cycle so you can store the daily backup off site. Also, if you have modified many files during a given day, you could make a daily backup before your next differential or incremental backup. If a problem occurs before your next differential or incremental backup, you can restore folders and files that otherwise would not have been backed up until your next scheduled backup.

TIP

A daily backup is not an automatic process performed by your backup utility, but rather one you initiate as an extra precaution.

Even if you combine a differential or incremental backup strategy with periodic full backups, remember that you have no backups of changes to files made between each differential or each incremental backup, so you may want to employ the use of a copy backup or a daily backup for added protection.

Keeping Multiple Backups

If you back up to an external hard disk, a network folder, or online Web site where you have plenty of storage space, then you can keep more backups for a longer period of time. However, if you are backing up to media such as a flash drive where the amount of storage space might be limiting, or if you are backing up to a DVD, CD, or any other type of media that you might want to reuse, you will probably want to delete older backups to free up storage space; however, it is a good habit to keep at least the last four of your most recent backup sets. When you start your next backup cycle, you can use the backup media from your oldest backup cycle. As you start the next backup cycle, you have backups from three previous backup cycles that are untouched. After you complete the next backup cycle, you now have backups from your four most recent backup cycles. With each new backup cycle, you repeat this same process. This approach guarantees that you have backups from the three most recent backup cycles in case you encounter a problem while performing a backup during the next backup cycle. If you attempt to restore files from your most recent backup cycle and discover that your most recent backup set is defective, then you can turn to the backup set from the previous backup cycle.

Another common approach for rotating backup media and protecting against data loss is the **Grandfather-Father-Son (GFS)** rotation scheme. This approach uses three sets of backups. An incremental or differential backup is performed for the first 6 days of the week, and each set is referred to as the *son*. The media for these daily backups are reused each week in the same sequence. The last backup of each week is a full backup and is referred to as the *father*. That backup media is reused each month. The last full backup on the last day of each month is the *grandfather*, and it is retained for a year (or perhaps a quarter) before the media is reused.

If you decide to record over backups from your previous, and only other, backup cycle, then you are taking an unnecessary risk. If the backup, drive, or computer fails during the next backup, you might lose an important backup from your previous backup cycle, and you might also lose everything on your hard disk. Then you would have no backups and would be forced to recreate all your files from scratch, if possible.

PROSKILLS

Decision Making: Using Multiple Types of Backups

You should not rely on just one backup or even one type of backup media or backup strategy. You might, for example, want to back up important files on your computer to one type of removable storage (such as DVD, CD, or flash drive) and perform the same backup to an external hard disk drive, shared network folder, or online Web site so you can restore the same set of files in one of two or more different ways. As part of your backup process, you should keep a log of what backups you have made—including the date of the backup, the backup utility (and version) you used, what's included in the backups, and where the backups are stored. As noted earlier, it is a good idea to store at least one set of a backup off site. In fact, your insurance company might require you to store backups off site before they will insure your data.

Furthermore, in the public sector, the federal Sarbanes-Oxley Act of 2002 mandates that publicly held companies and accounting firms maintain and properly store financial data for not less than 7 years and maintain documentation on data integrity necessary for auditing the financial practices of firms and validating data integrity. If you're employed as a network administrator or an assistant network administrator and are responsible for guaranteeing that your firm meets these federal mandates, then you cannot afford any type of error that results in the loss of valuable backed-up data.

Understanding the Importance of the Archive Attribute

When you perform a full or normal backup, you select the drive(s), folder(s), and file(s) that you want to back up and then you back up everything you selected. When you perform a differential or incremental backup, the backup utility automatically selects only those folders or files that have been modified or created from the locations specified for the full or normal backup. The question is, "How does the backup utility know which files to select for a differential or incremental backup?" When you create or modify a folder or file, Windows 7 turns on the archive attribute or setting for that folder or file. The Backup utility then uses that attribute to determine what to include in a backup. Only files with the archive attribute enabled are selected for differential or incremental backups. The archive attribute is actually a bit that can be turned on or off.

If you want to view the status of the archive attribute of a file, or if you want to turn on or turn off the archive attribute of a file, view the properties of that file and choose the Advanced button on the General property sheet to open the Advanced Attributes dialog box, as shown in Figure 10-3.

| Figure 10-3 | Viewing the status of a file's archive attribute |

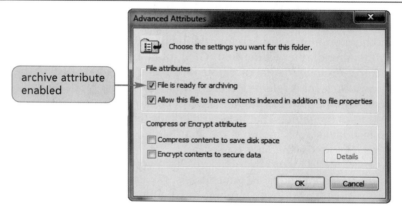

If the archive attribute is turned on, then you will see a check mark in the "File is ready for archiving" check box. If there is no check mark in this check box, then a Backup utility has backed up the file and turned off the archive attribute (or you have deliberately turned it off).

During a full or normal backup, a Backup utility backs up all the folders and files you've selected—whether the archive attribute is on or off. Once all the folders and files are backed up, the Backup utility turns off the archive attribute of any file that previously had the archive attribute enabled, as shown in Figure 10-4. The net result is that all the files that are backed up after a full or normal backup no longer have the archive attribute enabled.

Figure 10-4 Archive attribute of a new or modified file before and after a full backup

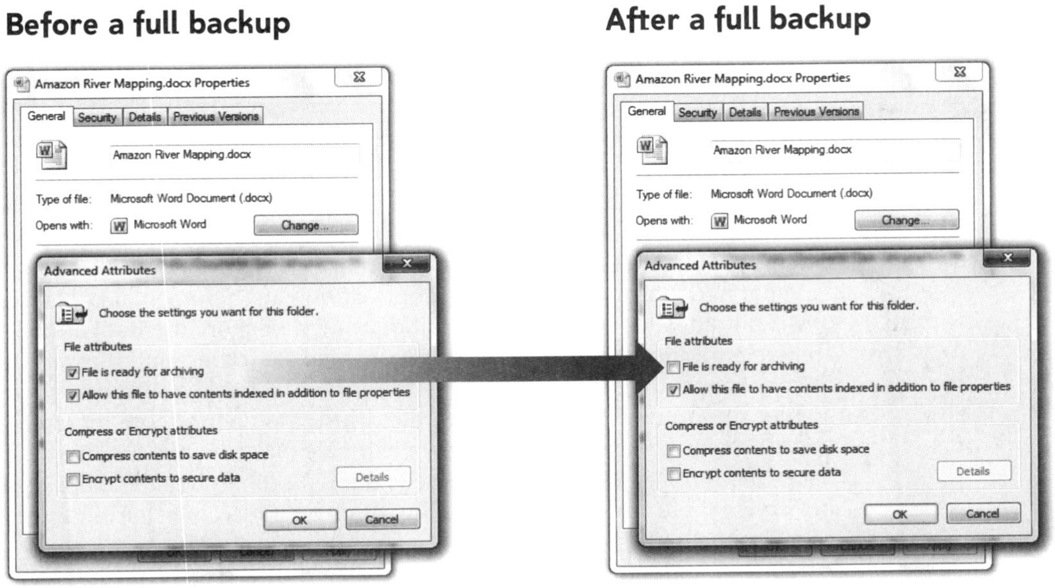

If you create a new file or folder or change an existing file after a full or normal backup, Windows 7 turns on the archive attribute when you save the file. If you then perform a differential backup, the backup utility selects all folders and files that have the archive attribute turned on (they are either new or modified files) and backs them up. The backup utility does not include folders or files that have the archive attribute turned off (they have already been backed up). Unlike a full or normal backup, the backup utility does not change the archive attribute of the files that it backed up during your first differential backup. See Figure 10-5.

Figure 10-5 Archive attribute of a new or modified file before and after a differential backup

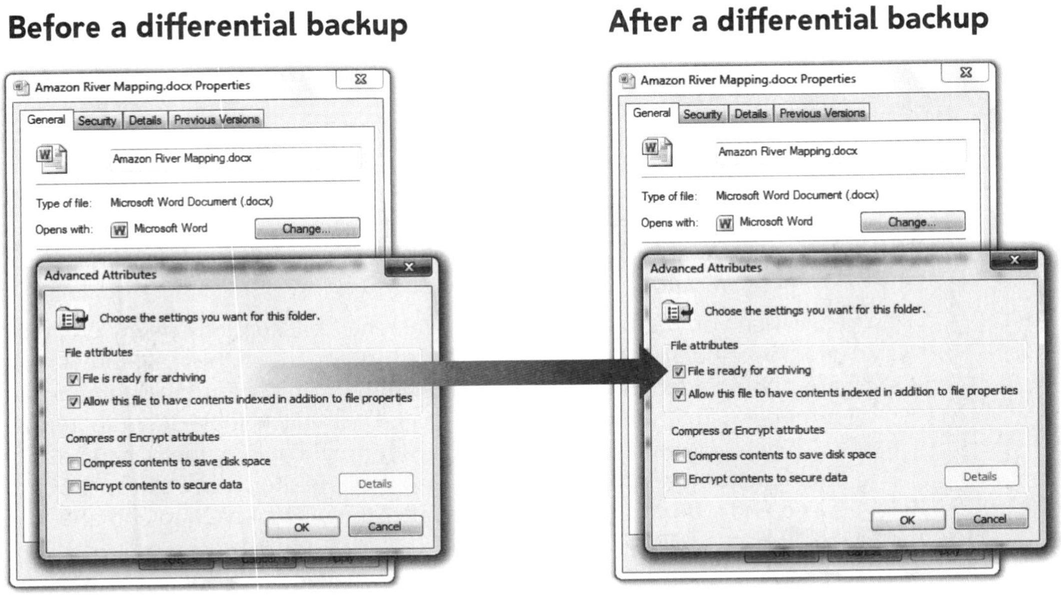

When you perform your next differential backup, any newly created or modified folders and files are backed up because their archive attribute is enabled. All files backed up in the previous differential backup are also included in this next differential backup because their archive bits are still enabled. That process is repeated with each differential backup so all differential backups contain all new or modified files since your last full or normal backup.

When you perform your next full or normal backup, the backup utility turns off the archive attributes that were previously enabled for folders and files. The only time archive attributes are turned off with a backup strategy that combines a full or normal backup with differential backups is when you do the full or normal backup. Therefore, differential backups do not change the archive attribute.

What happens to the archive attribute during an incremental backup? As in the previous example, after you perform a full or normal backup, the Backup utility turns off all archive attributes that were previously enabled for folders and files. If you create a new file or change an existing file after a full or normal backup, Windows 7 turns on the archive attribute when you save the file. If you then perform an incremental backup, the backup utility selects all those folders and files that have the archive bit enabled and backs them up—just like what happens during a differential backup. However, after an incremental backup, the Backup utility turns off the archive attributes of all the folders and files that were backed up. See Figure 10-6.

| **Figure 10-6** | **Archive attribute of a new or modified file before and after an incremental backup** |

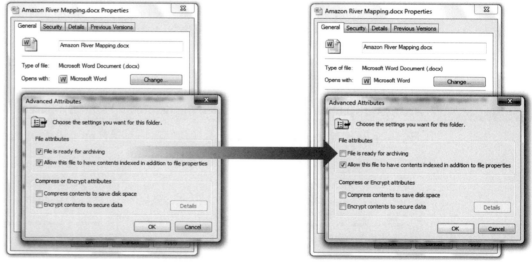

When you perform your next incremental backup, any newly created or modified files are backed up because their archive attributes are enabled. All previously backed-up files are not included in the next incremental backup because their archive attributes were turned off. That same process is repeated with each subsequent incremental backup.

When you perform your next full or normal backup, the Backup utility turns off the archive attributes of all the folders and files. As shown in Figure 10-6, archive bits are turned off with this backup strategy after the normal backup and after each incremental backup.

Figure 10-7 summarizes the status of the archive attribute before and after a full, differential, and incremental backup.

Figure 10-7   **How full, differential, and incremental backups handle archive attributes**

Type of Backup	Archive Attribute	
	Before backup	**After backup**
Full backup		
Already backed up files	Off	Off
New files	On	Off
Modified files	On	Off
Differential	On	On
Incremental	On	Off

Both full and incremental backups turn off the archive attribute of any new or modified folders and files that are backed up. Differential backups do not change the archive attribute of any new or modified folders and files that are backed up. Full backups also back up folders and files with the archive attribute off. Differential and incremental backups do not back up files with the archive attribute off.

When you perform a copy or daily backup, the Backup utility does not modify the archive attribute of files selected for the backup. So that means a copy or daily backup does not interfere with the use of differential or incremental backups.

The use of the archive attribute therefore provides a simple but powerful technique for determining the status of a file for backup operations.

Using Backup and Restore

You can use the Windows 7 Backup and Restore feature to perform two types of backups of your data:

TIP

Windows 7 does not offer a differential backup option.

- **File backup**—You can use this incremental backup option to back up your user folders and files as well as folders and files for other users on the same computer. You can let Windows Backup choose what to include in the backup, or you can choose. You can back up to a second hard disk drive and to removable media (i.e., a writeable DVD or CD formatted for the UDF Live File System), a flash drive with a storage capacity over 1 GB, Compact Flash (CF) memory card, or Secure Digital (SD) memory card. If you are using a version other than Windows 7 Starter, Home Basic, and Home Premium editions, you can also back up to a shared network folder (also called a network share). You cannot back up to the drive that you are creating a backup for. In other words, if you are backing up drive C, you cannot store your backup on that drive. If you are backing up to a drive locked with BitLocker Drive Encryption, then you must first unlock the drive. Windows Backup makes backups on a regular schedule, but you can change this schedule, and you can create a manual backup at any time.

  The first time you perform a backup of your folders and files, Backup and Restore performs a full backup of all your files. After that, you perform selective backups that include only specific groups of files. The backed-up files are stored in Compressed (zipped) Folders on the backup media. Subsequent backups are incremental backups that back up only changes within files, not the entire files themselves, so backups are faster.

  This type of backup does not back up system files, program files, encrypted files, user profile settings, and other files like temporary files or deleted files in the Recycle Bin. You can back up to disks that use the NTFS, FAT, and UDF (Universal Disk Format) file systems.

  If you have already used Windows Backup to back up folders and files, then it is set to automatically perform an incremental backup of all your folders and files on your computer. If you open a file and make a change to it, then during the next scheduled or manual backup, Windows Backup only backs up the changes within the file—not the entire file. This feature reduces the amount of storage space required for incremental backups. It's also important to remember that regularly scheduled backups only happen if the backup device is connected to the computer. If you use the same external hard disk to back up different computers, then you need to reconnect that external hard disk to the computer you are currently using so that a regularly scheduled backup can occur, and you need to power on the backup drive.

- **System image backup**—During this type of backup, Windows Backup creates a complete image of your entire hard disk so you can restore your computer if you experience a major problem. The system image backup includes the system volume that contains the files used to boot Windows, and the boot volume that contains the Windows folder. If you have a single-boot system with only one operating system installed on it, then the system volume and boot volume are one and the same. If you have a multiboot system with two or more operating systems installed on different partitions, then a system image backup will include the partition that contains the files for booting Windows 7 and the partition with the Windows folder. For example, the computer used for this textbook is set up as a dual-boot computer with Windows Vista installed on the first partition and Windows 7 installed on the second partition. A system image backup of this computer would include the first partition, which includes the files for booting Windows 7 and Windows Vista, as well as the second partition which includes the Windows folder for the Windows 7 operating system files.

A system image backup is stored on the backup media in a virtual hard disk file with the .vhd (for virtual hard disk) file extension. Windows Backup compacts the system image file by removing empty space so your backup uses disk storage space more efficiently. During a system image backup, Windows Backup reads block by block on the hard disk, not file by file, which would require moving from one file to another file that might be stored in a different location on disk. Therefore, a system image backup is faster than you might otherwise expect. However, because of the amount of data backed up, and because you might be backing up multiple volumes, system image backups might take time and require far more storage space on your backup media. Also, because a system image can easily exceed the 4 GB file size limit for FAT volumes, you cannot create a system image on a FAT volume.

If you use a system image backup to restore your computer, you cannot pick and choose what you want to restore. If you have a dual-boot system with two different Windows versions installed on two different partitions, and decide to restore your computer from a system image backup, then that restore operation affects both partitions. If you opt for a scheduled file backup, you also have the option of including a system image in that backup.

Windows 7 Backup and Restore simplifies, and provides an option for automating, the process for making backups, thus ensuring that you have backups of your valuable data.

Backing Up Folders and Files

In this section of the tutorial, you will create a scheduled backup, and then back up folders and files on your computer, including the Gaia Cartographics folder.

If you have not set up Windows Backup on your computer, then you can complete the following steps to initiate that process. If you have already set up Windows Backup on your computer, then read but do not keystroke the following steps.

To set up Windows Backup:

1. From the Start menu, click **Control Panel**, and then click the **Back up your computer** link under System and Security. Windows 7 opens the Backup and Restore window. See Figure 10-8.

| Figure 10-8 | Using Backup and Restore to set up Windows Backup |

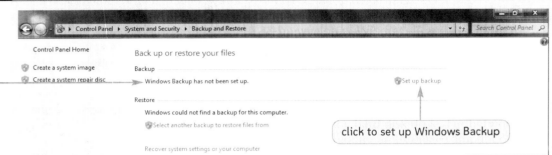

status of Windows Backup

click to set up Windows Backup

This window consists of two basic sections—one for backing up folders and files, and the other for restoring folders and files or your entire computer. What you see in this window depends on whether you have already backed up your computer. On the computer used for this figure, Windows Backup has not yet been set up. If your computer system is already set up for a scheduled backup, then Windows Backup reports on the date and time of the next and the last scheduled backup.

▶ 2. If Windows Backup has not been set up on your computer yet, click the **Set up backup** link under the Backup section. Then you briefly see a "Set up backup" dialog box asking you to wait while Windows Backup starts. In the next "Set up backup" dialog box, you are prompted to select where you want to save your backup. See Figure 10-9.

| Figure 10-9 | Selecting a local or network location for saving a backup |

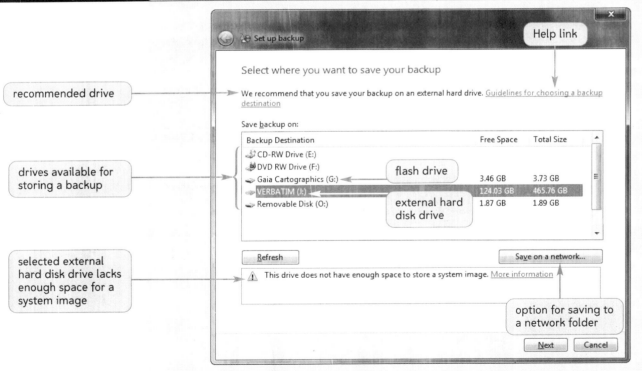

recommended drive

Help link

drives available for storing a backup

flash drive

external hard disk drive

selected external hard disk drive lacks enough space for a system image

option for saving to a network folder

Windows Backup recommends that you save your backup on an external hard drive. In the "Save backup on" box, Windows Backup identifies locations on your computer where you can save a backup. On the computer used for this figure, Windows Backup can back up to a CD or DVD rewriteable drive, a flash drive (identified as drive G on this computer), an external hard disk drive (identified as drive J on this computer), and a Secure Digital (SD) memory card from a digital camera (identified as drive O on this computer). Windows Backup also shows the free space and total size for each drive that contains media. If you have a DVD or CD disk in the corresponding drive, then Windows Backup reports on the free space and total size of the disc. You can use the Refresh button to update this list of backup locations, and you can use the "Save on a network" button to provide network credentials and specify a network location so Windows Backup can access the network location when saving your backup. You can only save backups on a network if you are using Windows 7 Professional, Windows 7 Ultimate, and Windows 7 Enterprise.

If you select a backup destination that has a limited amount of storage space, Windows Backup may display a warning informing you the drive does not have enough storage space for a system image, such as is the case in Figure 10-9. If you click the More information link next to the warning, then Windows Backup reports on how much storage space is needed on that backup destination.

The "Guidelines for choosing a backup destination" link opens a Windows Help and Support topic that provides extensive details on choosing a backup destination. Windows Help and Support points out that saving to an external hard drive is safer than saving to another partition on the same drive because if the hard disk fails, you will lose your backup on that other partition as well as what is stored on the partition that you backed up. Likewise, Windows Help and Support recommends that you do not save backups to the drive that contains the files you're backing up because a problem, such as an infection by malicious software, might arise on that drive or the hard disk might fail. That's why removable drives or disks are recommended. In fact, Windows Help and Support also points out that you can store a removable drive or disks in a fireproof safe to further protect your backups. In the case of DVDs and CDs, Windows Help and Support warns that these types of disks can become corrupted over time, and therefore you might not be able to access your backups

To continue setting up Windows Backup:

1. Select a backup destination, and then click the **Next** button. Windows Backup prompts you on what you want to back up. See Figure 10-10.

Figure 10-10	Specifying the approach for backing up files

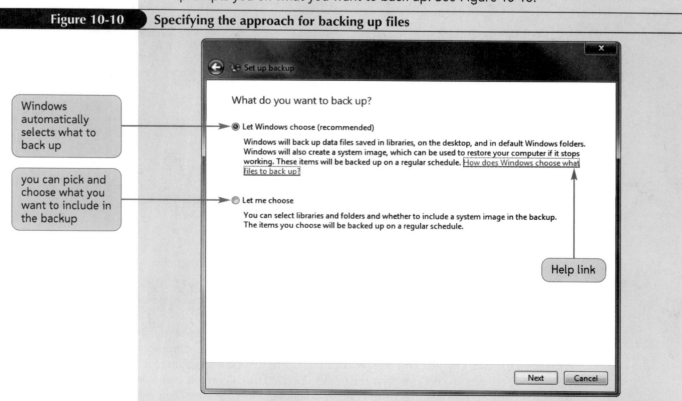

Windows automatically selects what to back up

you can pick and choose what you want to include in the backup

Help link

The default and recommended option is to let Windows choose for you. Windows Backup notes that this option backs up data files in libraries, the contents of the desktop, and files in user account folders for all users with an account on a computer. Default Windows folders include the AppData, Contacts, Desktop, Downloads, Favorites, Links, Saved Games, and Searches folders for each user. It also notes that it will create a system image, but only if you are backing up to an NTFS drive that has enough space for the system image backup. Furthermore, it notes that these items are backed up on a regular schedule. If you choose the first option, make sure you have enough storage space on your backup media for ongoing backups. Of course, the backup will take longer because it also creates a system image with each new backup. However, this option guarantees that all your data files are backed up periodically and that you also have a recent system image if you need to restore your computer. If you click the "How does Windows choose what files to back up" Help link, then Windows Help and Support further explains that only local files are backed up, not network files or files stored on the Internet. Files on a drive that does not use NTFS are not included in the backup.

The "Let me choose" option allows you to select those libraries and folders that you want to back up and decide whether you want to include a system image. If you expand a user account's libraries, such as those shown for Thiago in Figure 10-11, then Windows Backup identifies those locations and notes that additional locations are included in the backup. These additional locations are the same default Windows folders described in the previous paragraph.

| Figure 10-11 | Selecting what you want to back up |

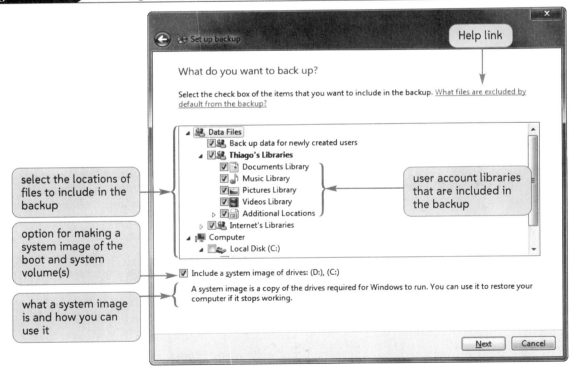

If you expand the folders for drive C under Computer, then you can locate and select specific folders on that drive that you want to include in your regular backups. By default, none of them are selected, but you can step down, or "drill down" to whatever folder level you want.

If you click the "What files are excluded by default from the backup?" Help link, Windows Help and Support notes that Windows Backup does not back up program files, files stored on hard disk drives that use the FAT file system, Recycle Bin files, and temporary files on drives with less than 1 GB of storage space.

The primary advantage of the "Let me choose" option is that it provides more flexibility. You can pick and choose those locations you want to back up, and you can exclude the option for making a system image. As a result, regularly scheduled backups of your data files are faster. You always have the option of creating a system image at any time from the Backup and Restore window.

The next set of steps set up a backup schedule for selecting and backing up the Gaia Cartographics folder and its contents on the computer you are using. If you are working on your own personal computer or a college computer, the following steps will describe how to back up your user account. To save time and backup media, whether you are working in a computer lab or on your own personal computer, the steps will recommend that you only back up the Gaia Cartographics folder. As an example of how much time a more comprehensive backup might take, a backup that included all user account folders and the Public user account folder on the computer used for this tutorial took 4 hours 17 minutes to back up 59.40 GB of data.

To specify what you want to back up:

▶ **1.** Choose one of the following three options:

    a. If you are working in a computer lab where the computers restore their original configuration and settings at the next boot, and if you want to create a backup of just the Gaia Cartographics folder and its contents and then later restore that folder and its contents, click the **Let me choose** option button, and then click the **Next** button. Windows Backup displays a "Set up backup" dialog box where you can specify which folders and files you want to back up, and whether you also want to include a system backup.

    b. If you are working on your own personal computer and want to choose what folders and files to back up on an ongoing basis, and want to decide whether to create a system image, click the **Let me choose** option button, and then click the **Next** button. Windows Backup displays a "Set up backup" dialog box where you can specify which folders and files you want to back up, and whether you also want to include a system backup.

    c. If you are working on your own personal computer and want to follow the Windows Backup recommended option for what to back up, and if you have enough storage space on your backup media to support this option on an ongoing basis, make sure the "Let Windows choose (recommended)" option is selected, and then click the **Next** button. Windows Backup then displays a "Set up backup" dialog box where you can review your backup settings.

> If time is a limiting factor, be sure you turn off the option for making a system image.

▶ **2.** If you selected the "Let me choose" option and if you are working on your own personal computer or on a computer in a computer lab and want to exclude the option to create a system image (to save time and backup media storage space), and if the "Include a system image of drives" check box has a check mark, click the **Include a system image of drives** check box to remove the check mark from this check box.

▶ **3.** If you selected the "Let me choose" option and if you are working on your own personal computer or on a computer in a computer lab with multiple user accounts and want to exclude other users of that same computer (again, to save time and backup media storage space), then click the check box next to each of the other users libraries check boxes (and remove the check mark). You can always later add other user accounts to the regularly scheduled backup.

4. To select the contents of the Gaia Cartographics folder in the Public Documents folder, click the **expand** icon ▷ to the left of Computer, click the **expand** icon ▷ to the left of Local Disk (C:), click the **expand** icon ▷ to the left of Users, click the **expand** icon ▷ to the left of Public, click the **expand** icon ▷ to the left of Documents, and then locate and if necessary, add a check mark to the check box for the Gaia Cartographics folder.

TIP

Make sure your backup device is on and ready so Windows Backup can perform a backup.

5. Click the **Next** button. In the next "Set up backup" dialog box, you are prompted to review your backup settings. See Figure 10-12. Windows Backup identifies your backup location, what items are included in your backup, and the backup schedule.

Figure 10-12   Reviewing backup settings for a backup

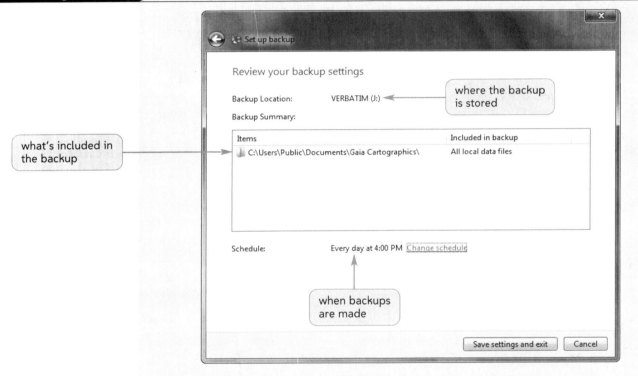

On the computer used for this figure, Windows Backup is set to back up the Gaia Cartographics folder every day at 4 PM. You can use the "Change schedule" link to change the default schedule. If you chose the "Let Windows choose" option earlier, or if you included the option for making a system image, and assuming in both cases that the backup media contained space for a system image, then Windows Backup also notes that a system image is included and that you may need to create a system repair disc to boot your computer so you can restore a system image. Your settings will differ.

6. Click the **Save settings and run backup** button. If Windows 7 is already set to perform a scheduled backup on your computer, and if you want to perform a manual backup, click the **Save settings and exit** button, and then click the **Back up now** button in the Backup and Restore window. The Backup in progress indicator in the Backup and Restore window provides a general idea of how far you are in the backup process. See Figure 10-13.

Figure 10-13   **Viewing the status of a backup in progress**

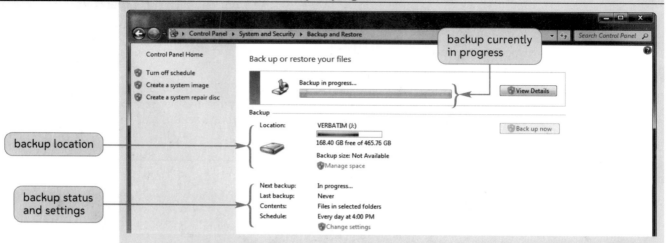

backup location

backup status and settings

Under Backup, Windows Backup identifies the backup drive, the amount of available and total storage space on the backup drive, the contents included in the backup, and the backup schedule. Windows 7 also shows the progress of the backup by a green progress indicator on the Backup and Restore taskbar button.

After the backup is complete, Windows Backup displays a Windows Backup dialog box indicating that the backup has completed successfully.

▶ **7.** Click the **Close** button, if necessary. The Backup and Restore window now shows the amount of storage space remaining on the backup media, the size of the backup, and the date and time of the next and the last backups. See Figure 10-14. Your details will differ.

Figure 10-14   **Viewing backup settings after a backup is complete**

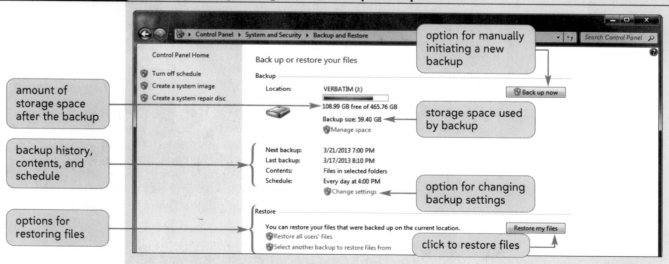

amount of storage space after the backup

backup history, contents, and schedule

options for restoring files

▶ **8.** Keep the Backup and Restore window open for the next set of tutorial steps.

After you perform a full backup of your files (and those of any other users) and set a schedule for periodic incremental backups, you can examine your backup storage media if you want to understand how Windows Backup organizes your backups.

REFERENCE

Setting Up a Regularly Scheduled Backup

- From the Start menu, click Control Panel, and then click the "Back up your computer link" under System and Security.
- If you have not set up Windows Backup on your computer, click the "Set up backup" link under the Backup section in the Backup and Restore window, and if necessary, provide Administrator credentials.
- In the first "Set up backup" dialog boxes, select a backup destination, and then click the Next button.
- Choose the "Let Windows choose (recommended)" option button or the "Let me choose" button to specify what you want to back up, and then click the Next button.
- If you chose the "Let me choose" option in the last "Set up backup" dialog box, check the items you want to include in your backup by indicating under Data Files whether to back up data for newly created users, and which user accounts you want to include in the backup. If you want to include additional folders on one or more hard disk drives, click the check box for each drive you want to include or expand the folder structure for each drive, and then navigate the folder structure while clicking the check box for each additional folder you want to include in the backup. If you do not want to create a system image for one or more drives, remove the check mark from the "Include a system image of drive(s)" check box. Then, click the Next button.
- In the next "Set up backup" dialog box, review your backup settings for your backup location, items included in the backup under Backup Summary, your backup schedule, and any other information provided by Windows Backup. If you want to change your schedule, use the Change schedule link.
- To start the backup, click the "Save settings and exit" button or the "Save settings and run backup" button, and monitor the status of the backup in the Backup and Restore window. Use the View Details button to determine the percent complete for the backup and to check which files are included in the backup.
- Verify that the backup completed successfully, and then close the Backup and Restore window.

Thiago recommends you examine your backup so you can ensure that you have backed up all the files you might need. He also notes that you must provide Administrator credentials to view the contents of the folder with your backup.

To examine your backed-up files:

1. Open a Computer window, and then open a window onto your backup drive. As shown in Figure 10-15, your backup media contains a folder with a custom icon and the name of your computer system and a MediaID.bin file. The folder with the name of your computer system contains your current backup and any future backups that you create. The name of the folder with your backup will differ.

Figure 10-15 | Viewing the contents of the backup media

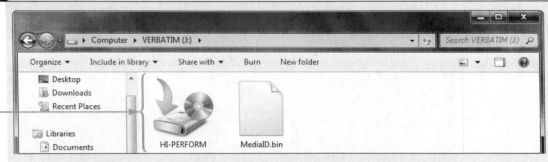

this folder with a custom icon, and named after your computer, contains your backups

▶ 2. If you can provide Administrator credentials, right-click the **backup folder** named after your computer system, and click **Open**. In the dialog box for the backup folder click the **Continue** button (if necessary), and then provide Administrator credentials (if necessary). If you cannot provide Administrator credentials, read this and subsequent steps and examine the figures. As shown in Figure 10-16, the backup folder contains your backup set or sets (if you have previously backed up your computer).

Trouble? If Windows Backup displays a Windows Backup dialog box with options for restoring your files from this backup, restoring files for all users of the same computer, and managing space used by this backup, you clicked the backup folder icon instead of right-clicking the icon. Close that Windows Backup dialog box, and repeat Step 2.

Figure 10-16 | Viewing the backup set (or sets) on your backup media

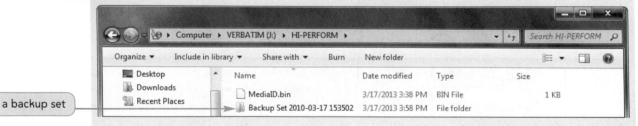

a backup set

The folder is named "Backup Set" followed by the current date in the format YYYYMMDD followed by the current time in hours, minutes, and seconds in the format HHMMSS. Your backup set name will differ, and you may have more than one backup set.

▶ 3. Click the **Backup Set** folder icon for the backup you just performed or for another backup set. If you open a Backup Set folder, you will find one or more Backup Files folder and a single Catalogs folder. See Figure 10-17.

Figure 10-17 | Identifying the folder with the backed up files

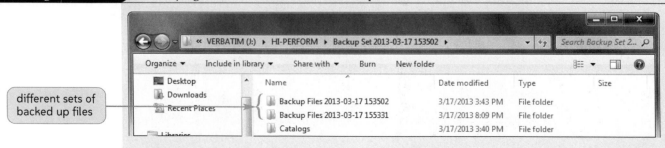

different sets of backed up files

Each Backup Files folder is an incremental backup, and the date and time included in the Backup Files folder name identifies when the backup was made. To open the Catalogs folder, you must provide Administrator credentials. As shown in Figure 10-18, the Catalogs folder contains a Windows Backup Catalog File named GlobalCatalog.wbcat, which contains an index (or list) of all the files that are included in this backup. Windows Backup uses this catalog to find the location of a file that you want to restore.

Figure 10-18	Viewing the contents of the Catalogs folder

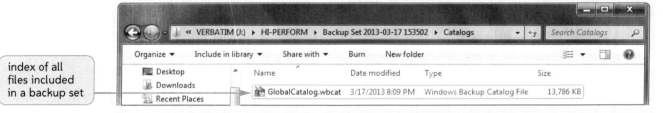

index of all files included in a backup set

▶ **4.** Click the **Backup Files** folder icon for your recently created backup or another backup. As shown in Figure 10-19, each Backup Files folder contains a set of Compressed (zipped) Folder files. Each file with the .zip file extension contains a set of files. Because Windows 7 treats these files as folders, you can open them and examine their contents and even copy backed-up files from these folders. On the computer used for this full backup, there are 336 Compressed (zipped) Folder files, each of which includes multiple files for a single backup. Your details will differ.

Figure 10-19	Backup .zip files for storing backed up files

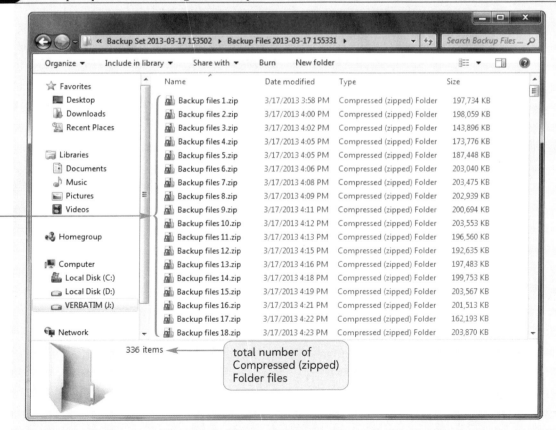

Compressed (zipped) Folder files with backed up files

total number of Compressed (zipped) Folder files

5. Click **Backup files 1.zip**. In this Compressed (zipped) Folder is a folder with the name of the drive that contained the files that were backed up. See Figure 10-20. *C* is the drive letter for drive C.

Figure 10-20 **Viewing the contents of a backup zip file**

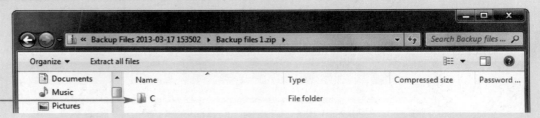

folder for the drive containing the files that were backed up

6. Click the **folder** icon for the drive that contains the files you backed up. Within the drive C folder is a Users folder that contains all user account folders, including the Public folder which in turn contains the Gaia Cartographics folder. See Figure 10-21.

Figure 10-21 **Viewing the Users folder for all backed-up user accounts**

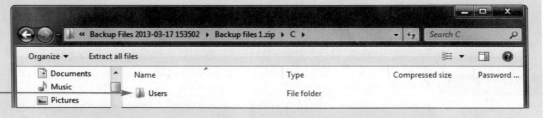

folder contains all backed-up user account folders

7. Click the **Users** folder icon, click the **Public** folder icon, click the **Documents** folder icon, click the **Gaia Cartographics** folder icon, and then click the **Mapping** folder icon. The Mapping folder contains two backed-up files. See Figure 10-22.

Trouble? If you are not able to locate a backup of the Public folder in this backup file, then read Step 7 and Step 8 and examine the figures.

Figure 10-22 **Viewing the backed up files from the Mapping folder**

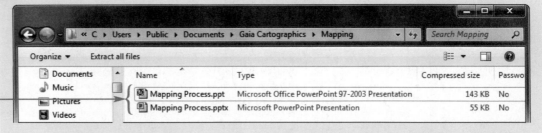

files backed up from the Mapping folder on drive C

In this step, you stepped or drilled down through multiple folders that included backed-up files.

8. Close the window onto the backup, but keep the Backup and Restore Center open for the next session.

Even though compression varies by file type, Microsoft notes that Compressed (zipped) Folders typically take up about half the storage space of the original files, thus enabling you to take maximum advantage of the backup storage media that you use for backups.

REVIEW

Session 10.1 Quick Check

1. The interval of time between each full or normal backup is called the _____.

2. What type of backup always includes all new and modified files since your last full or normal backup?

3. What type of backup includes only those files that you created or changed since your previous backup—whether it was a full or normal backup or a partial backup?

4. When you create a file or modify and then save an existing file, Windows 7 turns on the _____ attribute for that file.

5. True or False. Windows Backup stores backed-up files in Compressed (zipped) Folders with the .zip file extension.

6. What is the difference between a copy backup and a daily backup?

7. What is a system image backup?

8. At which point in a backup cycle does an incremental backup differ from a differential backup?

SESSION 10.2 VISUAL OVERVIEW

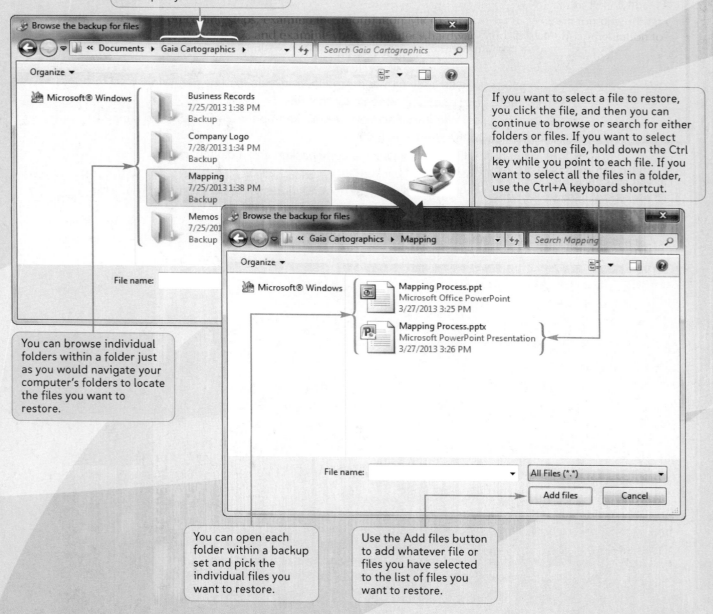

You can browse or search your backup set to locate a specific folder that contains the files you want to restore from your backup to your hard disk drive.

If you want to select a file to restore, you click the file, and then you can continue to browse or search for either folders or files. If you want to select more than one file, hold down the Ctrl key while you point to each file. If you want to select all the files in a folder, use the Ctrl+A keyboard shortcut.

You can browse individual folders within a folder just as you would navigate your computer's folders to locate the files you want to restore.

You can open each folder within a backup set and pick the individual files you want to restore.

Use the Add files button to add whatever file or files you have selected to the list of files you want to restore.

RESTORING FILES

If you need to examine another backup for a specific version of a file, you can use the "Choose a different date" link for each specific backup set, depending on how you set up the backup schedule (such as daily or weekly).

These restored files were selected from different folders and restored to a single folder.

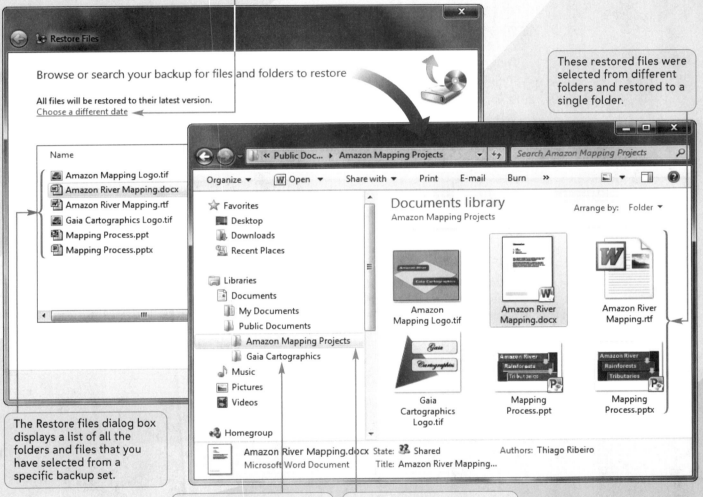

The Restore files dialog box displays a list of all the folders and files that you have selected from a specific backup set.

If you restore specific files to an alternate location, you can compare the restored files with the current versions of those files to determine which files meet your needs.

You can perform a test restore and restore a backup to an alternate location, such as a new folder, to make sure that the backup set and backup media are working properly.

Restoring Folders and Files

Occasionally, a file on your hard disk becomes corrupted or damaged, making it impossible to use the file. A **corrupted file** is a file whose contents have been altered as the result of a hardware or software error, power failure, damage caused by malicious software, or a problem with the file system itself. If you find that a file is corrupted, or if you accidentally permanently delete a folder or file, or if your hard disk fails, you can restore folders and files from your backups once you have resolved the problem that occurred with your computer. If your hard disk fails, you have to replace the drive and reinstall Windows 7. Then you can restore your personal folders and files on the computer.

In the following steps, you will delete the Gaia Cartographics folder and then restore it from your backup using the Restore Files wizard.

To restore a folder and its files:

1. Open the **Documents** library, click the **Documents library expand** icon ▷ , click the **Public Documents** folder, point to the **Gaia Cartographics** folder, press the **Delete** key, verify that you want to move this folder to the Recycle Bin, and then minimize the Public Documents folder window.

2. If necessary, open the Backup and Restore window. Under Restore, Windows 7 lists the options "Restore my files," "Restore all users' files," "Select another backup to restore files from," and "Recover system settings or your computer." You can use the "Select another backup to restore files from" option to restore files from a backup created on another computer with Windows 7 or Windows Vista.

3. Click the **Restore my files** button. Windows 7 opens a Restore Files dialog box where you can search for specific files to restore (using search criteria you examined in Tutorial 3), browse for specific files to restore, or browse for folders to restore. See Figure 10-23. You can use all of these options to find any combination of folders and files you want to restore.

Trouble? If Windows Backup does not display a "Restore my files" button on the computer you are using for this session, you can click the "Restore all users' files" link and continue with the following discussion and steps. However, be aware that this option affects all other individuals who have user accounts on the same computer.

Figure 10-23   **Options for selecting the files and folders to restore**

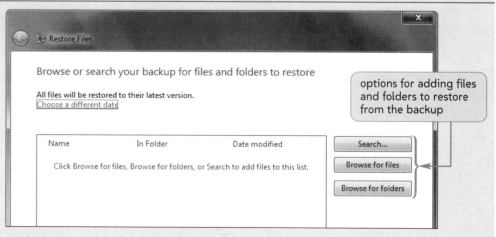

If you click the "Choose a different date" link, then a Restore Files dialog box shows the date and time of backups from the last week. See Figure 10-24. You can use the "Show backups from" button to select backups from the last week, last month, last 6 months, last 12 months, or from all backups. Windows Backup will restore all files on the date of the backup you select.

Figure 10-24   Choosing a backup set for a specific date

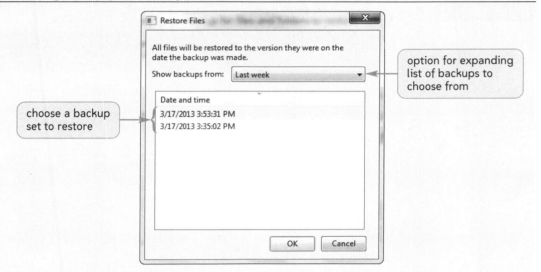

Because you want to restore the Gaia Cartographics folder and all its contents, you will use the option to browse for folders.

4. Click the **Browse for folders** button. In the "Browse the backup for folders or drives" dialog box, you can click the Backup of C: folder to navigate to the exact backup you want to restore. See Figure 10-25.

Figure 10-25   Browsing the backup for files to restore

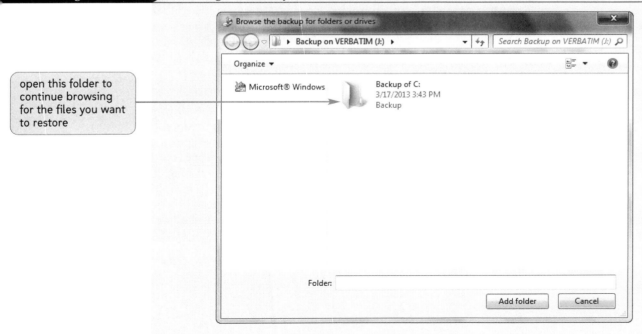

▶ **5.** Click the **Backup of C:** folder icon, click the **Users** folder icon, click the **Public** folder icon, click the **Documents** folder icon, point to the **Gaia Cartographics** folder icon, and then click the **Add folder** button. After you select the folder, the Restore Files dialog box shows the name of the Gaia Cartographics folder you want to restore. See Figure 10-26. You can repeat this process to restore any combination of folders and files.

Figure 10-26   **Gaia Cartographics folder added from backup set**

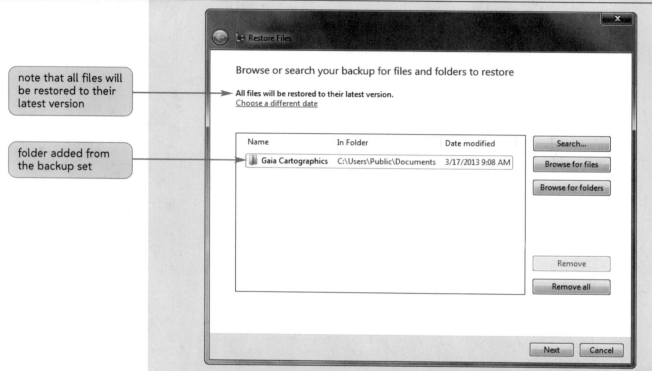

note that all files will be restored to their latest version

folder added from the backup set

This Restore Files dialog box also shows the Gaia Cartographics folder, its path, and date and time it was modified. If necessary, you can use the Remove or Remove All button to remove an individual folder or file, or all folders and files that you select. The Restore Files dialog box also notes that all files will be restored to their latest version.

If you want to browse for files, you follow the same process in the "Browse the backup for files" dialog box to browse the folder structure of your backup media for the files to restore, and then you select the file or files you want to restore, and click the Add files button. If you are using Search to locate folders or files to restore from your backup, you enter search criteria in the Search for box within the "Search for files to restore" dialog box. After the search is complete, you can use the folder and filenames, folder and file paths, and date and time modified to locate and then click the check box or check boxes for the folders or files you want to restore. You can also use the Select all button if you want to select all the folders and files in the search results. See Figure 10-27.

Figure 10-27   **Folders and files located by searching**

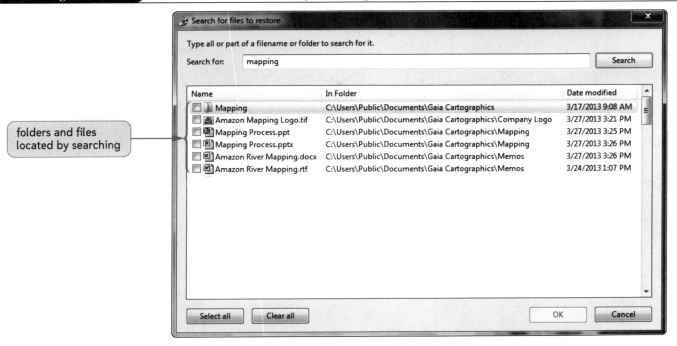

folders and files located by searching

Once you click OK, you return to the Restore Files dialog box and verify that you have selected the right set of folders and files to restore. See Figure 10-28.

Figure 10-28   **Specific files and folder selected for restoring**

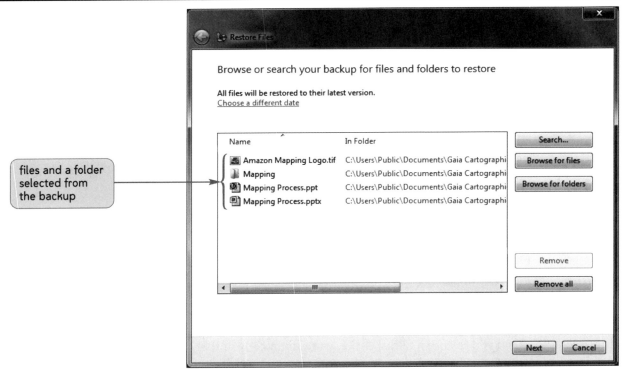

files and a folder selected from the backup

To complete and verify the restore operation:

1. Click the **Next** button. You can specify whether you want to restore the folder to its original location or to an alternate location. See Figure 10-29.

Figure 10-29   Deciding where to restore the files and folder selected from the backup

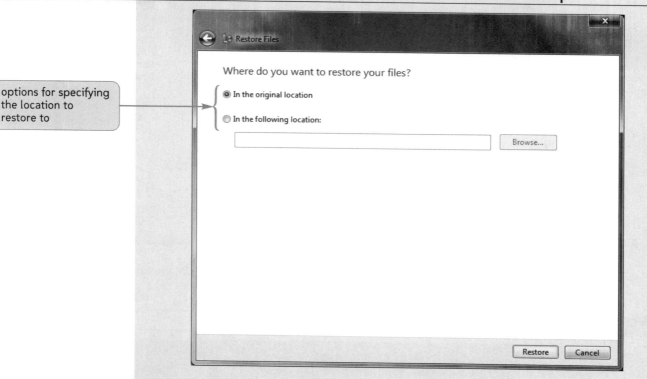

options for specifying the location to restore to

If you choose an alternate location, you can use the Browse button to locate the folder where you want to restore your folders and files. You can either select an existing folder or create a new folder. One advantage of restoring to an alternate location (for example, a new folder in the same location as the original folder and files) is that you can verify that the backup contains the folders and files you need without affecting your existing folder and files. If the backup contains what you need, then you can delete the original folder and change the name of the restored folder to the original folder name. Or you can keep both folders, and copy those restored files that you may need later to your original folder.

Because you deleted the original folder, you will restore the backed-up folder to its original location.

2. Click the **Restore** button. The Restore Files wizard informs you that your files have been restored.

3. Click the **Finish** button, and then use the **Windows Explorer** taskbar button to open the Public Documents folder from the Jump List. The Restore Files wizard has restored the Gaia Cartographics folder. The date shown under Date modified is the date the folder was last modified, not the date the folder was restored. When you restore a folder or file, you want a copy of that folder and file as of the date it was last modified so you can work with a previous version of that folder or file, not a copy of that folder or file with a new date and time stamp.

4. Open the Gaia Cartographics folder. All four folders within this folder are now restored.

5. Open the Mapping folder. The two files you examined earlier on your backup media are now restored.

6. Close the Mapping folder window.

If the Restore Files wizard discovers one or more filenames that match the files you want to restore, it informs you in a Copy File dialog box that there is already a file with the same name as a file you want to restore. See Figure 10-30.

Figure 10-30	Deciding how to handle a file conflict during a restore operation

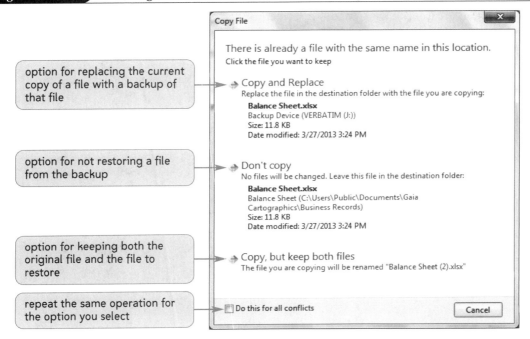

This dialog box displays "Copy and Replace," "Don't copy," and "Copy, but keep both files" options. You can compare the size, date modified, and time modified to determine which file, if any, is the latest version or newest copy of the file you want to restore. If you choose the "Copy, but keep both files" option, then the file you are copying will be renamed to include (2) at the end of the main part of the filename so you can distinguish the two copies. You can use the "Do this for all conflicts" check box to use the same option for every other conflict that is encountered, rather than respond to one prompt after another for each file that has a filename identical to the one that is being restored.

INSIGHT

Verifying Backups

A test restore is a good way to check your backup and your backup media to ensure that you can restore files from that backup and that backup media. You should not wait until a serious problem occurs before you attempt to restore files from a backup. You can select an alternate location for a test restore, or you can select and rename the original folder (or file) before you restore a copy of the original folder (or file) from your backup. After you verify that the restore and your backup media worked, you can delete the original folder, and rename the restored folder to the original folder name. By verifying backups, you ensure they are reliable.

When you browse for the folders or files you want to restore, remember that the folders or files may be under a user account name that is different than the one for the computer where you want to restore the folders or files, and you will therefore need to browse to a different location. You also have the option of browsing for a network location where you have an alternate backup you want to restore.

You can also restore files from a backup made on another computer system; however, it must be a backup that you created with Windows 7 or Windows Vista; both versions use the same approach for creating backups.

REFERENCE

Restoring Files and Folders

- Open the Control Panel, and then click the "Back up your computer" link under System and Security.
- In the Backup and Restore window, click the "Restore my files" button or "Restore all users' files" button.
- In the Restore Files dialog box, click the Search button, "Browse for files" button, or "Browse for folders" button.
- In the "Browse the backup for folders or drives" dialog box or the "Browse the backup for files" dialog box, browse the folder structure of your backup media for the folders or files to restore, and then click the Add folder button. If you are browsing for files in the "Browse the backup for files" dialog box, browse the folder structure of your backup media for the files to restore, select the files you want to restore, and then click the Add files button.
- Verify your selection, and then click the Next button.
- Choose whether to save the restored files in the original location or an alternate location that you specify, and then click the Restore button.
- If necessary, select an option in the Copy File dialog box to resolve conflicts where a file being restored has a name identical to an existing file.
- After the restore operation is complete, click the Finish button, and then close the Backup and Restore window.

Creating a System Image and a System Repair Disc

The option in Windows 7 for creating a system image copies the drives required for Windows to run properly block by block (rather than file by file) to a virtual hard disk file with the .vhd file extension. The first backup is a full backup, but each backup after that is a partial backup that backs up incremental changes *within* files, so subsequent system image backups are fast.

After you create a system image, you can use it to restore your computer if you encounter a serious problem that calls for rebuilding your computer. Because everything on the volume or volumes is restored from the system image, you must have a recently backed-up system image that includes all changes to your computer, including newly installed software and device drivers. The system image backup also contains copies of all your personal files, but you need to rely on scheduled backups so you have the most recent versions of your personal files that you can restore after you restore the system image.

After creating a system image backup, you can then create a system repair disc. A **system repair disc** is a boot disk that you can use to start up your Windows 7 computer; it also contains Windows 7 system recovery tools that can help you recover from a serious error or restore your computer from a system image.

The following steps take you through the process of creating a system image. If you have not yet created a system image, but have enough time and enough backup media, then you can perform the operations described in the following steps. You will also need a blank CD or DVD to create a system repair disc. If you have neither time nor sufficient backup media for creating a system image backup and a system repair disc, then read the tutorial steps and examine the figures. You must provide Administrator credentials to create a system image. On the dual-boot computer used for the following steps, it took 1 hour 5 minutes to create a system image backup by backing up two volumes—the boot volume and the system volume.

To create a system image backup:

 1. Open the Control Panel, click the **Back up your computer** link under System and Security, click the **Create a system image** link on the left side of the Backup and Restore window, and if necessary, provide Administrator credentials. Windows 7 opens two "Create a system image" dialog boxes; the smaller dialog box scans for backup devices. Once Windows 7 locates backup devices, the smaller dialog box closes, and you are prompted for where to save the system image backup. You can save it on a hard disk, one or more DVDs or CDs, or a network location. See Figure 10-31.

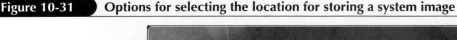

Figure 10-31   Options for selecting the location for storing a system image

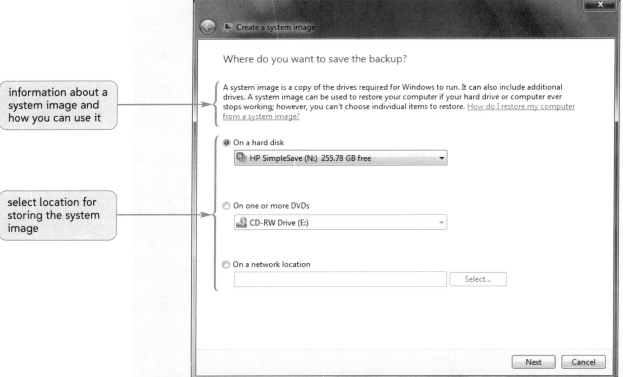

information about a system image and how you can use it

select location for storing the system image

If you have both a CD and DVD drive, then both drives are identified as CD drives, so you need to know the drive letter for your DVD drive to select the proper drive to back up to.

2. Select the drive or network location where you want to store the system image, and then click the **Next** button. At the next step, you specify which drives to include in the backup. See Figure 10-32.

Trouble? If Windows Backup does not prompt you to choose which drives to include in a backup, but instead asks you to confirm your backup settings (as described in Step 3), then read this step so you are familiar with the options for including additional drives in a backup, and then continue with Step 3.

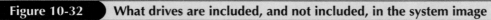

Figure 10-32   **What drives are included, and not included, in the system image**

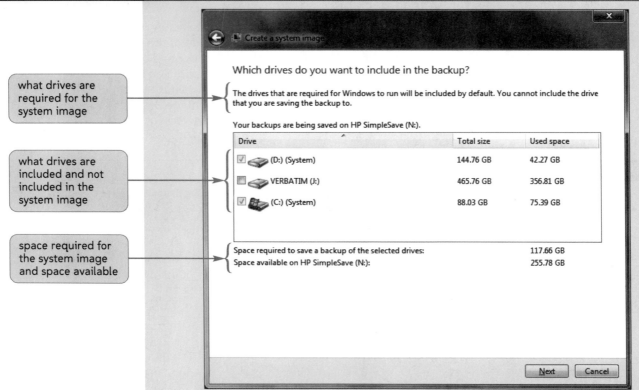

what drives are required for the system image

what drives are included and not included in the system image

space required for the system image and space available

The drives required by Windows to run properly are automatically included in the backup; however, at this point, you can also include other drives. But you cannot include the drive used to store the system image backup. The "Create a system image" dialog box also informs you how much storage space is required for the system image. On the dual-boot computer used for this figure, drive C (where Windows 7 is installed) and drive D (where Windows Vista is installed) are both included because drive C contains the Windows folder for Windows 7 and drive D contains the files needed to boot Windows 7.

3. If Windows Backup offers the option to include additional drives in the system image backup, select any other drives you want to include in this backup, and then click the **Next** button. The next "Create a system image" dialog box prompts you to confirm your backup settings, and shows the amount of storage space required for the system image backup. See Figure 10-33.

Figure 10-33 | Viewing your backup settings for a system image

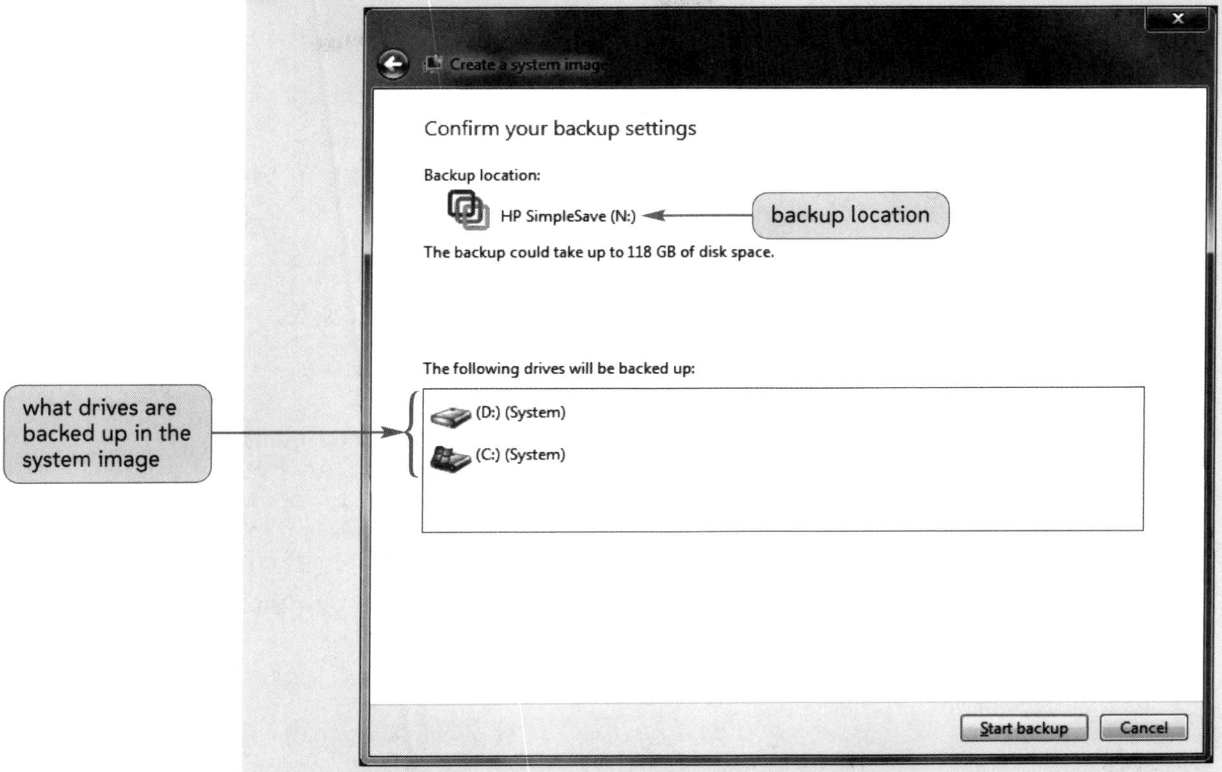

what drives are backed up in the system image

4. After confirming your backup settings, click the **Start backup** button. In the next "Create a system image" dialog box, Windows 7 shows a progress indicator for saving the backup. It also identifies each drive that is backed up to the system image, and at the end of this process, it asks you if you want to create a system repair disc. See Figure 10-34.

Figure 10-34 | Option for creating a system repair disc

important reasons for creating a system repair disc

Create a system image

Do you want to create a system repair disc?

A system repair disc can be used to boot your computer. It also contains Windows system recovery tools which can help you recover Windows from a serious error or re-image your computer from a system image.

☐ Don't show this message again   Yes   No

5. If you want to create a system repair disc, click the **Yes** button. Then you are prompted to select a CD or DVD drive and insert a blank disc into that drive, as shown in Figure 10-35.

Figure 10-35 **Choosing a drive for the system repair disc**

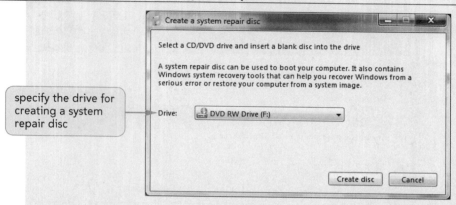

specify the drive for creating a system repair disc

6. Click the **Drive** button, select either a CD or DVD drive, insert a blank disc into the appropriate drive, and then click the **Create disc** button. After creating the system repair disc, you are prompted to label your disc. The dialog box also states that you can use the system repair disc to boot your computer and to access system recovery options for recovering your computer after a serious error occurs.

7. Remove the CD or DVD from the CD or DVD drive, and label your disc as shown in the "Create a system repair disc" dialog box.

8. Close the "Create a system repair disc" dialog box, and then close the "Create a system image" dialog box.

If you don't create a system repair disc after creating a system image backup, you can use the "Create a system repair disc" link in the Backup and Restore window at any time to prepare this type of disc.

REFERENCE

Creating a System Image and a System Repair Disc

- Open the Control Panel, click the "Back up your computer" link under System and Security, click the "Create a system image" link on the left side of the Backup and Restore window, and if necessary, provide Administrator credentials.
- In the "Create a system image" dialog box, select the drive or network location where you want to store the system image, and then click the Next button.
- In the next "Create a system image" dialog box, select any other drives you want to include in the system image backup (if available), and then click the Next button.
- In the last "Create a system image" dialog box, confirm your backup settings, and then click the Start backup button.
- After the system image backup is complete, click the Yes button in the "Create a system repair disc" dialog box if you want to make this disc, click the Drive button in the next dialog box, insert a blank CD or DVD into the appropriate drive, and then click the Create disc button.
- After creating the system repair disc, remove the CD or DVD, record the recommended label on your CD or DVD, close the "Create a system repair disc" dialog box, and then close the "Create a system image" dialog box.

After you create a system image backup, you can examine your backup storage media so you are familiar with the folder and file structure of your system image backup. You will discover that the folder and file structures are similar to those used for a backup of folders and files described earlier. To view the contents of the folder that contains the system image, you will need to provide Administrator credentials.

To examine your system image backup:

▶ **1.** Open a Computer window, and then open the drive that contains your system image backup. The WindowsImageBackup folder contains the system image backup. See Figure 10-36.

Figure 10-36	Viewing the folder with the system image and related folders and files

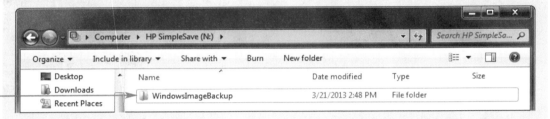

folder that contains the system image and related folders and files

▶ **2.** Click the **WindowsImageBackup** folder icon, and then provide Administrator credentials. After you open the WindowsImageBackup folder, you will see a folder with the name of your computer.

▶ **3.** Click the **folder** with your computer name, and then provide Administrator credentials. Within the folder with your computer name are three folders—a Backup folder with your backup set, a Catalog folder, a SPPMetadataCache folder, and a MediaID file. See Figure 10-37.

Figure 10-37	Viewing the folder with the system image

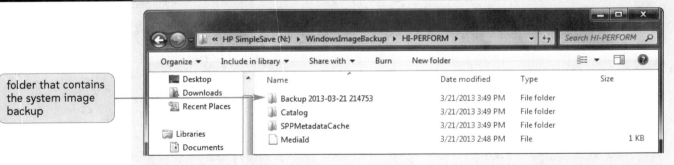

folder that contains the system image backup

The Catalog folder contains two catalog files—GlobalCatalog and BackupGlobalCatalog for keeping track of the system image backup versions. The Backup folder name includes the current date in the format YYYYMMDD followed by the current time in hours, minutes, and seconds in the format HHMMSS. The folder with the name of your computer also contains a MediaID file that identifies the disk image. If you open the Backup folder, you will find a virtual hard disk image file (or files) with the .vhd file extension that contains a complete backup of the volume or volumes on your computer. See Figure 10-38.

Figure 10-38   **Viewing the virtual hard disk image file(s) and supporting XML files**

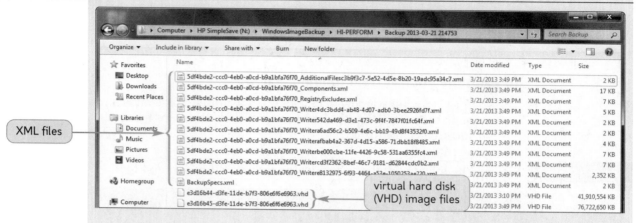

On the computer used for this figure, there are two virtual hard disk image files, one for each drive that was backed up. Note that these files are large in size. You will also see XML (Extensible Markup Language) files that store configuration settings for the system image backup file.

4. Close the window onto your system image backup.

If you have Virtual PC (a software environment for running up to four additional operating systems under an existing operating system) installed on your computer, you can mount the virtual hard disk image with the .vhd file extension as a secondary hard disk drive. You first modify Virtual PC settings in the Virtual PC console for an existing OS (such as Windows XP, Windows Vista, or another edition of Windows 7), and then you start that operating system, and access the secondary hard disk drive from a Computer window in the virtual environment. Next, you access the individual files in your system image backup as you would folders and files in your Documents library.

Restoring a System Image Backup

If you need to restore your computer from a system image backup, then you must boot from your Windows 7 DVD and open the System Recovery Tools because a complete restore of your computer overwrites everything on the drives backed up to the system image file.

Because restoring a computer from a system image is time consuming and only necessary if you have to rebuild your computer, the following discussion describes the process for restoring a system volume (or system volumes) using a system image backup. *Do not attempt to perform these steps for practice because doing so overwrites everything on your computer with the contents of a previous system image of your computer.*

- If necessary, connect the backup media with the system image to your computer.
- Insert your Windows 7 DVD, and reboot your computer in one of two ways:
  - During booting, press the key for displaying the boot menu for your computer, and then choose the option for booting from your DVD drive, or
  - During booting, open the BIOS Setup utility, change the boot sequence so your computer boots from the drive with your Windows 7 DVD, exit the BIOS Setup utility and save your boot settings, and then during booting, press a key when prompted to boot from your Windows 7 DVD.

- As your computer boots from the Windows 7 DVD, verify the "Language to install," "Time and currency format," and "Keyboard or input method" settings in the first Install Windows dialog box.
- In the next Windows dialog box, choose the "Repair your computer" option to work in the Windows Recovery Environment. This option opens the program RecEnv.exe.
- In the System Recovery Options dialog box, choose the "Restore your computer using a system image that you created earlier" option button, and if the system image backup is on a DVD, insert the DVD disc, and then click the Next button.
- In the "Re-image your computer" dialog box, the option for automatically using the latest system image backup is already selected, and you see the location and the date and time for the system image backup as well as the computer name. You also have an option of selecting a system image.
- After you select the system image backup you want to use, you advance to the next step where you have the option of repartitioning and formatting the disk if the disk is not already partitioned and formatted. In the case of a dual-boot system, that may mean partitioning and formatting two volumes.
- After you advance to the next step, you click Finish, and then Windows System Image Restore rebuilds each disk using the system image backup.
- After your computer is restored with the system image backup, then your computer restarts.

You can restore a system image backup to another hard disk on the same or another computer, even if it's a different size; however, you have to make sure that there is enough storage space on that drive to restore everything from your system image backup.

If you open the Backup and Restore window, and click the "Recover system settings or your computer" link, Windows 7 opens a Recovery window where you have the option to use System Restore to restore your computer to an earlier point in time. If you then click the "Advanced recovery methods" link in this window, you can choose between one of two advanced recovery methods, as shown in Figure 10-39.

Figure 10-39   Advanced recovery methods

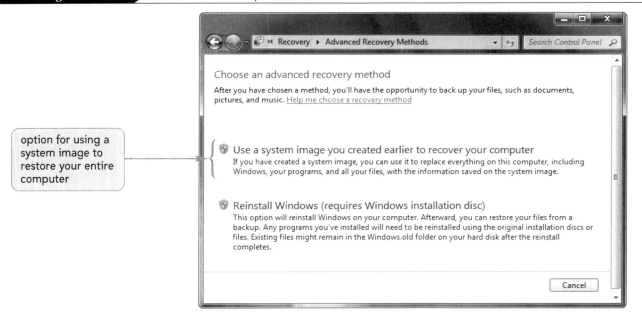

option for using a system image to restore your entire computer

You can choose between using a system image to recover your computer, and an option for reinstalling Windows 7 using the Windows 7 installation disc. This latter option requires you to reinstall any programs from their original installation discs, or from downloaded files. After the install is complete, any existing files might be in the Windows.old folder on your hard disk. After you chose an advanced recovery method, you have the option to back up your files first.

Using Previous Versions and Shadow Copies

You can use a Windows 7 feature called Previous Versions to restore files, folders, or even your entire hard disk drive from either a backup or a shadow copy. A **shadow copy** is a copy of a folder or file that Windows 7 creates for a restore point or for a backup.

Windows 7 uses System Protection (covered in Tutorial 8) to periodically create restore points that include shadow copies of new files or files that you've modified since the last restore point. If you back up your computer with Backup and Restore, then Windows 7 uses its Volume Shadow Copy service to take a snapshot of any files that you have open so Windows Backup can back up the files (rather than skipping the open files and excluding them from the backup). You can continue to work on an open file while Windows Backup uses the shadow copy of the files for the current backup. The shadow copy, which is kept in reserve by the Volume Shadow Copy, then becomes a previous version of the files you're backing up.

You can use the VSSADMIN command (the Volume Shadow Copy Service administrative tool), in a command-line window to display the storage space reserved on disk for Shadow Copy Storage. On the computer used for Figure 10-40, the amount of storage space used on drive C for the Shadow Copy Storage space is 4% of the volume's storage capacity. On the computer used for this figure, Volume Shadow Copy is creating and storing shadow copies on another partition of the same drive (i.e., drive D) and on an external hard disk drive.

| Figure 10-40 | Viewing details on Shadow Copy Storage space |

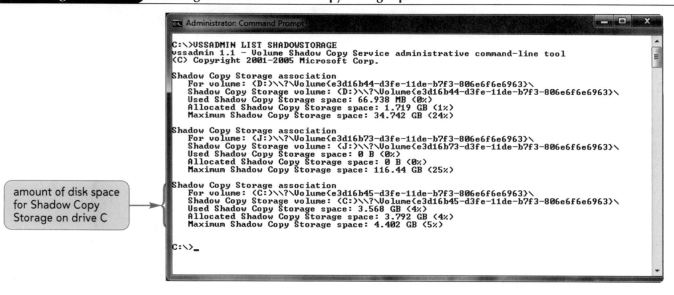

amount of disk space for Shadow Copy Storage on drive C

To use the VSSADMIN command, open an Administrator: Command Prompt window by right-clicking Command Prompt on the Accessories menu, click "Run as administrator" on the shortcut menu, and finally provide administrator credentials, even if you are already logged on under an Administrator account.

Viewing Previous Versions of Folders and Files

Windows 7 can use shadow copies and backup copies of files to restore previous versions of files. However, to view and work with the Previous Versions feature of folders and files, the Windows 7 Volume Shadow Copy must first make shadow copies of files on your computer. The Volume Shadow Copy service does not automatically make a shadow copy (or previous version) of each file right after you make a change to a file, which means you will not have every version of a file that you've worked on and saved.

Thiago asks you to check his Amazon Mapping River file in the Memos folder to determine whether there are any previous versions of the file and if so, restore the most recent version of the file so he can check a change he made in the file.

To complete the following steps, Windows 7 or Windows Backup and Restore must have already created either shadow copies or backups that include the file you examine in this section of the tutorial. If Windows 7 informs you that there are no previous versions for the file, then continue to read the following steps so you are familiar with the use of previous versions.

To check for previous versions of a file:

▶ **1.** Click the Windows Explorer taskbar button 📁 to open a view onto your computer's libraries, click the **expand** icon ▷ to the left of Documents, click **Public Documents**, click the **Gaia Cartographics** folder, and then click the **Memos** folder.

▶ **2.** Right-click the **Amazon River Mapping.docx** file icon, click **Properties** on the shortcut menu, click the **Previous Versions** tab, and after Windows 7 searches for previous versions of this file, drag the **Location column** button in the File versions box to the left of the Date modified column button so you can identify where previous versions come from. At the top of this property sheet, Windows 7 informs you that previous versions come from restore points or from Windows Backup. See Figure 10-41.

Trouble? If no previous versions of the Amazon River Mapping.docx file appear in the Properties dialog box for this file, open the Properties dialog box for another file that you opened, changed, and saved within the last several days.

Figure 10-41 **Viewing previous versions of a Microsoft Office Word file**

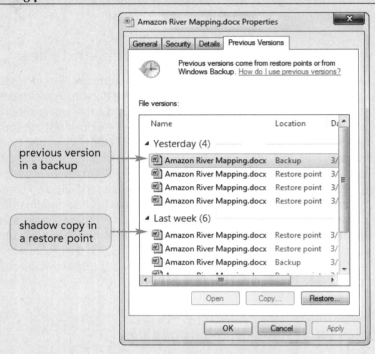

previous version
in a backup

shadow copy in
a restore point

On the computer used for Figure 10-41, Windows 7 found four previous versions
of this file listed under Yesterday, and six previous versions listed under Last Week
(although not all of them are available). These previous versions are shadow copies created during a backup or a restore point over a 2-week period. Your previous versions will differ. If Windows 7 does not find any previous versions of a file,
it informs you that there are no previous versions.

3. If you have a previous version of this file, select the previous version, and then
click the **Restore** button. A Restore Files dialog box opens followed by a Copy File
dialog box. On the computer used for the previous figure and this step, the copies
are identical (because no changes were made to this file).

4. In the Copy File dialog box, click **Copy, but keep both files**. In the Restore Files
dialog box, the Restore Files wizard notes that it successfully restored the file.

5. Click the **Finish** button in the Restore Files dialog box, and then click the **OK**
button in the Amazon River Mapping.docx Properties dialog box. In the Memos
folder window, you have two versions of this file—the original file and a previous version named Amazon River Mapping (2).docx. You can use this approach
to restore a previous version of a file and examine it before you delete the more
recent version.

6. To remove the restored previous version of this file, right-click the **Amazon River
Mapping (2).docx** file, click **Delete**, and in the Delete File dialog box, click the
Yes button.

If the previous version of a file is stored in a backup, then the only option you have for restoring the file is the Restore button. If there is a previous version of a file created by a restore point, then you can choose the option to restore, copy, or open the file. If you choose the copy option, you are then prompted in a Copy Items dialog box to select the location for the copy of the previous version of a file.

You can also create a new folder for the copied file. After the previous version of the file is copied to the location you specify, you have an earlier version of that same file. If you choose the Open option, then the previous version of the file is opened in an application on your computer, and you have the choice of saving that file in a different location, under a different filename, or both.

You can also restore previous versions of a folder and even a drive. Thiago recommends you examine these options so you are aware of the possibilities available with Previous Versions.

To restore a previous version of a folder:

TIP

You can also access previous versions of a folder from within the folder by right-clicking its background and then viewing its properties.

▶ 1. Click **Public Documents** in the Address bar to open the parent folder of Gaia Cartographics.

▶ 2. Right-click the **Gaia Cartographics** folder, click **Properties**, and then click the **Previous Versions** tab. On the computer used for Figure 10-42, there is one previous version that was made the current day (identified as Today), five previous versions made the previous day (identified as Yesterday), and eight versions made the previous week (identified as Last week). Your previous versions will differ.

Figure 10-42   **Viewing previous versions of a folder**

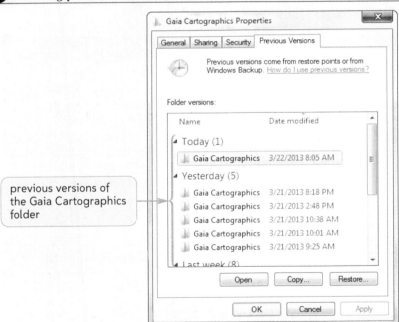

previous versions of the Gaia Cartographics folder

3. Scroll down the Folder versions box, locate and select the oldest previous version, and then click the **Open** button. Windows 7 opens the previous version of that folder in a new window, as shown in Figure 10-43.

Figure 10-43 **Viewing the contents of a previous version of a folder**

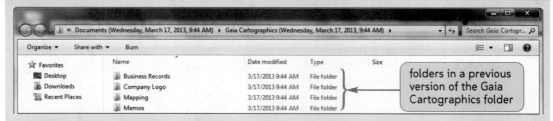

Notice that the Address bar includes the name of the Gaia Cartographics folder followed by the date of the previous version you opened. This folder with previous versions of Gaia Cartographic folders and files is *completely* separate from the original folder with newer versions. Once you open a previous version of a folder, then you can examine all the files previously contained in that folder and copy specific files that you need to another location.

If you had chosen to restore the previous versions of these folders and their files, then the dates and times for the restored folders and files would be identical to those at the time the previous version was made. If you do not make changes to a set of folders and files over a long period of time, you will find that previous versions made on different dates contain the identical folders and files with the identical dates and times.

4. Close the Gaia Cartographics window with previous versions of the Gaia Cartographics folders and files, and then close the Gaia Cartographics Properties dialog box.

5. In the Navigation pane, click **Computer**, right-click **Local Disk (C:)**, click **Properties**, and then click the **Previous Versions** tab. Windows 7 displays previous versions of your hard disk drive. On the computer used for Figure 10-44, there is one previous version that was made the current day (identified as Today), five previous versions made the previous day (identified as Yesterday), and nine versions made the previous week (identified as Last week), showing you that you can have multiple copies of the contents of your hard disk drive that you can restore. Your previous versions will differ.

Figure 10-44   **Viewing previous versions of a drive**

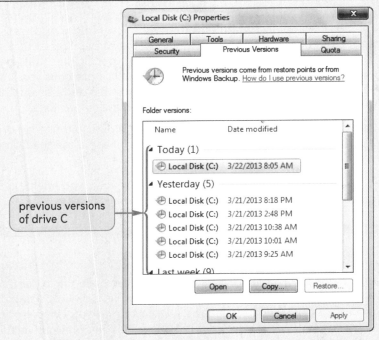

previous versions
of drive C

> **6.** Scroll down the Folder versions box, locate and select the oldest previous version, and then click the **Open** button. Windows 7 opens the previous version of the folders and files on your hard disk drive in a new window. See Figure 10-45.

Figure 10-45   **Viewing the contents of a previous version of a drive**

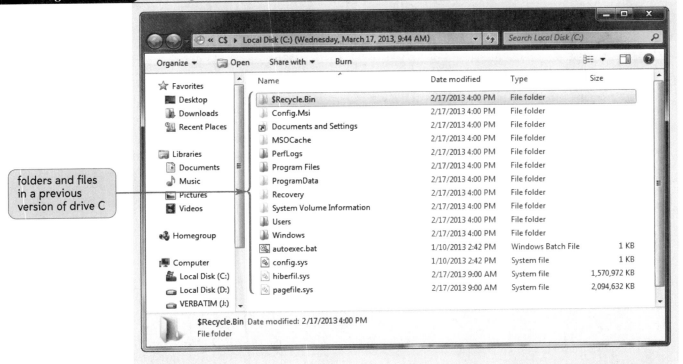

folders and files
in a previous
version of drive C

Notice that the Address bar includes the name of the Local Disk (C:) folder followed by the date of the previous version you opened. Your previous version of drive C will differ. This folder with previous versions of the folders and files on drive C is *completely* separate from the top-level folder of drive C with the most recent contents of the folders and files on that drive. You can open folders from this previous version, and examine and copy specific files that you need to another location. Note that this folder not only contains a previous version of the Windows and Program Files folders, but also the Recycle Bin and Users folders. In addition, there is a previous version of the hibernation file (hiberfil.sys).

▶ **7.** Close the window with previous versions of folders and files on drive C, and then close the Local Disk (C:) Properties dialog box, and close the Computer window.

In addition to recovering files using Previous Versions, you might be able to recover a file manually from a regular backup or a system image backup.

REFERENCE

Restoring Previous Versions of Files, Folders, and Drives

- If you want to restore a previous version of a file, open the folder that contains the most recent version of that file, right-click the file, click Properties, click the Previous Versions tab, and wait for Windows 7 to locate previous versions of that file. If there is a previous version created by a backup, select that previous version, and then use the Restore button to restore previous versions of the file over the current version of the same file. If there is a previous version created by a restore point, then you can restore, copy, or open the previous version. After selecting a previous version, you can use the Copy button to copy the contents of that previous version to a different or a new folder. Or you use the Open button to open a previous version of a file, then save it to a new location, under a new filename, or both.

- If you want to restore a previous version of a folder, you open the library or folder that contains the folder that you want to locate previous versions for. Then you right-click the folder icon, click Properties, click the Previous Versions tab, and wait for Windows 7 to locate previous versions of the folder. You can select a previous version of the folder and then use the Restore button to restore the previous version of the folder over the current version of that same folder. Or, you can use the Copy button to copy the contents of that previous version of the folder to a new location. Or, you use the Open button to open the previous version of that folder, and then examine and copy files of the previous version of that folder to wherever you want.

- If you want to restore a previous version of a drive, you open a Computer window, right-click the drive, click Properties, click the Previous Versions tab, and wait for Windows 7 to locate previous versions of the drive. You can select a previous version of the drive and then use the Copy button to copy the contents of that previous version of the drive to a new location. Or you use the Open button to open the previous version of the drive, and then examine and copy files of the previous version of that drive to wherever you want.

By combining backups with restore points automatically created by System Protection, you enhance the chance that you can recover an important file you need to meet an important deadline.

PROSKILLS

Problem Solving: Using Previous Versions to Recover Folders and Files

In addition to restoring a previous version of a file, folder, or hard disk drive, there are other ways to use Previous Versions:

- **Recovering deleted files**—If you delete one or more files in a folder, you can right-click the background of the folder window and choose the option for viewing properties of the folder. Then, from the Previous Versions property sheet, you can use the Restore option to restore copies of the deleted files. If you cannot find a previous version of a file, you can create an empty file using the exact same filename, and view Previous Versions of the file to determine if you can recover a previous version.
- **Recovering deleted folders**—If you delete one or more folders within another folder, you can right-click the background of the folder window and choose the option for viewing properties of that folder. Then, from the Previous Versions property sheet, you can use the Restore option to restore copies of the deleted folders and all the files in those folders. Or, you can create a new folder with the name of the original folder, open the empty new folder, right-click the background of the folder window and choose the option for viewing properties of the folder. Then, from the Previous Versions property sheet, you can use the Restore option to restore copies of the deleted subfolders within this folder and all the files in those folders.

The Windows 7 Previous Versions feature can be a powerful problem-solving tool if you accidentally delete or overwrite an important file, or if you need to recover a previous version of a file rather than reconstruct the file from scratch or from an existing file.

Restoring Your Computer's Settings

Complete the following steps to restore your computer to its original settings.

1. Use the Start menu to turn off the display of the Computer icon on the desktop.
2. Open the Folder Options dialog box and enable double-click activation (if necessary); turn off the display of hidden folders, files, and drives; and hide protected operating system files.
3. Open the Public Documents folder, delete the Gaia Cartographics folder, and then close the Public Documents folder window.

REVIEW

Session 10.2 Quick Check

1. If you want to restore a folder from a backup, but keep the original folder until you can verify whether the restored files meet your needs, what option can you choose when you restore files from that backup?
2. What type of file does Windows Backup create for a system image, and what file extension does it use for that file?
3. What type of boot disk can you use to restore a system image on your computer?
4. True or False. A shadow copy is a copy of a folder or file that Windows 7 creates for a restore point or for a backup.
5. What two types of previous versions can Windows 7 use to restore files to a computer?
6. Describe two ways you can use Previous Versions to restore a deleted folder.
7. How can you verify that a new backup will work if you later need to restore folders and files from that backup?
8. The first system backup is a full backup, but each backup after that is a partial backup that backs up _____ changes within files.

Practice the skills you learned in the tutorial using the same case scenario.

PRACTICE

Review Assignments

For a list of Data Files in the Review folder, see page 641.

Recently, a representative of the local community college contacted Thiago to discuss the possibility of Gaia Cartographics hiring a student intern as part of an independent work-study program. Through a federal program, the college pays half of the student intern's salary. Thiago interviewed the student and decided to hire him to work on the new expansion of the Amazon River mapping project. Thiago asks you to review and demonstrate options for backing up and restoring files with this intern.

As you complete each step in these Review Assignments, record your answers to the questions so you can submit them to your instructor. Use a word-processing application such as Word or WordPad to prepare your answers to these questions. If you change any settings on the computer you are using, note what the original settings were so you can restore them later. Complete the following steps:

1. Open the Tutorial.10 folder that contains your original copy of the Windows 7 for Power Users Data Files, and copy the Review folder from the Tutorial.10 folder to the Public Documents folder. Change the name of the Review folder to **Mapping Projects**.

2. Use System Protection to create a restore point named "Manual Restore Point." Then restart your computer, and log on under your user account.

3. What edition of Windows 7 is installed on your computer?

4. Describe techniques or strategies you use to ensure that you have backup copies of important files on your hard disk drive. Include in your discussion how many backups you retain, what type of backup media you use, and how frequently you back up. Do you store any backups off site?

5. Open Backup and Restore. What options are available for backing up files on your computer and for restoring files? If Windows Backup has recently backed-up files on your computer, what schedule did you specify for each of your next backups? Where does the Backup and Restore store your backups?

6. What other features available from the Backup and Restore window do you use, and why?

7. Open the Public folder, open the Public Documents folder, view properties of the Mapping Projects folder, and then select the Previous Versions tab. Do you have any previous versions of this folder and, if so, when were those previous versions made?

8. Select the most recent previous version, and then click Open. What name does Windows 7 show for this folder in the Address bar? List the date and time under the Date modified column for all the folders in the Mapping Projects folder.

9. Open the Memos folder within the window you opened from the Previous Versions property sheet. What files does this folder contain? Close the Memos folder window, and close the Mapping Projects Properties dialog box.

10. In the Public Documents folder, open the Mapping Projects folder. What is the date and time for all the folders in the Mapping Projects folder? How much time elapsed between the point when you copied the Review folder from the Tutorial.10 folder to the Public Documents folder and the point at which Windows 7 created the previous versions you examined in Step 8? How might this previous version prove useful?

11. Open the Memos folder. What does this folder contain? How does this Memos folder differ from the one that you opened from the Mapping Project Properties Previous Versions property sheet?

12. Right-click the Contract Income Projection.docx file, choose the option to view Properties, and then select the Previous Versions property sheet. What types of locations contain previous versions of this file (if any)? Close the Contract Income Projection.docx Properties dialog box.

13. From the Memos folder, return to the Mapping Projects folder.

14. Submit your document to your instructor either in printed or electronic form, as requested.

Use your skills to develop a backup strategy for a law firm.

APPLY

Case Problem 1

There are no Data Files needed for this Case Problem.

Grayson, Sables & O'Toole   Morgana Courey, an attorney in the law firm of Grayson, Sables & O'Toole, prepares new bond documents for funding rural water projects. Because most projects require essentially the same type of bond document, she adapts bond documents she prepared for previous projects to prepare new bond proposals. Morgana asks you to develop a backup strategy that will guarantee that she can retrieve an earlier version of a bond document and adapt it to a new funding project.

As you complete each step in this case problem, record your answers to the questions so you can submit them to your instructor. Use a word-processing application such as Word or WordPad to prepare your answers to these questions. If you change any settings on the computer you are using, note the original settings so you can restore them later. Complete the following steps:

1. What would be the best backup strategy for Morgana to use so she could easily recover earlier versions of other bond documents?

2. Assume that her assistant uses backup software that supports full, differential, and incremental backups. Prepare a table that describes how to implement this backup strategy using a backup cycle of 1 week. (Assume a 5-day workweek.) Name the table "Proposed Backup Schedule" and include the following three columns: Stage of Backup Cycle, Type of Backup, and Backup Includes. Identify each stage in the backup cycle, the type of backup, and what types of folders and files are included in the backup. Also identify when the next backup cycle begins.

3. How many copies of each backup set would you recommend that Morgana's assistant keep, and where should he store those backup sets?

4. What other Windows 7 features might Morgana's assistant use to recover earlier versions of previously created bond documents?

5. How might Morgana benefit from a system image backup?

6. Submit your document to your instructor either in printed or electronic form, as requested.

Use your skills to determine the best backup strategy for a consulting firm.

APPLY

Case Problem 2

There are no Data Files needed for this Case Problem.

Thaxton Consulting, Inc.   The Middlesworth County's Board of Directors recently contracted with Christopher Thaxton to develop a comprehensive growth management plan for the county. Christopher wants to implement a backup strategy that guarantees access to the most recent version of documents that he prepares. Because each revision of Middlesworth County's comprehensive growth management plan undergoes extensive analysis, review, and public comment, Christopher only needs to keep the most recent versions of files. Also, because the development of a comprehensive growth management plan takes several years, he works on the same documents each day. Christopher asks you to develop a backup strategy that will meet his needs for this project.

As you complete each step in this case problem, record your answers to the questions so you can submit them to your instructor. Use a word-processing application such as

Word or WordPad to prepare your answers to these questions. If you change any settings on the computer you are using, note the original settings so you can restore them later. Complete the following steps:

1. What would be the best backup strategy for Christopher to use?

2. Assume that Christopher's assistant uses backup software that supports full, differential, and incremental backups. Prepare a table that describes how to implement this backup strategy using a backup cycle of 1 week. (Assume a 5-day workweek.) Name the table "Proposed Backup Schedule" and include the following three columns: Stage of Backup Cycle, Type of Backup, and Backup Includes. Identify each stage in the backup cycle, the type of backup, and what types of folders and files are included in the backup. Also identify when the next backup cycle begins.

3. How many copies of each backup set should his assistant keep, and where should he store those backup sets?

4. What can Christopher do in advance to guarantee that he can restore his entire computer should he encounter a serious problem with his computer?

5. If Christopher wants to only perform a full backup at the beginning of the month, how might he effectively combine the use of full, differential, and incremental backups?

⊕ **EXPLORE**
6. If you've never performed a full backup of your user files on your own computer, if you have enough time and storage media to perform a full backup of your user files, and if you have access to an Administrator account, then open Backup and Restore, create a backup schedule with Windows Backup, and then perform a full backup. If you have already specified a backup schedule and performed a previous full backup, and if you want to back up changes to folders and files since that previous backup, open the Backup and Restore and then start a backup.

7. Describe the process that Christopher would initially follow if he decided to use Windows Backup to back up his user files every day. Then describe how he would perform subsequent backups.

⊕ **EXPLORE**
8. Create a new folder named **Test Restore** in your Documents folder. Then use the Backup and Restore option for restoring a folder from the backup to the Test Restore folder.

9. Submit your document to your instructor either in printed or electronic form, as requested.

Extend your skills to examine previous versions for a shipping firm.

CHALLENGE

Case Problem 3

There are no Data Files needed for this Case Problem.

CalBay International Shipping, Inc.   Iloai Tuilagi works as an accountant for CalBay International Shipping, Inc., which handles shipping for well-known import/export businesses. As part of her job, Iloai occasionally requests copies of financial and supporting documents from company's clients. She asks you to help her with the new Previous Versions feature of Windows 7 so she can view previous copies of the company's financial documents. You decide to show her how you access previous versions of files using your computer.

As you complete each step in this case problem, record your answers to the questions so you can submit them to your instructor. Use a word-processing application such as Word or WordPad to prepare your answers to these questions. If you change any settings on the computer you are using, note the original settings so you can restore them later. Complete the following steps:

1. What edition of Windows 7 is installed on your computer?

⊕ **EXPLORE**   2. Open a Computer window and then select and view previous versions of your hard disk drive. How many previous versions do you have, and how are they broken down by date? What options are available for using a previous version (i.e., Open, Copy, and/or Restore)? Describe the contents of the window that opens. What does Windows 7 display in the Address bar as the name of this folder? Close the window you opened from the Previous Versions property sheet, and then close the Properties dialog box for your hard disk drive.

⊕ **EXPLORE**   3. In the Computer window, open a window onto drive C, open the Users folder, open your user account folder, right-click the My Documents folder, choose the option to view its Properties, and then select the Previous Versions property sheet. How many previous versions do you have, and how are they broken down by date? What options are available for using a previous version? Click the most recent previous version. Describe the contents of the window that opens. What does Windows 7 display in the Address bar as the name of this folder? Close the window that you opened from the Previous Versions property sheet, and then close the My Documents Properties dialog box.

⊕ **EXPLORE**   4. Use the Address bar to return to the Users folder, open the Public folder, view properties of the Public Documents folder, and then select the Previous Versions property sheet. How many previous versions do you have, and how are they broken down by date? What options are available for using a previous version? Click the most recent previous version. Describe the contents of the window that opens. Close the window that you opened from the Previous Versions property sheet, and then close the Public Documents Properties dialog box.

5. Open the Public Documents folder, open a subfolder (if necessary) select a file, view its properties, and then select the Previous Versions tab. Describe the types of previous versions available and their location(s).

6. If a shadow copy is available, select that previous version, and choose the option to make a copy of it. When prompted for the location for the shadow copy, open the Public Documents folder, create a new folder for the shadow copy, and then copy the shadow copy to the new folder. If you do not have a shadow copy but you do have a Backup Copy, select that Backup Copy and then click the Restore button. In the Copy File dialog box, choose the option to copy the file, but keep both files (the original and the previous version). Then close the Restore Files dialog box and the Properties dialog box for the file you selected.

7. Comment on your impression of the value of the Previous Versions feature, and note whether you would find it useful on your computer.

8. Submit your document to your instructor either in printed or electronic form, as requested.

Extend your skills to back up and restore files for a book publisher.

Case Problem 4

CHALLENGE

For a list of Data Files in the Case4 folder, see page 641.

Vejar Press, Inc.   Miguel Vejar's publishing firm publishes books written by Latin American writers. As head of the firm, he frequently reviews manuscripts, contracts, and company documents at home and while traveling. At the end of a particularly busy day, he asks you to make a backup of his business files rather than wait for the next scheduled backup. Afterwards, he wants you to do a test restore to verify that there are no problems with the backed-up files and his backup media.

To complete this case problem, you must have available a backup drive and, if necessary, backup media, as well as sufficient time for performing a backup. If you have not already set up Windows Backup, you will need to perform that process first and then perform a full backup of your computer. The latter will require not only sufficient storage space on the backup media, but also time. You will also have to provide Administrator credentials.

As you complete each step in this case problem, record your answers to the questions so you can submit them to your instructor. Use a word-processing application such as Word or WordPad to prepare your answers to these questions. If you change any settings on the computer you are using, note the original settings so you can restore them later. Complete the following steps:

1. Copy the Case4 folder in the Tutorial.10 folder to the Public Documents folder, and then change the name of the Case4 folder to **Vejar Press**.

2. Right-click the Vejar Press folder, and choose the option to view properties of this folder. What is the size of the folder in KB and bytes, and how many files and folders are contained with this folder. Also, what is the path of this folder?

3. If you have not already set up Windows Backup, open Backup and Restore, and then use the instructions in this tutorial to not only set up Windows Backup but also to perform your first full backup. If you have already set up Windows Backup, then use the Back up now button to initiate a backup. As your backup progresses, click the View Details button, and provide Administrator credentials so you can monitor the progress of the backup.

⊕ **EXPLORE** 4. In the Backup and Restore window, choose the option to restore your files. In the Restore Files dialog box, click the Search button, type **Vejar Press** in the Search for box in the "Search for files to restore" dialog box, and then click the Search button. Locate the Vejar Press folder with the path identified in Step 2, click the check box to restore that folder, and then click the OK button to close the "Search for files to restore" dialog box. In the Restore Files dialog box, verify that you selected the Vejar Press folder, and then advance to the next step.

⊕ **EXPLORE** 5. When prompted as to where you want to restore these files, choose the "In the following location" option button, and turn off the option for restoring the files to their original subfolders. Open the Browse For Folder dialog box, and navigate to the Public Documents folder of Local Disk (C:). Click the "Make New Folder" button, name the new folder **Vejar Press Test Restore**, and then click the OK button. What is the path for restoring these files? Choose the Restore button, and after the files are restored, close the Restore Files dialog box.

6. Open the Public Documents folder (if necessary), right-click the Vejar Press Test Restore folder, and choose the option to view properties of this folder. What is the size of the folder in KB and bytes, and how many files and folders are contained with this folder. What is the path of this folder? Compare this information to that in Step 2 for the Vejar Press folder, and explain how you can tell whether the restore worked properly.

⊕ **EXPLORE** 7. In the Backup and Restore window, click the Manage space link and provide Administrator credentials. What is your backup location? List the information reported for Space usage summary. Under Data file backup, use the View backups button to determine if you can free up disk space by deleting data file backups. What information does Windows Backup report in the "Manage Windows Backup disk space" dialog box? What would happen if you deleted a set of backups for a backup period? Is there advantage to removing older backups? Close each of the two "Manage Windows Backup disk space" dialog boxes without making any changes, and then close the Backup and Restore window.

8. Delete the Vejar Press and Vejar Press Test Restore folders in the Public Documents folder.

9. Submit your document to your instructor either in printed or electronic form, as requested.

ENDING FILES

There are no ending Data Files needed for this tutorial.

WINDOWS

OBJECTIVES

Session 11.1
- Prepare for an operating system upgrade
- Install and use the Windows 7 Upgrade Advisor
- Evaluate ways to install Windows 7
- Examine Windows Easy Transfer
- Assess Windows XP Mode

Session 11.2
- Turn Windows Features on or off
- Examine how to install and upgrade software
- Use the Program Compatibility troubleshooter
- Uninstall software
- Add and remove Microsoft Office components
- Set program defaults

Installing, Upgrading, and Configuring Software

Optimizing the Use of Software

Case | NanoAssets, Inc.

NanoAssets, Inc. provides capital to emerging industries and research groups that develop new products using nanotechnology, such as automobile fuel cells, nanoparticle delivery of medications, nanoparticle textile coatings, and solar panels. In her role as venture capital analyst, Kai Acoya evaluates funding proposals submitted by new companies and research groups and tracks the progress of these entrepreneurs. Like other staff members at NanoAssets, Kai relies on state-of-the-art operating systems and software technologies. She realizes the importance of updating her operating system software, her Microsoft Office suite, her project management software, and the other software products she uses every day.

In this tutorial, you examine how to prepare for and perform an upgrade to Windows 7, use the Windows 7 Upgrade Advisor to evaluate the feasibility of upgrading your computer to another Windows version or edition, examine ways to install Windows 7, and examine how to transfer files and settings from an older computer to a new computer using Windows Easy Transfer. You also examine how to turn Windows features on or off, install and uninstall software, use the Program Compatibility troubleshooter to correct program compatibility problems, examine how to add and remove Microsoft Office components, and review options for setting program defaults.

STARTING DATA FILES

There are no starting Data Files needed for this tutorial.

SESSION 11.1 VISUAL OVERVIEW

At its Web site, Microsoft lists 32-bit and 64-bit system requirements for each new version of Windows. Windows 7 supports 32-bit and 64-bit processors with a minimum 1 GHz clock speed, but has different 32-bit and 64-bit requirements for RAM and hard disk storage space.

Microsoft offers an upgrade advisor program that evaluates your computer system to determine whether there are any system, program compatibility, or device driver issues that could prevent or affect an upgrade to a new Windows version.

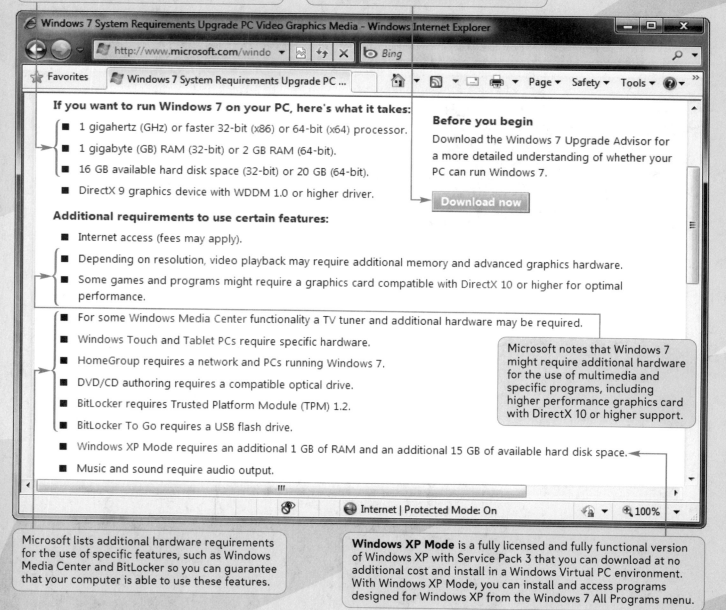

Windows 7 System Requirements Upgrade PC Video Graphics Media - Windows Internet Explorer

http://www.microsoft.com/windo ▾ | Bing

☆ Favorites | Windows 7 System Requirements Upgrade PC ... | 🏠 ▾ 🔊 ▾ 🖂 🖶 ▾ Page ▾ Safety ▾ Tools ▾ 🔞 ▾ »

If you want to run Windows 7 on your PC, here's what it takes:

- 1 gigahertz (GHz) or faster 32-bit (x86) or 64-bit (x64) processor.
- 1 gigabyte (GB) RAM (32-bit) or 2 GB RAM (64-bit).
- 16 GB available hard disk space (32-bit) or 20 GB (64-bit).
- DirectX 9 graphics device with WDDM 1.0 or higher driver.

Additional requirements to use certain features:

- Internet access (fees may apply).
- Depending on resolution, video playback may require additional memory and advanced graphics hardware.
- Some games and programs might require a graphics card compatible with DirectX 10 or higher for optimal performance.

- For some Windows Media Center functionality a TV tuner and additional hardware may be required.
- Windows Touch and Tablet PCs require specific hardware.
- HomeGroup requires a network and PCs running Windows 7.
- DVD/CD authoring requires a compatible optical drive.
- BitLocker requires Trusted Platform Module (TPM) 1.2.
- BitLocker To Go requires a USB flash drive.
- Windows XP Mode requires an additional 1 GB of RAM and an additional 15 GB of available hard disk space.
- Music and sound require audio output.

Before you begin

Download the Windows 7 Upgrade Advisor for a more detailed understanding of whether your PC can run Windows 7.

Download now

🌐 Internet | Protected Mode: On | 🔒 ▾ | 🔍 100% ▾

Microsoft notes that Windows 7 might require additional hardware for the use of multimedia and specific programs, including higher performance graphics card with DirectX 10 or higher support.

Microsoft lists additional hardware requirements for the use of specific features, such as Windows Media Center and BitLocker so you can guarantee that your computer is able to use these features.

Windows XP Mode is a fully licensed and fully functional version of Windows XP with Service Pack 3 that you can download at no additional cost and install in a Windows Virtual PC environment. With Windows XP Mode, you can install and access programs designed for Windows XP from the Windows 7 All Programs menu.

UPGRADING WINDOWS

There are two basic options for upgrading Windows—a custom install and an upgrade. A **custom install** requires that you back up all important folders and files, reformat your hard disk, install Windows 7, reinstall all your other software programs, upgrade and reinstall device drivers (where necessary), and then restore folders and files from a backup.

Microsoft posts at its Web site the **upgrade path**, which identifies whether you can upgrade from any earlier version or edition of Windows to a Windows 7 edition.

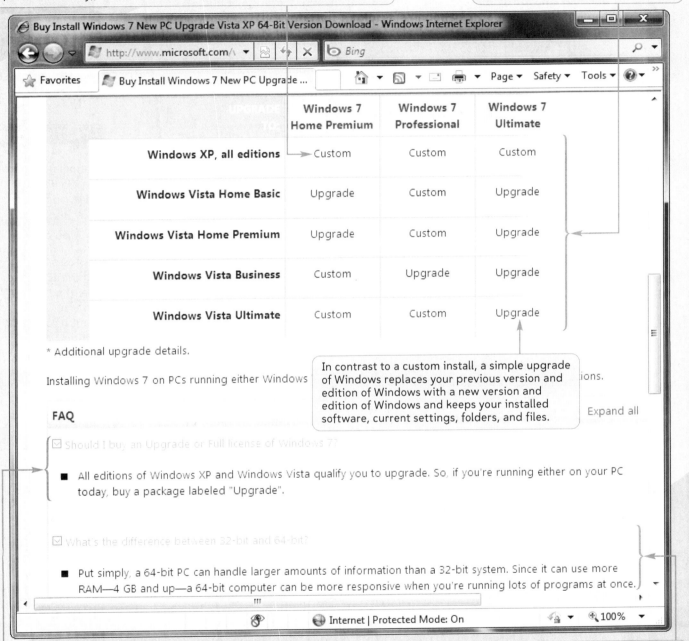

Buy Install Windows 7 New PC Upgrade Vista XP 64-Bit Version Download - Windows Internet Explorer

http://www.microsoft.com/\   Bing

Favorites   Buy Install Windows 7 New PC Upgrade ...   Page ▼   Safety ▼   Tools ▼

UPGRADE	Windows 7 Home Premium	Windows 7 Professional	Windows 7 Ultimate
Windows XP, all editions	Custom	Custom	Custom
Windows Vista Home Basic	Upgrade	Custom	Upgrade
Windows Vista Home Premium	Upgrade	Custom	Upgrade
Windows Vista Business	Custom	Upgrade	Upgrade
Windows Vista Ultimate	Custom	Custom	Upgrade

* Additional upgrade details.

Installing Windows 7 on PCs running either Windows   ions.

In contrast to a custom install, a simple upgrade of Windows replaces your previous version and edition of Windows with a new version and edition of Windows and keeps your installed software, current settings, folders, and files.

FAQ   Expand all

☑ Should I buy an Upgrade or Full license of Windows 7?

■ All editions of Windows XP and Windows Vista qualify you to upgrade. So, if you're running either on your PC today, buy a package labeled "Upgrade".

☑ What's the difference between 32-bit and 64-bit?

■ Put simply, a 64-bit PC can handle larger amounts of information than a 32-bit system. Since it can use more RAM—4 GB and up—a 64-bit computer can be more responsive when you're running lots of programs at once.

Internet | Protected Mode: On   100%

If you are performing a simple upgrade to a new version and edition of Windows, you can purchase an upgrade copy at a lower price and install Windows 7 over your current version of Windows. If you are installing Windows on a computer for the first time, or if you have to perform a custom install, you must purchase the more expensive full version of Windows 7.

Evaluate the information Microsoft provides on the advantages and differences between using a 32-bit versus a 64-bit Windows 7 version to determine how best to upgrade your computer.

Getting Started

To complete this tutorial, you must display the Computer icon on the desktop and switch your computer to single-click activation. In the following steps, you will check, and if necessary, change these settings.

To set up your computer:

▶ **1.** If necessary, use the Start menu to display the Computer icon on the desktop.

▶ **2.** If necessary, open the Folder Options dialog box and enable single-click activation.

Now, you are going to examine how to prepare for an operating system upgrade.

Preparing for an Operating System Upgrade

Microsoft continually develops new versions and editions of its Windows operating system and enhances the capabilities of existing Windows versions and editions via Windows updates. These new Windows versions, editions, service pack upgrades, and updates take advantage of the rapid emergence of new hardware and software technologies critical to businesses and home users; they also increase computer security and privacy for Windows users.

Installing or upgrading to a new version of the Windows operating system represents a significant change not only in the way that you use your computer, but also in the configuration of your computer and the operating system's support for existing and new software. Before you install or upgrade to Windows 7 or any other operating system, you should take certain steps to protect the integrity of your computer system and data. These steps also improve the chances that a new Windows operating system will install properly. Once you complete these preparatory steps, you can install the new Windows operating system.

You should perform the following steps before installing or upgrading to Windows 7 (or a future version of the Windows operating system):

- **Compare editions**—Windows 7 includes different editions with different features for different types of users. When upgrading to Windows 7 or its successors, you should examine the different editions to find out which one contains the features you need. That information, in turn, helps you make a decision when purchasing a computer and computer hardware.
- **Check system requirements**—Operating systems, as well as software applications, utilities, and games, have specific requirements that you should check before purchasing and attempting to install the software, including specific requirements for the processor, RAM, hard disk drive storage capacity, and graphics memory.
- **Consider the upgrade path**—The upgrade path identifies whether you can upgrade from your current version or edition of Windows to the next version of Windows or to another edition of Windows, or whether you need to perform a custom install.
- **Check hardware and software compatibility**—If you are buying a new computer, you need to know whether the hardware and software provided with that computer support a newer version or edition of Windows. Also, if you are buying new hardware for a computer, you need to know whether your existing version and edition of Windows supports that hardware.

- **Understand the differences between Windows 32-bit and 64-bit versions**—When deciding whether you want to have a 32-bit computer system or a 64-bit computer system, you will need to consider the following factors:
  - **Processor**—If you are using a computer with a 32-bit processor that is not 64-bit capable, you must purchase and install a 32-bit edition of Windows. If you are using a computer with a 32-bit processor that is 64-bit capable, you can purchase and install either a 32-bit or 64-bit edition of Windows.
  - **Applications**—If you use or install a 32-bit edition of Windows, you will need to purchase and install 32-bit applications, utilities, and other types of software. If you use or install a 64-bit edition of Windows, you should purchase and install software products designed for use under a 64-bit edition of Windows. In some instances, software products designed for use under a 32-bit edition of Windows may work under a 64-bit edition of Windows, but you should verify this information before purchasing the product. Also, even if you are able to use a 32-bit program with 64-bit Windows, the software is limited to using 4 GB of RAM. If upgrading from a 32-bit edition to a 64-bit edition of Windows, you will have to purchase new 64-bit versions of your Internet security or antivirus software, and perhaps other utilities as well.
  - **Hardware and device drivers**—If you install or use a 32-bit edition of Windows, you must purchase hardware that has 32-bit device drivers. If you install or use a 64-bit edition of Windows, you must purchase hardware that has 64-bit device drivers. If you want to use hardware that you purchased and used previously under a 32-bit edition of Windows with a newly installed 64-bit edition of Windows, you must visit the hardware manufacturer's Web site and verify that there are 64-bit device drivers available because you cannot use 32-bit device drivers with a 64-bit edition of Windows.
  - **RAM**—When deciding how much RAM your computer needs, consider these Windows edition requirements:
    - All 32-bit editions of Windows 7, except for Windows 7 Starter, support up to 4 GB of RAM. The 32-bit edition of Windows 7 Starter only supports up to 2 GB of RAM.
    - The 64-bit editions of Windows 7 Professional, Ultimate, and Enterprise support up to 192 GB of RAM.
    - The 64-bit edition of Windows 7 Home Premium supports up to 16 GB of RAM, the 64-bit edition of Windows 7 Home Basic supports up to 8 GB of RAM, and the 64-bit edition of Windows 7 Starter supports up to 2 GB of RAM.

    When buying a computer or adding more RAM to a computer, you need to know this information so you buy only up to the amount of RAM supported by a specific version and edition of Windows 7. You will also want to know the amount of RAM already installed in a computer you purchase or upgrade, and you will want to know the computer manufacturer's limit on the amount of RAM supported by that particular computer system.

The management at NanoAssets has decided to replace the company's current computer systems with high-performance computers that take advantage of the newer features in Windows 7 Ultimate. At Kai's request, they also agreed to provide higher performance laptops for use by employees who frequently travel on company business. Kai asks you to visit the Microsoft Web site and examine information on how best to upgrade Windows.

Remember that Web sites and software change over time, so the views shown in the following figures may differ from what you see when you visit the Microsoft Web site. Also, because Web sites change and update their Web pages frequently, you may have to use a Web site's search feature to locate information.

To compare Windows 7 editions:

1. Open Internet Explorer (or another Web browser), type **microsoft.com** in the Address bar of your Web browser, and press the **Enter** key. At the Microsoft home page, point to the **Windows** link, and then click the **Windows 7** link on the drop-down menu. You are now at the Windows 7 home page (*www.microsoft.com/windows/windows-7/default.aspx*).

Trouble? If you experience problems locating the Web page for a specific version of Windows, go to the Microsoft Web site at *www.microsoft.com*, and use the search box to locate the Web page for the version of Windows of interest to you.

TIP
You can press F11 to view the Web page full screen, and then press it again to exit full-screen view.

2. On the Windows 7 Web page, click the **Compare** link near the top of the page, and adjust your view so you can see the comparison of features found in the Windows 7 Home Premium, Professional, and Ultimate Editions, as shown in Figure 11-1. This Web page also has a link to the Web page that covers the Starter Edition.

Trouble? If the Web page does not contain a Compare link, click inside the *Search Microsoft.com* search box, type *compare Windows 7 editions*, press the Enter key, and examine the search results for a link to the Windows 7 Web page that showcases Windows 7 editions.

Figure 11-1   **Comparison of features in different Windows 7 editions**

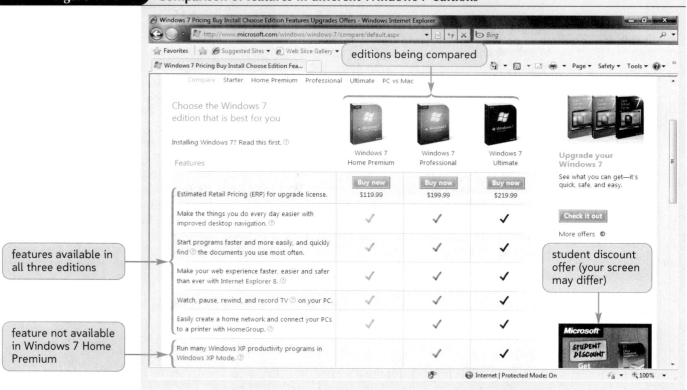

TIP

The check marks in Figure 11-1 are color coded to match the package color of the different Windows 7 editions.

As shown in Figure 11-1, Microsoft Corporation lists the estimated cost of upgrading to each of these editions, and in the table it compares specific features (although not all features) of these editions. All three editions support the option for watching, pausing, rewinding, and recording TV broadcasts on your computer and the use of a new Windows 7 feature called HomeGroup (covered in the next tutorial) for setting up a home network and sharing files and printers. If you want to use Windows XP Mode (covered later in this tutorial) for running older Windows XP programs, you have to purchase either the Windows 7 Professional Edition or Windows 7 Ultimate Edition. If you purchase Windows 7 Home Premium, you will not have access to this feature. Likewise, if you want BitLocker Drive Encryption, you have no choice but to purchase the more expensive Windows 7 Ultimate Edition. Before you purchase a Windows 7 edition or purchase a computer that comes with a specific Windows 7 edition, make sure that it will meet your immediate and future needs. For the more serious computer professional who needs access to all of the features in Windows 7, as well as more advanced technologies, the Windows 7 Ultimate or Professional Editions are the obvious choices.

If you scroll to the bottom of this page and click the "Windows 7 Disclaimer" link, Microsoft notes that some Windows 7 product features are only available in certain editions of Windows 7, and those product features may also require new hardware. Also, features may vary by country.

INSIGHT

Taking Advantage of Educational Discounts

When purchasing a computer, many people focus solely on the cost of the computer system. However, after purchasing a computer, people quickly discover the high cost of software needed for the tasks they want to perform on the computer as well as the software to protect the security of their computer system. These costs can easily exceed the total cost of the computer. If you are a student enrolled in a university, college, community college, or one of its extensions, you may be able to purchase Microsoft Windows and Microsoft Office at discount prices. For example, at the time this textbook was released, Microsoft offered 70% off the Windows 7 Professional Upgrade and 90% off the full version of Microsoft Office Ultimate 2007 (a premium edition with multiple applications).

To qualify for these and other educational discounts that you might find online or at retail stores (remember to ask), you must provide proof that you are currently enrolled in a college. You can usually prove that you are a student by providing the email address of your free college email account, or by providing a copy of your current class schedule. It really does pay to check for educational discounts you can benefit from by virtue of being a student.

Before you purchase or upgrade your computer, you must verify whether that computer supports the requirements of a new Windows version or edition.

To compare Windows 7 system requirements:

▶ 1. Click your Web browser's **Back** button ⬅ to return to the Windows 7 home page.

▶ 2. Scroll to the bottom of this page, and under the "Windows 7 Help and How-to" section, click the **Windows 7 system requirements** link, and if necessary, adjust your view so you can view the details. Microsoft itemizes the requirements for running Windows 7 on your PC as well as additional requirements for the use of specific features of Windows 7. See Figure 11-2.

Figure 11-2   Windows 7 system requirements

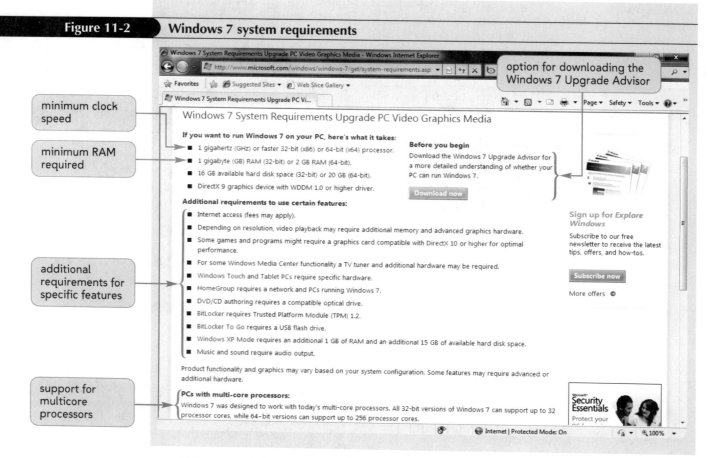

When examining system requirements for Windows 7 or any other operating system upgrade, you want to consider the following factors:

- **Processor**—Microsoft recommends a 1 GHz 32-bit (also referred to as x86) or 64-bit (also referred to as x64) processor for all editions of Windows 7. Prior to the introduction of present-day 32-bit and 64-bit processors, the earlier 80286, 80386, and 80486, and early Pentium 32-bit processors were referred to as x86 processors, so x86 became associated with 32-bit.

  As a practical measure, you have to evaluate whether you can expect reasonable performance with your current processor when you upgrade to Windows 7 or to a new Windows 7 edition. Even if your processor meets the minimum or recommended requirements, an older and slower processor might act as a bottleneck and affect the overall performance of the computer.

- **RAM**—Microsoft recommends that you have at least 1 GB of RAM for a 32-bit version of Windows 7 and at least 2 GB of RAM for a 64-bit version of Windows 7. If you have the Windows 7 Professional, Ultimate, or Enterprise edition and want to use Windows XP Mode, you will need an additional 1 GB of RAM. To ensure optimal performance of Windows 7 and the other software on your computer, you will need far more than the minimum requirements. If you do not have enough RAM for the Windows 7 operating system and the software that you use, Windows 7 will rely more heavily on the use of virtual memory, which slows down the performance of your computer and can result in error conditions. You should purchase enough RAM to support everything you need to do on your computer.

- **Hard disk drive storage capacity**—To accommodate the demands of users and rapidly emerging hardware and software technologies, the Windows 7 operating systems require a computer with an ever-increasing amount of hard disk drive storage capacity. As shown in Figure 11-2, Microsoft recommends that your hard disk drive have at least 16 GB of available storage space for a 32-bit version of Windows 7 and 20 GB for a 64-bit version of Windows 7. To support all the operations that Windows 7 performs, and to support additional software that you add to your computer over time as well as all the files you create and download, you should purchase a hard disk with as much storage capacity as you can afford. Also, consider that the Windows operating system and your other software will be downloading and installing updates on a regular basis, thus increasing the need for more storage space on the hard disk drive. Furthermore, certain types of files, such as video and audio files, require an extensive amount of storage space.
- **Graphics memory**—Although Microsoft does not specify the amount of graphics memory you need for Windows 7, it is as important a factor today as any other component in your computer. Microsoft does point out on this Web page that playing videos on your computer may require additional memory and advanced graphics hardware. Microsoft recommends that your computer support DirectX 9 graphics devices and Windows Display Driver Model (WDDM) 1.0 driver. Microsoft introduced DirectX 10 in Windows Vista and DirectX 11 in Windows 7. DirectX updates for different versions of Windows are available from the Microsoft Download Center (*www.microsoft.com/downloads*).
- **Other components**—If you want to record TV broadcasts and take advantage of all the features in Windows Media Center on your computer, Microsoft notes that you will need a TV tuner and additional hardware. It further notes that the Windows Touch and Tablet PC components of Windows 7 require specific hardware, including a touch screen. If you want to use Windows 7 Ultimate BitLocker Drive Encryption, you need a computer with a TPM (Trusted Platform Module) 1.2 chip (covered in Tutorial 5) as well as a USB flash drive for BitLocker to Go.

Microsoft also notes on this Web page that Windows 7 was designed to work with multicore processors. It further notes that 32-bit versions of Windows 7 can support up to 32 processor cores, and 64-bit versions can support up to 256 processor cores. Furthermore, the Windows 7 Professional, Ultimate, and Enterprise editions support computers with two physical processors whereas the other editions only support one physical processor.

Kai also emphasizes the importance of checking upgrade paths before purchasing a Windows 7 edition.

To examine information on upgrade paths:

▶ **1.** Click your Web browser's **Back** button ⊙ to return to the Windows 7 home page.

▶ **2.** Click the **How to upgrade your PC** link under *Get the answers you need*, and then scroll down to locate the table shown in Figure 11-3 that shows upgrade options from Windows XP and Windows Vista.

Figure 11-3   Windows 7 upgrade path options

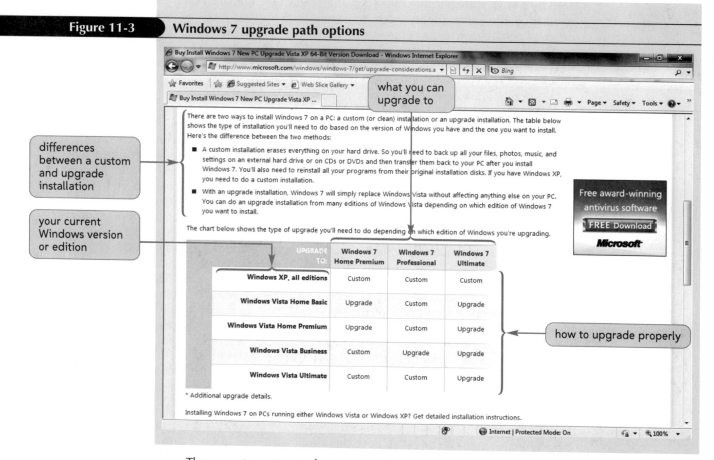

There are two approaches to upgrading. If you want to install a new version or edition of Windows over your existing Windows version and edition and keep your installed software, Windows settings, and personal files, you perform an **upgrade-in-place** (identified in the table as *Upgrade*). To perform an upgrade-in-place, you purchase an upgrade copy of Windows. An **upgrade copy** is a less expensive version of a software product that checks for a previous version already installed on a computer before installing itself. The existence of a previous copy is a prerequisite for installing the upgrade.

In contrast, a clean install is a custom install that requires careful preparation and forethought because, as noted in the Session 11.1 Visual Overview, you must reformat your hard disk drive, install Windows 7, and install all your own software as well as any needed device drivers, and then of course, restore all your personal folders and files. To perform a clean install, you must purchase a full version of Windows. A **full version** is a more expensive version of a software product, and it does not require that you already have a previous version of that software product installed on your computer. Your first purchase of a software product requires the more expensive full version; however, if you continue to update that version, you can purchase less expensive upgrade copies.

Before a clean install, it's important to make sure that you have copies of any device drivers that you might need for your hardware and, if necessary, to also have a backup of your email messages and email addresses. If you are upgrading Windows from a 32-bit to a 64-bit edition, or performing a clean install of a 64-bit Windows edition, you must acquire and install new 64-bit device drivers for your hardware. Also, you need to locate your original software disks for all other software products installed on your computer so you can reinstall those programs after the clean install.

A clean install is also useful if your computer has no operating system, if you want to completely replace the current operating system and all the other content on your hard disk drive with a new version or edition of the same operating system, restore default Windows settings, repartition your hard disk, remove malware that cannot be removed in any other way, or if you want to remove everything from your hard disk drive and rebuild your computer system. A clean install is time consuming, and requires that you antici-pate everything that you might need before and after the clean install.

As shown in Figure 11-3, you must perform a custom install if you are upgrading from any edition of Windows XP to the Windows 7 Home Premium, Professional, or Ultimate editions. To upgrade from Windows Vista Home Basic or Windows Vista Home Premium to Windows 7 Home Premium or Windows 7 Ultimate, you can perform a simple upgrade, but to upgrade to Windows 7 Professional, you must perform a custom install. If you want to upgrade from Windows Vista Business to Windows 7 Home Premium, you must perform a custom install, but if you want to upgrade to the Windows 7 Professional or Windows 7 Ultimate edition, you can perform a simple upgrade. If you want to upgrade from Windows Vista Ultimate to either Windows 7 Home Premium or Windows 7 Professional, you must perform a custom install, but if you want to upgrade to the Windows 7 Ultimate edition, you can perform a simple upgrade.

Microsoft recommends that you use the Windows 7 Upgrade Advisor, a Web applica-tion, to determine whether your computer supports Windows 7, and if so, what Windows 7 edition best suits your computer, as well as what features your computer supports. Microsoft notes that you can use the Windows 7 Upgrade Advisor to determine whether you can upgrade to another edition of Windows 7. If you already have a version of Windows 7 on your computer that meets your needs, you can also use the Windows 7 Upgrade Advisor to check for hardware or software problems.

Now, you're ready to locate information on the Windows 7 Upgrade Advisor and then download a copy for use in the second session of the tutorial.

To locate information on the Windows 7 Upgrade Advisor:

▶ **1.** Scroll to the bottom of the current Microsoft Web page, and under the "Windows 7 Help and How-to" section, click the **Windows 7 Upgrade Advisor** link. At the Windows 7 Upgrade Advisor Web page, Microsoft notes that the Windows 7 Upgrade Advisor scans your computer and identifies problems with hardware, devices, installed programs, and Windows settings. Microsoft also notes that before you use the Windows 7 Upgrade Advisor, you should plug in and power on any USB devices or other hardware devices, such as external hard disks, printers, and scanners, which you regularly use.

▶ **2.** Click the **Download the Windows 7 Upgrade Advisor** button to open the Download details Web page. Microsoft provides a brief overview of the Windows 7 Upgrade Advisor, how you can use the Windows 7 Upgrade Advisor, and the sys-tem requirements for running the Windows 7 Upgrade Advisor. You can use the Windows 7 Upgrade Advisor on computers that use Windows 7, Windows Vista, or Windows XP with the Service Pack 2 upgrade (or a later upgrade). The Windows 7 Upgrade Advisor also requires that you have .NET Framework 2.0 installed on your computer. If it's not installed, the installation program for the Windows 7 Upgrade Advisor will install it for you.

▶ **3.** Click the **Download** button, click the **Start download** link on the Download Confirmation Web page if the download does not start immediately, and in the File Download - Security Warning dialog box, click the **Save** button. Click **Downloads** under *Favorites* in the Navigation pane, click the **New folder** button on the toolbar, type **Windows 7 Upgrade Advisor** for the new folder name, press the **Enter** key, click the **Open** button (or press the **Enter** key a second time), and then click the **Save** button in the Save As dialog box to start the download.

▶ **4.** After Internet Explorer displays a Download complete dialog box and informs you that the download is complete, click the **Close** button.

▶ **5.** Close your Web browser.

TIP

If you right-click a down-loaded file, you may see an option for scanning the file with your Internet security or antivirus software.

Now, you're ready to install the Windows 7 Upgrade Advisor.

Installing the Windows 7 Upgrade Advisor

Because Kai wants to upgrade her laptop from Windows 7 Home Premium to Windows 7 Ultimate, she decides to download and install the Windows 7 Upgrade Advisor so she can check whether her laptop is compatible with Windows 7 Ultimate. Before she installs the Windows 7 Upgrade Advisor, she decides to create a restore point.

If you are working in a computer lab, ask your college's technical support staff if you can make a restore point because they may have turned off System Restore on computers in your computer labs. If you cannot make a restore point, read but do not keystroke the following steps.

To create a restore point:

▶ **1.** Right-click the **Computer** desktop icon, click **Properties**, and in the System window, click the **System protection** link, and provide Administrator credentials (if necessary).

▶ **2.** Click the **Create** button on the System Protection property sheet in the System Properties dialog box, type **Before Installing Windows 7 Upgrade Advisor** in the System Protection dialog box to identify the new restore point, and click the **Create** button. After System Protection successfully creates a restore point, click the **Close** button in the System Protection dialog box.

▶ **3.** Click the **OK** button to close the System Properties dialog box, and then close the System window.

If you encounter a problem after installing software on your computer, you can attempt to uninstall the software first, but if that fails, you can use System Restore to roll back your computer to a restore point automatically created by Windows 7 before you installed that software product or to a manual restore point that you created before you installed that software product.

Now, you're ready to install the Windows 7 Upgrade Advisor.

If you want to install the Windows 7 Upgrade Advisor on your computer and check for upgrade options, complete the following steps. If you do not want to install the Windows 7 Upgrade Advisor on your computer and check for upgrade options, read the steps for downloading and then installing this software in the next two sections and examine the figures, but do not keystroke the steps. If you are working in a computer lab and want to download and install the Windows Upgrade Advisor on a computer in your computer lab, ask your instructor or technical support staff for permission.

As noted earlier, the Windows 7 Upgrade Advisor may need to download and install additional software from the Microsoft download Web site before it can install itself properly. If you do not want to install that software, or if you don't want to modify your computer system, then read but do not keystroke the following steps.

To install the Windows 7 Upgrade Advisor:

▶ **1.** From the Start menu, click your **user account name**, click the **Downloads** folder, and then open the **Windows 7 Upgrade Advisor** folder. The name of the file you downloaded is Windows7UpgradeAdvisorSetup.exe.

▶ **2.** Click the **Windows7UpgradeAdvisorSetup.exe** file icon, and then provide Administrator credentials. Windows 7 welcomes you to the Windows 7 Upgrade Advisor Setup Wizard and prompts you to read and accept the license terms for using the Windows 7 Upgrade Advisor. Be sure to read the license terms that comes with a software product so you know what is actually installed with a software product.

▶ **3.** After you read the license terms, click the **I accept the license terms** option button, and then click the **Install** button. Windows 7 installs the Windows 7 Upgrade Advisor and then informs you that the software was successfully installed.

▶ **4.** Click the **Close** button, and then close the Windows 7 Upgrade Advisor window.

Now, you can use the Windows 7 Upgrade Advisor to evaluate your computer.

To examine a computer with the Windows 7 Upgrade Advisor:

▶ **1.** Attach any devices that you regularly use, such as a printer, scanner, or USB external hard disk, to your computer system before you open the Windows 7 Upgrade Advisor.

▶ **2.** From the left pane of the Start menu, click **Windows 7 Upgrade Advisor**, and then provide Administrator credentials by clicking the **Yes** button in the User Account Control dialog box to allow this program to make changes to your computer. The Windows 7 Upgrade Advisor dialog box explains what the Windows 7 Upgrade Advisor does, reassures you that no information will be used to identify or contact you, and then reminds you to connect and turn on all of your devices so the Upgrade Advisor can check them. It also notes that it will provide you with upgrade options and guidance on fixing system, program, and device issues.

▶ **3.** Click the **Start check** button. The Windows 7 Upgrade Advisor scans your computer for compatibility. When complete, it provides reports for upgrading to either a 32-bit or a 64-bit edition of Windows 7. The reports break out issues and compatibility information into three categories—System, Devices, and Programs. See Figure 11-4. Your issues and Windows upgrade recommendation will differ.

Figure 11-4   **Viewing a Windows 7 Upgrade Advisor summary**

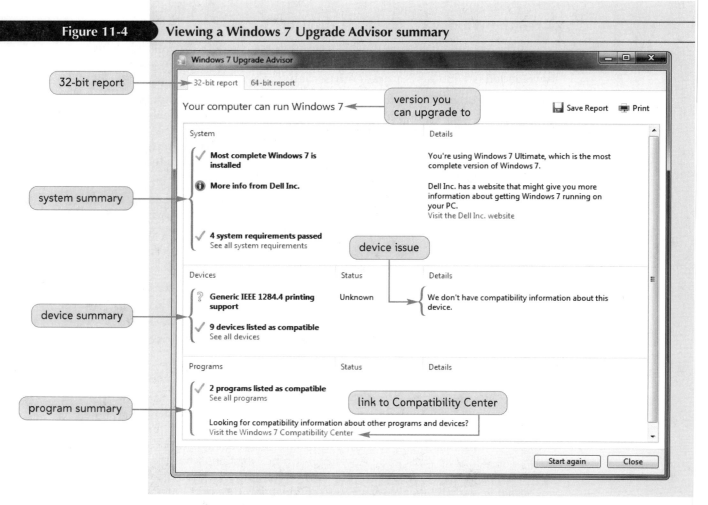

On the 32-bit report tab, the Windows 7 Upgrade Advisor notes under the System section that this computer is already using the most complete version of Windows 7, namely, Windows 7 Ultimate. The Windows 7 Upgrade Advisor also provides a link to the Dell Web site for additional information in upgrading to Windows 7 on this Dell computer. If there are any issues, the Windows 7 Upgrade Advisor flags those issues and provides details on how to resolve them. Your Windows upgrade recommendation will differ.

Under the Devices section, the Windows 7 Upgrade Advisor notes that eight devices on the computer used for this figure are compatible, and identifies an unknown device for which it does not have compatibility information. Under Programs, the Windows 7 Upgrade Advisor notes that there are two compatible programs.

To examine 32-bit compatibility details:

▶ **1.** In the System section, click the **See all system requirements** link. The Windows 7 Upgrade Advisor provides more details on System issues and compatibility. See Figure 11-5.

Figure 11-5	Reviewing system issues

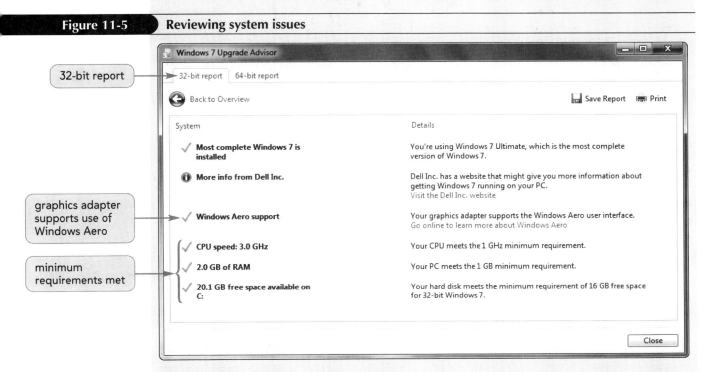

In addition to information previously provided on the summary, the Windows 7 Upgrade Advisor verifies that the graphics adapter supports the Windows Aero user interface, an important consideration when upgrading. It also notes that the CPU speed meets the 1 GHz minimum requirement, that the computer meets the 1 GB minimum requirement for RAM, and that the hard disk drive meets the 16 GB minimum requirement for free space. Your system details will differ.

▶ **2.** Click the **Back** button ⬅, and under the Devices section, click the **See all devices** link. In addition to information previously provided on the summary, the Windows 7 Upgrade Advisor identifies other devices as compatible with Windows 7. Your device details will differ.

▶ **3.** Click the **Back** button ⬅, and under the Programs section, click the **See all programs** link. In addition to information previously provided on the summary, the Windows 7 Upgrade Advisor Adjust identifies programs that have earned Microsoft's Compatible with Windows 7 logo. See Figure 11-6. Your program details will differ.

Figure 11-6 Reviewing program compatibility

32-bit report

programs rated
Compatible
with Windows 7

4. Click the **Back** button ⬅, and then click the **64-bit report** tab to view an upgrade compatibility summary for 64-bit editions of Windows 7. As shown under the System section for the computer used in Figure 11-7, the Windows 7 Upgrade Advisor indicates that a custom installation to a 64-bit edition of Windows 7 is required.

That means that you will have to reinstall all your programs and make a backup of your important files before upgrading. Except for the custom installation requirement, all the details for the Devices and Programs issues on the 64-bit report for the computer used for the figures are identical to those for the 32-bit report. Your System, Devices, and Programs issues and details will differ.

Figure 11-7 Reviewing a 64-bit report

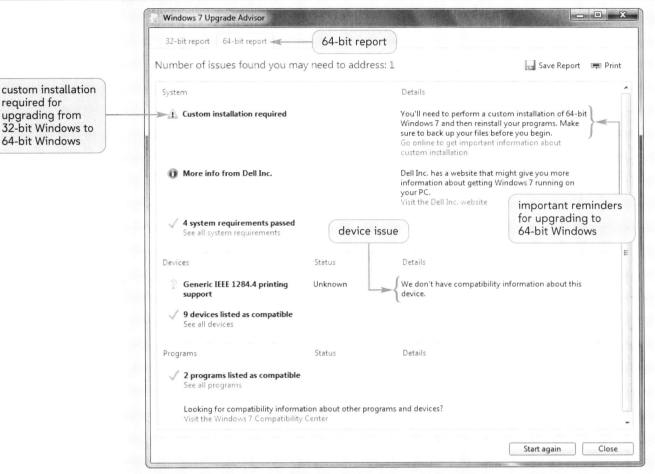

custom installation required for upgrading from 32-bit Windows to 64-bit Windows

important reminders for upgrading to 64-bit Windows

device issue

5. To save your 32-bit and 64-bit reports in one file, attach your flash drive (if necessary), close the AutoPlay dialog box, click the **Save Report** button in the Windows 7 Upgrade Advisor window, and navigate to the Tutorial.11\Tutorial folder on your flash drive. Type **Windows 7 Upgrade Advisor Reports** in the File name box, note that the report is saved as a "Web archive, single file" with the .mht file extension, and then click the **Save** button. If you click on the file icon for this file, Windows 7 will open the file in Internet Explorer so you can view the report. The report contains two sections labeled *Information* about upgrading to 32-bit Windows 7 and about upgrading to 64-bit Windows 7.

6. If you want to print your report, click the **Print** button in the Windows 7 Upgrade Advisor window, select a printer, and then click the **Print** button.

7. Close the Windows 7 Upgrade Advisor window.

PROSKILLS

Decision Making: Evaluating Recommendations for Upgrading Windows

Whenever Microsoft releases a new version of the Windows operating system, check its Web site for an Upgrade Advisor, which can save you valuable time and money by identifying problems that might otherwise interfere with an upgrade to a new version or edition of Windows and by recommending ways to correct those problems so an upgrade goes as smoothly as possible. If an Upgrade Advisor recommends that you upgrade your hardware device drivers, check the manufacturer's Web site for newer device drivers and install them on your computer. Then, use the Upgrade Advisor again to make sure that the new device drivers have resolved the problems that prevent you from upgrading to a newer version or newer edition of Windows before you actually install that new version or edition of Windows. By using this approach, you can reduce the chances of a major problem during installation and guarantee as smooth an upgrade as possible.

If the Windows 7 Upgrade Advisor informs you that you have to do a custom install, you can click the "Go online to get important information about custom install" link to make sure you do the necessary preparation required to successfully install Windows and ensure that you can reinstall software and restore your data files.

REFERENCE

Evaluating a Computer with the Windows 7 Upgrade Advisor

- Attach any devices that you regularly use, such as a printer, scanner, or external hard disk, to your computer system before you open the Windows 7 Upgrade Advisor.
- Open the Start menu, point to All Programs (if necessary), and then click Windows 7 Upgrade Advisor.
- Click the Start check button, and after the scan is complete, examine information on issues and compatibility in the System, Devices, and Programs sections on the overall summary.
- Use the See all system requirements link, See all devices link, and See all programs link to examine System, Devices, and Programs details for the 32-bit report.
- Click the 64-bit tab, and then examine the summary of System, Devices, and Programs issues and compatibility.
- Use the See all system requirements link, See all devices link, and See all programs link to examine System, Devices, and Programs details for the 64-bit report.
- To save your report, click the Save Report button, select the folder where you want to store the report, enter a report filename, and then click the Save button.
- If you want to print your report, click the Print button, select a printer, and then click the Print button.
- Close the Windows 7 Upgrade Advisor window.

Next, you can complete the upgrade preparation.

TIP

To verify your Windows edition, computer name, and workgroup or domain name, right-click the Computer desktop icon, and select Properties.

Completing the Upgrade Preparation

Before installing a Windows 7 upgrade, prepare your computer for the upgrade as follows:

- **Document hardware, software, and network settings**—Before installing an operating system upgrade, you should compile important information about your computer's hardware and software settings. You can use Device Manager (covered in Tutorial 12) to document hardware configuration settings on your computer and the System Information utility (covered in Tutorial 8 and Tutorial 12) to document hardware, software, and system settings. If your computer is part of a network, you should know your computer name, your workgroup or domain name, and your IP address unless it is automatically assigned. An IP address is a unique address that identifies a computer on a network or the Internet. You can use Network and Sharing or the IPCONFIG command-line utility to obtain your IP address.

- **Check the available storage space on your hard disk drive**—Make sure you have enough storage space on the drive where you intend to install Windows 7. Also make sure this drive contains enough available storage space for installing periodic service pack upgrades and other important updates. Take into account the storage space required for the virtual memory paging file (covered in Tutorial 9) and the Internet cache (covered in Tutorial 6 and Tutorial 7), as well as updates to all your other software.
  To free up storage space, you can perform the following tasks:
  - **Empty the Internet cache**—Use your Web browser to empty the contents of the folder used to cache files downloaded from the Internet and World Wide Web. You can also use the Disk Cleanup Wizard to help you find these files for Internet Explorer as well as other files, including temporary files.
  - **Archive personal files**—If your computer contains important files that you no longer use but want to keep in case you need them in the future, consider archiving them. Make sure you have backup copies of these files, and then move them off your hard disk drive onto a permanent storage medium, such as an external hard disk drive. If you want to keep them on your hard disk drive, you can create and store them in a Compressed (zipped) Folder so they require less storage space or you can compress these files using NTFS compression.
  - **Uninstall unneeded software applications and utilities**—Examine the software installed on your computer and decide whether you still need all these applications, utilities, and games. If not, uninstall them.
- **Scan for computer viruses and other types of malicious software**—Verify that your Internet security software, antivirus software, and antispyware software download daily updates, and then perform a full scan of your computer with your Internet security software or antivirus software (and, if necessary, your antispyware software) prior to installing a new operating system.
- **Back up important files on your hard disk drive**—Use the backup software in your version of Windows to back up all your important files. As you discovered in Tutorial 10, you can use Windows Backup to create a system image, back up all your personal user files the first time you use Windows Backup, and then perform regular scheduled backups of your personal files.
- **Check the hard disk drive for errors**—Before you install or upgrade a new operating system, application, or utility, use a disk analysis and repair utility, such as the Error-checking tool or the command-line Check Disk utility that you examined in Tutorial 5 to verify the integrity of the file system, and if necessary, repair errors in the file system.
- **Optimize hard disk drive storage space**—If necessary, use Disk Defragmenter in your version of Windows (or a third-party utility) to optimize the storage space on your hard disk drive. After upgrading Windows, it's a good idea to use the Disk Defragmenter again to optimize the hard disk drive. Although the Disk Defragmenter under Windows 7 is scheduled to defragment the hard disk drive once a week, you can initiate a manual defragmentation at any time.
- **Turn off background programs**—Programs, such as Internet security software or anti-virus software, might interfere with the installation of an operating system. If your anti-virus software places an icon in the notification area, you can right-click this icon and close or disable the program. Remember, however, to reenable your Internet security software or antivirus software after you install an operating system upgrade.

- **Unencrypt folders and files**—If you have encrypted folders and files on your computer, unencrypt them so you do not encounter a problem accessing those folders and files after your Windows installation. Once you've installed or reinstalled Windows 7, you can reencrypt those folders and files.
- **Reboot your computer**—Prior to installing or upgrading an operating system, close all open applications, utilities, and windows, and then reboot your computer to clear memory.

TIP

IT administrators can use the Windows 7 Resource Kit to help deploy and install Windows 7 (including customizing and automating installations).

Then, you're finally ready to install the operating system upgrade. Although it takes time to prepare your computer for an operating system upgrade, it's far more time consuming to rebuild your computer from scratch if a serious problem arises during installation. *The more carefully you prepare for an installation of a new operating system, the less likely you will encounter problems during the installation.* Follow the preceding steps, examine the information Microsoft posts at its Web site on upgrading to Windows 7, and examine your computer's hardware and software documentation to ensure a reliable and problem-free installation of Windows 7.

Installing Windows 7

Once you have assured yourself that your computer is ready for Windows 7 or an upgrade to another edition of Windows 7, you can use one of the following approaches for obtaining and installing Windows 7:

- **Download Windows 7**—You can download a copy of Windows 7 from the Microsoft Store Web site using either Download Manager or your Web browser. If you acquire Windows 7 from the Microsoft Store Web site, you download an ISO file. An ISO file is a disc image that you can burn to a DVD (or CD). You can then use the Windows 7 USB/DVD Download Tool to burn the ISO file to a DVD or to copy the ISO file to a flash drive so that you can boot Windows 7 from the DVD or flash drive.
- **Windows 7 DVD**—If you purchase a Windows 7 DVD, you can install Windows 7 by booting your computer from that disc.

If you are installing Windows 7 by booting from a DVD drive or a USB flash drive (if that option is available in your BIOS), you may need to open the BIOS Setup utility and specify these devices in your Boot Device menu. If you are installing Windows 7 over your current Windows version, an autorun.inf Setup Information file opens the Setup program for installing Windows 7. Figure 11-8 shows the contents of this autorun.inf file.

Figure 11-8 **Windows 7 Ultimate autorun.inf file**

The open key in autorun.inf specifies the program to run (in this case, setup.exe), and the icon key specifies the location of the icon in the program file (*0* for the first icon in the file). If a path is not included with the open key, Windows assumes the program is in the top-level folder (or root directory) of the disk.

If you purchased Windows 7 online and then downloaded your licensed copy, locate the downloaded file and click (or double-click) to start the Windows 7 installation.

The following information on installing Windows 7 describes a Custom (advanced), or clean install, on an empty partition. The Windows 7 installation program takes you through the following operations in one Install Windows dialog box after another.

However, depending on how you install Windows 7, you may not need to perform some of the following steps.

- **Specify language and other preferences**—In the first Install Windows dialog box, Setup prompts you to specify the language to use for the installation (for example, *English*), the time and currency format (for example, *English (United States)*), and the keyboard or input method (for example, *United States*).
- **Option to install**—In the next Install Windows dialog box, Setup provides the option for starting the installation of Windows 7. It also provides a "What to know before installing Windows" link and a "Repair your computer" link. The latter is useful if you want to initiate Startup Repair from your Windows DVD.
- **Get important updates for installation**—For a successful installation and to help protect your computer against security threats, Microsoft recommends that you get the latest updates before continuing the installation of Windows 7. However, you can wait and install those updates after you install Windows 7.
- **Review and agree to the license terms**—After you choose the option to install Windows 7, Setup prompts you to read the license terms and displays an "I accept the license terms" option. You must accept the conditions of the license agreement before you can continue. This contract is a legally binding agreement, and you should read and understand all its components before you accept the agreement.
- **Choose the type of installation**—After you agree to the license terms, Setup prompts you for the type of installation you want to perform—Upgrade or Custom (advanced), and includes a "Help me decide" link for information on these two options. Setup notes that the Upgrade option allows you to upgrade to a newer version of Windows and keep your files, existing settings, and programs. It also points out that the option to upgrade is only available when an existing version of Windows is already running. It also recommends that you back up your files before installing Windows 7.
  - **Upgrade**—If your current version of Windows supports an upgrade to Windows 7, you will likely choose the Upgrade option so you can keep your current files, settings, and programs. However, even if your current version of Windows supports an upgrade, you can still perform a clean install if you prefer.
  - **Custom installation**—If you choose Custom (advanced), Setup notes that it will install a new copy of Windows. Setup points out that this option does not keep your files, settings, and programs. It further notes that, if you choose this option, you can make changes to disks and partitions. If your computer contains a version of Windows that does not support an upgrade to Windows 7, you must choose the Custom (advanced) option and perform a clean install of Windows 7. If you already have a 32-bit edition of Windows 7 installed on your computer and want to upgrade to a 64-bit edition of Windows 7 (or vice-versa), you must perform a clean install.

    If you choose the Custom (advanced) option for a clean install, Setup will display a list of disks and partitions on your computer where you can install Windows 7, along with each partition's total size and amount of free space. Setup also includes each partition's type, such as OEM (Reserved), System, and Primary (the same partition types you examined in Disk Management in Tutorial 5). You can then select the partition where you want to install Windows 7. If Setup does not detect any disks, you can choose the option for loading drivers for your hard disk drive(s).

    If you choose the "Drive options (advanced)" link, you can format the partition you selected and apply a file system to that drive; however, Setup warns you that this option erases everything on the partition. If you don't format the drive on which you are going to install Windows 7, Setup informs you in the next Install Windows dialog box that the partition you selected contains files from a previous Windows installation, and that it will move these folders and files to a folder named Windows.old. It further points out that you can access the contents of the Windows.old folder, but you will not be able to use your previous version of Windows. Once you select "Drive options (advanced)," other options, such as extending a partition, are available. If you deliberately or inadvertently select an OEM (Reserved) partition,

Setup warns that the partition may contain recovery files, system files, or important software from your computer manufacturer, and if you format this partition, you will lose any data stored on it.

- **Restart computer and start installation**—In the next Install Windows dialog box, Setup notes that it has all the information it needs, and informs you that your computer will restart several times during installation. Then, it identifies the steps that are part of the installation: Copying Windows files, Expanding Windows files, Installing features, Installing updates, and Completing installation. After these steps are complete, Setup informs you that Windows needs to restart to continue. During the reboot, Windows displays an OS choices menu if you have a multiboot computer so you can choose the version of Windows to use. After Windows 7 starts, Setup updates Registry settings and starts Windows services. Then Windows 7 switches to the native resolution for your LCD monitor and continues to complete the installation. After the next reboot, Windows 7 starts again and Setup starts the process of preparing your computer for first use, and it checks video performance.

- **Prompt for user name and computer name**—In the next Setup Windows dialog box, Windows 7 identifies the edition installed on your computer (such as Windows 7 Ultimate), and prompts you to choose a user name for your user account, which will be an Administrator account. Windows 7 also prompts you to name your computer to distinguish it from other computers on your network.

- **Prompt for user password**—Windows 7 prompts you for a password and password hint for your user account.

- **Provide Product ID**—Windows 7 next prompts for your Windows Product Key so Setup can activate Windows 7 after it is installed. You can find the sticker with the Product Key inside the plastic DVD holder within the product package. Windows Help and Support notes that if you purchased and downloaded Windows 7 online, you can find your product key in a confirmation email. Windows 7 also notes that you can enter the Product Key without typing the dashes (they are automatically added). The "Automatically activate Windows when I'm online" check box is already enabled so this essential step is performed after you install Windows 7. There is also a link for viewing information about activation.

- **Help protect your computer and improve Windows automatically**—Windows 7 next provides two options—"Use recommended settings," and "Install important updates" only. If you go with "Use recommended settings," Windows 7 will install important and recommended updates, check online for solutions to problems, and help Microsoft improve Windows. Windows 7 notes that, if you use this option, it will send some information to Microsoft, but that information is not used to either identify you or contact you. It further notes that you can locate the link for turning off these settings by searching for "Turn off recommended settings" in Help and Support.

  If you select "Install important updates only," Windows 7 will only install security updates and other important updates for Windows. There is also a "Learn more about each option" link for you to compare the two options before selecting the option you want to use.

- **Review your time and date settings**—At this point, you can review and, if necessary adjust, your date, time, and time zone settings. The option for automatically adjusting your computer's clock for Daylight Savings time is enabled.

- **Select your computer's network location**—Windows 7 points out that your computer is connected to a network, and notes that it will automatically apply the correct settings for the network location. However, you should verify that the option Windows 7 selects is not only appropriate but also the one you want to use. Windows 7 provides three network options—Home network, Work network, and Public network. For the Home network option, Windows 7 notes that if all the computers on your network are located in your home, and you recognize them, your network is a trusted home network. It also recommends that you do not choose this option for public places, such as coffee shops or airports.

For the Work network option, Windows 7 notes that if all the computers on your network are located in your workplace, and you recognize them, your network is a trusted work network. As with the Home network option, Windows 7 recommends that you do not choose this option for public places, such as coffee shops or airports.

For the Public network option, Windows 7 notes that if you do not recognize all the computers on the network to which you are connected, or if you have mobile broadband, your network is a public network, and therefore is not trusted.

Windows 7 notes that if you are not sure which option to choose, then you should choose Public network. Once you select a network location, Windows 7 connects to your network and applies the appropriate network settings.

- **Preparing your desktop**—After preparing your desktop, Windows 7 installation is complete. At this point, you want to check and make sure there are no problems. For example, if Windows 7 does not detect your sound system, you may need to go to the Web site of the company for your sound system and download updated Windows 7 device drivers.

After you install Windows 7, take the following steps, if necessary, to update your computer and protect its security:

- **Obtain Windows Updates**—Check for any additional Windows updates for Windows 7 and for your other Microsoft software.
- **Update device drivers**—Whether you performed an upgrade or a clean install, you may need to check for more recent device drivers for your hardware and Windows 7.
- **Install software applications and utilities**—If you performed a clean install of Windows 7, you will need to reinstall those software applications and utilities you want to use and obtain updates for those applications and utilities. If you performed an upgrade to Windows 7, and if you use Windows Mail or Outlook Express, then you will need to locate and install a new email program.
- **Restore your files**—If you performed a clean install of Windows 7, then you will need to restore your folders and files from your most recent backup or backups.
- **Enable your Internet security software, antivirus software, and/or antispyware software**—If you turned off these software products prior to performing an upgrade to Windows 7, then remember to reenable them after the Windows 7 installation is complete.
- **Remove the Windows.old folder**—If you restored your files from a backup after installing Windows 7, you can delete the Windows.old folder to regain valuable storage space.
- **Reencrypt folders and files**—If you removed encryption from folders and files prior to installing Windows 7 and want to restore that encryption, then reencrypt those folders and files.

Although the Setup installation program performs a hardware performance assessment near the end of installing Windows 7, you may need to open the System window, open the Performance Information and Tools window, and use the "Re-run the assessment" link to update your Windows Experience Index base score and subscores.

Over the years, Microsoft has simplified and automated the process for installing Windows, and has reduced the amount of time required for installation.

Using Windows Easy Transfer

When Kai upgraded her computer, the company's tech support staff used Windows Easy Transfer to transfer her user account, user settings, and files from her old computer to her new computer. That not only saved Kai valuable time and effort, but it also allowed her to begin working on her new computer within a short period of time; in addition, her new computer was set up in the same way as her old computer.

You can use Windows Easy Transfer to copy all your user files and user account settings, as well as those of all other users on the same computer, from a Windows XP, Windows Vista, or Windows 7 computer to a Windows 7 computer. User and computer settings include Start menu and taskbar options, desktop settings, screen saver settings, accessibility settings, and network settings. As shown in Figure 11-9, Windows Easy Transfer transfers everything within the Documents, Music, Pictures, and Videos folders; email settings, contacts, and messages; Internet settings and favorites; shared items; and program configuration settings.

Figure 11-9   **What's transferred with Windows Easy Transfer**

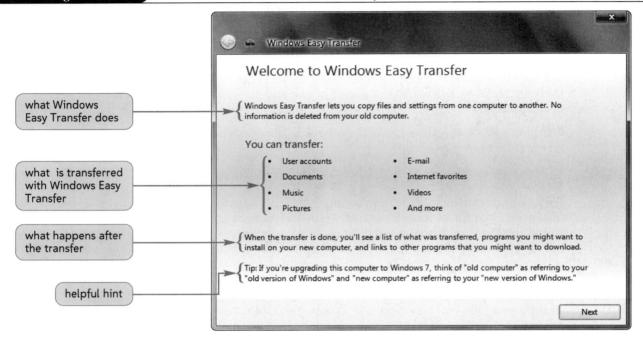

Although it does not transfer installed software, it does transfer program settings thereby reducing the time it takes to customize software. You must reinstall software that you want to continue to use on the new computer. During this process, you can pick which user accounts to transfer, as shown in Figure 11-10.

Figure 11-10   **Choosing user accounts to transfer**

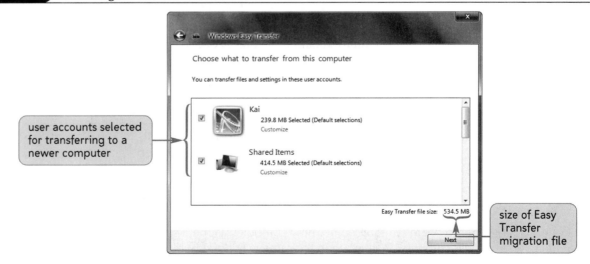

As shown in Figure 11-11, you can use one of the following methods to make the transfer.

Figure 11-11   **Choosing the method for transferring items to a new computer**

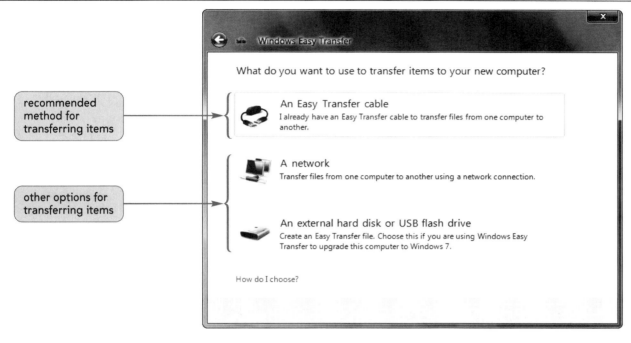

recommended method for transferring items

other options for transferring items

- **Easy Transfer Cable**—The simplest way to transfer files and settings from one computer to another is to use an Easy Transfer cable, which you can purchase online or at a local computer or electronics store. An Easy Transfer cable is a special type of USB cable (you cannot use a standard USB cable), so you need to use USB ports for the transfer. You can then transfer files and settings from your old computer to your new computer over the Easy Transfer cable by using Windows Easy Transfer on your new computer. When performing this operation, you start Windows Easy Transfer on your new computer, and then when prompted, attach the Easy Transfer cable to the new computer. Before you attach the cable to your older computer, you may need to insert a CD on the older computer to install Windows Easy Transfer on that computer.
- **Networked connection**—If your new and older computers are on the same network, you can transfer files and settings over the network connection by using Windows Easy Transfer on the new computer.
- **External hard disk drive or USB flash drive**—You can use an external hard disk drive or a USB flash drive to transfer files and settings from computer to computer.

TIP

The .mig file extension identifies a file as an Easy Transfer file.

You initiate the processing for transferring files by starting Windows Easy Transfer on your new computer, and Windows Easy Transfer copies whatever you selected to a file named "Windows Easy Transfer - Items from old computer.MIG". Then you switch to your new computer and use Windows Easy Transfer to copy everything from the migration file to the new computer.

After completing the transfer, Windows Easy Transfer provides reports that show what was transferred, what programs you might need to install on your new computer, and links to other programs you might want to download and install on your computer.

Windows Easy Transfer simplifies the process of gathering all your user settings and files and copying those to your new computer so it is ready for you to use. You do not need to reconfigure the new computer unless you want to specify even newer user settings.

Supporting Older Programs Using Windows XP Mode

Windows 7 Professional, Ultimate, and Enterprise support the use of Windows XP Mode for older programs designed for Windows XP. Using Windows XP Mode, you can access and use Windows XP programs on a computer running Windows 7. Once you set up your computer for Windows XP Mode, the All Programs menu will have a group folder called Windows Virtual PC, and under that group folder are options for opening Windows Virtual PC, opening Windows XP Mode, and selecting a program from the Windows XP Mode Applications folder.

TIP

Processors with the AMD-V, Intel VT, and VIA VT (VIA Technologies, Inc.) support hardware-assisted virtualization.

To use Windows XP Mode, your computer must meet certain system requirements. First your computer's processor must support **hardware-assisted virtualization**, which refers to the inclusion of additional microcode (called hardware extensions) in the processor, which enables it to better support the use of virtual environments. A virtual environment relies on the use of software to create a virtual machine that mimics a real-life computer. To determine whether your processor meets this requirement, you can download the Hardware-Assisted Virtualization (HAV) Detection Tool from the Microsoft Web site. If your computer supports this feature, the HAV Detection Tool displays a dialog box that informs you that your computer is configured with hardware-assisted virtualization, and that it meets the processor requirements to run Windows Virtual PC if your computer runs a supported edition of Windows 7 (as noted at the beginning of this section). See Figure 11-12.

Figure 11-12 **Using the Hardware-Assisted Virtualization Detection Tool**

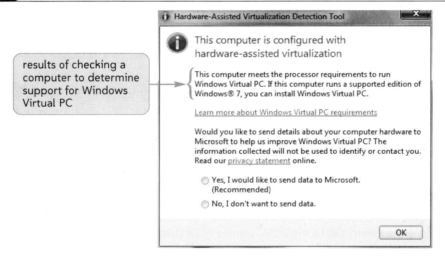

results of checking a computer to determine support for Windows Virtual PC

If your computer supports hardware-assisted virtualization, this feature must also be enabled in your computer's BIOS. If it's not enabled, the HAV Detection Tool will inform you that hardware-assisted virtualization is disabled, and you must then enable it in the BIOS. If your computer does not support hardware-assisted virtualization, you cannot use Virtual PC or Windows XP Mode on your computer.

The HAV Detection Tool requires specific Windows versions, editions, and service packs before it checks your computer; otherwise, it reports that this tool does not run on your operating system. Also, if your computer supports Intel's Trusted Execution Technology (or Intel TXT), and if that feature is enabled in the BIOS, the HAV Tool reports that the configuration of your computer is not compatible with Virtual PC. You must turn off Intel's Trusted Execution Technology if you want to use Virtual PC and Windows XP Mode. Intel's Trusted Execution Technology provides enhanced security for executing software and protecting data.

If your computer supports hardware-assisted virtualization, and after you enable this feature in the BIOS, you can download and install Windows Virtual PC and Windows XP Mode on your computer. If you search for Windows XP Mode in Windows Help and Support, you will find links to the appropriate sites for downloading Windows Virtual PC and Windows XP Mode. After installation, Windows XP Mode opens in a separate window, and then you can insert a program installation disc in your DVD or CD drive, and install that program. Microsoft also recommends that you download and install antivirus software within Windows XP Mode as well, even if your Windows 7 computer already has antivirus software.

Session 11.1 Quick Check

REVIEW

1. When evaluating whether a new operating system or software product will work on your computer, you need to examine its _____ requirements.

2. The _____ determines whether you can upgrade your current version or edition of Windows to a newer version or edition, or whether you must perform a custom install.

3. True or False. You can perform an upgrade-in-place from 32-bit Windows to 64-bit Windows (and vice versa).

4. Name four important computer components that determine whether you can upgrade your computer to Windows 7.

5. What program can you use to identify hardware, software, and other compatibility problems before upgrading your computer to Windows 7 or to a new edition of Windows 7?

6. What program can you use to copy files and settings from an older computer with a previous version of Windows to a newer computer that contains Windows 7?

7. If you are using the Windows 7 Professional, Ultimate, or Enterprise Edition and want to use an older program designed for Windows XP, you may be able to use _____.

8. True or False. Hardware-assisted virtualization refers to the inclusion of additional microcode (called hardware extensions) in the processor to provide support for the use of virtual environments.

SESSION 11.2 VISUAL OVERVIEW

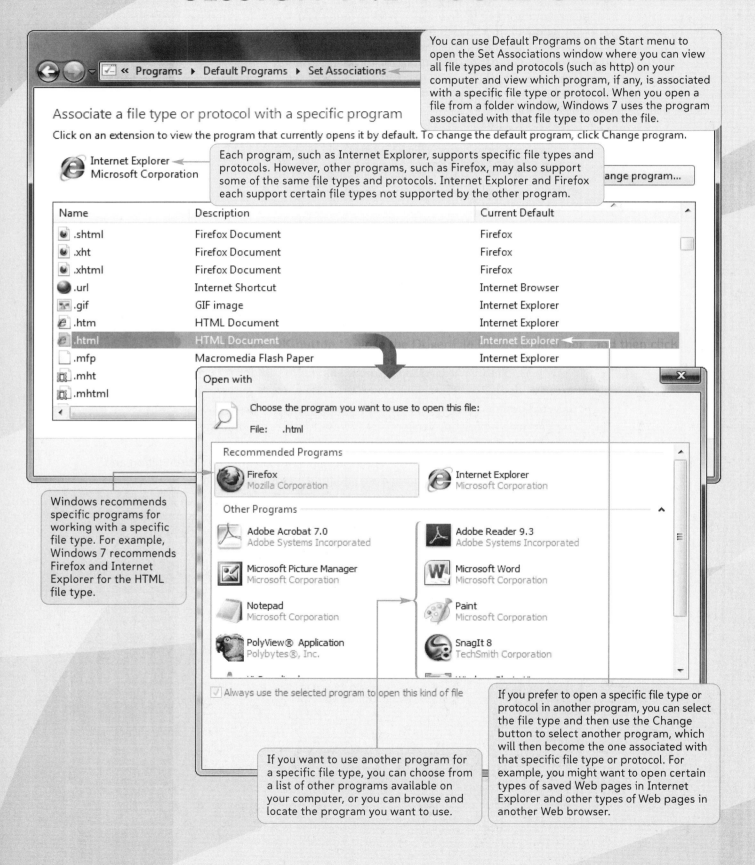

You can use Default Programs on the Start menu to open the Set Associations window where you can view all file types and protocols (such as http) on your computer and view which program, if any, is associated with a specific file type or protocol. When you open a file from a folder window, Windows 7 uses the program associated with that file type to open the file.

« Programs ▸ Default Programs ▸ Set Associations

Associate a file type or protocol with a specific program

Click on an extension to view the program that currently opens it by default. To change the default program, click Change program.

Internet Explorer
Microsoft Corporation

Each program, such as Internet Explorer, supports specific file types and protocols. However, other programs, such as Firefox, may also support some of the same file types and protocols. Internet Explorer and Firefox each support certain file types not supported by the other program.

...ange program...

Name	Description	Current Default
.shtml	Firefox Document	Firefox
.xht	Firefox Document	Firefox
.xhtml	Firefox Document	Firefox
.url	Internet Shortcut	Internet Browser
.gif	GIF image	Internet Explorer
.htm	HTML Document	Internet Explorer
.html	HTML Document	Internet Explorer
.mfp	Macromedia Flash Paper	Internet Explorer
.mht		
.mhtml		

Open with

Choose the program you want to use to open this file:

File: .html

Recommended Programs

Firefox
Mozilla Corporation

Internet Explorer
Microsoft Corporation

Other Programs

Adobe Acrobat 7.0
Adobe Systems Incorporated

Adobe Reader 9.3
Adobe Systems Incorporated

Microsoft Picture Manager
Microsoft Corporation

Microsoft Word
Microsoft Corporation

Notepad
Microsoft Corporation

Paint
Microsoft Corporation

PolyView® Application
Polybytes®, Inc.

SnagIt 8
TechSmith Corporation

☑ Always use the selected program to open this kind of file

Windows recommends specific programs for working with a specific file type. For example, Windows 7 recommends Firefox and Internet Explorer for the HTML file type.

If you want to use another program for a specific file type, you can choose from a list of other programs available on your computer, or you can browse and locate the program you want to use.

If you prefer to open a specific file type or protocol in another program, you can select the file type and then use the Change button to select another program, which will then become the one associated with that specific file type or protocol. For example, you might want to open certain types of saved Web pages in Internet Explorer and other types of Web pages in another Web browser.

SOFTWARE SUPPORT

If you right-click a program file or its shortcut, you can access the Compatibility property sheet for that program and customize its compatibility settings so it runs properly under your version and edition of Windows.

Windows 7 identifies the Windows 7 Upgrade Advisor installation program as a Win32 Cabinet Self-Extractor. A **cabinet file** is a file that contains multiple application files in a compressed format.

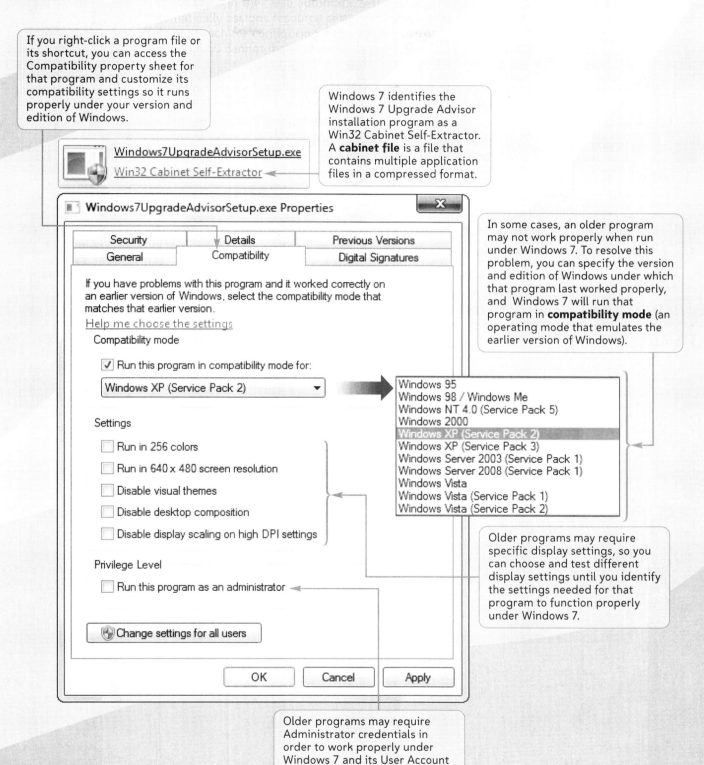

Windows7UpgradeAdvisorSetup.exe
Win32 Cabinet Self-Extractor

In some cases, an older program may not work properly when run under Windows 7. To resolve this problem, you can specify the version and edition of Windows under which that program last worked properly, and Windows 7 will run that program in **compatibility mode** (an operating mode that emulates the earlier version of Windows).

Windows7UpgradeAdvisorSetup.exe Properties

| Security | Details | Previous Versions |
| General | Compatibility | Digital Signatures |

If you have problems with this program and it worked correctly on an earlier version of Windows, select the compatibility mode that matches that earlier version.

Help me choose the settings

Compatibility mode

☑ Run this program in compatibility mode for:

Windows XP (Service Pack 2) ▼

Settings

☐ Run in 256 colors
☐ Run in 640 x 480 screen resolution
☐ Disable visual themes
☐ Disable desktop composition
☐ Disable display scaling on high DPI settings

Privilege Level

☐ Run this program as an administrator

🛡 Change settings for all users

OK   Cancel   Apply

Windows 95
Windows 98 / Windows Me
Windows NT 4.0 (Service Pack 5)
Windows 2000
Windows XP (Service Pack 2)
Windows XP (Service Pack 3)
Windows Server 2003 (Service Pack 1)
Windows Server 2008 (Service Pack 1)
Windows Vista
Windows Vista (Service Pack 1)
Windows Vista (Service Pack 2)

Older programs may require specific display settings, so you can choose and test different display settings until you identify the settings needed for that program to function properly under Windows 7.

Older programs may require Administrator credentials in order to work properly under Windows 7 and its User Account Control feature.

Turning Windows Features On or Off

Like Windows Vista, Windows 7 takes a different approach than earlier versions of Windows for the installation of Windows components, such as Windows Media Player. When you install Windows 7 on a computer, all Windows components are installed, but not all of them are available because they are turned off by default. If you want to remove a Windows feature, you do not uninstall that Windows feature; instead you turn off the Windows feature. The component remains installed on your computer, so you can always turn the feature back on later.

You can use the Control Panel to determine which features are enabled and disabled in your Windows 7 edition, and if necessary, make and apply changes to your computer. You may want to turn on or off certain features, such as Windows Media Player, Internet Explorer, Windows Media Center, Tablet PC components, and Windows Fax and Scan, to name a few. If you do not need certain features, you can turn those features off and optimize the performance of your computer in the process.

Kai recommends you examine the status of Windows features on your computer.

In the next set of steps, you will need to provide Administrator credentials. If you turn on or turn off Windows features, you will need to restart your computer to apply those changes. If you are working in your college's computer lab, and if lab policy does not permit you to modify software, do not keystroke the following steps, but rather read the steps and examine the figures so you are familiar with how to turn Windows features on and off. Note that in some computer labs, any settings you specify are restored to the original settings during the next boot.

To examine the status of Windows features:

1. From the Start menu, open **Control Panel**, click the **Programs** link, and under Programs and Features, click the **Turn Windows features on or off** link. Provide Administrator credentials, and then use Aero Snap to expand the Windows Features window vertically so you can see the complete list of Windows features available on your computer. In the Windows Features window, Windows 7 explains how to turn on or off a Windows feature.

The Windows Features dialog box lists Windows features or components in alphabetical order by name. Some features, such as Media Features, are expandable categories that enable you to turn on or off related features. Features that are enabled have a check mark in the check box, and features that are not enabled do not have a check mark in the check box. Check boxes with a blue fill indicate that one or more components or features within that category are turned on and others are turned off. See Figure 11-13. Your Windows feature settings will differ.

TIP

If you want to send and receive faxes using your computer, enable the Windows Fax and Scan feature under Print and Document Services.

Figure 11-13	Viewing the status of Windows Features

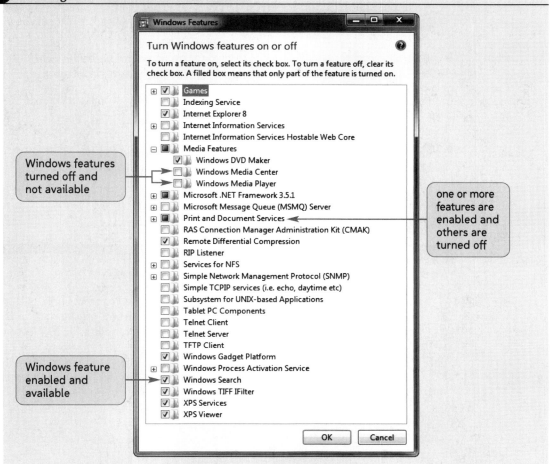

Windows features turned off and not available

one or more features are enabled and others are turned off

Windows feature enabled and available

2. Point to **Indexing Service** and pause. Windows 7 displays a ToolTip with informa-tion about this feature. The ToolTip explains that this feature "turns the indexing service that was available in previous versions of Windows on or off." This feature is independent of the Windows 7 indexing service (which is listed as Windows Search and automatically enabled).

3. Click the **expand** icon ⊞ to the left of Media Features. Under Media Features, you can turn on or off Windows DVD Maker (if available in your Windows edition), Windows Media Center (if available in your Windows edition), and Windows Media Player. If you do not use Windows Media Player, but rather use one or more other players, then you can turn off Windows Media Player. If Windows Media Center is available in your Windows edition, and if you are interested in exploring this feature, you can enable it; however, Windows Media Player must also be enabled.

> **4.** Click the **expand** icon ⊞ to the left of Print and Document Services. Under Print and Document Services, you can turn Internet Printing Client on or off. The Internet Printing Client allows you to connect to a Web print server over the Internet and print documents.

> **5.** If you have made changes to Windows features on your computer you wish to keep, click the **OK** button; otherwise, click the **Cancel** button.

> **6.** If a Microsoft Windows dialog box informs you that you must restart your computer to apply these changes, click the **Restart Now** button or the **Restart Later** button.

> **7.** Close the Programs window.

You should examine each category of Windows 7 features to determine whether you need to turn on any additional components that might prove useful to you or turn off components that you do not need and do not use.

REFERENCE

Turning Windows Features On and Off

- From the Start menu, open Control Panel, click the Programs link, click the "Turn windows features on or off" link, provide Administrator credentials, and then resize the Windows Feature window so you can see the complete list of Windows features available on your computer.
- If you want to turn a feature on or off, expand a set of related features (if necessary), click the check box of the feature, and then click the OK button.
- After Windows 7 configures the feature and prompts you to restart your computer, click the Restart Now button or click the Restart Later button, and close the Programs window.

Next, you turn your attention to installing software on your computer.

Installing Software

Kai relies on the applications included in Microsoft Office, and she also uses other applications, such as project management software. As she has discovered from installing software on her home computer, acquiring and installing software is easier than ever thanks to the Internet. If Kai discovers she needs a specific type of software product, she searches for reviews in online technical magazines and then evaluates different products. Once she's decided on which product to use, she downloads the software she needs from the vendor's Web site, installs the software, and within minutes she is using that software.

Currently, many software products are designed for use under a 32-bit Windows operating system, such as the 32-bit editions of Windows 7, Windows Vista, and Windows XP, as well as even earlier versions of Windows. These types of applications are referred to as **Win32 applications** (or more generally, **32-bit applications**), and Microsoft requires that these applications include an Uninstall program so a user can remove the software from a computer. **Win64 applications**, or **64-bit applications**, are now available for use under 64-bit versions of Windows.

The Windows 7 Compatibility Center (*www.microsoft.com/windows/compatibility/ windows-7/en-us/default.aspx*) identifies whether a software product is compatible under 64-bit Windows 7 or 32-bit Windows 7, or both. If the software product is identified as "Compatible - Windows 7 Logo," as shown in Figure 11-14 for the Microsoft Office suite, then it has passed the Microsoft compatibility tests for 64-bit Windows or 32-bit Windows 7, or both.

Figure 11-14	**Viewing 32-bit compatibility of Microsoft Office 2010 versions**

With earlier versions of the Windows operating systems, individuals also installed and used two other types of applications:

- **Win16 applications**—These types of applications were originally developed for use in **16-bit Windows operating environments**, such as Windows 3.1, where MS-DOS or PC-DOS, 16-bit operating systems, were installed. A 16-bit operating system was designed for 16-bit processors that handled 16 bits of data at a time and that, in theory, supported up to 2^{16} or 64 KB of RAM, but in practice, supported up to 2^{20}, or 1 MB, of RAM (due to the design of early 16-bit processors).
- **DOS applications**—Like Win16 applications, DOS applications were developed for 16-bit operating environments where MS-DOS or PC-DOS was installed as the operating system.

Support for Win16 applications and DOS applications under the Windows operating systems varies, especially in the case of DOS applications. However, by now, most people use more reliable and readily obtainable 32-bit applications or applications that work with both 32-bit and 64-bit Windows.

Decision Making: Choosing 32-bit or 64-bit Applications

Many software developers are now releasing 64-bit versions of their software products for 64-bit Windows operating systems. For example, starting with Microsoft Office 2010, Microsoft is making available a 32-bit and 64-bit edition of Microsoft Office. You can install a 32-bit edition of Microsoft Office with a 32-bit version of Microsoft Outlook on a computer that uses either a 32-bit or 64-bit version of Windows. In contrast, you can only install a 64-bit edition of Microsoft Office with a 64-bit version of Microsoft Outlook on a computer that uses a 64-bit Windows operating system. According to Microsoft, the 64-bit version of Microsoft Office 2010 will enable users and businesses to work with much larger sets of data. Microsoft also notes that the 32-bit version of Microsoft Office 2010 is installed by default, even on 64-bit systems. If you want to install the 64-bit version of Microsoft Office, you must choose that installment option. If you use a 32-bit version of an application under a 64-bit edition of Windows, then that application is limited to 4 GB of RAM. If you want to determine whether the 64-bit version of Microsoft Office 2010 will meet your needs, you can visit the Microsoft Office Web site (*http://office.microsoft.com*) and search for information on 64-bit Office versions.

Before you purchase software, or download and install software, you should verify that it will work with Windows 7 and you should decide whether you want the 32-bit or 64-bit version. You should also be aware of any limitations with backward compatibility in the 64-bit version of that software product. You can check the software vendor's Web site or use the Microsoft Windows 7 Compatibility Center Web site to determine whether the software is compatible with 64-bit Windows 7. You can also check the Web site of the company that makes the software to determine which versions and editions of Windows support that product. By carefully evaluating your present and future needs and by reviewing the availability of 32-bit and 64-bit software, you can plan wisely for the present and the long-term.

Preparing for a Software Installation or Upgrade

Kai has discovered that the guidelines that apply for preparing for an operating system upgrade are also useful when installing new software products on her computer.

Before you install software on your computer, you should prepare your computer system, using the guidelines described earlier for installing or upgrading an operating system. You should make sure that you have a recent backup of your document files before installing a new software product or a major upgrade to an existing software product. You should also use the Error-checking tool or the command-line Check Disk utility to check for and repair file system problems. Although Disk Defragmenter automatically defragments your hard disk drive under Windows 7, you can manually optimize storage space on your hard disk drive with Disk Defragmenter before installing a new software product.

When you install an application, the Setup program performs the following types of operations:

- **Application installation**—The Setup program creates a folder for the application on the hard disk drive and creates any subfolders needed for installing the product's program files and supporting files. When you install an application, you can use the default path and folder name that the Setup program proposes, or you can choose your own folder name. Setup programs typically install software in a folder under the Program Files folder (as recommended by Microsoft). For example, when you installed the Windows 7 Upgrade Advisor earlier, the software for this program was installed in the Microsoft Windows 7 Upgrade Advisor folder under the Program Files folder. If the Setup program indicates that it will install the software product elsewhere, you can override this option and designate the Program Files folder so all installed software is stored in one central location.

- **Registry updates**—The Setup program copies software settings and other information, such as the full path for program files, registration information, and file extension associations, to the Windows Registry.
- **Group folder and shortcuts creation**—The Setup program either adds a group folder or a program shortcut to the All Programs menu. After a Setup program creates a group folder for the software product, such as Microsoft Office, it creates shortcuts to the programs included with the software product. It may also create a shortcut to an Uninstall program as well as shortcuts to Help and Readme files that contain information and documentation on using the software product.
- **Uninstall program installation**—As required by Microsoft, Win32 and later applications include an Uninstall program that you can use to remove that application from your computer system. In fact, as just noted, the Uninstall program might be one of the options in the application's group folder on the Start or All Programs menu. In contrast, Win16 and DOS applications typically did not include an Uninstall program or option, and that often created problems for users because they were unable to uninstall Win16 applications.

You can install a Win32 application in one of the following ways:

TIP

The installation program file for many software products is named Setup.exe.

- **Use a software product's DVD or CD**—If you purchase a software product online or from a store, you can easily install the software by using the product's DVD or CD. As soon as you insert the DVD or CD in your computer, Windows 7 starts the installation program. If the installation program doesn't start, you can open a window on the DVD or CD, and then locate and click (or double-click) Setup.exe to start the installation of the software product.
- **Use a downloaded ISO file**—If you purchase and download software as an ISO file, you can use DVD- or CD-writing software to write the disc image to a blank DVD or CD so you can install the software from that disc.
- **Use a self-extracting executable file**—When you download a program from a Web site, the downloaded program might be stored in a self-extracting executable file with the .exe file extension. A **self-extracting executable file** is a file that contains one or more files stored in a compressed format, plus a program for extracting the contents of the self-extracting executable file itself. When you click (or double-click) the self-extracting executable file, a program within the downloaded file extracts the contents of this downloaded file and then starts the Setup program for installing the software product.
- **Use a Windows Installer package**—Other programs that you download from the Internet are stored in a file with the .msi file extension (for Windows Installer Package). You can click (or double-click) the file icon to start Windows Installer on your computer, and it will monitor the installation of the software product.
- **Use a Compressed (zipped) Folder**—If the program you download is stored in a file with the .zip file extension, it contains one or more files stored in a compressed format. The Zip file format is commonly used for compressing files for downloading from the Internet or a Web site, or for compressing files that are then included as an attachment to an email message (though not all email software allows these types of attachments for security reasons). Because Windows 7 treats a file with the .zip file extension as a Compressed (zipped) Folder, you can open the Compressed (zipped) Folder like any other folder, and then extract the files.

Downloading software from Web sites is becoming increasingly common. In fact, in most cases, you can quickly obtain and install software by downloading self-extracting executable files.

Earlier, you installed the Windows 7 Upgrade Advisor, so you are already familiar with the process for installing a Win32 application. The process for installing other software is very similar to that shown for the Windows 7 Upgrade Advisor. However, if you are installing an office suite like Microsoft Office, you are installing multiple applications, and therefore, you can choose which components within each application to install as well as decide which shared components you want to install. **Shared components** are modules of program code used by two or more programs.

Next, you examine how to add and remove components for Microsoft Office, an application that many business and home users depend on.

Adding and Removing Microsoft Office Components

People who use the Microsoft Office suite often find that they do not have access to all the features and components included in the software suite because they originally choose the default install option. Or perhaps someone else installed the software on their behalf and did not do a full install because they decided that the individual did not need certain features. As a result, those Microsoft Office users discover that they do not always have access to the features they need. However, you can open the Setup installation program for Microsoft Office, examine what's installed, and add or remove individual components.

When installing software on her laptop, Kai always makes a point of performing a full install or choosing the option that permits her to pick and choose which program components to install. That way her laptop is set up with everything she needs. She suggests that you do the same on your office laptop.

In the next section of the tutorial, you will open Microsoft Office Setup and examine installed components. To complete this section of the tutorial, Microsoft Office must be installed on the computer you are using. If Microsoft Office is not installed on that computer, then do not keystroke the tutorial steps in this section of the tutorial, but rather read the steps and examine the figures so you are familiar with the process for adding and removing program components.

If you are working on a computer in a computer lab that does not permit you to install or remove software, do not keystroke the following steps, but rather read the steps and examine the figures so you are familiar with how to add and remove program components within an installed application. The following steps illustrate the use of Microsoft Office Professional 2010. If you have a different version, you will notice differences in the availability of features.

If you are using your own computer, make sure you have your Microsoft Office CD or DVD before you start the tutorial steps in case you need to reinstall Microsoft Office.

To complete the following tutorial steps, you must provide Administrator credentials. If you cannot provide Administrator credentials, or if your college's computer lab does not permit you to modify installed software on lab computers, do not keystroke the following steps, but instead read the steps and examine the figures so you are familiar with the use of the features described in this section of the tutorial

To examine installable Microsoft Office components:

Make sure you point to but do not click your installed Microsoft Office version; otherwise, you will initiate the process for removing this software from your computer.

▶ **1.** From the Start menu, open the Control Panel, click the **Programs** link, click the **Programs and Features** link, *point to* your **Microsoft Office version**, click the **Change** button on the toolbar, and then provide Administrator credentials.

As shown in Figure 11-15, the Microsoft Office Professional Plus 2010 dialog box displays options for adding or removing features, repairing this version of Microsoft Office, removing (or uninstalling) this version of Microsoft Office, and entering a Product Key. Your Microsoft Office version options may differ.

Figure 11-15 **Modifying a Microsoft Office installation**

options for changing a Microsoft Office installation

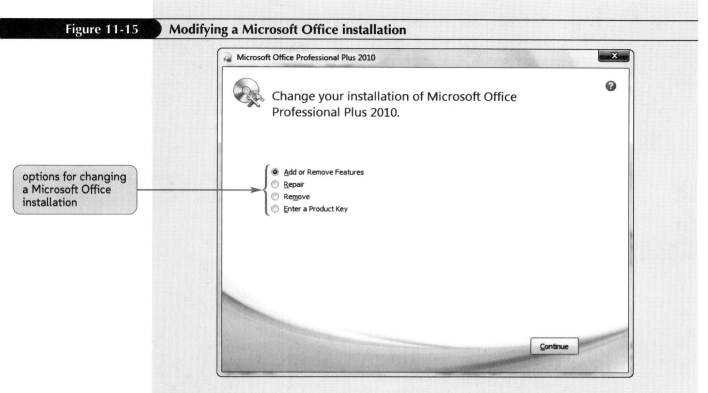

▶ **2.** Click the Add or Remove Features option button (if necessary), and then click the **Continue** button. You can now choose Installation Options for your version of Office. See Figure 11-16.

Figure 11-16 **Examining options for installing Microsoft Office components**

categories of Microsoft Office components

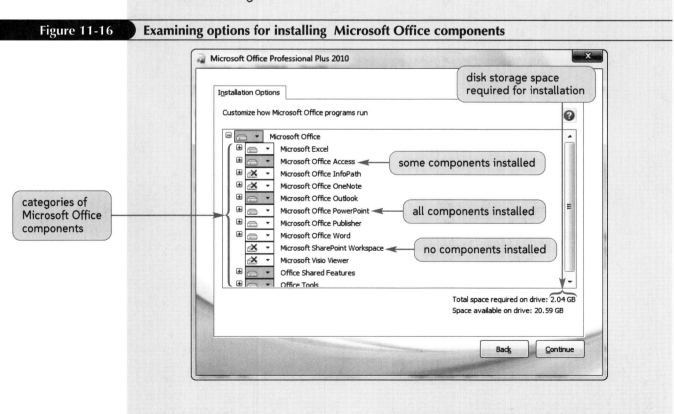

Note that the features are divided into categories for each application and include Office Shared Features and Office Tools. Your Microsoft Office program options may differ. If a component has a white button with a hard disk drive icon, that means all the components within that category are installed. If a component has a gray button with a hard disk drive icon, that means that only some of the components within that category are installed. If a component has a white button with a red *X* over the hard disk drive icon, that means none of the components within that category are installed. You can click the expand icon ⊞ next to any category or subcategory to view specific options. The dialog box also shows the total amount of hard disk drive storage space used by the components that are currently installed as well as the total hard disk drive storage space available.

▶ **3.** Click the **Microsoft Word** button. Setup displays a drop-down menu with options for modifying the installation of this feature. See Figure 11-17.

Figure 11-17   **Viewing options for installing a Microsoft Office component**

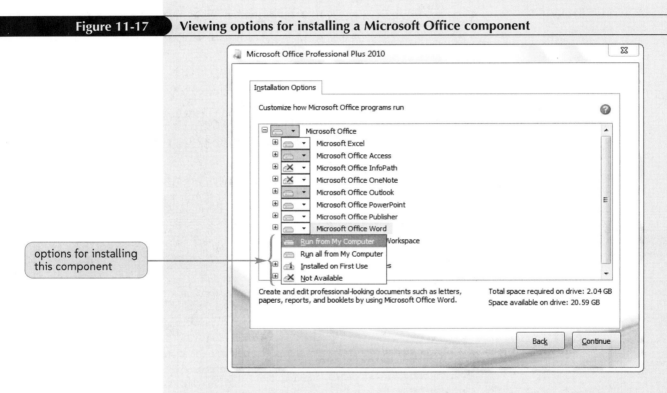

options for installing this component

If you choose "Run from My Computer," Setup installs the component on your hard disk drive. If you choose "Run all from My Computer," Setup installs the feature and all its components on your hard disk drive. (Some features do not have components.) If you choose "Installed on First Use," Setup installs the component when first needed. If you choose "Not Available," Setup does not install the component, or it removes the component if it is already installed.

If storage space on your hard disk drive is limited, or if you prefer to keep as much of your hard disk drive as free as possible, you can review these options to determine which ones you actually need. Then, only install the ones that you will be using and save disk space by not installing components you'll never use. If you have plenty of storage space on your hard disk drive, and if you want to install components on your computer, or if you want to remove components, you can review these options and decide which ones to install and which to uninstall.

4. If you do not want to make changes to your installed version of Office, click the **Close** button [x], click the **Yes** button in the Setup dialog box to cancel setup, and then click the **Close** button in the Microsoft Office dialog box. If you made changes to the selections for your version of Microsoft Office and want to keep those changes, click the **Continue** button. Setup will configure your installed version of Microsoft Office and make the changes you specified, and then it will inform you that the configuration of your version of Microsoft Office was completed successfully so you can close the Setup installation program. If you made changes that you want to access immediately, exit any Office programs and open them again.
5. Keep the Programs and Features window open for the next section of the tutorial.

If your computer comes with installed software, or if you or someone else opted for a standard, typical, or default installation of a software product on your computer, you may want to open the Setup program for that software product, examine the list of installed and uninstalled components, and change options so you have all the tools you need for your work.

REFERENCE

Adding or Removing Microsoft Office Components

- From the Start menu, open the Control Panel, click the Programs link, and then click the Programs and Features link.
- Do not click the version of Microsoft Office installed on your computer, but rather point to that version to select it, click the Change button on the toolbar, and then provide Administrator credentials.
- In the Microsoft Office dialog box, choose the "Add or Remove Features" option button, and then click the Continue button.
- Click the expand icon to expand a category and examine which options are available under that category. Click the button to the left of each category of options or to the left of a specific component to choose "Run from My Computer," "Run all from My Computer," "Installed on First Use," or "Not Available." Then, click the Continue button to install and uninstall options you've selected. Then, close the Microsoft Office dialog box after the configuration changes are made.
- If you want to exit Setup at any time without making changes, click the Close button and verify that you want to cancel Setup. Then, close the Microsoft Office dialog box.

If you select Microsoft Office in your list of installed programs, you can use the Repair button on the toolbar to troubleshoot and repair any problems you encounter with your version of Microsoft Office.

Using the Program Compatibility Troubleshooter

After upgrading to Windows 7, Kai encountered problems with an older program on her computer. At the suggestion of her IT staff, she decided to use the Program Compatibility troubleshooter to determine whether she could resolve the problems.

You can use the Program Compatibility troubleshooter to specify different settings for running an older program that does not otherwise run properly under Windows 7. If the program worked with an earlier version of Windows, you can specify that Windows 7 simulate the conditions under which that program would have run in the earlier version of Windows. Microsoft recommends that you do not use the Program Compatibility troubleshooter with an older antivirus program, older disk utilities (such as software for burning a CD), or older system utilities, because you might lose data or adversely affect your computer's security. Instead, you need to upgrade these older types of programs. Also, the Program Compatibility troubleshooter does not work with Windows Installer Package files with the .msi file extension, but only works with programs with the .exe file extension (other than the exceptions already noted).

Even though the Windows 7 Upgrade Advisor works fine on your computer, Kai suggests that you test the Program Compatibility troubleshooter on the Windows 7 Upgrade Advisor so you are familiar with the use of this feature.

To use the Program Compatibility troubleshooter:

▶ **1.** In the Programs and Features window, click **Programs** in the Address bar, and then click the **Run programs made for previous versions of Windows** link, and then click the **Next** button in the Program Compatibility dialog box. The Program Compatibility troubleshooter compiles a list of programs so you can select the one that's causing a problem. You can also select *Not Listed* to manually browse for a program.

▶ **2.** Scroll to the bottom of the list of programs, click **Windows 7 Upgrade Advisor**, and then click the **Next** button. The Program Compatibility troubleshooter displays two troubleshooting Options. With the "Try recommended settings" option, you can test run the program using Windows 7 recommended compatibility settings. The "Troubleshoot program" option allows you to select compatibility settings based on problems you've observed.

▶ **3.** Click the **Try recommended settings**. The Program Compatibility troubleshooter applies a Windows compatibility mode setting. On the computer used for Figure 11-18, the Program Compatibility troubleshooter is recommending that Windows 7 run this program as if it were designed for Windows XP (Service Pack 2). Your compatibility mode might differ. It also notes that you need to start the program and test the new settings applied to this program.

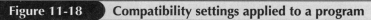

Figure 11-18 **Compatibility settings applied to a program**

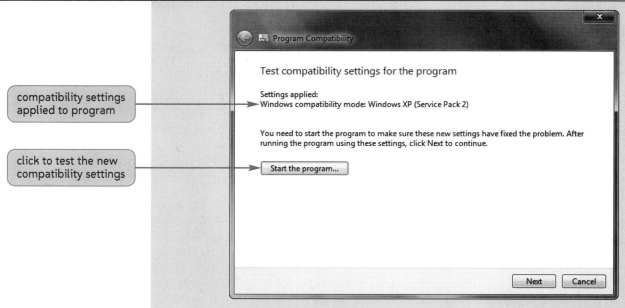

compatibility settings applied to program

click to test the new compatibility settings

▶ **4.** Click the **Start the program** button, and provide Administrator credentials.

▶ **5.** After the Windows 7 Upgrade Advisor window opens, click the **Windows 7 Upgrade Advisor** taskbar button to bring that window to the foreground.

▶ **6.** In the Windows 7 Upgrade Advisor window, click the **Start check** button so you can verify whether this program works with this compatibility mode setting, and then provide Administrator credentials.

▶ **7.** After the Windows 7 Upgrade Advisor produces a 32-bit and 64-bit report, click the **Close** button, and then click the **Next** button in the Program Compatibility troubleshooter dialog box. You have just verified that the Windows 7 Upgrade Advisor works with the compatibility mode settings applied by the Program Compatibility troubleshooter. The Program Compatibility troubleshooter informs you that troubleshooting is completed, and asks you if the problem is fixed. If so, you can save the compatibility mode settings for this program. If not, you can try again using different settings, or you can report the problem to Microsoft and check online for a solution.

▶ **8.** Click the **Cancel** button to close the Program Compatibility dialog box without applying compatibility mode settings.

In the next set of steps, you will open the Program Compatibility Wizard and manually apply compatibility mode settings for the Windows 7 Upgrade Advisor so you can examine an alternate approach to troubleshooting program compatibility problems.

To examine other troubleshooting options:

▶ **1.** In the Programs window, click the **Run programs made for previous versions of Windows** link, and then click the **Next** button in the Program Compatibility dialog box.

▶ **2.** Press the **End** key to select **Windows 7 Upgrade Advisor** (or manually select it, if necessary), click the **Next** button, and then click the **Troubleshoot program** option. The Program Compatibility troubleshooter now asks you to identify problems you've noticed. See Figure 11-19.

| **Figure 11-19** | **Identifying the types of observed problems** |

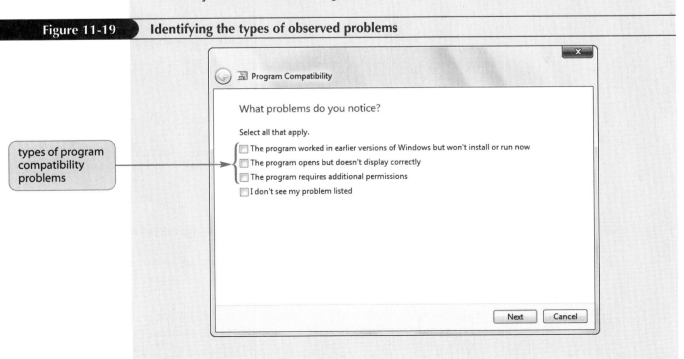

types of program compatibility problems

Notice that the Program Compatibility troubleshooter identifies three common program problems, namely, programs that worked in an earlier version of Window but that don't work in Windows 7, programs that do not display correctly once opened, and programs that require additional permissions. Assume the problem you encountered is not listed or that you're not sure which of the first three to choose.

▶ 3. Click the **I don't see my problem listed** check box, and click the **Next** button. The Program Compatibility troubleshooter identifies different versions and different service pack upgrades for specific versions of Windows so you can select the version, edition, service pack, or some combination to troubleshoot the problem.

▶ 4. If the Program Compatibility troubleshooter automatically selected Windows XP (Service Pack 2) when you ran it automatically earlier, then click **Windows XP (Service Pack 2)** and click the **Next** button; otherwise, select the version of Windows that the Program Compatibility troubleshooter previously chose, and then click the **Next** button. The Program Compatibility troubleshooter asks you to identify display problems you've noticed, as shown in Figure 11-20.

| **Figure 11-20** | **Identifying the types of display problems** |

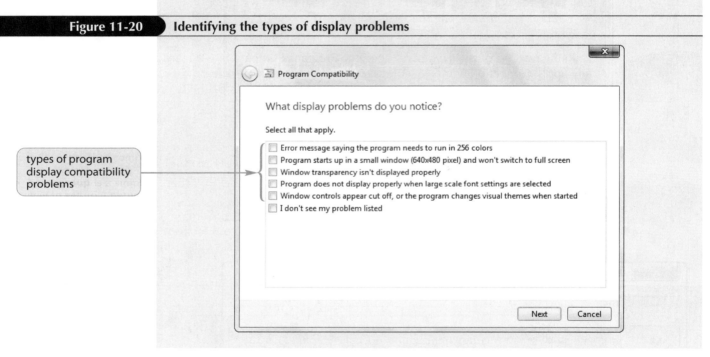

types of program display compatibility problems

The following bulleted list describes each of these options:

- **Error message saying the program needs to run in 256 colors**—An older program might need to run with a low color depth setting (256 colors).
- **Program starts up in a small window (640 × 480 pixel) and won't switch to full screen**—An older program might require a low resolution of 640 × 480 in order to render the graphical user interface properly.
- **Windows transparency isn't displayed properly**—This option turns off Windows Aero desktop composition.
- **Program does not display properly when large scale font settings are selected**—This option disables display scaling that uses high DPI settings.
- **Windows controls appear cut off, or the program changes visual themes when started**—This option disables the use of visual themes on your computer so Windows controls appear properly.

If you are not sure which, if any, settings are the ones required for the program, you can advance to the next step and test the program with the compatibility mode for an earlier version of Windows. If the program still does not work properly, you can choose one display setting at a time until you locate the setting (or settings) needed by the program to work properly under Windows 7.

To continue with the Program Compatibility troubleshooter:

▶ **1.** Click the **I don't see my problem listed** check box, and then click the **Next** button. The Program Compatibility troubleshooter applies the compatibility mode you selected and sets program compatibility settings so that the program runs with Administrator credentials.

▶ **2.** Click the **Start the program** button, and in the User Account Control dialog box click the **Yes** button when prompted to allow this program to make changes to your computer.

▶ **3.** Close the Windows 7 Upgrade Advisor dialog box, click the **Cancel** button in the Program Compatibility dialog box, and then close the Programs window.

You can also specify compatibility settings by changing properties of the program file itself or its shortcut on the All Programs menu.

To change compatibility settings for a program file:

▶ **1.** From the Start menu, right-click **Windows 7 Upgrade Advisor**, and then click **Properties**.

▶ **2.** Click the **Compatibility** tab. Compatibility mode settings, display settings, and privilege level settings are organized into one location. See Figure 11-21.

Figure 11-21 **Viewing compatibility options on a Compatibility property sheet**

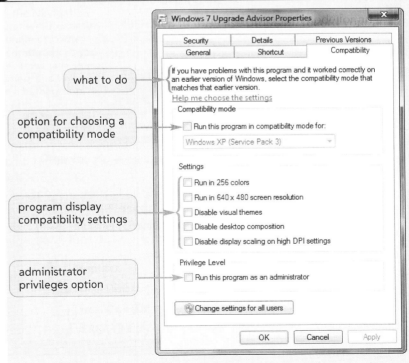

If you enable the option for the "Run this program in compatibility mode for" check box, and then click the Compatibility mode list button, you will find that you have access to the same Windows versions, editions, and service packs. Under Settings, you have the same options that are available in the Program Compatibility troubleshooter, although the options are more concise. You can also specify the privilege level for the program, and change settings for all users. The settings you choose become a property of this object on your computer, and Windows 7 uses these settings when you open the program. To test these settings, you must open and work with the program.

Microsoft recommends the following approaches for each of the following five settings:

- **Run in 256 colors**—Use this option if you think that an older program is designed for a lower color depth setting.
- **Run in 640 × 480 screen resolution**—Use this option if you notice problems with displaying the graphical user interface.
- **Disable visual themes**—Use this option if you notice problems with menus or buttons on the program's title bar.
- **Disable desktop composition**—Use this option if you notice that window movements appear erratic.
- **Disable display scaling on high DPI settings**—Use this option if high DPI settings affect the appearance of fonts within a program and objects on the desktop.

Another issue that affects compatibility of older programs is Administrator privileges. Programs designed for earlier versions of Windows assume they have Administrator privileges, and they attempt to modify system settings by writing to system folders or the Windows Registry. To guarantee the security of your computer, Windows 7 does not allow programs to perform these operations. That means that software developers must upgrade their software so the software works properly with Standard user privileges and with User Account Control. If you enable Administrator privileges for an older program that requires those privileges to work properly, then you are side-stepping the additional security and protection provided by Windows 7. Rather than compromise the security of your computer, you need to upgrade your software.

To close the Windows 7 Upgrade Advisor Properties dialog box:

▶ **1.** Click the **Cancel** button to close the Windows 7 Upgrade Advisor Properties dialog box without making any changes to your installed version of the Windows 7 Upgrade Advisor.

If the Program Compatibility troubleshooter does not correct the problem, check the Web site of the manufacturer of the software to determine if there is an update that enables the program to work properly under Windows 7, or upgrade to a program that does work under Windows 7.

REFERENCE

Using the Program Compatibility Troubleshooter to Specify Compatibility Settings

- From the Start menu, open the Control Panel, click the Programs link, and then click the "Run programs made for previous versions of Windows" link.
- In the Program Compatibility dialog box, click the Next button to compile a list of programs on your computer, select the program that you've experienced problems with, and then click the Next button.
- When prompted to select a troubleshooting option, choose "Try recommended settings" to use recommended compatibility settings, or choose "Troubleshoot program" to manually choose compatibility settings.
- If you choose "Try recommended settings," the Program Compatibility troubleshooter applies one or more compatibility mode settings, and prompts you to Start the program. After you test the program and then close it, click the Next button in the Program Compatibility dialog box, and choose the option for saving compatibility settings for the program, trying again using different settings, or reporting the problem to Microsoft and checking online for a solution.
- If you choose "Troubleshoot program," identify which problems you've noticed to apply specific compatibility settings to the program, or indicate that you do not see the problem you've encountered listed, and then click the Next button. If prompted, identify which version of Windows this program previously worked with, or choose the "I don't know" option, and then click the Next button. If prompted to identify specific display problems, select the display problem options you've encountered with the program, or select "I don't see my problem listed," and then click Next.
- After the Program Compatibility troubleshooter applies compatibility settings to your program, choose the option to start the program. After you test the program and then close it, click the Next button in the Program Compatibility dialog box, and choose the option for saving compatibility settings for the program, trying again using different settings, or reporting the problem to Microsoft and checking online for a solution.

TIP

There is no manual option for running the Program Compatibility Assistant.

Windows 7 also has a Program Compatibility Assistant that is different from the Program Compatibility troubleshooter. Windows 7 runs the Program Compatibility Assistant automatically when it detects a known compatibility problem with a program. The Program Compatibility Assistant adjusts compatibility settings for a program based on known compatibility issues for the program in question. Figure 11-22 shows a Program Compatibility Assistant dialog box for the installation of a downloaded software product.

Figure 11-22 **Program Compatibility Assistant identifies a problem with installing a program**

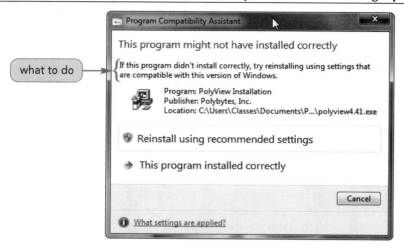

what to do

As shown in this figure, the Program Compatibility Assistant might prompt you to reinstall a program using recommended settings, or verify that you installed the program (or device driver) correctly. (The latter option was the case for the software installation shown in Figure 11-22.) Also, the Program Compatibility Assistant can resolve conflicts a program may encounter with User Account Control. If the Program Compatibility Assistant detects a serious compatibility problem, it might warn you, or it might completely block the program from running. Your next step is to check the vendor's Web site for information on this problem or, better yet, for an upgrade that resolves the problem.

Uninstalling Software

If you no longer need a program, you can uninstall it from your computer. If you are experiencing a problem with a program, you can choose the option for repairing the problem. If the problem still remains, you can uninstall the software, and then reinstall it.

Now that you have examined your computer with the Windows 7 Upgrade Advisor, Kai recommends that you uninstall the Windows 7 Upgrade Advisor.

If you want to uninstall the Windows 7 Upgrade Advisor, complete the following steps. If you do not want to uninstall the Windows 7 Upgrade Advisor, read the following steps and examine the figures, but do not keystroke the steps. If you uninstall the Windows 7 Upgrade Advisor and later need to check your computer again, you can always download it (or the most recent update of this program) from the Microsoft Web site. Also, you will need to provide Administrator credentials to uninstall the Windows 7 Upgrade Advisor.

To uninstall a program:

1. From the Start menu, click **Control Panel**, then click the **Uninstall a program** link under Programs.

Do not click the program, but rather make sure you point to the program to first select it.

2. In the Programs and Features window, locate and *point* to **Windows 7 Upgrade Advisor**. The toolbar now contains the Uninstall, Change, and Repair options. If you right-click an installed program, the shortcut menu shows options for uninstalling, changing, and repairing the program.

3. Click the **Change** button on the toolbar. The Windows 7 Upgrade Advisor Setup Wizard displays two options, one for repairing the installation of this software and another for removing the software.

▶ **4.** Click the **Remove Windows 7 Upgrade Advisor** option button, click the **Finish** button, click the **Yes** button in the User Account Control dialog box that asks whether you want to allow the program to update software on your computer, and then wait for Windows 7 to uninstall this program.

▶ **5.** A Windows 7 Upgrade Advisor dialog box appears, informing you that removal is complete. Click the **Close** button. The program no longer appears in the list of installed programs. That program also no longer appears on the All Programs menu.

Trouble? If Windows 7 still shows the Windows 7 Upgrade Advisor in the list of installed software, press the F5 (Refresh) key to update your view.

▶ **6.** Close the Programs and Features window.

The Uninstall option on the toolbar is a quicker way to remove a software product if you do not need to see what other options are available for changing the installation of a specific software product.

REFERENCE

Uninstalling Software

- From the Start menu, click Control Panel, and then click the "Uninstall a program" link under Programs.
- Locate and select the program you want to uninstall, click the Uninstall button on the toolbar (or right-click the program and click Uninstall), and provide Administrator credentials. If you want to view more options for managing the installed software, including an option for uninstalling the software, click the Change button, and follow the instructions for removing the software.
- Close the Programs and Features window.

Although it's easy to identify which software is installed on your computer by using the All Programs menu, the Programs and Features window provides more detail on the installed software and may include options (such as plug-ins, video display adapter drivers, software dictionaries, and even utilities) not shown on the All Programs menu.

INSIGHT

Reviewing Installed Software

You should periodically review the software on your computer by using the Programs and Features windows to identify software that you never use. Then, you can uninstall it from your computer system to free up valuable disk storage space. However, before you uninstall it, verify that you have the original installation DVDs or CDs for that software so you can reinstall it if you find that you need it later. Likewise, if you download software from a Web site, store the downloaded file in your user account's Downloads folder so you can easily reinstall it later. Another option is to download the software again from the Internet and, at the same time, determine whether there is a newer version with improved features.

Another way to configure the software on your computer is to set program defaults, which you'll do next.

Setting Program Defaults

During the installation of software on a computer, the installation program specifies default settings and file types for the software product. When you initiate a certain type of activity, such as browsing the Web, watching video, or playing music, Windows 7 opens a specific program to handle the operation. However, you might have several different programs that you use for the same purpose. For example, you might use both Windows Internet Explorer and Mozilla Firefox to browse the Web, and you might use Windows Media Player and another player, such as VLC Media Player, QuickTime Player, or RealPlayer, to watch videos or listen to music. In each case, you might prefer to use one of two or more programs for a specific activity.

When you install or set up software for use on your computer, the installation program or software might prompt you to choose whether you want to make that program the default program for a specific activity, and it might also prompt you to specify which file types that software product uses. In other cases, the installation program installs itself as the default program for a specific type of activity or for use with specific file types without asking you, or worse yet, provides you with no other option than to use that program as the default program with its file type settings. Then, you discover that the program that Windows 7 opens is not the one that you want to use for a specific activity (at least most of the time). However, under Windows 7, you can change program defaults and settings and specify how you want Windows 7 to handle programs by choosing Default Programs on the Start Menu.

You can specify default programs and settings in four ways:

- **Set your default programs**—You can use this option to make a specific program the default for all file types and protocols. For example, you might want to specify Mozilla Firefox as your default Web browser. Examples of protocols include HTTP (for Web connections) and HTTPS (for secure Web connections).
- **Associate a file type or protocol with a program**—You can specify which program is associated with a specific file extension. For example, you might want to specify that all HTM or HTML files open in a specific Web browser.
- **Change AutoPlay settings**—You can specify default settings for different types of media and media devices. For example, you might want to specify how Windows 7 handles DVD movies and Blu-ray disc movies.
- **Set program access and computer defaults**—You can use this option to specify the default Web browser, email program, media player, instant messaging program, and the virtual machine for Java. **Java** is a hardware-independent Web programming language for creating interactive and animated content on Web pages. When you visit a Web site that has interactive and animated content, Java programs are downloaded so you can view and use that content. However, for these Java programs to run on your computer, Windows 7 must use a virtual machine (VM) environment to translate Java program code into processor-specific instructions. These options apply to all users on the same computer. Furthermore, the programs you install must register themselves when you install them; otherwise, you cannot specify them as default programs.

Kai asks you to check the default settings used by your Web browser so you can verify that Windows 7 uses the program and settings you prefer.

You cannot open "Set Program access and computer defaults" by providing Administrator credentials. Instead, you must be logged on under an Administrator account. If you are not logged on under an Administrator account, do not keystroke the following steps, but rather read the steps and examine the figures so you are familiar with this feature. If you are working in your college computer lab, make sure you have permission to examine default computer and program settings (if they are available).

To check and specify program access and computer defaults:

▶ **1.** If necessary, log on under an Administrator account, and from the Start menu, click **Default Programs**. In the Default Programs window, you can specify default settings for the four options previously described.

▶ **2.** Click the **Set program access and computer defaults** link, and then click the Microsoft Windows **expand** icon ⨈ to view these settings. In the Set Program Access and Computer Defaults window, Windows 7 notes that a program configuration specifies default programs for certain activities, such as Web browsing, and determines which programs are accessible from the Start menu, desktop, and other locations. See Figure 11-23.

Figure 11-23   **Options for customizing a computer configuration**

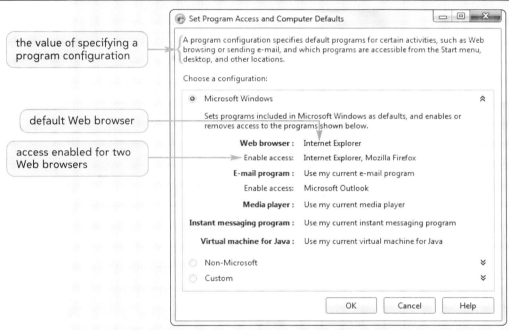

On the computer used for this figure, Internet Explorer is set as the default Web browser; however, access is enabled for both Internet Explorer and Mozilla Firefox so either can be selected from the Start menu. Access to Microsoft Outlook is enabled for E-mail program; however, that program is not currently used, and Windows 7 is set to use the current email program. The other options are also set for the currently used program. Your settings will differ.

If the Non-Microsoft option is enabled on this computer, the default Web browser becomes Mozilla Firefox, and Windows 7 removes access to Internet Explorer and Microsoft Outlook. Again, your options will differ.

To examine the Custom option:

▶ **1.** Click the Custom **expand** icon ⨈. With this configuration, you can choose which program you want to use, and which other programs you want to enable access to by displaying them on the Start menu and All Programs menu. See Figure 11-24.

Figure 11-24 **Examining custom configuration options**

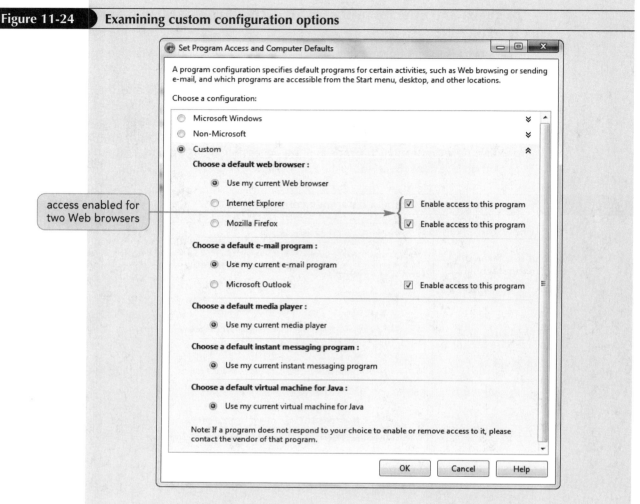

Note that, for example, this option uses the current Web browser, and enables access to both Web browsers on this computer. The other options are similar to the Microsoft Windows options. Although your Custom options may differ, this feature allows you to mix Microsoft and non-Microsoft programs as default programs for different uses.

2. If you are working on your own computer, and if you have made changes that you want to keep, click the **OK** button, and Windows 7 will display an Applying Settings dialog box as it applies the new settings you specified. If you do not want to change the default settings for your computer, or if you are working in a college computer lab, click the **Cancel** button to close the Set Program Access and Computer Defaults window without making any changes to the computer you are using.

3. Keep the Default Programs window open for the next set of tutorial steps.

If you see a Computer Manufacturer configuration option, the manufacturer of your computer installed Windows on your computer and specified program access and computer defaults settings. You can use this option to restore your settings to those selected by the manufacturer of your computer.

This feature allows you to quickly identify the default programs that you want to use for the most common types of operations you perform on your computer in one step. You can also set a specific program as the default program for all file types and protocols it can open.

To set default programs:

▶ **1.** In the Default Programs window, click the **Set your default programs** link and in the Programs box, click **Internet Explorer**. Windows 7 lists specific programs for which you can specify file types and protocols. See Figure 11-25.

Figure 11-25 **Options for customizing a computer configuration**

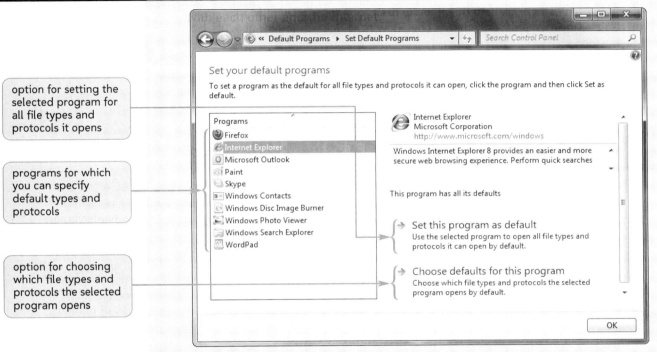

option for setting the selected program for all file types and protocols it opens

programs for which you can specify default types and protocols

option for choosing which file types and protocols the selected program opens

---

To the right of the Programs box, Windows 7 displays information about Internet Explorer, identifies how many defaults are currently set for this program (in this case, all its defaults), and allows you to set this program as the default for all file types and protocols it can open, or you can pick and choose which file types and protocols it opens by default. Your number of defaults may differ.

▶ **2.** Click the **Choose defaults for this program** link. In the Set Program Associations window, Windows 7 identifies which file extensions open with this program and which protocols it opens. On the computer used for Figure 11-26 (which has both Internet Explorer and Mozilla Firefox installed), Internet Explorer is set as the default program for opening all the file extensions and all the protocols.

Figure 11-26 **Viewing Internet Explorer default settings**

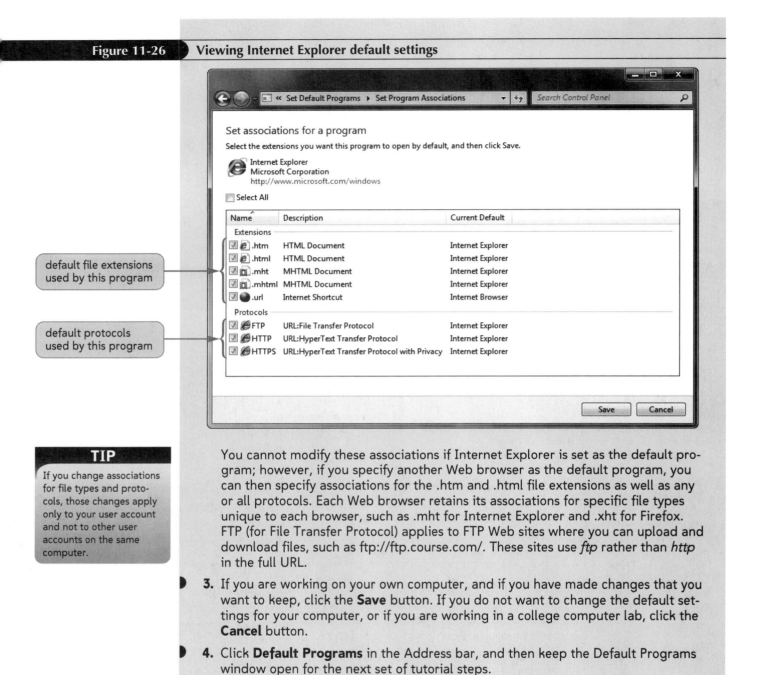

default file extensions used by this program

default protocols used by this program

You cannot modify these associations if Internet Explorer is set as the default program; however, if you specify another Web browser as the default program, you can then specify associations for the .htm and .html file extensions as well as any or all protocols. Each Web browser retains its associations for specific file types unique to each browser, such as .mht for Internet Explorer and .xht for Firefox. FTP (for File Transfer Protocol) applies to FTP Web sites where you can upload and download files, such as ftp://ftp.course.com/. These sites use *ftp* rather than *http* in the full URL.

3. If you are working on your own computer, and if you have made changes that you want to keep, click the **Save** button. If you do not want to change the default settings for your computer, or if you are working in a college computer lab, click the **Cancel** button.

4. Click **Default Programs** in the Address bar, and then keep the Default Programs window open for the next set of tutorial steps.

If you want to set default file types or protocols for a program and if that program does not appear in this list, you must open "Associate a file type or protocol with a program" first, and specify a file type or protocol for that program. This option for setting defaults for using file types and protocols is also useful when you want to customize the use of commonly used programs on your computer. You can associate individual file types and protocols with a specific program. For example, you might want to specify which program opens different types of graphics file formats (such as Bitmap, JPEG, GIF, and PNG) so you can use a specific program to perform a specific type of operation on a specific type of image. If you are designing Web pages, you might want to be able to open each of the different image types that you will put on that Web page with Internet Explorer so you can view how an image appears under that Web browser.

To associate a file type or protocol with a specific program:

1. In the Default Programs window, click the **Associate a file type or protocol with a program** link. Windows 7 displays a list of all file extensions on your computer, provides a description or name for each file type, and identifies the program currently assigned as the default program for opening that file type. However, certain file extensions and protocols might not be associated with a program, and the program is therefore identified as "Unknown application." See Figure 11-27.

Figure 11-27   Program associations for different file types

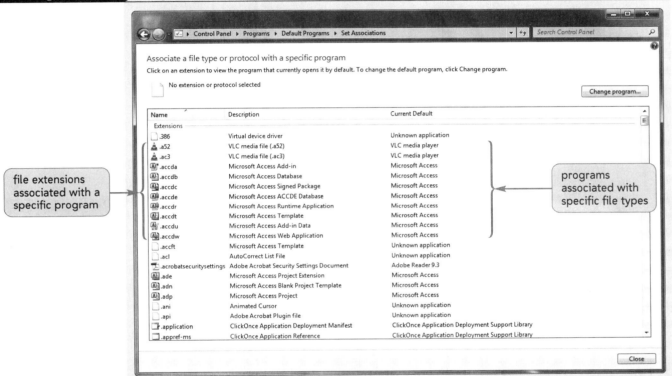

file extensions associated with a specific program

programs associated with specific file types

2. Locate the .jpg file extension (or file type) and note that, by default, this file type opens in Windows Photo Viewer (unless you or someone else has already changed this association). If you locate the .gif, .png, and .bmp file extensions, you will discover that files with GIF images open with Internet Explorer, and that PNG images and Bitmap images open with Windows Photo Viewer, by default. If you prefer to open these file types in another program, you can change the default file type by selecting the file extension, clicking the Change program button, and then selecting a program on your computer. Also, you cannot remove an association so the file type or protocol is no longer associated with any program; in other words, you must designate an association.

3. In the Name column, click the **.jpg** file extension, click the **Change program** button, and then click the **expand** icon ⌄ for the Other Programs section. Windows 7 displays an Open with dialog box and lists recommended programs and other programs that you can use to open this specific file type. See Figure 11-28. Your options may differ.

Figure 11-28 **Choosing a different program for opening a file type**

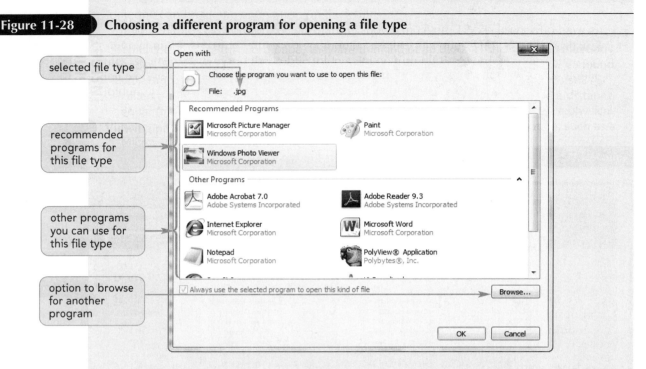

You can also use the Browse button to browse the Program Files folder and locate another graphics program (or a Web browser) for viewing or working with this file type. Note that Windows 7 is set to use any program you select as the default program for that file type; however, you can always change it again.

▶ **4.** Click **Cancel** to close the Open with dialog box, click **Close** in the Set Associations window, and then close the Default Programs window.

The ability to modify individual file extensions and protocols provides the greatest control for customizing the use of programs on your computer by enabling you to pick and choose which program opens which file type. You can combine the use of these three different ways for specifying program defaults and settings to meet your specific needs.

Specifying default programs as well as programs for specific file types guarantees that Windows 7 opens specific file types in the programs you prefer to use.

REFERENCE

Specifying Program Defaults and Settings

- Log on under an Administrator account if you want to make changes to "Set Program Access and Computer Default," and from the Start menu, click Default Programs.
- To specify defaults programs for certain types of activities and to specify which programs are accessible from the Start menu, desktop, and other locations, click the "Set program access and computer defaults" link, and choose a computer configuration. If you choose Custom, you can further customize defaults by program and enable access to programs on the Start Menu, desktop, and other locations. Click OK to save your computer configuration.
- To specify defaults for certain programs, click the "Set your default programs" link, select a program in the Programs box, click "Set this program as default" to use this program for all file types and protocols that it can open, or click "Choose defaults for this program" to specify file extensions and protocols for this program. Click the Save button to save your settings and close the Set Program Associations window. Then close the Set Default Programs window.
- To specify a program for each file type or protocol on your computer, click the "Associate a file type or protocol with a program" link, locate and select a file extension, click the Change program button, choose a recommended program, expand the Other Programs section and choose a program, or use the Browse button to locate a program that's not listed in the Open with dialog box, click OK to save your changes, and then click Close to close the Set Associations dialog box.
- Close the Default Programs window.

Restoring Your Computer's Settings

Complete the following steps to restore your computer to its original settings.

1. If necessary, use the Folder Options dialog box to turn off single-click activation, and then use the Start menu to turn off the display of the Computer icon on the desktop.

REVIEW

Session 11.2 Quick Check

1. What is the difference between Win32 and Win64 applications?
2. True or False. You can use a Win64 application with a 32-bit version of Windows.
3. What is a self-extracting executable file?
4. What is the difference between the Program Compatibility troubleshooter and the Program Compatibility Assistant?
5. True or False. When you install Win32 software on your computer, the Setup program copies software settings and other information, such as the full path for program files, registration information, and file extension associations, to the Registry.
6. What are shared components?
7. Name two ways in which you can specify file associations for a program.
8. How does Windows 7 handle the installation of Windows components?

Practice the skills you learned in the tutorial using the same case scenario.

PRACTICE

Review Assignments

There are no Data Files needed for the Review Assignments.

Now that Kai has upgraded her laptop to Windows 7 Ultimate, she's ready to upgrade the software on her home computer so it is similar to her office computer and her laptop. Then, when the need arises, she can work at home and have access to the same features she has on her office computer. Because the Windows 7 Home Premium Edition is currently installed on her home computer, her first step in upgrading her home computer is to determine whether she can upgrade to Windows 7 and which Windows 7 edition is the best possible edition. Kai also wants to make sure that the Windows 7 edition she upgrades to supports Windows Media Center.

Some of the following steps require Administrator credentials. As you complete each step in these Review Assignments, use a word-processing application, such as Microsoft Word or WordPad, to record your answers to the questions so you can submit them to your instructor. If you change any settings on the computer you are using, note the original settings so you can restore them later. Complete the following steps:

1. Kai's first step is to review the information on Windows 7 at the Microsoft Web site.
   a. Open your Web browser and go to the Microsoft Web site (*www.microsoft.com*).
   b. Locate and examine the information on comparing different Windows 7 editions. Which edition or editions of Windows 7 best fits your specific needs, and why?
2. Locate and examine the system requirements for Windows 7:
   a. What type(s) of processors are supported by Windows 7, and what is the minimum clock speed?
   b. How much RAM and graphics memory must a computer have in order to upgrade to Windows 7 Ultimate?
   c. How much disk space is required for installing the 32-bit or 64-bit edition of Windows 7?
   d. Are there any other requirements and, if so, what are they?
   e. What tool can you use to determine whether your computer hardware and software is compatible with Windows 7, and what types of information does it provide on Windows 7 compatibility?
3. Kai has a second, older computer with Windows XP Professional on her home network, and she wants to know what editions of Windows 7 she can use to upgrade that computer.
   a. From the Microsoft Windows 7 home page, locate information on Windows 7 upgrade paths.
   b. What Windows 7 edition or editions can she upgrade to, and how would she perform the upgrade?
4. Outline the steps that Kai should take prior to installing Windows 7 on these two computers. Include any steps Kai should take to improve the chances of a successful installation or upgrade and, if necessary, to restore her computers to their original state.
5. If Kai decides to replace her older Windows XP Professional computer with a new computer, can she transfer her files and computer settings from that computer to her new computer, and if so, how, and what type of media can she use?
6. Explain how Kai would examine and choose only those Windows features that she needs on each of her two computers after upgrading.
7. Kai also wants to check her installed version of Microsoft Office to make sure all the features she needs are installed and to also remove features she does not need. How can she perform this task?

8. Examine the installed software on your computer. How many programs are installed on your computer, and how much disk storage space do they use? Describe how you would remove an application or program that you no longer need from your computer.

9. Describe how Kai can use Windows 7 to set her computer's configuration so she can use another software product as her default Web browser and email program.

10. Explain how Kai can modify default program settings for Internet Explorer and her other Web browser so they work with specific files and protocols.

11. Describe how Kai can modify her program settings so files with graphic images automatically open in a specific program installed on her computer. Assume she works with GIF, JPEG, PNG, and Bitmap image files.

12. If necessary, restore any default settings on the computer you used for the review assignments.

13. Submit your answers to the review assignments to your instructor, either in printed or electronic form, as requested.

Use your skills to evaluate a proposed Windows 7 upgrade.

APPLY

Case Problem 1

There are no Data Files needed for this Case Problem.

Reflection Recording, Ltd.   Alaric Richardson works as a marketing associate for Reflection Recording, Ltd. He depends on the use of his company laptop when traveling on business, meeting with clients, and working at home on special projects. Before he upgrades his laptop from Windows 7 Professional Edition to Windows 7 Ultimate Edition, he wants to make sure that the upgrade will go smoothly and that his computer meets the requirements for using Windows 7 Ultimate. He asks you to identify the approach he should use for this upgrade.

As you complete each step in this case problem, use a word-processing application, such as Microsoft Word or WordPad, to record your answers to the questions so you can submit them to your instructor. If you change any settings on the computer you are using, note what the original settings were so you can restore them later. Complete the following steps:

1. Open the System window and view properties of your computer so you can document your computer system for a possible upgrade. Identify your Windows version and edition, your Windows Experience Index rating, your processor and its clock speed, the amount of system memory (or RAM), the System type (i.e., 32-bit or 64-bit operating system), your computer name, and your workgroup name (if applicable).

2. Open a Computer window. What is the storage capacity of your hard disk drive(s)? If you have multiple drives, identify each drive by name and list each drive's storage capacity. How much storage space is available on the drive where you would install a Windows upgrade? Is there sufficient storage space for an upgrade?

3. Open a window onto drive C and view the properties of the Windows folder. What is the total size on disk required for the contents of the Windows folder? View properties of the Program Files folder. What is the total size on disk for the contents of the Program Files folder? Close the drive C window.

4. View a list of the installed software on your computer. What type of applications do you use on your computer (Win32, Win64, or Win16 applications)? How many programs are installed on your computer, and how much disk storage capacity do all these programs require? Sort the list of installed software by size. What program requires the most amount of disk storage space? Sort the list of installed software by name.

5. If Microsoft Office is installed on your computer, what version of Microsoft Office do you use? How much storage space does Microsoft Office require?

6. Visit the Microsoft Web site and locate information on features available in different editions of Windows 7. If you wanted to use Windows XP Mode, what edition(s) could you use?

7. What edition or editions of Windows 7, if any, can you upgrade to? Would you have to purchase an upgrade copy or a full version of Windows 7? Would you need to upgrade the hardware on your computer, and if so, what would you need to do? Would you need or prefer to perform a clean install or an upgrade-in-place? From your perspective, what advantages do each of these types of upgrades offer, and what disadvantages do each of these types of upgrades pose?

8. Before upgrading your computer to a new edition of Windows 7, what Microsoft tool could you use to determine the compatibility of hardware and software on your computer?

9. What precautions would you take before installing a new edition of Windows 7 or a new version of the Windows operating system?

10. What precautions would you take before installing a new edition of a major software application like Microsoft Office?

11. Submit your answers to your instructor, either in printed or electronic form, as requested.

Use your skills to evaluate an upgrade to a new edition of Windows.

APPLY

Case Problem 2

There are no Data Files needed for this Case Problem.

McDaniel & Atkins Financial Services Leah McDaniel owns and manages McDaniel & Atkins Financial Services. As a member of her IT Department, you are going to assist in the process of evaluating the company's desktop computers and laptops for an upgrade to Windows 7 Ultimate so all staff members have access to all the features available in Windows 7.

This case problem requires that you download and install the Windows 7 Upgrade Advisor and any additional software needed to support the use of the Windows 7 Upgrade Advisor on the computer you are using for this case problem. You must provide Administrator credentials to install the Windows 7 Upgrade Advisor.

As you complete each step in this case problem, use a word-processing application, such as Microsoft Word or WordPad, to record your answers to the questions so you can submit them to your instructor. If you change any settings on the computer you are using, note what the original settings were so you can restore them later. Complete the following steps:

1. From the Microsoft Web site (*www.microsoft.com*) and the Microsoft Download Center Web site (*www.microsoft.com/downloads*), locate the most recent version of the Windows 7 Upgrade Advisor and download it to your computer. Save the down-loaded file in a subfolder within your user account's Downloads folder.

2. Open the folder that contains the program you downloaded. What is the name of the file that you downloaded? What is its file extension and file type? How do you install this type of file on a computer?

3. Install the Windows 7 Upgrade Advisor. Identify the names of any additional Microsoft software you have to install to use the Windows 7 Upgrade Advisor.

4. Run the Windows 7 Upgrade Advisor. What edition of Windows 7 does it recom-mend for the computer you are using? Are you viewing a 32-bit or 64-bit report? In the summary of its findings, what does the Windows 7 Upgrade Advisor report for System, Devices, and Programs?

5. View report details for any compatibility problems. What are the most significant system, device, and program compatibility problems (if any), and what does it rec-ommend you do to resolve each problem?

6. If you are using a 32-bit system, view the 64-bit report. If you are using a 64-bit sys-tem, view the 32-bit report. Do these reports differ and, if so, how?

7. Choose the option for saving a report for your 32-bit or 64-bit system as **Windows 7 Upgrade Advisor Report** in the Tutorial.11\Case2 folder on your flash drive.

8. Uninstall Windows 7 Upgrade Advisor from your computer. Provide a brief overview of how you uninstalled this software.

9. Submit your answers to the questions in this case problem and your Windows 7 Upgrade Advisor Web archive report to your instructor, either in printed or electronic form, as requested.

Use your skills and the Internet to prepare for a Microsoft Office upgrade.

RESEARCH

Case Problem 3

There are no Data Files needed for this Case Problem.

Estuary Restoration Foundation   Jarrod Terrell and Ian Douglas are codirectors of a foundation devoted to restoring estuaries in the United States. Thanks to the generosity of several prominent donors, their foundation now has two state-of-the-art Windows 7 computer systems that the foundation will use to track the status of restoration projects and funding. Jarrod asks you to evaluate the different editions of Microsoft Office and prepare the computers for an Office upgrade. He also reminds you that they will need an Office suite that contains Microsoft Access, Microsoft PowerPoint, and Microsoft Outlook.

As you complete each step in this case problem, use a word-processing application, such as Microsoft Word or WordPad, to record your answers to the questions so you can submit them to your instructor. If you change any settings on the computer you are using, note what the original settings were so you can restore them later. Complete the following steps:

1. Open your Web browser and visit the Microsoft Office Online Web site: *http://office.microsoft.com*

2. Choose the option for viewing information about products, and then choose the option for comparing suites (or finding the best suite for you). List the names of the Microsoft Office suites, and identify which version of Microsoft Office you are examining, such as Microsoft Office 2010.

3. Which Office suites contain Microsoft Word, Microsoft Excel, Microsoft PowerPoint, and Microsoft Access? Which Office suites also contain Outlook?

4. Which Office suites contain Microsoft Word, Microsoft Excel, Microsoft PowerPoint, and Microsoft Outlook?

5. Click the product name link for viewing details of one of the Office suites, and then choose the link for viewing system requirements of Microsoft Office suites. Which Microsoft Office suite did you examine, and what are the processor, memory, hard disk drive, display, and operating system requirements of this Office suite?

6. Outline the steps you would follow to upgrade your computer to a newer Microsoft Office suite.

7. Submit your answers to the questions in this case problem to your instructor, either in printed or electronic form, as requested.

Use your skills to specify default program settings for a Web design firm.

APPLY

Case Problem 4

There are no Data Files needed for this Case Problem.

Web Arts Design, Inc.   Devon Flynn designs Web pages for her company Web Arts Design, Inc. She wants to check program default settings for her computer and make any adjustments that would simplify her use of her computer while permitting her to use those programs she prefers. Because she has not yet worked with these settings, she asks you to assist her in this process and point out any options of particular benefit to her line of work.

To complete this case problem, you will need to provide Administrator credentials to view and make changes to program access settings and computer defaults.

As you complete each step in this case problem, use a word-processing application, such as Microsoft Word or WordPad, to record and print your answers to the questions so you can submit them to your instructor. If you change any settings on the computer you are using, note what the original settings were so you can restore them later. Complete the following steps:

1. Choose the option for examining Default Programs from the Start menu, and then choose the option for setting program access and computer defaults. Is the computer you are using set for a Microsoft, non-Microsoft, or custom configuration? What are this computer's default Web browser, email program, and media player settings, and what programs are enabled for access? Under what circumstances might you use a Custom computer configuration, and what benefits would you derive? Close the Set Program Access and Computer Defaults window without making changes to the computer you are using.

2. Choose the option to set default program settings. What Web browser(s) are installed on your computer? Select Internet Explorer, and then select the option for choosing defaults for this program. What is the default program for files with the .htm, .html, and .url file extensions? What protocols are set for Internet Explorer?

3. If you want to specify another Web browser as the default for all extensions, protocols, and Internet link, how would you make this change?

4. In the Set Default Programs window, choose Windows Photo Viewer, and then select the option for choosing defaults for this program. What file extensions are set as defaults for Windows Photo Viewer? Which file extensions are set by other programs, and what are the names of those programs? Return to the Default Programs window without making any changes to default file extensions for Window Photo Viewer.

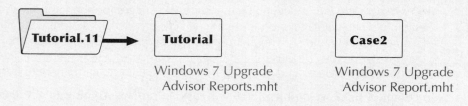 **EXPLORE**

5. In the Default Programs window, choose the option for associating a file type or protocol with a program. What is the description for each of the following file extensions, and what program on your computer is associated with each of these file extensions?

   a. .chk   i. .img   q. .rtf
   b. .com   j. .inf   r. .sfcache
   c. .cpl   k. .ini   s. .vbs
   d. .dll   l. .iso   t. .xps
   e. .docx (or .doc)   m..mig   u. MAILTO
   f. .eml   n. .msi   v. SEARCH
   g. .gadget   o. .msrcincident
   h. .hlp   p. .rdp

6. How would you change the association of a file extension so the file type opens in a different program?

7. Close the Set Associations window without making any changes to extension and protocol settings on the computer you are using.

8. Submit your answers to the questions in this case problem to your instructor, either in printed or electronic form, as requested.

ENDING DATA FILES

Tutorial.11 → **Tutorial**   **Case2**

Windows 7 Upgrade   Windows 7 Upgrade
Advisor Reports.mht   Advisor Report.mht

OBJECTIVES

Session 12.1
- Learn about Plug and Play hardware
- Examine Windows 7 support for newer types of hardware
- Examine the importance of hardware resource assignments
- View hardware configuration settings in Device Manager
- Troubleshoot hardware problems

Session 12.2
- Check your computer name and workgroup or domain name
- View networked computers in the same workgroup
- Use the Network and Sharing Center
- Compare three ways to share folders on a network
- Create a mapped drive
- Create, join, and leave a homegroup

Managing Hardware and Networks

Troubleshooting Hardware and Setting Up a Workgroup

Case | *Alexander Medical Research Institute*

The Alexander Medical Research Institute in Atlanta, Georgia, uses specialists in different disciplines to tackle the most pressing medical problems today. Remy Besson, a technical support specialist, evaluates new software and hardware technologies for use by research and administrative staff. In addition to setting up, configuring, customizing, and troubleshooting computers, he also advises staff on how to set up home computer networks that connect to the institute's network so they have access to the resources they need any time of the day.

In this tutorial, you will compare Plug and Play and legacy hardware and discover the advantages that Plug and Play computer systems offer. You will also survey Windows 7 support for newer types of hardware devices. After learning about the importance of hardware resource assignments, you will open Device Manager and examine the hardware configuration of your computer. Next you look at the process for checking your computer name and workgroup or domain name, and view networked computers in the same workgroup. You open the new Network and Sharing Center to view network settings, compare three different ways to share folders on a network, and create a mapped drive to a shared network folder. You will also examine how to create, join, and leave a homegroup, and learn how to share homegroup resources.

STARTING DATA FILES

There are no starting Data Files needed for this tutorial.

SESSION 12.1 VISUAL OVERVIEW

Device Stage is a new Windows 7 feature that displays links for working with, and accessing information about, devices that support this feature. The primary advantage of Device Stage is that it gathers and provides information about all of a device's features and options in one location.

HP Photosmart 8200 Series

See what's printing
View, pause, or cancel your print jobs

Customize your printer
Change the name, security settings, or other properties

Adjust print options
Change color, layout, or paper settings

You can use Device Stage or Devices and Printers to view printers and to access the print queue for a printer. A **print queue** contains a list of all the documents that are scheduled to print. You can then change the status of a print job or cancel a print job.

NVIDIA GeForce 7900 GTX (Microsoft Corporation - WDDM) Pro...

General | Driver | Details | Resources

NVIDIA GeForce 7900 GTX (Microsoft Corporation - WDDM)

Resource settings:

Resource type	Setting
Memory Range	DD000000 - DDFFFFFF
Memory Range	C0000000 - CFFFFFFF
Memory Range	DE000000 - DEFFFFFF

Setting based on:

☑ Use automatic settings   Change Setting...

Conflicting device list:

No conflicts.

If you need to troubleshoot a hardware device or verify that it is properly installed, you can use Device Manager to view information about resources required by, or assigned to, that hardware device by Windows 7.

Windows 7 automatically detects and assigns resources to devices during booting or when a device is attached to a computer. If you override Windows 7 and configure resources for a hardware device manually, you are creating a **forced hardware configuration** that Windows 7 will always use; as a result, Windows 7 will have less flexibility in assigning resources to other devices that you might later add to your computer.

The Resources property sheet for a hardware device identifies whether that hardware device and another hardware device are in conflict with each other. If a conflict occurs, then one or both hardware devices may not work properly or at all.

Cancel

DEVICE MANAGER

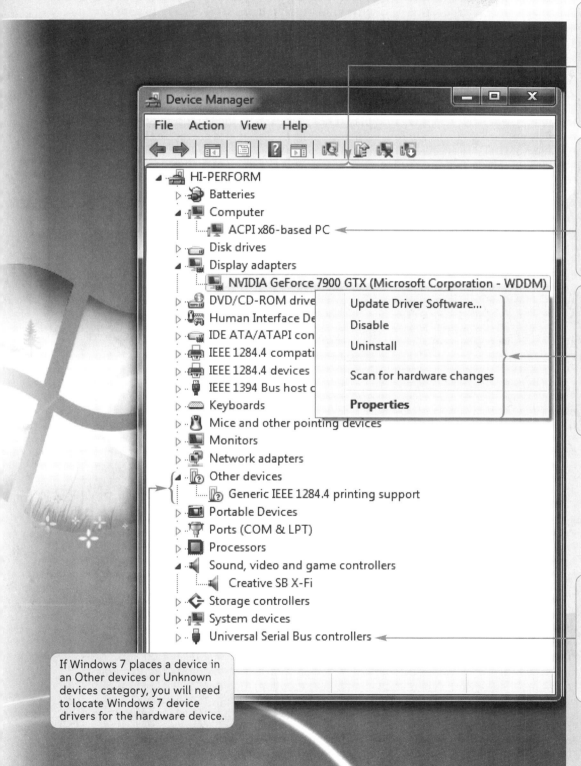

When you open Device Manager, it displays a hardware tree that organizes devices by category and type of device. You can expand a hardware category to view the individual hardware devices in that category.

An **ACPI (Advanced Configuration and Power Interface) BIOS** performs the initial steps of identifying and configuring hardware devices during the early stages of booting, and Windows 7 uses this information to complete device configuration.

You can right-click a hardware device in Device Manager to display a shortcut menu with options for searching for updates to that hardware's device drivers, disabling a device you no longer use, uninstalling a device, scanning for changes to the hardware in your computer, and viewing device properties and settings.

If Windows 7 places a device in an Other devices or Unknown devices category, you will need to locate Windows 7 device drivers for the hardware device.

You can use the Universal Serial Bus controllers category to view information about the use of USB devices on your computer, including information on what types of USB devices your computer supports and power usage by device.

Comparing Types of Hardware Devices

The Director of the Alexander Medical Research Institute has asked Remy to supervise a group of technical staff and managers in identifying and implementing new hardware technologies critical to the future growth of the institute. Remy's 15 years of experience in the computer industry has helped him realize the importance of choosing hardware technologies that are reliable, stable, easy to install and use, and designed to meet the future needs of his company.

One of the major problems computer users faced in the past was the overly complex process for installing and configuring new hardware devices. To reduce the problems and support costs that often resulted from installing new hardware components, hardware manufacturers now produce **Plug and Play (PnP)** hardware so the Windows operating system immediately detects a hardware device, installs device drivers for that device, and configures the device during booting or, if the computer is already up and running, when the device is attached to the computer. The goal of Plug and Play is simple: You plug in the device, Windows detects and installs support for the device, and you are ready to "play." Hardware devices that do not support Plug and Play are called **non-Plug and Play** or **legacy devices**. They require manual installation and configuration and often extensive troubleshooting. However, Plug and Play hardware has been the standard for some time.

Each time you boot your computer or attach a hardware device to your computer, Windows 7 checks for any new hardware. If Windows 7 detects a new hardware component that supports Plug and Play, it installs and loads the device drivers for that component and then configures the device to work properly. If Windows 7 does not have a device driver for that Plug and Play component, it prompts you to insert a disk with the software that includes the device driver(s) and any other software important to the use of that hardware device.

A *bona fide* Plug and Play computer system has the following features:

- **ACPI BIOS**—In addition to performing a Power-On Self Test and locating and loading the operating system from disk during booting, an ACPI BIOS (Advanced Configuration and Power Interface BIOS) identifies and activates hardware devices, determines their resource requirements, creates a nonconflicting hardware configuration, loads device drivers, passes configuration information to the operating system, and notifies it of any configuration changes. An ACPI BIOS also determines the power management capabilities of hardware devices, and supports the use of power saving modes such as sleep and hibernation. The Windows 7 operating system, not the BIOS, is responsible for configuring a computer system and managing power to devices and the computer itself once a computer is up and running.
- **Plug and Play hardware devices and device drivers**—For a hardware device to be automatically detected and configured with the proper device drivers, it must be a Plug and Play device. Plug and Play hardware devices have a Plug and Play ID that uniquely identifies the hardware device to the operating system. Today a wide range of devices fully support Plug and Play, so there's no need to use legacy devices. Windows 7 also uses Plug and Play drivers for legacy devices, such as motherboard legacy hardware, which improves support for the device.
- **Plug and Play operating system**—Like its predecessors, Windows 7 is a Plug and Play operating system. Windows 7 stores configuration information on Plug and Play devices in the Registry. When you install a new Plug and Play device, it checks the resources used by other Plug and Play devices in the Registry and configures the new device without introducing conflicts between hardware devices.

Windows 7 also uses **Universal Plug and Play (UPnP)** to detect and configure wired and wireless devices in a networking environment, consumer electronics equipment (such as home entertainment systems and appliances connected to a Windows 7 computer), and Internet gateways. A **gateway** consists of hardware and software that provide an access point to another network. UPnP relies on Internet and Web protocols (TCP/IP, HTTP, and XML) to enable devices to configure themselves, announce themselves on the network, discover or locate other devices on the network, communicate directly with other devices, and direct the operation of other devices. **TCP/IP (Transmission Control Protocol/Internet Protocol)** is a standard protocol for transferring data in packets with a source and destination address over the Internet or a private network. A **packet** consists of a set of data (such as part of a file), as well as a source address and destination address, sent from one location to another over the Internet or other network. **HTTP (Hypertext Transfer Protocol)** is a standard protocol for transferring files from a Web server to your browser so you can view the contents of a Web page over the World Wide Web. Like HTML (Hypertext Markup Language), XML (Extensible Markup Language) describes the layout of a Web page and your ability to interact with that content, but unlike HTML, XML can also describe data to support the transfer and sharing of information.

Increased Hardware Support in Windows 7

For the Alexander Medical Research Institute, the increased support that Windows 7 provides for new hardware technologies is one of its most important features.

Not only does Windows 7 provide support for newer types of hardware devices while maintaining support for existing hardware devices, Windows 7 also provides ongoing and enhanced support for the following important technologies:

- **Universal Serial Bus (USB)**—Universal Serial Bus is an external, bidirectional, Plug and Play bus for connecting up to 127 high-speed serial devices to your computer either using a USB port, USB hubs, or another USB device. USB hubs are useful when attaching multiple USB devices to your computer. A **bus** is a path for transferring data between computer components. Today, USB is the dominant technology used for hardware devices that you connect to your computer. In the early years of the Windows operating system, each type of device typically required a separate port, which required you to figure out how to assign resources to each device; to complicate matters, resources were limited. With USB and IEEE 1394 hardware devices (covered in the next bulleted point), you no longer need to deal with limited resources such as IRQ settings, DMA channels, and I/O addresses (covered later in the tutorial). For certain types of devices, such as a mouse or keyboard, you do not need extra power cables because the USB connection provides power to those devices.

    The first-generation USB bus, identified as USB 1.*x* (USB 1.0 and USB 1.1) supported two data speeds: **Full-Speed** at 12 Mbps (12 megabits per second or 12 million bits per second) for devices that require large amounts of bandwidth, such as devices that process video and audio; and **Low-Speed** at 1.5 Mbps (1.5 megabits per second or 1.5 million bits per second) for devices such as keyboards and mice. **Bandwidth** refers to the amount of data that can be transmitted over a device in a fixed amount of time; digital devices measure bandwidth in bytes per second or bits per second. Second-generation USB devices (USB 2.0) supported a data transfer rate of 480 Mbps (480 megabits per second) called **Hi-Speed**. The new generation of USB 3.0 devices combines a **SuperSpeed** bus (or pathway) for data transfers at a speed of 5 Gbps (gigabits per second) with a USB 2.0 bus (also called non-SuperSpeed) that retains support for Hi-Speed, Full-Speed, and Low-Speed. SuperSpeed is almost 11 times faster than USB 2.0's High-Speed. Plus, USB 3.0 supports multiple data stream transfers. USB 3.0 cables do not work with USB 2.0 hardware.

    USB also supports Plug and Play, power management, and **hot swapping** (also called **hot plugging** or **hot insertion and removal**), which means that you can connect or disconnect a USB device while the computer is running. You do not need to power down your computer before adding or removing the USB device; however, it is a good idea to check your hardware manual to verify its ability to support hot swapping.

TIP

Be careful when comparing data transfer speeds, as Mbps refers to mega*bits* per second while MBps refers to mega*bytes* per second.

- **IEEE 1394**—First-generation **IEEE 1394** (for Institute of Electrical and Electronics Engineers) is another high-speed Plug and Play bus with data transfer rates of 100, 200, and 400 Mbps. Second-generation IEEE 1394b supported data transfer rates of 800 Mbps. Faster data transfer speeds of 1.6 and 3.2 Gbps are expected in the future. Apple originally developed this technology and called it **FireWire**; however, this technology is now also available on the PC. IEEE 1394 supports the connection of up to 63 devices via one bus. IEEE 1394 supports high-bandwidth devices and thereby plays an important role in digital imaging, video teleconferencing, and as a bridge for connecting consumer electronics to computers. Like USB, IEEE 1394 supports Plug and Play, power management, and hot swapping. IEEE 1394 is also referred to as i.Link on SONY computers.
- **SATA and eSATA**—The SATA (Serial ATA, or Serial Advanced Technology Attachment) and eSATA (external SATA) buses provide fast connections for hardware devices, such as internal and external hard disk drives, solid-state drives, and optical drives. SATA now supports data transfer speeds up to 6 Gbps, and eSATA supports data transfer speeds of up to 3 Gbps. Like USB and IEEE 1394, SATA also supports hot swapping.
- **Sensors**—**Sensors** are hardware components that provide information about the location and surroundings of your computer. Some sensors are built into a computer while others are connected to your computer via a wired or wireless connection. For example, a light sensor on a mobile computer detects the ambient light in your surroundings and then adjusts the brightness of your monitor's image accordingly. This feature is called Adaptive Brightness. To check for sensors that might be available on your computer, open Location and Sensors in the Control Panel.
- **Device Stage**—This Windows 7 feature simplifies the process for working with newer types of hardware devices that support Device Stage. For example, if you connect a cell phone that supports Device Stage to your computer, Windows 7 opens a window that displays information about the device, such as the number of text messages, new photos, amount of free space, the quality of the cell phone signal, the battery level, and whether the device is charging. Windows 7 also displays options for synchronizing content, such as contacts, appointments, music, video, movies, and recorded TV shows between the mobile phone and the computer; for managing media on the phone; for locating and viewing files; for setting ring tones; for importing pictures and videos; for changing device settings; for downloading software updates; for accessing customer support; and for learning more about your device.

While you may wonder how you might use and benefit from these new technologies, consider that CD drives were novelties when they were first introduced. Within a few years after their appearance in the marketplace, CD drives were standard components on new computers, and became the primary medium for installing software. Now DVD drives are replacing CD drives and are automatically included with most new computers. Within a few years even newer hardware technologies will become indispensable to the way you work and play with your computer.

Getting Started

To complete this tutorial, it is recommended that you display the Computer icon on the desktop, switch your computer to single-click activation and display hidden folders and files, as well as protected operating system files. In the following steps, you will check and, if necessary, change these settings.

To set up your computer:

▶ **1.** If necessary, use the Start menu to display the Computer icon on the desktop.

▶ **2.** If necessary, use the Folder Options dialog box to enable single-click activation; display hidden folders, files, and drives; and display protected operating system files.

▶ **3.** If Windows 7 does not display the Devices and Printers or the Network options on your Start menu, right-click the **Start** button 🌚, click **Properties**, and click the **Customize** button on the Start Menu property sheet.

▶ **4.** In the Customize Start Menu list of options, locate and click **Devices and Printers** to add a check mark, and then locate and click **Network** to add a check mark. Click the **OK** button to close the Customize Start Menu dialog box, and click the **OK** button to close the Taskbar and Start Menu Properties dialog box.

Next you are going to view an important Windows tool for managing hardware—Devices and Printers.

Viewing Devices and Printers

To view, use, and, if necessary, troubleshoot hardware devices, you can open and use the new Windows 7 Devices and Printers window. Devices and Printers replaces the Printers folder available in earlier versions of Windows, and provides more options for working with devices on your computer. In addition to displaying an icon for your computer, Devices and Printers also identifies and displays icons for your monitor; portable devices, such as digital cameras, music players, and mobile phones; a webcam, a keyboard, and a mouse. In addition, Devices and Printers identifies USB devices, such as flash drives, all-in-one multicard readers for flash memory cards, and external hard disk drives. You will also see printer configurations for physical printers and virtual printers (such as Microsoft XPS Document Writer, which saves printed output to a file) and network devices.

Devices and Printers does not include icons for components inside the system unit, such as the processor, RAM, a video card (or cards), a sound card, internal hard disk drive (or drives), DVD drive, or CD drive. In addition, Devices and Printers does not identify certain external devices, such as speakers. If you have older hardware devices that do not use a USB connection, such as a mouse connected to a serial port, those older hardware devices are not displayed in Printers and Devices.

Remy suggests you open the new Printers and Devices window on your computer so you can examine options for working with hardware devices.

To view devices and printers on your computer:

TIP

To create a desktop shortcut, drag Devices and Printers from the Start menu to the desktop.

▶ **1.** Open the Start menu, and then click **Devices and Printers**. As shown in Figure 12-1, Windows 7 identifies and displays icons for devices and for printers. Windows 7 may also display a light yellow Information bar under the toolbar informing you that it can display enhanced device icons and information from the Internet. If you click this Information bar, Windows 7 then displays a menu where you can authorize Windows to get device information from the Internet.

Trouble? If Devices and Printers is not available on the Start menu, open the Control Panel from the Start menu, and under Hardware and Sound, click "View devices and printers."

Figure 12-1   **Viewing devices and printers**

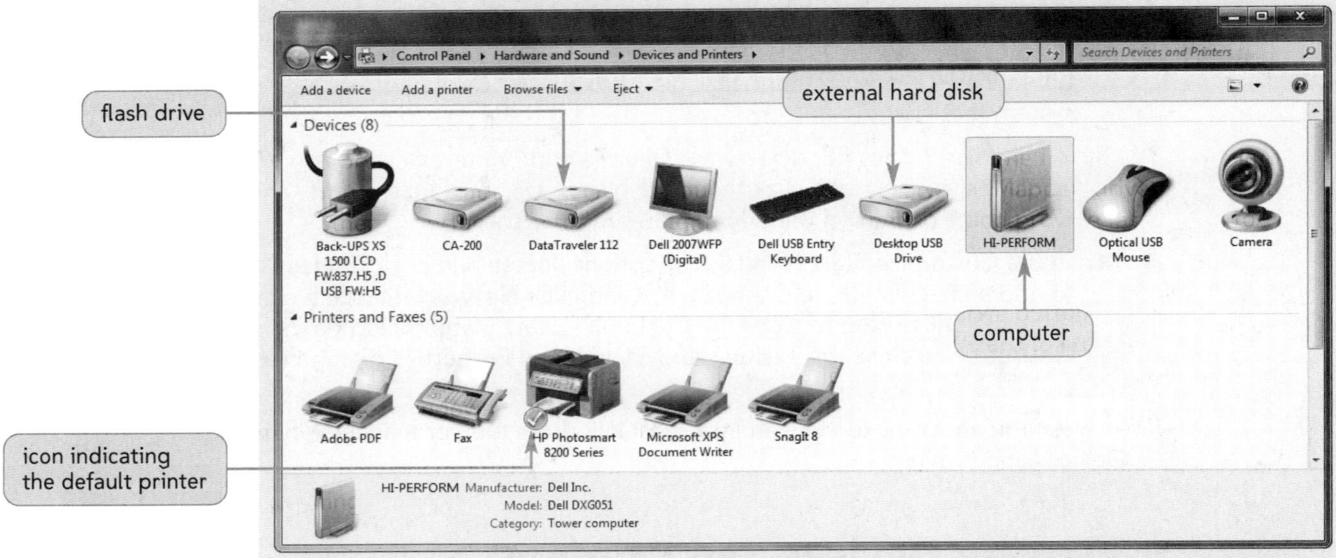

flash drive

external hard disk

computer

icon indicating the default printer

Among the hardware devices identified under Devices for the computer used for this figure, Windows 7 identifies a Back-UPS XS device (an uninterruptable power supply unit) and a CA-200 internal USB flash card reader. HI-PERFORM is the name assigned to the computer, and Data Traveler 112 is a flash drive. Your devices and printers will differ.

2. Under Devices, click your **computer name** icon. Windows 7 opens either a Device Stage window for your computer model or a Properties dialog box for your computer. The window for your computer model may contain links for changing system settings, adding hardware or changing hardware settings, exploring your computer, locating computer accessories, accessing product support, and browsing disks and drives. If a Properties dialog box opens, Windows 7 identifies the manufacturer, the model, model number (if available), the category (such as Tower computer), and description (if available) on the General property sheet.

3. Click the **Hardware** tab. Under Device Functions, Windows 7 identifies devices in the system unit and on the system board or motherboard.

4. Click the **OK** button to close the Properties dialog box for your computer.

You can use the "Add a device" button on the Devices and Printers toolbar to search your computer for hardware devices to add to Printers and Devices. You can use the "Add a printer" button on the toolbar to open the Add Printer dialog box, where you can install either a local printer or a network, wireless, or Bluetooth printer. The "Add a local printer" option in the Add Printer dialog box is designed for printers that are not USB printers because Windows 7 automatically detects USB printers and installs device drivers for them. A Bluetooth printer is one that uses short-range Bluetooth wireless technology to communicate between hardware devices and your computer.

If you right-click a device under Devices in the Devices and Printers window, you will see a shortcut menu with options for creating a desktop shortcut, opening a Printers and Devices troubleshooter to assist you with troubleshooting hardware problems, and for displaying hardware device properties. If the device is a flash memory card reader, an external hard disk drive, or a flash drive, there is also an option on the shortcut menu for viewing files on the device and for ejecting the media. The shortcut menu may also include device-specific options, such as accessing display settings for a monitor, keyboard settings and region and language settings for a keyboard, and mouse settings for your installed mouse. The icon for your computer may contain options for opening AutoPlay for a drive, browsing files on a drive, or ejecting a removable drive. You may also have options for examining network, sound, modem, mouse, keyboard, and region and language settings as well as system properties, device installation settings, and power settings. Plus, you can open Windows Update, create a desktop shortcut to access the same menu options, troubleshoot a problem, and view properties of your computer.

If you right-click a printer icon and then click the "See what's printing" link, Windows 7 opens a print queue. The print queue contains information about each print job, including the program, document name, the status of the document, the owner (or user name of the person who submitted the print job), the number of pages that have printed and the total number of pages, the document size, the time and date the print job was submitted, and the port used by the printer. Figure 12-2 shows a print queue after a print job was sent to a network printer. The Status column identifies the current status of the print job (such as whether it's spooling, printing, or paused).

Figure 12-2	Viewing a print queue for an installed printer

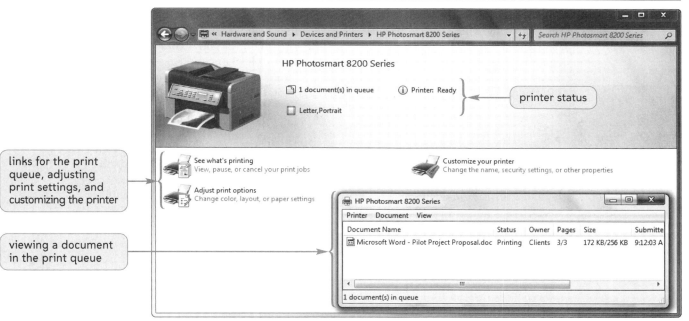

If you select a print job in the print queue, you can use the Document menu to pause the print job, resume the print job, restart the print job (from the beginning), cancel the print job, or change its properties (such as its priority or schedule). To pause printing of a print job, you select the print job, and then choose Pause on the Document menu. To pause all jobs, you choose Pause Printing on the Printer menu. To resume printing, you select a print job, and choose Resume on the Document menu. Or if you want to resume printing of all print jobs, you remove the check mark from Pause Printing on the Printer menu. To cancel a print job, you select the print job, and then choose Cancel on the Document menu. To cancel all print jobs, you choose Cancel All Documents on the Printer menu. If you choose the option to pause or cancel a print job, the document might be printed before the request to pause or cancel the job is completed because the printer's buffer might be able to store an entire document. Once you send a document to the printer, you cannot use the print queue to change printer settings and printing preferences for that document. If you need to select multiple print jobs in the print queue, hold down the Ctrl key while you click each job; then you can change the settings for all the print jobs at the same time. You can only control your own print jobs, not those of other users, unless you are assigned the Manage Documents permission. In Figure 12-2, the printer window shown behind the print queue window is an example of **Device Stage**, a new Windows 7 feature for assembling in one location all the resources you need for a device. As you can see from this figure, there are links not only for viewing what's printing but also links for adjusting print options and for customizing the printer. Your options may differ.

If you right-click a printer under Printers and Faxes, the shortcut menu allows you to see what's printing, set a printer as the default printer, specify printing preferences, examine printer properties for printer-specific features and settings, create a desktop shortcut to a printer, troubleshoot a printer, remove the printer, and view general device properties of the printer. Printer preferences allows you to specify a wide variety of printing options, such as page layout options (orientation and pages per sheet), page order, paper source, and color or black-and-white printing, to name a few. The Troubleshoot option opens the Printer Troubleshooter, which in turn attempts to identify and resolve any printer problems, and which can also recommend ways to optimize the use of your computer, such as providing access to the same printer on other computers.

As shown in Figure 7-1, if there is more than one printer under Printers and Faxes, Windows 7 displays a circle with a green background and white check mark on the icon of the printer that is the default printer. The default printer is the printer that Windows 7 uses every time you print. Although only one printer can be the default printer, you can select another printer when you print a specific document. If you want to change the default printer, you can right-click a printer icon under Printers and Faxes, and then choose "Set as default printer."

Remy suggests you examine device installation settings for your computer.

To examine device installation settings:

▶ **1.** Under Devices, right-click your **computer name** icon, and then click **Device installation settings**. Windows 7 opens a Device Installation Settings dialog box, and prompts you to choose whether you want Windows 7 to download driver software and realistic icons for your devices automatically or let you choose what to do.

If you prefer to choose what to do, you can specify that Windows 7 install the best driver software from Windows Update, (only) install driver software from Windows Update if it is not found on my computer, or never install driver software from Windows Update. If you choose the last option, you are responsible for checking for updates to the device drivers for your hardware. You also have the option as to whether you want to replace generic device icons with enhanced icons that display detailed information about your hardware devices, such as the manufacturer, product name, and model number.

To continue with your examination of Device Installation Settings:

▶ **1.** If you want to change options for your computer, make the changes you want, and then click the **Save Changes** button. If you are working in a computer lab or if you do not want to make changes to your computer, click the **Cancel** button.

▶ **2.** Close the Devices and Printers window.

Next you are going to view another important Windows tool for managing hardware—Device Manager.

PROSKILLS

Decision Making: The Importance of Device Drivers

One of the main problems individuals face with hardware, whether it is new hardware or older hardware that is still useful, is the availability of necessary device drivers and device driver updates. When you purchase new hardware for your computer, first verify that the manufacturer provides device drivers for the 32-bit or 64-bit version of Windows on your computer, and verify that your Windows edition supports that hardware. Make sure that you can return the hardware within a reasonable time in the event you encounter an unexpected problem. After installing the hardware, make sure you obtain device driver updates for all your hardware. One way to do so is to use Windows Update to locate and download device drivers for your hardware. Another option is to check the Web sites of manufacturers of hardware for new updates. If you have set up your computer for automatic updates, you may still have to use Windows Update to identify optional updates that include device driver updates. The obvious disadvantage of having Windows 7 automatically download driver software is that you may encounter a problem with a device driver update, which would require you to use the Roll Back Driver option (covered later in this tutorial) to restore your previous functioning device driver. If you have older hardware from manufacturers that no longer provide device drivers for that hardware with newer versions of Windows, do a little research because you might be able to configure your hardware device as a different model from the same or a different manufacturer and thereby continue to use it. By careful planning and research in advance and by staying on top of device driver updates, you can not only retain useful hardware but also have access to newer features provided by newer device driver updates.

Understanding Hardware Resource Assignments

Windows 7 can allocate the following four types of resources to hardware devices that require them:

- **Interrupt request (IRQ) resources**—An **interrupt** is a signal transmitted by hardware or software to the processor or operating system for some type of service. Hardware devices and software constantly interrupt the processor and operating system with requests for specific services. An **interrupt request** might require the processor to perform a function, handle an error condition, or move data. For example, when you press a key on the keyboard, you generate a **hardware interrupt**, and the operating system interprets the scan code generated by the keystroke. When you issue a command to save a document, the software application you are using generates a **software interrupt** for recording the contents of the file on disk. An interrupt request from a hardware device is transmitted to the processor via an IRQ hardware line. Typically, each hardware device that requires an IRQ line is assigned its own line. In the past, the number of available IRQs was a limiting factor in adding new hardware to a computer. However, today that is far less of an issue for three reasons. First, USB and IEEE 1394 devices bypass this limitation by supporting more than one device on the same port. Second, Windows has for many years supported the sharing of IRQs between hardware devices. Third, Windows 7 can assign virtual IRQs to hardware devices.
- **Input/Output (I/O) resources**—Each hardware device that handles I/O, such as ports and disk drives, must have a unique address in memory, a system resource called its **I/O address**. This I/O address uniquely identifies a hardware device and serves as a channel for communicating with the device.
- **Direct Memory Access (DMA) resources**—**Direct Memory Access** is a channel for transferring data between two devices without the intervention of the processor. For

example, by using a DMA channel, your computer can transfer data from a hard disk drive into system memory without the processor. If the processor handles the data transfer, the overall process is much slower than a direct transfer to memory. DMA channels are important in the transfer of video, audio, and graphics data.

• **Memory resources**—**Memory resources** refer to specific regions of memory allocated to a hardware device. For example, one or more regions of memory might be designated for the video display adapter that generates the image you see on the monitor. These memory resources are identified as a range of memory addresses assigned to a device.

Windows 7 assigns a unique combination of hardware resources to each hardware device during booting or when the device is attached to the computer.

Using Device Manager

Device Manager provides an important source of information about the hardware components on a computer, and it shows the configuration settings that Windows 7 uses for both Plug and Play and non-Plug and Play devices. You can use Device Manager to document hardware settings, verify the installation of a hardware device, check for hardware conflicts, troubleshoot hardware problems, change the configuration of a hardware device, update device drivers for a hardware device, roll back device drivers for a hardware device, and remove a hardware device.

If you use Device Manager to change a configuration setting for a hardware device, you might create a conflict with another hardware device, or there might already be a conflict between hardware devices. A **hardware conflict**, **device conflict**, or **resource conflict** occurs when two hardware devices attempt to share the same resource. When a hardware conflict exists, one or both devices might not work properly or at all. Worse yet, the computer might become unstable or stop functioning. Before you examine or make changes to the hardware configuration settings in Device Manager, you should document the current hardware configuration settings that you intend to change and make sure that you understand how changes to the configuration of your computer will affect your computer's operation.

The instructions in the tutorial steps request that you view, but not change, hardware configuration settings in Device Manager. Only users with expert knowledge of computer hardware and hardware configuration settings should change resource settings for hardware devices. At the same time, there are ways in which you can use Device Manager to find important information about hardware devices, verify the installation of a hardware device, and identify existing hardware problems that require troubleshooting. You must provide Administrator credentials before you can make changes to resource settings in Device Manager. However, you can open Device Manager and examine hardware settings without providing Administrator credentials.

Remy depends on Device Manager to provide him with important information about the hardware configuration of each employee's computer. If an employee experiences a problem with a hardware device, the first tool Remy turns to is Device Manager. Remy recommends that you open Device Manager and examine information about your computer and hardware devices.

To open Device Manager and view information about hardware devices:

▶ 1. If your flash drive is attached to the computer you are using, click the **Show hidden icons** button ▲ in the notification area (if necessary), click the **Safely Remove Hardware and Eject Media** icon 📷, select the option for removing your flash drive, and after Windows 7 displays a Safe to Remove Hardware dialog box informing you that you can now safely remove the device, remove your flash drive.

TIP

You can also press the Windows key, type *dev* in the Search programs and files box, and then click Device Manager in the Search results.

2. Right-click the **Computer** desktop icon, click **Properties** on the shortcut menu, click the **Device Manager** link on the left side of the System window, and if Windows 7 displays a Device Manager dialog box and informs you that you are logged on as a standard user with Administrator privileges, click the **OK** button. Windows 7 opens Device Manager and displays categories for different types of hardware components installed on your computer, as shown in Figure 12-3.

Trouble? If you cannot see all the hardware categories in the Device Manager window, use Aero Snap to adjust the height of the Device Manager window so it extends from the top of the desktop to the taskbar.

Figure 12-3	Viewing the hardware tree in Device Manager

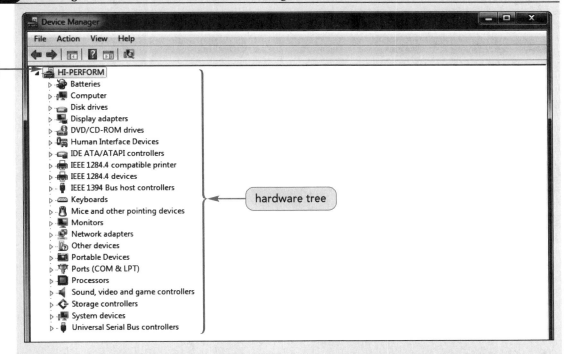

This view is referred to as a hardware tree, and by default, it displays devices by type. Each device category contains one or more hardware devices. Hardware devices include the computer itself, peripherals (external hardware devices), adapters and controllers connected to the system board, ports, and components on the system board itself as well as portable devices. Your hardware tree will differ.

3. Keep the Device Manager window open for the next set of tutorial steps.

Once you open Device Manager, you can view properties of a hardware device and determine whether the device is working properly. The video display adapter is not only a standard hardware component; it takes on added importance in Windows 7 by providing support for Windows Aero. Remy asks you to examine properties of your video display adapter.

To view properties of the display adapter:

1. Click the **expand** icon ▷ to the left of the Display adapters category. Windows 7 expands the category to show the type of display adapter used on your computer. On the computer used for Figure 12-4, Device Manager identifies the display adapter as an NVIDIA GeForce 7900 GTX display adapter that uses the Windows Display Driver Model (WDDM) to provide support for Windows Aero features. Your display adapter will differ.

Figure 12-4 Viewing the Display adapters category

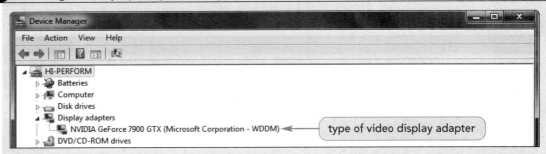

TIP

To view device properties, you can also select the hardware device and then click the Properties button on the Device Manager standard toolbar.

2. Double-click your **display adapter type**. Device Manager opens a Properties dialog box for your display adapter type. On the computer used for Figure 12-5, Device Manager opens an NVIDIA GeForce 7900 GTX (Microsoft Corporation – WDDM) Properties dialog box.

Figure 12-5 Properties dialog box for a video display adapter

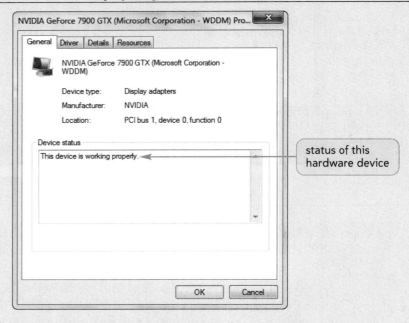

Each hardware device has one or more property sheets. The General property sheet, common to all hardware devices, identifies the device type, the manufacturer (if known), and the location of the device. The most important information on this property sheet is shown in the Device status box. If there are no problems with the hardware device, Device Manager reports that "This device is working properly." If there is a hardware problem or conflict, Device Manager briefly describes the problem, displays a problem code, and suggests a solution. Microsoft technical support can use the problem code to help you troubleshoot your hardware problem.

▶ **3.** Click the **Driver** tab. Device Manager provides information about the driver used for this device, including the driver version and whether the driver is digitally signed and therefore certified for use with Windows 7. See Figure 12-6. Your details will differ.

Figure 12-6 **Viewing the Driver property sheet for the video display adapter**

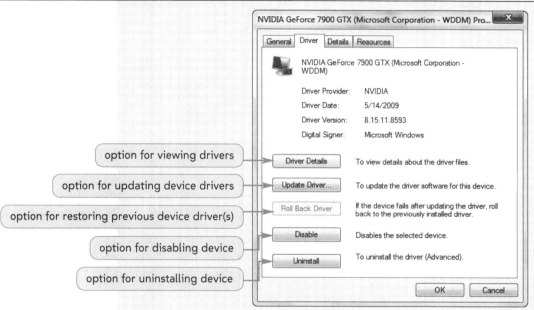

You can click the Driver Details button to view information about the device drivers for a hardware device. The Update Driver button opens the Update Driver Software dialog box, which then steps you through the process of checking for an update to the device driver either on the Internet or on your local computer.

If you install a new driver and then discover that it doesn't work or that it creates a problem on your computer, you can use the Roll Back Driver button to restore the previously used device driver (a one-time change only). You can use the Disable button to disable the device, and you can use the Uninstall button to remove the device driver for the hardware device and thereby uninstall the hardware.

▶ **4.** Click the **Driver Details** button. In the Driver File Details dialog box, Windows 7 displays the name of the driver files used for this hardware device. On the computer used for Figure 12-7, Device Manager lists three driver files for the video display adapter. If you select a driver file in the Driver files box, Device Manager provides information on the provider, file version, copyright, and digital signer (if known) underneath the Driver files box.

Figure 12-7 Viewing device drivers for the video display adapter

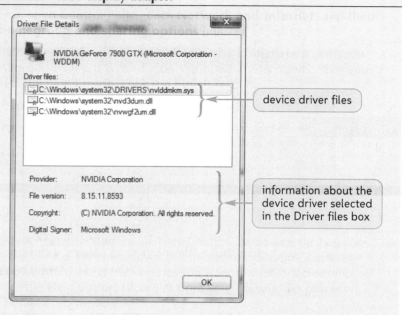

5. Click the **OK** button to close the Driver File Details dialog box, and then click the **Resources** tab. Under Resource settings on the Resources property sheet, Device Manager lists the types of resources assigned to a specific hardware device. On the computer used for Figure 12-8, Device Manager lists eight resource settings used by this video display adapter—one IRQ, four Memory Ranges, and three I/O Ranges—although not all are visible in the figure. Your resource settings may differ.

Figure 12-8 Viewing hardware resources for the video display adapter

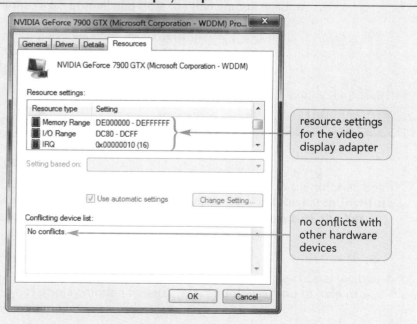

A check mark in the "Use automatic settings" check box indicates that Windows 7 automatically assigns resource settings to this hardware device, which is the best approach for configuring a hardware device. If "Use automatic settings" is dimmed, you cannot make changes to resource settings.

The most important information in the Resources property sheet is in the Conflicting device list box. Device Manager either reports no conflicts with other hardware devices, or it identifies the devices and the resource or resources involved in the hardware conflict.

▶ **6.** Click the **Cancel** button to close the Properties dialog box for your video display adapter without inadvertently making changes to your hardware configuration settings.

▶ **7.** Keep the Device Manager window open for the next set of tutorial steps.

If you right-click a hardware device under a category in the hardware tree, Windows 7 displays a shortcut menu with options for updating the driver software, disabling the hardware device, uninstalling the hardware device, scanning for hardware changes, and viewing hardware device properties.

Remy notes that some hardware devices, such as the mouse and keyboard, have a Power Management property sheet where you can specify whether the device wakes up a computer from a sleep state. You decide to examine that type of property sheet.

To examine the mouse's Power Management property sheet:

▶ **1.** Click the **expand** icon ▷ to the left of the Mice and other pointing devices category, double-click your **mouse device** (which may be identified as a HID-compliant mouse), and then click the **Power Management** tab.

On the Power Management property sheet for the computer used for Figure 12-9, Device Manager provides an option that allows the mouse to wake the computer from a sleep state. For other hardware devices, such as a network adapter, there may be an option for Windows 7 to turn off the hardware device in order to save power.

Trouble? If your mouse does not have a Power Management tab, then read this step and examine the figure so you are familiar with this option.

Figure 12-9 | Viewing power management options for a mouse

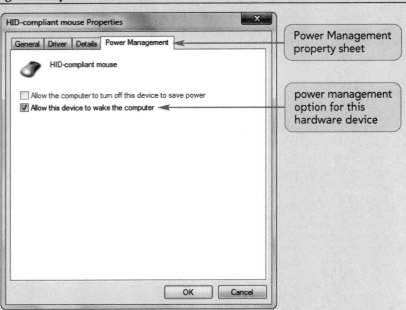

2. Click the **Cancel** button to close the Properties dialog box for your mouse without making changes to your mouse hardware configuration settings.

3. Click the **collapse** icons ◢ to the left of the Mice and other pointing devices category and the Display adapters category.

4. Keep the Device Manager window open for the next set of tutorial steps.

INSIGHT

Human Interface Devices

HID stands for **Human Interface Devices** (a broad category of input devices). These consist of devices for interacting with and controlling computers. HID devices include not only the standard types of devices that people use on their computers, such as the keyboard, mouse, trackball, joystick, and wireless pointing devices used for presentations, but they also include devices used to control home entertainment systems, smart appliances, and virtual reality simulations (such as head-mounted displays).

Remy asks you to view the devices in the Disk drives category, and then attach your flash drive and watch Device Manager dynamically update the list of devices under the Disk drives category in the hardware tree.

To examine the Disk drives category:

▶ **1.** Click the **expand** icon ▷ to the left of the Disk drives category. Windows 7 expands the category to show the type of disk drives used on your computer. This category includes any internal or external hard disk drive, USB flash drives, and media card readers for one or more types of memory cards.

▶ **2.** Watch the hardware tree as you attach your flash drive to the computer you are using and, if necessary, close the AutoPlay dialog box for your flash drive. Device Manager will update the hardware tree and include your flash drive in the Disk drives category. On the computer used for Figure 12-10, Device Manager identifies the flash drive as a USB Device. Your disk drives may differ.

| Figure 12-10 | Hardware tree updated to include flash drive |

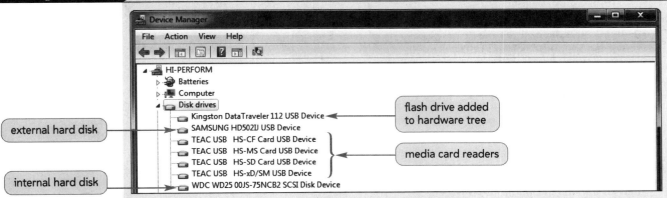

▶ **3.** Under the Disk drives category, double-click your **flash drive**. Device Manager opens a Properties dialog box for your flash drive. On the General property sheet, Device Manager identifies the device type, manufacturer (if known), and location. Device Manager also reports that the device is working properly.

▶ **4.** If available, click the **Policies** tab. Device Manager reports on the setting for two removal policies.

As shown on the Policies property sheet in Figure 12-11, the "Quick removal (default)" setting disables write caching on the flash drive and in Windows, and you can remove the flash drive without using the Safely Remove Hardware and Eject Media icon. The "Better performance" setting enables write caching to improve disk (and system) performance; however, you must use the Safely Remove Hardware and Eject Media icon in the notification area to safely disconnect the device.

Trouble? If your flash drive's Properties dialog box does not have a Policies tab, then read but do not keystroke this step and read the following discussion so you are familiar with this option.

Figure 12-11   **Reviewing a flash drive's write caching policies**

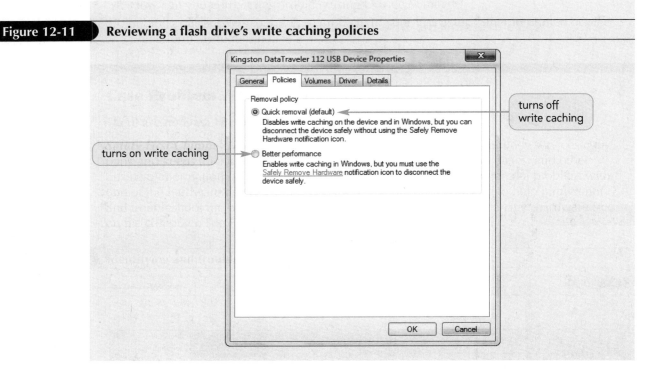

Write caching is a process by which changed data is held in the system cache in RAM and then written to disk by Windows 7 at periodic intervals so as to improve system performance, rather than writing data to disk immediately. That's why the second option, which enables write caching, is identified as a Better performance option. However, if you enable the Better performance setting, and then remove a flash drive without first using Safely Remove Hardware and Eject Media option, changed data still stored in the system cache, but not yet written to disk, is lost. Likewise, you can lose data with write caching enabled if a power outage or hardware failure occurs.

If you use the default Quick removal option, you can remove your flash drive without using the Safely Remove and Eject Media option because data is written to disk immediately rather than held in the system cache. While that guarantees that you have any changes you've made written to disk, it also affects the performance of your computer. The Safely Remove Hardware and Eject Media icon guarantees that all data is written to a flash drive before you remove that disk.

To continue your examination of your USB device properties:

▶ **1.** Click the **Driver** tab and then click the **Driver Details** button. On the computer used for Figure 12-12, the flash drive has two driver files. Note that both driver files have a .sys file extension—typical of files that are device drivers.

Figure 12-12	Viewing drivers for a newly attached flash drive

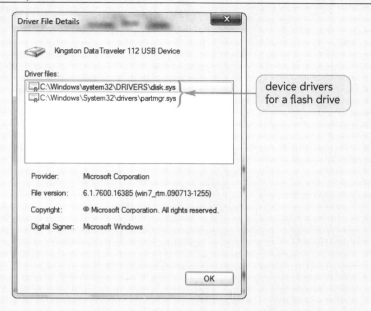

device drivers
for a flash drive

2. Click the **OK** button to close the Driver File Details dialog box, and then click the **Cancel** button to close the Properties dialog box for your flash drive without making any changes to hardware configuration settings for the flash drive.

3. Keep the Device Manager window open for the next set of tutorial steps, but do not remove your flash drive.

Now watch how Device Manager updates the hardware tree when you choose the option to remove a flash drive but not physically detach it from your computer.

To examine changes to the hardware tree when removing a flash drive:

Make sure you do not physically remove your flash drive from your computer after using the Safely Remove Hardware and Eject Media icon.

1. Click the **Show hidden icons** button ▲ in the notification area (if necessary), click the **Safely Remove Hardware and Eject Media** icon 🖥, select the option for ejecting your flash drive, and after Windows 7 displays a Safe to Remove Hardware dialog box informing you that you can now safely remove the device, *do not physically remove your flash drive yet*.

Device Manager updates the hardware tree and removes the flash drive from the Disk drives category.

2. If necessary, adjust your view of the hardware tree so you can see the Universal Serial Bus controllers category. Notice that one of the listings for USB Mass Storage Device displays a Warning icon ⚠ overlaying part of the icon for the hardware device to indicate a problem with the hardware device. See Figure 12-13.

Figure 12-13 **Device Manager reports a device problem**

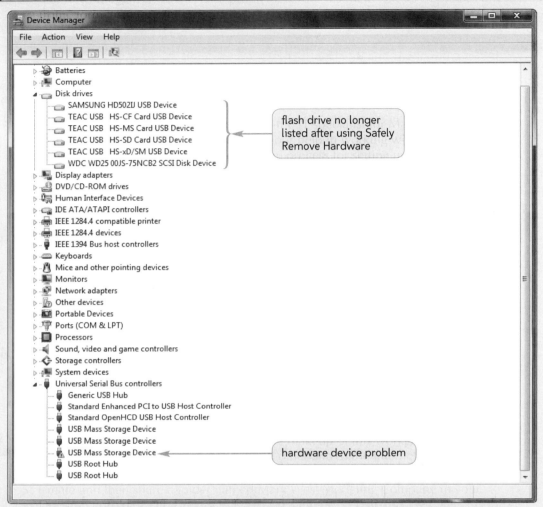

3. Double-click the **USB Mass Storage Device** with the Warning icon. In the Device status box on the General property sheet, Device Manager informs you that "Windows cannot use this hardware device because it has been prepared for 'safe removal,' but it has not been removed from the computer. (Code 47)." See Figure 12-14. Device Manager then informs you that you can fix this problem by unplugging the device from your computer and then plugging it in again.

Figure 12-14	Viewing the status of a device with a hardware problem

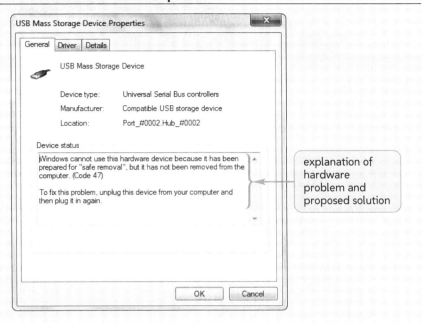

4. Leave the USB Mass Storage Device dialog box open, but physically remove the flash drive from your computer. Device Manager updates the hardware tree in the background, updates the information in this dialog box, and then informs you that "Currently, this hardware device is not connected to the computer. (Code 45)." See Figure 12-15.

Figure 12-15	Viewing the updated status of a device with a hardware problem

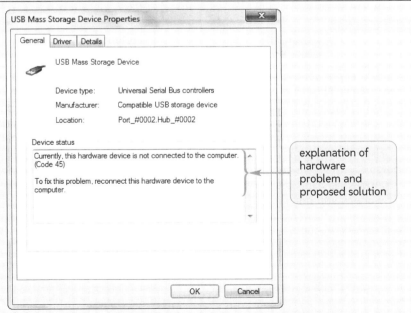

> To correct this problem, it suggests that you reconnect this hardware device to your computer. Notice also the USB Mass Storage Device listing with the error icon was removed from the hardware tree (though you may need to adjust the window to see that part of the hardware tree).
>
> **5.** Click the **OK** button to close the USB Mass Storage Device Properties dialog box.

Each **USB Host Controller** listed under the Serial Bus controllers category consists of one or more computer chips that identifies a USB hardware device and determines its bandwidth requirements. The USB Host Controller also mediates the transfer of data to and from USB devices. An **Enhanced Host Controller Interface (EHCI)** is one that supports the use of second-generation Hi-Speed USB 2.0 devices with data transfer rates of 480 Mbps. This type of host controller also supports the use of first-generation Low-Speed and Full-Speed USB 1.x devices with data transfer rates of 1.5 and 12 Mbps. If you see *Enhanced* in a Host Controller name, you know that your computer supports the use of USB 2.0 devices. The **Universal Host Controller Interface (UHCI)** and the **Open Host Controller Interface (OHCI)** support the use of first-generation USB 1.x devices with data transfer rates of 1.5 and 12 Mbps. USB 3.0 controllers include USB 3.0 in the controller name.

The **USB Root Hub** detects the attachment or removal of a USB device, manages power to USB devices, and handles the distribution of signals to USB devices attached to the same USB Root Hub. Each USB Root Hub contains one or more USB ports for attaching USB devices to your computer. If you examine properties of a USB Root Hub, the Power property sheet shows the number of attached devices, their power usage, and the number of available ports. The Advanced property sheet shows whether a USB 2.0 Hub is operating at Hi-Speed (480 Mbps) or Full-Speed (12 Mbps).

To end your examination of device properties:

> **1.** Close the Device Manager window, and then close the System window.

REFERENCE

Viewing Device Properties

- If you want to change device properties using Device Manager, you must log on under an Administrator account first; otherwise, if you are using a Standard user account, you can only view information on device properties in Device Manager.
- Right-click the Computer desktop icon, or right-click Computer on the Start menu, click Properties and in the System window, click the Device Manager link.
- Click the expand icon next to the hardware category that contains the device you want to examine, and then double-click the hardware device name to view its properties.
- Check the Device status section on the General property sheet to determine if the device is working properly.
- Click the Resources tab (if available) to view information on the resource settings for a device, and examine the Conflicting device list to determine if there are any hardware conflicts with other devices.
- Click the Driver tab and use the Roll Back Driver button if you want to restore the previously used device driver (a one-time change only).
- Close the device's Properties dialog box, and then close the Device Manager window.

To create a desktop shortcut for Device Manager, use one of the following paths: %SystemRoot%\System32\devmgmt.msc or %windir%\System32\devmgmt.msc. If necessary, modify the shortcut properties to specify that Windows 7 run the program with Administrator credentials.

As you will see later when you examine how to troubleshoot hardware conflicts, resources are a precious commodity, and Windows 7 attempts to assign resources without creating hardware conflicts. In the past, the limited number of IRQs was the primary source of problems for PC users who wanted to add more hardware devices than their computer can support. As noted earlier, Window's 7 support for newer hardware technologies and the way in which Windows 7 assigns resources to hardware devices overcomes these limitations.

Troubleshooting Hardware Problems

Remy relies on Device Manager to help him troubleshoot hardware configuration problems and reconfigure devices so they do not conflict with each other. At your next meeting with him, he describes how to recognize and troubleshoot hardware conflicts with Device Manager.

If there is a problem with the configuration of a hardware device, Windows 7 expands that portion of the hardware tree category where the problem occurs, shows the configured hardware devices within the category, and then displays one of three error icons over the hardware device icon to identify a problem. Device Manager detects three types of hardware problems:

- **Disabled device**—If a device is disabled for some reason, Windows 7 displays the device category's icon overlaid with a white circle that has a black arrow pointing down ⊕ to indicate that the hardware device has been disabled for some reason. On the computer used for Figure 12-16, Windows 7 detected the presence of a DVD drive; however, it is not included in the configuration of the computer because it is disabled.

| Figure 12-16 | Device Manager reports a problem with a disabled device |

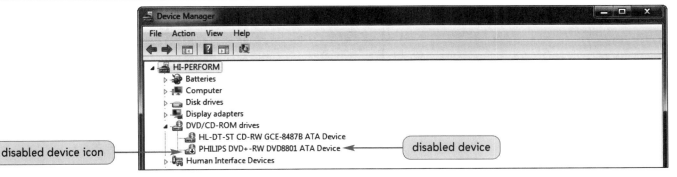

To correct this problem, you open Device Manager, double-click the disabled hardware device, and then check the Device status section on the General property sheet for information about the problem. See Figure 12-17. Windows 7 reports that the device is disabled and includes the hardware code (Code 22). If a device is disabled, Windows 7 does not load the device drivers for the hardware device. To enable this device, Device Manager recommends you click the Enable Device button.

Figure 12-17 Viewing the status of a disabled device

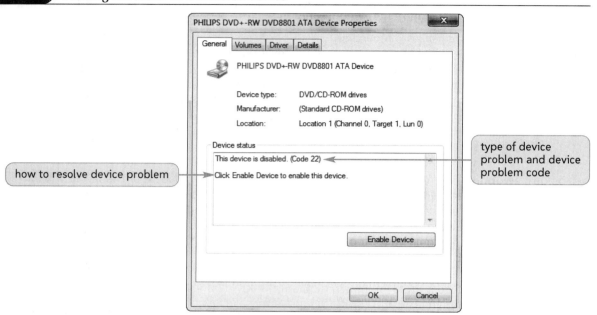

how to resolve device problem

type of device problem and device problem code

If you click the Enable Device button, Windows 7 opens the Device Problems Troubleshooting Wizard, and explains why a device might be disabled. As shown in Figure 12-18, the device might not be working properly or it might be causing a resource conflict.

Figure 12-18 Using the Device Problems Troubleshooting Wizard

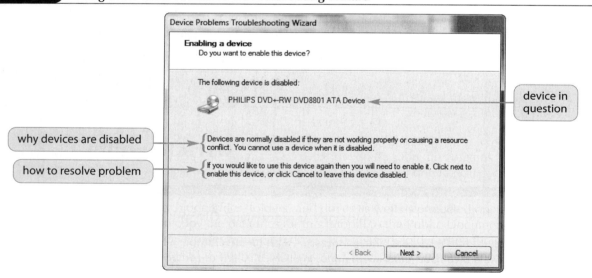

device in question

why devices are disabled

how to resolve problem

If you click the Next button, the Device Problems Troubleshooting Wizard tells you that it successfully enabled the device. Once you enable a device, Windows 7 loads that device's device drivers.

After you click the Finish button, Windows 7 closes the Device Problems Troubleshooting Wizard and returns you to the Properties dialog box for the hardware device. The Device status box now informs you that the device is working properly. After you close the hardware device's Properties dialog box, Windows 7 updates Device Manager and removes the icon overlay that indicated a problem with the device.

If you recognize this type of problem as a disabled device, you can right-click the disabled device, and then click Enable on the shortcut menu.

- **Resource conflict**—Thanks to the widespread use of USB and IEEE 1394 hardware devices, a far less frequent type of problem that you might encounter is a resource conflict—one in which two hardware devices use the same resource, such as the same IRQ or I/O address. If there is a resource conflict, Device Manager displays a yellow triangle with a black exclamation mark ⚠ over the icon for the hardware device icon. If you then check the Conflicting device list on the Resources property sheet for that device, Device Manager identifies the names of the devices and the resources that are causing the conflict. As noted earlier, a check mark in the "Use automatic settings" check box on the Resources property sheet means that Windows 7 chooses resource settings for the hardware device. If you can remove the check mark, you can manually configure the device by choosing another combination of resource settings from the "Setting based on" box. The configuration settings for a hardware device includes Current configuration and also includes one or more other configurations identified by names, such as "Basic configuration 0000," "Basic configuration 0001," and "Basic configuration 0002." An example of these settings is shown in Figure 12-19 for Communications Port (COM1). These basic configurations are combinations of resource settings that work for this particular hardware device and that are not used by any other device. Other devices have different combinations of configuration settings. Choosing another combination of configuration settings might resolve the conflict. After you select another combination of configuration settings, Device Manager updates the Conflicting device list and might report that the new configuration creates no conflicts.

Figure 12-19   **Viewing configuration options for a hardware component**

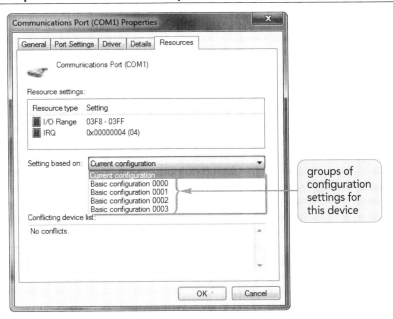

- **Other devices**—Windows 7 places a hardware device in an Other devices category if the device is not fully supported. In Figure 12-20, Windows 7 displays a white circle with a blue question mark ⓘ over the Other devices category icon and also over the device icon because Windows 7 did not find one of the device drivers needed to provide full support for this hardware device (an inkjet printer). The problem was eventually resolved by installing support for the printer using a compatible device driver for another type of inkjet printer manufactured by the same company.

Figure 12-20 **Problem with a device missing a device driver**

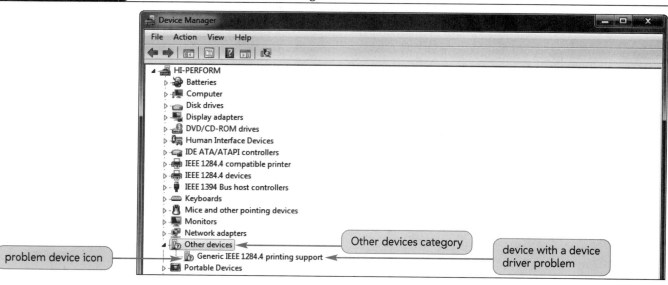

In another example shown in Figure 12-21, Device Manager lists EPSON Scanner under the Other devices category, but in this case, Device Manager displays a warning icon over the icon for the hardware device, indicating that Windows 7 was able to identify the specific type of EPSON scanner and that the device needs updated device drivers. In this case, updated software for using the scanner under Windows 7 was also needed.

Figure 12-21 **Problem with device drivers for a scanner**

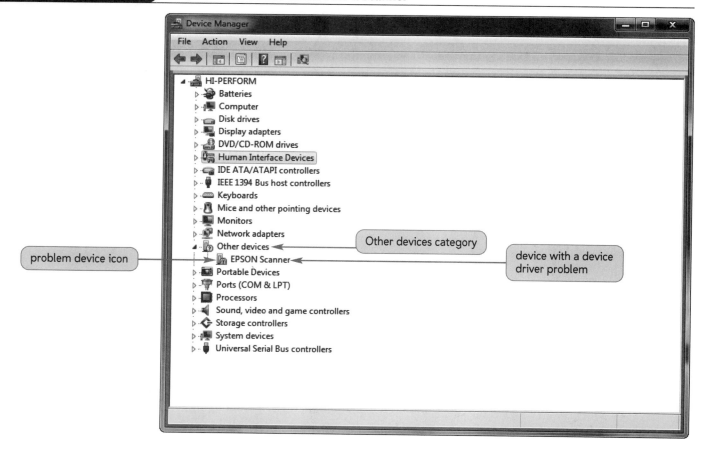

Checking Device Manager on a New Computer

Before you buy a computer on display in a store, open Device Manager on the computer and check the hardware configuration. If Windows 7 reports a hardware problem, don't buy that computer. If you do purchase it, you might find it difficult to resolve the problem or your computer might not perform optimally. If you purchase a computer online, check Device Manager immediately after you receive the computer while the computer is under warranty. If you spot hardware problems, you may be able to return the computer within a short time period for a full refund.

Windows 7 provides better support, more hardware resources, and better configuration of hardware devices than past Windows versions. However, Microsoft depends on manufacturers to update their device drivers for newer Windows versions and thereby continue support for their hardware devices. Obviously, as newer hardware devices appear in the marketplace, hardware manufacturers have to provide new device drivers that provide support for 32-bit and 64-bit Windows editions, and Microsoft therefore has to continually update Windows to provide ongoing support for these new technologies.

Session 12.1 Quick Check

1. Windows 7 can automatically detect and configure a(n) _____ hardware device.
2. _____ is an external, bidirectional, Plug and Play bus for connecting up to 127 high-speed serial devices via one port on your computer.
3. _____ refers to the amount of data that can be transmitted over a device in a fixed amount of time.
4. You can use _____ to document hardware settings, verify the installation of a hardware device, check for hardware conflicts, troubleshoot hardware problems, change the configuration of a hardware device, and update device drivers for a hardware device.
5. What is a resource conflict?
6. To restore the previously used device driver for a hardware device, you use _____.
7. What is write caching?
8. True or False. You can connect or disconnect devices that support hot swapping while the computer is up and running.

SESSION 12.2 VISUAL OVERVIEW

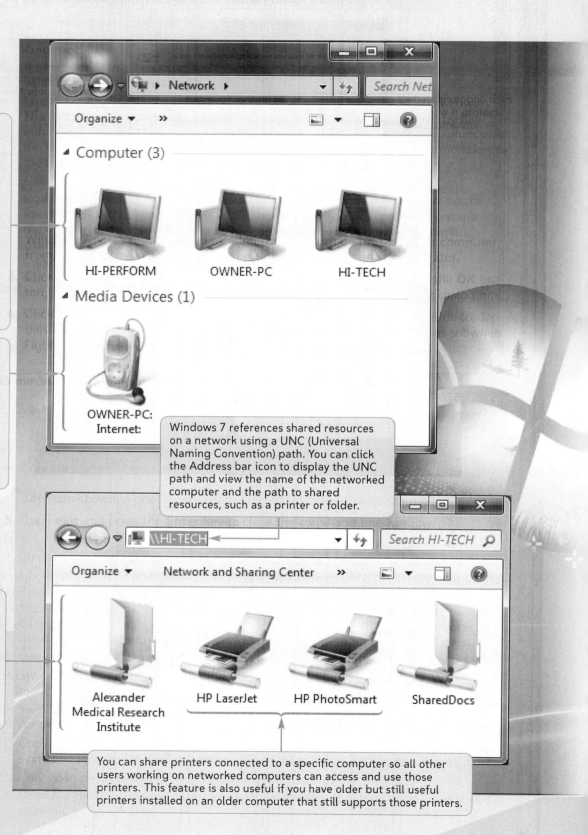

You can use the Network window to view networked computers in your peer-to-peer network and access shared resources, such as printers, folders, and files. A **peer-to-peer network** is a network in which each computer communicates directly with each other computer, and users decide which resources to share. Each computer's name distinguishes it from other computers on the same network.

Media devices available in a homegroup permit users to stream media, such as videos, to other computers over the network. A **homegroup** is a simpler way to set up a network between computers; however, each computer in a homegroup must be running Windows 7.

Windows 7 references shared resources on a network using a UNC (Universal Naming Convention) path. You can click the Address bar icon to display the UNC path and view the name of the networked computer and the path to shared resources, such as a printer or folder.

You can create a **mapped drive** by assigning a shared network folder a drive name. Then you can access the shared network folder by opening the mapped drive in a Computer window or by dragging the mapped drive to the desktop to create a shortcut to the mapped drive.

You can share printers connected to a specific computer so all other users working on networked computers can access and use those printers. This feature is also useful if you have older but still useful printers installed on an older computer that still supports those printers.

NETWORKING

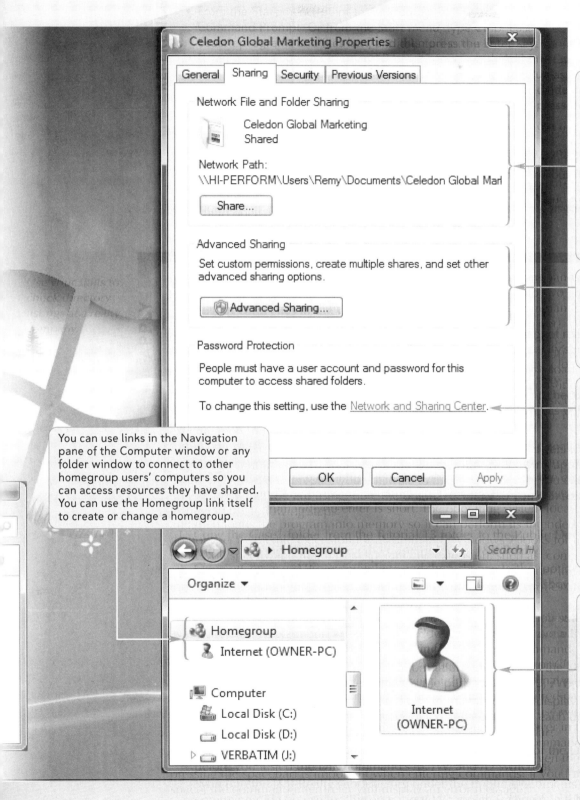

One simple way to share folders and files on a network is to use the File Sharing Wizard, which is enabled by default in Windows 7. The Sharing property sheet identifies whether a folder or file is shared, and it displays the UNC path for that network resource. You can use the Share button to enable sharing if a folder or file is not currently shared.

Another way to share folders and files is to use Advanced Sharing, which provides more options for sharing a resource, including specifying who may share a network resource and how they can share.

You can use the Network and Sharing Center to view basic information about your network and its connections, including a network map, as well as to configure your network as a Home, Work, or Public network. You can also set up new connections, connect to a network, create a homegroup, change a homegroup's settings, and just as importantly, trouble-shoot network problems.

You can use links in the Navigation pane of the Computer window or any folder window to connect to other homegroup users' computers so you can access resources they have shared. You can use the Homegroup link itself to create or change a homegroup.

A third way to share network resources is to create a homegroup and decide what resources you want to share. Other users on Windows 7 computers can join that homegroup and decide what they want to share. Then each user can access shared resources allowed by all other users in the homegroup.

Windows 7 Networking Capabilities

Over the last several months, the Alexander Medical Research Institute has hired additional technical support staff to keep up with its rapid growth and its customers' needs. Remy and his staff work with these new employees to set up network connections on their computers so they can access the resources they need to perform their jobs.

Many computer users in a business environment need a networked computer to access important applications and documents, shared hardware devices (such as printers), and resources on their company's network and the Internet. More people are also beginning to set up small networks at home so more than one person can use a computer and access network resources as well as consumer electronics devices in the home itself.

If you are connected to a network, it is either a server-based network or a peer-to-peer network. In a server-based network, the **server** is the computer that manages the network and provides shared resources to network users within a domain. A **domain** consists of a group of networked computers that share a common directory database and security policy as well as network resources and that are managed as a unit by a network administrator. A domain may consist of thousands of computers that are located on different networks. Network administrators also use a domain to apply and standardize settings across all computers in the domain. Your user account gives you access to all of the domain resources, such as shared folders and files and printers, for which you must also have permission. To connect to a domain, you must provide a password or other credentials. Only the Windows 7 Professional, Ultimate, and Enterprise editions support the option for joining a domain.

In contrast, a **workgroup**, or peer-to-peer network, is a network in which each computer is an equal. No server manages network resources and provides network users access to those resources. Each computer in a workgroup might have multiple users, or just a single user, and those users decide what resources to share on the network. Peer-to-peer networks are typically home or small office networks with two to 20 computers, and include shared hardware devices such as shared printers and perhaps a shared Internet connection. Although workgroups permit you to share resources, such as files and printers, you have to actually specify what you want to share.

Windows 7 introduces the use of the **HomeGroup** feature that allows each Windows 7 computer to share libraries, documents, pictures, music, videos, and printers more easily. All users on a single computer, except the Guest account, belong to the same homegroup, and each user controls access to their own libraries. To join a homegroup, users must be part of a workgroup of networked computers. All editions of Windows 7 support the use of a homegroup, and each computer in a homegroup must be running some edition of Windows 7. If you are using Windows 7 Starter or Windows 7 Home Basic, you cannot create a homegroup, but you can join a homegroup. A homegroup is also password-protected for security reasons. Networked computers that are part of a domain can also join a homegroup, and they can access shared files, but they cannot share files. You will examine the HomeGroup feature in more detail later in this session.

The steps in this next section of this tutorial assume that you are part of a workgroup. If you examine network settings on your own computer network, make sure you document settings that you intend to change so you can restore them later if a problem develops. If you are working in a computer lab at your college, network restrictions may prevent you from modifying network settings, and you may need to read, but not keystroke, certain sections and steps in this session of the tutorial.

Viewing Your Computer's Name

Each computer in a workgroup has a unique name that identifies the computer on the network. The computer name is important because it determines how Windows 7 identifies a computer when you are viewing network connections, and therefore makes it easier for you to locate a specific computer on a network.

Microsoft Help and Support recommends that you keep computer names short, and only use names with 15 characters or less. It also recommends that the computer name only include letters of the alphabet (such as the lowercase and uppercase letters *A* through *Z*), numbers (*0* through *9*), and a hyphen. A computer name cannot consist of only numbers. Also, you cannot use spaces, and you cannot use certain symbols, such as those not allowed in filenames and folder names:

   < > ; : " * + = \ | ?

Next, you're going to examine your computer's name and other information about your peer-to-peer network.

To view your computer's name:

TIP

The default workgroup name is WORKGROUP.

▶ **1.** Right-click the **Computer** desktop icon and then click **Properties**. Windows 7 opens the System window, and under "Computer name, domain, and workgroup settings," Windows 7 displays your computer's name and any description you've provided for the computer as well as the workgroup name.

▶ **2.** If you can provide Administrator credentials, click the **Change settings** link under the "Computer name, domain, and workgroup settings" section, and then provide Administrator credentials. Windows 7 opens the System Properties dialog box with the Computer Name tab displayed in the foreground, as shown in Figure 12-22, and then explains that it uses the information on this property sheet to identify your computer on a network.

Figure 12-22   **Viewing computer network settings**

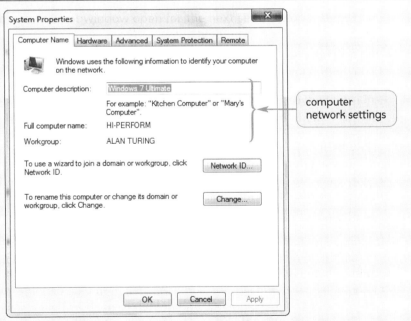

You can also specify a friendly computer description to more easily identify your computer, such as the examples shown on this property sheet. You can use the Network ID button on the Computer Name property sheet to start the Join a Domain or Workgroup Wizard, which allows you to specify whether your computer is part of a business network that you use to connect to other computers at work, or whether it is part of a small home computer network. On the computer used in this figure, the Change button was used to change the default WORKGROUP name to ALAN TURING (a British mathematician who was one of the earliest and foremost pioneers in the development of present-day computers).

3. Click the **Change** button. Windows 7 opens the Computer Name/Domain Changes dialog box where you can not only change the name of your computer but also indicate whether you are a member of a domain or workgroup. See Figure 12-23.

Figure 12-23	Viewing the computer name and workgroup name

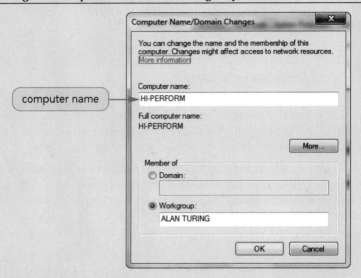

computer name

If you make changes in this dialog box, you must restart your computer so those changes are applied to your computer. If you click the OK button but have not made any changes in this dialog box, Windows 7 will still inform you that you must restart your computer to apply changes. Although you do not have to restart your computer immediately, any changes you've made may affect your access to network resources, and you must restart your computer so Windows 7 can apply the changes.

> Double check any changes you have made, and make sure you really do want to apply them.

4. If you have applied any changes that you want to keep, click the **OK** button in the Computer Name/Domain Changes dialog box; otherwise, if you do not want to apply any changes, click the **Cancel** button.

Trouble? If Windows 7 displays another Computer Name/Domain Changes dialog box and informs you that you should save any open files and close all programs before restarting your computer and applying changes, click the OK button. If you clicked the OK button in the Computer Name/Domain Changes dialog box, Windows 7 displays a warning at the bottom of the Computer Name property sheet, and notes that changes will take effect after you restart your computer.

Trouble? If Windows 7 displays another Computer Name/Domain Changes dialog box welcoming you to your new workgroup, click the OK button.

5. Click the **Close** button or the **OK** button to close the System Properties dialog box.

6. If Windows 7 displays a Microsoft Windows dialog box informing you that you must restart your computer to apply changes you made, click the **Restart Now** button or the **Restart Later** button. Note also Windows 7 recommends that you save any open files and close all programs before restarting your computer.

7. Close the System window.

In the past, if you had a peer-to-peer network at home, each computer used the same workgroup name to make it easier to access other computers on a home network. In Windows 7, different computers on a network can have different workgroup names. However, if your network includes one or more Windows XP computers, you should change the workgroup name on those Windows XP computers so they match the one on your Windows 7 computer. That in turn enables you to view and connect to those computers on your network.

REFERENCE

Viewing and Changing Your Computer's Name, Description, and Workgroup Name

- Right-click the Computer desktop icon, click Properties, and then examine the information shown under "Computer name, domain, and workgroup settings" in the System window.
- If you want to make changes to any of these settings, click the Change settings link and provide Administrator credentials.
- On the Computer Name property sheet in the System Properties dialog, click the Change button to open the Computer Name/Domain Changes dialog box to change your computer name or workgroup name, or to specify whether you are a member of a domain or workgroup.
- If you have applied any changes that you want to keep, click the OK button. Otherwise, click the Cancel button.
- If Windows 7 displays another Computer Name/Domain Changes dialog box and informs you that you should save any open files and close all programs before restarting your computer and applying changes, click the OK button.
- If Windows 7 displays another Computer Name/Domain Changes dialog box welcoming you to your new workgroup, click the OK button.
- Click the Close button or the OK button to close the System Properties dialog box.
- If Windows 7 displays a Microsoft Windows dialog box informing you that you must restart your computer to apply changes you made, click the Restart Now button or the Restart Later button.
- Close the System window.

Viewing Computers in a Workgroup

If you have a peer-to-peer network, you can view other computers that are part of that network by opening the Network folder. Then you can browse those computers for shared network resources.

Remy suggests you examine computers in your workgroup, and view and browse shared network resources.

TIP

You can add a network printer or wireless device from the toolbar in this window.

To view networked computers in a workgroup:

1. Open the Start menu, and then click **Network**. Windows 7 opens the Network window, identifies networked computers by computer name, and then identifies other network devices, such as media devices. On the computer used for Figure 12-24, the computer network consists of two computers—one identified as HI-PERFORM (a computer with Windows 7 Ultimate) and the other as HI-TECH (a computer with Windows XP Professional). These two computers are part of the same workgroup on a peer-to-peer network. Your networked computers and computer names will differ.

Figure 12-24 **Viewing networked computers in the Network window**

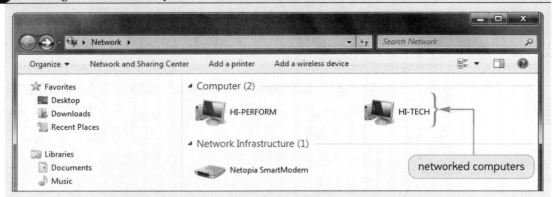

2. In the Network window, click a **network computer** icon for another computer on your network. Windows 7 opens a window that shows the shared devices on that computer. In Figure 12-25, Windows 7 shows a shared Alexander Medical Research Institute folder (shared specifically by the user of that networked computer), a shared HP LaserJet printer, a shared HP PhotoSmart printer, and the SharedDocs folder on the computer named HI-TECH. Your shared network resources will differ.

Figure 12-25 **Viewing shared network resources on a Windows XP Professional computer**

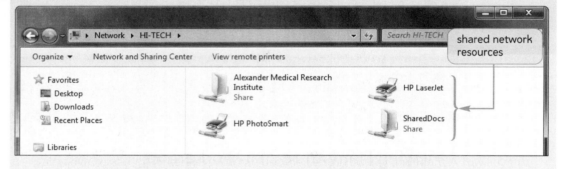

SharedDocs is the network name for the Shared Documents folder on the Windows XP Professional computer. Any user on that Windows XP Professional computer can share a file with any other user on that same computer by copying or moving a file into the Shared Documents folder. You can open a shared folder and access any shared files in that folder from another computer in the same workgroup. You can also print to a shared printer on another computer in the same network. In Windows Vista and Windows 7, Public Documents is the name of a shared folder that is comparable to the Shared Documents folder in Windows XP.

You can open a shared folder (such as the Alexander Medical Research Institute folder) from another computer in the same workgroup, and access any shared files in that folder. You can also print to a shared printer on another computer in the same network by first opening the Print dialog box in the program you are using and then choosing the shared printer from a printer name box. The printer name box may show a friendly name for the networked printer, or it may show the UNC path for the networked printer. As noted in Tutorial 1, the UNC (Universal Naming Convention) path identifies the location of a computer or a shared resource on a network. When identifying a computer, the UNC path consists of two backslashes followed by the computer name. Unlike URLs, which use forward slashes, the UNC path uses backslashes.

To continue your examination of this networked computer:

TIP

To create a Network desktop shortcut, drag Network from the Start menu to the desktop.

▶ **1.** Click the **Address bar** icon 🖳 to the left of Network. Windows 7 displays the UNC path for the networked computer. On the computer used for Figure 12-25, the UNC path is \\HI-TECH. Your network path will differ.

▶ **2.** If there is a shared network folder on this computer, click the **shared network folder** icon. Windows 7 opens the network folder and displays its contents. On the computer used for Figure 12-26, Windows 7 displays two subfolders— Interdisciplinary Resources and Research Projects—in the shared Alexander Medical Research Institute folder.

Figure 12-26   Viewing shared network folders

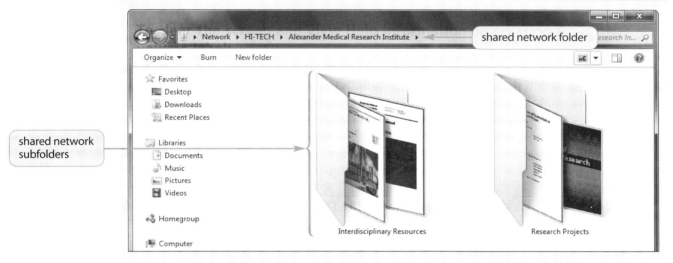

Because the parent folder of these subfolders is shared, these folders are also shared. Your network folders will differ. The UNC path for this network folder is \\HI-TECH\Alexander Medical Research Institute. Your network path will differ.

▶ **3.** Click a **folder** icon. Windows 7 opens the folder and displays files on that network computer that you can access. On the computer used for Figure 12-27, Windows 7 displays two files—a Medical Personnel Directory and a Pilot Project Proposal file—in the Interdisciplinary Resources folder.

Figure 12-27 **Viewing files in a shared network folder**

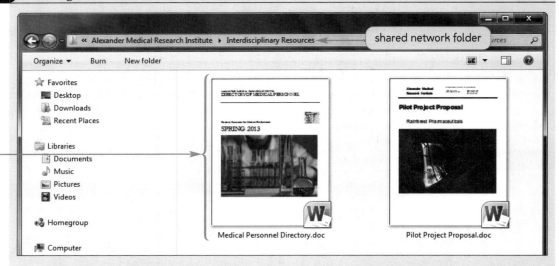

Because the parent folder of this subfolder with these files is shared, these files are also shared. The UNC path for the folder shown in the figure is \\HI-TECH\ Alexander Medical Research Institute\Interdisciplinary Resources. The UNC path for the Pilot Project Proposal.doc file is \\HI-TECH\Alexander Medical Institute\ Interdisciplinary Resources\Pilot Project Proposal.doc. Your network paths will differ.

4. Close the current window.

If you click the Address bar icon in a shared network folder window, or if you examine the General property for any file in that shared network folder, Windows 7 displays the path to the current folder.

REFERENCE

Viewing Computers and Shared Resources in a Workgroup

- From the Start menu, click Network to view networked computers.
- To view shared resources of a network computer, click the network computer icon, and then browse and examine shared folders and files.
- When finished browsing network resources, close the current window.

While the Network option on the Start menu provides easy access to all shared network computers, folders, files, and devices, the Network and Sharing Center displays your network settings.

Using the Network and Sharing Center

The Network and Sharing Center displays your current network settings and a simple network map that visually illustrates the setup of your network. From the Network and Sharing Center, you can change network settings, view a full network map, and access other tools for displaying other network settings and for troubleshooting networks.

Remy uses the Network and Sharing Center to verify that network settings on new computers are correct and, when necessary, to resolve problems. He asks you to check the Network and Sharing Center on an employee's computer who recently reported a network problem.

To open the Network and Sharing Center:

TIP

You can also open the Networking Sharing Center from the Network window.

▶ **1.** Click the **Network** icon in the notification area for your wired or wireless connection, and then click the **Open Network and Sharing Center** link. Windows 7 opens a Network and Sharing Center window, as shown in Figure 12-28. At the top of the window, Windows 7 displays a simple map of your network. If you click the "See full map" link, Windows 7 displays a more detailed diagram of your network setup, including the names of each PC on the network and how they connect with each other and the Internet.

Figure 12-28 Network and Sharing Center

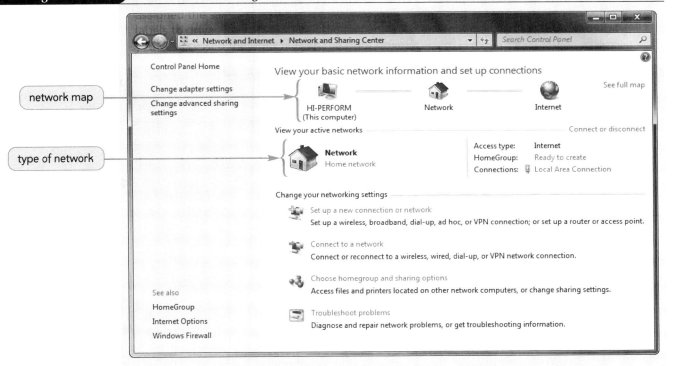

▶ **2.** Keep the Network and Sharing Center window open to examine more features.

Under the section labeled "View your active networks" in the Network and Sharing Center window, Windows 7 identifies whether your network is a Home network, Work network, Public network, or Domain. If you click a link for your type of computer network under the "View your active networks" section, Windows 7 opens a Set Network Location dialog box, as shown in Figure 12-29, so you can change your network type or specify that you want to treat all future networks that you connect to as a Public network (for greater security). The Public network option is one you would use if you are accessing the Internet on a network in a public place, such as an Internet café or airport.

Figure 12-29 Choosing a network location

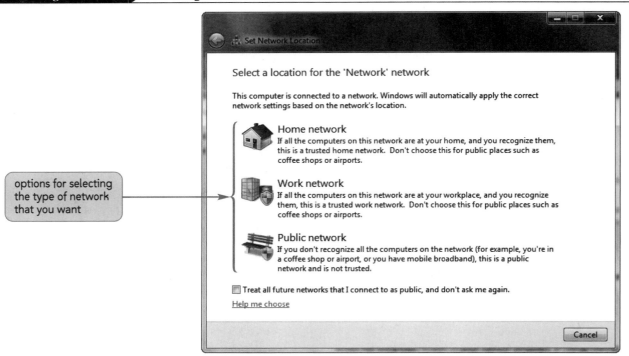

options for selecting the type of network that you want

In the Network and Sharing Center window, under "Change your networking settings," you can set up a new connection or network, connect to a network, choose homegroup and sharing options, and troubleshoot network problems.

If you click the Network icon in the network map, you open the Network folder where you can view and browse computers on your network. If you click the Internet icon in the network map, you open your Web browser and connect to the Internet. If you click the icon for your network computer (labeled "This computer"), you open a Computer window.

To view advanced sharing settings:

1. In the upper-left corner of the Network and Sharing Center window, click the **Change advanced sharing settings** link. Windows 7 opens the Advanced sharing settings window where you can create a separate network profile, or combination of network settings, for each of your networks. See Figure 12-30.

| Figure 12-30 | Viewing advanced sharing settings for network discovery and printer, folder, and file sharing |

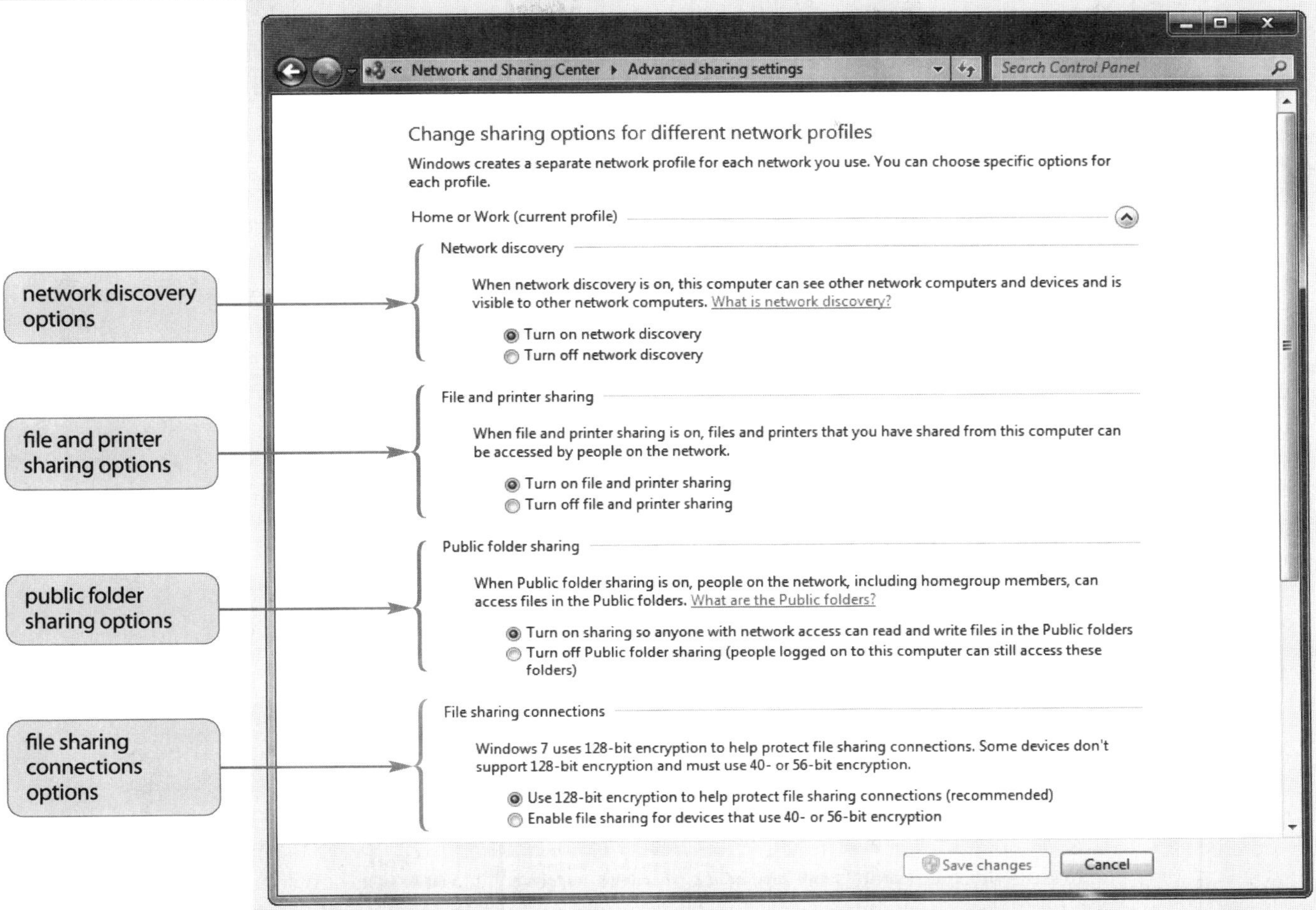

network discovery options

file and printer sharing options

public folder sharing options

file sharing connections options

Windows 7 also expands the profile for your type of network: Home or Work, and Public. On the computer used for this figure, Windows 7 displays profile settings for the Home or Work network type. Your network type and profile settings will differ.

Under the Network discovery section for the computer used for this figure, Windows 7 points out that the computer you are currently using can detect other network computers and devices if network discovery is enabled. Also, the computer you are currently using is visible to other computers on the same network. When enabled, you can share files and printers. The Network discovery option that you choose also affects your firewall settings. Network discovery works more quickly if all computers on the network are in the same workgroup.

Under the "File and printer sharing" section, you can enable this option if you want to share files and printers with other users on the same network. Under "Public folder sharing," Windows 7 notes that when you enable this option, other users on the same network, including homegroup members, can read and modify files in the Public folders. If you turn off Public folder sharing, only users who have accounts on the same computer can work with files in the Public folders.

Under "File sharing connections," Windows 7 notes that it uses 128-bit encryption to protect file sharing connections, and it notes that you must use either 40-bit or 56-bit encryption for devices that don't support 128-bit encryption. If Windows 7 uses more bits to encrypt your files, your files are more secure, and there is less likelihood that someone can break the encryption on those files.

If you enable Password protected sharing, shown in Figure 12-31, users who have an account and password on the same computer are the only ones who can access shared files, shared printers, and the Public folders. If you turn off Password protected sharing, you are providing other users access to shared files, shared printers, and the Public folders.

Figure 12-31   **Viewing password protected sharing and HomeGroup connection settings**

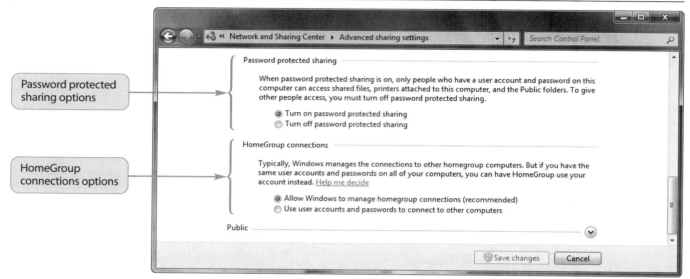

Password protected sharing options

HomeGroup connections options

Under "HomeGroup connections," Windows 7 is set to manage connections to other computers on your network that are part of your homegroup. That is the easiest and best way to share files and printers. Windows 7 also notes that if you have the same user accounts and passwords on all the computers in your network, you can specify that the HomeGroup feature use your user account and password instead to access other computers.

The Public profile is similar to the default settings for the Home or Work profile except that Network discovery and file and printer sharing are both set to off by default to protect your computer and its content.

From the Network and Sharing Center, you can also examine settings for your Local Area Connection. To view properties of your Local Area Connection, you will need to provide Administrator credentials.

To view shared network folders and files:

1. Click **Network and Sharing Center** in the Address bar, and then under "View your active networks," click the **Local Area Connection** link. Windows 7 opens the Local Area Connection Status dialog box, which contains information about your current connection, including the status of IPv4 Connectivity and IPv6 Connectivity (described below), the speed of your connection, and the number of bytes sent and received. You can use the Diagnose button to troubleshoot problems with your Local Area Connection.

   Trouble? If you have a Wireless Network Connection link instead of a Local Area Connection link, then click the Wireless Network Connection link to open the Wireless Network Connection Status dialog box.

▶ **2.** Click the **Properties** button at the bottom of the Connection Status dialog box for your network connection, and then provide Administrator credentials (if necessary). Windows 7 opens the Local Area Connection Properties dialog box, and displays information about your network settings, as shown in Figure 12-32. In the Connect using box, Windows 7 identifies your network adapter.

Trouble? Your Wireless Network Connection dialog box may also have a second tab labeled Sharing for implementing Internet Connection Sharing, which allows other computers to use the same Internet connection as the computer where you are viewing network properties.

Figure 12-32   Viewing the Connection Properties dialog box for a network connection

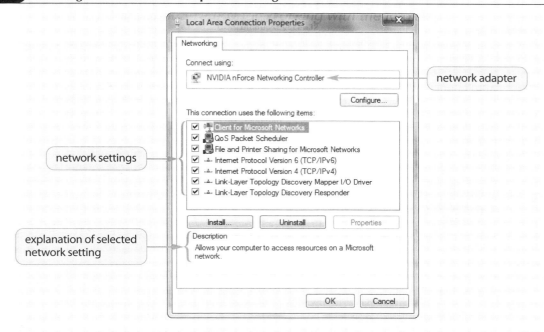

Under "This connection uses the following items," Windows 7 lists the services used by this connection:

- **Client for Microsoft Networks** (a required networking component) is **client software** for accessing resources on a Microsoft network. A **client** is a computer or a program that connects to, or requests services of, another computer or program.
- **QoS (Quality of Service) Packet Scheduler** provides for the efficient flow of data on a network by handling the scheduling of packets of data over a network.
- **File and Printer Sharing for Microsoft Networks** is **service software** that enables users of other computers within the same network to access your files and printer.
- **Internet Protocol Version 6 (TCP/IPv6)** and **Internet Protocol 4 (TCP/IPv4)** are a set of protocols for the transmission of data over the Internet as well as business and home networks. One important feature of the newer Internet Protocol Version 6 (TCP/IPv6) over TCP/IPv4 is that it increases the number of bits used for network addresses from 32 bits to 128 bits, thus providing support for more Internet and network addresses necessary for the inevitable growth of the Internet while also providing enhanced security.
- **Link-Layer Topology Discovery Mapper I/O Driver** and **Link-Layer Topology Discovery Responder** are two network components that discover computers devices on a network as well as components of the network infrastructure. These two components also determine the network bandwidth.

Now that you have examined these network settings, you can close the Network and Sharing Center.

To close the Connection Properties dialog box for your type of network connection and to close the Network and Sharing Center:

▶ **1.** Click the **Cancel** button in the Connection Properties dialog box for your network connection, and click the **Close** button in the Connection Status dialog box for your network connection.

▶ **2.** Close the Network and Sharing Center window.

If you want a desktop shortcut to the Network and Sharing Center, you can drag the icon on the left side of the Network and Sharing Center Address bar to the desktop.

REFERENCE

Using the Network and Sharing Center

• Click the Network icon in the notification area, and then click Open Network and Sharing Center.
• To view a full network map, click the "See full map" link.
• To change the network type, click the link under "View your active networks," and then select a network location.
• To view or change sharing options for different network profiles, click the "Change advanced sharing settings" link, and then click the Save changes button if you made any changes to these settings.
• To view the status of your type of network connection, click the link for your type of network connection under "Connect or disconnect." To view properties of your local area connection, click the Properties button in the Connection Status dialog box for your type of network connection. When finished examining the status and properties of your local area connection, close the Connection Properties dialog box for your type of network connection, close the Connection Status dialog box for your type of network connection, and if necessary, close the Network window.
• Close the Network and Sharing Center window.

Sharing Folders

The simplest way to share folders and files among different users of the same computer is to place the folders and files in the Public Documents folder. However, you may want to share folders and files located in other folders so other network users can access and use those folders and the files within those folders. The object that you make available to other users on a network is called a **share** or **network share**. When you share folders, you are granting permission for everyone or for specific designated users and groups to access and use those folders in a specific way. A **permission** is a setting that determines who can access a network resource and how they can use it. For example, you might grant one or more users permission to read a document, but not permission to change that document. Once shared, anyone who has access to the computer network also has access to the shared folder or file using whatever permission level you specified. You can also share hardware, such as network printers.

Remy asks you to create an Alexander Medical Research Institute folder on a new computer, and then compare two different approaches for sharing folders. He also notes that if you turn on sharing for a folder, all files you place in that folder are shared.

To view sharing properties of a newly created folder:

▶ **1.** Right-click the **Windows Explorer** taskbar button, click **Windows Explorer** on the Jump List, click the **expand** icon ▷ to the left of the Documents library in the Navigation pane, and then click **My Documents**.

▶ **2.** Click **Organize** on the toolbar, click **Folder and search options**, click the **View** tab, and scroll to the bottom of the Advanced settings box. As shown in Figure 12-33, Windows 7 automatically enables the Use Sharing Wizard setting to simplify the process of sharing folders and files. Your Use Sharing Wizard setting may differ.

Figure 12-33   Checking the Use Sharing Wizard setting

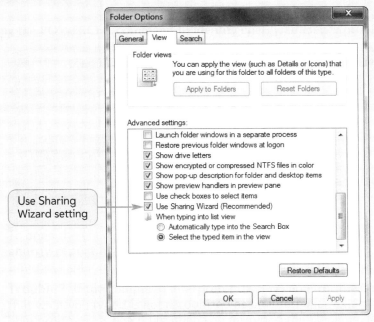

Use Sharing Wizard setting

▶ **3.** If you have turned off the Sharing Wizard, click the **Use Sharing Wizard (Recommend)** check box to add a check mark.

▶ **4.** Click the **OK** button to close the Folder Options dialog box.

▶ **5.** Click the **More options** arrow on the Change your view button to switch to Large Icons view (if necessary).

▶ **6.** Click the **New folder** button on the toolbar, type **Alexander Medical Research Institute**, and then press the **Enter** key.

▶ **7.** Right-click the **Alexander Medical Research Institute** folder, click **Properties**, and in the Alexander Medical Research Institute Properties dialog box, click the **Sharing** tab. On the computer used for Figure 12-34, Windows 7 lists the network path to that folder. You can use the Share button to share the folder with additional users; however, with the Sharing Wizard, there is an alternate and easier approach.

Figure 12-34 Viewing options on the Sharing property sheet for a folder

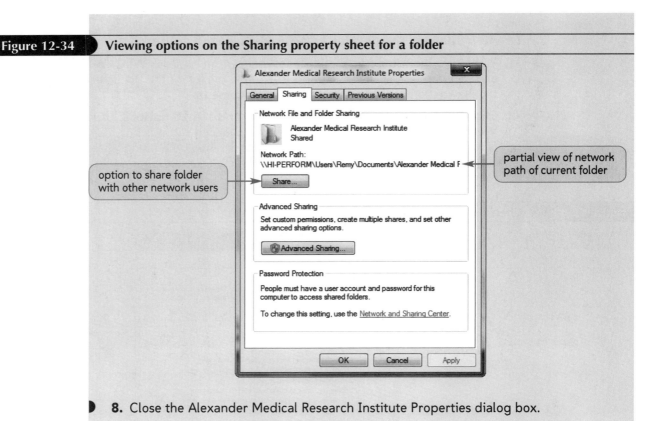

8. Close the Alexander Medical Research Institute Properties dialog box.

Next, share this folder with everyone on your network.

To share this folder:

1. Right-click the **Alexander Medical Research Institute** folder, and point to **Share with**. As shown in Figure 12-35, you can select Nobody, Homegroup (Read), Homegroup (Read/Write), or Specific people.

Figure 12-35 Choosing a sharing option

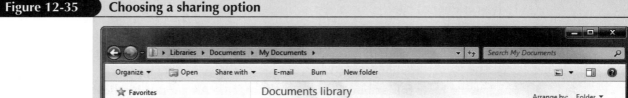

The Nobody option makes the folder private, and only you will have access to the folder. The Homegroup (Read) option makes the folder available to other users joined to your homegroup; however, those users can only view the contents of the folder. The Homegroup (Read/Write) option makes the folder available to other users joined to your homegroup, and those users can view and modify the contents of the folder. The Specific people option opens the File Sharing Wizard so you can choose with whom you want to share the folder.

▶ **2.** On the Share with menu, click **Specific people**. Windows 7 opens the File Sharing dialog box. On the computer used for Figure 12-36, Windows 7 lists the Permission Level of Remy, an Administrator account, as Owner. Your user account name and permission level will differ.

Figure 12-36 File Sharing dialog box for choosing a person to share a folder with

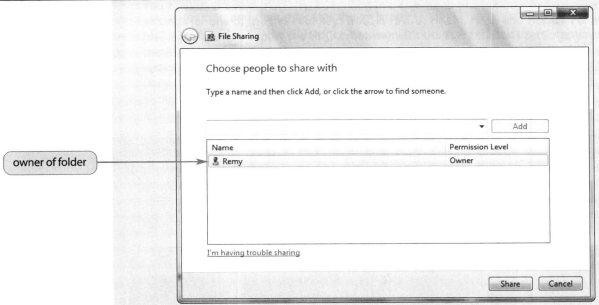

owner of folder

A user with Owner permission can view, edit, delete, or add a shared file. Plus that user can configure sharing, or remove sharing from, the folder. To share this account with other users, you can type the name of the user or group with whom you want to share the folder or file, or you can choose the user or a group from a drop-down list.

▶ **3.** Click the **Choose people to share with** arrow, and then click **Everyone**. If you choose Everyone, the folder is shared with all users on the same computer. The "Choose people to share with" box includes the names of other user accounts on the same computer as well as Homegroup and Everyone.

▶ **4.** Click the **Add** button. The File Sharing Wizard adds the user or group under "Name" and assigns the user or group the Read permission level, the default permission level. See Figure 12-37. The Read permission level indicates that a user or group can open a folder (or file) and view its content, but not change or delete it.

Figure 12-37 Users sharing the same folder

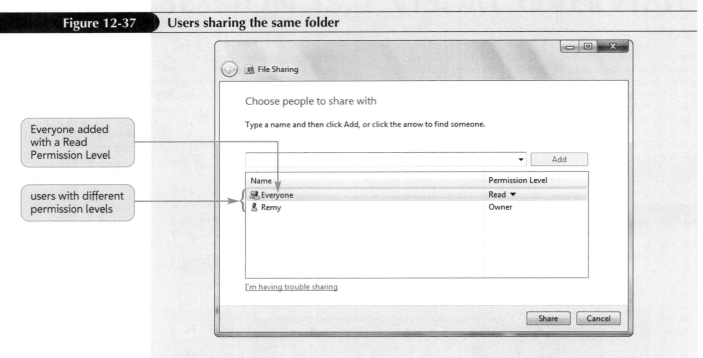

Everyone added with a Read Permission Level

users with different permission levels

5. Under Permission Level, click the **Read** arrow. From this list, you can choose one of three permissions—Read, Read/Write, or Remove. With the Read/Write permission level, a user can view, edit, delete, or add a shared file.

6. Click **Read** (the already-selected default option), and then click the **Share** button. As shown in Figure 12-38, the File Sharing Wizard reports that the folder is shared and shows the UNC path to the folder. Your UNC path will differ.

Figure 12-38 File sharing operation completed

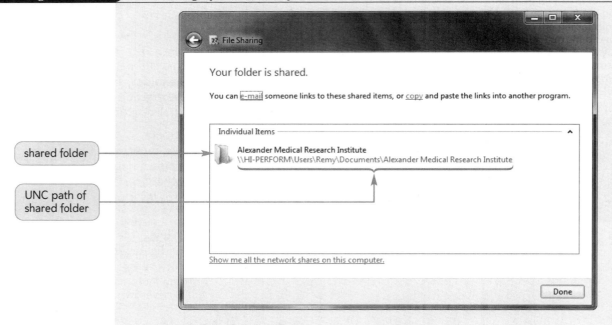

shared folder

UNC path of shared folder

7. Click the **Done** button. Windows 7 closes the File Sharing dialog box.

To access this file, other users open a Network window, open a window onto the networked computer where the shared folder is located, open the Users folder, open the user account folder, and then open the Documents folder. For faster access later, you can create a desktop shortcut to this folder. Any file you put or create in the Alexander Medical Research Institute folder will be shared so everyone on the same network can open the file.

To remove sharing from a folder:

▶ **1.** Right-click the **Alexander Medical Research Institute** folder, point to **Share with**, and then click **Nobody**. The File Sharing Wizard removes permission for all users and groups except the owner.

Now, other users on the network cannot open the Alexander Medical Research Institute folder or its files.

REFERENCE

Sharing a New Folder with Specific People

- To view sharing properties of a newly created folder, open the folder where you want to create a new folder.
- Click Organize on the toolbar, click Folder and search options, click the View tab, and scroll to the bottom of the Advanced settings box, and if necessary, enable the Use Sharing Wizard (Recommended) by adding a check mark to the check box, and then click OK to close the Folder Options dialog box.
- Click the New folder button on the toolbar, type a name for the new folder, and then press the Enter key.
- Right-click the folder, point to Share with, and then Specific people.
- Click the "Choose people to share with" arrow button, click Everyone (or specify individual users), and then click the Add button.
- Under Permission Level, click the Read arrow for the user or group you just added, choose Read or Read/Write, click the Share button, and then click the Done button.
- If you later want to remove sharing for all users and groups except the owner, right-click the folder, point to Share with, and then click Nobody.

You can also use Advanced Sharing to share a folder. To use Advanced Sharing, you must supply Administrator credentials.

To use Advanced Sharing:

▶ **1.** Right-click the **Alexander Medical Research Institute** folder, click **Properties**, and then click the **Sharing** tab in the folder's Properties dialog box. Under Advanced Sharing, Windows 7 notes that you can set custom permissions, create multiple shares, and set other advanced sharing options. See Figure 12-39.

Figure 12-39 | **Viewing the Advanced Sharing option**

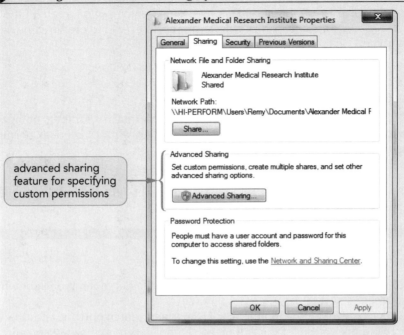

advanced sharing
feature for specifying
custom permissions

2. Click the **Advanced Sharing** button, provide Administrator credentials (if necessary), and in the Advanced Sharing dialog box, click the **Share this folder** check box to select it. As shown in Figure 12-40, Windows 7 enables options in the Advancing Sharing dialog box, lists the folder name as the Share name, and limits the number of simultaneous users to 20. You can change the Share name if you prefer, and you can also change the number of users who can access this folder at the same time.

Figure 12-40 | **Enabling sharing for a folder**

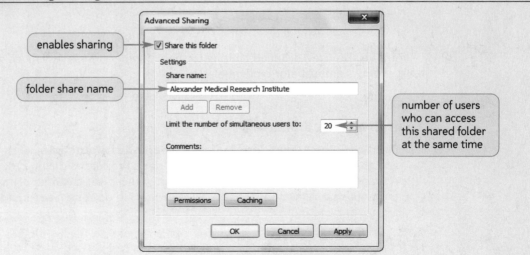

enables sharing

folder share name

number of users
who can access
this shared folder
at the same time

3. Click the **Permissions** button. Windows 7 shows share permissions in the Group or user names box for Everyone. See Figure 12-41.

Figure 12-41   Viewing permissions for a shared folder

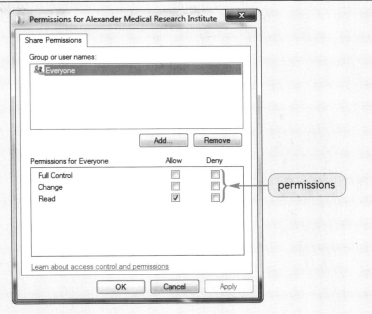

In the Permissions for Everyone box, you can specify Full Control (equivalent to the owner) or Change (so users can modify the file), or you can keep the default Read permission. You can also use the Add button to add users or groups, and the Remove button to remove users or groups. Remember that if you grant access to the Everyone group, anyone who accesses the computer from a domain or workgroup has access to the folder at the permission level you specified.

4. In the Permissions for Alexander Medical Research Institute dialog box, click the **OK** button to keep the default Read permission for Everyone.

5. In the Advanced Sharing dialog box, click the **Caching** button. In the Offline Settings dialog box, you can specify whether users can access this shared resource when they are working offline, and how. See Figure 12-42.

Figure 12-42   Specifying offline settings

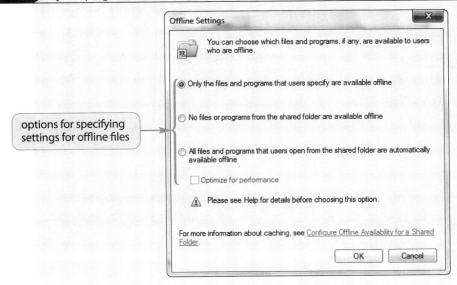

Offline files are copies of files on the network that are stored locally (see the "Working with Offline Files" Insight box for more information on the Offline Files feature). You can specify that Offline Files include only the files and programs that users designate as available offline, you can specify that no files or programs from the shared folder are available offline, or you can specify all files and programs opened by the user are available in Offline Files. The first option is useful in cases where the user needs access to files when not connected to the network, such as when traveling with a mobile laptop, or when experiencing a slow network connection. The second option ensures that documents containing sensitive information are available only via a network connection. The third option is useful when a user needs to work with all the files in a shared folder on a frequent basis. If you choose the third option, you can enable the "Optimize for performance" option, which caches and makes available executable files in a local cache.

6. Click the **OK** button in the Offline Settings dialog box, click the **OK** button in the Advanced Sharing dialog box, and then click the **Close** button in the Alexander Medical Research Institute Properties dialog box.

To make files available offline, you need to enable Offline Files by opening the Control Panel and then searching for the link for managing offline files in the Sync Center. On the General property sheet in the Offline Files dialog box shown in Figure 12-43, you click the Enable offline files button, provide Administrator credentials, and then restart your computer. When you decide to make a file available offline, you right-click the file, and then you click "Always Available Offline." To access offline files, you can click "View offline files" button on the General property sheet of the Offline Files dialog box. Also, if you are using a shared network folder and want to work with a file offline, you can select the file, and then click the "Work Offline" button on the toolbar.

Figure 12-43 **Managing offline files**

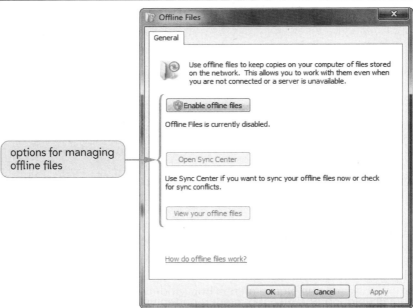

Working with the Offline Files Feature

By using the Offline Files feature, you can work with files even when not connected to the network (such as when you are traveling or working at home). Once you reconnect to that network, Windows 7 automatically updates the files on the network (or vice versa). Also, by working offline, you free up network resources, reduce network traffic, and guarantee better network performance, all of which are especially important in a workplace environment.

If you change your mind later about sharing a folder, you can remove advanced sharing from that folder.

To remove advanced sharing from a folder:

▶ **1.** Right-click the **Alexander Medical Research Institute** folder, click **Properties**, click the **Sharing** tab, and click the **Advanced Sharing** button and if necessary, provide Administrator credentials.

▶ **2.** In the Advanced Sharing dialog box, click the **Share this folder** check box to deselect it, click the **OK** button in the Advanced Sharing dialog box, and then click the **Close** button in the Alexander Medical Research Institute Properties dialog box.

Trouble? If Windows 7 displays a Sharing dialog box and informs you that there are one or more files open by one or more users connected to this folder and also informs you that if you stop sharing, the files will close and you might lose data, click the Yes button.

▶ **3.** Close the My Documents window.

Now, other users on the same network cannot open the Alexander Medical Research Institute folder or its files.

Using Advanced Sharing to Share a Folder

- Right-click the folder you want to share, click Properties, and in the folder Properties dialog box, click the Sharing tab.
- Click the Advanced Sharing button, provide Administrator credentials, and in the Advanced Sharing dialog box, click the "Share this folder" check box to select it.
- To specify permissions, click the Permissions button, adjust permissions for the group or user, click the Add button to add new users (and then adjust their permissions), and then click the OK button.
- In the Advanced Sharing dialog box, click the Caching button, choosing the caching option you want to use, and then click the OK button.
- Click the OK button in the Advanced Sharing dialog box, and then click the Close button in the folder's Properties dialog box to apply your share settings.
- To enable offline caching, open the Control Panel, search for *offline files*, click the Manage offline files link, click the Enable offline files button on the General property sheet, provide Administrator credentials, and then restart your computer.

Sharing of folders on a network enables selected users or all users to access and work with the same files and thereby improves productivity.

Creating a Mapped Drive

To simplify access to shared folders on a network, you can create mapped drives to provide easy access to network resources.

Remy suggests you create a mapped drive to the shared Alexander Medical Research Institute folder on the network.

In the following steps, you will create a mapped drive on another computer in your network. That means the other computer must have a shared network folder. If you are working in a computer lab and are not able to perform this operation, read the following steps and examine the figures, but do not keystroke the steps.

To create a mapped drive:

1. From the Start menu, click **Network**, and in the Network window, click the **icon** of a computer on your network, and if Windows 7 displays a Windows Security dialog box, enter the user name and password for the user account open on the other network computer, and then click the **OK** button. Windows 7 displays shared folders and devices on that networked computer.

2. Right-click a **shared network** folder icon of your own choice, and then click **Map network drive**. Windows 7 opens a Map Network Drive dialog box, as shown in Figure 12-44.

Figure 12-44 ▶ **Specifying settings for mapping a network drive**

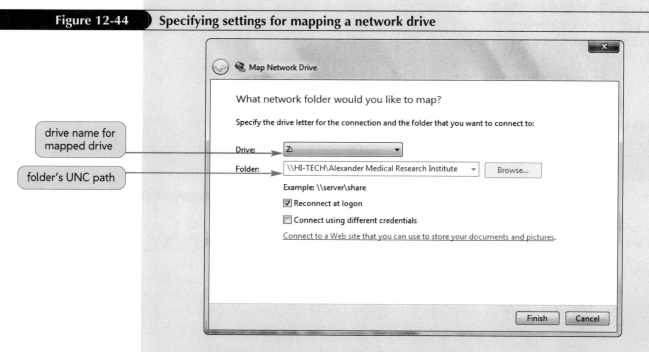

In the Drive box of the Map Network Drive dialog box, you can select a drive name to map to the shared folder. Drive names are listed and used in reverse alphabetical order. The Folder box shows the UNC path to the shared folder. You also have the options of reconnecting to the mapped drive at logon and connecting under different credentials.

3. To use drive Z (or the next available drive name), click the **Finish** button, and after Windows 7 opens a window onto the mapped drive, switch to Extra Large Icons view or Large Icons view (whichever you prefer) and widen the Navigation pane so you can see the mapped drive listed under Computer. See Figure 12-45. If you examine the Address bar, you will notice that the mapped drive is accessible from the Computer window, and you can view the UNC path. Your shared folder name and path will differ.

Figure 12-45　　Viewing the contents of a mapped drive

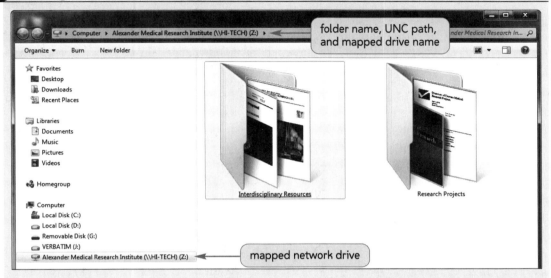

4. Click **Computer** in the Address bar. Under Network Location in the Computer window, Windows 7 displays a new drive Z for the shared network folder. See Figure 12-46. As part of the drive's friendly name, Windows 7 also shows the UNC path to the network computer that contains the shared folder.

Figure 12-46　　Viewing a mapped drive in the Computer window

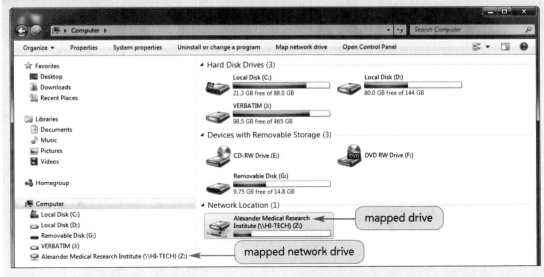

5. Keep the Computer window open for the next set of steps.

Like regular shortcuts, mapped drives provide quick access to shared folders on a network. Furthermore, you can create desktop shortcuts to the mapped drives.

PROSKILLS

Problem Solving: Using Mapped Drives and Network Locations to Access Network Resources

You probably already rely on the use of bookmarks to navigate the Internet, another important network that is connected to your computer and network. Mapped drives represent another important way to automate the use of your network and provide fast access to network resources without the need to enter a network address, navigate your network, or search for those resources. You can also create network connections to FTP sites. If you open the Computer window, you can use the Map network drive button on the toolbar to create a mapped drive or open the Add Location Network Wizard to create a connection to an FTP site for uploading and downloading files. After you create a connection to an FTP site, Windows 7 places a custom icon for a file folder under Network Locations in the Computer window. You can then create a desktop shortcut to either a mapped drive or an FTP network location for even faster access to interconnected network resources. By combining techniques you've already learned, you can streamline your work environment and improve your productivity.

If you no longer need a mapped drive, you can disconnect it.

To disconnect a mapped drive:

▶ **1.** In the Computer window, right-click the **mapped drive**, and then click **Disconnect**. Windows 7 no longer displays the mapped drive in the Computer window and in the Navigation pane. The shared folder still exists; however, there is no mapped drive for that shared folder.

▶ **2.** Close the Computer window, and then close the window for the other computer on your network.

Mapped drives simplify access to shared networked folders.

REFERENCE

Creating and Disconnecting a Mapped Drive

- From the Start menu, click Network, and in the Network window, click the icon of a computer on your network.
- If Windows 7 displays a Windows Security dialog box, enter the user name and password for the user account open on the other network computer, and then click the OK button.
- Right-click a shared network folder icon, and then click Map network drive, click the Drive list button, select a mapped drive name, and then click the Finish button.
- To disconnect a mapped drive, open a Computer window under your user account on your computer, right-click the mapped drive, and then click Disconnect.

Using the HomeGroup Feature to Share Network Resources

Windows 7 introduces the new HomeGroup networking feature so users on different Windows 7 computer systems can easily share libraries and printers with other computers in the same homegroup. Each computer in a homegroup must be set up as a Home network. When a user creates a homegroup, it is automatically password protected, and other users who want to join the homegroup must know its password. After a user creates or joins a homegroup, all other user accounts on that same computer, except for the Guest account, are members of the same homegroup.

If a user on a different computer wants to access files or printers on another computer that already has a homegroup, that user must first join that computer's homegroup. When a user creates or joins a homegroup, that user decides what libraries they want to share and whether to share printers. Then each user can easily access other homegroup computers from the Navigation pane; however, those homegroup computers are not available (or displayed in the Navigation pane) if they are turned off or if they are in a sleep state or in hibernation. A user can leave a homegroup at any time, and if all users leave a homegroup, the homegroup no longer exists.

All Windows 7 editions support the use of the HomeGroup feature. However, users on a Windows 7 Starter or Windows 7 Home Basic computer cannot create a homegroup; they can only join a homegroup. Also, computers that belong to a domain can join and access files shared by other users, but they cannot share files with a homegroup.

When you first install Windows 7 on a computer, the Setup installation program includes an option for setting up a homegroup near the end of the installation process.

Remy suggests that you set up a homegroup on your computer so your coworker can join that group and share files that you both need for your job.

To complete the steps in this section of the tutorial, your Windows 7 computer must be set up as a workgroup on a Home network, and there must be at least one other Windows 7 computer also set up as a workgroup on the same Home network. If your computer is set up as a Public network, you cannot create or join a homegroup. Also, to create a homegroup, your Windows 7 computer must use an edition of Windows 7 other than Windows 7 Home Starter or Windows 7 Home Basic.

If you do not have a homegroup on your Home network and want to create a homegroup, complete the following steps. If you already have a homegroup on your computer and do not want to change that homegroup, do not keystroke the following steps, but instead read the steps and examine the figures. If you are working in a computer lab at your college, ask your instructor or lab support staff whether you can create a homegroup.

To create a homegroup:

TIP

You can click Homegroup in the Navigation pane or choose HomeGroup in the Control Panel to create a new homegroup.

▶ **1.** Click the **Network** icon for your wired or wireless connection in the notification area of the taskbar, click the **Open Network and Sharing Center** link, and then click the **Choose homegroup and sharing options** link in the Network and Sharing Center window. In the HomeGroup window, Windows 7 notes that there is currently no homegroup for the computer used in Figure 12-47.

Trouble? If you already have a homegroup, Windows 7 opens a HomeGroup window where you can change homegroup settings. Read the discussion for this step, read but do not keystroke Steps 2–6, and then complete Steps 7–9.

Trouble? If there is only an option for joining a homegroup, read but do not keystroke the steps in this section of the tutorial. The explanatory text after these steps describe the process for joining an existing homegroup.

Figure 12-47 Creating a homegroup

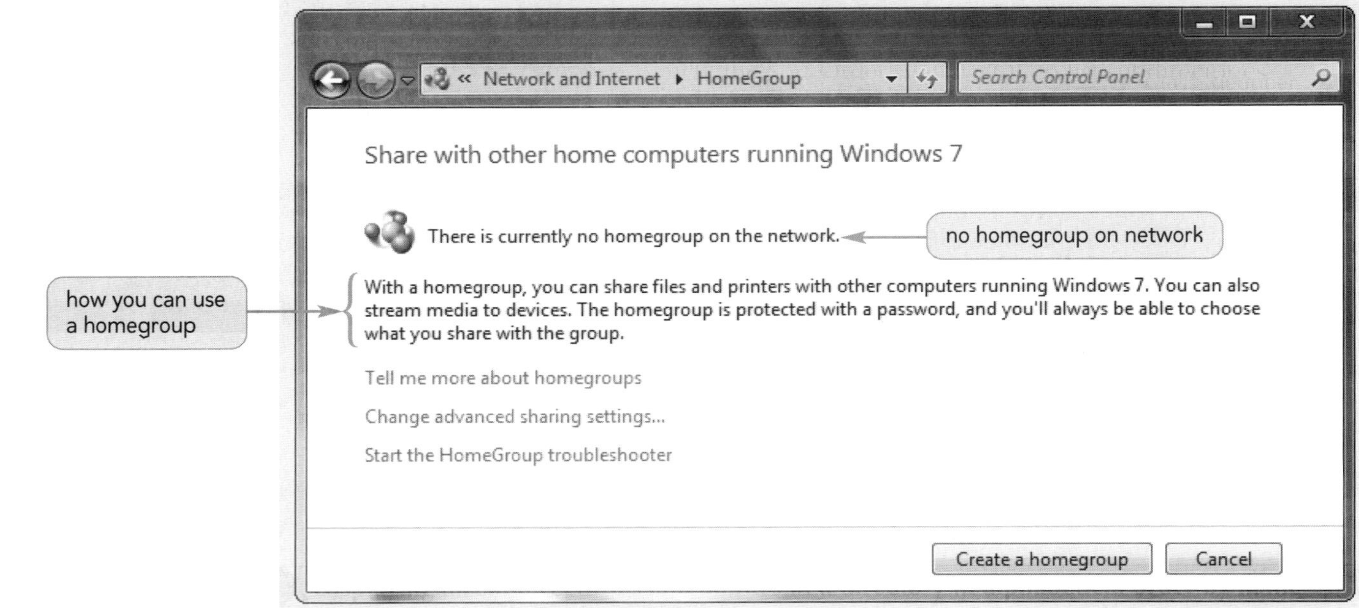

<< Network and Internet ▸ HomeGroup   ▾ ↕⁷   Search Control Panel

Share with other home computers running Windows 7

There is currently no homegroup on the network. ◄—— no homegroup on network

how you can use a homegroup ——►

With a homegroup, you can share files and printers with other computers running Windows 7. You can also stream media to devices. The homegroup is protected with a password, and you'll always be able to choose what you share with the group.

Tell me more about homegroups

Change advanced sharing settings...

Start the HomeGroup troubleshooter

Create a homegroup   Cancel

Windows 7 notes that you can share files and printers with other Windows 7 computers if you have a homegroup, and that you can also stream media to devices in that homegroup. Each homegroup is password protected, and you can decide what to share with other computers in the same homegroup when you create or join a homegroup. This window also includes a link to the Start the HomeGroup troubleshooter.

▶ 2. Click the **Create a homegroup** button. In the Create a Homegroup dialog box, you select what you want to share. You can share any or all of the Documents, Pictures, Music, Videos, and Printers folders. See Figure 12-48.

Figure 12-48 Selecting folders to share in a new homegroup

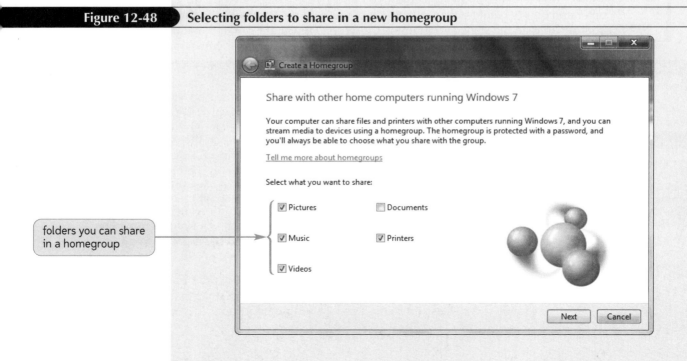

Create a Homegroup

Share with other home computers running Windows 7

Your computer can share files and printers with other computers running Windows 7, and you can stream media to devices using a homegroup. The homegroup is protected with a password, and you'll always be able to choose what you share with the group.

Tell me more about homegroups

Select what you want to share:

folders you can share in a homegroup ——►

☑ Pictures   ☐ Documents

☑ Music   ☑ Printers

☑ Videos

Next   Cancel

Windows 7 selects all these libraries except the Documents library, so you have to decide whether you also want to share that library. The Public Documents folder in the Documents library is automatically shared, so you may not need or want to share your My Documents folder within that same library.

▶ **3.** Click the **Next** button. After Windows 7 creates a homegroup, the next Create a Homegroup dialog box identifies the password others need to use to add other computers to your homegroup and then to access files and printers located on those other computers. See Figure 12-49.

Figure 12-49 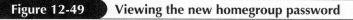 **Viewing the new homegroup password**

why you need this homegroup password

new homegroup password

what to do if you forget the homegroup password

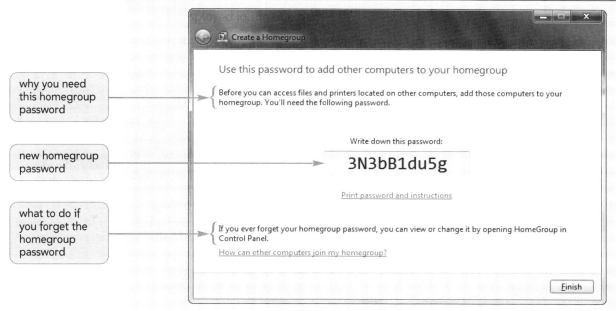

Windows 7 recommends you write down this password; however, it also notes that if you ever forget your homegroup password, you can view or change it by opening HomeGroup from the Control Panel. To guarantee that you have this password, you can print it. You may also want to change your homegroup password to make it easier to remember; however, if you do so, choose a strong password to protect your homegroup.

▶ **4.** If you want to print your homegroup password, click the **Print password and instructions** link. The "View and print your homegroup password" window opens and lists the steps for joining a homegroup. It also notes that computers that are turned off or sleeping do not appear in the homegroup. Sleeping includes a Hybrid Sleep or Standard Sleep state as well as Hibernation.

▶ **5.** To continue the process for printing a homegroup password, click the **Print this page** button. If you want to print this page to an XPS document file, click **Microsoft XPS Document Writer** under Select Printer, click the **Print** button, type **HomeGroup Password**, and then click the **Save** button. If you want a printed copy of this page, select a printer (if necessary), and then click the **Print** button.

6. If necessary, close the "View and print your homegroup password" window, and then click the **Finish** button. In the HomeGroup window, Windows 7 notes that your computer now belongs to a homegroup, identifies shared libraries and printers, lists links for sharing additional libraries and excluding files and folders, includes an option for sharing media with devices, and includes links for other homegroup actions—viewing and printing the homegroup password, changing the homegroup password, leaving the homegroup, changing advanced settings, and starting the HomeGroup troubleshooter. You examined advanced settings earlier in the Network and Sharing Center.

7. Close the HomeGroup window.

8. From the Start menu, click **Network**, and then click **Homegroup** in the Navigation pane. In the Homegroup window on the computer used for Figure 12-50, Windows 7 notes that there are no other people in the homegroup, and it lists the steps that a user on another Windows 7 computer must complete to join the homegroup. From this window, you can also view the homegroup password and view homegroup settings.

| Figure 12-50 | How other users can join a homegroup |

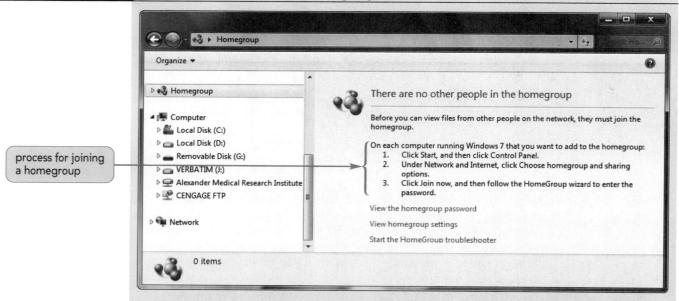

9. Close the Homegroup window.

If a user later wants to share additional folders and files, or a custom library they've created, that user can use the Share with button on the toolbar of a folder window, and then choose either Homegroup (Read) or Homegroup (Read/Write), as shown in Figure 12-51. Later, if that user decides to no longer share those folders and files, the user can choose the Nobody option on the Share with menu.

Figure 12-51   Sharing a folder on a homegroup

options for sharing a folder on a homegroup

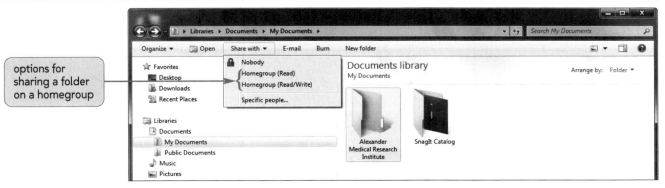

If a user on another Windows 7 computer wants to join an existing homegroup, that user can click the Network icon in the taskbar notification area, click the "Open Network and Sharing Center" link, and then click the "Choose homegroup and sharing options" link in the Network and Sharing Center window. Windows 7 then displays a HomeGroup window where that user can choose the option to share with other home computers running Windows 7, as shown on the Windows 7 Home Premium laptop (with Windows Aero turned off) used for Figure 12-52. Windows 7 also notes that Remy on HI-PERFORM has created a homegroup on the network.

Figure 12-52   Accessing a homegroup from another computer

homegroup creator

what you can do by joining a homegroup

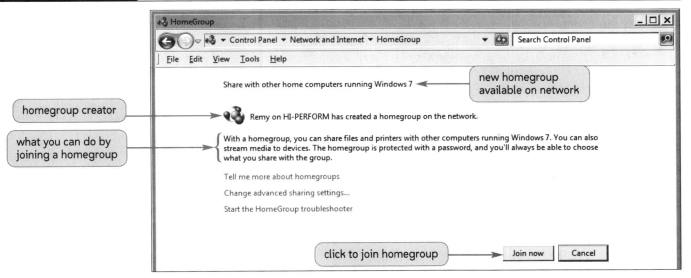

To join this homegroup, the user of that computer clicks the Join now button, and then on that computer, Windows 7 displays a Join a Homegroup dialog box where that user selects the options for sharing specific libraries as well as printers (with the same choices shown in the earlier Figure 12-48). Windows 7 also informs you that it detected a homegroup on your network, and notes that you can not only share files and printers with other computers running Windows 7, but you can also stream media to devices.

After the Windows 7 Home Premium user advances to the next step, Windows 7 prompts for the homegroup password, as shown in Figure 12-53, and notes that the other user can get the password from Remy on HI-PERFORM or from another member of the homegroup.

Figure 12-53 Joining a homegroup by specifying its password

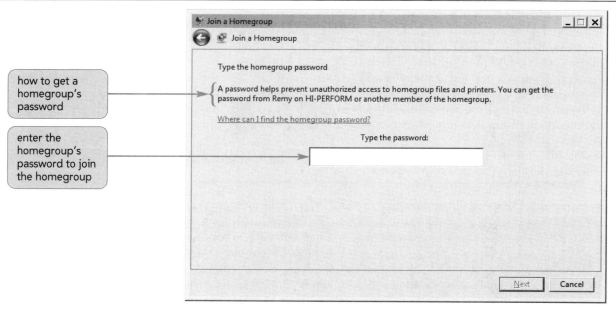

how to get a homegroup's password

enter the homegroup's password to join the homegroup

The next Join a Homegroup dialog box informs that user he or she has joined the homegroup, and that he or she can now access files and printers shared by other people in the homegroup. That user can then click the Finish button in the Join a Homegroup dialog box. (On the computer where the homegroup was created, Windows 7 informed Remy that it detected a homegroup printer and offered the option to install that printer.)

After joining the homegroup, Windows 7 displays another HomeGroup window where the new homegroup user has the option of changing the homegroup settings, including which libraries and printers to share, and whether to stream pictures, music, and videos to all devices on the home network. Windows 7 also notes that shared media is not secure, and that anyone connected to your network can receive your shared media. If that new homegroup user opens a Homegroup window on the Windows 7 Home Premium laptop, as shown in Figure 12-54, that user has the option of browsing Remy's shared libraries. In the Navigation pane, Windows 7 provides a link to Remy's computer and its shared libraries.

Figure 12-54 Viewing links to a homegroup member

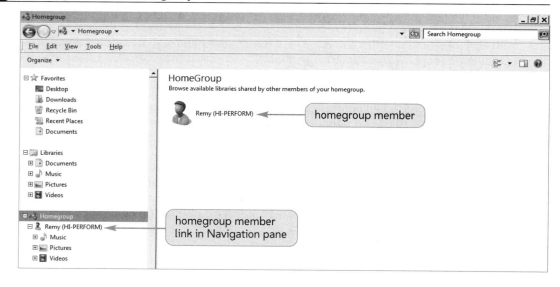

homegroup member

homegroup member link in Navigation pane

If Remy opens his Homegroup window, Windows 7 displays an icon for the networked computer of the new member of the homegroup (namely, Remy's coworker Betty). See Figure 12-55. If Remy opens a window onto that user's HomeGroup connection, he has access to her shared folders—Music, Pictures, and Videos—and the folders and files within those shared folders.

Figure 12-55   Viewing a new homegroup member

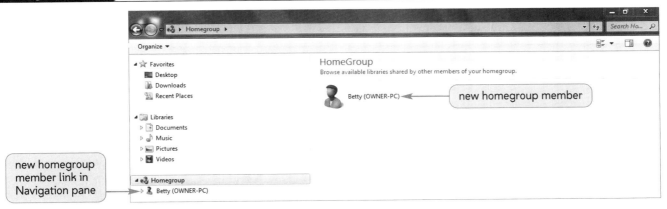

If Remy's coworker wanted to leave the HomeGroup, she could open the Network and Sharing Center and use the "Choose homegroup and sharing options" link to open a HomeGroup window. That coworker would then use the "Leave the homegroup" link to open the Leave the Homegroup dialog box shown in Figure 12-56 where she can then choose the "Leave the homegroup" option. Windows 7 notes that this option disconnects all homegroup connections and that if that user leaves the homegroup, they cannot access homegroup files and printers.

Figure 12-56   Options for leaving or remaining in a homegroup

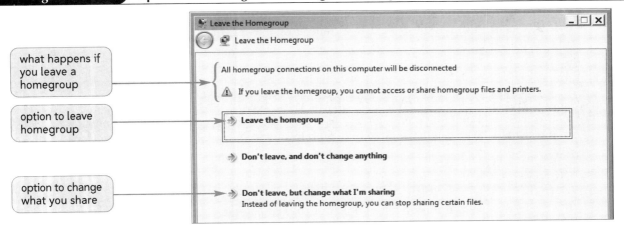

After leaving a homegroup, Windows 7 verifies that the operation was successful and that the user's files are no longer shared with the homegroup.

If you want to leave the homegroup on the computer you are using, complete the following steps. If you do not want to change that homegroup, do not keystroke the following steps, but instead read the steps and examine the figures.

To leave a homegroup:

▶ **1.** From the Start menu, open Control Panel, click **Network and Internet**, and then click the **Choose homegroup and sharing options** link.

▶ **2.** Click the **Leave the homegroup** link, click the **Leave the homegroup** option in the Leave the Homegroup dialog box, and after Windows 7 informs you that you have successfully left the homegroup, click the **Finish** button.

▶ **3.** Close the Homegroup window.

The HomeGroup feature is yet another important way that you can share resources on a Home network.

REFERENCE

Creating, Joining, and Leaving a HomeGroup

- To create a homegroup, open the Start menu, click Control Panel, click the Network and Internet link in the Control Panel window, click the HomeGroup link, click the "Create a homegroup" button, select the libraries you want to share, decide whether to share printers, click the Next button, record or print your homegroup password, and then close the HomeGroup window.
- To access resources in a homegroup, click Network on the Start menu, click HomeGroup in the Navigation pane, and then select and open a shared resource on another HomeGroup computer.
- If another user wants to join the homegroup, that user opens the Control Panel, clicks the "Choose homegroup and sharing settings" link, clicks the Join now button, selects the libraries that user wants to share, decides on whether to share printers, enters the homegroup password, and clicks Finish.
- To leave a homegroup, open the Control Panel, click the Network and Internet link, click the "Choose homegroup and sharing options" link, click the "Leave the home-group" link, click the "Leave the homegroup" option in the Leave the HomeGroup dialog box, click the Finish button, and close the Homegroup window.

Restoring Your Computer's Settings

If you are working in a computer lab, or if you want to restore your desktop computer to the settings that existed prior to working on this tutorial, complete the following steps.

To restore your computer's settings:

▶ **1.** To remove the shared network folder that you created earlier in the tutorial, open the **My Documents** folder, right-click the **Alexander Medical Research Institute** shared folder, click **Delete**, and in the Delete Folder dialog box, click the **Yes** button.

▶ **2.** Close the My Documents window.

▶ **3.** If necessary, use the Folder Options dialog box to turn off single-click activation (or Web style); to not display hidden folders, files, and drives; and to hide protected operating system files.

▶ **4.** If you changed your computer setting for the Sharing Wizard, enable or turn off the "Use Sharing Wizard (Recommended)" option, and then click the **OK** button to close the Folder Options dialog box.

▶ **5.** If you want to remove the Devices and Printers option or the Network option from your Start menu, right-click the **Start** button ⊕, click **Properties**, click the **Customize** button on the Start Menu property sheet, locate and click **Devices and Printers** in the Customize Start Menu list of options (to remove the check mark from the check box), locate and click **Network** in the Customize Start Menu list of options (to remove the check mark from the check box), click the **OK** button to close the Customize Start Menu dialog box, and click the **OK** button to close the Taskbar and Start Menu Properties dialog box.

▶ **6.** If necessary, use the Start menu to remove the Computer icon from the desktop.

After your examination of network tools in Windows 7, you are now ready to assist Remy in setting up, configuring, customizing, and troubleshooting computers at the Alexander Medical Research Institute and to help users connect to the Institute's network so they have access to the resources they need.

REVIEW

Session 12.2 Quick Check

1. What is a peer-to-peer network or workgroup?
2. The _____ identifies the location of a networked computer as well as shared resources on a network.
3. If _____ is enabled, your computer can detect other computers and devices on the same network, and those other computers can also detect your computer.
4. Explain what the following notation means: \\HI-TECH\Alexander Medical Research Institute
5. True or False. One advantage of the Offline Files feature is that you can work with files even when not connected to the network (such as when you are traveling or working at home).
6. Briefly describe three ways in which you can share a folder.
7. A(n) _____ is a shared network folder that is assigned a drive name.
8. True or False. A homegroup can include computers with Windows 7 as well as computers with other Windows versions.

Practice the skills you learned in the tutorial using the same case scenario.

PRACTICE

Review Assignments

There are no Data Files needed for the Review Assignments.

Remy asks you to assist him with documenting hardware and network settings on a new set of computers that were purchased for use by a research group at Alexander Medical Research Institute.

As you complete each step in these Review Assignments, record your answers to the questions so you can submit them to your instructor. Use a word-processing application, such as Word or WordPad, to prepare your answers to these questions. To save time in reporting or recording information, use Alt+Print Scrn to capture images of property sheets and paste the images into your Word or WordPad document. If you change any settings on the computer you are using, note the original settings so you can restore them later.

To open Device Manager and view all the properties of a device, you must provide Administrator credentials. To complete some of the network steps, the computer you are using must be connected to a workgroup set up as a Home network.

Complete the following steps:

1. From the Start menu, open Devices and Printers. What types of devices does Windows 7 identify on your computer? What is the default printer? Are there any network printers and, if so, how do you know they are network printers? Close the Devices and Printers window.

2. Open Device Manager. Does Device Manager identify any hardware problems? If so, what types of hardware problems are they, and how you might resolve them?

3. Expand Computer in the hardware tree. How does Device Manager identify your computer?

4. Expand Disk drives. List the names of your disk drives, and identify the type of each drive. Which drive is your internal hard disk drive? View properties of your hard disk drive. What write-caching policy does your hard disk drive use, and how does Windows 7 handle write caching? Are there any other options for handling write caching, and if so, what are they? Close the Properties dialog box for your hard disk drive.

5. Expand the Network adapters category. How does Device Manager identify your network adapter? View properties of your network adapter. What resource settings are assigned to your network adapter? Are there any device conflicts? What power management options are available for your network adapter? Close the Properties dialog box for your network adapter.

6. Expand the Processors category. What type of processor or processors does your computer have? Does your computer have multiple processors or a multicore processor?

7. Expand the Universal Serial Bus controllers category. Does your computer support USB 3.0, USB 2.0, and USB 1.x? Explain how you arrived at this conclusion using information in Device Manager. Close Device Manager.

8. Open the System window. What is your computer's name, and is the computer you are using part of a workgroup or a domain? Close the System window.

9. From the Start menu, open the Network window. What computers does Windows 7 identify as part of your network? Open a window onto one of the network computers, and identify what types of shared resources (if any) are available, and then return to the Network window.

10. Open the Network and Sharing Center. Draw a diagram of your computer network using the network map provided by Windows 7. Is your network a Home, Work, or Public network?

11. Use the Network and Sharing Center's link to open the HomeGroup window. Does your computer belong to a homegroup, and if so, what resources does your homegroup share?

12. Describe two ways in which you can share a folder with and without a homegroup. How can you remove sharing from a folder with and without a homegroup?

13. Open a Computer window. Are there any mapped drives, and if so, what is the drive name, and what is the UNC path for one of the mapped drives? What process can you use to create a mapped drive? Close the Computer window and any other open windows.

14. Submit your answers to the questions in the review assignments to your instructor, either in printed or electronic form, as requested.

Use your skills to identify a hardware configuration problem.

APPLY

Case Problem 1

There are no Data Files needed for this Case Problem.

WTI Insurers, Inc.   Eunice Lyons works as technical support specialist and troubleshooter for WTI Insurers, Inc. During a job interview for a position as her assistant, she asks you to identify and describe how you would resolve a hardware device problem. To assist you with this task, she hands you a printed copy of the Device Manager hardware tree shown in Figure 12-57.

Figure 12-57   **Evaluating a hardware device problem**

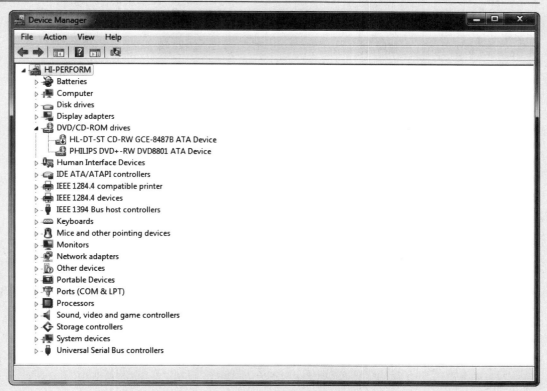

As you complete each question, record your answer so you can submit them to your instructor. Use a word-processing application, such as Word or WordPad, to prepare and then print your answers to these questions. If you change any settings on the computer you are using, note the original settings so you can restore them later. Use Figure 12-57 to answer the following questions:

1. What device does Device Manager identify as a problem?

2. What type of hardware configuration problem has occurred?

3. How can you use Device Manager to obtain information about this problem?

4. How can you correct this problem using Device Manager?

5. Submit your answers to this case problem to your instructor, either in printed or electronic form, as requested.

Use your skills to troubleshoot a hardware problem.

APPLY

Case Problem 2

There are no Data Files needed for this Case Problem.

Safety First Chimney Services Ruben Dickson operates his own chimney services company and keeps track of all his clients, billing, financial information, taxes, and other business information on his networked laptop. Recently, he encountered a problem with one of the hardware devices on his computer, and he has asked you to help him identify and troubleshoot the problem. You start by examining the Device Manager hardware tree on his computer. See Figure 12-58.

Figure 12-58 **Identifying and troubleshooting a hardware device problem**

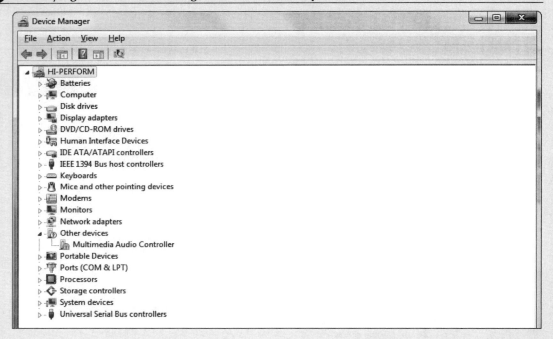

As you complete each question, record your answer so you can submit them to your instructor. Use a word-processing application, such as Word or WordPad, to prepare your answers to these questions. If you change any settings on the computer you are using, note the original settings so you can restore them later. Use Figure 12-58 to answer the following questions:

1. What device does Device Manager identify as a problem?

2. What type of hardware configuration problem has occurred?

3. How can you use Device Manager to obtain information about this problem?

EXPLORE

4. How can you use System Information to obtain information about this problem?

5. What is the most likely cause of this problem, and what approaches can you use to resolve this problem?

6. Submit your answers to this case problem to your instructor, either in printed or electronic form, as requested.

Use your skills to troubleshoot a hardware installation problem.

APPLY

Case Problem 3

There are no Data Files needed for this Case Problem.

Specialists To Go   Antwan Bourdon works for a temporary employment agency that places network specialists and technical support personnel on temporary assignments for businesses in the greater Chicago metropolitan area. At Antwan's latest temporary job assignment, Device Manager reports a hardware problem when he attempts to install an inkjet printer on a computer for his client, as shown in Figure 12-59. Antwan asks you to help him figure out the best approach to take in resolving this problem.

Figure 12-59	Troubleshooting a hardware problem after installing a printer

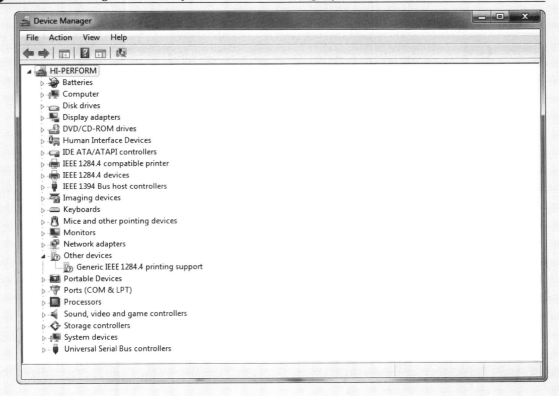

As you complete each question, record your answer so you can submit them to your instructor. Use a word-processing application, such as Word or WordPad, to prepare your answers to these questions. If you change any settings on the computer you are using, note the original settings so you can restore them later. Use Figure 12-59 to answer the following questions:

1. What device does Device Manager identify as a problem?
2. What do you think caused this hardware problem?

⊕ **EXPLORE**

3. After examining the General property sheet for this device, you discover that Windows 7 reports that the device is working; however, you are unable to print with this device. When you examine the Driver property sheet, Windows 7 notes that the Driver Provider is unknown, the Driver Date and Driver Version are not available, and that the driver is not digitally signed. When you open the Driver File Details dialog box, Windows 7 reports that no driver files are required or have been loaded for this device. You also discover that System Information does not report any problems with hardware devices. Does this additional information confirm your initial conclusion? Explain.

⊕ **EXPLORE**

4. How would you correct this problem using the information found in Device Manager?

5. Submit your answers to this case problem to your instructor, either in printed or electronic form, as requested.

Extend your skills to set up a small home network.

Case Problem 4

CHALLENGE

There are no Data Files needed for this Case Problem.

Mark West Modeling Company Rex Soliz is the IT specialist for Mark West Modeling Company in New York City. He has enlisted your help in working with two employees who have asked for assistance in reviewing the process for setting up a home network for when they are working from home.

To complete this case problem, you must be working on a networked computer that is part of a workgroup. As you complete each step in this case problem, record your answers to the questions so you can submit them to your instructor. Use a word-processing application, such as Word or WordPad, to prepare your answers to these questions. If you change any settings on the computer you are using, note the original settings so you can restore them later. Complete the following steps:

1. Locate the Computer name, Computer description, and Workgroup for your computer. How did you find this information?

⊕ **EXPLORE**

2. Assume you have to set up two different home networks so users can easily access network resources on other computers in the same network. Assume the first home network includes computers that are running different versions of Windows, and assume that all computers in the second home network are using Windows 7. Explain how you would set up the two networks.

3. What are the names of the computers in your workgroup, and what operating system is installed on each computer?

⊕ **EXPLORE**

4. Draw a diagrammatic representation of the makeup of this workgroup, and indicate how each computer is connected to each other and to the Internet. Include any networked printers in your diagram.

5. Create and then share a folder named Mark West Modeling Company in your Documents folder with Everyone. Describe the process that you used. What is the UNC path to this shared folder?

6. Remove sharing from this folder, and then described the process that you used.

7. Create a Mark West Modeling Company folder on another computer in the same workgroup, change the permission level so users can read and write to the folder, and then share the folder.

⊕ **EXPLORE**

8. Create a mapped drive to the shared Mark West Modeling Company folder on the other computer in the same workgroup, and note the UNC path and drive name. Describe how you created the mapped drive. What is its UNC path and drive name?

9. Remove the mapped drive, and then describe the process that you used.

10. Remove the shared Mark West Modeling Company folder you created on the other computer in your network, and then remove the Mark West Modeling Company folder you created on your own computer.

11. Submit your answers to this case problem to your instructor, either in printed or electronic form, as requested.

ENDING FILES

There are no ending Data Files for this tutorial.

Using the Command-Line Environment

Developing Command-Line Skills

OBJECTIVES

Session 13.1
- Learn about the importance of command-line skills
- Use internal and external commands
- Customize a command-line window
- Pipe output to the More filter
- Compile information about a computer and its power usage

Session 13.2
- Display a directory tree, change directories, and view directory listings
- View file attributes
- Create a directory and copy files
- Use wildcards to streamline command operations
- View the Windows environment and create an environment variable

Case | *Assets First Credit Union*

As the IT administrator for Assets First Credit Union in Appleton, Wisconsin, Eve Larsen relies on the Windows 7 command-line environment to configure and troubleshoot problems as well as perform operations not possible from the graphical user interface. Eve recently hired you as a network technician. In this tutorial, you will examine the importance of the command-line environment and command-line skills. You will open a Command Prompt window, use internal and external commands, customize the Command Prompt window, assign a volume label, and evaluate your computer. You will view and navigate a directory tree, view the contents of directories, view file attributes, create a directory, copy files, and view and customize the Windows environment.

STARTING DATA FILES

Tutorial.13

Tutorial
- Business Records
- Client Projects
- Company Performance
- Company Projections
- Contract Training
- Personal Records
- Sales Analyses

Review
- Business Records
- Client Projects
- Company Performance
- Company Projections
- Contract Training
- Personal Records
- Sales Analyses

Case1
- Business Records
- Client Projects
- Company Performance
- Company Projections
- Contract Training
- Personal Records
- Sales Analyses

Case2
- Business Records
- Client Projects
- Company Performance
- Company Projections
- Contract Training
- Personal Records
- Sales Analyses

Case3
- Business Records
- Client Projects
- Company Performance
- Company Projections
- Contract Training
- Personal Records
- Sales Analyses

SESSION 13.1 VISUAL OVERVIEW

When you use the **Help switch (/?)** to view Help information for a command, the program displays information on how to use the command (or the **syntax**) and includes all the various required and optional parameters for using a command.

To work in the command-line environment, you type a command after the operating system prompt (C:\Users\Eve in this figure) displayed by Windows, and then press the Enter key to execute the command. The **operating system prompt** acts as a reference point for interacting with the operating system in the command-line window. In this example, the internal COLOR command changes the background color of the window and the color of the text.

The TITLE command, an internal command, changes the window name on the title bar to text that you specify. An **internal command** is a command that is stored in the **command interpreter**, a program that interprets a command that you enter, locates the program code for the command, and then executes the program.

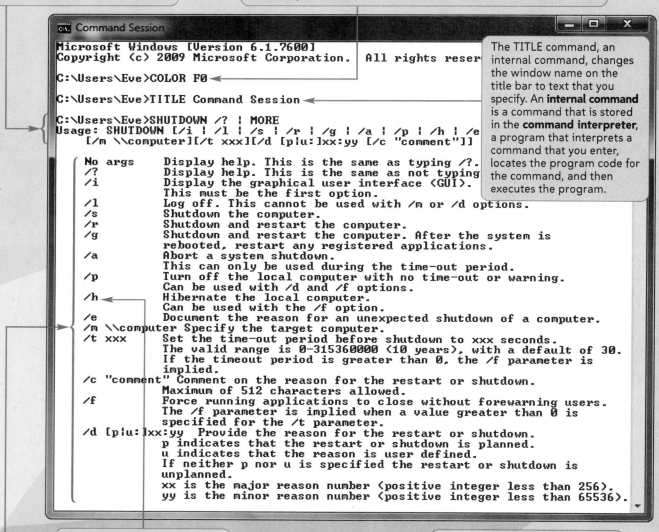

```
Command Session                                                    _  □  X

Microsoft Windows [Version 6.1.7600]
Copyright (c) 2009 Microsoft Corporation.    All rights reser

C:\Users\Eve>COLOR F0

C:\Users\Eve>TITLE Command Session

C:\Users\Eve>SHUTDOWN /? | MORE
Usage: SHUTDOWN [/i | /l | /s | /r | /g | /a | /p | /h | /e
       [/m \\computer][/t xxx][/d [p|u:]xx:yy [/c "comment"]]

    No args      Display help. This is the same as typing /?.
    /?           Display help. This is the same as not typing
    /i           Display the graphical user interface (GUI).
                 This must be the first option.
    /l           Log off. This cannot be used with /m or /d options.
    /s           Shutdown the computer.
    /r           Shutdown and restart the computer.
    /g           Shutdown and restart the computer. After the system is
                 rebooted, restart any registered applications.
    /a           Abort a system shutdown.
                 This can only be used during the time-out period.
    /p           Turn off the local computer with no time-out or warning.
                 Can be used with /d and /f options.
    /h           Hibernate the local computer.
                 Can be used with the /f option.
    /e           Document the reason for an unexpected shutdown of a computer.
    /m \\computer Specify the target computer.
    /t xxx       Set the time-out period before shutdown to xxx seconds.
                 The valid range is 0-315360000 (10 years), with a default of 30.
                 If the timeout period is greater than 0, the /f parameter is
                 implied.
    /c "comment" Comment on the reason for the restart or shutdown.
                 Maximum of 512 characters allowed.
    /f           Force running applications to close without forewarning users.
                 The /f parameter is implied when a value greater than 0 is
                 specified for the /t parameter.
    /d [p|u:]xx:yy  Provide the reason for the restart or shutdown.
                 p indicates that the restart or shutdown is planned.
                 u indicates that the reason is user defined.
                 If neither p nor u is specified the restart or shutdown is
                 unplanned.
                 xx is the major reason number (positive integer less than 256).
                 yy is the minor reason number (positive integer less than 65536). ▼
```

One useful switch for the SHUTDOWN command is the /H switch, which places the local computer in hibernation.

You can use the Help information for a command to create a desktop shortcut that performs the same action from the desktop that the SHUTDOWN command performs in a command-line window, such as placing your computer into hibernation.

Help information includes a more detailed explanation of the switches available for a command and any required or optional parameters for a switch. A switch modifies the way in which a command works.

Hibernate Computer

COMMAND HELP

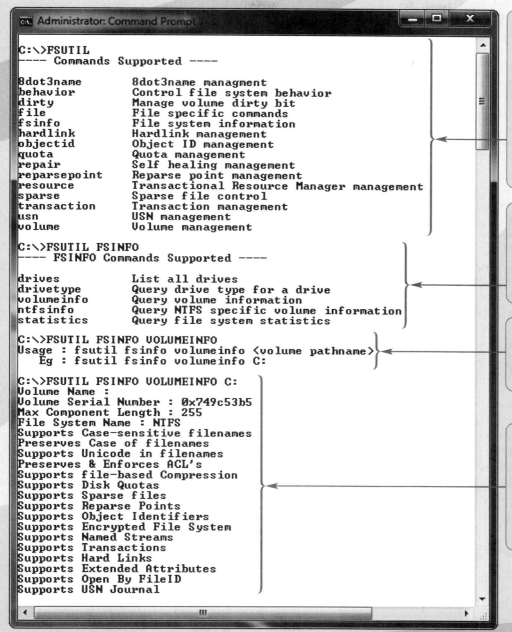

You can use the FSUTIL (File System Utility) command, an external command that requires Administrator credentials, to display technical information about the file system. To display Help information on this command, you type FSUTIL at the operating system prompt to display a list of supported commands. An **external command** is a command for a program that is stored in a file on disk.

To step down to the next level of Help and view Help information on the FSINFO, or file system command, you type FSUTIL FSINFO and then press the Enter key. You can use the VOLUMEINFO to display information about a volume.

To step down to the next level of Help and view the syntax for using FSINFO, you type FSUTIL FSINFO VOLUMEINFO and then press the Enter key.

Once you know the full syntax of the FSUTIL FSINFO VOLUMEINFO command, you can use it to view detailed technical information about the file system on a specific volume, as shown here for drive C, an NTFS volume, and find out which file system features are supported.

The Importance of Command-Line Skills

After the introduction of the first Windows operating system in 1995, there was a dramatic shift from working in a command-line environment (namely, the DOS operating system) to different Windows operating systems that rely on a graphical user interface. However, command-line skills are still essential, especially for those who administer networks and for those who provide technical support and troubleshooting. Furthermore, many concepts and features incorporated into the DOS operating system are important for understanding the Windows operating system and how it works. For example, when working with the DOS operating system, you had to know how to navigate a computer system by specifying the MS-DOS path to drives and directories (or folders). The DOS operating system also relied on the path for locating and loading applications and other programs stored in different directories. Likewise, Windows 7 and all previous versions of the Windows operating system rely on the paths (now stored in the Registry) to specific programs to locate and load applications and other programs. However, instead of navigating your computer in a command-line environment by specifying the path of each and every location you want to access, you now use a point-and-click approach to select and open folders and subfolders.

If you are a network administrator, specialist, technician, or troubleshooter, you must know command-line skills and concepts because you may need to use them to set up, configure, and troubleshoot a network or to resolve other types of problems. These same skills and concepts may also be important if you need to troubleshoot operating system, hardware, and software problems on a client's computer or even your own computer. If you experience a serious problem with starting Windows 7, you may have no other choice than to use the Safe Mode with Command Prompt option on the Advanced Boot Options menu to boot your computer and troubleshoot a problem in a command-line environment. If you contact technical support to help you with a problem, you might be guided through the process of working with commands from a command-line environment. Also, if you need to perform a task not possible in the graphical user interface, you will need to turn to a command-line environment.

To acquire professional certifications in certain specialties, such as networking, you must prove competency in the use of command-line skills. At many colleges, a command-line class is a requirement for networking courses that lead to certification in a specific area and that provide skills for a particular type of job. Also, as you will discover in this tutorial, you can perform operations in a command-line window far faster than in the graphical user interface.

Getting Started

To complete this section of the tutorial, you must display the Computer icon on the desktop, switch your computer to single-click activation, display extensions for known file types, and display hidden files, folders, and drives as well as protected operating system files. You will also copy the data files for this tutorial to the Public Documents folder from the Documents folder, your flash drive, or a network folder using the graphical user interface. In Session 13.2, you will examine how to use the command-line COPY command to copy folders and files.

To set up your computer:

▶ **1.** If necessary, display the Computer icon on the desktop, enable single-click activation, display extensions for known file types, and display hidden files, folders, and drives as well as protected operating system files.

▶ **2.** Make sure you have downloaded and extracted your copy of the Windows 7 for Power Users Data Files.

▶ **3.** Close all open windows, attach your flash drive (if necessary), open the Tutorial.13 folder, and copy the Tutorial folder to the Public Documents folder on your hard disk drive, or to the folder requested by your instructor or technical support staff.

▶ **4.** Select the newly copied Tutorial folder (if necessary), press the **F2** (Rename) key, type **Assets First** and then press the **Enter** key.

▶ **5.** Close the Public Documents folder window (or the window where you copied the data files to), and if necessary, close the folder window that contains the original copy of the Tutorial folder.

▶ **6.** If you do not know the drive name for your flash drive, open a Computer window, find the drive name of the flash drive, and then close the Computer window. You will need to know the drive name for this session of the tutorial.

Now you are ready to examine the command-line environment.

Working with the Command Interpreter

In Tutorial 6, you examined how to use the command-line Check Disk utility and the command-line DEFRAG utility from a Command Prompt window. In Tutorial 8, you learned how to boot your computer to a command prompt with the Advanced Boot Options menu. Therefore you are already familiar with the use of specific Windows 7 features that require a command-line environment.

To work in a command-line environment under Windows 7, you first open a command-line window. Windows 7 then executes the Windows Command Processor program from the file cmd.exe located in the System32 directory. Cmd.exe is the Windows 7 command interpreter. A command interpreter is a program that interprets commands entered at the command prompt, locates the appropriate program in memory or on disk, loads the program (if necessary), and then executes the program. The command interpreter is also responsible for displaying the command prompt that identifies where you enter commands in the command-line environment and identifies your current working position.

Because the process for working in a command-line environment is different from that used when working in a graphical user interface, and because this process relies on the precise use and entry of commands, the following conventions are used for this tutorial only:

- Commands that you type in the tutorial steps are displayed in lowercase and in boldface. However, you can use uppercase, lowercase, or mixed case when entering commands.
- Commands and switches that you type are displayed in uppercase in the explanatory text before, after, and in steps so they are consistent with how they are presented when viewing Help on a command in a command-line window. However, command names, such as Directory for the DIR command, and switch names, such as the Help switch for /?, are not displayed in uppercase. When entering the actual command with the switch, you typically use lowercase because it's easier than typing in uppercase.
- Punctuation, such as commas, semicolons, or periods, is not used in tutorial steps after commands you type to ensure that you do not inadvertently enter the command with that punctuation and thereby encounter an error condition.
- Commands that include the number *0* or *1* are identified as such (namely, zero or the number one), so you do not interpret the *0* or *1* as the uppercase letter *O* or the lowercase letter *l*.
- Commands listed in Reference boxes, which summarize operations you just completed, are displayed in all uppercase.

- Command options shown in italics within brackets, such as [*drive:*] and [*path*], are optional **parameters** or items of data. If you do not specify the drive and path for those commands that use them, Windows 7 uses the current drive and directory. Items shown in italics without brackets, such as *drive:* and *filename* are required parameters. You must enter a required parameter.

The following three points are guidelines you should keep in mind when working in a command-line environment:

- Although you might have some flexibility in entering certain commands, such as whether you include a space between a command and a switch, it is good practice to be consistent in the way you work to reduce the chances of accidentally entering a command in a format that produces an error condition.
- When entering commands from the keyboard, it's not uncommon to press the wrong key or keys and make mistakes. If you inadvertently mistype a command in the Command Prompt window, you might see the following type of message: '*Command*' is not recognized as an internal or external command, operable program or batch file. *Command* is the actual command you typed. If this occurs, enter the command again as shown with the proper spacing and optional parameters. If you type the command itself correctly, but make a mistake with the use of an optional parameter, the type of error message that you see will vary.
- To avoid error conditions when entering commands, and where noted in the command, type the spacing between parts of a command, quotation marks around a command or path, a colon after a drive letter in a drive name, the backslash symbol in a path, the regular slash symbol with switches, minus signs (or hyphens) with switches or part of a switch, and a dot (a period) or dots (two periods) that are used with a command or in a file specification.

After your initial orientation for your new job at Assets First Credit Union, Eve and you agree to spend a couple of hours each afternoon during your first week of work to review the basics of working with the Windows 7 command-line environment. Eve wants to start by showing you how to open a command-line session, enter and use some basic Windows 7 commands, navigate the directory structure of your computer, and customize system settings.

In the following steps, you are going to examine two approaches for opening a command-line session.

To open a Command Prompt window:

1. From the Start menu, point to **All Programs**, click **Accessories**, and then click **Command Prompt**. Windows 7 opens a Command Prompt window on the desktop and displays a command prompt (also called an operating system prompt) that identifies the default drive (in this case, drive C) and the path to your user account directory, followed by a blinking cursor to mark your current working position. See Figure 13-1. Note that *Command Prompt* appears on the title bar of the window.

| Figure 13-1 | Command Prompt window |

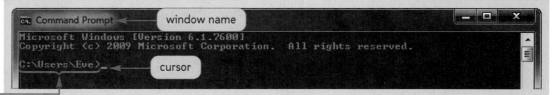

On Eve's computer, the command prompt in the Command Prompt window shows the full path to the directory for Eve's user account, namely C:\Users\Eve (your path will differ). After this path, the command interpreter displays a greater than symbol (>) to separate the path from any command that you enter. Note that the Command Prompt window also identifies the operating system (Microsoft Windows) and the version of Windows (Version 6.1.7600, the version number when Windows 7 was first introduced).

2. Type **exit** and then press the **Enter** key. The EXIT command closes a command-line window, but you can also use the window's Close button ▮ **X** ▮. After you enter a command at the command prompt, you must press the Enter key; otherwise, nothing will happen. The Enter key signals the operating system to execute, or carry out, the command you typed.

TIP

You can also type CMD.EXE in the Start menu Search programs and files box to open a command-line window.

3. Press the **Windows** key, type **cmd** in the Search programs and files box, and press the **Enter** key. Windows 7 opens a command-line window, but instead of displaying the label *Command Prompt* in the title bar, it displays the path to the program that it opened from the system32 directory, namely, cmd.exe. See Figure 13-2.

Figure 13-2	**Command-line window**

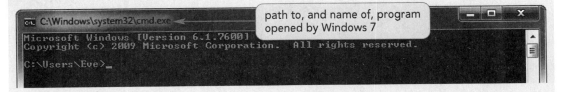

4. Type **exit** and press the **Enter** key to close the command-line window.

The Command Prompt window and the command-line window opened by using the CMD command are just two different ways of opening the same type of window so that you can work in a command-line environment. Only the window titles differ.

Because you will need to perform operations that require Administrator credentials, Eve recommends you create a Command Prompt shortcut with Administrator credentials.

To create a Command Prompt shortcut with Administrator credentials:

1. Display the All Programs menu, click **Accessories**, right-click **Command Prompt**, point to **Send to**, and then click **Desktop (create shortcut)**. Windows 7 creates a Command Prompt shortcut on the desktop.

2. Right-click the **Command Prompt** desktop shortcut, click **Properties**, and on the Shortcut property sheet, click the **Advanced** button. Windows 7 opens the Advanced Properties dialog box, as shown in Figure 13-3.

Figure 13-3 ▶ **Viewing advanced properties of a Command Prompt shortcut**

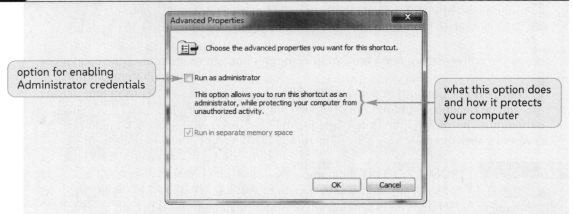

option for enabling Administrator credentials

what this option does and how it protects your computer

Windows 7 notes that the "Run as administrator" option protects your computer from unauthorized activity when you run this shortcut as an administrator.

▶ **3.** Click the **Run as administrator** check box to add a check mark, click the **OK** button, and then click the **OK** button in the Command Prompt Properties dialog box.

▶ **4.** Click the **Command Prompt** desktop shortcut and provide Administrator credentials. Windows 7 opens an Administrator: Command Prompt window, as shown in Figure 13-4.

Figure 13-4 ▶ **Command-line window opened with Administrator credentials**

command-line window with Administrator credentials

The path shown in operating system prompt is C:\Windows\system32.

▶ **5.** Type **exit** and press the **Enter** key to close the command-line window.

One advantage of this shortcut is that you won't forget to specify Administrator credentials before you open a Command Prompt window to perform operations that require those Administrator credentials. If you open a Command Prompt window by clicking Command Prompt on the Accessories menu, and then later decide to use a program that requires Administrator credentials, you have to close the Command Prompt window, and open a new window with Administrator credentials. So the shortcut sidesteps this common problem. You still have to specify the option to run the shortcut as an Administrator even if you are logged on under an Administrator account.

Opening and Closing a Command Prompt Window

- From the Start menu, point to All Programs, click Accessories, and then click Command Prompt. Or from the Start menu, type CMD (case does not matter) in the Search programs and files box, and then press the Enter key.
- If you want to open a Command Prompt window with Administrator credentials, right-click Command Prompt on the Accessories menu, click the Run as administrator check box (and add a check mark), and then specify Administrator credentials.
- To close the Command Prompt window, type EXIT and then press the Enter key.

If you modify the properties of the Start menu to show the Run command on the Start menu, you can choose Run, type CMD in the Open box, and then press the Enter key to open a command-line window. When you use the Run option, you are in effect working in a miniature command-line environment. You can also use the Windows+R keyboard shortcut to open a Run dialog box whether or not the Run command is on the Start menu.

Using Internal and External Commands

Once you open a Command Prompt window, you can enter commands at the command prompt to perform specific operations. These commands fall into two groups: internal commands and external commands. Internal commands are commands for common and important types of operations, such as creating a directory (or folder). When you open a Command Prompt window, Windows 7 loads cmd.exe into memory. Then cmd.exe performs specific functions, such as displaying a text user interface (TUI) with a command prompt and interpreting commands that you enter. Once cmd.exe loads into memory, you can access the program code for any of the internal commands it contains within itself. Because the operating system does not have to go back to disk to locate and load the program code for an internal command (it's already in memory), internal commands execute more quickly.

In contrast to internal commands, the program code for an external command resides in a specific file on disk. When you enter an external command, the command you type is actually the first part of the filename—the part before the file extension. And because command-line program filenames are typically limited to eight characters with no spaces, the command you enter is short. The operating system locates the file on disk and then loads the program into memory so it can perform its intended function. If you do not specify the file extension for a command, Windows 7 looks for files that have the name you specify and that have a specific file extension, such as .com, .exe, and .bat. The external commands are stored in the System32 directory under the Windows directory. As you examine different commands, you will learn which ones are internal commands and which are external commands.

To use internal and external commands, you must not only know what commands are available, but you also must know the syntax for entering each command. Syntax (pronounced "sin tax") refers to the proper format for entering a command, including how to spell the command (some are abbreviated, such as CHKDSK for *Check Disk*), how to use required parameters (such as specifying a drive), and optional parameters (such as a switch), as well as the spacing between the command, required parameters, and optional parameters. A switch is an optional parameter that you use with a command to change the way in which the command works. As you will discover in this tutorial, the command-line interface is syntax sensitive. You must type the command exactly as specified or the command interpreter will display an error message. Even the use of spaces (by pressing the spacebar) is important when entering commands. If you forget a required space, the command interpreter will display an error message.

To locate Help information about the use of the internal and external commands, you can use the Help switch (/?) or the HELP command (both of which you will examine in the next two sections) to extract Help information from the program code for a command. Note that the actual switch you type is a slash followed by a question mark (/?), and *Help switch* is the name of this particular switch.

Using Help to Specify Console Colors

The default background color for the console is black, and the default foreground color is white. In other words, when working in a command-line window, Windows 7 displays white text against a black background. The term **console** refers to the keyboard and monitor that are used for input and output. Although it is possible to use a mouse in a Command Prompt window for certain operations, such as copying text, your primary input device is the keyboard.

Prior to the Windows operating system, individuals used the DOS operating system with a **monochrome monitor** that was capable of displaying only one foreground color and one background color. There were monochrome monitors that could display black text on a white background, amber or green text against a black background, or white text on a black background.

Under Windows 7, you can use the COLOR command, an internal command, to change the background and foreground colors so it is easier to work in a command-line window.

Eve suggests that you use the COLOR command to customize the Command Prompt window to best suit your needs. Eve also recommends that you first use the Help switch (/?) to view the options available with this command.

To view Help information on the use of the internal COLOR command:

▶ **1.** From the Accessories menu, click **Command Prompt** to open a Command Prompt window without Administrator credentials.

▶ **2.** Point to the top border of the Command Prompt window, and when the mouse pointer changes to a double-headed white arrow pointing up and down ↕, drag the top border to the top edge of the desktop, and after Aero Snap extends the window from the top to the bottom of your monitor, release the left mouse button. If you maximize the window instead, the lower part of the window might be hidden behind the taskbar, making it difficult at times to view the contents of the window. If you try to widen the Command Prompt window, you will discover that you cannot widen it. To perform this operation, you have to change the properties of the Command Prompt window (by right-clicking the Command Prompt window frame and choosing Properties).

▶ **3.** Type **color /?** and then press the **Enter** key. Windows 7 displays Help information on the use of the COLOR command. See Figure 13-5.

TIP

You can also display Help information by typing HELP followed by a space and the command.

| Figure 13-5 | Viewing Help information on the COLOR command |

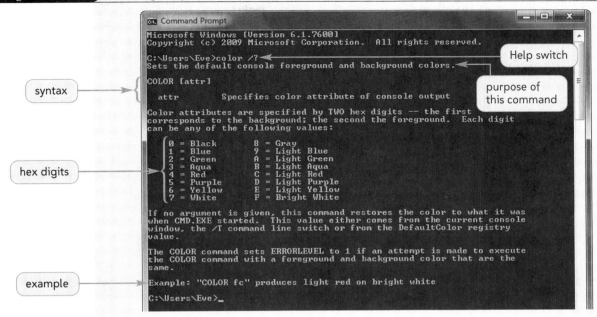

After completing the command, the command interpreter redisplays the command prompt so you can enter another command.

4. Keep the Command Prompt window open for the next set of tutorial steps.

As shown in the Help information, derived from the program file itself, the COLOR command changes the default console foreground and background colors. Then the Help information shows the syntax for the COLOR command: COLOR [attr]

The optional parameter *attr* specifies the color attribute of the console output. If you use the optional parameter and specify a color attribute, you must include a space between the command and the optional parameter.

As shown in the Help explanation for the use of this command, you use two hex digits to specify the color attribute. A **hex digit** is one of the 16 digits used in the hexadecimal number system (0 through 9 and A through F). The first hex digit is the color attribute for the background color and the second hex digit is the color attribute for the foreground color. This is logically backwards from the way in which individuals think of a user interface and even how they work in a text user interface. They typically think of text first and background next rather than vice versa. Note that the Help information explains that you use this command to set the default foreground and background color, but then later explains that you specify the background color first and the foreground color second. So the Help information is not consistent in the way that it approaches its explanation of the command. Help also lists the hex digits and their corresponding color assignments.

As described in the Help information, if you use the COLOR command without the optional color attribute parameter (which is also called an **argument**), the command restores the default background and foreground colors that were used when you first opened the Command Prompt window. As noted, the default settings it uses can be derived from three sources—the current console window (where you specify these settings with the COLOR command), the use of the /T switch with the CMD command, or from a setting stored in the Registry under the DefaultColor Registry value entry.

The Help information also includes an example. If you enter the COLOR FC command, the COLOR command changes the foreground and background colors so text is displayed in light red (the color attribute C) against a bright white background (the color attribute F). The default console color (white text on a black background) is the color attribute 07 (zero 7).

The Help switch works with almost every command. Like any other switch, it modifies the way in which the command works.

Eve recommends that you first try white text against a bright blue background, and then try bright white text against a bright red background.

To change the console colors:

▶ 1. Type **color 9f** and then press the **Enter** key. The COLOR command changes the foreground color to bright white and the background color to bright blue (called Light Blue in Help).

▶ 2. Type **color 4f** and then press the **Enter** key. The COLOR command applies the new color attribute, and displays bright white text against a bright red background.

▶ 3. Type **color** and then press the **Enter** key. The COLOR command restores the default console colors.

▶ 4. Keep the Command Prompt window open for the next set of tutorial steps.

You can change the console colors at any point. If you close the Command Prompt window and then later open it again, Windows 7 reverts back to the default console colors.

REFERENCE

Changing Console Colors

- From the All Programs menu, click Accessories, and then click Command Prompt.
- Type COLOR /? and press the Enter key to display Help information on the use of the COLOR command, including the hex digits that you can use to specify the background and foreground colors.
- To change the console colors, type COLOR followed by a space and then the two hex digit codes for the color attribute that you want to use, and then press the Enter key. For example, if you want to use white text on a blue background, type COLOR 9F and then press the Enter key.
- To restore the default console colors, type COLOR and press the Enter key.

When working in a Command Prompt window, you can recall previously entered commands by using the Up Arrow key; you can also use the F7 function key to display a command history. The **command history** is an area of memory that stores commands you previously entered.

To recall previously entered commands and view a command history:

TIP

You can also use the F3 key to recall the last command.

▶ 1. Press the **Up Arrow** key once. The command interpreter recalls the previously used COLOR command.

Trouble? If you also tried other combinations of hex digits, the command interpreter will recall another COLOR command. That's fine. The point is that the feature works.

2. Press the **Up Arrow** key again. Windows 7 recalls the command used before the COLOR command, namely COLOR 4F.

3. Press the **Up Arrow** key again. Windows 7 recalls the command used before the COLOR 4F command, namely COLOR 9F.

   Trouble? If you have tried other combinations of hex digits, use the Up Arrow (or Down Arrow) to locate the COLOR 9F command.

4. Press the **Enter** key. The COLOR command changes the console colors.

5. Type **color f0** (*F* and a zero), and press the **Enter** key. The COLOR command displays black text against a white background.

6. Press the **F7** function key. The command interpreter displays a command history. See Figure 13-6.

Figure 13-6 **Viewing the command history**

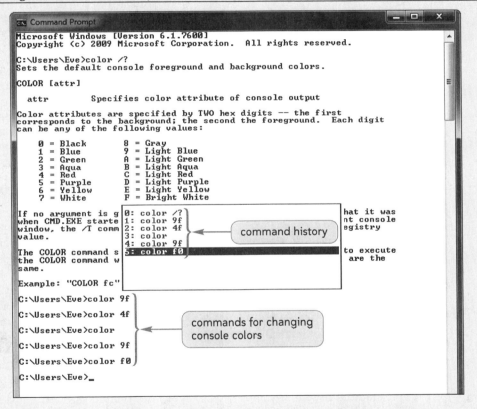

7. Press the **Up Arrow** key to select the **color 9f** command, and then press the **Enter** key. Windows 7 uses the previously entered command that you selected from the command history, and the COLOR command changes the console colors to white text against a bright blue background.

8. Press the **F7** function key, press the **Down Arrow** key to select the **color f0** command, and then press the **Enter** key to display black text against a white background.

9. Keep the Command Prompt window open for the next section of the tutorial.

You can use whatever colors you prefer for the rest of this tutorial; however, the remaining figures in the tutorial will use black text against a white background so it is easier to see the contents of the Command Prompt window in figures.

In addition to using the Up Arrow key and Down Arrow keys to scroll through the commands in the command history, you can also use the Esc key to close the command history and Alt+F7 to clear the command history but only after you close the command history first. You can also use the DOSKEY /HISTORY command to view a list of commands in the command history. When you close the Command Prompt window, all of the commands stored in the command history are erased.

REFERENCE

Recalling Commands from the Command History

- To recall the previously entered command in a Command Prompt window, press the Up Arrow key or press the F3 key.
- To display the command history, press the F7 function key, use the Up Arrow key or Down Arrow key to select the command you want to use, and then press the Enter key.

Under the DOS operating system, you had to use the DOSKEY command, an external command, to recall and edit previously entered commands and use a command history; however, under Windows 7, these features are available as soon as you open a Command Prompt window. The DOSKEY command is also available under Windows 7 so you have access to more advanced features, such as the ability to set the size of the **buffer** (or area of memory) used for the command history or the ability to create macros to automate operations that execute a series of commands.

INSIGHT

Techniques for Editing a Command Line

As you have just seen, when you work in a Command Prompt window, you have access to features that simplify the use of selecting and entering commands. After you enter or recall a command, you can also edit the command. If you make a mistake while entering a command, or if you want to change the parameters of a command, and if you have not already pressed the Enter key, you can use the Left Arrow key and Right Arrow key to move one character to the left or right on the command line. If you then type a character, it's automatically inserted where you type it because **insert mode** is the default mode when editing a command line. If you want to type over one or more characters, you first press the Insert key to switch to **overtype mode**, and then start typing. The Insert key is a toggle key, so you can press the Insert key again to switch back to insert mode. A **toggle key** alternates between two related uses each time you press the key. You can use the Backspace and Delete keys to delete part of a command, one character at a time. You can also press the Home key to move to the beginning of a command line, and the End key to move to the end of the command line. If you recall a command and then decide you do not want to use it, you press the Esc key to clear the command-line. You can also use the Esc key to clear all or part of a command that you've just typed but only if you've not pressed Enter first.

Using External Commands

You can use the LABEL command, an external command, to assign a volume label to a drive, such as a flash drive, and thereby more easily distinguish one drive for another. A **volume label** is an electronic label assigned to a drive.

Before you use the LABEL command or any other command, you can use the CLS (Clear Screen) command, an internal command, to clear the Command Prompt window of the output of any previous commands. Before each set of steps in each section of the tutorial, you will be asked to use this command so you can clear the Command Prompt window and then focus on just the output of the next command. This will also make it easier for you to compare your output with that shown in the figures.

Eve suggests that you use the HELP command first to display information on how to use the LABEL external command to assign an electronic label to your flash drive.

To clear the screen and view Help information on creating a volume label:

▶ 1. Type **cls** and then press the **Enter** key. The CLS (Clear Screen) command clears the window of any output and displays the command prompt in the upper-left corner of the window. Although you do not need to enter this command before you enter another command, this command does allow you to focus on the current command and its output, without also viewing output of previous commands.

TIP

You can also type LABEL /? to obtain Help on this command.

▶ 2. Type **help label** and then press the **Enter** key. The HELP command displays Help information on the LABEL command. See Figure 13-7.

Figure 13-7   Viewing Help information on the LABEL command

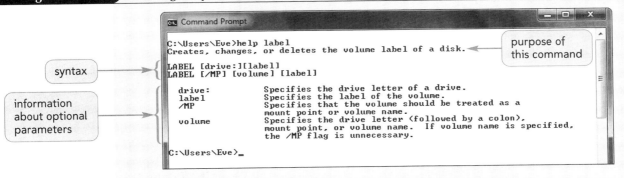

The Help information explains that the LABEL command creates, changes, or deletes the volume label of a disk (drive). Then the Help information displays two different ways for entering and using this command. With the first option, LABEL [drive:][label], you type the command LABEL with or without a drive name and with or without a new volume label. As noted earlier, the parameters included within square brackets are optional parameters that change the way the command works. You can use this option in one of four ways:

- If you type LABEL and press the Enter key, the program assumes you want to create, change, or delete the volume label for the default drive, which is the current drive (because you have not specified a drive with the command). The **default drive** is the one that Windows is currently using. When you open a Command Prompt, Windows 7 automatically uses drive C and that drive is the default drive. To change the label for drive C, you must open the Command Prompt window with Administrator credentials.
- If you type LABEL followed by a space and then a drive name, the program prompts you to create, change, or delete the volume label for the drive you specified.

- If you type LABEL followed by a space and a volume label, the program assigns the volume label you specified to the current drive (i.e., the default drive). Again, you must open the Command Prompt window with Administrator credentials before you can change the label for drive C.
- If you type LABEL followed by a space, the drive name, and a volume label (with or without a preceding space), the program assigns the volume label you specify to the drive you designated.

Now that you understand the syntax of this command, you're ready to assign the volume label *WINDOWS* to your flash drive. You will first use the internal VOL (Volume) command to display the current volume name of your flash drive. To complete the next set of tutorial steps, you must know the drive name for the flash drive.

To clear the screen and then assign a volume label to your flash drive:

1. Use the CLS command to clear the screen, type **vol** first, press the **spacebar**, and then type the **drive name** of your flash drive. For example, if your flash drive name is G: then you type: VOL G:

2. Press the **Enter** key. The VOL command displays the volume label for your flash drive (if any) and then displays its volume serial number. The flash drive used for Figure 13-8 does not have a volume label. Yours may differ.

Figure 13-8   **Checking the volume label for a flash drive**

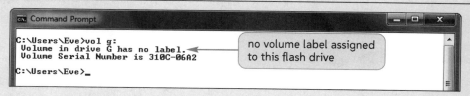

The serial number is created from the date and time when a disk or drive is first formatted. Before you change the volume label of your flash drive, make a note of its name so you can restore that name later.

3. Type **label** first, press the **spacebar**, type the **drive name** of your flash drive (such as G:), press the **spacebar**, type **windows**, and then press the **Enter** key.

4. Press the **Up Arrow** key *twice* to recall the VOL command that you entered previously and then press the **Enter** key. The VOL command displays the newly assigned volume label for your flash drive. See Figure 13-9. Even though you entered the volume label in lowercase, it was converted to uppercase because this flash drive uses the FAT32 file system. NTFS, on the other hand, is case-sensitive, so it retains the case you type as the volume name.

Figure 13-9   **Assigning and verifying a newly assigned volume label**

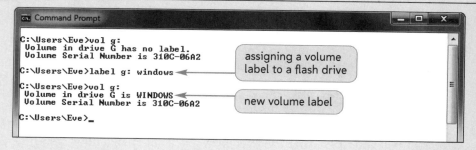

5. Keep the Command Prompt window open for the next set of tutorial steps.

You can use up to 11 characters for a volume label if the drive is formatted for the FAT file system or up to 32 characters if a drive is formatted for NTFS.

PROSKILLS

Problem Solving: Assigning Volume Labels to Drives

By assigning volume names to drives, you can quickly and easily distinguish between multiple hard disk drives (including internal and external drives) and multiple flash drives in a Computer window for all the types of file operations that you perform on your computer, such as saving, copying, archiving, and deleting files. If you are working in a command-line window, you can use the VOL command to quickly view the user-friendly volume label of a drive, including your flash drives, so you know you are using the correct drive. If you carry your flash drive around with you, say to work or to classes, you can assign all or part of your name as a volume label for your flash drive. If you then accidentally forget and leave the flash drive in a computer lab or at work, you and the lab staff or coworkers can quickly verify that the flash drive belongs to you. Furthermore, assigning user-friendly names to flash drives helps you distinguish them from drives for memory cards, all of which are assigned the same default name by Windows 7. If for no other reason, assigning volume labels to drives saves you time and effort and you can work more reliably, assured that you've accessed the right files on the right drive.

In the next set of steps, you restore the original volume label for your flash drive or just remove the volume label, whichever you prefer.

To restore the volume label on your flash drive:

▶ **1.** If your flash drive had another volume label before you assigned WINDOWS as the volume label, type **label**, press the **spacebar**, type the **drive name** of your flash drive (such as G:), press the **spacebar**, type your original flash drive name, and then press the **Enter** key. If your flash drive did not have another volume name before you assigned WINDOWS as the volume name, type **label**, press the **spacebar**, type the **drive name** of your flash drive (such as G:), press the **Enter** key, press the **Enter** key again when prompted for a volume label, and when prompted as to whether you want to delete the current volume label, type **Y** (case does not matter) for *Yes*, and then press the **Enter** key.

▶ **2.** To verify the operation, use the **Up Arrow** key to recall the last VOL command, and then press the **Enter** key.

▶ **3.** Keep the Command Prompt window open for the next section of the tutorial.

You may also want to assign a custom volume name to your hard disk drive or drives so you can more quickly identify the drive you want to use when you open a Computer window.

Checking, Assigning, and Removing a Volume Label for a Flash Drive

- If necessary, attach your flash drive to your computer and then close any dialog boxes or windows that open. If you do not know the drive name for your flash drive, open a Computer window, locate its drive name, and then close the Computer window.
- Open a Command Prompt window, type LABEL followed by a space, type the drive name for your flash drive followed by a space, type a volume label, and press the Enter key.
- To verify the volume name, type VOL followed by a space, type the drive name for your flash drive, and then press the Enter key.
- To remove a volume name from your flash drive, type LABEL followed by a space, type the drive name for your flash drive, press the Enter key, and when prompted for a volume name, press the Enter key, press the Enter key again when prompted for a volume label, and when prompted as to whether you want to delete the current volume label, type Y for *Yes*, and then press the Enter key.

Using the Pipe Operator to Display a Command-Line Reference List

If you want to locate a specific command or just find out what types of basic commands are available, you can display a list of commands from the Command Prompt window by using the external HELP command.

To view the commands for which Help is available, Eve suggests you use the HELP command by itself.

To display a command reference list:

1. Clear the screen, type **help** and then press the **Enter** key. The HELP command lists commands in alphabetical order and provides a brief description of each command. Because the window is not large enough to display all the commands in this command reference list, the first commands that were displayed scrolled off screen. Notice that for the VOL command, the HELP command explains that the VOL command "Displays a disk volume label and serial number."

2. Press the **Up Arrow** key to recall the **help** command you previously entered, press the **spacebar**, type I (a vertical bar typically found as the uppercase character on the key with the backslash character), press the **spacebar** again, and then type **more**. Your final command should read: **help I more**

   Trouble? Although the vertical bar appears as a single vertical bar in a document, it appears as a vertical bar with two separate smaller bars in a Command Prompt window. The key on your keyboard might show a single vertical bar or two separate smaller bars—identical to the way it appears in a Command Prompt window.

3. Press the **Enter** key. In the Command Prompt window, you can now see the first page of commands, followed by a *More* prompt at the bottom of the window. See Figure 13-10.

Figure 13-10 **Viewing a command reference list**

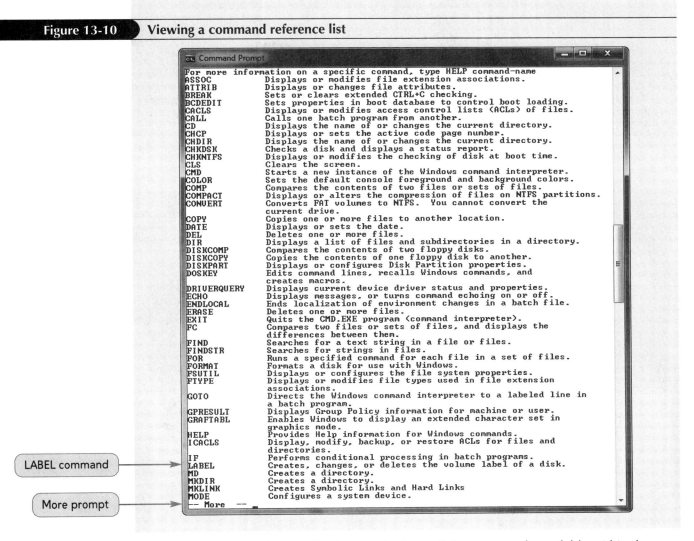

LABEL command

More prompt

This command reference list does not include all the commands available within the Windows 7 command-line environment; instead, it provides a list of only those commands for which Help information is available. You can, however, use Windows Help and Support to locate online information about the use of all available commands.

The HELP | MORE command relies on some important concepts and provides insight into the use of other command-line techniques.

The vertical bar is called the **pipe operator**, and it pipes the output of the HELP command to the MORE filter. When you **pipe** output, you are using the output of one command (e.g., HELP) as the input for another command (e.g., MORE). In this case, the HELP command outputs a list of commands for which Help information is available along with a brief description of the use of each command. Rather than displaying the output in the Command Prompt window, that output is passed to the MORE filter by the pipe operator. The MORE filter then produces **paged output**; in other words, it displays one window of output at a time. After each page of output, the MORE filter displays the prompt -- More -- so you know there is more output to view.

The MORE command (an external command) is called a **filter** because it modifies the output of another command. The entire command is called a **pipeline**. These techniques enable you to modify the use of one command with another command so it is easier to work within a command-line environment. Some commands (one of which you will examine later) include a Pause or Page switch (/P) for producing paged output, so in those instances, you do not need to use this technique with those commands (though this technique would work).

Understanding Computer Pages

When people use the word *page*, they are thinking of an 8½ × 11-inch regular sheet of paper. Even though monitors typically display only 1/3 to 1/2 of the viewable area found on a regular sheet of paper, the viewable area within a window on the screen is still called a page. When you press the Page Down key, for example, you advance a distance equal to the visible screen or window. Therefore, a page is a logical page, not a physical page. This same concept applies to working with a file in an Office application, such as a Microsoft Word document.

You can use two approaches to viewing the remainder of the output. If you press the Enter key, the MORE filter displays the next command. However, if you press the space-bar, the MORE filter displays the remainder of the output.

To view the remainder of the output:

▶ **1.** Press the **spacebar**. The MORE filter displays the remainder of the output. As noted at the bottom of the paged output by the MORE filter, the MORE program recommends that you see the command-line reference in online help for more information on command-line tools.

▶ **2.** Leave the Command Prompt window open for the next section of the tutorial.

You can use the pipe operator with other commands that produce more than one screen of output. Also, if you are using the Help switch with a command, and if the Help information exceeds more than the length of a window, you can recall the command and use the pipe operator and MORE filter to produce paged output.

Using the SystemInfo Command

SYSTEMINFO, an external command, displays configuration information about a computer and its operating system. This newer command does not follow the 8.3 file-naming conventions.

To become familiar with how to check employees' computers for information about the configuration of a computer system and its operating system, Eve suggests that you use the SYSTEMINFO command to check her computer system and then pipe the output of the command to the MORE filter.

To view system information about a computer:

▶ **1.** Clear the screen, type **systeminfo | more** and then press the **Enter** key. The SYSTEMINFO command compiles information for your computer and then displays that output. If the output consists of more than one page, the MORE filter displays the first page of output. See Figure 13-11. The details of your output will differ.

Figure 13-11 Viewing system information

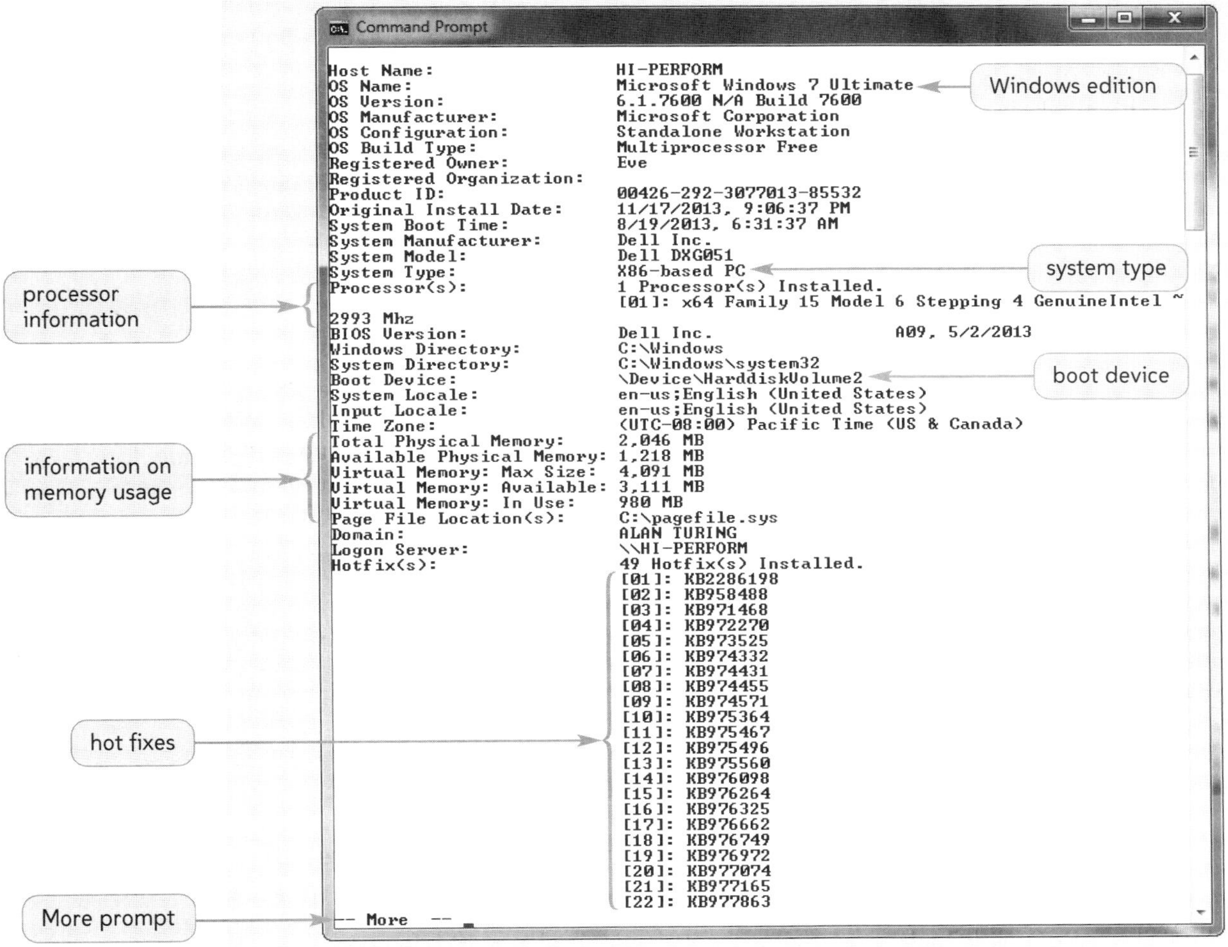

The Host Name identifies the name of the computer you are examining. The OS Name and OS Version identify the version and edition of Windows 7. The OS configuration identifies the computer used for Figure 13-11 as a stand-alone workstation (your OS configuration may differ). Another piece of information that might prove helpful in analyzing a computer is the Original Install Date, especially if you are checking dates and times on system files while troubleshooting a problem. System Model identifies the specific model of your computer. On the computer used for this figure, System Type identifies this computer as an x86-based PC; in other words, a 32-bit processor (that is also 64-bit capable). Processor(s) identifies the number of installed processors and provides you with the exact operating speed of your computer (though it may wrap around to the beginning of the next line).

The SYSTEMINFO command identifies the paths for the Windows Directory, System Directory, and Boot Device. It provides information on memory usage, including Total Physical Memory (or total RAM), the maximum size for virtual memory, the available virtual memory, and the amount of virtual memory currently in use as well as the path for the paging file. It also identifies **hot fixes**, or updates, that have been applied to a computer, and more importantly, it identifies the Microsoft Knowledge Base Article Number that identifies each hot fix. If you have a question about an update, you can use the Microsoft Knowledge Base to locate the article by the Article ID number, and then examine information about the hot fix.

To view the remainder of any output:

▶ **1.** If necessary, press the **spacebar**. The MORE filter displays the remainder of the output, which on this computer includes information about the network card.

▶ **2.** Keep the Command Prompt window open for the next section of the tutorial.

Instead of using the MORE filter with this command, you could also have adjusted your view by using the mouse and the vertical scroll bar in the Command Prompt window. However, the mouse may not always be available, or if you are skilled in the use of a command-line environment, you may prefer to use the keyboard.

If you want to examine other ways in which to use the SYSTEMINFO command, you can use the Help switch with this command.

Producing a Power Efficiency Diagnostics Report

The external POWERCFG (Power Configuration) command is a command-line tool for controlling power settings on a computer. You could use this command in a number of ways, including enabling or disabling hibernation on your computer. In Windows 7, the command includes a new switch (-ENERGY) that you can use to analyze your computer for common energy-efficiency and battery life problems and produce an HTML report (a Web page). Note that the switch uses a minus sign (-) before the word ENERGY.

To obtain accurate information about power usage on your computer, your computer must be up and running for at least 10 minutes, you must close all open windows, and you cannot interact with your computer while POWERCFG produces a Power Efficiency Diagnostics Report.

One of the company employees is experiencing battery problems with her laptop, so Eve asks you to produce a Power Efficiency Diagnostics Report for that laptop and analyze the information compiled on the battery.

To use the POWERCFG command with this new switch, you must provide Administrator credentials. If you cannot provide Administrator credentials, do not keystroke this section, but rather read the tutorial steps and examine the figures so you are familiar with the use of this command-line tool. Also, you should use this command when your computer is idle and with no other open programs or documents.

To open a Command Prompt window with Administrator credentials and produce a Power Efficiency Diagnostics Report:

▶ **1.** Close the current Command Prompt window, and then, if necessary, close all other open windows.

▶ **2.** Click the **Command Prompt** desktop shortcut to open an Administrator: Command Prompt window, and provide Administrator credentials (if necessary).

Trouble? If you no longer have a Command Prompt desktop shortcut, open the Accessories menu, right-click Command Prompt, click Run as administrator, and then provide Administrator credentials.

▶ **3.** Type **color f0** (*F* followed by a zero), and then press the **Enter** key to change the console colors, and then clear the screen.

▶ **4.** Type **powercfg -energy** (with a space before the switch), and then press the **Enter** key. The command notes that it is enabling tracing for 60 seconds and observing system behavior. On the computer used for Figure 13-12, POWERCFG reports that it found energy efficiency problems. Then it reports that these computer problems include 15 errors, one warning, and 13 informational problems. Your details will differ. It also recommends that you view the C:\Windows\ system32\energy-report.html for more details.

Trouble? If you see the error message "An unexpected error condition has occurred. Unable to perform operation. You may not have permission to perform this operation." That means you did not type the minus sign (or hyphen) before energy. Repeat this step and make sure you type the minus sign (or hyphen) before energy.

Figure 13-12	Using the POWERCFG command to identify energy efficiency problems

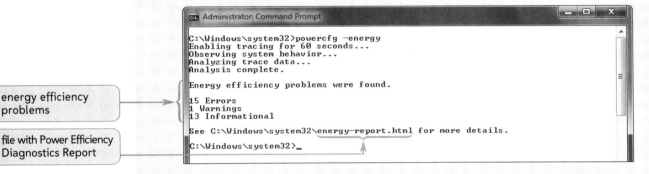

energy efficiency problems

file with Power Efficiency Diagnostics Report

TIP

This feature illustrates that you can open a file or a program from a command-line window.

▶ **5.** To open the energy report from the Command Prompt window, type **energy-report.html** and then press the **Enter** key. Windows 7 opens the report in Internet Explorer. See Figure 13-13. The details of your output will differ.

Trouble? If the command interpreter displays an error message and informs you that what you typed is not recognized as an internal or external command, operable program, or batch file, then you mistyped the filename. Repeat Step 5 using the correct filename.

Figure 13-13	Viewing a Power Efficiency Diagnostics Report in Internet Explorer

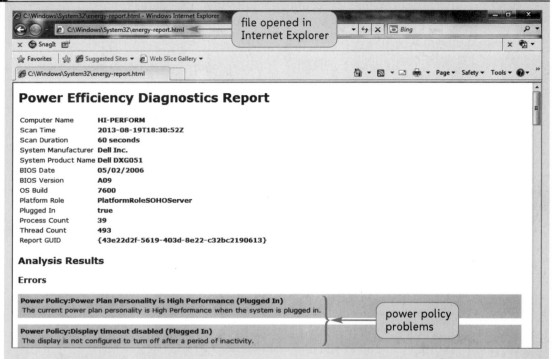

You were already in the directory where this file is stored; however, even if you were in a different directory, Windows 7 would be able to find this file and open it because the path of the directory where the report is stored is also included in the Windows path.

On the computer used for Figure 13-13, the first error notes that the power plan personality is High Performance, indicating that no power savings features are in effect in order to operate at the highest performance level. The next five errors (most of which do not appear in Figure 13-13) relate to the use of the High Performance power plan. The next nine errors note that nine USB devices did not enter a Suspend state, and that processor power management may be prevented if a USB device does not enter the Suspend state when not in use. The one warning for this computer notes that a wireless-compatible network adapter is not configured to use low-power modes.

Under Information, the report notes that the average processor utilization during the trace was very low (at 0.75%) and therefore the system consumes less power. Under Information, this report also notes the power plan is configured for optimal video quality, displays battery information for the UPS (uninterruptible power system), displays information on the sleep states supported by this computer, and finally displays processor power management capabilities of each execution core of the dual-core processor. Your details will differ.

From the Internet Explorer Page menu, you can choose the option to save a copy of this report. You can also use the Print button on the Internet Explorer command bar to create a high-fidelity XPS document to document the power efficiency of your computer.

To end this command-line session:

▶ **1.** Close your Web browser window with the Power Efficiency Diagnostics Report, and then close the Administrator: Command Prompt window.

Once you compile a Power Efficiency Diagnostics Report, you can then check the power management settings of your computer and decide how best to improve its power management.

REVIEW

Session 13.1 Quick Check

1. A(n) _____ is a program that interprets commands entered at the command prompt, locates the appropriate program in memory or on disk, loads the program, and then executes the program.
2. Briefly describe the difference between an internal and external command.
3. What is a switch?
4. True or False. You can use the VOL command to assign an electronic label to a drive, and you can use the LABEL command to view an electronic label for a drive.
5. Commands are stored in a(n) _____ so you can recall previously used commands.
6. True or False. When you pipe output, you are using the output of one command as the input for another command.
7. What is a filter?
8. What is the default drive in a command-line window?

SESSION 13.2 VISUAL OVERVIEW

You can use the DIR (Directory) command to display a **directory listing**, which contains information on directories and files in a directory or subdirectory. In a command-line environment, a subfolder is referred to as a subdirectory. You can also use various DIR command switches to specify the type of information you want to view. For example, the Attribute switch with the Directory attribute (/AD) displays all directories.

You can use the CD (Change Directory) command to navigate the directory structure of a disk and step down one directory level at a time from the root directory by specifying the name of the directory that you want to switch to. In a command-line environment, a folder is referred to as a directory. The root directory is the top-level directory (or folder) on a drive, and it is represented by the backslash (\) symbol.

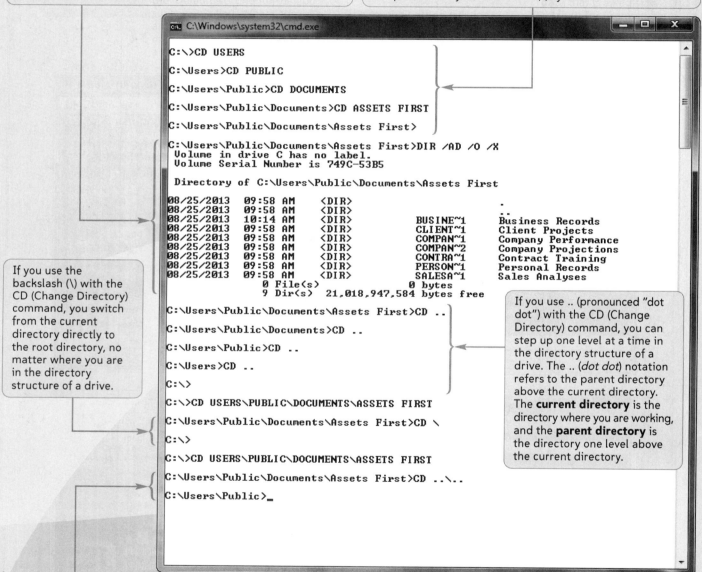

If you use the backslash (\) with the CD (Change Directory) command, you switch from the current directory directly to the root directory, no matter where you are in the directory structure of a drive.

If you use .. (pronounced "dot dot") with the CD (Change Directory) command, you can step up one level at a time in the directory structure of a drive. The .. (*dot dot*) notation refers to the parent directory above the current directory. The **current directory** is the directory where you are working, and the **parent directory** is the directory one level above the current directory.

You can use the .. (*dot dot*) notation to step up two or more levels in the directory structure by including a backslash delimiter or separator between each .. (*dot dot*). In this case, ..\.. switches up two levels in the directory structure.

NAVIGATION

The SET command, an internal command, displays all the environment variables and their settings in the Windows environment. Or, if you specify an environment variable name with the SET command, it shows you the setting for that environment variable. You can then use that environment variable as a replaceable parameter with the CD command to change directories. The Windows environment is an area of memory for storing environment variables and their settings.

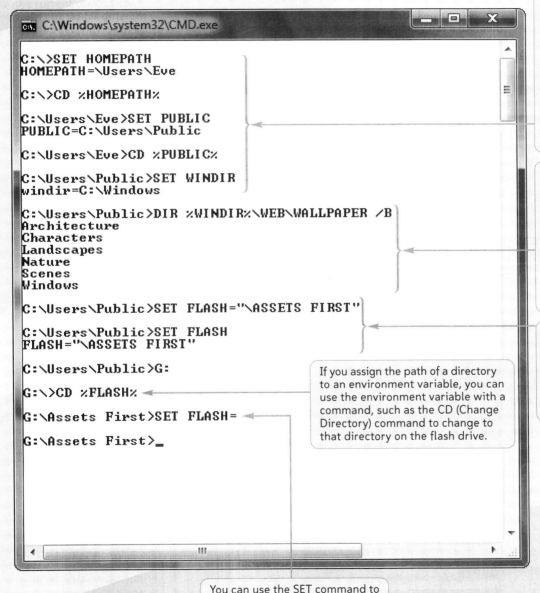

```
C:\>SET HOMEPATH
HOMEPATH=\Users\Eve

C:\>CD %HOMEPATH%

C:\Users\Eve>SET PUBLIC
PUBLIC=C:\Users\Public

C:\Users\Eve>CD %PUBLIC%

C:\Users\Public>SET WINDIR
windir=C:\Windows

C:\Users\Public>DIR %WINDIR%\WEB\WALLPAPER /B
Architecture
Characters
Landscapes
Nature
Scenes
Windows

C:\Users\Public>SET FLASH="\ASSETS FIRST"

C:\Users\Public>SET FLASH
FLASH="\ASSETS FIRST"

C:\Users\Public>G:

G:\>CD %FLASH%

G:\Assets First>SET FLASH=

G:\Assets First>_
```

You can use an environment variable as a **replaceable parameter** as part of the path for the DIR command to view the contents of a directory. The command interpreter then replaces the environment variable with its actual setting to display the directory referenced by that environment variable.

The SET command allows you to create your own environment variables, such as assigning the path to a flash drive directory to a new environment variable name of your own choosing (such as FLASH).

If you assign the path of a directory to an environment variable, you can use the environment variable with a command, such as the CD (Change Directory) command to change to that directory on the flash drive.

You can use the SET command to remove an environment variable from the Windows environment by assigning nothing to the environment variable.

Working with Directories and Files

When you work in the graphical user interface, you use the terms *folder* and *subfolder* to describe the file system components for organizing and tracking files. However, when working in a command-line environment, you use the comparable terms *directory* and *subdirectory* instead.

To effectively work with directories and files in a command-line environment, you must understand the directory structure of your computer and know how to navigate from the directory structure of a disk using a path. Once you open a directory, you can view information about the files included in that directory.

If you are working in a folder window under the graphical user interface, you can switch to a command-line window directly from that folder.

Eve recommends that you open a command-line window from the Public Documents folder where you have the Assets First folder, and then examine the directory structure of that folder.

To open a command-line window from a folder:

▶ **1.** Open the Public Documents folder under the Documents library.

▶ **2.** Right-click the **Assets First** folder, and examine the shortcut menu. Note that there is no option on the shortcut menu for opening a Command Prompt window.

▶ **3.** Press the **Esc** key to close the shortcut menu.

Eve suggests you use the Shift key to display additional shortcut menu options.

▶ **4.** Hold down the **Shift** key, right-click the **Assets First** folder, click **Open command window here**, and then release the **Shift** key. Windows 7 opens a command-line window, which displays the path to the Assets First directory in the command prompt to indicate your current location in the folder structure of your disk. In the title bar of the command-line window appears the path to the command interpreter, namely C:\Windows\system32\cmd.exe.

▶ **5.** Type **color f0** (*F* followed by a zero) to display black text against a white background, press the **Enter** key, and then clear the screen.

▶ **6.** Use Aero Snap to extend the command-line window from the top of the desktop to the taskbar.

This feature allows you to quickly open a command-line window from any folder and focus on that folder without having to type complex commands with long paths.

Displaying a Directory Tree

When you work in the Windows 7 graphical user interface, you use Windows Explorer to view the folders at any folder level within the hierarchy of your computer system and to also navigate from one folder level to another or one drive to another. You also use the Navigation pane to quickly switch to other folders and drives. If you want to view the directory structure in a command-line environment, you use the TREE command, an external command. The TREE command (without any parameters) displays the directory structure of the current directory and its subdirectories. The current directory is the directory displayed at the end of the path in the command prompt.

At Eve's prompting, you will examine your directory structure of the Assets First directory.

To view a directory tree for the current directory:

▶ **1.** Type **tree** and then press the **Enter** key. The TREE command produces a diagram-matic view of the directory structure under the Assets First directory (i.e., the current directory). See Figure 13-14.

Figure 13-14   ▶   **Viewing a directory tree**

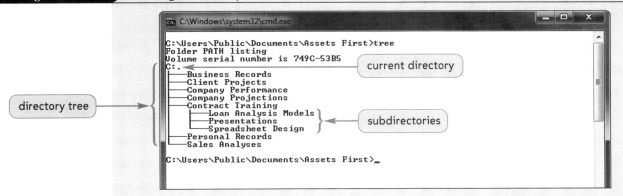

Because you did not specify where you wanted to start, the TREE command started at the current directory on the current drive. This use of the TREE com-mand does not list files under these directories and subdirectories.

As shown in this figure, the TREE command identifies the output as a "Folder PATH listing." Under the serial number, the notation C:. (pronounced *C colon dot*) marks the top of the directory tree, and the period (called a *dot*) after C: is a special notation used to denote the current directory. So, you interpret C:. as meaning the current directory on drive C.

Business Records, Client Projects, Company Performance, Company Projections, Contract Training, Personal Records, and Sales Analyses are subdirectories under the Assets First directory. Loan Analysis Models, Presentations, and Spreadsheet Design are subdirectories under the Contract Training directory.

INSIGHT

Understanding Directories and Subdirectories

After you open a Computer window and then select a drive, you are in the top-level folder of that drive. In a command-line window, the equivalent location is called the top-level directory or root directory. Within the top-level folder, top-level directory, or root directory of a drive, you have subfolders or subdirectories. For example, under the top-level folder of drive C, you have the Windows and Program Files subfolders. If you open the Windows subfolder in a command-line window, you refer to it as a directory, and you refer to its subfolders as subdirectories. If you need to refer to the directory above the current directory, that directory is called the parent directory. Thus, how you use the terms *directory* or *subdirectory* to describe your current location and what is included under that location depends in part on where you are located in the directory structure of a disk.

You can also view a list of files in these directories by using the Filename switch (/F).

To view filenames under each directory:

▶ **1.** Clear the screen, press the **Up Arrow** key twice to recall the TREE command, press the **spacebar**, type **/f** and then press the **Enter** key. The TREE /F command now displays the directory structure and lists files by subdirectory. See Figure 13-15.

Figure 13-15	Viewing a directory tree with filenames

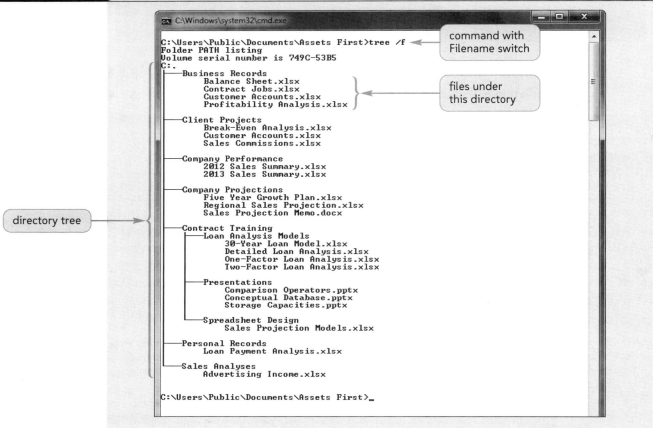

If you view the directory structure using the TREE command, and then decide that you want to save that directory tree in a file on disk, you use the **output redirection operator** (**>**) to redirect the output to a file using the following syntax:
TREE > [drive:]\[path]\filename /A

If you use the output redirection operator, that output is sent to another location, such as a file on disk, and you do not see the output on the screen.

The drive and path are optional, but a filename is required. The ASCII switch (/A) converts the vertical and horizontal lines in the directory tree to plus and minus signs as well as vertical bars and backslashes so you can see the relationships between directories in the text file. **ASCII** stands for **American Standard Code for Information Interchange**, and refers to the use of a set of codes to represent letters of the alphabet (uppercase and lowercase), numbers, symbols, and certain simple graphic symbols. (such as ╥). You can create the graphical symbol by typing 2566 followed immediately by Alt+X

So that you can become familiar with this option, you decide to redirect the output of the TREE command to a file on your flash drive.

The next set of steps assumes that G: is your flash drive name. If your flash drive name is different, you should type the name of your flash drive instead of G: in the commands.

> **TIP**
>
> ASCII files are simple text files.

To redirect output to a file using the output redirection operator:

▶ **1.** Type **tree > g:\AssetsFirst.txt /f /a** (substituting G: before the filename with your actual flash drive name), and then press the **Enter** key. The command interpreter displays a new command prompt after the output of the TREE command is redirected to the AssetsFirst.txt file.

Trouble? If the command interpreter displays the message "The device is not ready," then you did not specify the correct drive name. If necessary, open a Computer window to verify the correct drive name, and then enter the command again.

▶ **2.** Type **g:\AssetsFirst.txt** (substituting G: with your actual flash drive name), press the **Enter** key, and then use Aero Snap to vertically resize the window. Windows 7 opens the AssetsFirst file in Notepad, as shown in Figure 13-16. You now have a copy of this directory structure, along with filenames by directory. Notice the replacement of smooth lines in the directory tree with the ASCII characters for a plus sign, dash, vertical bar, and backslash.

Figure 13-16 **Viewing a directory tree in Notepad**

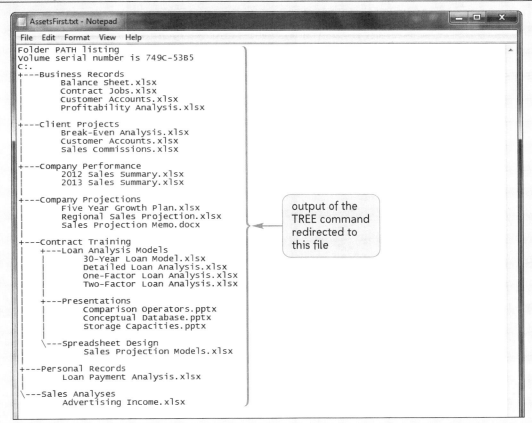

output of the TREE command redirected to this file

▶ **3.** Close the Notepad window.

You can also view the directory structure of any other part of a disk drive by specifying the path to the directory where you want to start. If you want to view all or part of the directory tree for your entire hard disk drive, you specify the backslash symbol (\) as the path to the top-level directory of that drive. However, because the directory structure is extensive and your output will comprise many pages, you should use the MORE filter to produce paged output, one screen at a time.

To view a directory tree of drive C:

1. Clear the screen, type **tree \ | more** (with a backslash before the pipe symbol) and press the **Enter** key. The MORE filter takes the output of the TREE command and displays the first part of the directory tree for drive C. The notation C:\ at the top of the directory tree indicates that the directory tree starts with the top-level directory (represented by the backslash symbol), or root directory, of drive C. In the command you entered, you used the backslash to instruct the TREE command to display the directory structure starting not from where you are currently located but at the top-level directory or root directory instead. Because you did not specify the drive, the TREE command displays a view of the directory structure of the current drive (presumably drive C, the default drive).

2. Press the **spacebar**. The MORE filter displays the next page of output. You can cancel this operation rather than examine the rest of the directory structure.

3. Press and hold down the **Ctrl** key while you press **C** on the keyboard, release **C**, and then release the **Ctrl** key. The command interpreter interrupts the output of the MORE filter, displays **^C^C** after the output (for Ctrl+C), and then redisplays the command prompt.

4. Keep the command-line window open for the next section of the tutorial.

Ctrl+C is called the **interrupt command** or cancel command because you use it to interrupt and cancel a command operation. You can also use Ctrl+Break to interrupt a command.

REFERENCE

Displaying a Directory Tree

- Click Command Prompt from the Accessories menu, or if you are in a folder window, hold the Shift key while you right-click a folder, and then click "Open command window here."
- If you want to display a directory tree for the current directory, type TREE, and then press the Enter key.
- If you want the directory tree to start with another directory, or on another drive, type TREE and then press the spacebar. Type the drive name (if needed), the full path to the directory, press the spacebar, type | (a vertical bar for the pipe operator), press the spacebar, type MORE and then press the Enter key.
- If you want the directory tree to start from the top-level directory of the current drive, type TREE and then press the spacebar followed by the drive name and a backslash symbol for the root directory (for example, TREE \ or TREE C:\).

If you want to examine the directory structure of another drive and start at that drive's top level folder, you must also specify the drive name. For example, if you are on drive C, and want to examine the entire directory structure of your flash drive in drive G, you enter this command: TREE G:\ | MORE

Changing to the Root Directory

To navigate from directory to directory in a command-line environment, you use the CD (Change Directory) command, an internal command. When you use this command, you also include the path to the directory that you want to use. If you want to switch to the root directory of the current drive, you specify the path for that directory, which is represented by a backslash (\).

Eve asks you to change to the root directory and then examine the contents of that directory.

To change to the root directory:

▶ **1.** Clear the screen, type **cd ** (a backslash symbol), and then press the **Enter** key. As shown by the path in the command prompt, you just changed from the Assets First directory under Public Documents to the root directory of drive C. See Figure 13-17.

Figure 13-17	Changing to the root directory

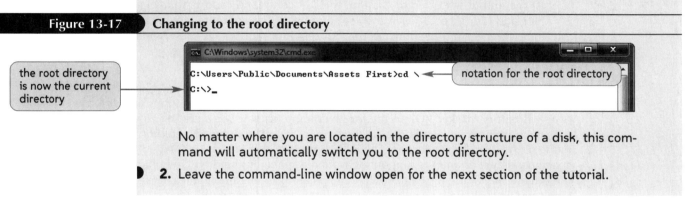

the root directory is now the current directory

No matter where you are located in the directory structure of a disk, this command will automatically switch you to the root directory.

▶ **2.** Leave the command-line window open for the next section of the tutorial.

Later you will examine other ways to use the CD command to change directories.

Once you switch to another directory, you often want to know what's stored in that directory.

Viewing the Contents of a Directory

You can use the DIR (Directory) command, an internal command, to display a list of subdirectories and files within a directory, along with information about the contents of the directory. In fact, the DIR command is one of the most commonly used commands, and when used with switches, it is very versatile.

Eve points out to you that you should become familiar with the contents of the root directory and with the different ways in which you can use the DIR command to view information about files on a disk.

To view the contents of the current directory:

▶ **1.** Clear the screen, and at the command prompt, type **dir** and then press the **Enter** key. The DIR (Directory) command displays the contents of the current directory—the root directory of the current drive (drive C). See Figure 13-18.

Figure 13-18 **Viewing a directory listing of the root directory**

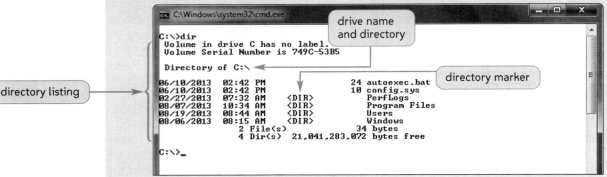

At the end of the directory listing, the DIR command reports that there are two files and four directories in the root directory. The contents of your root directory may differ from that shown in this figure. Note that the DIR command does not display the contents of each subdirectory under the root directory.

The first two columns of this directory listing show the date and time that each subdirectory or file was last modified, the third column identifies subdirectories with the use of the **directory marker** <DIR>, the fourth column displays file sizes in bytes (subdirectory sizes are not displayed because they are so small), and the fifth column displays the name of the subdirectory or file. The DIR command also reports on the total amount of space used by files and the amount of available space on the drive. If the file system on the drive is NTFS, the files and subdirectories are listed in alphabetical order, with files displayed first followed by subdirectories. If the file system on the drive is FAT, the directory listing is in the default disk order—the order in which each directory or file was created on the disk. The two files autoexec.bat and config.sys are DOS startup configuration files. Windows 7 keeps these files for backward compatibility with older programs.

The directory listing does not show hidden directories and hidden files. To view all subdirectories and files within a directory, you use the Attribute switch (/A) with the DIR command. The Attribute switch (/A) instructs the DIR command to list all subdirectories and files no matter what attributes are assigned to the subdirectories and files. If it makes it easier to remember, you can think of /A as meaning *all files*.

To view all subdirectories and files within the root directory:

1. Type **dir /a** and then press the **Enter** key. The DIR command displays a directory listing that now includes hidden directories and files in the directory listing. See Figure 13-19.

TIP

If you want to view information about other switches for the DIR command, type DIR /? and press the Enter key.

| Figure 13-19 | Modifying a directory listing to include hidden directories and files |

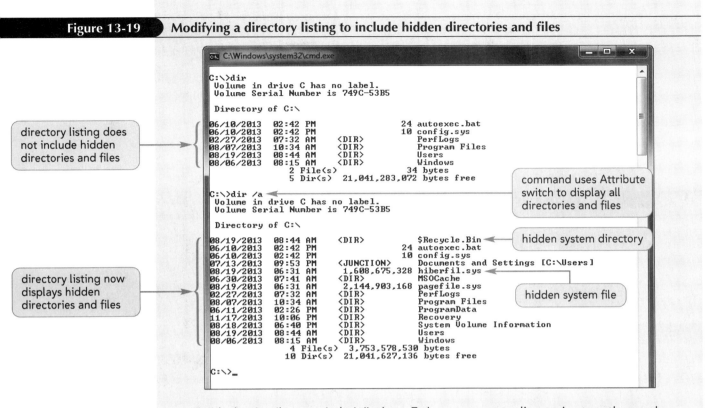

directory listing does not include hidden directories and files

command uses Attribute switch to display all directories and files

hidden system directory

directory listing now displays hidden directories and files

hidden system file

With the Attribute switch, Windows 7 does not group directories together and list them after files (as occurred when you did not use the Attribute switch). Note also the amount of storage space used by files is significantly greater now that the directory listing includes hidden files.

On the computer used for Figure 13-19, the DIR command reports that there are 4 files (2 of which are hidden files) and 10 directories (6 of which are hidden directories) in the root directory. The largest file is the virtual memory paging file with the filename pagefile. sys (which you examined in Tutorial 9 and which is hidden). If hibernation is enabled on your computer, you will also see a hibernation file named hiberfil.sys (which you examined in Tutorial 2 and which is hidden) with a file size close to the amount of installed RAM on your computer. This figure does not include bootmgr, the Windows Boot Manager file that you examined in Tutorial 8 that is hidden, and it does not include the Boot directory that contains boot configuration data and files that you also examined in Tutorial 8 and which is also hidden by default. Since the computer used for Figure 13-19 is set up as a dual-boot system, the bootmgr file and the Boot directory are on the first partition where Windows Vista is installed. The Windows 7 partition is identified as drive C even though it is the second partition. The contents of your root directory may differ from that shown in this figure.

The DIR command displays <JUNCTION> for the normally hidden Documents and Settings directory because, as shown in square brackets, it is an NTFS pointer to the C:\Users directory that contains the directories for each user account. Junctions provide backward compatibility with programs designed before the introduction of Windows Vista so they can work with the new folder names found in Windows 7 and Windows Vista. For example, in Windows XP, the Documents and Settings folder stored user accounts; however, under Windows 7, that folder no longer exists and instead user accounts are found in the Users folder. Junctions therefore redirect programs designed for versions of Windows before Windows 7 to the corresponding Windows 7 folders.

The Program Files subdirectory contains directories for operating system components (such as Internet Explorer) and directories for different software products installed on your computer. The hidden $Recycle.Bin folder contains deleted files in the Recycle Bin. The Windows directory contains the bulk of the installed software for the operating system.

You can also use another switch, the Sort Order switch (/O), to list subdirectories first in alphabetical order by directory name, followed by files in alphabetical order by filename. Note that the O in the Sort Order switch (/O) is the uppercase letter O, not the number 0 (zero).

To view all subdirectories and files within the root directory:

TIP

The order in which you list switches with this command does not affect the output.

1. Clear the screen, press the **Up Arrow** key to recall the previous **dir /a** command, press the **spacebar**, type **/o** (a lowercase o, not a zero), verify that your final command is **dir /a /o**, and then press the **Enter** key.

The DIR command displays a directory listing in alphabetical order, first by directory (including the JUNCTION which is a pointer to a directory), then by files. See Figure 13-20. Note the name of your Windows directory because you will need to know that name in the next set of tutorial steps.

Figure 13-20 | Displaying all subdirectories and all files in a directory in alphabetical order by name

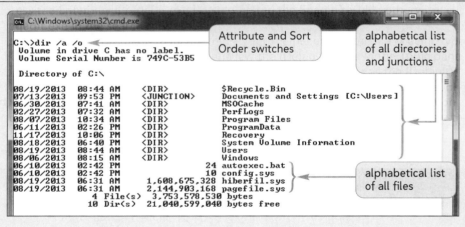

Eve suggests that you examine the Windows folder next, and because the Windows folder contains many different directories and files, she also suggests that you use the Page or Pause switch (/P) to display one screen of output at a time.

To view a directory listing of the Windows folder:

▶ **1.** Clear the screen, type **dir windows /a /o /p** (replacing *windows* with the name of your Windows directory if it is different), and then press the **Enter** key. Because you specified the path to the Windows directory, you are now viewing its contents rather than the contents of the root directory. Directories are listed first in alphabetical order, followed by files in alphabetical order, because you specified the Sort Order switch. You also specified the Page switch, so the DIR command produces paged output, and then displays the "Press any key to continue…" prompt at the bottom of the window. Because this command has its own switch for producing paged output, you do not need to use the pipe operator and the MORE filter (though they work). Note also that although the command you entered is not displayed in the window, it is displayed in the title bar.

When you specified the path to the Windows directory, you used a relative path by just identifying the name of the Windows folder. That **relative path** implied that the Windows directory is under the current directory (which is the case in this instance). You could have also typed \WINDOWS to indicate that the Windows directory is under the top-level directory of the current drive, or you could be more specific and use C:\WINDOWS, which is an **absolute path** that makes no assumptions about the location of the Windows folder.

The single period (called a *dot*) in the right column of the first directory marker (<DIR>) refers to the current directory—the one you are viewing (in this case, Windows). The two dots (called *dot dot*) to the right of the second directory marker refers to the parent directory of the current directory. In this case, the parent directory of the Windows subdirectory is the root directory of drive C; in other words, C:\. Windows 7 (and DOS) both use these directory markers to keep track of where they are in the directory structure of a disk and to navigate the directory structure. Every directory and subdirectory has a *dot* and a *dot dot* entry.

To view the next page of the directory listing:

▶ **1.** Press the **spacebar**. The next part of the directory listing for the computer used for this figure shows the names of files stored in the Windows folder, listed in alphabetical order.

▶ **2.** If necessary, keep pressing the **spacebar** to view the remainder of the output.

▶ **3.** At the next command prompt, clear the screen, type **cd windows** (replacing *windows* with the name of your Windows directory if it is different), and then press the **Enter** key. The CD command switches to the Windows directory. See Figure 13-21. The command interpreter updates the command prompt to show the path to the current directory—now the Windows directory.

| Figure 13-21 | Changing to the Windows directory |

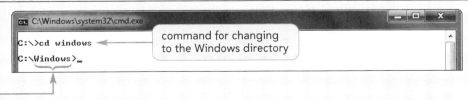

current directory

4. Type **dir /ad /o /p** and then press the **Enter** key. The DIR command displays only the subdirectories under the Windows directory because you added the *D* parameter for *directory* to the Attribute switch (/A). That changes the way in which the Directory command operates and specifies that it show only directories. You can use this technique to view and concentrate on subdirectories within a directory.

5. If necessary, press the **spacebar** to view the remainder of the directory listing.

6. Clear the screen, use the **Up arrow** key to recall the DIR /AD /O /P command, use the **Left arrow** key to position the cursor under the *D* in /AD, type a **minus sign**, verify that your final command is **dir /a-d /o /p** and then press the **Enter** key. The DIR command now displays only the files in the Windows directory.

If you place a minus sign before a parameter in a switch, you reverse its effect. The /A-D switch instructs the DIR command to exclude directories. By modifying the Attribute switch again, you changed the way in which the DIR command operates. You can use this technique to view and concentrate on files within a directory.

7. If necessary, use the **spacebar** to view the remainder of the directory listing and return to the command prompt, and then clear the screen.

8. Leave the command-line window open for the next section of the tutorial.

When using the DIR command, you can specify the path to the directory you want to examine or, if you prefer, you can use the CD command to first switch to that directory and then use the DIR command to view its contents.

Because the DIR command has an extensive list of switches, and because the switches can be combined and used in different ways, you can use the Help switch (/?) with the DIR command to refresh your memory about the types and uses of the DIR command switches.

As you can tell, the DIR command is quite versatile, and quite important, because it provides you with the information you need about the contents of a disk and directory.

Viewing File Attributes

Another important command is the ATTRIB (Attribute) command, an external command that lists attributes assigned to files by the operating system. You can also use this command to change file attributes. For example, if you need to edit a file assigned the read-only attribute, you must first turn off the read-only attribute so you can make changes to the file and then save the changes. Then you can turn on the read-only attribute again to protect the file from further modification.

Eve suggests that you return to the root directory and examine the attributes of Windows system files.

To change to the root directory and then view attributes of files:

1. Clear the screen (if necessary), type **cd ** and then press the **Enter** key to change to the root directory in one step. The command prompt now changes to the root directory of drive C.

2. Type **attrib** and then press the **Enter** key. The ATTRIB command lists the attributes of all the files in the root directory. On the computer used for Figure 13-22, all of the files are assigned the archive attribute (identified by the code *A*) indicating that they have been modified, but not yet backed up.

Figure 13-22 Viewing file attributes

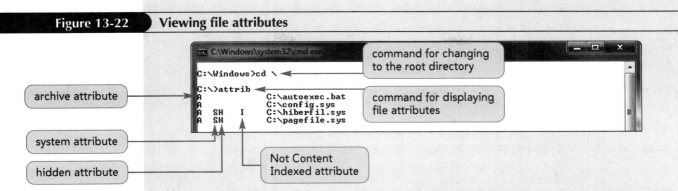

Hiberfil.sys and pagefile.sys are assigned the system attribute (identified by the code *S*) indicating that they are operating system files, and these files are also assigned the hidden attribute (identified by the code *H*) indicating that they are hidden files and therefore are not displayed in a directory listing, unless you specify otherwise. Hiberfile.sys is also assigned the Not Content Indexed attribute so it is not indexed by the Search Indexer. Because Windows 7 needs to write to pagefile.sys to use virtual memory and to write to hiberfil.sys before a computer switches to hibernation, these files cannot be read-only. Also, as you can tell from this list of file attributes, a file might be assigned more than one attribute.

Bootmgr, which is not visible in this figure because it's stored on another drive on this dual-boot computer, is also assigned the read-only attribute (identified by the code *R*) indicating that you cannot modify or delete this file.

▶ **3.** Type **attrib /?** and then press the **Enter** key. The Help information shows how to turn on and turn off an attribute. See Figure 13-23.

Figure 13-23 Viewing Help information on the ATTRIB command

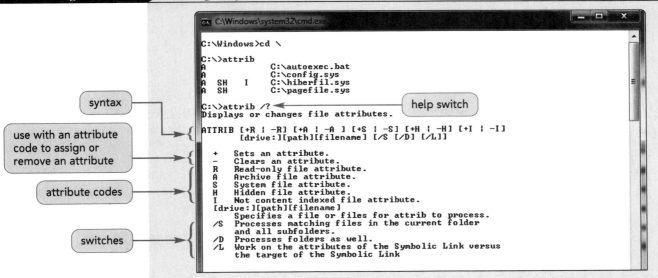

Note that you can also use the Subdirectory switch (*/S*) to view information or change attributes in the current directory as well as all subdirectories under the current directory. The Directory switch (*/D*) also includes directories in the operation.

▶ **4.** Leave the command-line window open for the next section of the tutorial.

To change file attributes, you type ATTRIB followed by a space and the filename, and then you specify which attributes you want to turn on or off. If you place a plus sign before the code for an attribute, you enable or turn on that attribute. For example, if you want to hide a file named Passwords.docx so it is not displayed in a directory listing (or in a folder), you enter the ATTRIB PASSWORDS.DOCX +H command. If you want to hide the file and make it read-only, you enter the ATTRIB PASSWORDS.DOCX +H +R command.

If you place a minus sign before the code for an attribute, you remove or turn off that attribute. For example, if you want to change the hidden file Passwords. docx so it is once again displayed in a directory listing or in a folder, you enter the ATTRIB PASSWORDS.DOCX -H command.

The ATTRIB command is often used with the DIR command when troubleshooting problems in a command-line environment. You use the DIR command first to view the contents of a directory with its Attribute switch (/A) to display all files. Then you use the ATTRIB command to view attributes of a specific file using its filename.

Creating a Directory

You can use the MD (Make Directory) command, an internal command, to create directories on a disk. When you use the MD command, you specify the name of the directory you want to create. If you want the directory created on another drive, you must also specify the drive name as part of the path with the new directory name. If a path, directory name, or filename contains one or more spaces, you enclose the path, directory name, or filename within quotation marks. Otherwise, Windows 7 might interpret the spaces as delimiters (like the backslash (\) in a full path) and assume that each space separates two different parameters within the command. For example, if you want to create a directory called Performance Measurements on the current drive, and assuming you were already at the root directory of that drive, you enter this command: MD "Performance Measurements"

If you do not use the quotation marks, the MD command creates two directories—one called Performance and the other called Measurements. It will not create a directory by the name of "Performance Measurements."

If you are working on drive C and want to create that same subdirectory on a flash drive in drive G, you enter one of the following commands:

MD "G:\Performance Measurements"
MD G:\"Performance Measurements"

(Note that the position of the quotation marks in each command differs.)

If you do not use quotation marks in this example, the MD command creates a directory on drive G called *Performance* and another directory *on drive C* called *Measurements*. (That also gives away the fact that you can use the MD command to create multiple directories at the same time.) For certain other commands, such as the CD command, which you examined earlier, you may not need to use quotation marks around subdirectory names or filenames that contain one or more spaces.

If a directory name or filename does not contain spaces, you do not need to use quotation marks even if the name is longer than eight characters. For example, to create a directory named *Performance* on drive G, and assuming you were already at the root directory of drive G, you enter this command: MD Performance

After asking Eve how to back up some important files on your computer and store the backups on your flash drive, she explains that one simple way is to copy the files individually or as a group. However, she notes that you first need to create a directory on your flash drive for the files you copy. If you switch to the subdirectory under the Public Documents directory that contains the files you want to copy, you can copy the files from that directory.

To create a subdirectory on a flash drive:

▶ 1. Clear the screen, type **cd users\public\documents\assets first\business records** and then press the **Enter** key. You switch from the root directory to the Business Records directory in one step. See Figure 13-24.

Trouble? If the command interpreter displays the message "The system cannot find the path specified," you mistyped the path. Repeat this step again and verify that you typed the full path correctly.

| Figure 13-24 | Changing to a new directory using a path |

specifying the path to a new directory

```
C:\Windows\system32\cmd.exe
C:\>cd users\public\documents\assets first\business records
C:\Users\Public\Documents\Assets First\Business Records>_
```

operating system prompt updated to show the current directory

Because you were already in the root directory, you do not need to include a backslash symbol in the path before *users* because the CD command assumes that you want to switch to a directory relative to the one where you are located, in other words, to a subdirectory under the current directory. However, you would need to specify the root directory if you were somewhere else in the folder structure (such as in the Windows directory). The advantage of using the first backslash symbol in the path is that you can change to any directory from *any* other directory on drive C. You do not need to be in the root directory first. You do, however, have to be on the right drive.

Make sure you enclose the drive and directory name within quotation marks.

▶ 2. To create a directory on your flash drive from drive C, clear the screen, type **md "g:\Assets First"** (substituting G: with the drive name for your flash drive), and then press the **Enter** key. If you want the directory name to use mixed case, with uppercase characters for the first character in each word, you must type it using the case you prefer. After the MD command creates the directory, you see another command prompt. To verify the operation, you can use the DIR command.

▶ 3. Type **dir** followed by a **space** and the **drive name** for your flash drive, and then press the **Enter** key. As shown for the flash drive in Figure 13-25, the MD command created a directory named Assets First.

Trouble? If the new directory name is displayed as *Assets*, you did not include quotation marks around the drive and directory name in the previous step. To correct this problem, you must first remove the two directories you created by using the RD (Remove Directory) command. Type RD G:\ASSETS (substituting your flash drive name for G:) to remove the Assets directory from your flash drive. Then type RD FIRST to remove the second directory created on the current drive. Repeat Step 2 and make sure you use quotation marks around the drive and directory name, and repeat Step 3 to verify the new directory name.

Figure 13-25   **Viewing a directory of a flash drive**

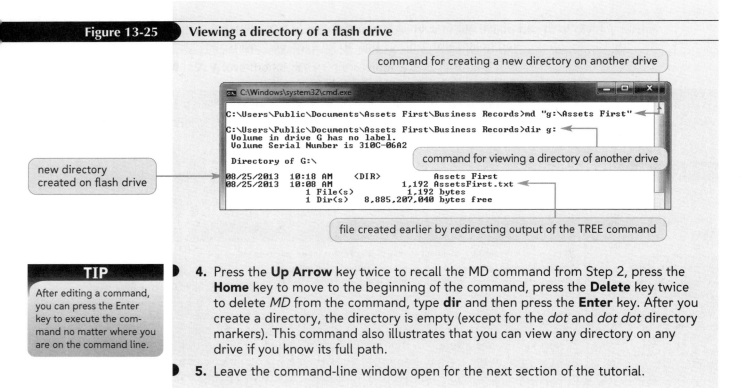

command for creating a new directory on another drive

new directory
created on flash drive

command for viewing a directory of another drive

file created earlier by redirecting output of the TREE command

4. Press the **Up Arrow** key twice to recall the MD command from Step 2, press the **Home** key to move to the beginning of the command, press the **Delete** key twice to delete *MD* from the command, type **dir** and then press the **Enter** key. After you create a directory, the directory is empty (except for the *dot* and *dot dot* directory markers). This command also illustrates that you can view any directory on any drive if you know its full path.

5. Leave the command-line window open for the next section of the tutorial.

If you merely want to create a subdirectory under the current directory, you do not need to specify the drive name or the path. However, if the new directory name includes a space, you must enclose it within quotation marks.

If you want to remove a directory, you can use the RD command. The syntax is similar to that of the MD command. If the directory that you want to remove contains other sub-directories and/or files, you must use the Subdirectory (/S) switch with the RD command to verify that you want to remove the directory and all its contents. For example, if you want to remove the Assets First directory on your flash drive, as well as any subdirecto-ries or files that are in that directory, you type RD "G:\ASSETS FIRST" /S and then press the Enter key and verify the operation.

Copying Files

You can use the COPY command, an internal command, to copy files from one location to another. The general syntax for the COPY command is as follows:
COPY *source destination*

The **source** is the directory, files, or file you want to copy. If you want to copy files from another drive and directory, you have to also specify the drive and path of the directory that contains the files you want to copy. The **destination** is the drive or direc-tory where you want to copy the files to. You can specify the full path of the source and destination so the COPY command knows exactly what to copy and where to copy it to. After a copy operation, you have two identical copies of the same file (or files) in two different locations.

Next Eve shows you how to use the COPY command to copy a single file to a direc-tory on your flash drive.

To copy files:

▶ **1.** Clear the screen, type **dir** and then press the **Enter** key. The file that you want to copy is Balance Sheet.xlsx.

▶ **2.** Clear the screen, type **copy "Balance Sheet.xlsx" "g:\Assets First"** (making sure you enclosed the filename and directory name within quotation marks and making sure you substituted your flash drive name for G: if it is different), and then press the **Enter** key. If the operation is successful, you will see the message *1 file(s) copied.* Because the command you enter is longer than the available space, the command interpreter will wrap the command around to the next line in the window, but it will still work.

> **Trouble?** If the command interpreter reports that the system cannot find the file specified, use the F3 key or Up Arrow key to recall the command you just entered, check to make sure your command is entered correctly, edit the command (if necessary), and then repeat Step 2. Also make sure you used the correct drive name for your flash drive.

▶ **3.** Press the **F7** function key to display the command history, use the **Up Arrow** key to locate the command DIR "G:\ASSETS FIRST", and then press the **Enter** key. The DIR command displays the contents of the directory on your flash drive, and that directory now contains the file you copied, as shown in Figure 13-26.

| Figure 13-26 | Copying a file to a directory on a flash drive |

command for copying a file to a directory on another drive

command for viewing the contents of a directory on another drive

file copied from drive C

▶ **4.** Leave the command-line window open for the next section of the tutorial.

If you specify a directory as the source, the copy command copies the contents of the directory (but not the directory itself) to whatever destination you specify. This feature is a simple way to specify that you want to copy everything within that directory.

Copying a File to a Flash Drive

- Attach the flash drive to your computer, close any dialog boxes or windows that open, and then open a Command Prompt window.
- To switch to the directory that contains the files you want to copy, type CD followed by a space and the full path of the directory that contains the files you want to copy.
- Type COPY, press the spacebar, type the name of the file you want to copy, press the spacebar, type the full path of the drive and directory you want to copy the files to, and then press the Enter key. If you are using directory names or filenames with one or more spaces, enclose the source and, if necessary, the destination, within quotation marks.
- To verify the copy operation, type DIR, press the spacebar, type the full path of the drive and directory that contains the copied files, and then press the Enter key.

The Copy command only copies files within a single subdirectory. If you need to copy files in several directories at once and create the same directory structure on a target disk, you would use the new ROBOCOPY (Robust File Copy) command.

Changing Drives

Another simple, but important, operation is changing from one drive to another drive. To perform this operation, you just type the drive name after the command prompt and press the Enter key. A drive name always consists of a letter of the alphabet followed by a colon. You must use the colon when typing a drive name.

Eve suggests you switch to your flash drive and then open the Assets First directory.

To change drives and open a directory:

1. Clear the screen, type **g:** (or the drive name for your flash drive if it is different) and then press the **Enter** key. Windows 7 changes to your flash drive and updates the command prompt. See Figure 13-27.

Figure 13-27 Changing from drive C to a flash drive

current drive and directory | command for changing to another drive

2. Type **cd Assets First** (you do not need to use quotation marks with the CD command, though they work as well), and then press the **Enter** key. Windows 7 changes to the Assets First directory on your flash drive and updates the command prompt to show your exact location.

3. Type **dir** and then press the **Enter** key. Windows 7 displays the file copied to the Assets First directory on your flash drive. See Figure 13-28. Unlike earlier, when you specified the path to this directory, you do not need to specify the drive name or directory name, because you have already switched to this drive and subdirectory before using the DIR command.

| Figure 13-28 | Switching to and viewing the contents of a new directory |

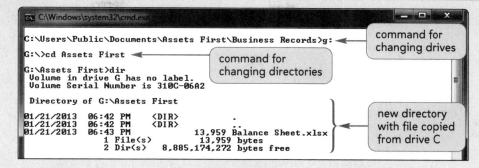

4. Type **c:** and then press the **Enter** key. You switch to the last directory that you were using on drive C; namely, the Business Records directory.

5. Leave the command-line window open for the next section of the tutorial.

When working in a command-line window, you depend on drive names and paths far more than you do when working the graphical user interface.

INSIGHT

Understanding the CD Command

You cannot use the CD command to change from one drive to another. For example, assume the current drive is drive C. If you enter the CD G: command to change to your flash drive, Windows 7 does not change to that drive. Instead, you remain on drive C. However, the CD command does show you which directory is the current directory on drive G. You can also use CD command to change to another directory on another drive and make it the current directory on that drive without actually switching to that drive. For example, you could enter the command CD G:\ASSETS FIRST to change to the ASSETS FIRST directory on your flash drive without actually switching to that drive. Then, if you copy files from a directory on drive C to your flash drive and only specify the drive to copy to, the files are copied to the ASSETS FIRST directory of that drive, and you do not need to specify the path for the directory (you just specify the drive name) as the destination.

Using Wildcards in File Specifications

When you perform certain types of operations, such as copying multiple files, you can streamline the process with the use of wildcards if the filenames have some feature in common, such as starting with the same set of characters or having the same file extension. You used wildcards in Tutorial 3 when searching for folders and files. In a command-line window, you can use a wildcard in a similar way as part of a file specification to select a group of files. A **file specification** is a notation for selecting one or more files in a command operation. The asterisk wildcard (*) substitutes for all or part of a filename, and the question mark wildcard (?) substitutes for a single character in a filename at the position of the wildcard.

The asterisk wildcard is the more commonly used wildcard because it makes it easier to select files using some common pattern in the filename. For example, if you want to copy all the Microsoft Word files in a folder to your flash drive (and assuming your flash drive name is G:), you enter the COPY *.DOCX G: command.

In this command, the file specification for the source is *.DOCX. The asterisk wildcard before the file extension substitutes for any filename, so the COPY command selects all files regardless of their filename. However, because you also specified that the file extension must be .docx, the COPY command only copies files with this extension. The net effect is that the COPY command copies all Microsoft Word files with the .docx file extension regardless of their filename. Using this approach, you can copy files as a group, rather than having to copy each separately by specifying each filename. Using wildcards, you can save yourself considerable time and effort.

If you want to copy Microsoft Word documents that contain either the .doc (for pre-Word 2007 files) or the .docx file extension, you can use two wildcards in the command in one of two ways:

COPY *.DOC* G:

COPY *.DOC? G:

The first of these two COPY commands uses the same asterisk wildcard twice. The second asterisk after .DOC specifies that the command select all files that have any character or characters after DOC as well as any files that have no character after DOC. The net effect is that it copies files with the .doc and .docx file extension. This command also copies files that have any other character after .doc in the file extension, such as files with the .docm file extension (for Word Macro-Enabled Documents). It also copies files that have more than one character after .doc in the file extension. If you only have files with the .doc or .docx file extension, it only copies those files.

The second of the two COPY commands shown above uses two wildcards, but the second wildcard is the question mark. This wildcard specifies that the COPY command select all files that have any character or no character after .doc in the file extension. That means that it copies files with the .doc or .docx file extension. Like the asterisk wildcard, it also copies files that have any other character after .doc in the file extension, such as files with the .docm file extension (Word Macro-Enabled Documents), but it does not copy files that have more than one character after .doc in the file extension. Both COPY commands illustrate that you can use more than one wildcard, that you can mix both wildcards in file specifications, and that there might be more than one approach that selects the right set of files.

Let's look at another example where you might use the asterisk wildcard. Assume you have a set of budget files for different fiscal years, such as budget reports and financial projections, each with different file extensions. Also assume you had anticipated that at some point you would need to copy all the files for a given fiscal year and that you named the files accordingly by using FY2013 as the first set of characters in each filename (for example, FY2013 Company Budget.xlsx). To copy all the files for a specific fiscal year by using the asterisk wildcard, you can enter the COPY FY2013* G: command.

This COPY command uses the file specification for the source, namely FY2013*, to select all files that have the same first six characters in the filename, no matter what the remainder of the filename is and no matter what the file extension is. This COPY command then, for example, would copy the files named FY2013 Company Budget.xlsx, FY2013 Budget Report.doc, and FY2013 Company Budget Presentation.ppsx to drive G in one step.

If you want to only copy Microsoft Excel files with filenames that start with FY2013 and not copy other files, such as Microsoft Word files, that start with the same six characters but have a different file extension, you can use the following variation of this command: COPY FY2013*.XLSX G:

In this instance, you are specifying that the first six characters of a filename must be FY2013 and the file extension must be .xlsx (for Microsoft Excel files). The asterisk wildcard means that any combination of characters can follow FY2013 and precede the file extension.

If you want to copy all the files in a directory, such as the Company Projections directory to your flash drive, and assuming you have already switched to that directory first, you can use the COPY *.* G: command. The file specification for the source is *.* (called *star dot star*). The asterisk wildcard before the dot (or period) selects all files, no matter what the main part of the filename is, and the asterisk wildcard after the dot selects all files, no matter what the file extension is. In other words, the file specification (*.*) selects all files.

If you are already in the directory that contains the files you want to copy, you can also use the COPY . G: command. The file specification for the source is represented by a dot, the directory marker for the current directory, and the COPY command therefore copies all files in the current directory. This Power Users tip simplifies the process for copying all files in a directory.

Although the asterisk wildcard is commonly used because of its ability to easily select groups of files, you might also find instances where you need to use the question mark wildcard in a file specification. Assume, for example, you might have five different versions of your resume stored in files with the filenames Resume #1.docx, Resume #2.docx, Resume #3.docx, Resume #4.docx, and Resume #5.docx. To copy these files to your flash drive, you can use the COPY "Resume #?.docx" G: command. In this case, the question mark wildcard substitutes for a single character at the ninth position in each filename, and therefore the COPY command copies all your resume files. If you also had a variation of Resume #1.docx named Resume #1A.docx, the COPY command would not copy that file because it does not meet the file specification (it has the letter *A* after the number represented by the wildcard rather than the required period indicated by the file specification). However, you could use the COPY RESUME* G: command.

Here's another example of when you might want to use the question mark wildcard. Again, assume you have created budget documents over the years and named the files so the first six characters identified the fiscal year. For example, you might have files named FY2012 Budget.xlsx, FY2013 Budget.xlsx, and FY 2014 Budget.xlsx. You can replace the sixth character in the filename with the question mark wildcard and use this file specification: COPY "FY201? Budget.xlsx" G:

This wildcard specification selects all Microsoft Excel files with the .xlsx file extension that have the same characters in the first through fifth positions and the seventh through thirteenth positions in the filename and have any character at the sixth position in the filename.

INSIGHT

Using Wildcards with Directory Names

You can also use wildcards in file specifications with directory names. For example, if you want to change to a directory named Company Projections under the current directory, you can enter the CD Company* command. If there is more than one directory with *Company* at the beginning of the directory name, this command switches to the first of those two directories (in alphabetical order). Depending on the names of the directories located under the current directory, you might also be able to use the CD C* or CD Co* or CD Com* or CD Comp* command. In other words, you only need to use enough characters in a file specification to distinguish one directory from all others with similar names.

Now that Eve has explained how to copy files in a command-line environment using wildcards, you want to copy all the files in the Company Projections directory. First, you will change to the Company Projections directory.

To copy files using a wildcard:

1. Clear the screen, type **cd ..\company projections** and then press the **Enter** key. The current directory is now the Company Projections directory. In this command, the .. (*dot dot*) instructs the CD command to first switch to the parent directory of the current directory (in other words, to Assets First) and then switch to the Company Projections directory next (under the Assets First) directory. Business Records and Company Projections are referred to as parallel directories because they are located at the same level in the directory tree. You can also type CD .. to step up one directory level and then type CD Company Projections to step down one directory level.

   Trouble? If the command interpreter reports that the system cannot find the path specified, then you did not include a space after typing *cd* or you included a space after typing ..(*dot dot*). Repeat this step and make sure you press the spacebar after *cd* and that you do not press the spacebar after .. (*dot dot*) in the path to the Company Projections folder.

2. Type **copy *.* "g:\Assets First"** (making sure you enclose the drive and filename within quotations and making sure you replace G: with the drive name of your flash drive if it differs), and then press the **Enter** key (or recall a previous COPY command from the command history, and then edit it). The COPY command uses wildcards to copy three files that match the file specification for the source to the Assets First directory on your flash drive (in other words, all the files in the Company Projections folder). You can also use . (*dot*) instead of *.* for the source.

3. To verify that the copy operation worked properly, type **dir "g:\Assets First"** (making sure you place quotation marks around the drive and filename and making sure you replace G: with the drive name of your flash drive if it differs) and then press the **Enter** key. The Assets First directory on your flash drive now has four files. See Figure 13-29.

Figure 13-29   Copying files to a subdirectory on a flash drive

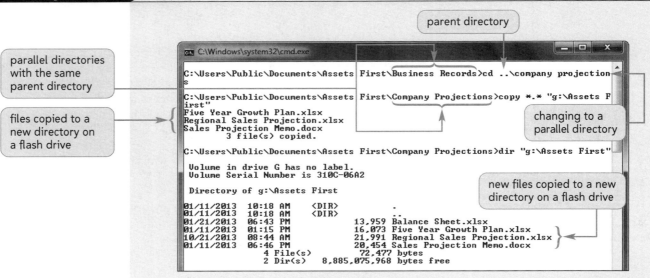

parent directory

parallel directories with the same parent directory

files copied to a new directory on a flash drive

changing to a parallel directory

new files copied to a new directory on a flash drive

---

4. Type **CD ..** (for *dot dot*) and press the **Enter** key to switch to the parent directory Assets First, and then clear the screen.

5. Keep the command-line window open for the next section of the tutorial.

Many commands use a file specification with or without wildcards to select one or more files for an operation. A file specification can refer to a specific directory or file, a group of directories, or a group of files selected with the use of wildcards.

Wildcards are quite powerful and save you time and effort. All you have to do is to formulate the file specification you need.

REFERENCE

Copying Files Using Wildcards

- Open a Command Prompt or command-line window.
- Use the CD (Change Directory) command to change to the directory that contains the files you want to copy.
- If you want to copy all the files in the directory to a flash drive (for example), type COPY *.* G: (where G: is the flash drive name) or type COPY . G: and then press the Enter key.
- If you want to copy all files with a specific file extension, such as .docx, to a flash drive, type COPY *.DOCX G: (where G: is the flash drive name), and then press the Enter key.
- If you want to copy all files that begin with the same set of characters in the filename, such as *Resume*, to your flash drive, type COPY RESUME* G: (where G: is the flash drive name), and then press the Enter key. If the source filenames contain one or more spaces, include the file specification for the source within quotation marks.
- If you want to copy files with identical filenames, except for one character, such as Resume #1.docx, Resume #2.docx, etc., type COPY "RESUME#?.DOCX" G: (where G: is the flash drive name), and then press the Enter key. If the source filenames contain one or more spaces, include the file specification for the source within quotation marks.

You can apply these power user techniques to other situations. For example, if you are extracting a program from a file downloaded from the Internet and want to extract it to the current directory rather than another directory that it is configured to use, you can type a *dot* for the current directory and then start the extraction.

PROSKILLS

Problem Solving: Careful Use of Wildcard Specifications

You must be careful with the use of wildcards because you might end up selecting far more files than you would have otherwise expected for an operation, such as a copy operation, or you might inadvertently end up deleting more files than you expected (including important files you need to keep). A safe strategy is to test wildcard file specifications first by using them with the DIR (Directory) command. This approach selects the files based on the wild-card file specification you use and displays them in the command-line window (but makes no changes to the files). Then you can check to make sure the correct set of files are selected before using that same wildcard file specification with another command, such as deleting all files using that wildcard specification. Also, files you delete in a command-line window are not placed in the Recycle Bin, so you cannot undelete them with Windows 7. To recover them, you would have to locate, download, and install a program for identifying deleted files on an NTFS volume and then restoring the files you want. While wildcards are powerful, you also must test them to make sure they produce the intended results.

Viewing the Windows Environment

In Tutorial 8, you examined environment variables and their settings stored in the Windows environment. You can also check settings for environment variables while working in a command-line environment. One particularly important setting is the one for the PATH environment variable. Windows 7 uses this setting, called the **Windows path**, to locate the program files for external commands.

Eve emphasizes the importance of understanding the Windows environment and path so you can more effectively troubleshoot problems and customize your use of the command-line environment. Eve also notes that you can create new environment variables to simplify the use of commands in a command-line environment. She recommends that you examine the Windows environment with the SET command and that you customize the Directory command by entering a new environment variable.

To view the contents of the Windows environment:

1. Type **CD ** and then press the **Enter** key to return to the root directory.

2. Clear the screen, type **set** and then press the **Enter** key. The SET command, an internal command, displays the contents of the Windows environment (which used to be called the DOS environment). See Figure 13-30. The environment variable names are listed in alphabetical order. Some of your environment variable settings may differ.

Figure 13-30 Viewing environment variables and their settings in the Windows environment

```
C:\Windows\system32\cmd.exe

C:\>set
ALLUSERSPROFILE=C:\ProgramData
APPDATA=C:\Users\Eve\AppData\Roaming
CommonProgramFiles=C:\Program Files\Common Files
COMPUTERNAME=HI-PERFORM
ComSpec=C:\Windows\system32\cmd.exe          ← path to command interpreter stored in
FP_NO_HOST_CHECK=NO                              ComSpec environment variable
HOMEDRIVE=C:
HOMEPATH=\Users\Eve
LOCALAPPDATA=C:\Users\Eve\AppData\Local
LOGONSERVER=\\HI-PERFORM
NUMBER_OF_PROCESSORS=2
OS=Windows_NT
Path=C:\Windows\system32;C:\Windows;C:\Windows\System32\Wbem;C:\Windows\System32
\WindowsPowerShell\v1.0\
PATHEXT=.COM;.EXE;.BAT;.CMD;.VBS;.VBE;.JS;.JSE;.WSF;.WSH;.MSC
PROCESSOR_ARCHITECTURE=x86
PROCESSOR_IDENTIFIER=x86 Family 15 Model 6 Stepping 4, GenuineIntel
PROCESSOR_LEVEL=15
PROCESSOR_REVISION=0604                        setting for PROMPT environment variable
ProgramData=C:\ProgramData                     used to customize the command prompt
ProgramFiles=C:\Program Files
PROMPT=$P$G          ←
PSModulePath=C:\Windows\system32\WindowsPowerShell\v1.0\Modules\
PUBLIC=C:\Users\Public
SAN_DIR=C:\Program Files\SiSoftware\SiSoftware Sandra Lite 2010.SP1d
SESSIONNAME=Console
SystemDrive=C:          ←              setting for SystemDrive environment variable
SystemRoot=C:\Windows
TEMP=C:\Users\Eve\AppData\Local\Temp
TMP=C:\Users\Eve\AppData\Local\Temp
USERDOMAIN=HI-PERFORM
USERNAME=Eve
USERPROFILE=C:\Users\Eve
windir=C:\Windows
```

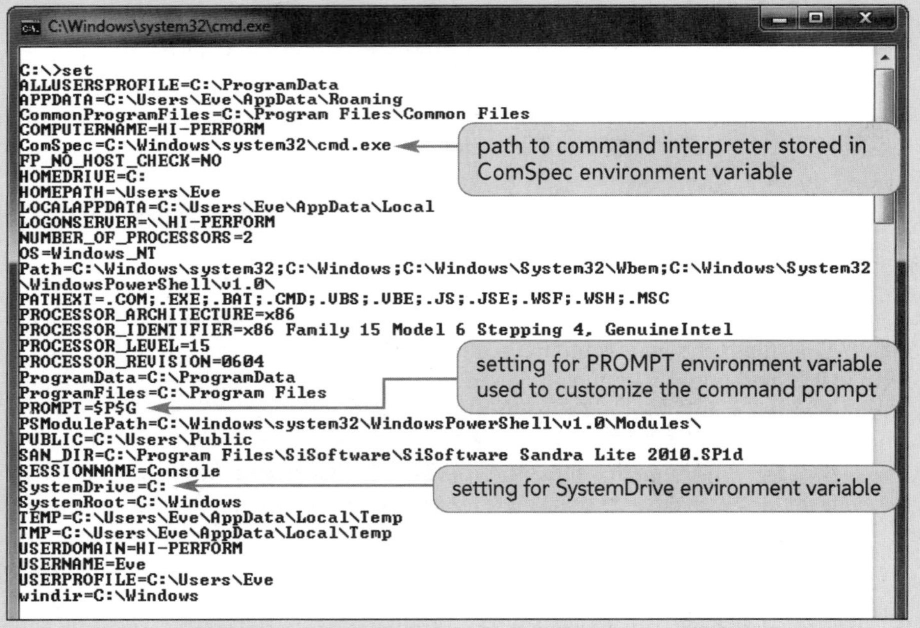

3. Locate the settings for the ComSpec, PROMPT, and SystemDrive environment variables.

The setting for the ComSpec environment variable is the full path of the program for opening a Command Prompt or command-line window. If Windows 7 needs to find cmd.exe so it can load it from disk, it checks the Windows environment for the ComSpec environment variable to determine the location and name of this program.

The PROMPT environment variable determines how the command prompt appears in a command-line window. The setting PG for this environment variable is called a **metastring** (or code) that instructs the command interpreter (cmd.exe) how to display the command prompt. $P (for *path*) instructs the command interpreter to display the full path of the current drive and current directory at the beginning of the command prompt. $G (for *greater than*) instructs the command interpreter to display the greater than symbol (>) after the full path. As noted earlier, the greater than symbol (>) separates the path of the current drive and directory from the command you enter. You can actually use the PROMPT command to design your own custom command prompts. To display the meta-string codes, use the Help switch (/?) with the PROMPT command.

Notice that the SystemDrive environment variable stores the setting for the drive where Windows 7 is installed.

You can also add new environment variables with new settings to the Windows environment. For example, when you first used the DIR command without any switches, it displayed directories and files in alphabetical order. You altered that by using the Sort Order switch (/O), so the DIR command first listed directories in alphabetical order followed by files in alphabetical order. You also used the Page or Pause switch (/P) to display the directory listing one screen at a time. If you frequently use certain switches for the DIR command, such as the Attribute, Sort Order, and Page switches, you can assign them to the DIRCMD environment variable in the Windows environment. Then, when you use the DIR command, you do not have to type the same switches every time you use the command.

Eve encourages you to try this power user's technique.

To assign switches to the DIRCMD environment variable:

▶ **1.** Check the list of environment variables and notice that there is no DIRCMD environment variable listed in the Windows environment (unless of course, you or someone else has already added it). If there is a DIRCMD environment variable, make a note of its setting so you can restore it later.

▶ **2.** Clear the screen, type **dir \windows** (replacing *windows* with the name of your Windows directory, if it is different), and then press the **Enter** key. Note that although the directory listing is in alphabetical order (on an NTFS volume only), directories and files are not grouped together, hidden files are not displayed, and the directory listing does not pause after one screen.

▶ **3.** Clear the screen, type **SET DIRCMD=/a /o /p** (*with no spaces before or after the equals sign*), and then press the **Enter** key. Although case does not matter when you type DIRCMD, uppercase is easier to spot when viewing environment variables and their settings. If you type a space after DIRCMD, that space becomes part of the environment variable name and then this environment variable will not work with the DIR command.

▶ **4.** Type **set** and then press the **Enter** key. The SET command in the previous step created a new environment variable called DIRCMD and assigned the /A, /O, and /P switches for the DIR command to that variable. See Figure 13-31.

Figure 13-31   **Viewing a new environment variable in the Windows environment**

new user-defined environment variable

Directory command switches assigned to the new environment variable

5. Clear the screen, type (or recall from the command history) **dir \windows** (replacing *windows* with the name of your Windows directory, if necessary), press the **Enter** key, view the directory listing, and if necessary, press the **spacebar** to view the remainder of the directory listing. Note that the directory listing is now in alphabetical order first by directory name and then by filename, directories are grouped together, files are grouped together, hidden files are displayed, and the directory listing pauses after each screen. You did not have to type the three switches to produce this type of directory listing; instead, the DIR command automatically used the switches you assigned to the DIRCMD environment variable. Every time you use the DIR command, it will use these switches.

Trouble? If the DIR command does not list directory names first and if there is no paged output, then repeat Steps 3–5, and make sure that you do not press the spacebar after typing DIRCMD in Step 3.

6. Close the Command Prompt window.

When you next open a Command Prompt window, you will need to specify a setting for the DIRCMD environment variable again because it is only retained for the current command-line session.

If you want to update the settings stored in the Windows environment for the DIRCMD variable, just use the SET command again to assign a new set of switches to the DIRCMD environment variable (it automatically overwrites the existing setting). If you want to remove this environment variable and its setting from the Windows environment, just type SET DIRCMD= followed by nothing (not even a space), and then press the Enter key. By not assigning anything to the environment variable, you remove it from the Windows environment. If you press the spacebar after the equals sign, you assign a space to the DIRCMD environment variable.

REFERENCE

Creating a DIRCMD Environment Variable

- From the All Programs menu, click Accessories, and then click Command Prompt.
- To assign switches to the DIRCMD environment variable, such as the switches /a /o /p (for example), type SET DIRCMD=/A /O /P and then press the Enter key.
- To verify the new setting for the DIRCMD environment variable, type SET and then press the Enter key.
- To remove the DIRCMD environment variable from the Windows environment, type SET DIRCMD= followed by nothing (*not even a space*), and then press the Enter key.

When you work in a command-line environment, you might need to execute specific programs to troubleshoot a problem. You can switch to the directory that contains those additional programs, or you can change the setting for the PATH environment variable to include that directory. That's why you should know how to check the settings in the Windows environment so you can verify, modify, or replace those settings. Without the correct path, Windows 7 cannot find and load programs—unless you just happen to be in the directory where the program is stored or unless the directory is included in the Windows path. You can speed up a search for a program by listing the directories in the order you want Windows 7 to search them (for example, the most frequently used, or most important, directory is listed first, and then less frequently used, or the least important, directory is listed last).

Before you change the path, you can record the current path in a batch file on disk by using the output redirection operator (>). You just enter the following command: PATH > OriginalPath.bat

A **batch program** or **batch file** (also called a **script**) is a user-defined program file with the .bat file extension that contains a list of executable commands that the command interpreter can process. Once created, you can use the OriginalPath.bat batch file, shown in Figure 13-32, to restore the original path at the end of a command-line session.

| Figure 13-32 | A batch file containing the PATH command for restoring the original path |

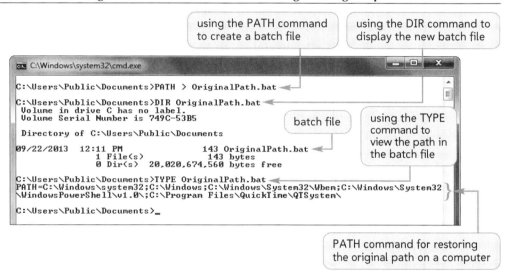

using the PATH command to create a batch file

using the DIR command to display the new batch file

batch file

using the TYPE command to view the path in the batch file

PATH command for restoring the original path on a computer

All you have to do is switch to the directory where you stored the OriginalPath.bat file, type the command OriginalPath and press the Enter key. Batch files are small in size, but are quite powerful tools for automating common types of operations. Because batch programs are simple ASCII text files, you can open them or create them with simple text editors such as Notepad and view their contents by using the TYPE command as shown in Figure 13-32.

Another advantage of storing a new path in a batch file such as this one is that you can automatically specify a different path every time you open a Command Prompt window by entering the name of the batch file. You can simplify access to this batch file if you store it in the directory opened by the Command Prompt or in one of the directories in the Windows path.

Restoring Your Computer's Settings

Complete the following steps to restore your computer to its original settings.

To restore your computer's settings:

▶ **1.** Open the Public Documents folder, delete the **Assets First** folder, and then close the Public Documents folder.

▶ **2.** Open a Computer window, open a window onto your flash drive, hold down the Ctrl key as you point first to the **Assets First** folder and then to the **AssetsFirst.txt** file to select both objects, click **Organize** on the toolbar, click **Cut** on the Organize menu, navigate to the Tutorial folder in your set of Data Files, click **Organize** on the toolbar, and then click **Paste**. Windows 7 moves the Assets First folder and AssetsFirst.txt file to the Tutorial folder.

▶ **3.** Turn off single-click activation; restore the option for hiding extensions for known file types; and then remove the Computer icon from the desktop.

▶ **4.** If you no longer need the Command Prompt desktop shortcut, delete that shortcut.

▶ **5.** If requested by your instructor, submit a copy of the Assets First folder and the AssetsFirst.txt file in the Tutorial folder, and then close the Tutorial folder.

REVIEW

Session 13.2 Quick Check

1. To refer to the root directory of drive C in a command, you type a(n) _____.

2. . (*dot*) refers to the _____.

3. .. (*dot dot*) refers to the _____.

4. When you perform a copy operation, you specify a(n) _____ and a(n) _____.

5. To change from drive C to drive G, you type _____.

6. A(n) _____ is a symbol used in a file specification to select a group of files.

7. True or False. CD .. changes to the root directory.

8. What is a batch file?

Practice the skills you learned in the tutorial using the same case scenario.

PRACTICE

Review Assignments

For a list of Data Files in the Review folder, see page 829.

Eve recommends that you practice the use of the commands and features that the two of you examined and use the SYSTEMINFO command to document your computer system's settings and the POWERCFG command to produce an updated Power Efficiency Diagnostics report. She also recommends that you examine and try different variations of these commands and features so you can apply your current skills to new ways of working.

As you complete each step in these Review Assignments, record your answers to the questions so you can submit them to your instructor. Use the Clear Screen command, as needed, to clear the output of previous commands so you can easily view the results for a new command. Use a word-processing application such as Word or WordPad to prepare your answers to these questions. If you change any settings on the computer you are using, note what the original settings were so you can restore them later. Complete the following steps:

1. If necessary, attach your flash drive to your computer and close any dialog boxes or windows that open.
2. What is the drive name for your flash drive?
3. Copy the Review folder from the Tutorial.13 folder to the Public Documents folder, and then change the name of the Review folder to **Assets First**.
4. Open a Command Prompt window, and then use Aero Snap to extend the Command Prompt window from the top of the desktop to the taskbar. What is the full path of the current directory in the command-line window?
5. Use the HELP command to display Help information about the COLOR command. What command did you enter? If you want to change the console colors so the command-line window uses a green background and a bright white foreground, what command would you enter at the command prompt? If you want to return to the default console colors without specifying hex digits for the color attribute, what command would you enter?
6. Customize the command-line window using console colors of your own preference. What command did you enter? What are your foreground and background colors now?
7. View information on the VOL command. What command did you enter to display Help information? What does the VOL command do? What is the syntax of the VOL command? Note which part of the command is required and which part is an optional parameter.
8. Use the VOL command to view the volume label for your flash drive. What command did you enter? What is the volume label for your flash drive (if any)?
9. Use the LABEL command to assign a volume label to your flash drive. What command did you enter, and what volume label did you specify?
10. Verify the volume label for your flash drive. What command did you use? What is the volume name of your flash drive?
11. Use the LABEL command to remove the volume label for your flash drive. What command did you enter, and how did you remove the volume label?
12. Verify that you removed the volume label for your flash drive. What command did you use?
13. Clear the screen, and then display a command reference list one screen at a time. What command did you enter to display the command reference list? What are the functions of the MOVE and REN commands? (View the next page of output if necessary). What is the function of the TYPE command? (View the next page of output if necessary).

14. Clear the screen, and use the SYSTEMINFO command to display information about your computer one screen at a time. What command did you enter? What is the OS Name, OS Version, OS Configuration, System Model, System Type, Processor Clock Speed, Windows Directory, System Directory, Boot Device, Total Physical Memory, and Page File Location(s) for your computer? View the remainder of the output of this command.

15. If necessary, close the Command Prompt window and open it again with Administrator credentials.

16. Use the POWERCFG command and its ENERGY switch to produce a new Power Efficiency Diagnostics report. Open the energy-report.html file produced by this command. Describe how you opened the energy-report.html file. Briefly summarize the results found by the POWERCFG command. Close your Web browser window or the Power Efficiency Diagnostics report.

17. Clear the screen and enter the following command: **TREE C:\ | MORE**

18. Explain what happened in the previous step. Where does the directory tree start? Interrupt the TREE command and return to the command prompt. What command did you use to interrupt and cancel this command? Explain how this command worked.

19. Clear the screen, and then change to the root directory. What command did you enter?

20. Change to the Assets First directory under the Documents directory for the Public user account. What command did you enter? What does the command prompt display?

21. Display a directory listing of the Assets First directory. What subdirectories are contained in the Assets First directory? How are the subdirectories listed? What do the . (dot) and .. (dot dot) entries in the directory listing refer to?

22. Display a directory tree of the Assets First directory. What command did you enter? What subdirectories are under the Contract Training directory?

23. Change to the Company Projections directory. What command did you enter?

24. Display a directory listing of the files in the Company Projections directory. What command did you enter? If this directory listing displayed more than one page of output, what command could you use to display only one screen at a time? If this directory listing contained both subdirectories and files, what command would you use to display a list of just subdirectories and what command would you use to display a list of just files?

25. View attributes of the files in this directory. What command did you use? What attributes are assigned to the files?

26. Create a directory named **Company Projections** on your flash drive, and then verify the operation by displaying the contents of your flash drive. What commands did you use?

27. Copy all the files in the Company Projections directory under Public Documents to the Company Projections directory on your flash drive. What command did you use?

28. Verify that the copy operation worked successfully. What command did you use?

29. Switch to the parent directory of the Company Projections subdirectory. What command did you enter?

30. Switch to the Client Projects subdirectory under the Public Documents folder. What command did you enter?

31. Copy the Break-Even Analysis.xlsx file in the Client Projects directory to the Company Projections directory on your flash drive. What command did you enter?

32. Change to the flash drive. What command did you use?

33. Display a directory listing of the Company Projections directory. What command did you use?

34. Change to the hard disk drive, and then change to the root directory. What commands did you use?

35. View the contents of the Windows environment. What command did you use? What are your settings for the SystemDrive, SystemRoot, and windir environment variables?

36. Add the DIRCMD environment variable to the Windows environment, and specify that it use the Page, Sort Order, and Archive switches for the DIR command. What command did you use to perform this operation?

37. Display a directory listing for the root directory. Describe how the DIR command listed directories and files in the root directory.

38. Remove the setting for the DIRCMD environment variable from the Windows environment. What command did you use?

39. Close the command-line window, delete the Assets First folder under the Public Documents folder, delete the Company Projections folder on your flash drive, and then restore any other settings you changed.

40. Submit your answers to the questions in the Review Assignments to your instructor, either in printed or electronic form, as requested.

Use your skills to check directory listings at a realty company.

APPLY

Case Problem 1

For a list of Data Files in the Case1 folder, see page 829.

J&B Realty, Inc. J&B Realty is a large firm that provides a variety of realty services to its clients in the greater New York City metropolitan area. As J&B Realty's network administrator, Alessandro Bolzoni uses his command-line skills to quickly locate and compile files for use by other employees in the firm and to examine directory information about installed software files and operating system files. He wants you to become familiar with the use of the various DIR (Directory) command switches, as well as wildcards, so you can assist him with troubleshooting.

As you complete each step in this case problem, record your answers to the questions so you can submit them to your instructor. Use a word- processing application such as Word or WordPad to prepare your answers to these questions. If you change any settings on the computer you are using, note the original settings so you can restore them later. Complete the following steps:

1. Copy the Case1 folder from the Tutorial.13 folder to the Public Documents folder and then change the name of the Case1 folder to **J&B Realty**.

2. Open a Command Prompt window, and then change to the root directory of drive C. What command did you use for this operation? What path is shown in the command prompt?

3. Use the SET command to view environment variables and their settings in the Windows environment. Does your Windows environment have a DIRCMD environment variable, and, if so, what is its setting?

4. Use the HELP command to display information on the use of the DIR command. What command did you enter? What is the purpose of the /B, /W, and /D switches?

5. Use the DIR command with the /B, /W, and /D switches to display the contents of the root directory. Describe the appearance and contents of each directory listing. In what way(s) are the /W and /D switches similar and dissimilar?

6. Why would you want to check the Windows environment for the DIRCMD variable before you tested the DIR command's /B, /W, and /D switches?

7. Switch to the J&B Realty subdirectory under the Public Documents folder. What command did you use for this operation? What path is shown in the command prompt?

8. View Help on the DIR command. What is the purpose of the /S switch?

9. Use the DIR command with the /S switch, and view all of the output. Describe the output of the DIR command. What advantage does this switch have over the other switches you've examined?

10. Change to the Company Performance subdirectory. What command did you use?

11. View Help on the DIR again. What is the purpose of the /X switch?

12. Use the DIR command with the /X switch. What additional information does the DIR command include in the directory listing?

13. Switch to the Presentations directory under the Contract Training directory. What command did you use?

14. What command can you use to display a list of only those files that have the letter C at the beginning of the filename?

15. What command can you use to display a list of only those files that have a .pptx file extension?

16. How can you customize the Windows environment so the DIR command always lists short filenames along with long filenames?

17. Close the Command Prompt window, delete the J&B Realty folder in the Public Documents folder, and restore any other settings that you changed for this case problem.

18. Submit your answers to the questions in this case problem to your instructor, either in printed or electronic form, as requested.

Use your skills to analyze a disk for fragmentation.

APPLY

Case Problem 2

For a list of Data Files in the Case2 folder, see page 829.

Golden Gate Wireless   Consuelo Orozco works as network specialist for Golden Gate Wireless on the West Coast and assists staff members in setting up, configuring, customizing, and troubleshooting wireless networks for clients. When you ask her how you can check for file system errors on your flash drive from a command-line window, Consuelo recommends that you use the command-line CHKDSK utility. She notes that if your flash drive uses the FAT file system and if there are any fragmented files, CHKDSK can provide information on those fragmented files.

As you complete each step in this case problem, record your answers to the questions so you can submit them to your instructor. Use a word-processing application such as Word or WordPad to prepare your answers to these questions. If you change any settings on the computer you are using, note the original settings so you can restore them later.

To complete this case problem, you must open a Command Prompt window with Administrator credentials. Complete the following steps:

1. Copy the Case2 folder from the Tutorial.13 folder to your flash drive, and then change the name of the Case2 folder to **Golden Gate Wireless**.

2. Open a Command Prompt window with Administrator credentials.

3. Display Help information on the use of the CHKDSK command. What command did you enter? What switch can you use to fix (file system) errors on a disk? What switch can you use to locate bad sectors on a hard disk and recover readable information?

4. Perform a diagnostic, or read-only, check of your flash drive by entering the CHKDSK command with the drive name for your flash drive. What command did you enter? What file system is used on your flash drive? If CHKDSK found problems, instruct CHKDSK to correct those errors. What types of errors did CHKDSK find, and how does it propose to resolve the problem?

5. If Windows reports file system errors on your flash drive, what command would you use to fix those errors?

6. View Help information on the CHKDSK command again. What does the filename switch do?

7. If your flash drive uses the FAT32 or FAT file system, perform the following steps. If your flash drive uses NTFS (the NT file system), skip this step.

   a. Switch to your flash drive by entering its drive name and, if there are no files in the root directory, switch to a subdirectory that contains files.

   b. Type CHKDSK *.* (the wildcard specification for all files), and then press the Enter key.

   c. The results may include additional information about file fragmentation for specific files after the information on the number of allocation units available on disk. If so, describe each fragmented file type and the number of noncontiguous blocks in each fragmented file.

8. Close the Command Prompt window, and then delete the Golden Gate Wireless folder from your flash drive.

9. Submit your answers to the questions in this case problem to your instructor, either in printed or electronic form, as requested.

Extend your skills to document computer settings.

CHALLENGE

Case Problem 3

For a list of Data Files in the Case3 folder, see page 829.

Lyang Surveying   Daeshim Lyang works as a computer troubleshooting specialist for his father's land surveying firm. He is particularly adept at using the command-line environment while working on projects for his father's employees. When setting up and configuring a computer, Daeshim checks and customizes computer system settings. He asks you to assist him by documenting the directory structure and settings on a new computer.

As you complete each step in this case problem, record your answers to the questions so you can submit them to your instructor. Use a word-processing application such as Word or WordPad to prepare your answers to these questions. If you change any settings on the computer you are using, note the original settings so you can restore them later. Complete the following steps:

1. Attach your flash drive to the computer you are using, and close any dialog boxes or windows that open.

2. Copy the Case3 folder from the Tutorial.13 folder to the Public Documents folder, and then change the name of the Case3 folder to **Lyang Surveying**.

3. Open a Command Prompt window, and change to the root directory of drive C.

4. Create a directory named **Documentation** on your flash drive. What command did you use?

5. To verify that you created the Documentation directory, display a directory listing of the root directory for your flash drive, and specify that you want to include only directories (not files) and that you want to view directories in alphabetical order. What command did you use?

6. Display an alphabetical listing of *all* directories and files in the root directory of drive C one screen at a time. What command did you use?

7. Recall the previous command from the command history, remove the switch for displaying the output one screen at a time, and then modify the command so it redirects its output to a file named **DriveCRootDir.txt** in the Documentation directory on your flash drive. What command did you use?

8. To verify that you created this file, display a directory listing for the Documentation directory on your flash drive. What command did you use?

9. Display a list of attributes assigned to all files in the root directory of drive C. What command did you use?

⊕ EXPLORE 10. Recall the previous command from the command history, and then modify it so the command redirects the output to a file named **DriveCRootAttributes.txt** in the Documentation directory on your flash drive. What command did you use?

11. To verify that you created this file, recall from the command history the command that you used to view a directory listing of the Documentation directory on your flash drive.

⊕ EXPLORE 12. Change to the Lyang Surveying subdirectory under the Public Documents directory. What command did you enter?

13. Use the TREE command with the Filename switch and the ASCII Switch to display a directory tree of the current directory and its subdirectories. What command did you use?

⊕ EXPLORE 14. Recall the previous command from the command history, and redirect the output to a file named **LyangSurveying.txt** in the Documentation directory on your flash drive. What command did you use?

15. To verify that you created this file, recall from the command history the command that you used to view a directory listing of the Documentation directory on your flash drive.

⊕ EXPLORE 16. Do not enter a command, but instead enter the full path to the LyangSurveying.txt file on your flash drive. Describe what happens? What is contained in this file?

17. Close any open windows, including the Command Prompt window, delete the Lyang Surveying folder in the Public Documents folder, and restore any other settings that you changed for this case problem.

18. Open a Computer window, open a window onto your flash drive, select the Documentation folder, click Organize on the toolbar, click Cut on the Organize menu, navigate to the Case3 folder in your set of data files, click Organize on the toolbar, and then click Paste. Windows 7 moves the Documentation folder to the Case3 folder.

19. If requested by your instructor, submit a copy of the Documentation folder in the Case3 folder, and then close the Case3 folder.

Extend your skills to prepare a workshop on the use of environment variables.

CHALLENGE

Case Problem 4

There are no Data Files for this Case Problem.

Brockmann Computer Outlet   Ursula Friedländer works as a network technician at Brockmann Computer Outlet in Indianapolis. Ursula relies on her command-line skills to quickly compile information about a computer so she can effectively troubleshoot problems encountered by customers. At the request of her supervisor, she presents workshops for coworkers where she demonstrates power user tips for working in a command-line environment.

As you complete each step in this case problem, record your answers to the questions so you can submit them to your instructor. Use a word-processing application such as Word or WordPad to prepare your answers to these questions. If you change any settings on the computer you are using, note the original settings so you can restore them later. Complete the following steps:

1. Open a Command Prompt window, and change to the root directory in one step. What command did you use? What is the path of the current directory?

2. Display the contents of the Windows environment. What command did you use? What setting is assigned to the OS and NUMBER_OF_PROCESSORS environment variables?

EXPLORE 3. Enter the following command: SET USERPROFILE
What setting is stored in this environment variable? Why might you prefer to use this variation of the SET command?

EXPLORE 4. Enter the following command: CD %USERPROFILE%
(Case does not matter, but you must type the percentage symbols.) What directory did the Change Directory command switch to? Explain why this happened.

EXPLORE 5. Use the SET command with each of the following variables: SystemRoot, HOMEPATH, ProgramFiles, and TEMP. What setting is stored in each environment variable?

EXPLORE 6. Use the CD (Change Directory) command with the SystemRoot, HOMEPATH, ProgramFiles, and TEMP environment variables. (*Hint*: Remember to use the percent sign symbols around the variable name.) List each command you entered and which directory you switched to.

EXPLORE 7. Are there any advantages to using these environment variables over specifying the path? Explain.

8. Enter the following command: DIR C:\Users\Public\Documents
What type of information does the Directory command display?

EXPLORE 9. Use the SET command to create a new environment variable named PublicDocs, and assign the full path (with the drive name) to the Public Documents directory to this environment variable. What command did you enter?

10. Change to your Public Documents subdirectory using the PublicDocs environment variable. What command did you enter to change to the Public Documents subdirectory? What advantage does this new environment variable offer?

EXPLORE 11. To restore your computer, remove the PublicDocs environment variable from the Windows environment, and then verify this operation. What command(s) did you use?

12. Close the Command Prompt window, and restore any other settings that you changed for this case problem.

13. Submit your answers to the questions in this case problem to your instructor, either in printed or electronic form, as requested.

ENDING DATA FILES

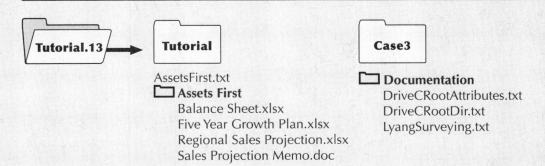

Tutorial.13 → **Tutorial**

AssetsFirst.txt
Assets First
    Balance Sheet.xlsx
    Five Year Growth Plan.xlsx
    Regional Sales Projection.xlsx
    Sales Projection Memo.doc

Case3

Documentation
DriveCRootAttributes.txt
DriveCRootDir.txt
LyangSurveying.txt

WINDOWS

OBJECTIVES

Session 14.1
- Learn about the role and importance of the Registry
- Create a restore point prior to using the Registry
- Open and examine the Registry with the Registry Editor
- Export Registry settings to a registration file

Session 14.2
- Examine the structure and organization of the Registry
- Trace information on registered file types
- View information on Class Identifiers
- Examine how to edit, create, and delete a Registry entry

Mastering the Windows Registry

Customizing Desktops with the Windows Registry

Case | *Mobile Software Center, Inc.*

Mobile Software Center, Inc., which develops software for mobile devices, is experiencing phenomenal growth due to the increasing popularity and dependence on mobile devices. Ian Caplinger, one of the company's programmers, modifies the Windows 7 Registry to customize and streamline the use of his computer so he is more efficient and productive. Ian also uses the Windows 7 Registry Editor to troubleshoot system configuration problems and remove malicious software.

In this tutorial, you will examine the role and importance of the Windows Registry. You will create a restore point prior to opening the Windows Registry. Then, you will export Registry settings so you have a backup of the Registry. You will also examine the structure of the Registry, trace information on a registered file type, examine Class Identifiers, and look at how to edit the Registry and add new Registry settings.

STARTING DATA FILES

There are no starting Data Files needed for this tutorial.

SESSION 14.1 VISUAL OVERVIEW

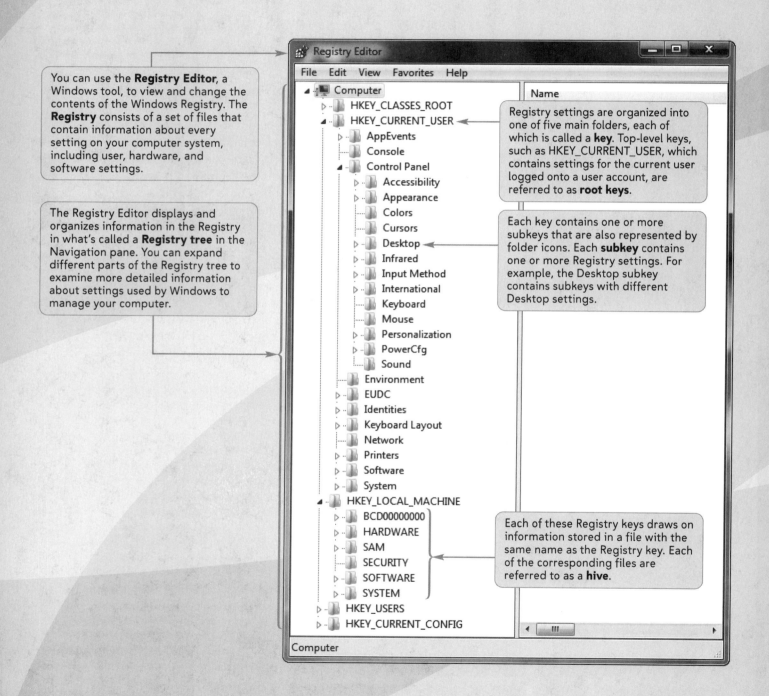

You can use the **Registry Editor**, a Windows tool, to view and change the contents of the Windows Registry. The **Registry** consists of a set of files that contain information about every setting on your computer system, including user, hardware, and software settings.

The Registry Editor displays and organizes information in the Registry in what's called a **Registry tree** in the Navigation pane. You can expand different parts of the Registry tree to examine more detailed information about settings used by Windows to manage your computer.

Registry settings are organized into one of five main folders, each of which is called a **key**. Top-level keys, such as HKEY_CURRENT_USER, which contains settings for the current user logged onto a user account, are referred to as **root keys**.

Each key contains one or more subkeys that are also represented by folder icons. Each **subkey** contains one or more Registry settings. For example, the Desktop subkey contains subkeys with different Desktop settings.

Each of these Registry keys draws on information stored in a file with the same name as the Registry key. Each of the corresponding files are referred to as a **hive**.

WINDOWS REGISTRY

You can use the Registry Editor to back up Registry settings to a **registration file** with the .reg file extension. Then you can open the registration file in Microsoft Word to view Registry settings. You can also **export**, or transfer, Registry settings to a text file.

A registration file shows the **Registry path** or location of each key in the Windows Registry. For example, the path to the Mouse key, which contains mouse settings for the current user, is HKEY_CURRENT_USER\Control Panel\Mouse.

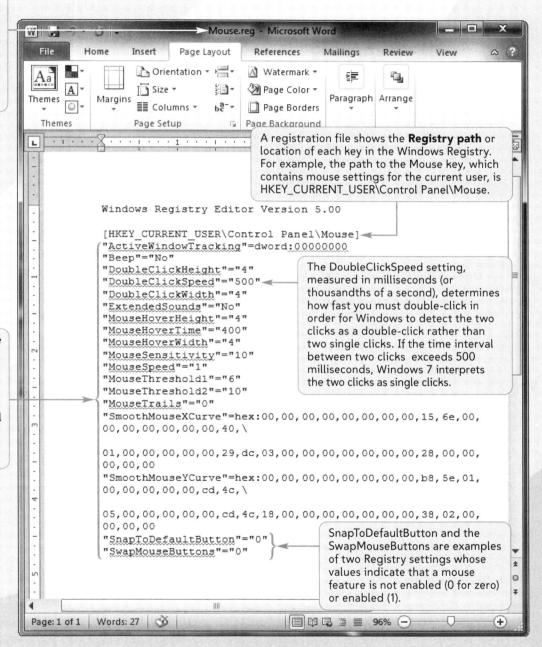

```
Windows Registry Editor Version 5.00

[HKEY_CURRENT_USER\Control Panel\Mouse]
"ActiveWindowTracking"=dword:00000000
"Beep"="No"
"DoubleClickHeight"="4"
"DoubleClickSpeed"="500"
"DoubleClickWidth"="4"
"ExtendedSounds"="No"
"MouseHoverHeight"="4"
"MouseHoverTime"="400"
"MouseHoverWidth"="4"
"MouseSensitivity"="10"
"MouseSpeed"="1"
"MouseThreshold1"="6"
"MouseThreshold2"="10"
"MouseTrails"="0"
"SmoothMouseXCurve"=hex:00,00,00,00,00,00,00,00,15,6e,00,
00,00,00,00,00,40,\

01,00,00,00,00,00,29,dc,03,00,00,00,00,00,00,00,28,00,00,
00,00,00
"SmoothMouseYCurve"=hex:00,00,00,00,00,00,00,00,b8,5e,01,
00,00,00,00,cd,4c,\

05,00,00,00,00,00,cd,4c,18,00,00,00,00,00,00,00,38,02,00,
00,00,00
"SnapToDefaultButton"="0"
"SwapMouseButtons"="0"
```

The DoubleClickSpeed setting, measured in milliseconds (or thousandths of a second), determines how fast you must double-click in order for Windows to detect the two clicks as a double-click rather than two single clicks. If the time interval between two clicks exceeds 500 milliseconds, Windows 7 interprets the two clicks as single clicks.

Within each key is one or more Registry entries with their corresponding setting. For example, this Mouse key contains 18 different mouse settings. When you modify a mouse setting in the graphical user interface, Windows 7 updates the corresponding setting in the Registry.

SnapToDefaultButton and the SwapMouseButtons are examples of two Registry settings whose values indicate that a mouse feature is not enabled (0 for zero) or enabled (1).

Understanding the Role of the Registry

Windows stores your computer's hardware, software, object, file associations, security, network, system performance, and user account settings in a database known as the Registry.

The Registry contains information on hardware devices and resources (such as IRQs, I/O addresses, and DMA channels) assigned to both Plug and Play and legacy devices. During booting, Windows 7 uses the Registry to load the appropriate device drivers, reconfigure hardware devices (if necessary), and update the Registry. Windows 7 also uses the Registry to load services and startup programs, and to configure your computer for one or more users and for applications. When you perform a normal boot of your computer, Windows 7 processes the information in the Registry to properly configure your computer. Malicious Web sites and malicious software that gain access to your computer can modify the Registry so Windows 7 loads a malicious program at each boot of your computer.

When you log on your computer, Windows 7 uses your **user profile** (or user account settings) in the Registry to customize your display of the desktop. Windows 7 updates the contents of the Registry when you change settings on your computer, such as when you customize your desktop with the Display Properties dialog box, when you install Plug and Play hardware devices, when you install or remove software, when you change settings using the Control Panel and Device Manager, and when you create, and specify settings for, user accounts. When you install software, the Setup installation program for that software product adds information about the software product to the Registry, including, for example, which file types (and therefore which file extensions) the application supports. If you click (or double-click) a file icon in a folder window, Windows 7 uses the Registry to locate the application associated with the file extension of the file that you selected. Then, it loads that application, and opens the document in the file. Using file associations stored in the Registry allows you to work in a document-oriented, or **docucentric**, environment. Not surprisingly, the Registry is constantly changing, and gradually increases in size as you, for example, install Windows updates and new software and when you add new users to your computer, so it can track all system, software, and user settings.

Microsoft recommends that you use tools, such as the Control Panel, Device Manager, and object property sheets, to make configuration changes whenever possible rather than opening and editing the Registry. If you open the Registry and make a mistake while you are changing a Registry setting, you may not be able to use your computer, or you may introduce errors that affect the hardware and software configuration of your computer so you cannot boot it. Windows 7 does not warn you if the change you made is incorrect, either at the time you make that change, or when you close the Registry. Instead, Windows 7 applies the change immediately. *Furthermore, there is no Undo option, so any changes you make to a Registry setting are final.*

The Windows 7 Registry database consists of a set of files named Default, SAM (Security Accounts Manager), Security, Software, System, and Components. Each of these files and its associated transaction log files (with the LOG, LOG1, and LOG2 file extensions) that contain information about changes to Registry keys and Registry settings, are called a hive. Each hive consists of a Registry tree. Each log file has a list of changes made to the keys and values of a hive. All of these hives are stored in the %SystemRoot%\system32\config folder, where %SystemRoot% is the path to your Windows folder. Because the log files are hidden files, you must specify that Windows 7 display protected operating system files and hidden files and folders to view the log files. Figure 14-1 lists the names of Registry files and the types of information stored in each file.

Figure 14-1   **Registry files**

Registry File	Contents
Components	Windows 7 component settings
Default	Default system settings
SAM (Security Account Manager)	Information on user and group accounts
Security	Security information, such as user rights, password policy, and local group membership
Software	Software configuration settings
System	Hardware and startup configuration settings

TIP

To view the contents of the Config folder, you may have to provide Administrator credentials.

Figure 14-2 shows the contents of the config folder on Ian's computer arranged in order by Type and without the Date Modified column. (This view includes hidden folders and files in the config folder, but not protected operating system files.) As just noted, the hives and supporting files are stored in the config folder. The path to that folder on the computer used for this figure is C:\windows\system32\config. The RegBack folder contains backup copies of the Default, SAM, System, Software, and Security Registry files for the current day.

Figure 14-2   **Viewing the contents of the Config folder**

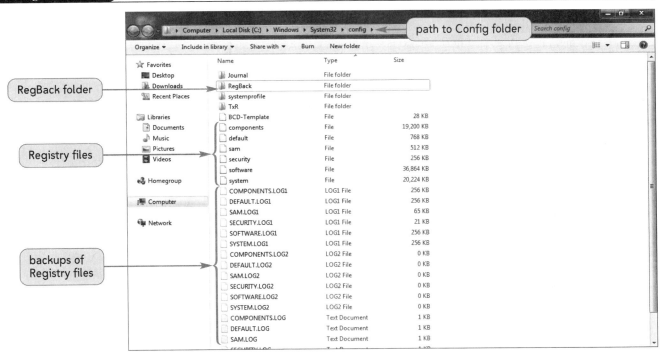

Although you generally make changes to your computer's hardware configuration and installed software, as well as user settings and preferences, using Windows tools such as the Control Panel, Device Manager, and property sheets, you may need to open the Registry to view, change, add, or troubleshoot settings. Therefore, it's important to become familiar with the structure of the Registry and its use.

PROSKILLS

Problem Solving: Working with the Registry

The Registry Editor is designed for the more advanced user, not a casual or inexperienced user. You must exercise caution when using the Registry Editor. Closely follow any instructions you may have for navigating, viewing, and modifying the Registry; double check and preferably triple check changes you make; and be prepared to restore your computer and its Registry if you run into a problem. If you want to create or modify a Registry setting, check the new setting at least twice before you apply it. If you want to delete a Registry setting, check at least twice to make sure you have selected the correct setting before you delete it. The well-known adage "Measure twice, cut once" especially applies to the use of the Registry.

Backing Up the Windows Registry

Ian emphasizes to you the importance of backing up the Windows Registry before making any changes to the Registry. Because the Windows Registry is critical to the booting and functioning of your computer, the backup strategies that you develop for your computer system should also take into account the Registry. You can back up the Registry in several ways:

- **Create a system image**—As you discovered in Tutorial 10, you can use Backup and Restore to back up your entire computer system. Because your computer's configuration and content are constantly changing as the result of Windows updates and other changes you make to your computer, you need to make and keep as recent a backup copy as is feasible. If you need to restore your computer from a system image backup, you must boot from your Windows DVD and open the System Recovery Tools because a complete restore of your computer overwrites everything on the system volume.
- **Use System Protection**—As you discovered in Tutorial 8, you can use System Protection to create a restore point for a fixed point in time, and then you can use System Restore to roll back your computer to that point should a problem arise later. *Before you make a change to the Windows Registry, you should always create a manual restore point because System Protection does not automatically create a restore point.*
- **Export the Registry**—You can also open the Registry Editor, a utility for viewing the contents of, and making changes to, the Registry, and then export (or transfer) a copy of the Registry to a registration file (with the .reg file extension) on disk. If you have a problem, you can import the contents of this registration file into the Windows Registry if you need to restore the Registry. *However, you must be careful not to double-click (or single-click in Web style) the exported registration file, because that will initiate the process of restoring the Registry with settings from the registration file, thereby overwriting your current settings.*

Windows 7 keeps a backup copy of the Windows Registry in the RegBack folder (C:\windows\system32\config\RegBack). To open this folder, you may need to provide Administrator credentials.

As you discovered in Tutorial 8, you can restore the Windows Registry using the Last Known Good Configuration on the Advanced Boot Options menu. Whenever Windows 7 successfully loads all its startup drivers and a user logs onto a computer, it copies those startup settings, now known as the Last Known Good Configuration, to the Registry. If a problem occurs after installing a new device driver or application, you can reboot your computer, press the F8 key during the initial stages of booting to display the Advanced Boot Options menu, and then choose the Last Known Good Configuration from that menu. However, when you choose the Last Known Good Configuration, you lose all of your other configuration changes since you last successfully booted your computer, and you may need to update your computer system afterwards.

You can also repair or restore the Windows Registry by booting from your Windows 7 DVD and choosing the option to repair your computer. Then, Windows 7 displays a System Recovery Options dialog box (covered in Tutorial 8) with various troubleshooting options. Startup Repair can fix missing or damaged system files, and it can also initiate System Restore (covered in Tutorial 8), or you can choose System Restore from the System Recovery Options dialog box, and roll back your computer (and the Registry) to an earlier functioning state. You can also restore your system volume and the Registry from a recent system image backup.

Because Windows 7 settings change over time (as you upgrade Windows 7, install new hardware and software, and reconfigure your system), *you must perform regular backups of the Windows Registry*.

INSIGHT

Using a Consistent Strategy for Working with the Registry

It is a good idea to develop a consistent strategy for working with the Windows Registry, including backing up the Registry, repeatedly verifying changes that you make before you commit those changes, and documenting any changes made to the Registry so you can effectively troubleshoot problems that might arise later. As Benjamin Franklin noted, "An ounce of prevention is worth a pound of cure."

Getting Started

To complete this tutorial, you must display the Computer icon on the desktop and switch your computer to single-click activation. In the following steps, you will check, and if necessary, change these settings.

To set up your computer:

▶ **1.** If necessary, use the Start menu to display a Computer icon on the desktop.

▶ **2.** If you need to enable single-click activation, open the Folder Options dialog box from a folder window and then enable and apply the options for single-click activation and underlining icon titles only when you point to them.

Now, you're ready to create a restore point before you open the Windows Registry.

Creating a Restore Point for the Windows Registry

Even though Windows 7 automatically creates restore points on a periodic basis or when you make significant changes to your system, you should *always* create a restore point before opening and working with the Registry. If you have not made a recent backup copy of your computer and your document files, this is the time to do it. Make these backups before you proceed with the remainder of this tutorial.

Next, Ian recommends that you manually create a restore point before you examine the Windows Registry.

To open System Protection in the following steps, you must provide Administrator credentials. *Do not skip the following steps as they are an important part of working with the Registry.*

To create a restore point:

▶ **1.** Right-click the **Computer** desktop icon, click **Properties**, and in the System window, click the **System protection** link in the left pane, and then provide Administrator credentials. After Windows 7 opens the System Properties dialog box, you may have to wait while System Protection searches for your existing restore points.

▶ **2.** Click the **Create** button, type **Registry Manual Restore Point** in the first System Protection dialog box, click the **Create** button in this same dialog box, wait for System Protection to create a restore point, and then click the **OK** button in the next and last System Protection dialog box.

▶ **3.** Click the **OK** button to close the System Properties dialog box, and then close the System window.

> **TIP**
>
> When creating Registry restore points on your computer, use a description that clearly identifies the purpose of the restore point.

You have successfully created a manual restore point.

Opening the Windows Registry

If you want to view the contents of the Registry or make changes to the Registry, either to customize your computer or to troubleshoot problems, you use a Windows 7 tool called the Registry Editor.

Because there is no option on the All Programs menu for opening the Registry Editor, you can either create a desktop shortcut to the Registry Editor (C:\Windows\regedit.exe), or use the Search programs and files box on the Start menu to enter the command for opening the Registry Editor. After the Registry Editor opens, the Registry Editor displays a Registry tree in the Navigation pane. The Registry Editor organizes settings in the Windows Registry by keys, each of which is represented by a folder icon in the Registry tree. Each key may have one or more subkeys (also represented by folder icons). When you work directly with a subkey, you refer to it as a key. The first set of keys you see after you open the Registry are the top-level keys, also referred to as root keys. You cannot add new root keys or delete root keys.

After you open the Registry, you are going to export your computer's Registry settings to a file on disk so you have an additional, alternate backup. You can then examine the structure and contents of the Registry, and if necessary, add new settings or modify existing settings in the Registry. *Remember that all accidental or deliberate edits are final and that the Registry Editor and Windows 7 do not ask for verification.*

Exporting Registry Settings

If you open the Registry Editor and then export, or transfer, Registry settings, the Registry Editor creates a registration file with the .reg file extension that contains a copy of all or part of the Registry's settings. This type of backup is the easiest and fastest to make. If necessary, you can restore the Registry, or a part of the Registry, from a registration file.

Ian recommends that you start by opening the Registry with the Registry Editor, and then export Registry settings to a registration file on disk so you have a backup of the Registry.

If your computer lab does not permit you to use the Registry Editor, or if you prefer not to use it on your computer until you better understand how it works, then read the remainder of the steps in this tutorial and examine the figures, but do not keystroke the steps.

In the next set of steps, you are going to open and export the contents of the Registry to a file on disk. *Do not skip the following steps as they are an important part of working with the Registry.*

To open the Registry Editor:

▶ **1.** Press the **Windows** key, and in the Start menu Search programs and files box, type **regedit** and, if regedit.exe is the first option in the Search results, then press the **Enter** key; otherwise, click **regedit.exe** in the Search results. If necessary, provide Administrator credentials. The Registry Editor displays the Registry tree in the Navigation pane. (Though it serves a similar purpose, this Navigation pane is different than the one you see in folder windows.) See Figure 14-3. As you can tell, even though the Registry consists of separate files, the Registry Editor combines the contents of those files into a single, unified view.

Figure 14-3 **Viewing the Registry Tree**

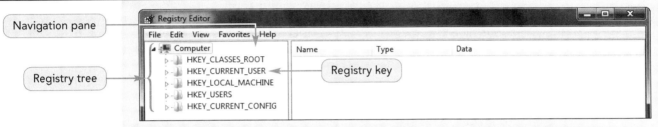

- Navigation pane
- Registry tree
- Registry key

▶ **2.** If Computer is not already selected in the Navigation pane on the left side of the Registry Editor window, click **Computer**. By selecting Computer first, you are guaranteeing that the Registry Editor will export *all* the Registry settings to a registration file. If you select a specific key, the Registry Editor exports only that portion of the Registry under that key.

TIP

You can also export all or part of the Registry to a simple text file.

▶ **3.** Click **File** on the menu bar, and then click **Export**. Windows 7 opens the Export Registry File dialog box. See Figure 14-4. The Save as type box identifies the file type as Registration Files (*.reg). Under Export range, the Registry Editor is set to export the entire range, not just a selected branch, to the Documents library.

Figure 14-4   **Exporting Registry settings to a registration file**

- file type
- exports entire Registry

4. Click the **Create New Folder** button 🗐 on the Export Registry File dialog box toolbar, type **Registry Backup**, and then press the **Enter** key twice to open the new Registry Backup folder.

5. In the File name box, type **Registry Backup (yyyy-mm-dd)** replacing *yyyy* with four digits for the current year, *mm* with two digits for the current month, and *dd* with two digits for the current day, click the **Save** button, and be patient while the Registry Editor exports all the Registry settings to a registration file on disk.

6. Right-click the Windows Explorer taskbar button 🗐, click **Windows Explorer** on the Jump List, open the Documents library, click the **Registry Backup** folder icon, if necessary click the **More options** arrow 🎛 ▾ on the Change your view button, and then click **Details**.

7. Click the **window background**, and then press the **Ctrl** and **+** keys (using the plus sign on the numeric keypad) to adjust all columns for a best fit, or if necessary, manually adjust column widths. On the computer used for this figure, the registration file is 110,935 KB (or approximately 108 MB). See Figure 14-5.

| Figure 14-5 | Viewing the exported registration file |

registration file

If you exported the Registry on the computer used for the figures in this tutorial to a text file, you would discover that the file is approximately 55,000 pages.

8. Close the Registry Backup folder window.

9. If you are going to continue with the tutorial, leave the Registry Editor window open for the next session of the tutorial; otherwise, close the Registry Editor window.

You have just successfully created a backup of the Registry by exporting Registry settings.

Exporting Registry Settings

- From the Start menu, type regedit in the Search programs and files box, and then press the Enter key if regedit.exe is listed first in the Search results; otherwise, click regedit.exe in the search results.
- If necessary, click Computer in the Registry tree shown in the Navigation pane.
- Click File on the menu bar, and then click Export.
- In the Export Registry File dialog box, locate the drive and folder where you want to store the exported Registry settings, then in the File name box, type a name for your registration file, and then click the OK button.
- Close the Registry Editor.

If you need to restore the Registry from this registration file, you open the Registry and use the Import command on the File menu. In the Import Registry File dialog box, you select the registration file to import. If the Registry Editor cannot import all of the data to the Registry, it will display a Registry Editor dialog box explaining that some keys are open by the system or by other processes. You can also open the folder that contains the registration file, and then click (or double-click) it to restore the Registry (because of the association of the .reg file extension with the Registry Editor). Windows 7 warns you in a Registry Editor dialog box that adding information can unintentionally change or delete values and thereby cause components to stop working properly. Windows 7 then points out that, if you do not trust the source, do not add the information in the registration file to the Registry.

INSIGHT

Exporting Registry Settings in a Command-Line Window

You can use the REG (Registry) command in a command-line window to export Registry settings for one of the five root keys (HKCR, HKCU, HKLM, HKU, and HKCC). For example, if you want to export the HKCU root key with the current user's settings, you enter the REG EXPORT HKCU command followed by a space and then the name of the text file where you want to store the exported Registry settings (such as HKCU.REG). The REG (Registry) command contains a number of useful options for working with the Registry, and like other commands, you can use the command-line Help switch to view the syntax and uses of the REG command.

Like other types of backups, you must periodically make new backups of the Registry because the Registry is constantly changing. If you restore the Registry from a registration file that is not recent, any configuration changes made since the date when you exported settings to a registration file are no longer in the Registry.

REVIEW

Session 14.1 Quick Check

1. Windows 7 stores your computer's hardware, software, object, file associations, security, network, system performance, and user profiles in the _____.
2. Default, SAM, Security, Software, or System and their associated log files are called _____.
3. The files that constitute the Windows Registry are stored in the _____ folder, and backups are stored in the _____ folder.
4. To restore the Windows Registry and your computer to its last working state using the Advanced Boot Options menu, you select _____.
5. True or False. The Registry Editor organizes settings in the Windows Registry by keys, each of which is represented by a folder icon in the Registry tree.
6. What type of file does the Registry Editor automatically create when you export the Windows Registry?
7. True or False. You can use the Undo option on the Edit menu to undo any changes you have made to the Registry.
8. List three ways to create a backup of the Registry.

SESSION 14.2 VISUAL OVERVIEW

Each specific Registry setting under a key or subkey, such as the (Default) setting for the .jpg subkey, is called a value entry, and each **value entry** consists of three parts. The first part of a value entry is the **value name**.

The second part of a value entry is the **value data type**, which identifies the type of data for each value entry.

The third part of a value entry is the actual **value data** that is a Registry setting. For example, the (Default) value entry for the .jpg subkey identifies this file type as a jpegfile.

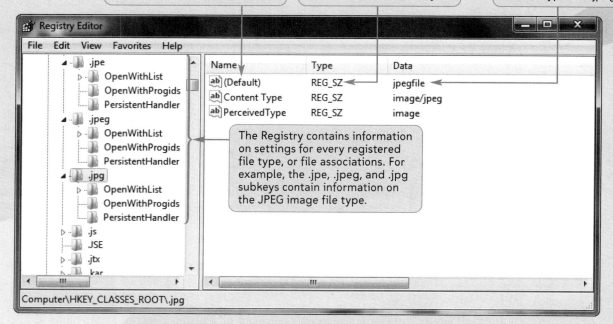

The Registry contains information on settings for every registered file type, or file associations. For example, the .jpe, .jpeg, and .jpg subkeys contain information on the JPEG image file type.

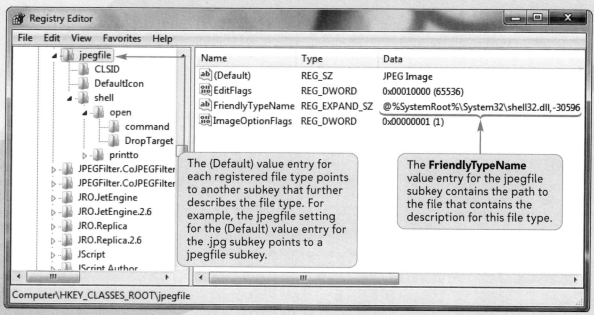

The (Default) value entry for each registered file type points to another subkey that further describes the file type. For example, the jpegfile setting for the (Default) value entry for the .jpg subkey points to a jpegfile subkey.

The **FriendlyTypeName** value entry for the jpegfile subkey contains the path to the file that contains the description for this file type.

REGISTRY DATA

The Desktop subkey for the current user contains value entries for different desktop settings, such as the path to the wallpaper setting.

Each Registry key or subkey has a (Default) value entry, whether or not it is assigned a setting.

The **REG_SZ** data type indicates that a Registry setting is a **fixed-length text string**, which is a nonnumeric value that contains a set of characters. A string can contain digits, but the digits are treated as text, not numeric values.

The **REG_DWORD** data type stores a 32-bit numeric value in binary, hexadecimal, or decimal format for a Registry setting.

The **REG_BINARY** data type is a binary value displayed in hexadecimal format, and it contains a numeric value for a Registry setting.

Examining the Structure of the Registry

The Registry consists of five major keys called root keys, each of which starts with HKEY. The *H* in HKEY stands for *Handle*, meaning each key is a handle for a specific group of settings. Within each key are sets of subkeys that contain groups of related settings. Under each subkey, there may be additional keys that break down the settings into even smaller groups. In other words, Registry keys and settings are organized using a hierarchical approach—similar in concept to how libraries, folders, and files are organized under Windows 7.

Before you examine specific keys, Ian suggests that you first examine the major Registry keys in the Registry tree structure.

To view the contents of the main Registry keys:

1. If you closed the Registry Editor after the first session, open the Registry Editor, and then maximize the Registry Editor window.

2. Click the **expand** icon ▷ to the left of the HKEY_CLASSES_ROOT key (commonly abbreviated as HKCR) and, if necessary, use the split bar to widen the Navigation pane to view the subkeys. As you can immediately tell from the Navigation pane, this key contains subkeys for each registered file type. Each subkey identifies the programs associated with each file type. See Figure 14-6.

> **TIP**
>
> Click View on the menu bar, and then click Split to adjust the width of the Navigation and Topic panes.

Figure 14-6 **Viewing subkeys in the HKEY_CLASSES_ROOT key**

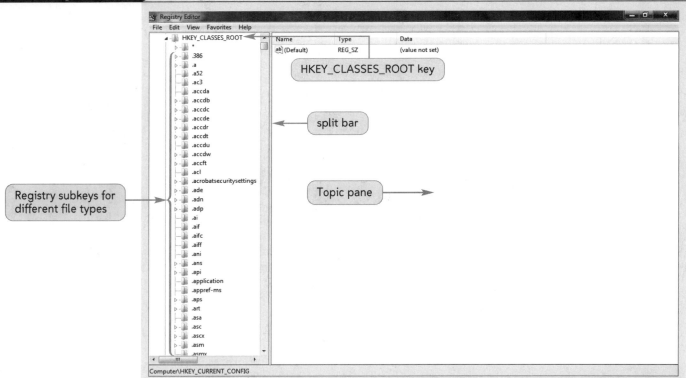

Your keys will differ from those shown in the figure because the types of subkeys found under this key depend on what file types are available on your computer system, and that, in turn, depends on the type of software installed on your computer. (Later in the tutorial, you will examine information on a file type.) This key also contains information on Windows objects, such as Computer and the Recycle Bin.

> **3.** Click the **collapse** icon ◢ to the left of the HKEY_CLASSES_ROOT key, and then click the **expand** icon ▷ to the left of the HKEY_CURRENT_USER folder icon, and then click the **expand** icon ▷ to the left of the Control Panel key. The HKEY_CURRENT_USER key (commonly abbreviated as HKCU) and its subkeys, such as Control Panel and Mouse, contain settings for the current user logged onto the computer. See Figure 14-7.

| Figure 14-7 | Viewing subkeys in the HKEY_CURRENT_USER key |

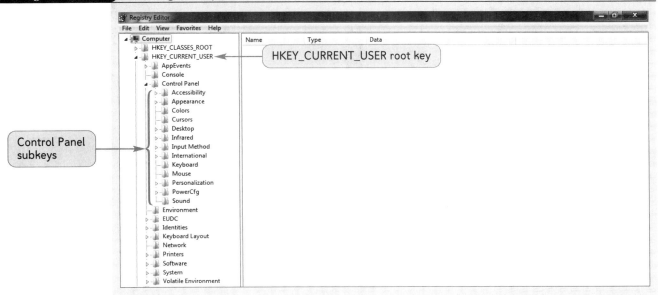

These Registry key settings guarantee that each user has access to her or his personal preferences as well as their software configuration settings, desktop settings, keyboard layout settings, printer connections, network settings, and environment variable settings. The information for a specific user in this key is derived from the HKEY_USERS key. Each user who logs on under their account on the same computer system has access to her or his personal settings via the HKEY_CURRENT_USER key.

> **4.** Click the **collapse** icon ◢ to the left of the HKEY_CURRENT_USER folder icon, and then click the **expand** icon ▷ to the left of the HKEY_LOCAL_MACHINE folder icon. The HKEY_LOCAL_MACHINE key (commonly abbreviated HKLM) contains all systemwide hardware and operating system configuration settings for the local computer system as well as user account information, security settings, user rights settings, and boot settings (including the previous driver and Registry settings in HKLM\SYSTEM\CurrentControlSet for booting with the Last Known Good Configuration). See Figure 14-8. Notice that there are keys for each of the Registry hives.

Figure 14-8   **Viewing subkeys under the HKEY_LOCAL_MACHINE key**

> **5.** Click the **collapse** icon ◢ to the left of the HKEY_LOCAL_MACHINE folder icon.

> **6.** Keep the Registry Editor window open for the next section of the tutorial.

The HKEY_USERS key (also abbreviated as HKU) contains user profile settings, or user account settings, for all users as well as a default profile. The HKEY_CURRENT_USER key is derived from a subkey of HKEY_USERS.

The HKEY_CURRENT_CONFIG key (also abbreviated as HKCC) contains configuration settings for the currently used hardware profile for the local computer at system startup. The settings determine which device drivers are loaded and what the final display resolution is.

The System Configuration utility that you examined in Tutorial 8 uses Registry key abbreviations (such as HKLM and HKCU) to identify where startup programs load from during booting.

Tracing a Registered File Type

By examining information on registered files in the Windows Registry, you can gain a better understanding of the organization of the Registry and how to work with the Registry, and you can also improve your understanding of how Windows 7 functions by drawing on information in the Registry.

When you select a key in the Registry Editor, Windows 7 displays the value entries associated with that key. As noted in this session's Visual Overview, each value entry is a Windows Registry setting that contains three parts: a value name, value data type, and the actual value data (or setting). For example, in the next set of steps you are going to examine the .bmp Registry key. The first value entry in the .bmp key has the name (Default), and the value for the (Default) value entry is Paint.Picture (all one word). Its data type is REG_SZ, which identifies Paint.Picture as a fixed-length text string.

Ian suggests that you next view information on file associations and registered file types so you become familiar with the process of navigating around the Registry.

To view information on registered file types:

> **1.** Click the **expand** icon ▷ to the left of the HKEY_CLASSES_ROOT key in the Navigation pane.

> **2.** Scroll down the Navigation pane and locate and double-click the **.bmp** key, adjust your view of the Registry tree so the .bmp key is near the top of the Navigation pane, and if necessary, adjust the width of the Navigation pane. Not only do you select this key and see its associated value entries or settings in the Topic pane on the right, but the Registry Editor also expands this part of the Registry tree in the Navigation pane, and displays the subkeys located below the .bmp key. See Figure 14-9.

| Figure 14-9 | Viewing value entries for the .bmp key |

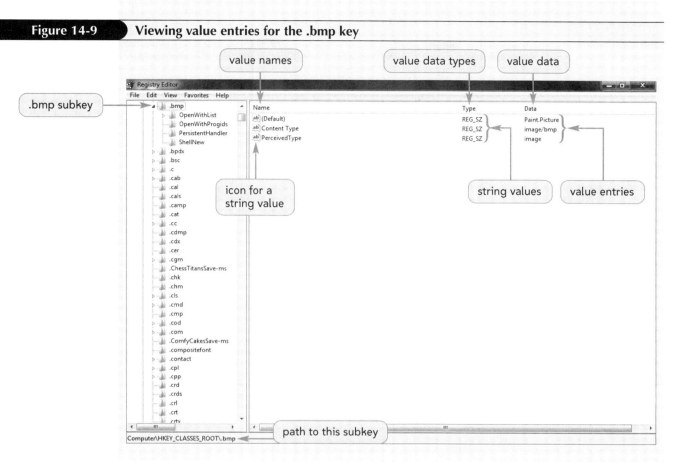

The settings shown in the Topic pane on the right are the value entries. As noted earlier, the value for the (Default) value entry is Paint.Picture, and its data type is REG_SZ (a string value). The REG_SZ values stores Unicode strings. **Unicode** is a coding scheme for assigning a unique number to each character, so all known characters in all known languages can be represented on a computer. Unicode is platform independent and application independent.

This value entry points to another key by the same name (the Paint.Picture key) that contains additional information about this file association. Notice also that the path to the current key, shown on the left side of the status bar at the bottom of the Registry Editor window, is Computer\HKEY_CLASSES_ROOT\.bmp. Like regular paths (such as the path to a folder) and UNC paths, this type of notation uses backslashes (\) rather than regular (or forward) slashes (/).

TIP

You can use the path on the status bar to verify that you are in the right location in the Registry.

To view information on the setting for the ShellNew subkey:

▶ **1.** In the Navigation pane, click the **ShellNew** subkey below the .bmp key, and then adjust the width of the columns in the Topic pane as necessary. The Registry Editor shows three value entries for the ShellNew subkey—a (Default) value entry, an ItemName value entry, and a NullFile value entry (explained in the next paragraph). See Figure 14-10. Also note on the status bar that the path to the current key is Computer\HKEY_CLASSES_ROOT\.bmp\ShellNew.

Figure 14-10 **Viewing the ShellNew's value entries**

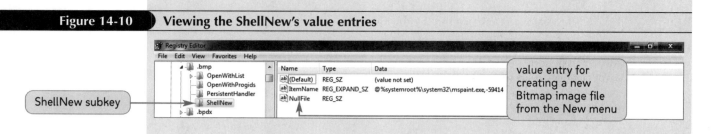

When you right-click the desktop or the background of a folder window (but not a library window), point to New on the desktop or folder's shortcut menu, you may see a Bitmap image option. If you click Bitmap image, Windows 7 uses the information in the .bmp key's ShellNew subkey to create a new, empty Bitmap image file that has no associated template (called a NullFile or **null file**) and that is zero bytes in size. You can open the file and create a new document using the application associated with this registered file type. Each menu option on the New menu has a corresponding ShellNew key in the Registry below that registered file type.

INSIGHT

Understanding the Concept of a Shell

In the Windows 7 operating system, the term **shell** refers to the software (Windows Explorer) that provides a graphical user interface for interacting with the operating system. In a command-line environment, the command interpreter (cmd.exe) is the shell that provides a text-user interface for interacting with the Windows operating system. The shell separates the user from the core operating system services referred to as the **kernel**. That also means that a shell is the "outermost layer," and the kernel is the "innermost layer."

Next, you and Ian decide to locate the Paint.Picture key. Although you could scroll through the Registry, it is faster to use Find to search for the key because of the extensive amount of information stored in the Registry.

To locate Paint.Picture:

1. Click **Edit** on the menu bar, and then click **Find**. In the Find dialog box, you can enter a search string, and specify what components of the Registry to examine during the search—keys, values, data, or some combination of those components. See Figure 14-11.

Figure 14-11 **Using the Find option for locating Registry content**

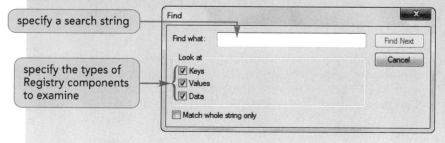

You can also specify that any matches found by the Registry Editor are ones that match your whole search string.

2. If necessary, click the **Keys** check box (and make sure it has a check mark), click the **Values** and **Data** check boxes to remove their check marks (if necessary), and click the **Match whole string only** check box (and make sure it has a check mark). The more specific you are when performing a search, the faster you locate what you want to find.

3. Type **Paint.Picture** (with the period between *Paint* and *Picture* and with no spaces) in the Find what box.

TIP

You can press the F3 key (the Find Next key) to continue a search with the same search string.

4. Click the **Find Next** button, and be patient. By limiting the search to just the keys and by specifying whole strings only, you speed up your search for this key.

5. After the Registry Editor finds the Paint.Picture key, adjust your view so the Paint. Picture key appears near the top of the Navigation pane, and then widen the width of the Navigation pane (if necessary).

6. Double-click **Paint.Picture** in the Navigation pane to expand this key, click **(Default)** in the Topic Pane, and adjust the column widths for a best fit. The (Default) value entry for this key identifies this object as a Bitmap Image (a REG_SZ data type, or string value). See Figure 14-12.

Figure 14-12	Viewing Paint.Picture key value entries

Class Definition subkey for the Bitmap image file type

file type displayed by Windows in Details view and on property sheets

When you switch to Details view in a folder window, and then sort the files in the folder by file type (by clicking the Type column button), Windows 7 uses this Registry setting to identify the file type, and to group related file types together using this description. However, Windows 7 does not preserve case; so it displays *Bitmap image* rather than *Bitmap Image*. If you right-click a Bitmap image file, and then choose the option to view its properties, Windows 7 uses the (Default) value from this Registry key to identify the file type as a Bitmap image on the property sheet. Notice also that the path on the status bar to this key is Computer\HKEY_CLASSES_ROOT\Paint.Picture.

TIP

If you do not see the status bar, click View on the menu bar, and then click status bar.

7. Under the Paint.Picture key in the Navigation pane, click the **DefaultIcon** subkey. The (Default) value in the Topic pane shows the path to the program file that is associated with this file type, namely %systemroot%\system32\imageres.dll. On the computer used for Figure 14-13, the icon for the Bitmap image file type is drawn from a dynamic link library file named imageres.dll. The negative value after the path is called a Resource ID, and it identifies the position of the icon within the file.

Figure 14-13 Viewing the path to the file with the icon for the Bitmap image file type

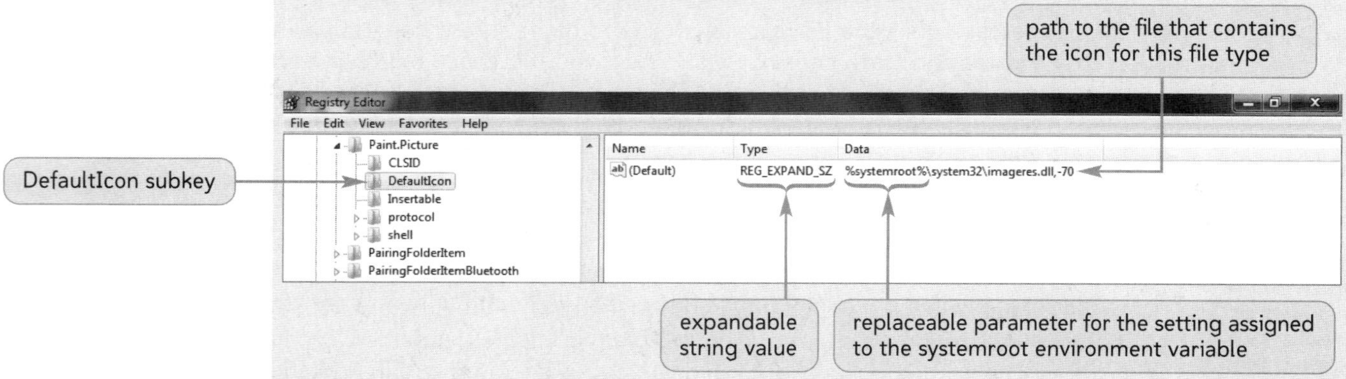

path to the file that contains the icon for this file type

DefaultIcon subkey

expandable string value

replaceable parameter for the setting assigned to the systemroot environment variable

If Windows 7 is installed on drive C in a folder named Windows, the path to the file with the icon is C:\Windows\System32\imageres.dll. Note that the path to the current key is Computer\HKEY_CLASSES_ROOT\Paint.Picture\DefaultIcon.

8. In the Navigation pane, double-click the **shell** subkey under the Paint.Picture key to open this key, double-click the **edit** subkey under the shell key, and then click the **command** subkey under the edit key. Below the shell key in the Navigation pane, the Registry Editor lists subkeys that represent different actions you can perform on this type of object: edit, open, and printto. See Figure 14-14.

Figure 14-14 Viewing the program path for editing .bmp files

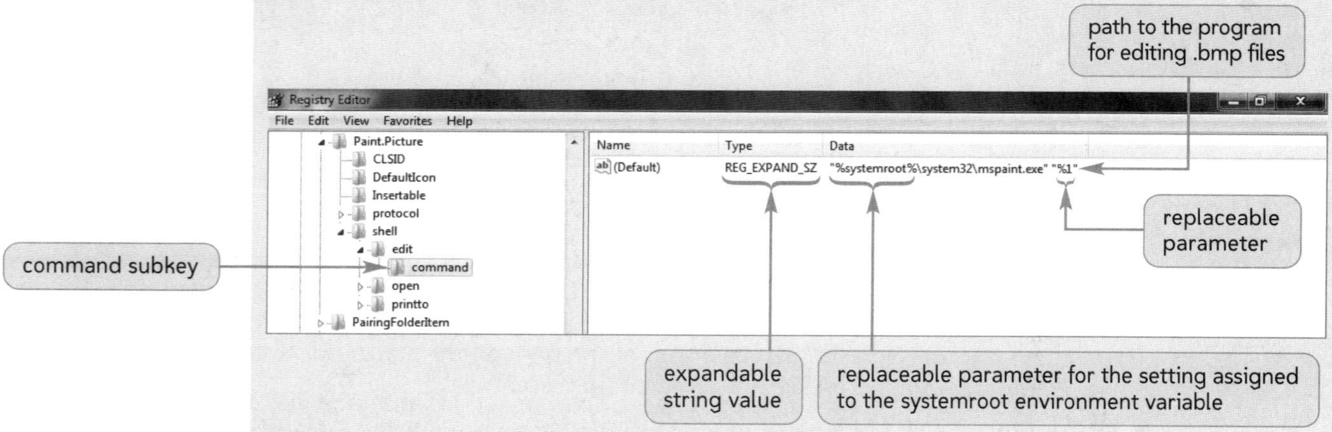

path to the program for editing .bmp files

replaceable parameter

command subkey

expandable string value

replaceable parameter for the setting assigned to the systemroot environment variable

These actions are displayed on a shortcut menu for a Bitmap image file as Preview (the default action shown in boldface), Edit, and Print. Notice on the status bar that the path to the current key is Computer\HKEY_CLASSES_ROOT\Paint.Picture\shell\edit\command.

REG_EXPAND_SZ is an **expandable string value** or **variable-length string** value because it contains a replaceable parameter for an environment variable or another type of variable value, each of which are converted into specific values when a program or service uses this Registry entry. Like a String Value, an Expandable String Value stores a string value; however, the value is expanded once the string is referenced and used.

On the computer used for this figure, the value for the Edit command is "%systemroot%\system32\mspaint.exe" "%1".

Your path may differ. This (Default) value contains the environment variable system-root as a replaceable parameter. If Windows 7 is installed in the Windows folder on drive C, Windows 7 expands this string to include the path to the Windows folder in the path to the Paint program, namely "C:\Windows\system32\mspaint.exe" on a computer with Windows installed on drive C.

The %1 after the path to the program file is another type of replaceable parameter. This replaceable parameter is a variable value that the command operates on and that is substituted when you invoke this command. For example, when you right-click a Bitmap image file, and then click Edit on the shortcut menu, Windows 7 replaces %1 with the filename of the Bitmap image file, and then opens that file. If you right-click a Bitmap image file named Hot Air Balloons.bmp and choose Edit on the shortcut menu, the Edit command is converted to "C:\Windows\system32\mspaint.exe" "Hot Air Balloons.bmp". Windows 7 then opens the Paint program and the file so you can edit the image in this file.

The quotation marks are included around the path to the program in the event the value for the systemroot environment variable is a long folder name with one or more spaces. Likewise, the replaceable parameter %1 is enclosed within quotation marks in case the file in question has a long filename with one or more spaces.

Next, examine the printto action.

To continue your examination of the Paint.Picture key:

1. In the Navigation pane, double-click the **printto subkey** folder icon under the shell key, click the **command** subkey folder icon under the printto subkey, click the **(Default)** value entry in the Topic Pane, and then adjust columns widths for a best fit. The (Default) value for printto is "%systemroot%\System32\mspaint.exe" /pt "%1%" "%2%" "%3%" "%4%". The *pt* in the /pt switch stands for "PrintTo." See Figure 14-15. Your path may differ.

Figure 14-15   **Viewing the command for printing .bmp files**

command subkey

printto switch

path to the program for printing .bmp files

This command is similar to the one for opening a Bitmap image file, except the /pt (Print To) switch instructs the Paint program to print the contents of the file (rather than open it for editing). Each of the replaceable parameters after the path to the program represent placeholders (replaceable parameters) for multiple files that you might select and print one right after the other. Each replaceable parameter is enclosed in quotation marks in a file in case a long filename includes one or more spaces. Notice on the status bar that the path to the current key is Computer\HKEY_CLASSES_ROOT\Paint.Picture\shell\printto\command.

2. Under the Paint.Picture key in the Navigation pane, click the **CLSID** (for Class ID, or Class Identifier) subkey. The Registry Editor shows the CLSID for Paint.Picture, namely {D3E34B21-9D75-101A-8C3D-00AA001A1652}. See Figure 14-16. Notice on the status bar that the path to the current key is Computer\HKEY_CLASSES_ROOT\Paint.Picture\CLSID.

Figure 14-16   **Viewing the CLSID for Paint.Picture**

CLSID subkey → [Registry Editor showing Paint.Picture with CLSID, DefaultIcon, Insertable, protocol subkeys. Name column shows (Default), Type REG_SZ, Data {D3E34B21-9D75-101A-8C3D-00AA001A1652}] ← Class Identifier

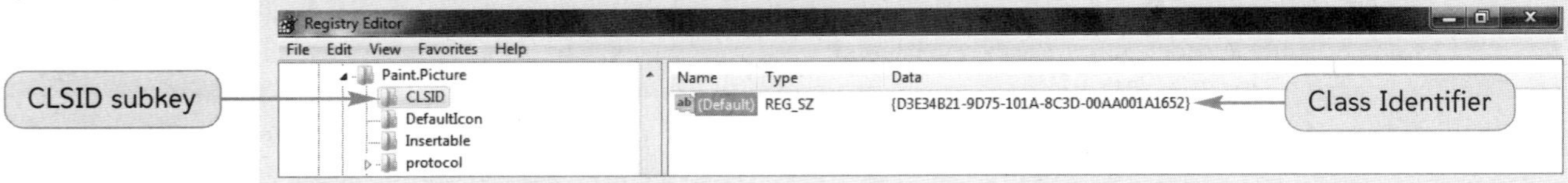

The **CLSID** (or **Class Identifier**) is a unique code called a GUID (globally unique identifier) that identifies a component as a COM class object in Windows 7. All other Windows versions use this same CLSID for Paint.Picture. The **Component Object Model (COM)** is a platform-independent approach to creating software components that can interact with each other. A **component** is an object that consists of program code and data as well as a set of services.

You can use this same strategy and approach to locate similar types of information on other types of registered files.

REFERENCE

Tracing Information on Registered File Types

- From the Start menu, type regedit in the Search programs and files box, and then press the Enter key if regedit.exe is listed first in the Search results; otherwise, click regedit.exe in the search results.
- Use Find on the Edit menu to locate the key for the file extension of a specific type of file type name (such as .bmp), and then view the (Default) value in the Topic pane.
- Use Find on the Edit menu to locate the key with the same name as the (Default) value entry (such as Paint.Picture), and then double-click that key to view its subkeys. Double-click the shell key to view actions for this file type. Double-click an action subkey (such as edit, open, or printto), and then click the command key to view the command for executing a specific action.
- Close the Registry Editor.

By examining information on registered files in the Windows Registry, you can get a better idea or "picture" of how Windows 7 handles routine operations that you perform every day.

Using CLSIDs

Windows 7 also assigns CLSIDs, or Class Identifiers, to system objects, such as Computer and the Recycle Bin. If you need to view or change properties of these objects, you need to know how to work with CLSIDs in the Registry. In some cases, the only way to change a property of a system object may be via the Registry. You can find the CLSIDs for these objects in the Registry's HKEY_CLASSES_ROOT key.

To search for an object's CLSID, you can search for the object name (such as Recycle Bin). However, in some cases, you may need to know the GUID (globally unique identifier) for the object to locate its CLSID key. A list of the CLSIDs for system components, such as the Recycle Bin, is included after the next set of tutorial steps.

So you can become familiar with the use of CLSIDs, Ian asks you to locate the CLSID for the Recycle Bin.

To locate the CLSID key for the Recycle Bin:

▶ 1. Click **Paint.Picture** (or any other key or subkey) in the Navigation pane to change the focus from the Topic pane to the Navigation pane, press the **Home** key to move to the top of the Registry tree, and make sure **Computer** is selected in the Navigation pane. Your search will start from this point in the Registry.

▶ 2. Click **Edit** on the menu bar, click **Find**, type **645FF** (case does not matter) in the Find what box, make sure the Keys check box has a check mark, make sure the Values and Data check boxes do not have a check mark, click the **Match whole string only** check box to remove the check mark, click the **Find Next** button, and then be patient while the Registry Editor locates the CLSID key for the Recycle Bin.

<table>
<tr><td>

TIP

Not all CLSIDs identify the friendly name of the object for the (Default) value entry.

</td><td>

▶ 3. Adjust your view in the Navigation pane so the {645FF040-5081-101B-9F08-00AA002F954E} key at the bottom of the Navigation pane is positioned near the top of the Navigation pane, click the **(Default)** value entry in the Topic Pane, and then adjust column widths for a best fit. For the (Default) value entry in the Topic pane, the Registry Editor identifies this key as the CLSID for the Recycle Bin. See Figure 14-17.

</td></tr>
</table>

Figure 14-17 Viewing value entries for the Recycle Bin CLSID

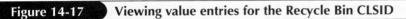
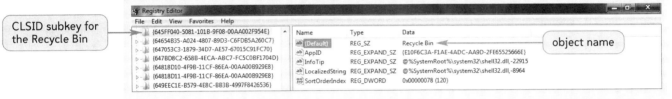

Notice on the status bar that the path to the current key is: Computer\ HKEY_CLASSES_ROOT\CLSID\{645FF040-5081-101B-9F08-00AA002F954E}.

▶ 4. Double-click the **{645FF040-5081-101B-9F08-00AA002F954E}** key in the Navigation pane, and then click the **DefaultIcon** subkey in the Navigation pane. The Empty value entry identifies the full path and name of the file that contains the icon that Windows 7 uses for the Recycle Bin when it is empty. It also identifies the location of the icon within that program file by using the icon's Resource ID. See Figure 14-18.

Figure 14-18 Examining Recycle Bin icon locations

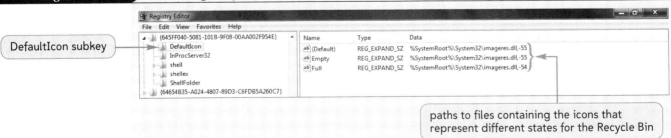

Because the setting for the SystemRoot environment variable is the path of the Windows folder determined during booting, the full path on this computer for the file that contains the icon for an empty Recycle Bin is C:\Windows\system32\imageres.dll.

The Full value entry identifies the full path and name of the file that contains the icon Windows 7 uses for the Recycle Bin when it contains deleted files. This icon is also derived from the same dynamic link library, imageres.dll, but the Resource ID for the icon number after the path is different. The (Default) value entry identifies the full path and name of the file that contains the icon Windows 7 uses to represent the current status of the Recycle Bin, and that changes depending on whether the Recycle Bin is empty or contains deleted folders and files. Notice on the status bar that the path to the current key is Computer\HKEY_CLASSES_ROOT\CLSID\ {645FF040-5081-101B-9F08-00AA002F954E}\DefaultIcon.

▶ **5.** Click the **collapse** icon ◢ to the left of the {645FF040-5081-101B-9F08-00AA002F954E} key in the Navigation pane, press the **Home** key to quickly navigate to Computer, and then click the **collapse** icon ◢ to the left of HKEY_CLASSES_ROOT.

▶ **6.** Keep the Registry Editor open for the next section of the tutorial.

Although you have just examined only a very small amount of the information stored in the Registry, the information that you did examine shows how Windows 7 uses Registry settings to support your use of registered file types and how Windows 7 handles objects, such as the Recycle Bin.

REFERENCE

Locating Information on CLSIDs

- From the Start menu, type regedit in the Search programs and files box, and then press the Enter key if regedit.exe is listed first in the Search results; otherwise, click regedit.exe in the search results.
- Click Edit on the menu bar, click Find, type part of the CLSID for the object you want to find (you may be able to search by object name, such as Recycle Bin, or you may have to know the CLSID), add a check mark to the Keys check box, remove the check marks from the Values, Data, and "Match whole string only" check boxes, and then click the Find Next button.

Figure 14-19 lists the CLSIDs for objects commonly found on a Windows 7 computer. These same CLSIDs are used in previous versions of Windows where the features were available. Also, some object names might have changed from an earlier version of Windows. For example, Control Panel changed to All Control Panel Items. You can use these CLSIDs to locate the key in the Registry for an object so you can customize your computer or correct an error condition. Although you could search for objects by name, not all objects are identified by name, so you may have to search for objects by using a part of their CLSID, and then examine different CLSIDs until you find the one you need.

| Figure 14-19 | Examples of CLSIDs for system objects |

OBJECT	CLASSID
All Control Panel Items	{21EC2020-3AEA-1069-A2DD-08002B30309D}
CompressedFolder	{E88DCCE0-B7B3-11d1-A9F0-00AA0060FA31}
Computer	{20D04FE0-3AEA-1069-A2D8-08002B30309D}
Computers and Devices	{F02C1A0D-BE21-4350-88B0-7367FC96EF3C}
Desktop	{00021400-0000-0000-C000-000000000046}
Explorer Navigation Bar	{056440FD-8568-48e7-A632-72157243B55B}
File Open Dialog	{DC1C5A9C-E88A-4dde-A5A1-60F82A20AEF7}
File Save Dialog	{C0B4E2F3-BA21-4773-8DBA-335EC946EB8B}
FileSystem Object	{0D43FE01-F093-11CF-8940-00A0C9054228}
Folder	{C96401CC-0E17-11D3-885B-00C04F72C717}
Help and Support	{2559a1f1-21d7-11d4-bdaf-00c04f60b9f0}
HomeGroup Network	{07700F42F-EEE3-443a-9899-166F16286796}
Installed Updates	{d450a8a1-9568-45c7-9c0e-b4f9fb4537bd}
Internet Shortcut	{FBF23B40-E3F0-101B-8488-00AA003E56F8}
Network	{208D2C60-3AEA-1069-A2D7-08002B30309D}
Network Map	{E7DE9B1A-7533-4556-9484-B26FB486475E}
Power Options	{025A5937-A6BE-4686-A844-36FE4BEC8B6D}
Printers	{2227A280-3AEA-1069-A2DE-08002B30309D}
Recycle Bin	{645FF040-5081-101B-9F08-00AA002F954E}
Search	{2559a1f0-21d7-11d4-bdaf-00c04f60b9f0}
Security Center	{E9495B87-D950-4ab5-87A5-FF6D70BF3E90}
Shortcut	{00021401-0000-0000-C000-000000000046}
Taskbar	{05d7b0f4-2121-4eff-bf6b-ed3f69b894d9}
Taskbar and Start Menu	{0DF44EAA-FF21-4412-828E-260A8728E7F1}
The Internet	{3DC7A020-0ACD-11CF-A9BB-00AA004AE837}
User Account Control Settings	{06C792F8-6212-4F39-BF70-E8C0AC965C23}
UsersLibraries	{031E4825-7B94-4dc3-B131-E946B44C8DD5}

As you select and examine keys for registered file types and objects, you will discover that you are already familiar with some or many of the settings because you access and work with these settings, using Windows 7 tools, property sheets, folder windows, and dialog boxes.

Viewing the Interaction Between Windows Tools and the Registry

When you make changes to your computer using Windows tools, such as the Control Panel, in the graphical user interface, Windows 7 immediately updates the corresponding Registry setting.

Ian suggests that you open the Mouse properties dialog box alongside the Registry Editor and make a change to a mouse setting while at the same time viewing the corresponding change in the Registry.

To compare a change to a Mouse properties setting to its corresponding Registry setting:

▶ **1.** Click the **expand** icon ▷ to the right of HKEY_CURRENT_USER (if necessary), click the **expand** icon ▷ to the right of the Control Panel key, click the **Mouse** subkey, and then click the **MouseTrails** value entry in the Topic pane. As shown in Figure 14-20, the MouseTrails value entry type is a string value (identified by REG_SZ), and the setting is *0* indicating that this feature is turned off. Your setting may differ if you have already activated this feature on your computer.

| **Figure 14-20** | **Viewing the current setting for MouseTrails** |

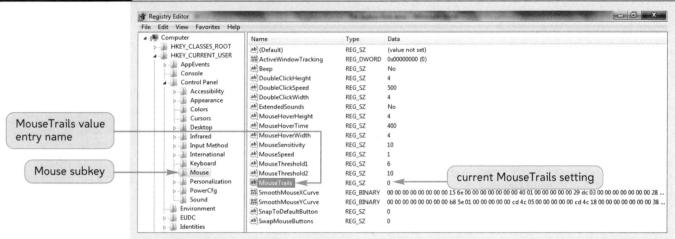

MouseTrails value entry name

Mouse subkey

current MouseTrails setting

Notice on the status bar that the path for the current key is: Computer\HKEY_CURRENT_USER\Control Panel\Mouse.

▶ **2.** Use Aero Snap to dock the Registry Editor window on the left side of the desktop, and then use the split bar to adjust the width of the Navigation and Topic panes so you can view the Registry tree in the Navigation pane and the corresponding Mouse settings in the Topic pane.

▶ **3.** From the Start menu, open the Control Panel, click **Hardware and Sound** in the Control Panel window, and under Devices and Printers, click the **Mouse** link. After Windows 7 opens the Mouse Properties dialog box, close the Hardware and Sound window in the background.

▶ **4.** Drag the Mouse Properties dialog box to the right of the Registry Editor window, click the **Pointer Options** tab in the Mouse Properties dialog box, and then note your current setting for the Display pointer trails check box under Visibility.

Make sure you click the Apply button so you can see the change in the Registry in the next step.

▶ **5.** On the Pointer Options property sheet, click the **Display pointer trails** check box under Visibility (and add a check mark to this check box), click the **Apply** button, and then move your mouse pointer and notice that it now displays pointer trails. Windows 7 immediately enables this feature and displays previous positions of the mouse pointer shape as you move the mouse so it is easier to locate the mouse. Notice that the MouseTrails setting in the Registry Editor window did not change.

▶ **6.** Click the **Registry Editor** title bar, click **View** on the menu bar, and then click **Refresh**. Windows 7 updates the view in the Registry Editor window, and then displays the new setting for MouseTrails, as shown in Figure 14-21.

Figure 14-21   Viewing the Registry change to the MouseTrails setting

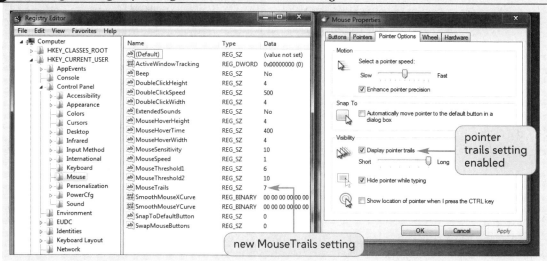

The setting you see depends on the position of the slider tab on the slider bar under the Display pointer trails check box. If you drag the slider tab to each notch along the slider bar, apply your new setting, and then update the view in the Registry Editor window, Windows 7 will display the new setting.

▶ **7.** Click the **Display pointer trails** check box under Visibility in the Mouse Properties dialog box (and remove the check mark from this check box), click the **Apply** button, click the background of the Registry Editor window, and then press the **F5** (Refresh) key to update your view. Windows 7 displays the original setting (zero) that corresponds to turning off this feature.

▶ **8.** If necessary, restore your original mouse setting for displaying pointer trails, and then click the **Apply** button.

Next, examine the corresponding change in the Registry setting when you enable and then turn off the Snap To feature that automatically moves the mouse pointer to the default button in a dialog box.

To compare a change in the Snap To feature to its corresponding Registry setting:

▶ **1.** In the Registry Editor window, note that the current setting for SnapToDefaultButton is 0 (zero), again indicating this feature is not enabled.

▶ **2.** Click the **Automatically move pointer to the default button in a dialog box** check box to select it, and then click the **Apply** button.

▶ **3.** Click the background of the Registry Editor window, and then press the **F5** (Refresh) key to update your view. The setting for SnapToDefaultButton is now 1, indicating that this setting is enabled.

▶ **4.** Click the **Automatically move pointer to the default button in a dialog box** check box, click the **Apply** button, click the background of the Registry Editor window, and then press the **F5** (Refresh) key to update your view. Windows 7 restores the original setting (of zero).

▶ **5.** If necessary, restore your original mouse setting for displaying pointer trails, and then click the **Apply** button.

▶ **6.** Click the **OK** button in the Mouse Properties dialog box to apply any further changes you have made and to close this dialog box.

▶ **7.** Close the Registry Editor window.

By examining the relationship between the Windows settings in the graphical user interface with the corresponding settings in the Registry Editor, you have a better idea of how Windows 7 uses the Registry.

Editing the Registry

Computer trade magazines, professional and personal Web sites, and even Microsoft's Knowledge Base abound with tips and information that allow you to customize your computer, improve its performance, increase security, improve network connectivity, enhance hardware and software support, and troubleshoot problems by making changes to the Registry. In every instance, these sources for Registry tips also warn you to be especially cautious when you make changes to the Windows Registry as errors may result in an unstable system or prevent you from even booting your computer. However, in certain cases, you may want or need to make changes to your computer system that require you to edit the Registry because you have no other option for making that change.

For example, if you open the Start menu and point to the Jump List button ▸ or if you point to Administrative Tools on the Start menu, there is a slight delay before Windows 7 displays the corresponding menu. If you want menus to be displayed more quickly, you can make a simple change in the Registry. The next section of the tutorial describes how you make this change. However, because changes to the Registry can adversely affect the performance of a computer, the next section of the tutorial does *not* include hands-on steps, but rather describes the process for making this change and illustrates it with figures.

If you are working in a computer lab, your technical support staff may limit access to the Registry Editor and Registry so someone cannot accidentally or deliberately modify configuration settings that, in turn, may adversely affect the performance of that computer. Also, some computer labs may be configured so a computer's settings are restored to their previous state after you log off or shutdown a computer, or when you (or someone else) reboots the computer, thereby eliminating any changes you may have made that would otherwise affect other users. Ask your instructor or technical support whether you are able to test the type of changes described in the remainder of this section of the tutorial on computers in your college lab.

Before you attempt to make this change on your own computer, make sure you have the necessary backups you need if you have to restore your computer, including recent backups of the Registry.

Locating the Correct Registry Key

After opening the Registry, the first step is to locate the correct key. Before you can edit the Registry, you must know the path to, and name of, the key. You also have to know the name of the value stored in the Registry, and if it is not present, you need to know how to add it to the Registry. You obviously also must know the setting that you are going to assign to this value. As noted earlier, many articles in computer magazines, Web sites, and blogs that specialize in Registry tips; reference books on Windows 7; and Microsoft's Online Support Web site and Knowledge Base provide you with step-by-step details on how to make a change to the Registry so you can customize or troubleshoot a computer. Also, as previously noted, these sources for Registry tips also always include a disclaimer warning you that making changes to the Registry may adversely affect the performance of your computer. *In other words, any changes you make are at your own risk.* As is the case with researching information on add-ons and startup programs (covered in Tutorials 7 and 8) as well as Browser Helper Objects (covered in Tutorial 7), you should not depend on just one source, but rather examine multiple sources of information and compare your findings before you make changes to the Registry. You should also verify whether the Web sites that provide Registry tips are legitimate Web sites and are providing you with the correct information. Examine information about the Web site itself and about the background of the individuals who are providing Registry tips. Obviously, if Microsoft provides you with information on how to make a change to the Windows Registry, you would consider their information reliable. But would you take the same approach with a Web site that you are totally unfamiliar with?

The Registry path to the Desktop key for modifying desktop settings is Computer\HKEY_CURRENT_USER\Control Panel\Desktop.

Once you locate the Desktop key, you should check the path on the status bar at the bottom of the Registry Editor window to verify that you have found the correct key. Figure 14-22 shows the Desktop subkey. This key contains a number of settings that you can customize. Your value entries and their settings may differ from those shown for the computer used for this figure.

Figure 14-22	**Viewing the Registry entry that controls the slight delay in displaying a menu**

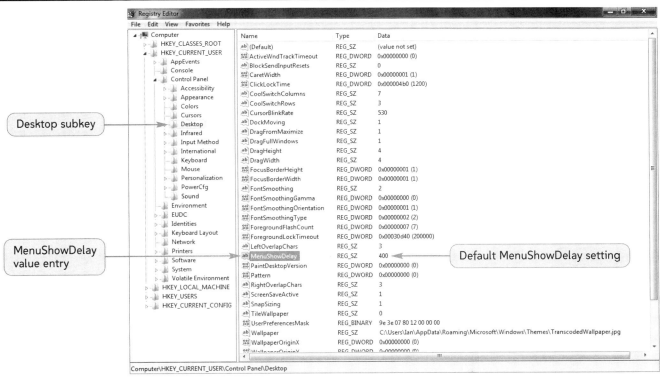

The value entry name for the menu delay settings is called MenuShowDelay, and its data type is REG_SZ, which identifies the setting as a string value.

The next logical step is to export the Desktop key to a registration file on disk, so if a problem occurs, you can double-click that registration file to restore the previous settings for this key. You first select the Desktop key in the Navigation pane. Then you click File on the menu bar, and select Export. In the Export Registry dialog box, Selected branch is already selected for the Export range, and the Registry Editor shows the full path to this key. Next, you select (or create) the folder where you want to store the registration file. After that, you enter a name for the registration file, and then save it to disk. You might, for example, use the filename Desktop.reg. This operation saves all the settings in the Desktop key and all its subkeys.

Editing a Registry Value

Before you make a change to a Registry setting like the ShowMenuDelay setting, you might want to test the current setting first by pointing to and displaying the Administrative Tools menu on the Start menu and by pointing to and displaying a Jump List for an application listed on the Start menu, so you have a sense of how much of a delay you experience with the default ShowMenuDelay setting.

Before you change the Registry key, make a note of the original setting. You can edit Registry settings in one of three ways:

- You can double-click the value entry's name in the Topic pane.
- You can single-click the value entry's name in the Topic pane, and then select Modify on the Edit menu.
- You can right-click the value entry name in the Topic pane, and then click Modify.

If you use any of these approaches to edit the MenuShowDelay value entry, the Registry Editor then displays an Edit String dialog box, as shown in Figure 14-23.

Figure 14-23	Editing a string value

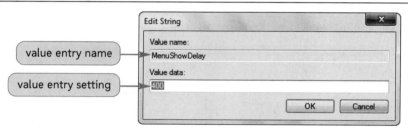

This dialog box shows the value name (MenuShowDelay), and the value data; in this case, 400, the default setting. That means there is a delay of 400 milliseconds before Windows 7 displays a menu. A millisecond is one-thousandth of a second, so 400 milliseconds would be four-tenths of a second. If you change this setting to 40, Windows 7 displays a menu after four-hundredths of a second. If you change it to 4, Windows 7 displays a menu after four-thousandths of a second (much faster). After you decide on a new setting, you type that setting and then click the OK button. Figure 14-24 shows a new setting of 4 for the MenuShowDelay value entry.

Figure 14-24	Modified setting for the MenuShowDelay value entry

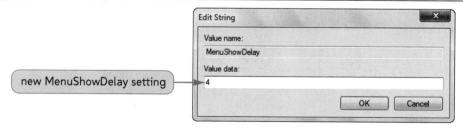

Windows 7 applies the settings immediately, as shown in Figure 14-25. For other types of changes you make to the Registry, you may have to log off your user account and then log back on, or you may have to restart your computer.

Figure 14-25   **Viewing the new setting for controlling the display of menus**

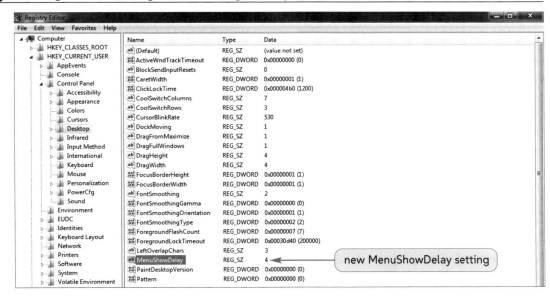

After changing this setting, you can test it again by displaying the Administrative Tools menu on the Start menu, or by displaying a Jump List for an application listed on the Start menu, so you have a sense of how much faster menus display.

Adding a Registry Key Location to the Favorites Menu

To quickly return to a specific key in the Registry, you use the Registry's Favorites menu to bookmark that Registry key. First, you select the key that you want to bookmark (for example, the Desktop subkey with the MenuShowDelay value entry and setting). Then, you open the Favorites menu and choose the Add to Favorites option, and provide a name for the bookmark, such as MenuShowDelay. The Registry Editor then displays an Add to Favorites dialog box, and prompts you for the Favorite name you want to use for this Registry key. After you click the OK button in the Add to Favorites dialog box and then view the Favorites menu, it now identifies this Registry location using the name you provided. See Figure 14-26.

Figure 14-26   **Viewing the new MenuShowDelay bookmark**

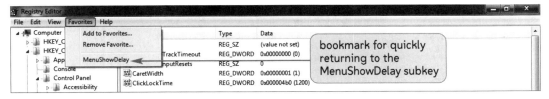

To return to this same Registry key, you open the Registry Editor, and from the Favorite menu click the bookmark name. You can use the Remove Favorite option on the Favorites menu to select and remove a bookmark that you no longer need.

To reverse the change to the MenuShowDelay setting, you repeat the same steps described previously for changing the MenuShowDelay setting, and then restore the original setting for this setting (namely, 400), or if you wait and then later forget what this setting should be on your computer, you can use the registration backup file you created to restore the previous Registry settings in the Desktop key.

Adding a New Entry to a Registry Subkey

After the introduction of an operating system like Windows 7, tips for modifying the Registry, adding new Registry keys, and removing Registry keys gradually appear over time at Web sites and blogs devoted exclusively to providing Windows 7 tips, Web sites for technical publications, and at Microsoft's Web sites, including its Support Web site (*http://support.microsoft.com*), TechNet Web site (*http://technet.microsoft.com*), and MSDN (Microsoft Developers Network) (*http://msdn.microsoft.com*). Verify that any tips that you discover and want to implement on your computer are in fact applicable to Windows 7.

If you need to add a new Windows 7 Registry key, use the following approach:

- Locate and select the exact key in the Registry where you want to add a new key or a new value entry (i.e., an entry under an existing key). To locate this key, you can use the Find option on the Edit menu to search for the existing key's name under which you want to create a new key or add a new value entry. To simplify this process, choose the options for searching for keys and matching whole strings only. If you have a bookmark to the existing key, you can select it from the Favorites menu. As mentioned earlier, compare the path recommended by the Windows 7 tip or fix to the path shown on the Registry status bar to make sure they match.
- To add a new key or subkey, you can use the New option on the Edit menu, select Key on the New menu, and then enter a name for the new key. You can also add a new key by right-clicking the background of the Topic pane in the Registry Editor window, pointing to New, and then choosing Key. Figure 14-27 shows the options on the New menu.

Figure 14-27   **Options for adding new types of value entries**

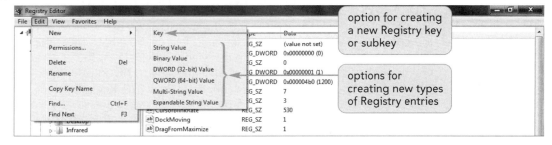

- To add a new value entry, you can use the New option on the Edit menu, select the appropriate value entry type on the New menu (such as String Value or Binary Value), and then enter a name for the new value entry. You can also add a new value entry by right-clicking the white background of the Topic pane on the right, pointing to New and selecting a value entry type, and entering a name for the new value entry. After adding a new value entry, you can double-click the value entry name to open an Edit dialog box for the value entry data type you specified, and then specify the setting for that value entry.

From the New menu, you can select one of the following value entry types:

- **String Value**—This option refers to the **REG_SZ** value data type, which, as you discovered earlier, consists of one or more characters that constitute a simple setting that is treated as text.
- **Binary Value**—This option refers to the **REG_BINARY** value data type, which stores numeric values as well as encrypted passwords. Binary values are numeric values displayed in **hexadecimal code** (a base-16 number system that uses the digits 0 through 9 and the uppercase and lowercase letters A through F to encode data). Hardware component information, such as a specific item of information about each processor execution core, is stored as a binary value.
- **DWORD (32-bit) Value**—This option refers to the **REG_DWORD** (or double word) value data type, which consists of a four-byte number (or 32-bit number) displayed in binary, hexadecimal, or decimal format. DWORDs store not only numeric values, but

also values that represent whether a setting is enabled (on) or not enabled (off). A **word** consists of 16 bits, so a **double word** consists of two sets of 16 bits for a total of 32 bits. A DWORD value can range from 0 (zero) to 4,294,967,295 (or 2^{32}). An example of a Registry value entry that uses a DWORD value type is the DefaultColor value entry that contains a setting for the default background and foreground color settings of a Command Prompt window.

- **QWORD (64-bit) Value**—This option refers to the **REG_QWORD** (or quadruple word) value data type, which stores a 64-bit number.
- **Multi-String Value**—This option refers to the **REG_MULTI_SZ** value data type, which is used to store lists or multiple values, such as the SystemBIOSVersion value entry that contains a list of details on the System BIOS version.
- **Expandable String Value**—This option refers to the **REG_EXPAND_SZ** value data type for Registry values that contain a replaceable parameter.

Three other data types found in the Registry but not available on the New menu are the following:

- **REG_FULL_RESOURCE_DESCRIPTOR**—This value data type contains a list of hardware resources used by a hardware device, such as the configuration data for a processor execution core.
- **REG_RESOURCE_LIST**—This value data type contains lists with categories and subcategories of information about resources for a device driver, including, for example, detailed settings or properties for physical memory.
- **REG_NONE**—This value data type is used for Registry entries that have no defined type.

Deleting a Registry Value Entry or Key

If you need to delete a Registry value entry or key, you should first export the Registry key to a registration file on disk. If you later discover that you need to restore that key, you can double-click the registration file you created and restore the Registry key to the Windows Registry.

To delete a Registry value entry or key, you select the value entry or key, and from the Edit menu, choose Delete. You can also right-click the value entry or key, and choose Delete from the shortcut menu. Or you can select the value entry or Registry key and press the Delete key. If you choose the option for deleting a value entry, the Registry Editor will display a Confirm Value Delete dialog box and inform you that deleting certain registry values could cause system instability and asks if you want to permanently delete the value. If you choose the option for deleting a Registry key, the Registry Editor displays a Confirm Key Delete dialog box and asks if you are sure you want to permanently delete the key and all of its subkeys.

PROSKILLS

Problem Solving: Connecting to a Remote Registry

If you need to make changes to or troubleshoot the Registry on another computer over a network, you can use the Registry Editor on your computer to connect to that other computer, provided network policy settings permit this option. To make the connection, you log on under an Administrator account on your computer, open the Registry Editor, choose the Connect Network Registry option on the File menu, specify Computers as the object type for the connection, and then select the specific computer on the network. Both computers must be running the Remote Registry service. If that service is not enabled on the remote computer, you can enable that service with your Administrator credentials. Once you complete your task, you can use the Disconnect Network Registry option on the File menu to disconnect from the other computer's Registry. This option for editing the Registry on another computer remotely offers yet another way of working efficiently and troubleshooting problems over a network.

Restoring Your Computer's Settings

If you are working in a computer lab, or if you want to restore your computer, you can delete the folder that contains the registration file you created earlier in the tutorial. If you decide that you want to keep the registration file, you can skip Step 2 in this section.

To restore your computer's settings:

▶ **1.** If necessary, close the Registry Editor window.

▶ **2.** If you do not want to keep, or no longer need, the registration file you created at the beginning of this tutorial, open the Documents library and then select and delete the Registry Backup folder.

▶ **3.** If necessary, restore double-click activation, and remove the Computer icon from the desktop.

By better understanding the structure and organization of the Windows 7 Registry, and by understanding the process for editing, adding, and removing Registry keys and value data entries, you can implement Registry tips and Registry fixes to streamline and troubleshoot your computer system.

REVIEW

Session 14.2 Quick Check

1. What three components are included in a Registry value entry?

2. A(n) _____ is a nonnumeric value that contains a set of characters that are treated exactly as they are typed or shown.

3. In the Windows 7 operating system, the term _____ refers to the software (Windows Explorer) that provides a graphical user interface for interacting with the operating system.

4. True or False. A null file is a file that is zero bytes in size.

5. *%systemroot%* is an example of a(n) _____.

6. *%1%* is an example of a(n) _____.

7. A(n) _____ value is a four-byte number (or 32-bit number) displayed in binary, hexadecimal, or decimal format.

8. What is an expandable string value or variable-length string?

Practice the skills you learned in the tutorial using the same case scenario.

PRACTICE

Review Assignments

There are no Data Files needed for the Review Assignments.

Because files saved as Rich Text Format can be opened by other applications, Ian recommends that you open the Registry and use the same approach that you used earlier for the .bmp file extension to examine information on the .rtf file association so you can become more familiar with this file type. He also suggests you look at information about files with the .zip file extension and locate information on the current theme used on your computer.

To create a restore point, you must provide Administrator credentials. As you complete each step in the Review Assignments, record your answers to the questions so you can submit them to your instructor. Use a word-processing application, such as Word or WordPad, to prepare your answers to these questions. If you change any settings on the computer you are using, note the original settings so you can restore them later. Complete the following steps:

1. If necessary, display the Computer icon on the desktop and enable single-click activation.

2. Use System Protection to create a restore point named **Registry Manual Restore Point**, and then close the System Protection dialog box, the System Properties dialog box, and the System window.

3. Open the Registry Editor using the Start menu Search programs and files box. If Computer is not already selected in the Registry Tree pane, select a key in the Navigation pane, and press the Home key.

4. Choose the option for exporting the Registry, create and then open a folder named **Registry Backup** (if necessary), and then save the Registry settings to a file named **Registry Backup** followed by the current date within parentheses using the date format yyyy-mm-dd (where *yyyy* is four digits for the current year, *mm* are two digits for the month, and *dd* are two digits for the day). Examine the registration file in the Registry Backup folder. What is its file size? Close the Registry Backup folder window.

5. What Registry key contains information on file types and file associations?

6. In the Registry Editor window, search for the following key: .rtf

7. What is the path to the .rtf key? What is the (Default) value entry data setting for this file type? Is this setting a string, binary, or DWORD value?

8. What is the .rtf key's Content Type? If you double-clicked this file, what program do you think Windows 7 would open?

9. Make a note of the (Default) value entry data for the .rtf key. Use Find to locate the subkey *under* the HKEY_CLASSES_ROOT key (*not* the subkey under the .rtf key) with this name. What is the (Default) setting that Windows uses to identify files of this type in Details view?

10. Open the shell subkey under this key. What types of actions or operations can you perform on the .rtf file type?

11. Open the subkey for creating a new document of this file type, select the command subkey, and then select the (Default) value entry data. What is the command for creating a new document of this file type?

12. Search for the CLSID key {E88DCCE0-B7B3-11d1-A9F0-00AA0060FA31}. (*Hint*: As in the tutorial, you can locate this key by using part of the CLSID.) What is the value data or setting for the (Default) value entry?

13. Expand this key and select the DefaultIcon subkey. What is the path to the file that contains the icon that Windows 7 uses for a Compressed (zipped) Folder? What is the value entry data type? Explain why Windows 7 uses this data type for this (Default) value entry.

14. Locate and open the following key:

    Computer\HKEY_CURRENT_USER\Software\Microsoft\Windows\
    CurrentVersion\Themes

15. What is the value data for the CurrentTheme value entry? What information does this value data setting provide?

16. Display the subkeys under Themes, expand the Installed Themes key, and then select the MCT subkey. If necessary, widen the Name column in the Topic pane. What type of country theme is used on your computer? *Note*: This path to the MCT folder allows you to locate themes for other countries.

17. Close the Registry Editor.

18. If you do not want to keep, or no longer need, the registration file you created at the beginning of this Review Assignment, open the Documents folder (or the folder that contains the registration file), and then select and delete the Registry Backup folder.

19. Restore your default computer settings.

20. Submit the results of the preceding steps to your instructor, either in printed or electronic form, as requested.

Use your skills to document registered files for a satellite and cable company.

APPLY

Case Problem 1

There are no Data Files needed for this Case Problem.

Internet Bypass, Inc.   Rosalyn McCullough works part-time as a computer and network troubleshooter for Internet Bypass, Inc., a satellite and cable company in Omaha, Nebraska. She also teaches part-time at nearby Locey Community College. For her next class, she wants to prepare a handout that lists different file types and the friendly name that Windows 7 displays for the file type in folders and on property sheets. Because she is quite busy with several tasks, she asks you to help her prepare this handout and provides you with a list of the file types. See Figure 14-28.

Figure 14-28   **Identifying file types using the Registry**

Class Definition	Data Value (Description of File Type)
anifile	
batfile	Windows Batch File
CABFolder	
CERFile	
chkfile	
cmdfile	
comfile	
cplfile	
Directory	
dllfile	
drvfile	
exefile	
ftp	
hlpfile	
htmlfile	
http	
https	
icofile	
inffile	
inifile	
lnkfile	
ocxfile	
RDP.File	
regfile	
SHCmdFile	
sysfile	
VBS	
zapfile	

To complete this case problem, you must provide Administrator credentials to create a restore point. As you complete each step in this case, record your answers to the questions so you can submit them to your instructor. Use a word-processing application, such as Word or WordPad, to prepare your answers to these questions. If you change any settings on the computer you are using, note the original settings so you can restore them later. Complete the following steps:

1. Use System Protection to create a restore point. Why should you perform this operation before using the Windows Registry? How might you use this restore point if you run into a problem after changing the Windows Registry?

2. Open the Registry Editor and export the contents of the Registry to a registration file on disk. If you want to make sure that the registration file contains a copy of all Registry settings, what must you first select before exporting Registry settings?

3. Using the information in the HKEY_CLASSES_ROOT key, prepare a table similar to that shown in Figure 14-28 to identify the friendly name for each of the file types in this figure. For example, the (Default) value entry for the Class-Definition *batfile* is *Windows Batch File*. (*Hint*: Use the Find feature to quickly locate keys.) If your Registry does not contain a file type listed in Figure 14-28, record N/A for "not available."

4. Close the Registry Editor.

5. Name at least three other places where you have seen some of the descriptions for these different file types.

6. If you do not want to keep, or no longer need, the registration file you created at the beginning of this case problem, open the Documents folder (or the drive and folder that contains the registration file), and then select and delete the Registry Backup folder.

7. Submit the results of the preceding steps to your instructor, either in printed or electronic form, as requested.

Use your skills to identify startup programs for a retail computer store.

APPLY

Case Problem 2

There are no Data Files needed for this Case Problem.

Computer Tech Center, Inc. Renaldo Urquidez works as a computer specialist for a large retail store that sells computers and electronic equipment, and he troubleshoots problems that customers encounter with new computers that they purchase from the Computer Tech Center.

To complete this case problem, you must provide Administrator credentials to create a restore point and to open the System Configuration utility.

As you complete each step in this case, record your answers to the questions so you can submit them to your instructor. Use a word-processing application, such as Word or WordPad, to prepare your answers to these questions. If you change any settings on the computer you are using, note the original settings so you can restore them later. Complete the following steps:

1. Use System Protection to create a restore point. Why should you perform this operation before using the Windows Registry? How might you use this restore point if you run into a problem after changing the Windows Registry?

2. Open the Registry Editor and export the contents of the Registry to a registration file on disk. If you want to make sure that the registration file contains a copy of all Registry settings, what must you first select before exporting Registry settings?

3. In the Registry Editor, locate and select the following key:
Computer\HKEY_LOCAL_MACHINE\SOFTWARE\Microsoft\Windows\
CurrentVersion\Run

⊕ **EXPLORE**

4. With the Run key selected, export the contents of this one Registry key to a registration file on disk.

5. List the value name, value type, and value data for each setting other than (Default) under the Run Registry key. (*Hint*: You can double-click a value entry to open its Edit dialog box, right-click the value data, click Copy, click the Cancel button, switch back to Word or WordPad, and then paste the long paths into the document with your answers to this case problem. By clicking the Cancel button, you cancel any accidental changes made to the Registry entry.)

6. Open Windows Task Manager, sort the program filenames on the Processes sheet in alphabetical order, and then widen the Description column. Which of the startup programs that you identified in Step 5 are listed as processes? Close Windows Task Manager.

7. Using Administrator credentials, open System Configuration and select the Startup tab. Which of the startup programs that you identified in Step 5 are listed on the Startup property sheet, and what is the path to the location from which these startup programs load? Close System Configuration.

8. From the Accessories menu, open System Tools, open System Information, expand the Software Environment category, select Startup Programs, and then adjust your view in the pane on the right so you can view the information in each column about each startup program. How does this information compare to the information you documented in Step 5? Close System Information, and then close the Registry Editor.

9. If you do not want to keep, or no longer need, the registration files you created in this case problem, open the Documents folder (or the drive and folder that contains the registration files), and then select and delete the Registry Backup folder.

10. Submit the results of the preceding steps to your instructor, either in printed or electronic form, as requested.

Use your skills to locate information on using Registry tips.

RESEARCH

Case Problem 3

There are no Data Files needed for this Case Problem.

Cutting Edge Graphics Services, Inc.   Talisha Vannoy works as a Help Desk technician for a large graphics services company in St. Louis, Missouri. She relies on Registry tips to customize, troubleshoot, and enhance the performance of her computer and other employee's computers. She asks you to use a search engine to locate information on Windows 7 Registry tips that she might be able to apply to employees' computers.

As you complete each step in this case, record your answers to the questions so you can submit them to your instructor. Use a word-processing application, such as Word or WordPad, to prepare your answers to these questions. If you change any settings on the computer you are using, note the original settings so you can restore them later. Complete the following steps:

1. Use a search engine to search for Windows 7 Registry tips. Examine information on at least three Windows 7 Registry tips. List the description or purpose for each Registry tip and provide the name and URL of the Web site where you found each tip. Also, explain the approach you used to locate these Registry tips.

2. Select a Windows 7 Registry tip of interest to you, note which Windows 7 tip you are describing, and provide the following information on how to implement the Registry tip:

   a. Describe how the Registry tip changes the way in which Windows 7 works if you implemented it.

   b. Identify the path of the Registry key where you would make the change.

   c. Describe how you make the change to a Registry value entry. Include in your description the value entry name, the value entry data type, and the value entry data.

   d. If available, explain whether the changes take effect immediately, whether you need to log off and then log back on your computer, or whether you need to restart your computer. Also include any other comments or observations about the Web site and the Registry tips.

   e. Does the Web site include any warning, and if so, what is the text of that warning?

   f. Explain how you can restore the original Registry setting.

3. Explain what precautions you would take before making a change to the Windows Registry.

4. Submit the results of the preceding steps to your instructor, either in printed or electronic form, as requested.

*Use your skills
to search the
Registry for
information.*

APPLY

Case Problem 4

There are no Data Files needed for this Case Problem.

Everhardt Computer Recycling Center   Wardell Weldin works as a computer specialist for a computer recycling company in Detroit, Michigan. After individuals donate used computers to the recycling center, Wardell examines the computers for any personal or product registration information, as well as personal folders and files that may remain on the computer, before he sets up the computer for reuse by another customer. He enlists your help to check a newly donated computer.

To complete this case problem, you must provide Administrator credentials to create a restore point.

As you complete each step in this case, record your answers to the questions so you can submit them to your instructor. Use a word-processing application, such as Word or WordPad, to prepare your answers to these questions. If you change any settings on the computer you are using, note the original settings so you can restore them later. Complete the following steps:

1. Use System Protection to create a restore point. Why should you perform this operation before using the Windows Registry? How might you use this restore point if you run into a problem after changing the Windows Registry?

2. Open the Registry Editor and export the contents of the Registry to a registration file on disk. If you want to make sure that the registration file contains a copy of all Registry settings, what must you first select before exporting Registry settings?

3. Make sure Computer is selected in the Registry Tree pane, and then use Find (with only the Values option enabled) to search for the value entry RegisteredOwner (one word with no spaces) under the Windows NT key. What is the path to the subkey that contains this value entry? What is the data type for the RegisteredOwner value entry? Who is listed as the RegisteredOwner?

4. Examine the other settings in this subkey and list the settings for the CurrentBuildNumber, CurrentVersion, EditionID, InstallationType, PathName, ProductName, RegisteredOrganization (if any), SoftwareType, and SystemRoot value entries.

5. Return to Computer at the top of the Navigation pane.

6. *Read this step completely before you start working on the step.* If you are working on your own computer, use Find to search for your first name, and to save time, specify that you only want to search for Data. If you are working on a college computer, search for the college's name. After Find locates the first instance of where your name is used, use the F3 key to continue the search from that point. List the path to five keys that identify you (or the college) by name, and list the corresponding value entry data for DisplayName (if available). (*Note*: You do not need to list your name.) If the name of the software product is not obvious from the name of the key, use the other value entries under that key to identify the software product. For very long paths, include enough of the path to identify the basic purpose of the key, such as a product key. (*Note*: For a comprehensive search, you can also search by just your last name.)

7. Close the Registry Editor.

8. If you do not want to keep, or no longer need, the registration file you created at the beginning of this case problem, open the Documents folder (or the folder that contains the registration file), and then select and delete the Registry Backup folder.

9. Submit the results of the preceding steps to your instructor, either in printed or electronic form, as requested.

ENDING FILES

There are no ending Data Files needed for this tutorial.

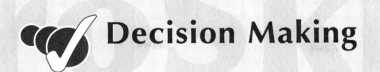

Decision Making

Optimizing the Productivity and Performance of Windows Computers

Decision making is the process of choosing between alternative courses of action using the results of a problem-solving process. The choice made is the actual decision. The decision-making activity starts after the analyzing of all potential alternatives. The steps involved in evaluating a given alternative include the following:

- Identify and evaluate approaches for different courses of action for reaching your goal, including weighing the pros and cons of each option.
- Predict the overall effect of each course of action and how each action might affect other actions you want to implement.
- Select the best combination of actions to achieve your goal.
- Prepare an action plan to implement your course of action.
- Implement your action plan and monitor the result.
- Evaluate and verify the effectiveness of your decision and actions, and if necessary, take corrective action,

Deciding on the Best Course of Action

When identifying, evaluating, and deciding on the best course of action, draw on your experience and knowledge so you can effectively weigh and implement different options available to you, including the strategy you use for making a decision. If you have reservations or questions about implementing a course of action, discuss your goals and decisions about the best approach to use with your department head, immediate supervisors, and other coworkers with experience in the same field. If implementing many different actions, create a decision tree that schematically lists or maps the options you want to implement, the most effective order for implementing these actions, and the checks you intend to use to verify the effectiveness of these actions. When making a decision that will affect multiple computers, such as changing which startup programs load during booting and which add-ons are used in employees' Web browsers, implement your course of action on a single computer, evaluate the use and productivity of that computer, and then, if necessary, adjust your action plan.

Draw on all other resources available to you. For example, you can use the Internet to locate and examine how other companies and professionals have implemented effective decisions that improve the overall productivity and performance of their staff. Develop a time table for implementing these changes and determine the most cost-effective approach for your company, including the time required to implement these changes, the personnel required for these tasks, and any impacts on the time and productivity of employees. Finally, anticipate the time, resources, and personnel required to provide ongoing support for the changes you intend on implementing. If necessary, decide on a project manager to oversee the implementation of your action plan. Identify key milestones in the action plan so the project supervisor can monitor and evaluate the success of your action plan.

ProSkills

Optimize the Use and Performance of Your Computer

Everyone wants to customize and optimize their computer to be sure they work efficiently, meet their ongoing needs without interruption, remain secure, and do not constantly require troubleshooting. By making careful decisions and taking the time you need up front, you create a more satisfying and productive working environment. Using the skills and features presented in Tutorials 1 through 14, document the following tasks that you perform on your computer. Complete the following tasks:

1. Start Windows 7 and log on your computer (if necessary). Open Windows Help and Support, and locate information on the Aero desktop experience. List the advantages of using Windows Aero, and list the Windows Aero features available on your computer.

2. View details on your computer's Windows Experience Index, and then view and print detailed performance and system information using the Microsoft XPS Document Writer.

3. Review your desktop theme, background, and window colors; taskbar and Start menu properties and custom options; resolution and color depth; and power management settings. Identify and list each of the settings you've selected for best productivity.

4. List how you use features, such as stacks, filters, and grouping that simplify access to files. List those search features that help you quickly locate folders and files on your computer.

5. List the desktop, Control Panel, Internet, and Navigation pane shortcuts that you use for fast navigation around your computer and for fast access to folders, files, and Web sites.

6. What tools do you use to verify and repair the file system on your computer's drives and to optimize your hard disk drive? What file system features do you implement for maximizing the use of disk storage space and protecting sensitive files? What scheduled tasks have you created on your computer?

7. Examine the Action Center for any pending problems or issues and verify the security of your computer. Review your firewall, Windows Update, virus protection, spyware settings, and User Account Control settings. Capture a screen of your current Action Center settings. List the Internet Explorer security features that you implement on your computer.

8. Use Reliability Monitor to analyze your computer's stability, and then briefly describe its performance over the last 15 days. Examine and describe your System Protection settings for creating restore points on different drives. Open Event Viewer, examine any Critical or Error event types in the Summary of Administrative Events, and then briefly summarize the types of problems your computer experienced during the last hour.

9. Use System Configuration to review startup programs on your computer, list the types of startup programs that load during booting, and use System Information to verify this information.

10. Use Task Manager, Resource Monitor, and Resource and Performance Monitor to examine memory usage. Briefly summarize your findings. Create a system health report, and examine and briefly summarize the Diagnostic Results in the System Diagnostics Report. Briefly describe how you might use Performance Monitor to periodically evaluate memory usage.

11. Describe how you use Windows Backup. What are the advantages of creating a system image and system repair disc? How do you benefit from using the Previous Versions feature?

12. Outline the process that you will use to upgrade your computer to the next version of the Windows operating system and the next version of Microsoft Office.

13. List the benefits of using Device Manager.

14. If you have a computer network, describe your type of computer network and how you access shared network resources.

15. Describe how you use the Command Prompt environment, and what types of features you benefit from in that environment. What two types of useful system reports can you create?

16. Describe the overall organization of the Windows Registry, and describe any ways in which you have customized your computer by using the Registry.

17. Submit your documentation and captured images to your instructor, either in printed or electronic form, as requested.

GLOSSARY/INDEX

Note: Boldface entries include definitions.

SPECIAL CHARACTERS

() (parentheses) A Boolean operator that selects all folders and files that match all of the words enclosed within parentheses; however, the words in the search results can be arranged in any order. WIN 198, WIN 214

/? The Help switch, an optional command parameter for displaying Help information on a command in a command-line environment. WIN 830

< (less than) A comparison operator that selects all folders and files that are less than a certain value that you specify. WIN 214, WIN 215

>> (append output redirection operator). *See* append output redirection operator

> (greater than) A comparison operator that selects all files that exceed a certain value that you specify. WIN 214, WIN 215

> (output redirection operator), WIN 858, WIN 859

~~ (contains wildcard), WIN 222

"" (quotation marks) A Boolean operator that selects all folders or files that match exactly what is typed within the quotation marks. WIN 199, WIN 214

* (asterisk wildcard) A symbol used as part of a file specification to substitute for any and all characters in the folder name, filename, or file extension, starting at the position of the asterisk. WIN 220, WIN 873–877

?\~(backslash) (1) The symbol for the top-level folder or root directory; (2) a delimiter that separates two directory names, or a directory name and filename, in a path or file specification. WIN 861

? (question mark wildcard) A symbol used as part of a file specification to substitute for a single character at the position of the wildcard in a filename or file extension when performing a search. WIN 220

>= (greater than or equal to) A comparison operator that selects all files that exceed a certain value or exactly match a certain value that you specify. WIN 214, WIN 215

<= (less than or equal to) A comparison operator that selects all folders and files that are less than a certain value or that exactly match the value you specify. WIN 214, WIN 215

. (dot) (1) The period that separates the main part of a filename (or perhaps even a folder name) from a file extension that in the case of a file identifies the file type and the application associated with that file type; (2) The period that acts as a directory marker and that denotes the current directory in a directory listing. WIN 16, WIN 188, WIN 865

.. (dot dot) The directory marker denoting the parent directory in a directory listing. WIN 854

. (range of values) A comparison operator that locates all folders and files that fall within a certain range and that

include the starting and ending values for that range. WIN 214, WIN 215

: (colon) A reserved symbol that is part of a drive name (such as C: for drive C). WIN 53

[ ] (no value, or null value) A comparison operator that locates files that do not have a value or setting for a property. WIN 214, WIN 215

% Processor Time A performance counter that monitors the level of processor activity. WIN 600, WIN 604–605, WIN 609

~*? (matches pattern, or pattern match) A search operator that uses the asterisk and question mark wildcards with text you type to locate any items that match a specific pattern. WIN 222

~< (begins with) A search operator that locates all folders and files that begin with the text you type. WIN 221

~> (ends with) A search operator that locates all folders and files that end with the text you type. WIN 221

~~ (contains) A search operator that locates all folders and files that contain the text you type. WIN 222

A

absolute path The complete path to the location of a folder, directory, subdirectory, or file that also includes the drive name. *See also* relative path. WIN 865

accelerator An Internet Explorer 8 feature that allows you to access features of another Web site (such as the option to perform a search) without first navigating to that Web site. WIN 474

access point, WIN 141, WIN 762

accessibility settings, WIN 137

ACPI. *See* Advanced Configuration and Power Interface (ACPI)

ACPI BIOS. *See* Advanced Configuration and Power Interface BIOS (ACPI BOIS)

action An operation you can perform on an object, such as opening an object. *See also* shortcut menu. WIN 14, WIN 391

default, WIN 14, WIN 205

Action Center A Windows 7 component that contains information about security settings and security problems on a computer. WIN 428, WIN 430–436

changing settings, WIN 455–456
firewall settings, WIN 432–436
opening, WIN 430–431

Action Center button, WIN 38

Action Center icon, WIN 116, WIN 429, WIN 430, WIN 439

activation A process by which you verify that you have a legitimate and fully licensed version of Windows on your computer. WIN 50

Active Directory network A network that manages user logons and provides access to network and shared resources. WIN 519

active partition The partition that contains the files for booting a computer. *See also* primary partition. WIN 329

active window The window that is currently selected and that you are currently using. *See also* inactive window. WIN 23

ActiveX control A module of program code that is downloaded from a Web site and run locally on your computer to provide access to interactive Web content. WIN 364

Add Counters dialog box, WIN 606

add-on A program used with a Web browser to enhance your browsing experience or extend its functionality. WIN 373

Internet Explorer, managing, WIN 471–476

Address bar A bar at the top of a system or folder window that identifies the current location on your local computer or network, and in which you can enter an address for or choose another location on your local computer, network, or URL for a Web site. WIN 55

Administrative Tools option, placing on Start and All Programs menus, WIN 406

Administrator account An account that provides you with complete access to your computer. You can change system settings (including security settings); manage user accounts (your account and other user's accounts); install, configure, update, troubleshoot, and uninstall software and hardware; and access all folders and files on a computer (including folders and files of other users). WIN 101, WIN 445

Advanced Attributes dialog box, WIN 340

Advanced Boot Options menu A menu that contains a list of options for booting Windows and troubleshooting boot, hardware, and software problems. WIN 528, WIN 538–545

Advanced Configuration and Power Interface (ACPI) A set of power management specifications that allow the operating system to manage the power state of each hardware device and control the amount of power that each device receives. WIN 138, WIN 761

Advanced Configuration and Power Interface BIOS (ACPI BIOS) A type of BIOS that identifies and activates hardware devices, determines their resource requirements, creates a nonconflicting hardware configuration, loads device drivers, passes configuration information to the operating system, notifies it of any configuration changes, and determines the power management capabilities of hardware devices. WIN 762

Advanced Sharing, WIN 807–810

adware (1) Software originally designed to display advertising in pop-up windows; (2) spyware that displays unsolicited advertising (usually in pop-up windows), monitors your activity on the Internet, and reports that information to a third party without your authorization or knowledge. *See also* spyware. WIN 443

C

cabinet file A file that contains multiple application files in a compressed format. WIN 727

cache (pronounced cash) A folder on disk or an area of memory where a program or Windows temporarily stores data. WIN 366

cached memory A portion of RAM that stores program code as well as data that has been modified or is currently not being used. WIN 572, WIN 582, WIN 585, WIN 592

cathode ray tube (CRT). *See* CRT (cathode ray tube)

CD The Change Directory command, an internal command used in a command-line window to change and navigate from directory to directory. WIN 854, WIN 855, WIN 861, WIN 865, WIN 868, WIN 869, WIN 872–873, WIN 875, WIN 876, WIN 877

CD drive, WIN 52
    viewing properties, WIN 327–328

CDFS (Compact Disc File System) A file system used on CDs. WIN 308

Center option, Picture location box, WIN 84

central processing unit. *See* CPU (central processing unit)

certificate (also called a digital certificate or digital ID) Information issued by a certification authority to verify the authenticity of a program, a device, a service (such as secure email), an operation (such as encrypting files), a server, a client (computer) connecting to a server, a Web site, or a person. WIN 157, WIN 354

chain A sequence of lost clusters that once belonged to a single file. *See also* file fragment. WIN 382
    lost, WIN 383

Change graph type button, Performance Monitor toolbar, WIN 624

Check Disk utility. *See* CHKDSK

CHKDSK The Check Disk command, an external command used in a command-line window to (1) examine a disk for file system errors and repair those errors where possible, (2) to check the integrity of sectors on a disk, and (3) to move data in defective sectors to good sectors. *See also* Error-Checking Tool, Fix switch (/F), and Repair switch (/R). WIN 374–381, WIN 837
    command-line Check Disk utility, WIN 386–389
    Error-checking tool compared, WIN 388

class identifier. *See* CLSID (class identifier)

Classic style A way of working in Windows where you use double-clicking to open an object and single-clicking to select an object. *See also* Web style. WIN 41

clean install (or custom install) A process whereby you install (or reinstall) an operating system on the same partition or a new one after reformatting and erasing the partition. Then you reinstall all your applications and restore your documents from backups. WIN 25, WIN 701, WIN 708–709

ClearType A font-smoothing technology designed for displaying fonts as clearly and smoothly as possible on LCD monitors. WIN 97

ClearType Text Tuner A Windows 7 feature that allows you to improve the sharpness and readability of text in windows and dialog boxes. WIN 79, WIN 96–100

client A computer or a program that connects to, or requests services of, another computer (called a server) or a program. WIN 801

Client for Microsoft Networks Client software for accessing resources on a Microsoft network. WIN 801

client software Software for accessing resources on a network. WIN 801

clock speed The speed at which a processor executes instructions, typically measured in gigahertz (GHz), or billions of cycles per second on newer computers, and in megahertz (MHz), or millions of cycles per second, on older computers. WIN 51

CLS The Clear Screen command, an internal command for clearing a command-line window of output. WIN 843

CLSID (class identifier) A unique GUID that identifies a component as a COM class object, such as for the Recycle Bin. *See also* GUID (globally unique identifier). WIN 911–915
    list, WIN 914–915
    locating information on, WIN 914

cluster (also called an allocation unit) One or more sectors of storage space on a disk allocated by an operating system as a single unit or block to all or part of a file. *See also* sector. WIN 309
    bad, WIN 309
    determining number of sectors, WIN 315
    lost, WIN 382–383
    NTFS, size, WIN 315

CMD An external command for opening a command-line window. WIN 835, WIN 837, WIN 839

cold boot A full boot of your computer that starts from the moment you power on your computer and that also includes the BIOS Power-On Self-Test (POST). *See also* warm boot. WIN 4

collection A group of selected objects that may or may not be located adjacent to each other in a window or on the desktop. WIN 249

color
    console, specifying, WIN 838–842
    display settings, WIN 124, WIN 129–131
    windows, specifying, WIN 85–88

COLOR An internal command used to change or restore the background and foreground colors of a command-line window. WIN 838–841

color depth (or color depth setting) The monitor setting that determines the total number of colors that can be displayed for each pixel, such as Highest (32-bit), which determines the quality of the image. WIN 124, WIN 129–131

color hot-track A new Windows 7 feature that displays a glowing effect on a taskbar button when you point to the taskbar button. The glowing color matches the predominant color of the icon on the taskbar button. WIN 22, WIN 36

color palette. *See* palette

COM (Component Object Model) A platform-independent approach to creating software components that can interact with each other. WIN 912

command An instruction to the operating system (or other software) to perform a specific task. WIN 2. *See also* specific commands
    displaying reference list, WIN 846–848
    DOS, WIN 12
    editing, WIN 842
    external, WIN 831, WIN 837–838, WIN 843–846
    internal, WIN 830, WIN 837–838
    recalling from command history, WIN 840–842

command history An area of memory where Windows 7 keeps track of the commands that you enter in a Command Prompt or command-line window. WIN 840–841

command interpreter The command-line program that displays a command prompt, interprets commands entered at the command prompt, locates and loads the appropriate program from memory or disk, and then executes the program. WIN 558, WIN 830, WIN 833–838

command prompt. *See* operating system prompt

command-line environment The command-line window in which you work. *See also* command-line interface. WIN 269, WIN 829–882
    changing drives, WIN 872–873
    changing to root directory, WIN 861
    CHKDSK, WIN 386–389
    command interpreter, WIN 833–838
    copying files, WIN 870–872
    creating directories, WIN 868–870
    creating shortcuts with Administrator credentials, WIN 835–836
    Defrag utility, WIN 400–404
    displaying a directory tree, WIN 856–860
    displaying command-line reference lists, WIN 846–848
    ending sessions, WIN 403
    exporting Registry settings, WIN 901
    external commands, WIN 843–846
    importance of skills for using, WIN 832
    opening a session, WIN 834–835
    POWERCFG command, WIN 850–853
    specifying console colors, WIN 838–842
    SystemInfo command, WIN 848–850
    viewing contents of a directory, WIN 861–866
    viewing file attributes, WIN 866–868
    viewing Windows environment, WIN 878–881
    wildcards in file specifications, WIN 872–877

command-line interface A text or character-based user interface with an operating system prompt at which you enter commands to interact with the operating system and perform tasks. WIN 2

command-line operating system An operating system that uses a command-line interface through which you interact with the operating system by manually entering and executing commands. WIN 2, WIN 12

comma-separated values (CSV) A common file format with the .csv file extension for storing exported data in a format where each item of data is stored as text and separated from other items of data by a comma. WIN 157

F

Fast User Switching A feature of all Windows 7 editions, except the Starter edition, that enables you to switch back to the Welcome screen without logging off your user account and without closing any open programs or documents so you or someone else can log into another user account. Later, you can log back into your account and continue where you left off. WIN 25

FAT (file allocation table). *See* file allocation table (FAT)

FAT0 A duplicate copy of FAT1 that is updated by the TFAT (Transaction-Safe FAT) file system after changes to FAT1 are completed. WIN 323

FAT1 (1) The first of two copies of the file allocation table on a FAT volume; (2) The first of two copies of the file allocation table in the TFAT (Transaction-Safe FAT) file system. WIN 319

FAT2 A duplicate copy of the first file allocation table (FAT1) on a FAT volume. WIN 319

FAT12 The FAT file system used for floppy disks and small media. WIN 319

FAT16 A FAT file system used on smaller volumes and on some flash drives. WIN 320
    slack, WIN 321

FAT32 A variation of the FAT16 file system that supports larger volume sizes than FAT16, that more efficiently uses storage space on a disk than FAT16 by working with small cluster sizes and thereby reducing slack, that supports the use of more clusters on a disk than FAT16, and that keeps a backup of critical data structures in the boot record. WIN 320–321
    slack, WIN 321–322

FATFS (FAT file system or file allocation table file system). *See* file allocation table (FAT)

fault tolerant A type of disk that provides a mechanism, such as an error-checking feature, so the operating system can recover data in the case of a disk failure. WIN 307

favorite An Internet shortcut to a Web site. WIN 286–291

Favorites folder, WIN 157

Favorites menu, adding Registry key locations, WIN 921

Federal Deposit Insurance Corporation (FDIC), WIN 465

feed. *See* RSS feed

field The name of a specific type of BIOS setting and the setting itself. WIN 533

file A collection of data, such as a program or a document, stored in a folder on a disk under a unique filename and, in most cases, with a file extension. WIN 52
    attributes, viewing in command-line environment, WIN 866–868
    backing up. *See* backup; Backup and Restore
    compressed, WIN 229
    compressing and uncompressing. *See* compression
    copying. *See* copying a file
    corrupted, WIN 672
    creating shortcuts to files, WIN 258–260
    cross-linked, WIN 383–384
    decrypting, WIN 353
    deleted, recovering, WIN 693

    discarded by Windows upgrade, WIN 368
    downloading, WIN 166
    encrypted, copying to unencrypted folder, WIN 352–353
    executable, WIN 166
    extracting, WIN 166, WIN 349–350
    filtering, WIN 194–196
    fragmentation analysis report, WIN 403
    fragmented. *See* fragmented file
    grouping, WIN 196–197
    null, WIN 908
    offline, WIN 810–811
    organization, WIN 54, WIN 156–158, WIN 165
    organizing, WIN 154, WIN 191–194
    organizing for backup, WIN 647
    orphaned, WIN 376
    paging, WIN 572, WIN 577–578
    posting on FTP sites, WIN 346
    registered. *See* registered file
    registration, WIN 893
    Registry, WIN 894–895
    restoring. *See* restoring files and folders
    searching for, WIN 203–206
    shortcuts, WIN 8
    sparse, WIN 317
    stacking, WIN 154, WIN 191–194
    unencrypting before upgrading Windows, WIN 718
    verification, WIN 376

file allocation table (FAT) (also called file allocation table file system [FATFS]) A table in the system area of a FAT volume that keeps track of which clusters (or allocation units) are available or unused, which ones store the contents of files and are therefore used, which are defective and unusable, and which are reserved for use by the operating system. WIN 309, WIN 317–322
    boot record, WIN 317–318
    directory table, WIN 319
    FAT12, FAT16, and FAT32 compared, WIN 319–322
    file allocation tables, WIN 318–319
    slack in, NTFS compared, WIN 321–322

File and Printer Sharing for Microsoft Networks
Service software that enables users of other computers within the same network to access your files and printer. WIN 801

file extension The characters that follow the main part of a filename and a separator (a period) and that identify the type of application that produced the file or the type of data in the file. WIN 16

file fragment A chain of lost clusters that once belonged to a single file. WIN 382

file fragmentation A condition in which the clusters for one or more files are located in one or more nonadjacent blocks in different locations on a disk. WIN 392–404

file property Characteristic or setting of a single file or characteristic or setting common to a set of files. WIN 155

file record segment (FRS) A unique ID assigned to each folder and file in the Master File Table on an NTFS volume. WIN 376

file sharing An option and setting that lets users on other computers connected to the same network as your computer access any files or printers that you choose to share. WIN 789, WIN 799, WIN 805–812
    offline files, WIN 810–811

File Sharing dialog box, WIN 805

file specification A notation for selecting one or more files in a command operation, either using Search in the graphical user interface or with a command in a command-line environment. WIN 873
    wildcards, WIN 873–877

file system The operating system components and data structures that the operating system uses for naming, organizing, storing, and keeping track of disks, drives, folders, files, and data as well as the file system itself. WIN 3, WIN 5, WIN 305–356
    checking, WIN 323–328
    Disk Management, WIN 328–335
    errors, checking for and repairing, WIN 374–386
    exFAT, WIN 308, WIN 322–323
    FAT. *See* file allocation table
    Live File System, WIN 308, WIN 328
    NTFS. *See* NTFS
    TexFAT, WIN 323
    TFAT, WIN 323
    UDF, WIN 308, WIN 328

File Transfer Protocol (FTP) A standard Internet protocol for transferring files between computers on the Internet and as such, is commonly used to download programs and other types of files from FTP servers to your computer. WIN 346, WIN 750

file type A characteristic of a file that associates a file extension with a specific application on a computer and that indicates the type of content or data contained within the file. WIN 155

filename
    8.3, WIN 54, WIN 188
    long, WIN 16, WIN 53–54

Filename switch (/F) An optional switch used with the TREE command in a command-line window to display filenames under each directory and subdirectory. *See* TREE and ASCII switch (/A). WIN 857, WIN 858

files area The area on a FAT volume that follows the system area for storing folders and files. WIN 317

Fill option, Picture location box, WIN 84

filter (1) To select one or more criteria for displaying files in a folder window, such as displaying only Microsoft Word Document files; (2) To specify one or more criteria for selecting events in Event Viewer so you can focus on one specific type of event; (3) A command-line program that modifies the output of another command. WIN 194–196, WIN 497, WIN 847
    search, WIN 199, WIN 208–209
    SmartScreen Filter, WIN 459, WIN 464–468

Filter Current Log dialog box, WIN 523

firewall Software that protects a computer from hackers and Internet worms and from malicious software that has already gained access to your computer by monitoring incoming traffic from the Internet or a network and by

also monitoring outgoing traffic from your computer to the Internet or a network. WIN 428
    settings, WIN 432–436

FireWire A high-speed Plug and Play bus with data transfer rates of 800 Mbps to 3.2 Gbps (gigabits per second); equivalent to IEEE 1394a. WIN 764

firmware A hardware device, such as the BIOS, that contains embedded software that controls how the hardware interacts with the operating system. WIN 530

first-party cookie A cookie placed on your computer by a Web site that you visit. WIN 458

first-party Web site A Web site whose Web page you are currently viewing. WIN 477

Fit option, Picture location box, WIN 84

Fix switch (/F) A switch used with the CHKDSK command to repair file system problems (if possible) on a disk. *See also* CHKDSK. WIN 388

fixed-length text string A nonnumeric value that contains a set of characters. WIN 903

flash drive. *See* USB flash drive

folder A file that keeps track of a group of related objects, such as other folders (called subfolders) and files that are stored at different locations on a disk. WIN 52
    backing up. *See* backup; Backup and Restore
    compressed (zipped), using, WIN 345–350
    compressing and uncompressing. *See* compression
    creating shortcuts to folders, WIN 254–258
    deleted, recovering, WIN 693
    encrypting, WIN 351–352
    fragmentation analysis report, WIN 403
    fragmented, WIN 390
    group, WIN 733
    opening command-line windows from, WIN 856
    organization, WIN 54, WIN 156–158, WIN 163–165
    organizing for backup, WIN 647
    renaming, WIN 170
    restoring. *See* restoring files and folders
    sharing folders, WIN 802–811
    shortcuts, WIN 8
    uncompressing, WIN 344, WIN 345
    unencrypting before upgrading Windows, WIN 718
    viewing contents. *See* viewing folder contents
    virtual, WIN 154, WIN 158, WIN 159, WIN 160, WIN 191–192, WIN 198, WIN 200, WIN 218–219

Folder Options dialog box, WIN 42

folder window, initiating searches, WIN 200

font (1) A design style for a set of characters; (2) A combination of a specific typeface, point size, and weight or style. WIN 13, WIN 96

font smoothing A Windows 7 feature for improving the appearance of characters on a monitor by filling in pixels adjacent to a diagonal or curved line with increasingly lighter colors to simulate a smooth curve. WIN 97–100

forced hardware configuration A configuration created by manually changing the resource assignment(s) for a hardware device. *See also* Device Manager. WIN 760

formatting Preparing a disk for use on a computer. WIN 12
    hard disks, WIN 308–310

high-level, WIN 310
low-level, WIN 310

fragmented file A file that is stored in two or more non-contiguous clusters on a disk. WIN 390, WIN 392–404
    defragmenting using command-line Defrag utility, WIN 400–404
    defragmenting using Disk Defragmenter, WIN 396–400

fragmented folder A folder that is stored in two or more noncontiguous clusters on a disk. WIN 390

free memory The amount of memory that can be immediately used by the operating system, drivers, and processes. WIN 592

free space fragmentation A condition in which there are noncontiguous blocks of unused disk storage space. WIN 390
    fragmentation analysis report, WIN 403

friendly name A label or name assigned to a drive to identify the type of drive, such as Local Disk (C:) for drive C. WIN 55

FTP site An Internet site for uploading and downloading files. WIN 346, WIN 750

full backup A type of backup that marks the start of a backup cycle and that includes all or part of the contents of a hard disk (or in some cases, all selected files). WIN 642
    archive attribute, WIN 655, WIN 657
    combining with incremental backup, WIN 650–652

full version A more expensive version of a software product that does not require that you already have a previous version of that software product installed on your computer. WIN 708

Full-Speed (or Full-Speed USB) The speed of the initial first generation USB bus, identified as USB 1.x (USB 1.0 and USB 1.1), which supports speeds of 12 Mbps (12 megabits per second) for devices that require large amounts of bandwidth, such as devices that process video and audio, and which supports Low-Speed USB at 1.5 Mbps (1.5 megabits per second) for devices such as keyboards and mice. WIN 763

G

G. *See* gigabyte (G, GB, or gig)

gadget A miniprogram that provides easily accessible useful tools and information on the desktop. WIN 29

Gadget Gallery, WIN 46–47

Game Statistics File A file created by Windows 7 for tracking information about your use of games. WIN 369

gateway The hardware and software that provide an access point to another network. WIN 762–763

GB. *See* gigabyte (G, GB, or gig)

GFS. *See* grandfather-father-son (GFS)

gibibyte (GiB) 1,024 mebibytes, or 230 bytes (approximately one billion bytes), of storage space in RAM, according to the International Electrochemical Commission. WIN 57

GIF. *See* Graphics Interchange Format (GIF)

gig. *See* gigabyte (G, GB, or gig)

gigabyte (G, GB, or gig) (1) 1,024 megabytes, or 230 bytes (approximately one billion bytes) of storage space in RAM; (2) 1,000 megabytes, or 109 bytes (exactly one billion bytes), of storage space on disk, according to the International Electrochemical Commission. WIN 56

gigahertz (GHz) One billion cycles per second. WIN 61

globally unique identifier. *See* GUID (globally unique identifier)

grandfather-father-son (GFS) A backup rotation scheme that uses three sets of backups-incremental or differential backups performed for the first 6 days of the week (each of which is referred to as the son) and which are reused each week in the same order, a full backup at the end of each week (referred to as the father) that is reused each month, and a full backup on the last day of each month (referred to as the grandfather) that is retained for a year (or perhaps a quarter) before reusing the media. WIN 653

graphical user interface (GUI) A type of user interface that uses a combination of features, including icons, windows, menus with task-related lists, dialog boxes, toolbars, colors, and fonts, as well as special screen elements, such as shading, shadows, animation, and translucency, to provide a visually rich working environment as well as provide on-screen clues that simplify interaction with the operating system. WIN 3, WIN 13
    customizing. *See* customizing the GUI

Graphics Interchange Format (GIF) (pronounced jiff or gif) A bitmapped graphics file format that stores an image at a compression of 1.5:1 to 2:1 without any loss of detail in the image. WIN 82–83

graphics memory, Windows 7 requirements, WIN 707

graphics mode A video display mode for displaying graphic images as well as text in a variety of fonts and colors, and that supports the use of graphics, animation, and video. WIN 14

greater than operator (>) A comparison operator that selects all files that exceed a certain value that you specify. WIN 214, WIN 215

greater than or equal to operator (>=) A comparison operator that selects all files that exceed a certain value or exactly match a certain value that you specify. WIN 214, WIN 215

group To organize folders and files in a folder window using specific criteria (such as file type). WIN 868, WIN 873, WIN 874, WIN 875, WIN 877

group folder A folder on the All Programs menu that contains one or more programs for an installed software product. WIN 39, WIN 733

group properties Common properties of one or more folders, one or more files, or one or more folders and files. WIN 182–183

grouping
    files, WIN 196–197
    taskbar buttons, WIN 112–113

Guest account An account designed for a user (such as a visitor or friend) who needs temporary access to the features on your computer, such as the ability to use software, connect to the Internet, and browse the Web. WIN 446

GUI. *See* customizing the GUI; graphical user interface (GUI)

GUID (globally unique identifier) A unique randomly generated 128-bit (or 16 byte) number assigned to an object. WIN 316

H

handle An ID that uniquely identifies a resource, such as a file or Registry setting, so a program can access that resource. WIN 582

hard disk
checking for errors, WIN 717
checking storage space, WIN 717
copying files to external hard disk or network folder for backup, WIN 646
copying files to removable storage for backup, WIN 646
diagnostic check, WIN 377–381
dynamic, WIN 329
formatting, WIN 308–310
fragmentation analysis report, WIN 401–403
optimizing. *See* optimizing your hard disk
optimizing storage space, WIN 717
virtual, WIN 335
Windows 7 requirements, WIN 707

Hard Disk Partition Table A table within the Master Boot Record of a hard disk that identifies where each partition starts and ends, and that also identifies which partition is the partition for booting a computer. WIN 310

hard fault (or hard page fault or page fault) A condition in which the operating system must retrieve a page from the paging file on the hard disk because the page is no longer available in physical memory. WIN 587

hard link A link to a file on an NTFS volume that appears as a separate file (with the same or different filename) and that provides an additional way for opening and working with a file. WIN 316–317

hard page fault. *See* hard fault

hardware. *See also specific hardware devices*
comparing types, WIN 762–764
Device Manager. *See* Device Manager
resource assignments, WIN 769–770
troubleshooting problems, WIN 783–787
viewing, WIN 765–769
viewing device properties, WIN 782
Windows 7 support, WIN 763–764

hardware conflict A problem that results when two hardware devices attempt to share the same resource, such as the same IRQ (interrupt request line). WIN 770. *See also* Device Manager

hardware interrupt A signal transmitted from a hardware device to the processor when the device is ready to send or accept data. WIN 769

hardware reserved memory Memory reserved for us by the BIOS and some hardware drivers. WIN 592

hardware tree The Device Manager view that displays categories of hardware components installed on your computer. WIN 761

hardware-assisted virtualization (HAV) The inclusion of additional microcode called hardware extensions in a processor to enable it to better support the use of virtual environments. WIN 724

HAV. *See* hardware-assisted virtualization (HAV)

HELP An external command used in a command-line window to display a command reference list with Help information on commands. WIN 838–840, WIN 843, WIN 846–847. *See also* Help switch (/?)

Help and Support. *See* Windows Help and Support

Help link A link in Windows Help and Support that is similar to a link on a Web page and that opens a specific Help topic or dialog box, displays a definition or explanation of a feature, or opens a Web site with Help information. WIN 44

Help switch (/?) An optional parameter for displaying Help information on a command used in a command-line environment. WIN 830

Help system, WIN 10

hertz One cycle per second. WIN 61

hex digit A digit in the hexadecimal number system (0 through 9, and A through F) used with the COLOR command to customize the background and foreground colors of a Command Prompt or command-line window. WIN 839

hexadecimal code A base-16 number system that uses the digits 0 through 9 and the uppercase and lowercase letters A through F to encode data. WIN 922

hibernation A power-saving feature in which Windows 7 saves the contents of RAM to a hibernation file on disk, shuts down the computer, and places it in hibernation. When you next power on the computer, Windows 7 restores the contents of RAM from the hibernation file so the computer returns to its previous operating state before you manually implemented hibernation or it automatically implemented hibernation. WIN 69

hibernation file A system file that Windows 7 uses to store a copy of the contents of RAM before it switches the computer to a hibernation state. WIN 69

HID. *See* human interface device (HID)

hidden attribute An attribute (or setting) assigned to a folder or file to indicate that a folder or file should not be displayed in a folder window (unless you choose the option to display all hidden folders and files). WIN 312, WIN 313, WIN 314

hierarchy An ordered structure, or view, of system components, such as the disks, drives, folders, and files that form part of the file system of a computer system, and that shows and describes the logical relationship between those system components and folders. WIN 7

High Color A 16-bit color setting for a video display adapter that allows it to display 216 or 65,536 colors. WIN 130

High Performance power plan A Windows 7 power plan for maximizing power usage on mobile computer even if it results in shorter battery life. *See* power plan and power management. WIN 138

high-level formatting The process for creating a file system on a disk. WIN 310

Hi-Speed (or Hi-Speed USB) Second-generation USB devices (USB 2.0) that support a data transfer rate of 480 Mbps (480 megabits per second). WIN 763

history, Windows Update, checking, WIN 439–442

hive A Registry database file (Default, SAM, Security, Software, System, and Components) with Registry settings and its associated log file (Default.log, SAM.log, Security.log, Software.log, System.log, and Components.log). WIN 892

HKCC. *See* HKEY_CURRENT_CONFIG (HKCC)

HKCR. *See* HKEY_CLASSES_ROOT (HKCR)

HKCU. *See* HKEY_CURRENT USER (HKCU)

HKEY_CLASSES_ROOT (HKCR) A Registry root key that contains subkeys for each registered file type. WIN 904, WIN 906–908, WIN 912

HKEY_CURRENT_CONFIG (HKCC) A Registry root key that contains configuration settings for the currently used hardware profile for the local computer at system startup. WIN 906

HKEY_CURRENT_USER (HKCU) A Registry root key that contains subkeys for the current user logged onto the computer. WIN 905

HKEY_LOCAL_MACHINE (HKLM) A Registry root key that contains subkeys for all systemwide hardware and operating system configuration settings as well as user account information, security settings, user rights settings, and boot settings. WIN 905–906

HKEY_USERS (HKU) A Registry root key that contains user profile settings, or user account settings. WIN 906

HKLM. *See* HKEY_LOCAL_MACHINE (HKLM)

HKU. *See* HKEY_USERS (HKU)

hoax An email message sent from a family member, friend, or coworker warning of a nonexistent problem that poses a risk to your computer and recommending that you send an email message to everyone you know and warn them of the threat, and have them in turn send an email message to everyone they know, in order to overload the Internet with email traffic and even shut down email servers. WIN 468

HomeGroup A new Windows 7 feature that permits Windows 7 users on a home network to share documents, pictures, music, videos, and one or more printers. WIN 160, WIN 788, WIN 790, WIN 815–822
accessing from another computer, WIN 819
creating homegroups, WIN 160, WIN 788, WIN 790, WIN 815–818
joining, WIN 820, WIN 822
options for leaving or remaining in, WIN 821–822
viewing links to members, WIN 820
viewing new members, WIN 821

hot fix An update for operating system software. WIN 849

N

NAP. *See* Network Access Protection (NAP)

native resolution The resolution set by an LCD monitor manufacturer that is typically the highest and best resolution available for the LCD monitor. WIN 126

navigation, WIN 52–60
    to personal user account folders, WIN 60

Navigation pane A pane in a folder window that contains links to frequently used locations on a computer as well as other locations, including libraries, a homegroup, drives, and a network. WIN 55
    customizing, WIN 277–280

Network Access Protection (NAP) A Windows service that checks a computer's security settings and installed software to make sure it is secure before it is connected to a network and that, if necessary, updates that computer's software and security settings. WIN 428, WIN 455

Network and Sharing Center A Windows 7 component that displays your current network settings and a network map that visually illustrates the layout of a network. WIN 796–802
    opening, WIN 797
    viewing shared network folders and files, WIN 800–801
    viewing sharing settings, WIN 798–799

network file, copying, WIN 166

Network Locations, accessing network resources, WIN 814

network share (or share) A network object made available to other users on a network. WIN 657, WIN 802

network shortcut, WIN 240

networking, WIN 788–823
    creating mapped drives, WIN 812–814
    HomeGroup feature, WIN 815–822
    Network and Sharing center, WIN 796–802
    operating system, WIN 9
    sharing folders, WIN 802–811
    viewing computers in workgroup, WIN 793–796
    viewing computer's name, WIN 790–793

new computer user training, WIN 27

New Technology File System. *See* NTFS (NT File System or New Technology File System)

no value, or null value operator ([ ]) A comparison operator that locates files that do not have a value or setting for a property. WIN 214, WIN 215

noncontiguous Clusters of folders and files stored in non-adjacent blocks on disk. WIN 392, WIN 394, WIN 395

nonpaged kernel memory Memory that is available only to the operating system and that cannot be paged to disk. WIN 582

non-Plug and Play device (or legacy device) An older type of hardware device that does not support the Plug and Play specifications for hardware devices, and that requires manual installation, configuration, and frequently troubleshooting. WIN 16, WIN 762

nonresponding program, shutting down, WIN 548

normal backup A type of backup that marks the start of a backup cycle and that includes all or part of the contents of a hard disk (in other words, all selected folders and files). WIN 648
    combining with differential backup, WIN 648–650

NOT A Boolean operator that combines two criteria and selects all folders or files that meet the first condition but not the second condition. WIN 214

Not Content Indexed An attribute (or setting) assigned to folders and files for the purpose of excluding them from indexing. WIN 314

notification area The area on the right side of the taskbar that contains an Action Center icon, a Power icon, a Network icon, a Volume icon, and the current time, day, and date as well as a Show hidden icons button for accessing other notification area icons for specific Windows 7 features or other open programs. Windows 7 also displays notifications, or messages, about problems or successfully completed operations in the notification area. WIN 38, WIN 116–117
    checking settings, WIN 116–117
    customizing, WIN 113

NT File System. *See* NTFS (NT File System or New Technology File System)

NTFS (NT File System or New Technology File System) The native file system for Windows 7 and for the Windows NT product line that uses a Master File Table (MFT) to track information about folders and files on disk, that supports larger storage media than the FAT file systems, that supports disk compression and encryption, and that includes security features that determine access to folders and files by users. WIN 307, WIN 308, WIN 311–317
    CHKDSK error-checking tool, WIN 375–381
    cluster sizes, WIN 315
    MFT attributes, WIN 312–314
    slack, WIN 322
    volume sizes, WIN 315

NTFS compression. *See* compression

NTFS directory. WIN 378

NTFS encryption. *See* encryption

null file (or NullFile) An empty file for a specific file type that contains no template and that is zero bytes in size. WIN 908

null value operator ([ ]) A comparison operator that locates files that do not have a value or setting for a property. WIN 214, WIN 215

O

object (1) A component of the graphical user interface and your computer system, such as a hardware device, software application, folder, file, document, or part of a document; (2) A visible element of the graphical user interface that you can right-click. WIN 14

object-oriented interface The Windows 7 graphical user interface, which treats components of a computer as objects with actions and properties. WIN 14

OEM (original equipment manufacturer) A company that develops, or acquires, and subsequently sells a product. WIN 17

Offline Files Copies of network files that are stored locally. WIN 810–811

Offline Files cache A folder on a local computer that acts as a temporary storage location for copies of network files. WIN 200

Offline Files feature, WIN 810–811

Offline Webpages Web pages stored locally on your computer so you can view them without being connected to the Internet. WIN 367

OHCI. *See* Open Host Controller Interface (OHCI)

Old Chkdsk files Recovered file fragments with the .chk file extension that once belonged to a file. WIN 368

OLE registration, Software Environment information, WIN 560

online backup The use of a backup utility to back up folders and files to a Web site. WIN 646

Online Help Help information provided at a Web site by the manufacturer of the software you are using on your computer. WIN 10, WIN 43, WIN 45–49

online privacy, WIN 476. *See also* cookies

online profiling Techniques used by Web sites to gather information about your personal preferences without your knowledge or consent . WIN 476

Open dialog box, initiating searches, WIN 201

Open Host Controller Interface (OHCI) A host controller that supports the use of first-generation USB 1.x devices with data transfer rates of 1.5 and 12 Mbps. WIN 782

operating environment A software product that performs many of the same functions as an operating system, but requires an operating system to boot the computer and manage disks, drives, folders, and files. WIN 2

operating system (OS or OpSys) A software product that manages all the operations on your computer from the time that you power on your computer until you shut it down, including managing the interaction of software and hardware to guarantee that they work together (where possible), and providing support for the use of other software, such as application software, Web browsers, email software, utilities, games, and even customized software for special tasks required in a business. WIN 3, WIN 4–21
    DOS, WIN 10–13
    Linux, WIN 21
    locating and loading, WIN 4–5
    Mac OS, WIN 21
    operations, WIN 4–10
    Plug and Play, WIN 762
    Unix, WIN 21
    Windows, WIN 13–20

operating system prompt (or command prompt) A set of characters displayed by a command-line operating system or in a command-line window to identify the current drive and directory and to provide a reference point for interacting with the operating system's command interpreter (or program), which interprets commands that you enter from the keyboard. WIN 11, WIN 561, WIN 830

operator. *See* Boolean operator, comparison operator, logical operator, and relational operator

OpSys. *See* operating system (OS or OpSys)

Program Defaults A Start menu option for (1) specifying default programs for all file types and protocols, (2) associating a file type or protocol with a program, (3) changing AutoPlay settings, and (4) setting program access to certain programs as well as specifying computer default settings. WIN 746–753

program group, Software Environment information, WIN 560

Programs and Features A Control Panel component for viewing, organizing, uninstalling, repairing, and changing installed software as well as viewing installed updates and turning Windows features on and off. WIN 728, WIN 734, WIN 737, WIN 738, WIN 744, WIN 745

PROMPT An internal command that uses a metastring to determine the appearance of the operating system prompt, or command prompt, in a command-line window. WIN 879

Properties button, Performance Monitor toolbar, WIN 625

property (1) A characteristic or setting of an object; (2) A setting, such as a trigger, action, and history of events, for a scheduled task. WIN 14, WIN 391

creating searches using file properties, WIN 206–208, WIN 212

shortcuts, viewing, WIN 250–254

property sheet A group of related object settings displayed on a sheet in a dialog box. WIN 41

Protected Mode A security feature of Internet Explorer that protects Web sites from making changes to system files on your computer and from installing malicious software on a computer. WIN 459

protocol The rules and conventions for transmitting data over a network. WIN 460, WIN 593

Q

QoS (Quality of Service) Packet Scheduler A network component that provides for the efficient flow of data on a network by handling the scheduling of packets of data over a network. WIN 801

question mark wildcard (?) A symbol used as part of a file specification to substitute for a single character at the position of the wildcard in a filename or file extension when performing a search. WIN 220

quotation mark Boolean operator ("") A Boolean operator that selects all folders or files that match exactly what is typed within the quotation marks. WIN 199, WIN 214

QWORD A quadruple word that stores a 64-bit number. WIN 923

R

RAID (Redundant Array of Independent Disks) The use of use of multiple hard disks to store data in order to improve performance or reliability. WIN 329

RAID-0 A striped volume on a dynamic disk. *See also* striped volume. WIN 329

RAID-1. *See* mirrored volume

RAID-5 A fault-tolerant volume that stores data and parity information in stripes across three or more physical hard disks. WIN 329

RAM (random access memory) (also called system memory) (1) The predominant and most important type of memory within a computer that consists of RAM memory chips stored on memory modules inside the system unit; (2) temporary, or volatile, high-speed memory used to store copies of the operating system, device drivers, open programs, open documents, and data as well as all input, processing, and output; (3) workspace for software, documents, data. WIN 4

Windows 7 requirements, WIN 706

random access memory. *See* RAM (random access memory)

range of values operator (..) A comparison operator that locates all folders and files that fall within a certain range and that include the starting and ending values for that range. WIN 214, WIN 215

read-only attribute An attribute (or setting) assigned to a file by the operating system to indicate that you can read from, but not write to, the file. WIN 312, WIN 313

read-only memory. *See* ROM

read-only mode A diagnostic mode of operation in which the command-line Check Disk utility checks a drive and, if it finds errors, reports the presence of these errors and identifies how it would correct the problem. *See also* CHKDSK. WIN 365

Really Simple Syndication Feed. *See* RSS feed

rebooting computer, upgrading Windows, WIN 718

recently opened programs list An area of the Start menu where Windows 7 lists your most recently used programs so you can quickly open a program you recently used. WIN 37, WIN 38

record Information within the Master File Table about a folder or file or about the Master File Table and its settings. WIN 311

recovered file fragment, *See also* Old Chkdsk files. WIN 368

Recycle Bin, removing folders and files, WIN 367

Redundant Array of Independent Disks. *See* RAID (Redundant Array of Independent Disks)

refresh rate The number of times per second that the image on the screen of a CRT monitor is redrawn by the video card (and thereby refreshed). WIN 132

REG_BINARY A Registry data type for a Registry setting that is a binary value displayed in hexadecimal format. WIN 903, WIN 922

REG_DWORD A Registry data type for a Registry setting for a DWORD (or double word) that consists of a four-byte number (or 32-bit number) stored in binary, hexadecimal, or decimal format. WIN 903, WIN 922–923

REG_EXPAND_SZ A Registry data type for a Registry setting that is an Expandable String Value or variable length string and that contains a replaceable parameter for an environment variable or another type of variable value, each of which are converted into specific values when a program or service uses the Registry setting. WIN 910, WIN 923

REG_FULL_RESOURCE_DESCRIPTOR A Registry data type for a Registry setting that contains a list of hardware resources used by a hardware device. WIN 923

registered file A file that is associated with an application on your computer via its file extension. WIN 176

tracing registered file types, WIN 906–912

registration file A file with the .reg file extension that contains a backup of the entire Registry, or a specific key within the Registry. WIN 893

Registry A database that consists of a set of files where Windows 7 stores your computer's hardware, software, security, network, system performance, and user settings (or user profiles). WIN 891–924

adding new entries to subkeys, WIN 922–923
backing up, WIN 896–897
CLSIDs, WIN 911–915
consistent strategy for working with, WIN 897
creating restore point for, WIN 897–898
editing, WIN 918
editing Registry values, WIN 920–921
exporting Registry settings, WIN 898–901
files, WIN 894–895
interaction with Windows tools, WIN 915–918
keys. *See* key
opening, WIN 898–901
overview of role, WIN 894–896
remote, connecting to, WIN 923
restoring, WIN 896–897
tracing registered file types, WIN 906–912

Registry Editor A Windows tool for viewing and changing the settings in the Windows Registry. WIN 892, WIN 918

opening, WIN 899–900

Registry path The path to the current Registry key shown on the status bar of the Registry Editor window. WIN 893

Registry tree A diagrammatic representation of the organization of Windows Registry settings by keys and subkeys in the Navigation Pane of the Registry Editor window. WIN 892

Registry update, WIN 733

REG_MULTI_SZ A Registry data type for a Registry setting that is a Multi-String Value used to store lists or multiple values. WIN 923

REG_NONE A Registry data type for a Registry setting denoting that there is no defined value type. WIN 923

REG_QWORD A Registry data type for a Registry setting that is a QWORD (or quadruple word), which stores a 64-bit number. WIN 923

REG_RESOURCE_LIST A Registry data type for a Registry setting that contains lists with categories and subcategories of information about resources for a device driver. WIN 923

REG_SZ A Registry data type for a Registry setting that consists of a fixed-length text string; in other words, a string value. WIN 903, WIN 922

relational operator. *See* comparison operator

relative path A partial path to a folder, directory, subdirectory, or file that implies a location as under the current folder or directory or under the current drive. WIN 865

relative search A search specification that selects all folders and files relative to a fixed reference, such as a day, month, or year; for example, date:today locates all folders and files with a folder or file date for the current day. WIN 222

Reliability Monitor A Windows 7 tool that gathers, analyzes, and reports on the reliability and stability of your computer using data collected by the Reliability Analysis Component (RAC) and that calculates and graphically produces a system stability chart, which illustrates the impact on problems on the stability of a computer. WIN 496, WIN 506–510

reliability rating. *See* stability index value

Remote Assistance A Windows 7 tool for connecting to another computer over the Internet or a network in order to offer help or work collaboratively with another person. WIN 44

remote computer A computer that is not physically connected to your computer, but one that you can access over a network or the Internet. WIN 519

renaming a folder, WIN 170

Repair switch (/R) A command-line Check Disk utility switch that examines each sector on disk to determine whether it can read from, and write to, sectors in each cluster and that, if necessary, moves data stored in defective sectors to another cluster. *See also* CHKDSK. WIN 376

Repair your computer A boot option displayed on the Advanced Boot Options menu that allows you to use system recovery tools for troubleshooting your computer. WIN 542

replaceable parameter A variable value that is replaced by a setting when processing a command that contains the replaceable parameter. WIN 558, WIN 855

reserved symbol A symbol, such as a colon, that is reserved for use by the operating system, and that cannot be used as part of a folder name or a filename. WIN 53

resizing buttons, WIN 26

resolution A monitor setting that determines the sharpness and quality of the image that appears on the monitor. WIN 124, WIN 126–129
  native, WIN 126

Resource and Performance Monitor A Windows tool used to produce a System Diagnostics Report that provides extensive information about the performance, security, and current status of your computer and that identifies problems and describes how to resolve them. WIN 573

resource conflict A problem that results when two hardware devices attempt to share the same resource, such as the same IRQ (interrupt request line). *See also* Device Manager. WIN 770, WIN 785

Resource Monitor A Windows tool that provides valuable information on the use of memory by the operating system, applications, Windows services, startup programs, and device drivers. WIN 572
  CPU usage details, WIN 588–590
  disk usage information, WIN 592–593
  evaluating system performance, WIN 586–594

examining memory performance, WIN 626–630
  opening, WIN 586–587
  services information, WIN 591–592

Resource Overview An administrative tool that displays information on the status, utilization, and details of four basic system components-the CPU, network, disk, and memory. WIN 573

Restart option, logging off, WIN 69

restore point A snapshot of a computer at a given point in time that enables System Restore to roll back the computer to an earlier working point. *See also* System Protection. WIN 497
  creating, WIN 515–516, WIN 644–645, WIN 710, WIN 897–898
  Registry, WIN 897–898
  viewing, WIN 516–519

restoring files and folders, WIN 670–693
  creating system image and system repair disc, WIN 678–684
  Previous Versions, WIN 686–687, WIN 693
  restoring system image backups, WIN 684–686
  shadow copies, WIN 686–687
  verifying backups, WIN 677

Restricted sites An Internet Explorer security zone that includes Web sites that you do not trust and therefore includes sites that could potentially damage your computer or its data. WIN 460, WIN 461, WIN 462

Rich Text Format (RTF) A document format that includes character formatting and tab codes that many types of word-processing applications recognize. Rich Text Files have the .rtf file extension. WIN 174, WIN 212

right-clicking, creating shortcuts, WIN 246

right-dragging, creating shortcuts, WIN 246

ROM Read-only memory. WIN 332

root directory (1) The first directory (or folder) created on a disk during the formatting of the disk; (2) The command-line or DOS name for the top-level folder on a disk. WIN 11, WIN 186
  changing to, command-line environment, WIN 861

root key One of five major top-level keys in the Registry, each of which starts with HKEY. WIN 892

root name The main part of a filename (i.e. the name you designate when you save a file, or the main part of a program filename). WIN 53

rootkit Malicious (or perhaps even legitimate) software that, when installed on your computer, uses stealth techniques to hide itself from the operating system, other software, and you. WIN 443

routine A small program executed during the booting process to check the availability and functioning of basic hardware boot devices, and to locate and load the operating system from disk. WIN 4

RSS feed Web site content (such as news, headlines, or digital content such as video) automatically delivered to your Web browser, other programs, or your desktop from a Web site. WIN 374

RTF. *See* Rich Text Format (RTF)

running task, Software Environment information, WIN 559

S

Safe Mode A Windows 7 boot option that loads the minimum set of files and drivers for the mouse, monitor, keyboard, mass storage, and video as well as default system services so you can troubleshoot problems that might be caused by device drivers, Windows services, startup programs, and video display problems. *See also* Advanced Boot Options menu. WIN 528, WIN 540–541, WIN 542–545

Safe Mode with Command Prompt A Windows 7 troubleshooting boot option on the Advanced Boot Options menu that boots to a command-line environment and, in the process, loads the minimum set of files and drivers for the mouse, monitor, keyboard, mass storage, video, as well as default system services. *See also* Advanced Boot Options menu. WIN 541

Safe Mode with Networking A Windows 7 troubleshooting boot option on the Advanced Boot Options menu that loads the minimum set of files and drivers for the mouse, monitor, keyboard, mass storage, video, and network as well as default system services. *See also* Advanced Boot Options menu. WIN 541

SATA (Serial ATA or Serial Advanced Technology Attachment) A bus technology for connecting a hard disk drive to a computer with data transfer speeds up to 6 Gbps (6 gigabits per second). WIN 534, WIN 764

saturation The amount of gray in a color, and therefore a determinant of the purity of a color. WIN 78

Save dialog box
  initiating searches, WIN 201

Saved Games folder, WIN 158

saving a theme, WIN 88–89

scaling plotted values, WIN 611

scheduled task A task that automatically starts a program or script at a scheduled time or when specific conditions are met and that performs a specific action on a computer. WIN 391, WIN 404–418
  deleting, WIN 417–418
  locating program names and paths, WIN 404–405
  placing Administrative Tools option in All Programs and Start menus, WIN 406
  setting up, WIN 409–414
  viewing information on scheduled tasks, WIN 406–409
  viewing settings, WIN 414–417

screen font A specific typeface used by Windows to display text on the monitor (or screen). WIN 96

screen saver A moving image that Windows 7 displays on your monitor when you have not used your computer for a specified period of time. WIN 79, WIN 88

ScreenTip A label displayed in an application window when you point to an object, such as a button, and that identifies the object or displays information about the object. WIN 30

script A file that contains a list of executable commands processed without user intervention. WIN 391

SDD. *See* solid-state drive (SDD)

TASK REFERENCE

TASK	PAGE #	RECOMMENDED METHOD
32-bit Windows upgrade options, use the Windows 7 Upgrade Advisor to identify	WIN 716	*See* Reference box: Evaluating a Computer with the Windows 7 Upgrade Advisor
64-bit Windows upgrade options, use the Windows 7 Upgrade Advisor to identify	WIN 716	*See* Reference box: Evaluating a Computer with the Windows 7 Upgrade Advisor
Action Center, change settings in	WIN 456	*See* Reference box: Changing Action Center Settings
Action Center, open	WIN 430	Click ▐▀ in the notification area, click Open Action Center
Add-ons, view and manage Internet Explorer 8	WIN 475	*See* Reference box: Examining Information on Add-ons
Address bar, navigate to drive using the	WIN 58	Click first ▶ , click Computer, click the drive icon
Address bar, navigate using the	WIN 58	Click ▶ , click a location from the drop-down menu
Administrative Tools, add to Start menu	WIN 330	Right-click 🪟, click Properties, click Customize, locate System administrative tools, click the Display on the All Programs menu and the Start menu option button, click OK
Advanced Boot Options menu, display the	WIN 539	Boot or restart the computer, press the F8 key before you see the Windows logo
Aero Flip 3D, use	WIN 29	*See* Reference box: Using Aero Flip 3D
Aero Peek, use	WIN 31	*See* Reference box: Using Aero Peek
Aero Shake, use	WIN 31	Rapidly shake the active window's title bar
Aero Snap, use	WIN 34	*See* Reference box: Using Aero Snap
Application, create shortcut to	WIN 263	*See* Reference box: Creating a Shortcut to an Application
Applications, view running	WIN 546	Right-click the taskbar, click Start Task Manager, click the Applications tab
ATTRIB command, use	WIN 866	In a command-line window, type ATTRIB and press the Enter key
Attribute switch, use the DIR command's	WIN 862	In a command-line window, type DIR /A and press the Enter key
Autorun.inf file, create	WIN 285	*See* Reference box: Customizing a Flash Drive Icon
Backup, create	WIN 665	*See* Reference box: Setting Up a Regularly Scheduled Backup
Basic task, create	WIN 414	*See* Reference box: Creating a Scheduled Task
BIOS Setup utility, open	WIN 536	*See* Reference box: Changing the Boot Sequence
Boot sequence, change	WIN 536	*See* Reference box: Changing the Boot Sequence
Browsing history, delete Internet Explorer 8's	WIN 487	*See* Reference box: Deleting Your Internet Explorer 8 Browsing History
Cancel command, use	WIN 860	In a command-line window, press the Ctrl+C keys, or press the Ctrl+Break keys
Capture image of a dialog box or active window	WIN 499	Press the Alt+Print Screen keys
CD command, use	WIN 861	In a command-line window, type CD, press the spacebar, type directory name or the path to the directory, and press the Enter key

TASK	PAGE #	RECOMMENDED METHOD
Check Disk utility, use command-line	WIN 389	*See* Reference box: Using the Check Disk Utility in a Command Prompt Window
Classic menu bar, display or hide	WIN 59	Press the Alt key
ClearType Text Tuner, use	WIN 100	*See* Reference box: Using the ClearType Text Tuner
CLSIDs, locate information on	WIN 914	*See* Reference box: Locating Information on CLSIDs
COLOR command, obtain Help on the use of	WIN 840	*See* Reference box: Changing Console Colors
COLOR command, use	WIN 840	*See* Reference box: Changing Console Colors
Color depth setting, view or change	WIN 131	*See* Reference box: Changing the Color Depth Setting
Colors, adjust Start menu, taskbar, and window	WIN 88	*See* Reference box: Adjusting Window Color Settings
Column widths in a window or dialog box, adjust for best fit	WIN 194	Click a folder or file in a window or an item in a list box, press the Ctrl key and the + key on the numeric keypad
Command history, display	WIN 842	*See* Reference box: Recalling Commands from the Command History
Command Prompt window, clear	WIN 843	In a command-line window, type CLS and press the Enter key
Command Prompt window, open and close	WIN 837	*See* Reference box: Opening and Closing a Command Prompt Window
Command Prompt window, specify administrator credentials to open	WIN 837	*See* Reference box: Opening and Closing a Command Prompt Window
Command reference list, display	WIN 846	In a command-line window, type HELP and press the Enter key
Command, display Help for	WIN 838	In a command-line window, type HELP, press the spacebar, type a command, press the Enter key
Command, recall a previous	WIN 842	*See* Reference box: Recalling Commands from the Command History
Command, use cancel or interrupt	WIN 860	In a command-line window, press the Ctrl+C keys, or press the Ctrl+Break keys
Compatibility settings, specify	WIN 743	*See* Reference box: Using the Program Compatibility Troubleshooter to Specify Compatibility Settings
Compressed (zipped) Folder, create or extract	WIN 350	*See* Reference box: Creating and Extracting a Compressed (Zipped) Folder
Compressed (zipped) Folder, view properties of	WIN 347	Right-click [ ], click Properties
Computer configuration, customizing	WIN 753	*See* Reference box: Specifying Program Defaults and Settings
Computer icon, display on desktop or hide	WIN 40	Click [ ], right-click Computer, click Show on Desktop
Computer Management, open	WIN 330	Right-click [ ], click Manage
Computer name and description, view	WIN 793	*See* Reference box: Viewing and Changing Your Computer's Name, Description, and Workgroup Name
Computer window, open	WIN 54	Press the Windows+E keys
Computer, display system information for	WIN 848	In a command-line window, type SYSTEMINFO I MORE, press the Enter key
Computer, navigate	WIN 61	*See* Reference box: Navigating Your Computer
Computer, use the Windows 7 Upgrade Advisor to evaluate	WIN 716	*See* Reference box: Evaluating a Computer with the Windows 7 Upgrade Advisor

TASK	PAGE #	RECOMMENDED METHOD
Computer, view properties of	WIN 62	Right-click 💻, click Properties
Computers, view workgroup	WIN 796	*See* Reference box: Viewing Computers and Shared Resources in a Workgroup
Console colors, change	WIN 840	*See* Reference box: Changing Console Colors
Console colors, restore default	WIN 840	*See* Reference box: Changing Console Colors
Contents view, change to	WIN 192	Click ▤ ▾ for the Change your view button, click Content
Control Panel, create a shortcut to an item in	WIN 272	*See* Reference box: Creating a Control Panel Shortcut
Cookies, manage Internet Explorer 8 usage of	WIN 481	*See* Reference box: Controlling Cookie Usage
COPY command, use	WIN 872	*See* Reference box: Copying a File to a Flash Drive
CPU usage, evaluate	WIN 585	*See* Reference box: Using Task Manager to Monitor System Performance
CPU usage, use Performance Monitor to evaluate	WIN 625	*See* Reference box: Using Performance Monitor to Track Performance
CPU usage, use Resource Monitor to evaluate	WIN 594	*See* Reference box: Using Resource Monitor to Evaluate Memory Usage and System Performance
Create Shortcut Wizard, create a desktop shortcut with	WIN 277	*See* Reference box: Creating a Desktop Shortcut with the Create Shortcut Wizard
Defaults, set program	WIN 753	*See* Reference box: Specifying Program Defaults and Settings
Desktop background, choose	WIN 85	*See* Reference box: Customizing a Theme's Desktop Background
Desktop icons, change and restore size	WIN 36	*See* Reference box: Changing and Restoring Desktop Icon Sizes
Desktop icons, use mouse scroll wheel to adjust size	WIN 35	Hold down the Ctrl key and move mouse scroll wheel one notch forwards or backwards
Desktop view, update	WIN 258	Press the F5 (Refresh) key
Desktop, display translucent	WIN 30	Point to Show desktop button ▮ on the taskbar
Desktop, minimize or maximize all windows	WIN 30	Click Show desktop button ▮ on the taskbar
Desktop, personalize	WIN 81	Right-click the desktop background, click Personalize
Device Manager, use	WIN 782	*See* Reference box: Viewing Device Properties
Devices, view properties of	WIN 782	*See* Reference box: Viewing Device Properties
Devices and printers, view	WIN 765	Click 🔵, click Devices and Printers
DIR command, use	WIN 861	In a command-line window, type DIR with or without switches, press the Enter key
DIRCMD environment variable, assign switches to	WIN 880	*See* Reference box: Creating a DIRCMD Environment Variable
DIRCMD environment variable, remove	WIN 880	*See* Reference box: Creating a DIRCMD Environment Variable
Directory listing, display	WIN 861	In a command-line window, type DIR and press the Enter key
Directory listing, display in alphabetical order	WIN 864	In a command-line window, type DIR /O and press the Enter key
Directory tree, display	WIN 860	*See* Reference box: Displaying a Directory Tree

TASK	PAGE #	RECOMMENDED METHOD
Directory, change to another	WIN 865	In a command-line window, type CD, press the spacebar, type directory name or the path to the directory, press the Enter key
Directory, create	WIN 868	In a command-line window, type MD, press the spacebar, type a directory name (with quotation marks for long directory names), press the Enter key
Directory, display contents of	WIN 861	In a command-line window, type DIR and press the Enter key
Disk activity, use Resource Monitor to evaluate	WIN 594	*See* Reference box: Using Resource Monitor to Evaluate Memory Usage and System Performance
Disk Cleanup utility, run	WIN 372	*See* Reference box: Using the Disk Cleanup Utility
Disk Defragmenter, open and analyze a disk with	WIN 400	*See* Reference box: Opening Disk Defragmenter
Disk I/O, use Performance Monitor to evaluate	WIN 625	*See* Reference box: Using Performance Monitor to Track Performance
Disk I/O, use Resource and Performance Monitor to view information on	WIN 598	*See* Reference box: Creating a System Health Report
Disk Management Tool, open	WIN 335	*See* Reference box: Using the Disk Management Tool
Disk, use Disk Defragment to analyze	WIN 400	*See* Reference box: Opening Disk Defragmenter
Disk, use Disk Defragmenter to manually defragment	WIN 400	*See* Reference box: Opening Disk Defragmenter
DPI scaling settings, view	WIN 137	*See* Reference box: Adjusting the DPI Scaling
Drive, check, assign, or remove volume label for	WIN 846	*See* Reference box: Checking, Assigning, and Removing a Volume Label for a Flash Drive
Drive, restore previous versions of	WIN 692	*See* Reference box: Restoring Previous Versions of Files, Folders, and Drives
Drive, view properties of	WIN 324	Right-click the drive icon in the Computer window, click Properties
Drives, change	WIN 872	In a command-line window, type a drive name, press the Enter key
Environment variables, view information on	WIN 560	*See* Reference box: Using System Information to View Information on Startup Programs and Environment Variables
Environment variables, view settings for	WIN 878	In a command-line window, type SET and press the Enter key
Error-checking tool, use	WIN 380	*See* Reference box: Using the Error-checking Tool to Check the File System on a Hard Disk Drive
Event Viewer, use	WIN 526	*See* Reference box: Using Event Viewer
Events, use Event Viewer to examine Application, Security, Setup, System, and Forwarded	WIN 526	*See* Reference box: Using Event Viewer
Events, use Event Viewer to filter	WIN 526	*See* Reference box: Using Event Viewer
Events, use Reliability Monitor to view information on critical, warning, and information	WIN 510	*See* Reference box: Using Reliability Monitor
Extra Large Icons view, change to	WIN 59	Click ▦ ▾ for the Change your view button, click Extra Large Icons
File attributes, view	WIN 866	In a command-line window, type ATTRIB and press the Enter key
File property, search by	WIN 210	*See* Reference box: Searching Using a File Property, File Type, or Tags

TASK	PAGE #	RECOMMENDED METHOD
File system, identify a drive's	WIN 324	Right-click the drive icon in the Computer window, click Properties
File system, use Check Disk utility to check for errors in a hard disk drive's	WIN 389	*See* Reference box: Using the Check Disk Utility in a Command Prompt Window
File system, use the Error-checking Tool to check for errors in a hard disk drive's	WIN 380	*See* Reference box: Using the Error-checking Tool to Check the File System on a Hard Disk Drive
File tags, search by one or more	WIN 210	*See* Reference box: Searching Using a File Property, File Type, or Tags
File type, search by	WIN 210	*See* Reference box: Searching Using a File Property, File Type, or Tags
File type, specify the default program for	WIN 753	*See* Reference box: Specifying Program Defaults and Settings
File, assign one or more tags to	WIN 212	*See* Reference box: Assigning a Tag or Tags to a File
File, copy	WIN 168	Select files, hold down the Ctrl key as you drag files to a new folder on the same (or different) drive
File, copy	WIN 872	*See* Reference box: Copying a File to a Flash Drive
File, create a shortcut to a	WIN 258	Right-click the file icon, point to Send to, click Desktop (create shortcut)
File, move	WIN 168	Drag the file (or files) from one folder window to another on the same drive
File, open the location for	WIN 205	Right-click the file icon, click Open file location
File, search for	WIN 204	Click the Search box in a folder window, type all or part of a filename
File, use a file property, tag, file type, or search filter to search for	WIN 210	*See* Reference box: Searching Using a File Property, File Type, or Tags
File, use Details pane to view information on	WIN 178	Select a file in a folder window, examine the Details pane
File, view actions for	WIN 205	Right-click the file icon
File, view properties of	WIN 184	*See* Reference box: Viewing Properties of Files
Files and folders, restore	WIN 678	*See* Reference box: Restoring Files and Folders
Files, back up	WIN 665	*See* Reference box: Setting Up a Regularly Scheduled Backup
Files, display only	WIN 866	In a command-line window, type DIR /A-D and press the Enter key
Files, group	WIN 197	*See* Reference box: Grouping Files in a Folder
Files, organize into stacks	WIN 194	*See* Reference box: Organizing Files into Stacks
Files, restore previous versions of	WIN 692	*See* Reference box: Restoring Previous Versions of Files, Folders, and Drives
Files, sort and filter	WIN 196	*See* Reference box: Sorting and Filtering Files in a Folder
Files, use wildcards to copy	WIN 877	*See* Reference box: Copying Files Using Wildcards
Filter, use	WIN 847	In a command-line window, type a command, type l, type a filter
Flash drive icon, customize	WIN 285	*See* Reference box: Customizing a Flash Drive Icon
Flash drive, create shortcut to	WIN 249	*See* Reference box: Creating a Shortcut to a Flash Drive
Folder sharing, turn off	WIN 807	*See* Reference box: Sharing a New Folder with Specific People
Folder view and behavior settings, view and change	WIN 174	Click the Organize button in a folder window, click Folder and search options, click the View tab
Folder, choose a custom view	WIN 171	Click ▦ ▾ for the Change your view button, drag the slider bar tab to select a custom view

TASK	PAGE #	RECOMMENDED METHOD
Folder, compress	WIN 345	*See* Reference box: Compressing and Uncompressing a Folder and Its Contents
Folder, copy	WIN 168	Select the folder, hold down the Ctrl key as you drag the folder to a new folder on the same (or different) drive
Folder, create a shortcut to	WIN 258	*See* Reference box: Creating a Shortcut to a Folder and Customizing the Shortcut Icon
Folder, encrypt and decrypt	WIN 354	*See* Reference box: Encrypting and Decrypting a Folder
Folder, move	WIN 168	Drag the folder (or folders) from a folder window to another folder on the same drive
Folder, open a Command Prompt window from	WIN 856	Hold down Shift key, right-click the folder icon, click Open command window here
Folder, rename	WIN 170	Right-click the folder, click Rename, edit or type over the folder name, press the Enter key
Folder, select everything in	WIN 181	Press the Ctrl+A keys
Folder, share	WIN 807	*See* Reference box: Sharing a New Folder with Specific People
Folder, uncompress	WIN 345	*See* Reference box: Compressing and Uncompressing a Folder and Its Contents
Folder, use advanced sharing to share	WIN 811	*See* Reference box: Using Advanced Sharing to Share a Folder
Folder, view properties of	WIN 185	*See* Reference box: Viewing Properties of Folders
Folders and files, back up	WIN 665	*See* Reference box: Setting Up a Regularly Scheduled Backup
Folders and files, restore	WIN 678	*See* Reference box: Restoring Files and Folders
Folders, restore previous versions of	WIN 692	*See* Reference box: Restoring Previous Versions of Files, Folders, and Drives
Font sizes, adjust screen	WIN 137	*See* Reference box: Adjusting the DPI Scaling
Fragmentation, use Disk Defragmenter to analyze a disk for	WIN 400	*See* Reference box: Opening Disk Defragmenter
Fragmentation, use the Defrag utility to analyze a disk for	WIN 404	*See* Reference box: Producing a Fragmentation Analysis Report Using the Command-Line Defrag Utility
Group of files, use Details pane to view information on	WIN 182	Select a group of files in a folder window, examine the Details pane
Groups, organize files into	WIN 197	*See* Reference box: Grouping Files in a Folder
Hardware device, view properties of	WIN 782	*See* Reference box: Viewing Device Properties
Help and Support, browse	WIN 47	*See* Reference box: Browsing Windows Help and Support
Help and Support, open	WIN 45	Press the F1 (Help) key
Help and Support, search	WIN 49	*See* Reference box: Searching Windows Help and Support
HELP command, use	WIN 843	In a command-line window, type HELP, press the spacebar, type a command, press the Enter key
Help switch (/?), use	WIN 840	*See* Reference box: Changing Console Colors
History, check Windows Update	WIN 442	*See* Reference box: Checking Your Windows Update History
Homegroup, access resources in	WIN 822	*See* Reference box: Creating, Joining, and Leaving a Homegroup
Homegroup, create, join, or leave	WIN 822	*See* Reference box Creating, Joining, and Leaving a Homegroup
Icon, customize flash drive	WIN 285	*See* Reference box: Customizing a Flash Drive Icon

TASK	PAGE #	RECOMMENDED METHOD
Icons, display hidden	WIN 38	Click ▲ for the Show hidden icons button in the notification area
InPrivate Browsing window, open an Internet Explorer 8	WIN 487	Open Internet Explorer 8, click Safety on the toolbar, click InPrivate Browsing
InPrivate Filtering, enable	WIN 485	*See* Reference box: Using InPrivate Filtering to Identify Content Tracking
InPrivate Filtering, view content tracking settings for	WIN 485	*See* Reference box: Using InPrivate Filtering to Identify Content Tracking
Internet cache, empty	WIN 373	Open Internet Explorer 8, click the Safety button on the command bar, click Delete Browsing History
Internet Explorer 8, check and change security settings for	WIN 463	*See* Reference box: Checking Internet Explorer 8 Security Settings
Internet Explorer 8, check and change SmartScreen Filter settings for	WIN 467	*See* Reference box: Using the SmartScreen Filter
Internet Explorer 8, delete the browsing history for	WIN 487	*See* Reference box: Deleting Your Internet Explorer 8 Browsing History
Internet Explorer 8, open an InPrivate Browsing window in	WIN 487	Open Internet Explorer 8, click Safety on the toolbar, click InPrivate Browsing
Internet Explorer 8, view and change cookie usage settings for	WIN 481	*See* Reference box: Controlling Cookie Usage
Internet Explorer 8, view and change privacy settings for	WIN 481	*See* Reference box: Controlling Cookie Usage
Internet Explorer 8, view and manage add-ons for	WIN 475	*See* Reference box: Examining Information on Add-ons
Internet Explorer 8, view the Privacy Policy for a Web site with	WIN 483	*See* Reference box: Viewing the Privacy Report and Privacy Policy for a Web Site
Internet shortcut, create	WIN 287	Drag icon for a URL in a Web browser Address bar to the desktop
Internet shortcut, use a Web page link to create	WIN 289	Drag a Web page link to the desktop
Internet shortcut, view properties of	WIN 287	Right-click the Internet shortcut icon, click Properties
Interrupt command, use	WIN 860	In a command-line window, press the Ctrl+C keys, or press the Ctrl+Break keys
Jump List, display a Start menu program's	WIN 39	Click 🌐, point to a program's Jump List arrow
Jump List, display a taskbar program	WIN 37	Right-click the taskbar button, or drag the taskbar button up
Jump List, unpin item from	WIN 274	*See* Reference box: Pinning a Desktop Shortcut to the Start Menu and Taskbar
LABEL command, use	WIN 846	*See* Reference box: Checking, Assigning, and Removing a Volume Label for a Flash Drive
Last Known Good Configuration, boot computer with	WIN 539	Boot or restart the computer, press the F8 key before you see the Windows logo, select Last Known Good Configuration, press the Enter key
Library, view locations and settings for	WIN 161	Right-click 📷, click Windows Explorer, click the Library icon, click Locations link in Library pane
Links, add or remove in the Navigation pane	WIN 280	*See* Reference box: Adding and Removing Links in the Navigation Pane

TASK	PAGE #	RECOMMENDED METHOD
Live Taskbar Thumbnail(s), display	WIN 37	Rest mouse pointer on the taskbar button
Local area connection, view properties of a computer's	WIN 802	*See* Reference box: Using the Network and Sharing Center
Mapped drive, create or disconnect	WIN 814	*See* Reference box: Creating and Disconnecting a Mapped Drive
Mapped drive, view	WIN 814	*See* Reference box: Creating and Disconnecting a Mapped Drive
MD command, use	WIN 868	In a command-line window, type MD, type a directory name, press the Enter key
Memory performance counters, use the System Diagnostics Report to examine	WIN 629	*See* Reference box: Using the System Diagnostics Report to Examine Memory Performance Counters
Memory usage, evaluate	WIN 585	*See* Reference box: Using Task Manager to Monitor System Performance
Memory usage, use Performance Monitor to evaluate	WIN 625	*See* Reference box: Using Performance Monitor to Track Performance
Memory usage, use Resource Monitor to evaluate	WIN 594	*See* Reference box: Using Resource Monitor to Evaluate Memory Usage and System Performance
Microsoft Office components, view, add, and remove	WIN 737	*See* Reference box: Adding or Removing Microsoft Office Components
Mouse, change properties of	WIN 96	*See* Reference box: Changing Mouse Properties
Navigation pane, add or remove links in	WIN 280	*See* Reference box: Adding and Removing Links in the Navigation Pane
Navigation pane, use	WIN 61	*See* Reference box: Navigating Your Computer
Network activity, use Resource Monitor to evaluate	WIN 594	*See* Reference box: Using Resource Monitor to Evaluate Memory Usage and System Performance
Network and Sharing Center, use	WIN 802	*See* Reference box: Using the Network and Sharing Center
Network connections, view status of	WIN 802	*See* Reference box: Using the Network and Sharing Center
Network type, change a computer's	WIN 802	*See* Reference box: Using the Network and Sharing Center
Nonresponding program, shut down	WIN 548	*See* Reference box: Using Task Manager to Shut Down a Nonresponding Program
Notification area, view and change settings for icons and icon behaviors in	WIN 118	*See* Reference box: Customizing the Taskbar
Offline caching, enable	WIN 811	*See* Reference box: Using Advanced Sharing to Share a Folder
Page switch, use the DIR command's	WIN 865	In a command-line window, type DIR /P and press the Enter key
Paged output, display	WIN 847	In a command-line window, type a command, press the spacebar, type l, press the spacebar, type MORE, press the Enter key
Paged output, display a directory listing as	WIN 865	In a command-line window, type DIR /P and press the Enter key
Paging file, use Performance Monitor to evaluate the use of	WIN 625	*See* Reference box: Using Performance Monitor to Track Performance
Parent directory, change from the current directory to the	WIN 876	In a command-line window, type CD .. and press the Enter key
Password Reset disk, create	WIN 450	*See* Reference box: Creating a Password Reset Disk
Path, view a folder	WIN 186	Click the folder icon in the Address bar
Performance Monitor, use	WIN 625	*See* Reference box: Using Performance Monitor to Track Performance

TASK	PAGE #	RECOMMENDED METHOD
Program, pin to Start menu	WIN 40	Right-click the program on the All Programs menu, click Pin to Start menu
Program, pin to taskbar	WIN 37	Right-click the program on the Start or All Programs menu, click Pin to Taskbar
Program, search for	WIN 201	Press the Windows key, type all or part of a program filename in the Search programs and files box
Program, unpin from Start menu	WIN 40	Right-click the Start menu program , click Unpin from Start menu
Program, unpin from taskbar	WIN 37	Right-click the program taskbar button, click Unpin this program from taskbar
Programs, specify default	WIN 753	See Reference box: Specifying Program Defaults and Settings
Properties of computer, view	WIN 62	Right-click [icon], click Properties
Properties, change mouse	WIN 96	See Reference box: Changing Mouse Properties
Properties, use Disk Management to view disk, partition, volume, and drive	WIN 335	See Reference box: Using the Disk Management Tool
Properties, view Internet shortcut	WIN 287	Right-click the Internet shortcut icon, click Properties
Properties, view Compressed (zipped) Folder	WIN 347	Right-click [icon], click Properties
Properties, view computer	WIN 62	Right-click [icon], click Properties
Properties, view drive	WIN 324	Right-click the drive icon in the Computer window, click Properties
Properties, view file	WIN 184	See Reference box: Viewing Properties of Files
Properties, view folder	WIN 185	See Reference box: Viewing Properties of Folders
Properties, view shortcut	WIN 254	See Reference box: Viewing Properties of a Shortcut
Protocol, specify the default program for	WIN 753	See Reference box: Specifying Program Defaults and Settings
RAM, view total amount of installed memory	WIN 62	Right-click [icon], click Properties
Refresh rate settings, view	WIN 134	See Reference box: Checking Video Display Settings
Registered file type, locate information on	WIN 912	See Reference box: Tracing Information on Registered File Types
Registry Editor, open	WIN 899	Press the Windows key, type REGEDIT in the Start menu Search programs and files box, click regedit.exe in the Search results
Registry search, to continue	WIN 909	Press the F3 key
Registry settings, export	WIN 900	See Reference box: Exporting Registry Settings
Reliability Monitor, use	WIN 510	See Reference box: Using Reliability Monitor
Resolution, view or change the screen	WIN 129	See Reference box: Changing the Screen Resolution
Resource assignments, view a hardware device's	WIN 782	See Reference box: Viewing Device Properties
Restore point, create	WIN 516	See: Reference box: Creating a Manual Restore Point
Root directory, change to	WIN 861	In a command-line window, type CD \ and press the Enter key
Run dialog box, open	WIN 837	Press the Windows+R keys
Safe mode, boot in	WIN 545	See Reference box: Booting in Safe Mode
Saved search, view	WIN 218	Click the saved search under Favorites in Navigation pane

TASK	PAGE #	RECOMMENDED METHOD
Scheduled task, create	WIN 414	*See* Reference box: Creating a Scheduled Task
Scheduled task, delete	WIN 418	*See* Reference box: Deleting a Scheduled Task
Scheduled task, view and change settings for	WIN 417	*See* Reference box: Checking Settings for a Scheduled Task
Scheduled task, view information on	WIN 409	*See* Reference box: Viewing Information on a Windows Scheduled Task
Search and Index settings, examine	WIN 228	*See* Reference box: Examining Search and Index Settings
Search filter, search for a file using	WIN 210	*See* Reference box: Searching Using a File Property, File Type, or Tags
Search options, customize	WIN 229	*See* Reference box: Customizing Search Options
Search, save	WIN 217	Click the Save search button, click the Save button
Search, view a saved	WIN 218	Click the saved search under Favorites in Navigation pane
Security settings, view for Action Center	WIN 431	Click ▣ in the notification area, click Open Action Center, click ⊙ for the Security section
Security zones, check and change Internet Explorer 8 settings for	WIN 463	*See* Reference box: Checking Internet Explorer 8 Security Settings
Services, control the loading of Microsoft and non-Microsoft	WIN 555	*See* Reference box: Using System Configuration
Services, use System Configuration to check Windows and non-Microsoft	WIN 555	*See* Reference box: Using System Configuration
SET command, use	WIN 878	In a command-line window, type SET and press the Enter key
Shared resources, view workgroup	WIN 796	*See* Reference box: Viewing Computers and Shared Resources in a Workgroup
Shortcut, add to Startup folder	WIN 292	*See* Reference box: Adding Shortcuts to Your Startup Folder
Shortcut, create a new shortcut from an existing	WIN 263	Right-click the shortcut icon, click Copy, right-click the desktop, click Paste
Shortcut, create a Control Panel	WIN 272	*See* Reference box: Creating a Control Panel Shortcut
Shortcut, create a folder or file	WIN 256	Right-click the folder or file icon, point to Send To, click Desktop (create shortcut)
Shortcut, create an application	WIN 263	*See* Reference box: Creating a Shortcut to an Application
Shortcut, customize the icon for a folder	WIN 258	*See* Reference box: Creating a Shortcut to a Folder and Customizing the Shortcut Icon
Shortcut, pin to the Start menu or taskbar	WIN 274	*See* Reference box: Pinning a Desktop Shortcut to the Start Menu and Taskbar
Shortcut, rename	WIN 248	Select the shortcut, press the F2 (Rename) key, type or edit the filename, press the Enter key
Shortcut icon, update	WIN 258	Press the F5 (Refresh) key
Shortcut, using the Create Shortcut Wizard to create a desktop	WIN 277	*See* Reference box: Creating a Desktop Shortcut with the Create Shortcut Wizard
Shortcut, view properties of	WIN 254	*See* Reference box: Viewing Properties of a Shortcut
Shut Down Windows dialog box, open	WIN 70	Click the desktop background, press the Alt+F4 keys
Single-click activation, enable	WIN 43	*See* Reference box: Using the Control Panel to Enable Single-Click Activation

TASK	PAGE #	RECOMMENDED METHOD
Sleep power management settings, view and change	WIN 144	*See* Reference box: Managing Power Management Settings
SmartScreen Filter, check and change settings for Internet Explorer 8's	WIN 467	*See* Reference box: Using the SmartScreen Filter
Snap, use	WIN 34	*See* Reference box: Using Aero Snap
Software, uninstall	WIN 745	*See* Reference box: Uninstalling Software
Sort Order switch, use the DIR command's	WIN 864	In a command-line window, type DIR /O and press the Enter key
Spyware and unwanted software protection, view Action Center settings for	WIN 431	Click ▶ in the notification area, click Open Action Center, click ⌄ for the Security section
Stability index, use Reliability Monitor to view	WIN 510	*See* Reference box: Using Reliability Monitor
Stacks, organize files into	WIN 194	*See* Reference box: Organizing Files into Stacks
Start menu color, adjust	WIN 88	*See* Reference box: Adjusting Window Color Settings
Start menu, add Administrative Tools to	WIN 330	Right-click ⊛, click Properties, click Customize, locate System administrative tools, click Display on the All Programs menu and the Start menu option button, click OK
Start menu, open or close	WIN 40	Press the Windows key
Start menu, pin a desktop shortcut to	WIN 274	*See* Reference box: Pinning a Desktop Shortcut to the Start Menu and Taskbar
Start menu, view and change settings for the	WIN 112	*See* Reference box: Customizing the Start Menu
Startup folder, add a shortcut to	WIN 292	*See* Reference box: Adding Shortcuts to Your Startup Folder
Startup programs, use Resource and Performance Monitor to view information on	WIN 598	*See* Reference box: Creating a System Health Report
Startup programs, use System Configuration to check	WIN 555	*See* Reference box: Using System Configuration
Startup programs, view and control the loading of	WIN 555	*See* Reference box: Using System Configuration
Startup programs, view information on	WIN 560	*See* Reference box: Using System Information to View Information on Startup Programs and Environment Variables
Startup Repair, troubleshoot computer with	WIN 542	Boot or restart the computer, press the F8 key before you see the Windows logo, select Repair your computer, press the Enter key
Startup, customize with shortcuts	WIN 292	*See* Reference box: Adding Shortcuts to Your Startup Folder
Subdirectories and files, display all	WIN 862	In a command-line window, type DIR /A and press the Enter key
Subdirectories, display only	WIN 866	In a command-line window, type DIR /AD and press the Enter key
System Configuration, use	WIN 555	*See* Reference box: Using System Configuration
System files, scan and remove unneeded	WIN 372	*See* Reference box: Using the Disk Cleanup Utility
System health report, create a	WIN 598	*See* Reference box: Creating a System Health Report

TASK	PAGE #	RECOMMENDED METHOD
System image, create	WIN 682	*See* Reference box: Creating a System Image and a System Repair Disc
System information, display	WIN 848	In a command-line window, type SYSTEMINFO	MORE, press the Enter key
System Information, use	WIN 560	*See* Reference box: Using System Information to View Information on Startup Programs and Environment Variables
System performance, use Performance Monitor to evaluate	WIN 625	*See* Reference box: Using Performance Monitor to Track Performance
System Protection settings, view	WIN 514	*See* Reference box: Checking System Protection Settings
System repair disc, create	WIN 682	*See* Reference box: Creating a System Image and a System Repair Disc
System Stability Report, use Reliability Monitor to produce a	WIN 510	*See* Reference box: Using Reliability Monitor
System window, open	WIN 62	Press the Windows+Pause keys
System window, open	WIN 512	Press the Windows+Break keys
SYSTEMINFO command, use	WIN 848	In a command-line window, type SYSTEMINFO	MORE, press Enter key
Tags, assign to a file	WIN 212	*See* Reference box: Assigning a Tag or Tags to a File
Tags, search files by one or more	WIN 210	*See* Reference box: Searching Using a File Property, File Type, or Tags
Task Manager, open	WIN 546	Right-click the taskbar, click Start Task Manager
Task Scheduler, open	WIN 409	*See* Reference box: Viewing Information on a Windows Scheduled Task
Taskbar toolbar, display or create	WIN 122	*See* Reference box: Displaying and Creating Taskbar Toolbars
Taskbar color, adjust	WIN 88	*See* Reference box: Adjusting Window Color Settings
Taskbar, customize	WIN 118	*See* Reference box: Customizing the Taskbar
Taskbar, pin a Control Panel shortcut to	WIN 275	*See* Reference box: Pinning a Control Panel Desktop Shortcut to the Taskbar
Taskbar, pin a desktop shortcut to	WIN 274	*See* Reference box: Pinning a Desktop Shortcut to the Start Menu and Taskbar
Theme, choose desktop	WIN 85	*See* Reference box: Customizing a Theme's Desktop Background
Theme, save	WIN 89	*See* Reference box: Saving a Theme and Creating a Themepack
Themepack, save	WIN 89	*See* Reference box: Saving a Theme and Creating a Themepack
Tiles view, change to	WIN 54	Click ⊞ ▼ for the Change your view button, click Tiles
Toolbar, display or create a taskbar	WIN 122	*See* Reference box: Displaying and Creating Taskbar Toolbars
TREE command, use	WIN 860	*See* Reference box: Displaying a Directory Tree
Undo a task or operation	WIN 279	Press the Ctrl+Z keys
Update, remove	WIN 442	*See* Reference box: Checking Your Windows Update History
Updates, check for hidden	WIN 442	*See* Reference box: Checking Your Windows Update History
Updates, view installed Windows and Microsoft Office	WIN 442	*See* Reference box: Checking Your Windows Update History
User Account Control settings, check	WIN 455	*See* Reference box: Checking User Account Control Settings
Video display adapter, view memory usage of	WIN 134	*See* Reference box: Checking Video Display Settings
Video display adapter settings, view	WIN 134	*See* Reference box: Checking Video Display Settings
Video display modes, view	WIN 134	*See* Reference box: Checking Video Display Settings
Virtual memory settings, view	WIN 580	*See* Reference box: Viewing Virtual Memory Settings

TASK	PAGE #	RECOMMENDED METHOD
Virus protection, view Action Center settings for	WIN 431	Click 🏴 in the notification area, click Open Action Center, click ⊗ for the Security section
Visual effects, adjust	WIN 105	*See* Reference box: Adjusting Visual Effects
VOL command, use	WIN 846	*See* Reference box: Checking, Assigning, and Removing a Volume Label for a Flash Drive
Volume label, view, assign, or remove	WIN 846	*See* Reference box: Checking, Assigning, and Removing a Volume Label for a Flash Drive
Web style, change to	WIN 43	*See* Reference box: Using the Control Panel to Enable Single-Click Activation
Wildcards, copy files with	WIN 877	*See* Reference box: Copying Files Using Wildcards
Window colors, adjust	WIN 88	*See* Reference box: Adjusting Window Color Settings
Window, clear Command Prompt	WIN 843	In a command-line window, type CLS and press the Enter key
Window, dock	WIN 34	*See* Reference box: Using Aero Snap
Window, maximize vertically	WIN 34	*See* Reference box: Using Aero Snap
Windows 7 Upgrade Advisor, identify upgrade options with	WIN 716	*See* Reference box: Evaluating a Computer with the Windows 7 Upgrade Advisor
Windows Backup, set up	WIN 665	*See* Reference box: Setting Up a Regularly Scheduled Backup
Windows environment, view environment variables in	WIN 730	Type SET and press the Enter key
Windows Experience Index, view the base score and subscores of the	WIN 68	*See* Reference box: Viewing the Windows Experience Index Base Score and Subscores
Windows features, turn on and off	WIN 730	*See* Reference box: Turning Windows Features On and Off
Windows Firewall, view and change settings	WIN 435	*See* Reference box: Verifying Windows Firewall Settings
Windows Flip, use	WIN 28	*See* Reference box: Using Windows Flip
Windows Help and Support, browse	WIN 47	*See* Reference box: Browsing Windows Help and Support
Windows Help and Support, open	WIN 45	Press the F1 (Help) key
Windows Help and Support, search	WIN 49	*See* Reference box: Searching Windows Help and Support
Windows operating systems, view a computer's installed	WIN 555	Open System Configuration, click the Boot tab
Windows services, examine events for	WIN 526	*See* Reference box: Using Event Viewer
Windows Update, check history of	WIN 442	*See* Reference box: Checking Your Windows Update History
Windows Update, check settings for	WIN 439	*See* Reference box: Checking Your Windows Update Settings
Windows version and edition, view	WIN 62	Right-click 🖼, click Properties
Windows, minimize all other	WIN 31	Rapidly shake the active window's title bar
Windows, minimize or maximize all desktop	WIN 30	Click Show desktop button ▮ on the taskbar
Windows, show side by side	WIN 31	Right-click the taskbar, click Show windows side by side
Workgroup name, view a computer's	WIN 793	*See* Reference box: Viewing and Changing Your Computer's Name, Description, and Workgroup Name

DATE DUE